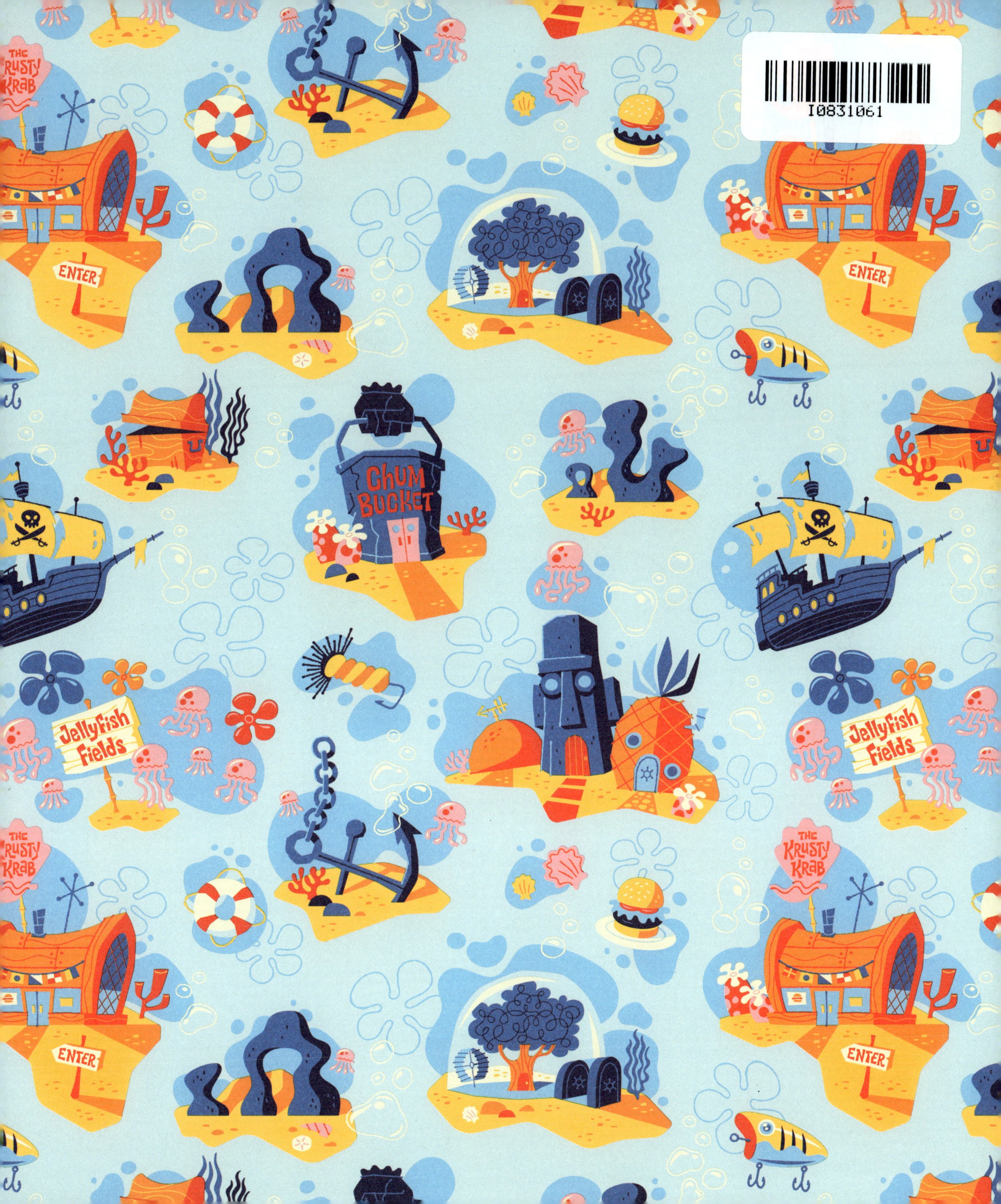
I0831061
THE KRUSTY KRAB
ENTER
CHUM BUCKET
Jellyfish Fields

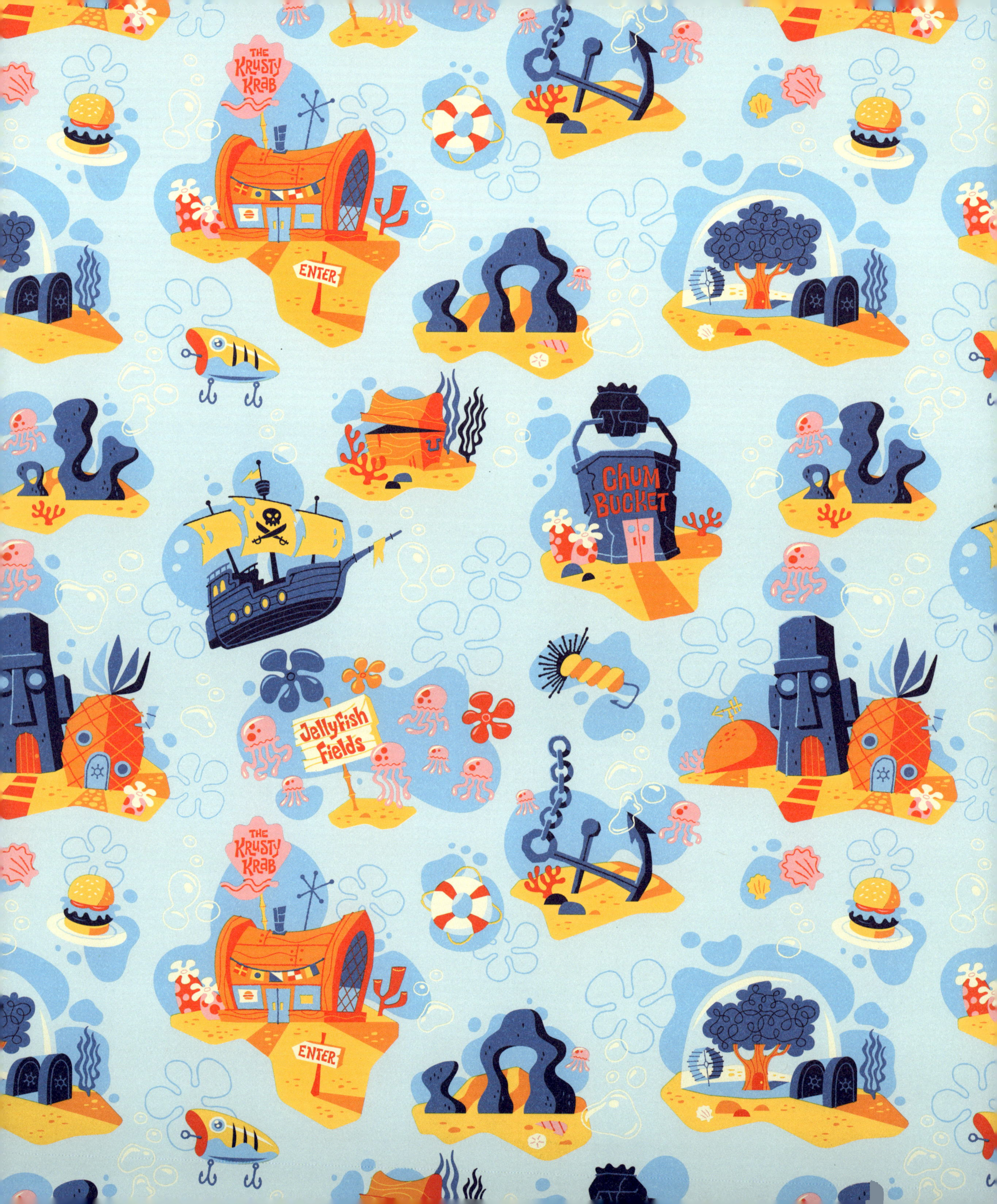

THE
KRUSTY
KRAB
ENTER
Chum
Bucket
Jellyfish
Fields
THE
KRUSTY
KRAB
ENTER

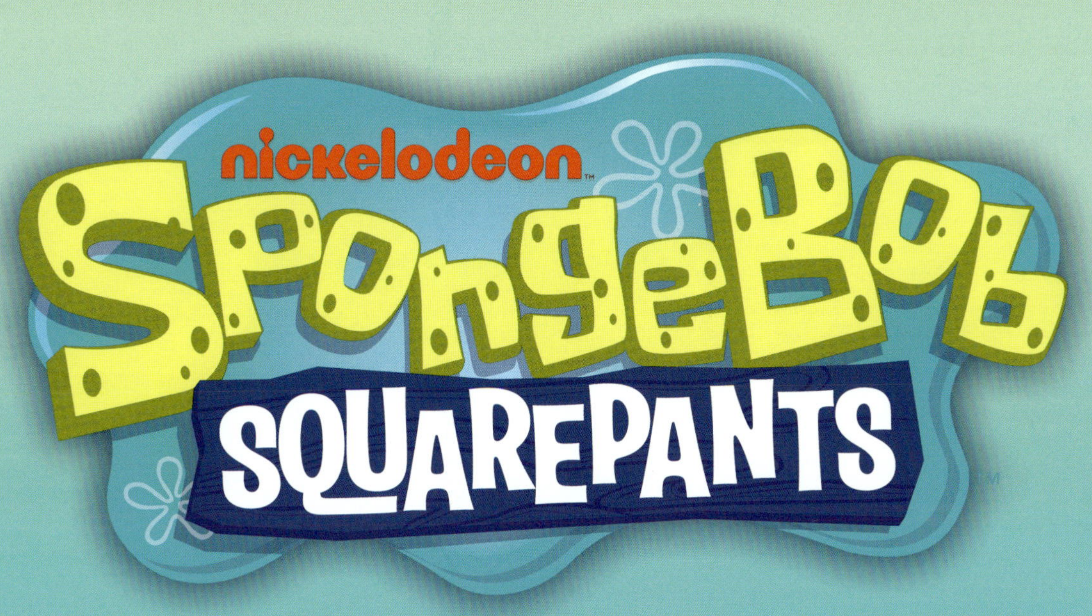

THE ART OF AN UNDERSEA WORLD

TRACEY MILLER-ZARNEKE

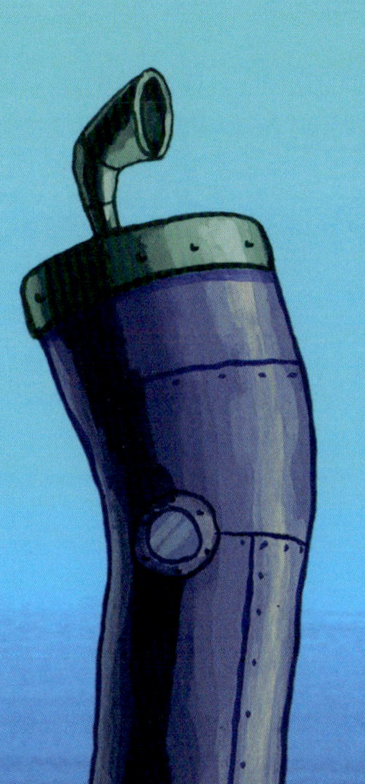

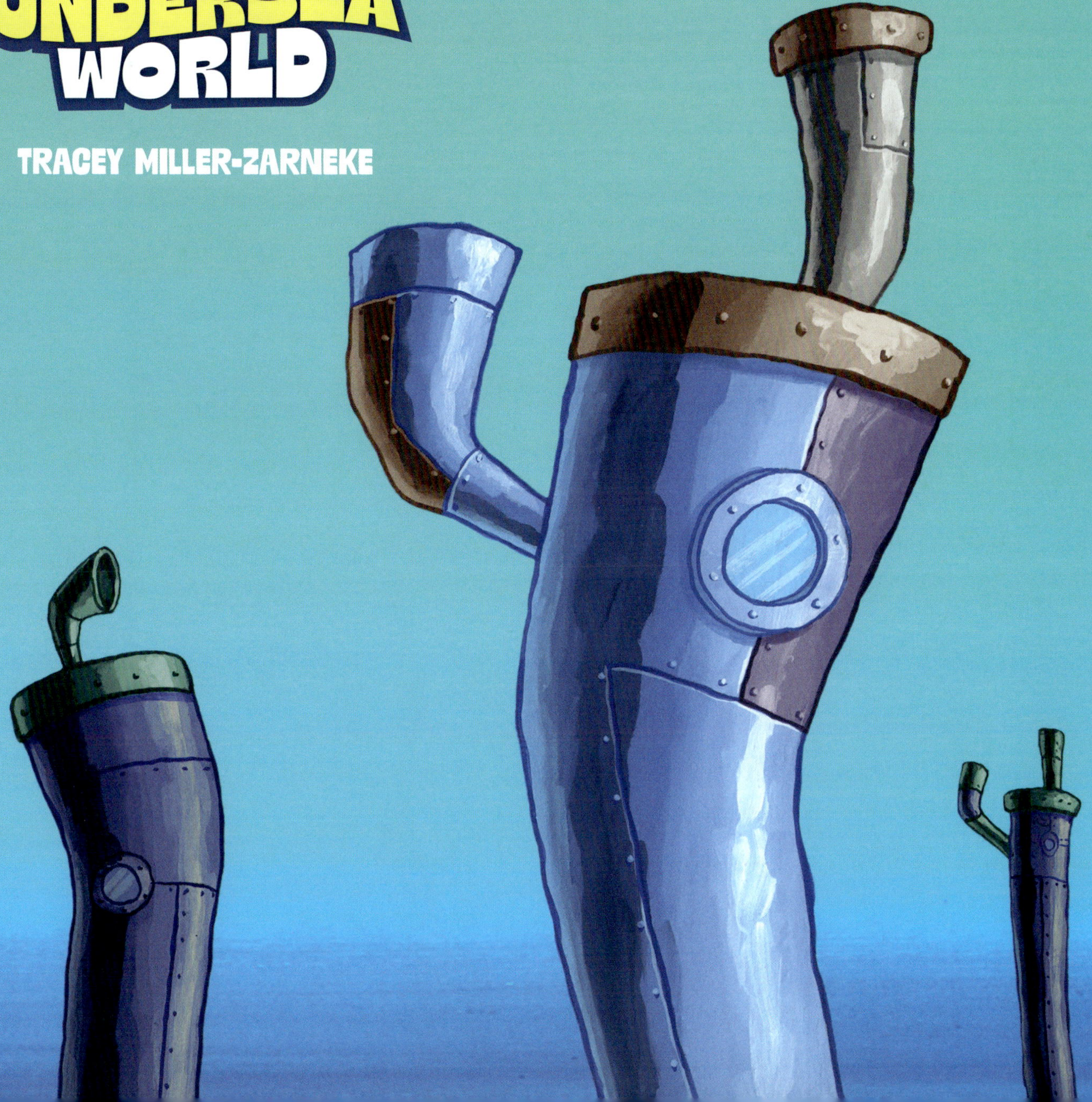

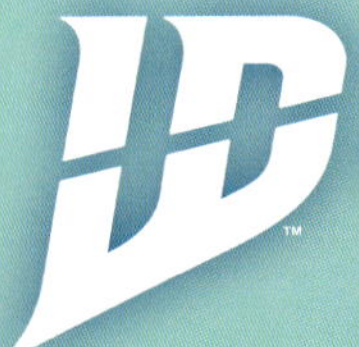

@IDWPUBLISHING
IDWPUBLISHING.COM
nickelodeon

979-8-88724-441-9 29 28 27 26 1 2 3 4

COVER ARTISTS:
Pablo R. Mayer, Adam Paloian

EDITORS:
Alonzo Simon
Anna Wostenberg

DESIGNER:
Darran Robinson

For international rights, contact licensing@idwpublishing.com

EU RP (for authorities only)
eucomply OÜ
Pärnu mnt. 139b – 14
11317 Tallinn, Estonia
hello@eucompliancepartner.com
+33757690241

Contracting Partner: Tara McCrillis, IDW Publishing
EU RP Partner: Marko Novkovic, CEO

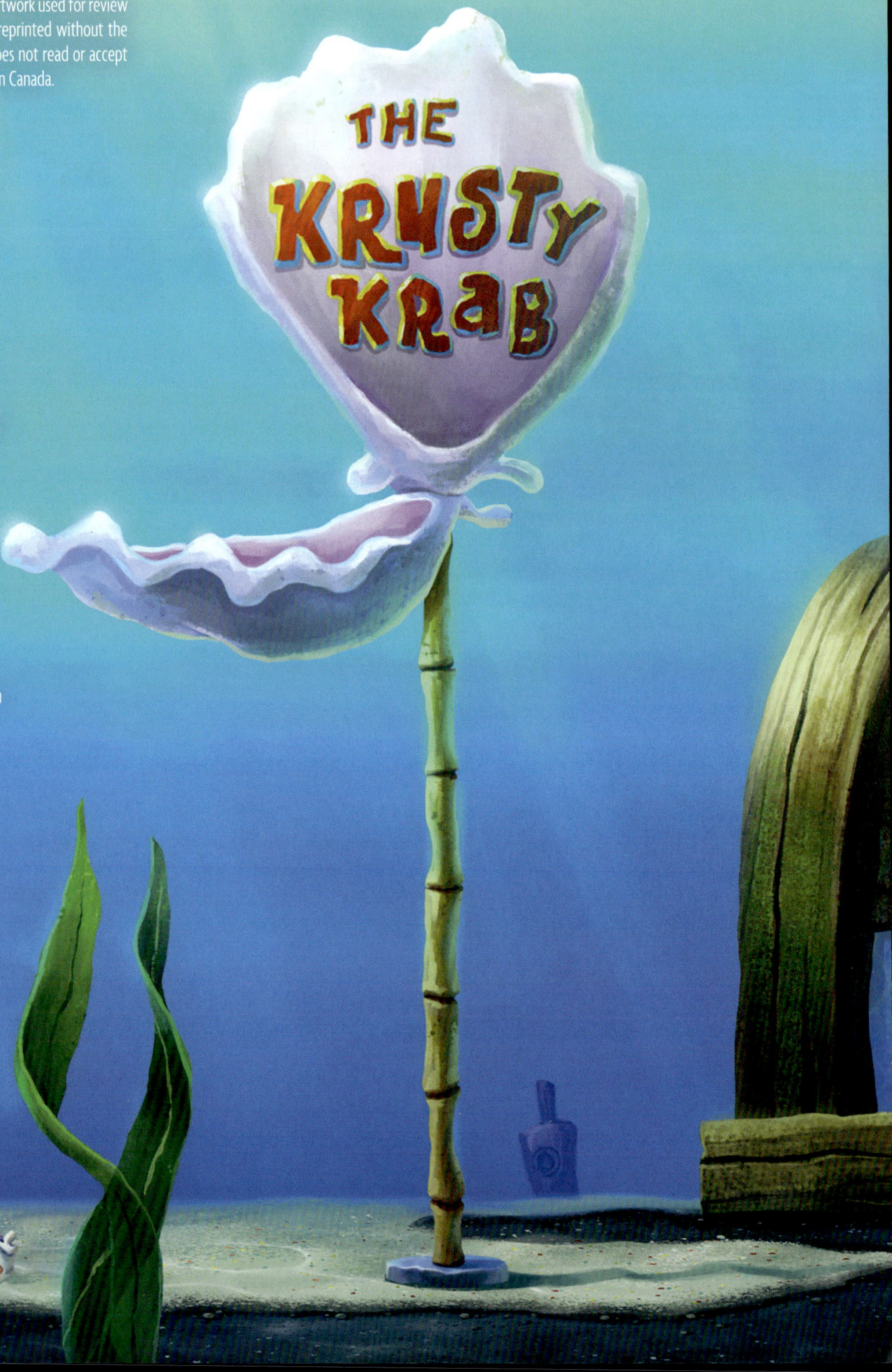

CONTENTS

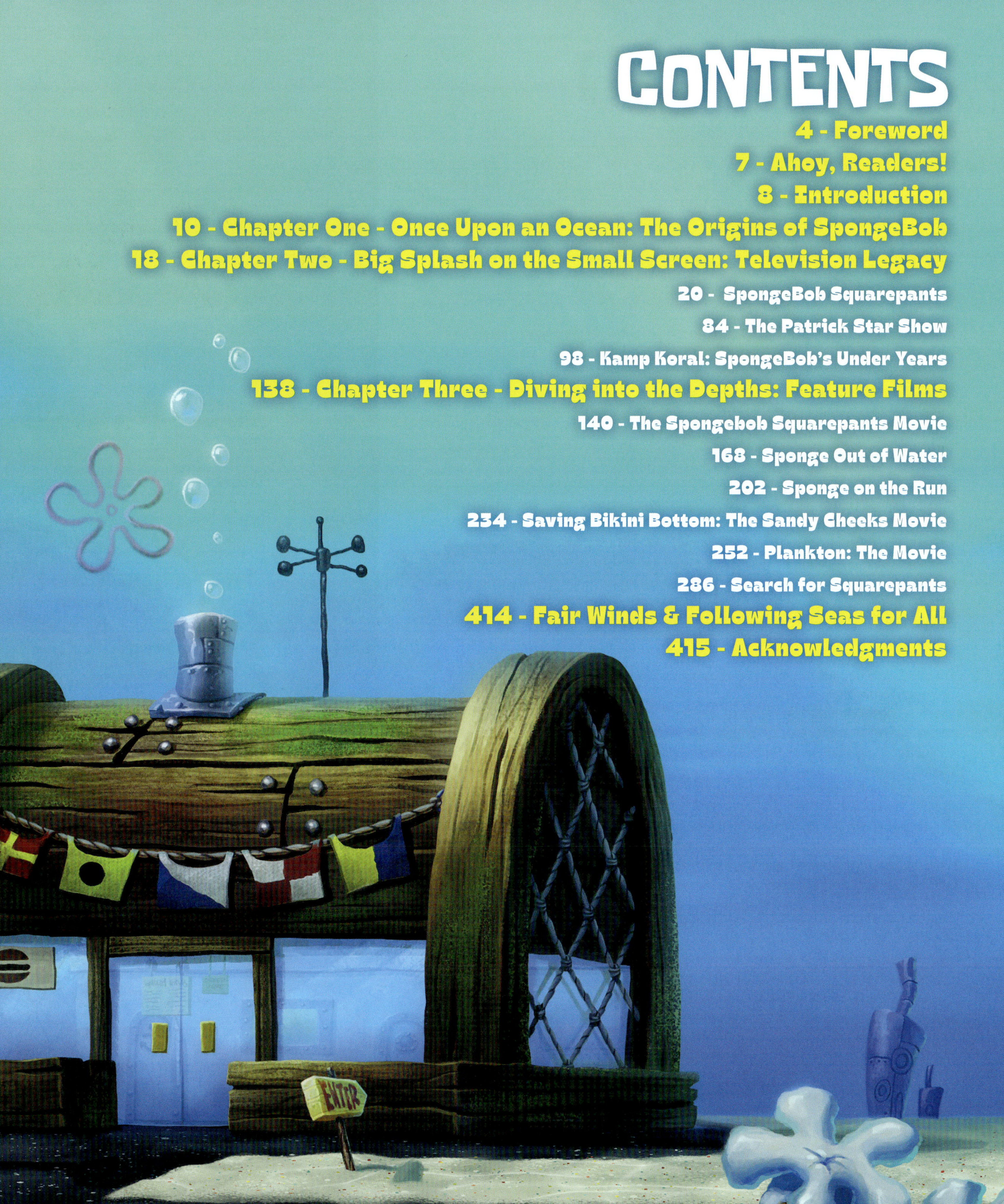

FOREWORD

I first became aware of Stephen Hillenburg when I was a student at CalArts in the early '90s. I was enrolled in the Live Action portion of the film school, and he was in the Experimental Animation program. When I saw the amazing shorts he was producing, like "The Green Beret," I was blown away by his creativity and offbeat humor. Around the same time, *Ren & Stimpy* premiered on Nickelodeon, and I realized I was probably in the wrong program. It took me another ten years working in adjacent industries before I made the transition to animation. But once I arrived, I knew I was where I belonged.

It was the art of *SpongeBob SquarePants* that first attracted me to the show when I joined the crew in 2010 as a board writer. I gravitated to animation as a career because I've always had a deep affection for cartoon surrealism. At the time, *SpongeBob* was one of the best examples of that kind of visual humor (and still is in my opinion). It's a show that has always fully embraced the comic potential of a drawn image. Where anything is possible with "IMAGINATION," and reactions and emotions are exaggerated and caricatured for maximum comic effect.

It makes sense that the show would appeal to my inner-weirdo art spirit. Steve's cartooning influences were similar to mine. We both enjoyed independent animators like Paul Driessen, George Dunning, Terry Gilliam, and Sally Cruikshank. Artists whose bizarre and imaginative styles helped rewire our brains to the limitless possibilities of the medium. We also found inspiration in underground and independent comics, especially *Raw* magazine from the '80s (where Steve discovered Kaz). Cartooning sources that were visually inventive and viscerally funny.

I'm sad that I missed the early developmental years of *SpongeBob*. From what I've heard from those who were there, it sounded like the best kind of intensely creative environment. Late nights and marathon rewriting and reboarding sessions. And lots of laughter while the crew was crafting and pitching some of the smartest stupid jokes ever told. But there's no space for regret, as our workdays are currently full to the brim, using the same silly spirit to fill the franchise with more *SpongeBob SquarePants* episodes and multiple simultaneous spinoffs and movies. Steve and his initial handpicked crew of super talented artists left us a wonderful box of toys to play with. A surplus of crazy characters and their bizarre, yet somehow familiar locations in and around the Bikini Bottom cargo cult. All the elements we'd need to mix and match in as many comic situations as our zany brains can fabricate.

I feel a close kinship with all of the immensely talented and skillful artists that Vincent Waller (my co-showrunner) and I work with each day. We all try to wring every last drop of humor from each crazy idea that is born in the writers' room, which then works its way through scripting, storyboarding, editing, design, animation, and finally music and sound effects. Each artist, along the way, tries to top the last until we feel comfortable unleashing our creations into the world at large. And it's been such a pleasure over the years seeing how our audiences have enjoyed what we've made. I hope you all enjoy the peek behind the scenes that this book offers. And here's hoping we continue to make you all laugh in this silly surreal cartoon paradise called Bikini Bottom.

Marc Ceccarelli
Executive Producer, *SpongeBob SquarePants* and *The Patrick Star Show*

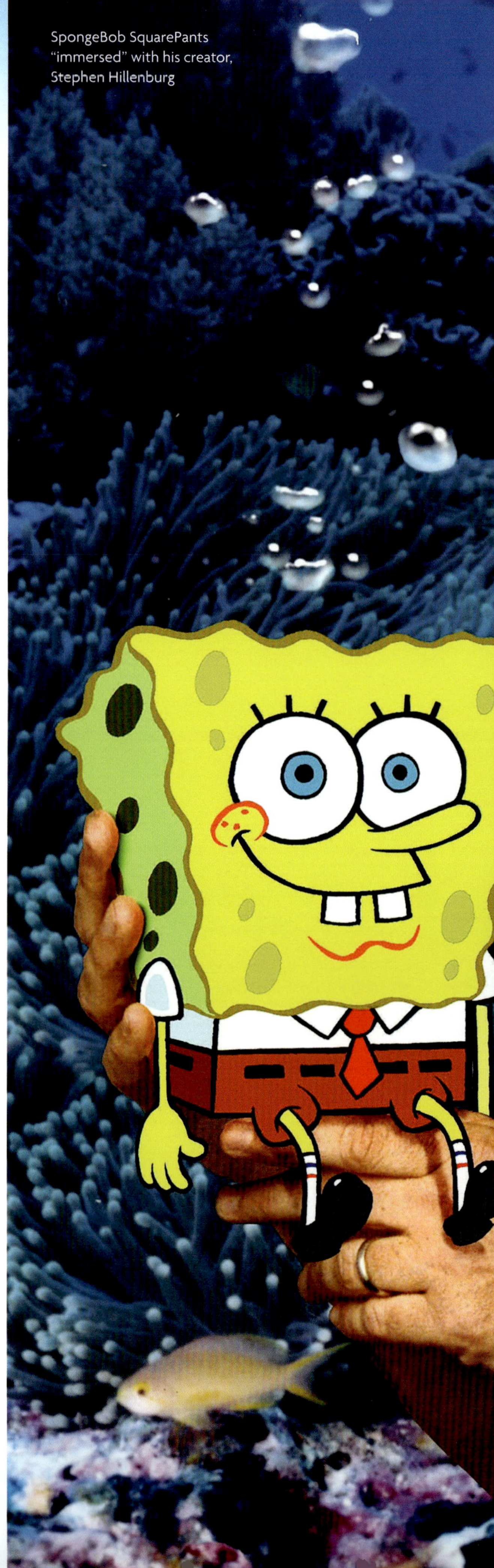

SpongeBob SquarePants "immersed" with his creator, Stephen Hillenburg

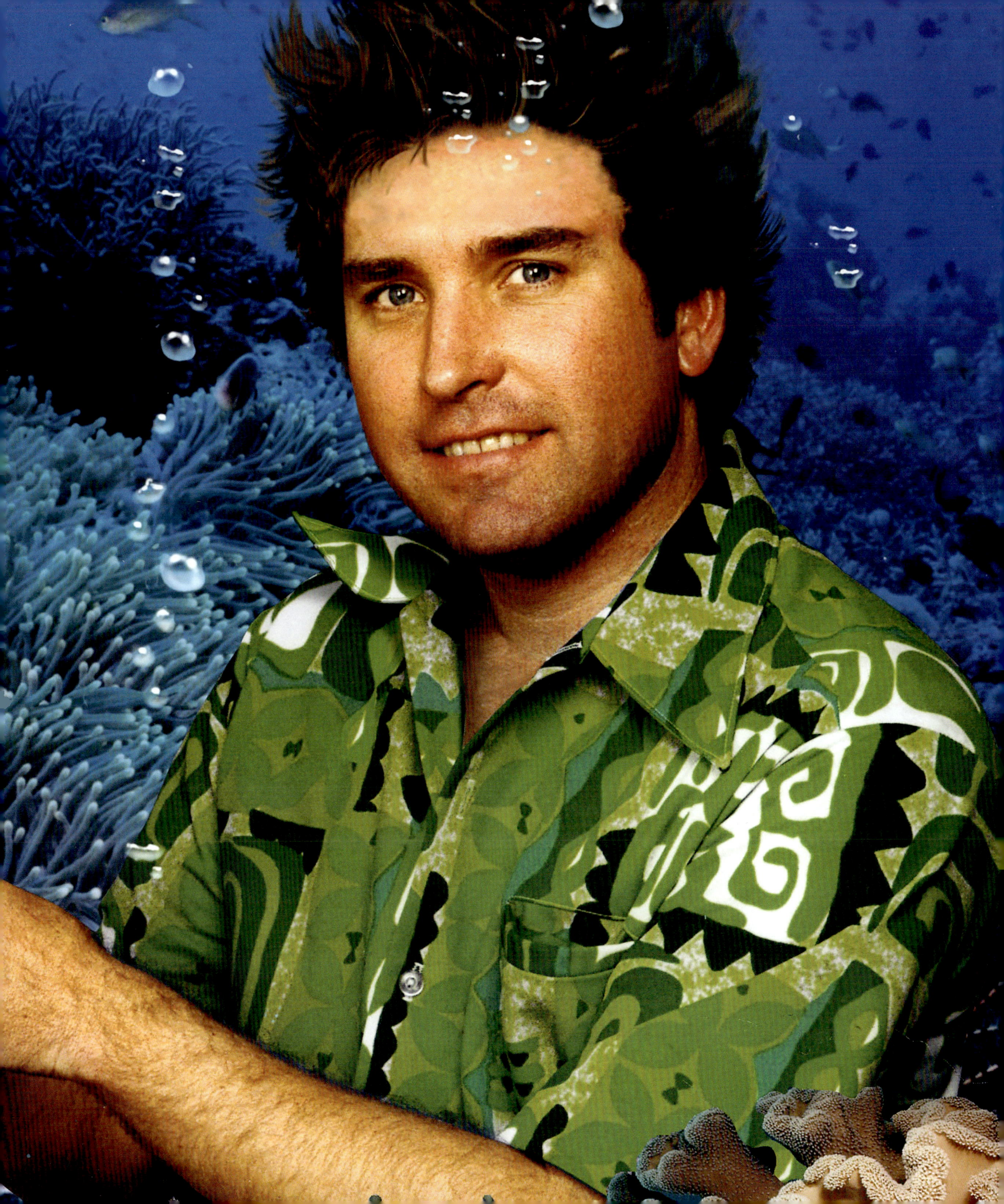

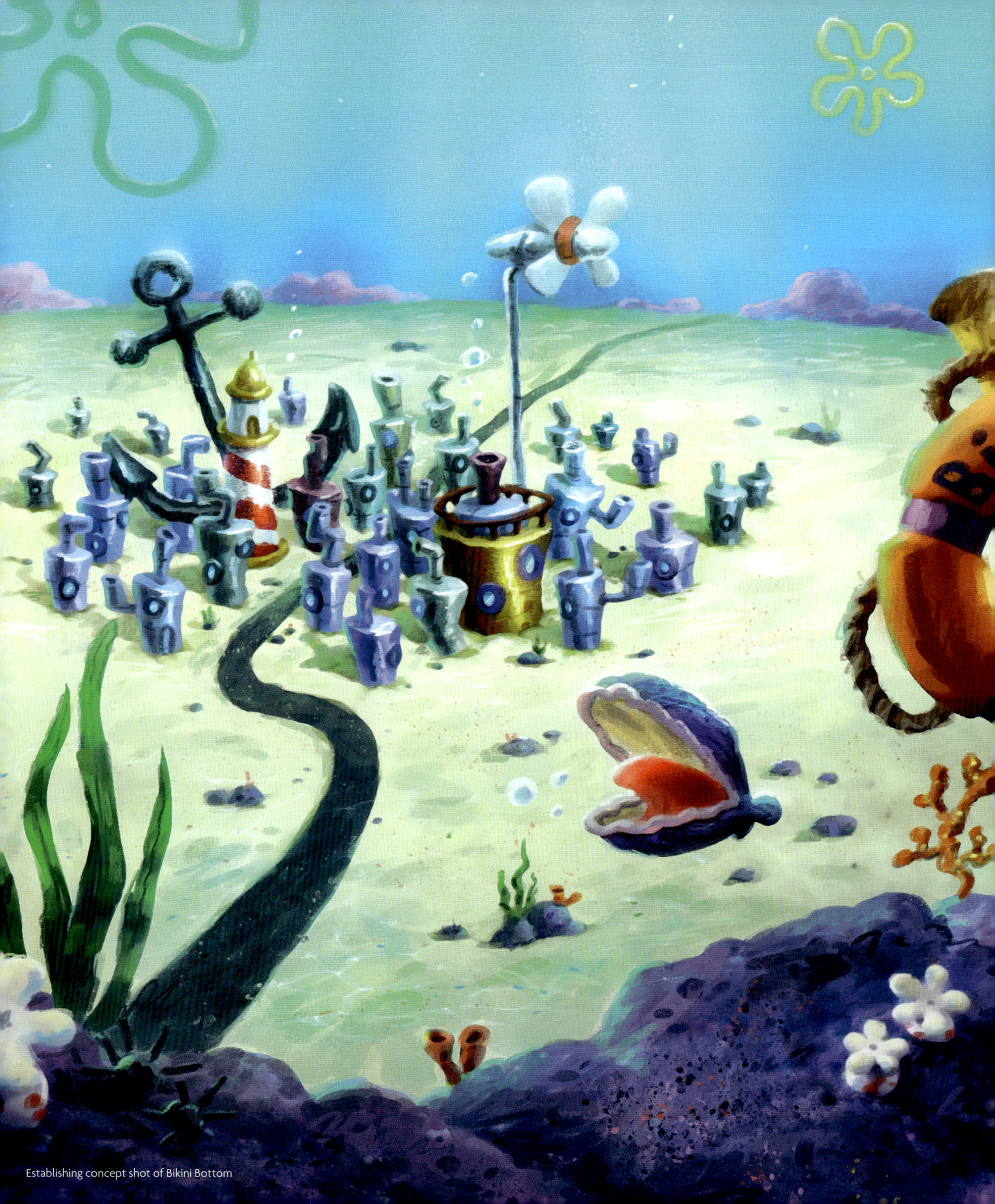
Establishing concept shot of Bikini Bottom

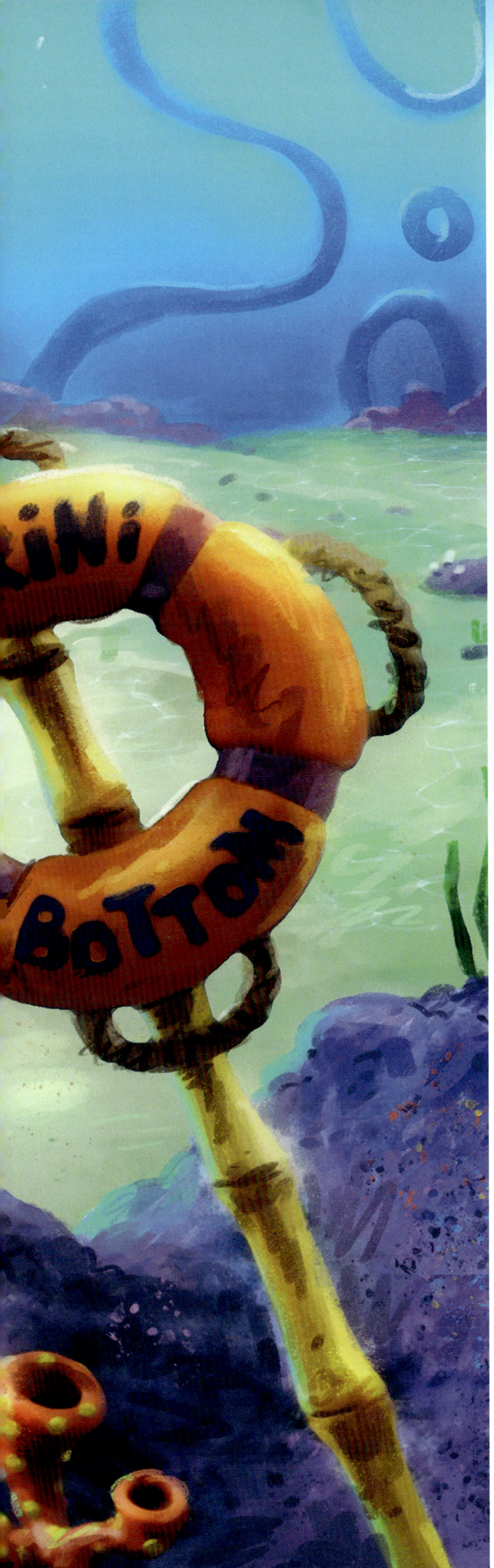

AHOY, READERS!

It's hard to believe, but there was a time when SpongeBob SquarePants didn't exist.

Back in 1996, Stephen Hillenburg and I were on different shows but worked in the same building on Vineland Avenue. I'd drop by his office every once in a while to say hi. I knew Steve was working on an idea for a show, but everybody was working on an idea for a show back then.

It wasn't unusual for his desk to be covered with drawings sketched on Post-it Notes. That's how he worked: patiently, methodically, one idea at a time until he figured out whatever problem he was trying to crack. In those days, he was working on his main character, an amorphous sea sponge. A blobby little guy named SpongeBoy wearing pants and a tie. Funny and weird, like Steve.

But he wasn't happy with it yet, so he kept sketching and sketching (and sketching).

I had never met anyone like Steve. Everyone else I knew in animation was heavily inspired by things like Disney and Looney Tunes, but Steve was very different. He was somewhere between a funny fine artist and a serious cartoonist. His drawings were smudgy, and his student films were weird and experimental, not anything like you'd see on Saturday morning at the time.

He had a vision for an animated show that took place in a tide pool. It wasn't completely formed yet, but the word he kept coming back to was DIFFERENT. He wanted to create something new, something unique, something he hadn't seen on TV before.

Later, original *SpongeBob SquarePants* production designer Nick Jennings would tap into that spirit as well. Before getting into animation, Steve had spent a couple years painting. They were impressionistic canvases painted with thick brush strokes. The one I remember best had a human figure standing in a kitchen. On the table was a fish. (Of course there was a fish!)

Nick had the idea to use Steve's painting style as the basis for the show's backgrounds. One of Nick's countless contributions to *SpongeBob* was developing a painterly look to the backgrounds that set them apart from anything else on TV at the time.

Again, different.

The work in this book was born from Steve's desire to make something truly unique. The artists represented here shared Steve's vision and carried it further than even he could have imagined. *SpongeBob* is known for its silly and irreverent humor, but it's a beautifully designed show too. So deceptively simple, the art never gets in the way of the jokes. Nick always said that if he does his job right, then no one will notice. But it's worth noticing because the world Steve, Nick, and the entire *SpongeBob* crew created is gorgeous.

Going back to 1996 and that building on Vineland, I vividly remember the day I popped by Steve's office when he called me over to look at something he drew. People always ask me if I had any idea back then how big the show would become, and it always brings me back to that moment.

There, on a Post-it, he had doodled a square dish sponge wearing pants and a tie. So silly, so different—he nailed it.

And just like that, SpongeBob existed.

Derek Drymon
Director of *The SpongeBob Movie: Search for SquarePants*

INTRODUCTION

As SpongeBob SquarePants swims toward his third decade as an exuberant, omnipresent pop-culture bellwether, it almost seems like he's always been there—a permanent fixture. (For a whole swath of millennials and Gen Z-ers, he HAS!) But long before he existed as pixels on a screen, he existed on paper, in a dreamer's desk drawer.

The first time I ever looked SpongeBob in the eye was in the form of the expressive, idiosyncratic, deeply silly drawings of Stephen Hillenburg. It was love at first sight. Steve had assembled his "series bible" and was ready to pitch it to Nickelodeon. Steve observed that SB and I shared certain characteristics, and he cast me as the voice of his peppy poriferan protagonist right out of the starting gate. As a result of that, I count myself preternaturally lucky to have had a snail's-eye view of SB's creation and to have become close friends with Steve and the dedicated doulas he assembled to birth his briny brainchild.

And, man, what a talented team of graphic geniuses he put together! One picture is indeed worth a thousand words, and the artistry on view in this book speaks for itself. When *SpongeBob SquarePants* first premiered in 1999, none of us knew what we were in for. We were (and still are) a bunch of goofball artists, tasked with helping bring to life the world that Steve dreamed up: the colorful, sincere, supremely silly subaquatic suburb called Bikini Bottom.

The ear-to-ear grin on SpongeBob's face (which often resembles STEVE'S face, if you ask me) just radiates joy. Fans across the entire globe have responded to that and continue to do so. To paraphrase the show's "French Narrator": "Twenty-six years, sixteen seasons, four feature films, and one Broadway musical later," the cultural footprint of SpongeBob's squeaky black shoes continues to expand. When people meet me, it's quite common for them to say, "Tom Kenny?! You're SpongeBob!" I know what they're trying to say, but I always explain that while I VOICE SpongeBob, and have shared a brain with him since 1999, Stephen Hillenburg CREATED him. The same people often ask me why I think SpongeBob has lasted this long, when so many other things have come and gone. The only answer I have is that he makes people feel good. I meet fans who watched SpongeBob as kids and now watch with their own children, along with said tykes' grandparents, and sometimes even great-grandparents! We've been through a lot together, and people really open up to me about it in myriad very affecting ways: "Thank you for my childhood." "SpongeBob was my comfort food during a tough time." "I first bonded with my best friend because we both loved SpongeBob." And this one hit me square in my heart: "Your voice was more present in my house than my parents' voices were." For that person, somewhere along the way SpongeBob "moved up" from being mere entertainment and became something more... companionship. It blows my mind when I think about the fact that SpongeBob has morphed into a Krabby Patty Combo Meal of multigenerational in-joke, secret language, and safe haven.

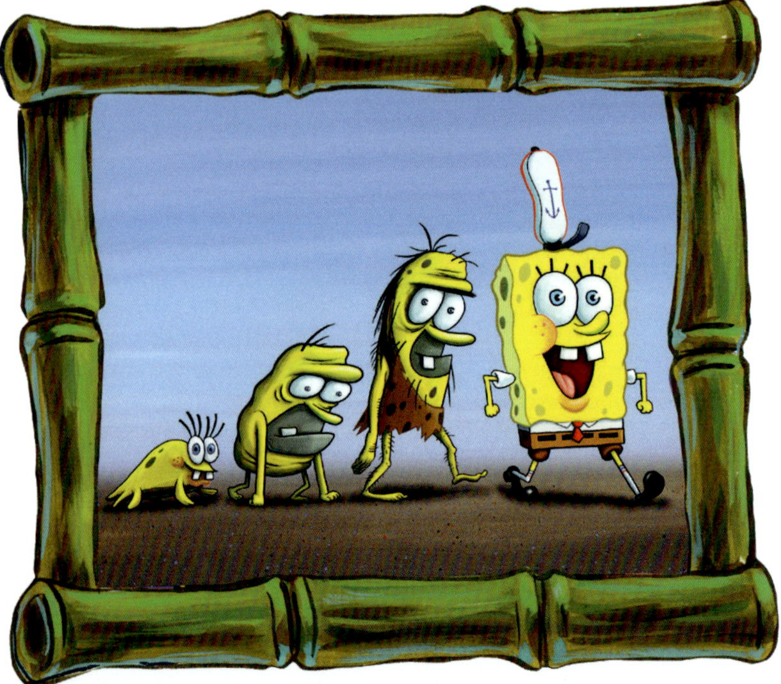

I assure you, I wake up every single day honored to be SpongeBob's voice box (and voice director), 100 percent certain that I indeed have the best job in the world. That's the gift Stephen Hillenburg handed to me, and I hear constantly about the gift he handed SpongeBob's still-developing viewers: A world where kindness is cool, and a hero whose superpower is jubilation. SpongeBob is optimism in dorky tube socks. SpongeBob believes that every day is going to be the "best day ever," and that even everyday mundanities are worth celebrating, loudly and without self-consciousness.

SpongeBob doesn't get steamrolled by naysayers and bullies; he disarms them with a firehose of unstoppable positivity and a belief in people's best instincts. SpongeBob is utterly incapable of being other than exactly who he is. I guess some of that has rubbed off on me over the years. I consider everybody who works in the "SpongeBob-iverse" to be part of one big creative family. Cast and crew bring their collective protean talents to the visual, aural, musical canvas of Bikini Bottom, making each character nuance and dumb joke live and breathe. This book is a tribute to the gift that Stephen Hillenburg gave the world, and the team he assembled to deliver it.

Steve's imagination built the ocean floor we're still walking on. His sunny high tide has raised ALL our boats. Despite the unavoidable daily horrors of this dysfunctional surface world, somewhere deep under the sea, HOPE is still alive and bubbling in Bikini Bottom.

As SpongeBob would say: "I-I-I-I'm READY!!!!"

Tom Kenny
Voice of SpongeBob SquarePants

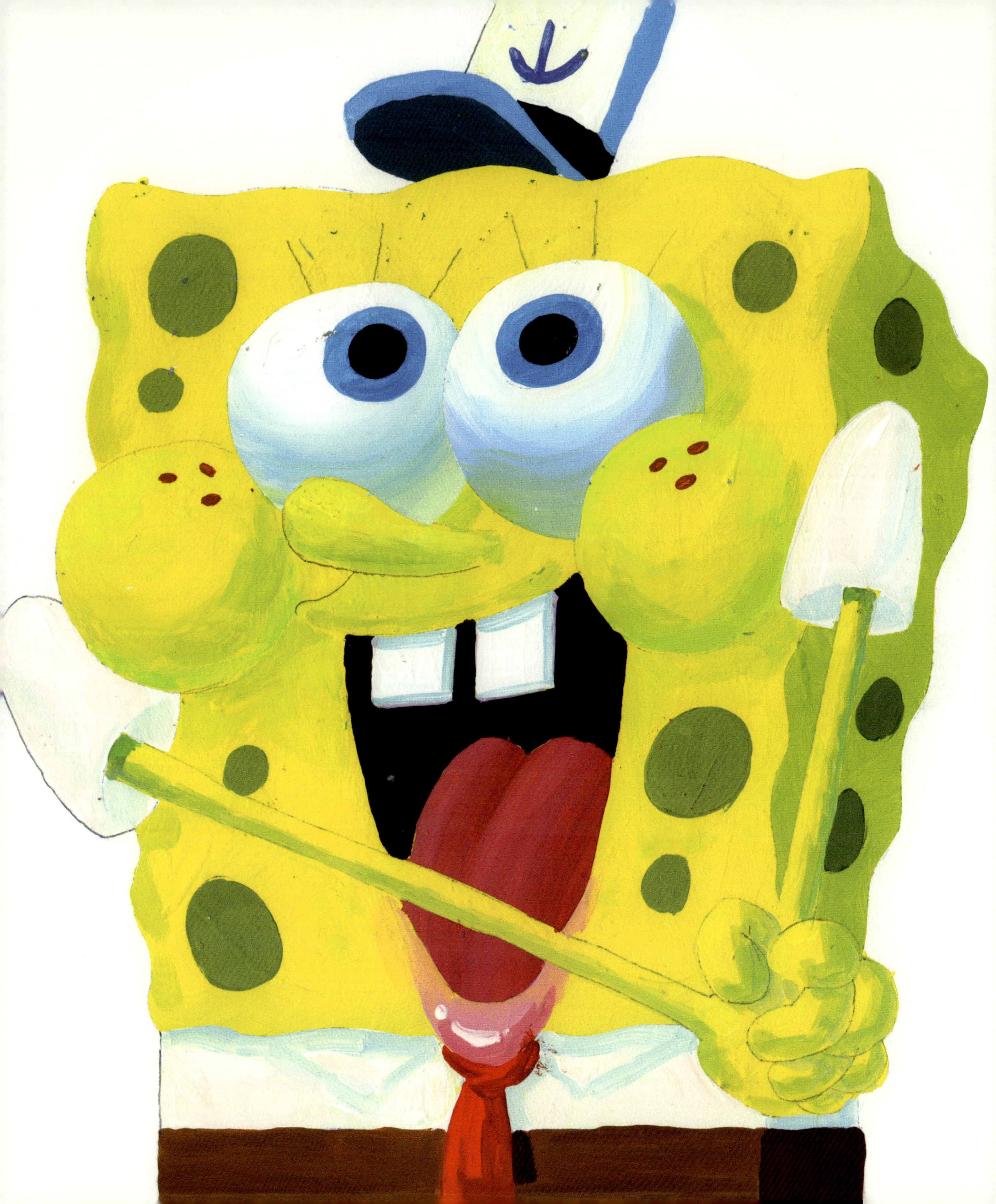

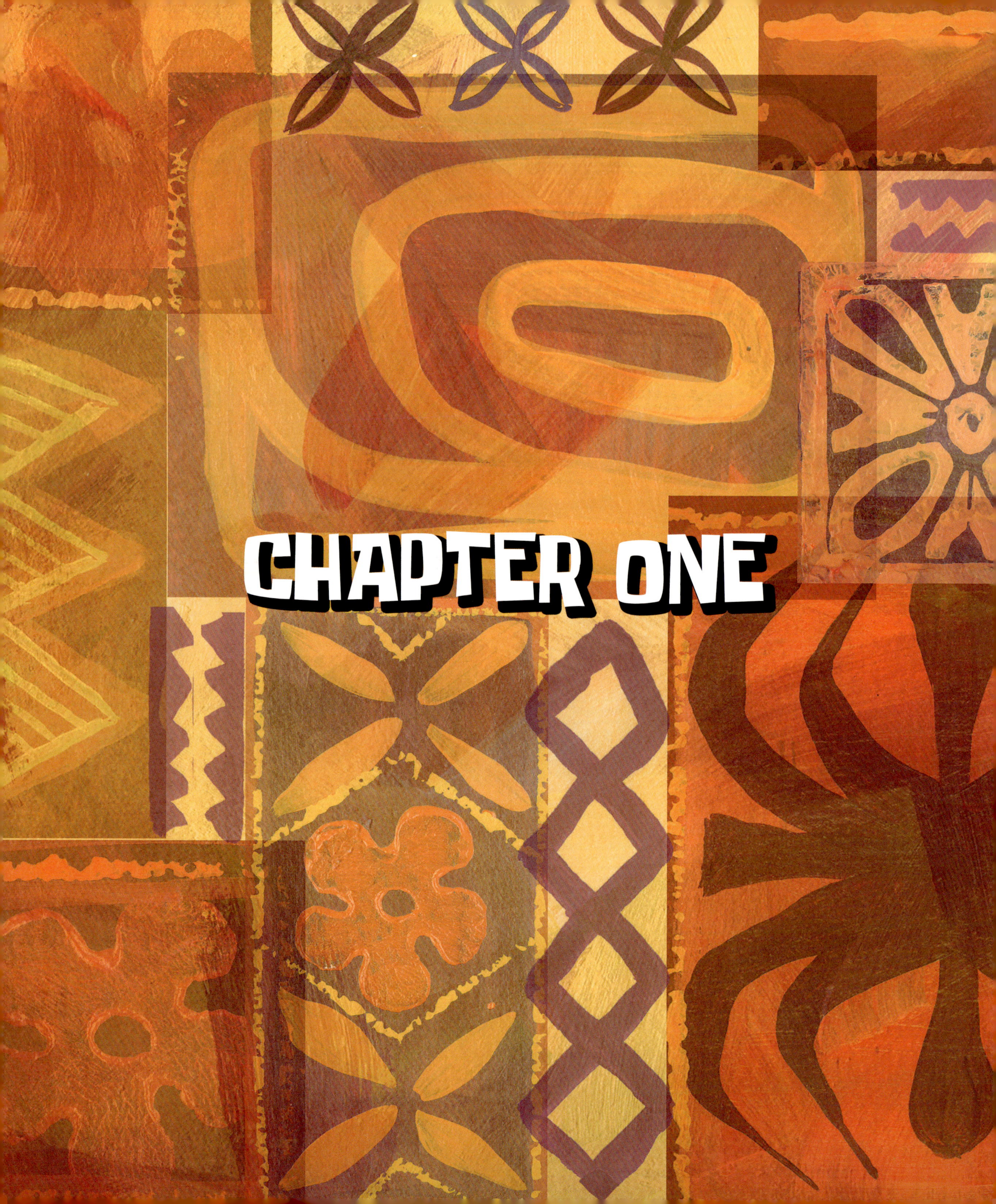

CHAPTER ONE

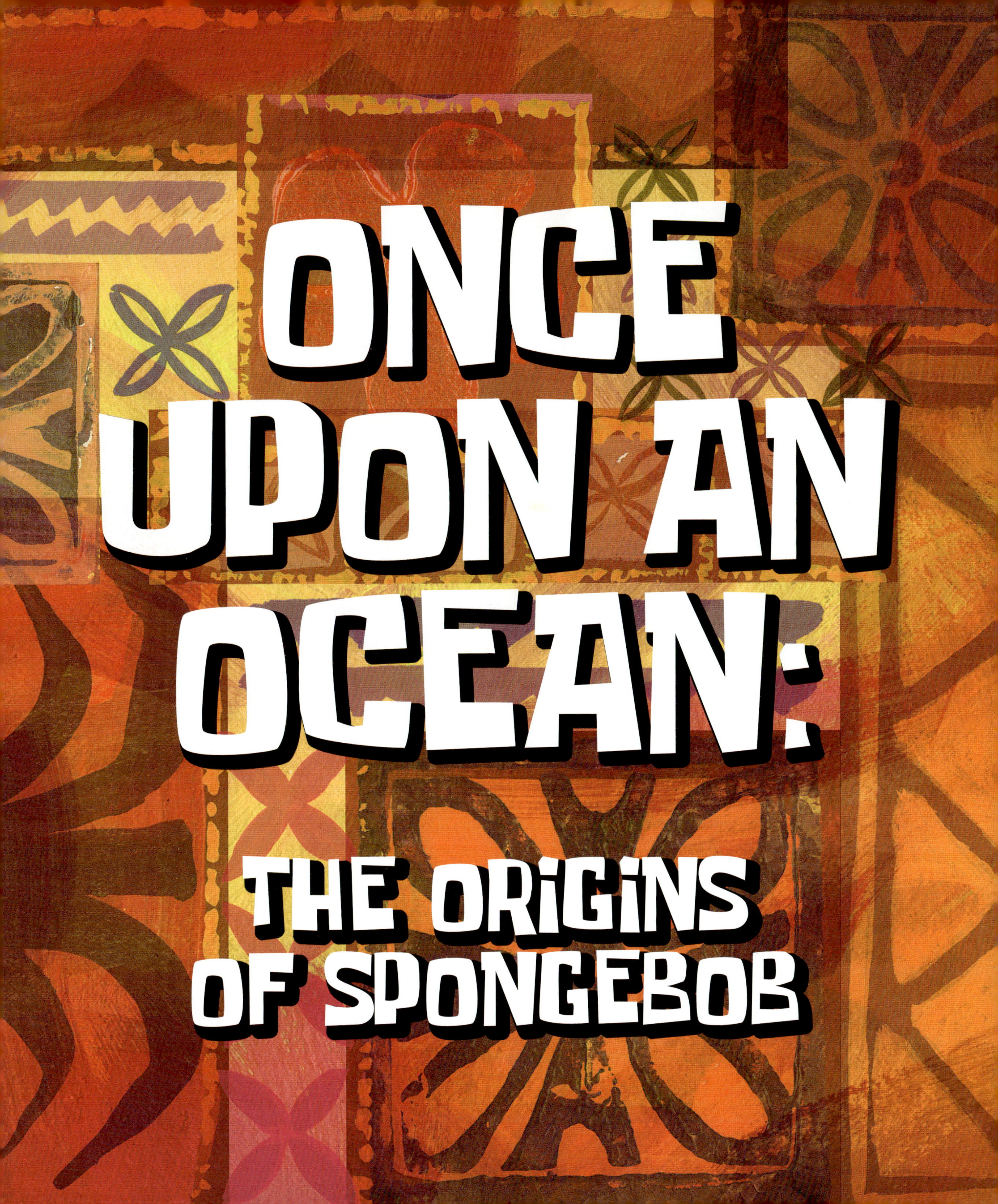
ONCE
UPON AN
OCEAN:
THE ORIGINS
OF SPONGEBOB

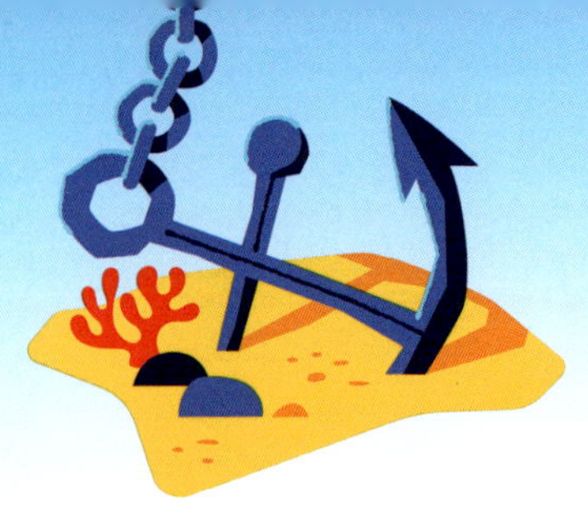

ARE YE READY, KIDS?

Multiple generations of audiences have been asked this simple question, and the clear answer has been a strongly energetic "YES!" ever since May 1, 1999, when Nickelodeon previewed three episodes of *SpongeBob SquarePants* during the Kids' Choice Awards. The legacy of animated, light-hearted fun that exists in Bikini Bottom and on infinite screens of all sizes around the globe still holds close to the wellspring that started it all—creative genius Stephen Hillenburg, whose unique love of both marine life and art continues to send ripples into today's culture over a quarter century later.

Tom Kenny, the voice of SpongeBob SquarePants, shares, "I had no idea it would still be around in twenty-five years. But I knew that I wanted to be involved in it because it was such good stuff coming from Stephen Hillenburg's brain and hand." *SpongeBob SquarePants* stands as one of the most widely distributed properties in Paramount International history, seen in more than 180 markets, translated into 30+ languages, and averaging more than 100 million total viewers every quarter as of 2025. Says executive producer Marc Ceccarelli, "We just try to keep a continuity of character and personality through all the mediums they're presented in. This can be difficult with such a large and popular franchise. But it's always been a mandate that was pushed by Steve from the very beginning."

Born far from the ocean in Oklahoma on August 21, 1961, Stephen Hillenburg moved to California with his family in the mid-1960s, a shift that gave him the opportunity to grow up playing on Southern California beaches and learning to snorkel and scuba dive. His immersive ocean experience, combined with all the eye-opening Jacques Cousteau television programming he watched in his youth, inspired Hillenburg to study marine biology at Humboldt State University (now called California State Polytechnic University, Humboldt).

Hillenburg's post-college journey started with employment at the Ocean Institute in Dana Point, California (previously known as the Orange County Marine Institute), where he did everything from teaching marine biology to working as a "sailor" on the tall ship *Pilgrim* to singing sea shanties with visiting youngsters to channeling

"Evolution Chart" leading to the creation of SpongeBoy

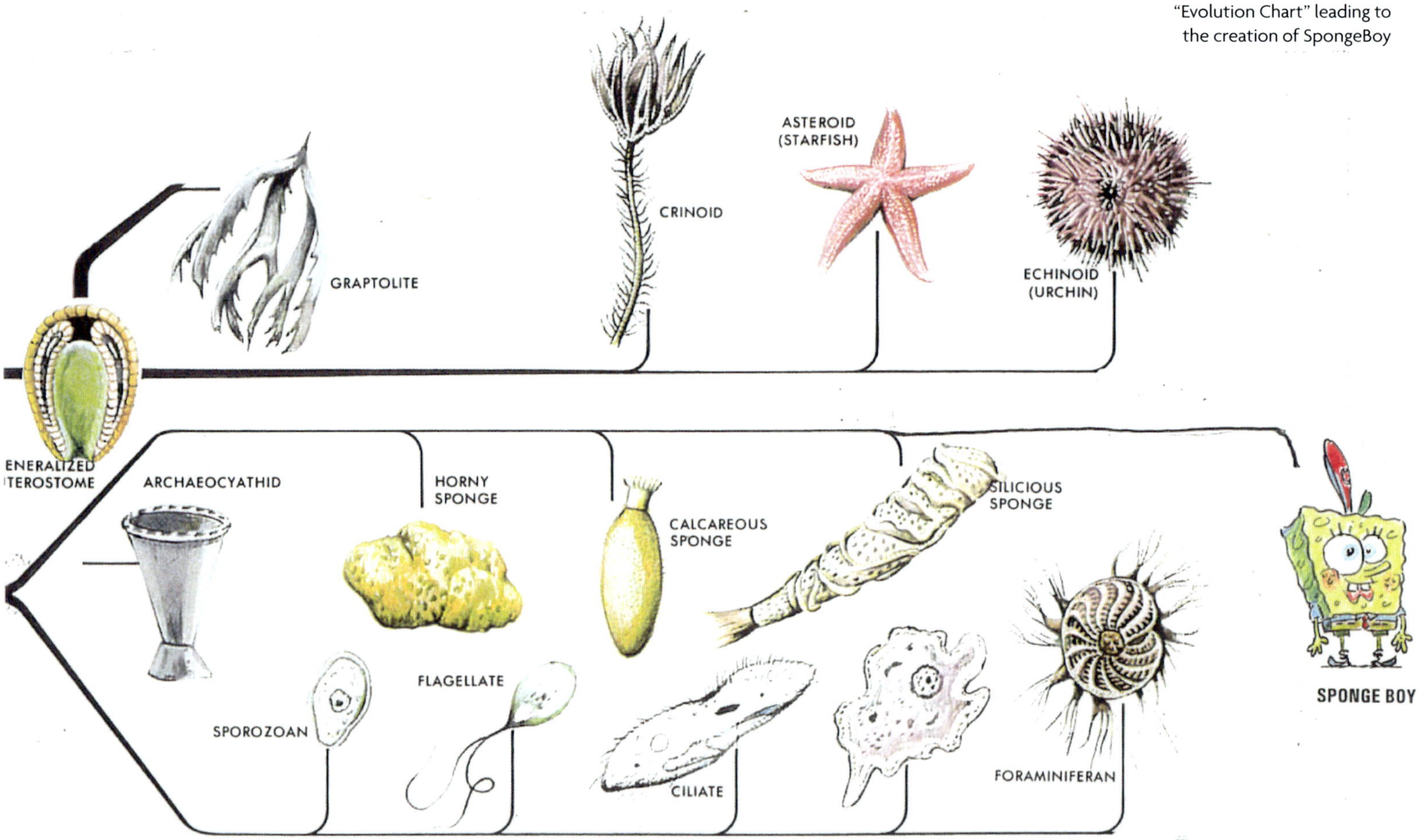

GRAPTOLITE
CRINOID
ASTEROID (STARFISH)
ECHINOID (URCHIN)
ENERALIZED TEROSTOME
ARCHAEOCYATHID
HORNY SPONGE
CALCAREOUS SPONGE
SILICIOUS SPONGE
SPOROZOAN
FLAGELLATE
CILIATE
FORAMINIFERAN
SPONGE BOY

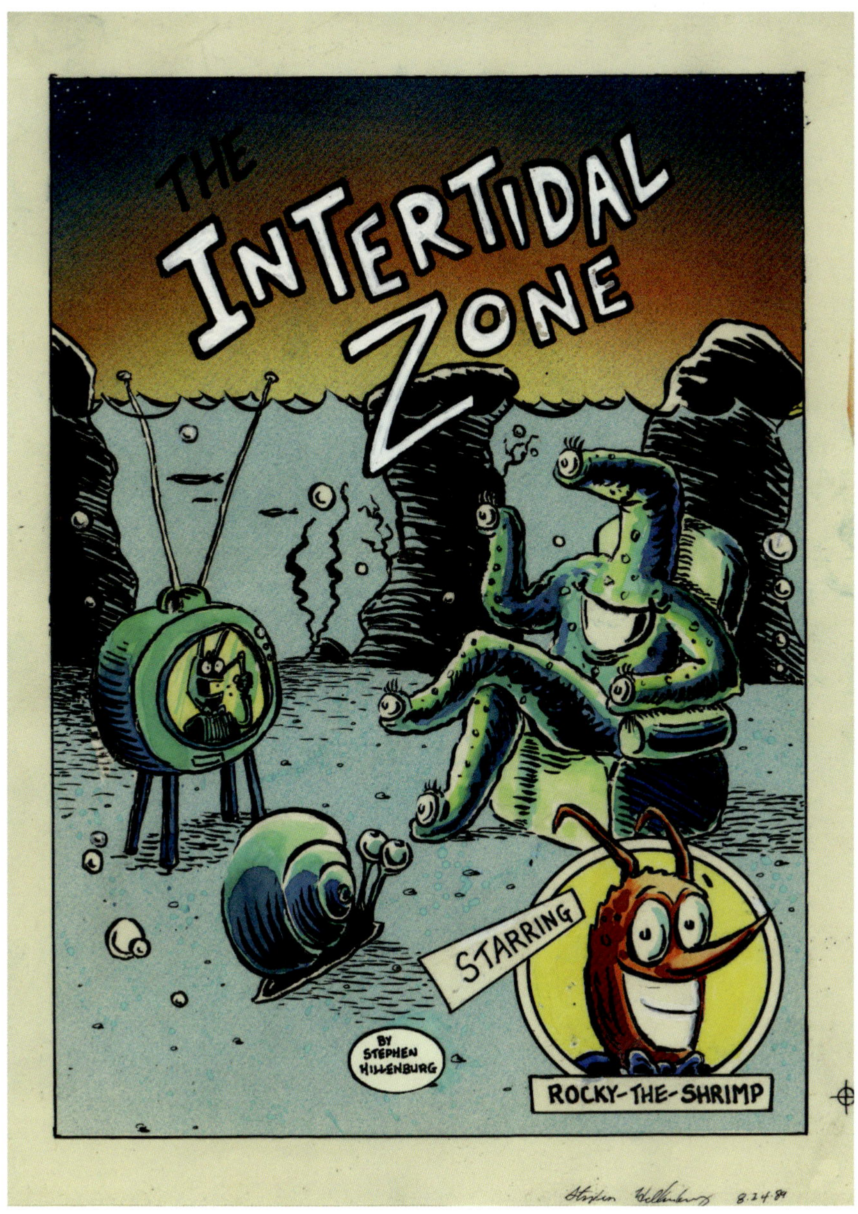

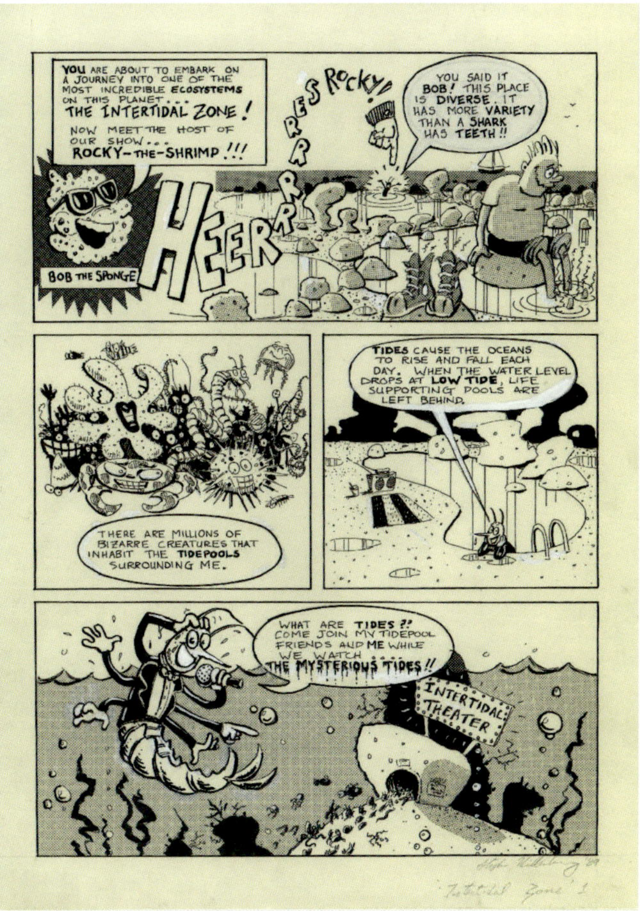

Layouts from Stephen Hillenburg's science comic adventure *The Intertidal Zone*

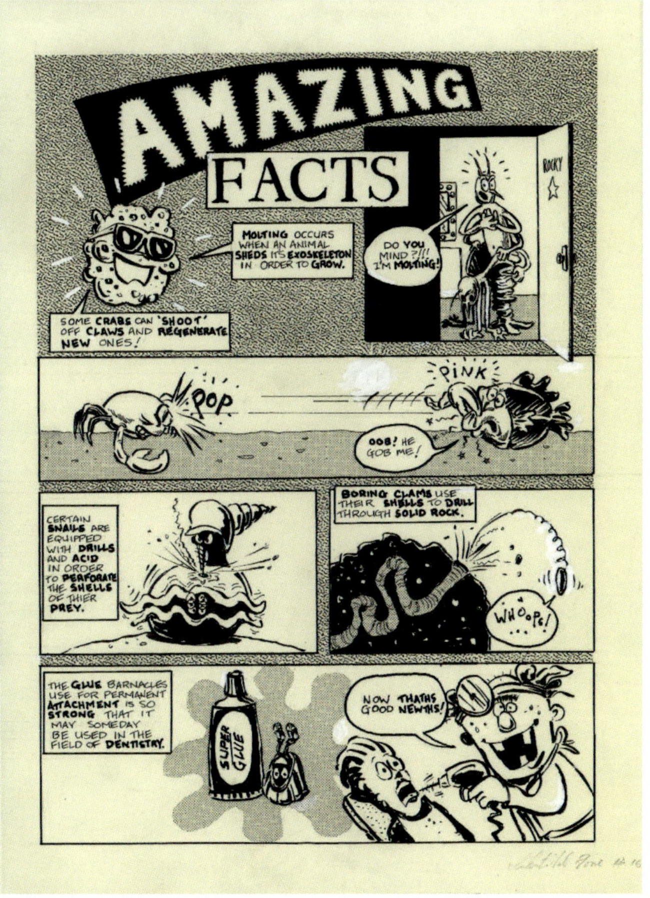

his artistic talents into crafting an educational comic book called *The Intertidal Zone*. Throughout his youth, Hillenburg had also enjoyed drawing and watching animation, with his attendance at the International Tournée of Animation festival in the 1970s making quite an impression on him, but he rationalized that perhaps it might be smarter to keep art as a passion and study something else for a career path.

Eventually, the siren call to art became stronger than he could ignore, luring Hillenburg to study at the California Institute for the Arts in 1989. During his MFA program in Experimental Animation, Hillenburg studied under the mentorship of pioneer Jules Engel and came to consider him as his "Art Dad." As his graduate thesis production, Hillenburg crafted a six-minute film, *Wormholes*, which opened the door for him to join the team of *Rocko's Modern Life* at Nickelodeon—a move that eventually brought all of his passions into focus at the right time and place. "Martin Olson [one of the *Rocko's* writers] saw that comic book that I made at the Marine Institute in a pile of stuff on my desk and started shouting, 'What are you, crazy? This is your show!' I finally saw, at age thirty-two, the possibility of dovetailing my love of both animation and marine biology," recalled Hillenburg.

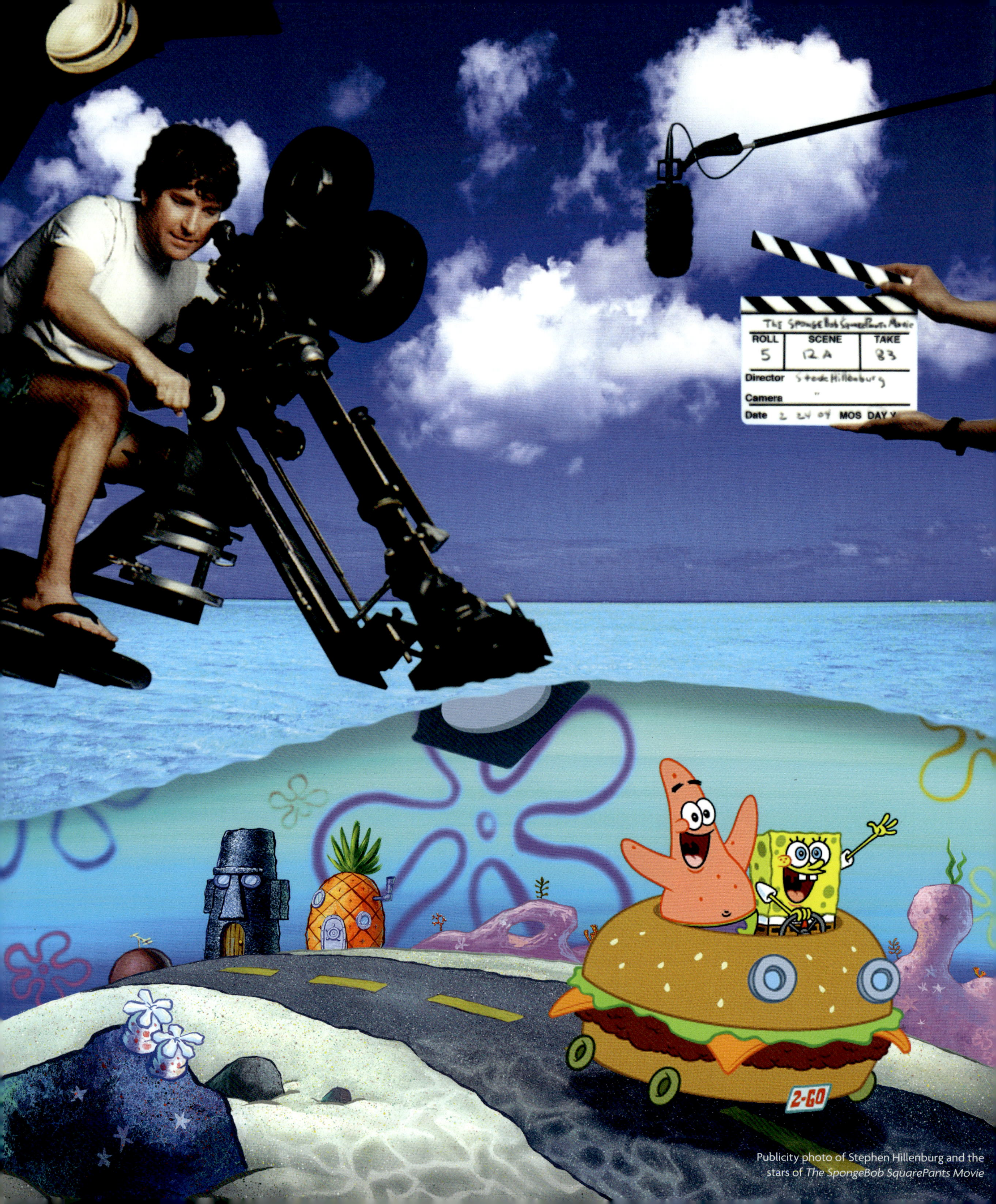

Publicity photo of Stephen Hillenburg and the stars of *The SpongeBob SquarePants Movie*

The *SpongeBoy, Ahoy!* pitch to Nickelodeon executives involved a thoughtfully crafted aquarium housing models of the characters, with Hawaiian music setting the tone and Hawaiian-shirt-sporting Hillenburg delivering the setup. As a result, a figurative treasure box opened, granting funding and two weeks to return with the blueprints for a pilot episode, the terms of which Hillenburg, Derek Drymon, Tim Hill, and Nick Jennings fulfilled to great laughter in their storyboard pitch for "Help Wanted." Former art director Nick Jennings shares, "The amount of talent, creativity, and imagination of everybody involved was unsurpassed. Steve Hillenburg was a true genius, whose passion for the sea and cartoons brought together one of the greatest animated series ever." Adds creative director Derek Drymon, "Steve was such a funny guy, such a good joke writer... and when you work with people that are really good, really better than you, it forces you to get your A game on."

With *SpongeBob SquarePants* greenlit, Hillenburg assumed the role of captain of a ship carrying charismatically crazy characters born out of loving, humor-centric simplicity, navigating unexpected twists and turns in timeless storytelling... and better yet, he created a space in which the boat has stayed afloat with a mix of artistic and well-voiced crew for decades, even when he was no longer manning the helm. "Steve was pretty careful not to compromise the integrity of the main characters he created, and that tradition has endured to this day," says former director Tim Hill. Adds Paul Tibbitt, former executive producer, "Hillenburg was very careful to make sure jokes and references came from the world he built and not our world or culture. The more insulated the better. However, if the joke was funny, he was always willing to stretch the boundaries of his own rules. If the joke made him laugh hard enough, it was in."

The longevity of visual and vocal talent aboard ship has supported creative buoyancy through the years. With Hillenburg keeping watch throughout the first two decades and recruiting other key creators and artists, including Derek Drymon, Nick Jennings, Tim Hill, Dave Cunningham, Alan Smart, Peter Bennett, Sherm Cohen, Aaron Springer, Kaz, Paul Tibbitt, Vincent Waller, Mr. Lawrence, Erik Wiese, Marc Ceccarelli, and others to go along for the journey, the characters and vibe of Bikini Bottom have had a vital tether back to their source all along. Background painter Lucy Tanashian-Gentry says, "Peter Bennett started as a background painter in 1999 on the series and then stepped into the role of art director around

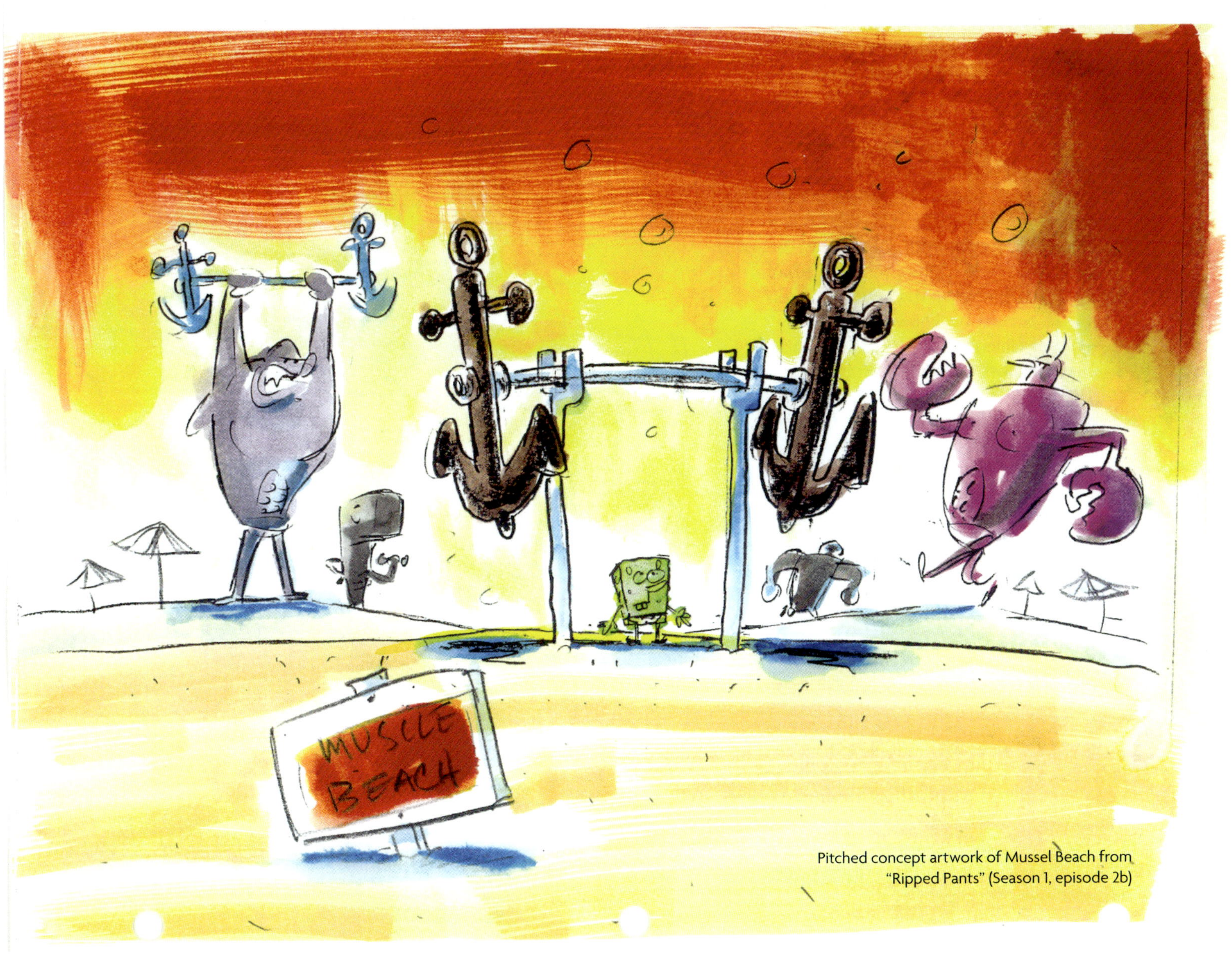

Pitched concept artwork of Mussel Beach from "Ripped Pants" (Season 1, episode 2b)

2005. Peter was truly the heart of SpongeBob visual identity. His work played a defining role in shaping the show's color world and artistic style. Peter wasn't just an incredible artist; he was a beautiful human being." Jennie Monica, vice president of animation production, adds, "Steve was so passionate and formed such an amazing crew that you could feel that passion and creativity in every phase. That energy made its way into every episode."

Meanwhile, the core cast of actor talent has given voice to key characters through multiple mediums since the last century, breathing life and consistency into their entertaining existence. Says Vincent Waller, executive producer, "Steve did an outstanding job of putting together our cast of characters and handpicking our actors who voice them. They are truly the gift that keeps on giving." The cast themselves all fondly recall their experiences being chosen by and working with Stephen Hillenburg, Tom Kenny in particular reminiscing about Steve saying "You kind of are SpongeBob: hyperactive, work your ass off, always trying to look at the sunny side of things. You laugh like him, you think like him, you cry like him. You're SpongeBob." Fellow vocal talent Bill Fagerbakke, who voices Patrick Star, says, "I was just blown away by this creation that Hillenburg had executed—this magic carpet of creativity and humor and wit and rhythm and characters weaving together to respond to each other in such a wonderful, engaging way." Rodger Bumpass, voice of Squidward, adds, "That was the cool thing about Steve—he had the concept. He had everything in his mind. And when the right execution came out from his actors, he knew it right away." Once in the studio, Hillenburg's process was also impactful, as Clancy Brown, voice of Mr. Krabs, notes, "Stephen started out in the booth. I'd never had a creator or a director sit in on the recording. In terms of having fun, it really did stand out... we had a lot of fun recording the pilot, and it's always been fun. It's never not been fun." The dual-duty creator and voice talent Mr. Lawrence shares a fun fact: "I actually read for SpongeBob with the Plankton voice—and I knew that wasn't going to be SpongeBob's voice. But Steve heard it, and we were laughing, and Steve said, 'If I had any guts at all, I would push to make that the voice of SpongeBob. That would be so silly and funny and a really over-the-top choice.' After we got a chance to refine what we wanted to do, Steve was like, 'You know, I think that might be Plankton.'" And Carolyn Lawrence, who provides the voice of Sandy Cheeks, observes, "The world that Steve Hillenburg created that is *SpongeBob* is so rich in loyalty and happiness and friendship. That's been a huge gift. It's really fun to play somebody who gets to be as fully capable as they are, because in real life, a lot of times, society limits whatever that capability is."

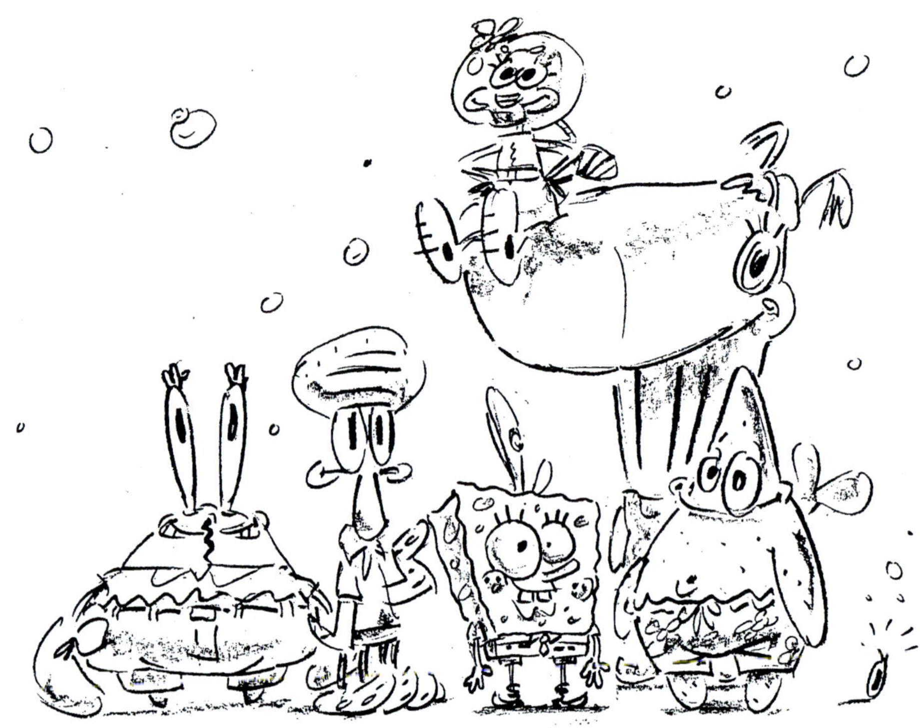

SpongeBoy, Ahoy! early character art of Sandy Cheeks, Pearl, Mr. Krabs, Squidward, SpongeBoy, and Patrick

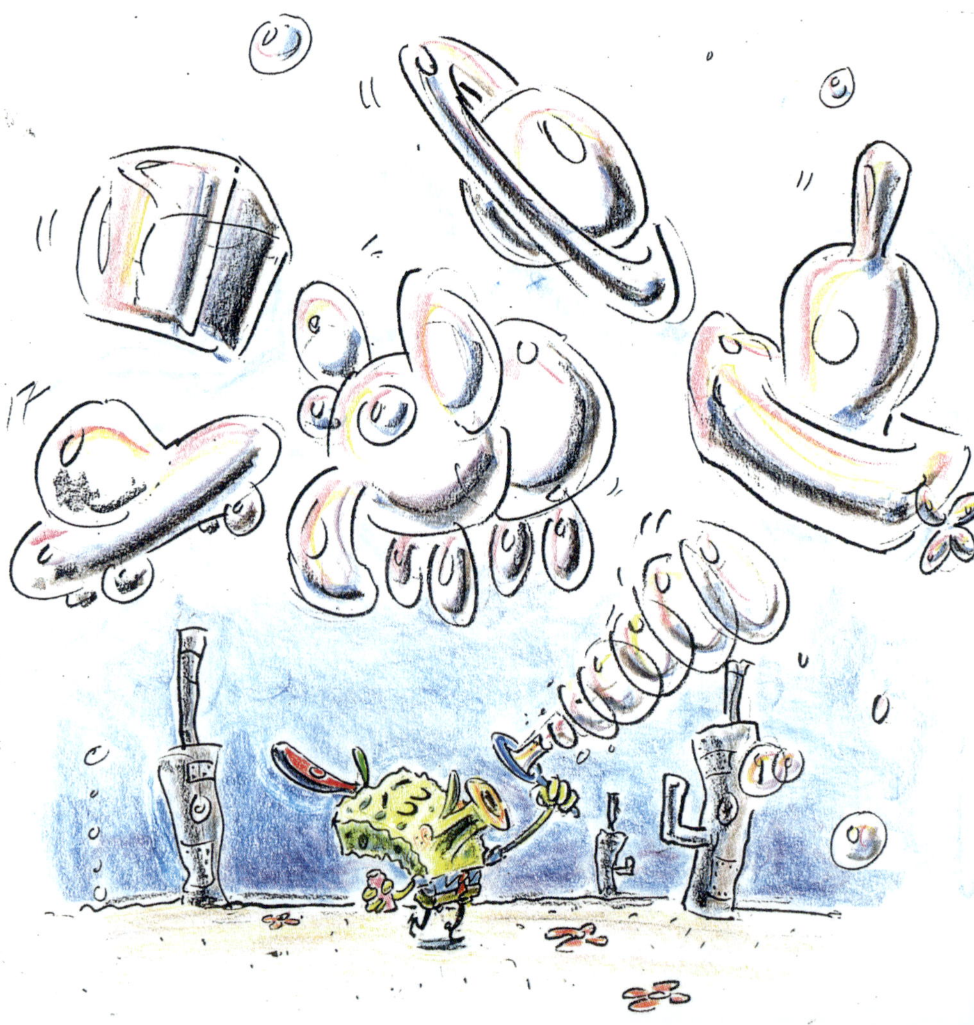

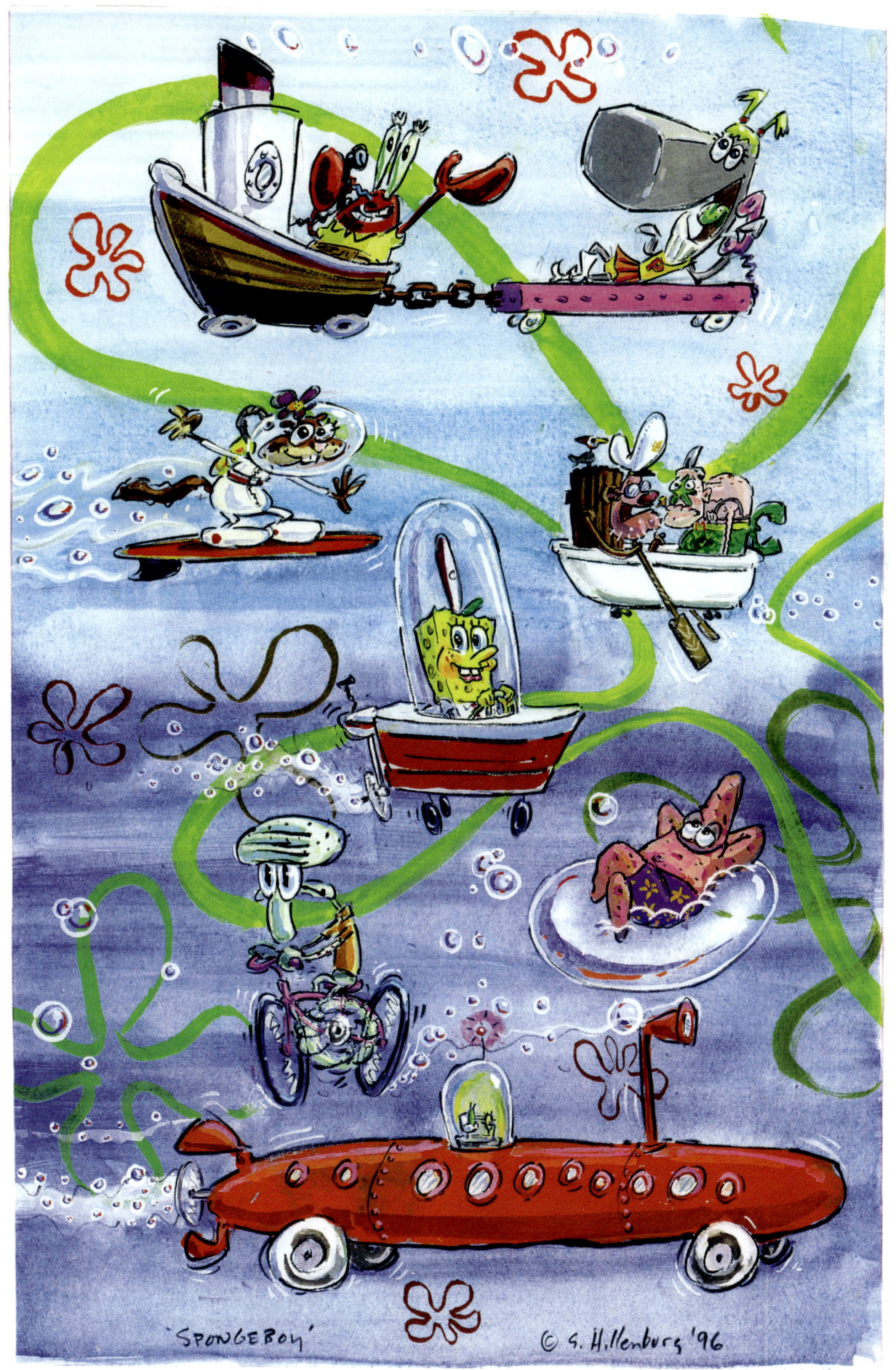

SpongeBoy, Ahoy! pitched character art of Mr. Krabs with Pearl, Sandy Cheeks, Barnacle Boy & Mermaid Man, SpongeBoy, Squidward, Patrick, and Plankton and Karen

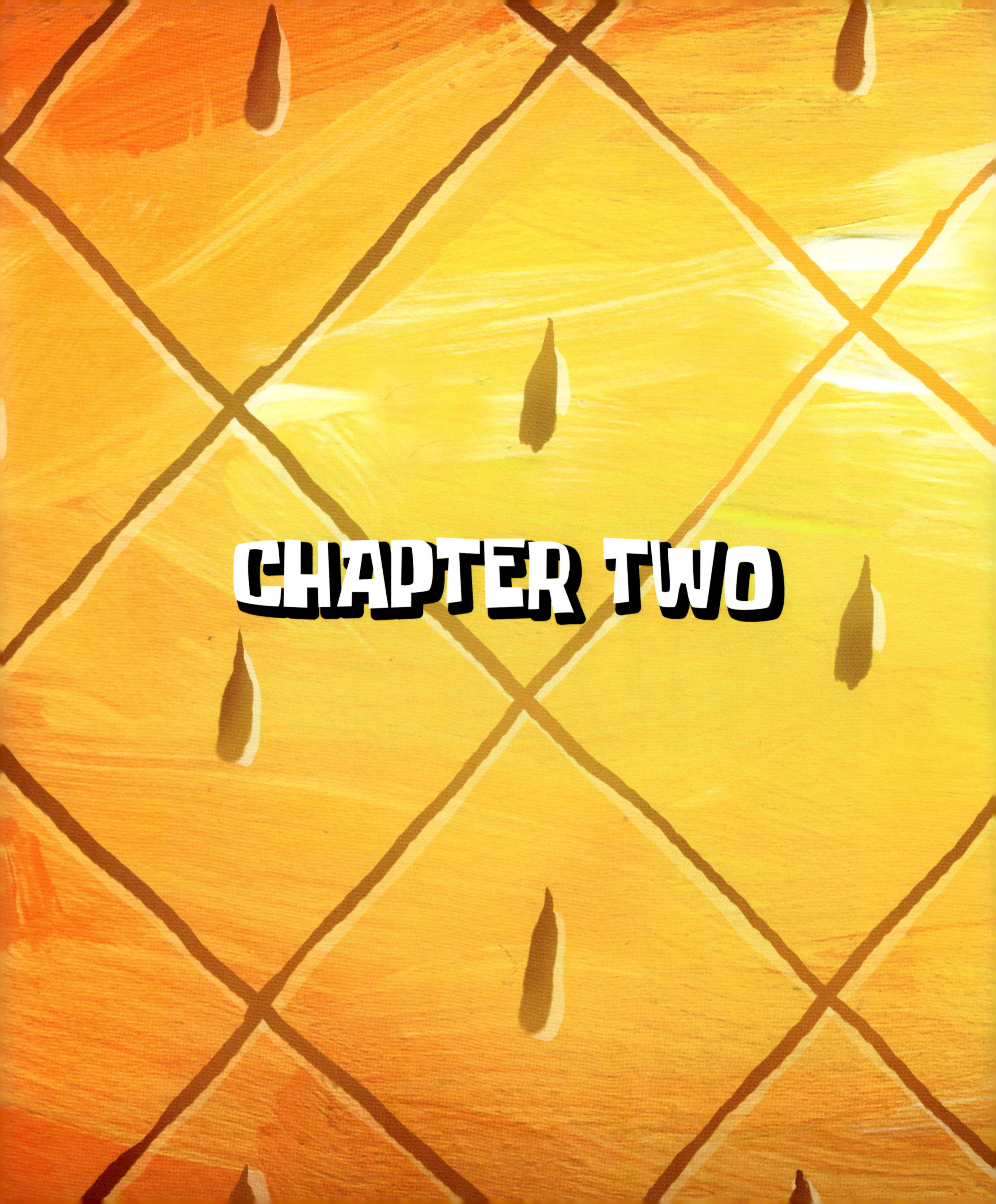

CHAPTER TWO

BIG SPLASH ON THE SMALL SCREEN:

TELEVISION LEGACY

nickelodeon™

SpongeBob

SQUAREPANTS™

“SpongeBob came from the mind and vision of Steve Hillenburg, whose distinctive sense of character, humor, tone, and world-building set a new standard in our industry. In many ways, it defined what Nickelodeon would become,” says Ramsey Naito, former president of Nickelodeon Animation & Paramount Animation. Former executive in charge Claudia Spinelli wholeheartedly agrees, adding that “*SpongeBob* became the quintessential Nicktoon. It was creator-driven, based on personal experiences and knowledge about the subjects, it broke from the herd and took creative risks, the characters were strongly defined, and they drove their stories while they simultaneously made us feel for them and care deeply about them.”

To date, more than three hundred episodes of *SpongeBob SquarePants* have aired, spanning sixteen seasons over the course of twenty-six years… and yet the show seems as timeless as ever. “I think overall, our characters have remained true to their original concepts. Where they have evolved is in their relationships to each other, as well as their backstories,” notes executive producer Vincent Waller. The cast of characters wear their emotions and motivations on their sleeves, even if they don’t technically have sleeves, playing out stories that lean into their innate complexity. “We know and anticipate what a character will say or how they will react—and that becomes part of the fabric of the show,” adds writer Mr. Lawrence. Agelessly, SpongeBob and his neighbors continue to explore new scenarios and occasionally encounter new characters, and while they consciously don’t encounter current worldly scenarios, stories may play out with undertones that speak to the heart of current world situations, treating them more like a parable. “SpongeBob is both very strange and very familiar. You recognize people and feelings you know, but the setting and rules of the world are otherworldly, so there is a slightly disorienting aspect to it,” says former executive producer Paul Tibbitt. Most importantly, the series is about fun, and trying to make people laugh. “It’s a cartoony cartoon that draws its humor, surreal gags, and deeply felt funny emotions from zany everyday conflicts,” explains writer Kaz.

As true as the ocean is deep, the creators of SpongeBob have done a great job with pacing themselves to the way that audiences may change, shifting with the tide to keep the show fresh and relevant, yet immersed in its essence, down to the brine. “There’s such an appreciation toward classic cartoons and gags, and after all this time, nobody is letting off the gas. They still want to make the best and funniest show possible,” adds prop designer Isaac Marzioli.

Part of the magic of keeping the series true to its essence springs from keeping its environment the colorful, welcoming space audiences new and old have come to love. “From the beginning, the phrase ‘nautical nonsense’ and the tiki aesthetic were always the guiding principles when it came to designing backgrounds on the show. But in every way, the world of SpongeBob SquarePants is simply fun,” explains supervising producer Kenny Pittenger. The setting “takes things we are familiar with and collides them with an underwater, beachy, surf style. All the designs are nautical based, emphasizing bright colors, loose linework, and rich, colorful textures. It reminds you of how you felt when you’d go to the beach as a kid. It’s not trying to be sophisticated, but instead confidently tries to be silly,” adds former art director Nick Jennings. Even the loose and colorful painting style has a subconscious effect on the viewer, since in “the alla prima style… with the squiggly linework, the environments look like you are viewing them underwater,” Jennings continues.

From a visual perspective, the artistic team keeps the spirit of experimentalism alive within the series, creating opportunities to weave in different mediums. Right from the start of using a realistic talking fish and Painty the Pirate in the theme song, live-action inserts have been woven into the fabric of the show. “Live-action inclusions go back to the Monty Python inspiration, plus other shows we grew up with that have the host dynamic [*Diver Dan, Mister Rogers’ Neighborhood*], or puppets [*Sesame Street, Electric Company*]… that’s where Patchy came from, wanting to have somebody who’s the host of a local show with as low production value as possible,” says writer Mr. Lawrence. “All the different formats—whether it be basic stick puppets, live-action photo collage, CG animation, stop-motion, or anything else—offer different benefits and are chosen based on the circumstance. Within the main show, we tend to use more live-action photo collage and basic ‘homemade’-looking mediums, because that is what the show has always done. But within the specials and spinoff series you see more stop-motion and CG,” explains supervising director Dave Cunningham. Regardless of what medium in which a SpongeBob story is told, “people seem to think that anything can happen in SpongeBob’s world, but that’s not true at all. It’s a semirealistic place that obeys the rules of gravity and physics; it’s actually very similar to the world we live in. There’s only one character that can make anything happen, and that’s SpongeBob,” adds creative director Derek Drymon.

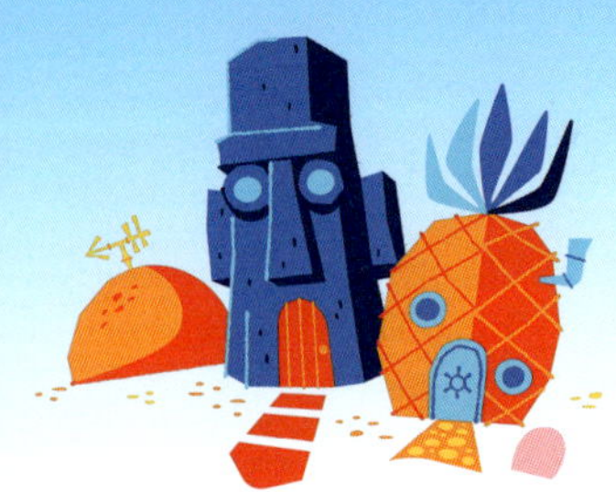

THE RESIDENTS OF BIKINI BOTTOM

SPONGEBOB SQUAREPANTS

Although the earliest version of Stephen Hillenburg's sponge-based character was more natural in shape, as was appropriate for Bob the Sponge in his original educational purpose in *The Intertidal Zone* comic book, the animated version found visual humor instantly when SpongeBoy was designed based on a kitchen sponge. "When Steve first designed SpongeBob I thought: I'm not sure this character will work. His legs are so skinny, would you even be able to see the stripes on his socks? His detached sleeves up on his body seemed strange and awkward to me. His big, flat face, will a three-dimensional mouth work on that? Well, Steve was right and I was wrong," admits former animation supervisor Alan Smart. Personality-wise, the association with something clean and square fit the nerdy profile Hillenburg had in mind. Nick Jennings helped assign the perfect hue of yellow to SpongeBob (name change due to trademark concerns), and former character designer Todd White recalls that "we went through several revisions on SpongeBob's design, even changing his shape in the second season. Stephen wanted him more rectangle than the original square."

While the flatness of SpongeBob's face might seem challenging from an animation standpoint, he is perhaps most appealing because he embodies the energy of his originator, channeling Hillenburg's vibrant spirit. "I love how SpongeBob looks like Steve. Steve was an incredibly sweet man—also very sharp and funny, obviously. But that wide-eyed, guileless quality is straight from him. When we designed the character, I used a lot of his mannerisms, even the way he would turn his body, in the model sheets," recounts former storyboard supervisor Erik Wiese.

Fun with the design of SpongeBob has continued through the years, with former prop and character designer Thaddeus Couldron recalling that "Steve assigned me the task of designing DoodleBob, a self-portrait that comes to life. He said he wanted it to be a bad drawing, that's why he assigned it to me, because he knew I could draw bad (his exact words: 'I know you can draw bad')." But every step of his evolution, the artistic team honors the fact that "SpongeBob was born out of 2D cel animation where the hand of the artist is always present. The most unique poses or expressions are still inspired by the artist who drew the storyboard and [then] elevated by the animator," says creative director Derek Drymon.

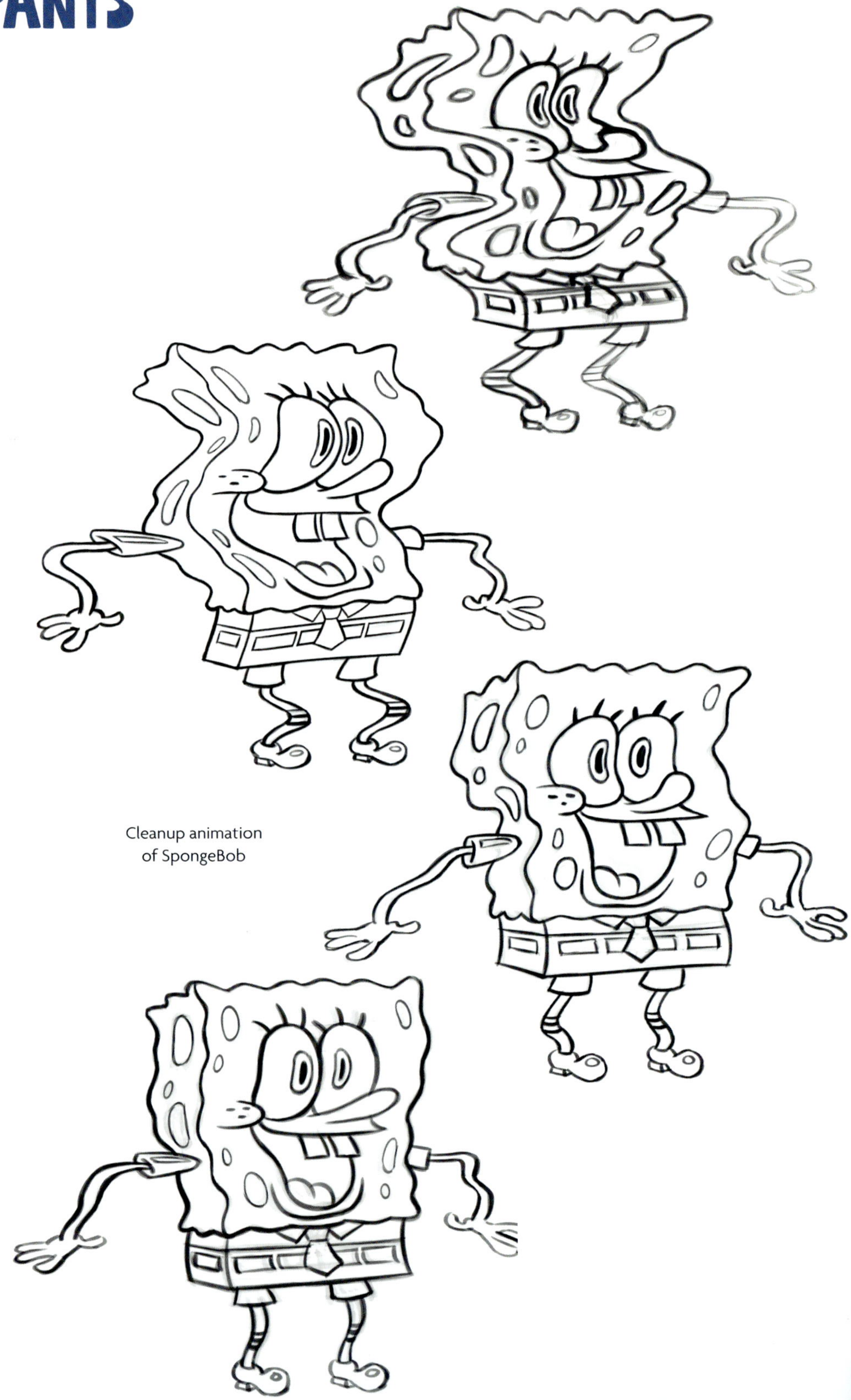

Cleanup animation of SpongeBob

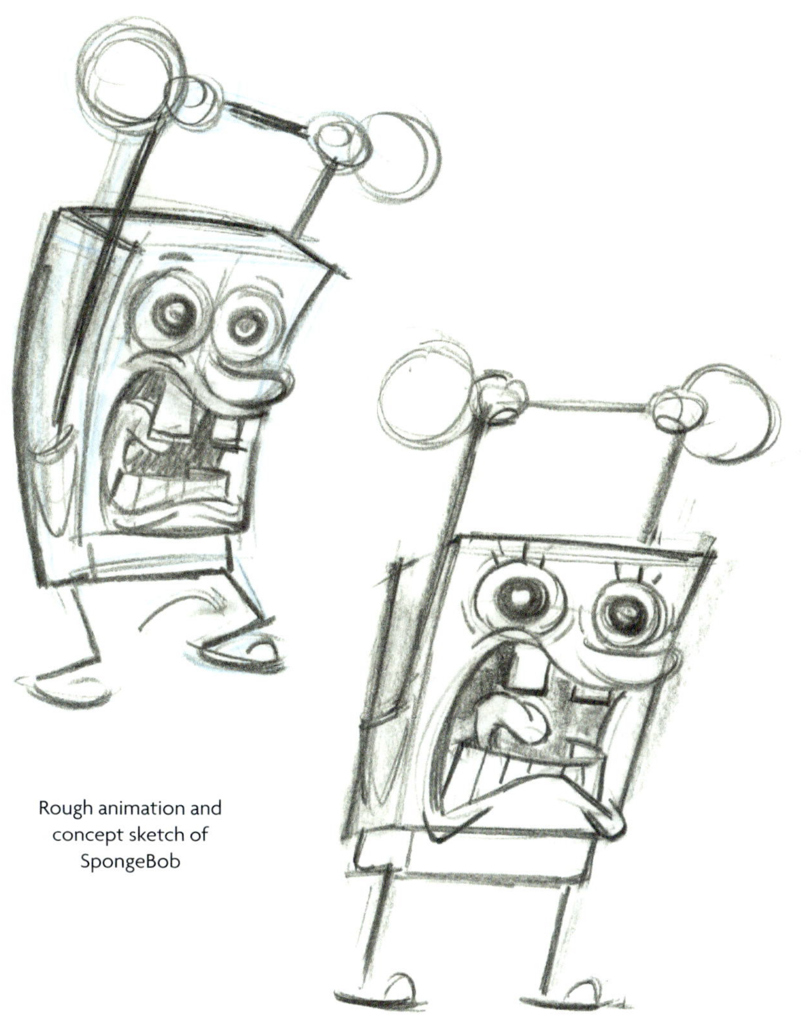

Rough animation and concept sketch of SpongeBob

"When SpongeBob wakes up, greets the day, and is completely ready for anything, that captures the spirit of the show perfectly," says Ramsey Naito. Innocent and inquisitive, aspirational and annoying, "there's a contradiction built into SpongeBob that makes him funny. His optimism is absurd; any other character would not be so buoyant (pun intended) when faced with life's problems and conflicts," says Kaz. SpongeBob is surprisingly complex, "sometimes childish or naive, sometimes obsessive. Has no cynicism or malice in him. Loyal to his boss and his crappy job. Loves his friends. (We should all have such appeal.) In short, he's a goofy goober," observes former director Tim Hill. SpongeBob is relatable and likable, "smart enough, sometimes blissfully unaware, and big on justice but not preachy about it," adds Mr. Lawrence. Just as sponges are quite resilient in nature, SpongeBob embodies persistence in physical endurance and especially in spirit. "He is true to himself and never lets the haters get him down, but when and if they do, he is not afraid to feel his feelings and let them out. It's a good way to live," says former executive producer Paul Tibbitt. At times, SpongeBob lets those feelings out in a big way, be that crying a fountain or melting down into a puddle, with the overdramatic outburst serving as a gag cartoon's hallmark of humor, rooted in his character's deepest identity. "SpongeBob has mastered the art of finding joy in life. He could be doing the most mundane thing—putting a patty on the grill, feeding Gary, picking up the mail—but he will bring so much enthusiasm that it becomes a celebration and, in turn, fun for us to watch," adds Claudia Spinelli.

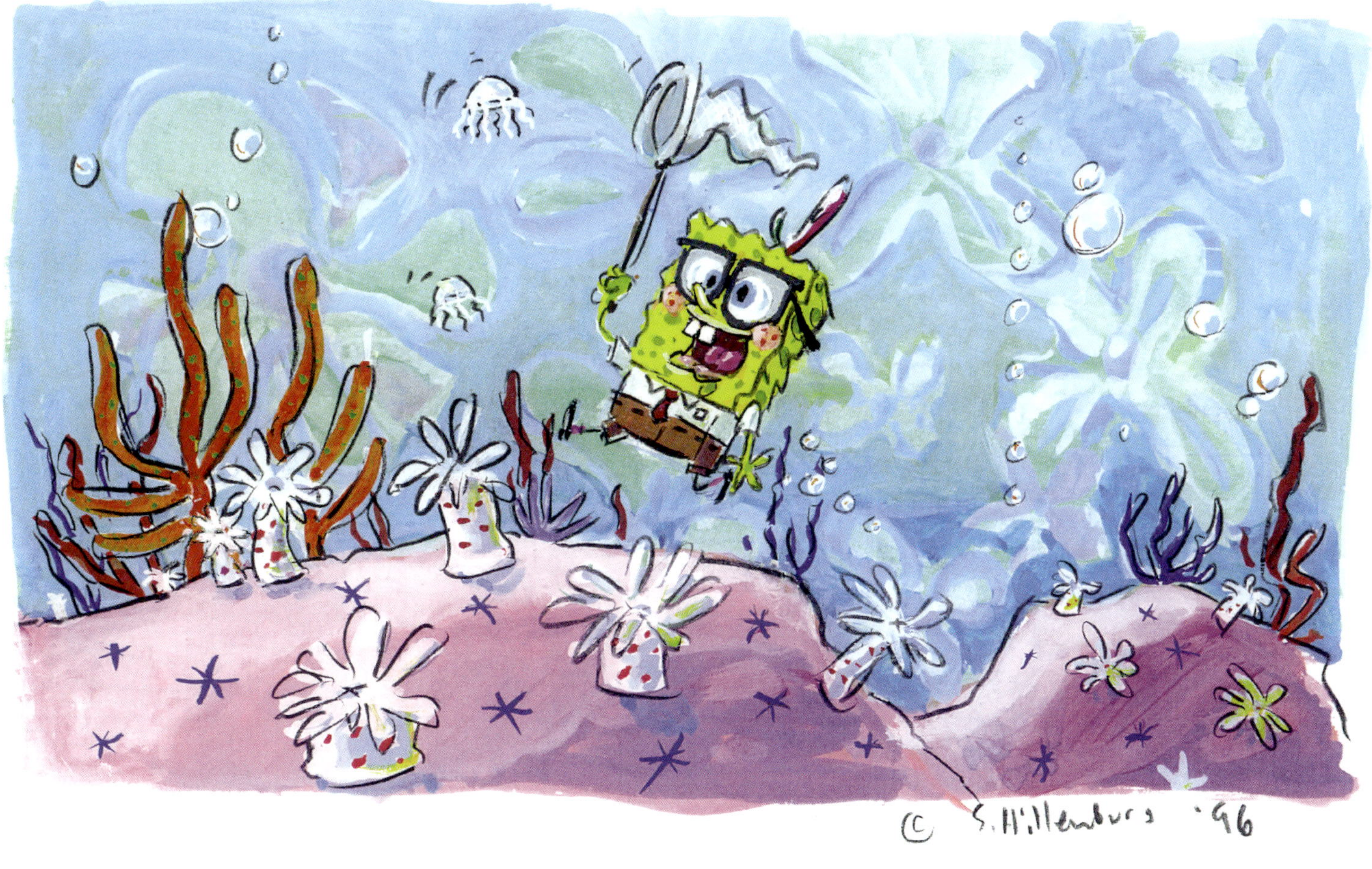

© S. Hillenburg '96

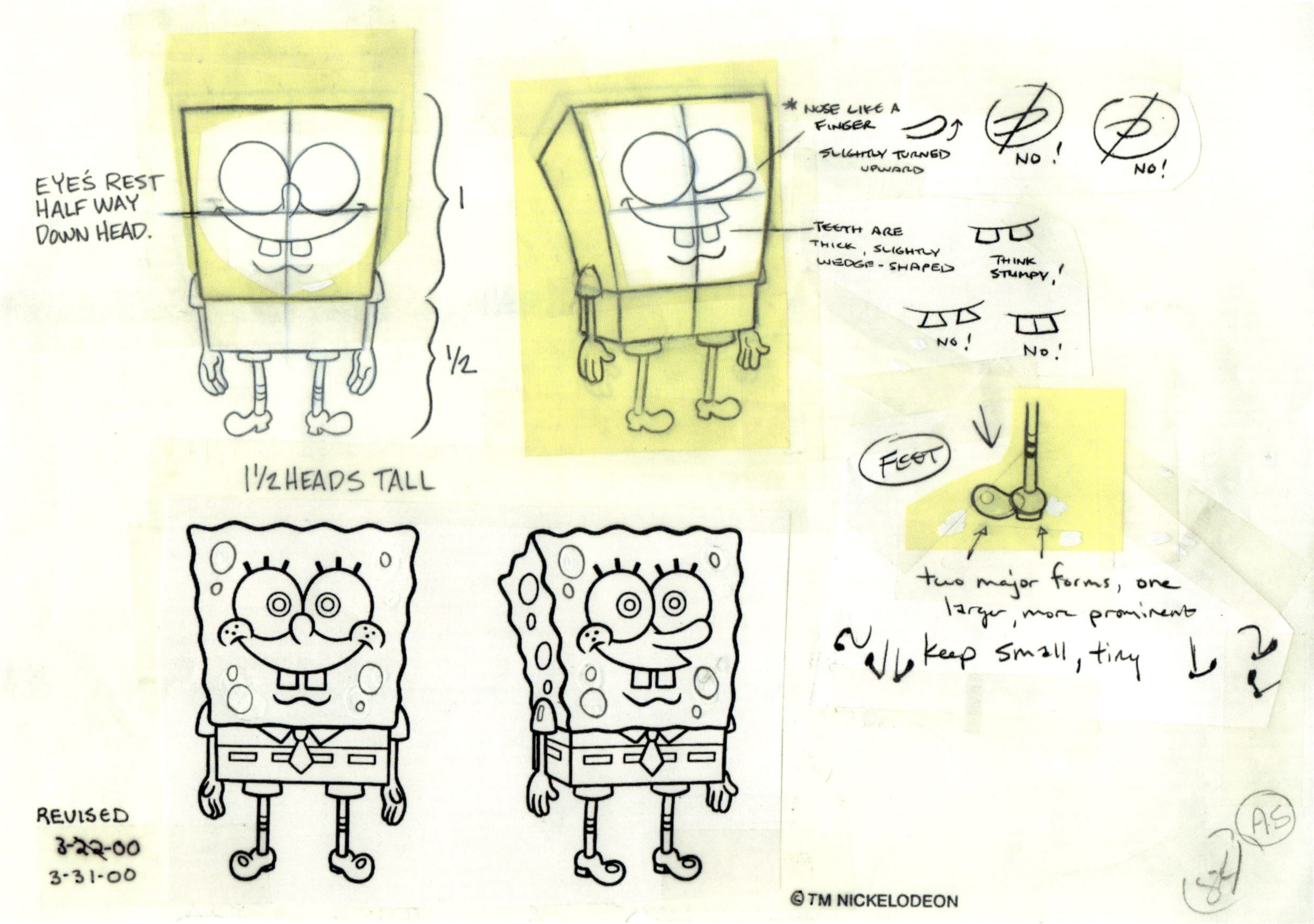

Style guide reference for SpongeBob [upper];
animation turnaround of SpongeBob [lower]

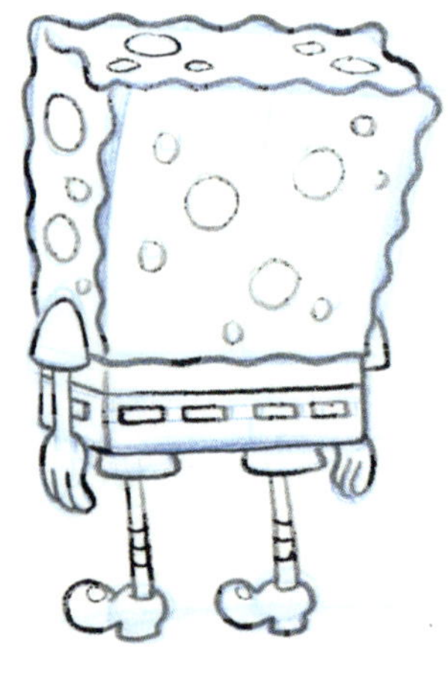
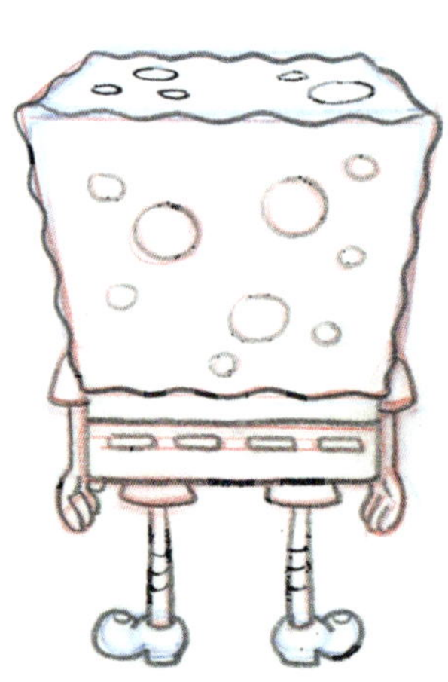
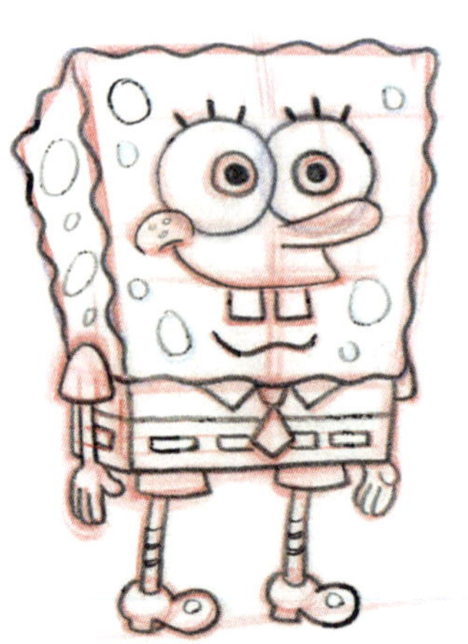
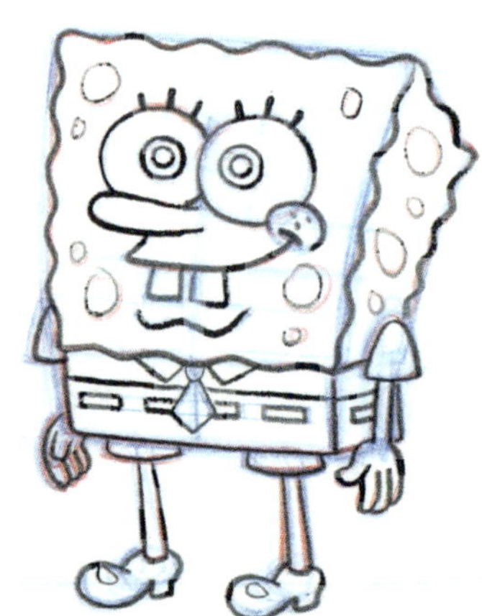

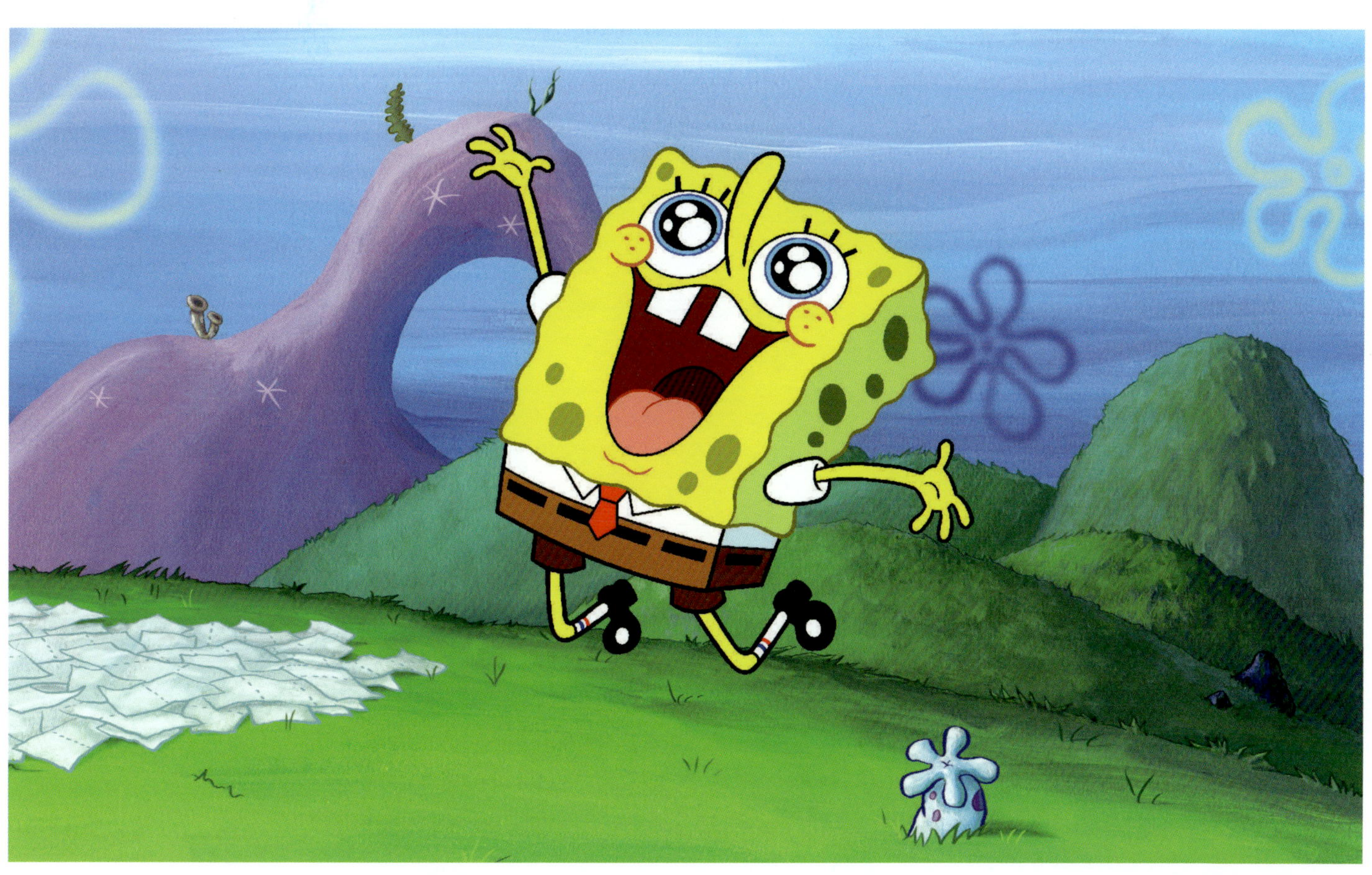

Final frame images of SpongeBob

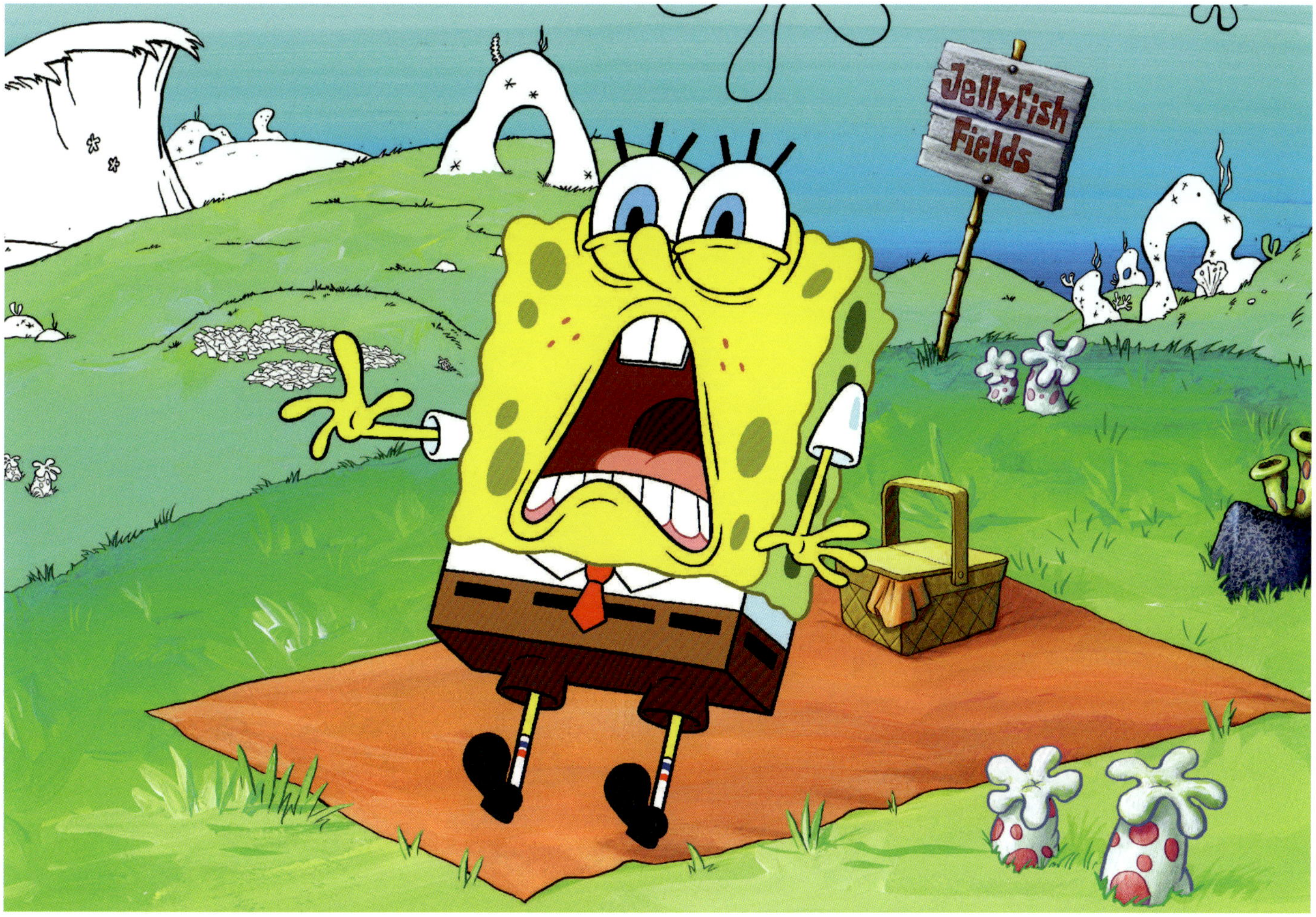

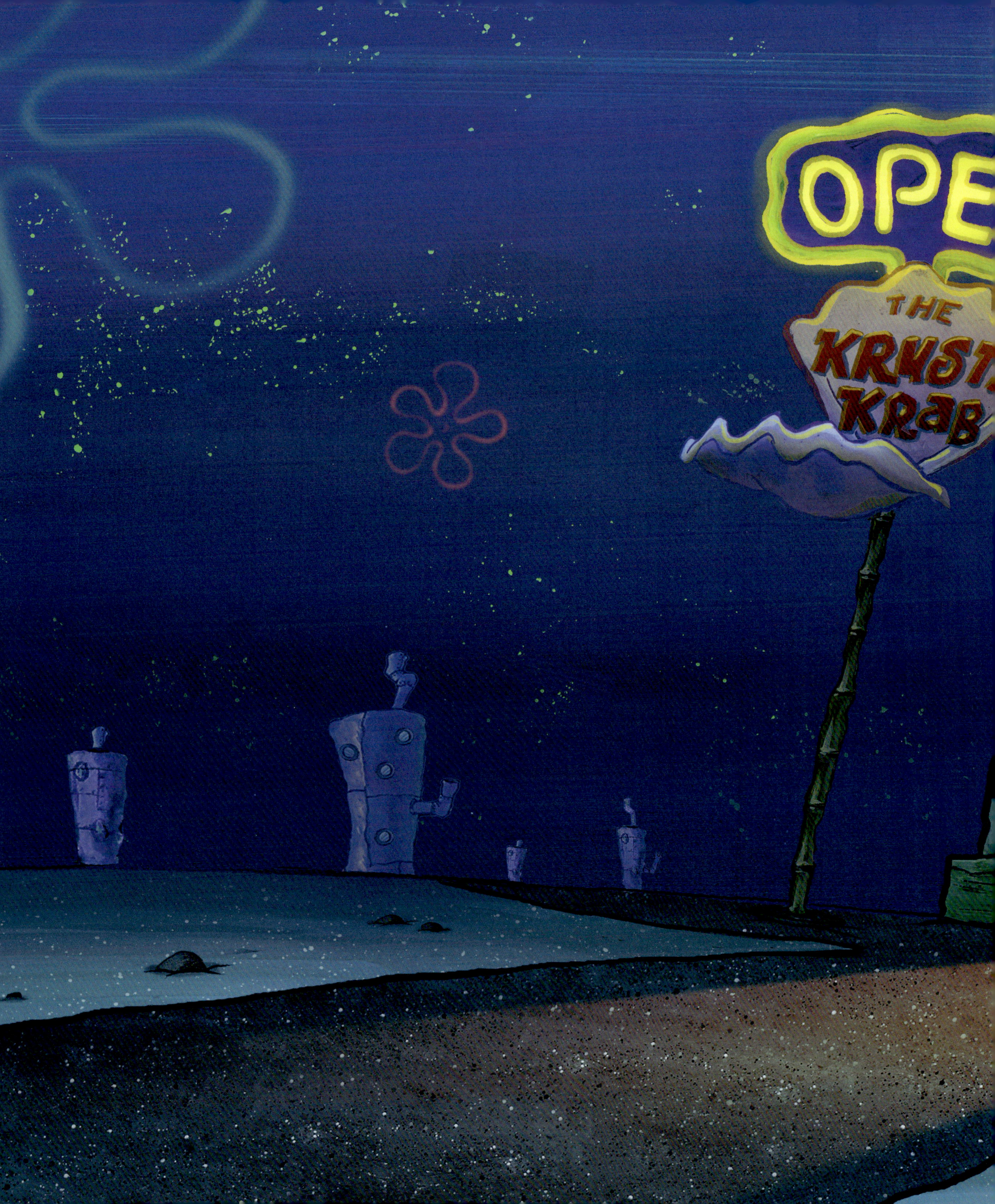
THE
KRAB

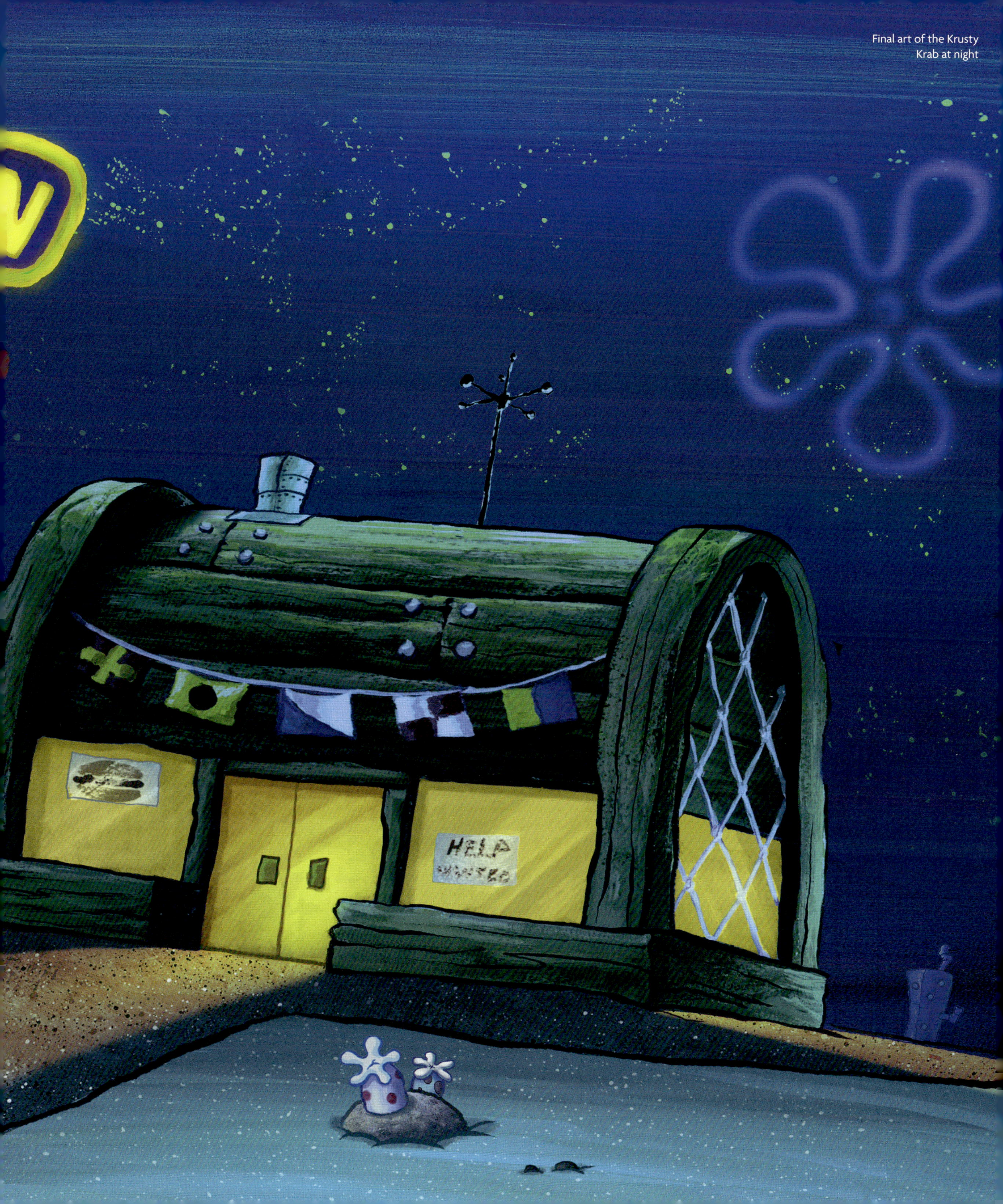

Final art of the Krusty
Krab at night

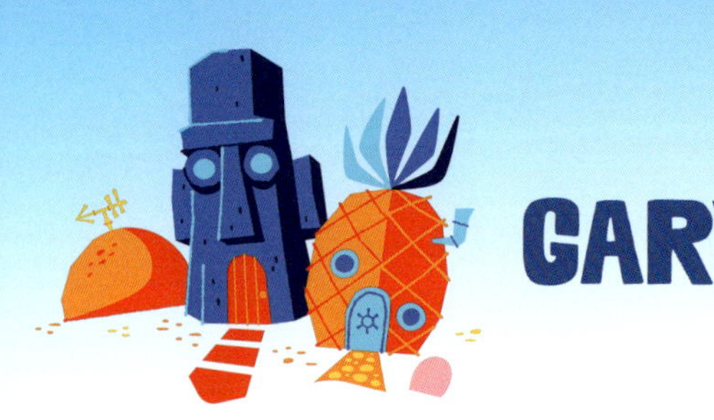

GARY

Gary has slid into the hearts of audiences as the most lovable domesticated house pet in Bikini Bottom, making his debut alongside SpongeBob in the pilot episode and keeping (a snail's) pace with him ever since. "Gary is a combination of understated, cute, and a little weird. While he has this baby palette and purrs like a cat, he leads so many secret lives and leaves a trail of blue slime wherever he goes," says former executive in charge Claudia Spinelli. Although he is a mollusk of few words—mainly a single word, MEOW—Gary participates in great conversations with SpongeBob, much to the story-development glee of his creators: He allows SpongeBob to spew great exposition and think out loud, responding in a purr-fectly efficient way while the audience can quickly follow the story beats as the writers intended.

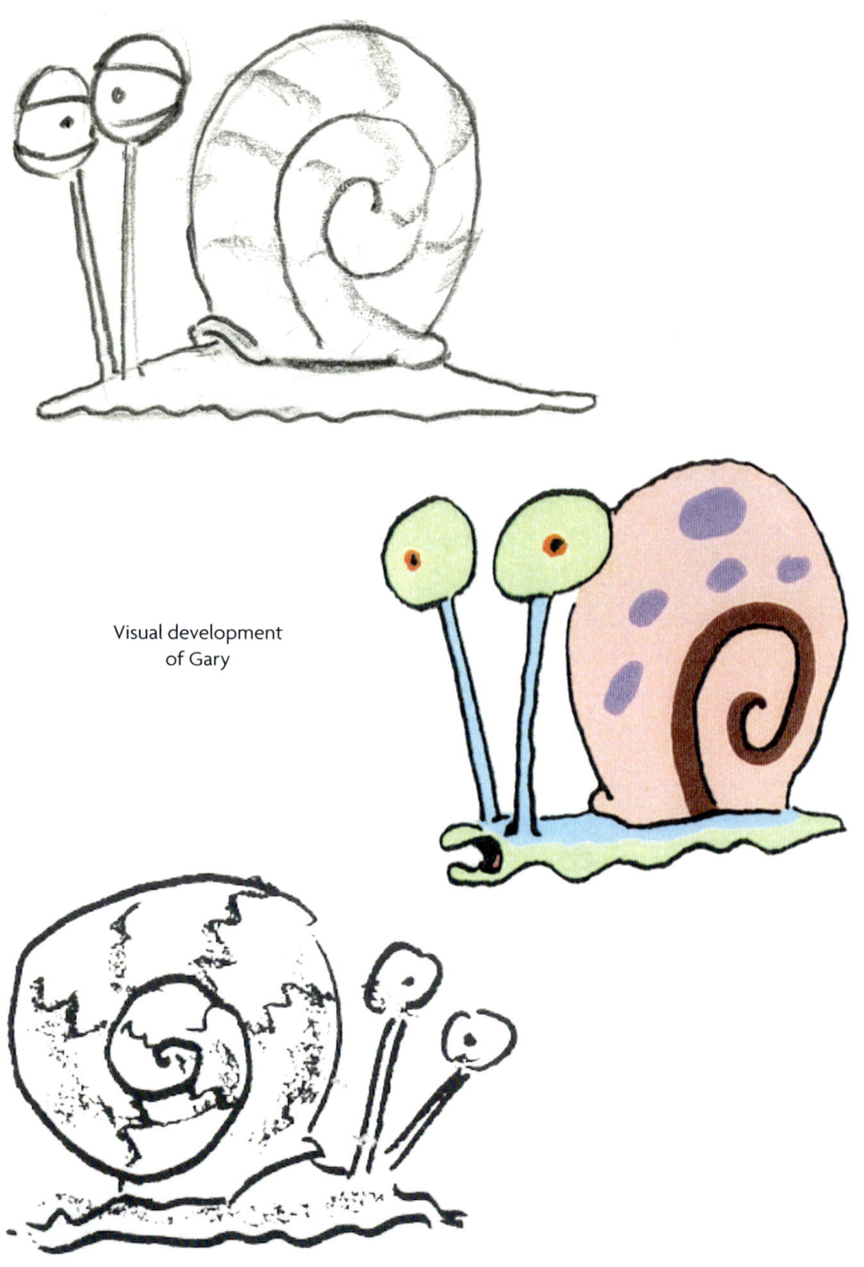

Visual development of Gary

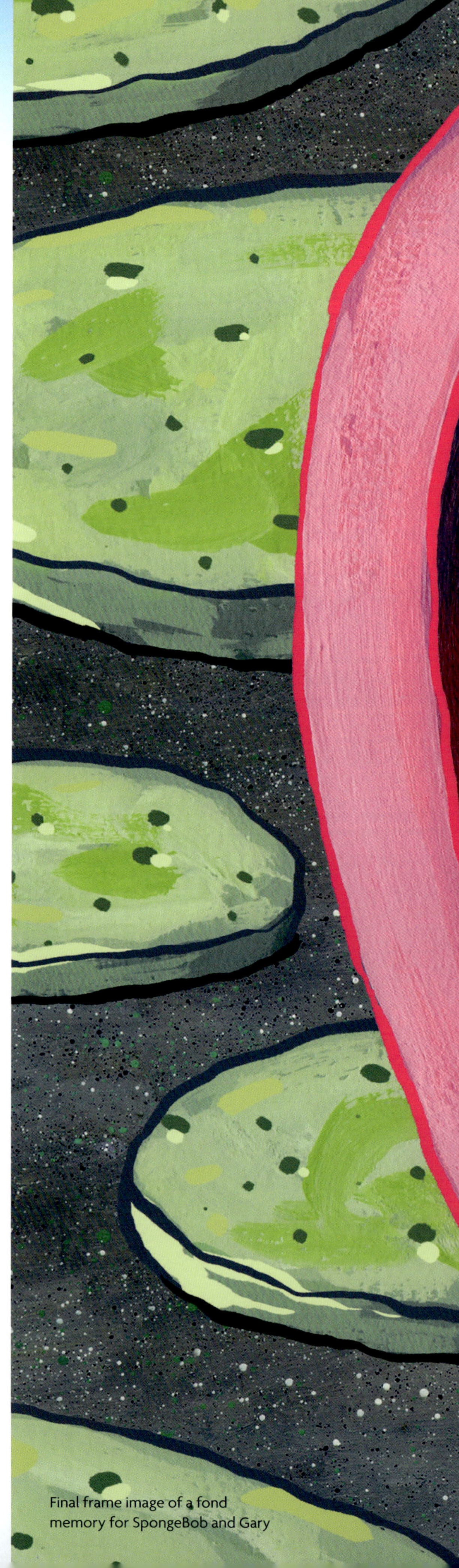

Final frame image of a fond memory for SpongeBob and Gary

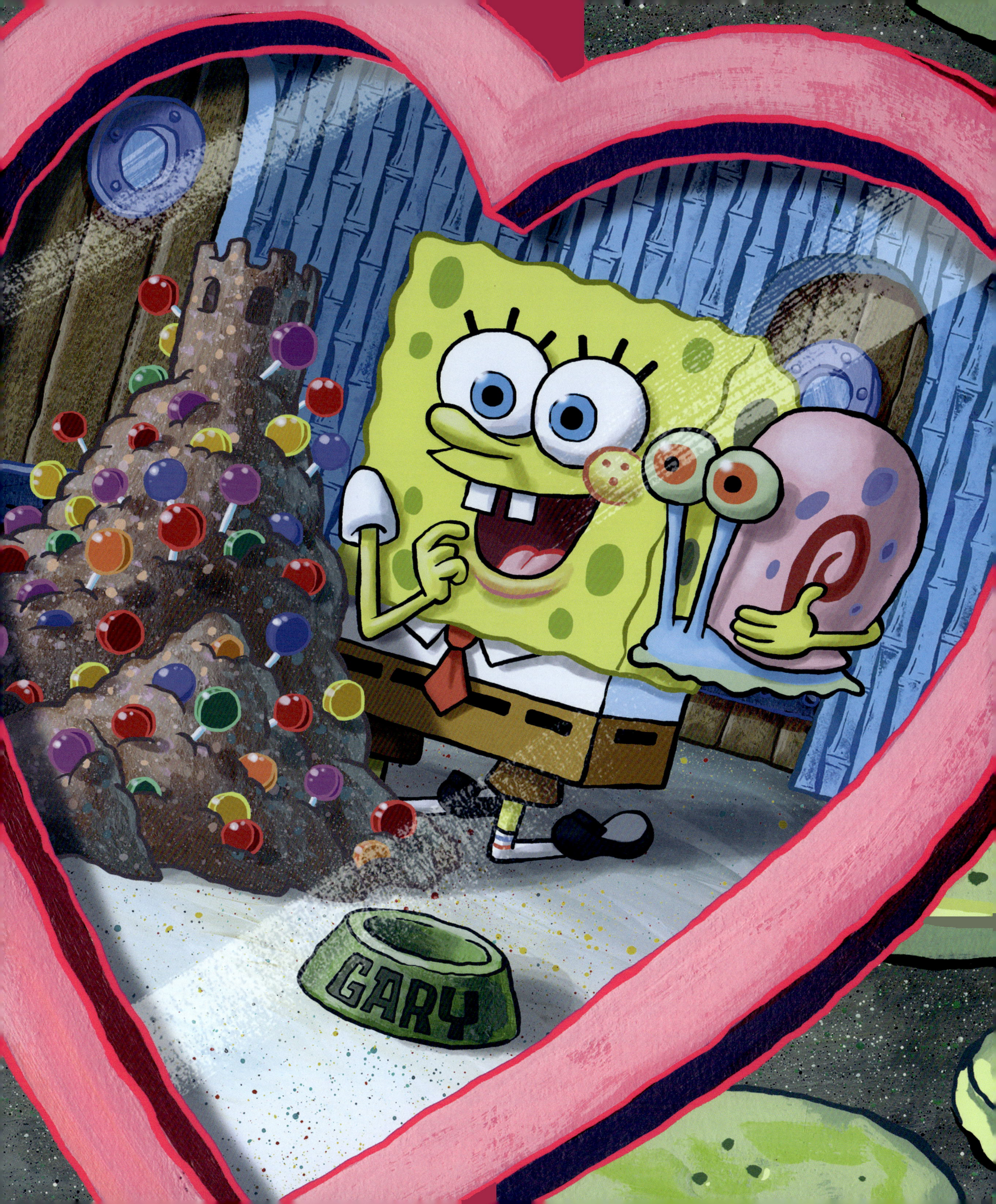
GARY

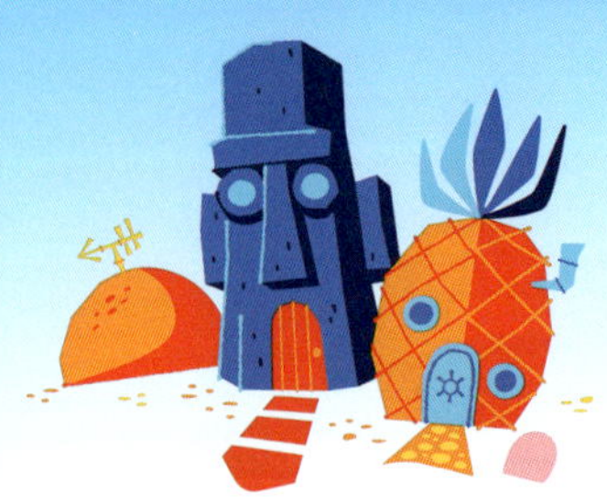

PATRICK STAR

Patrick Star means well but just doesn't have the intelligence to deliver on that most of the time... but it's not his fault, as a sea star does not have brains, a biological fact that fits his character perfectly, per the series bible created by Hillenburg. "I like Patrick because he's so simple, which means you can surprise the audience by having him quote Kant, or something. He's a good version of the 'big dumb guy,'" says former director Tim Hill. While his IQ may measure low, Patrick's loyalty to SpongeBob is off the charts, as are his enthusiasm and sense of wonder. It's hard to believe that in his early development, Patrick was an angry character who was really mad about being pink, acting more like a macho bully because he had this chip on his figurative shoulder about his appearance. Instead, the Patrick audiences know is "a lovable idiot. We often play him to be beyond dumb—psychedelically dumb. We take a given situation and carry it to its illogical conclusion," notes writer Kaz, who has found great joy in working with Patrick through the decades.

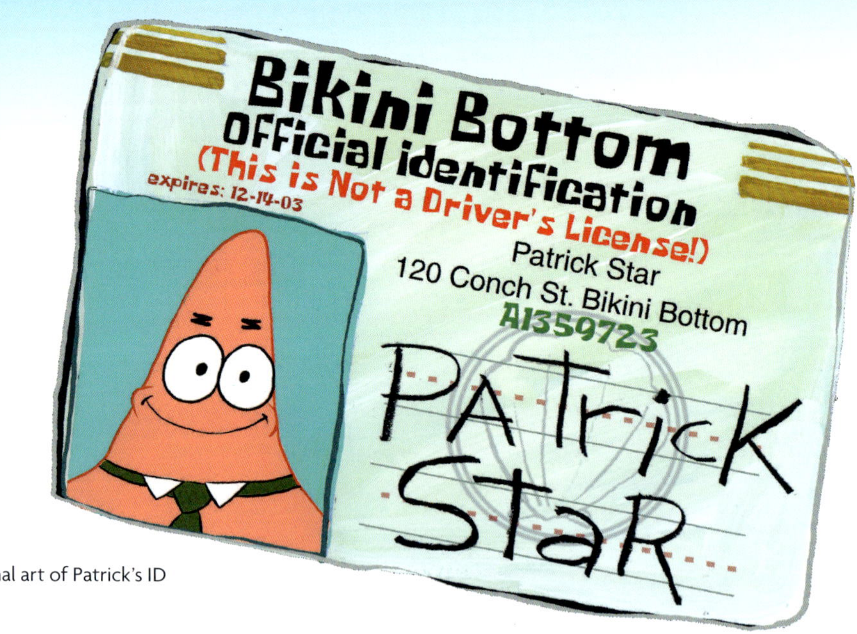

Final art of Patrick's ID

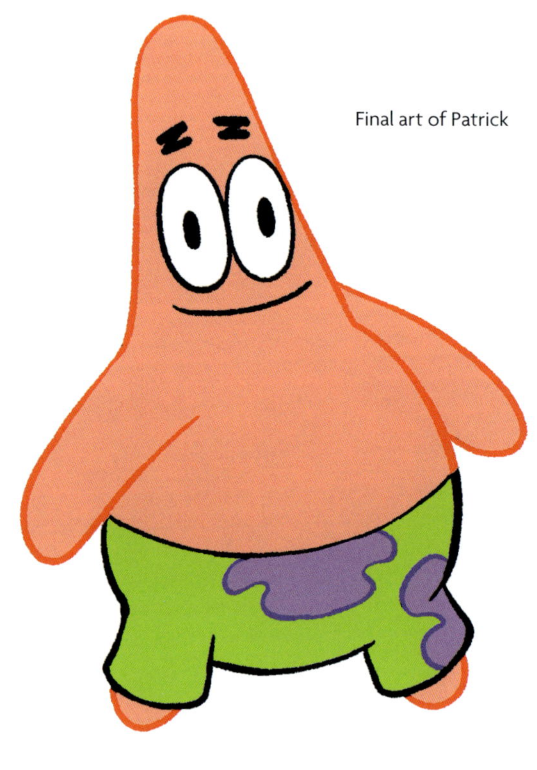

Final art of Patrick

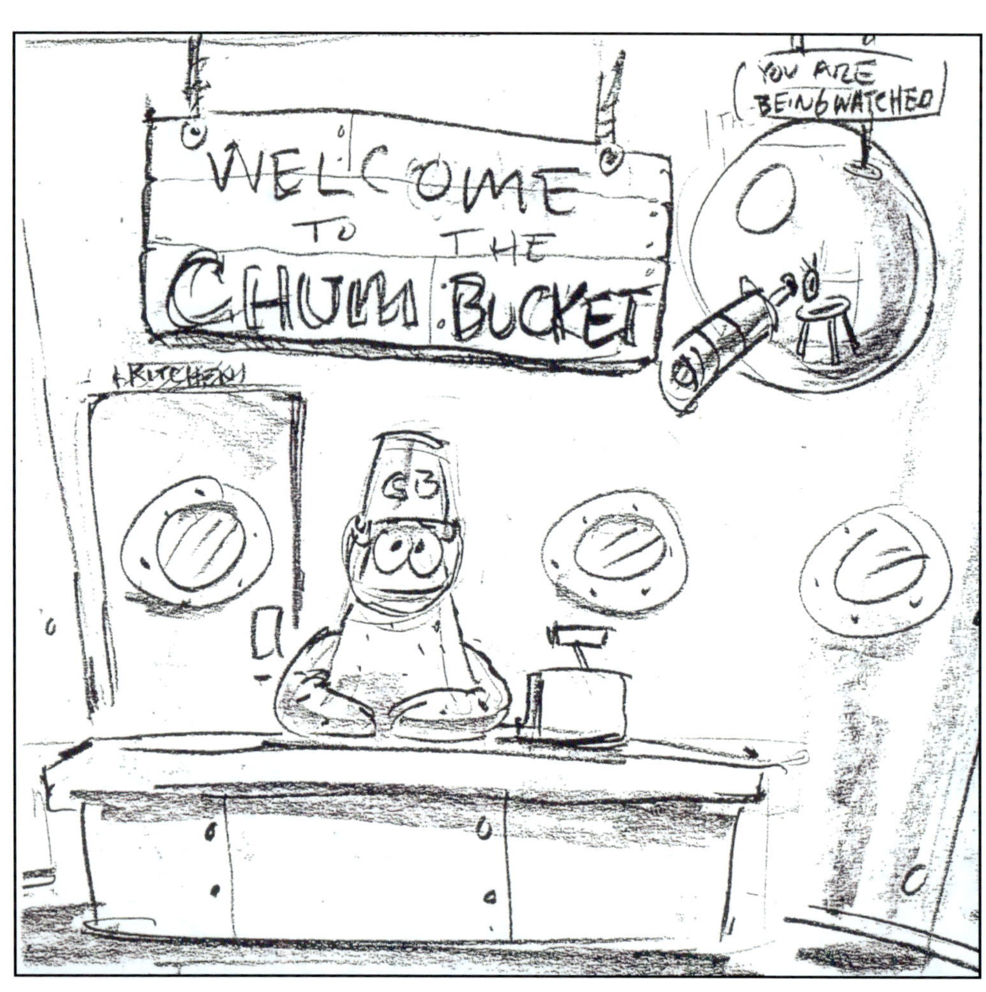

Character concept art of Patrick as a Chum Bucket employee

"PATRICK COMPLEMENTS SPONGEBOB PERFECTLY. THEY'RE A CLASSIC LAUREL AND HARDY COMBO."

ERIK WIESE,
FORMER STORYBOARD SUPERVISOR

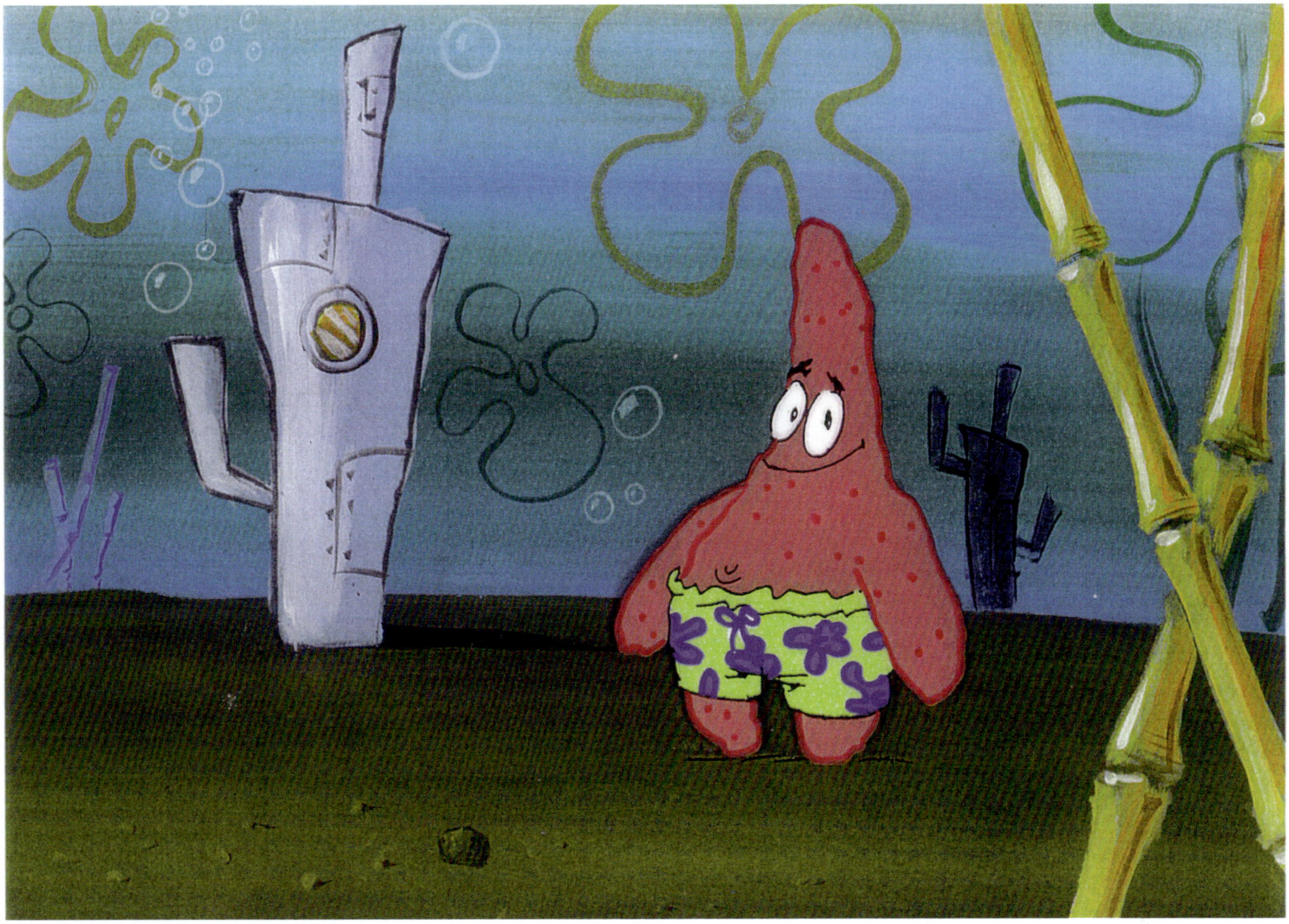

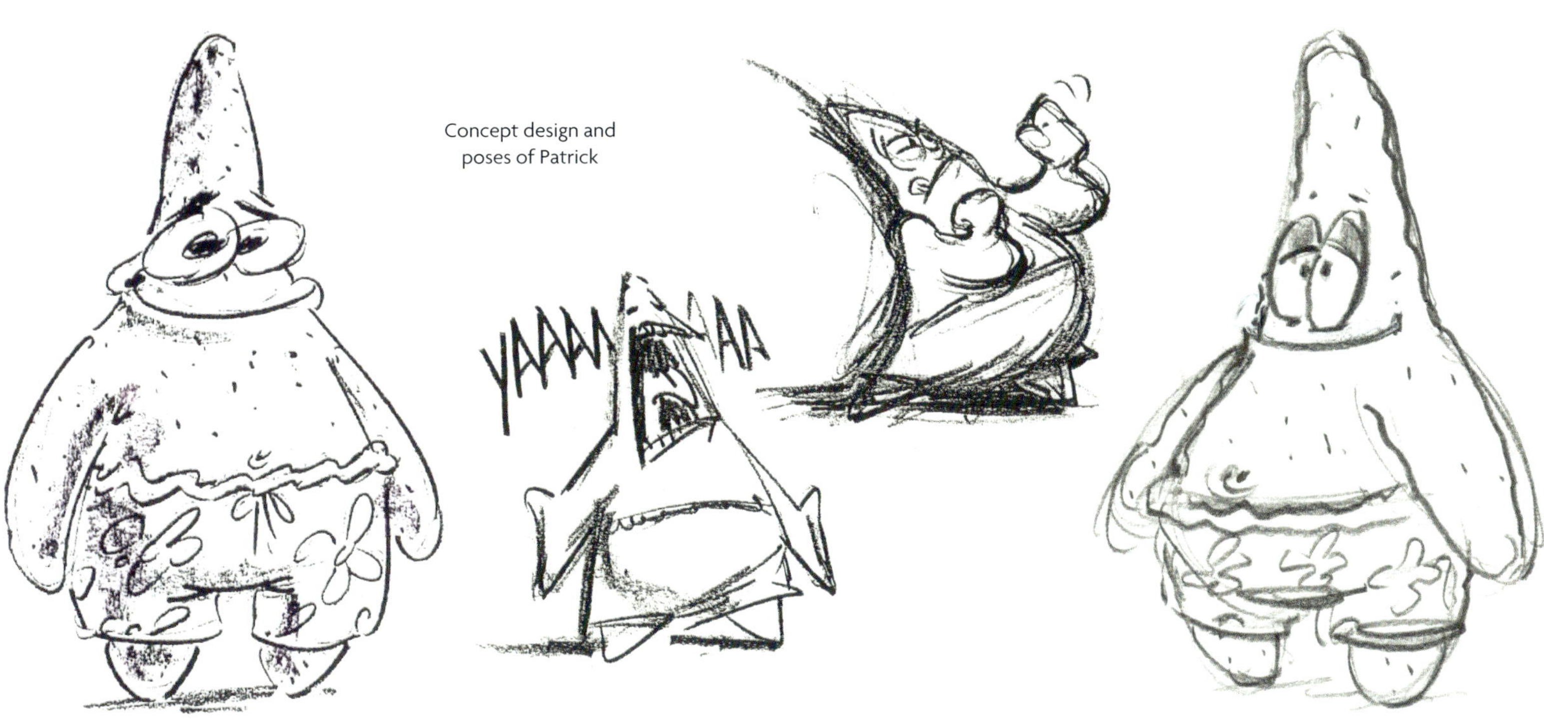

Concept design and poses of Patrick

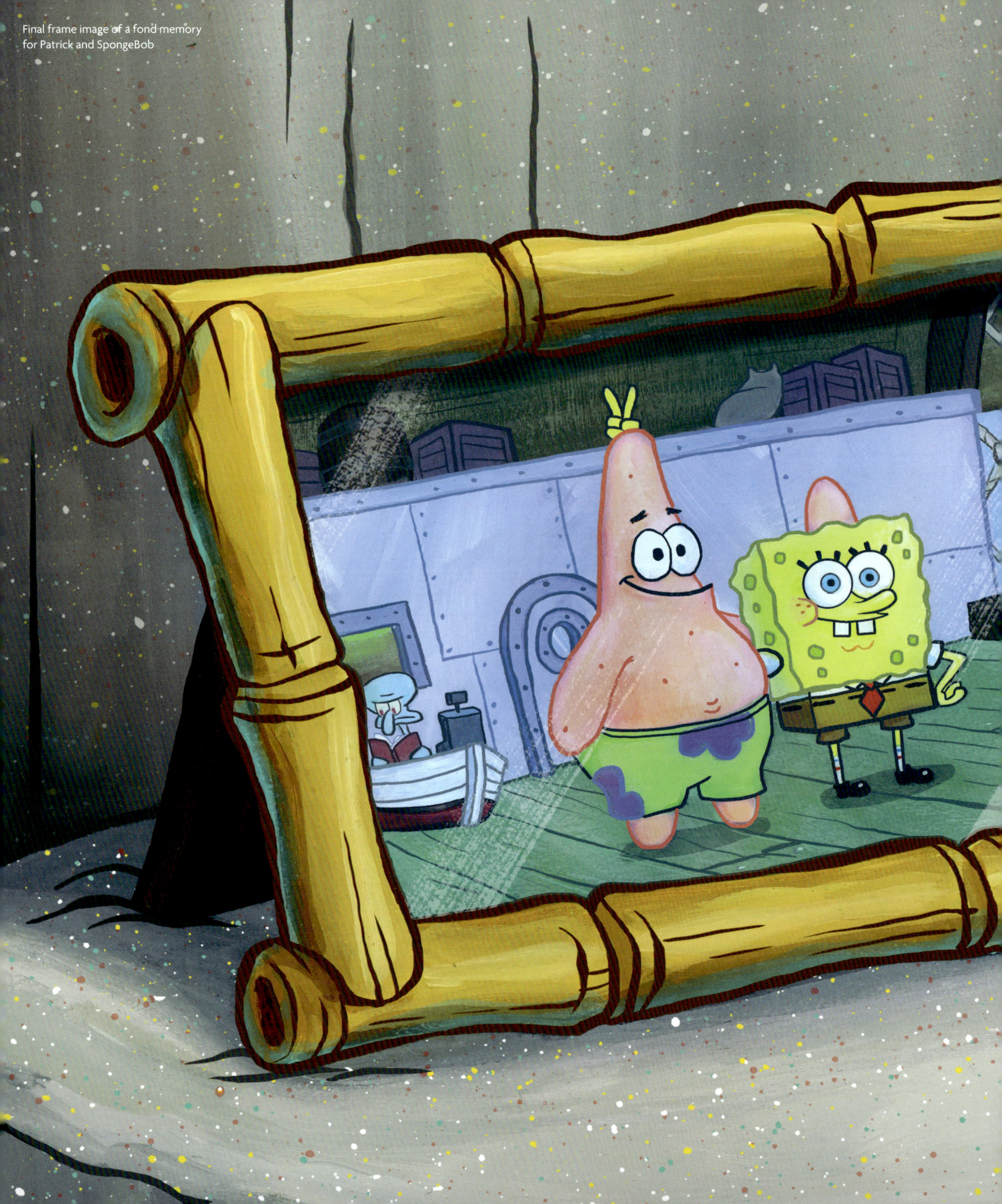

Final frame image of a fond memory for Patrick and SpongeBob

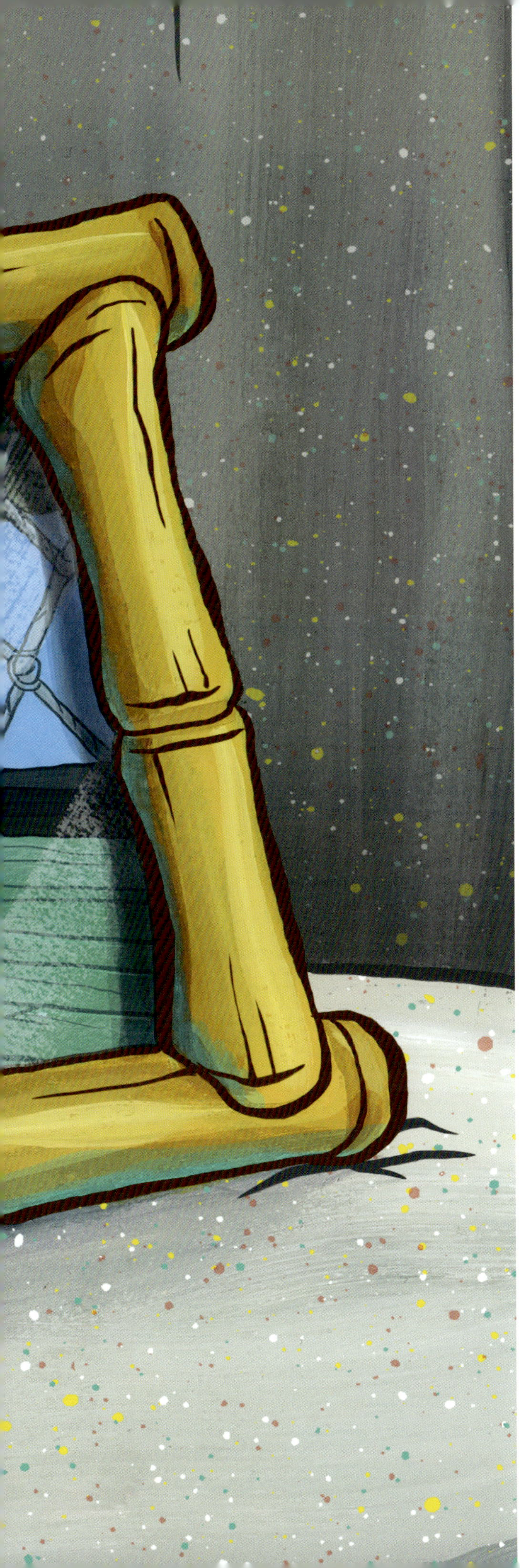

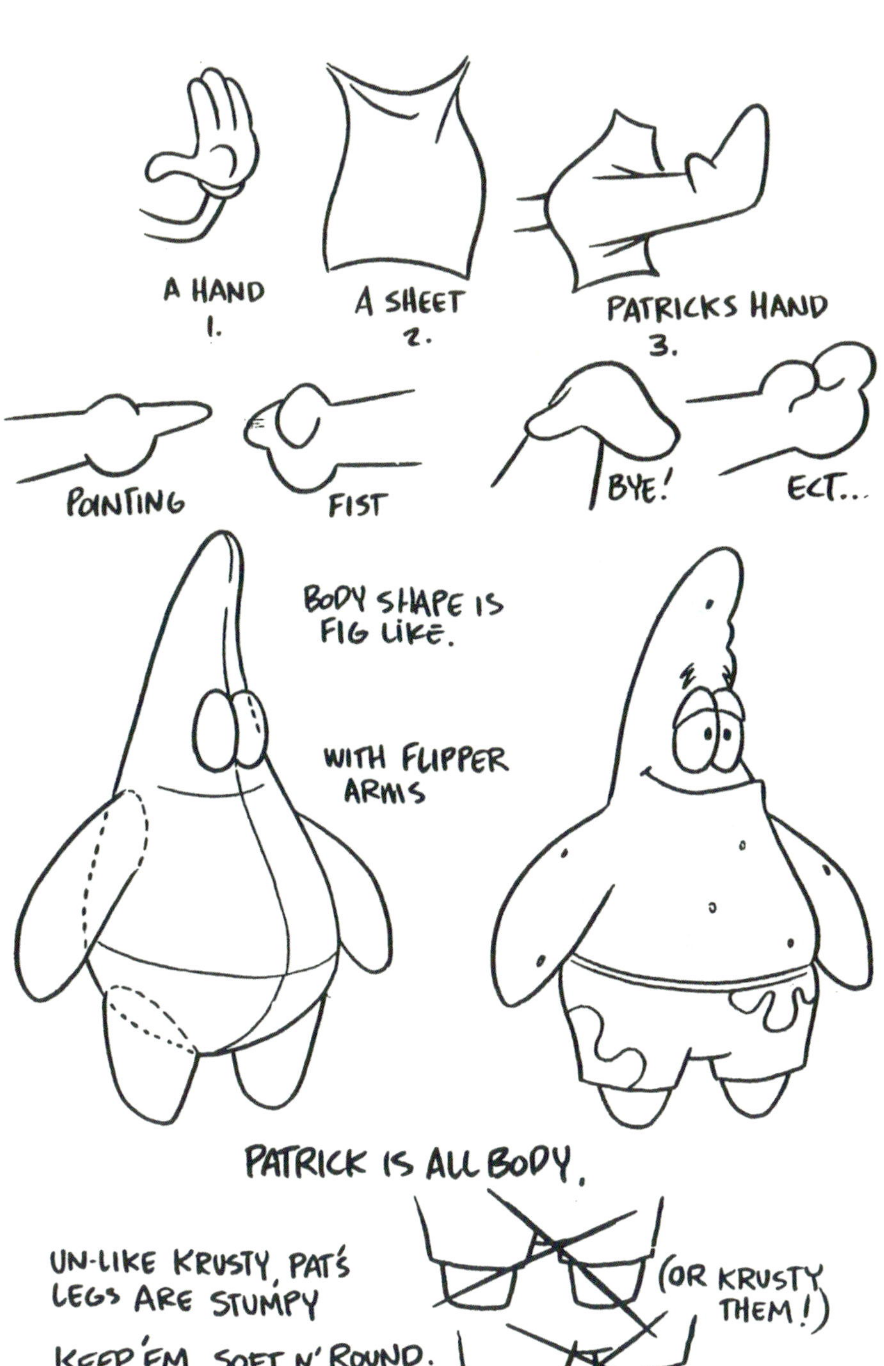

Style guide reference
for Patrick

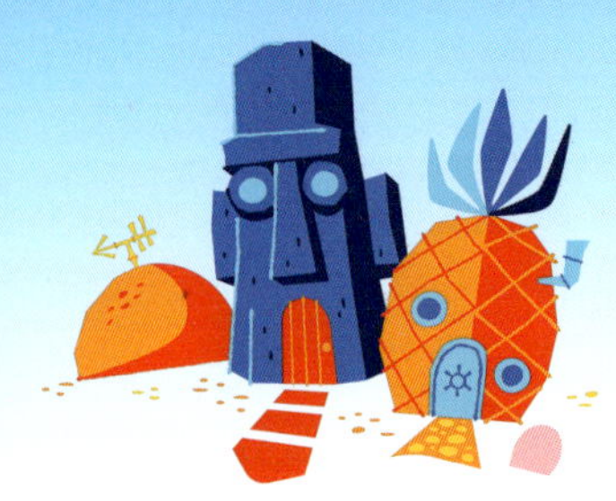

SQUIDWARD TENTACLES

An avid self-portrait painter and clarinet player, Squidward is quite unenthusiastic about being the neighbor of both SpongeBob and Patrick. Upon close inspection, it's notable that he's also innately un-squid-like in his actual octopus incarnation, even if he is only sporting six instead of the natural eight limbs. His narcissism is embodied in his big-headed design, while his grumpiness might be due to his geography: "Steve Hillenburg always said that Squidward represented the audience. It's how we would react if we were stuck living between two happy and—let's face it—annoying knuckleheads like SpongeBob and Patrick," recalls writer Kaz.

Character concept art of Squidward

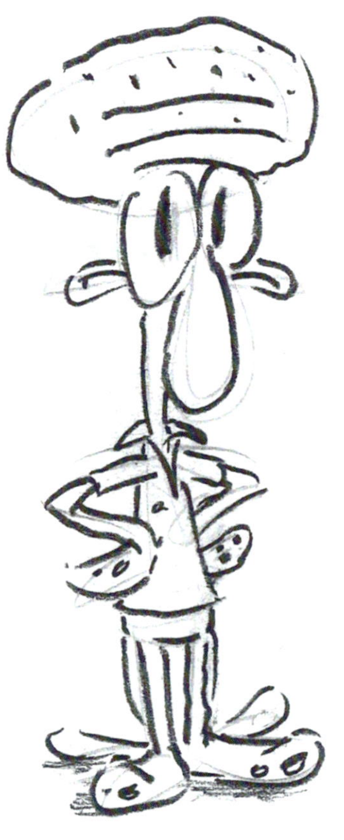

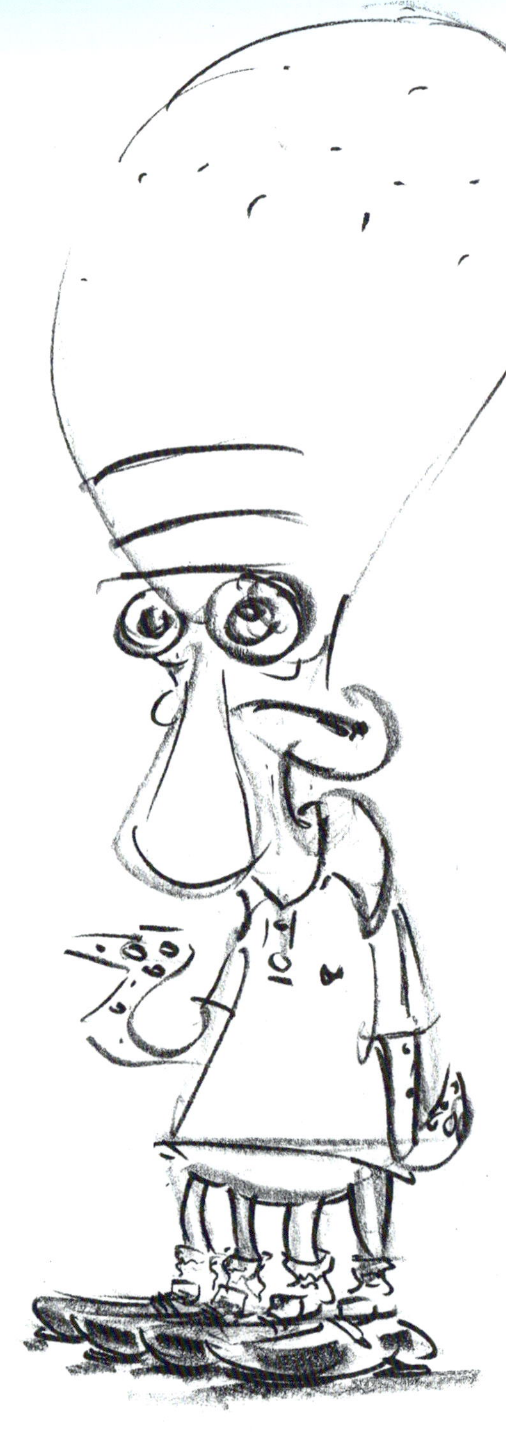

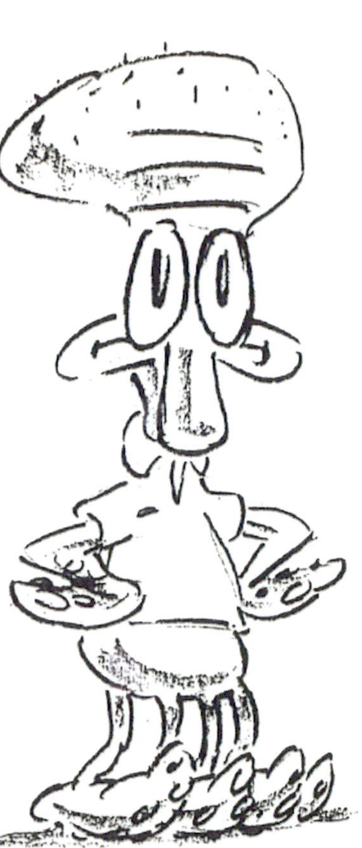

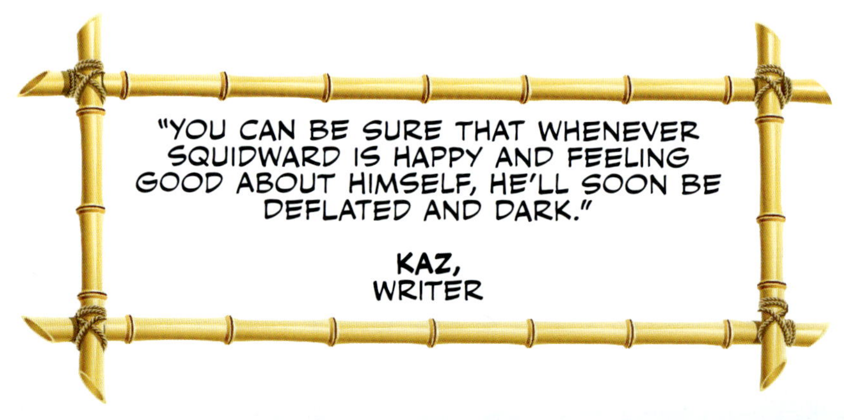

"YOU CAN BE SURE THAT WHENEVER SQUIDWARD IS HAPPY AND FEELING GOOD ABOUT HIMSELF, HE'LL SOON BE DEFLATED AND DARK."

KAZ,
WRITER

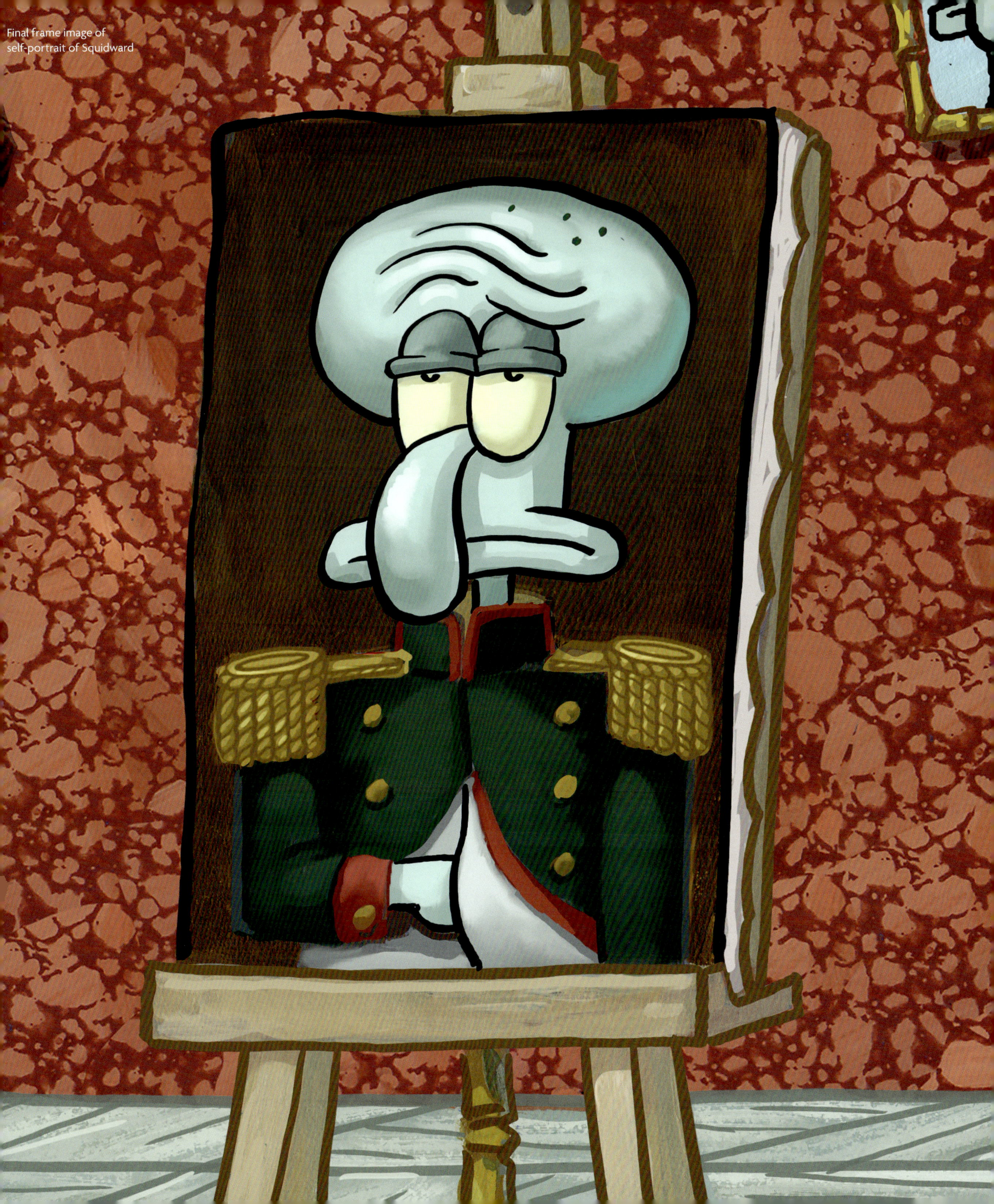

Final frame image of
self-portrait of Squidward

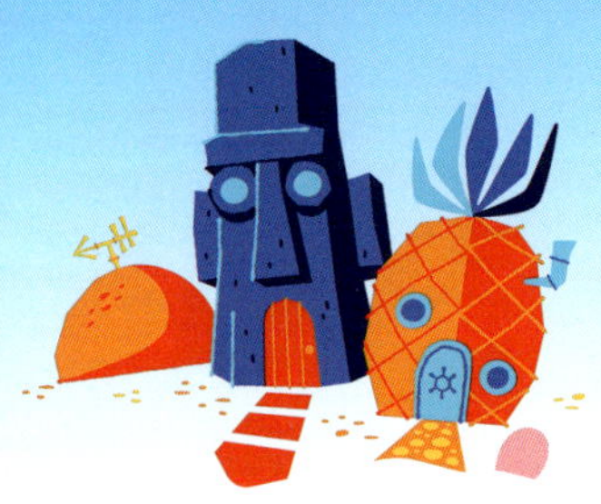

MR. KRABS

Eugene Harold Krabs is the proud but tight-wadded owner of the Krusty Krab restaurant, always looking to penny-pinch and seeing dollar signs, sometimes literally. His obsession with money is illogical, irrational, and inexpiable, but also the infinite source of humor in creating a hostile yet humorous work environment for both SpongeBob and Squidward.

Mr. Krabs is a caricature of a boss that Stephen Hillenburg had while working in a seafood restaurant in Maine, exaggerating the personality of that red-headed former-military cook but adding on the cheapskate and Krabby Patty secret-formula protection angles to turn up the heat on his personality. As hard-shelled as he is, Mr. Krabs exhibits a softness for both his (unpaid, good value) fry cook SpongeBob and also his daughter, Pearl.

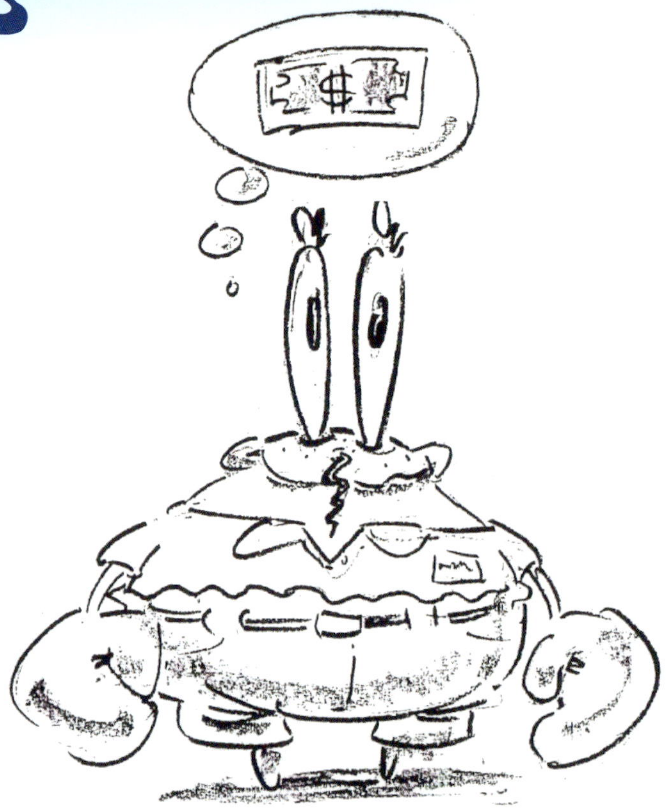

Original character design of Mr. Krabs [left]; and character construction drawings [below]

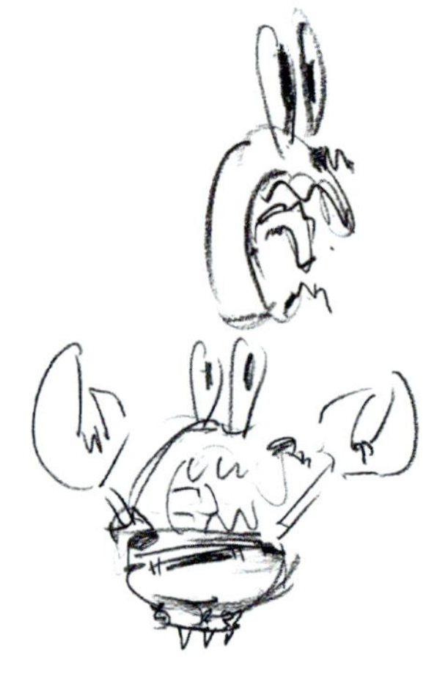

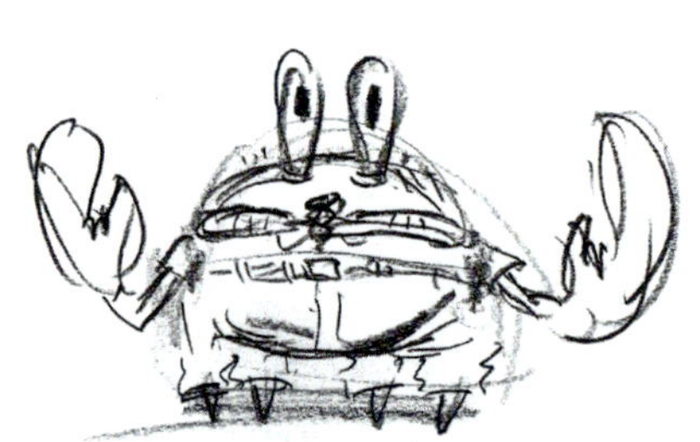

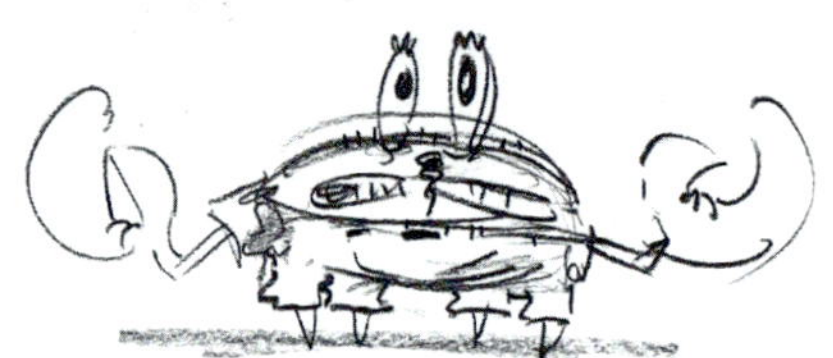

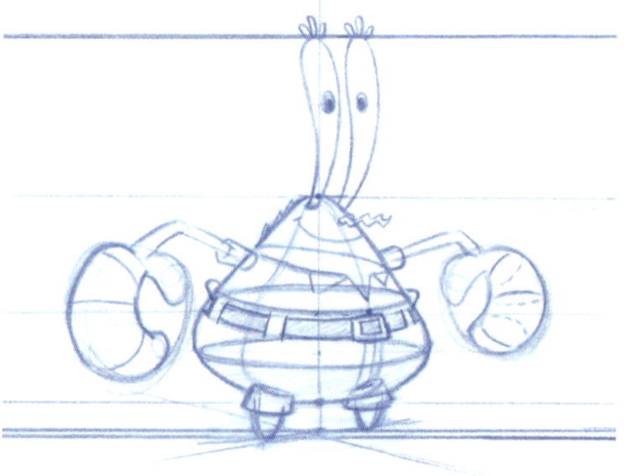

"KRUSTY KRAB IS UNFAIR! MR. KRABS IS IN THERE! STANDING AT THE CONCESSION, PLOTTING HIS OPPRESSION... WE ARE WORKERS UNITED! WE'RE TIRED OF YOUR SMELLY GREED, AND WE'RE GONNA SAW YOUR TABLES, AND WE'RE GONNA SMASH STUFF WITH A PEOPLE'S HAMMER, AND WE'RE GONNA... WE'RE GONNA... SQUIDWARD, WHAT WAS THAT OTHER PART?"

EXCERPT OF A RARE SPONGEBOB RANT AGAINST HIS EMPLOYER, MR. KRABS

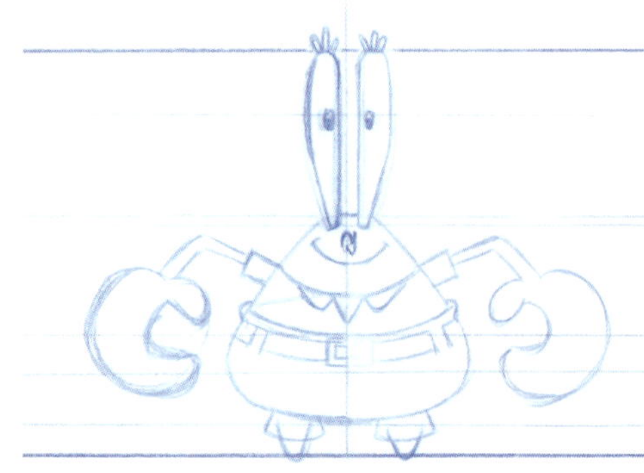

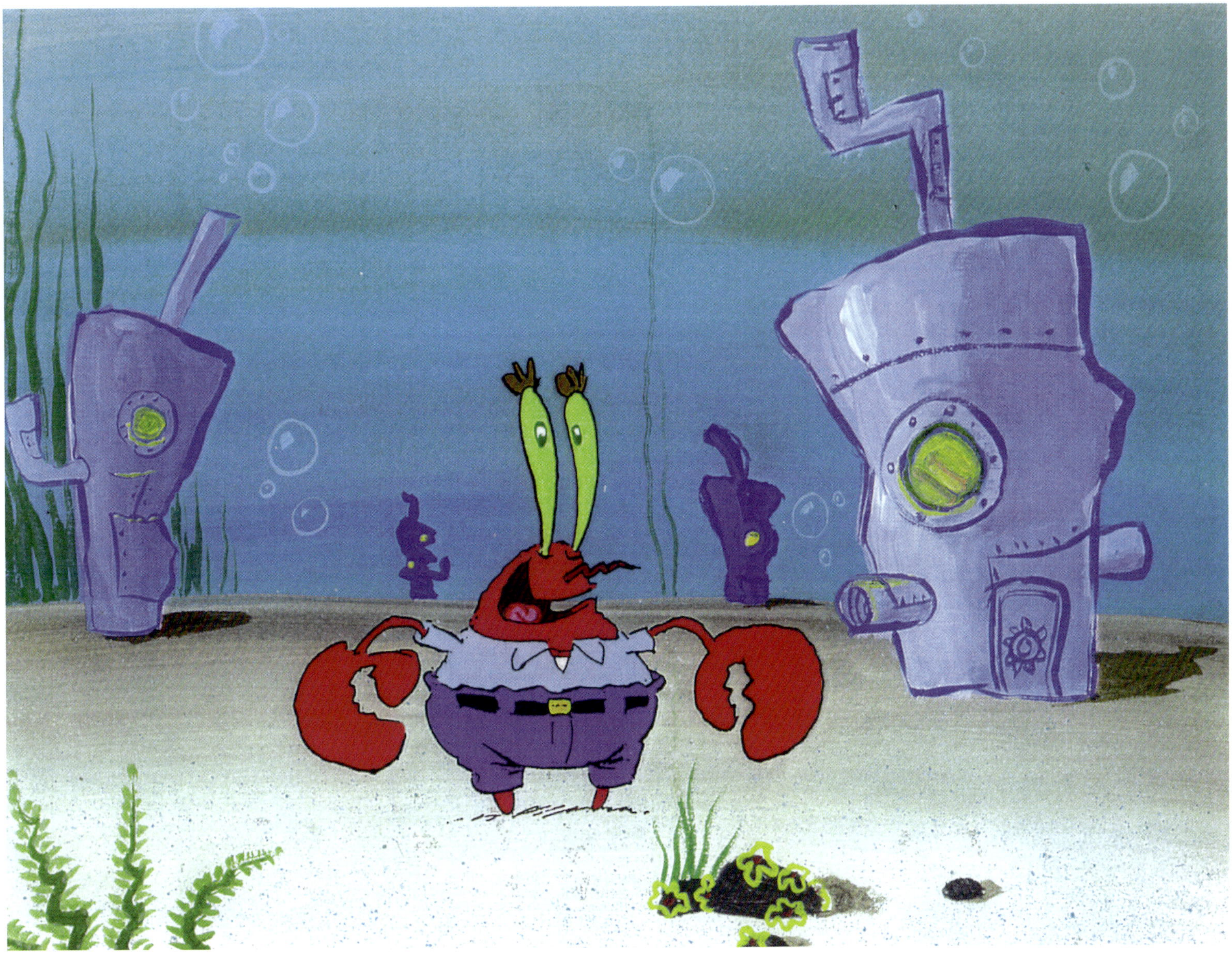

Krabs art inspired by "Jellyfish Hunter" (Season 2, episode 39a)

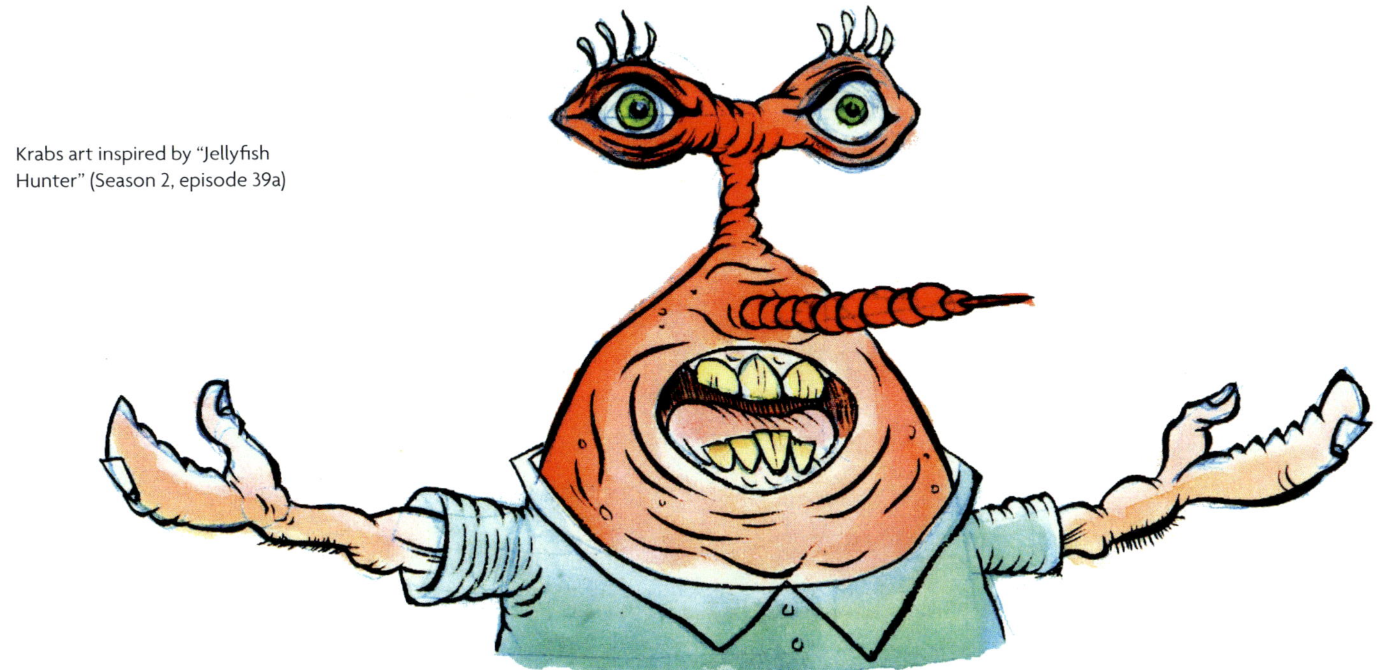

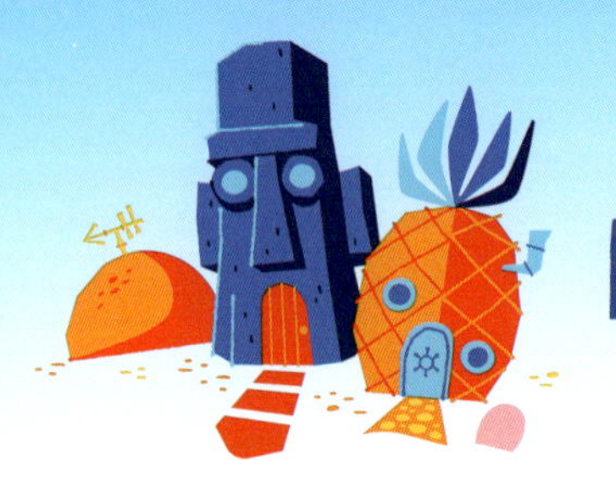

PEARL

The daughter of Mr. Krabs, Pearl Krabs is a generally happy teen sperm whale with an affinity for dressing in pink clothing and accessories. Unlike her father, who is tight with cash, Pearl enjoys shopping at Bikini Bottom Mall with her girlfriends. Occasionally her teenage emotions might overwhelm her large body and spring forth in a flood of tears or fountain from her spout, instigating her father to announce "Thar she blows!"

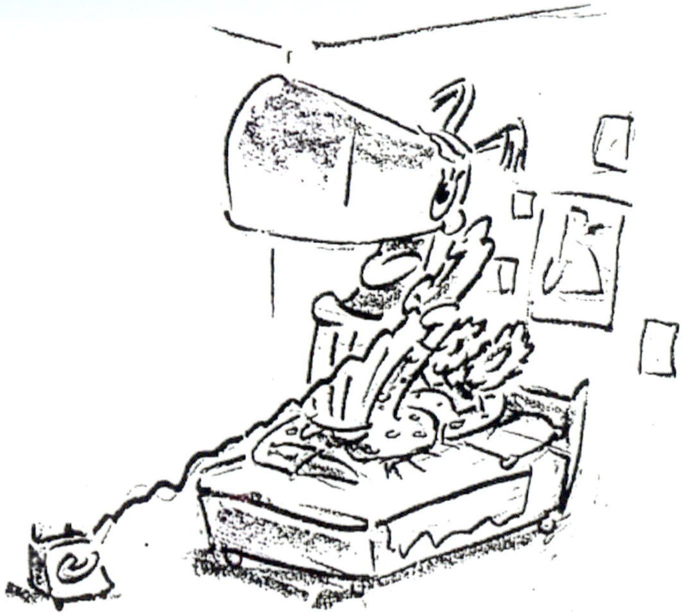

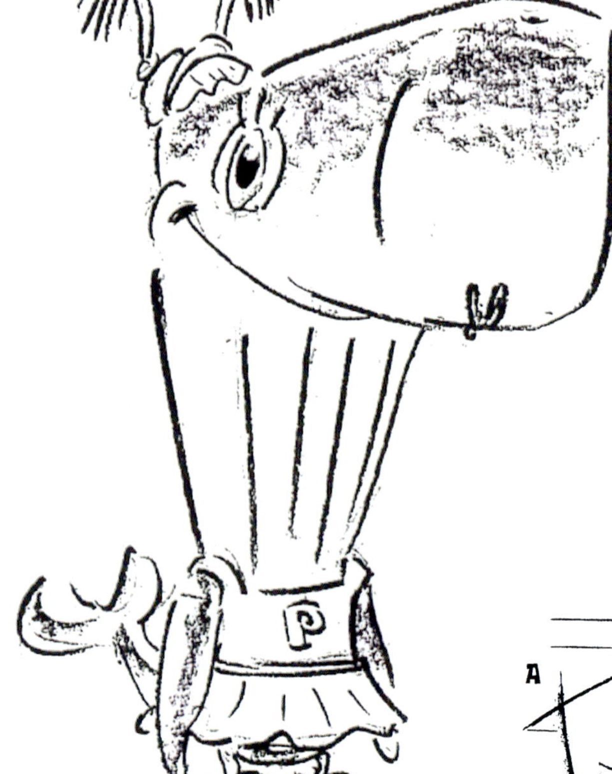

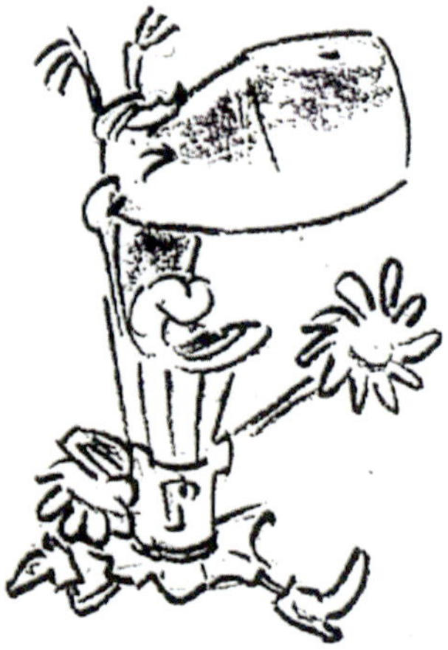

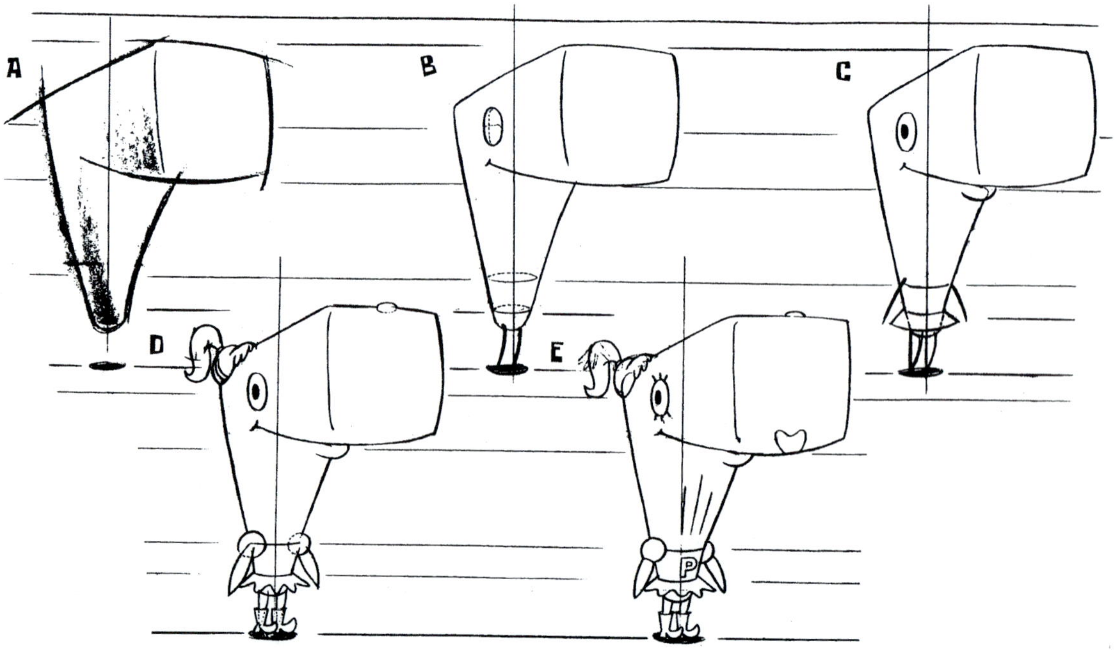

Early concept art of Pearl, plus "how to draw" guidance [lower right]

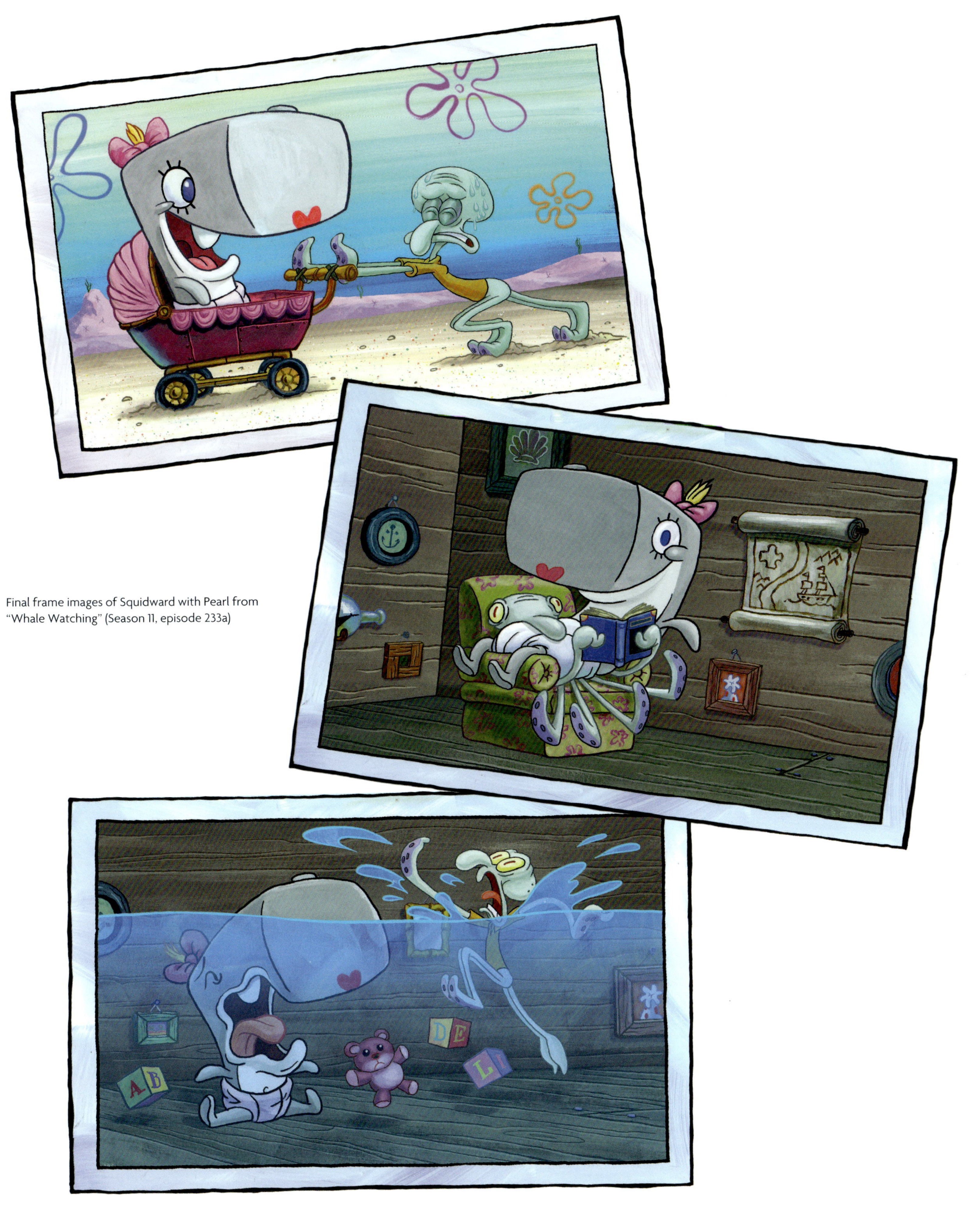

Final frame images of Squidward with Pearl from "Whale Watching" (Season 11, episode 233a)

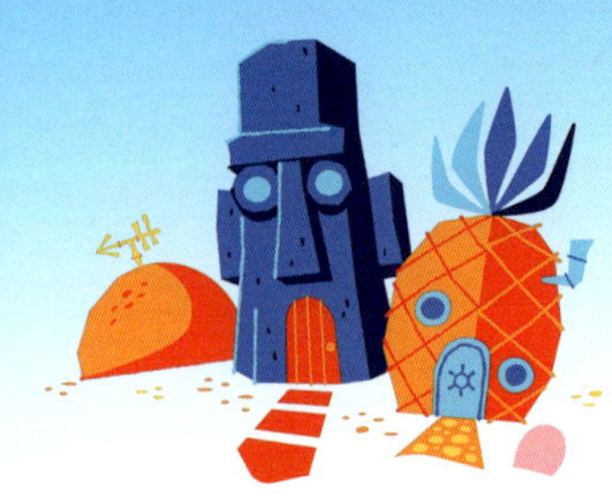

SANDY CHEEKS

The figurative "fish out of water" in Bikini Bottom is Sandy Cheeks, a strong-minded, science-focused squirrel from Texas. Outfitted in a diving suit and living in an air-filled "treedome" allows Sandy to cohabitate amongst her aquatic friends, a circle in which she often provides much-needed logic and problem-solving skills. Sandy's flower accent gives the slightest balance of a feminine touch to her persona while her talents for math, singing, athletics, guitar, and karate add to her overall impressive presence, giving her a skillset that can keep her "busier than a six-legged horse in tap shoes," as she might be so inspired to say herself.

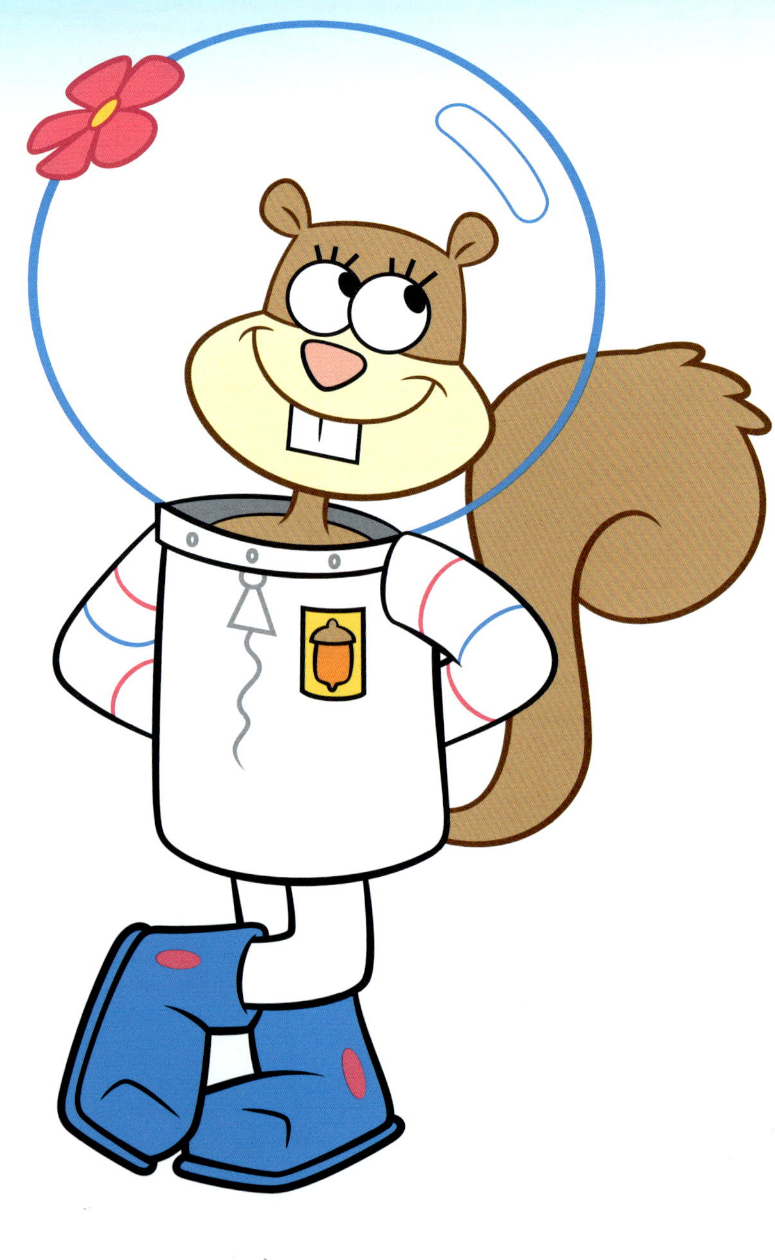

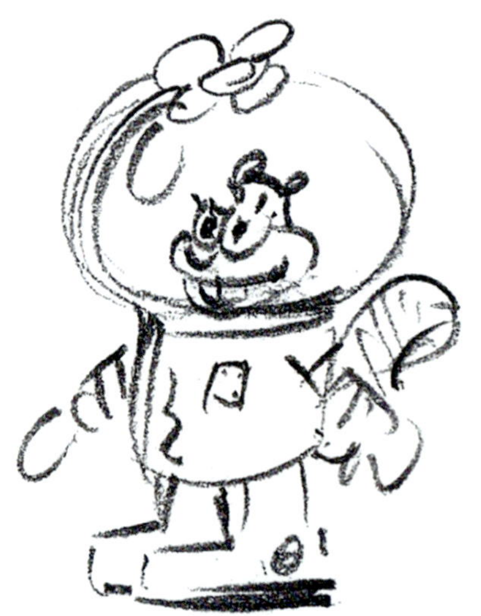

Concept sketches [lower left and lower right], plus storyboard sketch [upper right] of Sandy with multiple options for magnifying glass styling, and final charcter art [upper left]

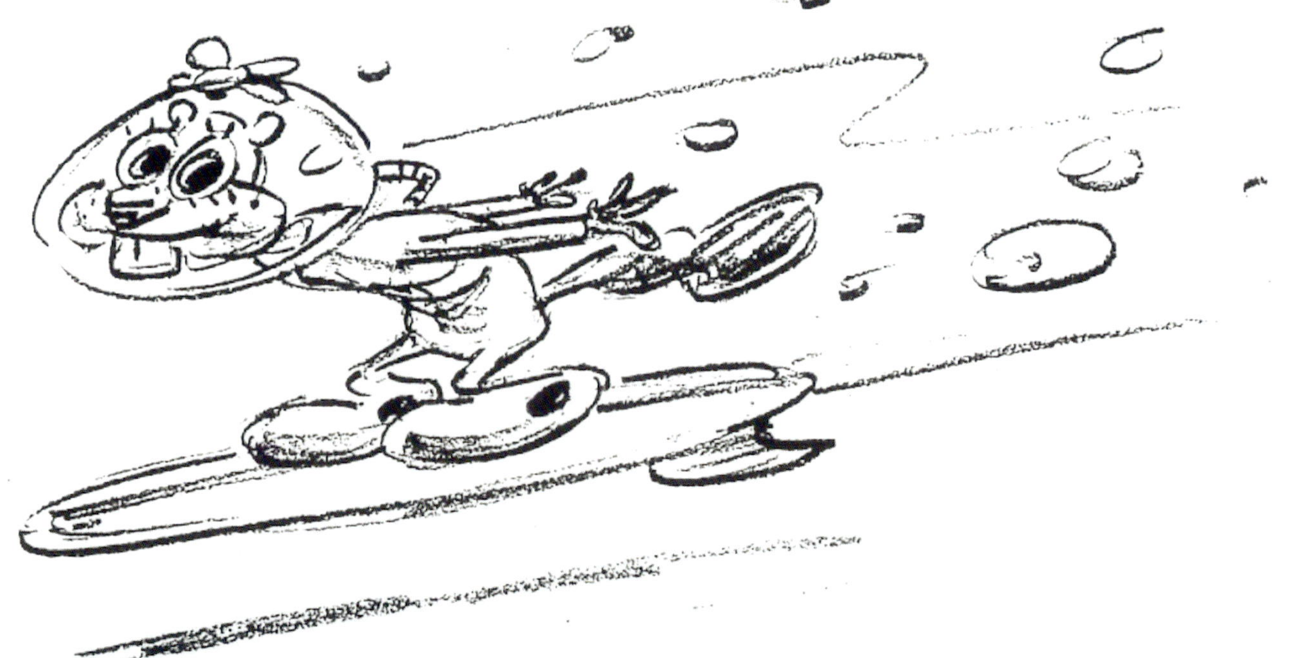

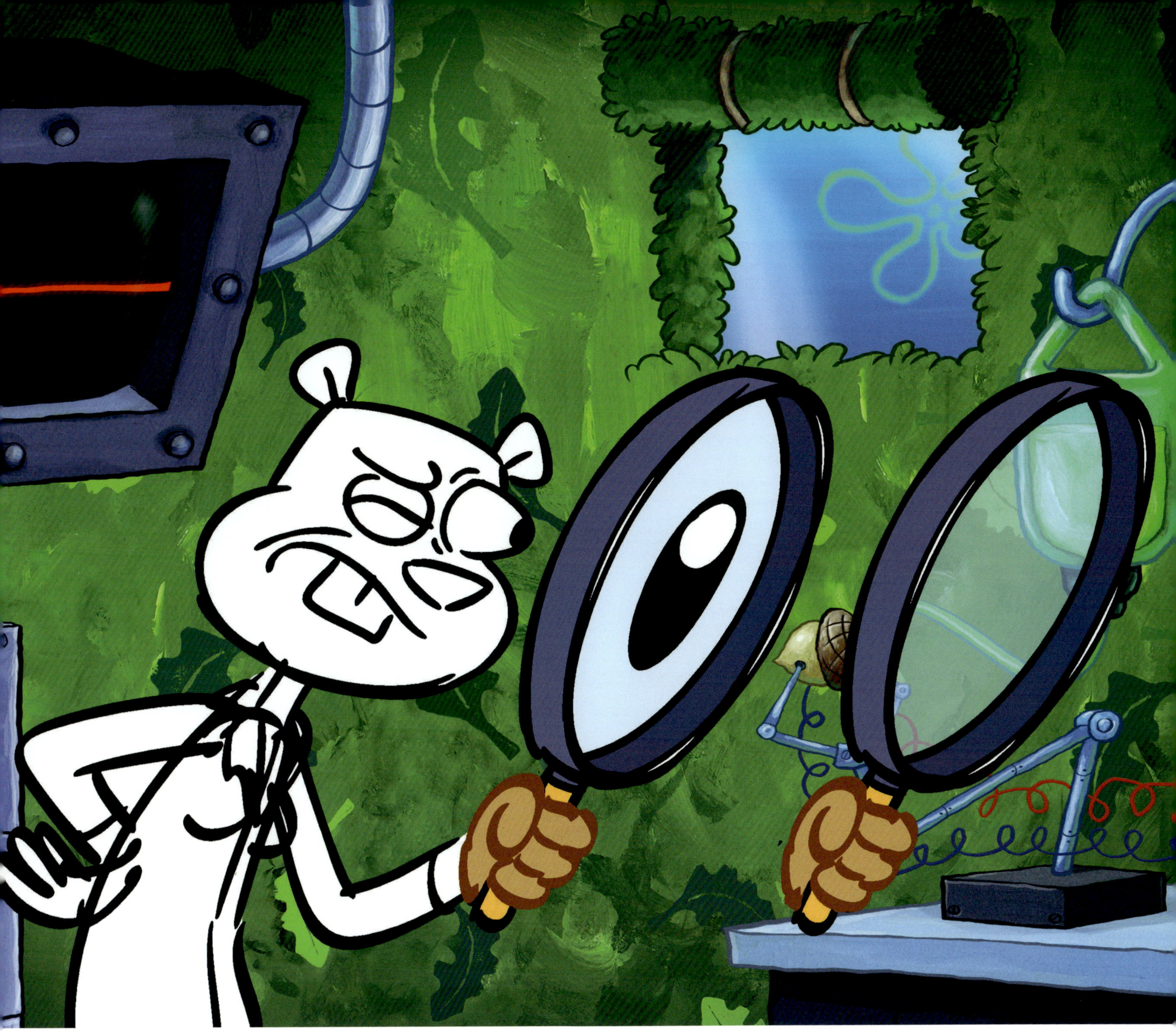

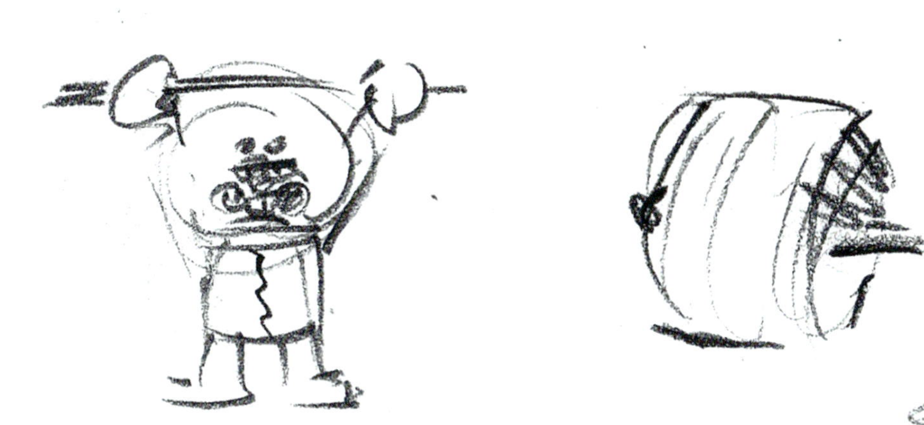

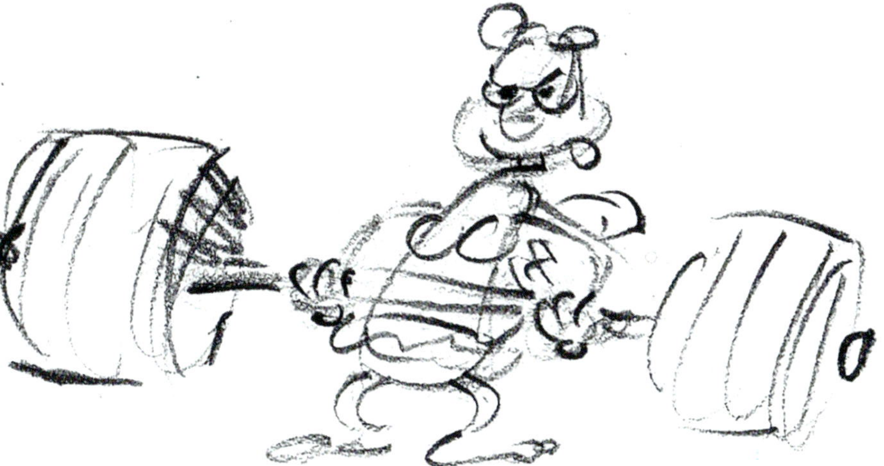

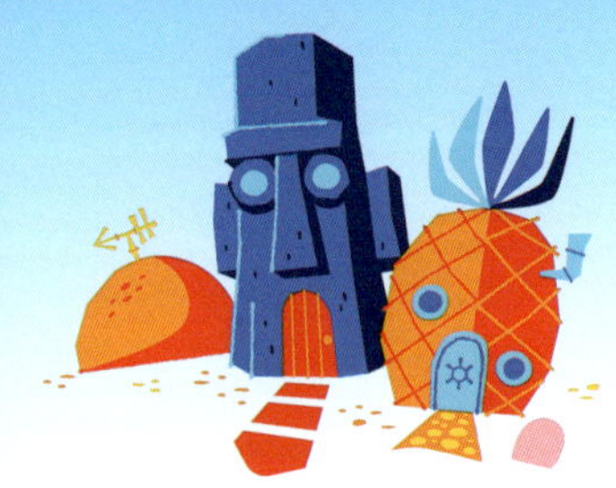

PLANKTON

Sheldon J. Plankton might be one of the smallest creatures in the ocean, but his ambitions make his presence much greater than that of the average copepod. "Plankton is a hapless villain. I love the fact that his grievance comes largely from his tiny size," says former director Tim Hill. Although he is the owner of the Chum Bucket restaurant, Plankton feeds on misplaced confidence and an unending obsession with obtaining the secret formula for the Krabby Patty, with a side of yearning for world domination for good measure. "His one eye (although scientifically accurate) is the perfect metaphor for his singular focus on destroying his competitor by sabotage and not innovation in his own recipes. If only he had another eye, maybe he could better see his folly," notes former executive producer Paul Tibbitt.

As both the writer and voice for Plankton, Mr. Lawrence feels that he "had to prove Plankton could survive as more than a one-note character trying to get that recipe. He's a more complex, wounded character who is really looking for a friend, in a way, but can't let that happen because of his evil front. He carries deep hurt underneath and doesn't want to let anybody know that." While his plans are entertaining in their massive failures time and again, Plankton often reasserts that "he's a genius up to a certain point, then the one brain cell he'd need to carry out his destructive plans just isn't there. He would be tragic if he weren't so funny," adds writer Kaz. Even as he ends up in the lowest of the low places often—being peeled off the bottom of many characters' feet after getting stepped on regularly due to his diminutive size—Plankton's persistence is never squashed for long. "Plankton comes from a long line of toothless-blowhard, paper-tiger villains in cartoons. The more assured he is of his place in the universe, the more satisfying it is when he fails. Napoleon complex taken to the extreme," adds Tibbitt.

Final frame image of Plankton after being squished

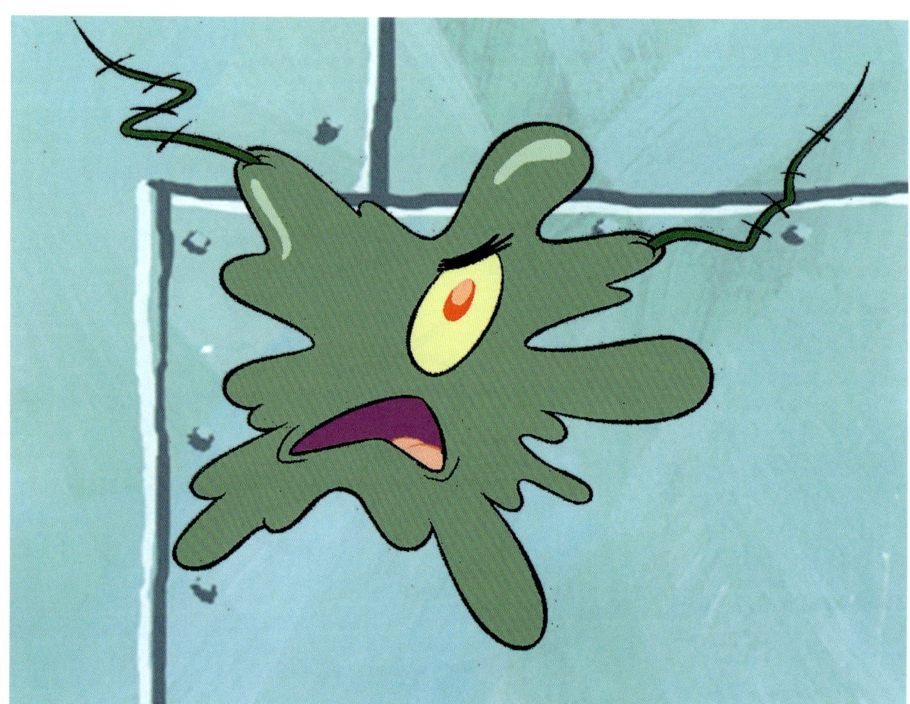

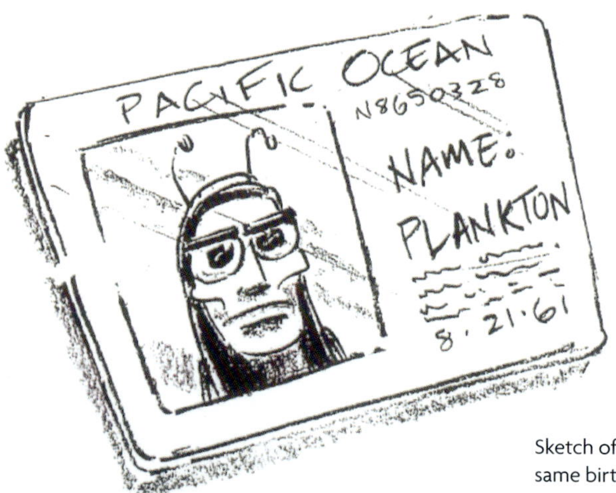

Sketch of Plankton's ID, exhibiting the same birthdate as Stephen Hillenburg

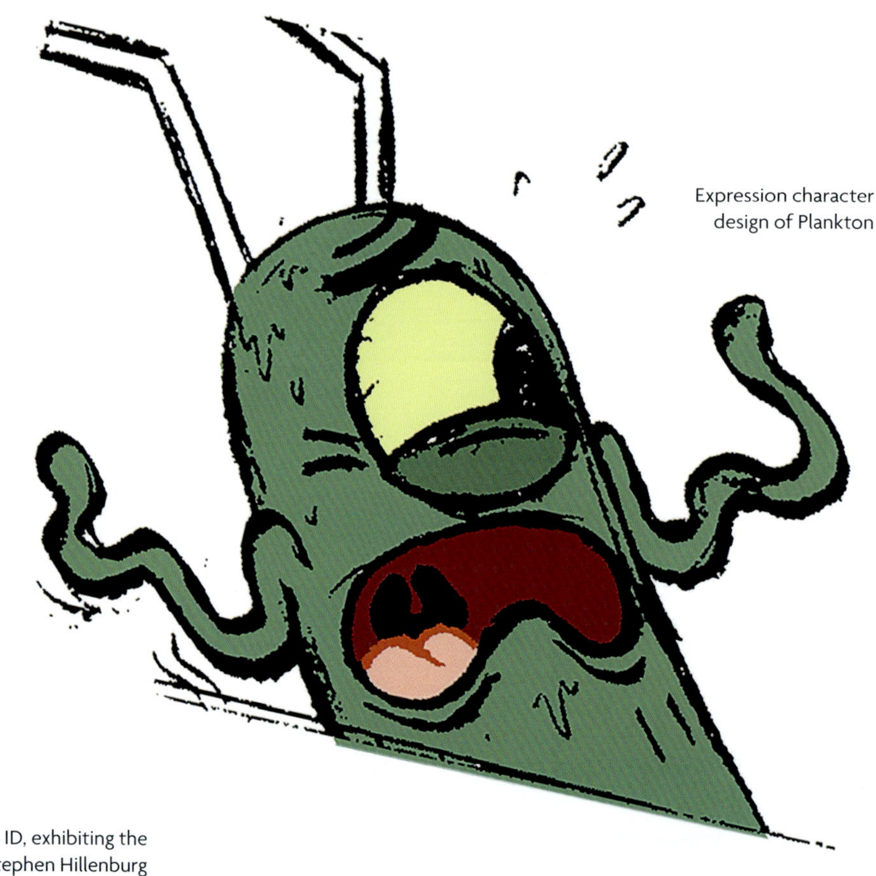

Expression character design of Plankton

Final frame image of Plankton from "Friend or Foe" (Season 5, episode 81)

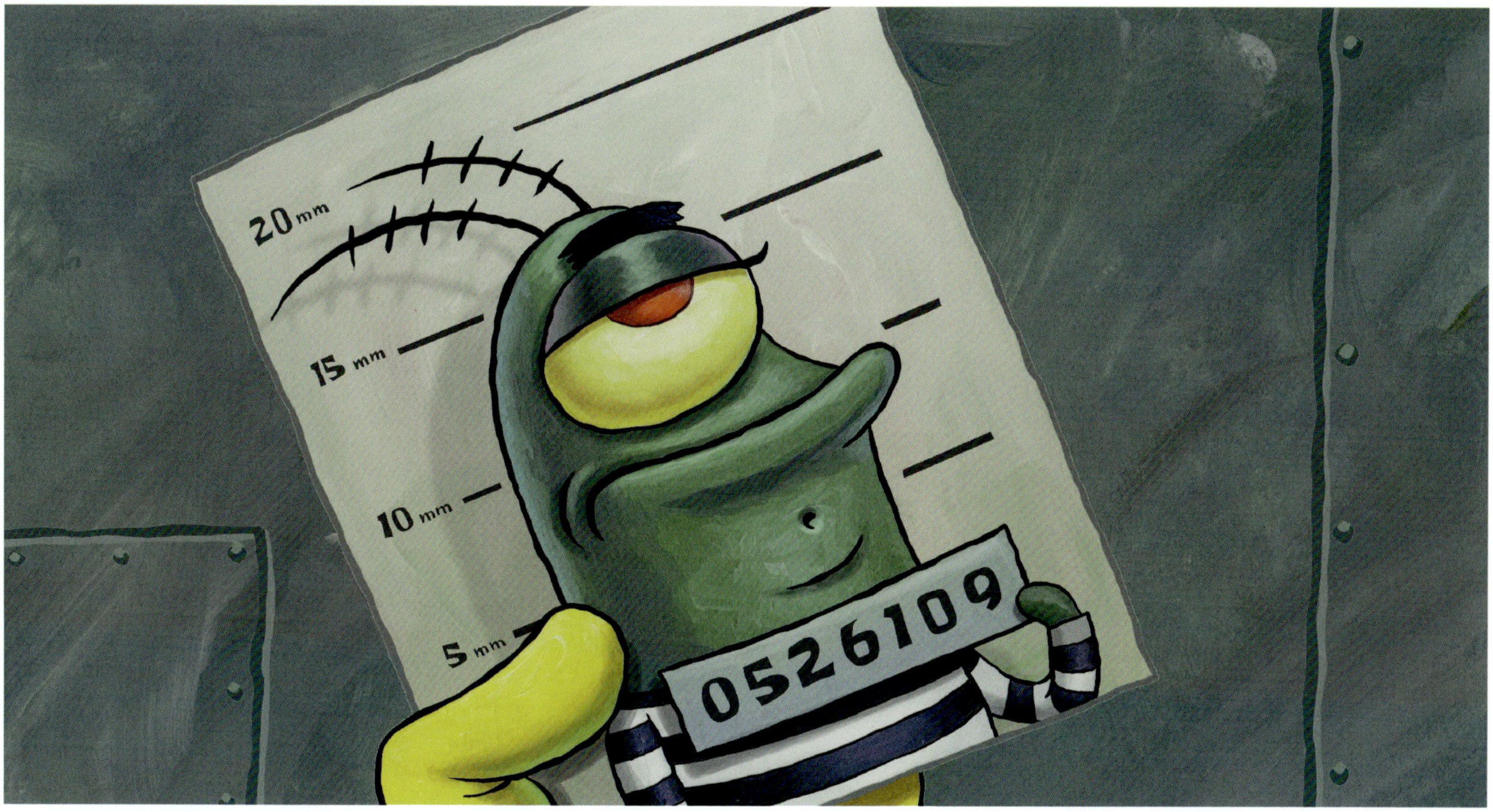

Final frame image of Plankton from "Lame and Fortune" (Season 9, episode 199b)

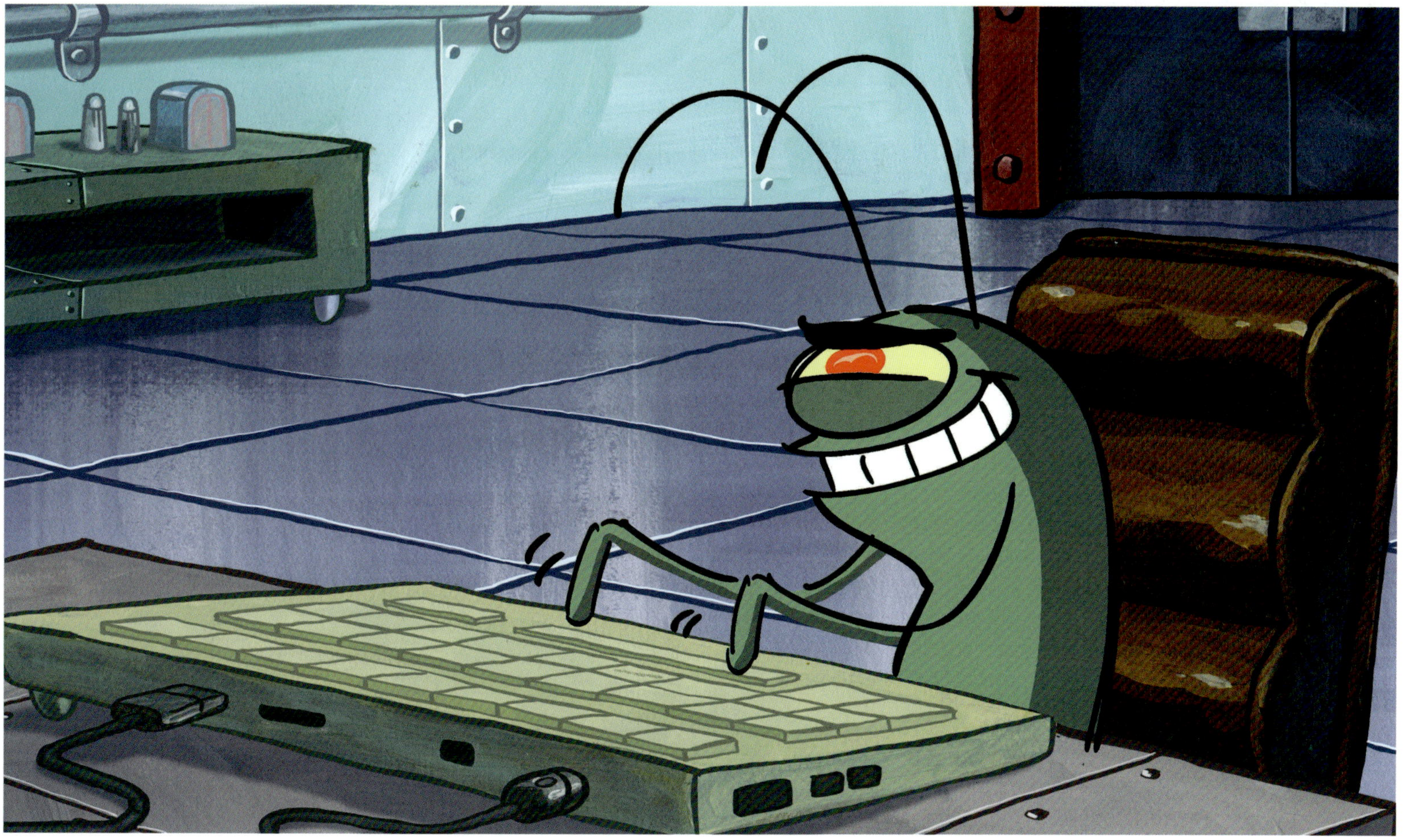

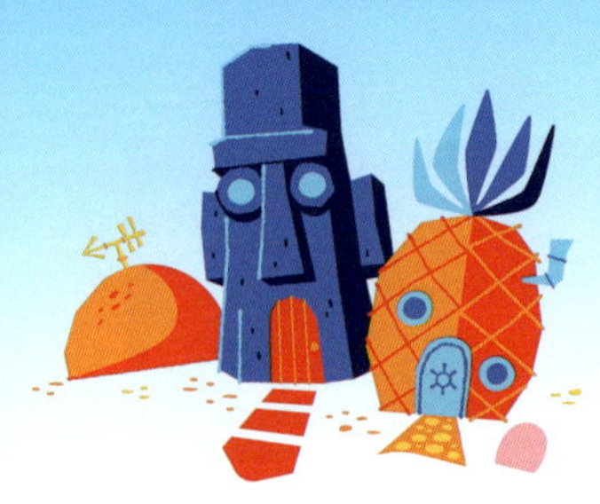

KAREN

Karen is a one-of-a-kind waterproof and sometimes mobile Mark II Surplus UNIVAC computer with more loyalty and patience than any human could ever muster when it comes to dealing with her creator and husband, Plankton. With a screen serving in place of a head, Karen's words and emotions are often clearly visualized in this space by expressive graphic lines, but she is also capable of displaying external images from this monitor as needed. Over the course of her existence, Karen has exhibited variations in her parts, an evolution not unlike the upgrades to electronics that come with never-ending waves of technological advances. But no matter what version of computer she exists as, Karen ultimately remains a dedicated spouse and partner to Plankton, even though she could easily achieve all his evil goals and desired success if only he and his many faulty plans would stand down and let her roll with her own.

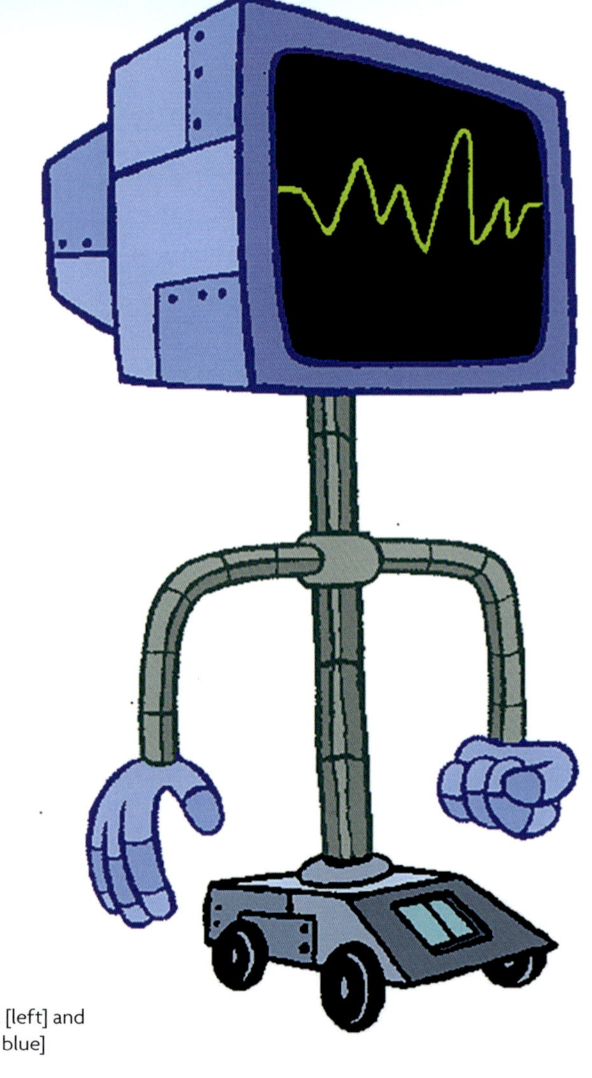

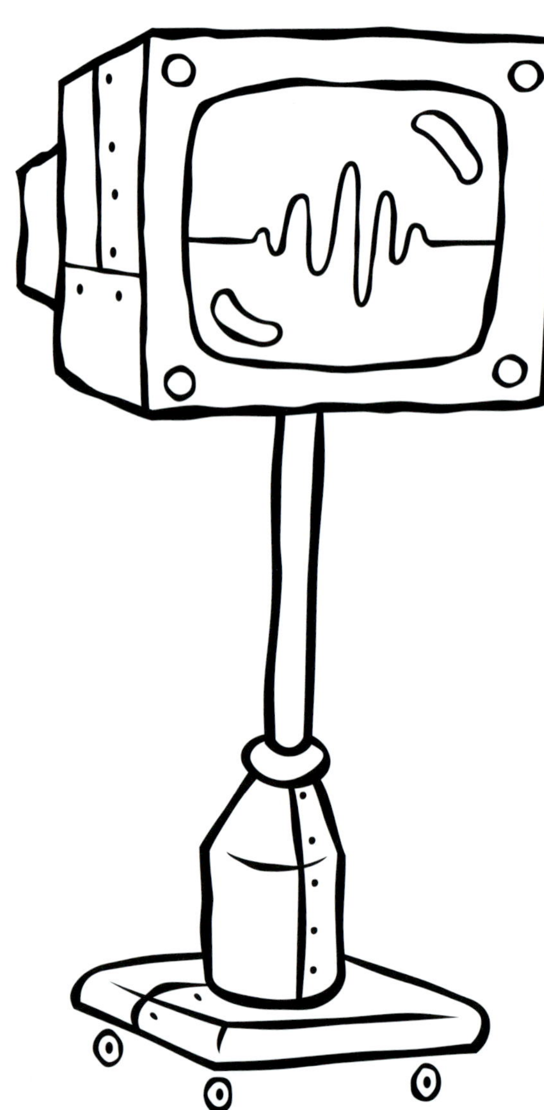

Line art character model [left] and final art of Karen [in blue]

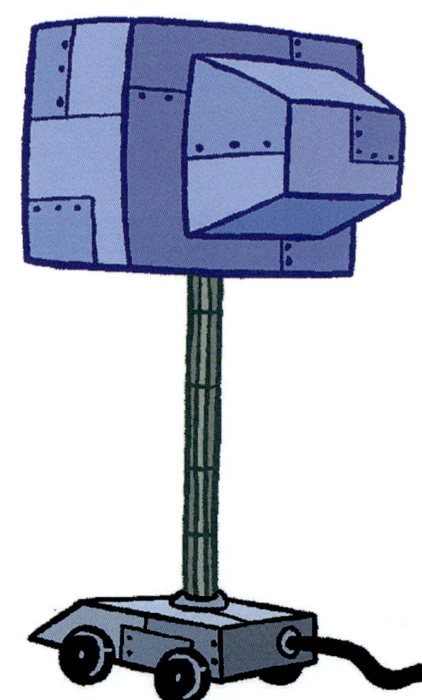

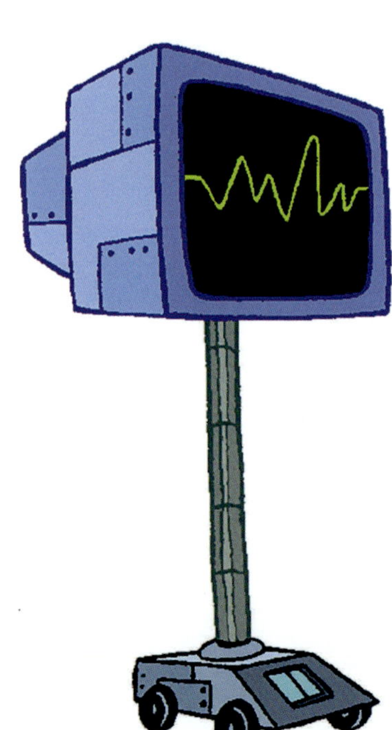

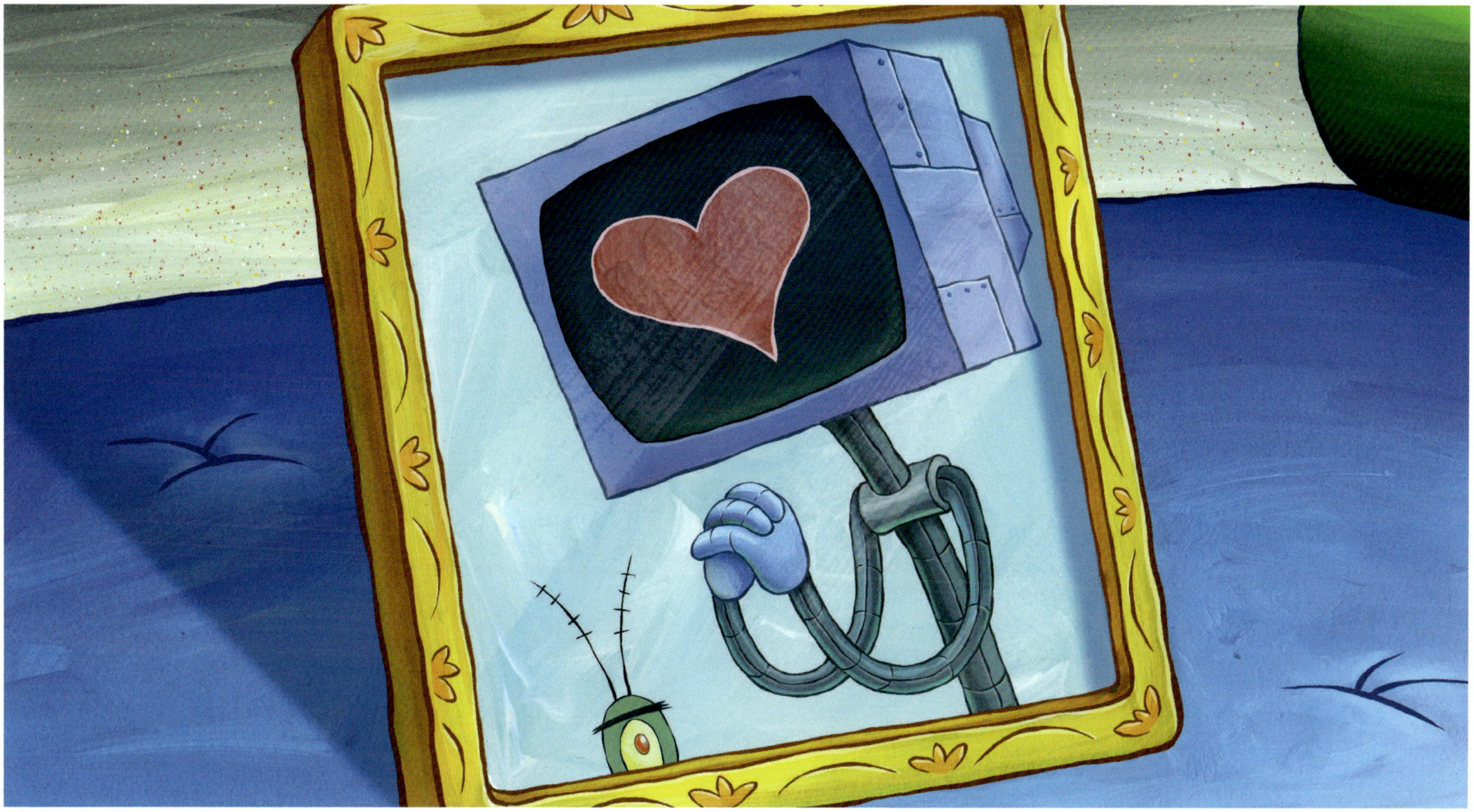

Final frame images of fond memories for Plankton and Karen

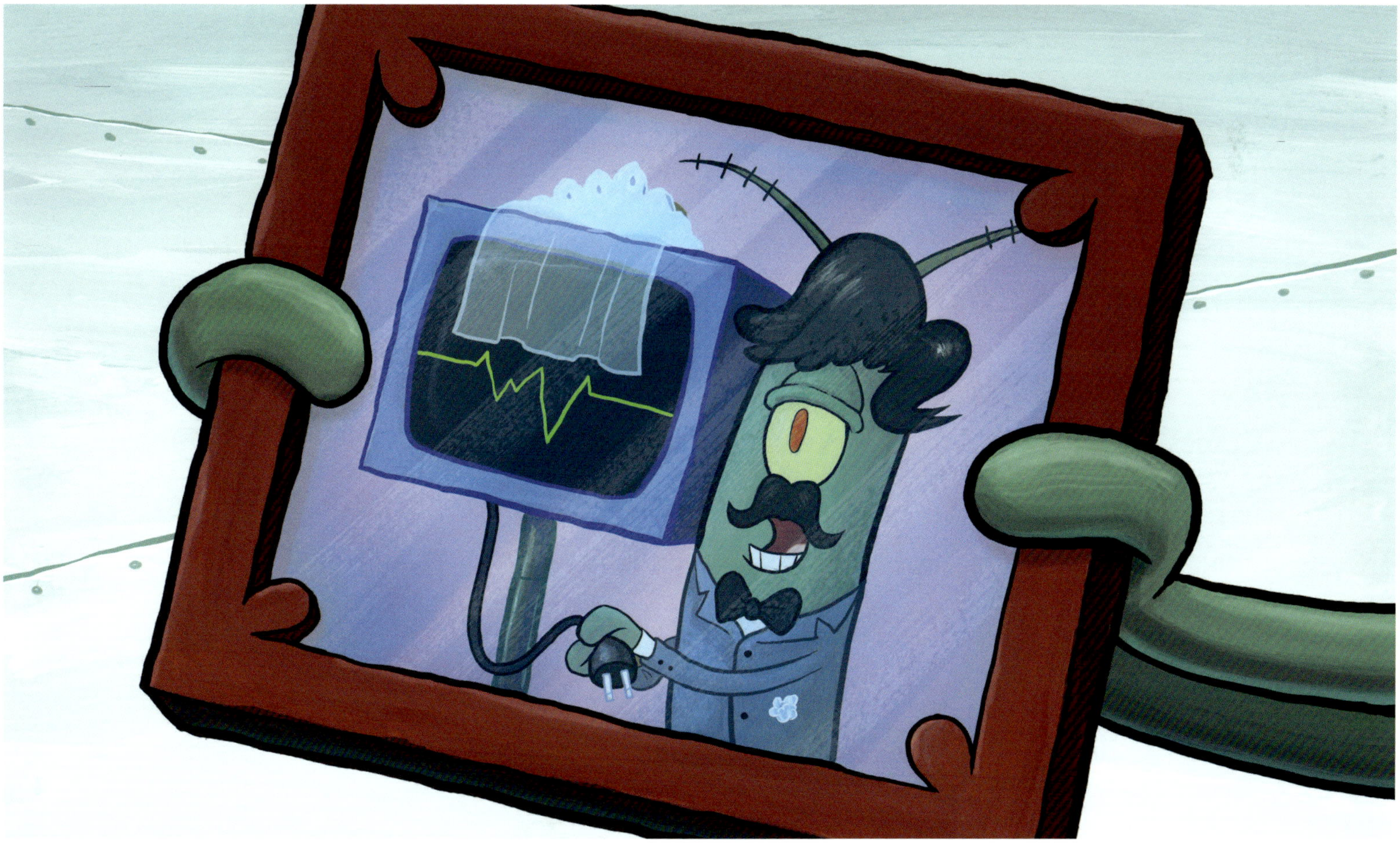

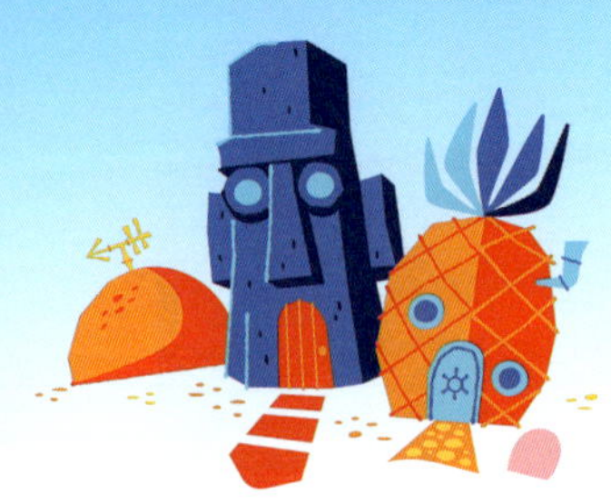

MRS. PUFF

Penelope Puff serves as the boating teacher in Bikini Bottom, similar to an automobile driving instructor in the out-of-water world. A sailor-suit clad pufferfish topped with a blond wig that has been known to fall off her head, Mrs. Puff is revered not only for her noble line of work but also for the fact she exists out of creative compromise: She was added to the Bikini Bottom cast of characters when having SpongeBob be a student became a studio mandate for series approval—thus Mrs. Puff's teaching about obeying traffic signals holds even deeper significance, since she can claim some authority in the greenlight for the SpongeBob SquarePants series. Many nods to her rich history exist within her appearances, but the way SpongeBob annoys Mrs. Puff is both humorous and as pointedly clear as her spikes.

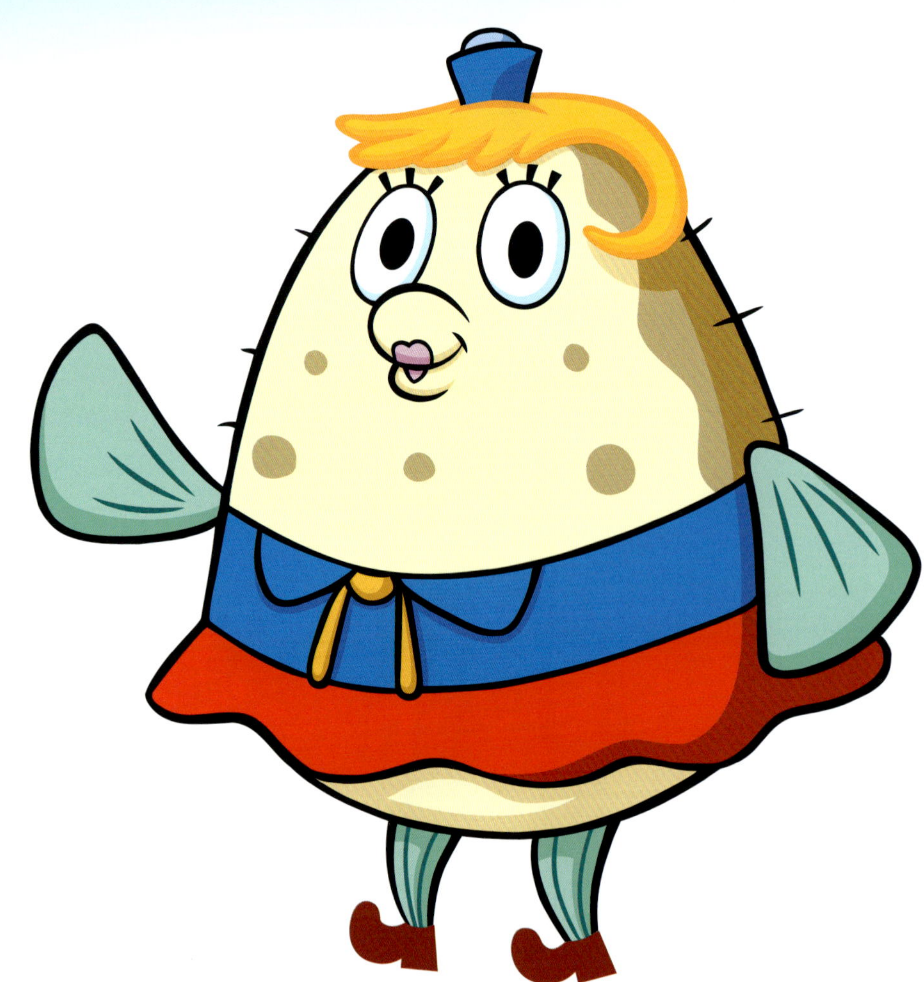

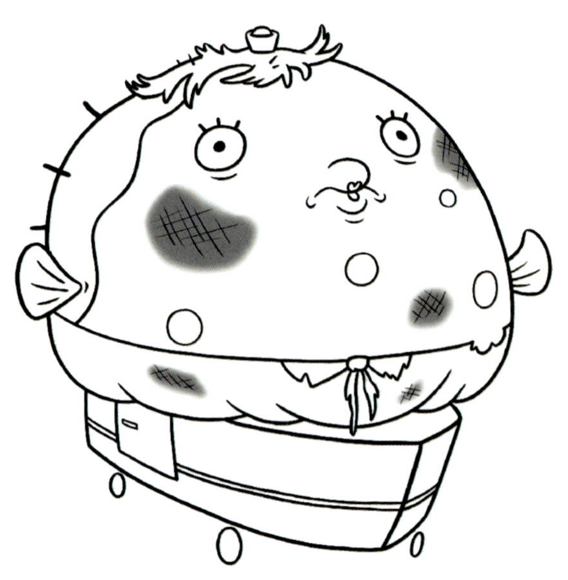

Final art [above] plus character effects and expressions of Mrs. Puff

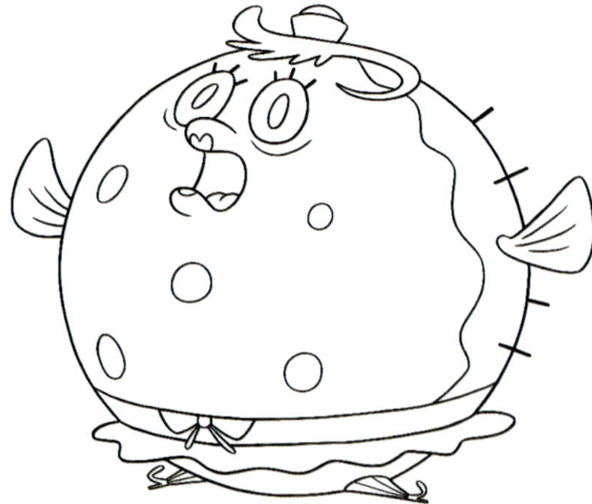

"CLASSMATES, WHO AM I TO DESERVE SUCH A GREAT HONOR? WHY, I WOULD BE NOTHING WITHOUT MRS. PUFF. AND TO MY PUBLIC, ALL I CAN SAY IS, I'M TOUCHED. AND FURTHERMORE, I WILL CARRY OUT MY DUTY. CRIME AND PUNISHMENT. PUNISHMENT AND CRIME. AND THE HALL, WHICH REMINDS ME OF AN EXTREMELY LONG SPEECH WRITTEN BY THE GREATEST HALL MONITOR OF ALL TIME. FRIENDS, STUDENTS, JUVENILE DELINQUENTS, LEND ME YOUR EARS. IN CONCLUSION, AND WITHOUT A MOMENT TO SPARE, I WILL PUT ON THIS UNIFORM AND ASSUME MY DUTIES AS... HALL MONITOR!"

SPEECH BY SPONGEBOB IN MRS. PUFF'S CLASS AFTER FINALLY BEING NAMED HALL MONITOR

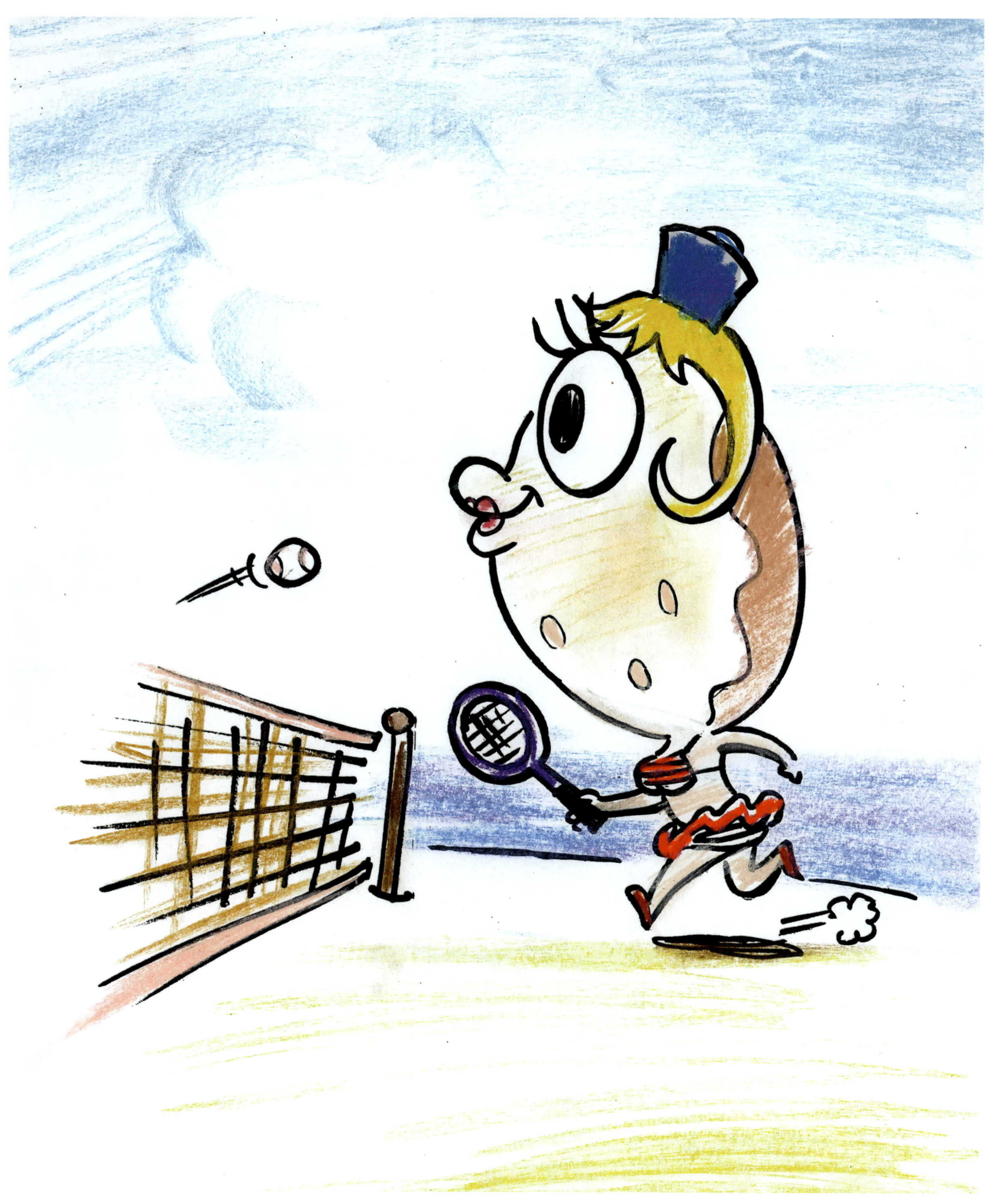

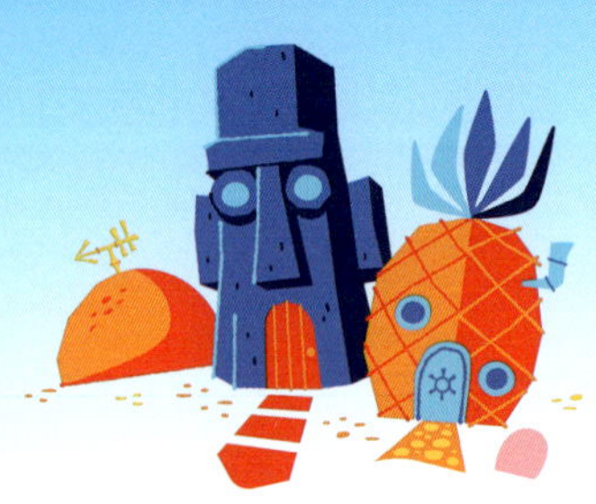

THE WIDER NET OF BIKINI BOTTOM CHARACTERS

With the realm of imagination in animation seemingly boundless, the opportunity for new and diverse characters to populate the world of SpongeBob SquarePants is as deep and wide as the sea. As former designer Todd White explains, "For a character designer, the show is a dream. I love creating the fast, odd shapes, and then building a character within those shapes." When he would show up for work at the start of the week, White recalls that "the script would be on my desk to create whatever cast was necessary for that episode. It could go anywhere from a biker fish to an amusement park to beach-goers to Captain Neptune. It was always great to see what new characters were going to pop up."

Executive producer Marc Ceccarelli really enjoys the challenge of introducing new characters into the franchise. "There's a lot of room to play with all the different styles of characters in Bikini Bottom, but you still need to make them feel like they are part of the visual language that the original crew set up. I love the fact that every character is designed for their own unique personality."

While there are not enough pages in this aquarium-on-paper book to collect all of the amazing sea life that exists in Bikini Bottom, here's a school of fish and other water-based folks that fit swimmingly.

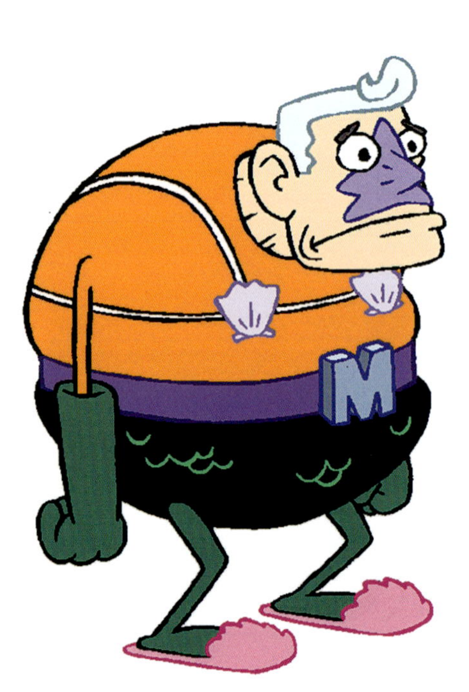

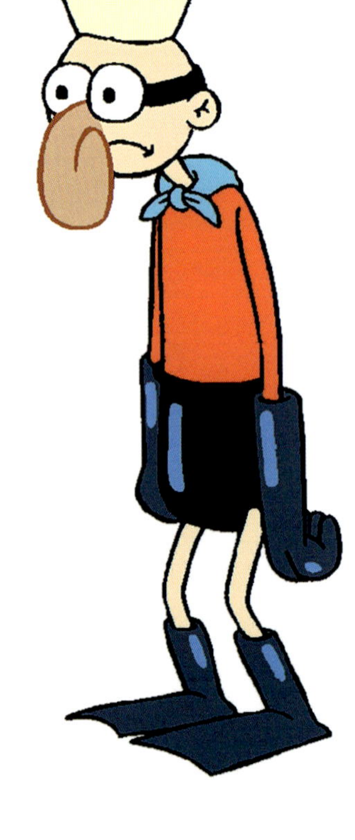

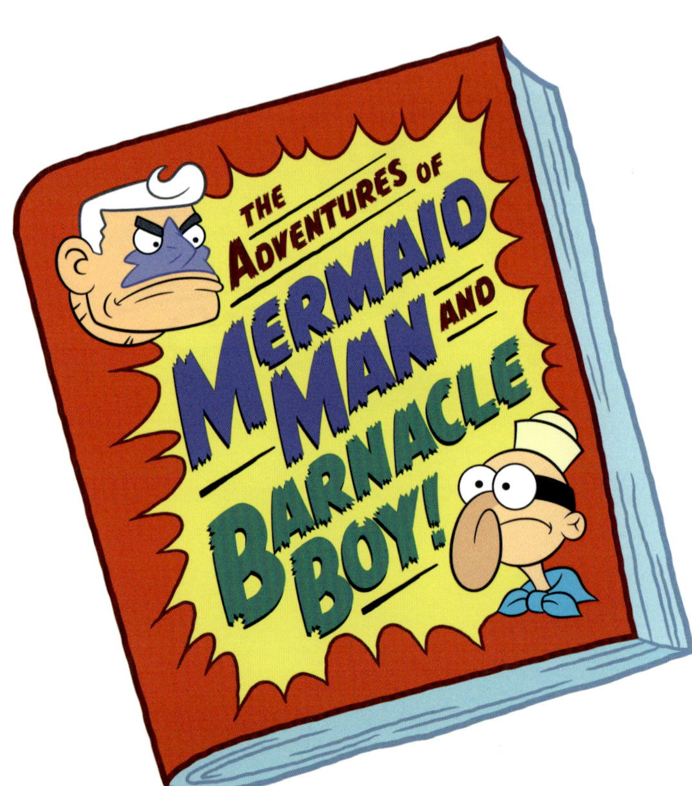

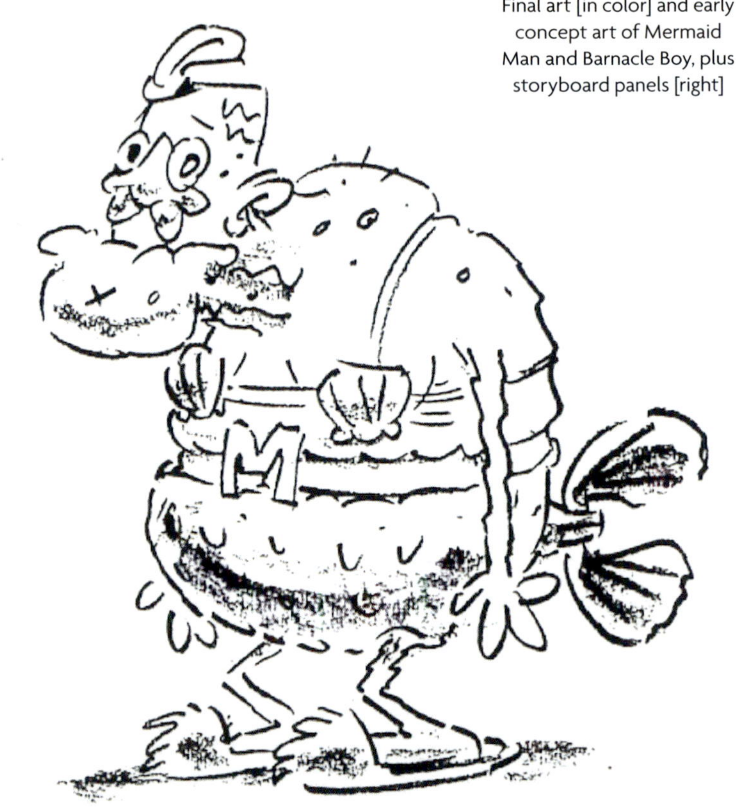

Final art [in color] and early concept art of Mermaid Man and Barnacle Boy, plus storyboard panels [right]

MERMAID MAN & BARNACLE BOY

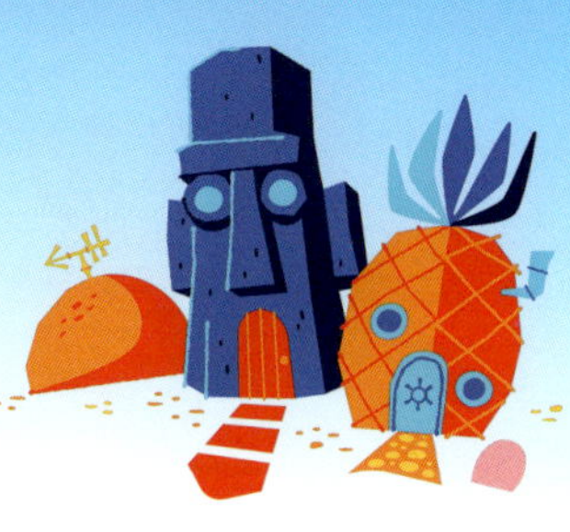

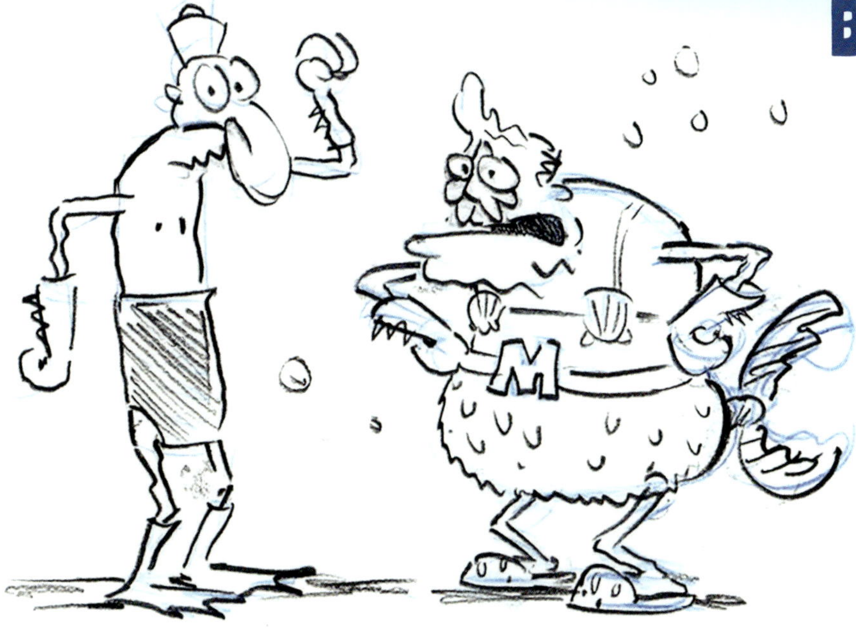

From the very start, Mermaid Man and Barnacle Boy were part of Stephen Hillenburg's vision, giving SpongeBob heroes to look up to, while also nodding to the Saturday morning cartoon superheroes of Hillenburg's own youth—an homage to the briny-but-buff pair Aquaman and Aqualad. The added twist of this beloved team being retired and geriatric when SpongeBob comes to interact with them adds to the salty fun but doesn't slow down the surge of humor and action. Adding another level of nautically translated nostalgia is the duo's voice casting: The younger versions featured the vocal talent of Adam West (classic Batman) as Mermaid Man and Burt Lord (classic Robin) as Barnacle Boy, while the retirees were voiced by classic television stars of *McHale's Navy* Ernest Borgnine as Mermaid Man and Tim Conway as Barnacle Boy... the "boy" factor still in play even when over the age of fifty.

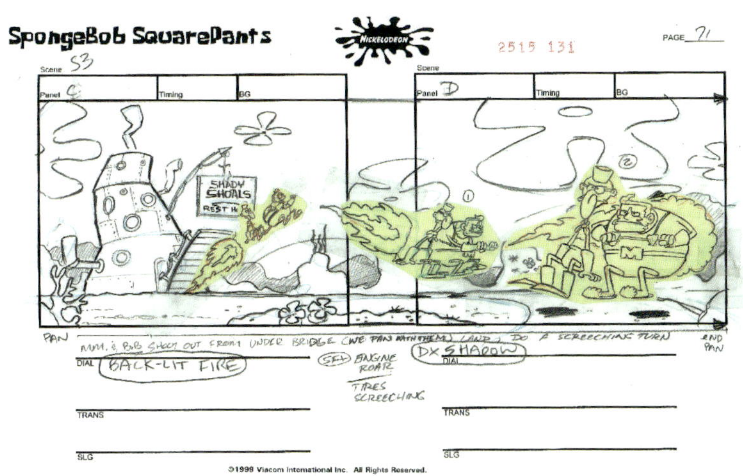

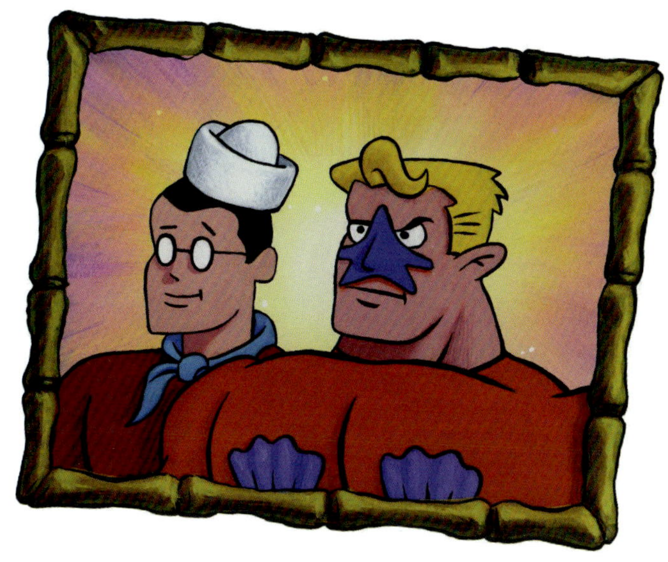

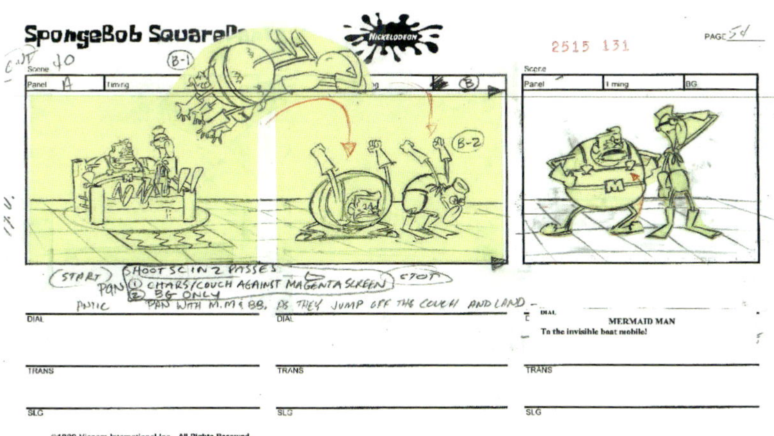

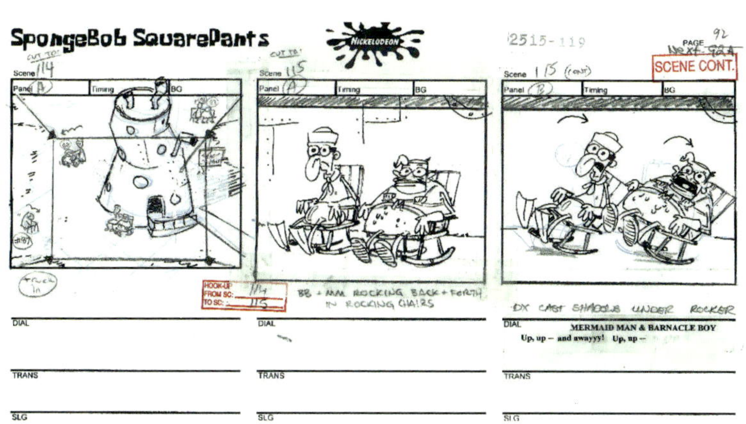

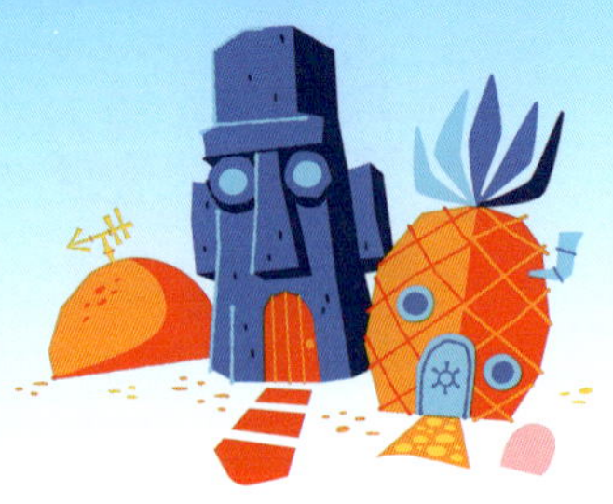

PATCHY THE PIRATE & POTTY THE PARROT

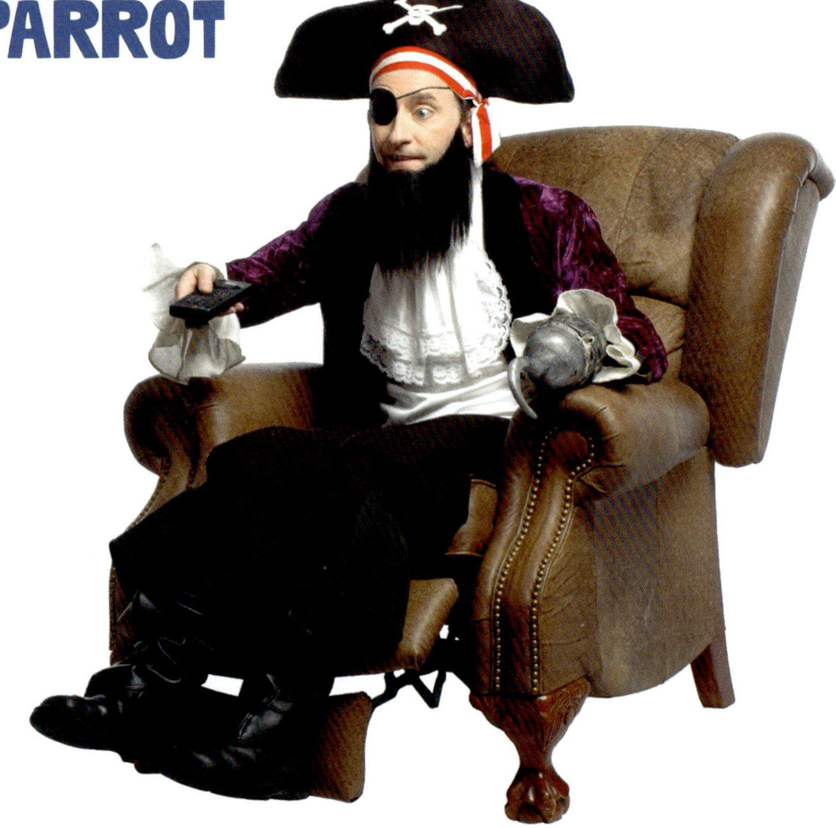

This pair live at the place where the SpongeBob SquarePants animated series takes a sharp turn into the live-action realm. Serving as the host of special episodes and other stand-alone appearances, the peg-legged, gap-toothed Patchy the Pirate broadcasts from his home in Encino, California, along with the sarcastic stringed puppet, Potty the Parrot. Patchy is the ultimate fan—proclaiming himself the president of the SpongeBob SquarePants fan club, owning all the merch, and cosplay dressing to the max—but his presence is a meta embodiment of the low-budget local TV show hosts that Stephen Hillenburg grew up watching on his own television set. Threatening folks with walking the plank or losing the lost episode has not cost Patchy his job... but then again, it's probably a low-paying job that no one else wants, not unlike SpongeBob's own employment situation. Perhaps the best figurative feather in this pirate's cap is the fact that Tom Kenny portrays Patchy.

Live-action images of Patchy the Pirate [upper] and Patchy with Potty the Parrot [lower]

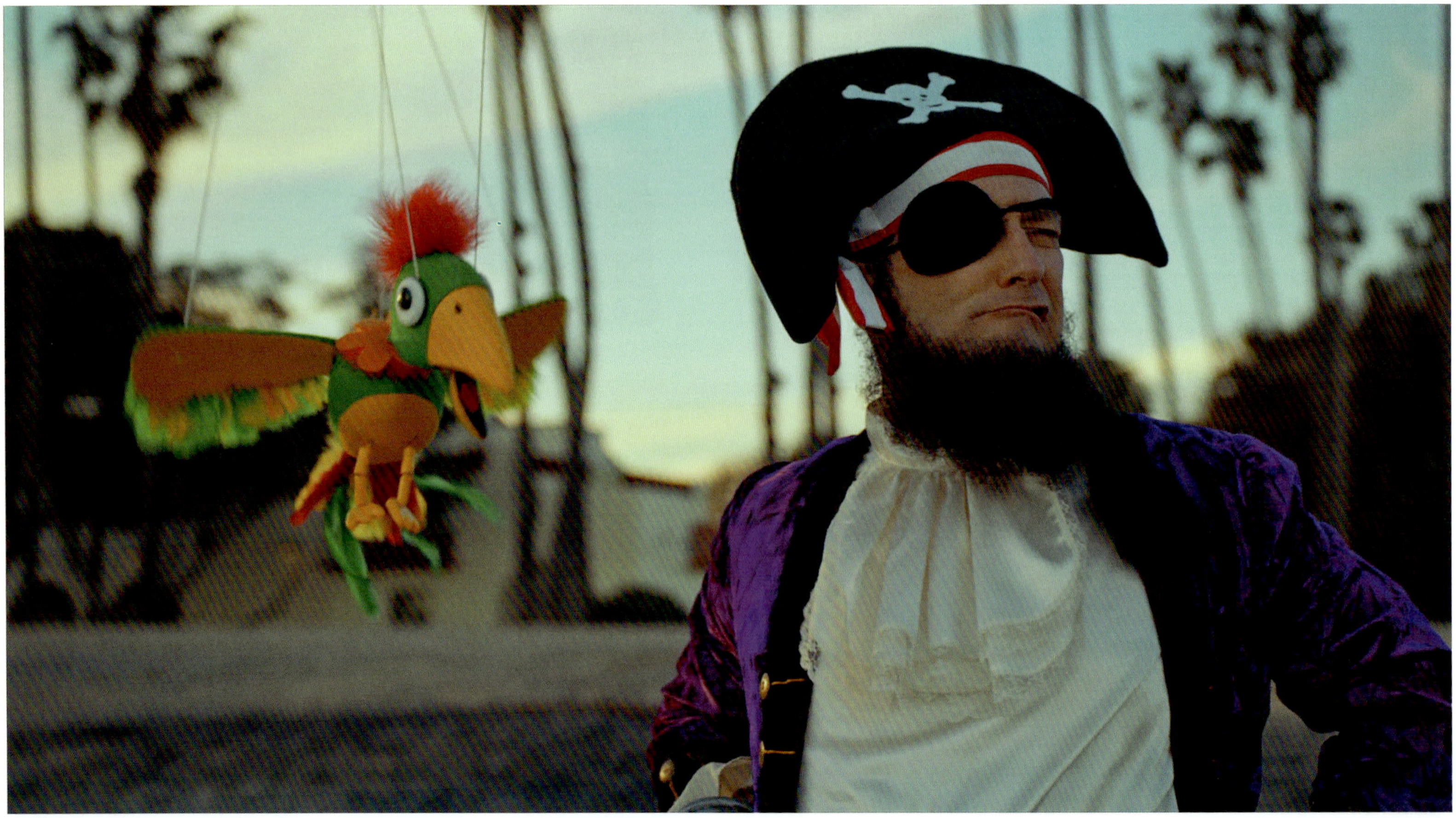

FLYING DUTCHMAN

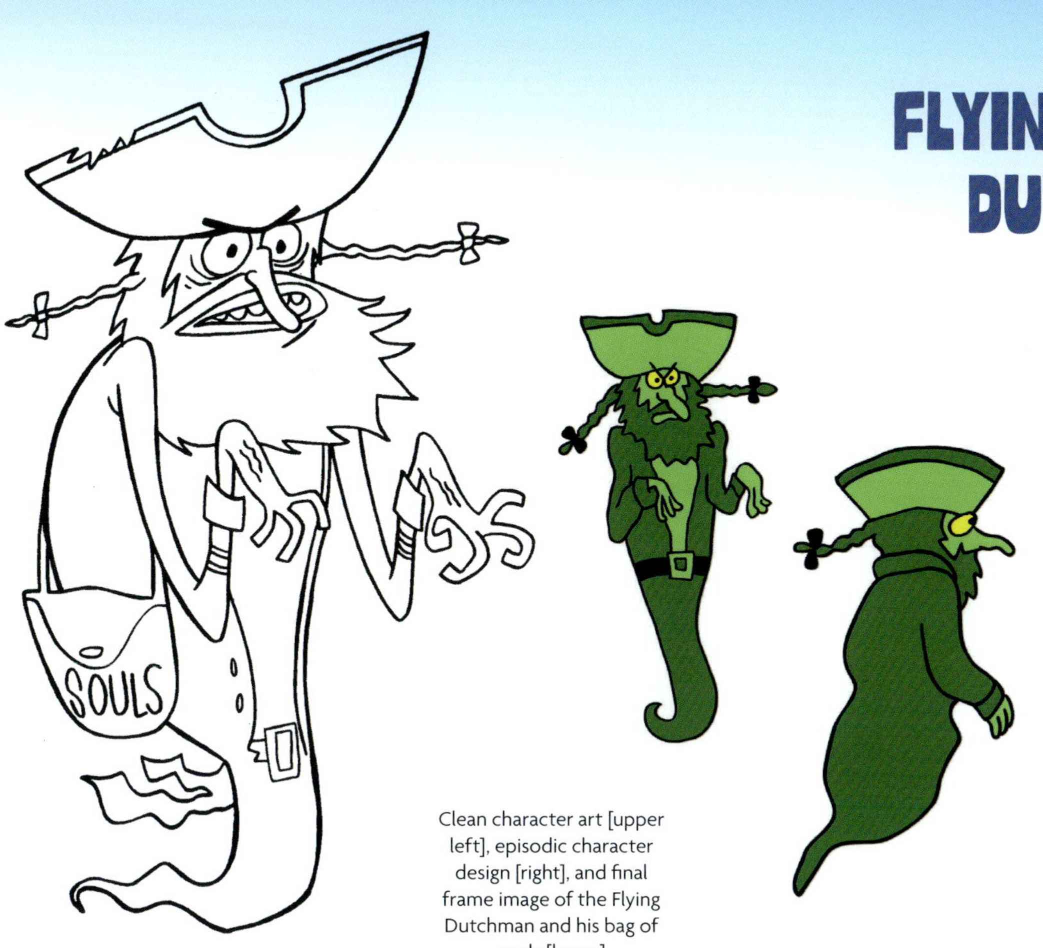

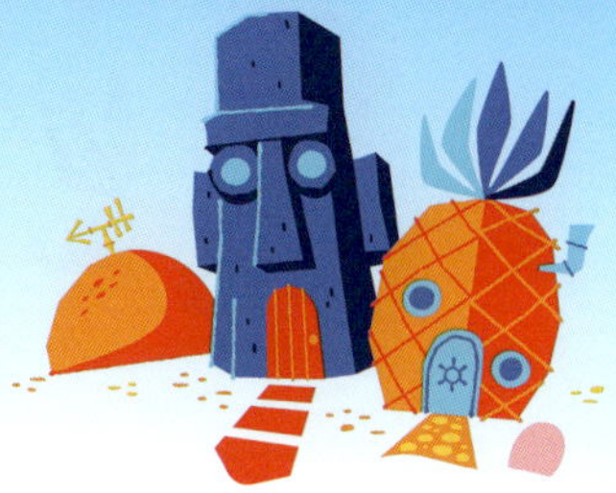

Clean character art [upper left], episodic character design [right], and final frame image of the Flying Dutchman and his bag of souls [lower]

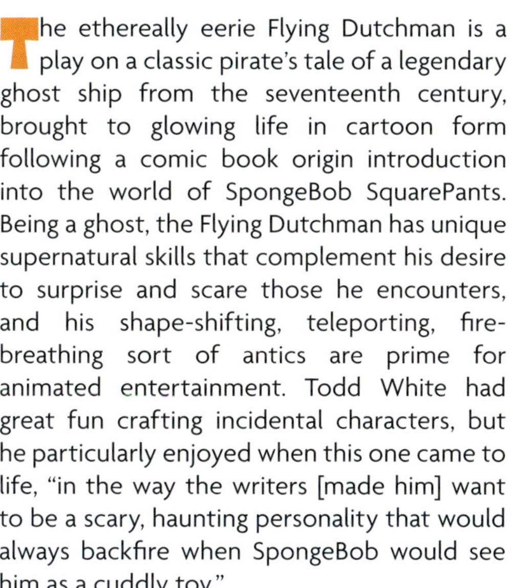

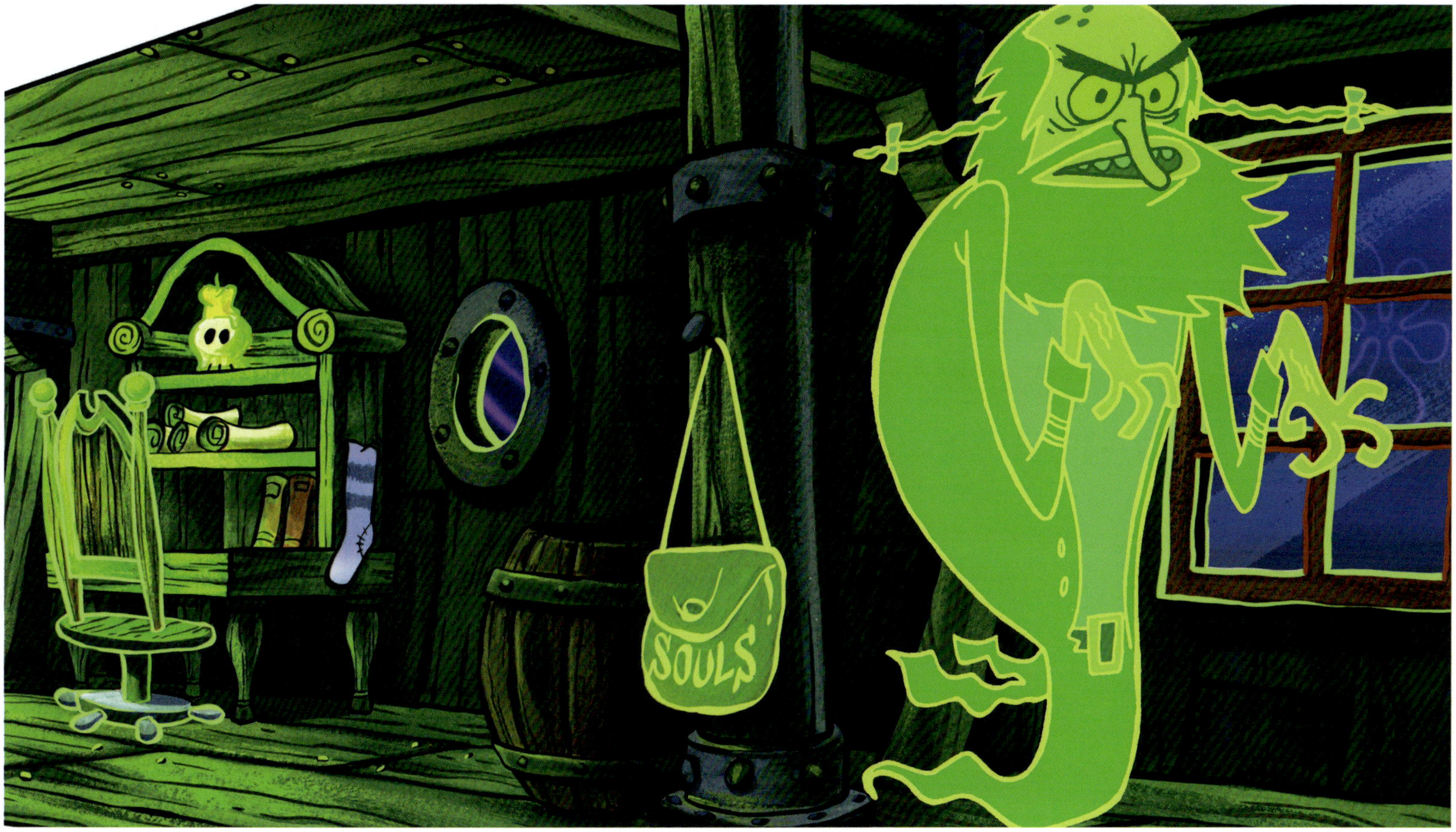

The ethereally eerie Flying Dutchman is a play on a classic pirate's tale of a legendary ghost ship from the seventeenth century, brought to glowing life in cartoon form following a comic book origin introduction into the world of SpongeBob SquarePants. Being a ghost, the Flying Dutchman has unique supernatural skills that complement his desire to surprise and scare those he encounters, and his shape-shifting, teleporting, fire-breathing sort of antics are prime for animated entertainment. Todd White had great fun crafting incidental characters, but he particularly enjoyed when this one came to life, "in the way the writers [made him] want to be a scary, haunting personality that would always backfire when SpongeBob would see him as a cuddly toy."

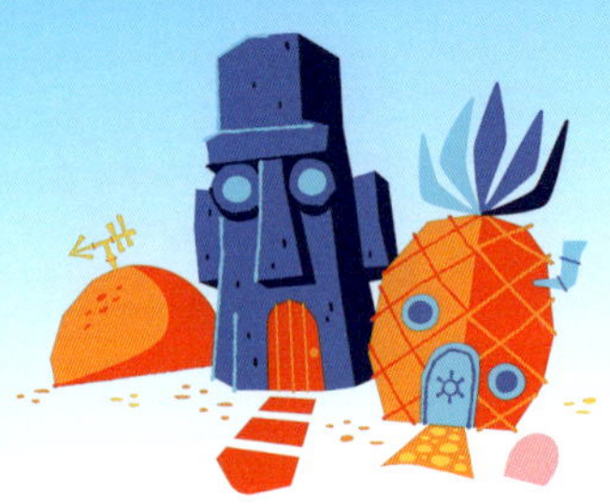

LARRY THE LOBSTER

An aquatic, athletic arthropod, Larry the Lobster spends his time working out and serving as a lifeguard at the Goo Lagoon. His coloring and shorts designs vary from time to time, but that's easy to rationalize if regular workouts and sun exposure may affect wardrobe changes and shell tones.

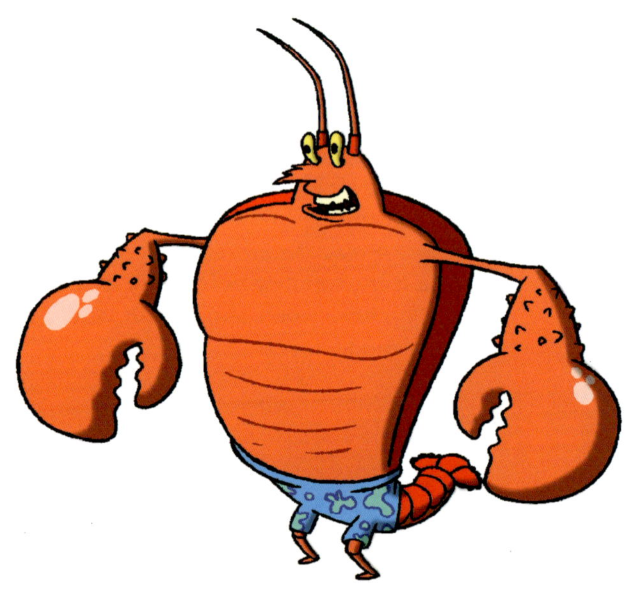

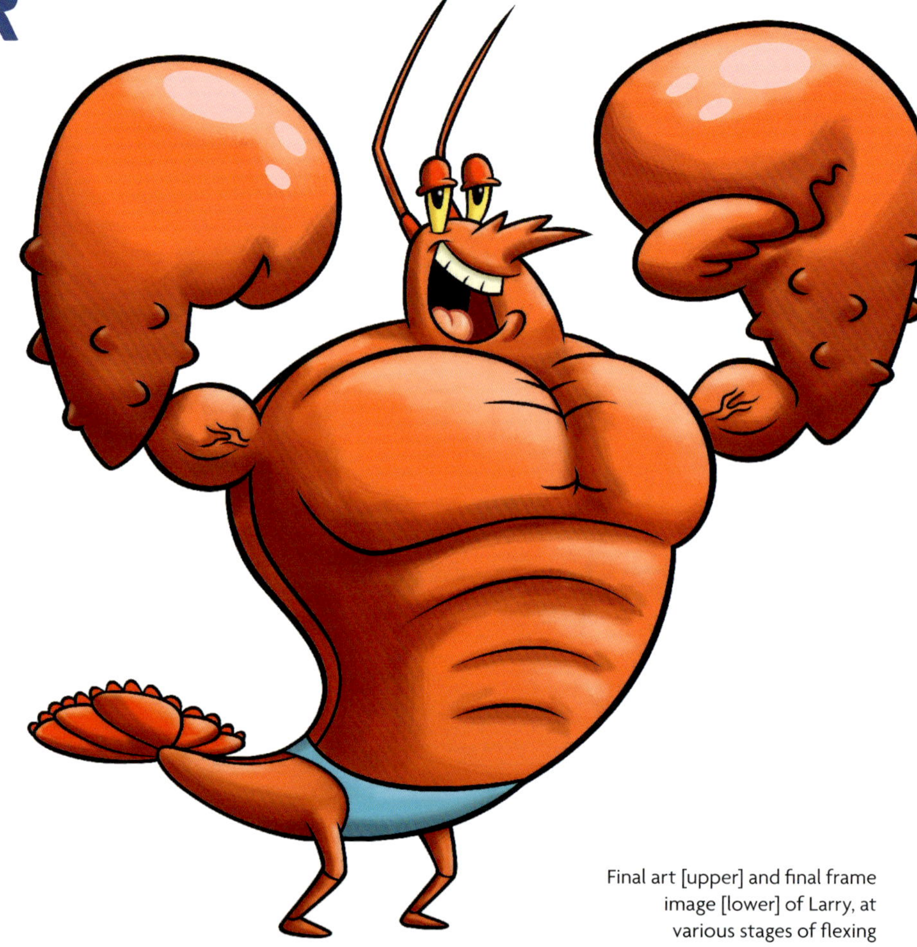

Final art [upper] and final frame image [lower] of Larry, at various stages of flexing

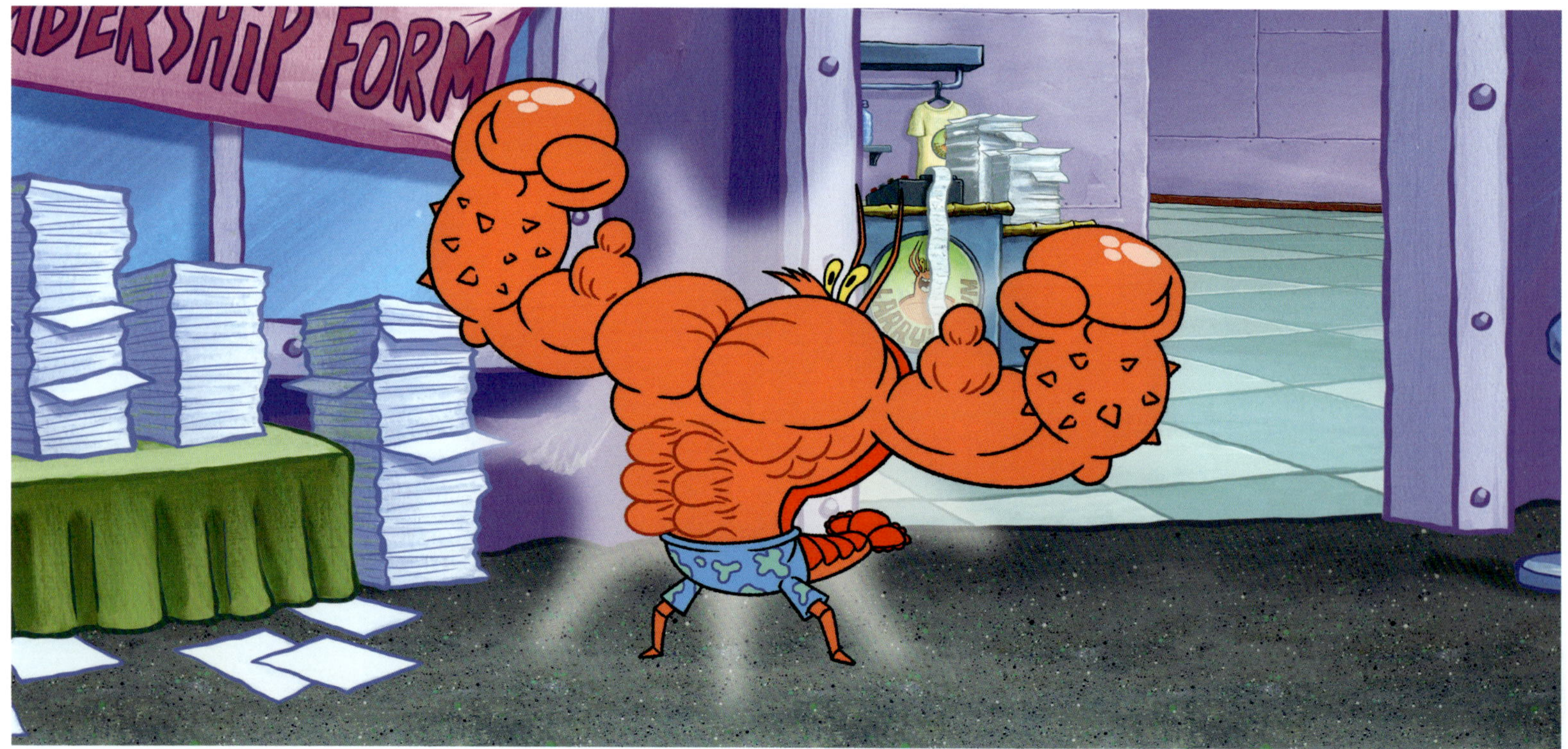

THE SQUAREPANTS FAMILY

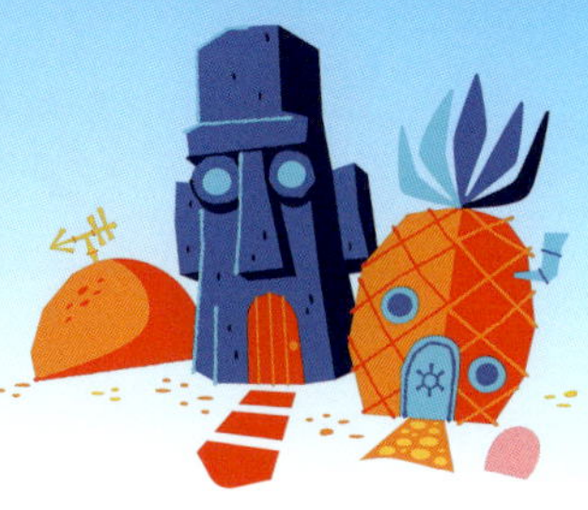

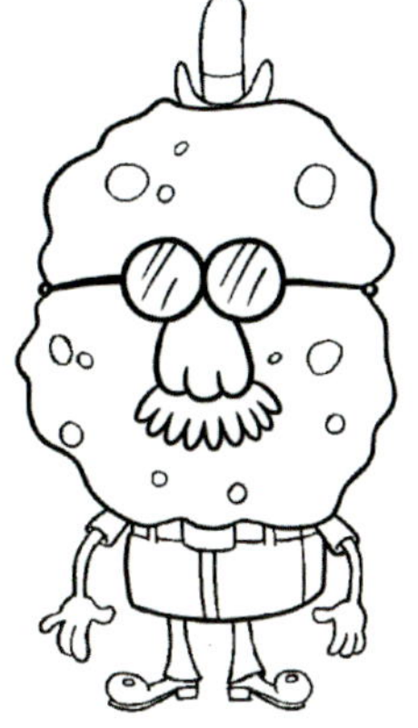

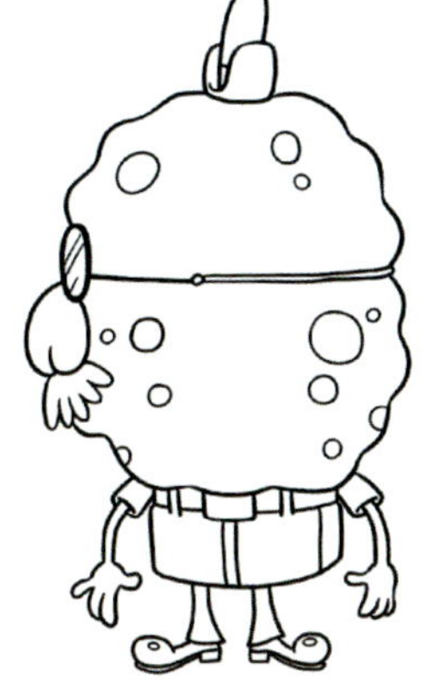

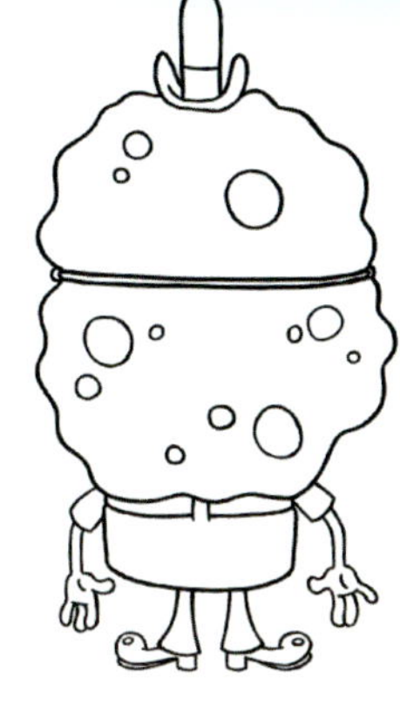

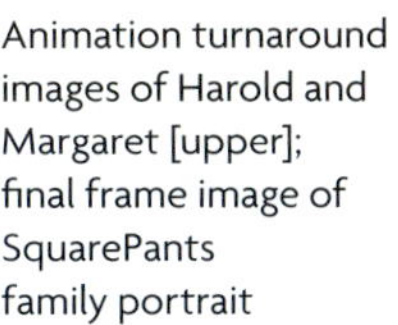

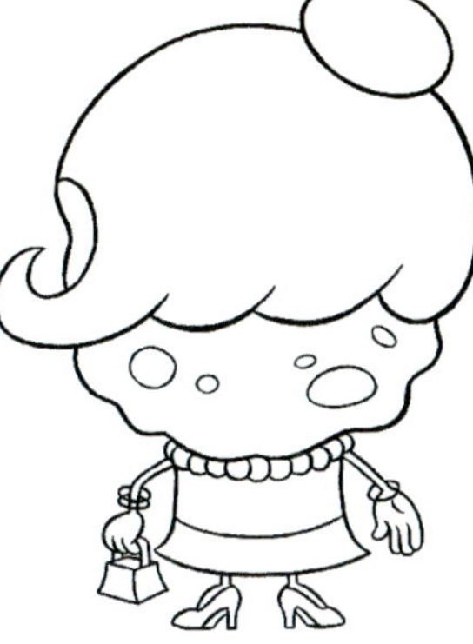

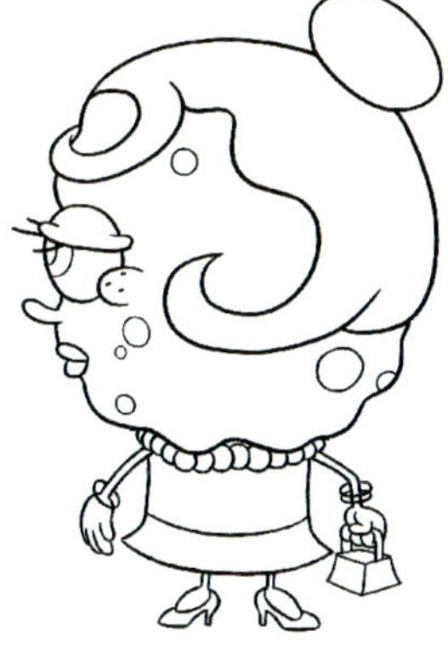

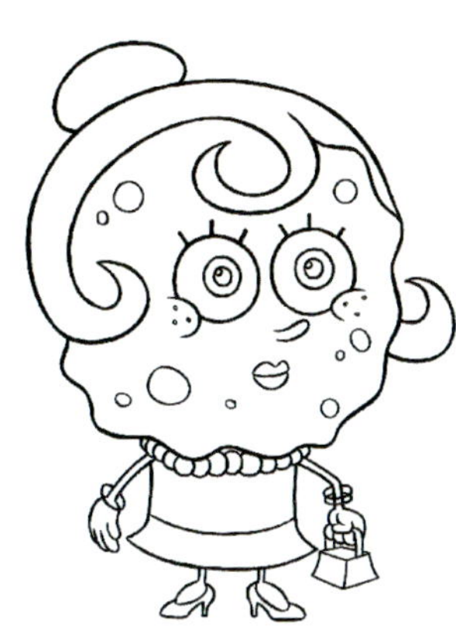

Animation turnaround images of Harold and Margaret [upper]; final frame image of SquarePants family portrait

Never has a pair of sponges been more loving to their offspring than Harold and Margaret are toward their son, SpongeBob... and that is saying a lot, since sea sponges technically have no hearts. From the belt up, Harold and Margaret look more rounded in appearance than their son, perhaps in homage to their original Bob the Sponge genetics. Grandma SquarePants shares a similar look to her son Harold, even if she's so old she can't remember how old she is, as does Harold's brother Captain Blue, a retired police officer. Harold's other known sibling, Sherm, projects the look of SpongeBob a bit more, proving that appearances may jump from different branches of the family tree into the next generation of offshoots.

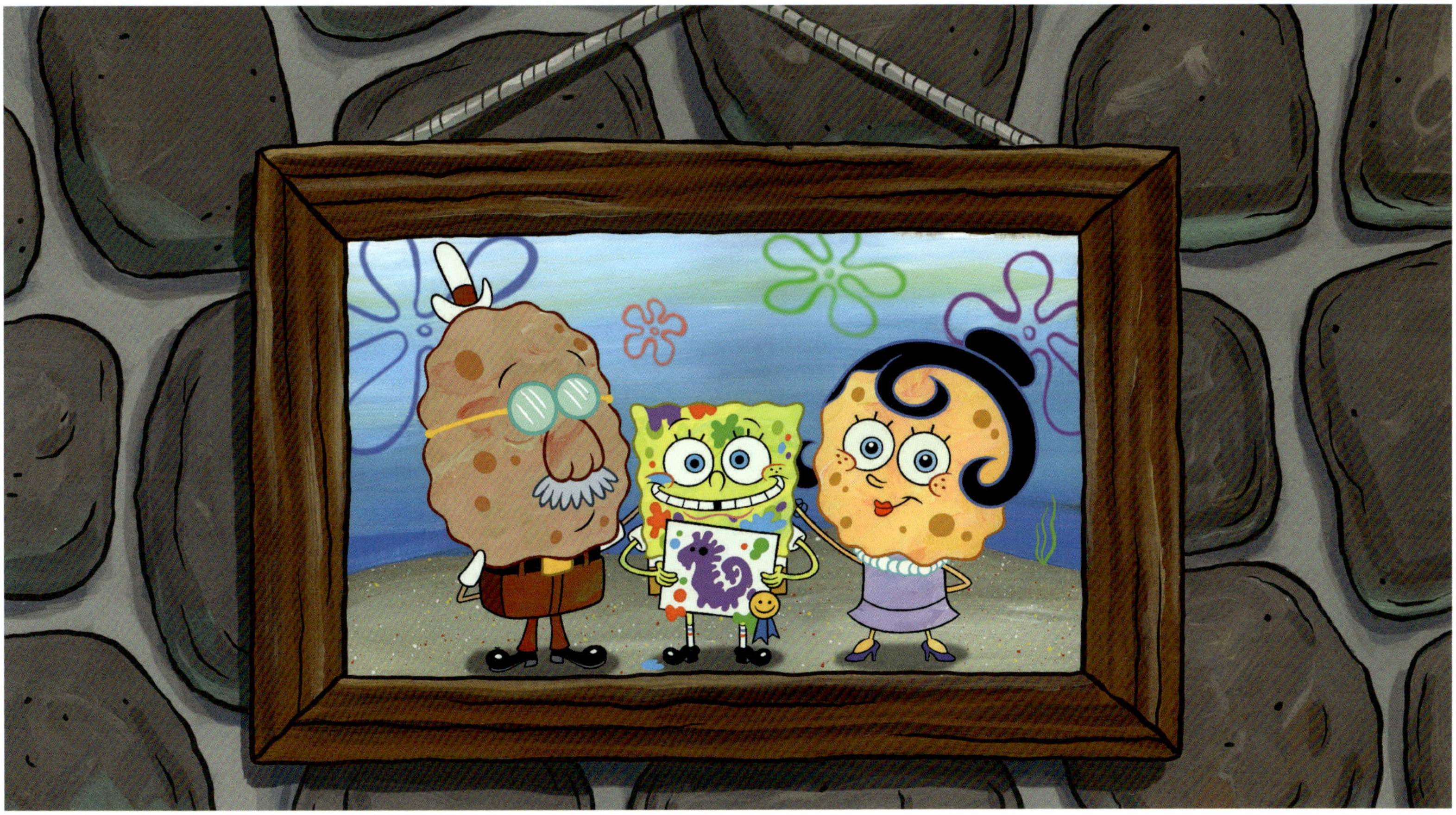

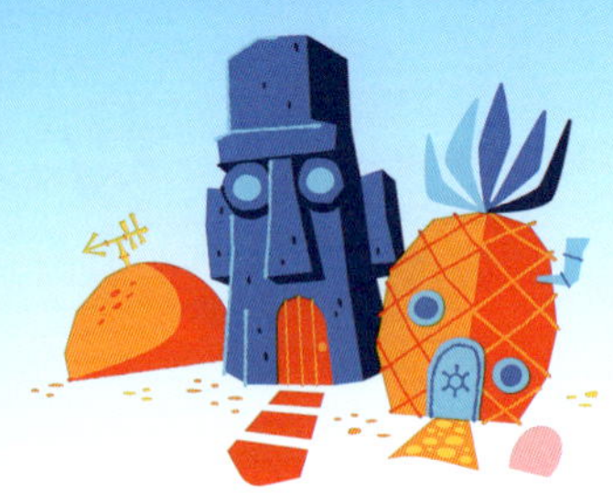

BUBBLE BASS

Perhaps not the most pleasant resident of Bikini Bottom, Bubble Bass exudes slovenliness and poor behavior. "He's a big slop of a nerdy adult who still lives at home with his mother but thinks very highly of himself as an expert on all subjects—especially Krabby Patties and comic books," explains writer Kaz. Despite his negative vibe, Bubble Bass does serve a good purpose, story-wise: He can be an "adversary, a friend, an obstacle, a good foil, definitely something more fun to play with," adds writer Mr. Lawrence.

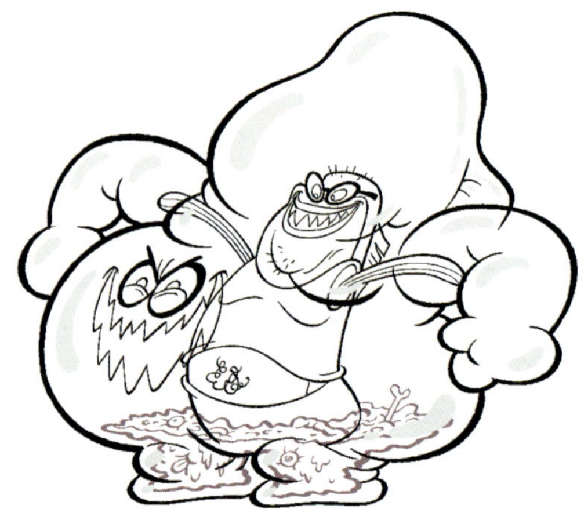

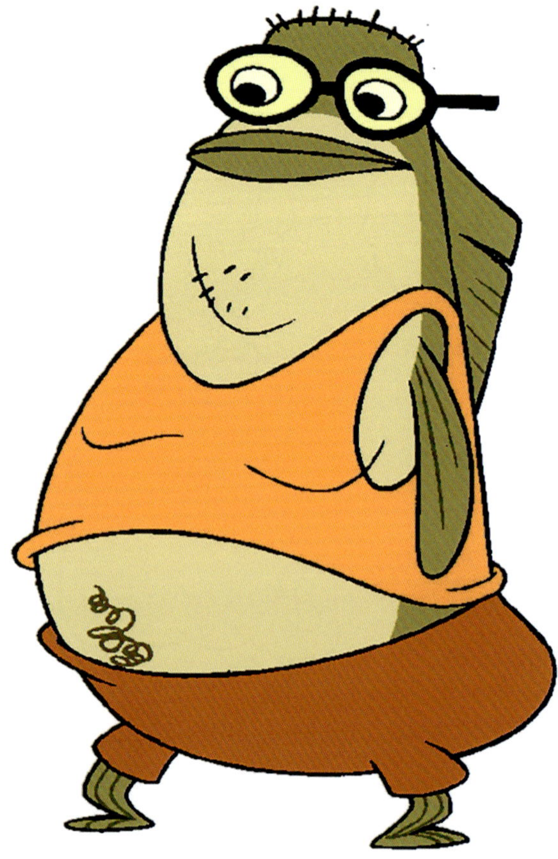

Cleanup animation drawings [black line, with some shading on Bubble Bass] and final art [full color] of various supporting characters

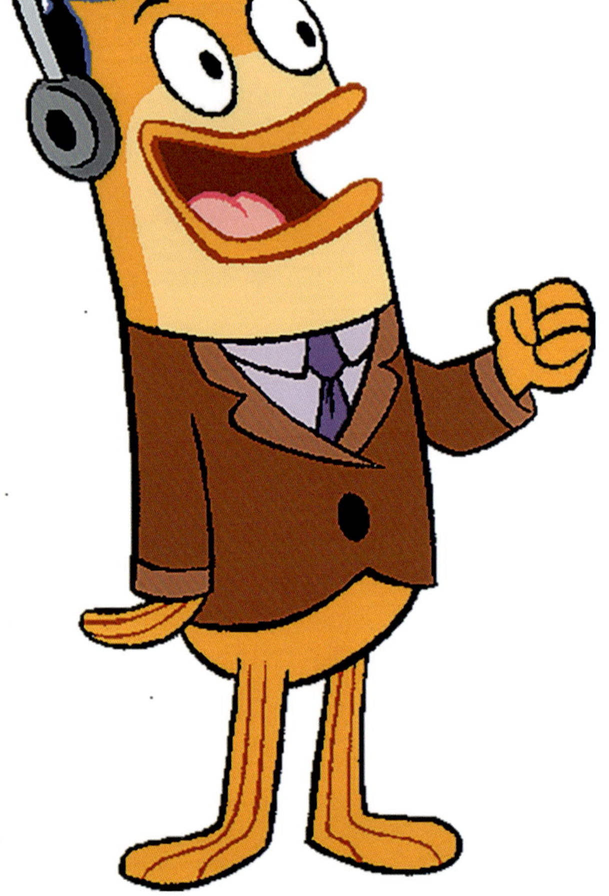

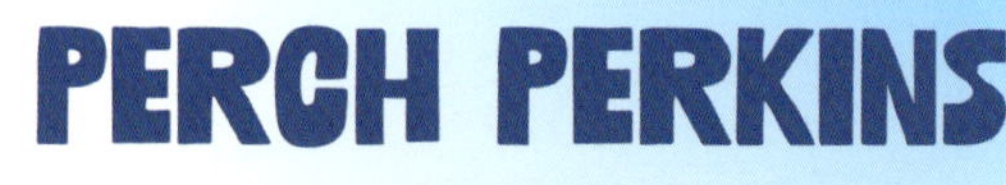

PERCH PERKINS

Perch is the well-dressed, well-spoken on-camera field reporter for Bikini Bottom News, announcing all the latest stories breaking in and around town.

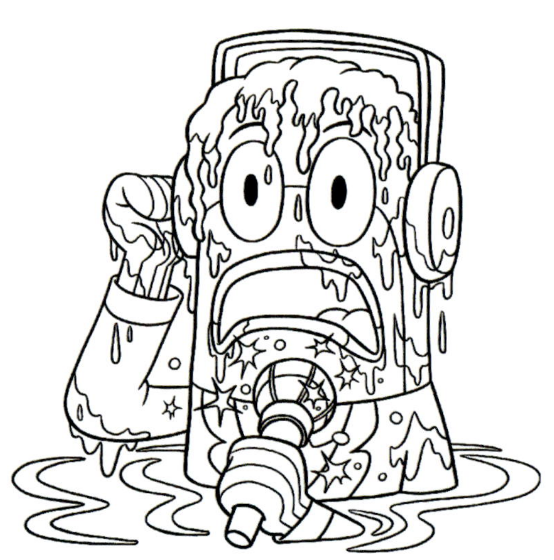

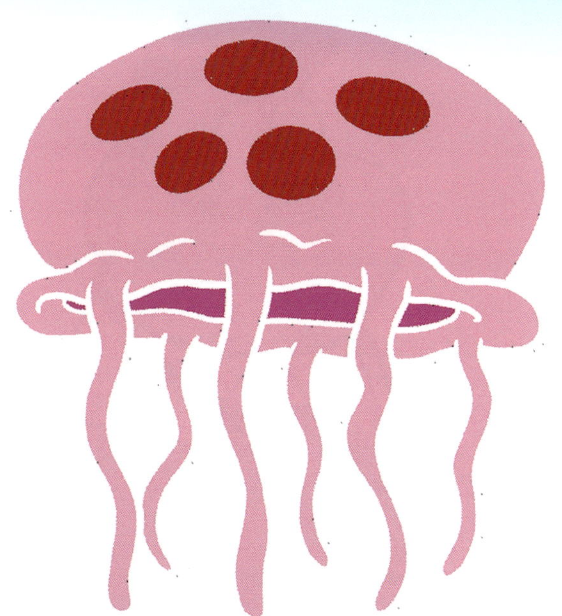

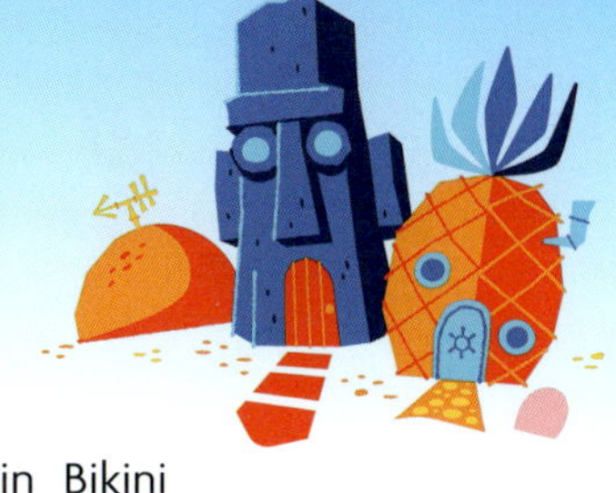

JELLYFISH

A wide variety of jellyfish inhabit the ocean space in Bikini Bottom, floating gently along in a nonverbal delicate way of adding atmosphere to the environment. They present in a variety of colors and patterns and can exhibit traits much akin to their real-world counterparts, or sometimes portray what bees and fireflies do in the above-water atmosphere.

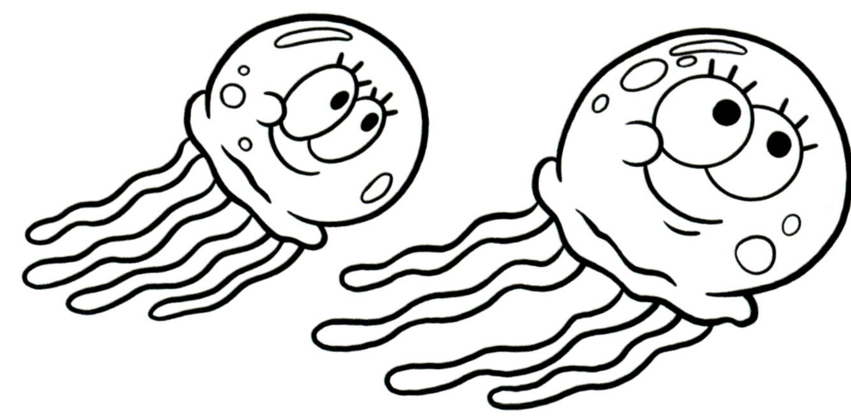

JEFF & MRS. TENTACLES

The family resemblance is crystal clear in Squidward's parents, Jeff and Mrs. Tentacles, in both look and behavior.

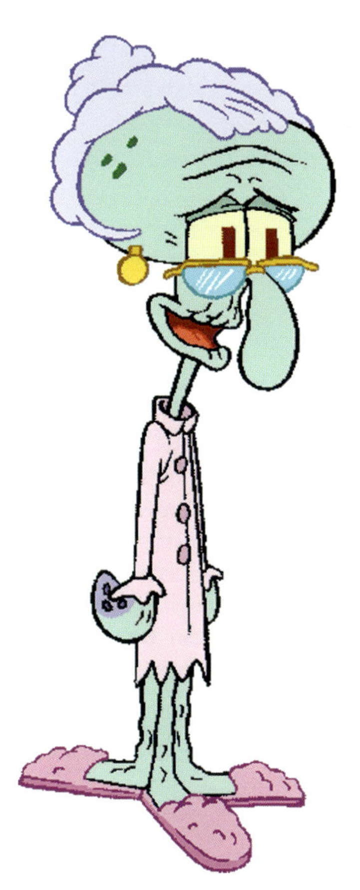

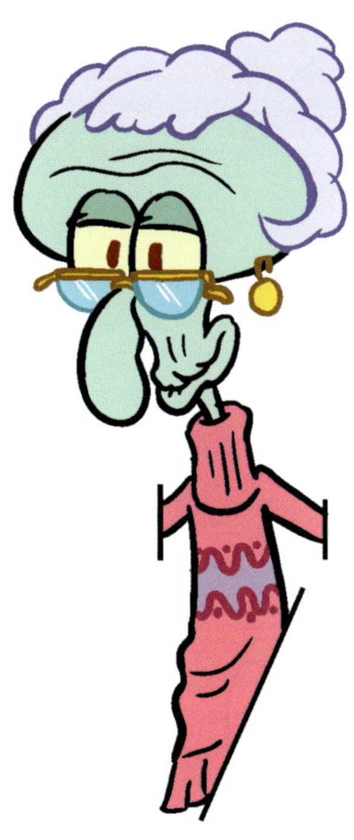

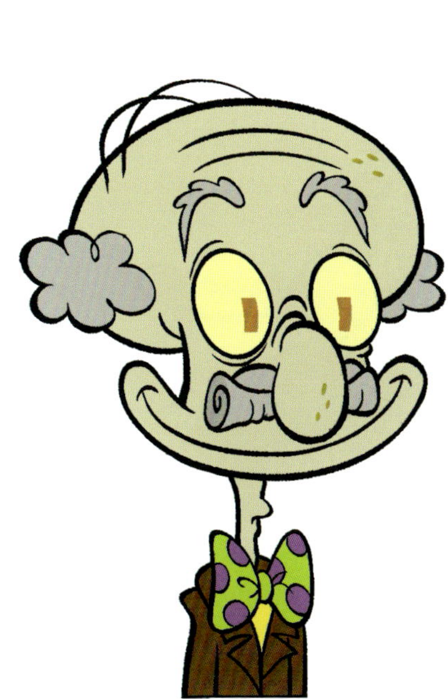

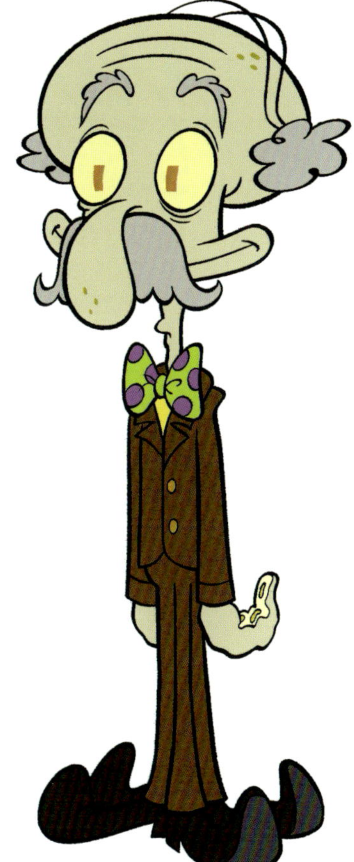

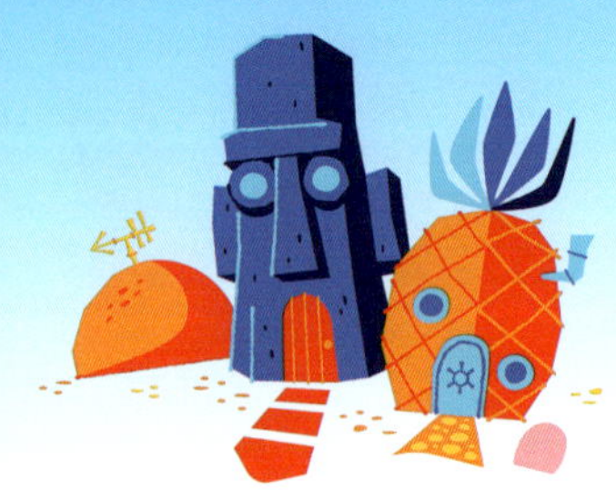

RUBE GOLDFISH

A relatively new addition to Bikini Bottom, Rube Goldfish "doesn't know how to be anything but polite and positive," says Mr. Lawrence. "His endless enthusiasm is a great counter to the bitter/grumpy demeanors of some of our main characters, being hopelessly optimistic while soft emotionally and physically," adds director Dave Cunningham.

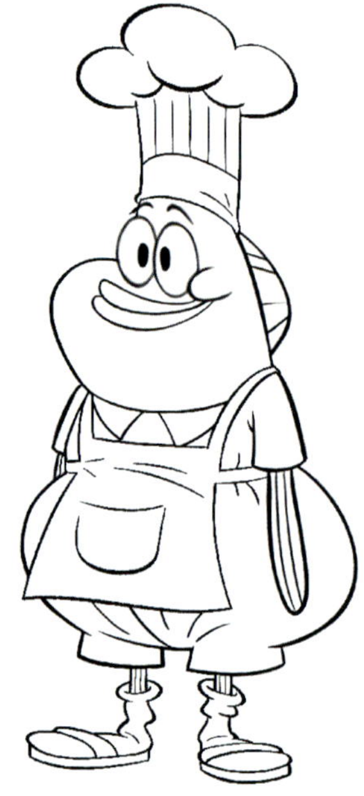

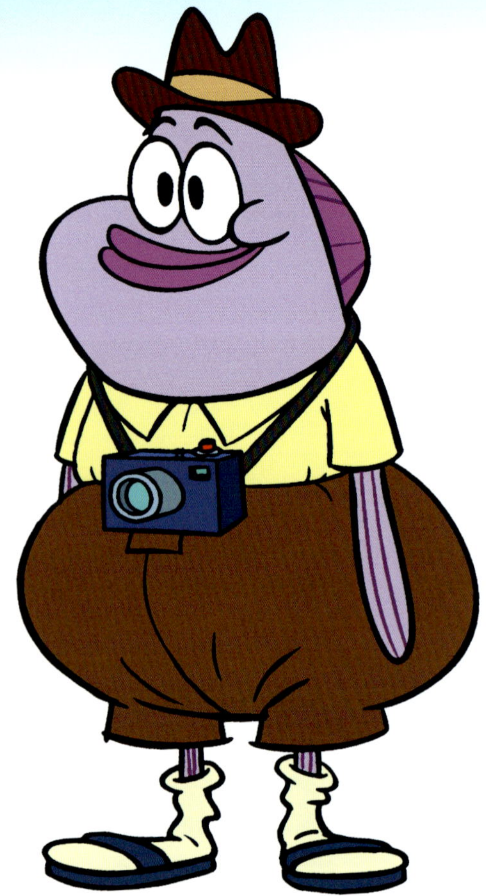

Cleanup animation drawings [single line color] and final art [full color] of various supporting characters

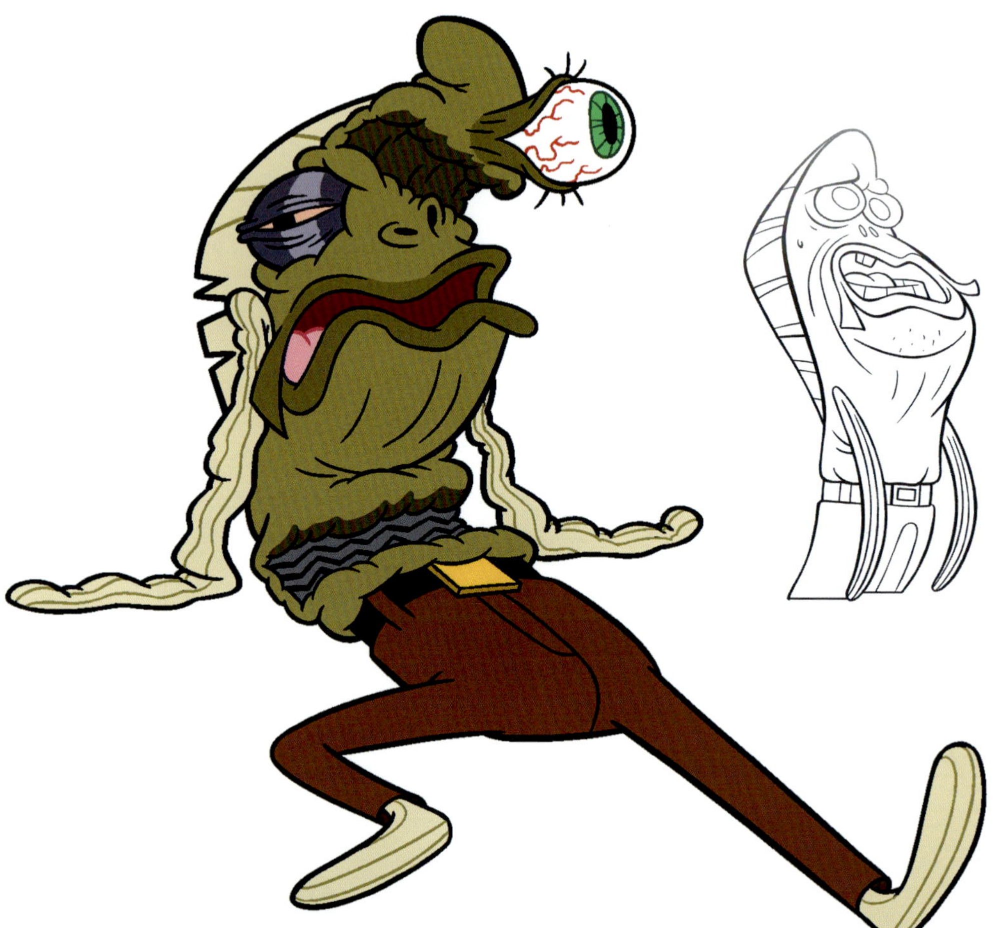

FRED

Sometimes random just works out, as the catchphrase "My leg!" did when yelled out during a crowd recording session, then placed into the mouth of Incidental Character #1, who has now become so popular he's been named Fred. "Fred was not always the only 'My leg!' character. Not until recent seasons did we single him out as THE character that says it. In earlier seasons, it would be whichever incidental male character the board artists chose," explains Dave Cunningham. But whatever character has been saying it, Mr. Lawrence gets requests to proclaim it at conventions and other public appearances… Who knew an imagined injury could be so popular that a crowd favorite and character upgrade could be made out of it?

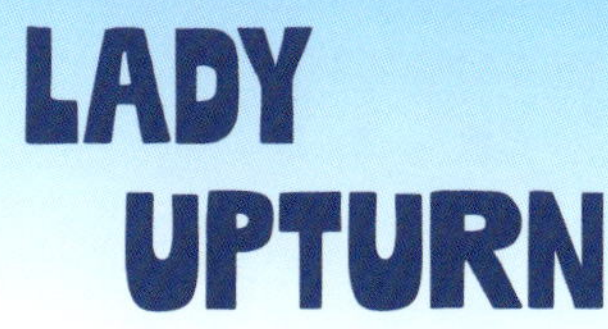

LADY UPTURN

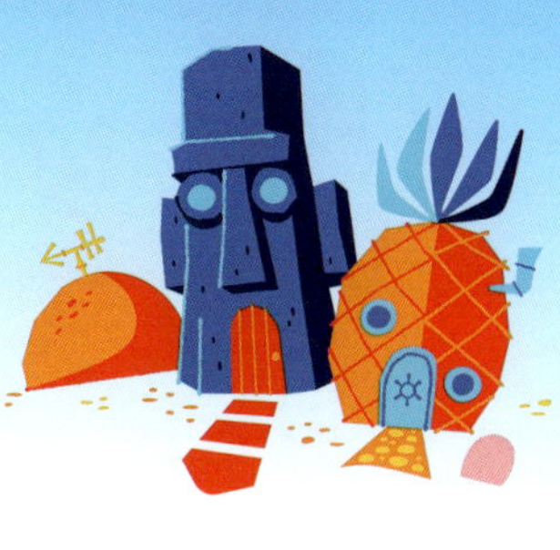

A bit snooty and posh, Lady Upturn is a high-pedigree resident of Bikini Bottom. "She's a blustery, funny character, like the Marx Brothers and Margaret Dumont," says Mr. Lawrence. Living in a mansion and owning a department store and an art museum seem like qualifications to be part of the high-class society, but Lady Upturn is not above going to the Krusty Krab for a bite, even if Mr. Krabs drops his "no pets" policy and charges her a premium to allow her pet worm, Fifi, to come into the restaurant: Since money talks in Mr. Krabs' world, it's a win-win for both ends of that transaction.

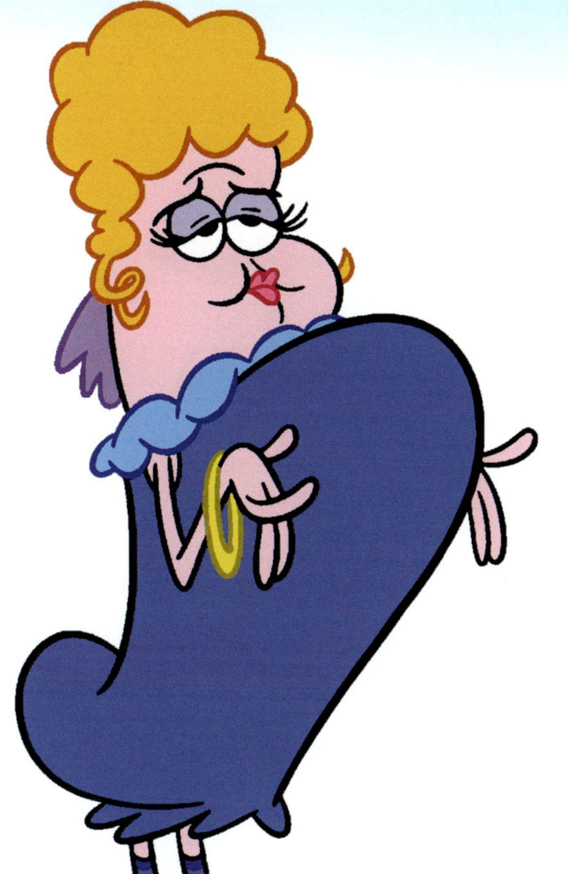

HELEN THE FELON

Perhaps the cutest member of E.V.I.L. (Every Villain Is Lemons, the name of a group of villains in the series), Helen the Felon displays a series of bad behaviors that range from selling cookies without a license to biting a lemonade vendor. Formerly referred to as Incidental #173, don't let the innocent-little-girl look lure you into letting your guard down around Helen.

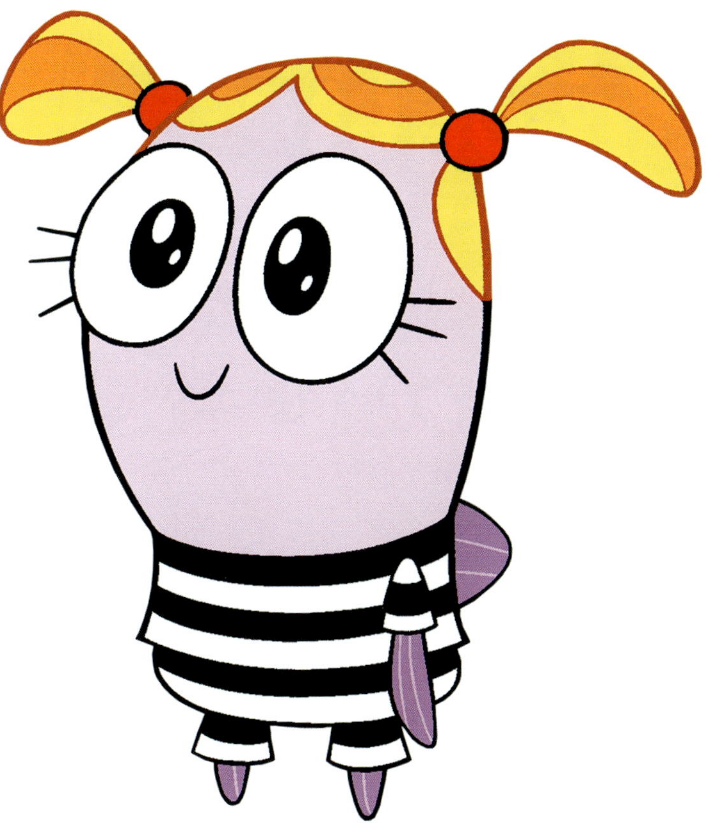

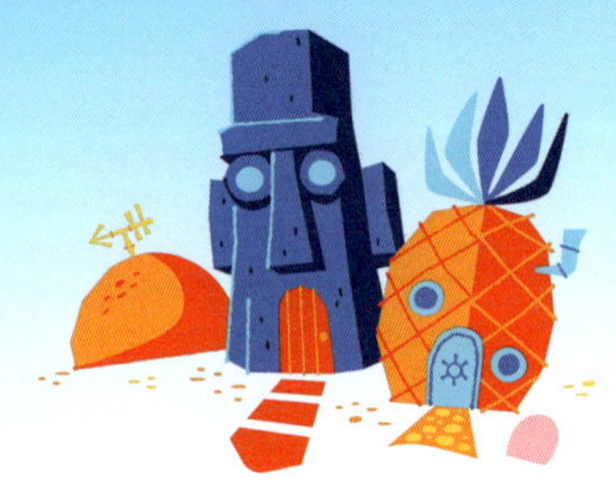

DIRTY BUBBLE

Floating and sucking his enemies into his body with "awesome surface tension," Dirty Bubble is another arch-enemy of Mermaid Man and Barnacle Boy. His weakness against pointy things suggests he should never take a class with Mrs. Puff, nor should he break into Squidward's home and encounter that squeaky-clean bathtub, as both water and soap could also pop his evil existence.

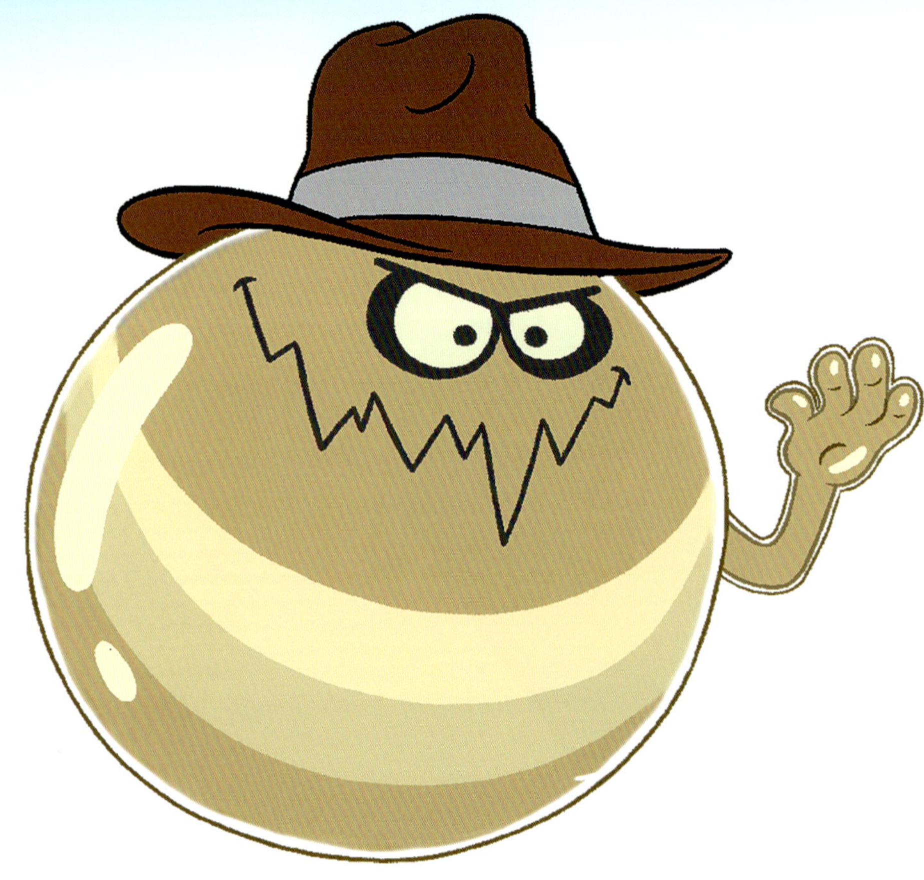

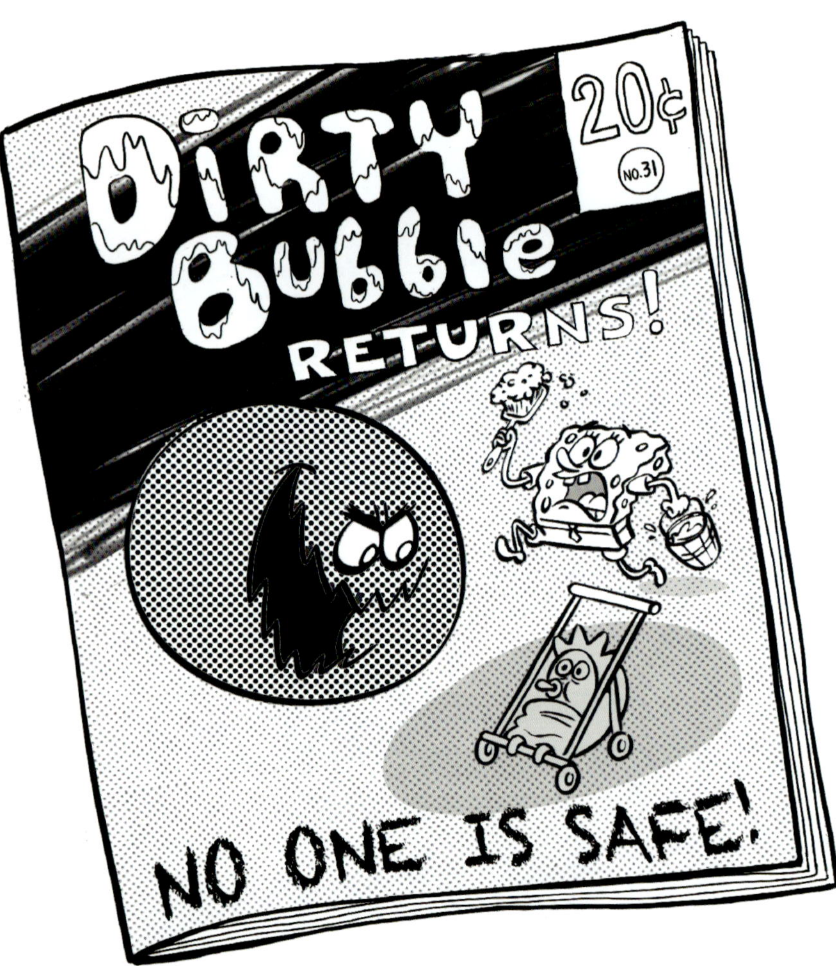

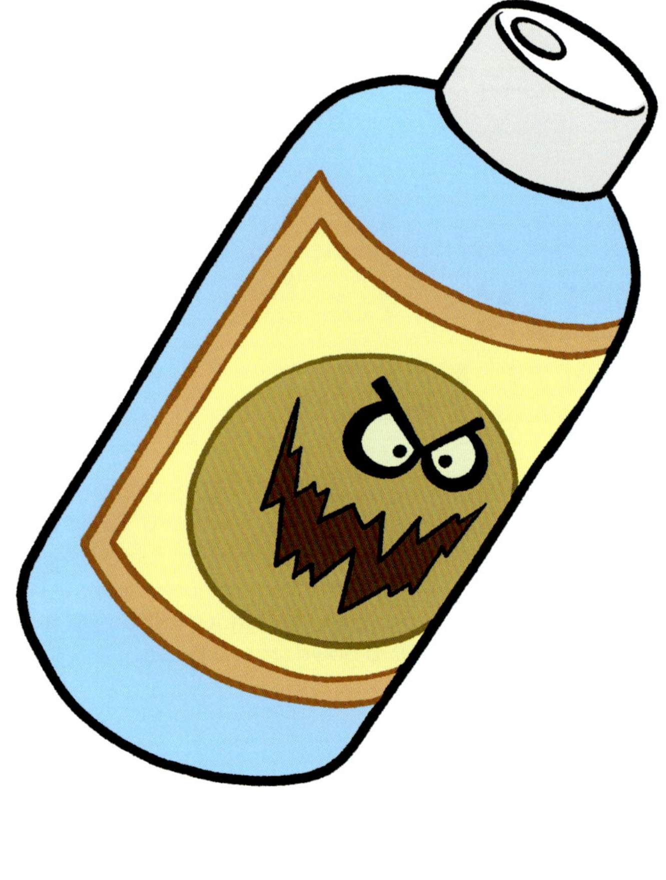

Final art of Dirty Bubble [upper]; cleanup animation drawing of Dirty Bubble comic book from "Dirty Bubble Returns" (Season 12, episode 252b), and bottle of Dirty Bubble

MAN RAY

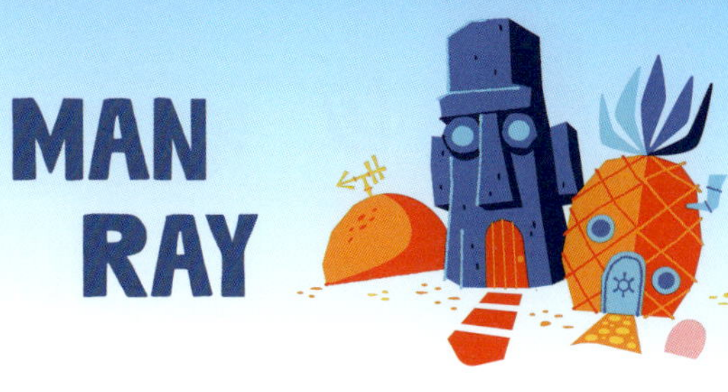

Staying in the realm of comic book characters in Bikini Bottom, Man Ray is the (also aging) foe of Mermaid Man and Barnacle Boy, but his fighting and tactical abilities have not lost their pep over time, perhaps due to the deep freeze he was kept in for a bit. A member of the villain squad better known as E.V.I.L., Man Ray is an homage to Aquaman's nemesis Black Manta and is not hesitant to command others under his supreme authority of wickedness, nor to put his laser ray gun to use.

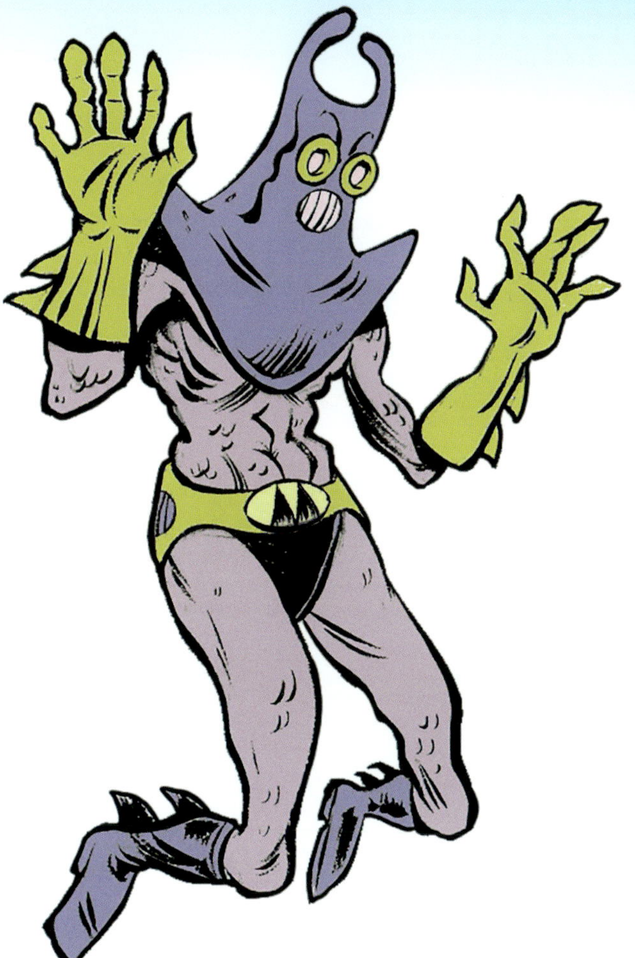

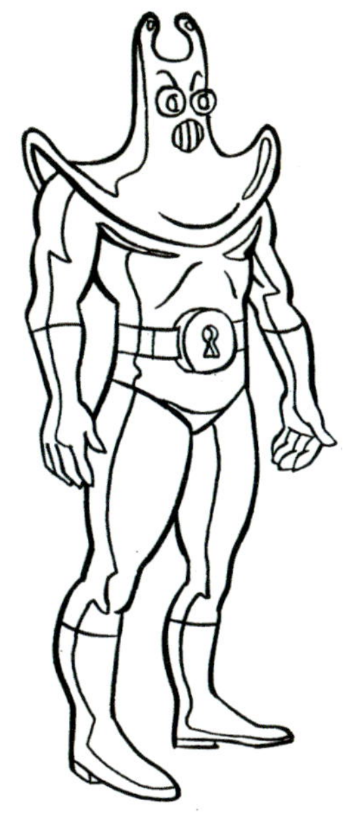

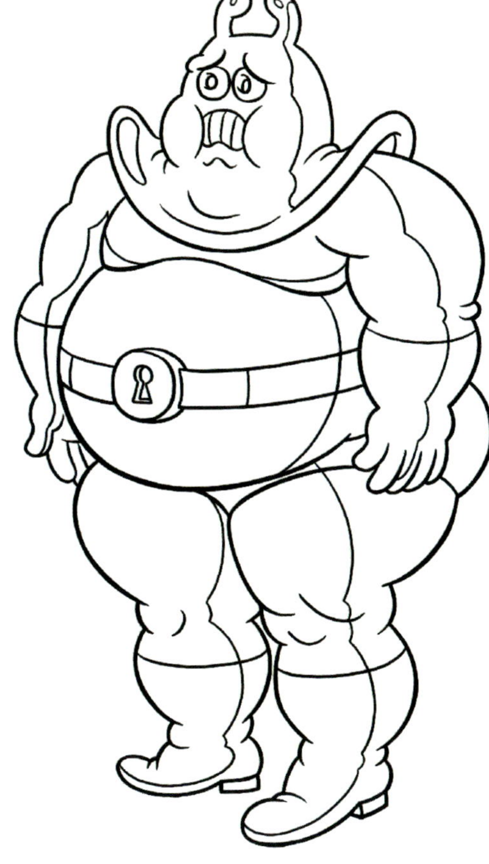

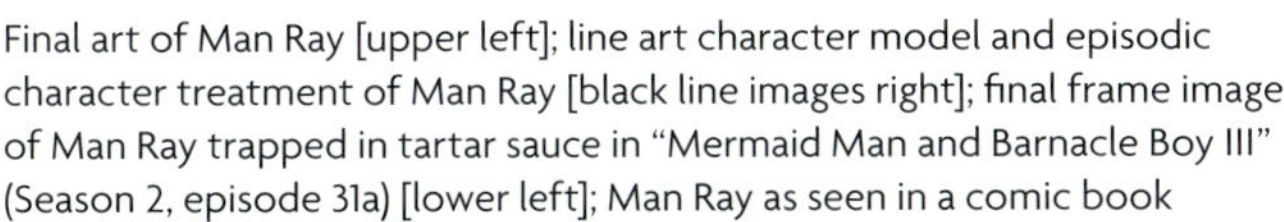

Final art of Man Ray [upper left]; line art character model and episodic character treatment of Man Ray [black line images right]; final frame image of Man Ray trapped in tartar sauce in "Mermaid Man and Barnacle Boy III" (Season 2, episode 31a) [lower left]; Man Ray as seen in a comic book

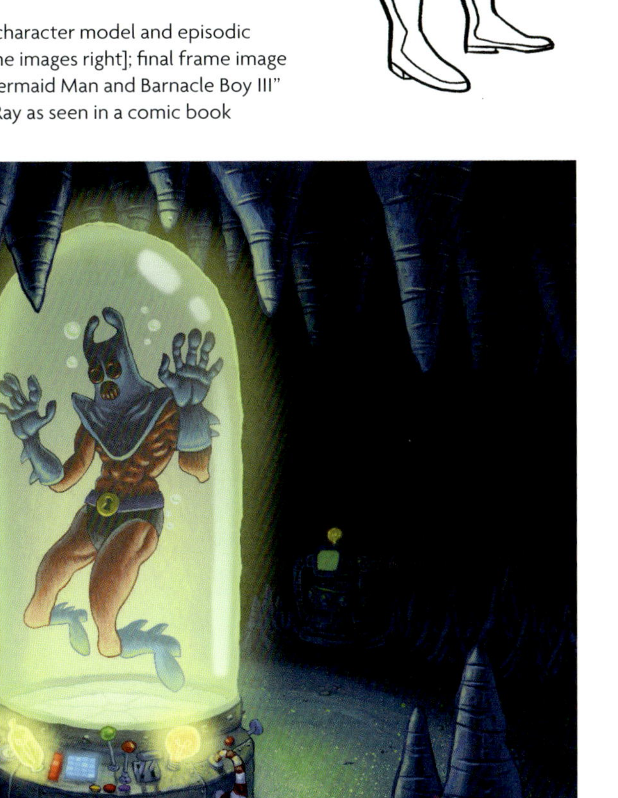

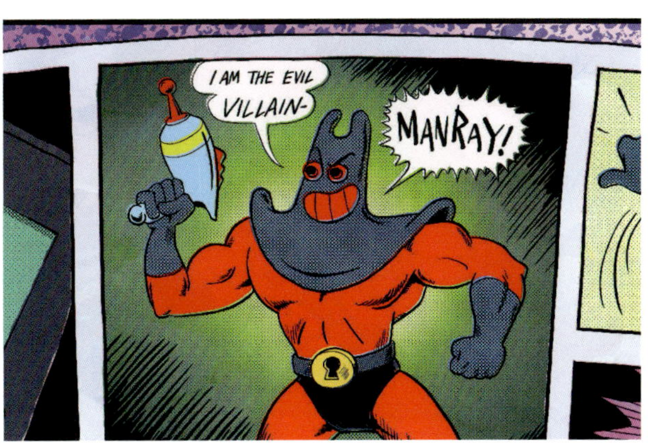

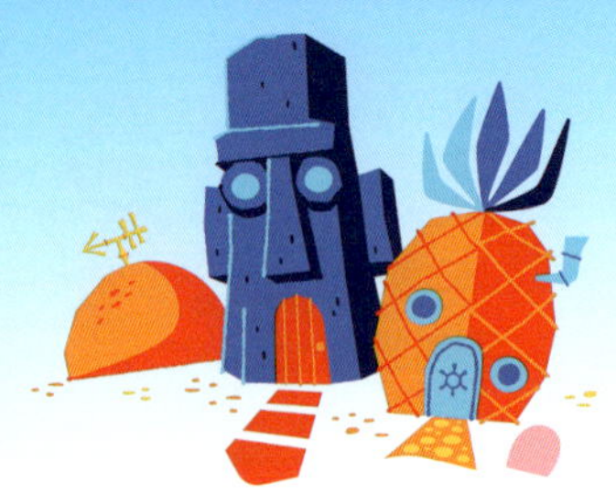

KEVIN C. CUCUMBER

Although he seems to share a love of jellyspotting like SpongeBob, Kevin C. Cucumber is just in it for the coolness factor, a choice that ends up coming around to sting him when he has an unfortunate encounter with the jellyfish.

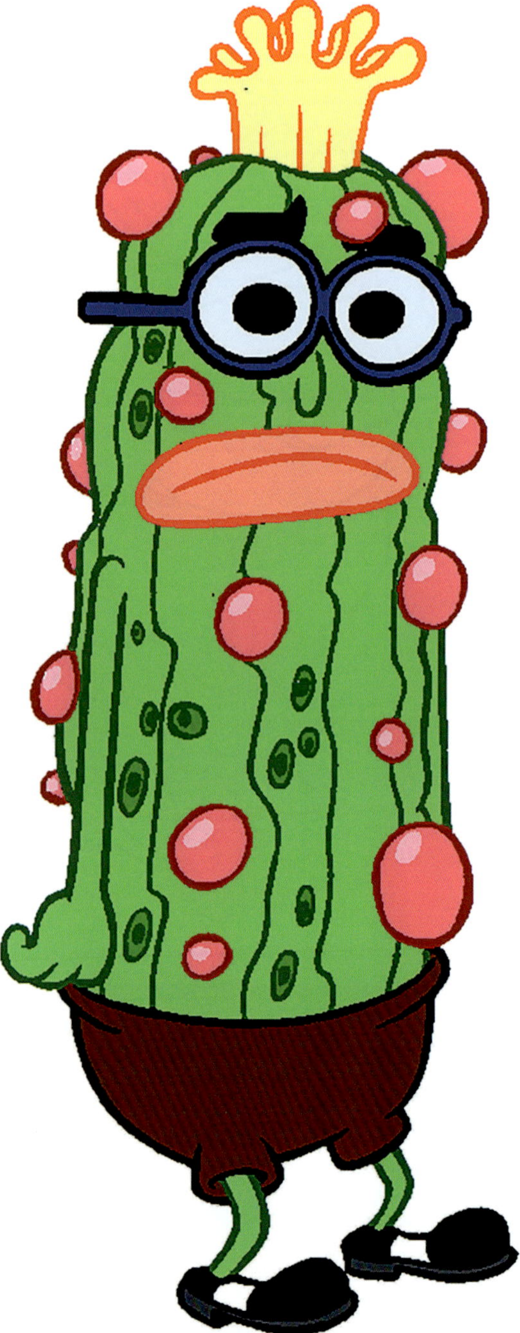

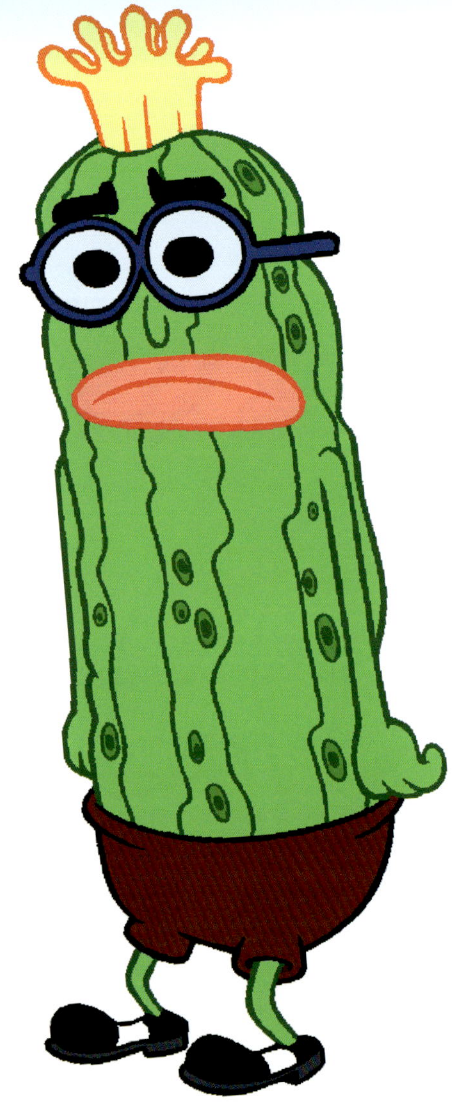

Final art [left and upper right] and final frame image [lower] of Kevin from "I'm Your Biggest Fanatic" (Season 2, episode 30b)

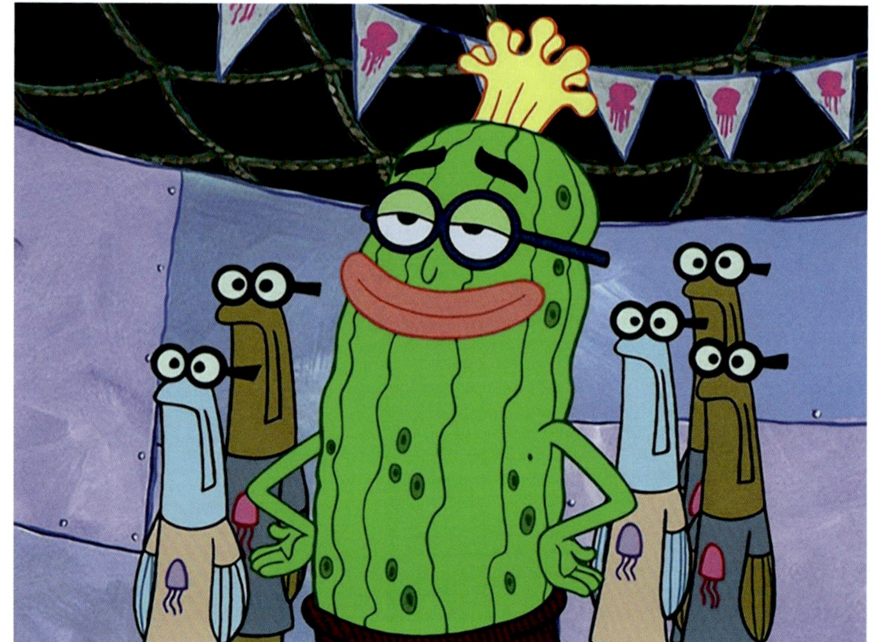

MERMAID PANTS & BARNACLE STAR

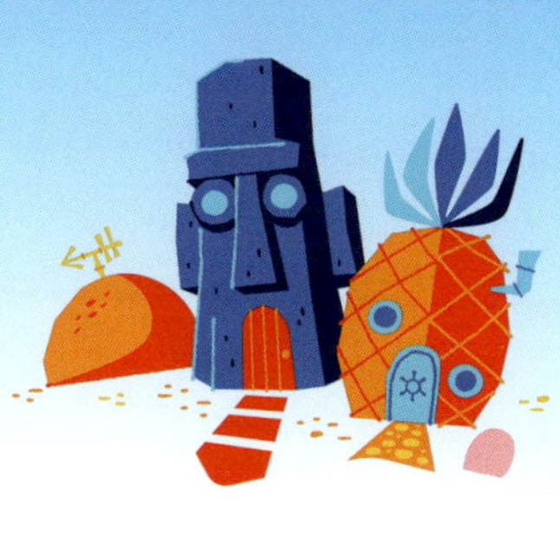

Fan Boys in action, SpongeBob and Patrick create hysterics instead of heroics when the less-than-dynamic duo don costumes and run amuck in Bikini Bottom, battling false threats until Captain Tightwad (a suited Mr. Krabs) shuts down their antics.

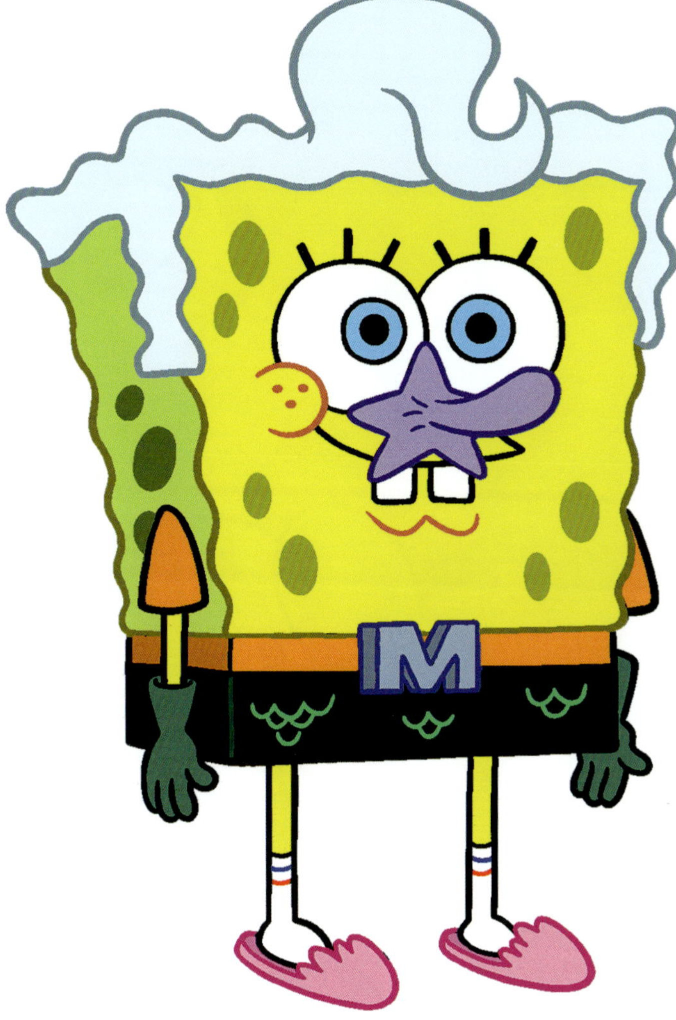

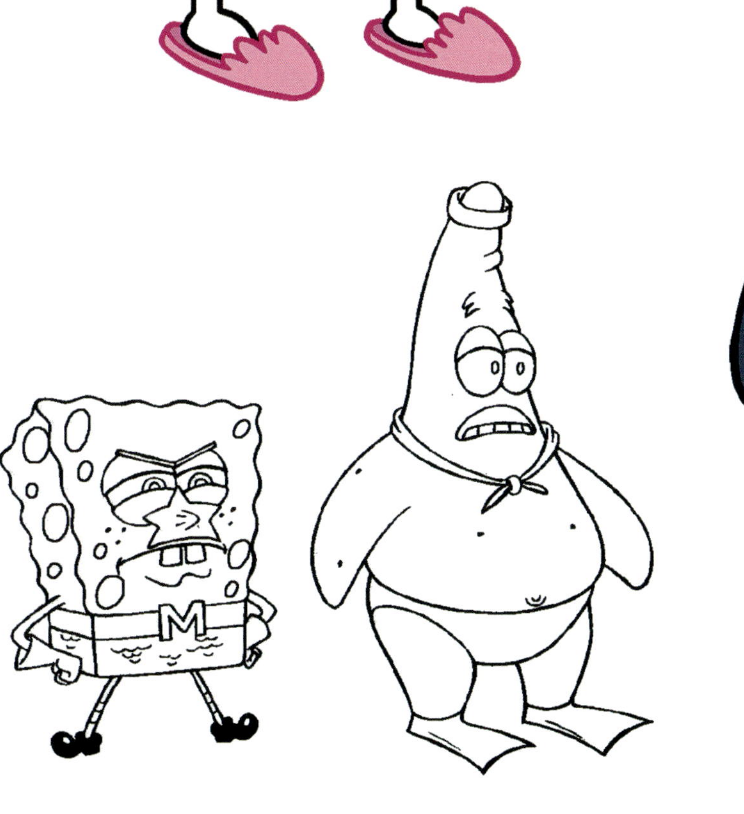

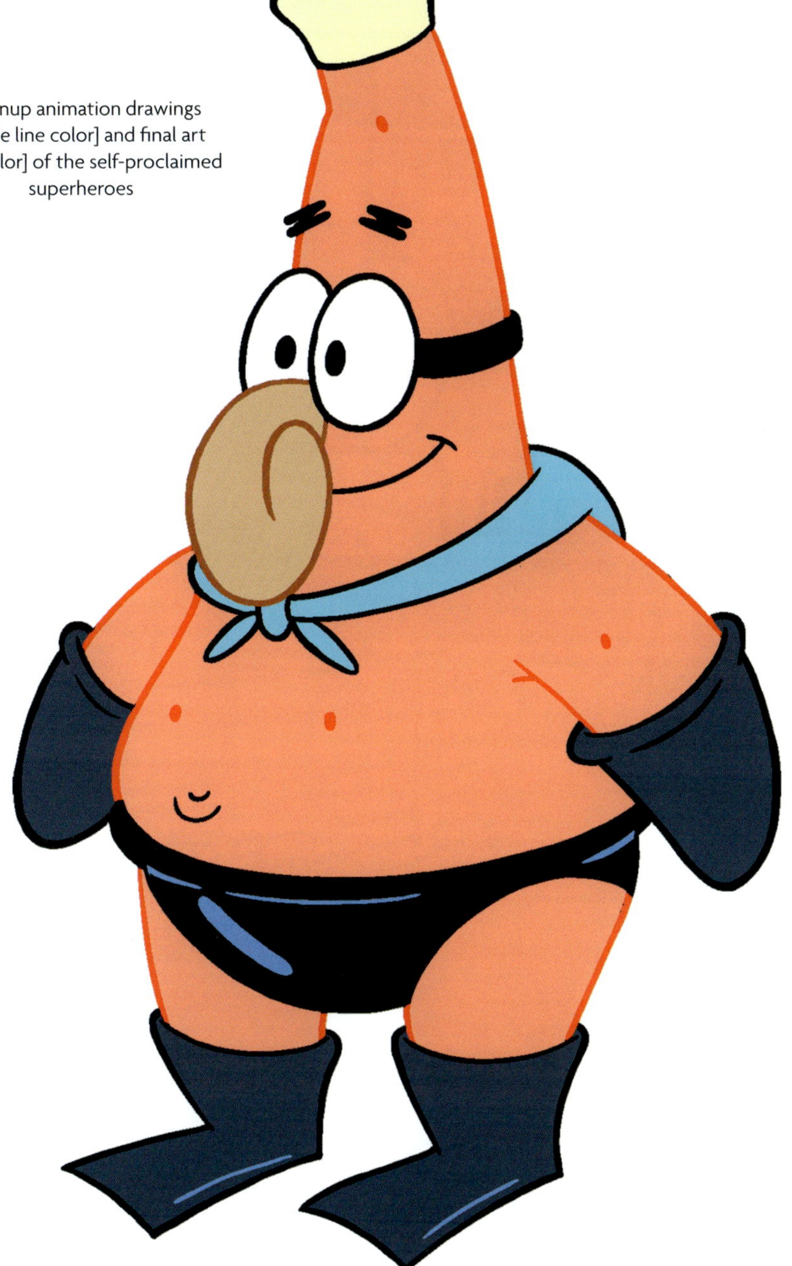

Cleanup animation drawings [single line color] and final art [full color] of the self-proclaimed superheroes

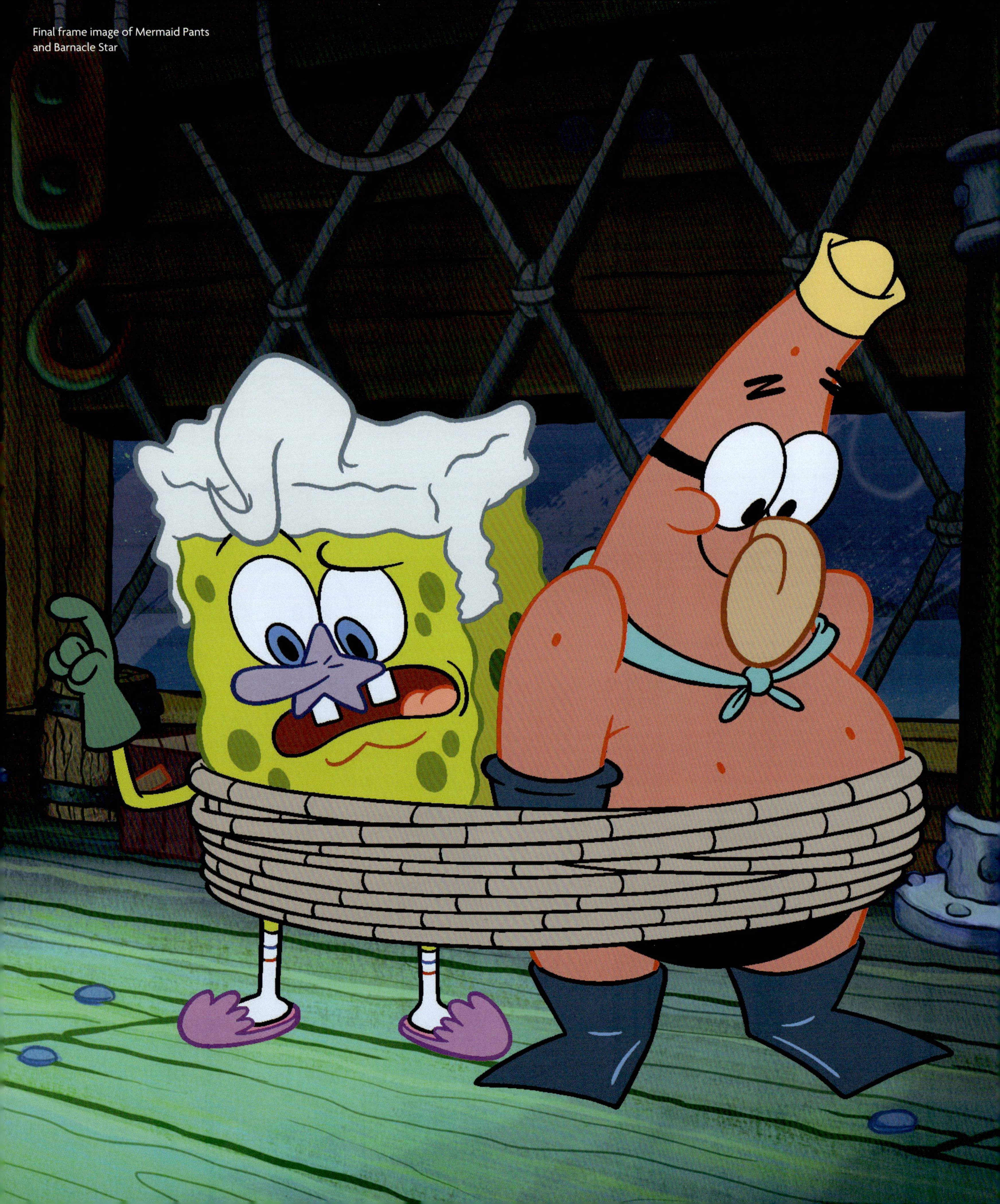

Final frame image of Mermaid Pants and Barnacle Star

CAPTAIN TIGHTWAD

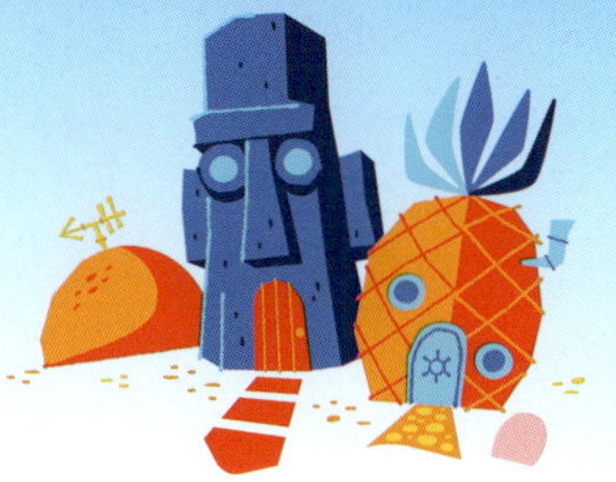

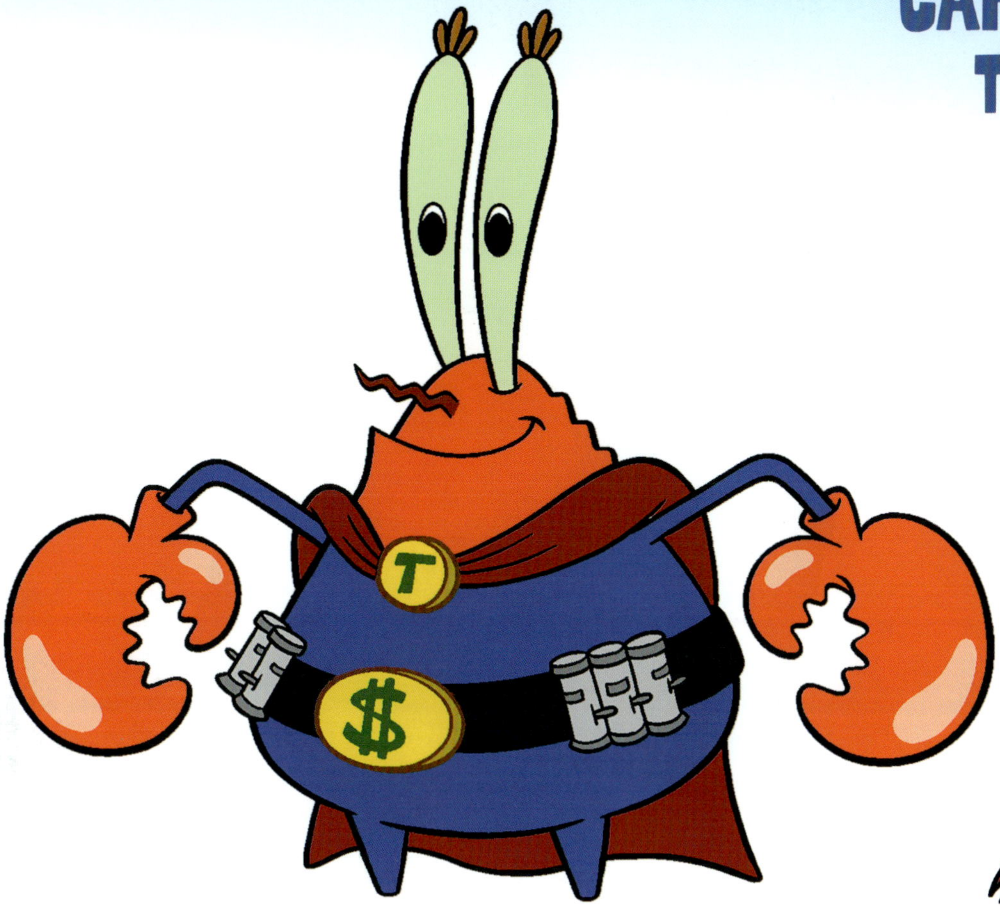

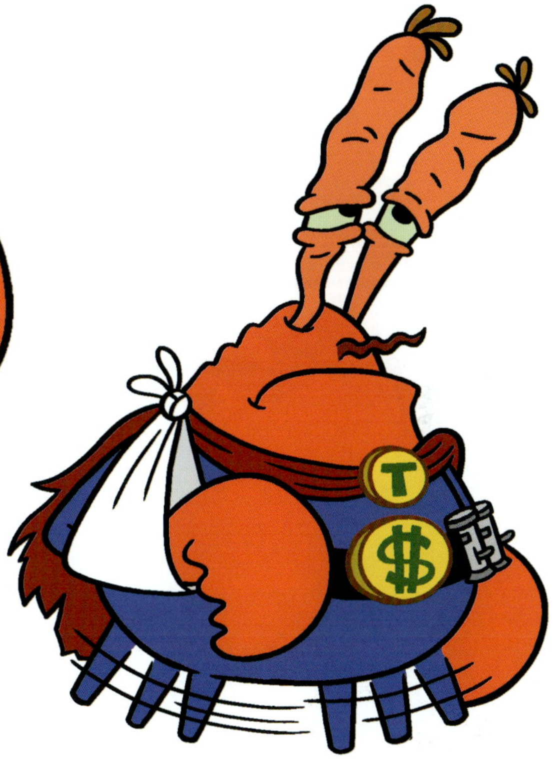

Final art of Mr. Krabs as Captain Tightwad [upper]; a peek into Mr. Krabs' secret room in "Mermaid Pants" (Season 10, episode 205b)

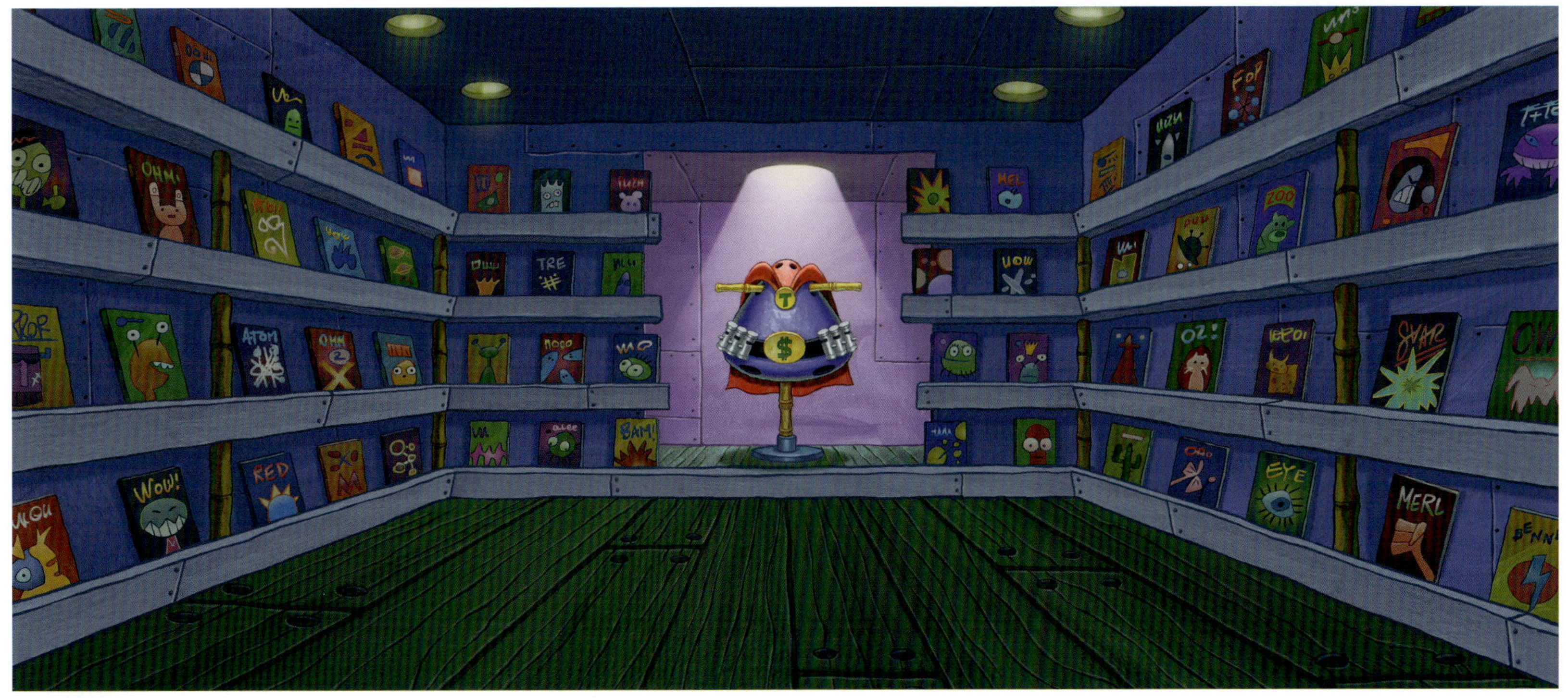

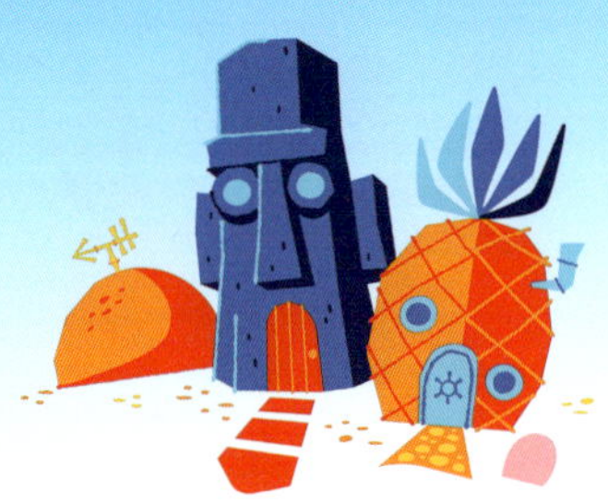

OLD MAN JENKINS & DOCTOR GILL GILLIAM

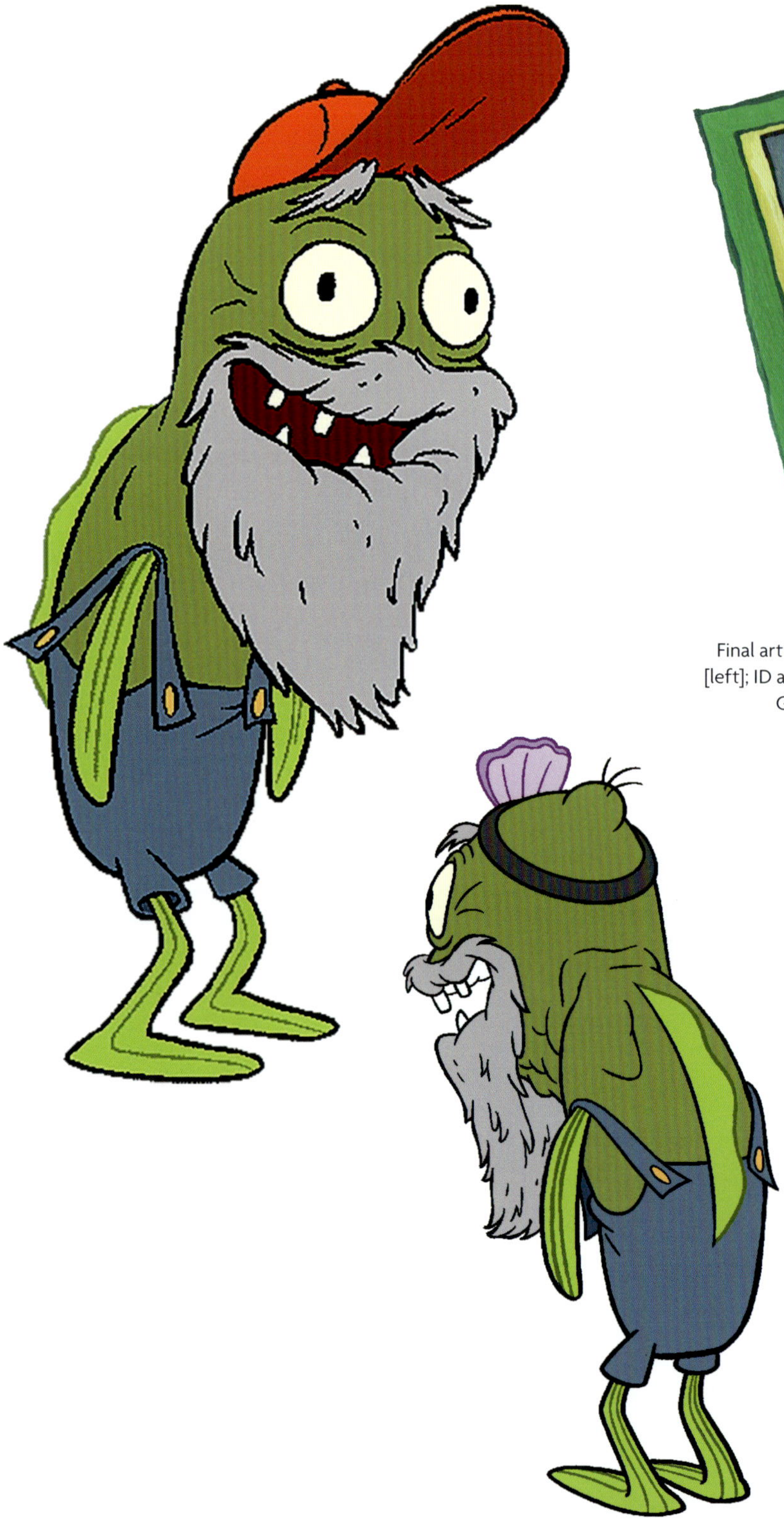

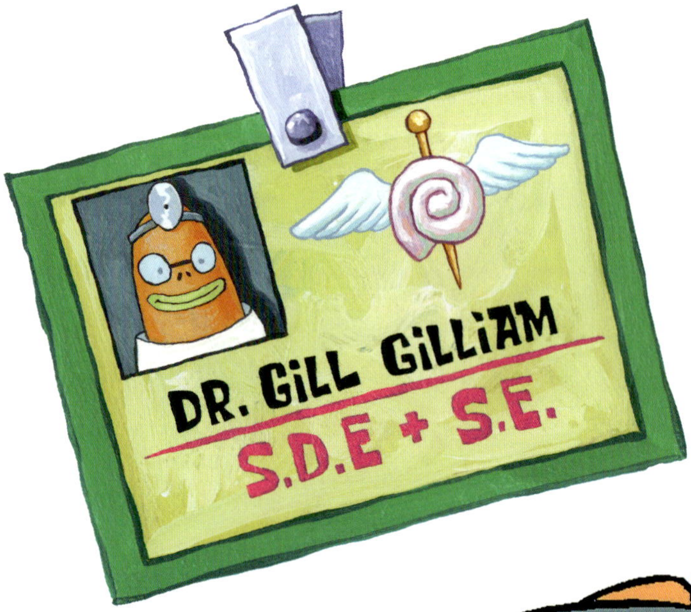

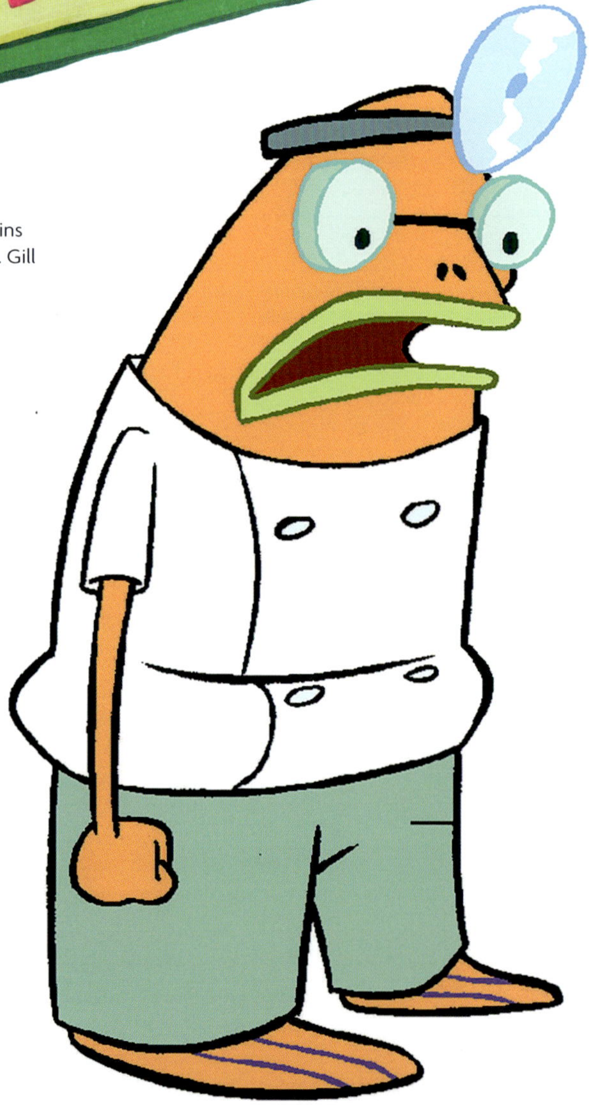

Final art of Old Man Jenkins [left]; ID and final art of Dr. Gill Gilliam [right]

FLATS THE FLOUNDER & SQUILLIAM FANCYSON

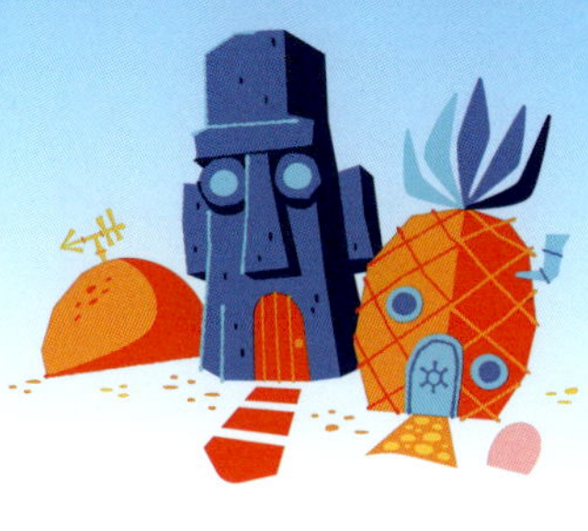

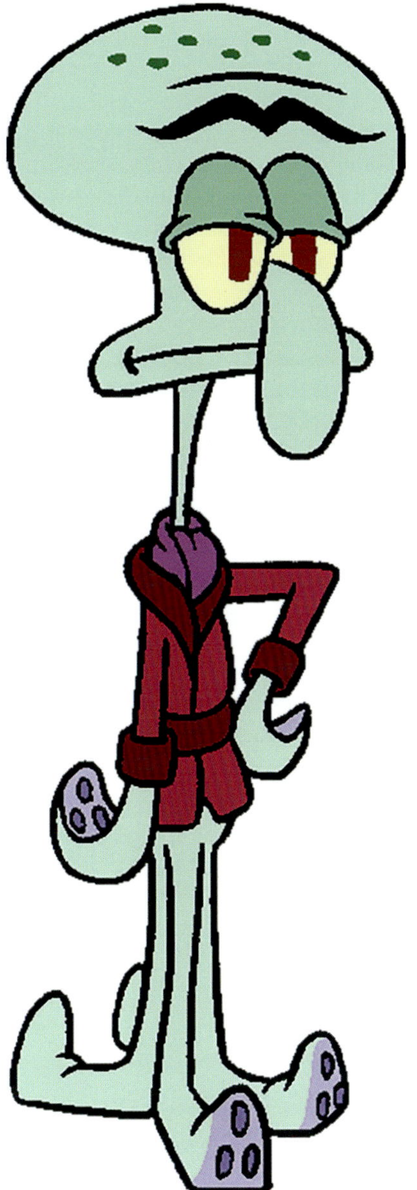

Former prop and character designer Thaddeus Couldron had fun creating all kinds of unique personalities to appear in Bikini Bottom over the years. "Steve and Derek gave me complete carte blanche when it came to doing concept art for weird characters and designs. I indulged myself completely; it was a whole lot of fun and extremely satisfying. They hired me to draw the weirdest s#!+ I could think of and I loved it," he notes.

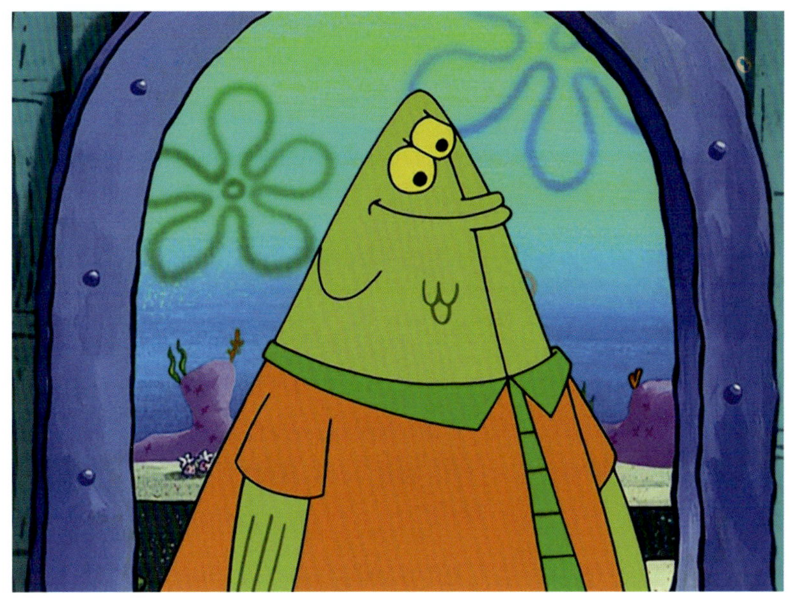

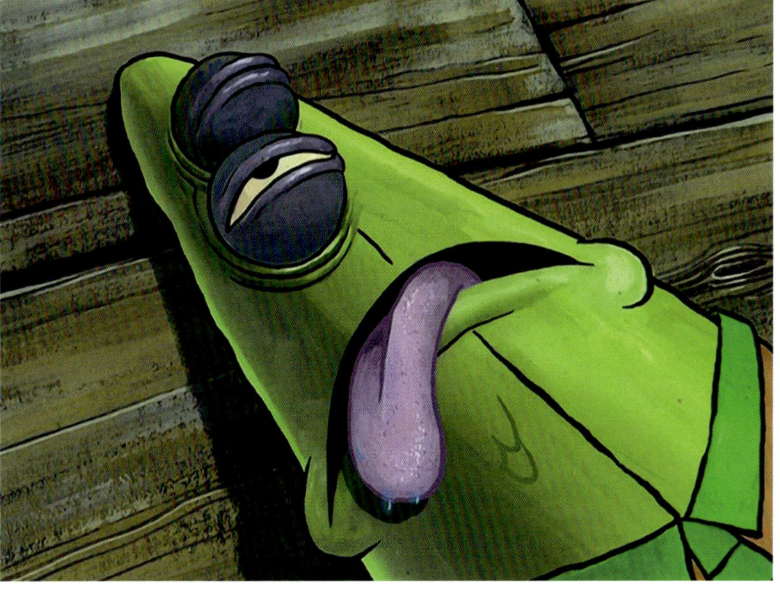

Final art of Squilliam (not to be confused with Squidward), Squidward's nemesis [left]; final frame images of Flats, a bully who first appeared at Mrs. Puff's Boating School

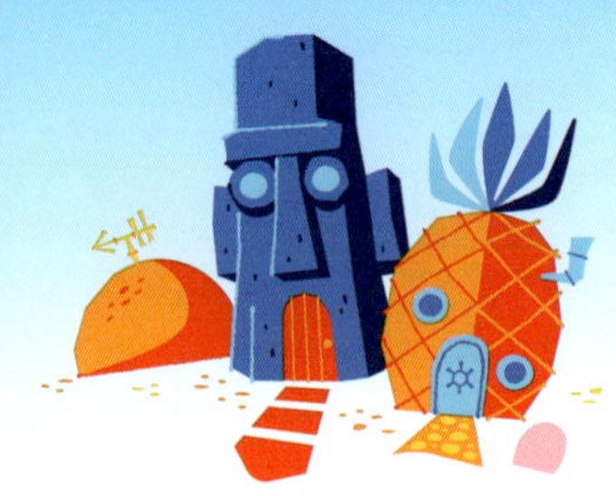

PLACES OF INTEREST IN BIKINI BOTTOM

The art direction of *SpongeBob SquarePants* is moored in a vibrant tiki and nautical environment. That décor vibe stems from the source, as former director Tim Hill recalls that before the show got started, "Steve Hillenburg used to live down the street from me with his wife, Karen, and their little house had a similar décor to SpongeBob's pineapple house. Bamboo trim here and there, sea shells and funny/tacky seascape art on the walls. I guess you could say Steve lived his art." Hillenburg's love of all things oceanic can be felt at even deeper depths of the art direction, since "anyone who has been scuba diving or snorkeling knows the ocean floor is a magical place. Just off the coast of California where Steve grew up, you can find many of the creatures that inspired him to create Bikini Bottom and all its inhabitants. All the colors of the creatures are brighter down there as they swim past each other with rays of wiggly sunlight dancing across their bodies," add executive producer Vincent Waller.

The show has a hang-loose painting style, adapting a Hawaiian tone wherein early art exploration involved using "potatoes cut out in little flower shapes and dipping them in paint, trying to mimic tiki-style influences," recalls former art director Nick Jennings. In more recent eras, the show has shifted to creating backgrounds in multiple painterly ways.

Art director Shane Richardson recognizes that a traditional paint foundation is the heart of the show's visual DNA, "so on the background paint side, we want to push ourselves to do as much as possible traditionally before relying on digital tricks." When digital painting first came into play in production, it posed a challenge to the art teams to maintain the show's impressionistic style "and the happy mistakes that come from traditional paint," explains background painter Lucy Tanashian-Gentry. "But that's why the visual style of today's *SpongeBob* means so much to me, with both traditional and digital painting. It brings together the best of both worlds, and for me, it's truly feels like coming home," she continues.

As audiences immerse themselves in Bikini Bottom, they can find it to be a wondrous yet familiar place, naturally working with the flow of the show. "The underwater vibes here feel like a secret getaway—somewhere I go to escape and just enjoy the magic of being in such a quirky, happy place," says former storyboard supervisor Erik Wiese.

"It's a collaboration between the writer/director/storyboard and myself to decide if an object can be nautical in some way, or if it needs bamboo/tiki touches. And since everything is under the sea, it's all waterlogged and soggy, which contributes to the wonky line quality," explains prop designer Isaac Marzioli. Every bit of the environment lends itself to welcome entanglement within the storyline, from pirate props to tropical tropes to surf stuff and tidal trivialities, inviting viewers to jump into the warm waters of friendly fantasy fun.

Final art of Bikini Atoll

BIKINI ATOLL

The slightly above sea-level marker for Bikini Bottom is the protrusion of Bikini Atoll, a small coral island outfitted with three palm trees. Because it exists in the middle of a vast ocean, the atoll may appear smaller than it actually is, or so the occasional episode and action on this spot suggest.

"When I dive into the world of SpongeBob, I'm immediately struck by the cool blues and the wide-open underwater space," notes Erik Wiese.

BIKINI BOTTOM

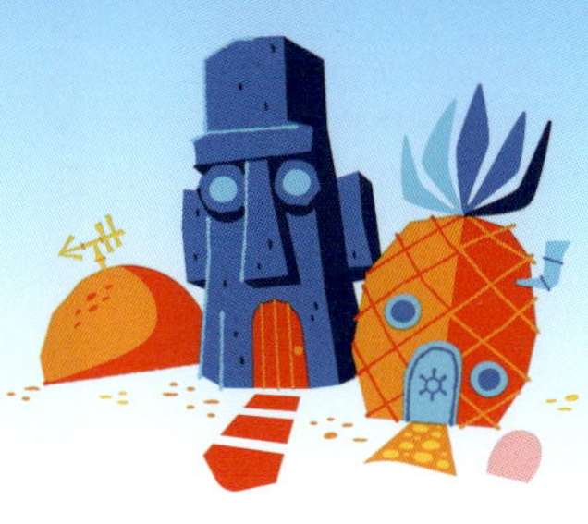

Below the atoll lies the community of Bikini Bottom, an underwater collection of dwellings and infrastructure that serves as home to SpongeBob SquarePants and a cast of interesting characters just as unique. Executive producer Marc Ceccarelli describes Bikini Bottom as a "cargo cult made up of debris that has sunk to the ocean floor," which explains perfectly that what is there is exactly what needs to be there, according to destiny. This community is "relatable to the world you live in with buildings, streets, cars, and people. But in *SpongeBob*, the icing is the style that smashes these typical things you know with a nautical theme," adds Nick Jennings.

"There's this playful silliness that makes me smile, but it's also really calming. The funny shapes of the houses and the gentle waves create a feeling of fun and relaxation all at once," says Erik Wiese. Bikini Bottom is "a great place to experiment visually," in the mind of art director Shane Richardson. "I want to maintain the continuity of what's come before—the nostalgic, colorful, painterly style—but also push the boundaries for what the audience expects from us in design, lighting, and color when traveling to new locations," he adds.

"The world of SpongeBob SquarePants is magical, heartwarming, delightfully silly, and completely original. There's truly nothing else like it in the world of animation. It truly is 'nautical nonsense' where anything and everything is possible," says Lucy Tanashian-Gentry.

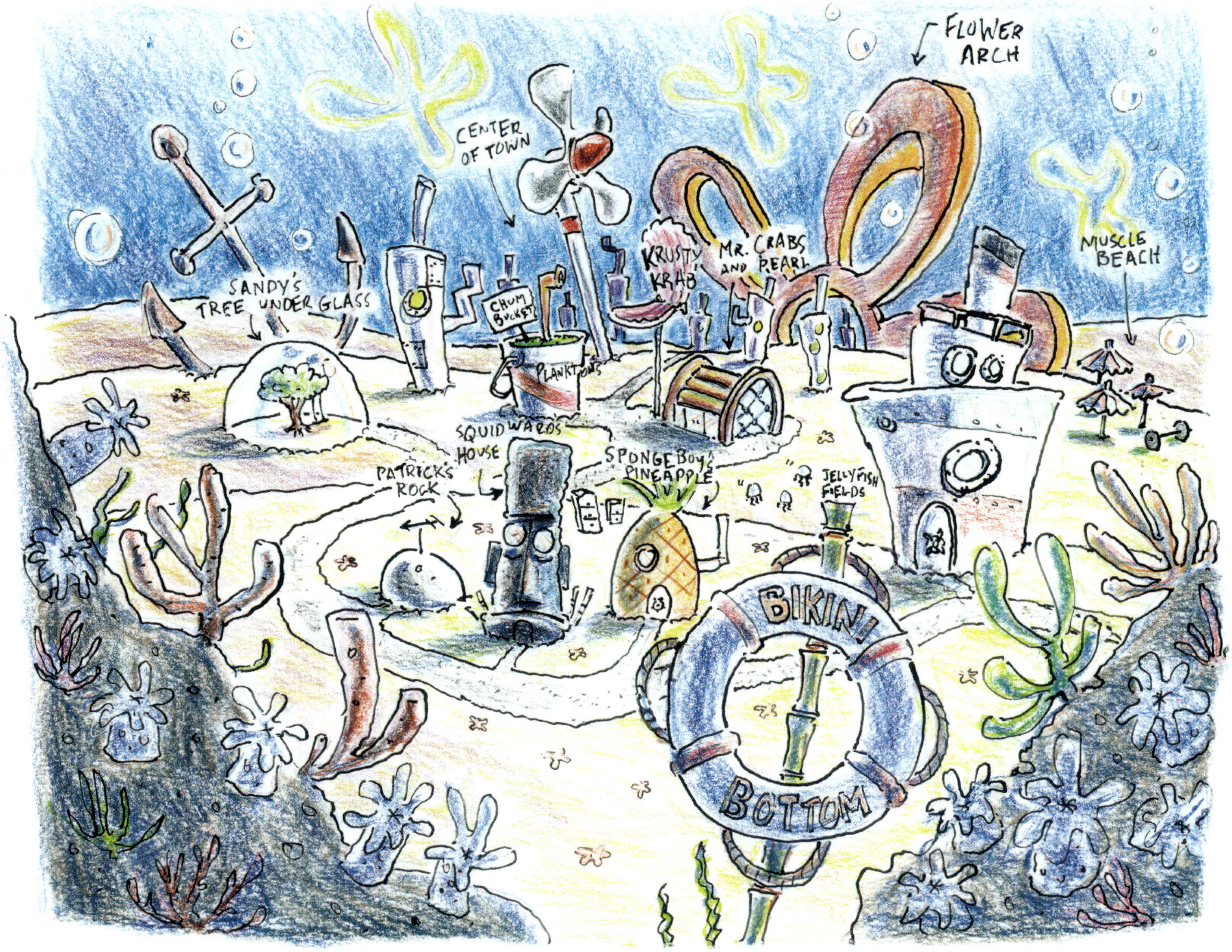

Rough color sketch of handy map of what's where in Bikini Bottom

Detailed final map of what's where in Bikini Bottom, plus how to navigate via the BBTS

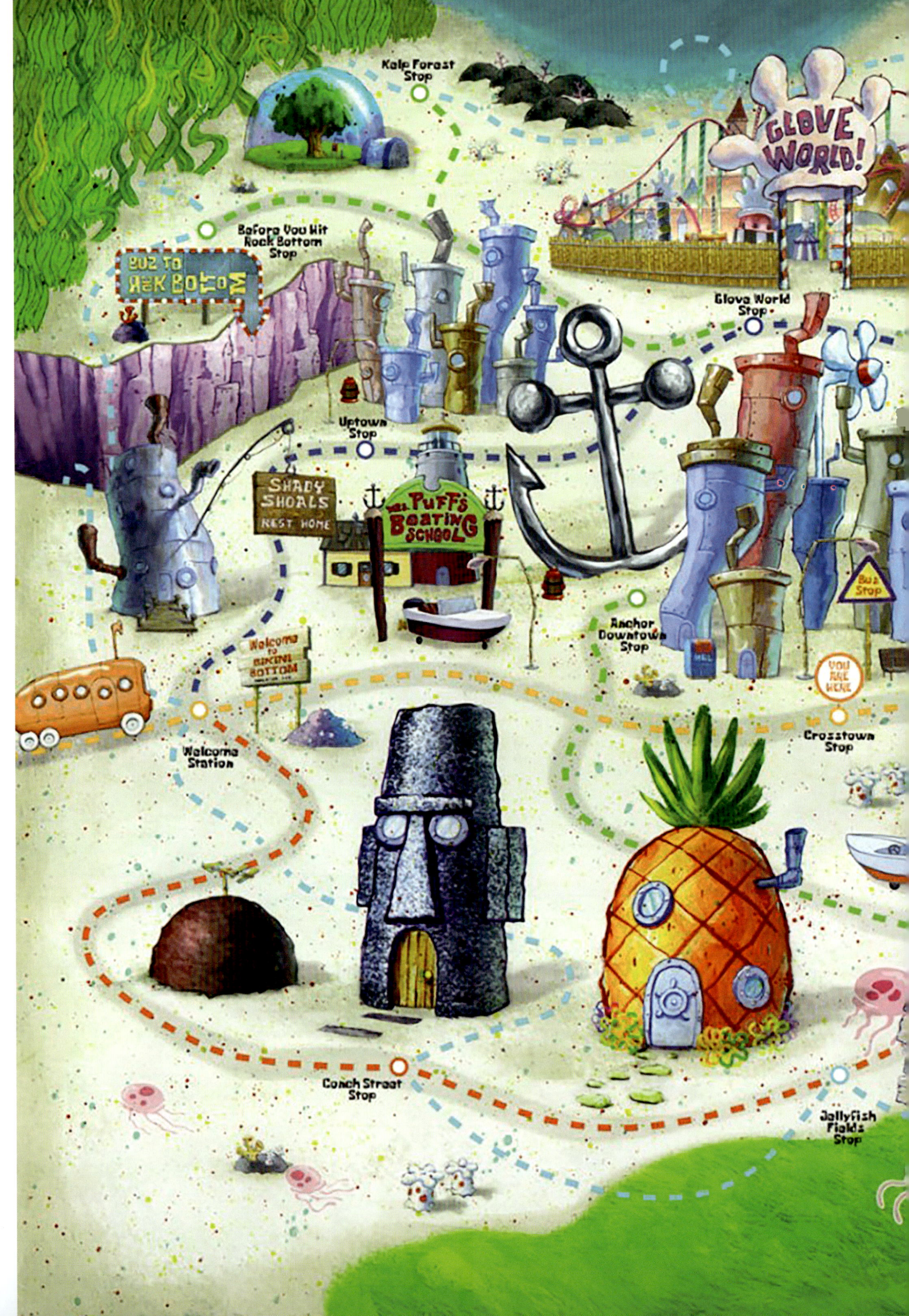

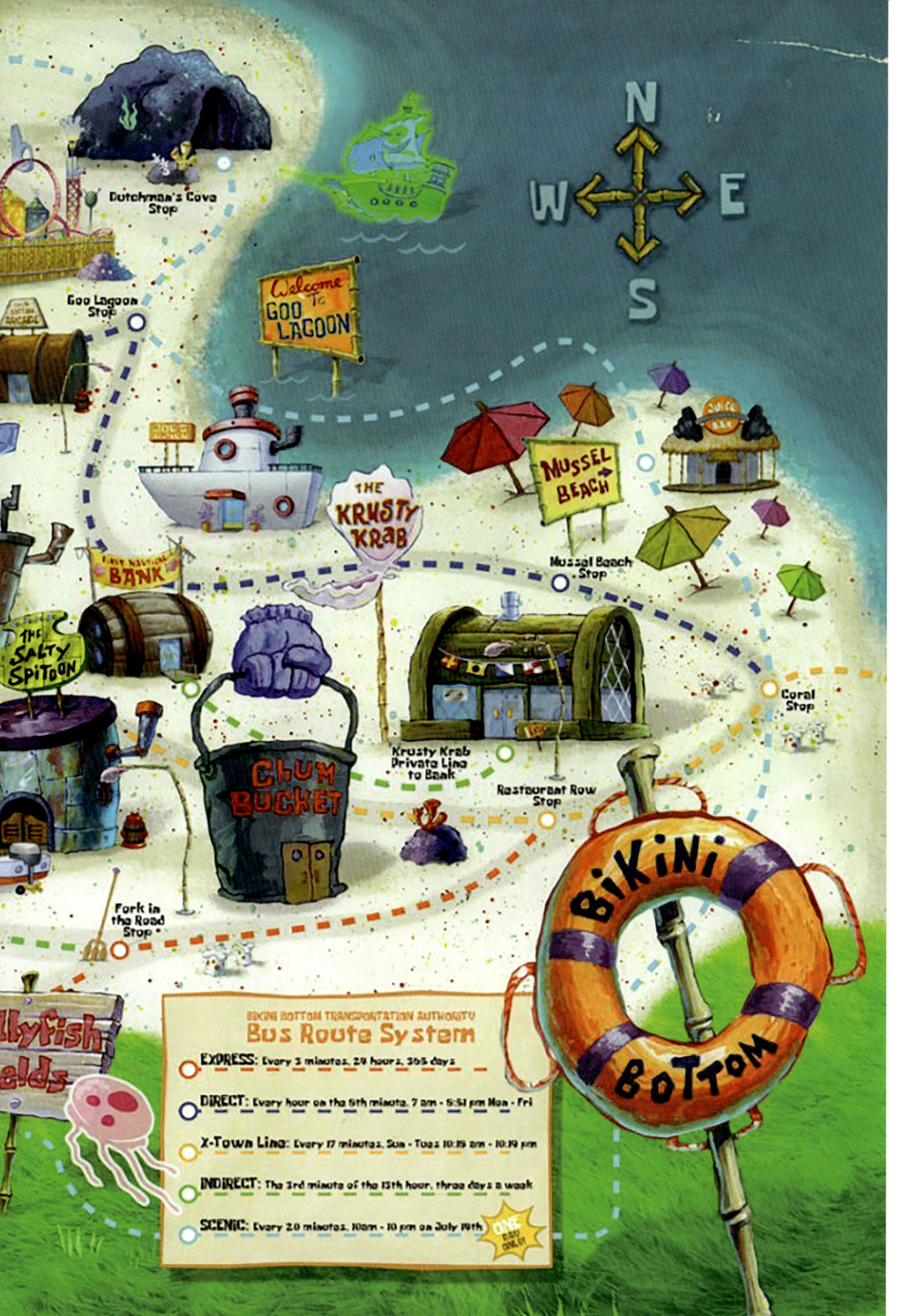

N
W
E
S
Dutchman's Cove Stop
Welcome To GOO LAGOON
Goo Lagoon Stop
MUSSEL BEACH
THE KRUSTY KRAB
BANK
Mussel Beach Stop
THE SALTY SPITOON
Coral Stop
CHUM BUCKET
Krusty Krab Private Line to Bank
Restaurant Row Stop
Fork in the Road Stop
BiKiNi BOTTOM
BIKINI BOTTOM TRANSPORTATION AUTHORITY
Bus Route System
EXPRESS: Every 3 minutes, 24 hours, 365 days
DIRECT: Every hour on the 5th minute, 7 am - 5:51 pm Mon - Fri
X-Town Line: Every 17 minutes, Sun - Tues 10:15 am - 10:19 pm
INDIRECT: The 3rd minute of the 13th hour, three days a week
SCENIC: Every 20 minutes, 10am - 10 pm on July 19th
ONE DAY ONLY!

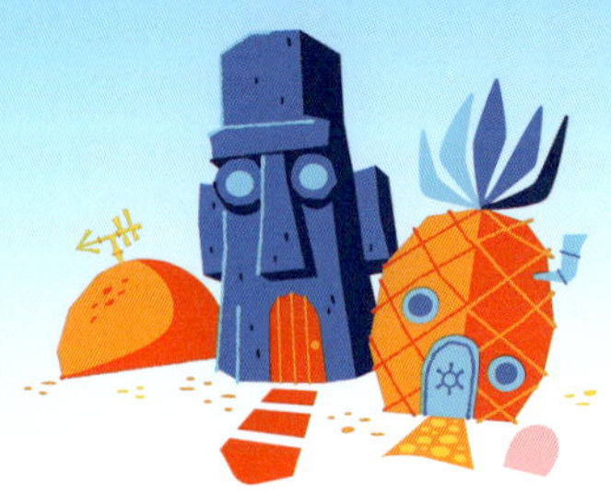

CONCH STREET

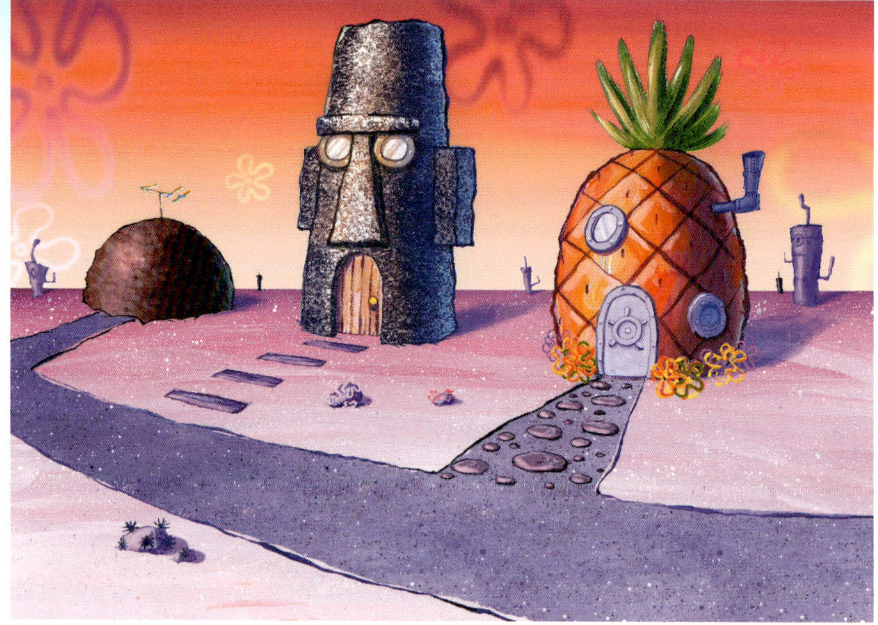

The homes of neighbors on Conch Street as rendered in various levels of design: Patrick's rock, Squidward's moai, and SpongeBob's pineapple

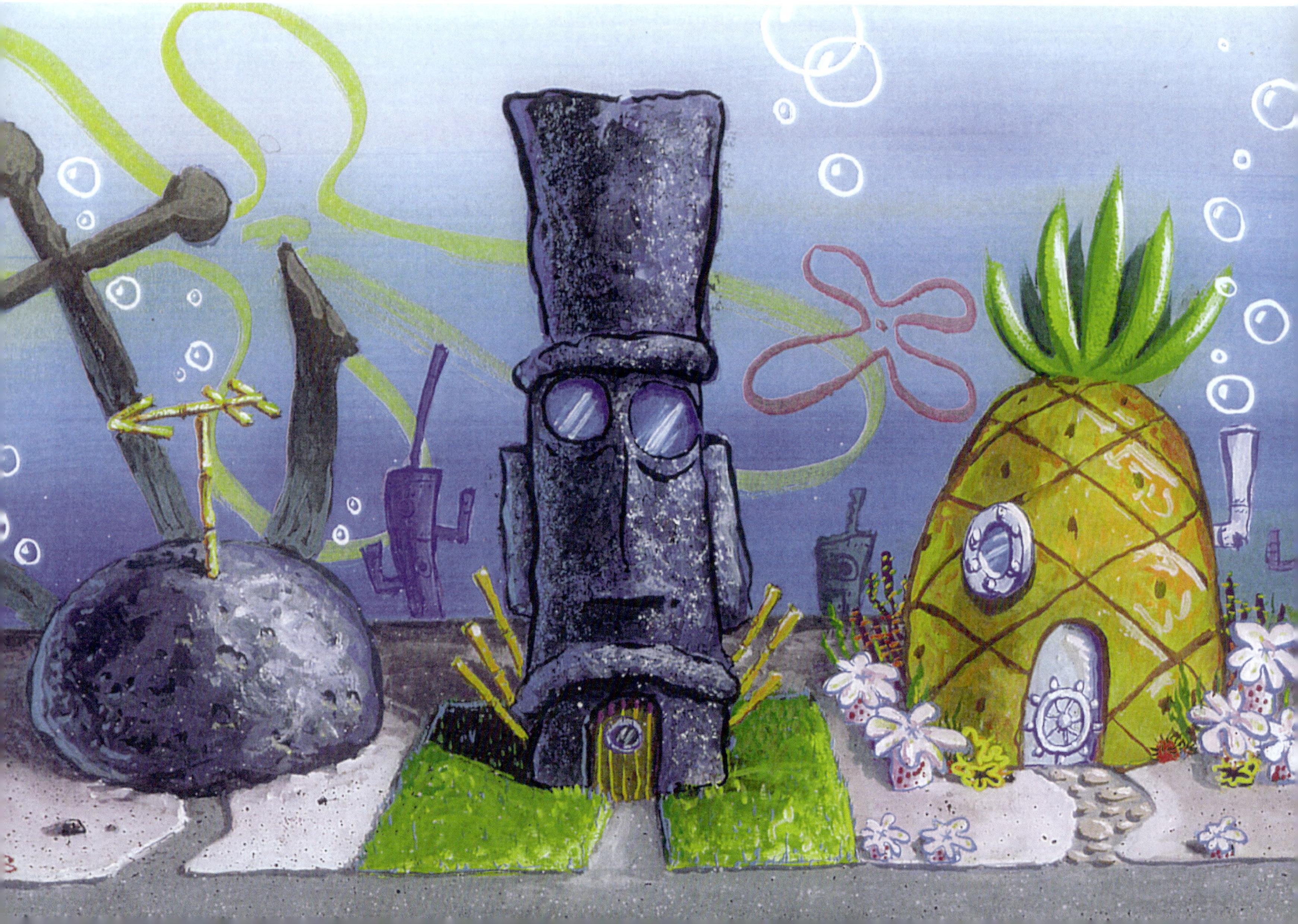

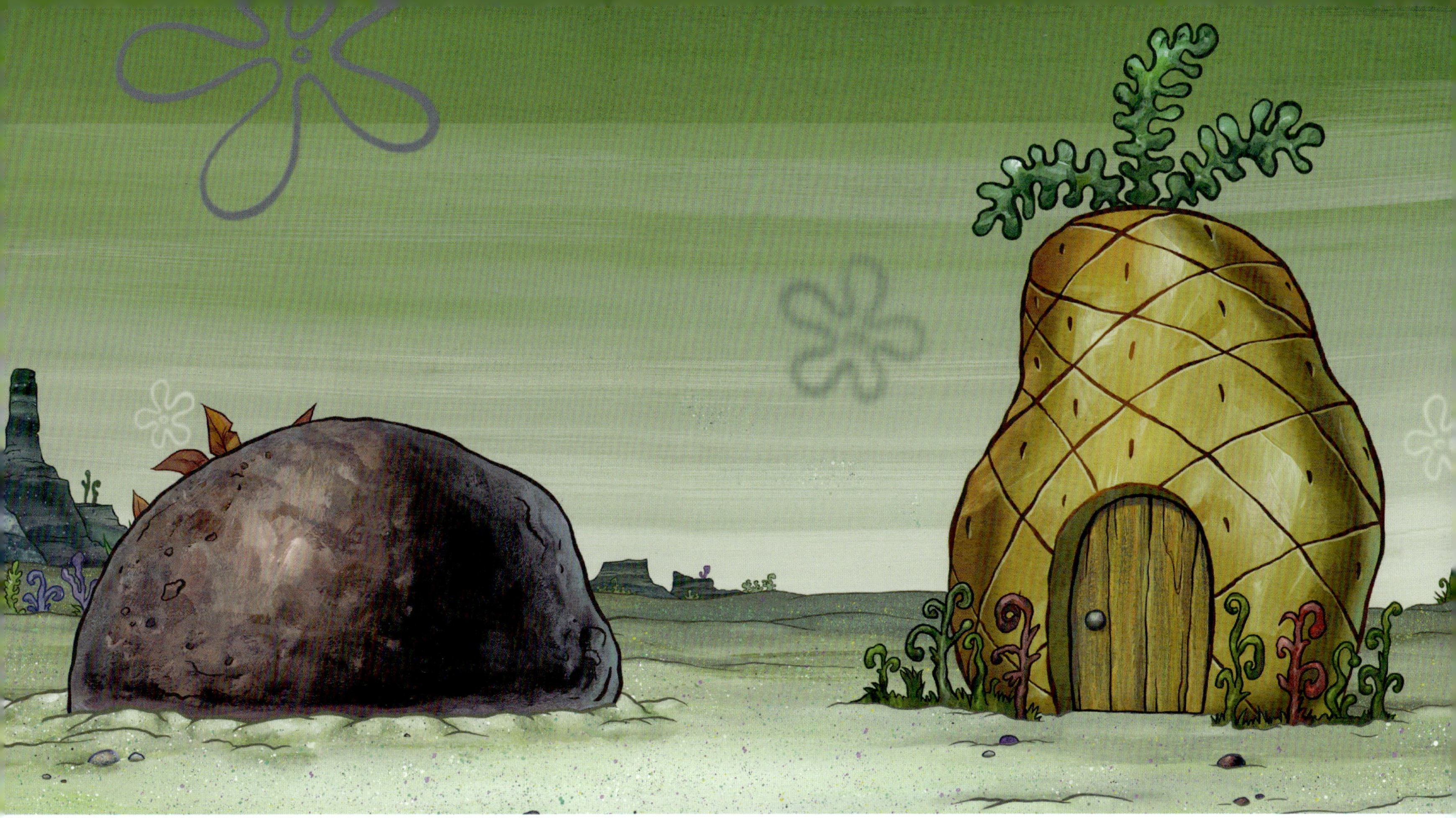

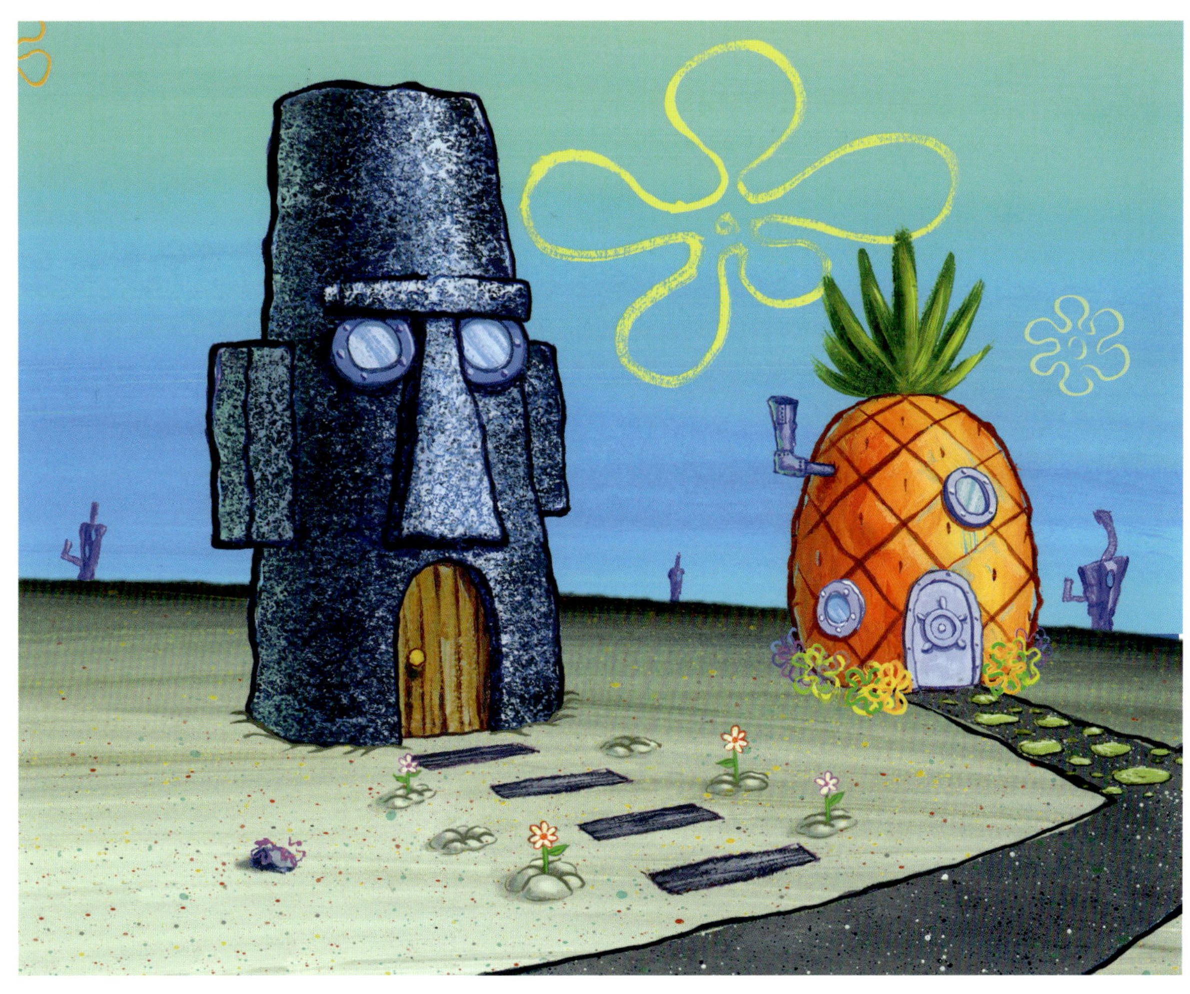

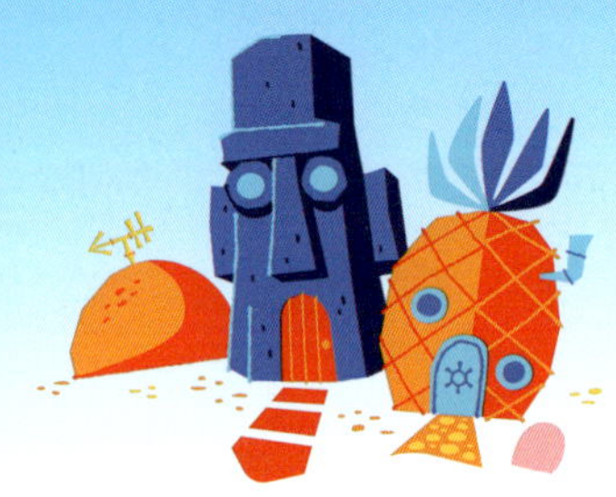

SPONGEBOB'S PINEAPPLE

Bikini Bottom is a place where anything that may fall into the ocean is fair game for being part of the environment, but thoughtful production design portrays that each home intentionally reflects its occupant. SpongeBob's pineapple house matches that he is "sweet, tangy, full of energy," says former executive producer Paul Tibbitt.

Through the magic of animation, the pineapple is "not only a kind of fantasy child-living-alone space, but there is no fixed floor plan. We are able to expand it and change it according to what an episode asks for," adds former storyboard supervisor Erik Wiese.

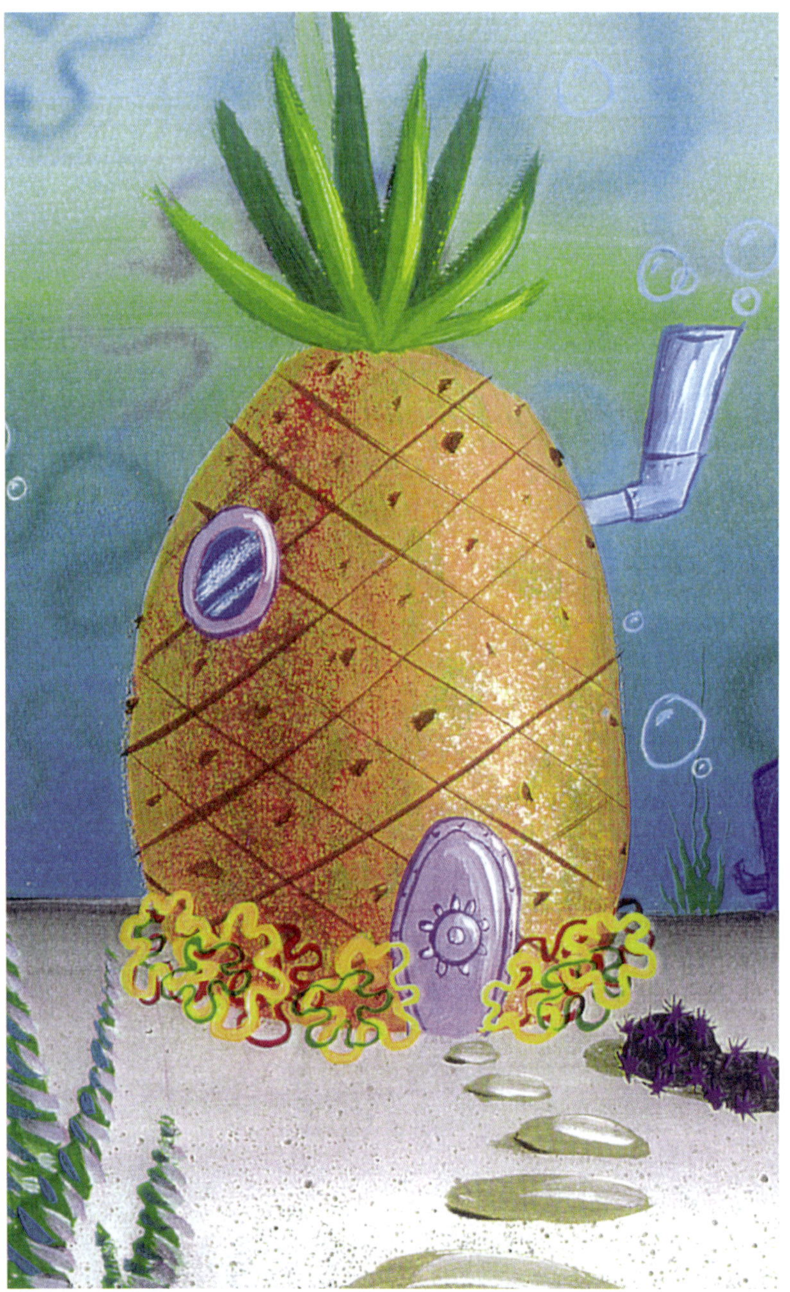

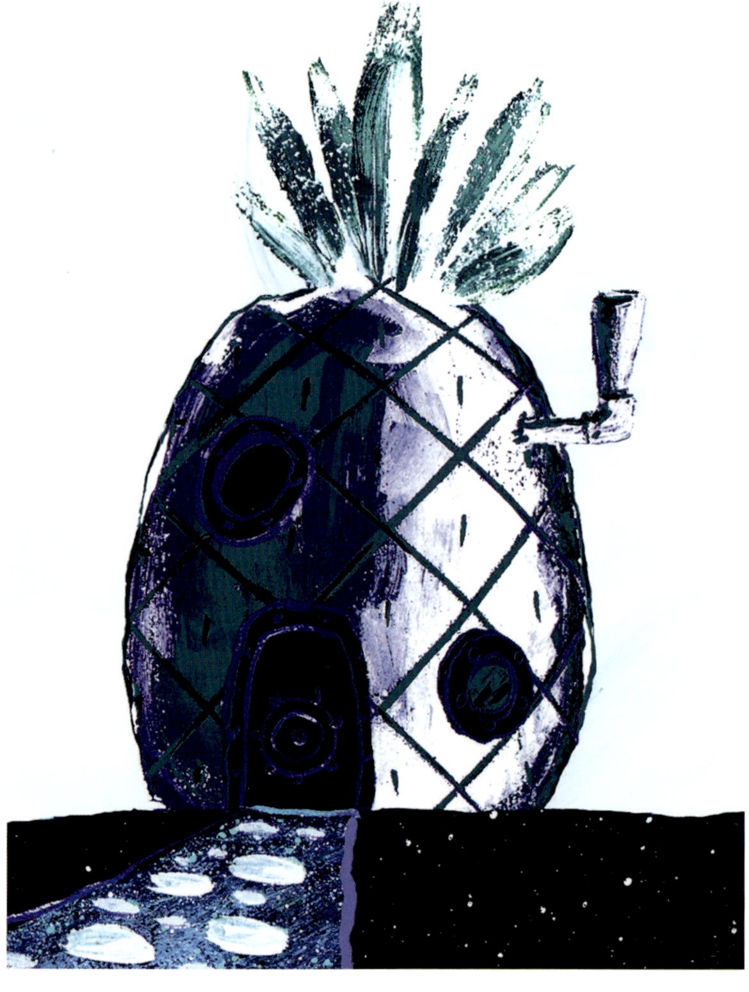

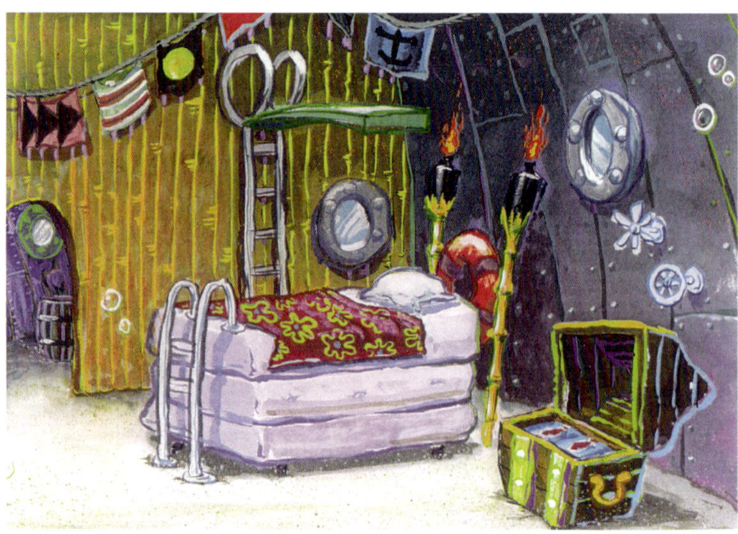

SpongeBob's pineapple home in visual development [left]; layout images from the SpongeBoy era [upper right]; and cleanup layout images [lower right]

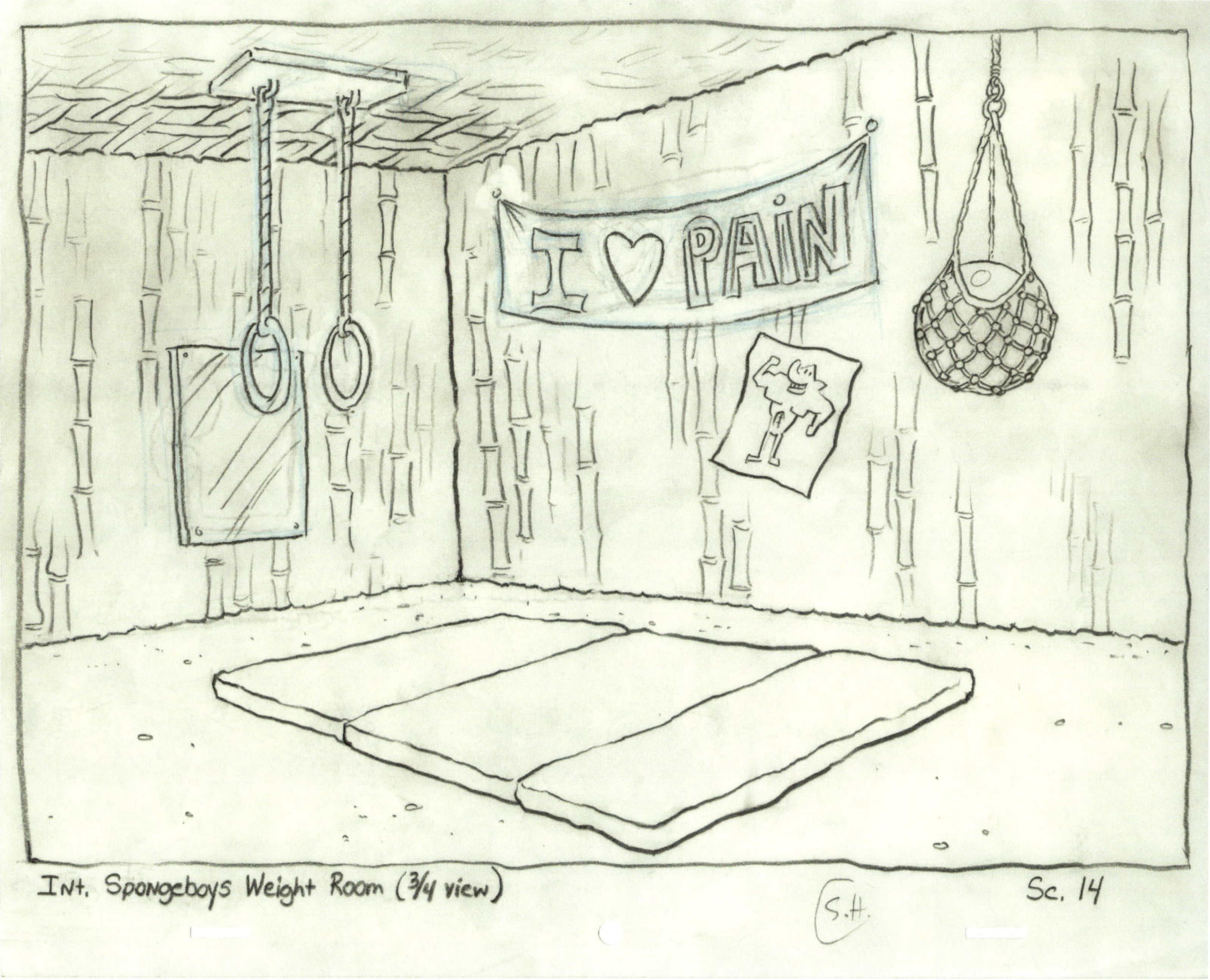

I ♥ PAIN

Int. Spongeboys Weight Room (3/4 view) S.H. Sc. 14

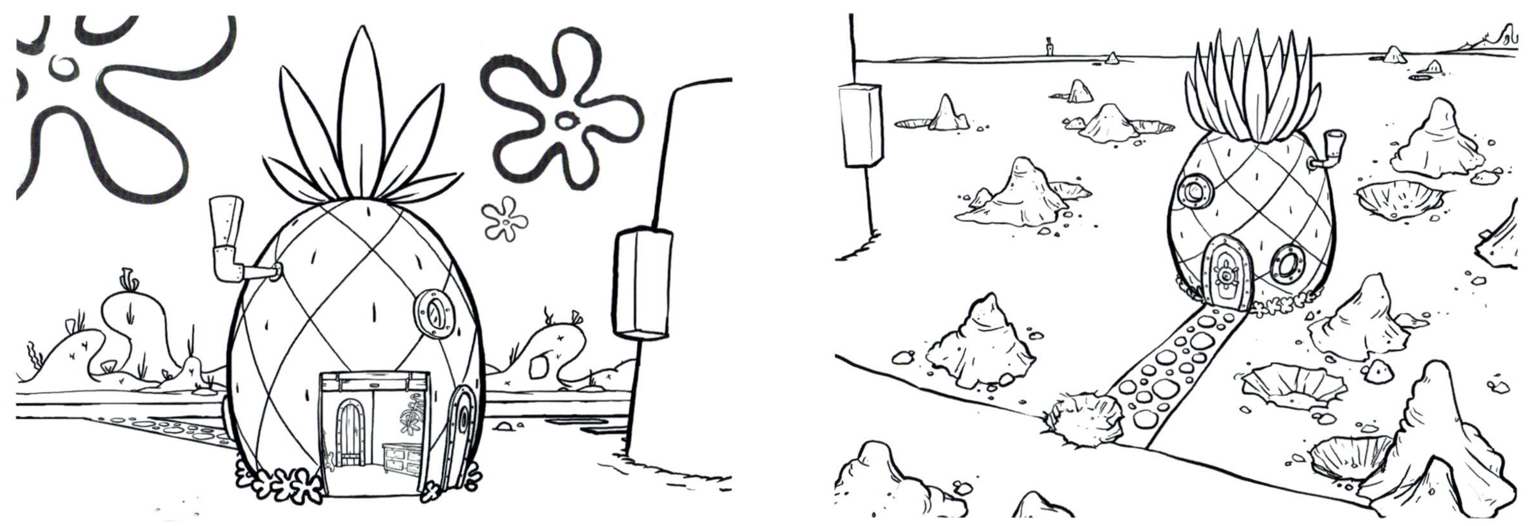

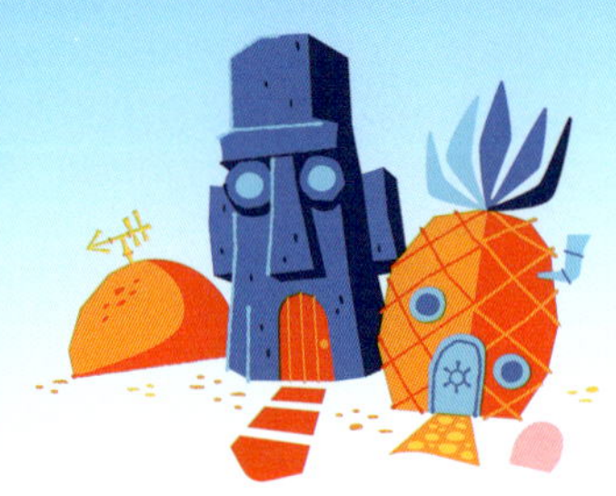

SQUIDWARD'S MOAI

A replica of an Easter Island head, Squidward's home was designed by Stephen Hillenburg to reflect its resident's expression. As an added layer of art direction, the moai also complements his nature, since Squidward has an exaggerated sense of self—a.k.a. letting his head get too big—plus he "is rigid and stuck in his ways like a statue," says former executive producer Paul Tibbitt. A look inside his home confirms Squidward's self-importance as it contains a wondrous gallery of self-portraits, most of which were created by Peter Bennett and "are integral [to] Squidward's backstory," according to executive producer Vincent Waller.

The placement of Squidward's home on Conch Street was an entirely intentional production design decision by Hillenburg, putting the three in a row so that there would always be conflicts with Squidward. "The fact that Squidward is such a crank and his house is stuck directly between the two most annoying people he knows is perfect cosmic justice," adds Tibbitt.

Tonal [black/gray] and final art [full color] images of Squidward's moai

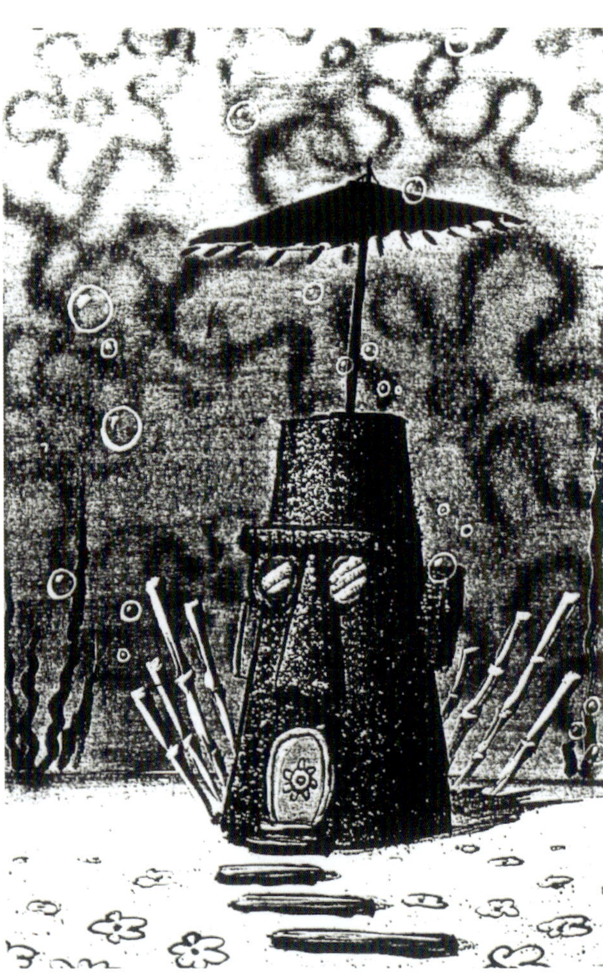

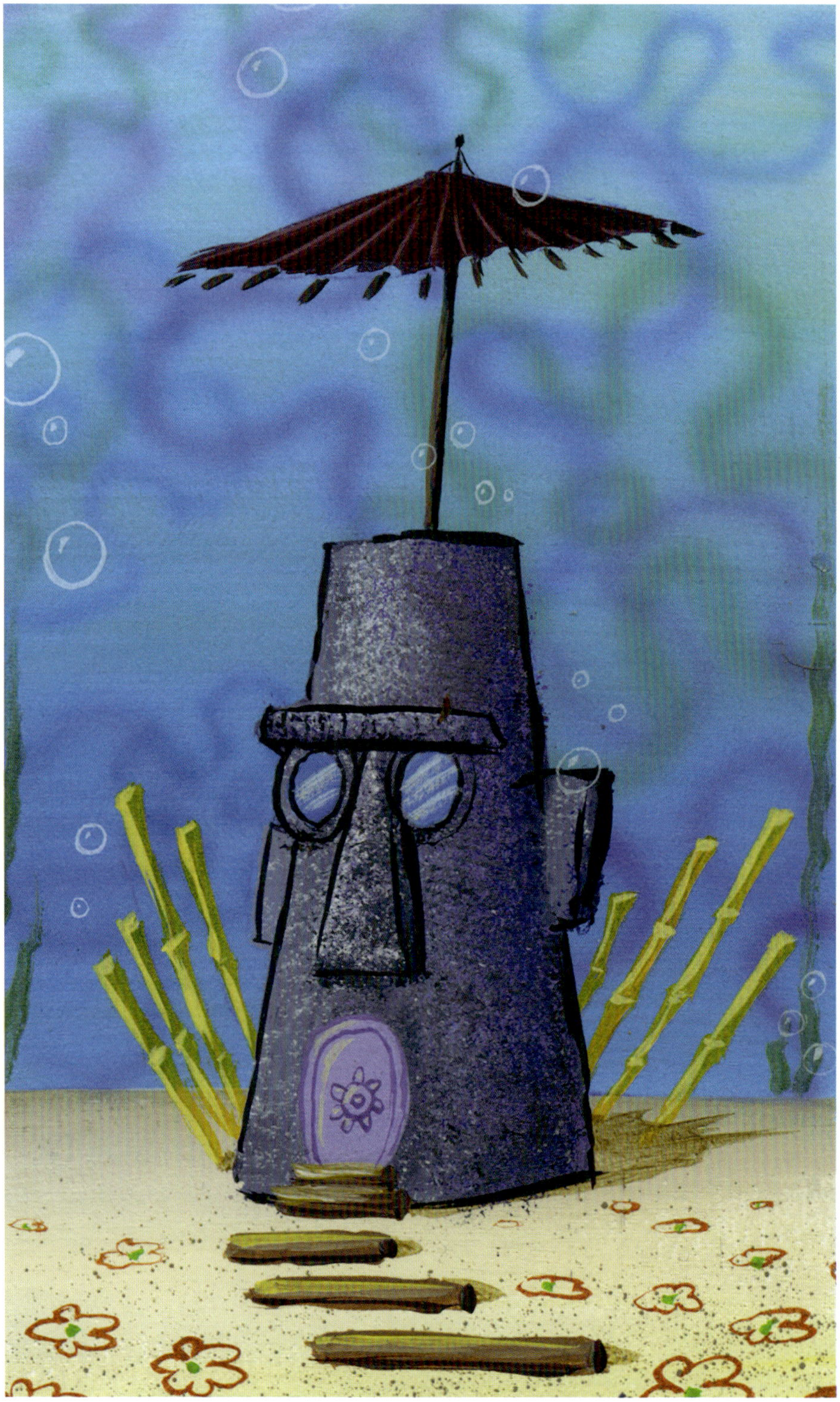

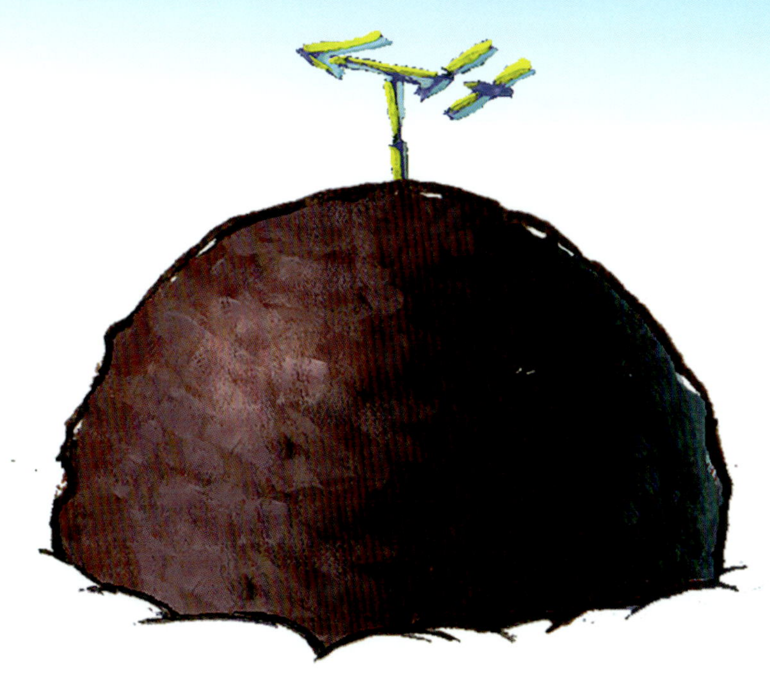

PATRICK'S ROCK

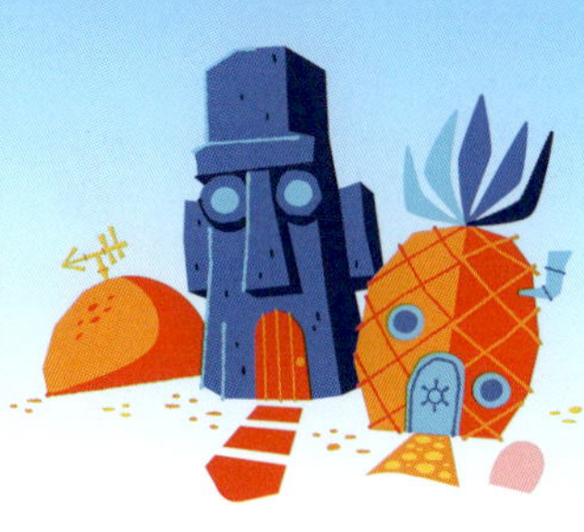

Perhaps the most logical ocean floor item along Conch Street is Patrick's home, a rock. This object perfectly befits his personality of being as dumb as a rock, adding a layer of art direction humor by visualizing the phrase for ignorance about "living under a rock."

Final art of Patrick's rock, with an interior view

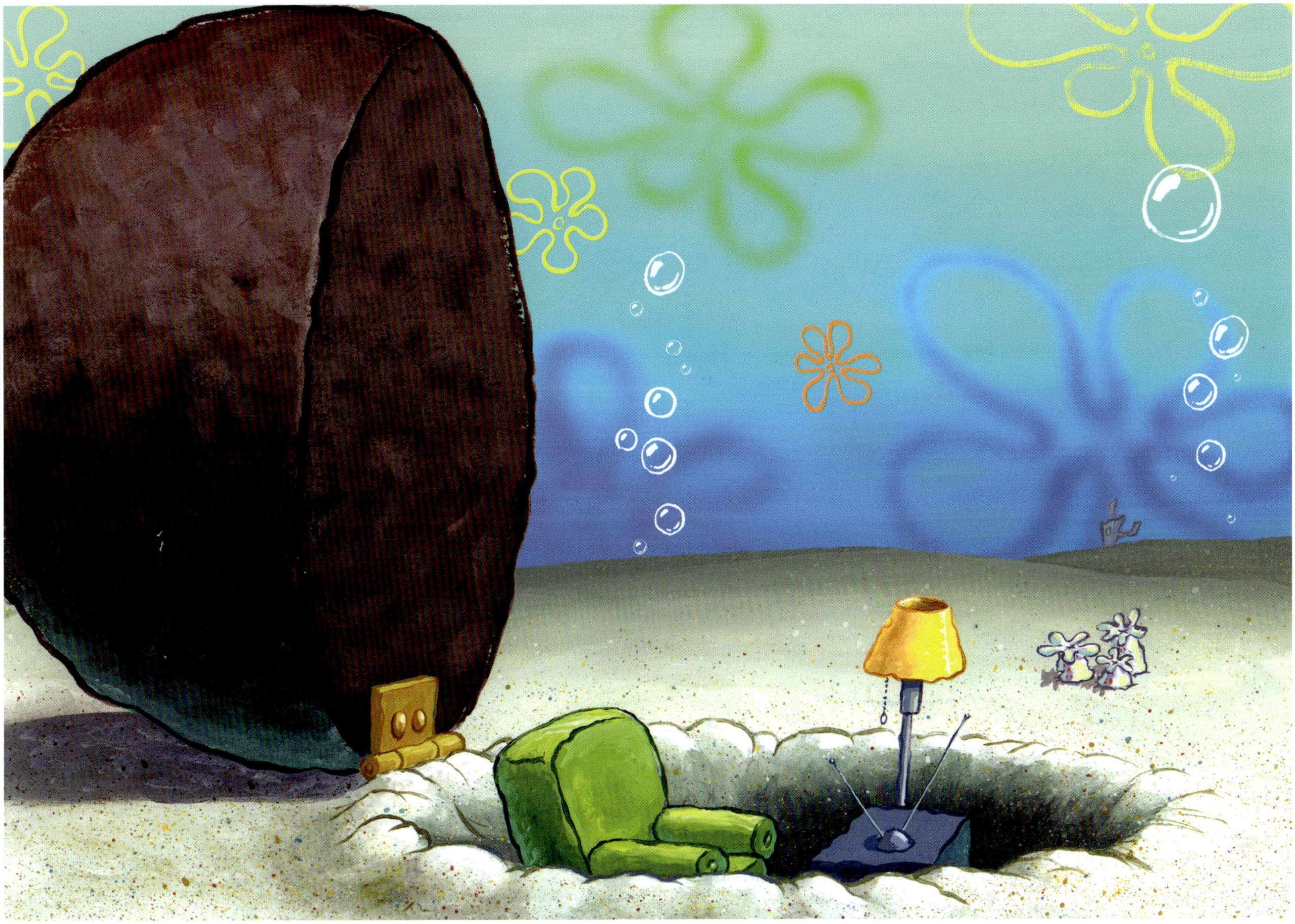

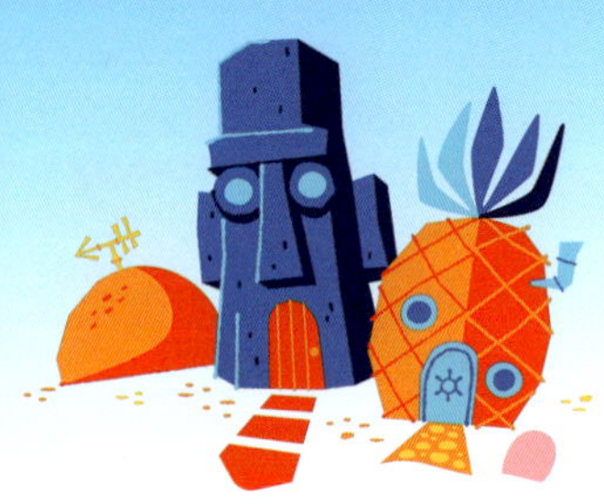

THE KRUSTY KRAB

This fast-food establishment owned and operated by Mr. Krabs is the most popular and frequented restaurant in Bikini Bottom. Its Galley Grub menu offers a variety of items to its patrons, but the Krabby Patty is the star of the food show, its secret formula kept under lock and key.

Design-wise, it's also fast fun to recognize that "the Krusty Krab is a lobster trap. It's a dead-end job," as pointed out by Paul Tibbitt. Employees Squidward and SpongeBob can attest to that, but it doesn't seem to bother the fry cook at all; he's happy to be part of the Krusty Krew.

Since the restaurant is perhaps the most detailed interior location in all of Bikini Bottom, supervising producer Kenny Pittenger appreciated the design challenges of so many specific elements in that space, and former painter Kit Boyce relished the environment that was "underneath the stove in the Krusty Krab kitchen. Filthy and dripping with grease."

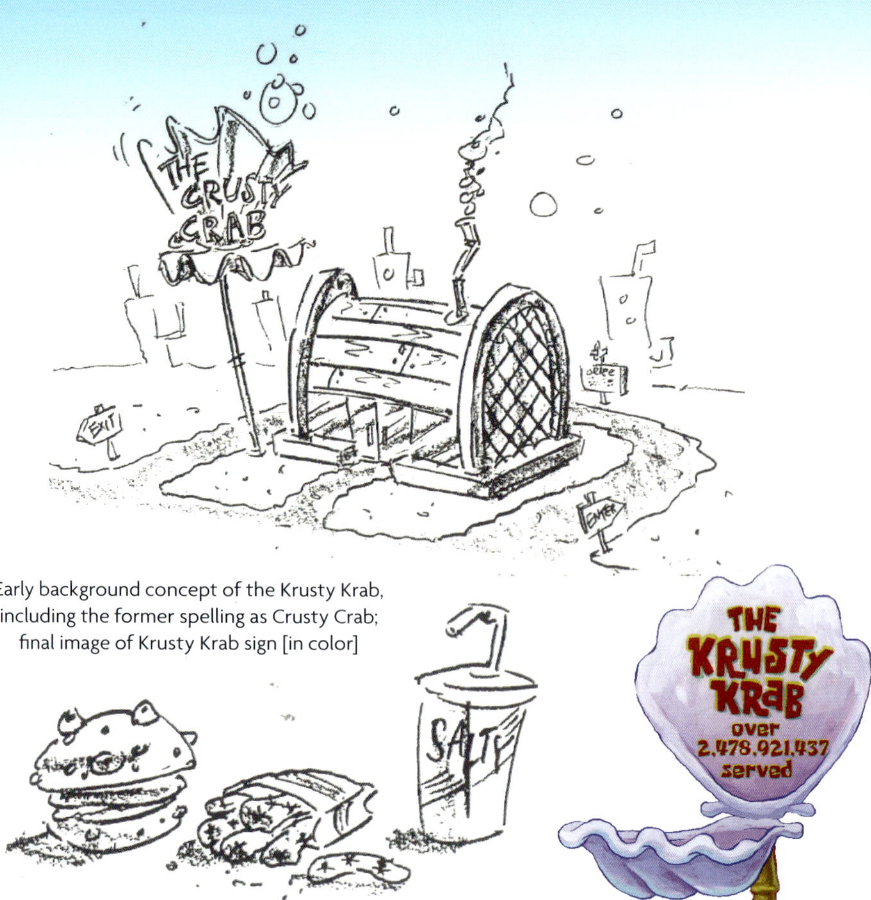

Early background concept of the Krusty Krab, including the former spelling as Crusty Crab; final image of Krusty Krab sign [in color]

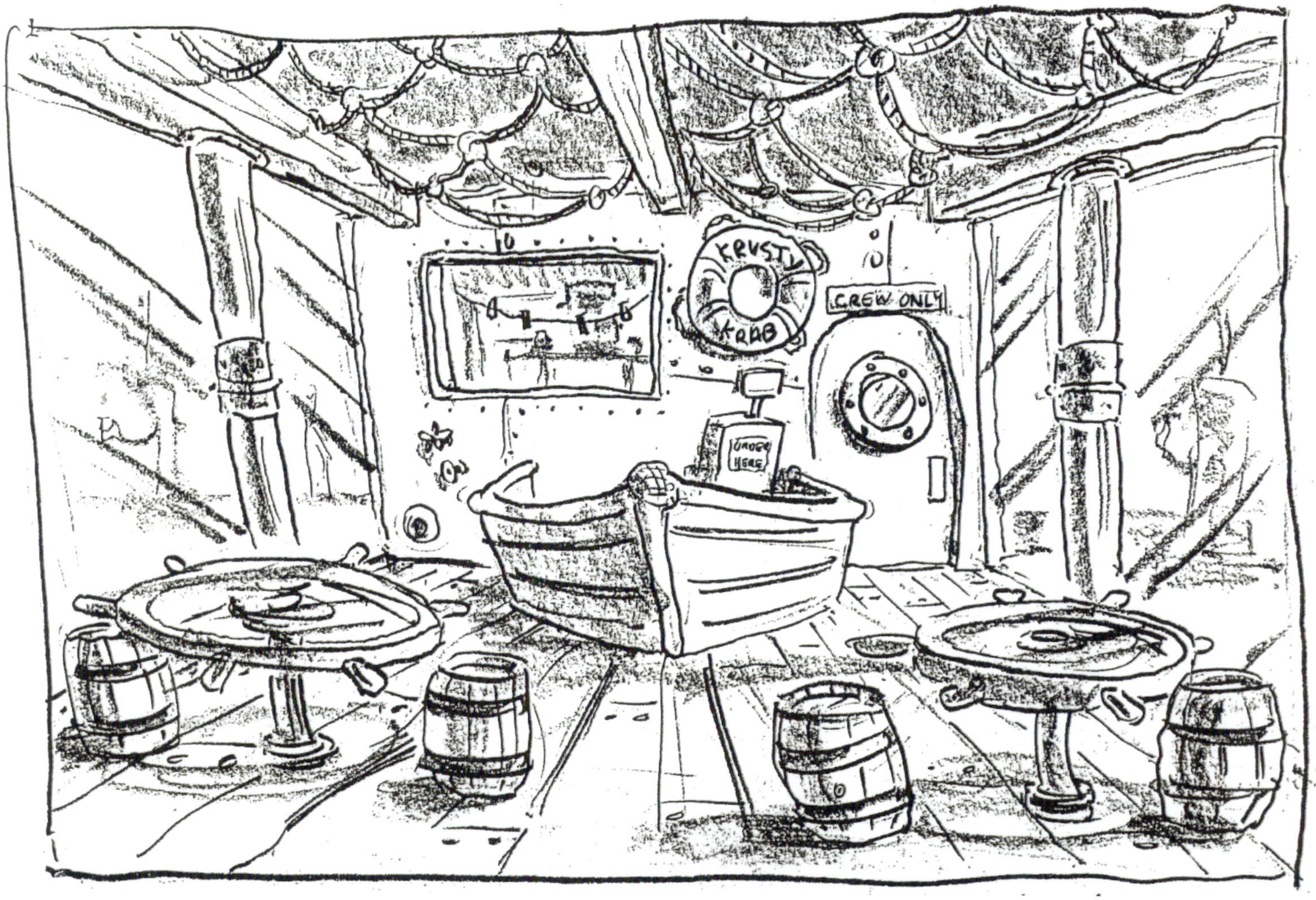

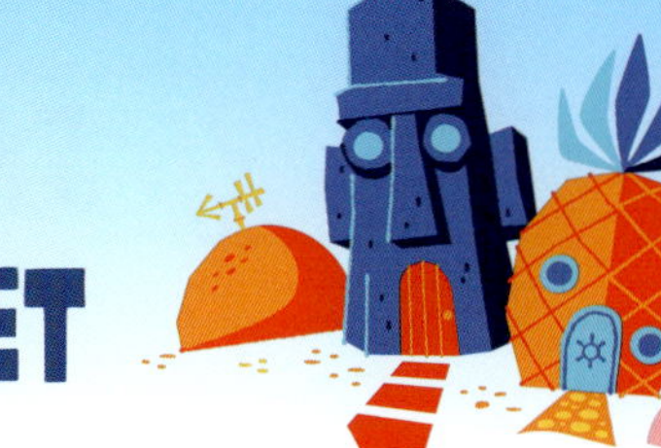

CHUM BUCKET

Directly across the street from the Krusty Krab is another fast-food establishment, but this one is perhaps the least popular and most rarely frequented restaurant in Bikini Bottom. Owned by Plankton, the Chum Bucket offers exactly what its name states, that mainstay being an oddly cannibalistic offering for a community of seemingly civilized fish. On the rare occasion that Karen gets to run the restaurant, it seems she would be the smarter partner in trying to make it a success, even without having access to the Krabby Patty secret formula that Plankton considers vital... but where's the fun in that, if Plankton doesn't continue to fail spectacularly?

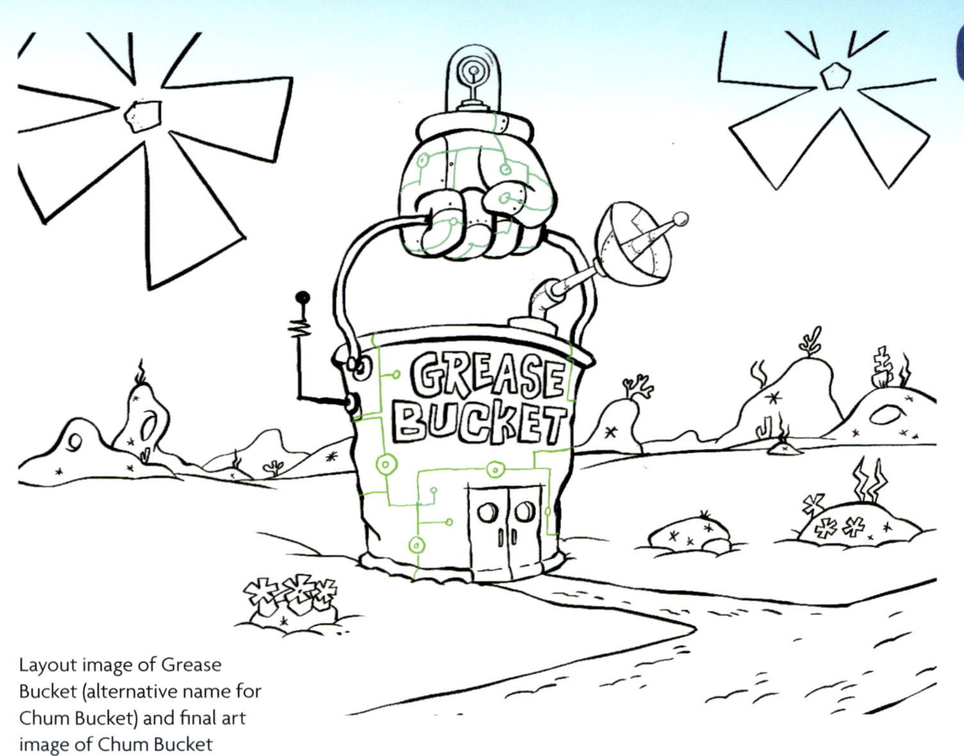

Layout image of Grease Bucket (alternative name for Chum Bucket) and final art image of Chum Bucket

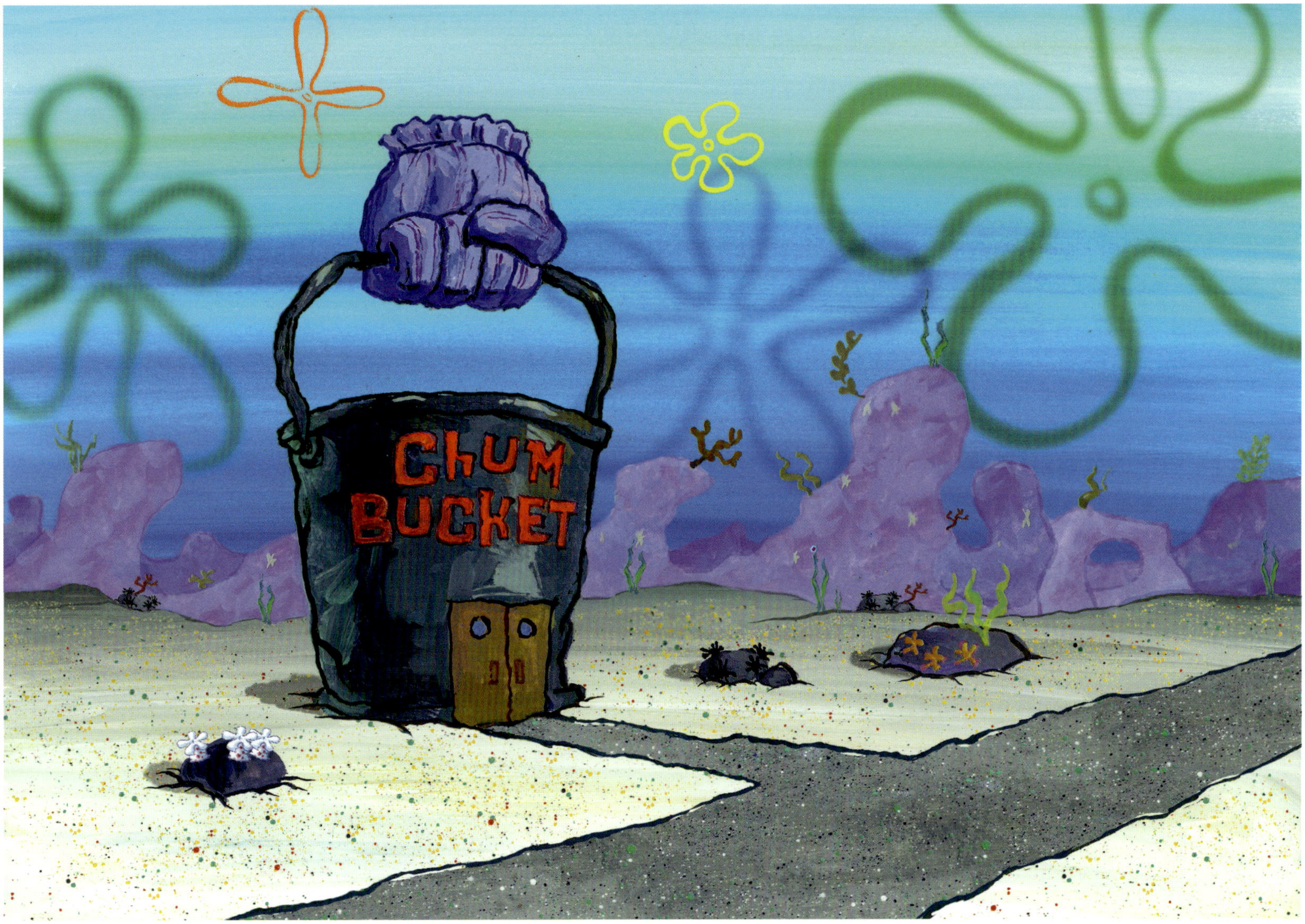

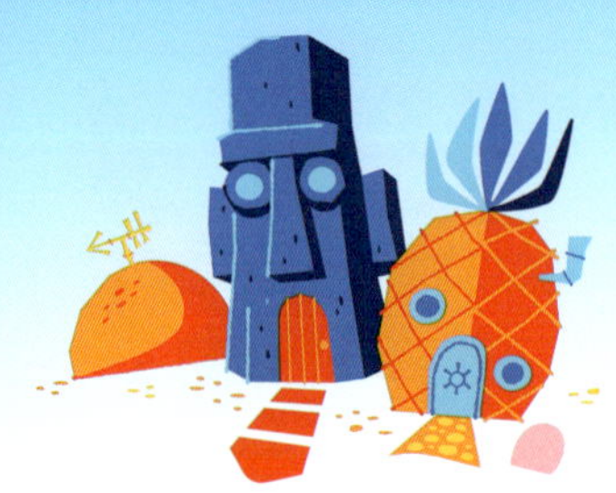

SANDY'S TREEDOME

In a slightly more remote area of Bikini Bottom, Sandy Cheeks lives in an airtight clear dome, which provides her a tree and some grass with an oxygenated environment in which they can subsist under the sea. Sandy has other amenities within the dome for her living and scientific needs, including a well-appointed home built within the trunk of the tree that features various wooden and acorn-accessorized household items. When residents of Bikini Bottom come to visit, she outfits them with proper fishbowl-like water helmets so that they don't wither and dry up like SpongeBob and Patrick did on their very first visit. Since then, Sandy has been more hospitable than a cast-iron pan full of butter is to popcorn, as she believes that "home is where you're surrounded by critters that care about ya."

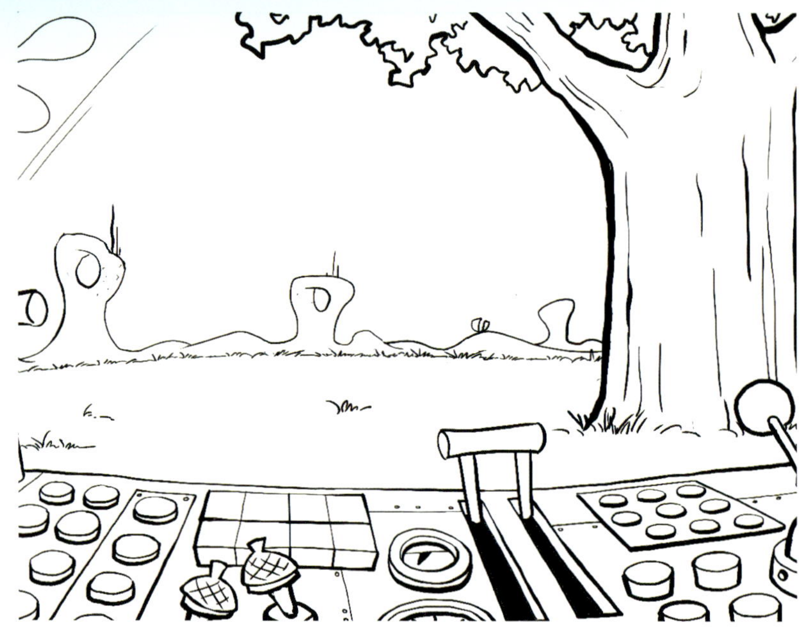

Layout image [upper] and final art of Sandy's home

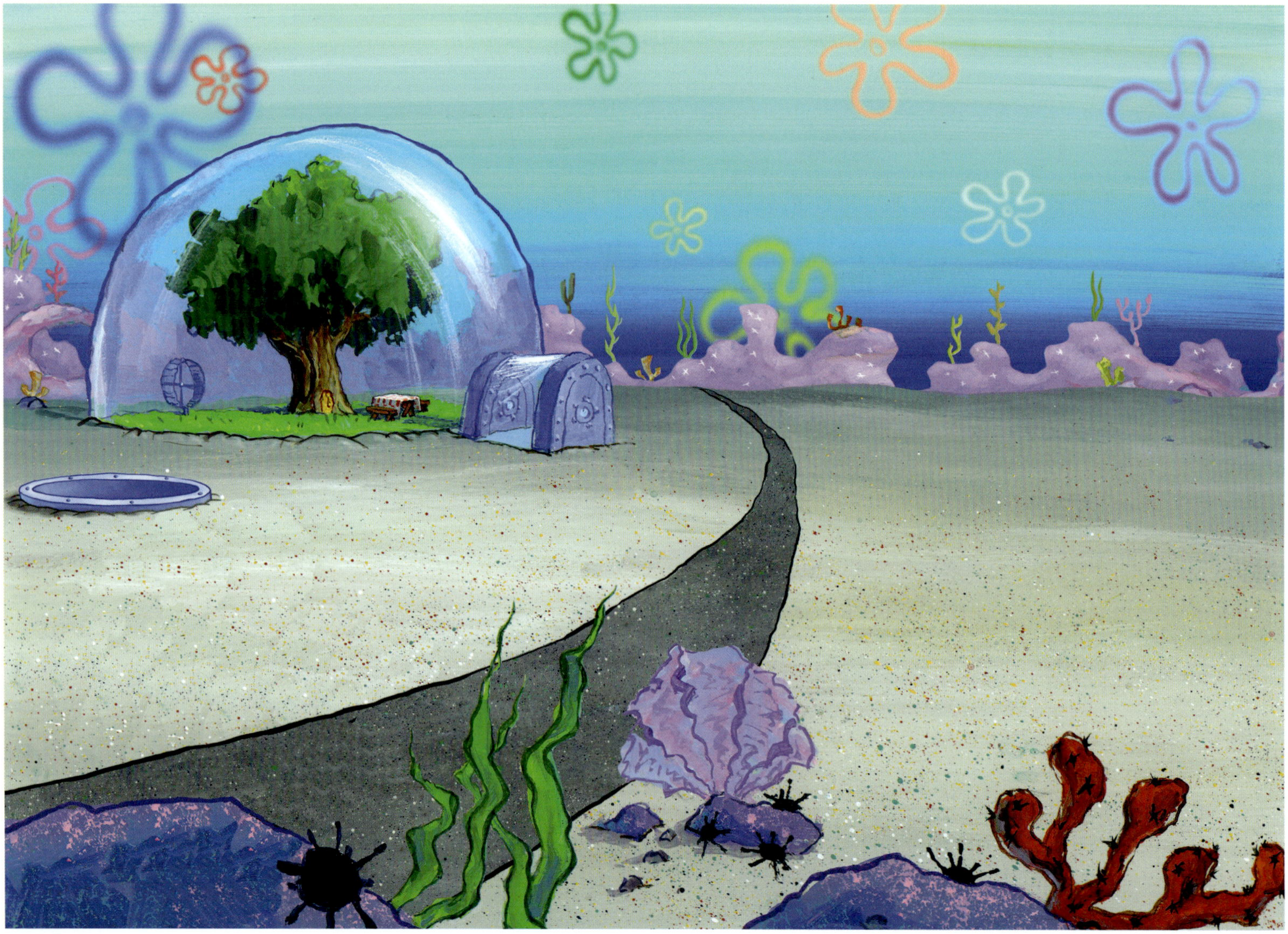

TOURING AROUND BIKINI BOTTOM

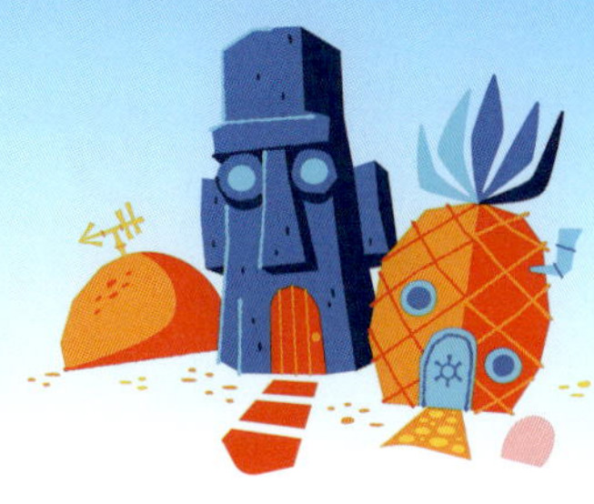

The city of Bikini Bottom contains many other interesting locations within its boundaries, and here's a visual visit to a few of them.

MRS. PUFF'S BOATING SCHOOL

Don't think too hard about the vehicles in Mrs. Puff's driving school—just go with the flow of fun. "Our boats in Bikini Bottom always float magically above their wheels, which adds a real sense of whimsy to the show," observes executive producer Vincent Waller.

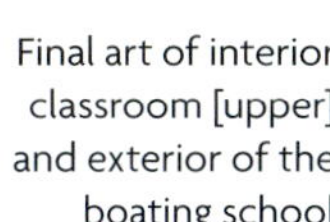

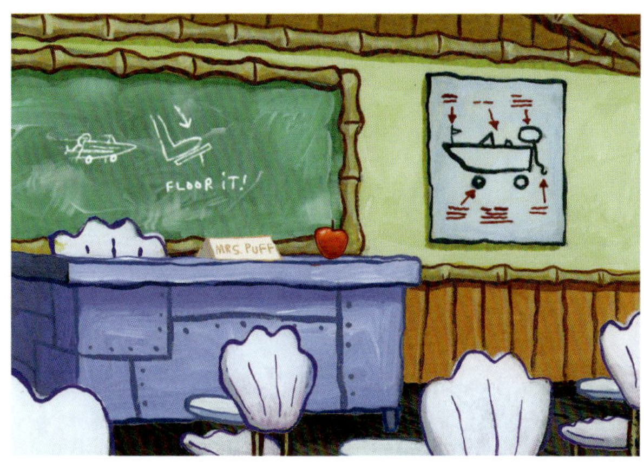

Final art of interior classroom [upper] and exterior of the boating school

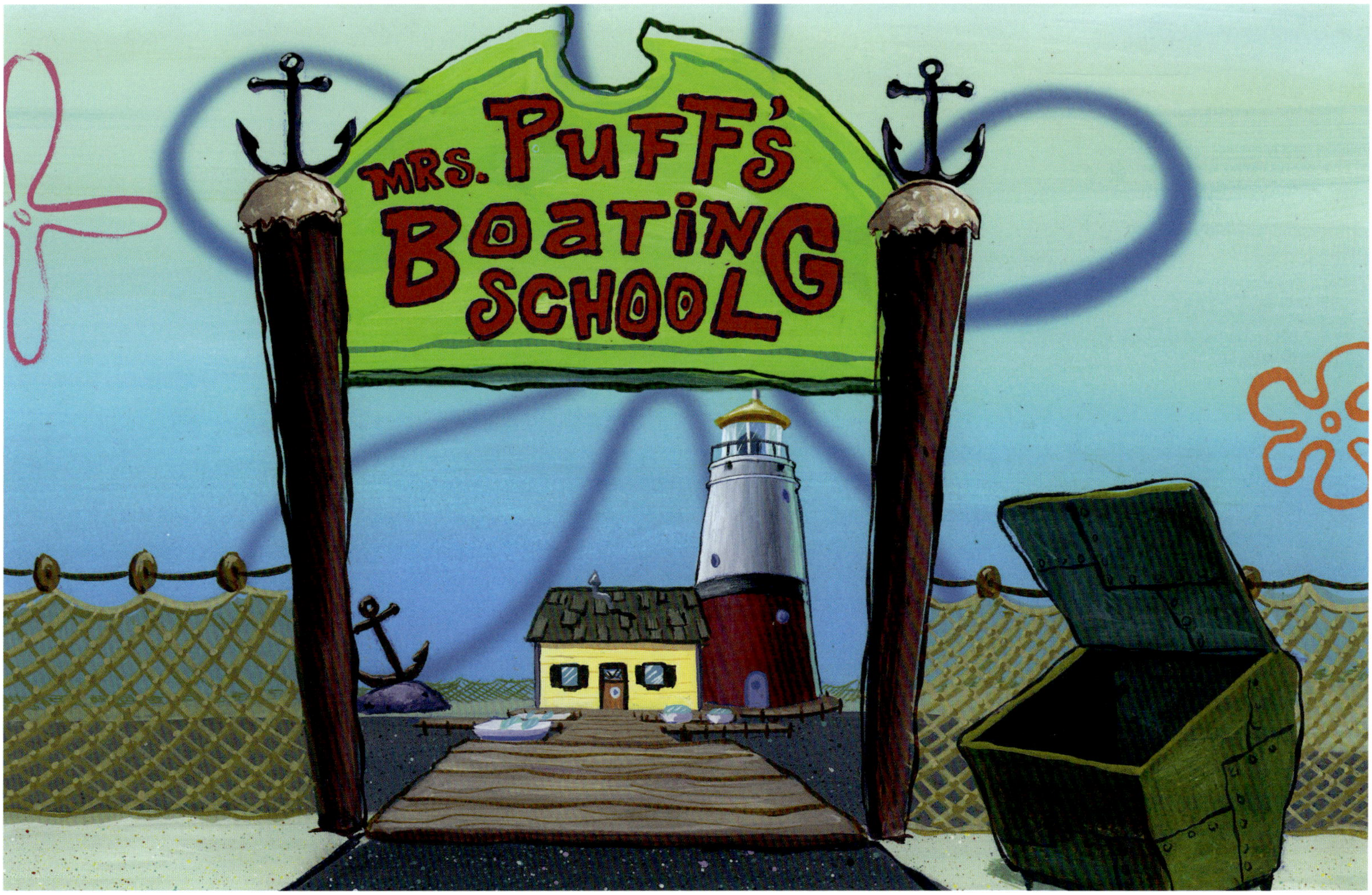

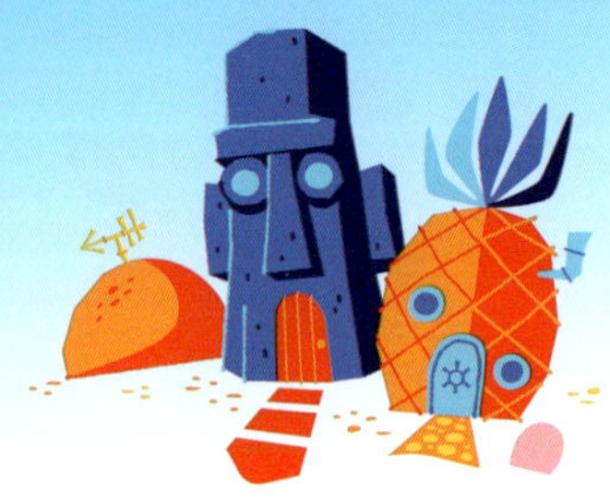

GOOFY GOOBER'S ICE CREAM PARTY BOAT

One of SpongeBob's favorite places to spend his free time is Goofy Goober's Ice Cream Party Boat. There's no doubt that any place with an abundance of ice cream guarantees a good time, whether you order a Triple Gooberberry Sunrise, Double Fudge Spinnies, Mount Razzleberries, or a good ol' Goober Meal. Just try to not overdo it, as an ice cream hangover is quite brain-freezingly hard to process... just ask Patrick or SpongeBob!

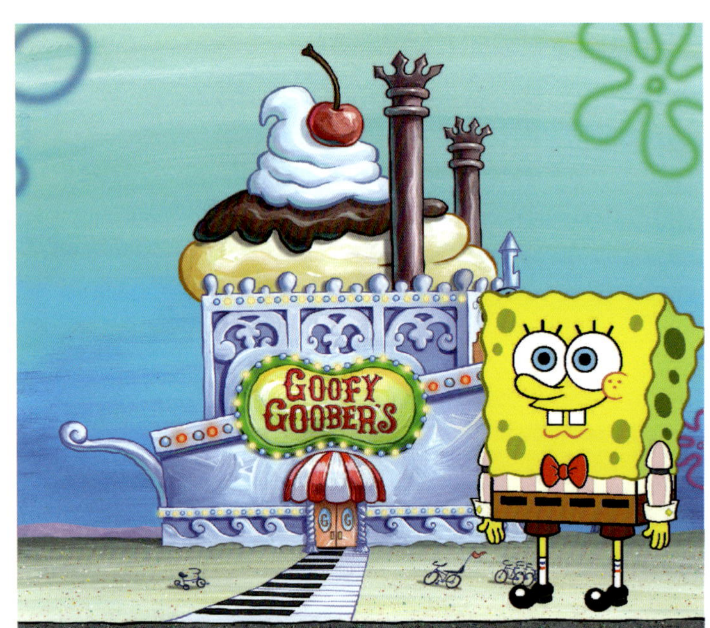

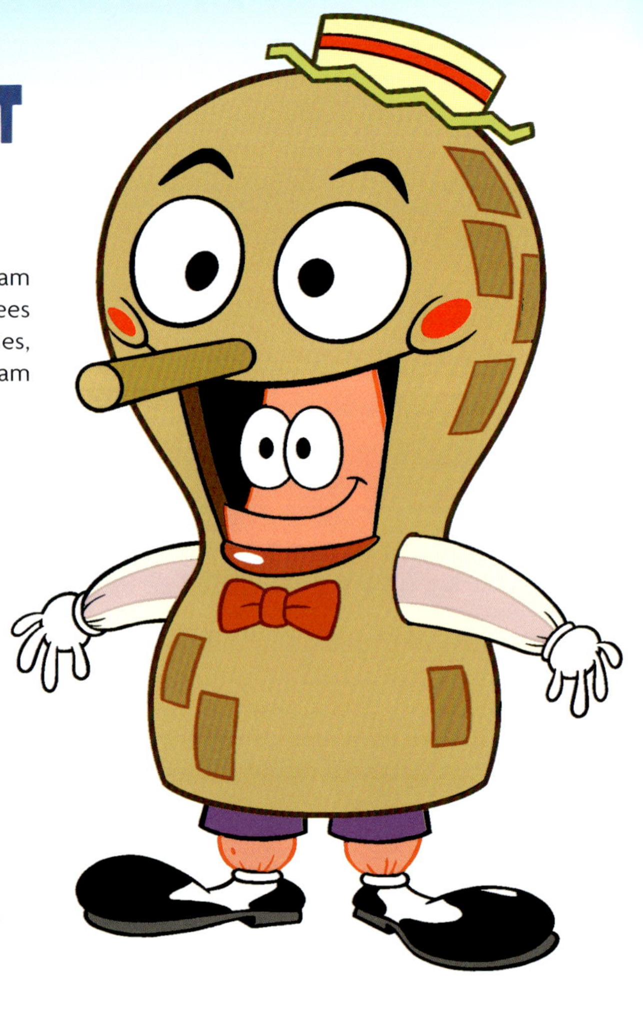

Final art of exterior and interior of the ice cream shop [left and lower] and Patrick as Goofy Goober himself [right]

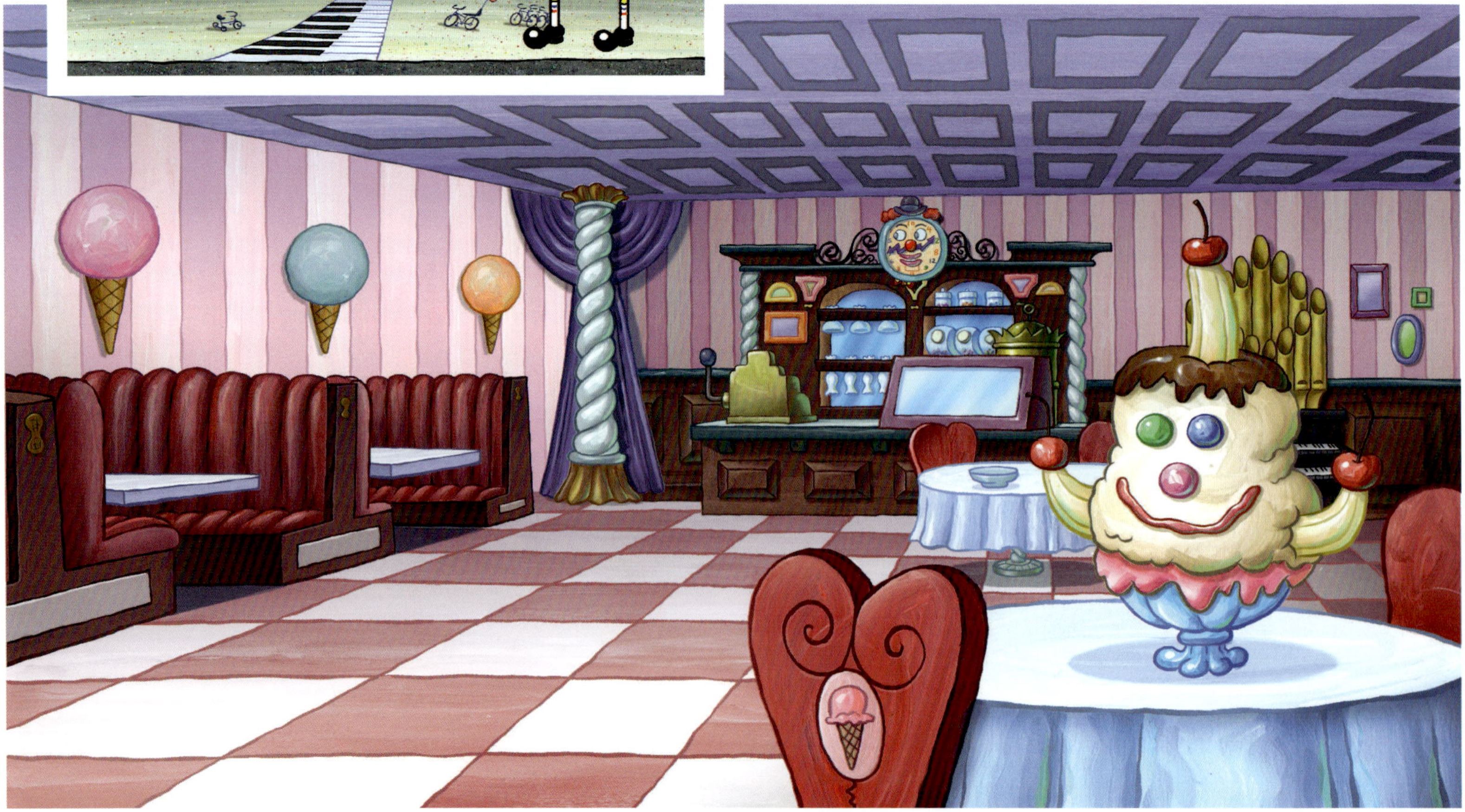

JELLYFISH FIELDS

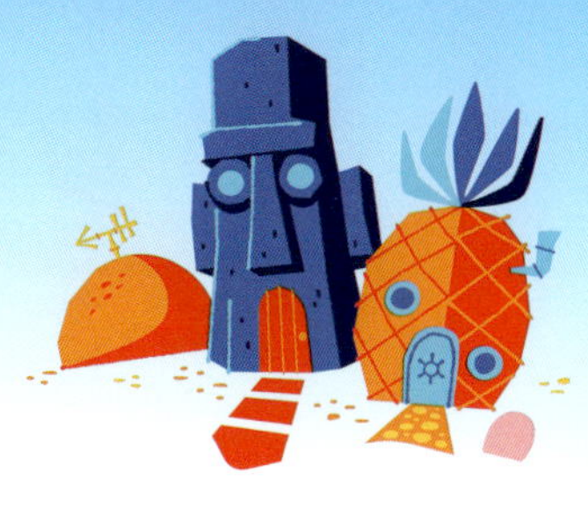

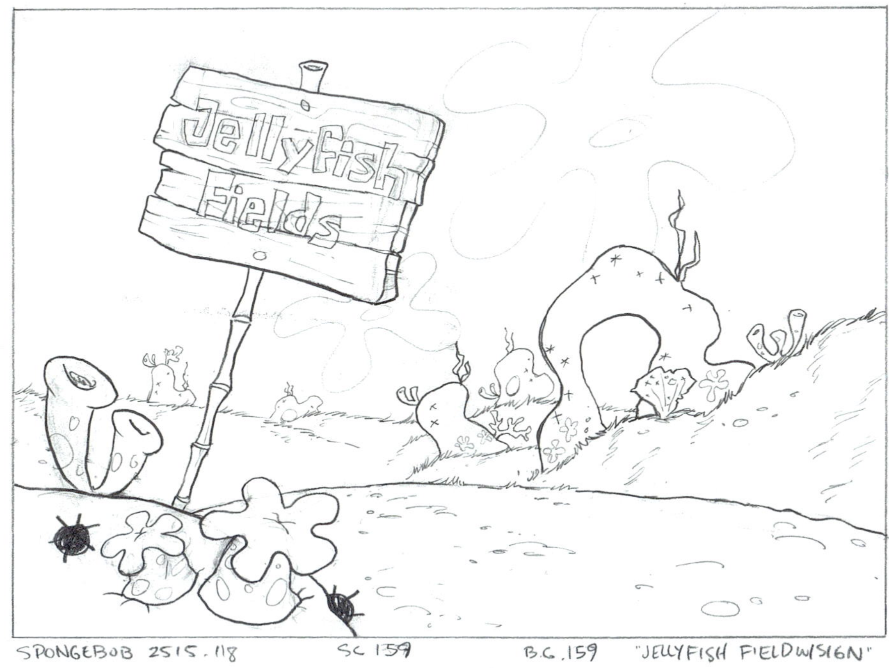

Another one of SpongeBob's favorite places to spend his free time is the Jellyfish Fields. "There's something magical about it. The color palette is lovely: It instantly lifts my mood. Watching SpongeBob and Patrick frolicking through the field, chasing jellyfish with pure, childlike wonder, makes me smile," notes background painter Lucy Tanashian-Gentry.

Layout image [upper] and final art [lower] of the Jellyfish Fields

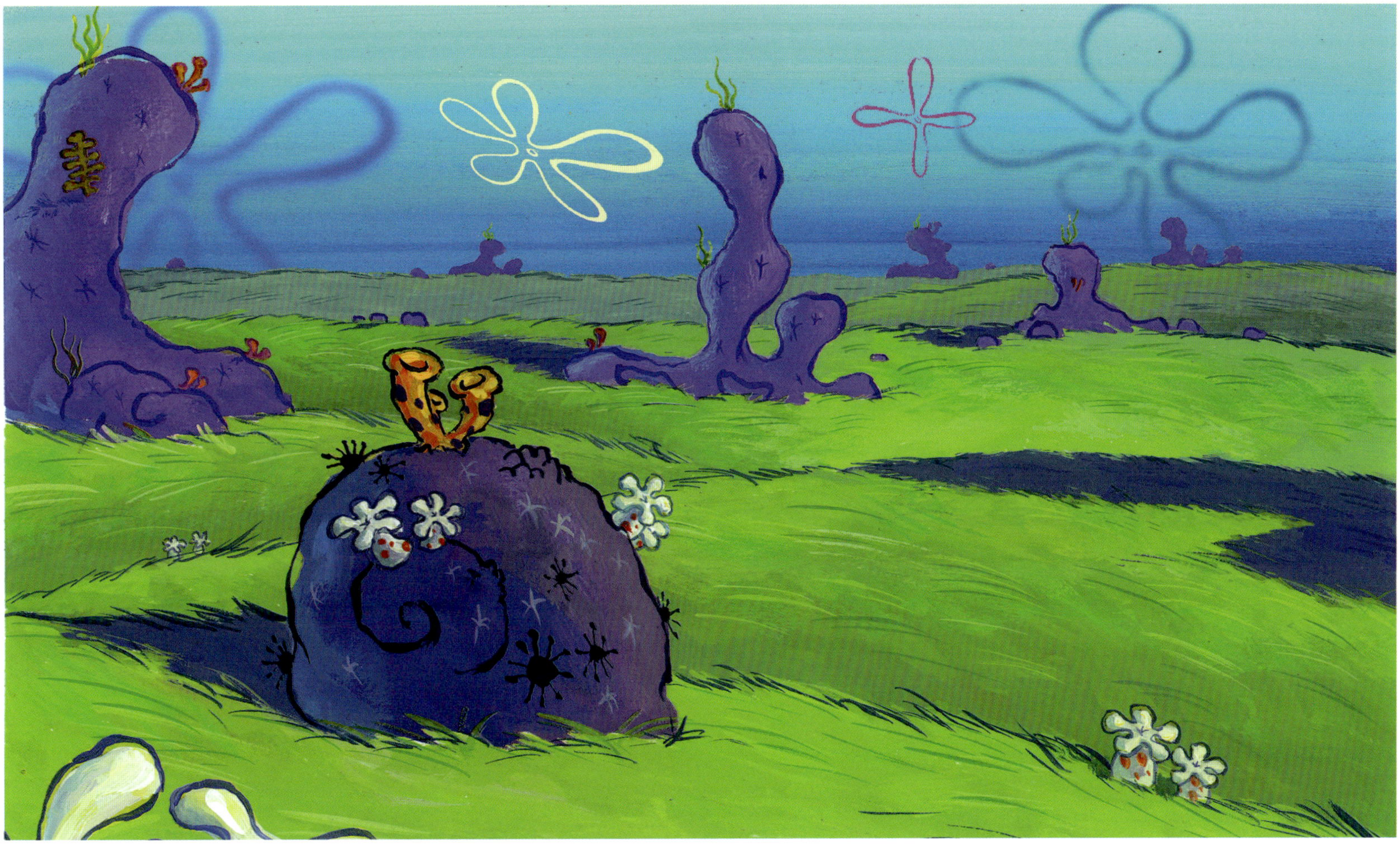

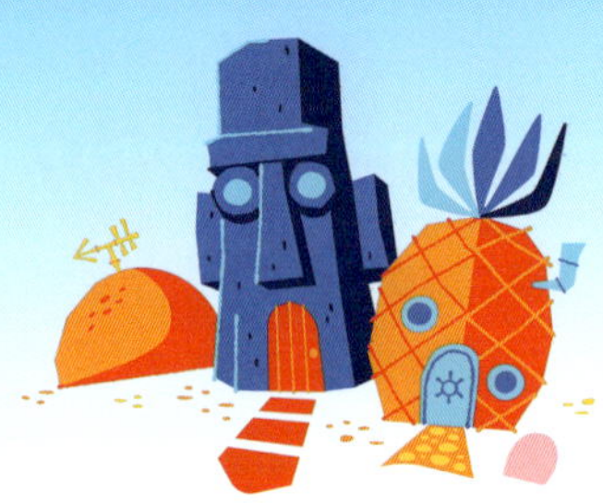

KRABS' ANCHOR HOUSE

Eugene and Pearl Krabs live in an anchor-shaped home, with his bedroom being in the right hook wing and hers being in the left side. You'd need a private tour to see features like the living/dining area in the center of the house, or the basement and root beer cellar down below.

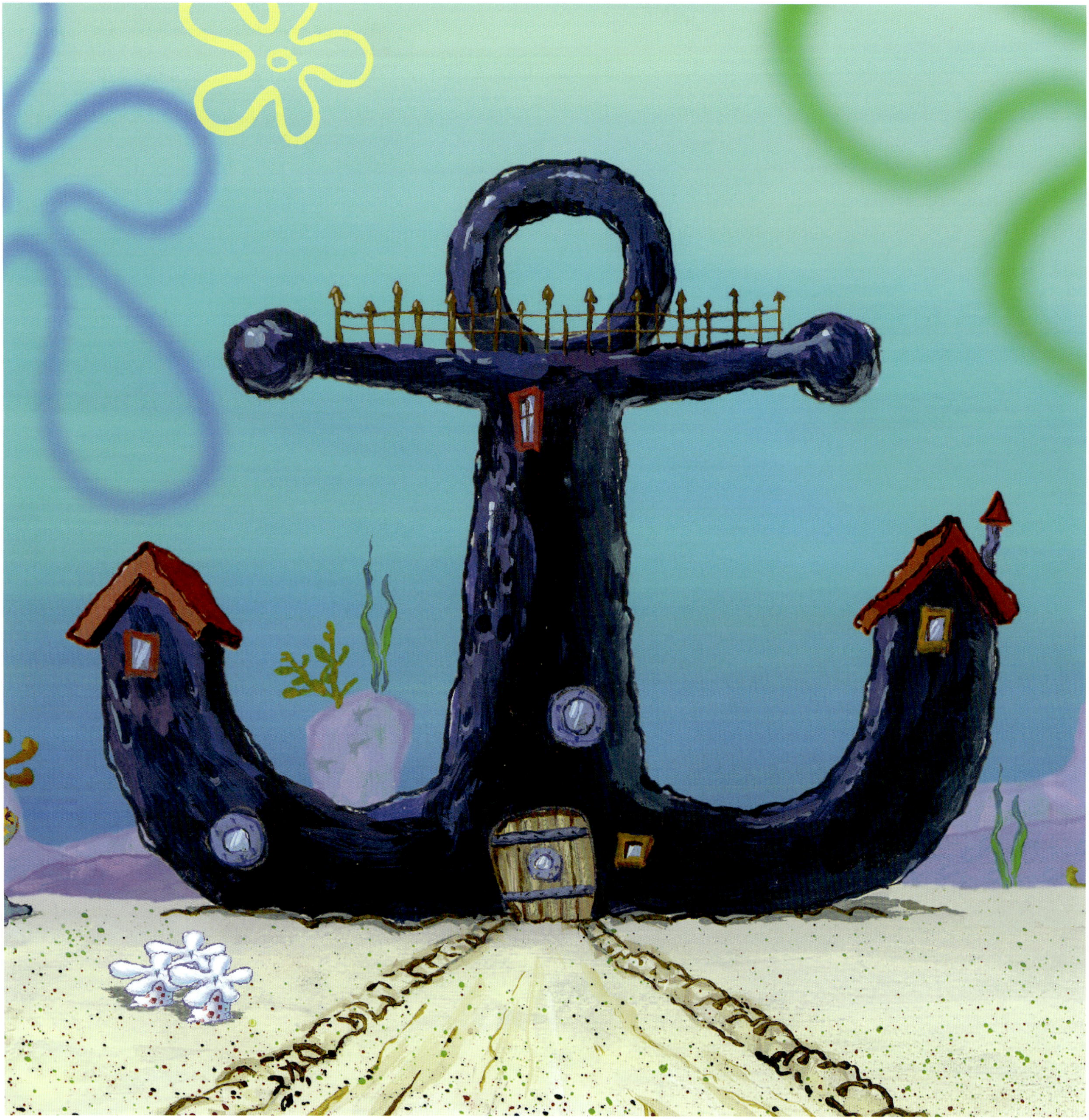

Final art of the Krabs residence

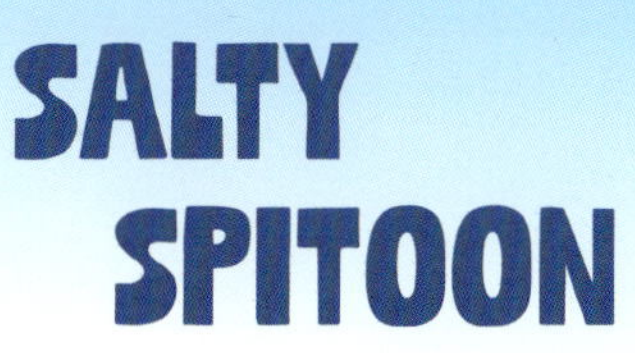

SALTY SPITOON

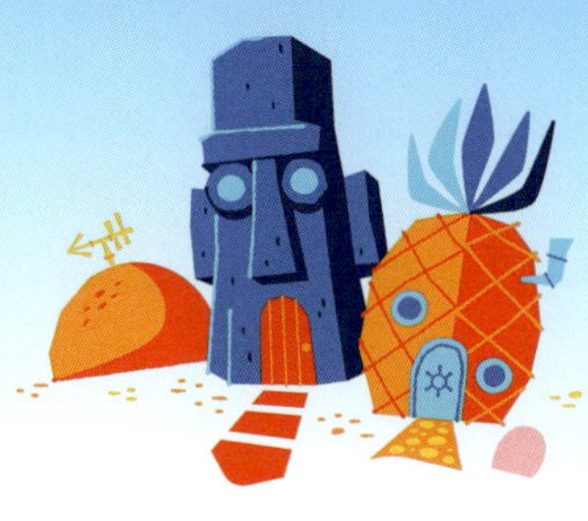

Accessible to tough guys only, the Salty Spitoon is a rough-and-tumble kind of establishment. "The Salty Spitoon is one of my favorite locations. It's got a lot of character, and it just feels very lived in. It's a tougher, grittier place than we usually see in *SpongeBob*, so it's a fun departure from the everyday Bikini Bottom," says art director Shane Richardson.

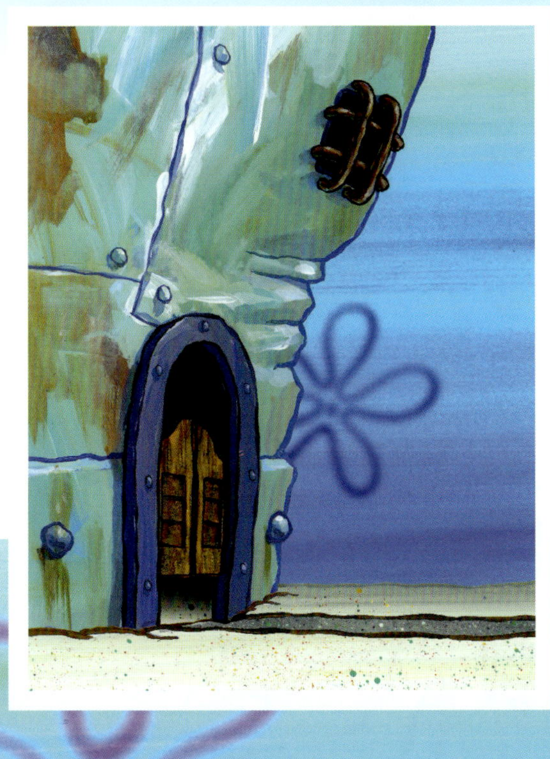

Final art of the Salty Spitoon

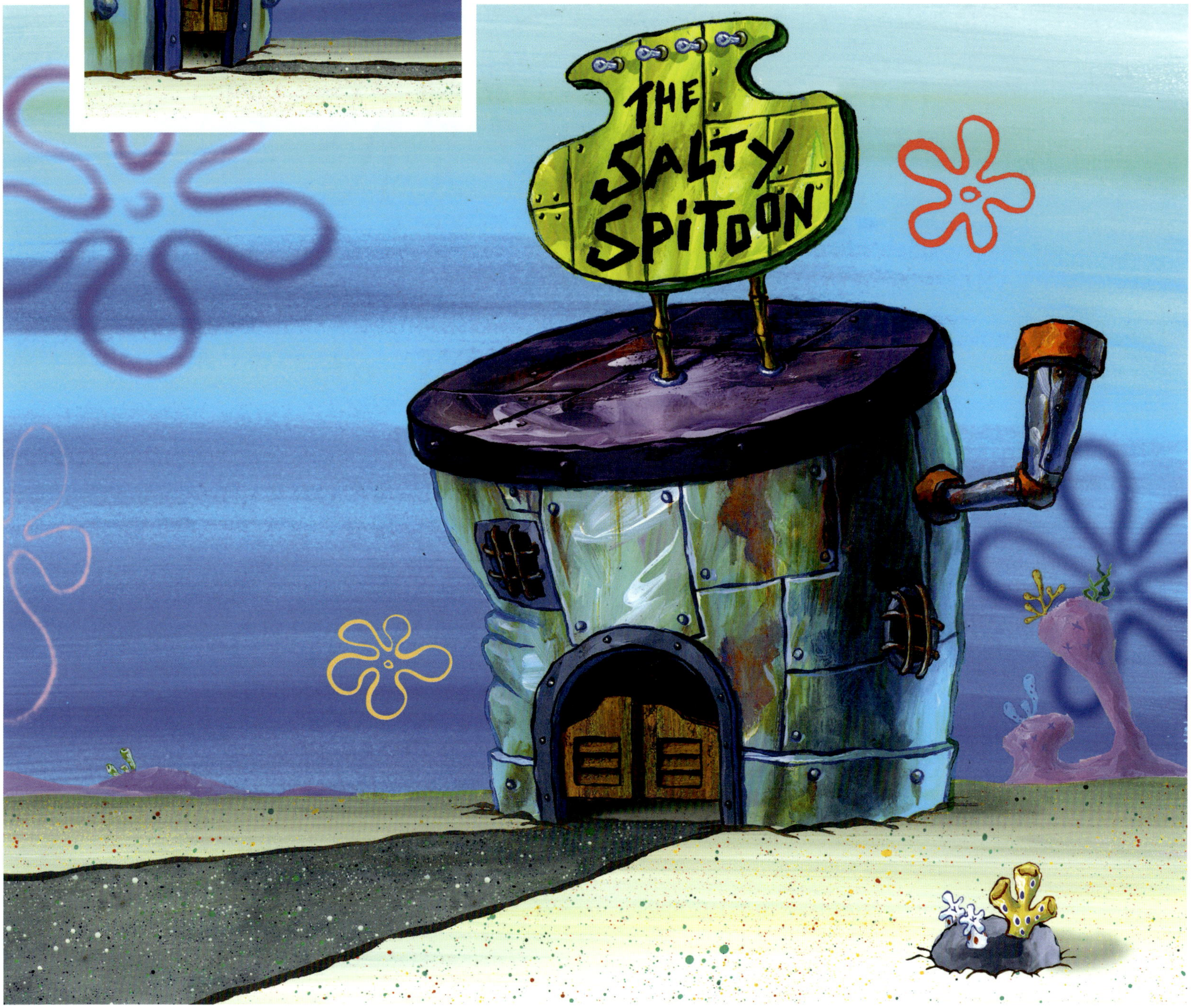

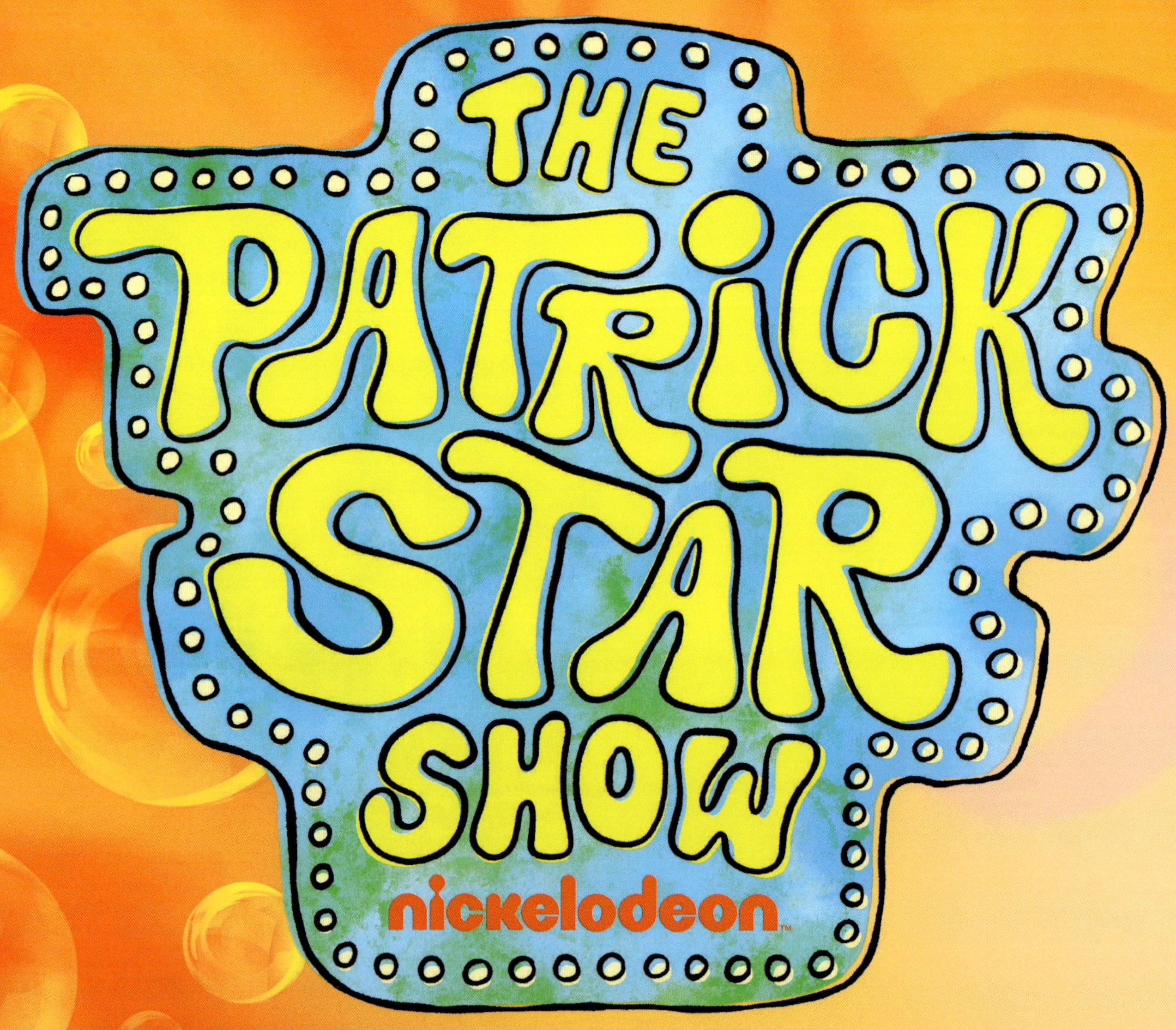

Ever wonder where Patrick Star came from, and how he might entertain himself if left to his own devices? *The Patrick Star Show* answers those questions and more, entertaining audiences since 2021.

The original concept for the show was to dive into what home life was like for Patrick, spending time with him and his family before he moved out on his own, but the creators knew they couldn't do just that. "What we were inspired to do was far more experimental, allowing our Monty Python and sketch comedy interests to drive the tone and pace in this new universe that lives alongside, but outside, that of *SpongeBob SquarePants*," explains writer Mr. Lawrence. The show cuts quickly from scene to scene in a distracted, frenetic style, conveying the short attention span of Patrick himself.

Set against a watercolor painterly look but reaching out into live action and stop-motion as well, *The Patrick Star Show* portrays its own unique blend of spoofs/sitcom/cooking show/time travel/variety hour in which anything can happen through the frame of Patrick's window as the television screen. Characters from the original *SpongeBob SquarePants* lineup make guest appearances from time to time, but for sure, the star power is all Patrick in this series.

"What makes every iteration and variation of the original SpongeBob SquarePants show so special are the characters. Over the years they've all become iconic, but from the start they've always been archetypal. Their personalities are all so well defined, and that's what drives the comedy—you can put them in the simplest of situations, and magic happens," says supervising producer Kenny Pittenger.

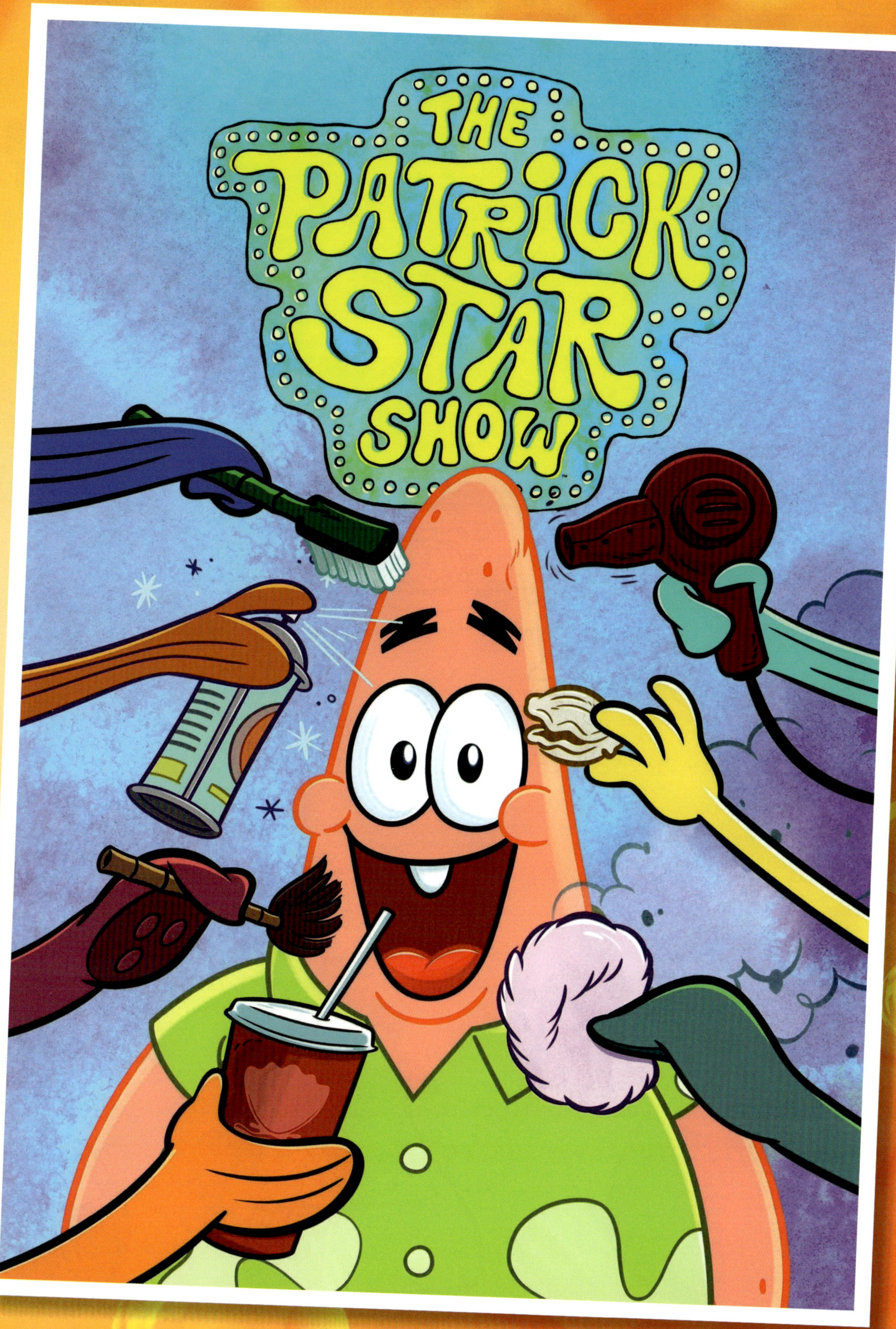
THE PATRICK STAR SHOW

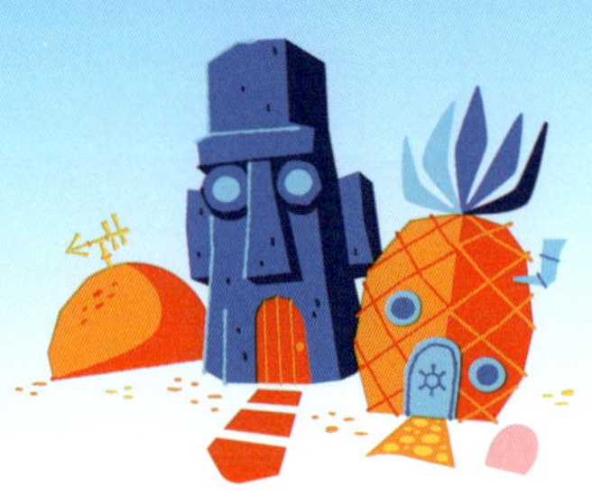

SUPPORTING CAST: BUNNY & CECIL

A loving, hard-working couple, Patrick's parents set the tone for a welcoming and supportive home for their family. Cecil is always happy to share his slightly inaccurate bits of wisdom, while Bunny tries her best to manage household chores without the advantage of having much common sense, her college studies having been in pseudoscience. They also sport some fabulous personal details, namely Cecil's muscular mustache and Bunny's animated tattoos.

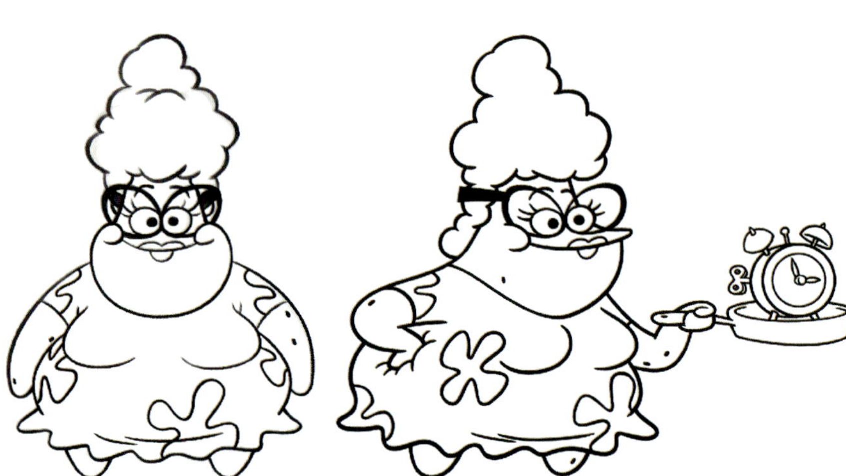

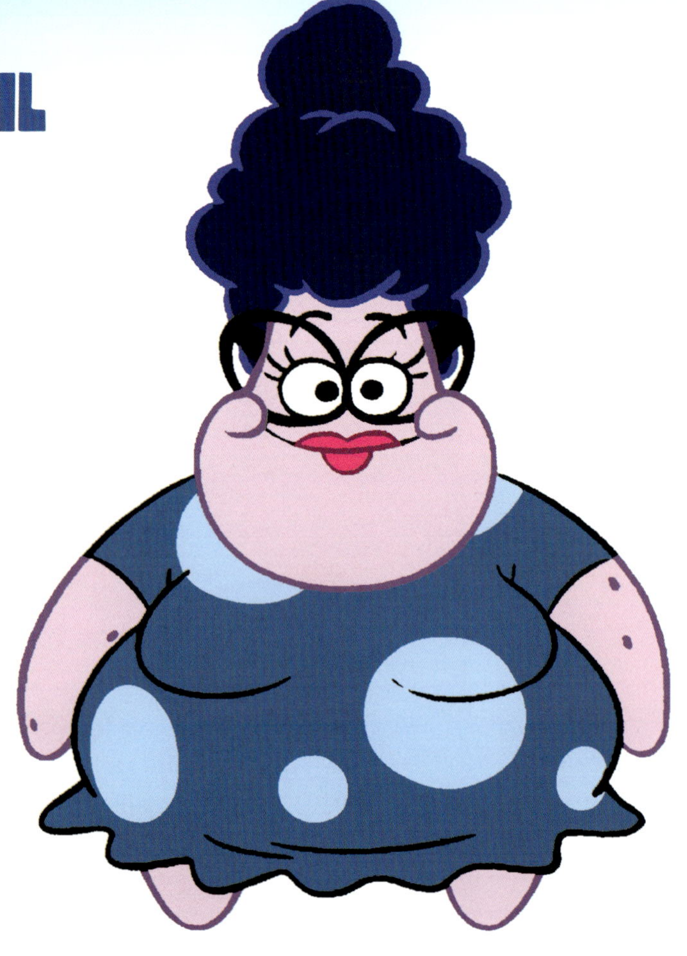

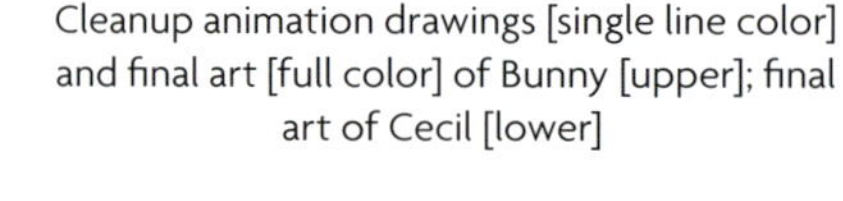

Cleanup animation drawings [single line color] and final art [full color] of Bunny [upper]; final art of Cecil [lower]

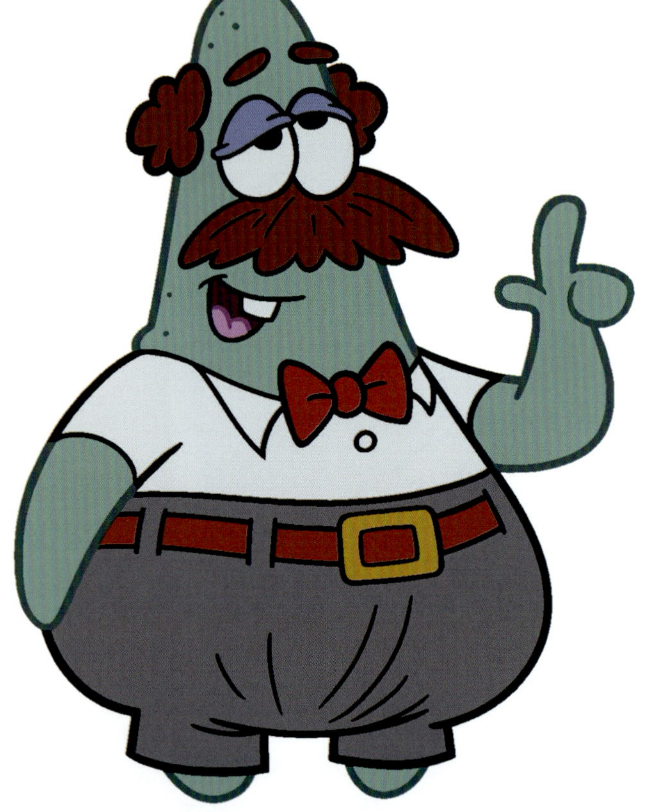

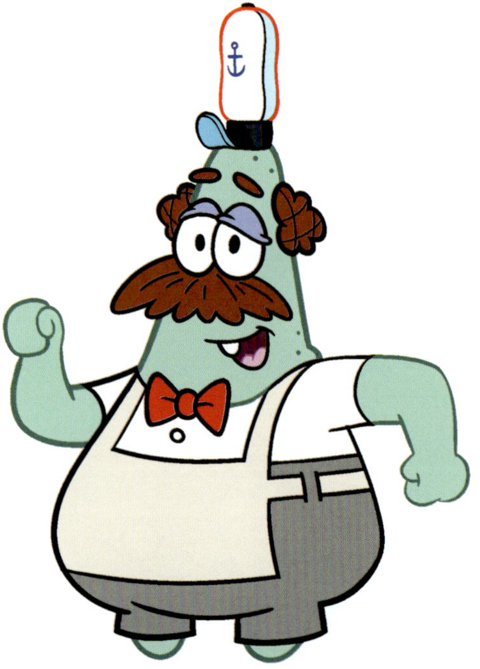

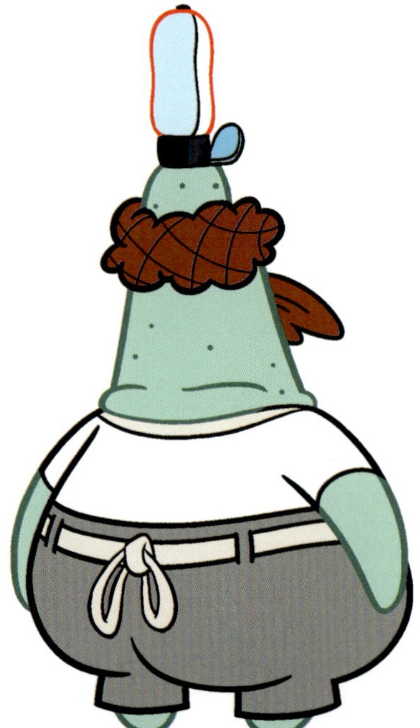

SQUIDINA

Patrick's preteen sister, who is actually a squid, appears to be the smartest member of the Star family, presenting in a cute but nerdy way. Squidina serves as the producer/director/camera operator/emcee of Patrick's show, while also participating in some of Patrick's adventures as well as shots that harken back to the 1970s broadcast television days, with actors popping out of opening frames on the wall à la *Laugh-In*.

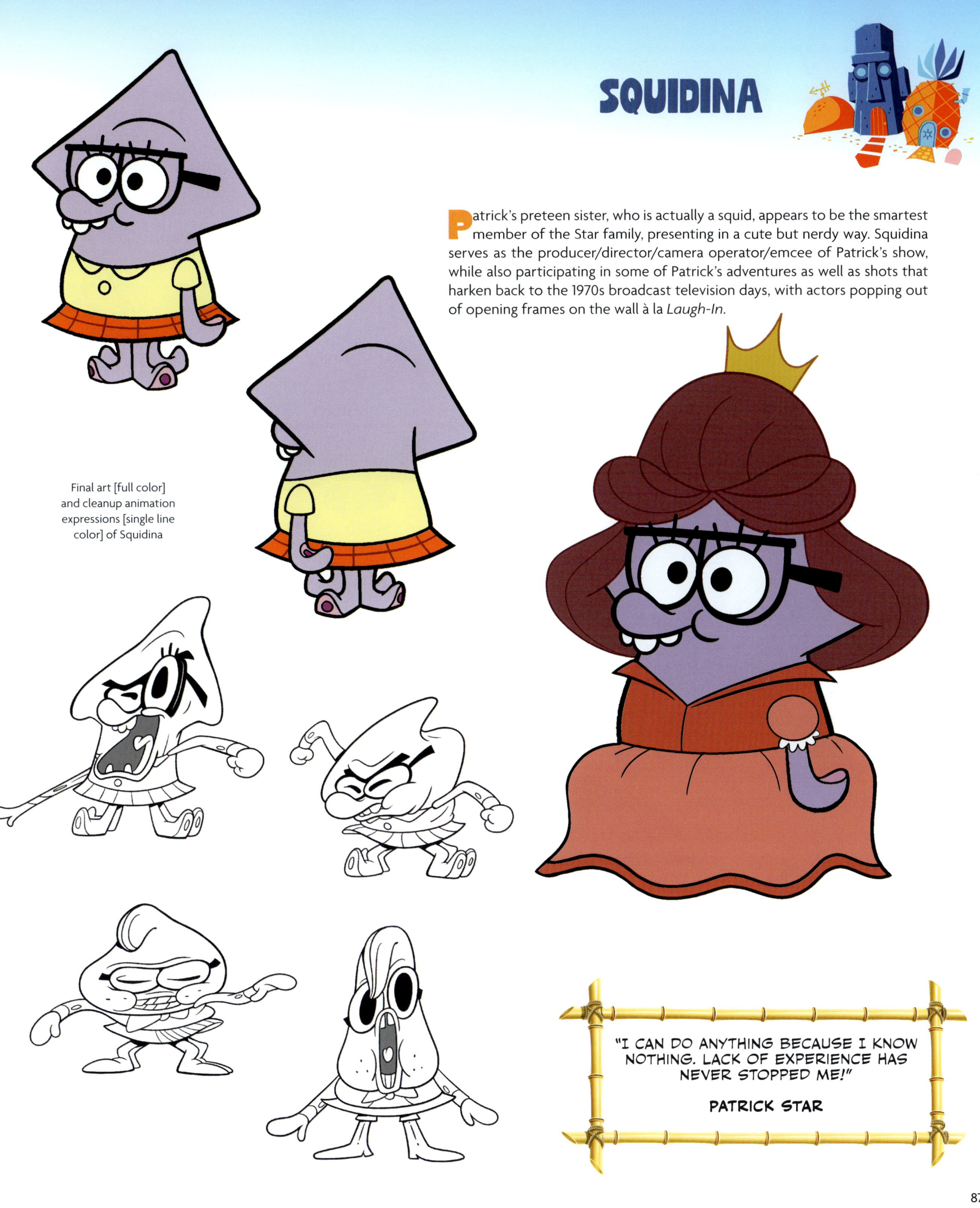

Final art [full color] and cleanup animation expressions [single line color] of Squidina

"I CAN DO ANYTHING BECAUSE I KNOW NOTHING. LACK OF EXPERIENCE HAS NEVER STOPPED ME!"

PATRICK STAR

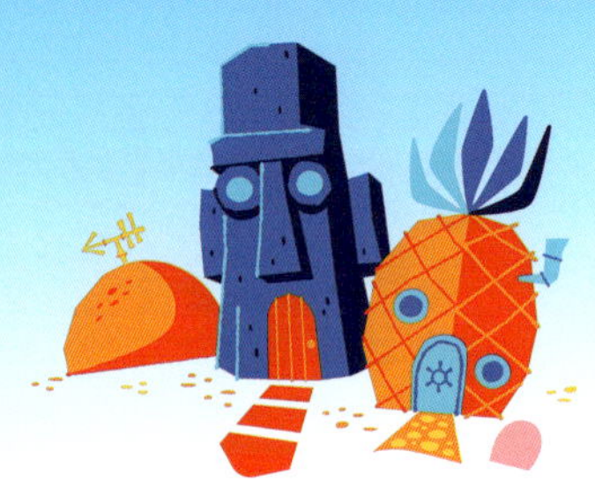

GRANDPAT

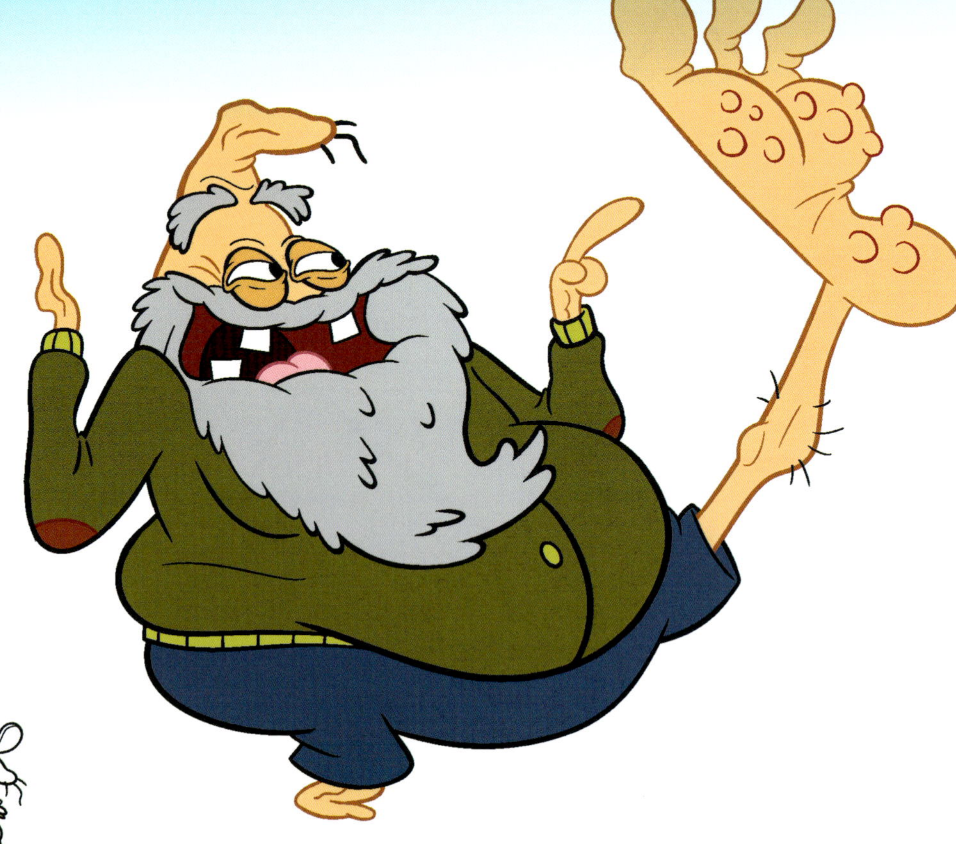

Patrick's paternal grandfather appears regularly, sometimes just moseying through the family kitchen, but sometimes pulling off a daredevil motorcycle act, or running a Pat-a-thon, or heckling the show from a very *Muppet Show*–like balcony, along with Grandma Tentacles.

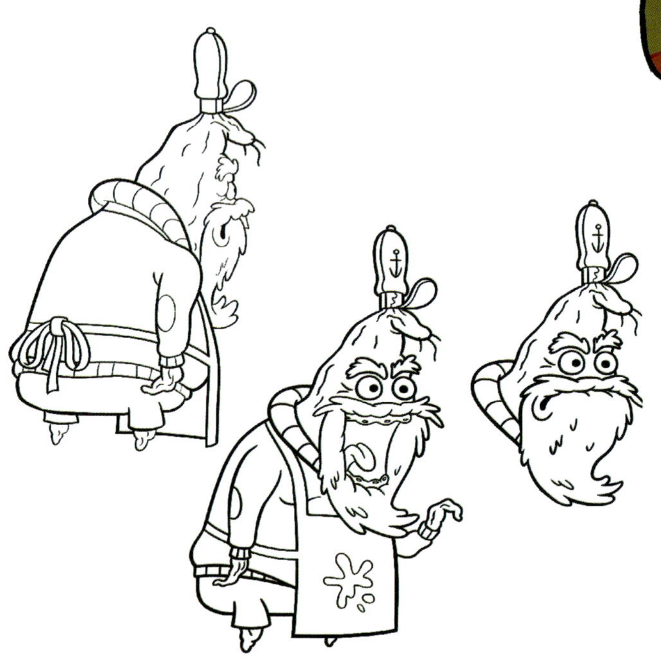

Cleanup animation drawings [single line color] and final art [full color] of Grandpat [upper]; tonal image [black/gray] and final art [full color] of Agnes Steelhead [lower]

AGNES STEELHEAD

Bunny's mother visits the Star family from time to time. She happens to be a squid and a witch, the latter detail being a lovely tribute to actress Agnes Moorehead of *Bewitched* fame.

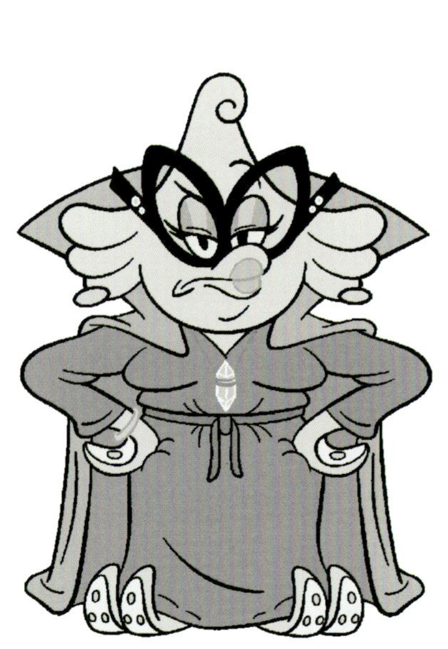

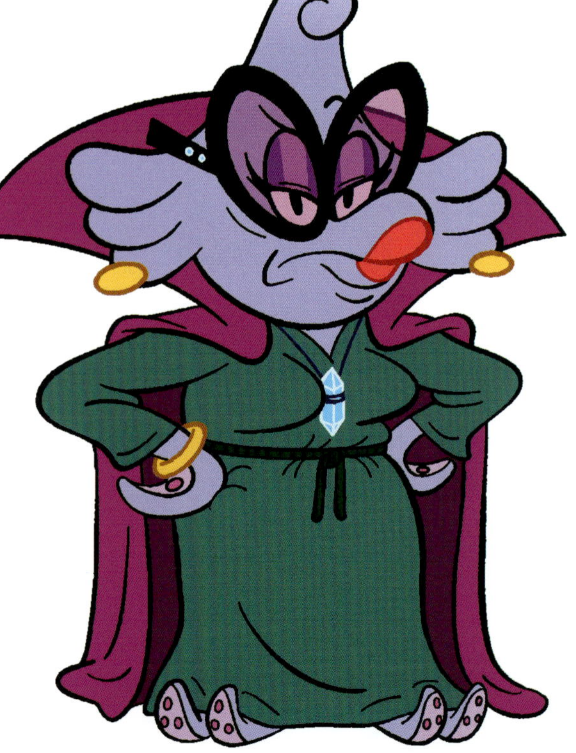

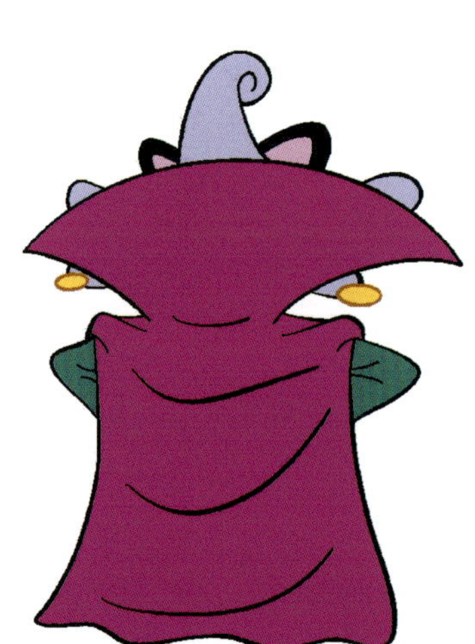

AUNT ESMERALDA

Bunny's sister also happens to be a squid and, in another *Bewitched* tribute, is named after a character in the classic television series.

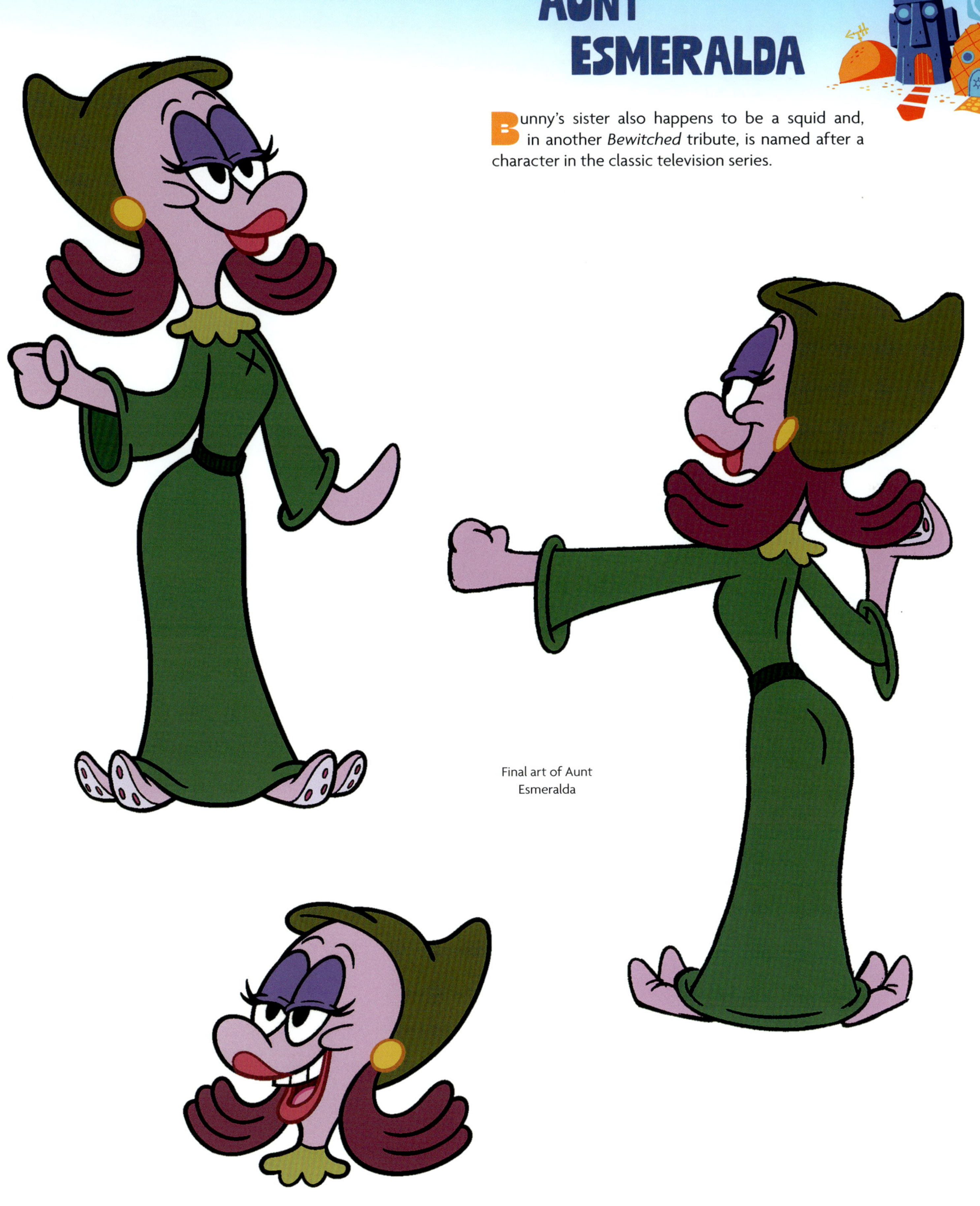

Final art of Aunt Esmeralda

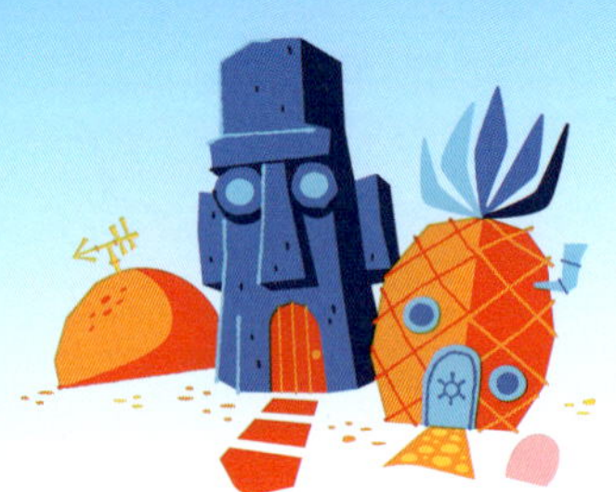

EXTENDED STAR FAMILY MEMBERS

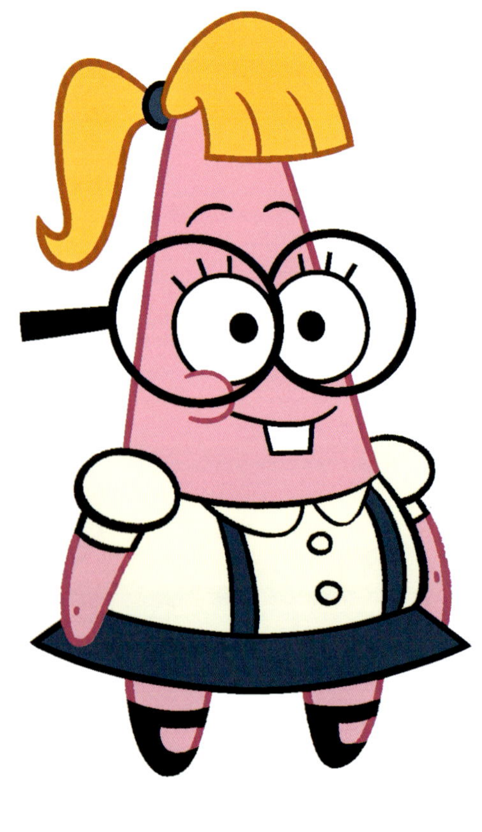

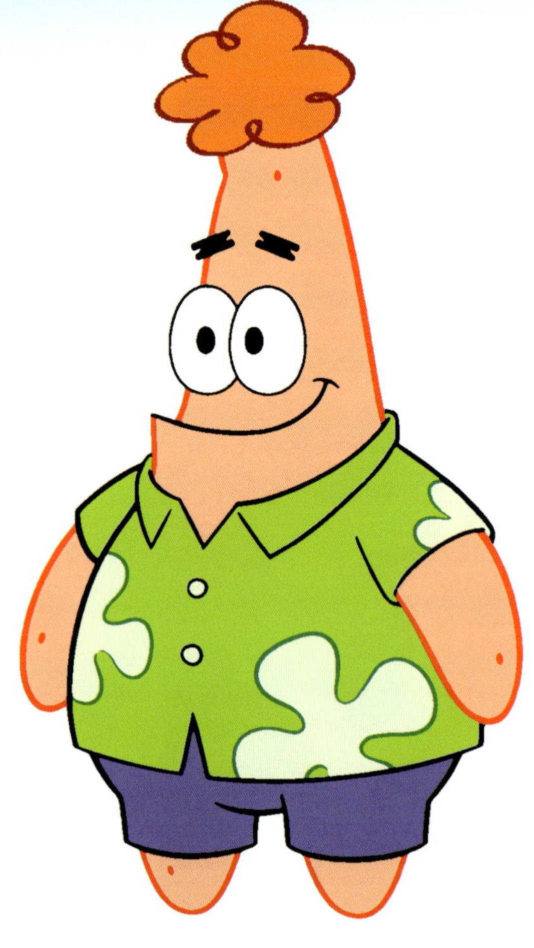

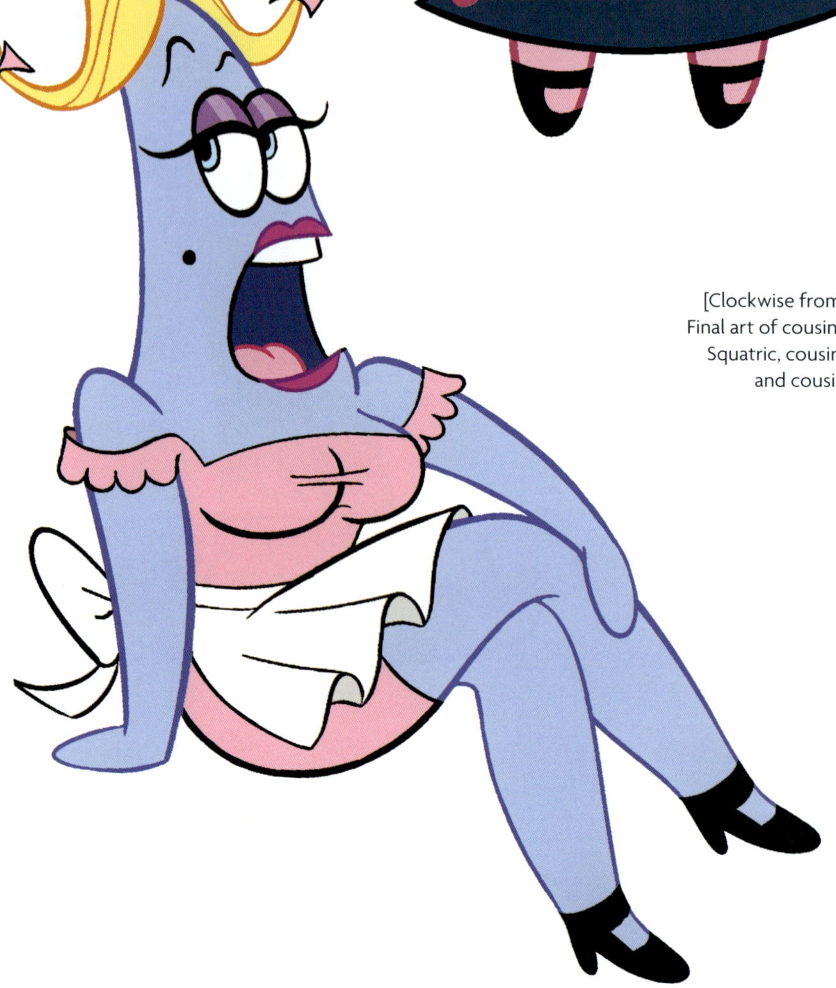

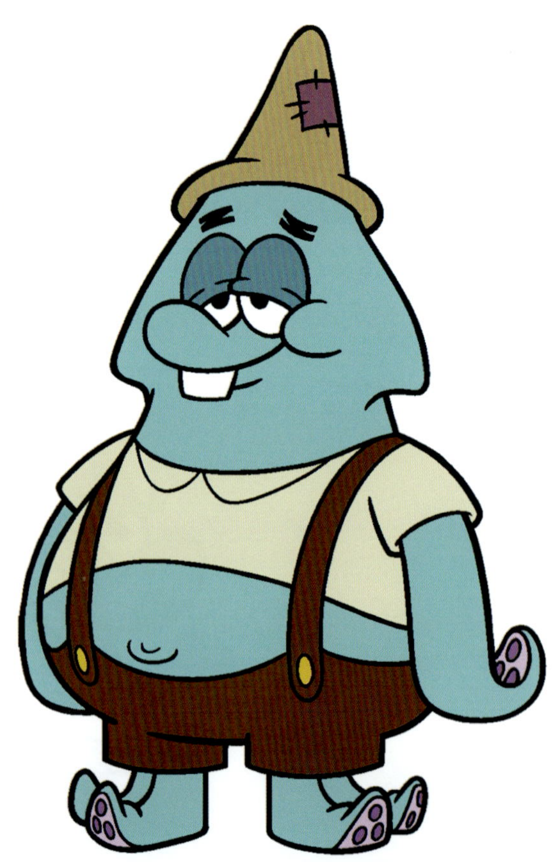

[Clockwise from upper left:] Final art of cousin Patina, cousin Squatric, cousin FitzPatrick, and cousin Inga.

THE DARTFISH FAMILY

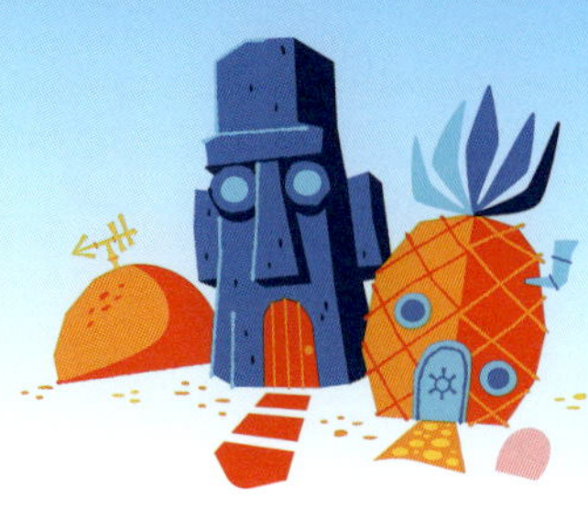

The Dartfish are a sweet, well-dressed, and well-mannered little family of four—Daddy, Mommy, Sister, and Teensy Tim—that live in the Star house and dine under the Stars' kitchen table.

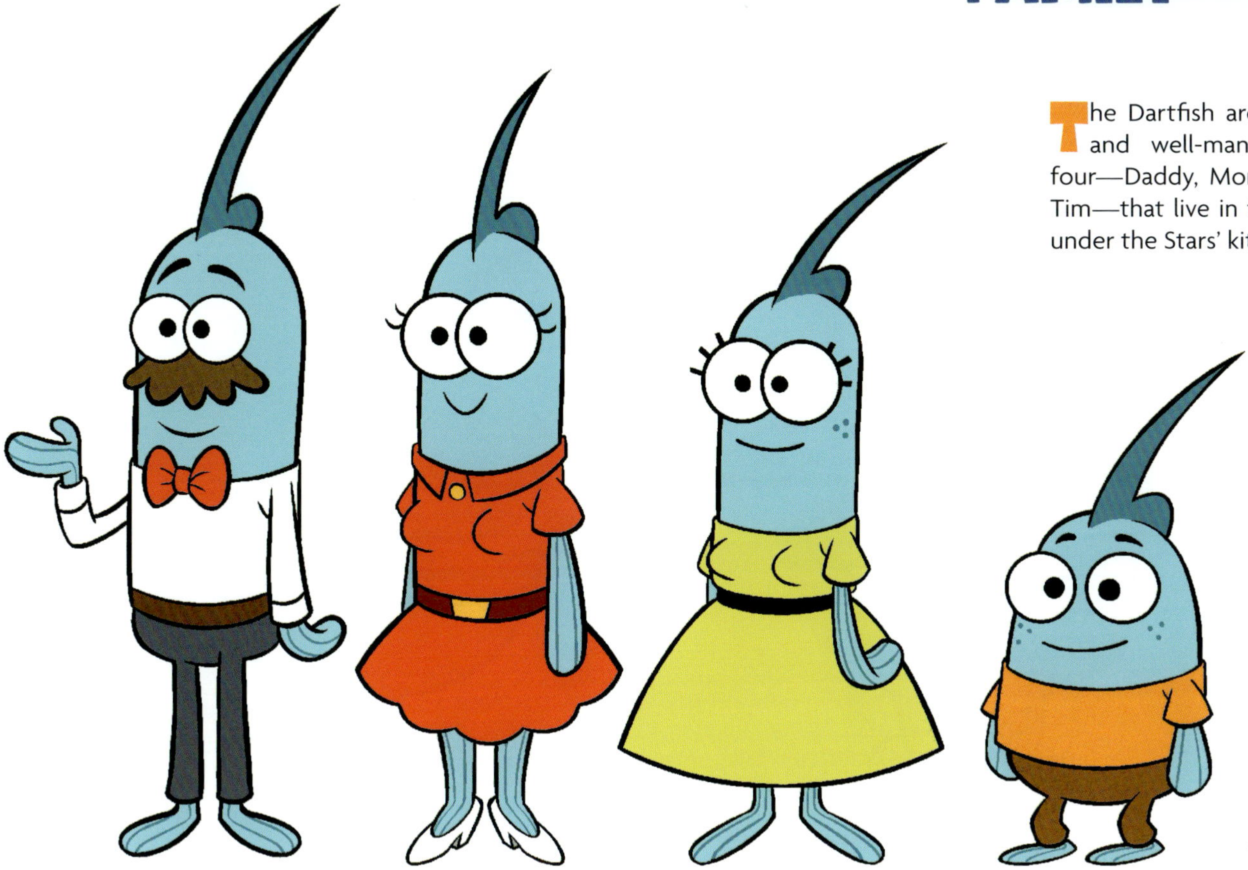

Final art of the Dartfish Family

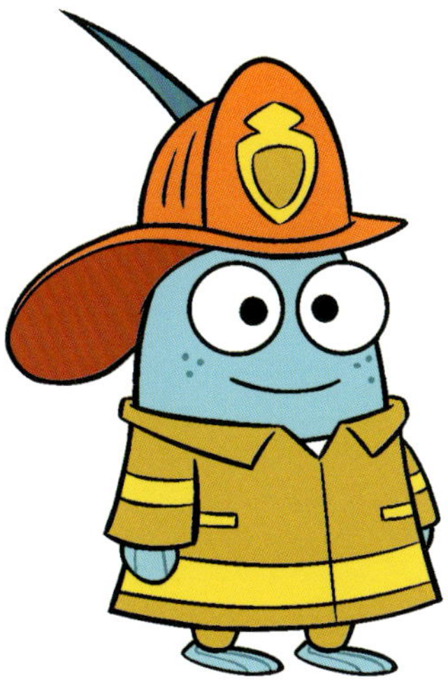

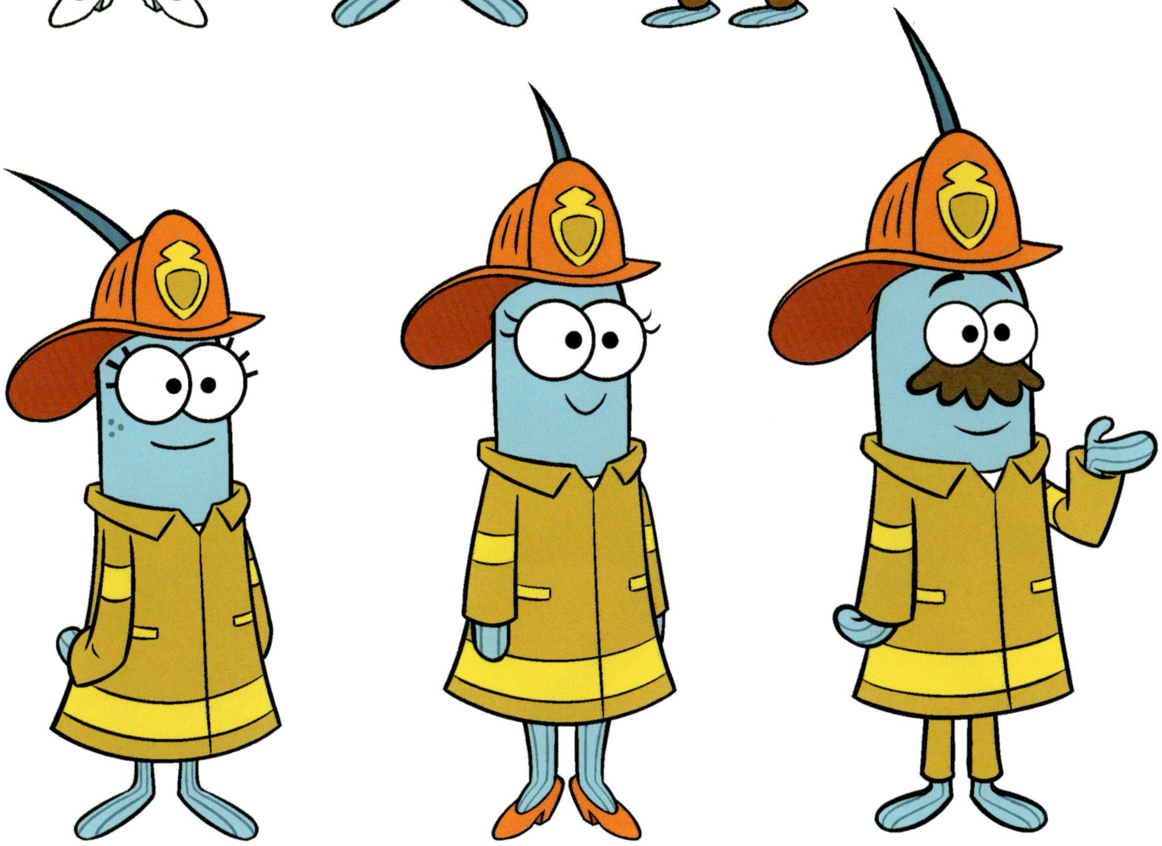

TINKLE

A sentient toilet that resides in the Star household, Tinkle might be more aggressive and toothier than most folks would dare to get near, especially when nature calls. Tinkle barks, wears a leash, plays fetch, and enjoys going for walks, much like a dog in the above-water world.

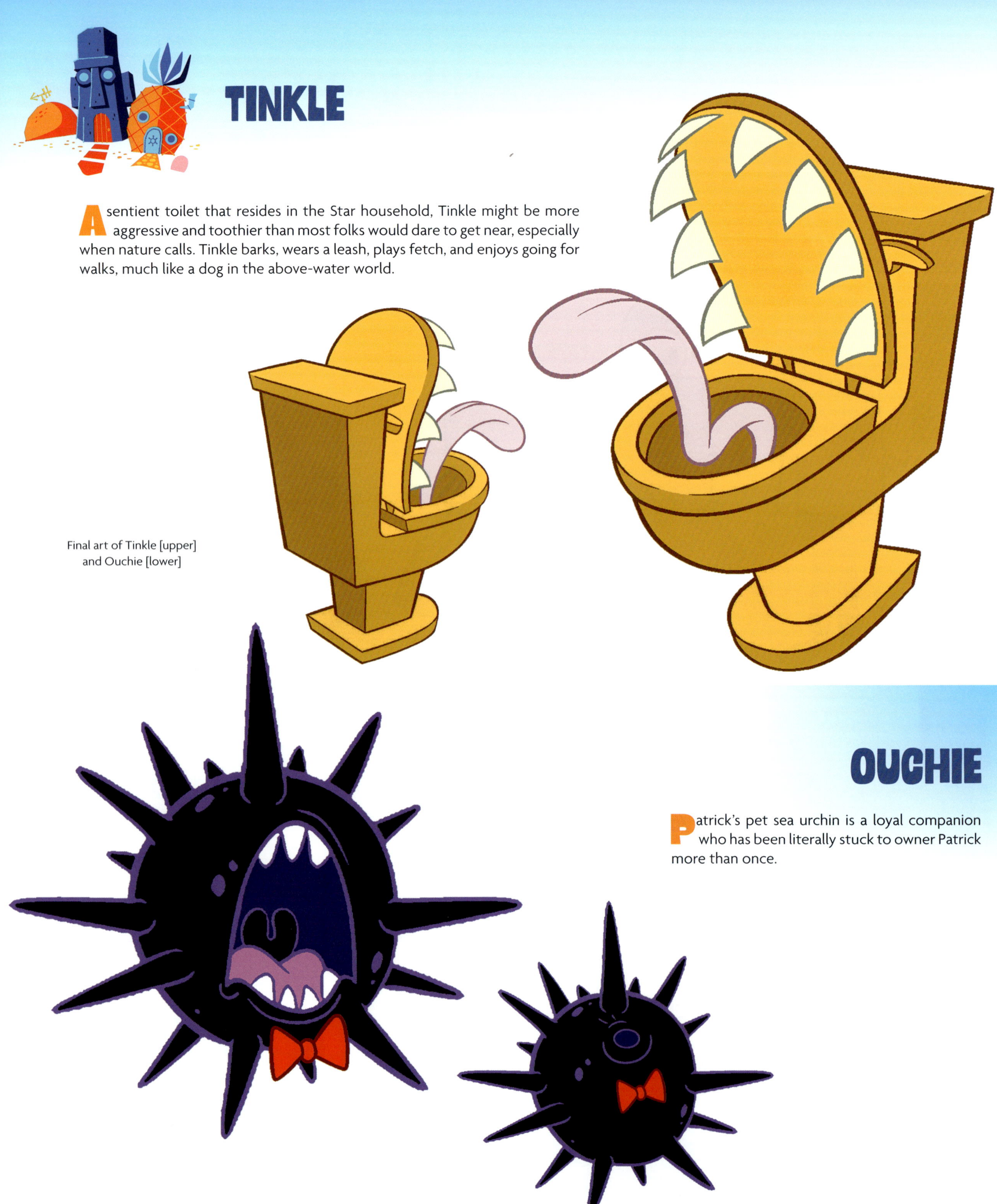

Final art of Tinkle [upper] and Ouchie [lower]

OUCHIE

Patrick's pet sea urchin is a loyal companion who has been literally stuck to owner Patrick more than once.

PINKEYE

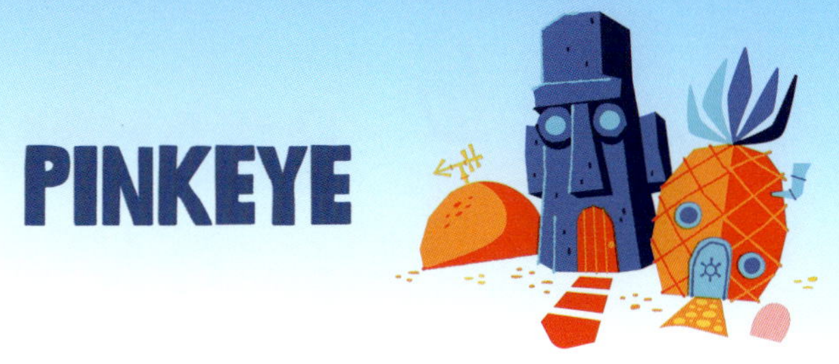

Ouchie's antagonistic playmate is a sea bunny that has also served as a guest host on Patrick's show.

Final frame image of Pinkeye

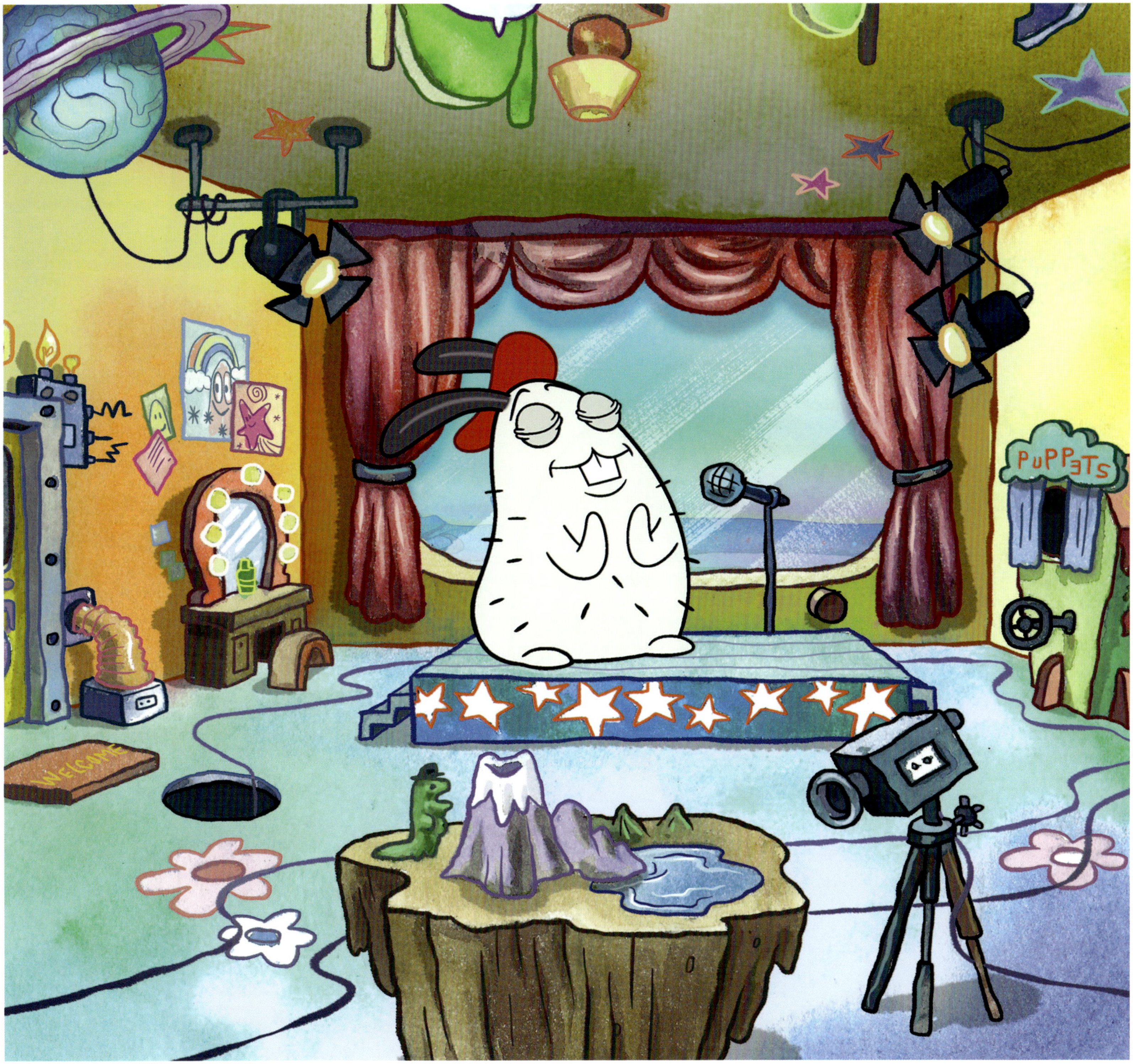

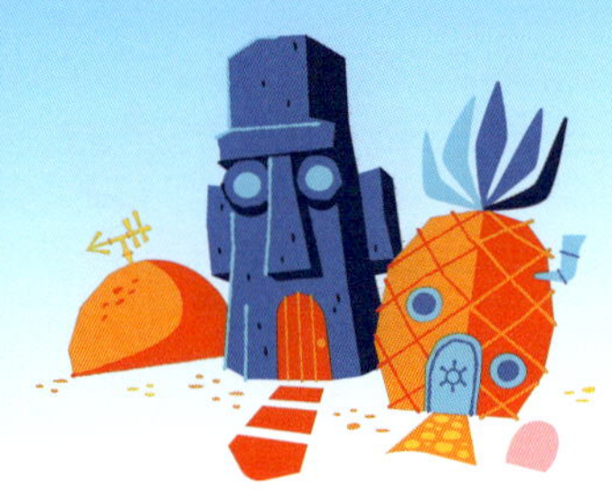

GRANDMA TENTACLES

Squidward's grandmother happens to live across the street from the Star family in a pink teapot house. Granny Tentacles is not too fond of Patrick's show interrupting her sleep... perhaps that's why she has been known to heckle him from the balcony.

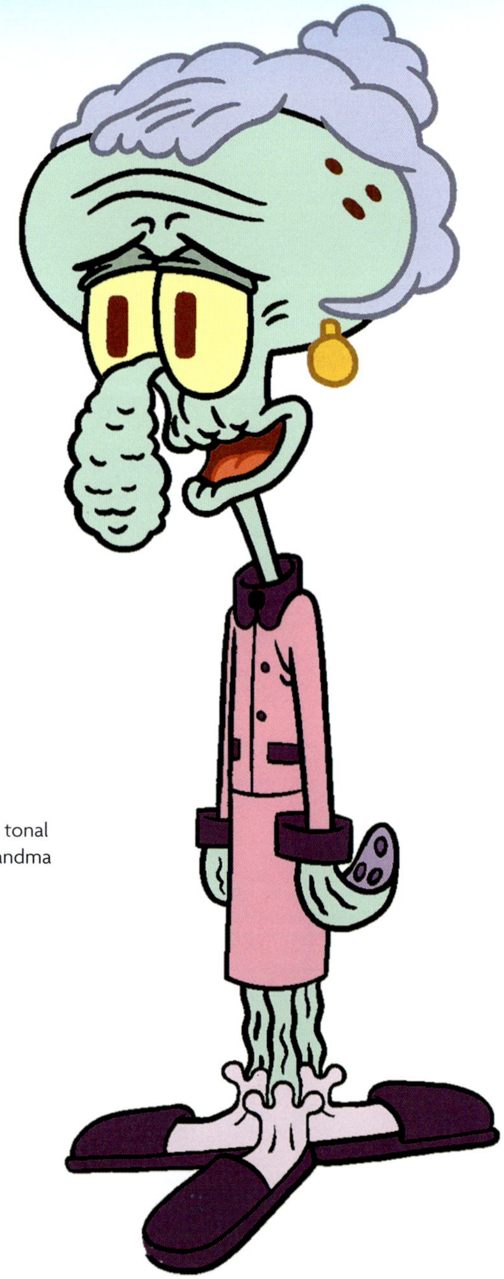

Final [upper] and tonal [lower] art of Grandma

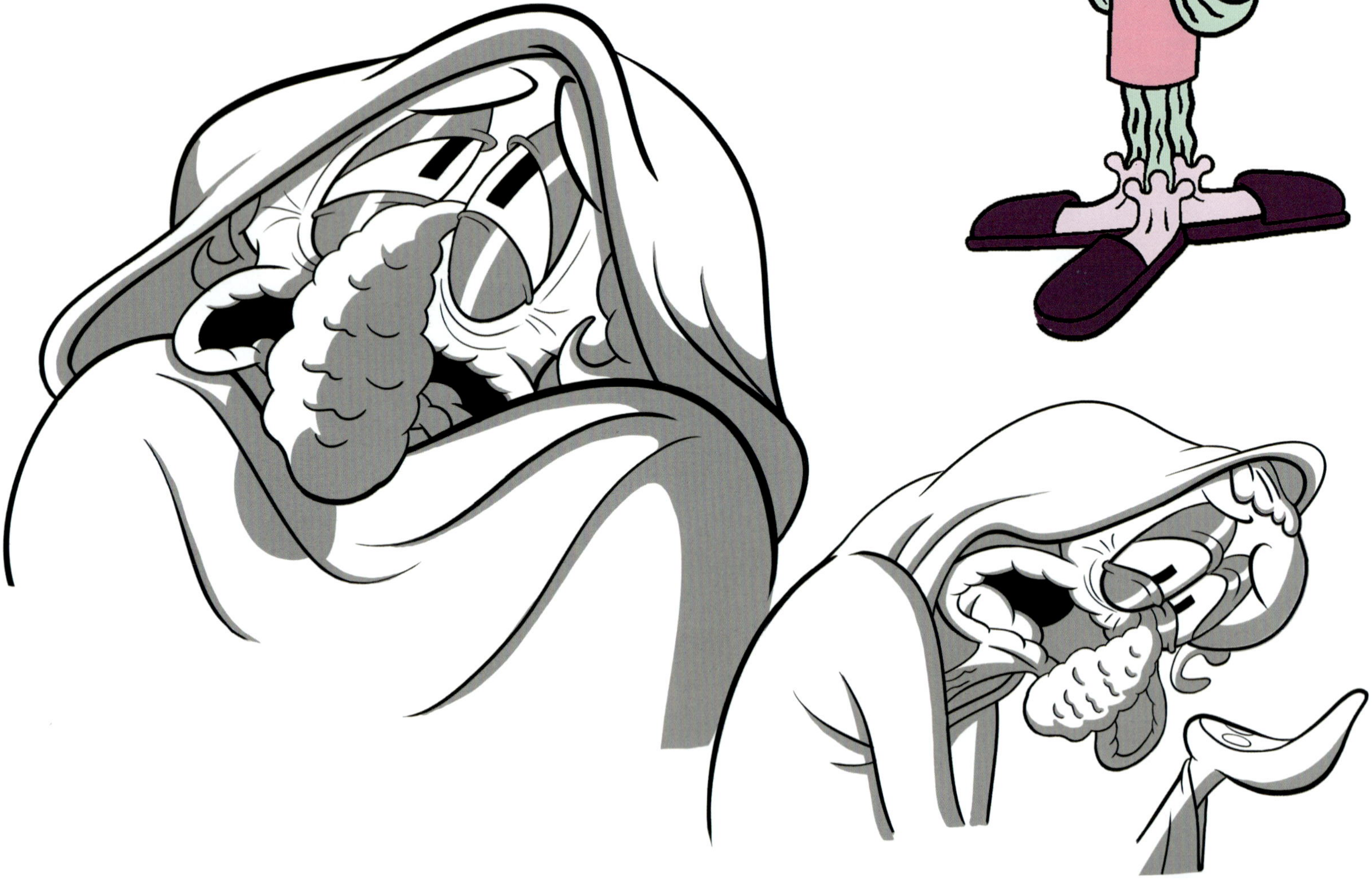

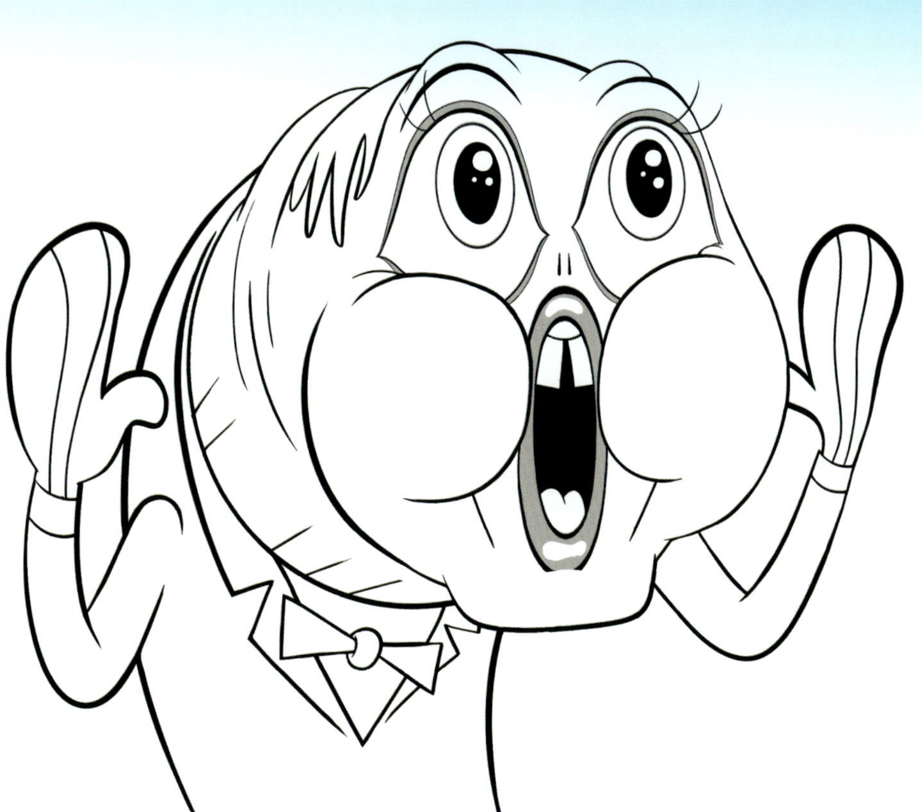

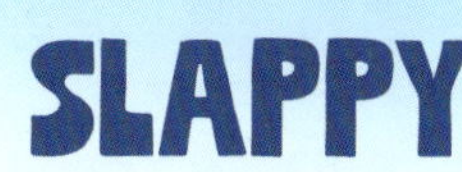

SLAPPY

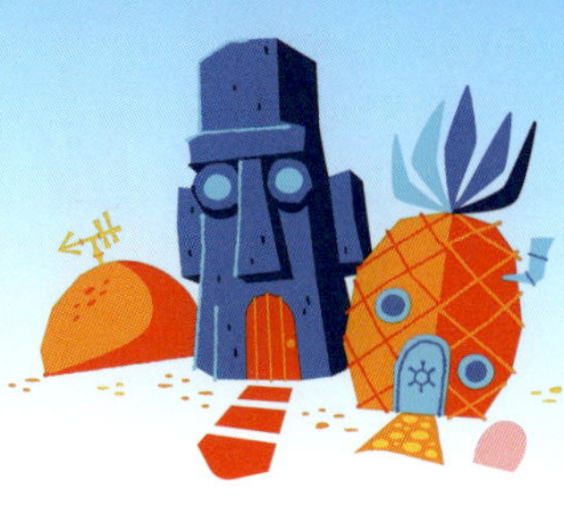

While Slappy has appeared on *SpongeBob SquarePants*, he's a regular presence on *The Patrick Star Show* as Patrick's #1 fan.

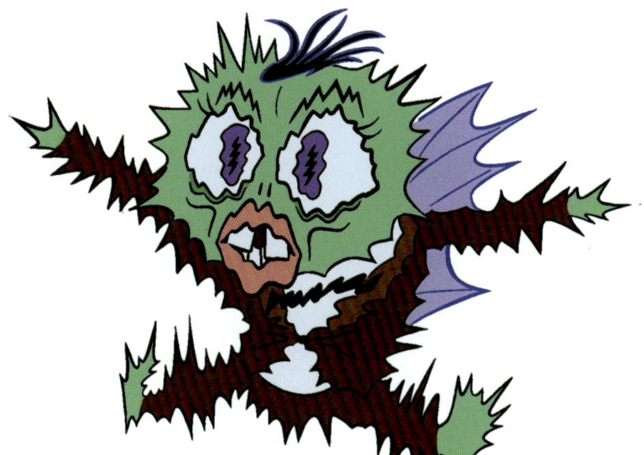

Tonal version of "normal" Slappy [black/gray] and final art of more extreme versions of him [full color]

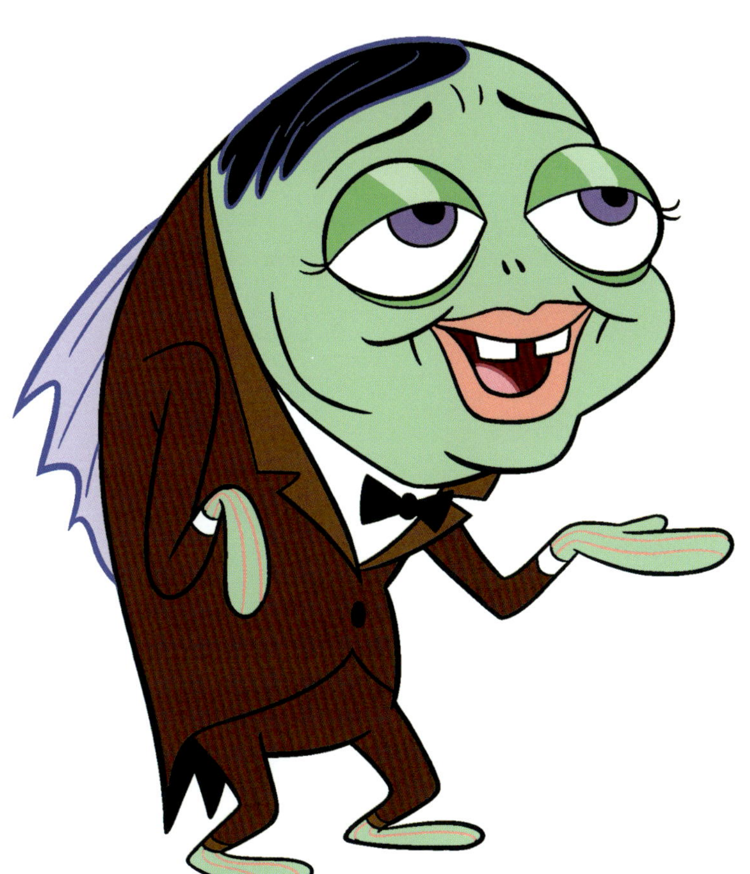

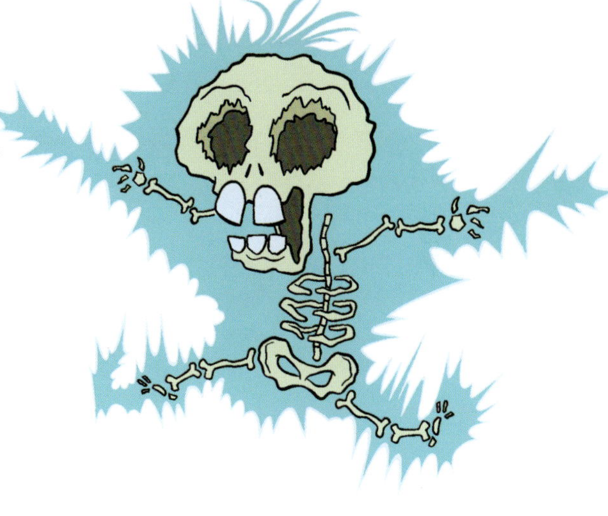

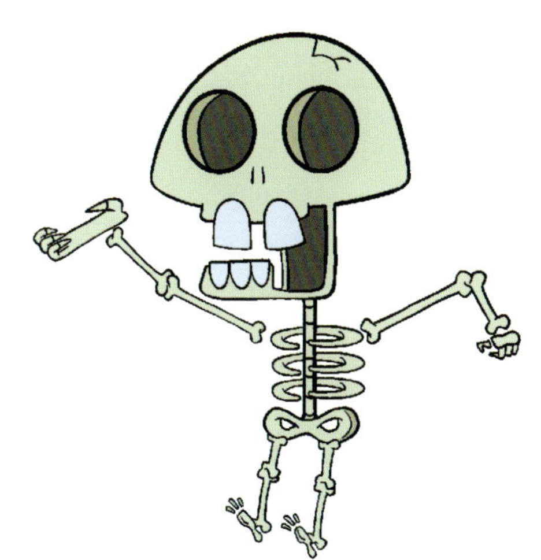

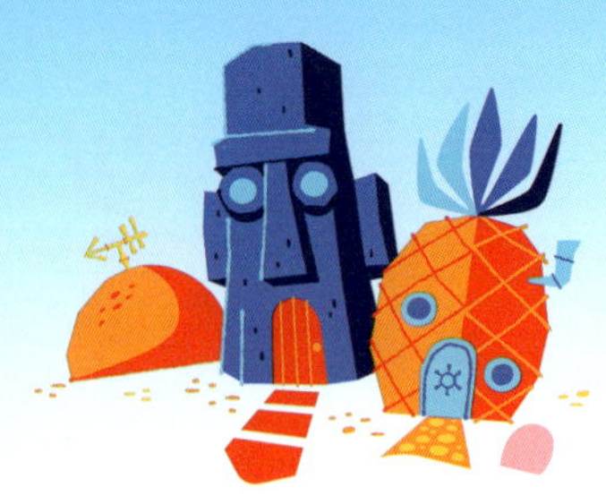

STAR HOUSE

The main location in this series, the Star house is where the family lives and Patrick's show takes place. It resembles an old-fashioned percolating coffee pot set next to an old tube television set and is located at 821 Anemone Lane in Bikini Bottom. Appropriately, Patrick "broadcasts" his show from his bedroom window, which happens to be in the TV set.

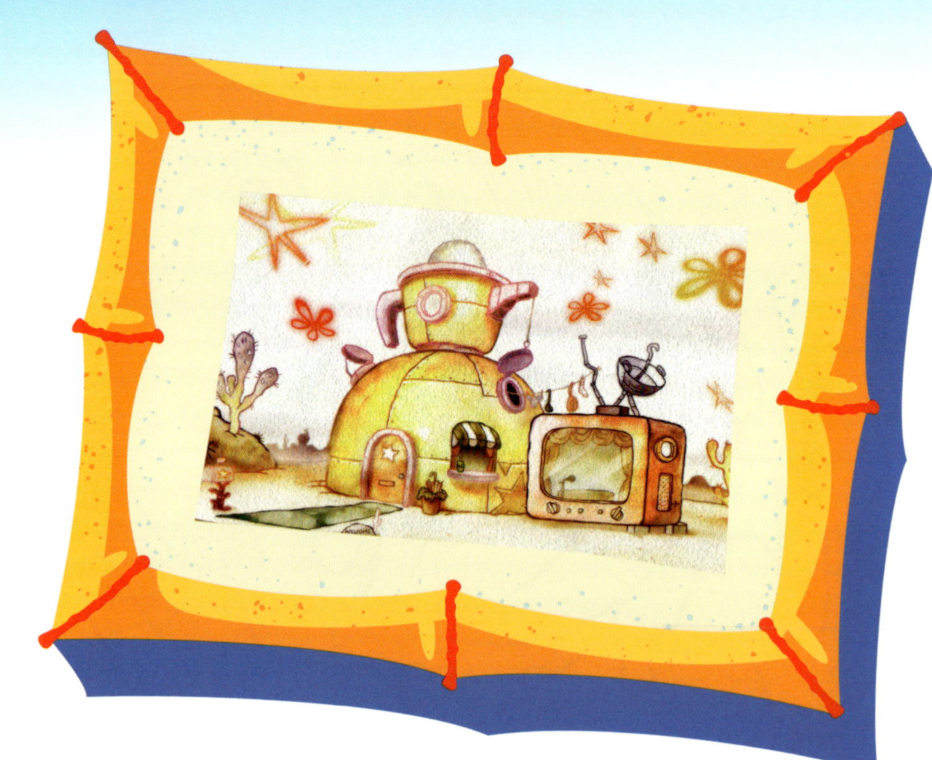

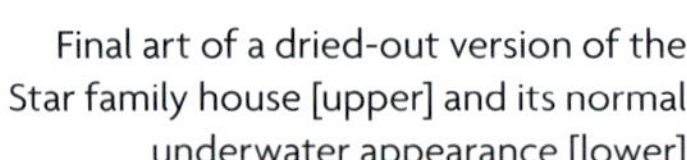

Final art of a dried-out version of the Star family house [upper] and its normal underwater appearance [lower]

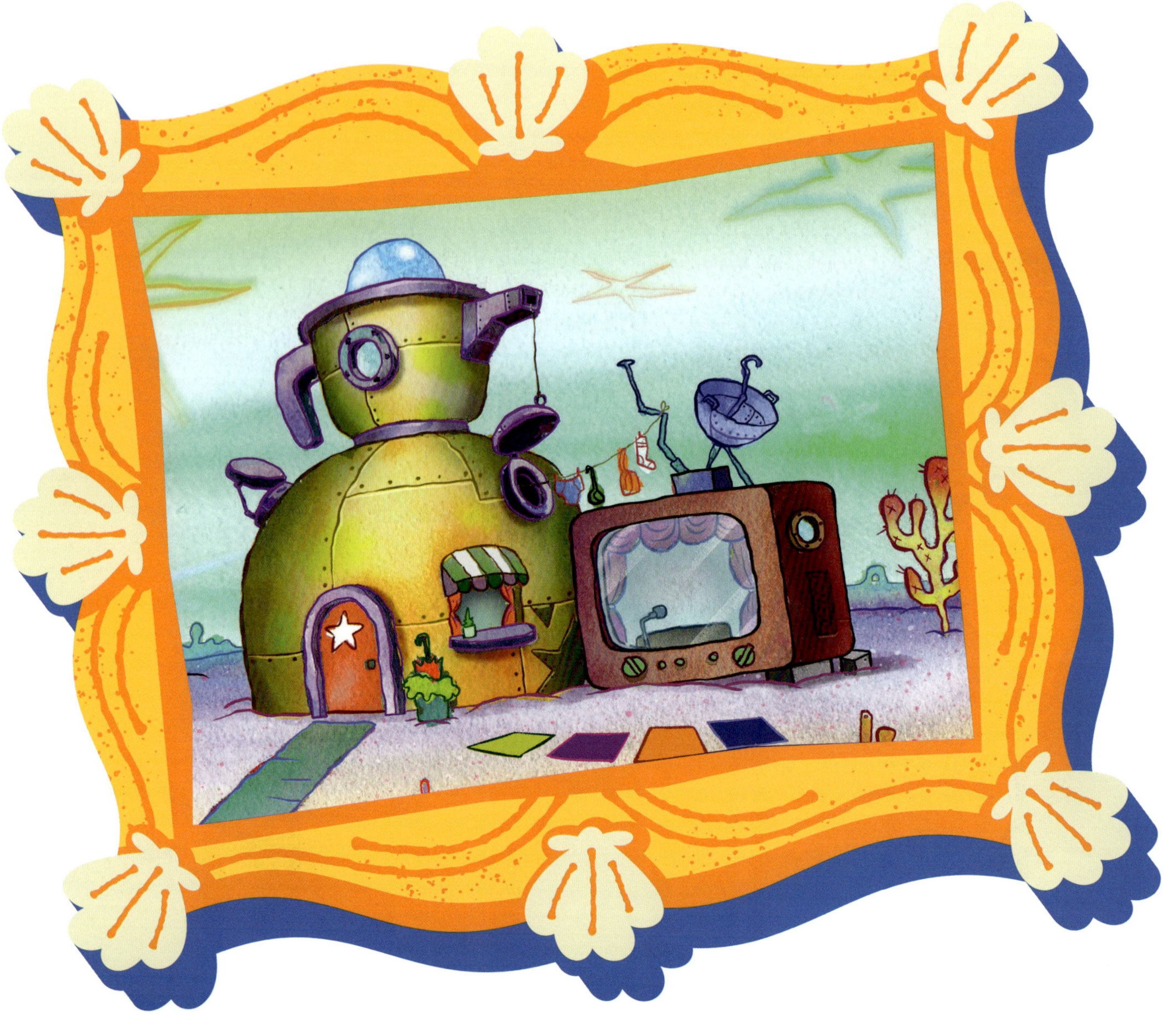

UKULELE BOTTOM

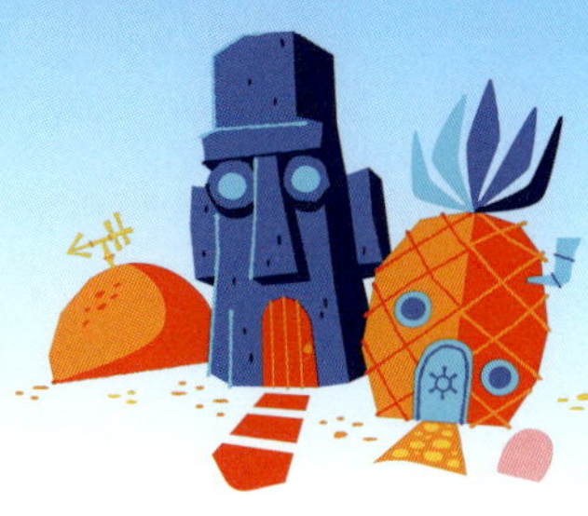

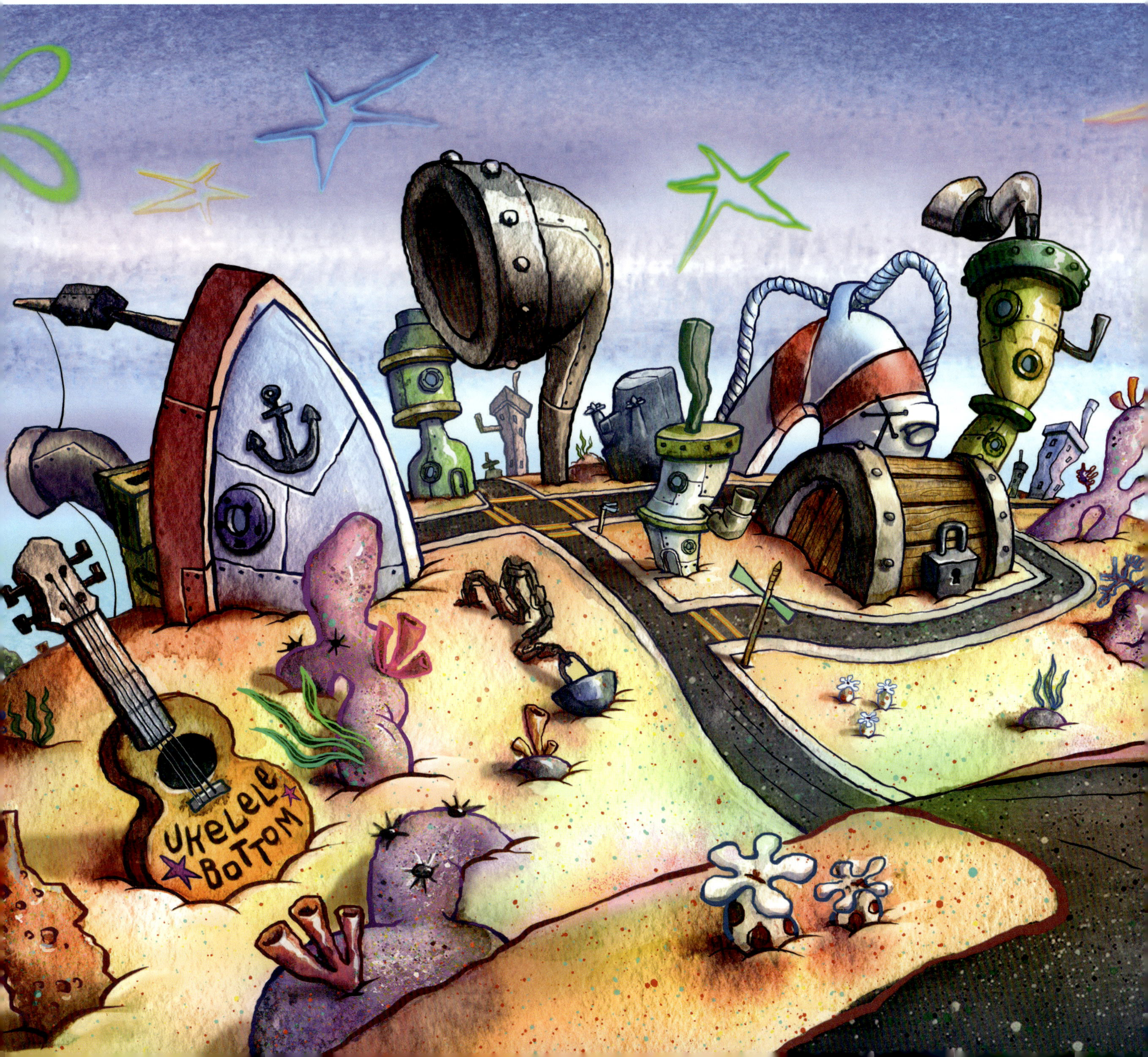

Final art of the suburb Ukulele Bottom, momentarily thought to be the setting for *The Patrick Star Show* but really just a briefly referenced location after its appearance in "I Was a Teenage Gary" (Season 1, episode 13b) of *SpongeBob SquarePants*

A suburb of Bikini Bottom, this location and its iconographically appropriate signage may not come into view often, but Ukulele Bottom's harmonious existence adds nice atmosphere to the friendly neighborhoods deep within the Pacific Ocean.

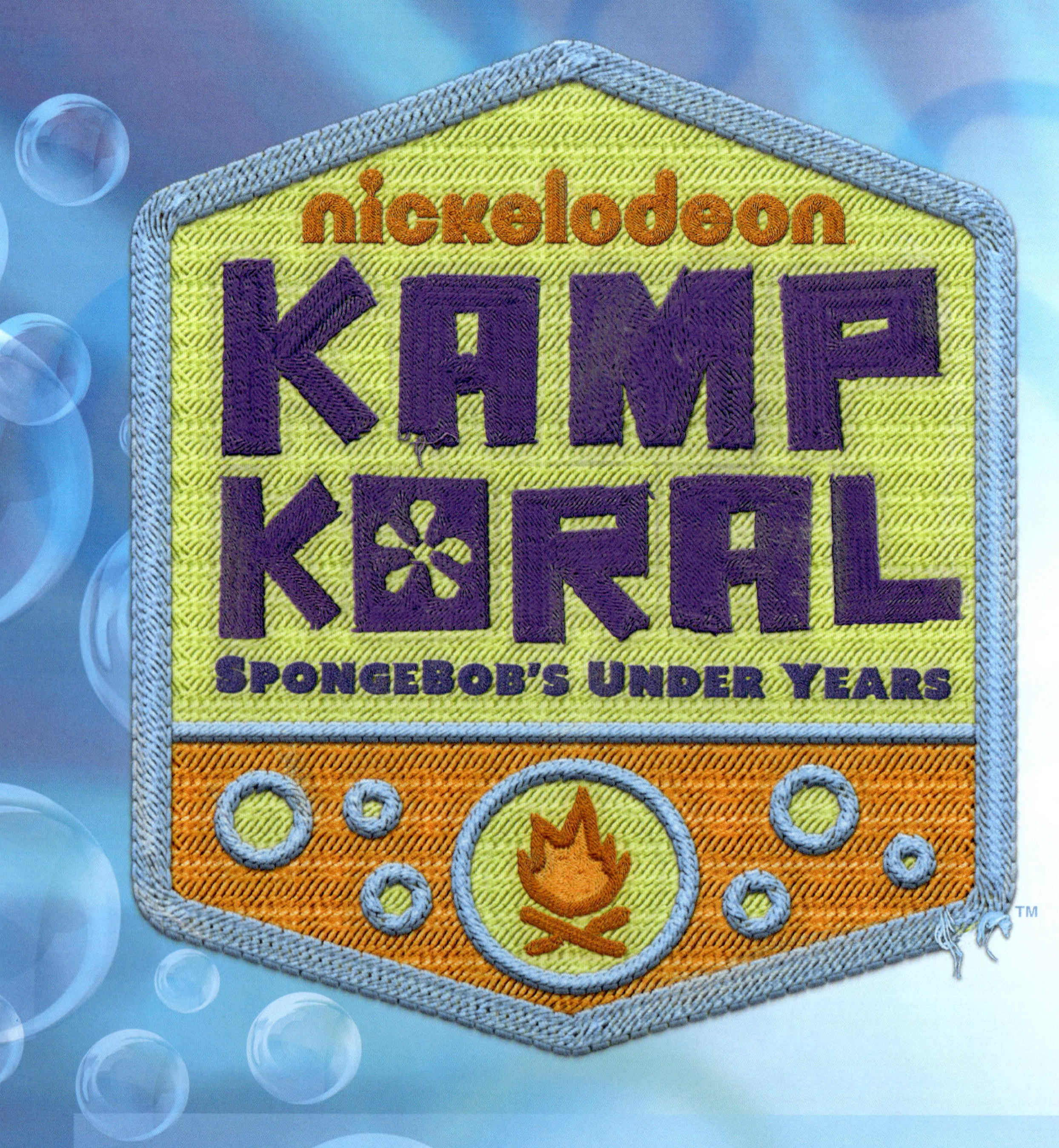

Taking the world of *SpongeBob SquarePants* back in time and into a computer-generated series space was a huge endeavor, worthy of earning a scout badge at the very least. "We did a group-think and went through a deep distillation period to get in the right space for *Kamp Koral*, wanting to make sure we played against the expectations of what it could be," recalls writer Mr. Lawrence. Needing to stay true to the well-established characters of Bikini Bottom, but wanting to explore an earlier part of their lives, the creative team leaned into memories of being away from their parents for the first time, for field trips, sleepaway camp, or summer vacation with another family. The creators made sure that this framework "would not change who SpongeBob is; he's the same exact guy except he hasn't found all his passions yet, but he's still going to react the same way to things and have the same personality," adds Mr. Lawrence.

Artistically speaking, shifting from 2D to CG series animation was a huge lift, but the crew "dove headfirst into the world of *SpongeBob SquarePants* learning curve to achieve the monumental task of giving fans something they'd never seen before, CG animation with expressions as big, crazy, and varied" as they'd come to expect from SpongeBob and everyone else in Bikini Bottom, says executive producer Vincent Waller.

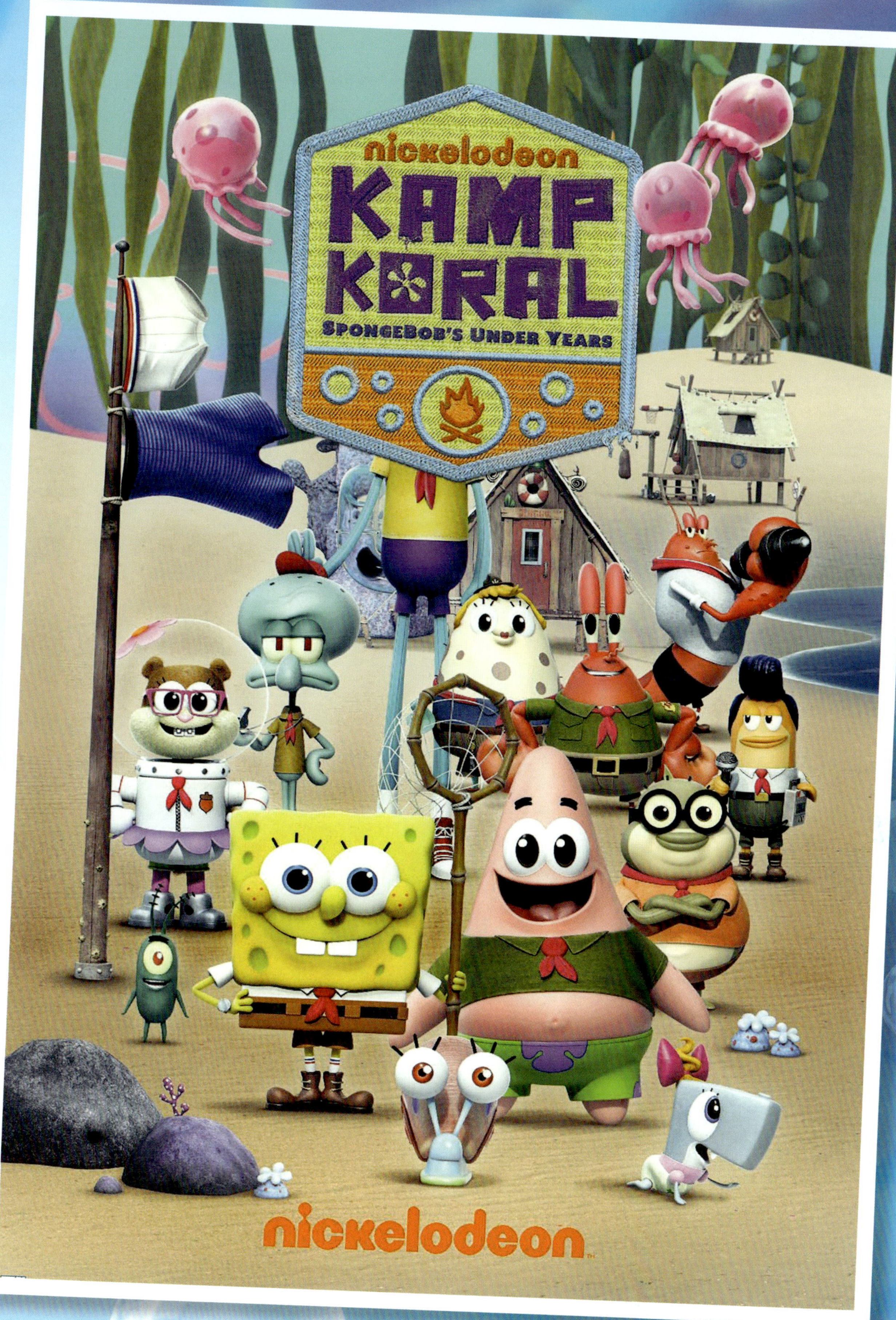
nickelodeon
KAMP
KORAL
SPONGEBOB'S UNDER YEARS
nickelodeon

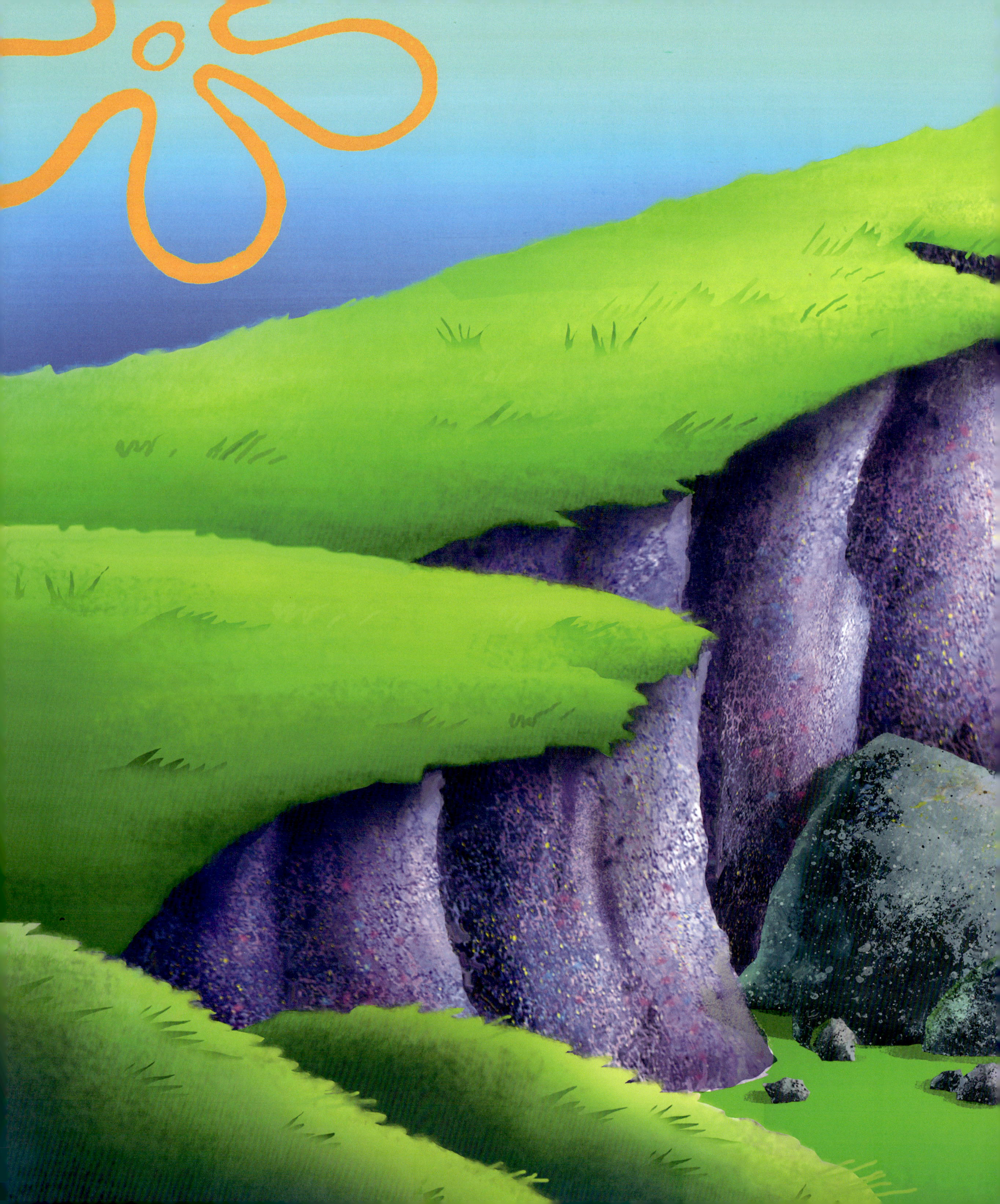

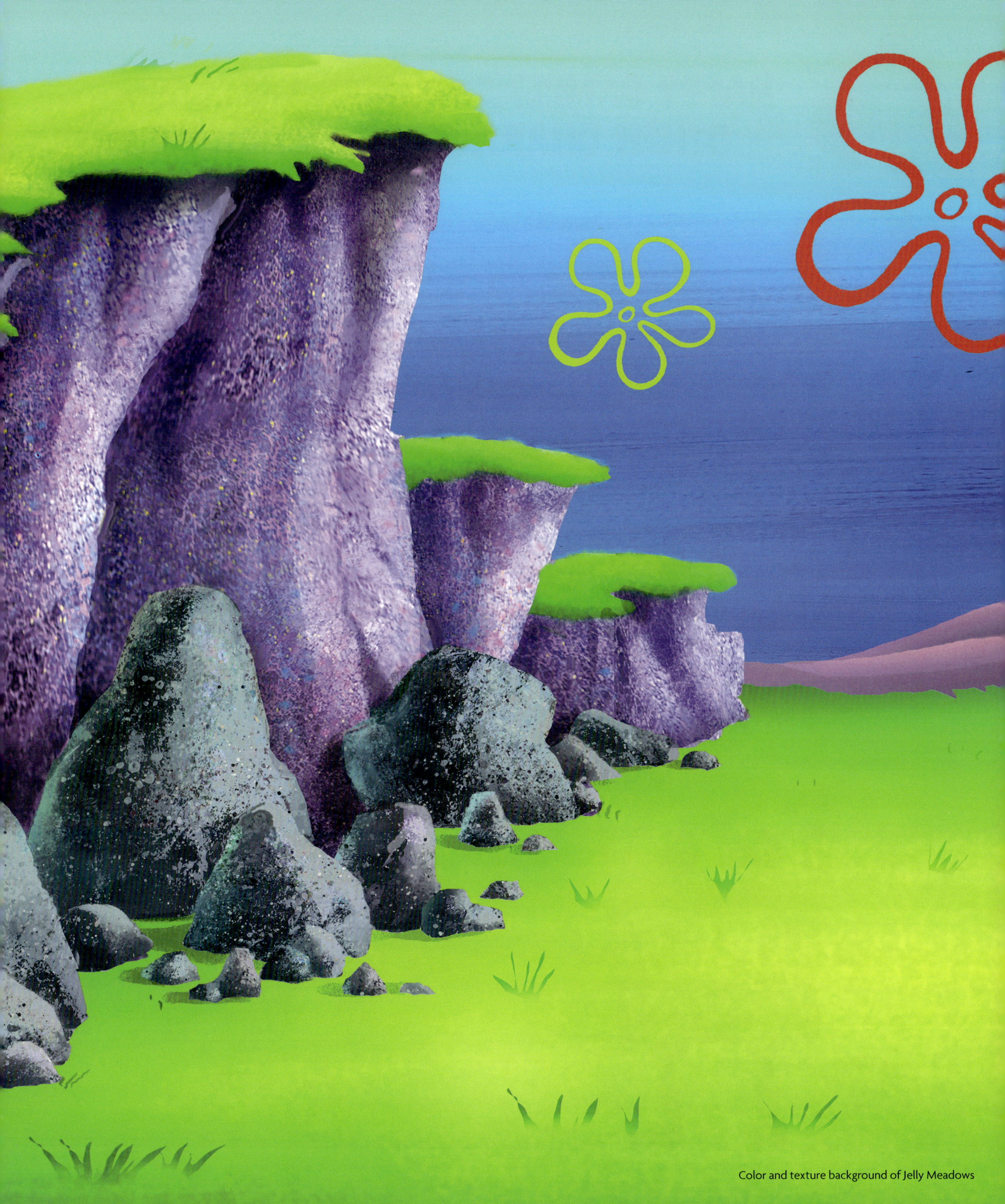

Color and texture background of Jelly Meadows

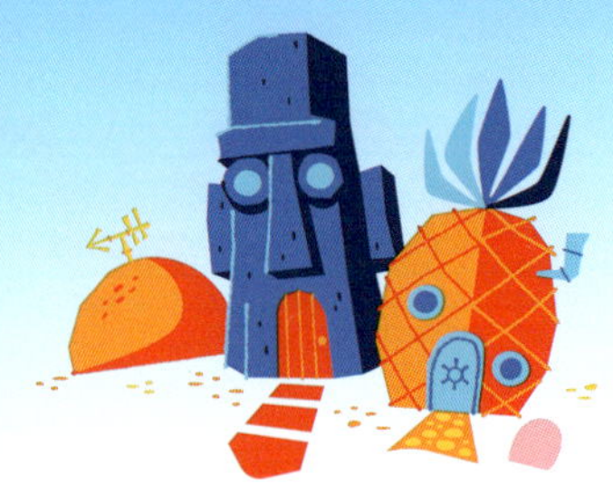

HAPPY CAMPERS & OTHER CHARACTERS

Most of the campers are recognizable from their older years as portrayed in the original series, but their younger versions are a whole new level of cute, and a few new faces add to the camper chaos. "I really enjoy the challenge of designing and introducing new characters into the franchise. There's a lot of room to play with all the different styles of characters in Bikini Bottom, but you still need to make them feel like they are part of the visual language that the original crew set up," notes executive producer Marc Ceccarelli.

In fact, "a lot of the campers were CG variations of designs done on the main show, many from the *SpongeBob SquarePants* episode 'Old Man Patrick,'" adds supervising director Dave Cunningham.

Stages of SpongeBob's translation from 2D final art into CG final form

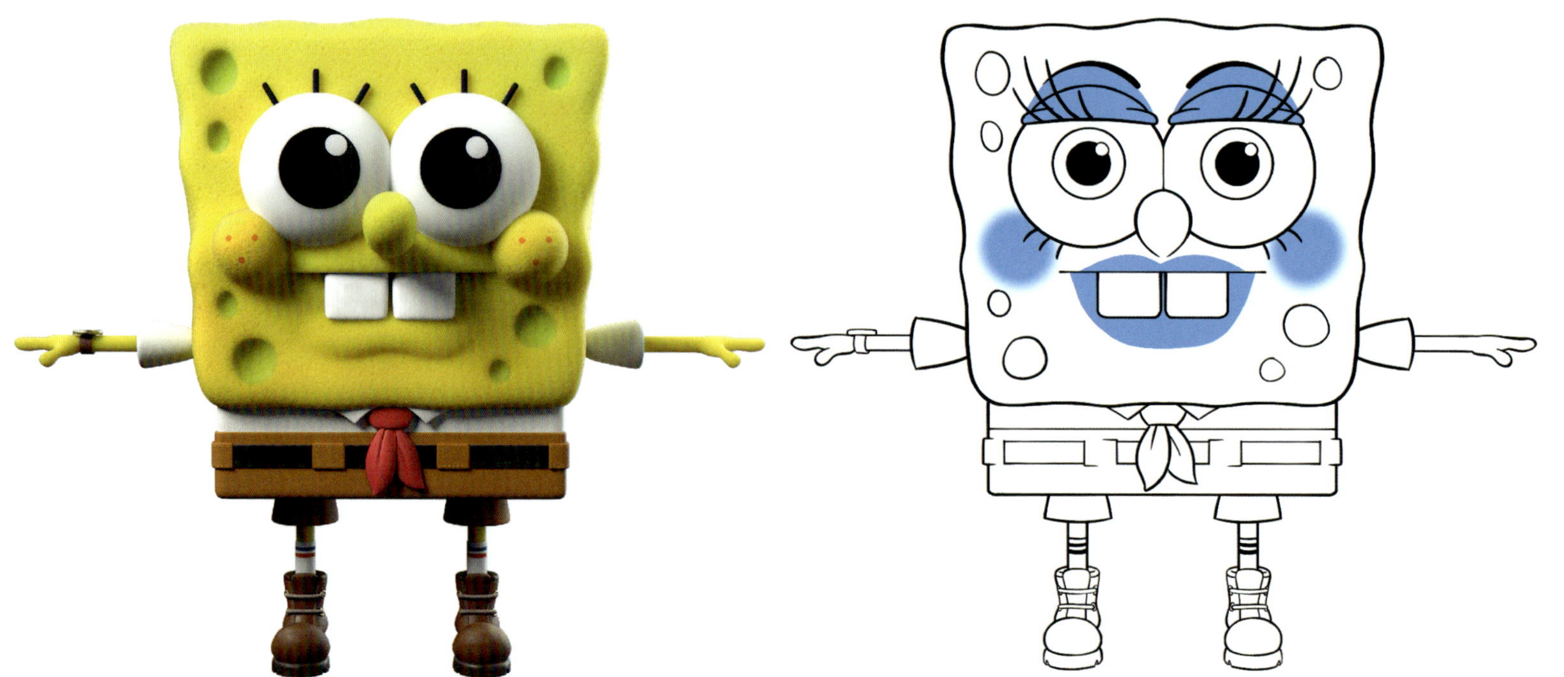

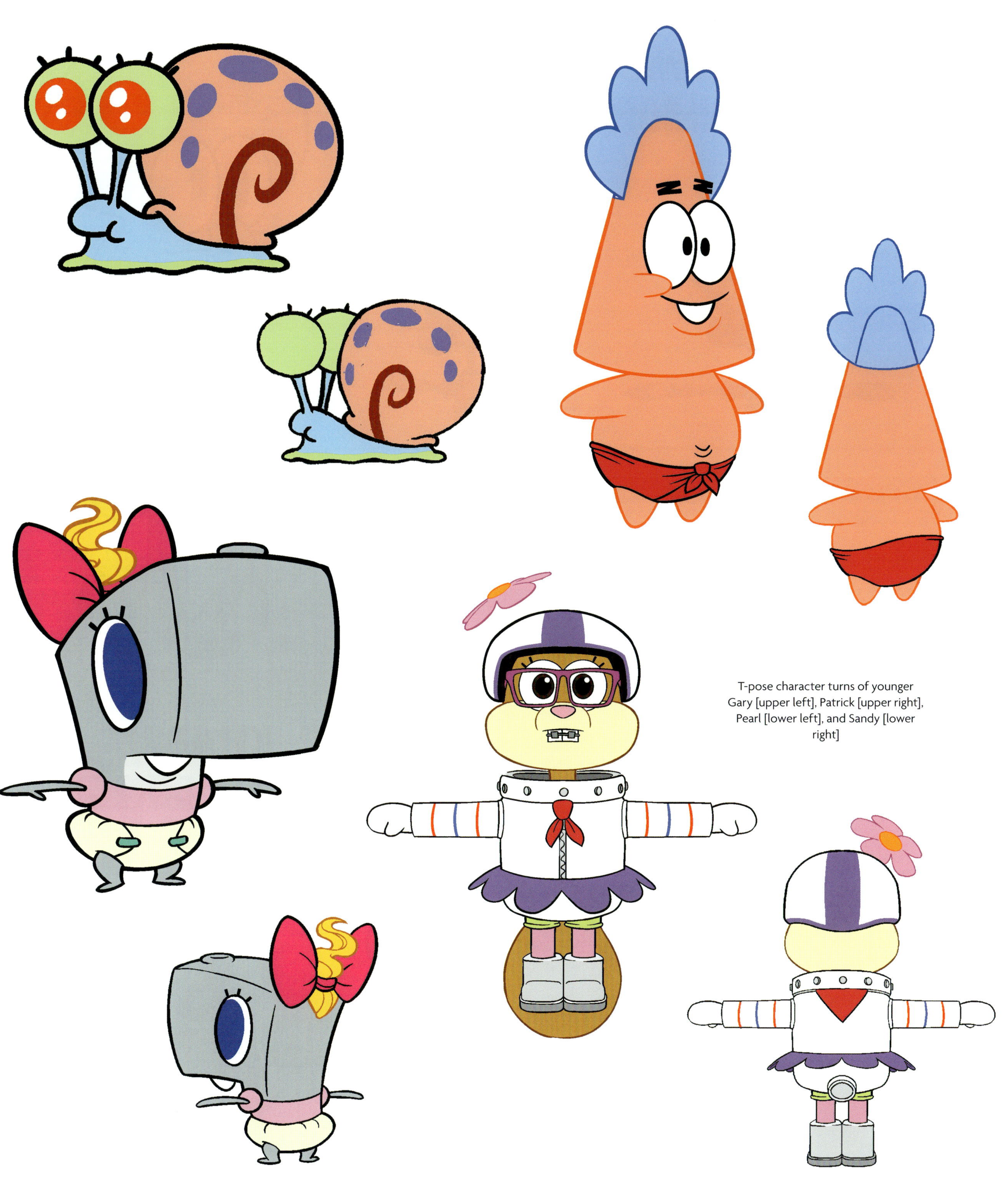

T-pose character turns of younger Gary [upper left], Patrick [upper right], Pearl [lower left], and Sandy [lower right]

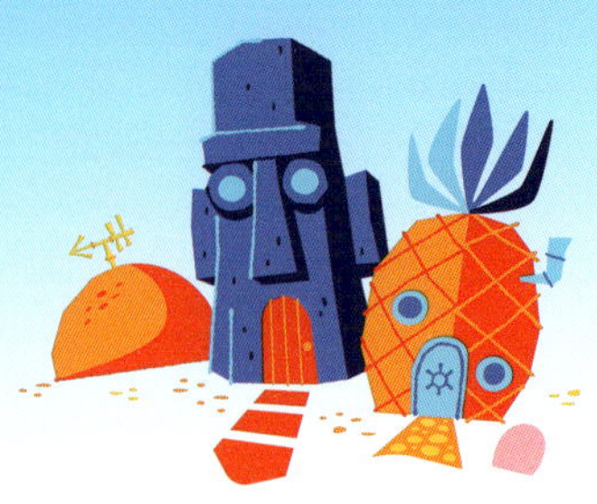

SQUIDWARD, JUNIOR COUNSELOR

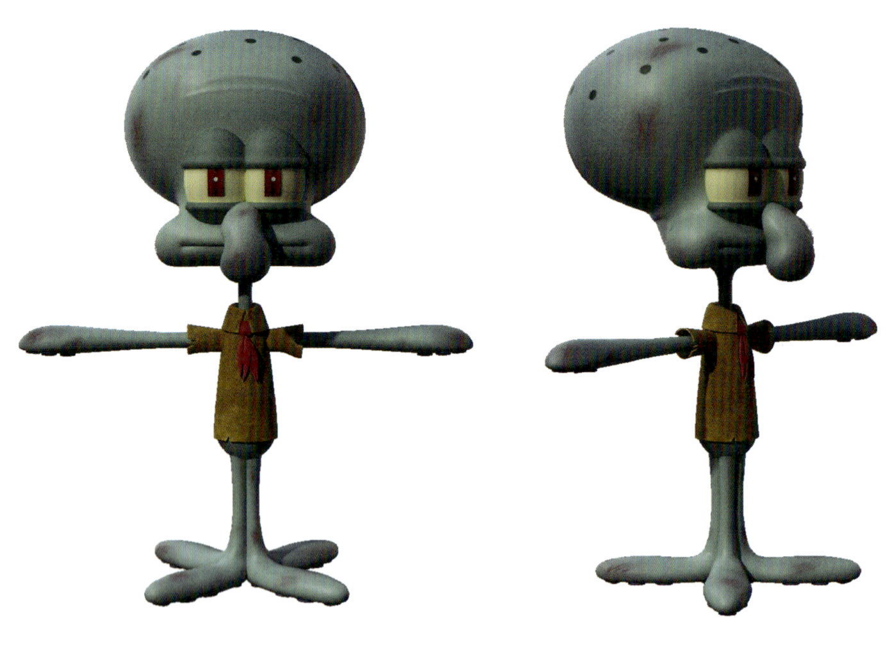

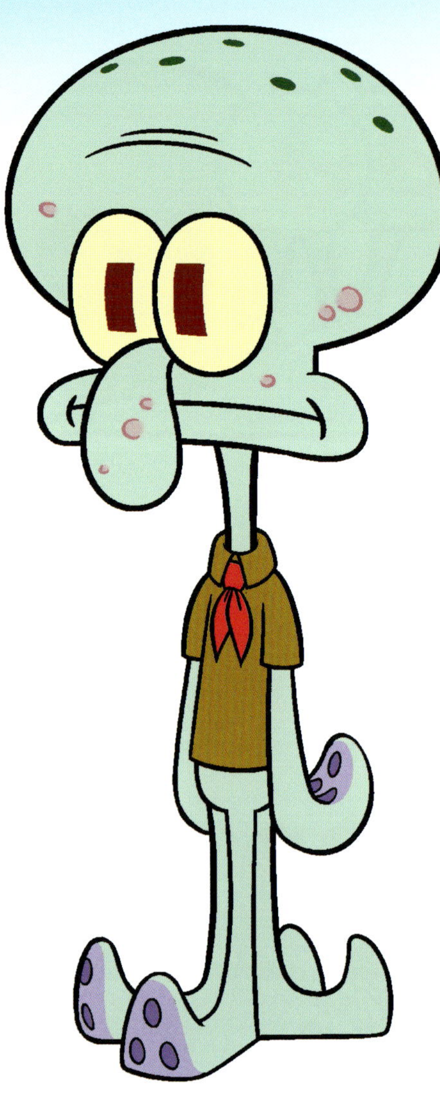

CG final [upper left] and 2D character design [upper right] of Squidward; 2D character breakdown of Mr. Krabs

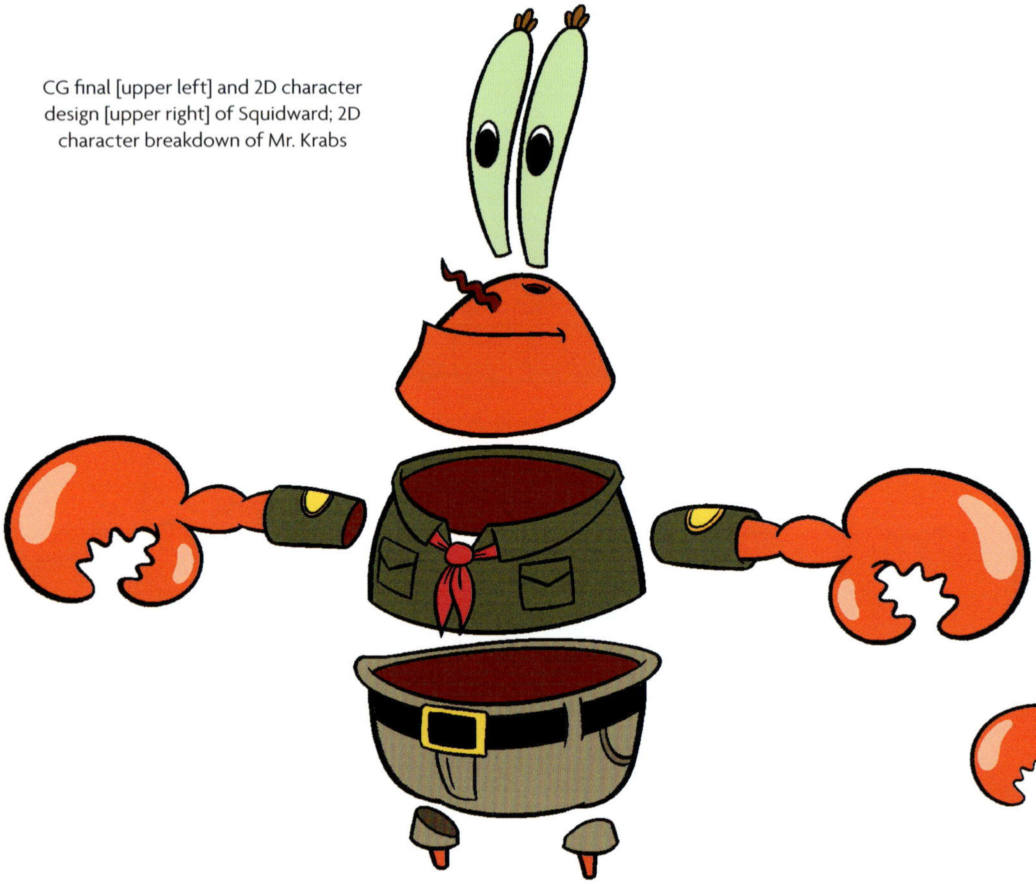

MR. KRABS, CAMP DIRECTOR

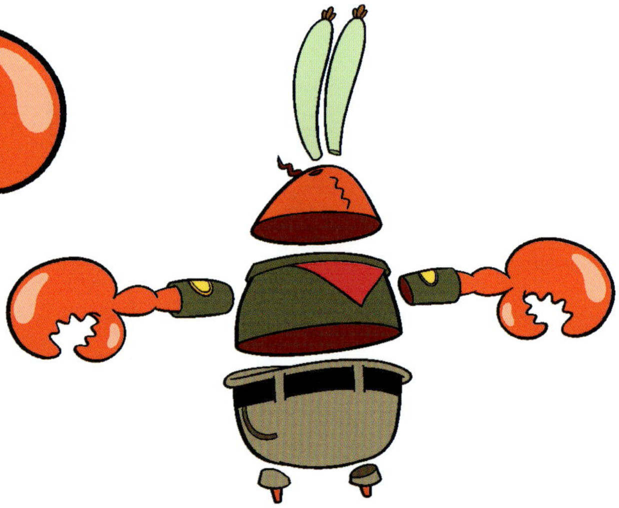

PLANKTON & KAREN, CAMP COOKS

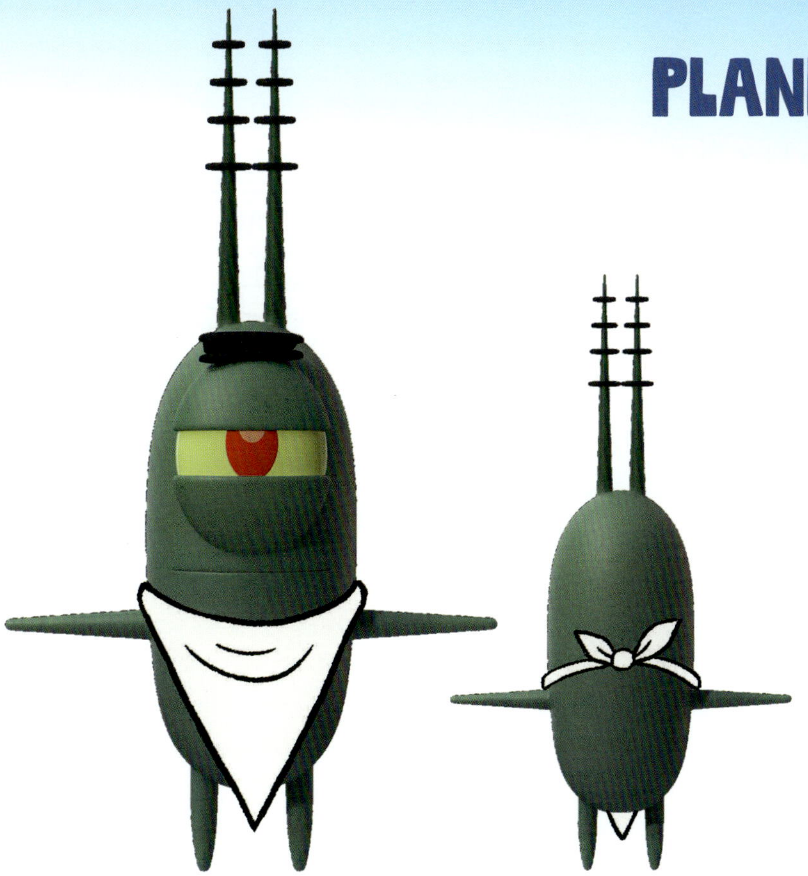

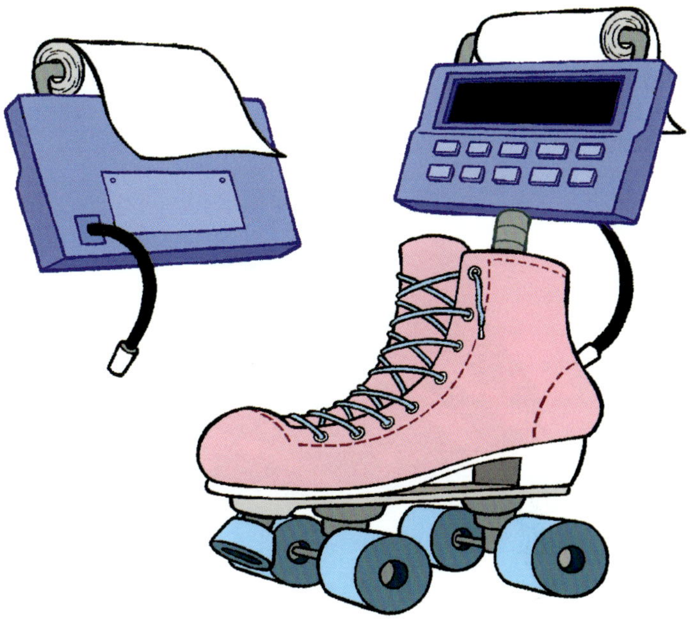

MRS. PUFF SCOUTMASTER & ACTIVITY TEACHER

CG rendered model of Plankton [upper left] and character designs of Karen [upper right] and Mrs. Puff [bottom]

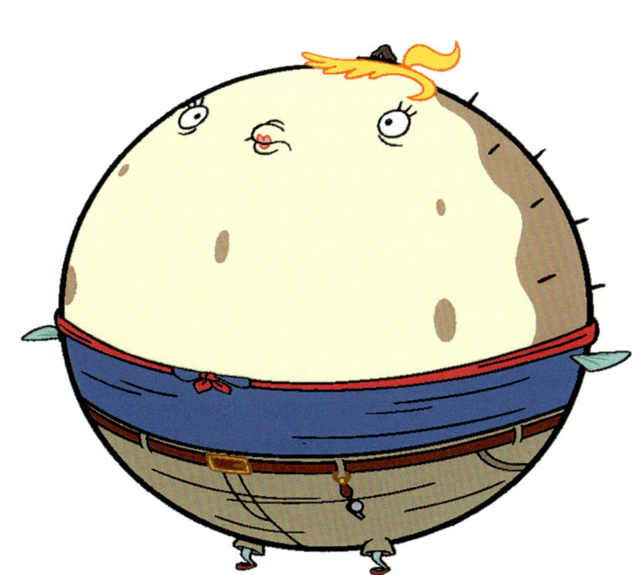

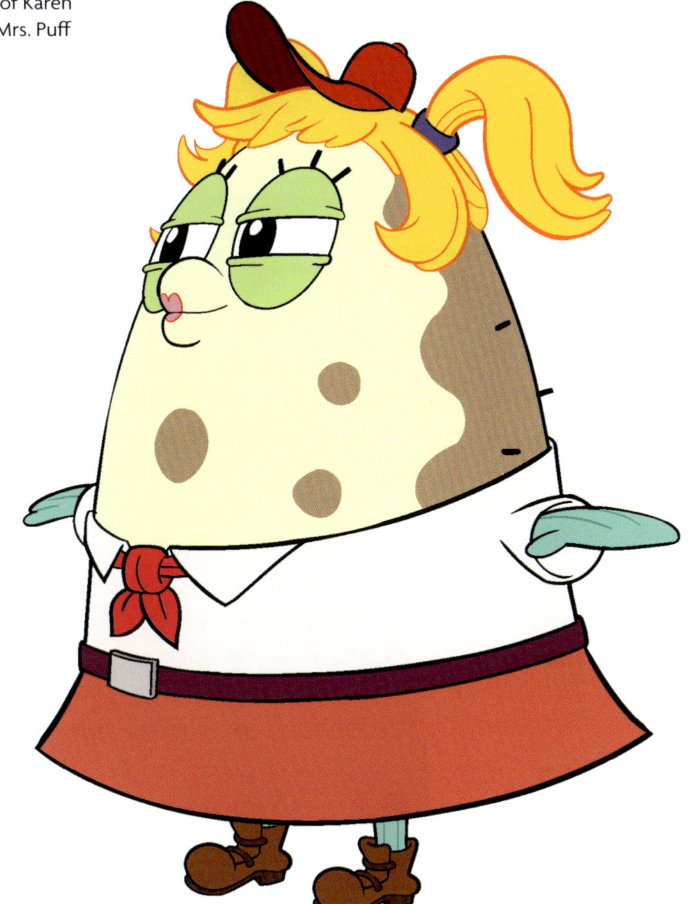

NARLENE & NOBBY NARWHAL

Residents of the Kelp Forest, these siblings are based on rough designs from Marc Ceccarelli and are so beloved that they have made their way into the other *SpongeBob* series as well.

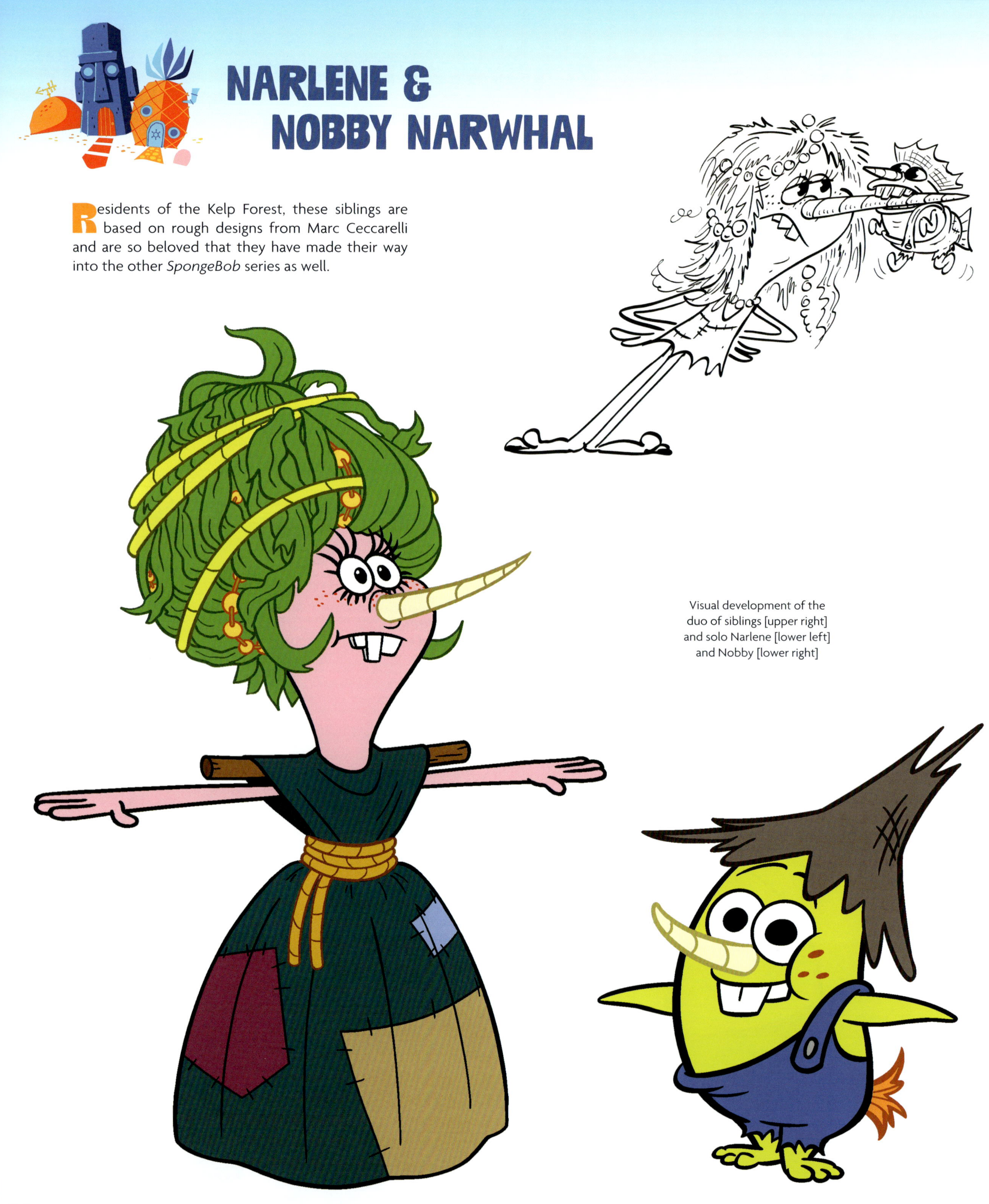

Visual development of the duo of siblings [upper right] and solo Narlene [lower left] and Nobby [lower right]

THE KRAKEN

The lake-dwelling and joke-telling Wise Kraken was created also in part to be an homage to late stand-up comedian Rodney Dangerfield.

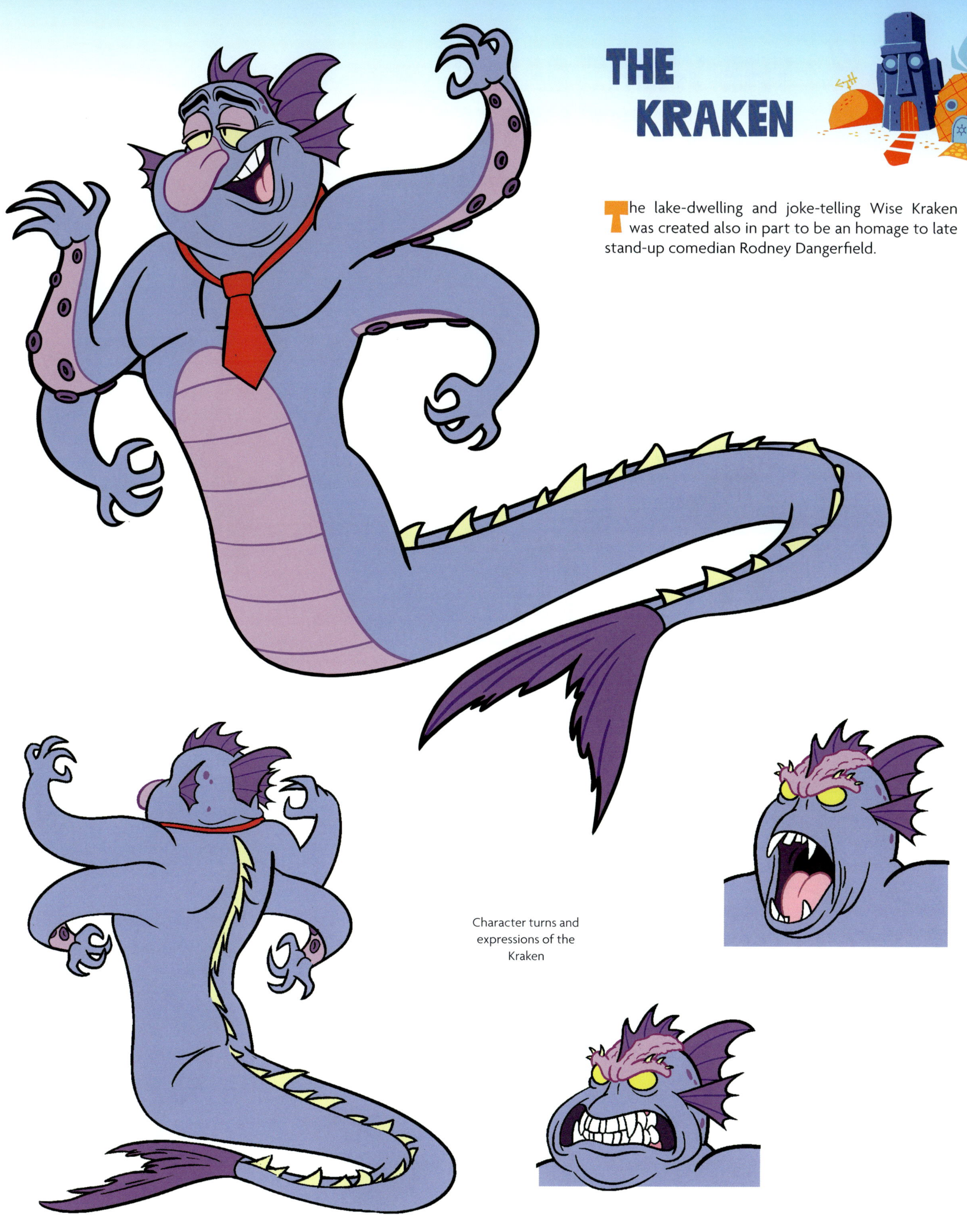

Character turns and expressions of the Kraken

THE YACHT CABIN: MISSY UPTURN, REA & ROH

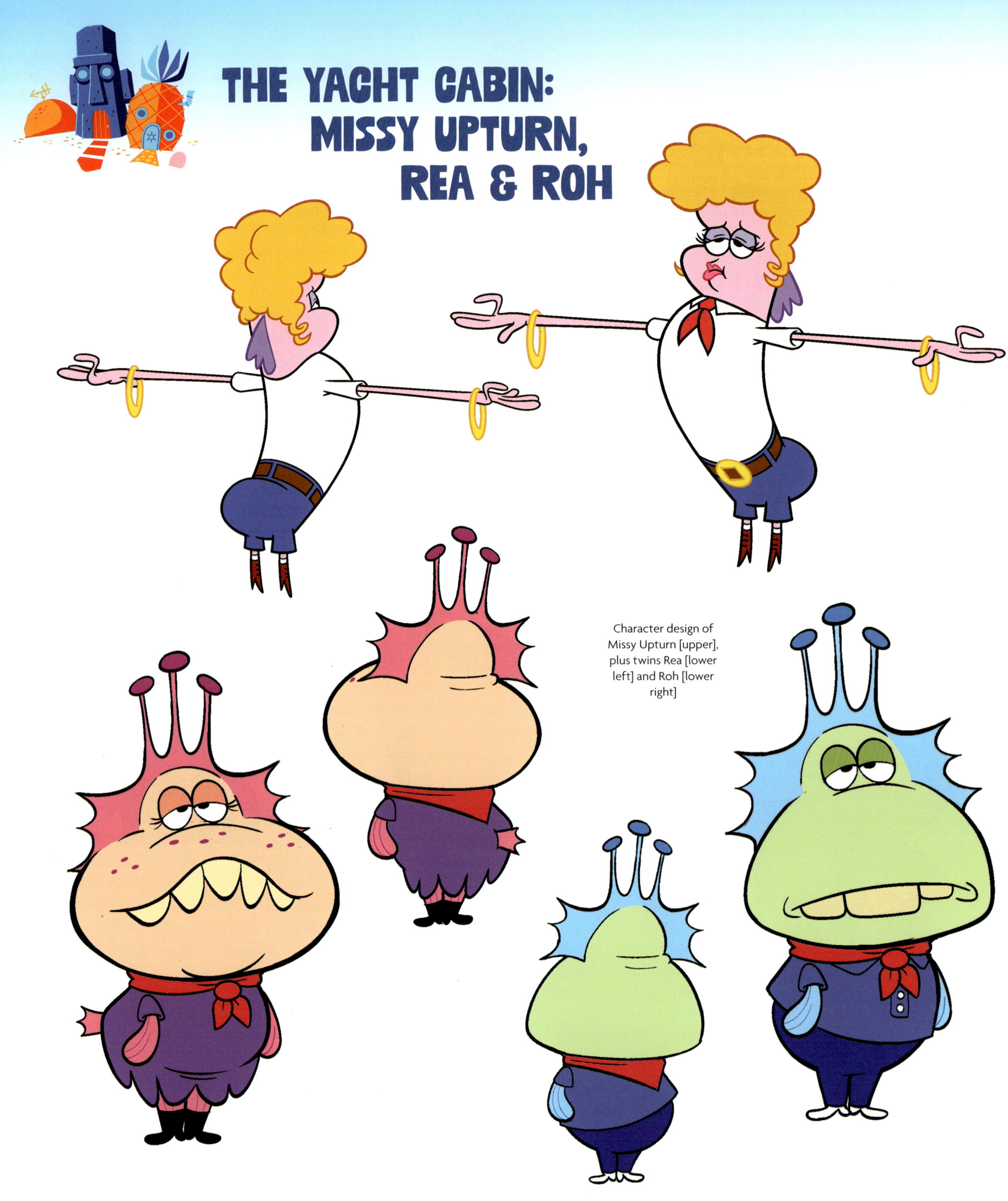

Character design of Missy Upturn [upper], plus twins Rea [lower left] and Roh [lower right]

THE PONTOON CABIN: BUBBLE BASS, KEVIN C. CUCUMBER & HARVEY

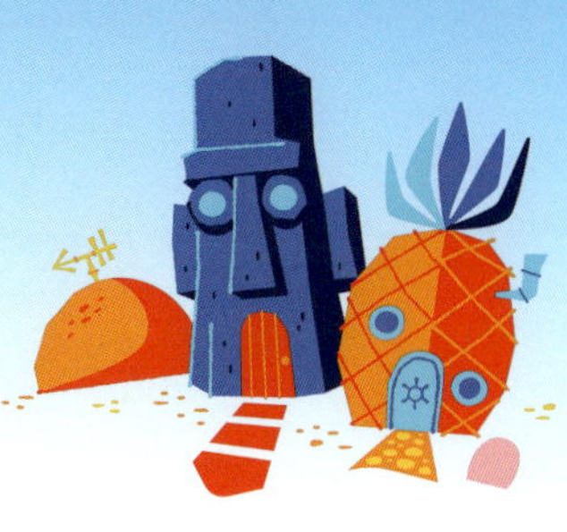

Kamp Koral has bunkloads of interesting attendees with unique personalities, but it's really Harvey's repeated conspiracy stories about Martians that test everyone's patience.

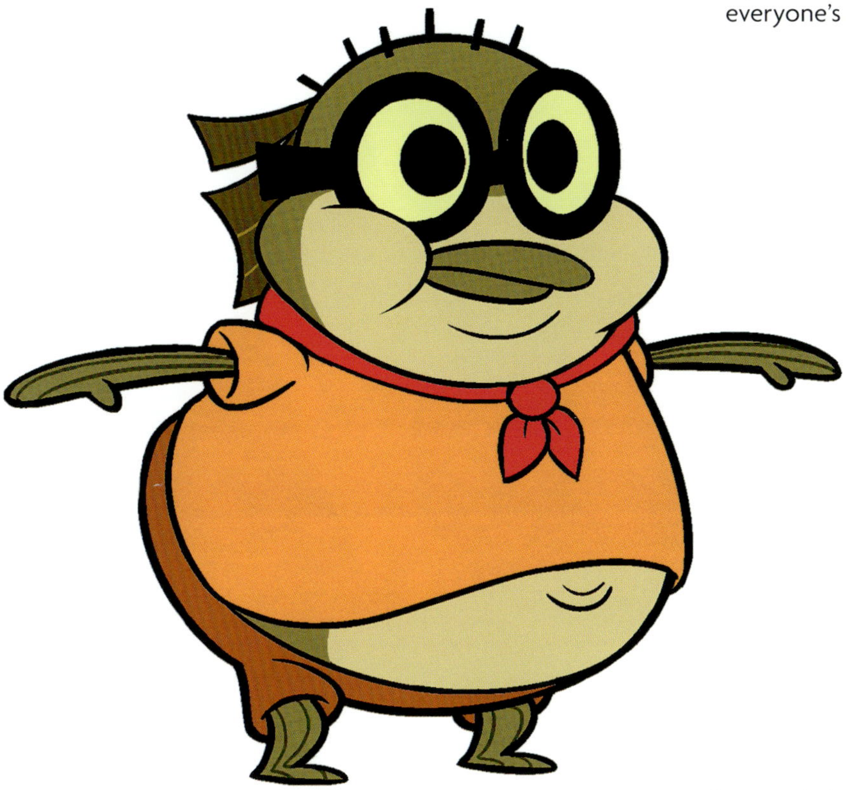

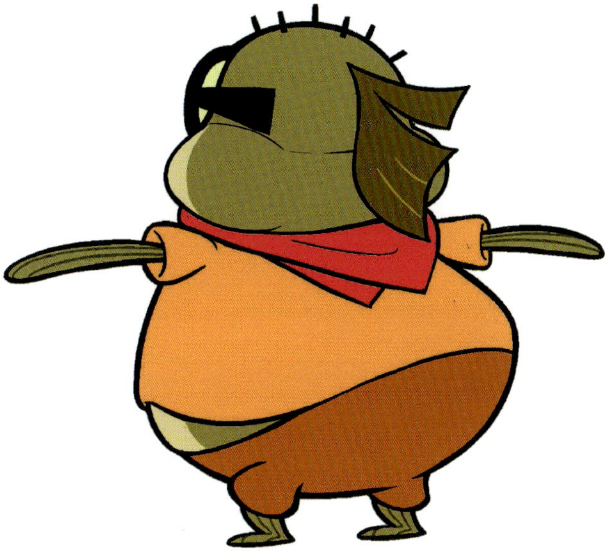

Character design of Bubble Bass [upper] and Kevin C. Cucumber [lower]

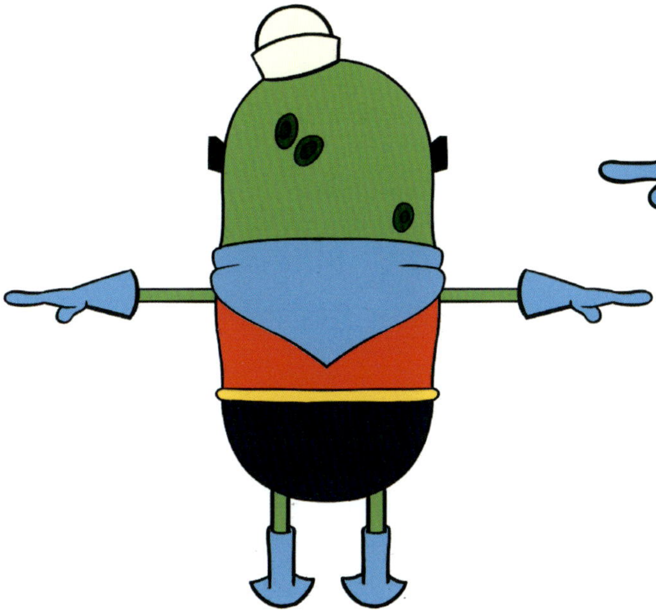

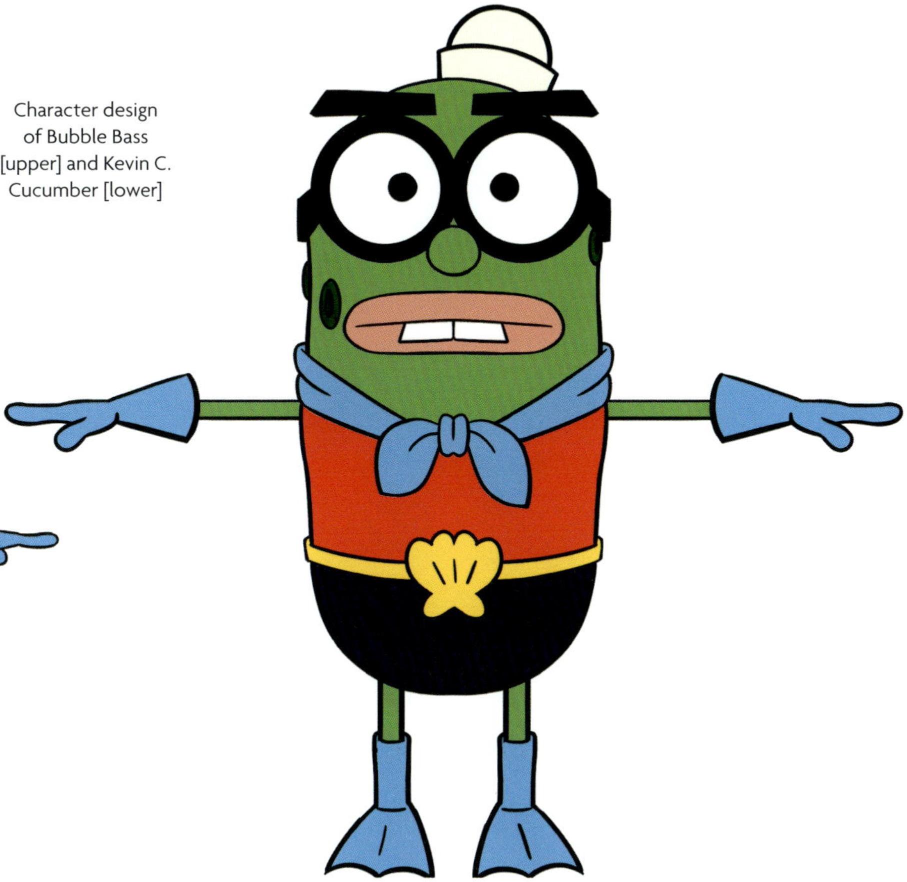

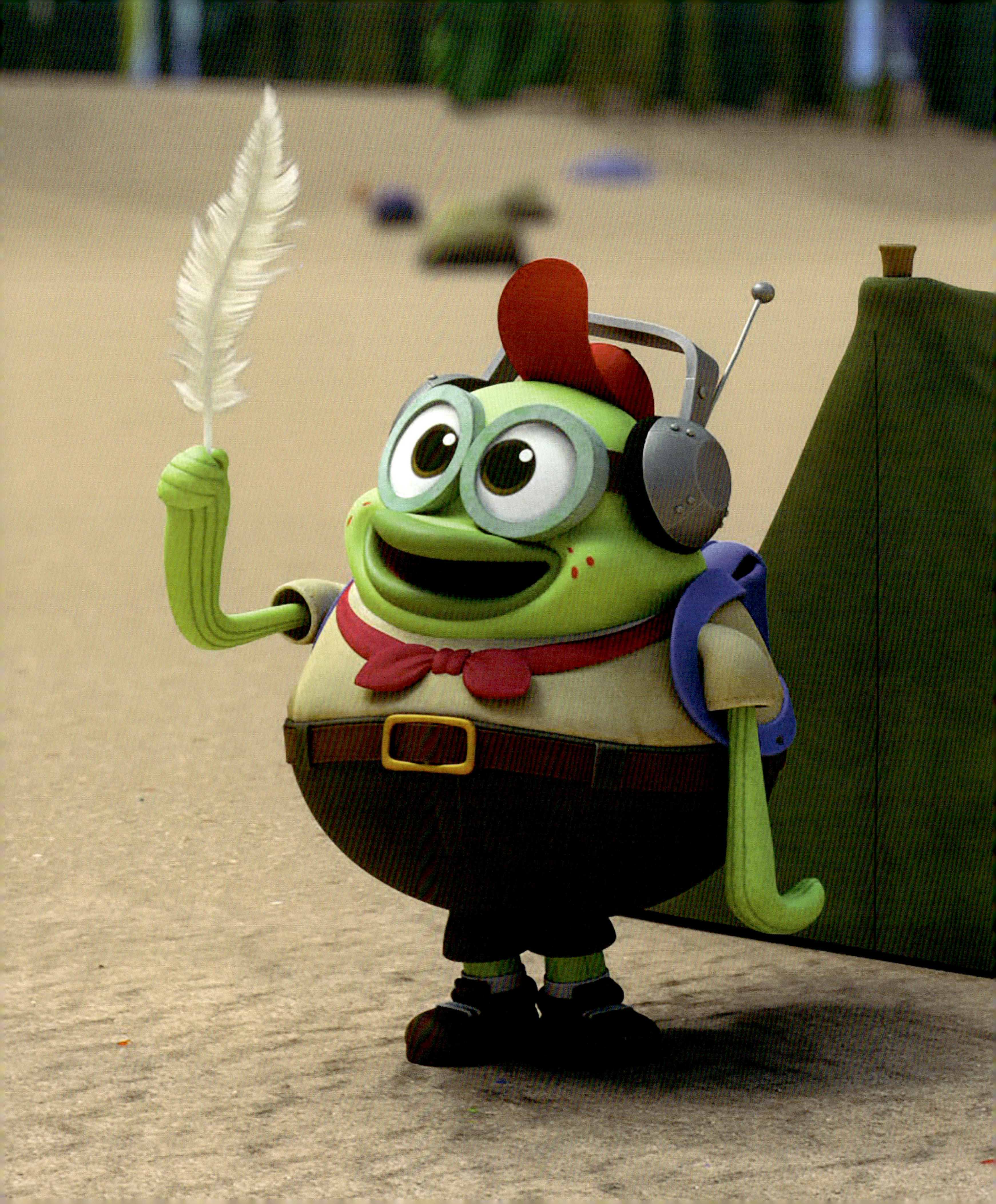

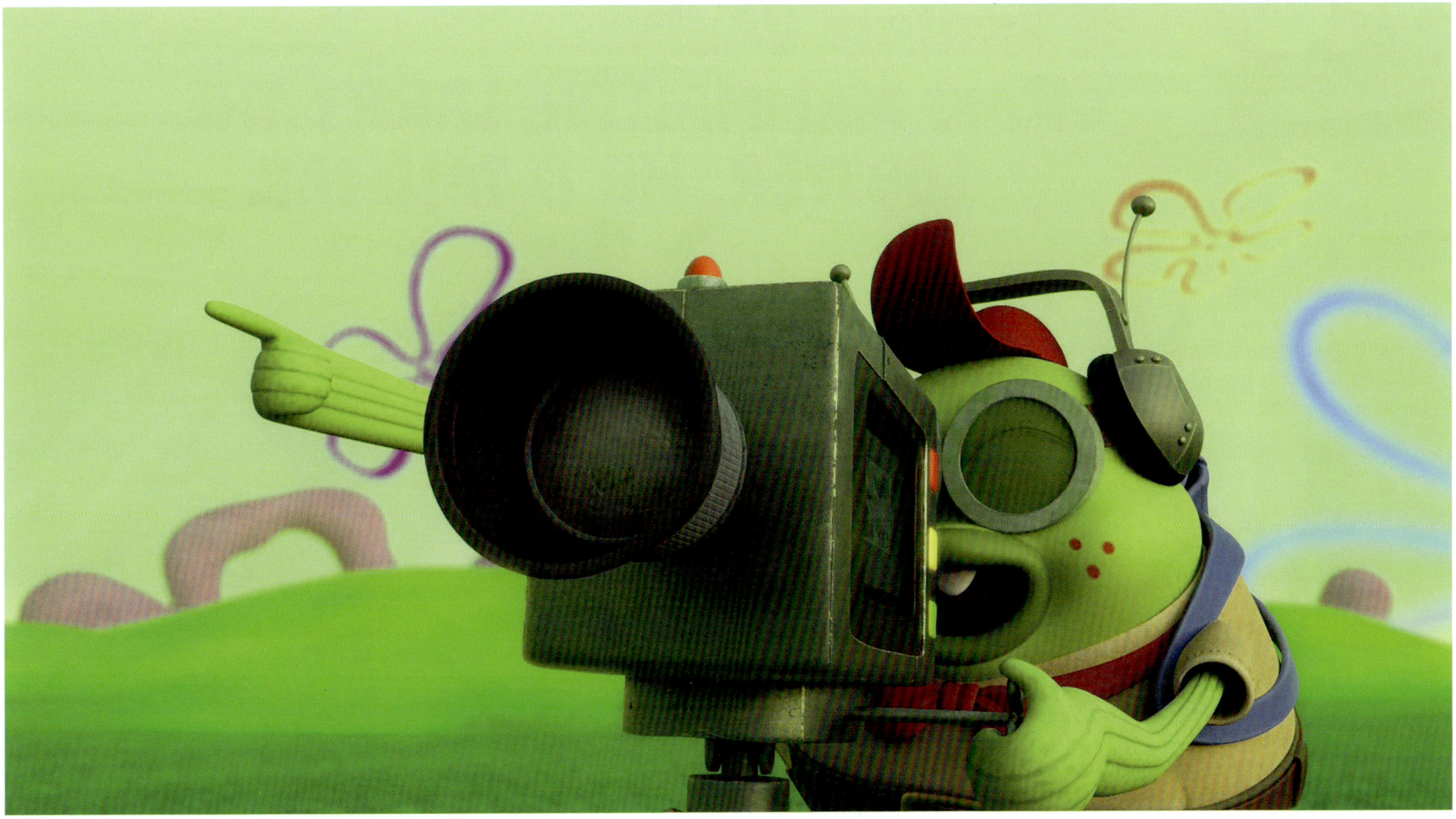

Final frame images of Harvey

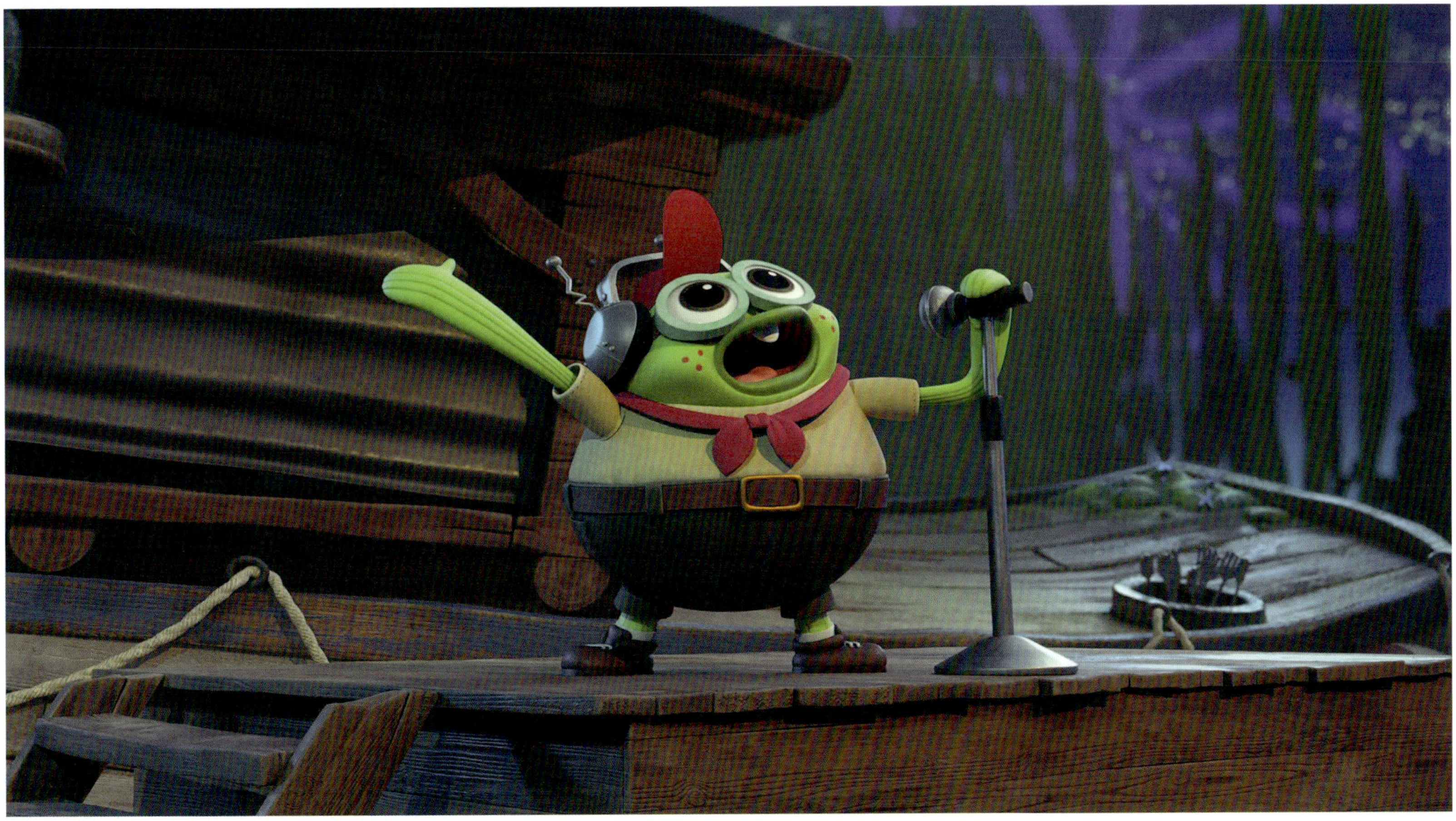

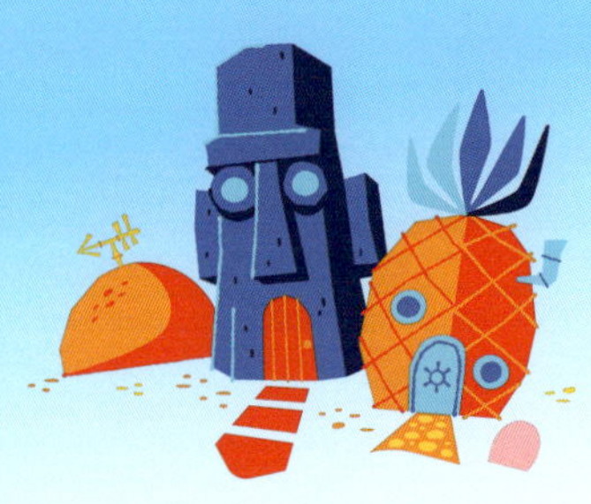

THE FRIGATE CABIN: CRAIG MAMMALTON, LARRY THE LOBSTER, MO & TALL TAIL

What might be referred to as the "Jock Cabin" houses the mohawk-sporting Mo, body builder Larry the Lobster, the ever-tanned Craig Mammalton, and also Tall Tail, but no one is quite sure where exactly that blue-toned super-sized camper sleeps.

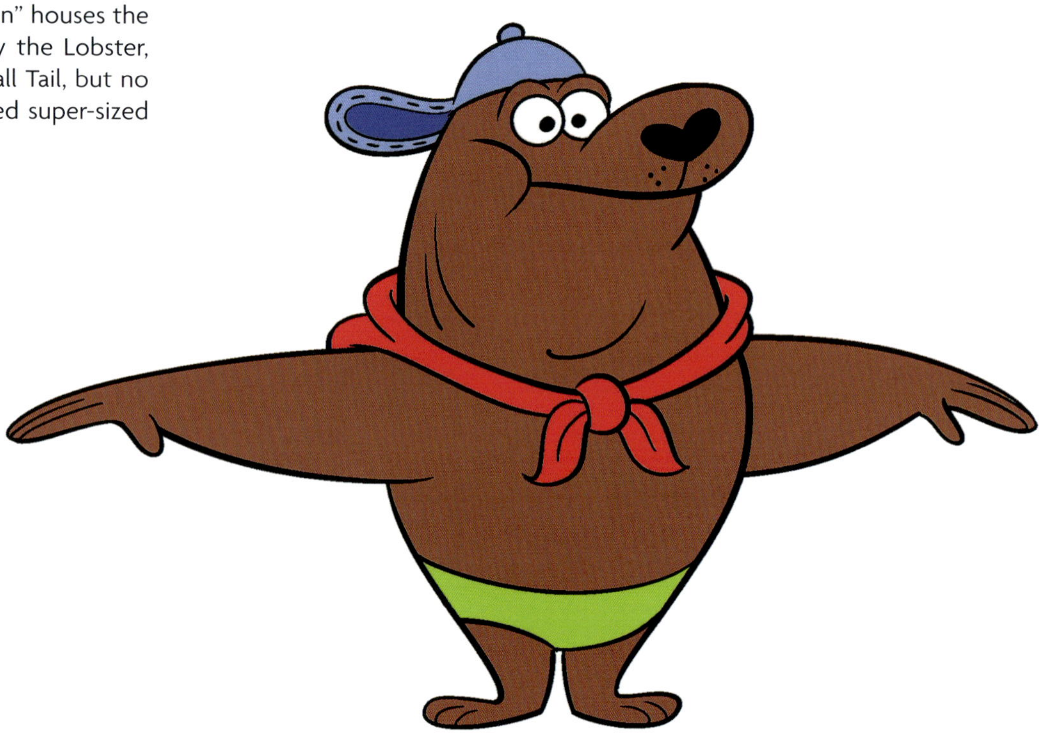

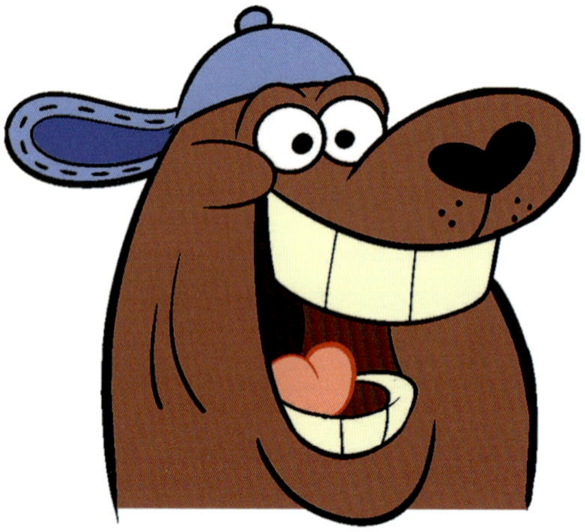

Character design and expressions of Craig Mammalton [upper] and Larry the Lobster [lower]

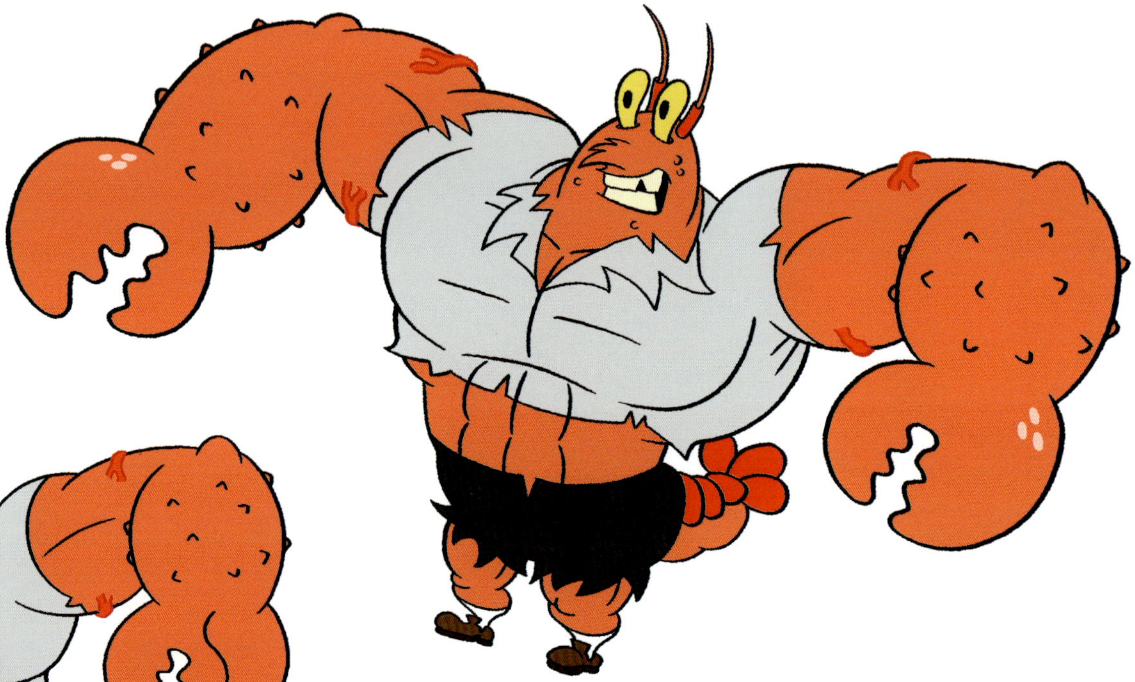

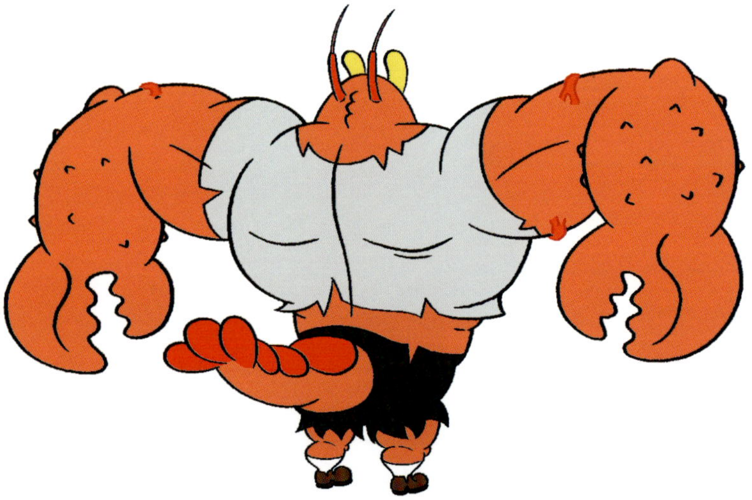

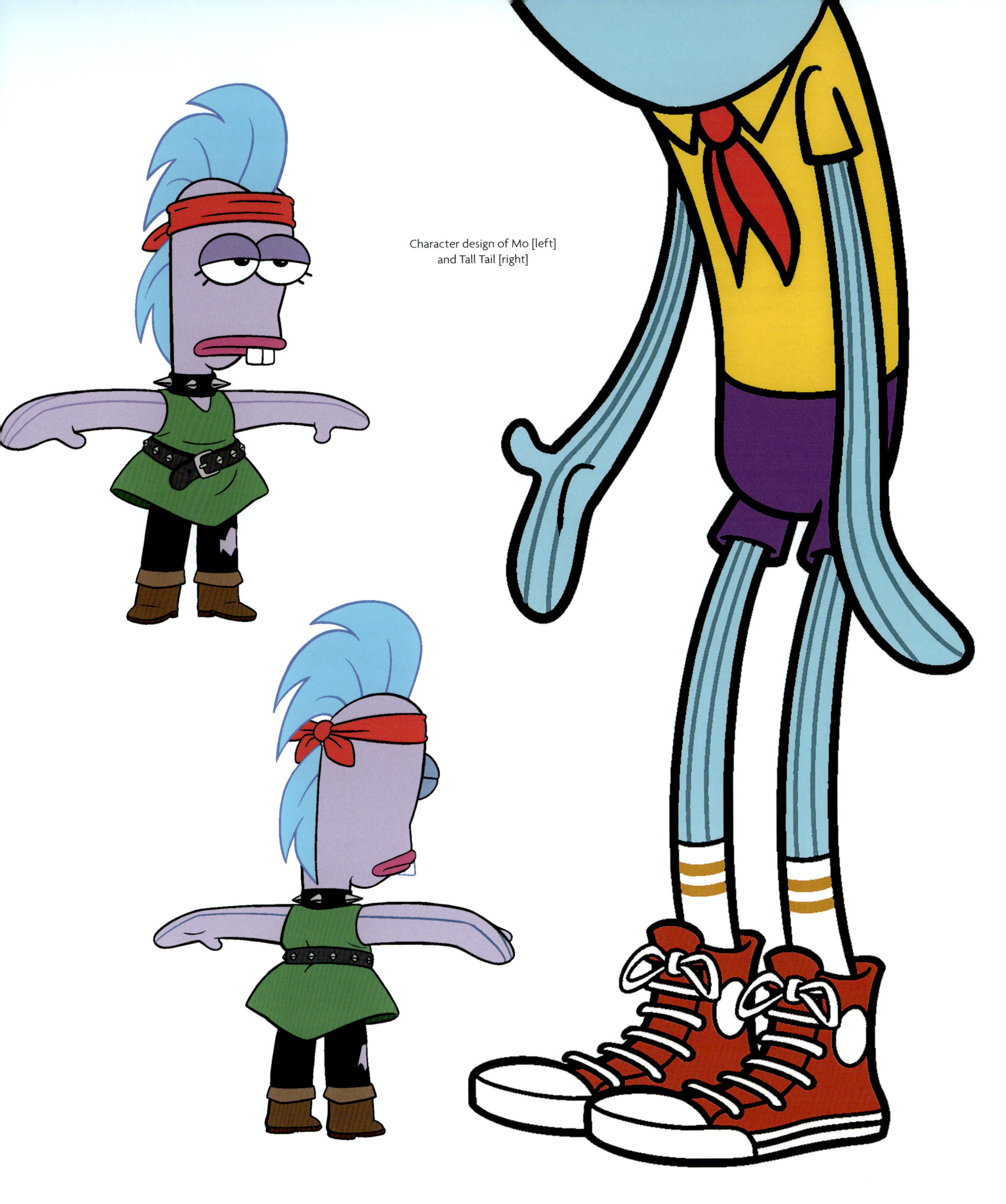

Character design of Mo [left]
and Tall Tail [right]

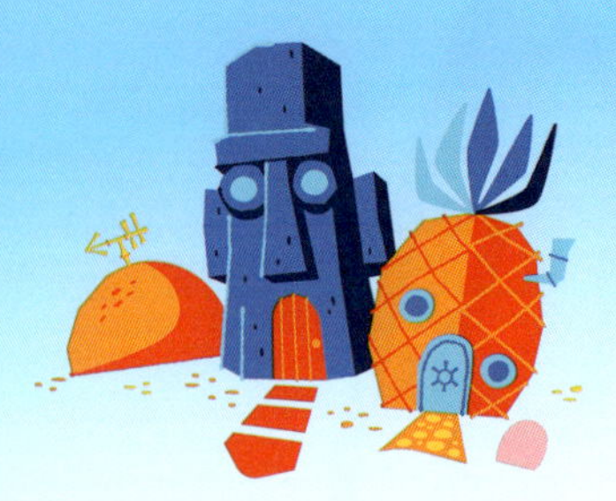

THE TRAWLER CABIN: ROXY (BIG & LITTLE), KIDFERATU, JIMMY BLOBFISH & PREDA TORY

This bunkhouse "is an homage to the monster shows we grew up with like *The Addams Family* and *The Munsters*," says Marc Ceccarelli. The combination of Roxy the angler fish(es), Preda Tory the sea spider, slimy Jimmy, and the humanistic yet slightly horrifying Kidferatu might also be unofficially labeled as residents of the "Weirdo Cabin."

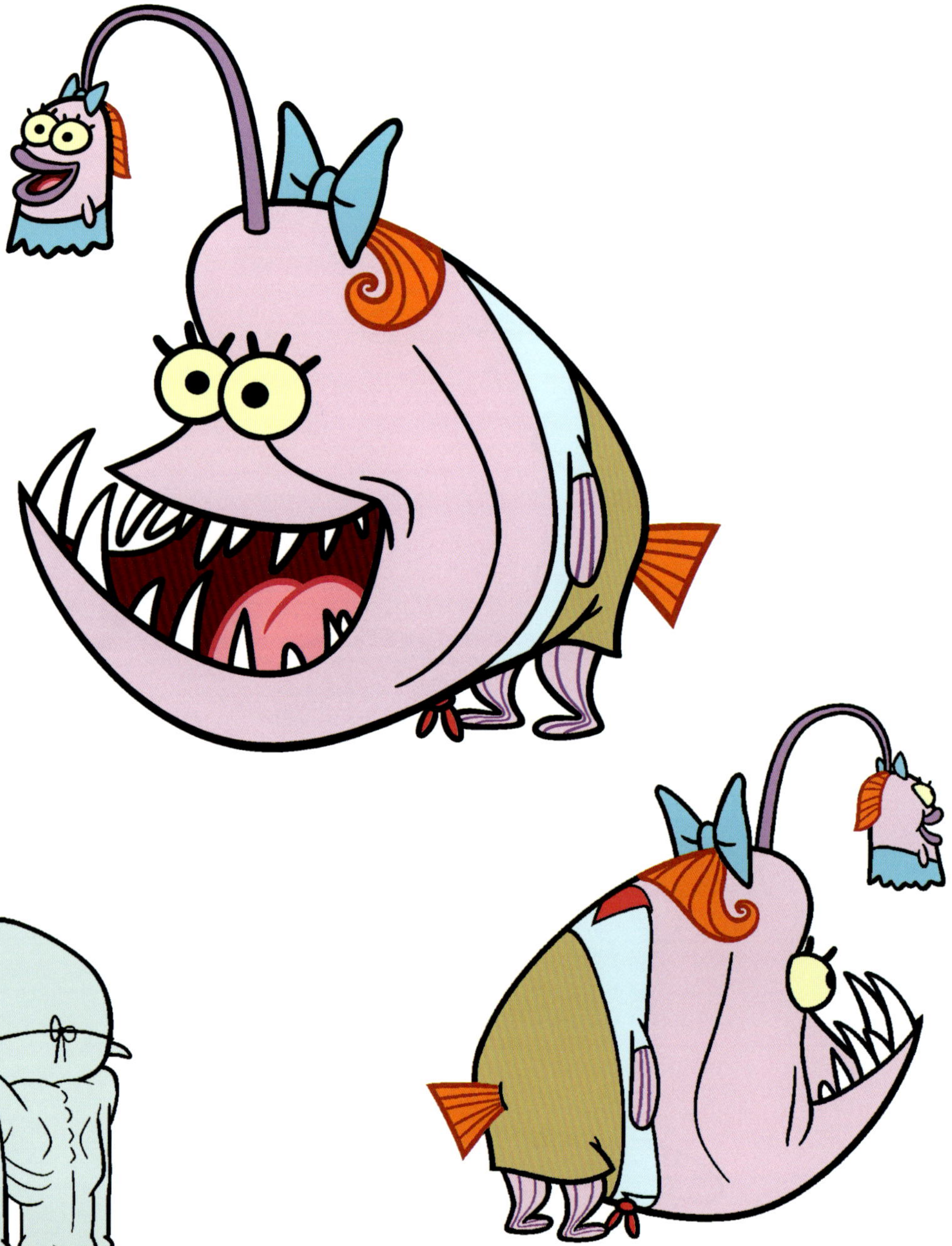

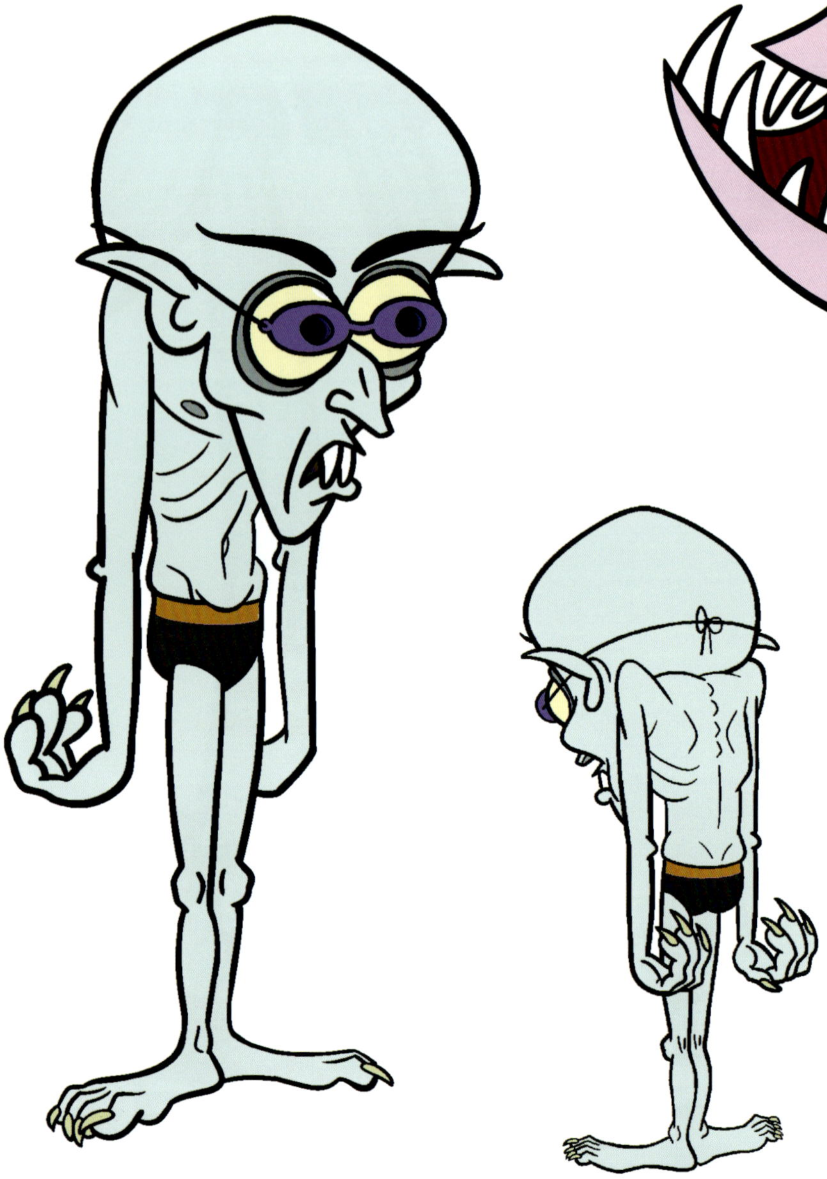

Character design of Kidferatu [left] and the Roxies [right]

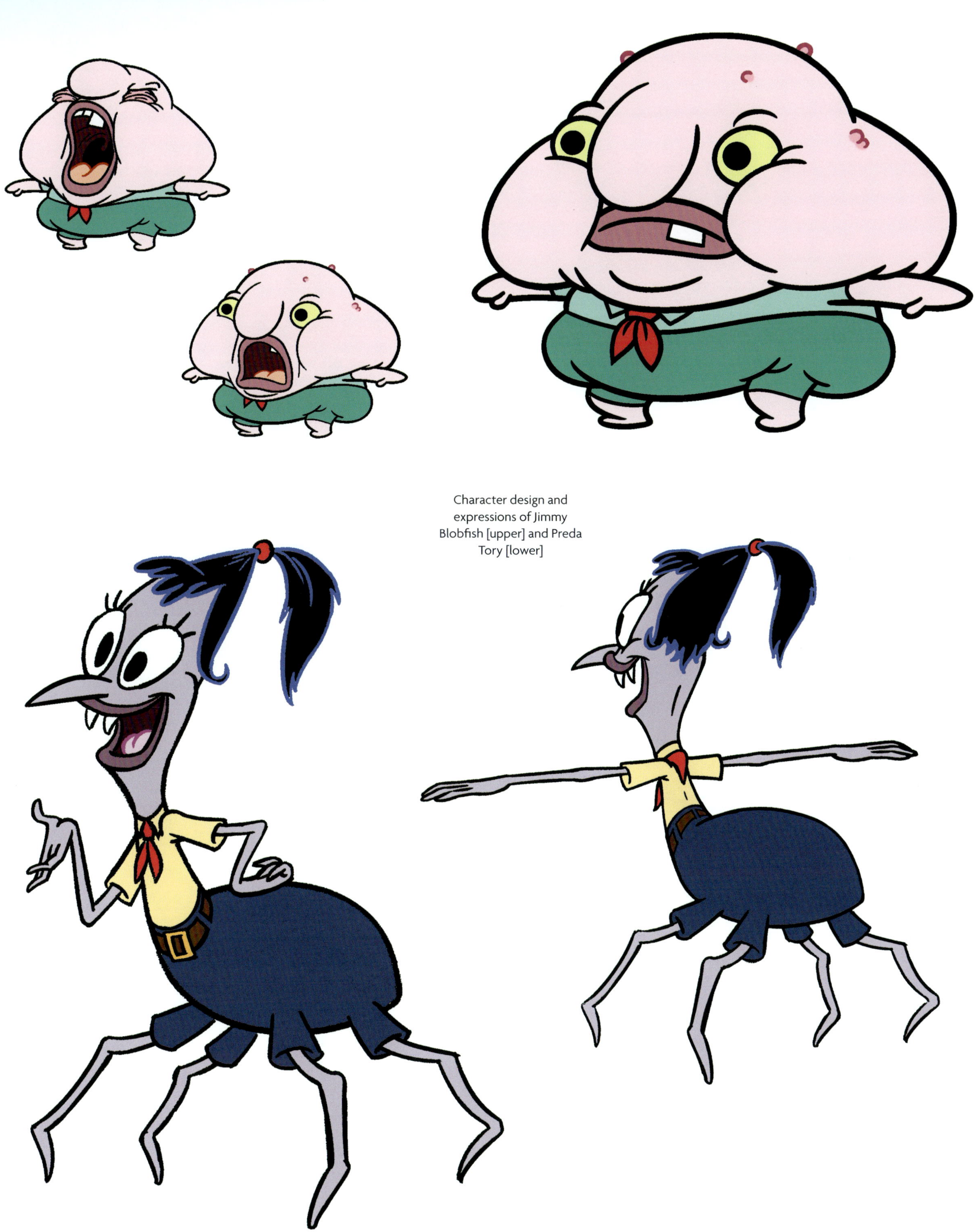

Character design and expressions of Jimmy Blobfish [upper] and Preda Tory [lower]

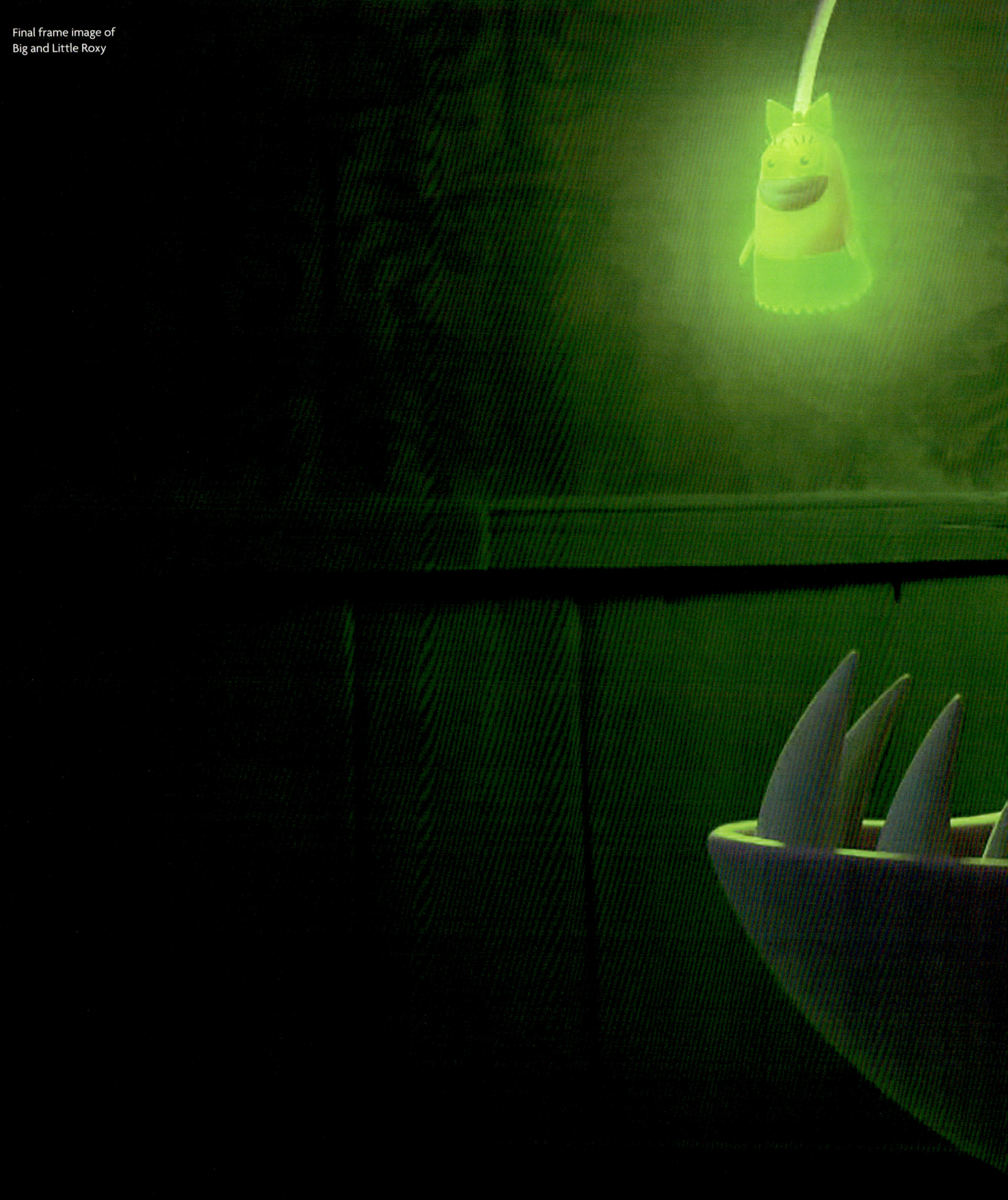

Final frame image of
Big and Little Roxy

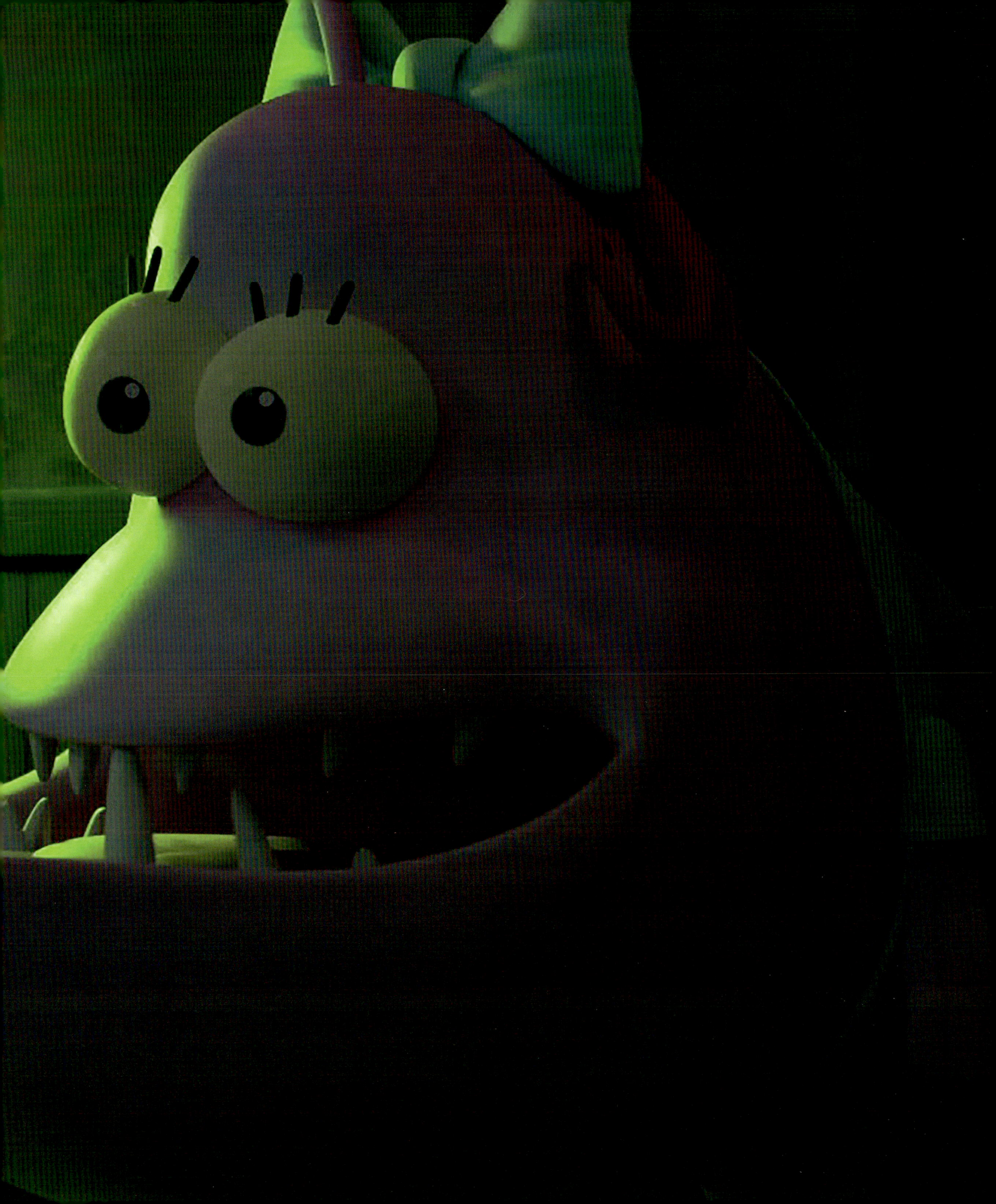

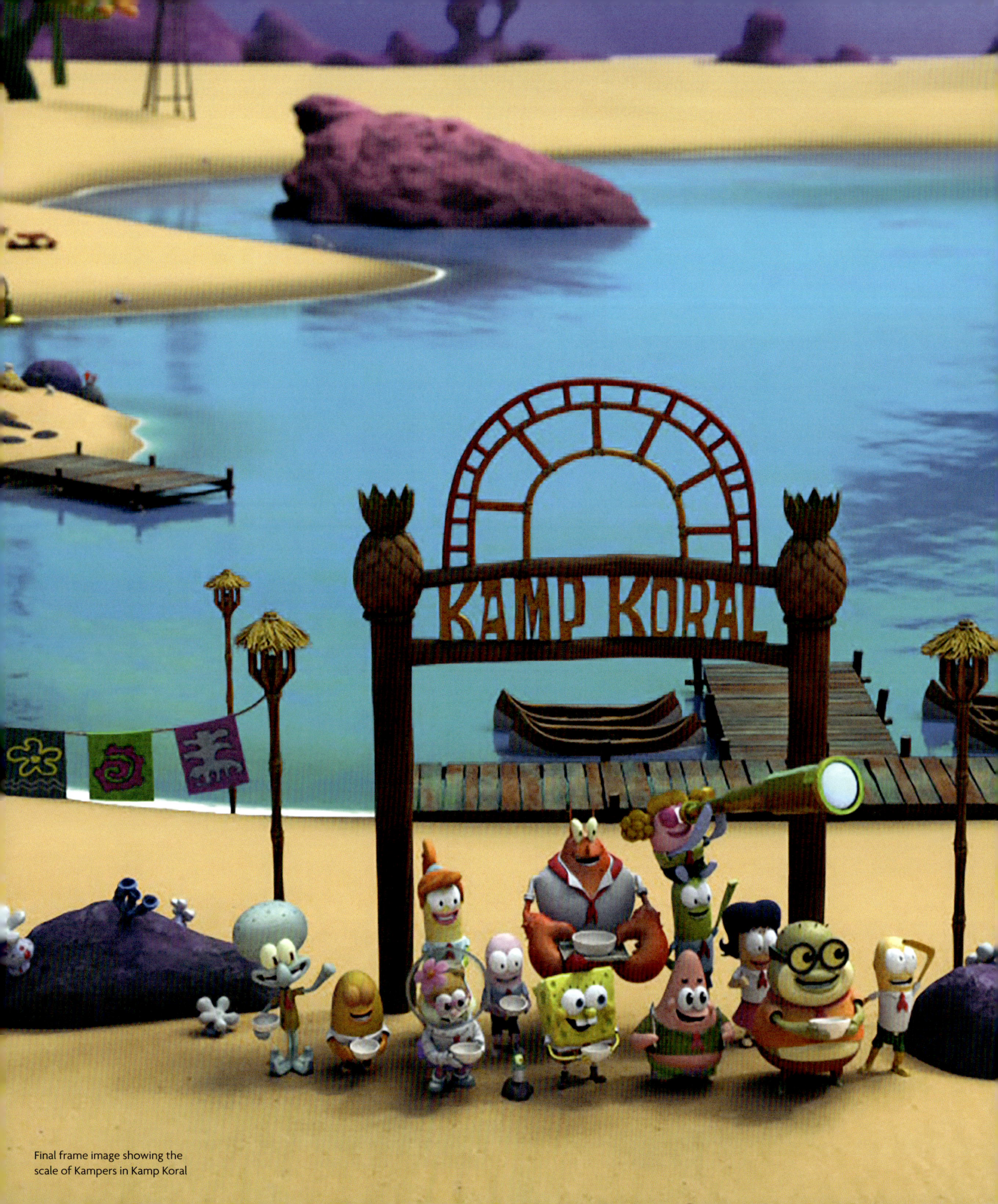

Final frame image showing the
scale of Kampers in Kamp Koral

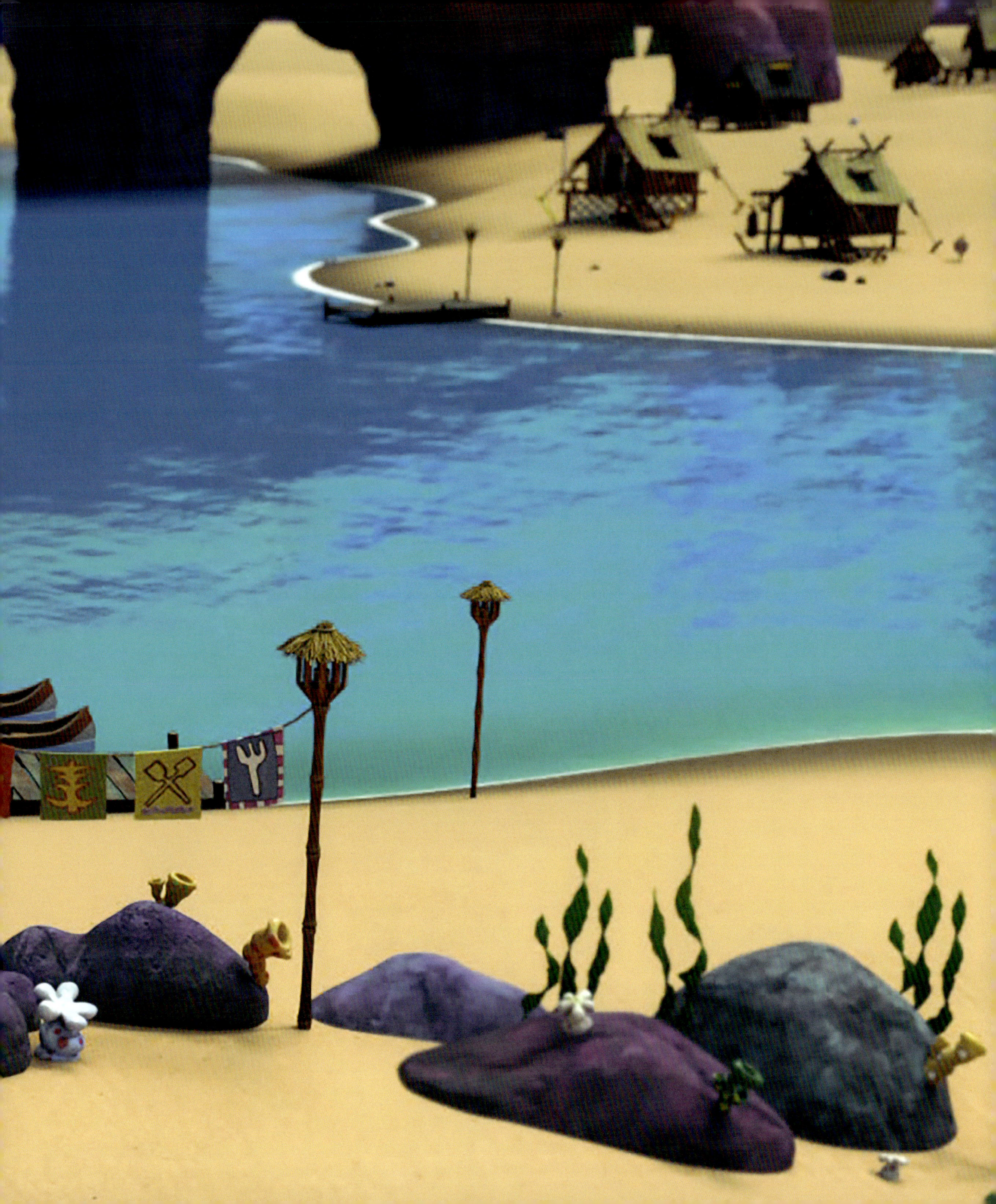

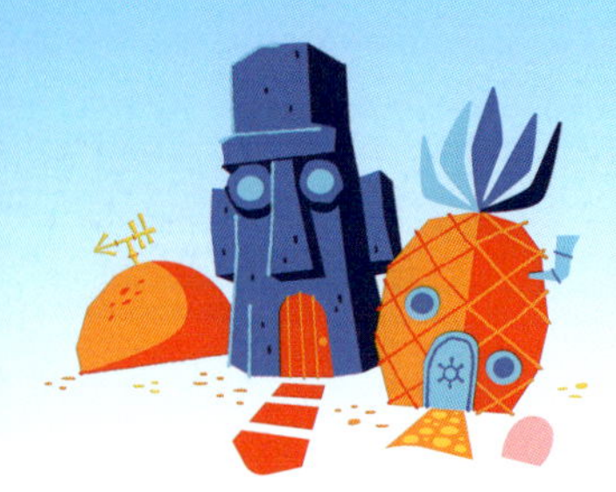

TOURING THE CAMPGROUNDS

Kamp Koral features a bounty of fun spaces, plenty to keep rambunctious campers entertained during their summer stays.

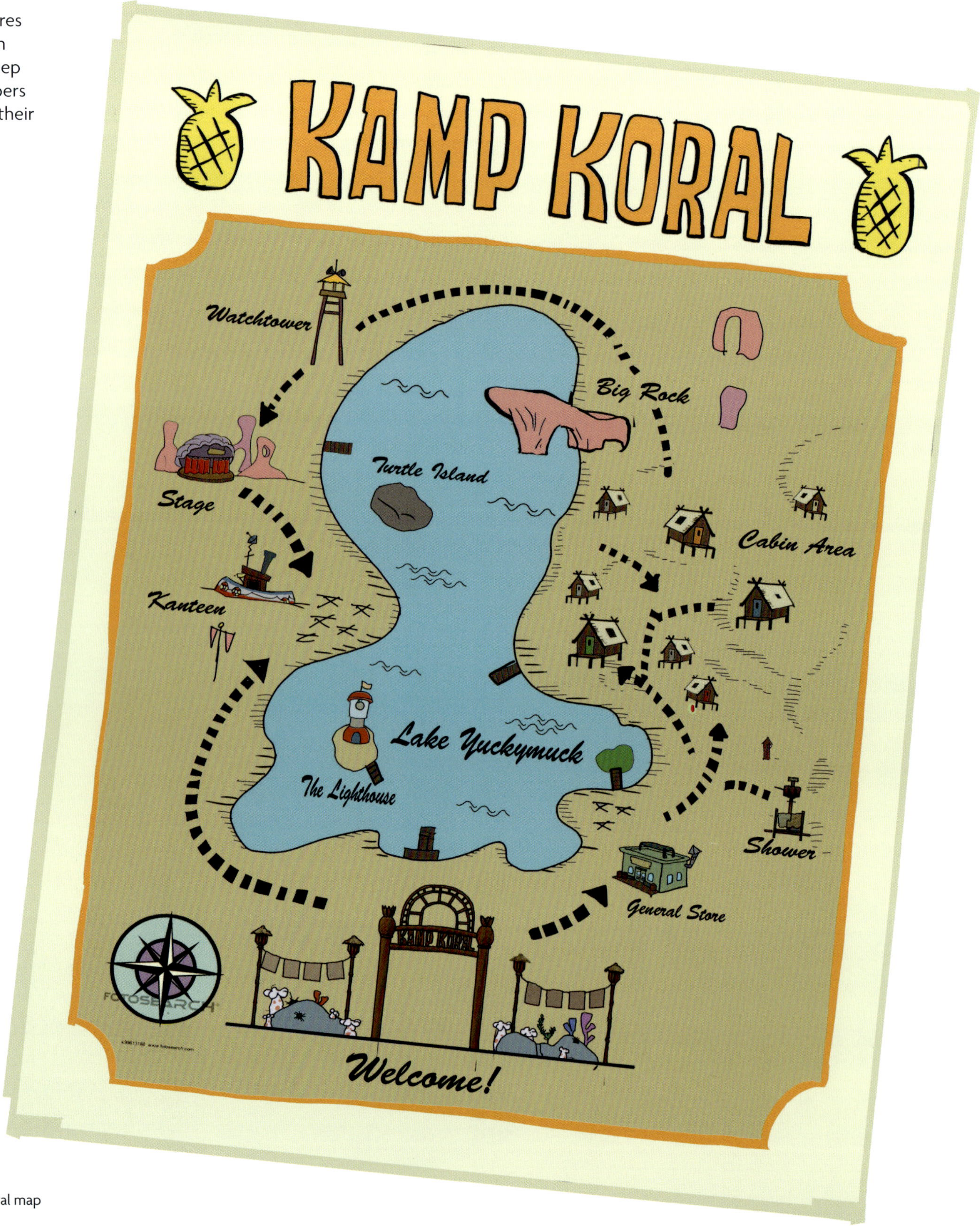

2D version of Kamp Koral map

THE KRUSTY KANTEEN

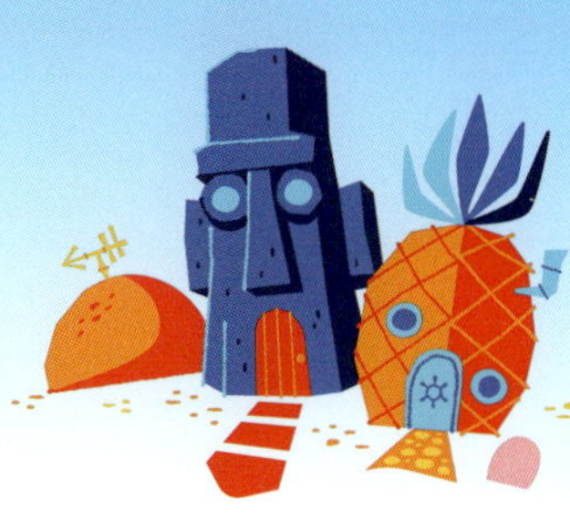

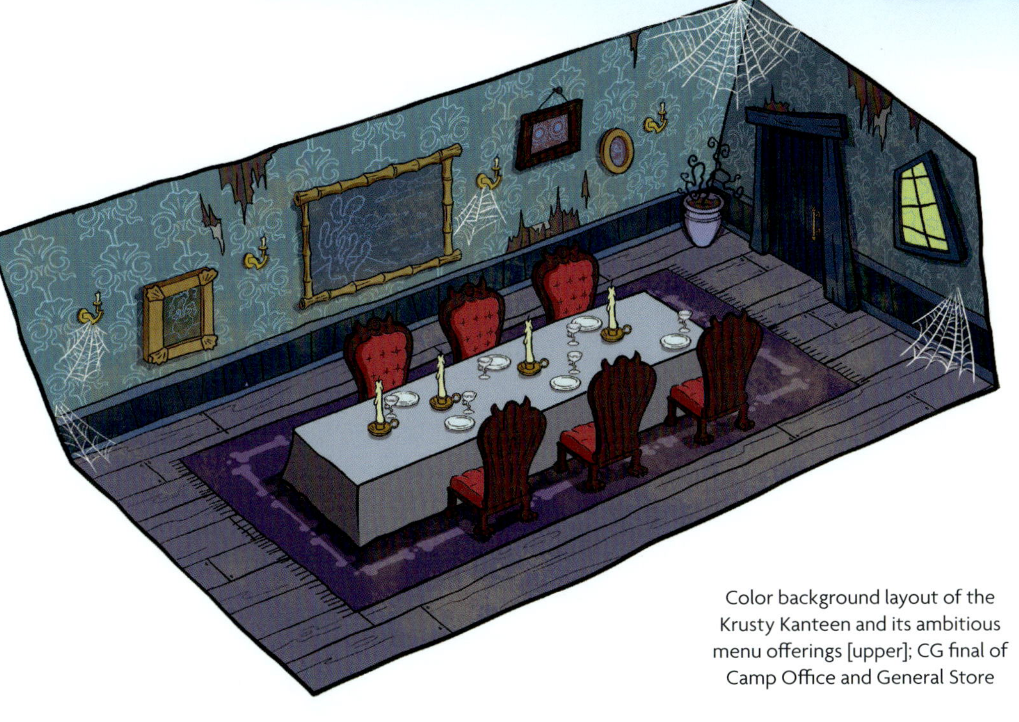

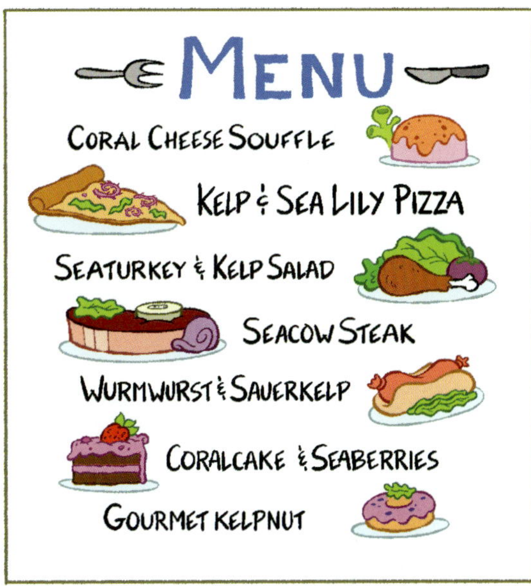

Color background layout of the Krusty Kanteen and its ambitious menu offerings [upper]; CG final of Camp Office and General Store

CAMP OFFICE & GENERAL STORE

The Camp Office is where Camp Director Krabs handles operations and discipline duties as needed, but the General Store is more his wheelhouse as it allows him to channel his true passion—making money—into the sales of snacks, toys, and other sundry items to his campers.

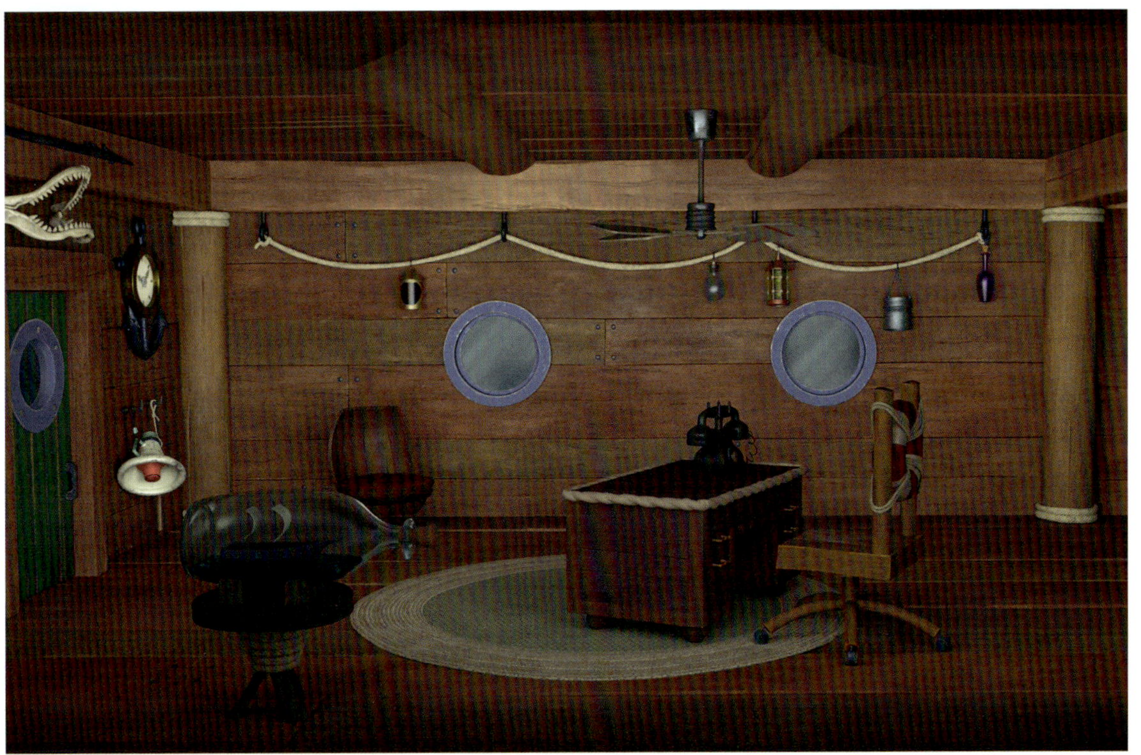

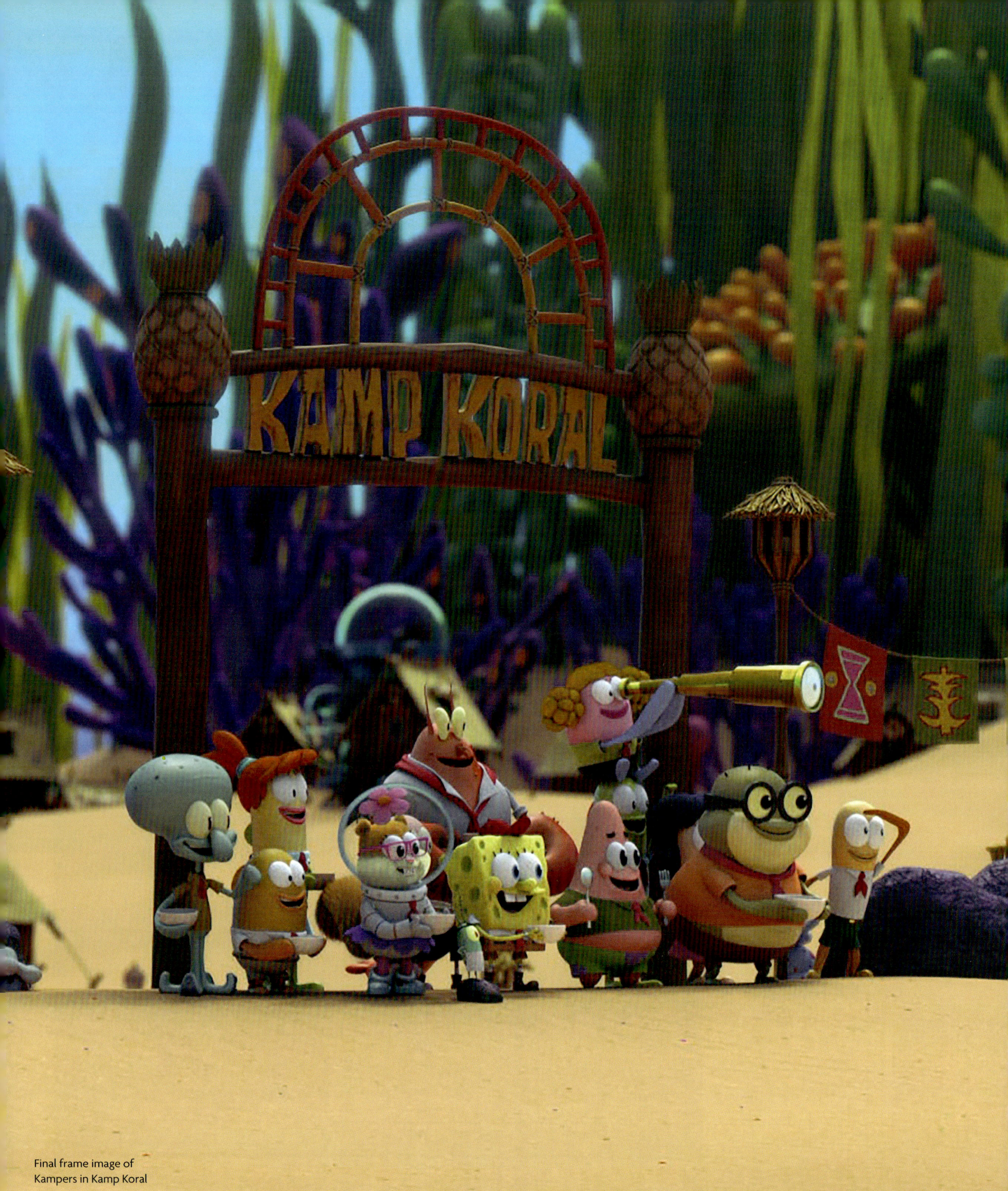

Final frame image of
Kampers in Kamp Koral

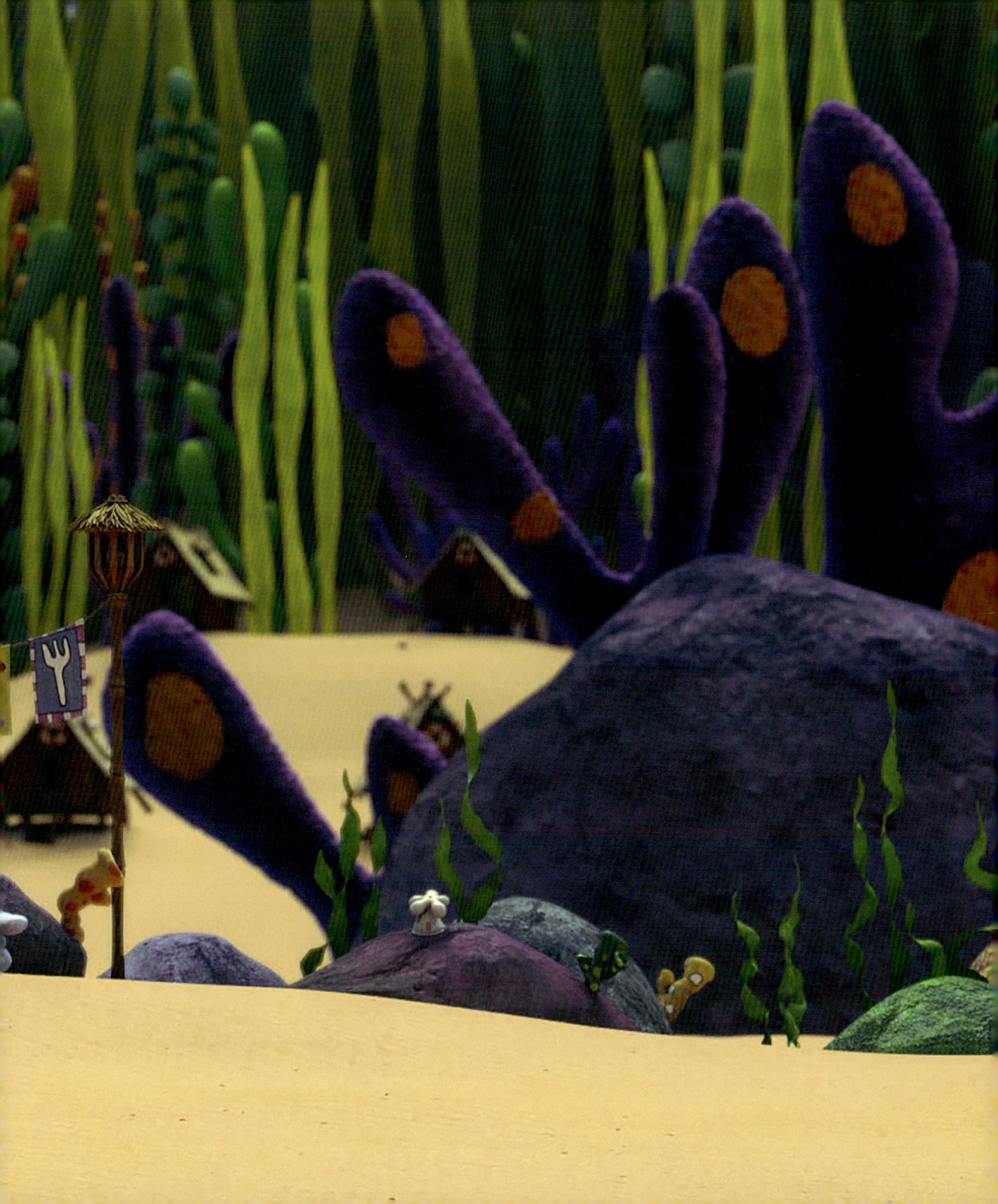

MRS. PUFF'S LIGHTHOUSE & GARDEN

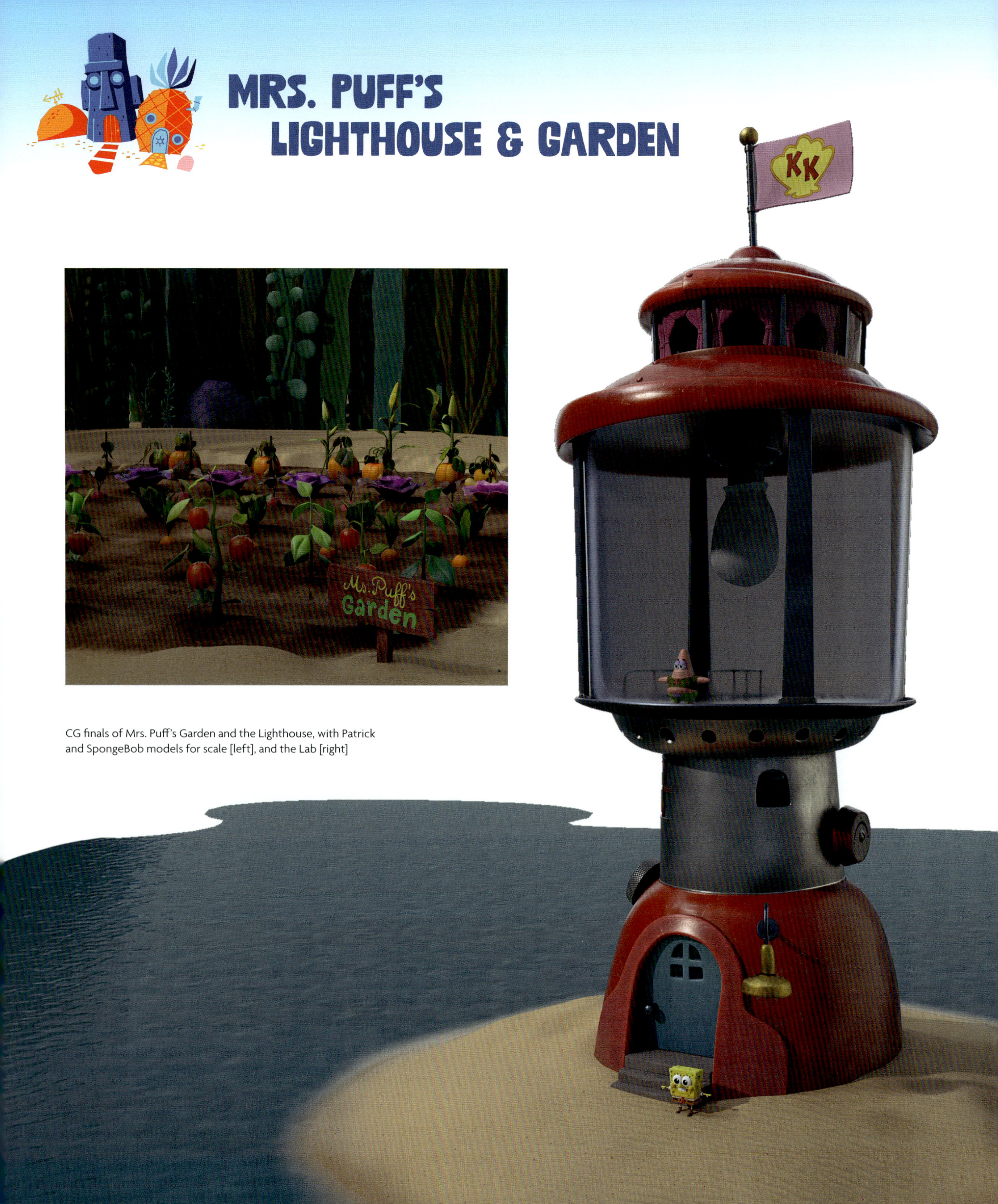

CG finals of Mrs. Puff's Garden and the Lighthouse, with Patrick and SpongeBob models for scale [left], and the Lab [right]

PLANKTON & KAREN'S LAB

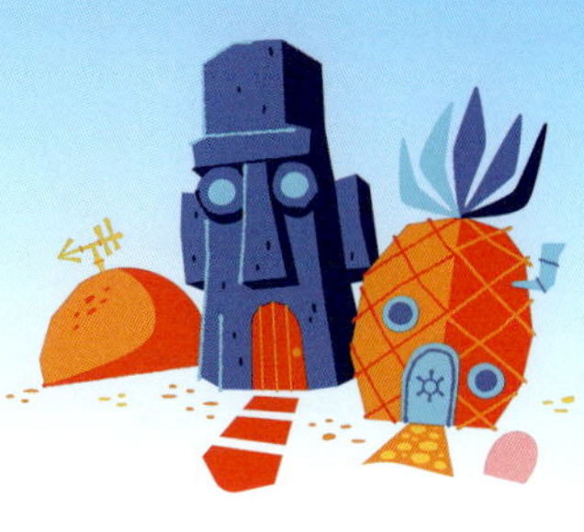

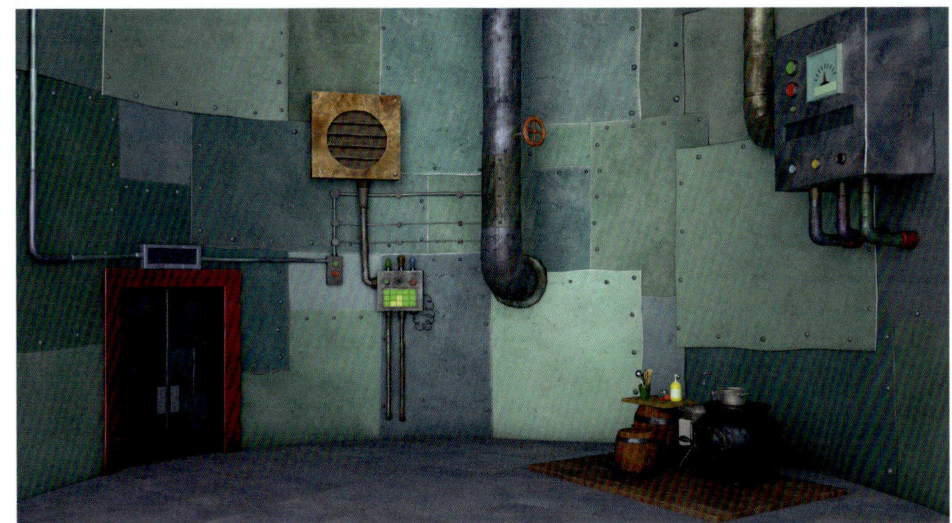

Young Plankton and Karen have their own secret laboratory underneath the cafeteria in Kamp Koral, giving them the space to cook up dastardly plans such as mutant snacks offered in the Blender Vender; even more concerning is the science project to try to create a Mr. Krabs clone. "Plankton's rivalry with Krabs apparently predates the origin of the Krabby Patty secret formula. Who knew?" wonders Marc Ceccarelli.

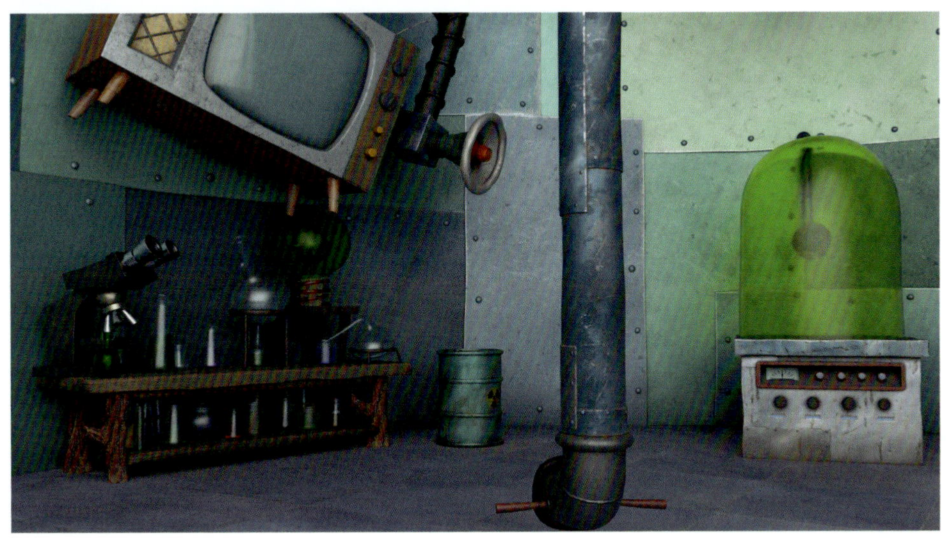

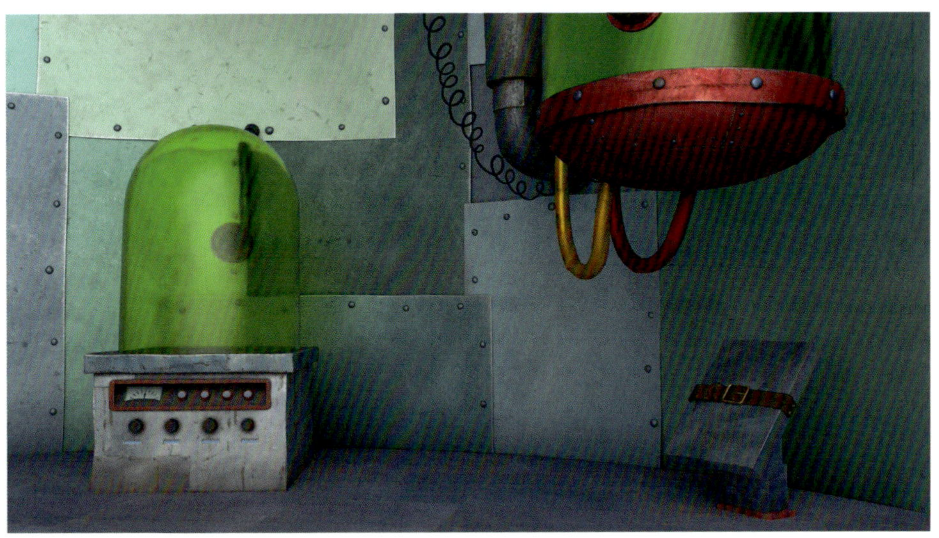

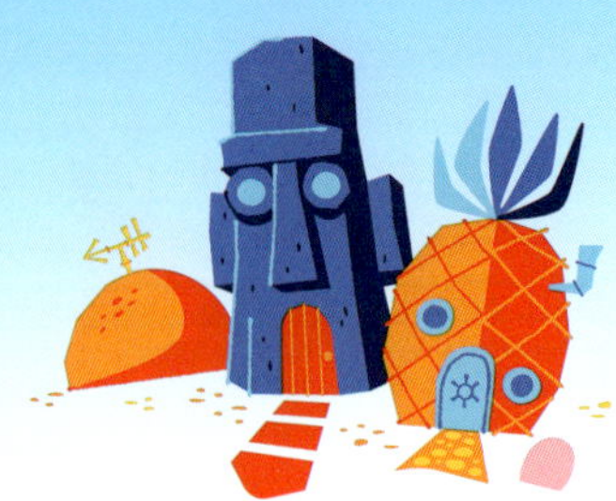

JELLY MEADOWS

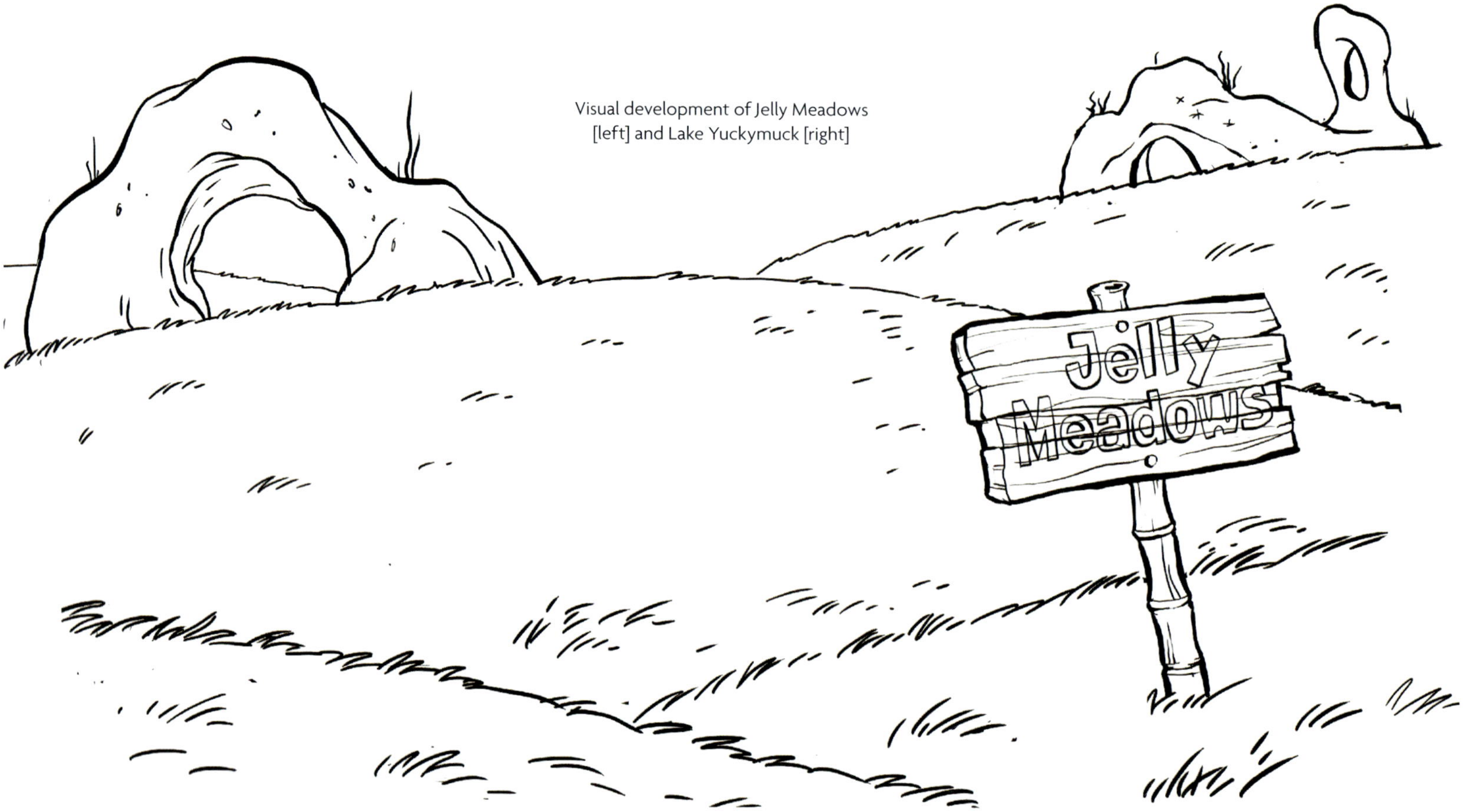

Visual development of Jelly Meadows [left] and Lake Yuckymuck [right]

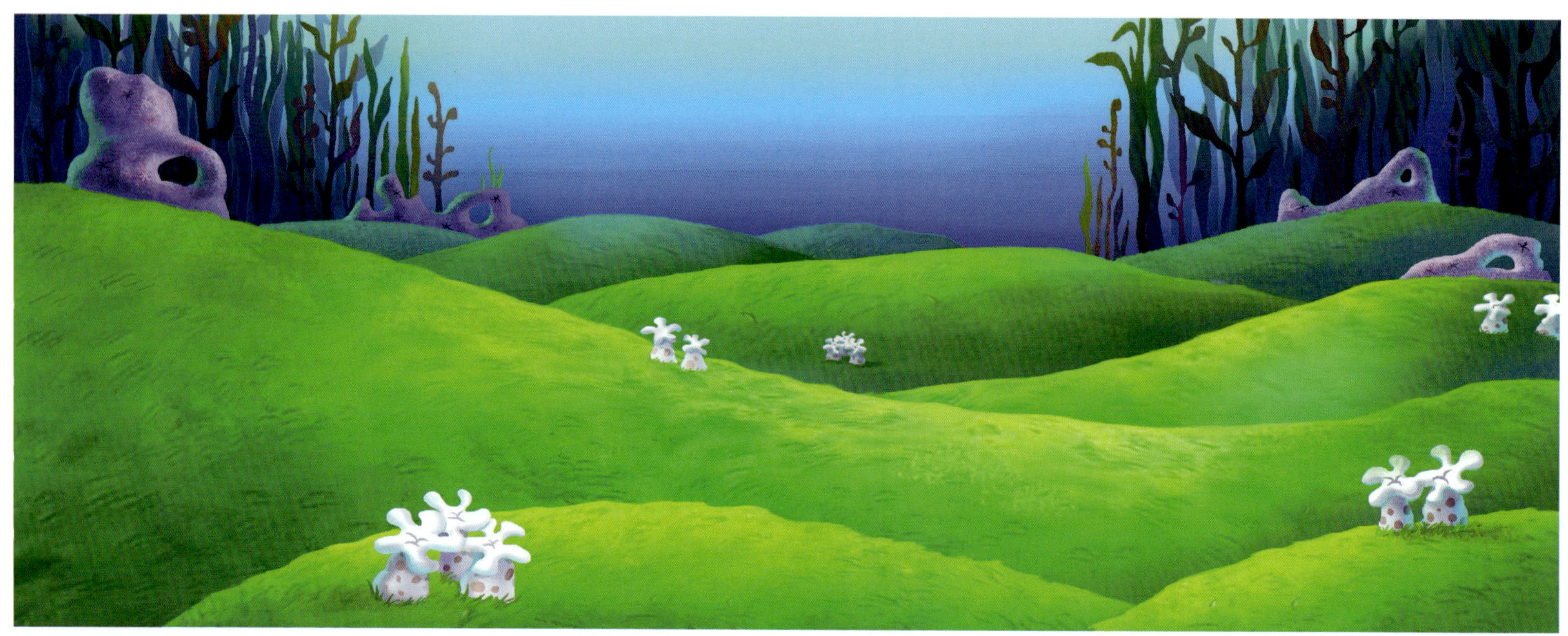

LAKE YUCKYMUCK

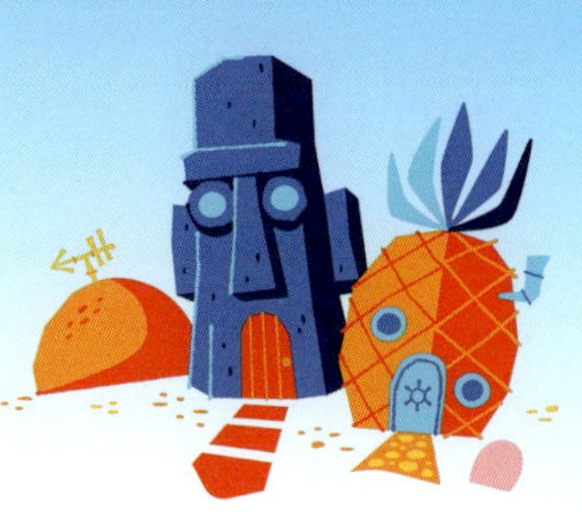

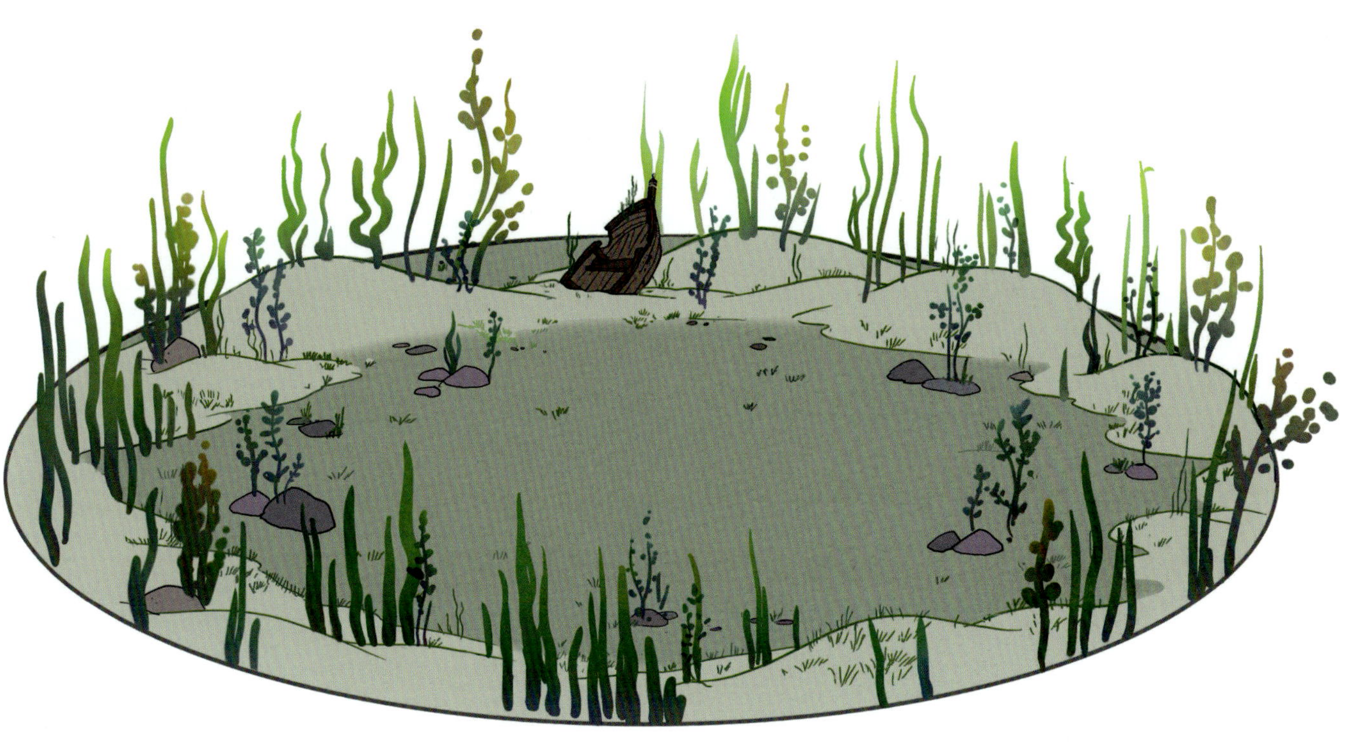

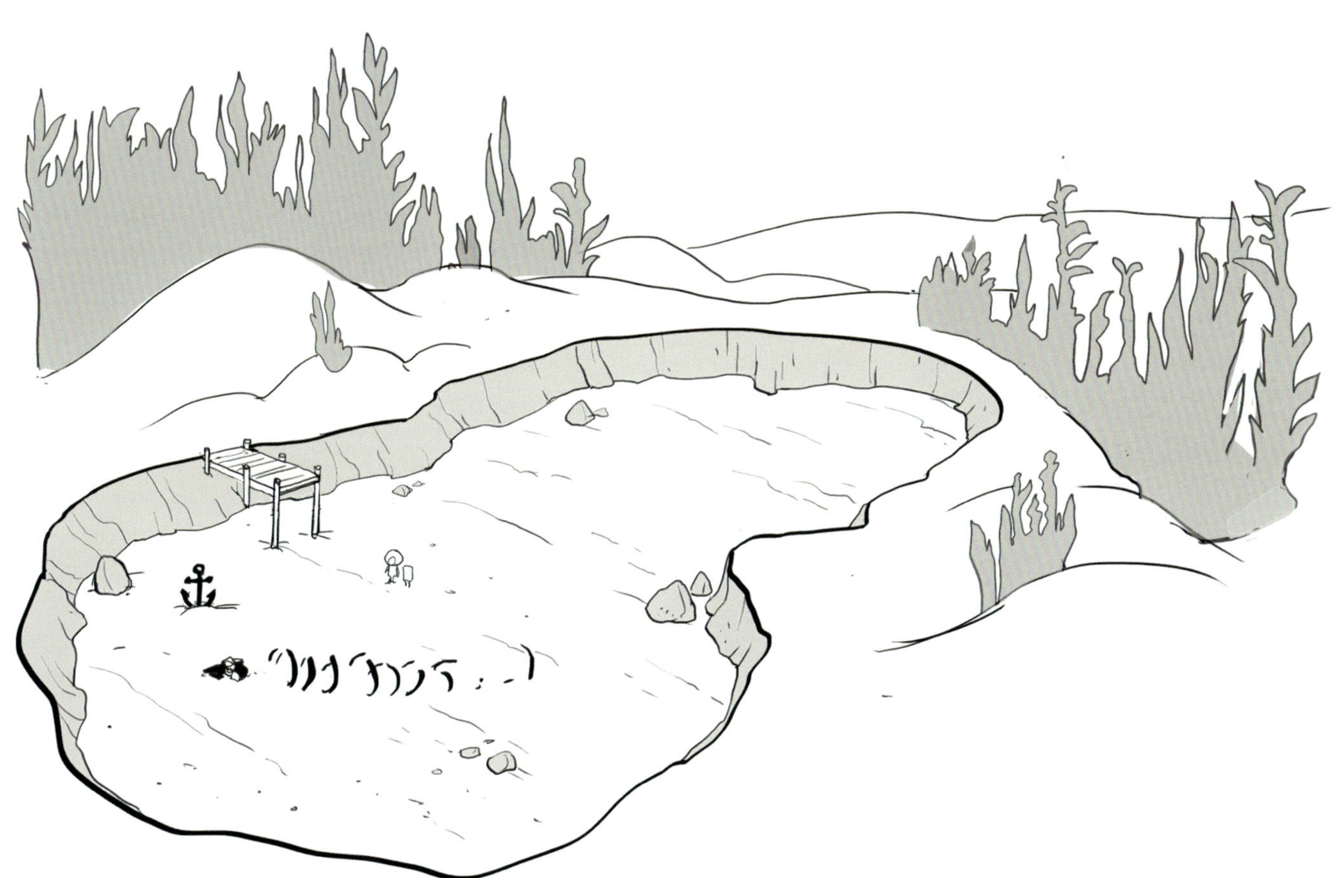

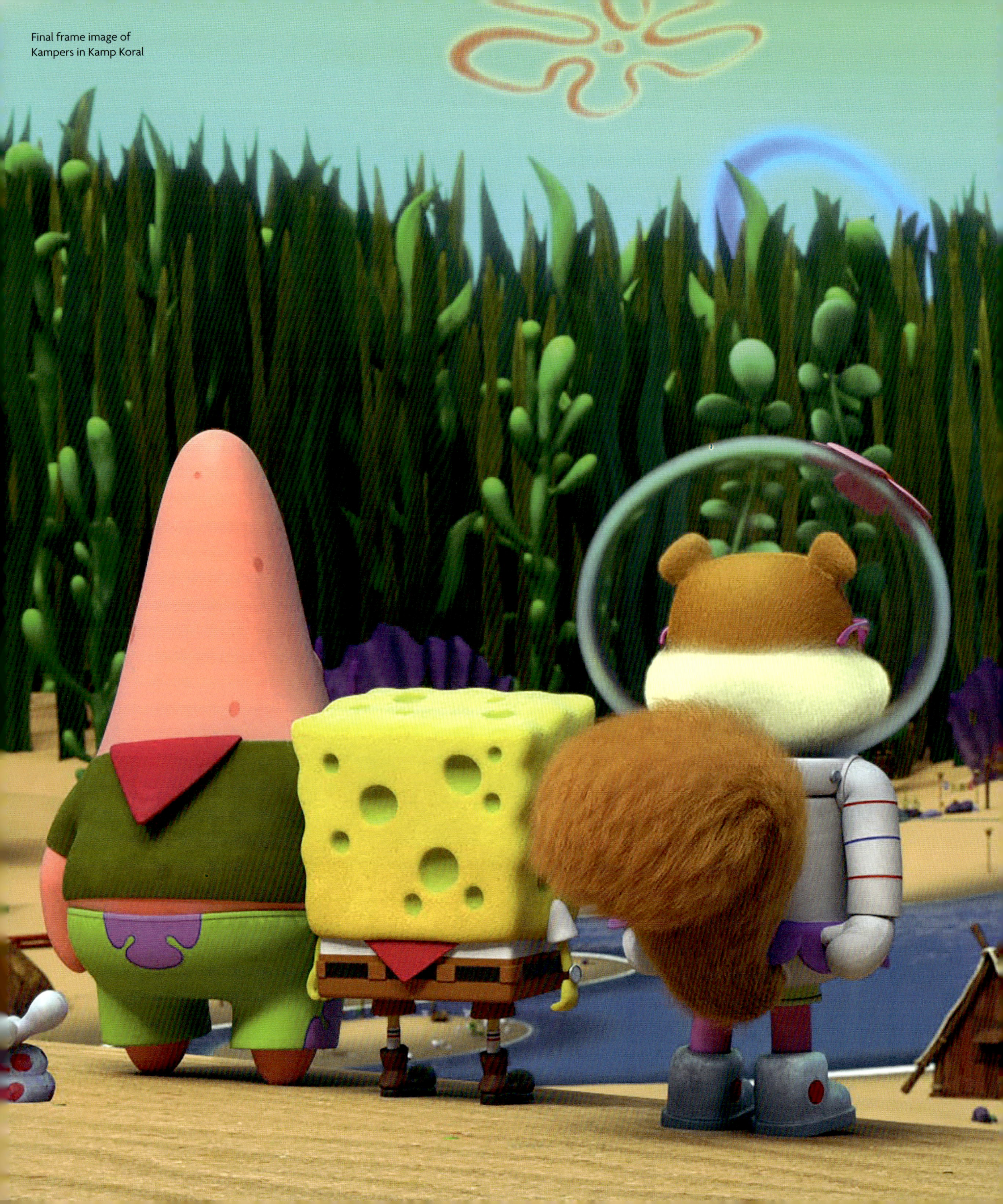

Final frame image of
Kampers in Kamp Koral

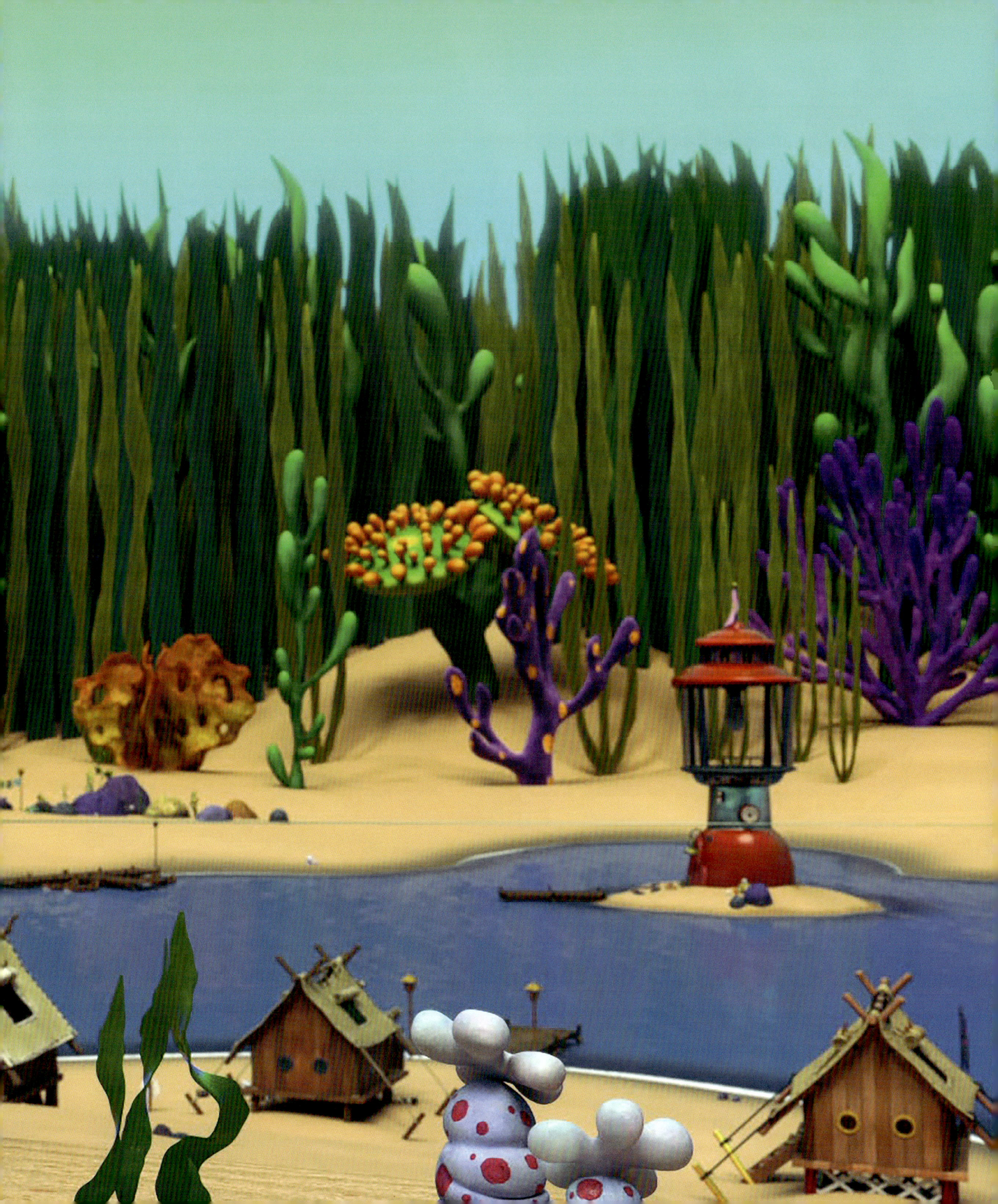

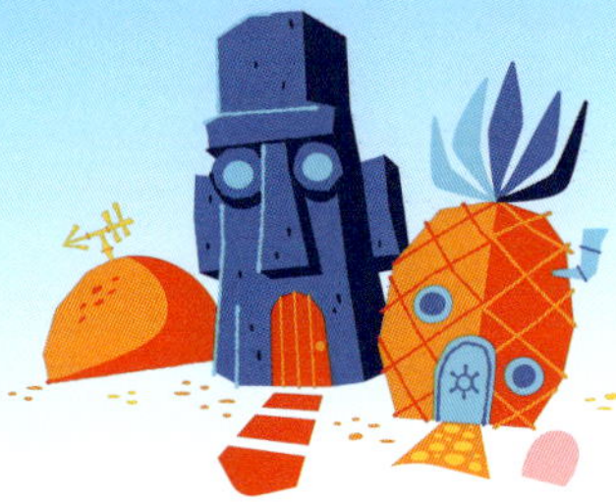

KELP FOREST

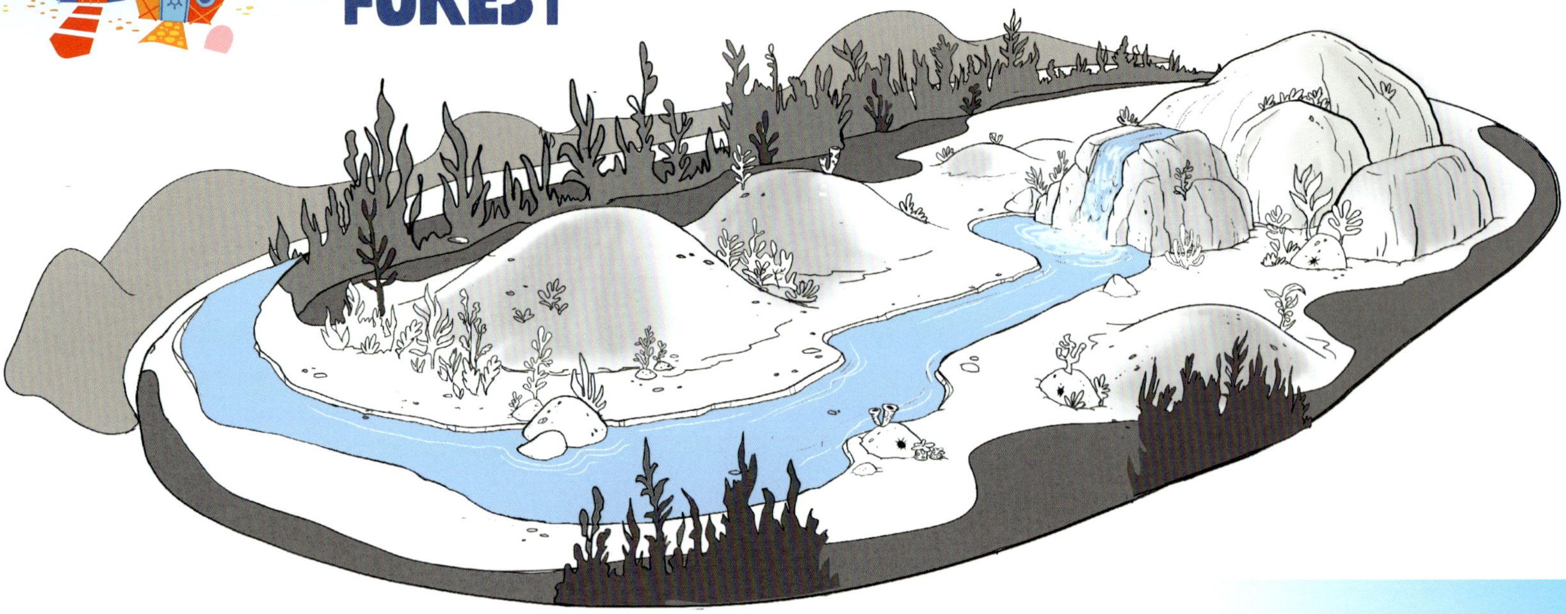

PORPOISE PARK

Visual development of Kelp Forest [upper] and Porpoise Park [lower]

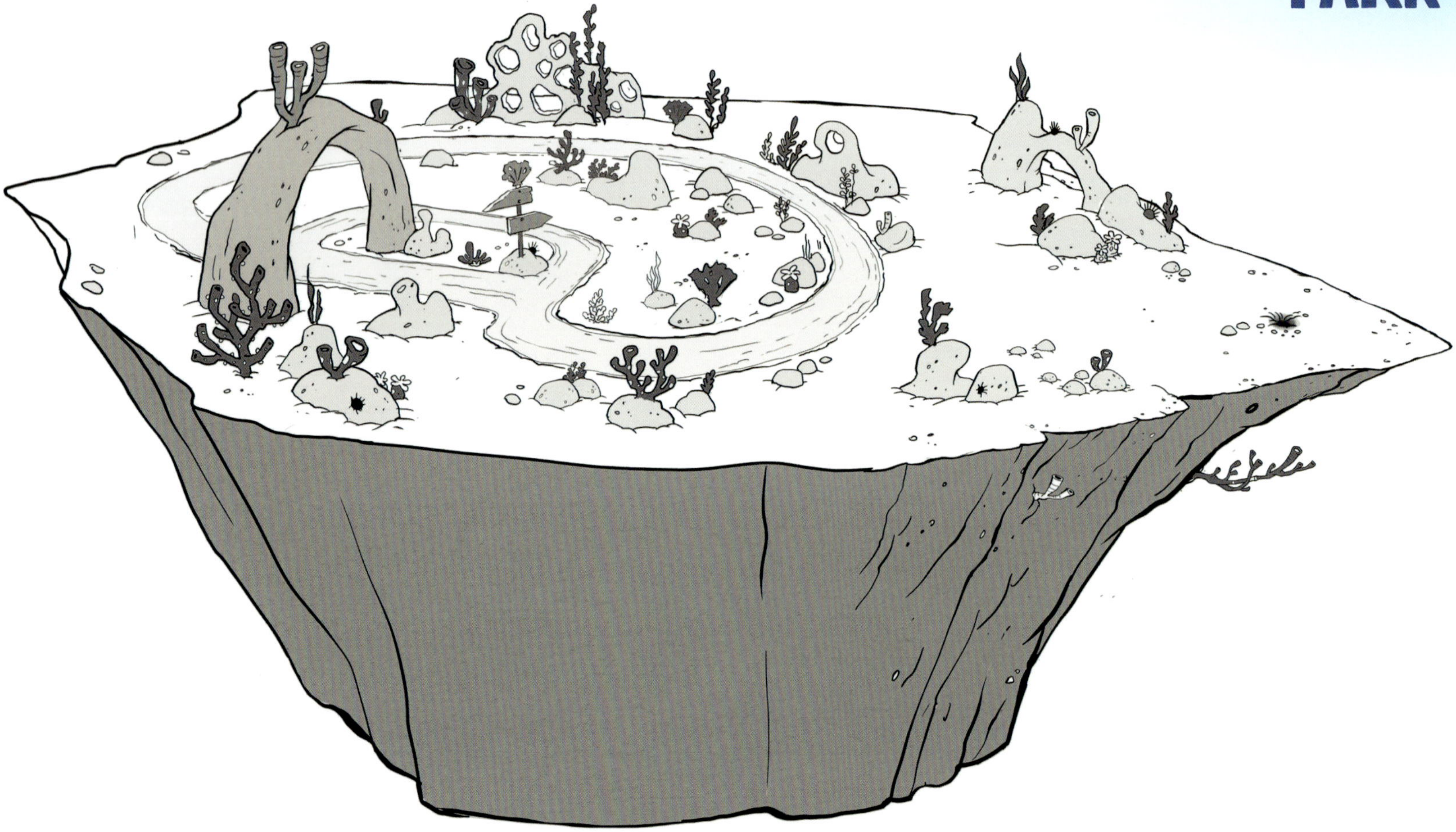

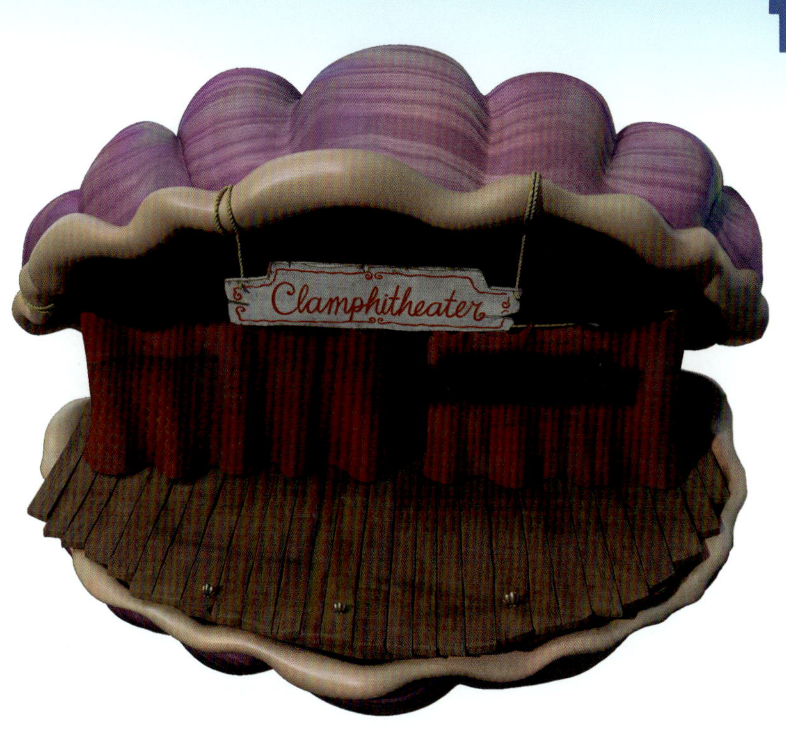

THE CLAMPITHEATER

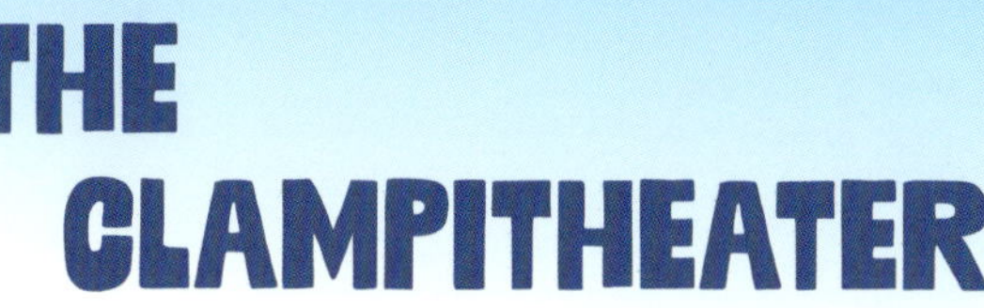

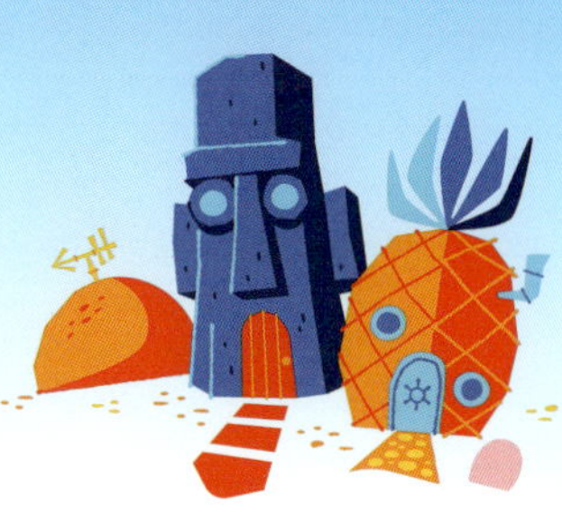

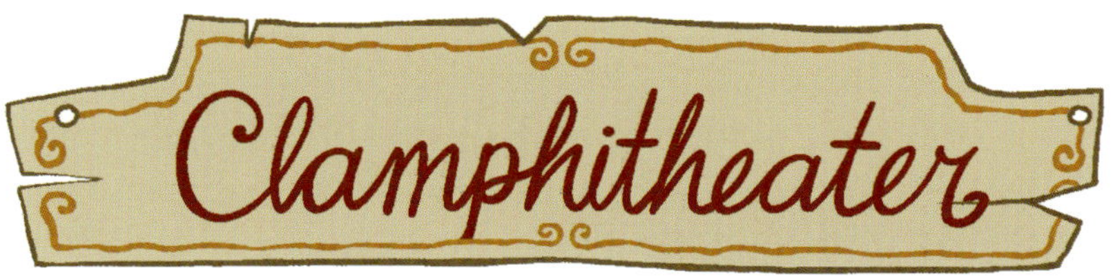

CG final of Clamphitheater and its 2D sign design [upper]; CG final [lower left] and 2D set elements, and CG rendered model [lower right] of Narlene and Nobby's shack

NARLENE & NOBBY'S SHACK

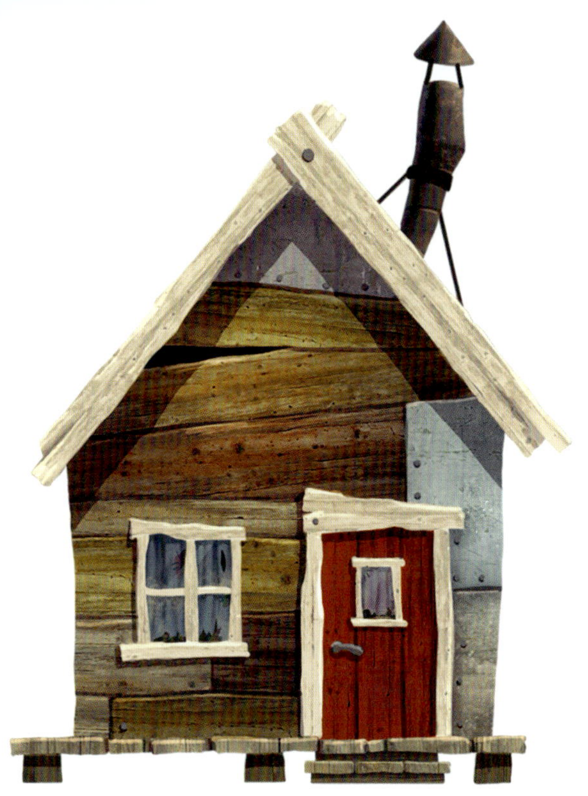

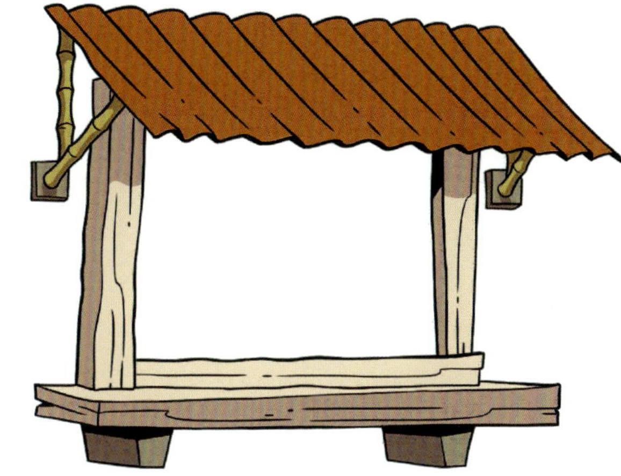

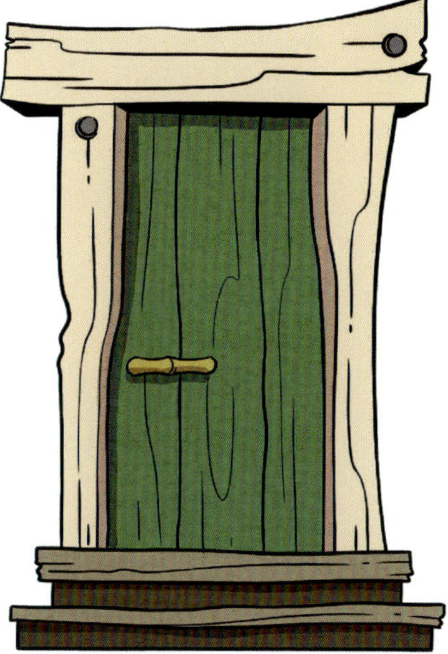

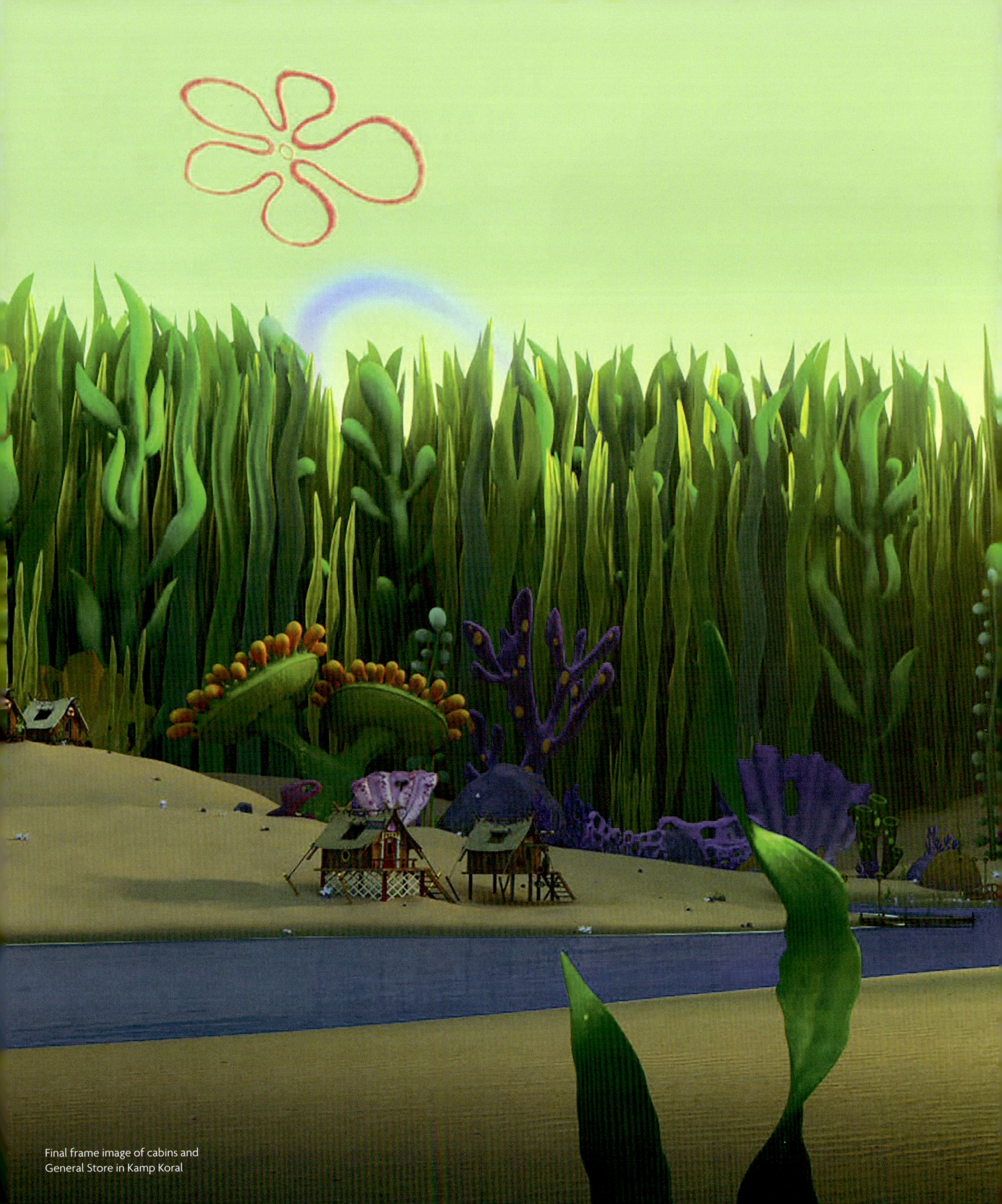

Final frame image of cabins and General Store in Kamp Koral

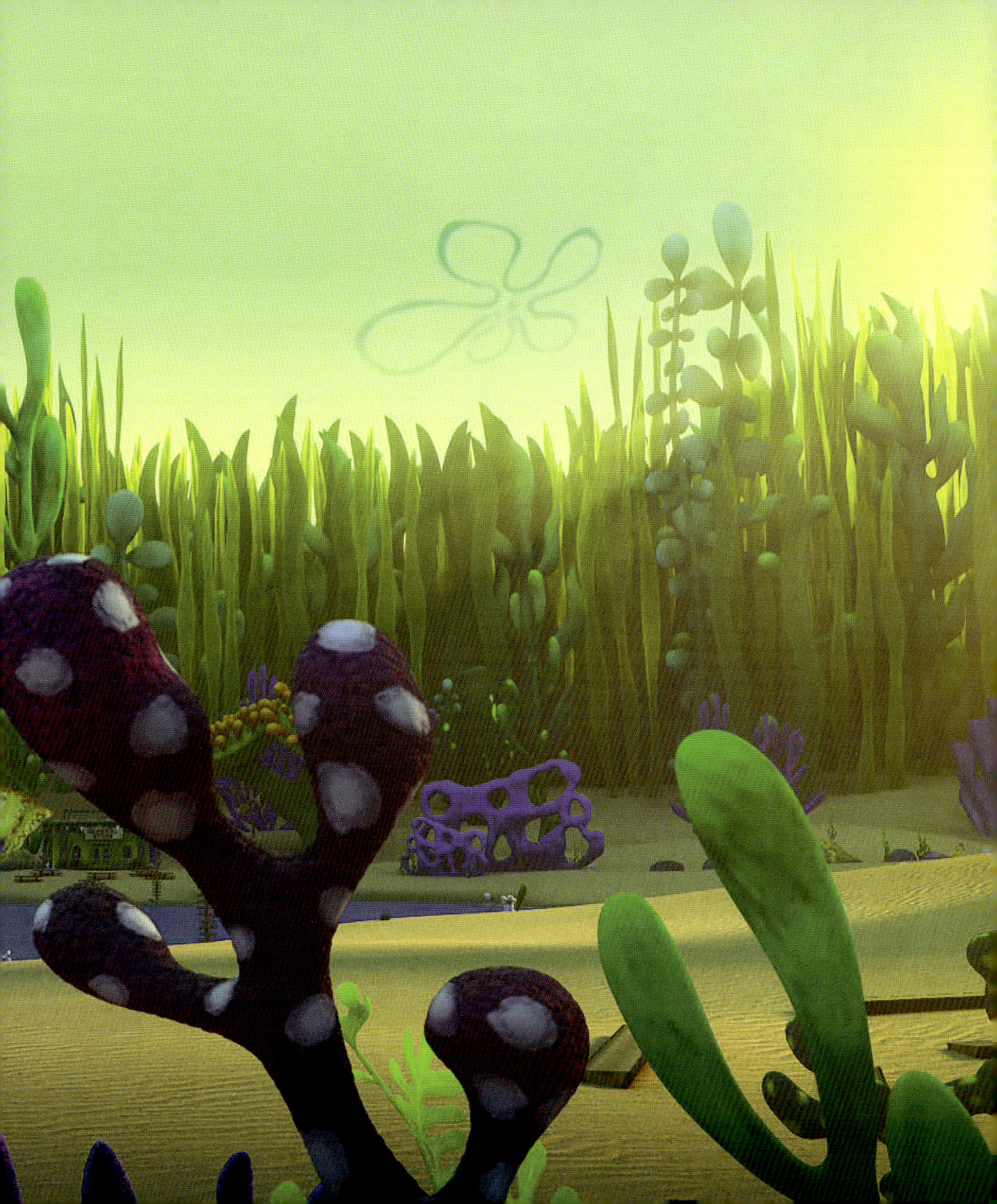

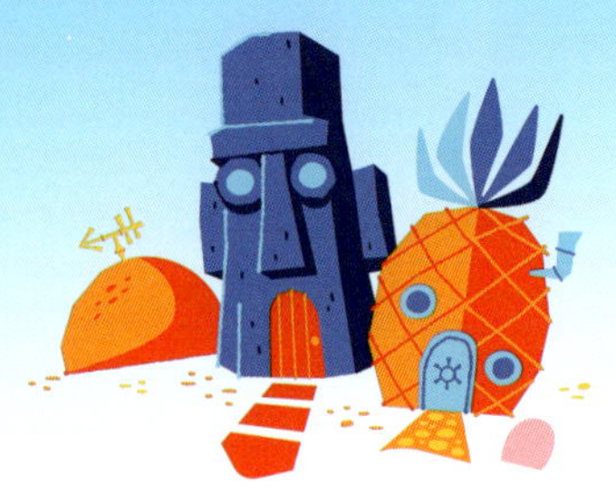

CABINS

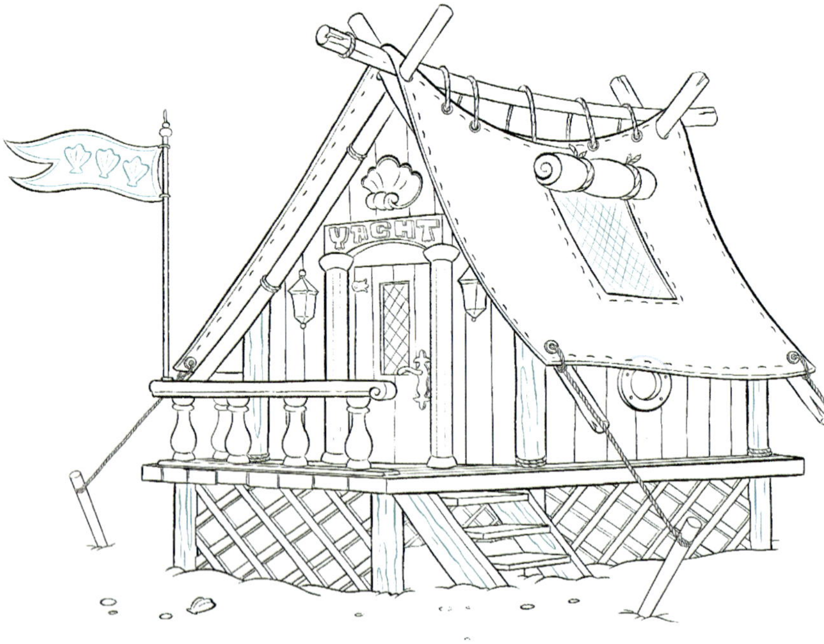

Line art concepts of Yacht [upper left] and Pontoon [lower left] cabins, plus cabin interior [right]

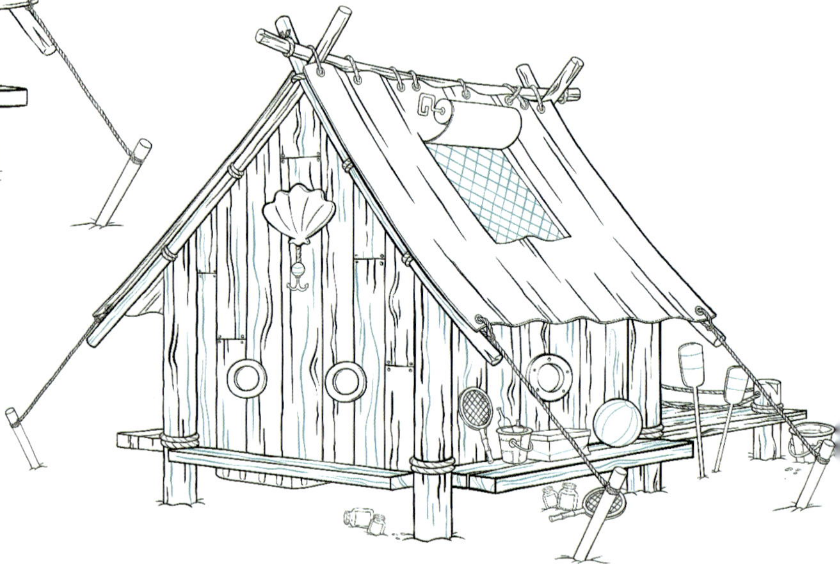

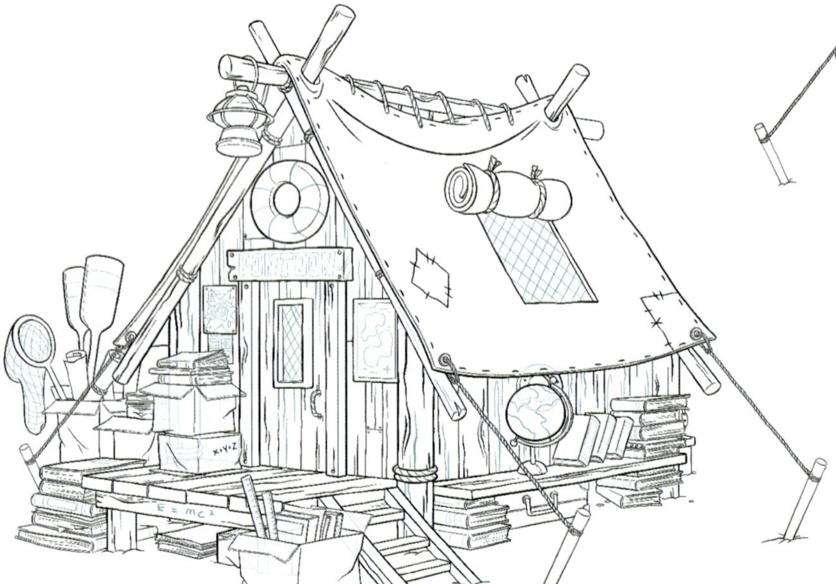

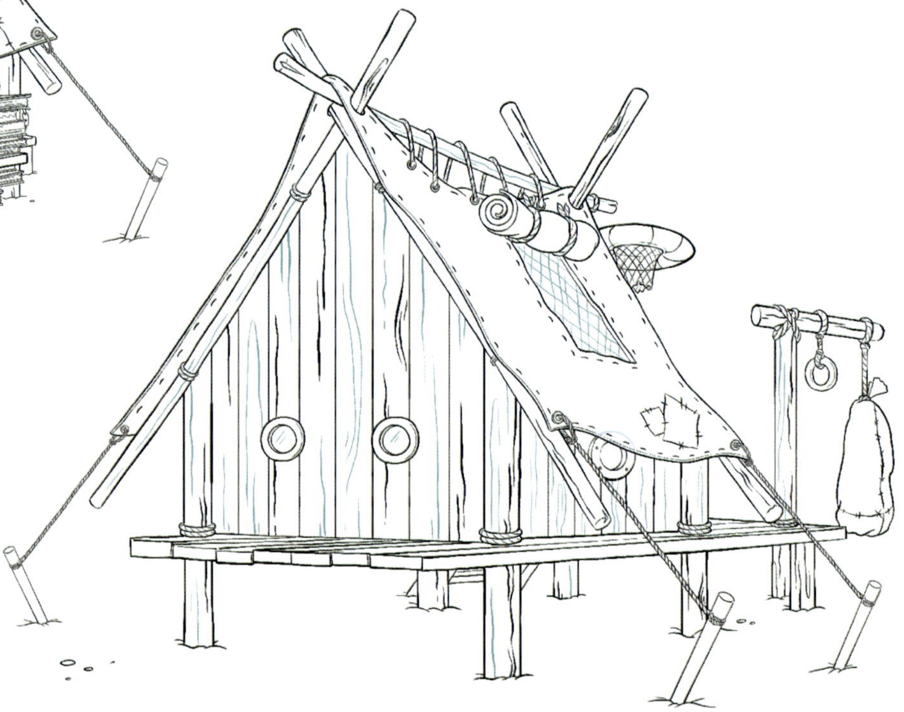

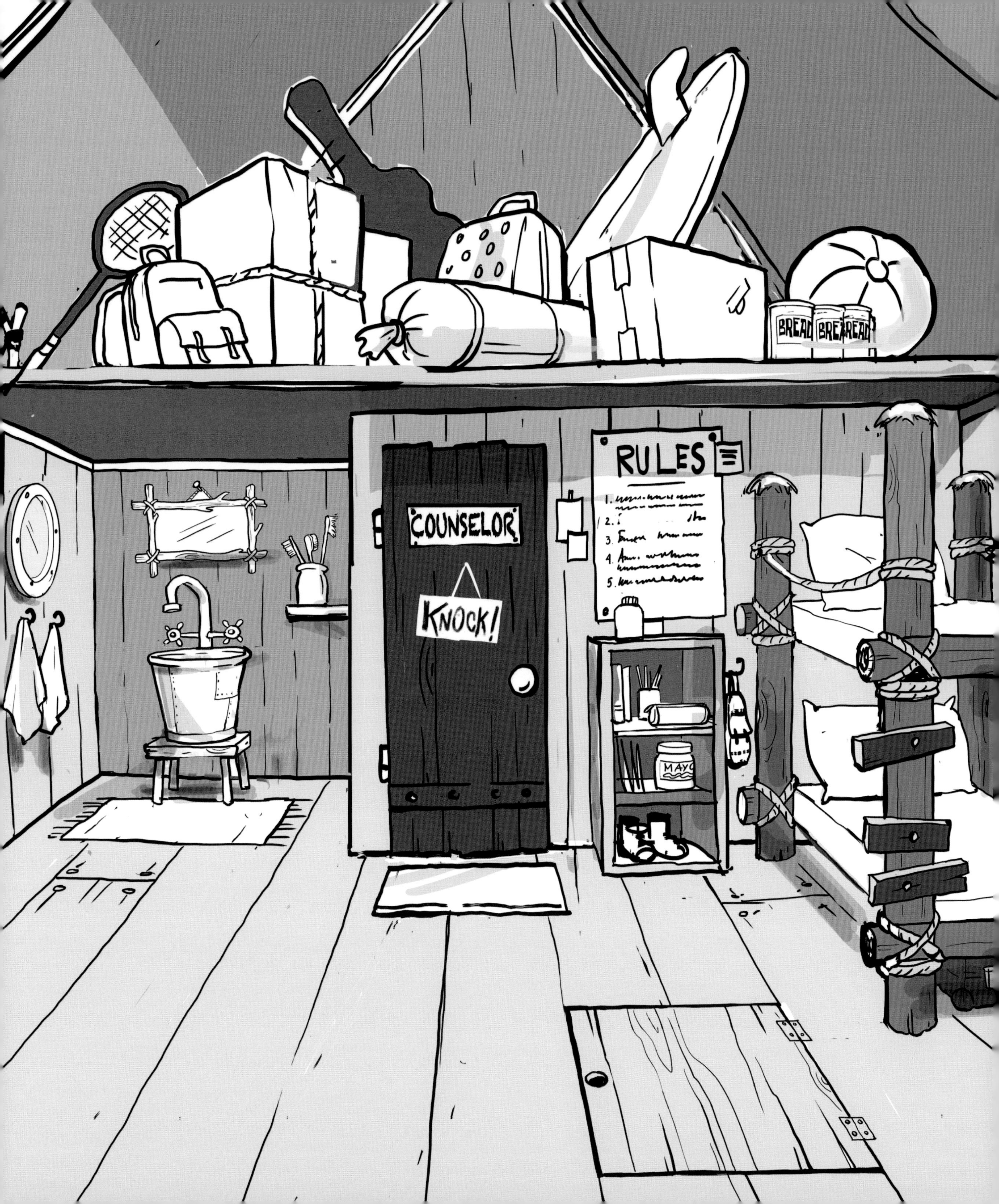
BREAD
COUNSELOR
KNOCK!
RULES
MAYO

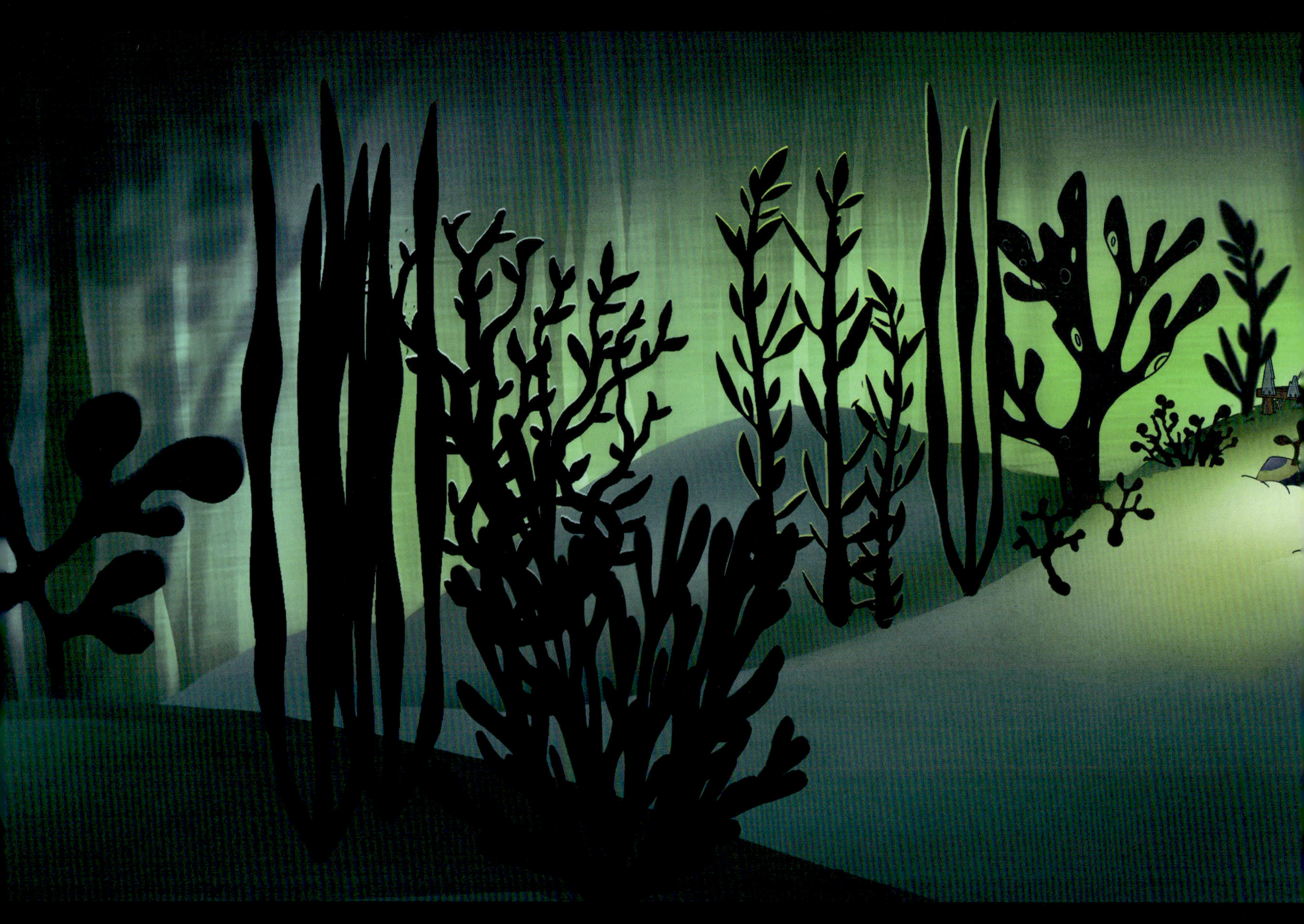

Background design

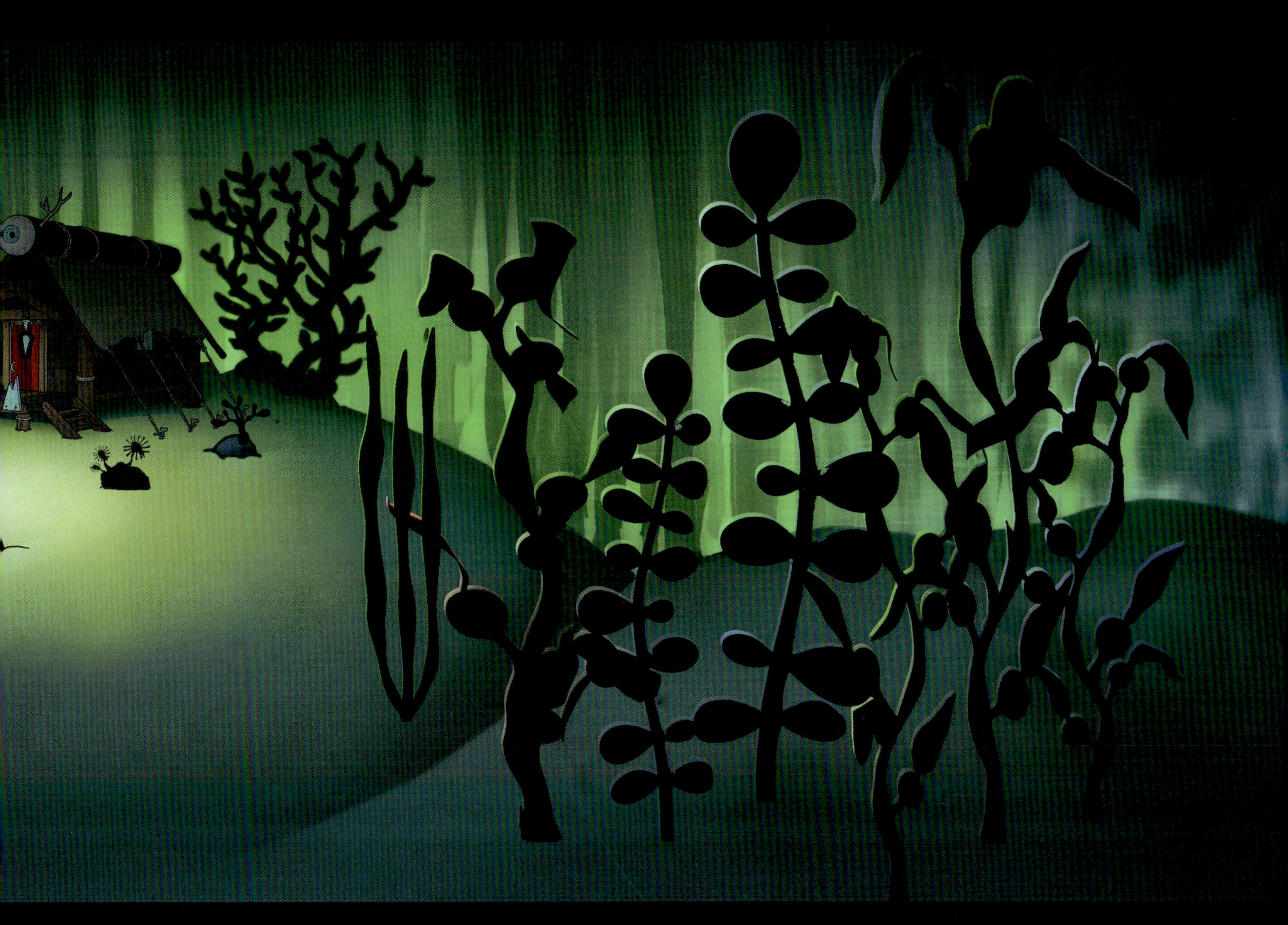

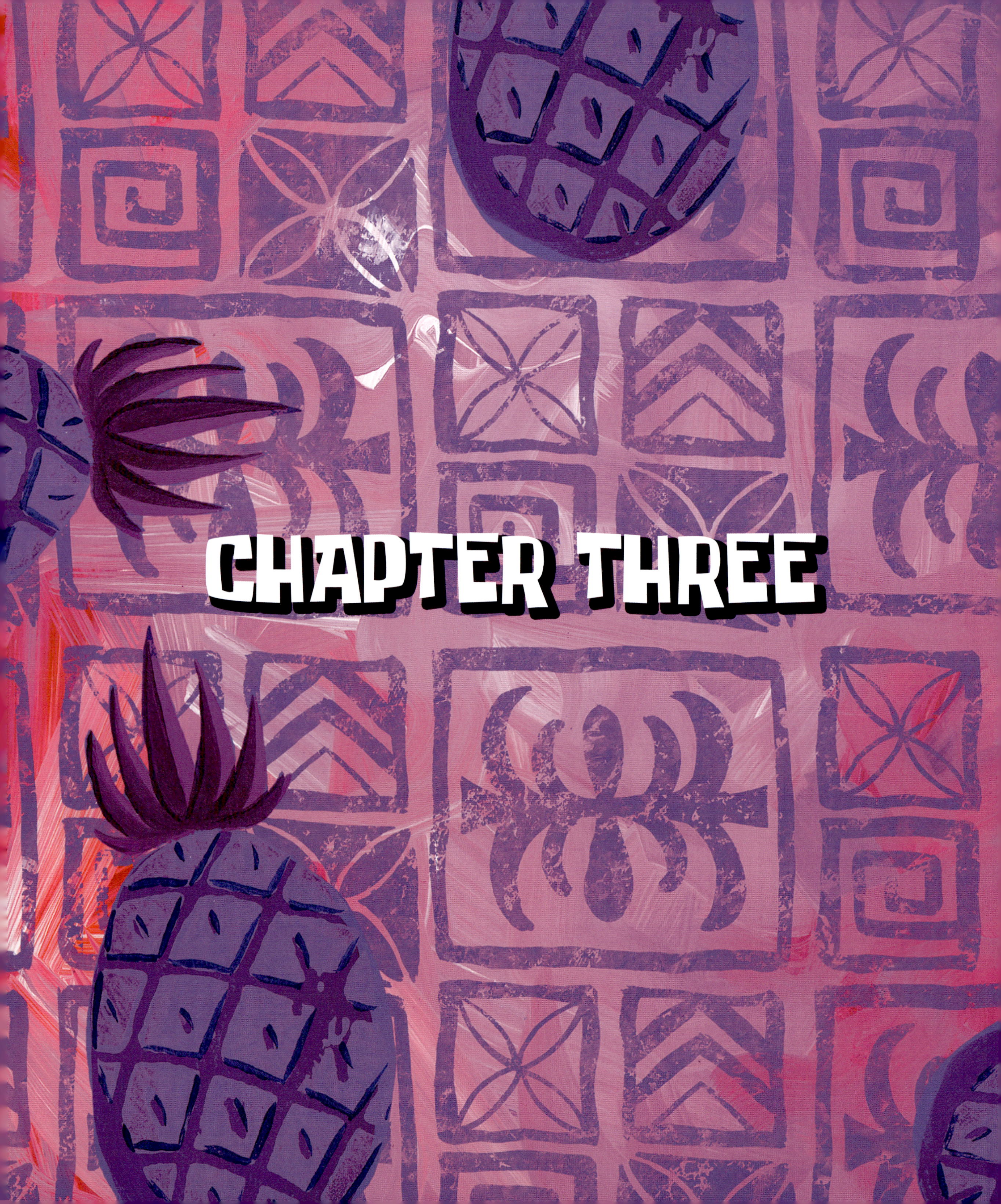

CHAPTER THREE

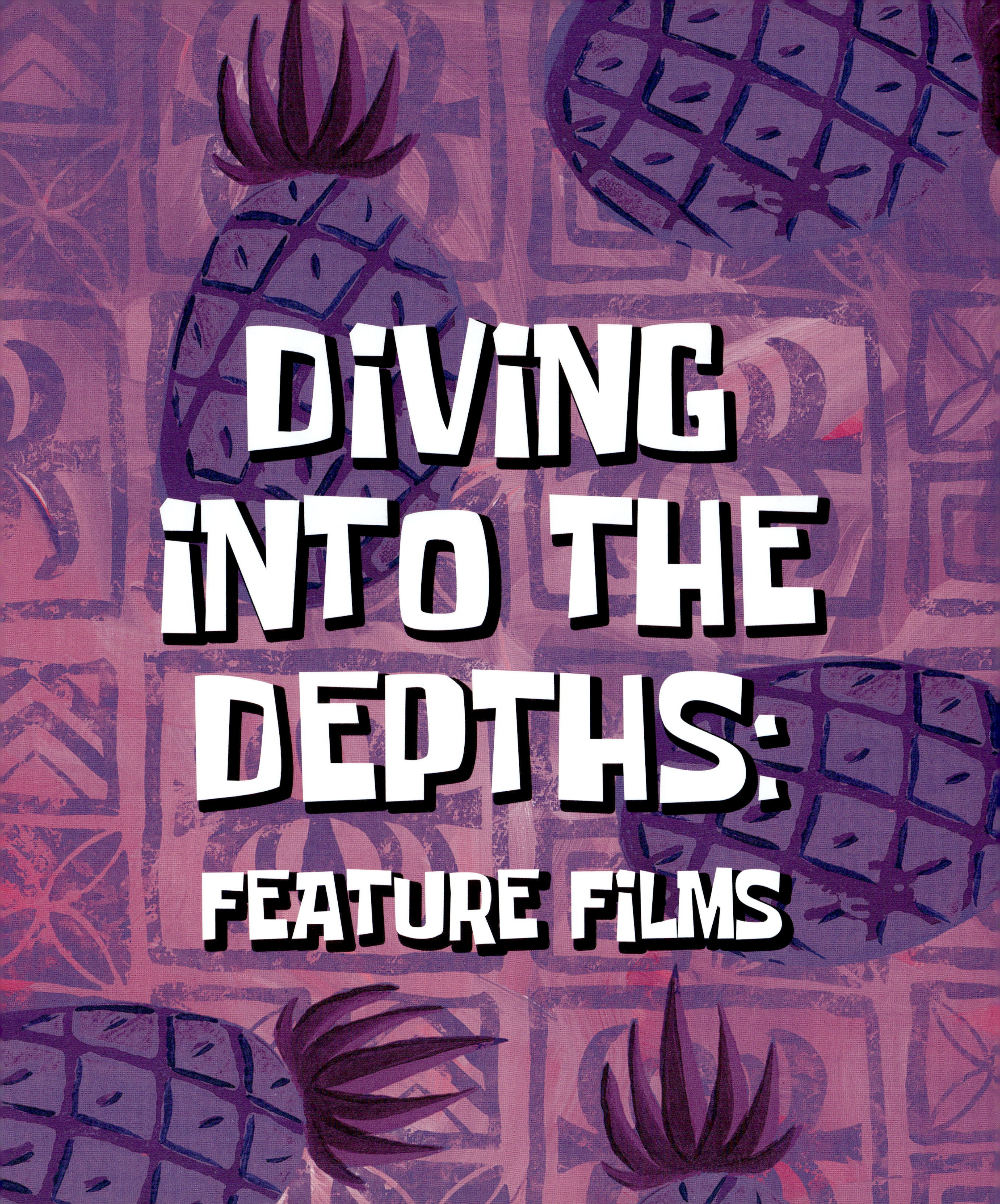
DIVING INTO THE DEPTHS:
FEATURE FILMS

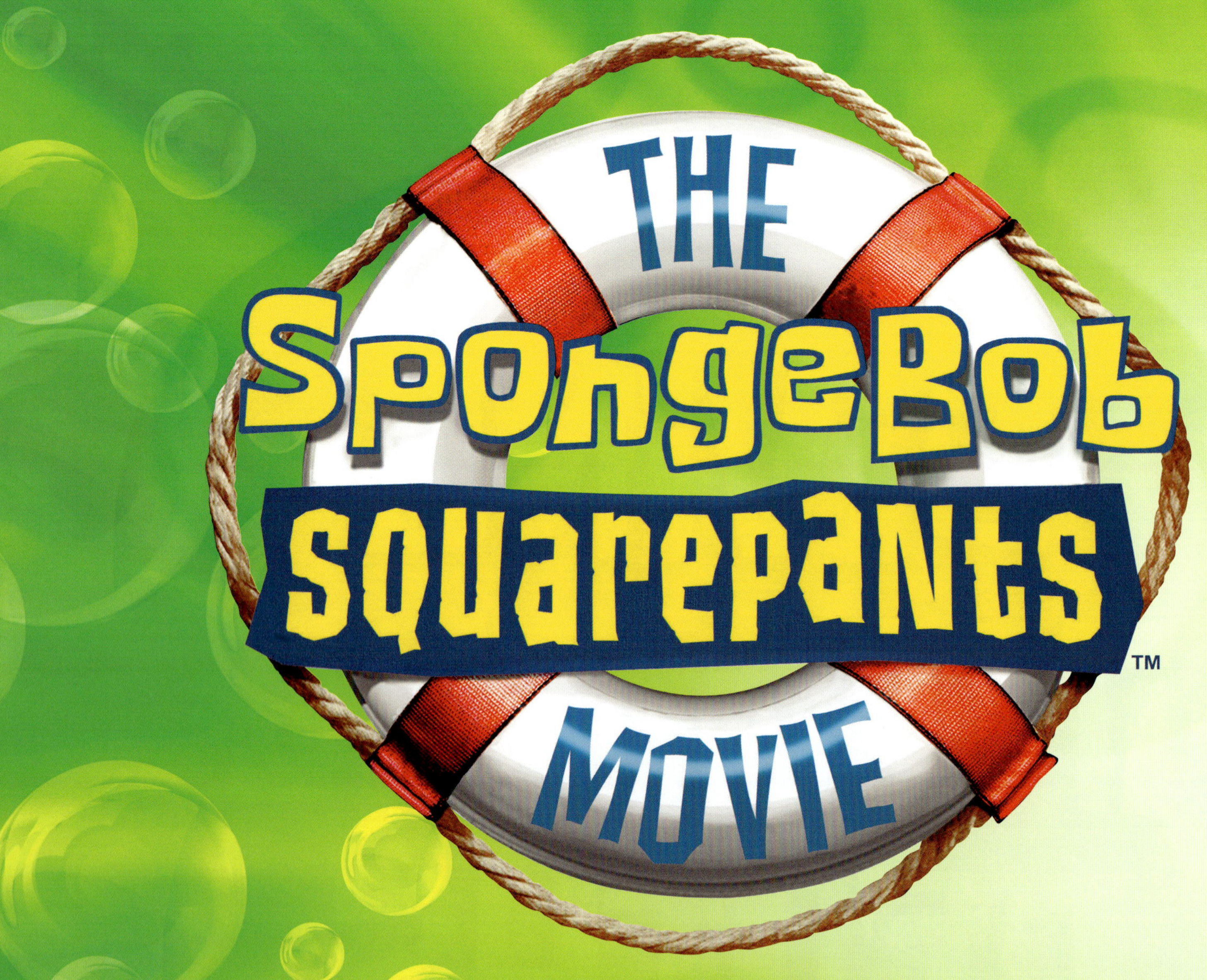

It's one thing to tell eleven-minute televised tales, but to stretch storytelling into feature-length films is a whole other ocean of reality! "In a movie, the audience expects a bigger scale. They want the story to have deeper stakes and need to feel the characters have grown due to the events of the story. As filmmakers, we need to respect those expectations but at the same time protect the characters so they aren't unfamiliar to the audience at the end of the movie," says executive producer Derek Drymon, also a writer on the film.

Creating a story big enough for the big screen was a challenge, but the crew rose to the occasion. After great deliberation and development, one idea floated to the top of the movie concept bucket: What if SpongeBob rose to the surface? This adventure would be technically and conceptually more ambitious than anything the team had ever attempted, but holding hands with Nickelodeon and Paramount Pictures, they all echoed SpongeBob's mantra of "I'm ready, I'm ready, I'm ready!"

The film told SpongeBob's story by blending 2D animation and live-action footage, recognizing "there is a visceral connection the audience makes to the hand-drawn style that always is at the core of SpongeBob, while pushing the medium to make something experimental and fun," notes former production designer Nick Jennings. The artists expanded the level of detail, effects, and animation while bringing in more live action than they had previously worked into the show. It was a win-win for both sides of the movie coin, offering new creative challenges for the artists while giving the audience something new and fun to watch.

The SpongeBob SquarePants Movie premiered on November 14, 2004, and was considered a box-office success, riding a tide of excitement over this next level adventure for SpongeBob and friends.

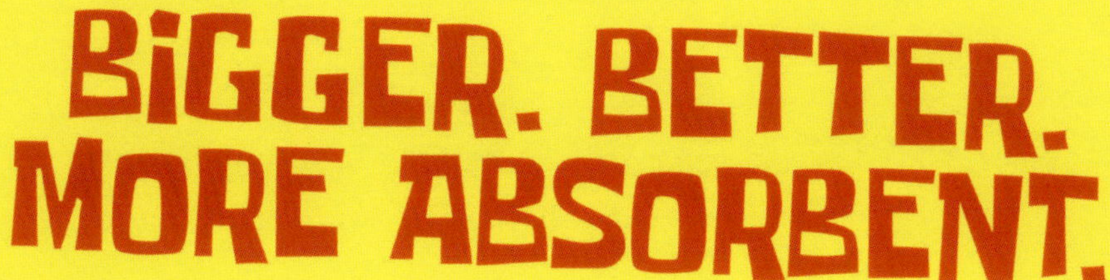

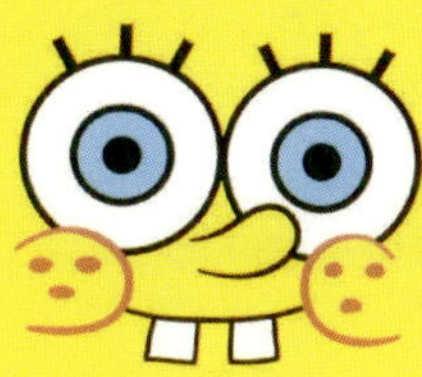

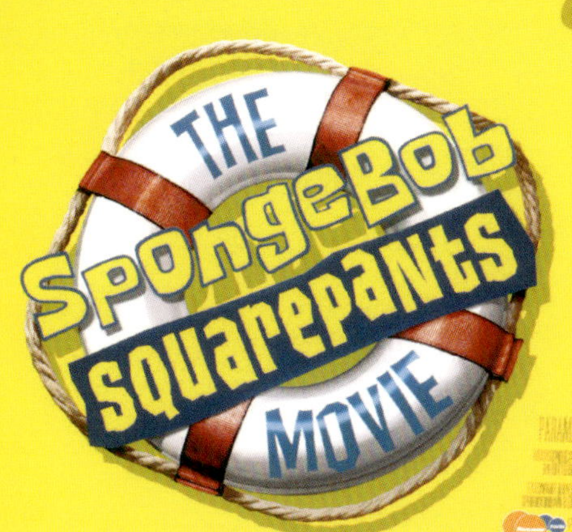

Teaser poster

Final frame image of Plankton spying out from the Chum Bucket

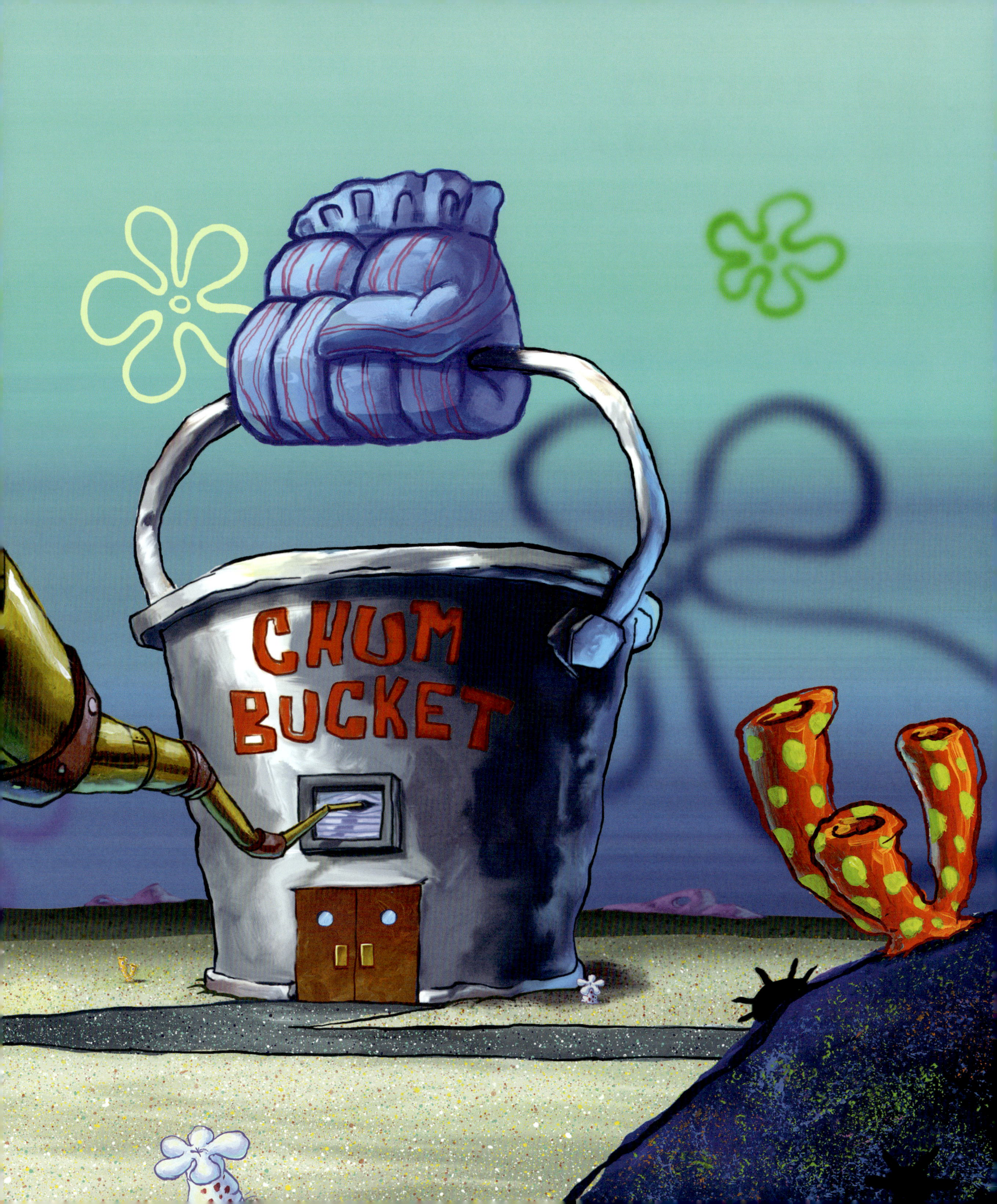
CHUM
BUCKET

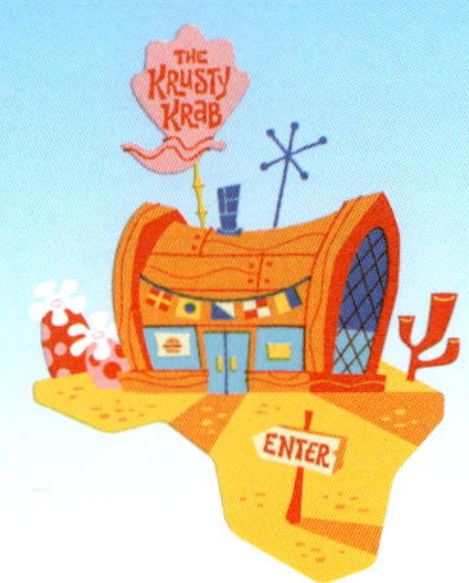

PLANKTON'S PLAN 2

Right on point for Plankton, he has an "evil, diabolical, and lemon-scented" plan to obtain the Krabby Patty secret formula.

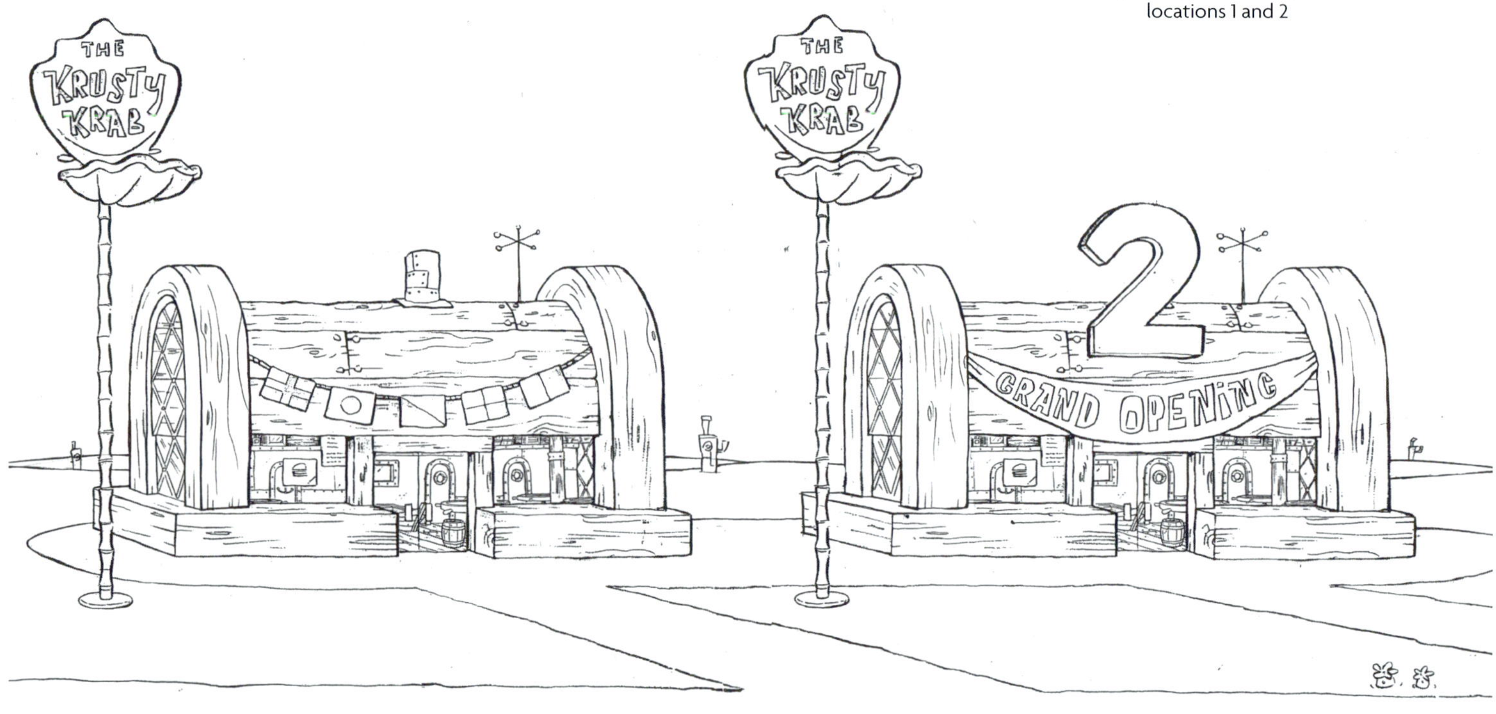

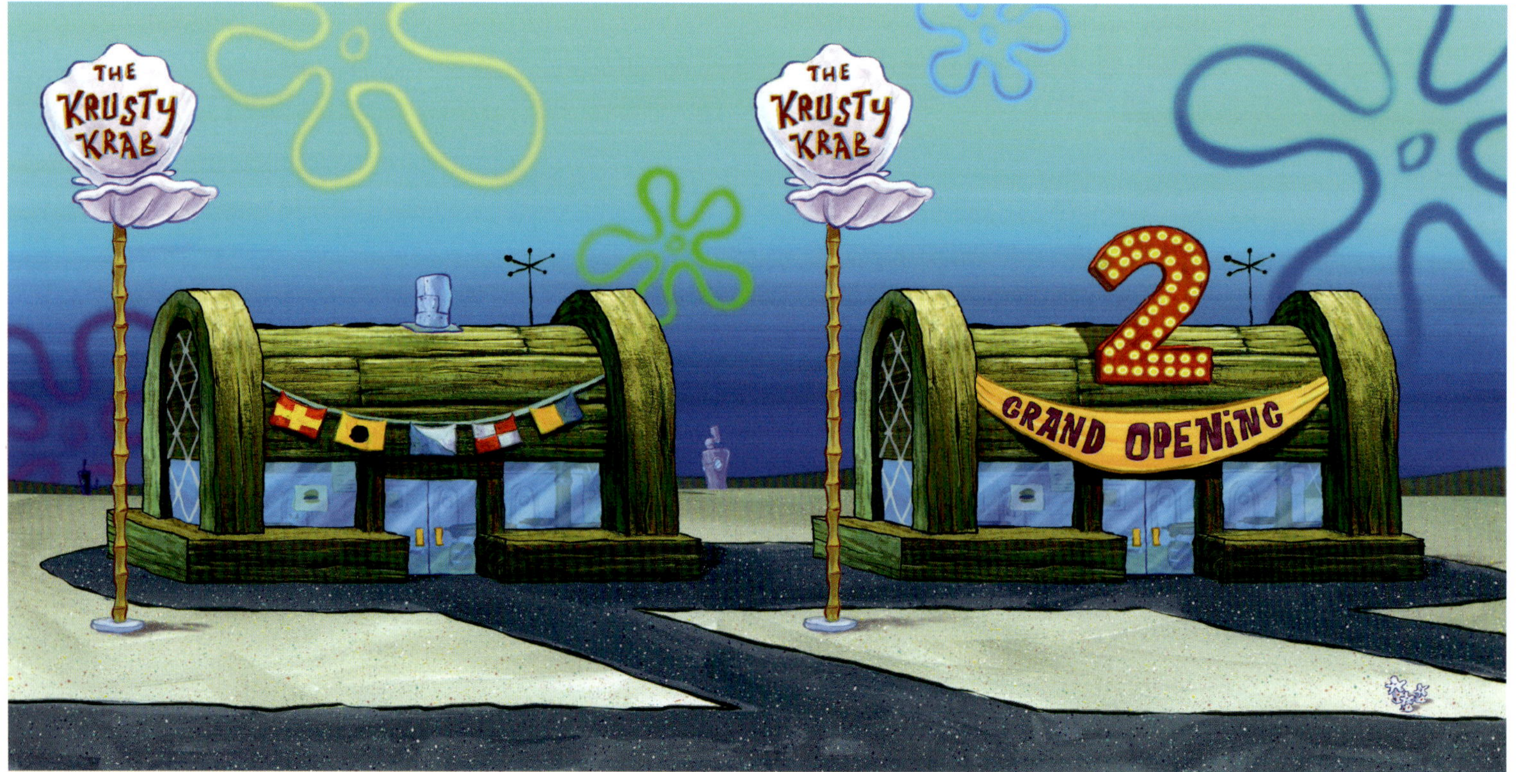

Layout image [upper] and final art [lower] of the Krusty Krab locations 1 and 2

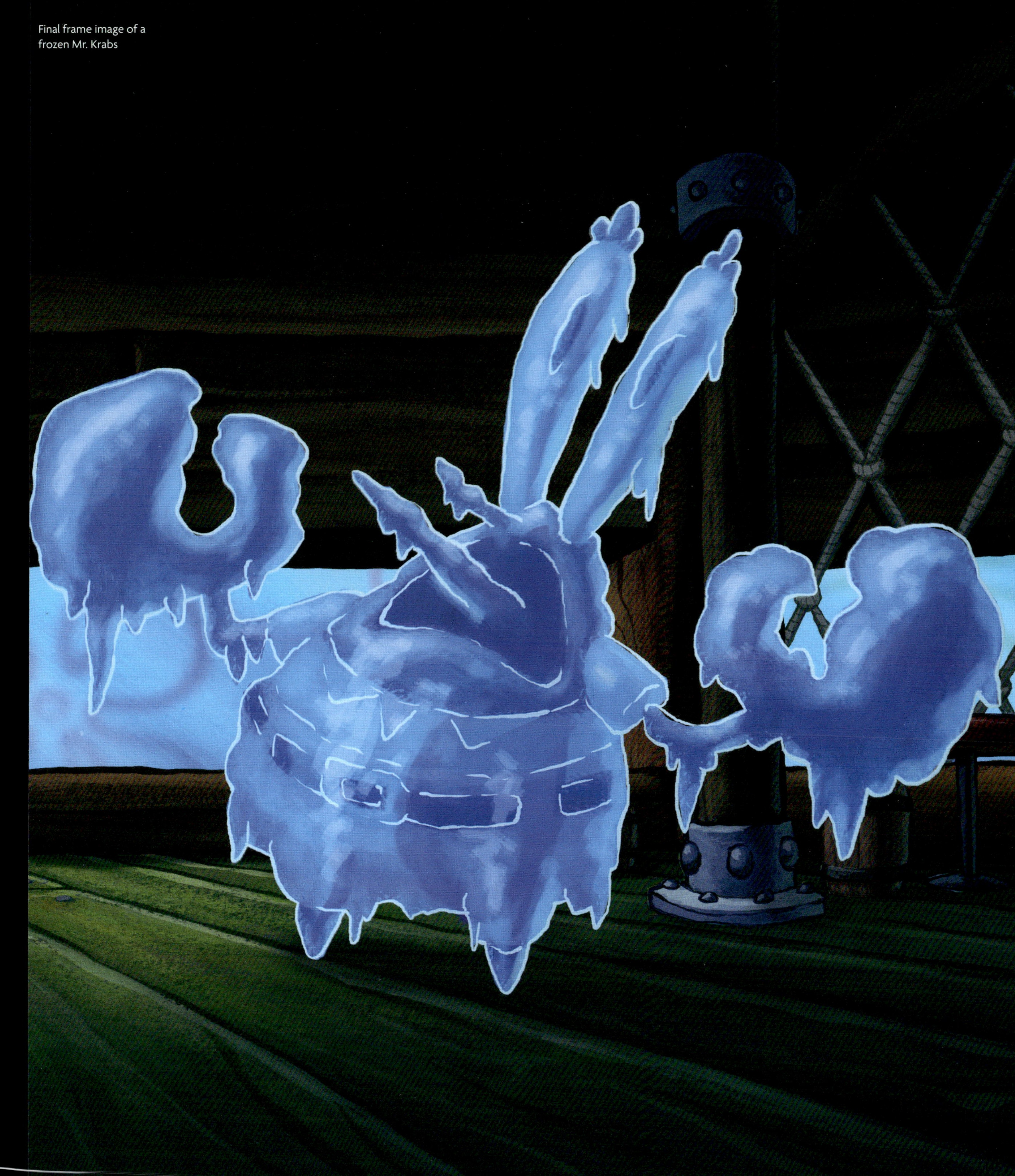

Final frame image of a
frozen Mr. Krabs

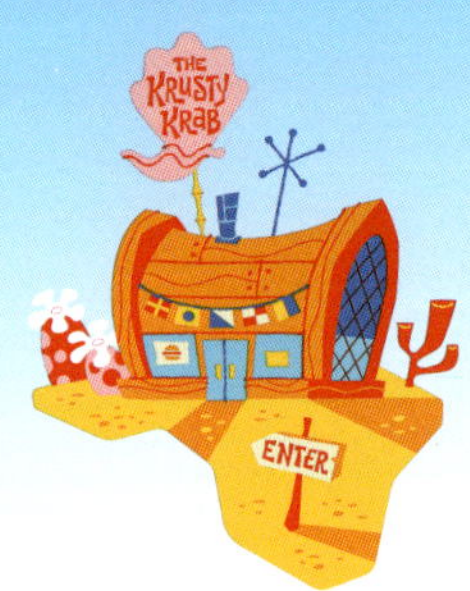

KING NEPTUNE & PRINCESS MINDY

This finned father and daughter pair add humor and royal stakes to the adventure in which the King's glaring baldness means death to whoever stole his crown.

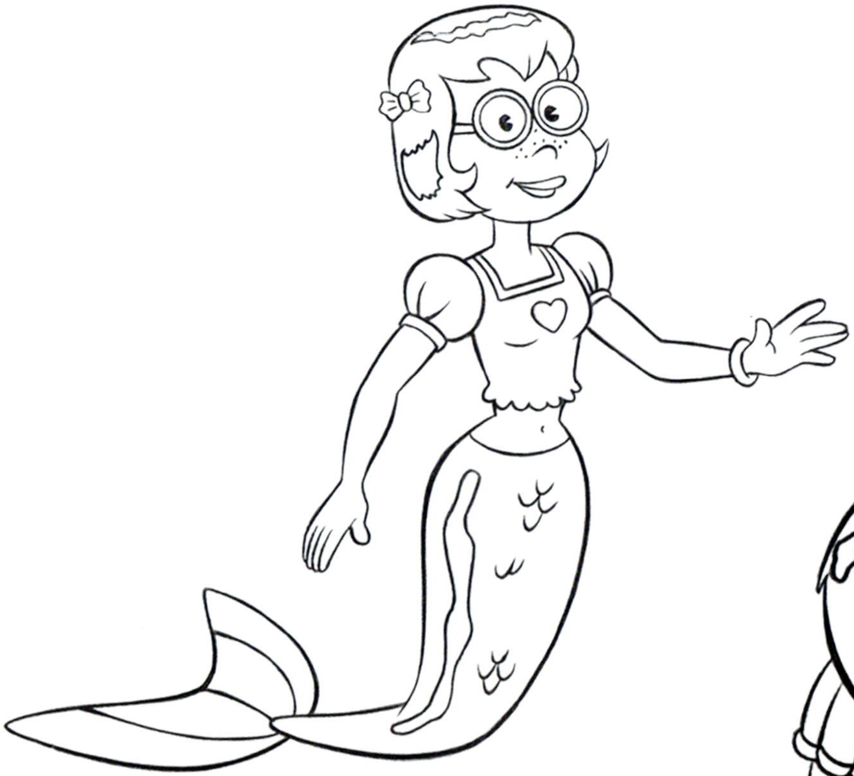

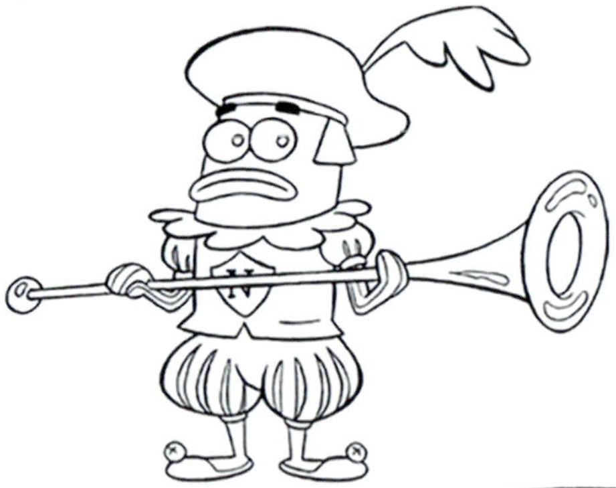

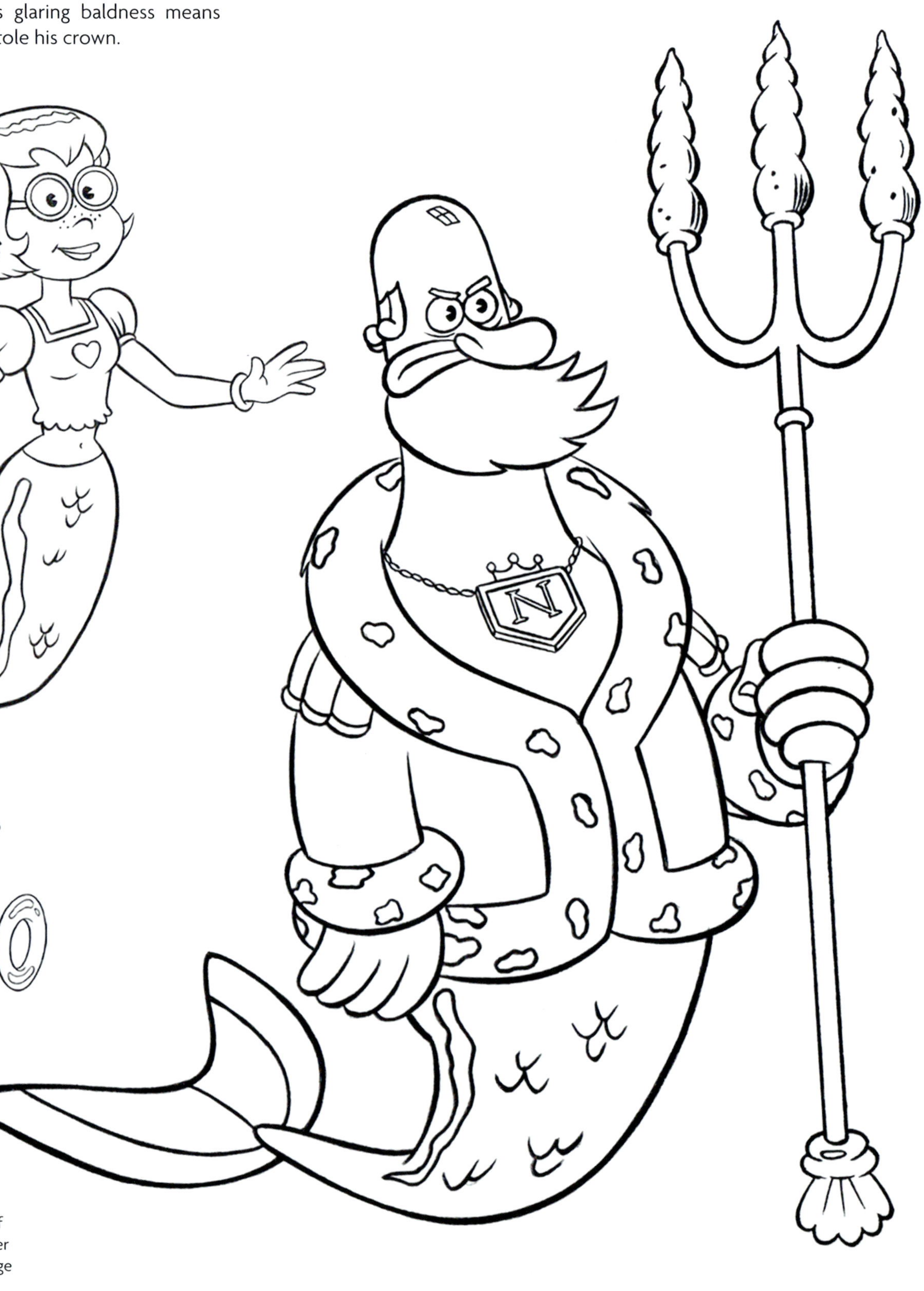

Cleanup animation drawings of Princess Mindy, King Neptune, and the royal squire [left]; look of picture [upper right] and final frame image [lower right] of a high-drama moment of Neptunian rage

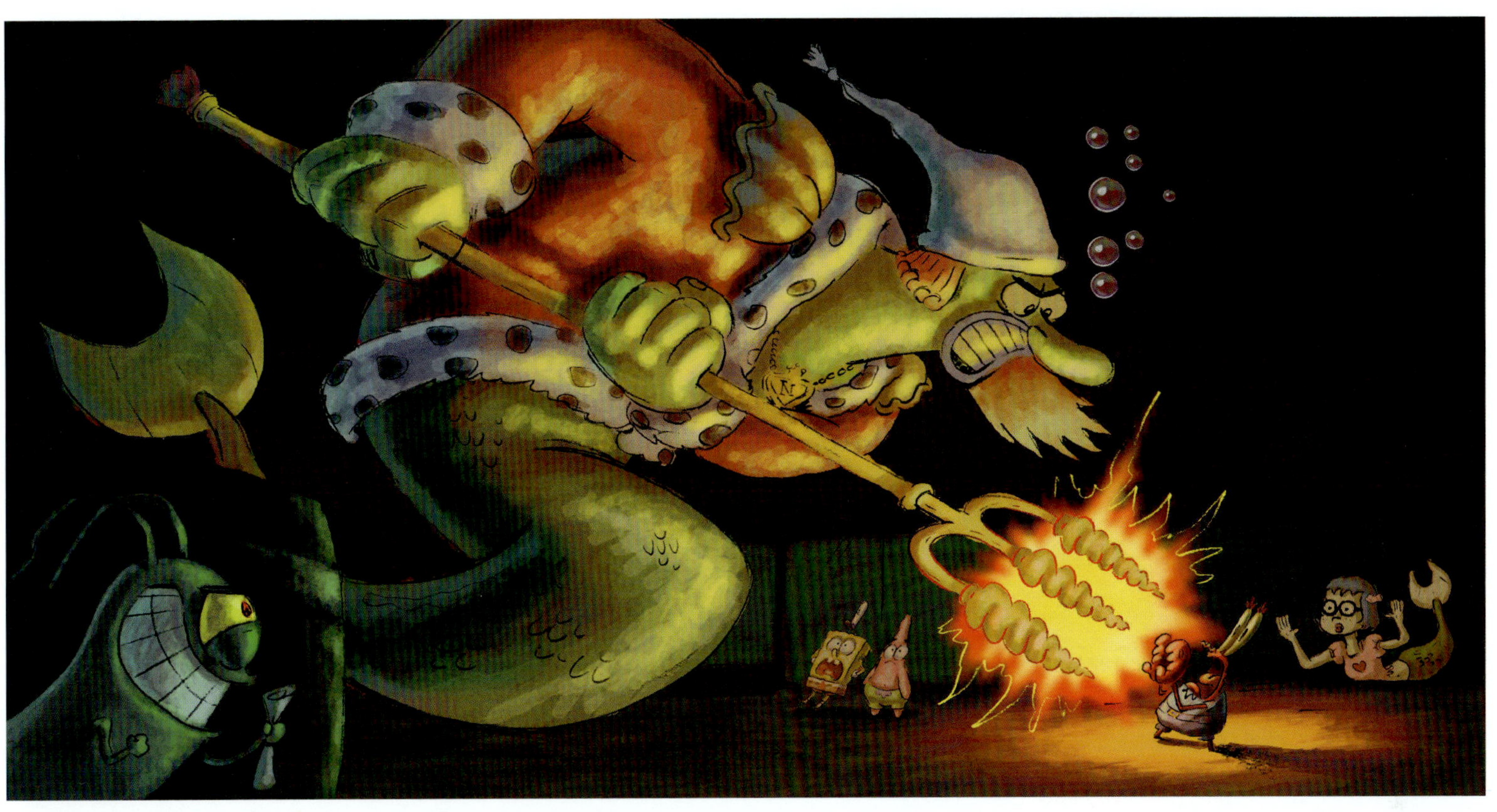

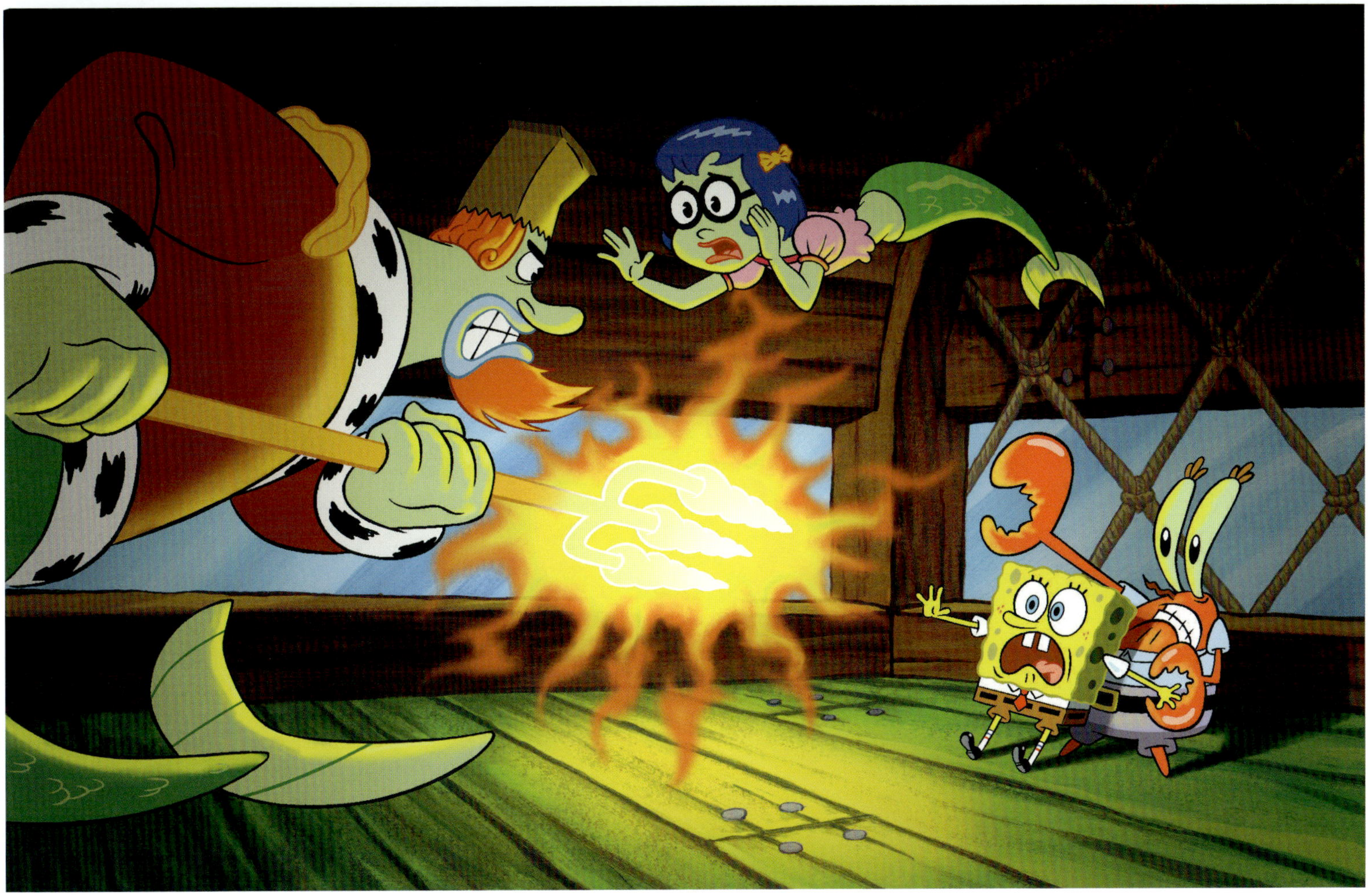

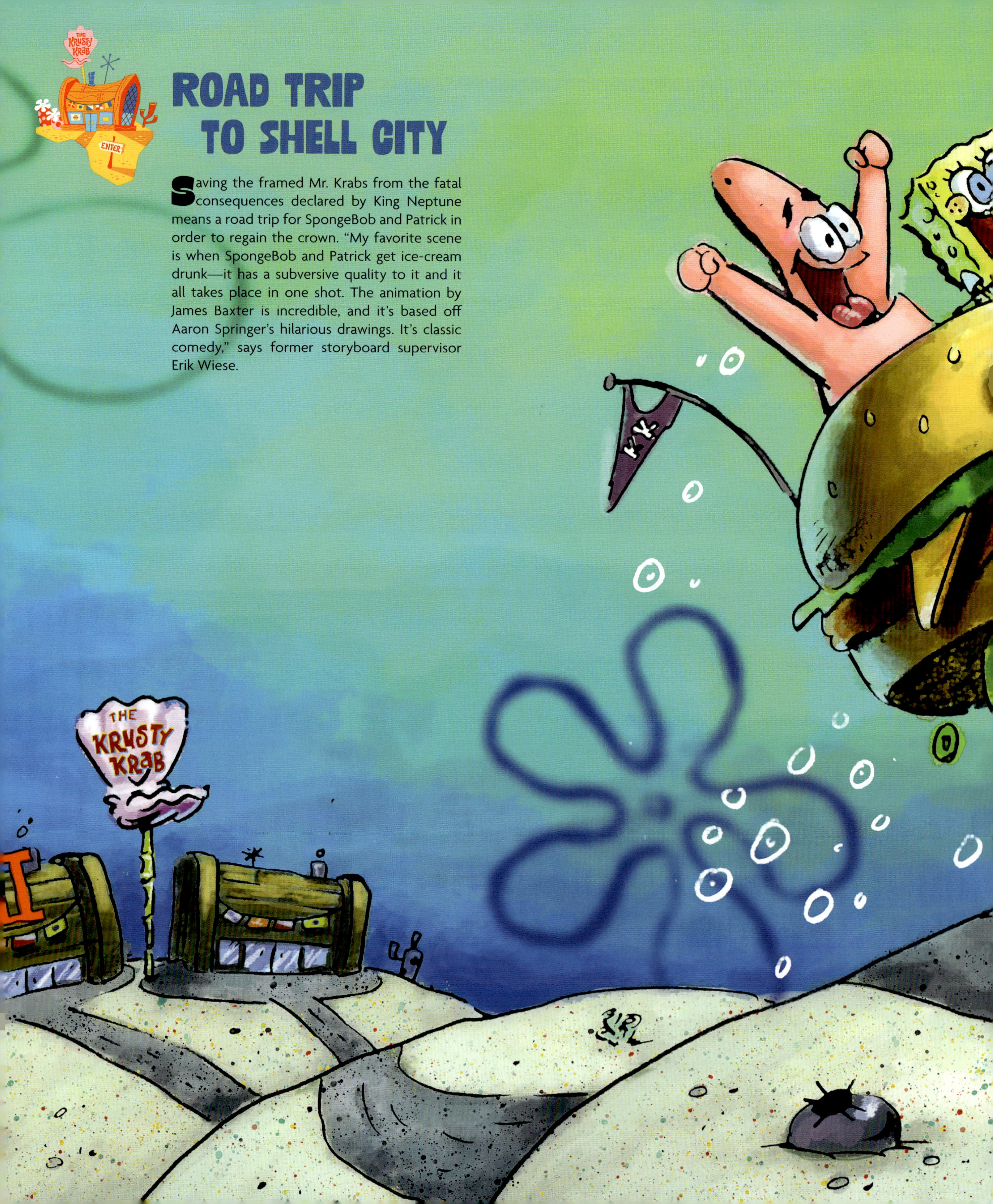

ROAD TRIP TO SHELL CITY

Saving the framed Mr. Krabs from the fatal consequences declared by King Neptune means a road trip for SpongeBob and Patrick in order to regain the crown. “My favorite scene is when SpongeBob and Patrick get ice-cream drunk—it has a subversive quality to it and it all takes place in one shot. The animation by James Baxter is incredible, and it’s based off Aaron Springer’s hilarious drawings. It’s classic comedy,” says former storyboard supervisor Erik Wiese.

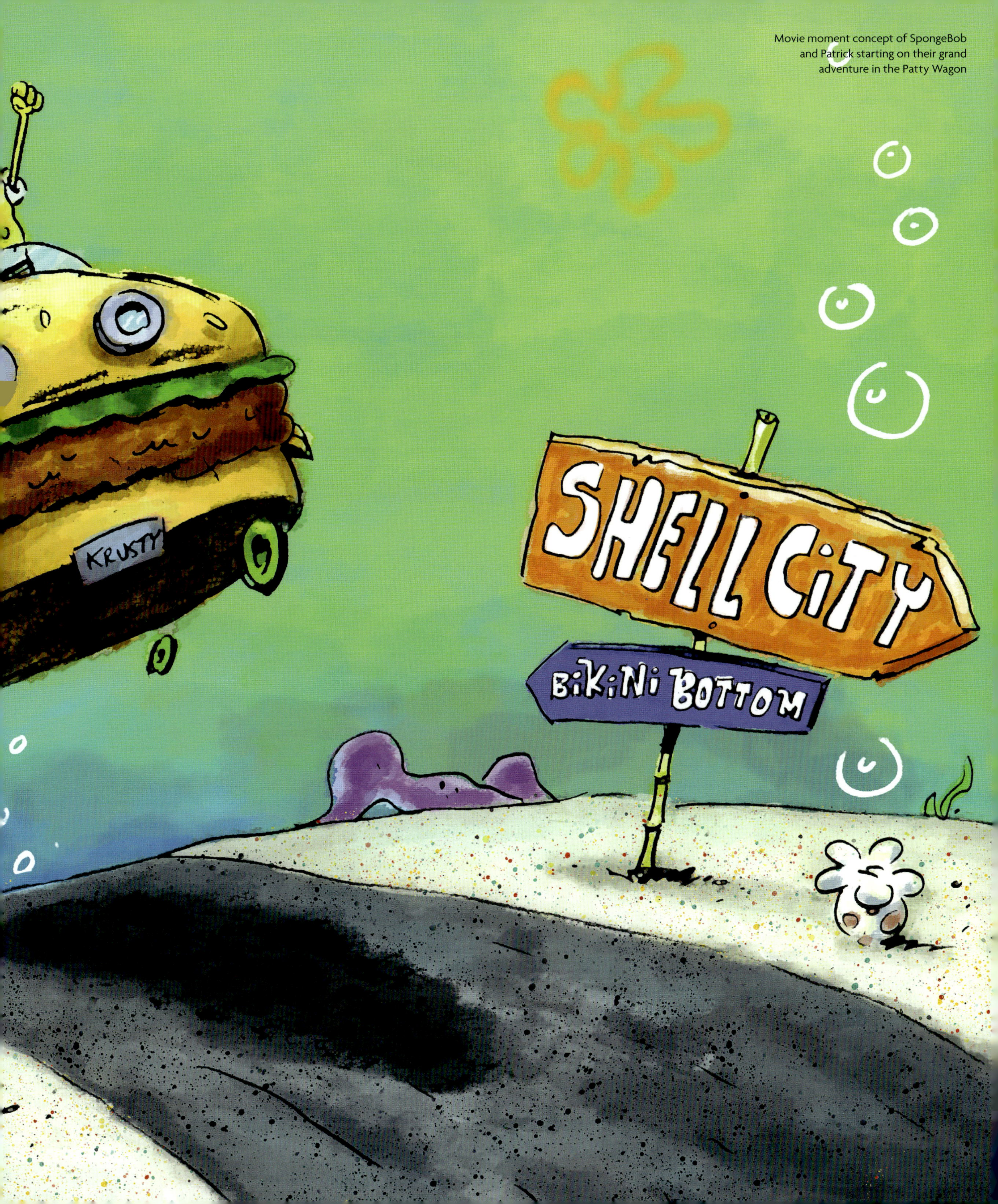

Movie moment concept of SpongeBob and Patrick starting on their grand adventure in the Patty Wagon

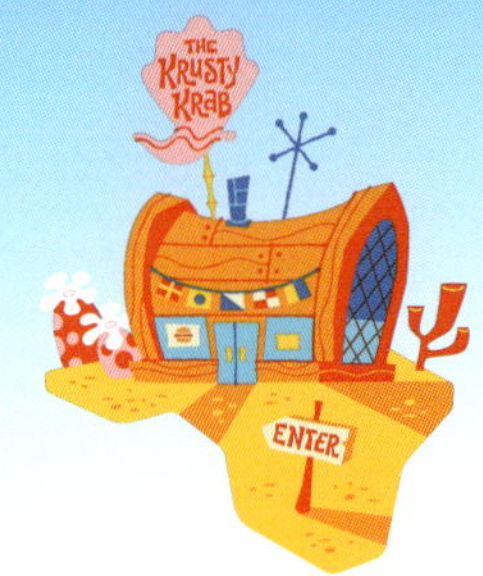

PATTY WAGON

The souped-up sandwich mobile is the perfect road-trip vehicle.

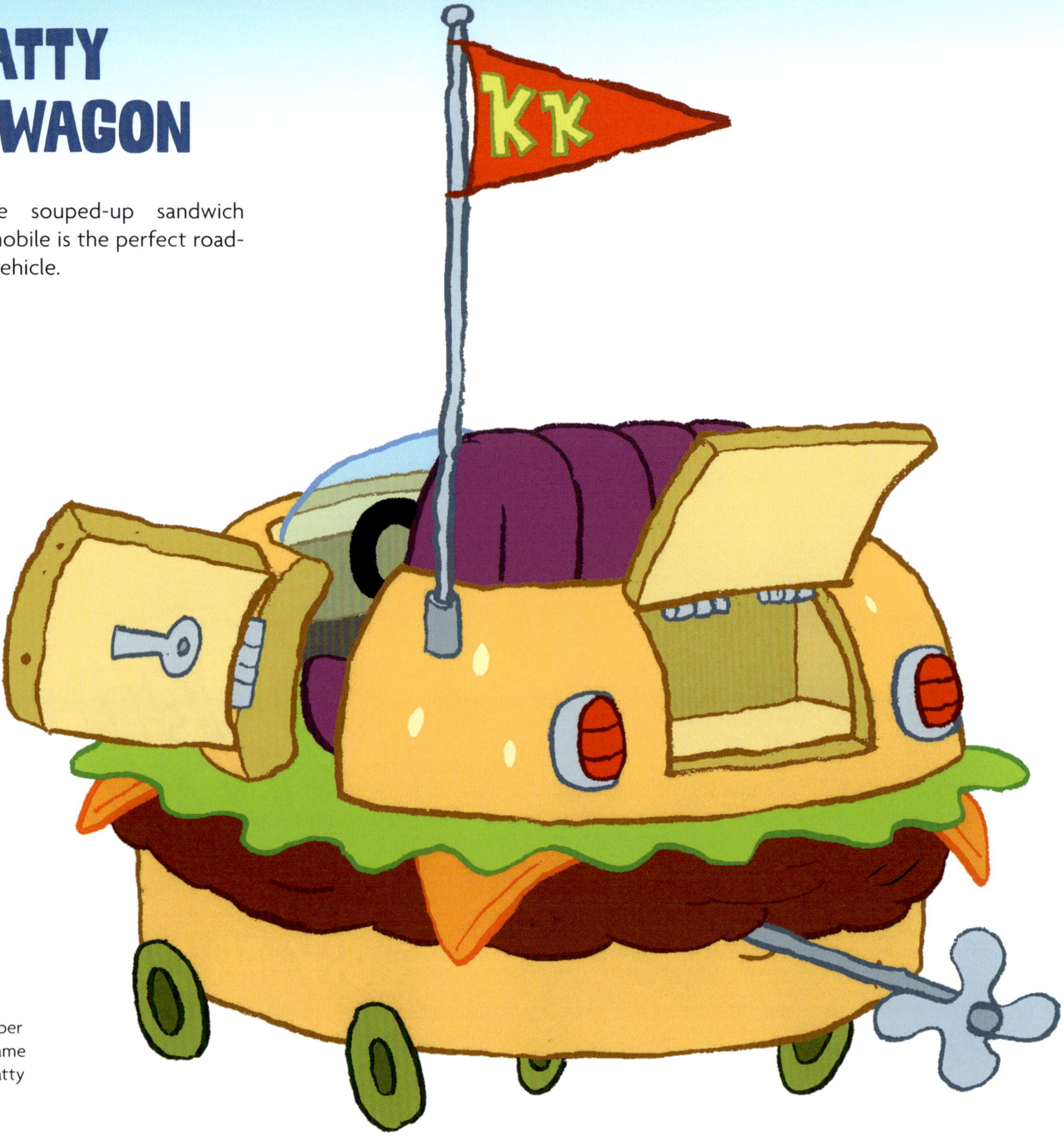

Prop design [upper left] and final frame images of the Patty Wagon

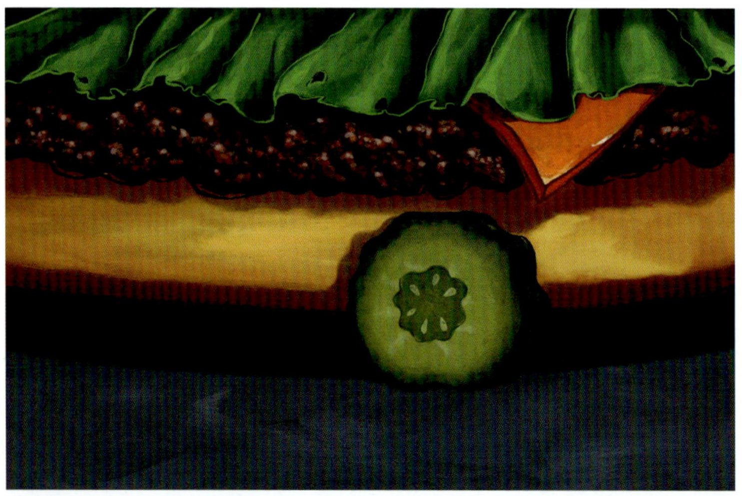

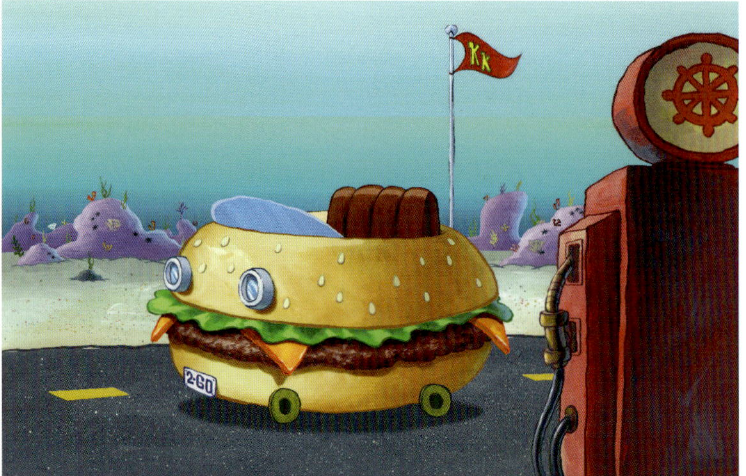

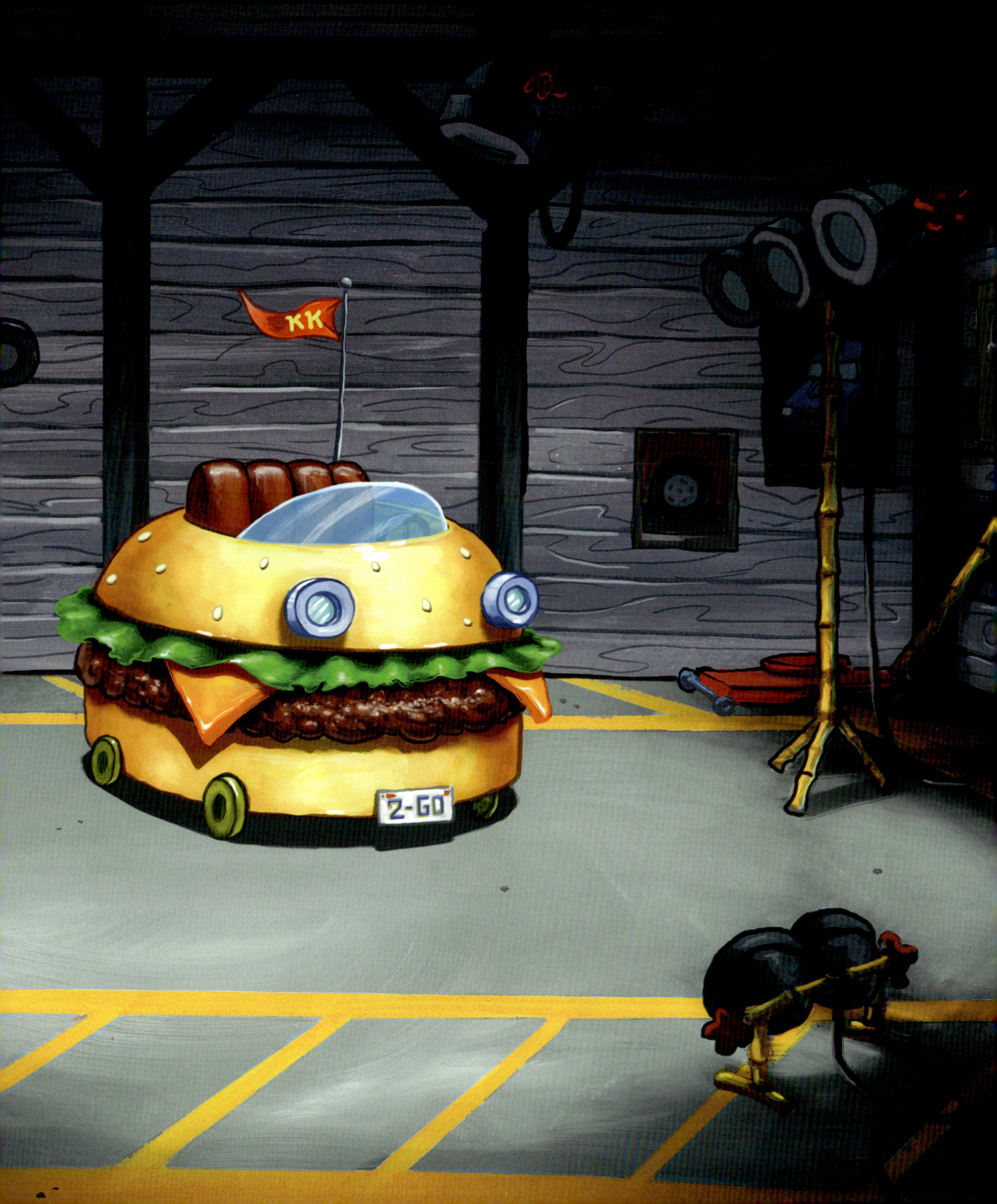
KK
2-GO

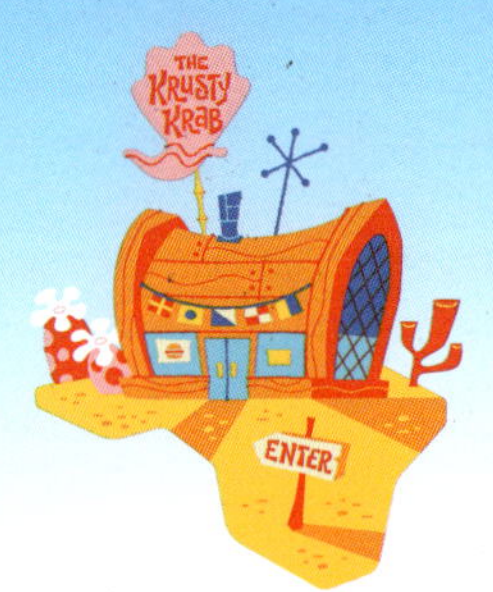

CROSSING THE COUNTY LINE

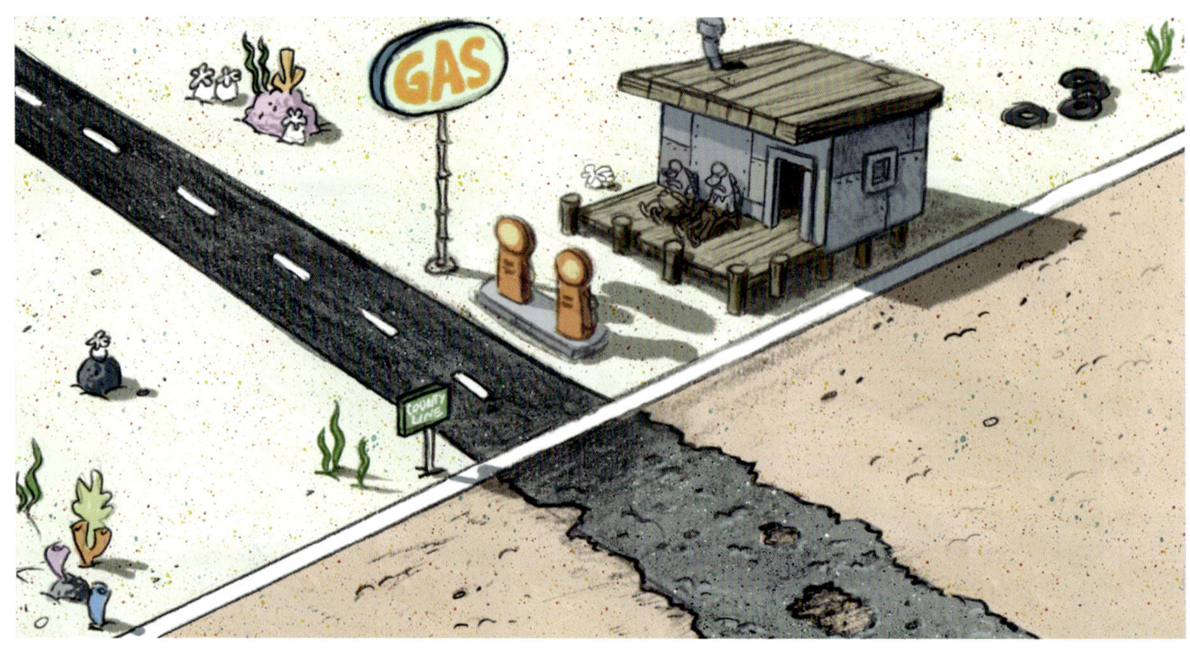

GAS STATION ATTENDANTS

Concept drawing of the gas station at the county line [upper] and final art of its gas station attendants Floyd [left] and Lloyd [right], who wonder what condiment the Patty Wagon takes for a fill-up

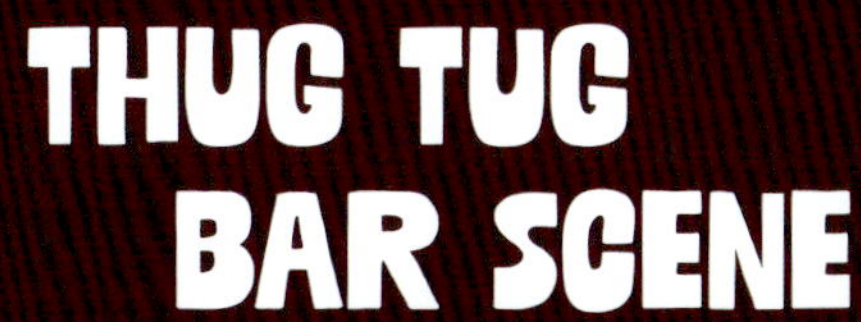

THUG TUG BAR SCENE

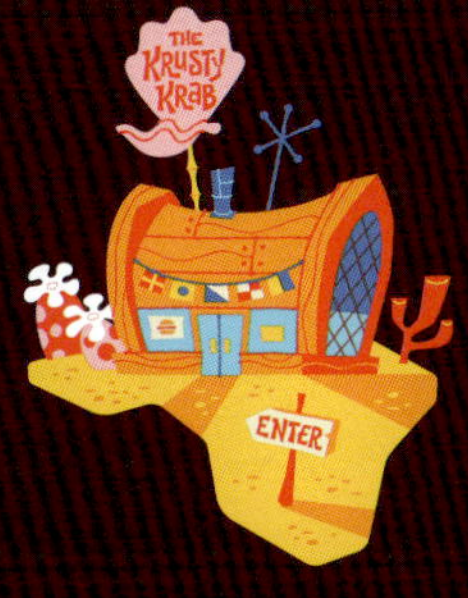

Another rare “tough guy” hangout under the sea is the Thug Tug. “There are so many environments I love, but one that stands out is the Thug Tug interior, which we did in reds and blacks. The simplicity of the color, the character designs, and what’s happening in the scene all come together nicely. It’s a fun scene to watch,” says former production designer Nick Jennings.

“I remember thinking about those little round glasses David Crosby used to wear when I designed the DJ in the bar. For that bar scene, I channeled an experience I had the first day at summer camp as a kid when a bigger kid lined us all up in the dorms and walked down the line like a drill sergeant, stopping in front of each terrified kid, clenching his fists, saying the words… ‘And YOU…’” adds director Aaron Springer.

Final frame image of the infamous Thug Tug bar

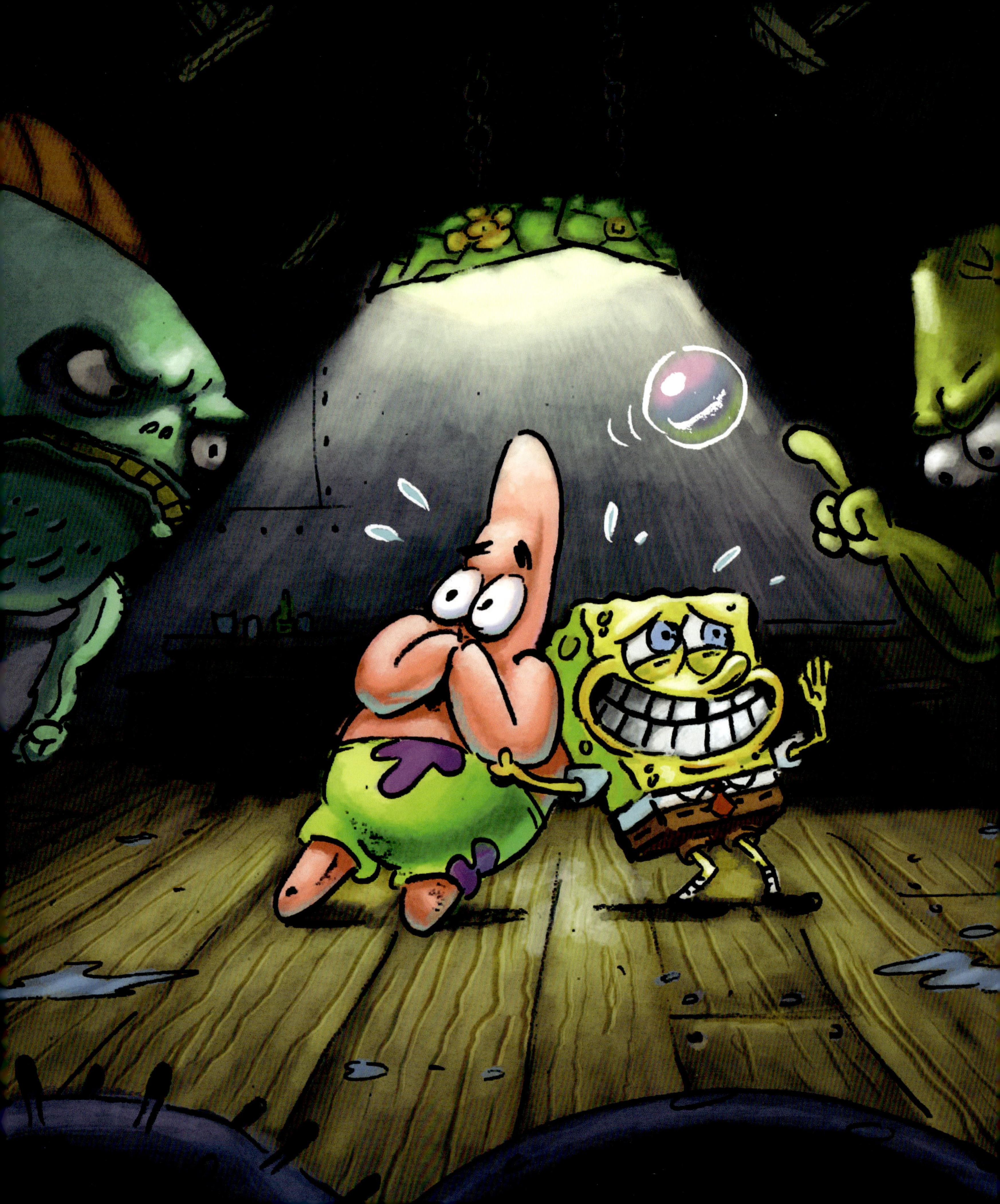

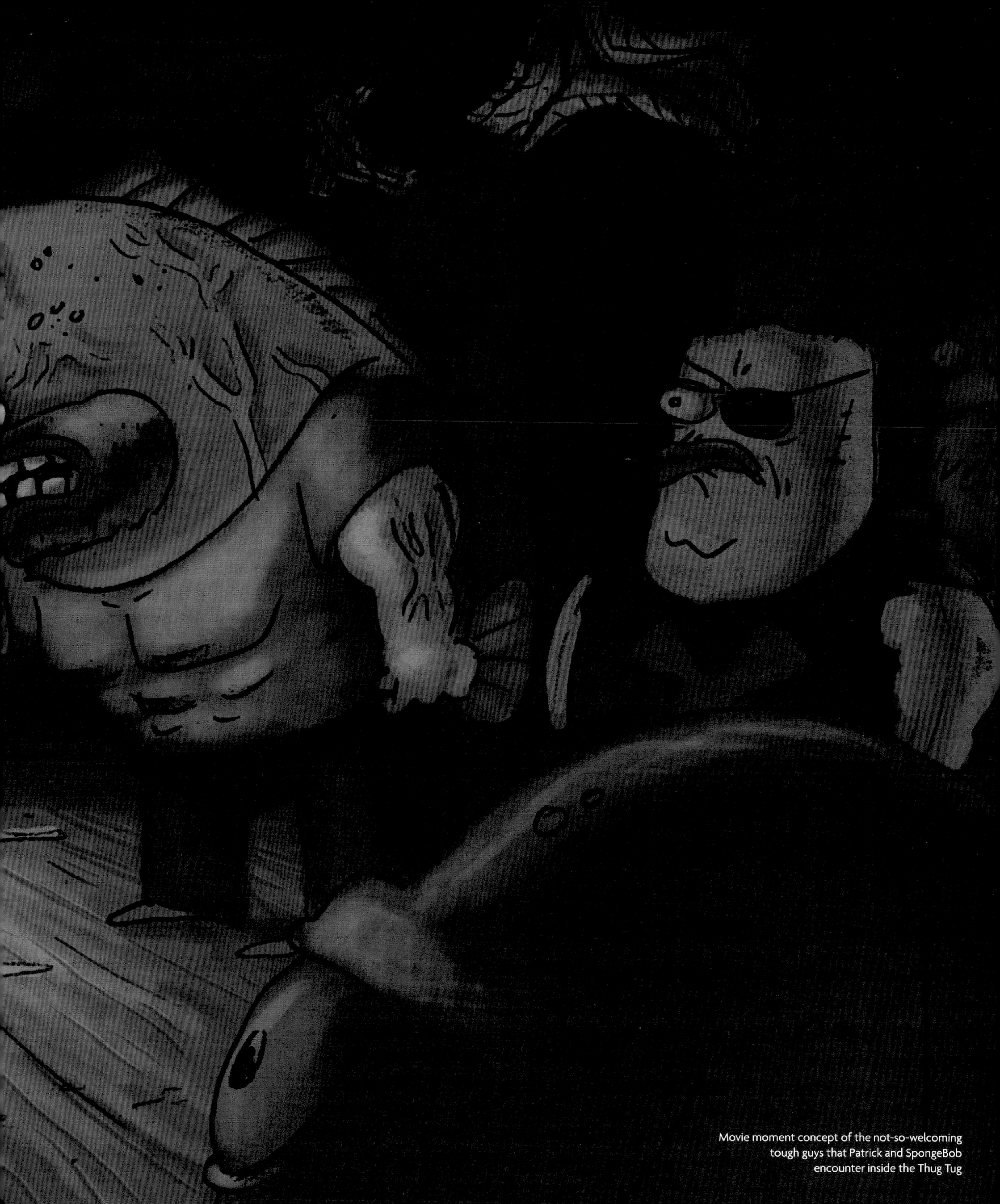

Movie moment concept of the not-so-welcoming tough guys that Patrick and SpongeBob encounter inside the Thug Tug

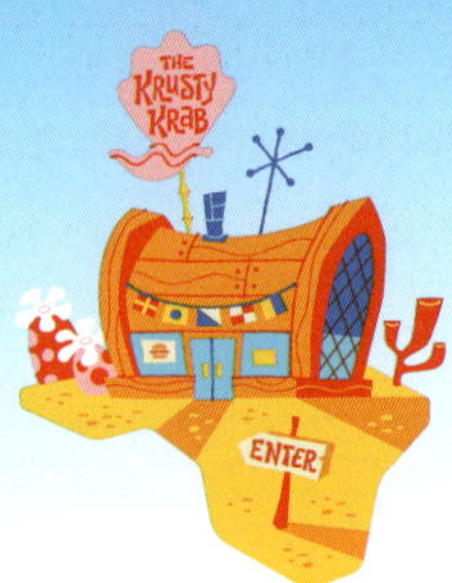

SKULL PILES & FROGFISH TRAP

Character concept [upper] and final frame image [lower] of the Frogfish Trap... and its scale to the Patty Wagon

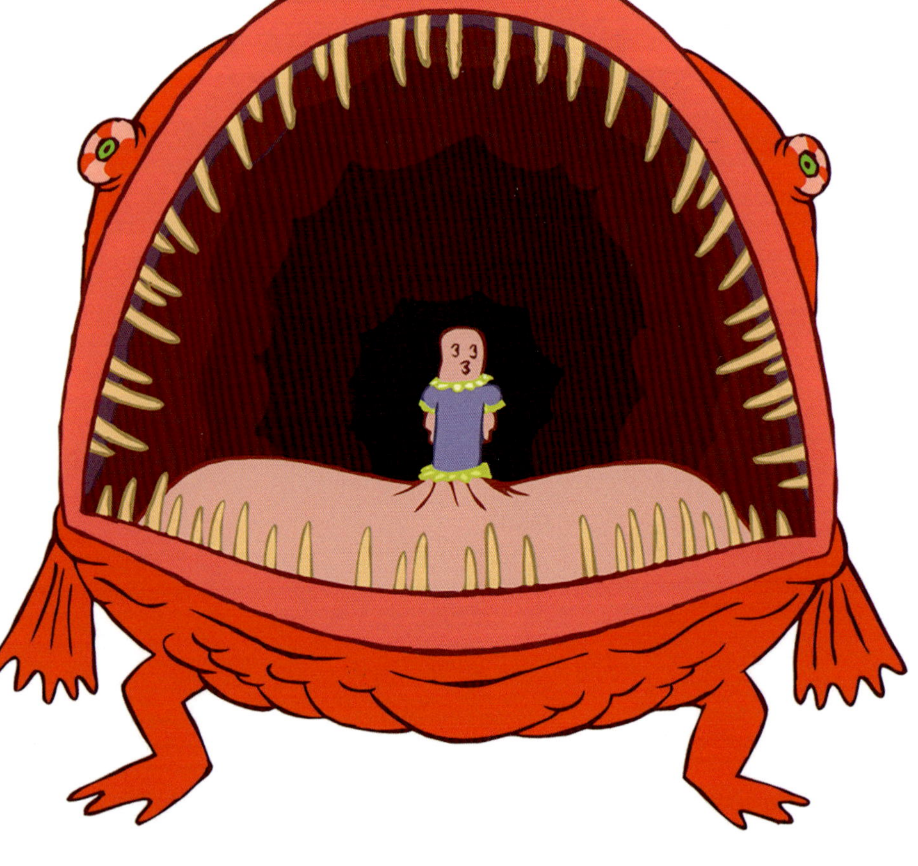

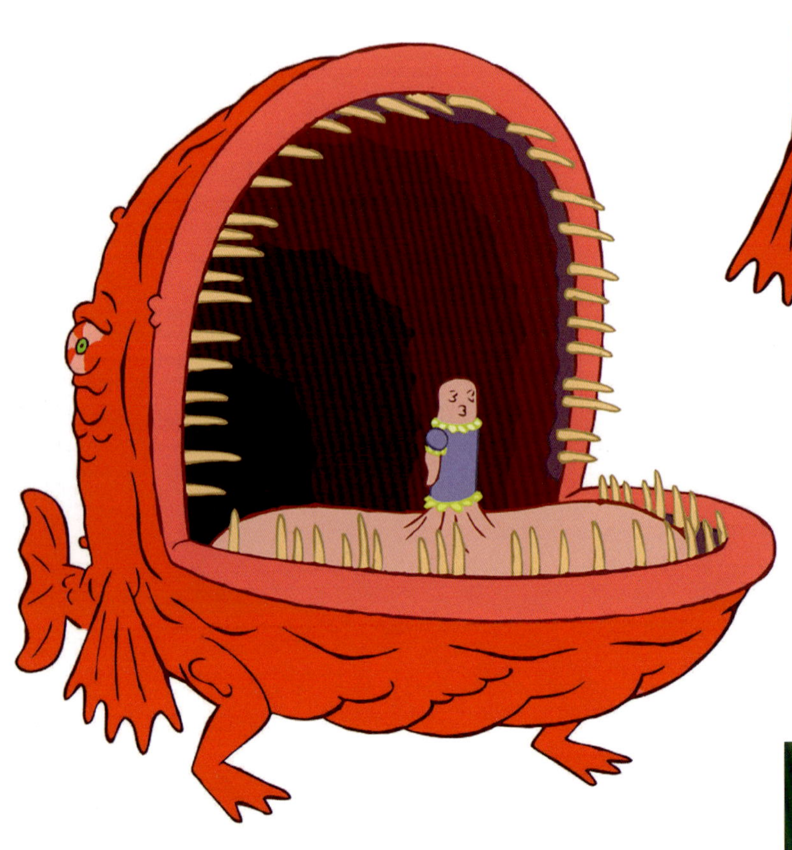

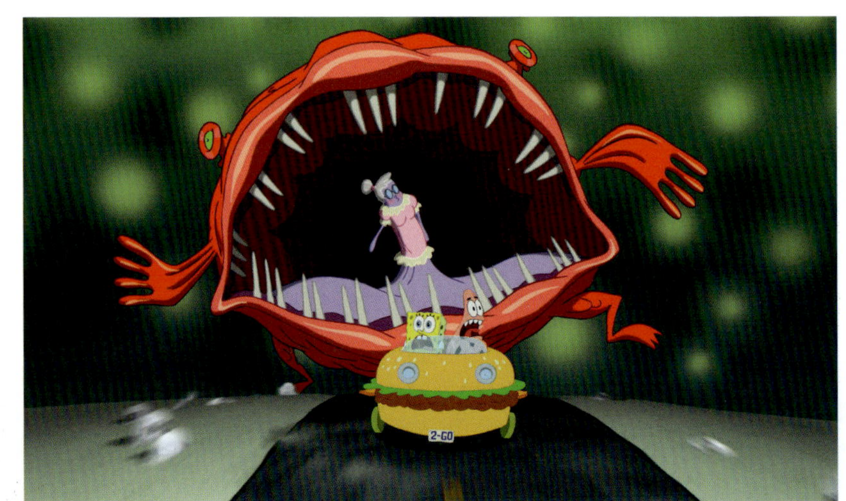

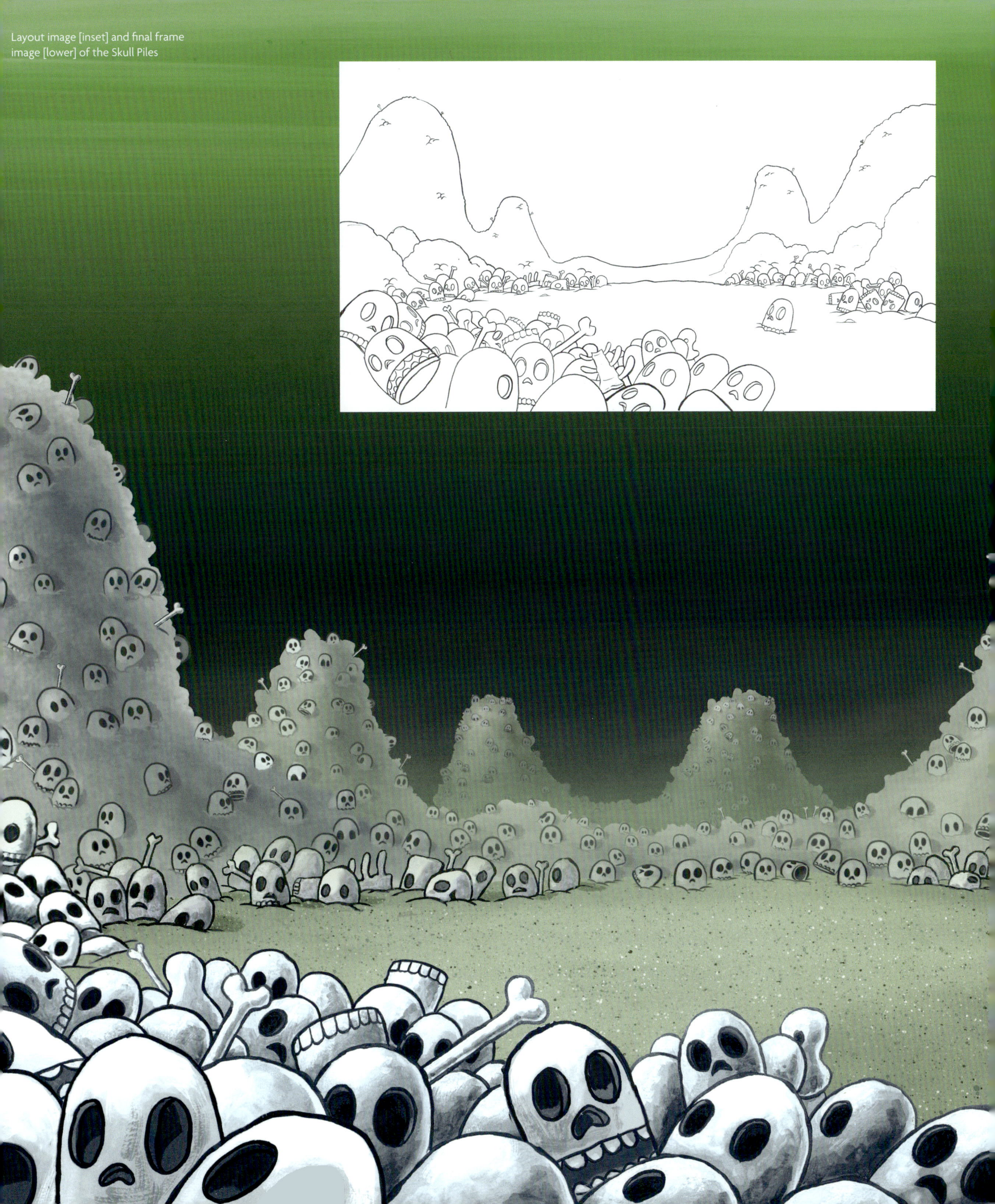

Layout image [inset] and final frame image [lower] of the Skull Piles

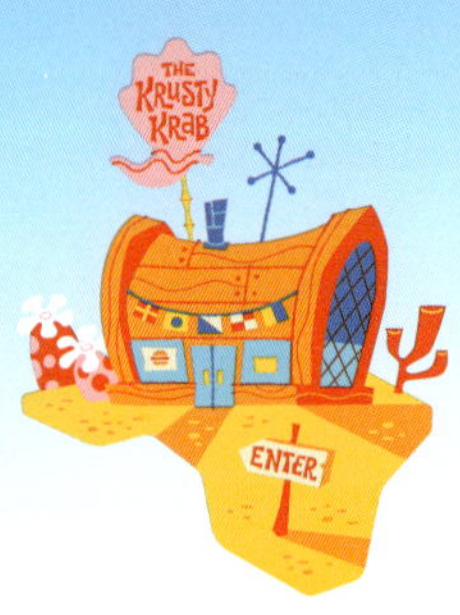

DENNIS THE HITMAN

Here's a guy you don't want to run into in a dark corner of the ocean. "When I storyboarded Dennis the Hitman sequences, I loosely based Dennis on Leonard Smalls, the hitman from *Raising Arizona*," says director Aaron Springer.

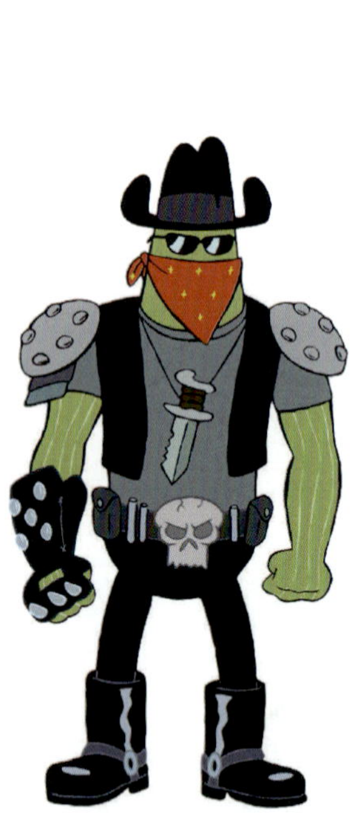

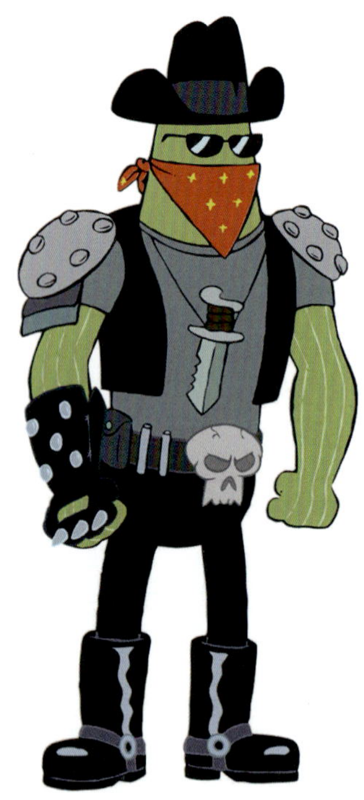

Final art [left] and final frame image [right] of Dennis

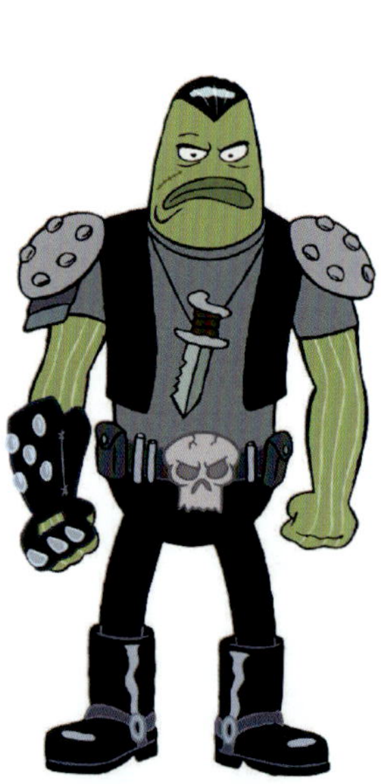

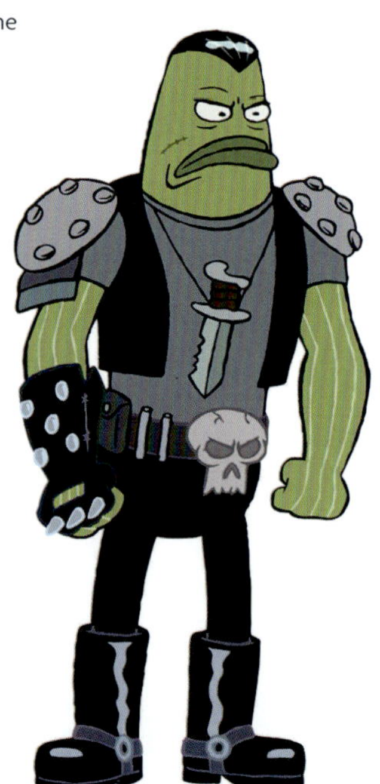

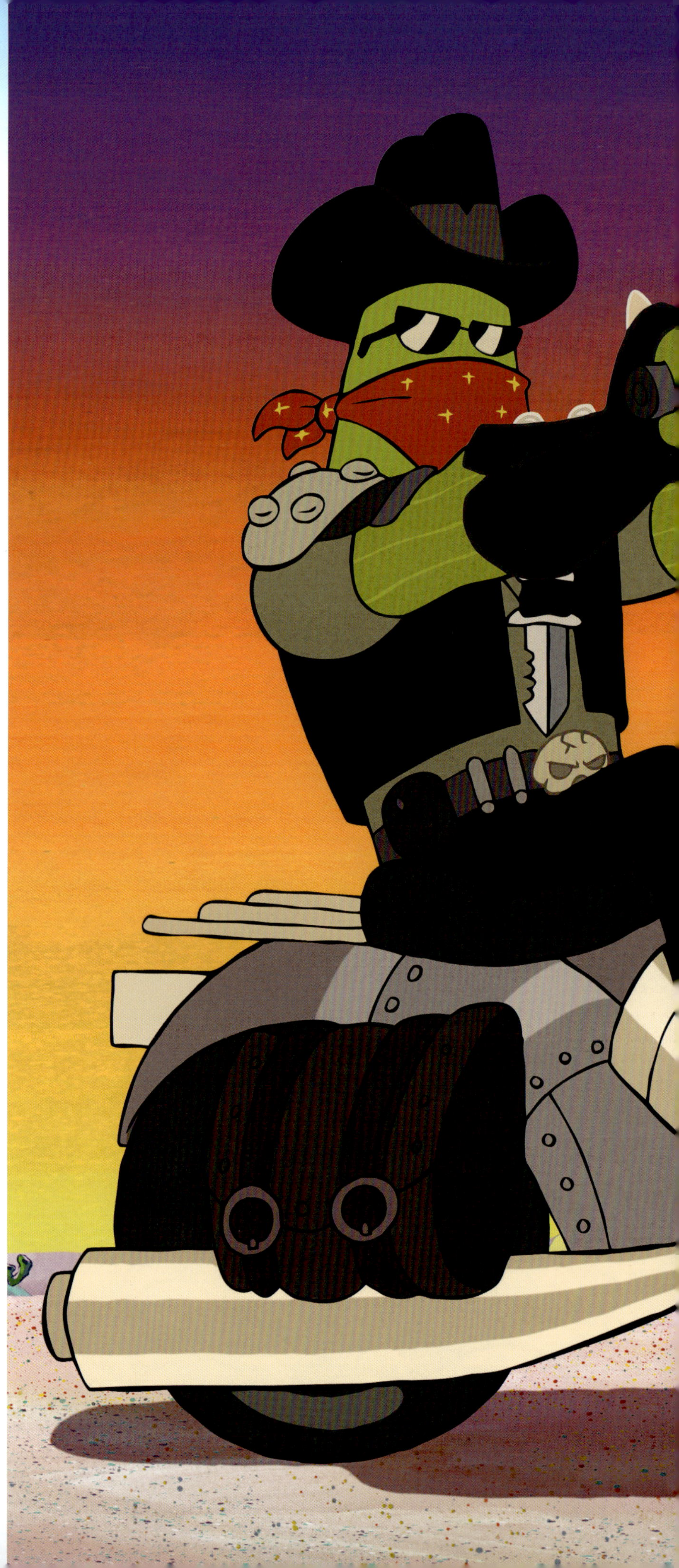

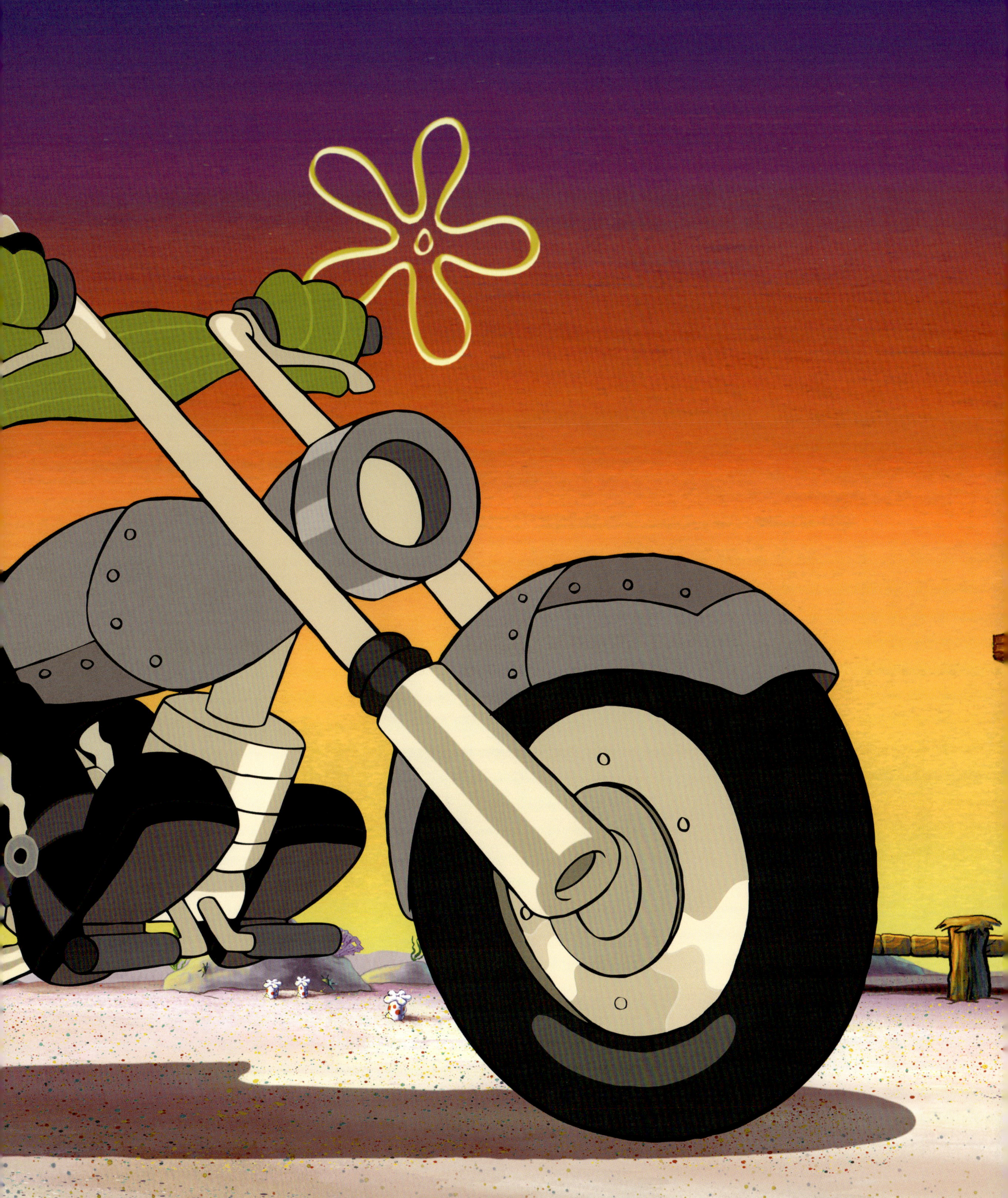

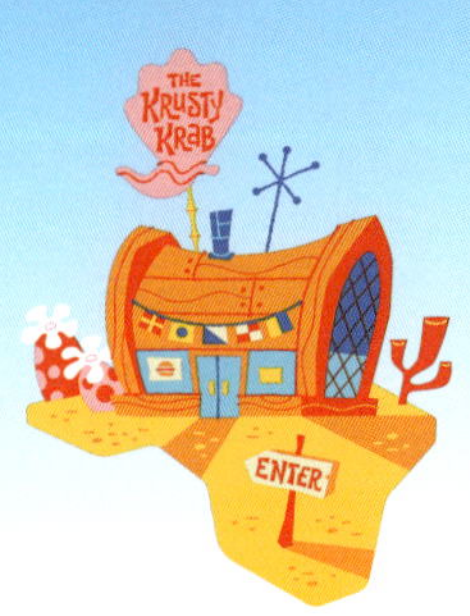

MEANWHILE... PLANKTOPOLIS

As part of his evil Plan Z, Plankton turns the residents of Bikini Bottom into mind-controlled citizens.

Layout image [upper] and final image [lower] of the Chum Bucket as it launches its Krabby Patty sales

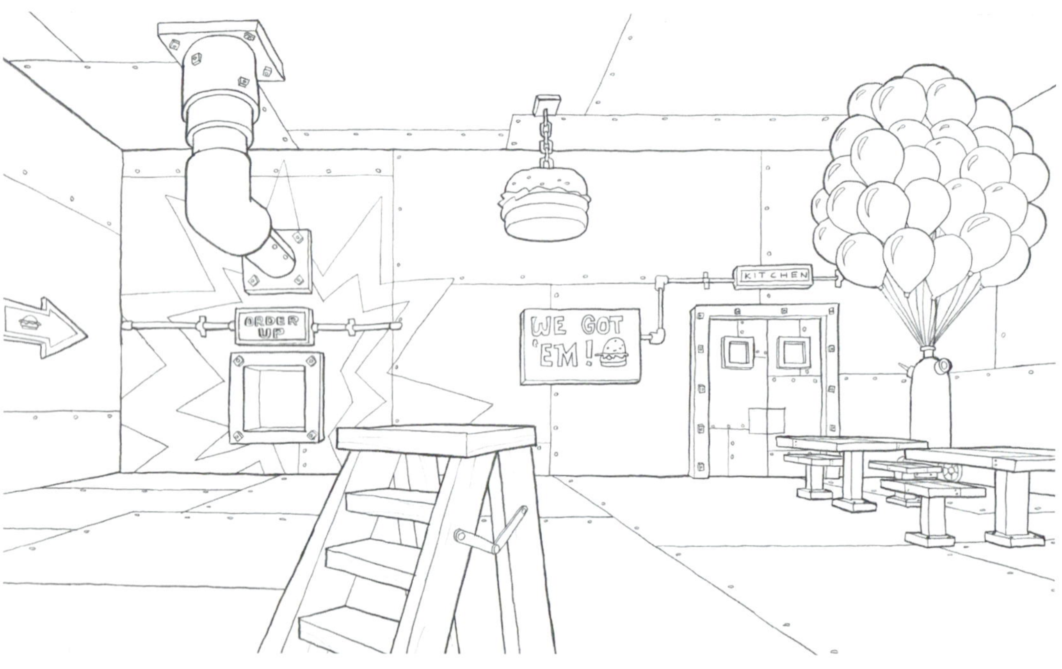

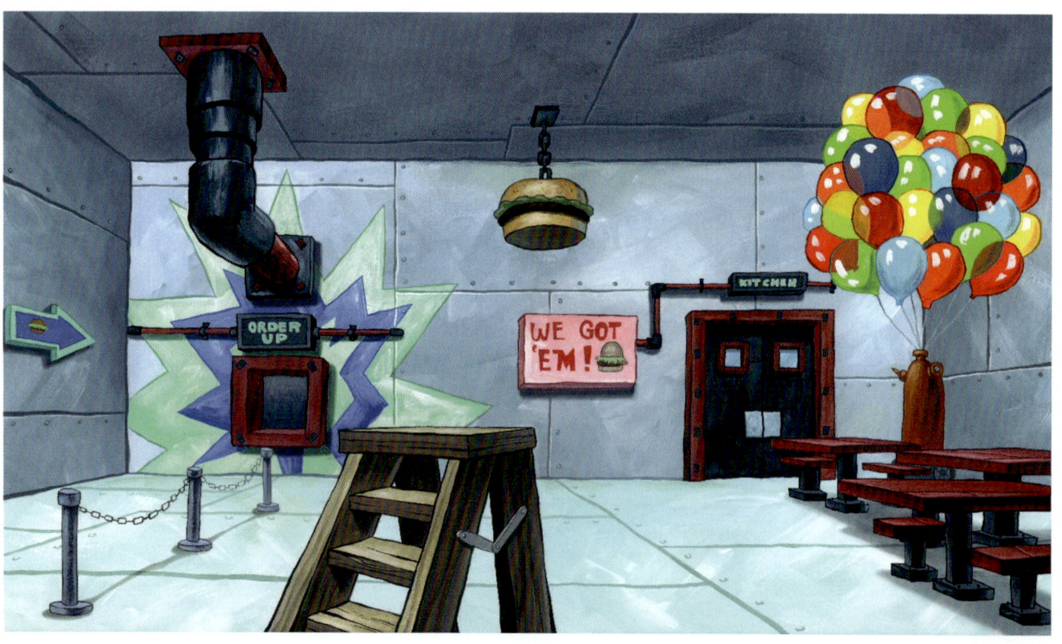

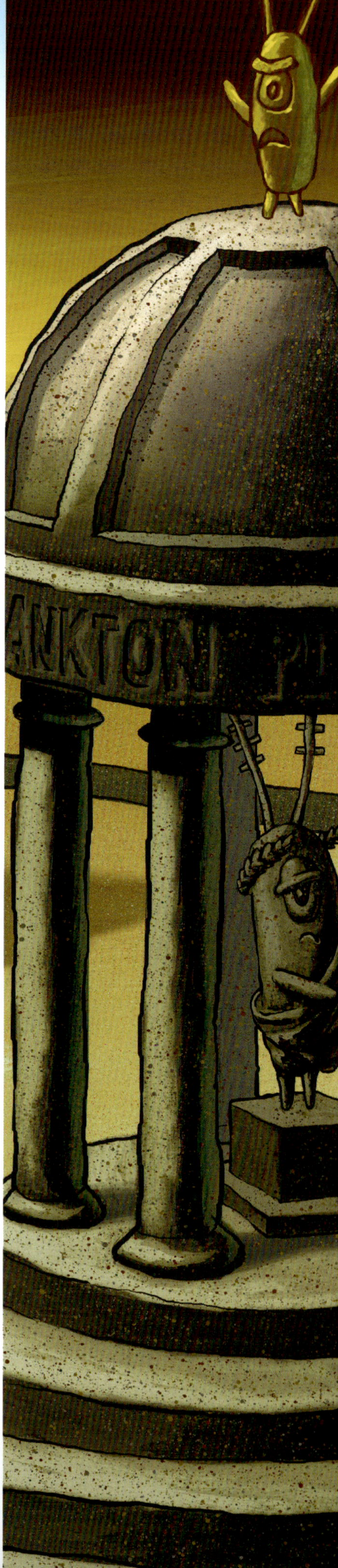

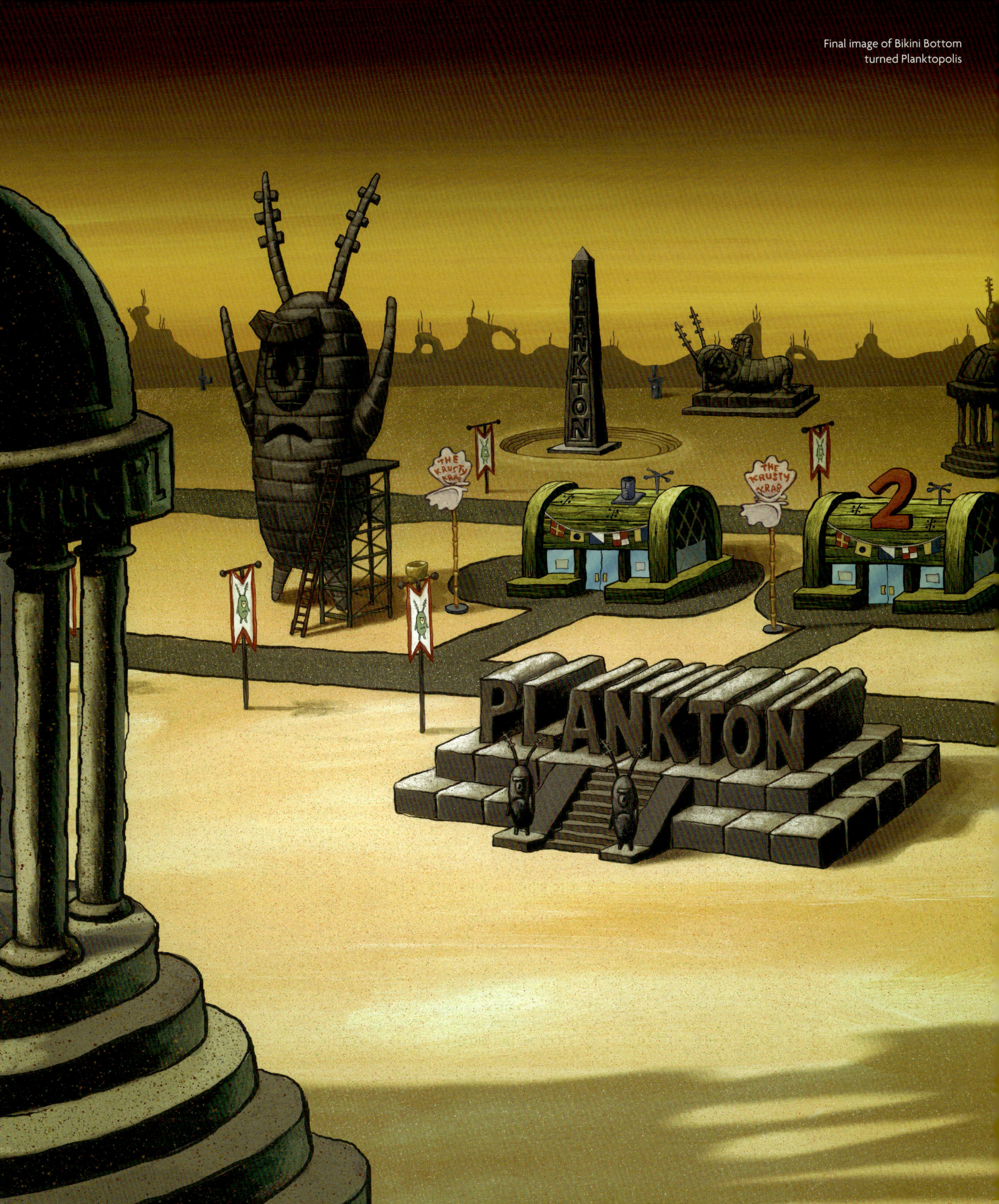

Final image of Bikini Bottom turned Planktopolis

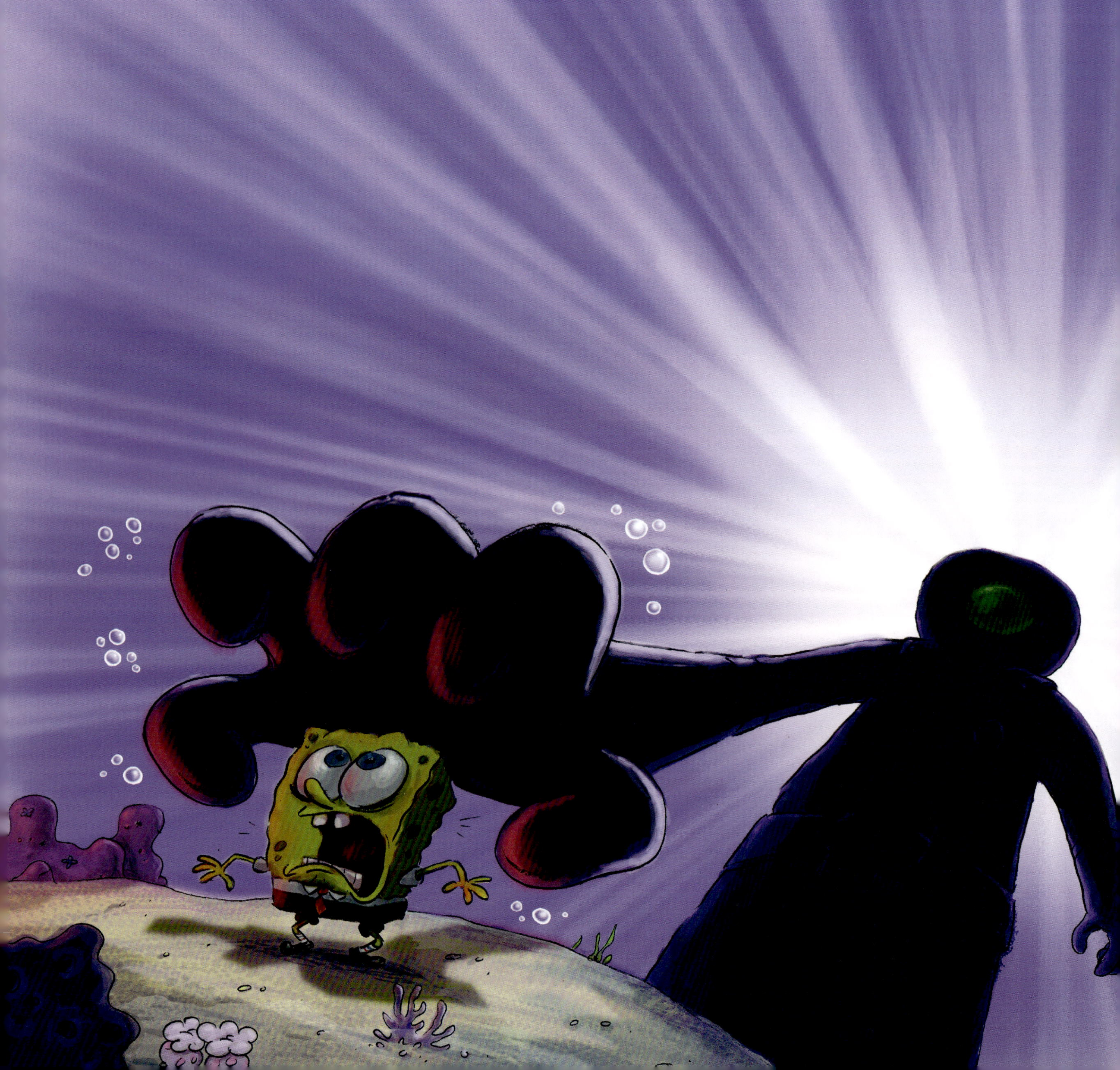

Movie moment concept of the Cyclops capturing SpongeBob

CYCLOPS

After SpongeBob is warned by Princess Mindy about a dangerous creature she calls a Cyclops, the deap-sea diver is his first interaction with humankind... and it's not a good one.

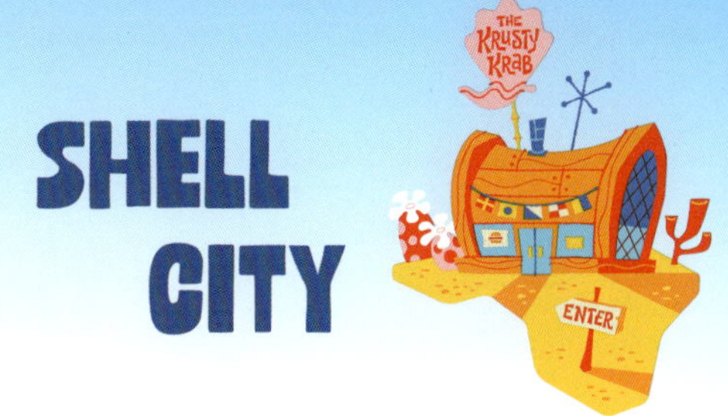

Tonal [upper] and final frame image [lower] of dehydrating Patrick and SpongeBob

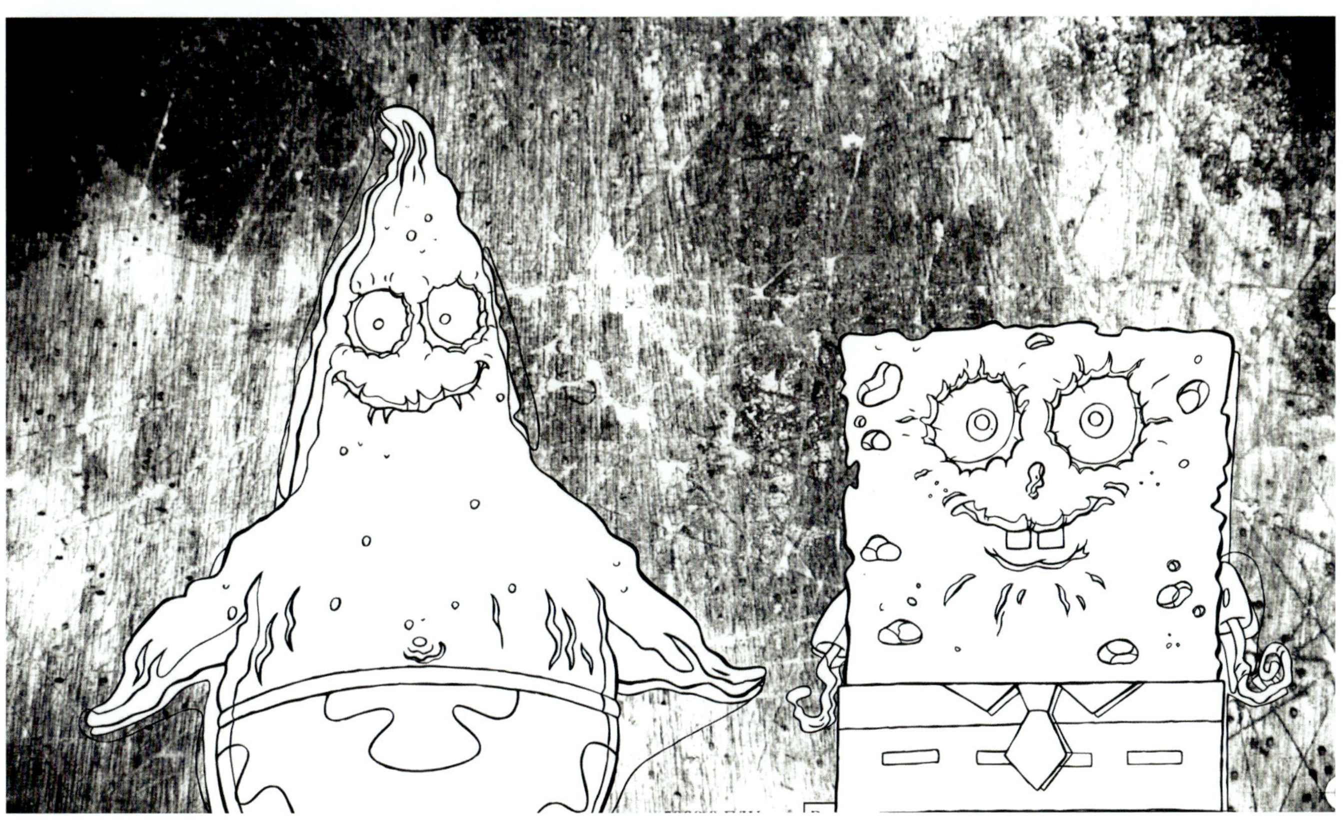

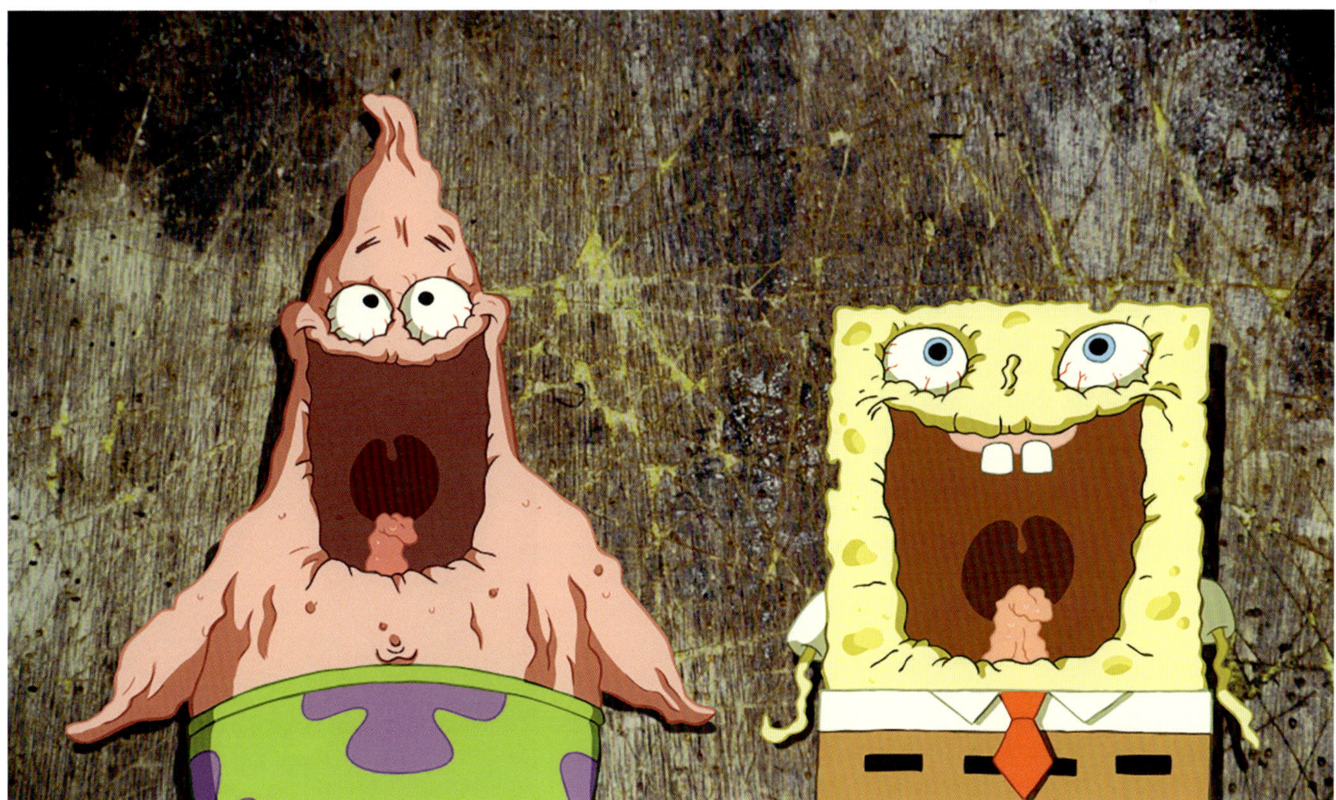

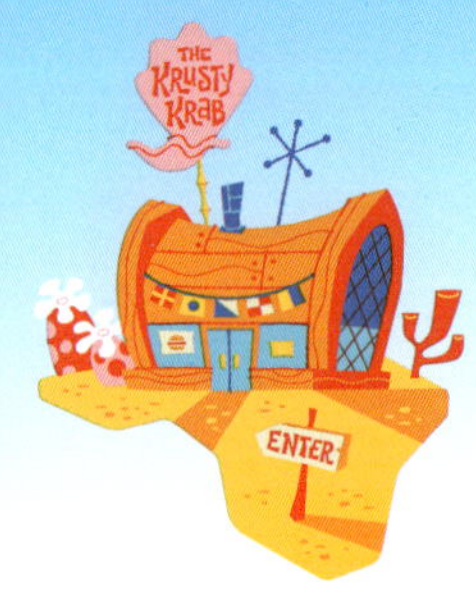

RESOLUTION AT THE KRUSTY KRAB

Amidst a victorious return of the crown and Mr. Krabs' rescue from death by Neptune, SpongeBob takes a moment to realize that he really has made a difference. He has confidence in himself, knows you can achieve great things despite your experience, and shares all of that learning out lengthily to his audience in one of his epic speeches.

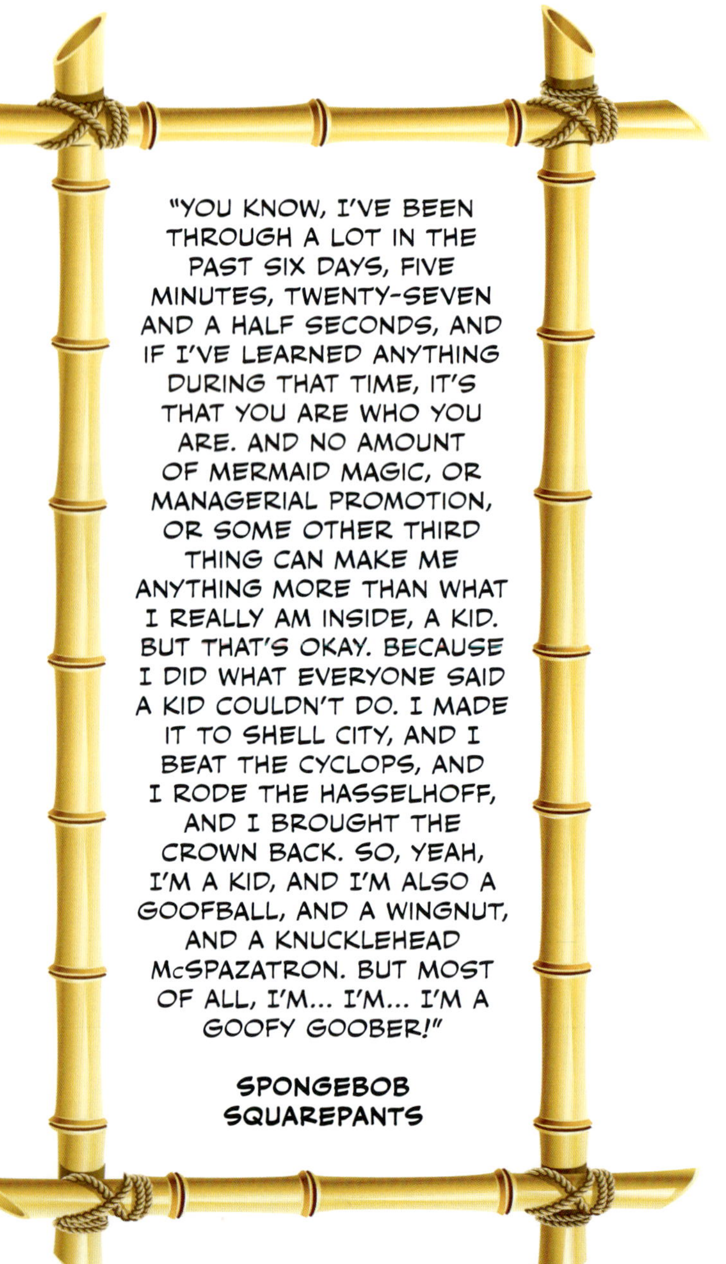

"YOU KNOW, I'VE BEEN THROUGH A LOT IN THE PAST SIX DAYS, FIVE MINUTES, TWENTY-SEVEN AND A HALF SECONDS, AND IF I'VE LEARNED ANYTHING DURING THAT TIME, IT'S THAT YOU ARE WHO YOU ARE. AND NO AMOUNT OF MERMAID MAGIC, OR MANAGERIAL PROMOTION, OR SOME OTHER THIRD THING CAN MAKE ME ANYTHING MORE THAN WHAT I REALLY AM INSIDE, A KID. BUT THAT'S OKAY. BECAUSE I DID WHAT EVERYONE SAID A KID COULDN'T DO. I MADE IT TO SHELL CITY, AND I BEAT THE CYCLOPS, AND I RODE THE HASSELHOFF, AND I BROUGHT THE CROWN BACK. SO, YEAH, I'M A KID, AND I'M ALSO A GOOFBALL, AND A WINGNUT, AND A KNUCKLEHEAD McSPAZATRON. BUT MOST OF ALL, I'M... I'M... I'M A GOOFY GOOBER!"

SPONGEBOB SQUAREPANTS

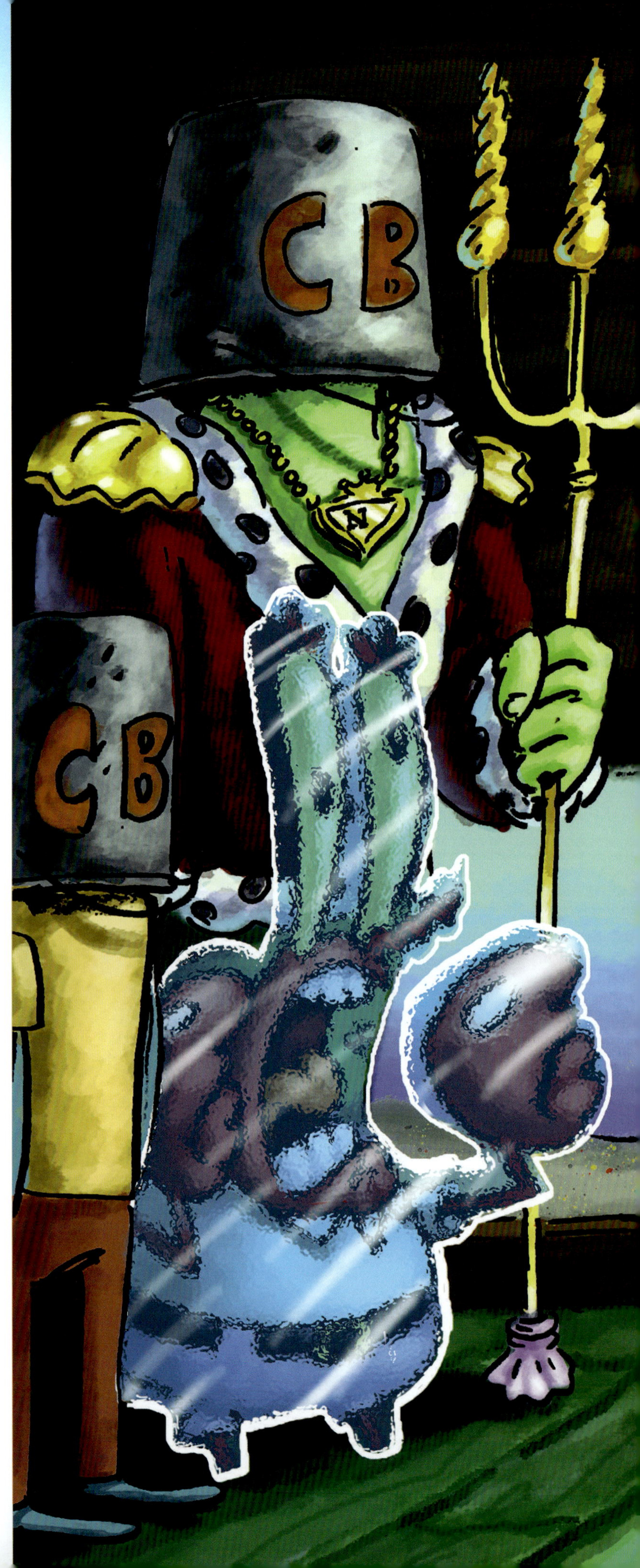

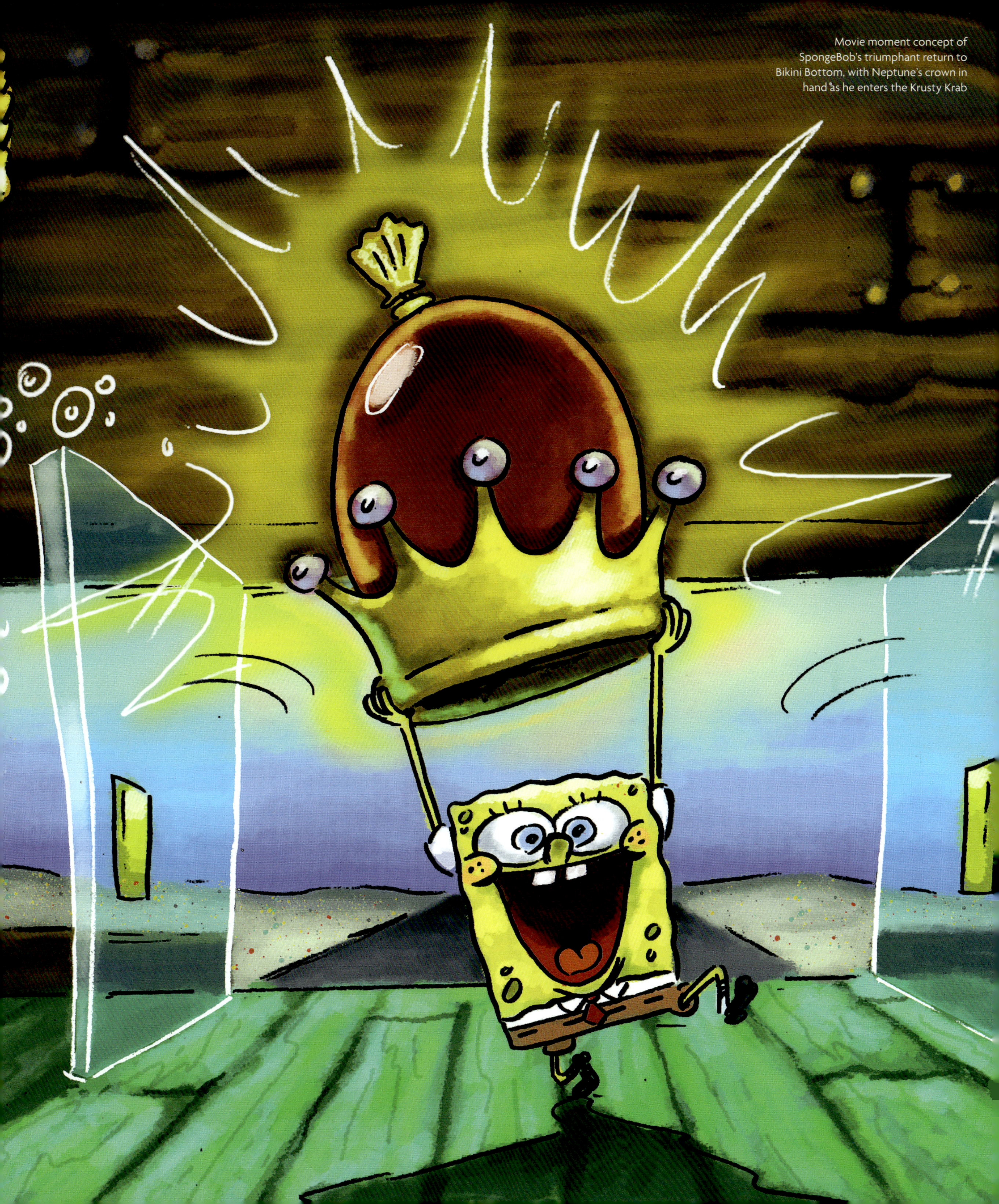

Movie moment concept of SpongeBob's triumphant return to Bikini Bottom, with Neptune's crown in hand as he enters the Krusty Krab

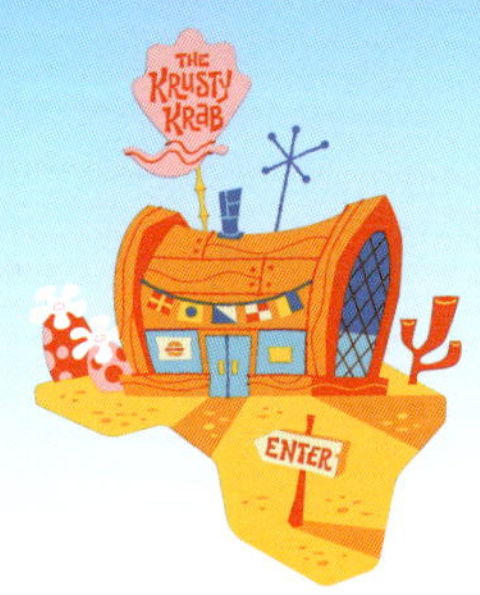

GOOFY GOOBER ROCK BALLAD

Musical fun is part of the SpongeBob joy, and this epic adventure wraps up with an epic rock ballad, just as smashing visually as it is sonically due to hilariously eye-burning imagery like Patrick in stilettos and fishnets, backup-dancing for wizard rock icon SpongeBob.

Movie moment concept of SpongeBob in song (right), and of SpongeBob and Patrick in song (below)

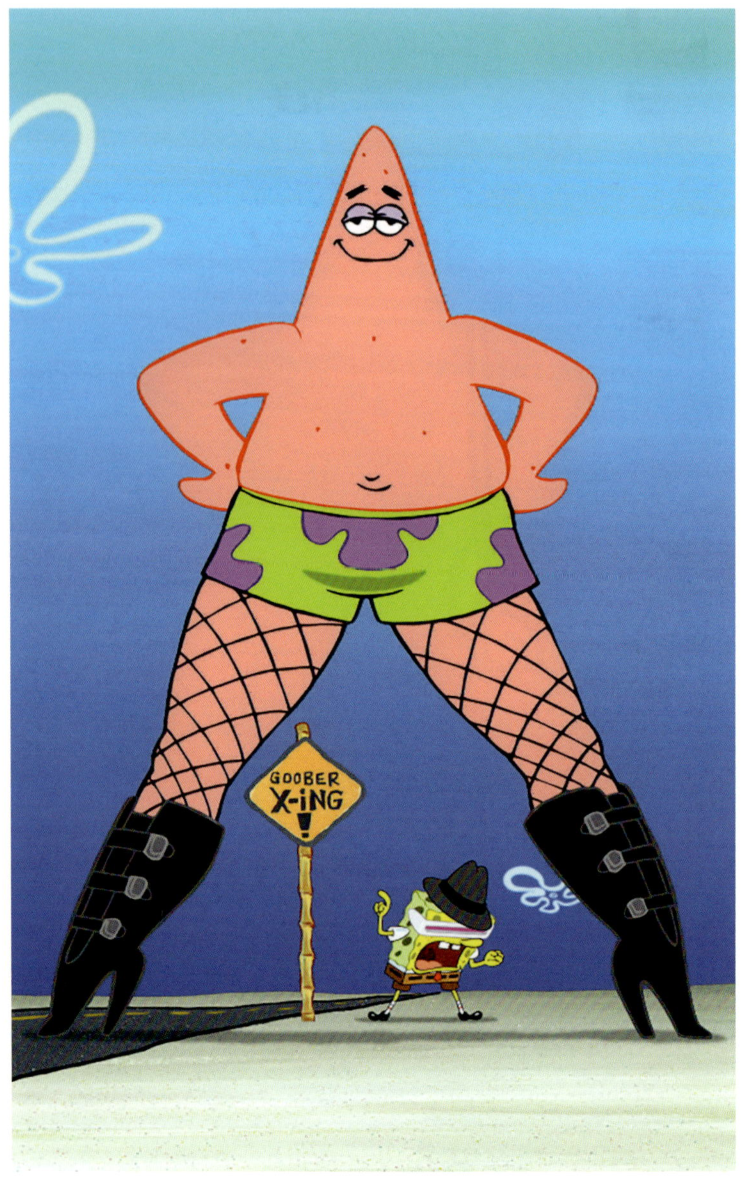

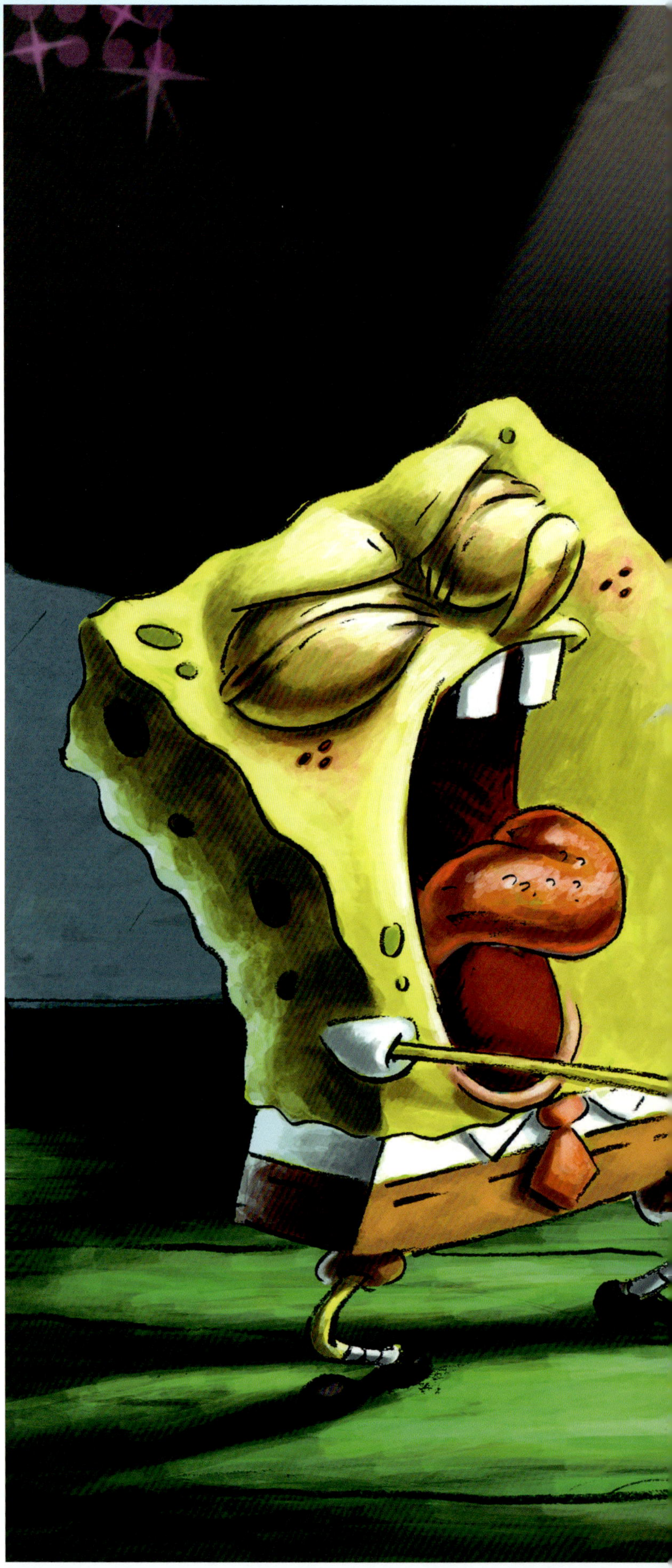

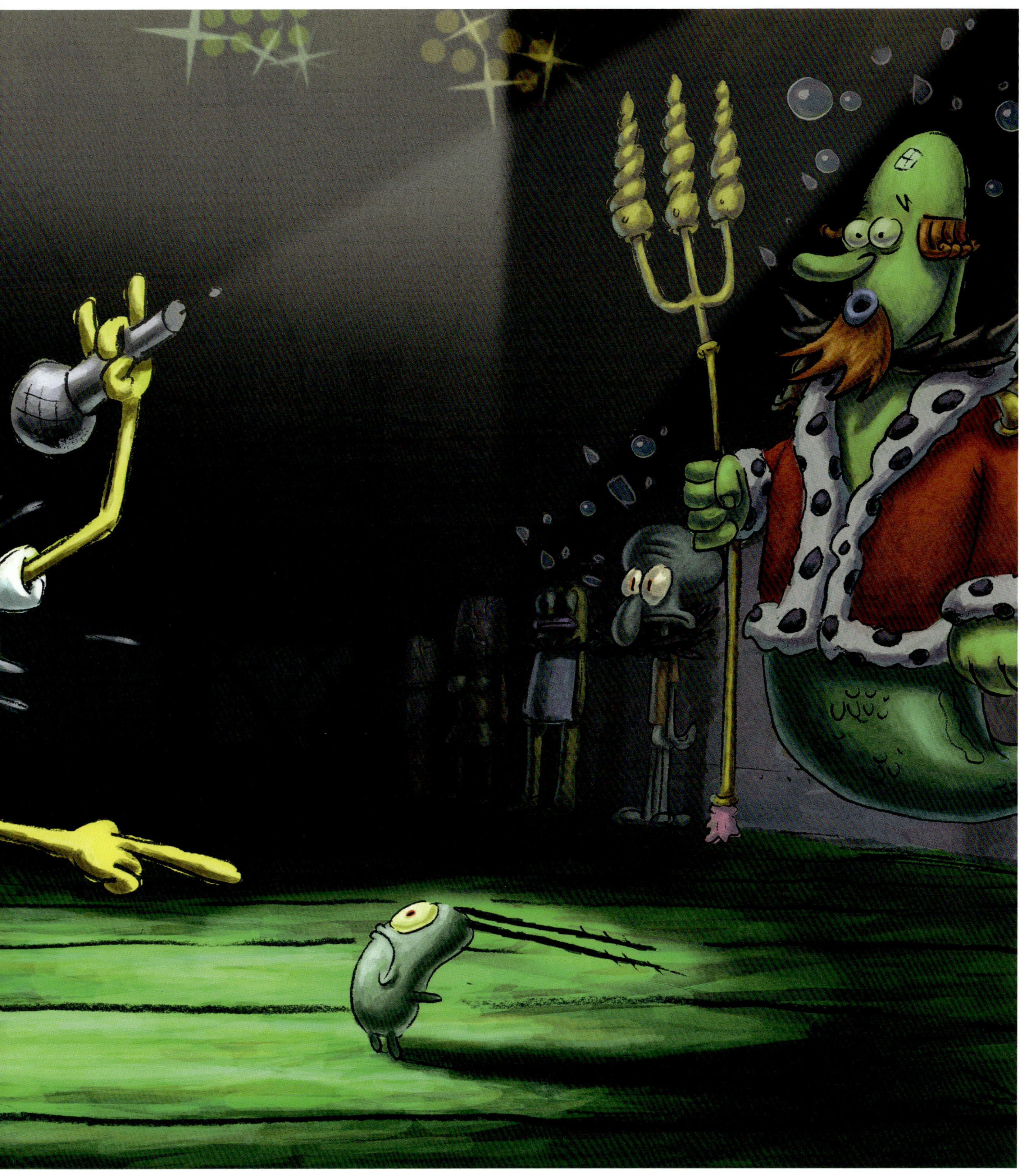

THE SPONGEBOB MOVIE™ SPONGE OUT OF WATER

The secret formula for the Krabby Patty is once again the anchor in a *SpongeBob* adventure, but this time, the real-world pirate Burger Beard is the recipe napper. *Sponge Out of Water*, the second animated/live-action feature-length film, premiered on February 5, 2015.

MAKING WAVES IN OUR WORLD

THE SPONGEBOB MOVIE
SPONGE OUT OF WATER

FEBRUARY 6
In Theatres & real D 3D

PARAMOUNT ANIMATION AND NICKELODEON MOVIES PRESENT A UNITED PLANKTON PICTURES PRODUCTION "THE SPONGEBOB MOVIE: SPONGE OUT OF WATER" ANTONIO BANDERAS
MUSIC BY JOHN DEBNEY EDITED BY DAVID IAN SALTER, ACE EXECUTIVE PRODUCERS STEPHEN HILLENBURG CALE BOYTER PRODUCED BY PAUL TIBBITT MARY PARENT LIVE ACTION DIRECTION MIKE MITCHELL BASED ON THE SERIES "SPONGEBOB SQUAREPANTS" CREATED BY STEPHEN HILLENBURG
STORY BY STEPHEN HILLENBURG & PAUL TIBBITT SCREENPLAY BY JONATHAN AIBEL & GLENN BERGER DIRECTED BY PAUL TIBBITT

nickelodeon MOVIES

PG PARENTAL GUIDANCE SUGGESTED MILD ACTION AND RUDE HUMOR
Some Material May Not Be Suitable for Children

SOUNDTRACK ALBUM ON I AM OTHER/COLUMBIA RECORDS

SpongeBobMovie.com

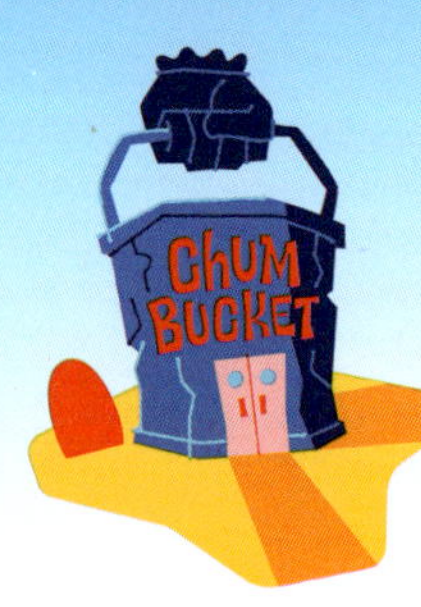

WARTIME BATTLE FOR THE SECRET FORMULA

When Krabby Patties are no longer available to sustain the residents of Bikini Bottom, the town turns into an apocalyptic war zone, but luckily Mr. Krabs has military experience and knows how to rally the troops to deal with the swell of insurgents. Meanwhile, SpongeBob breaks out in inspirational speech...

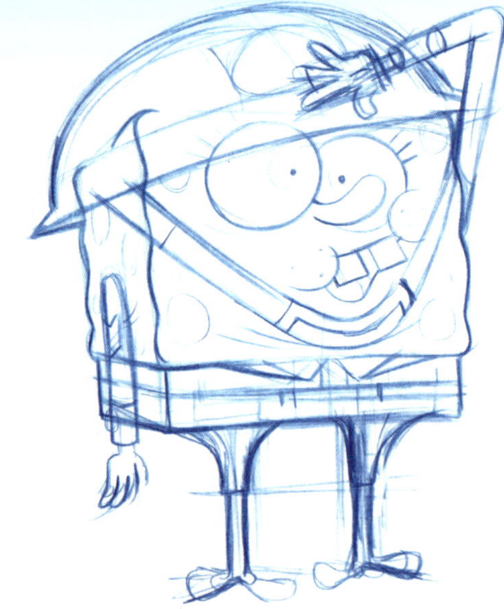

Cleanup [left] and rough animation [right] images of SpongeBob

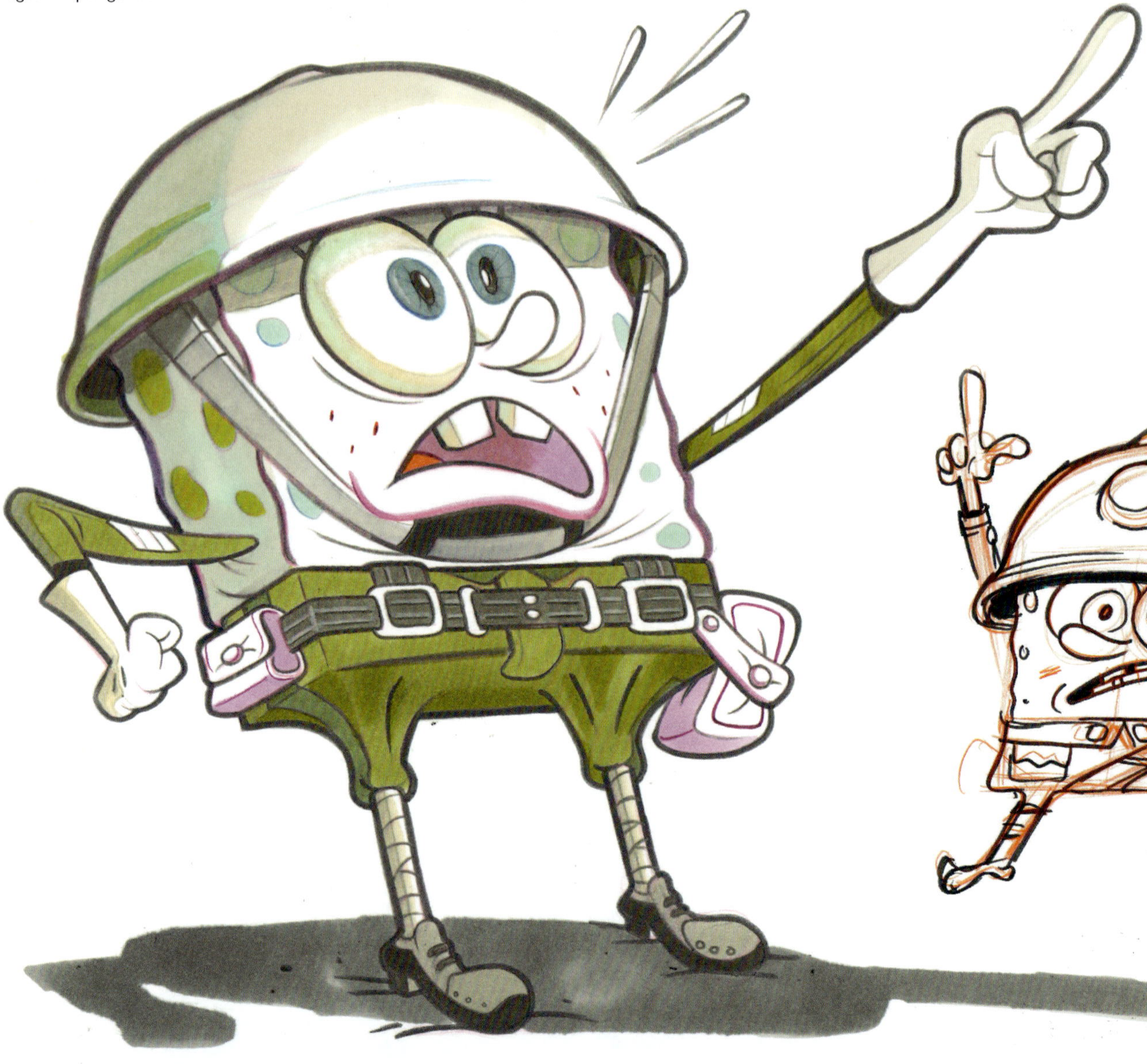

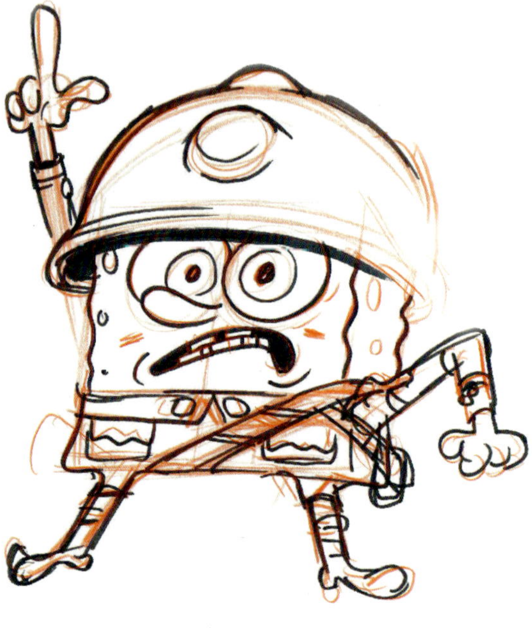

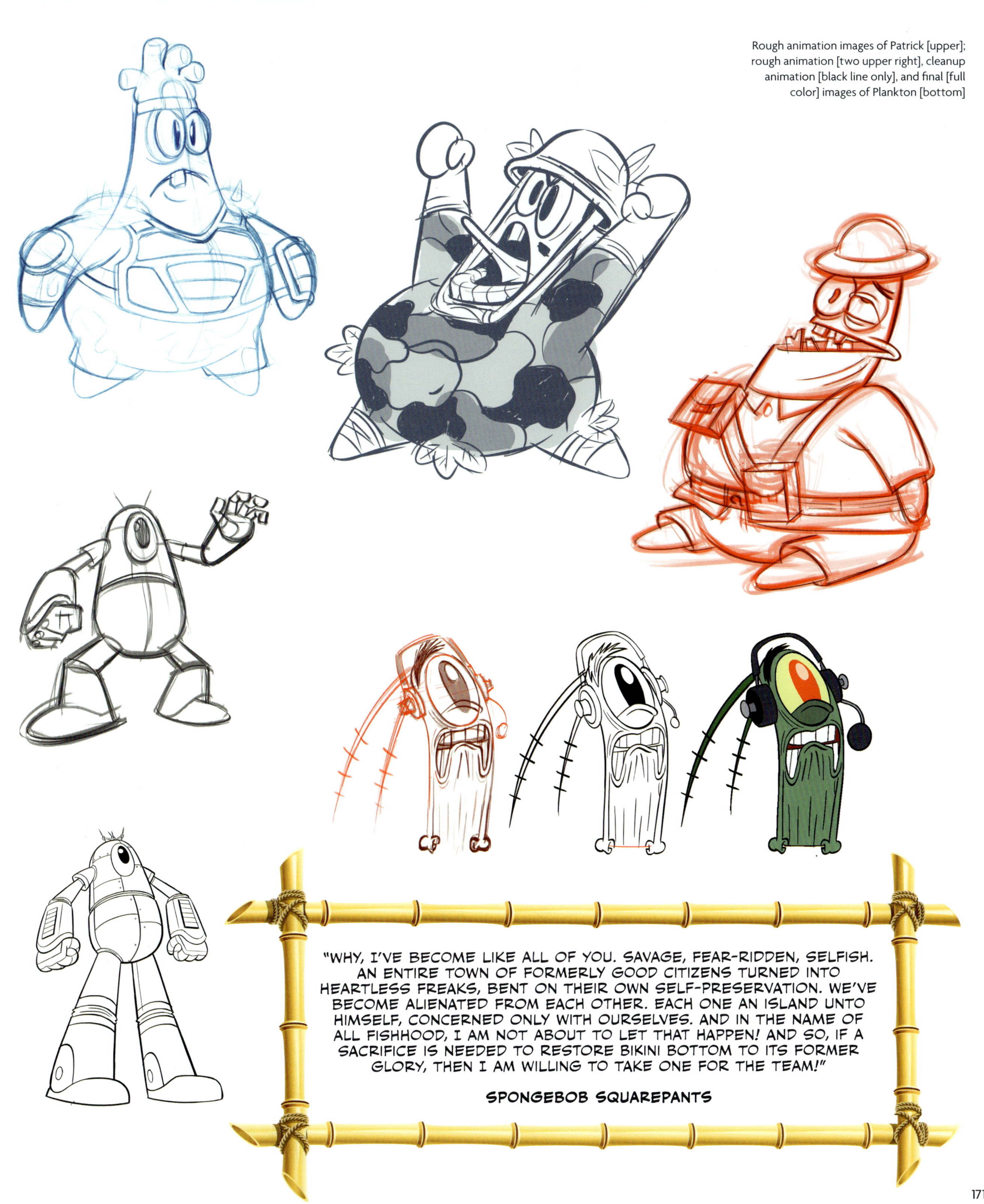

Rough animation images of Patrick [upper]; rough animation [two upper right], cleanup animation [black line only], and final [full color] images of Plankton [bottom]

"WHY, I'VE BECOME LIKE ALL OF YOU. SAVAGE, FEAR-RIDDEN, SELFISH. AN ENTIRE TOWN OF FORMERLY GOOD CITIZENS TURNED INTO HEARTLESS FREAKS, BENT ON THEIR OWN SELF-PRESERVATION. WE'VE BECOME ALIENATED FROM EACH OTHER. EACH ONE AN ISLAND UNTO HIMSELF, CONCERNED ONLY WITH OURSELVES. AND IN THE NAME OF ALL FISHHOOD, I AM NOT ABOUT TO LET THAT HAPPEN! AND SO, IF A SACRIFICE IS NEEDED TO RESTORE BIKINI BOTTOM TO ITS FORMER GLORY, THEN I AM WILLING TO TAKE ONE FOR THE TEAM!"

SPONGEBOB SQUAREPANTS

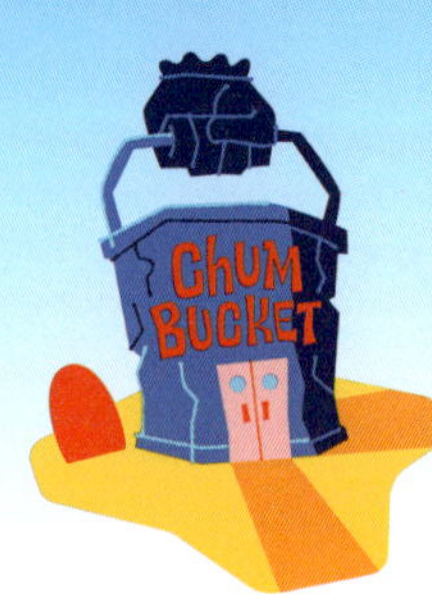

BIKINI BOTTOM TURNED DIRTY BOTTOM

Things get really bad, dropping down to cesspool level with the removal of Krabby Patties from Bikini Bottom's ecosystem.

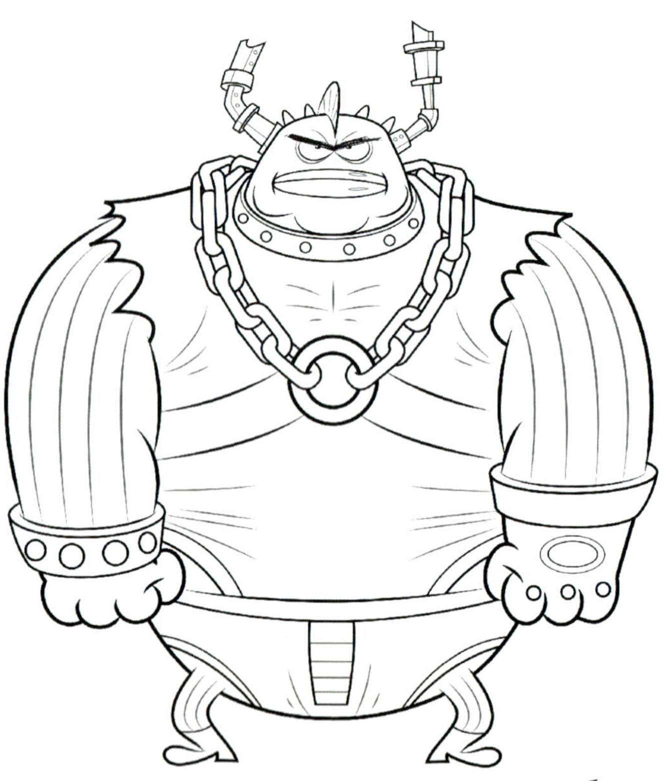

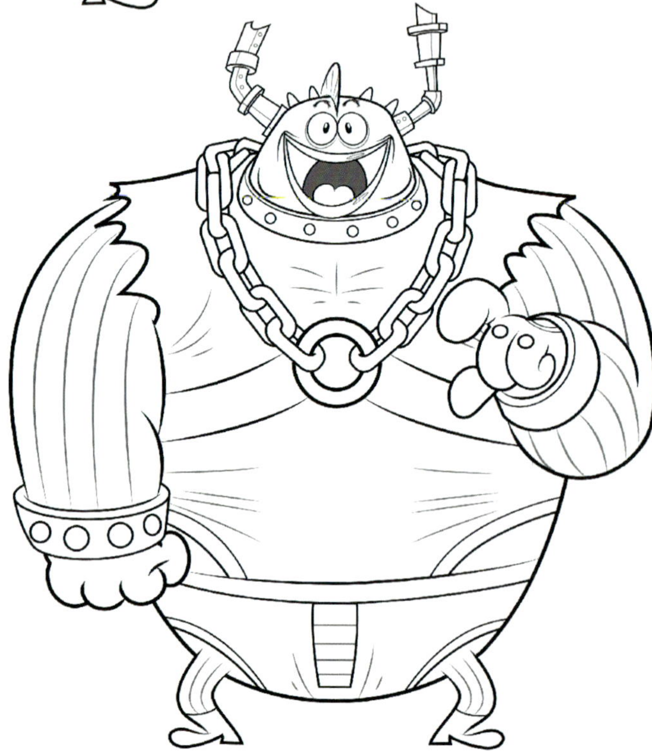

Cleanup animation drawings of post-apocalyptic character

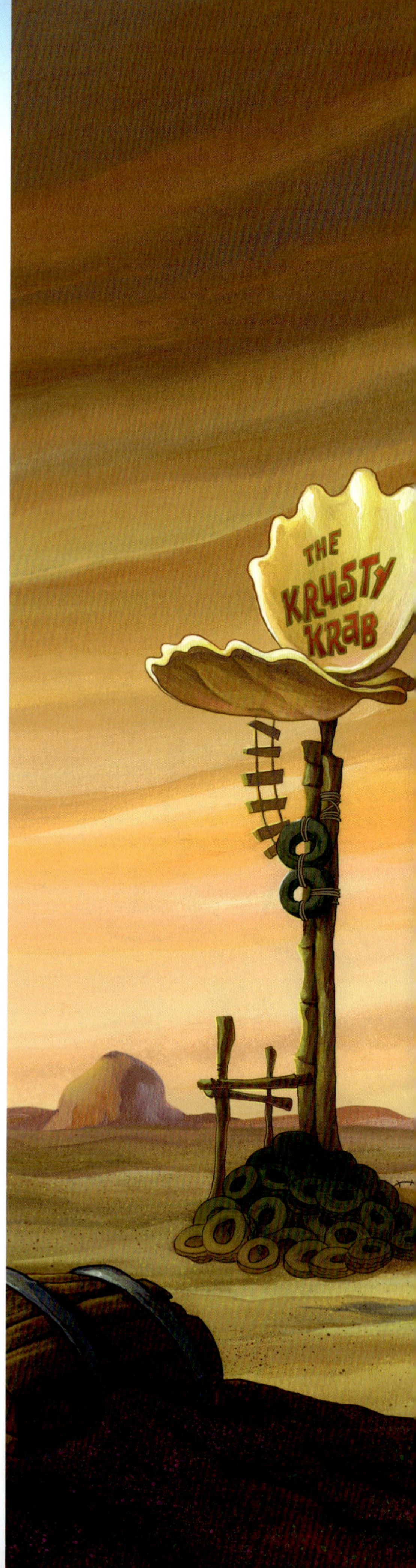

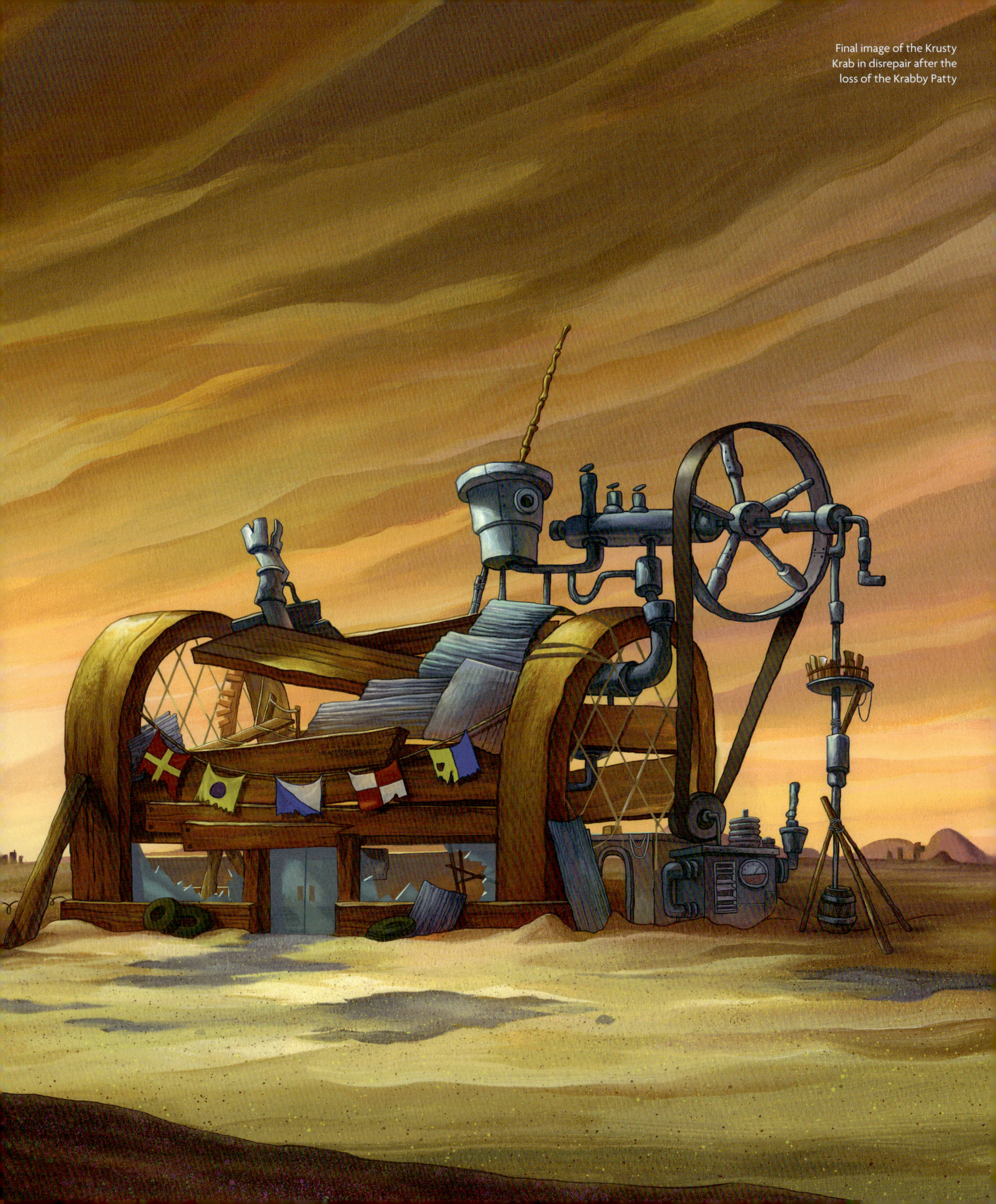

Final image of the Krusty Krab in disrepair after the loss of the Krabby Patty

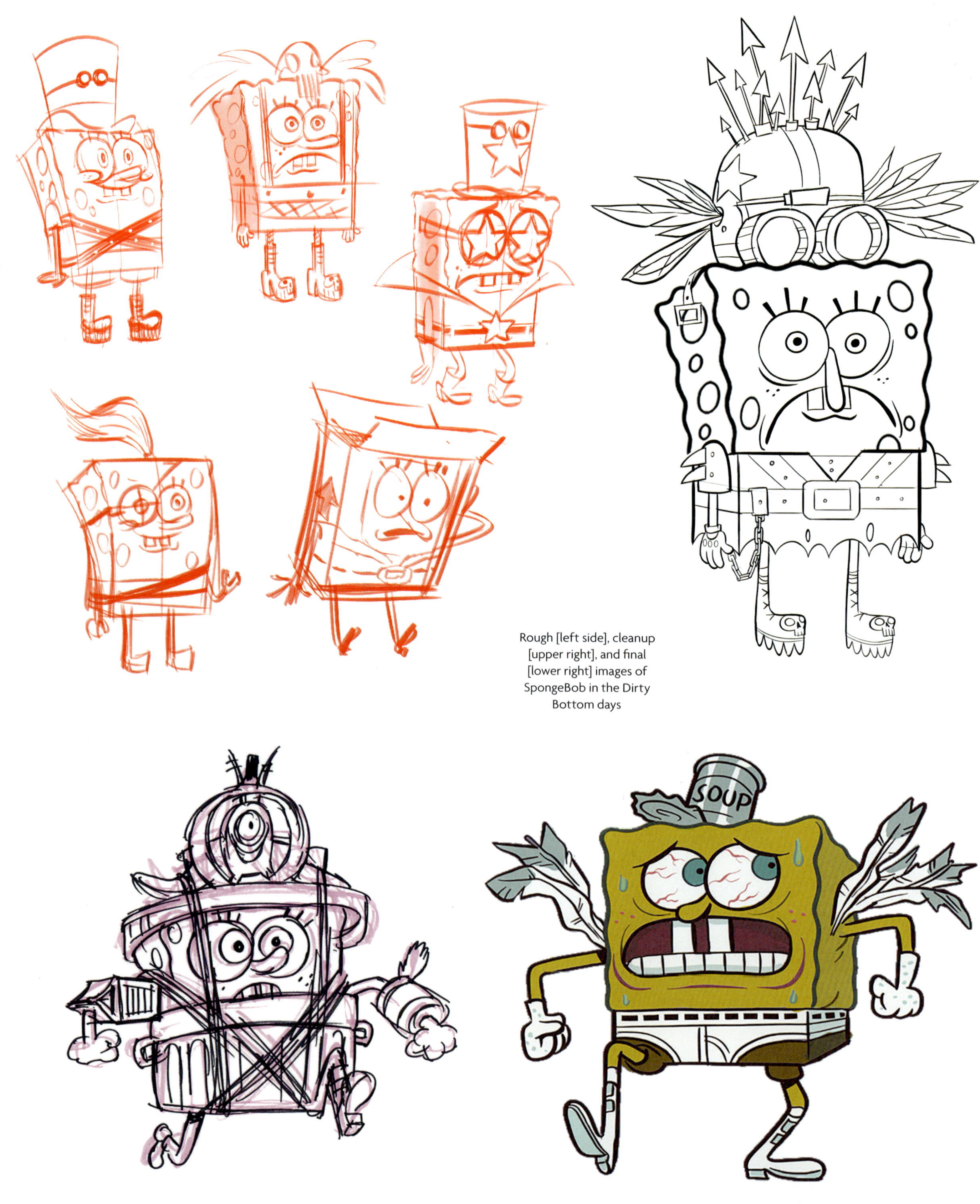

Rough [left side], cleanup [upper right], and final [lower right] images of SpongeBob in the Dirty Bottom days

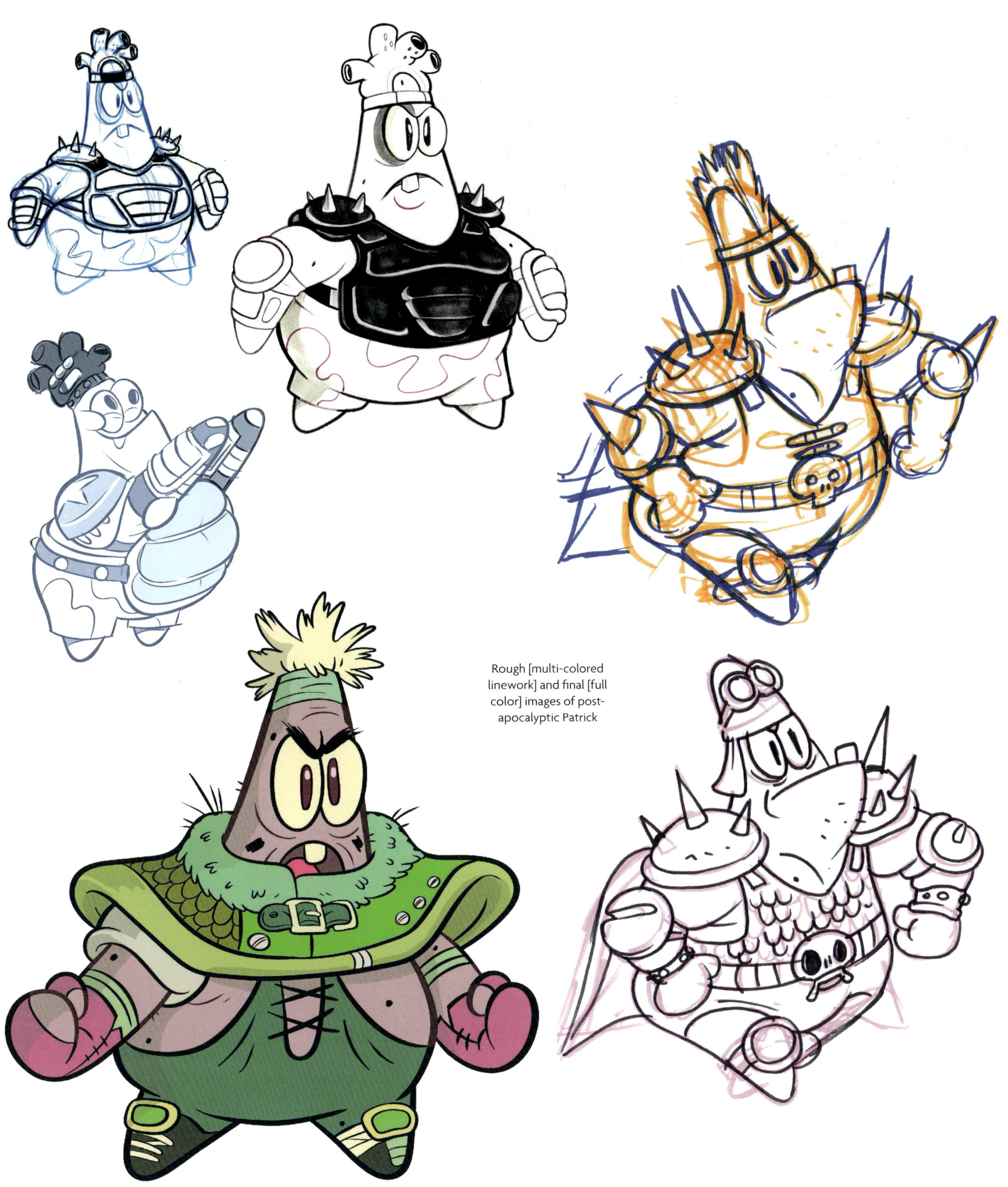

Rough [multi-colored linework] and final [full color] images of post-apocalyptic Patrick

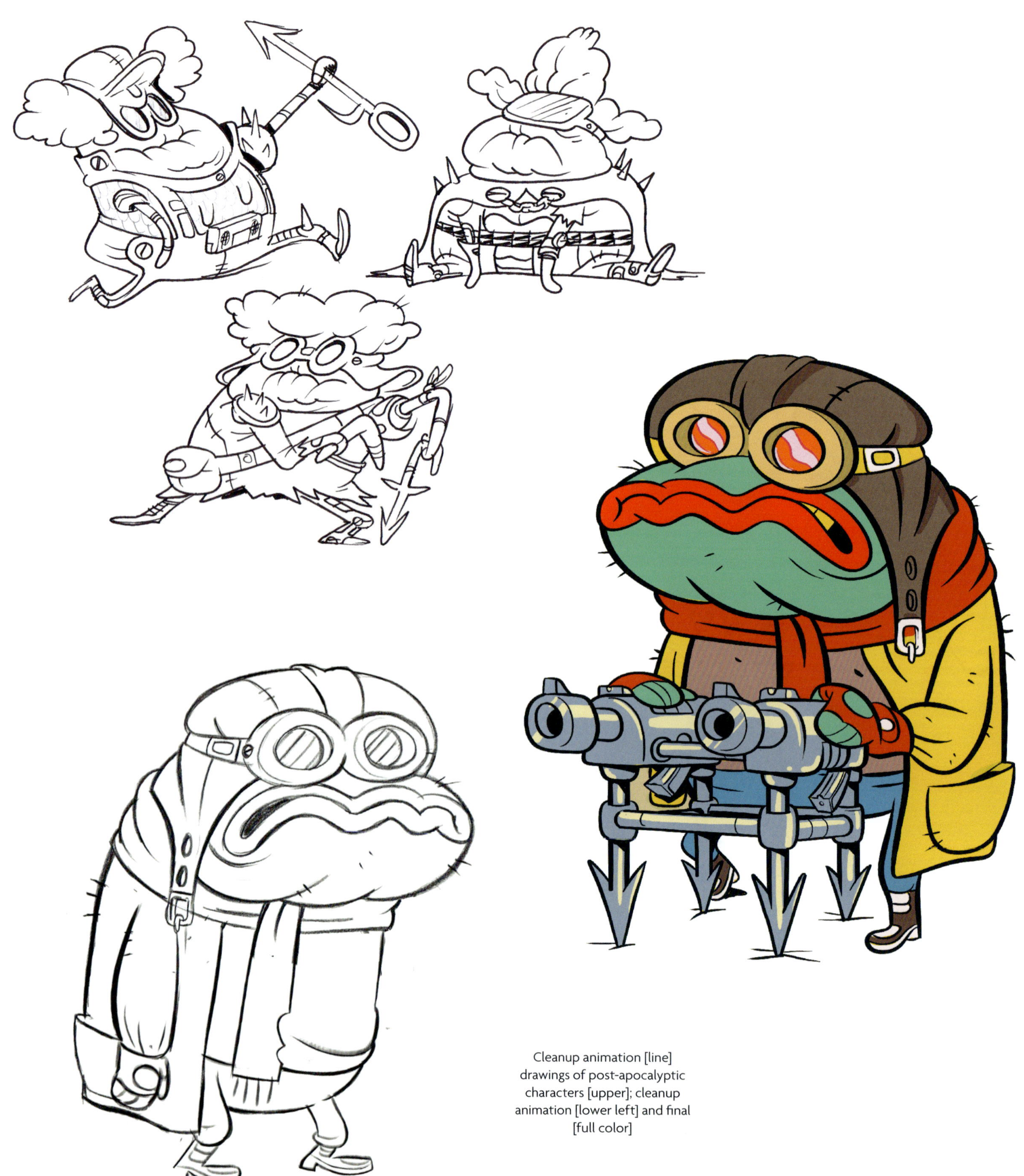

Cleanup animation [line] drawings of post-apocalyptic characters [upper]; cleanup animation [lower left] and final [full color]

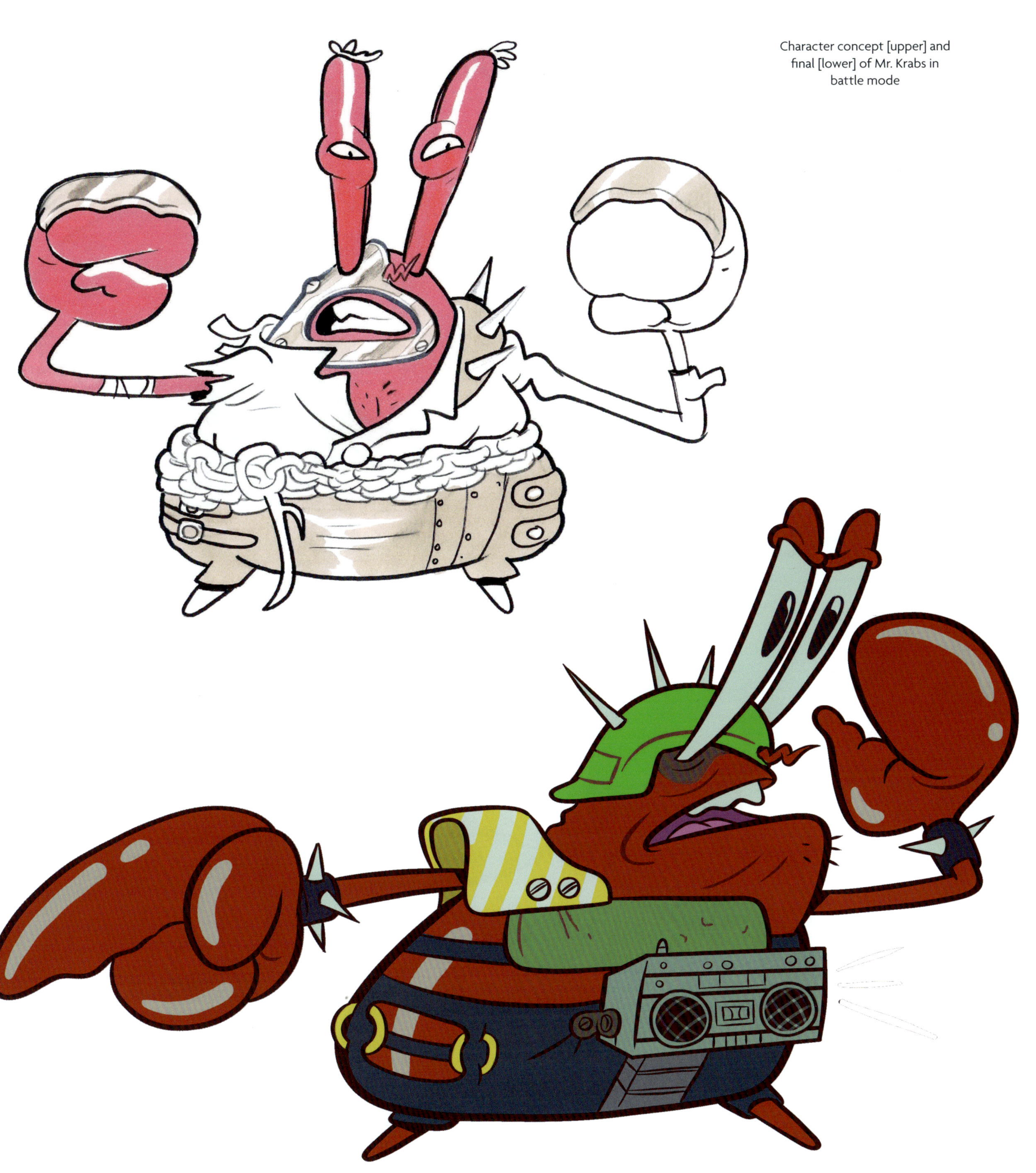

Character concept [upper] and final [lower] of Mr. Krabs in battle mode

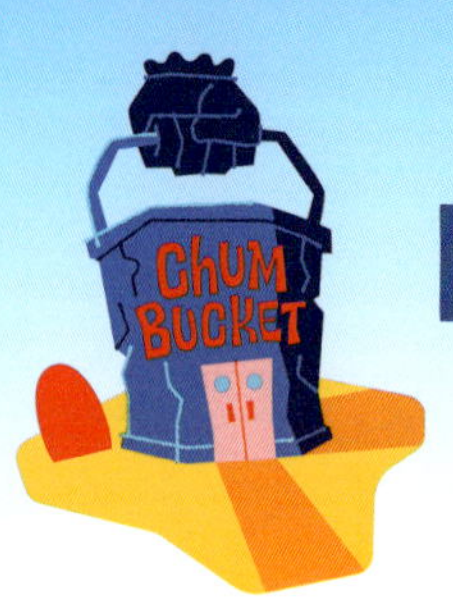

MEET SQUIDASAURUS REX

When Patrick travels back in time, he accidentally returns to the present with a primitive relative of Squidward in tow.

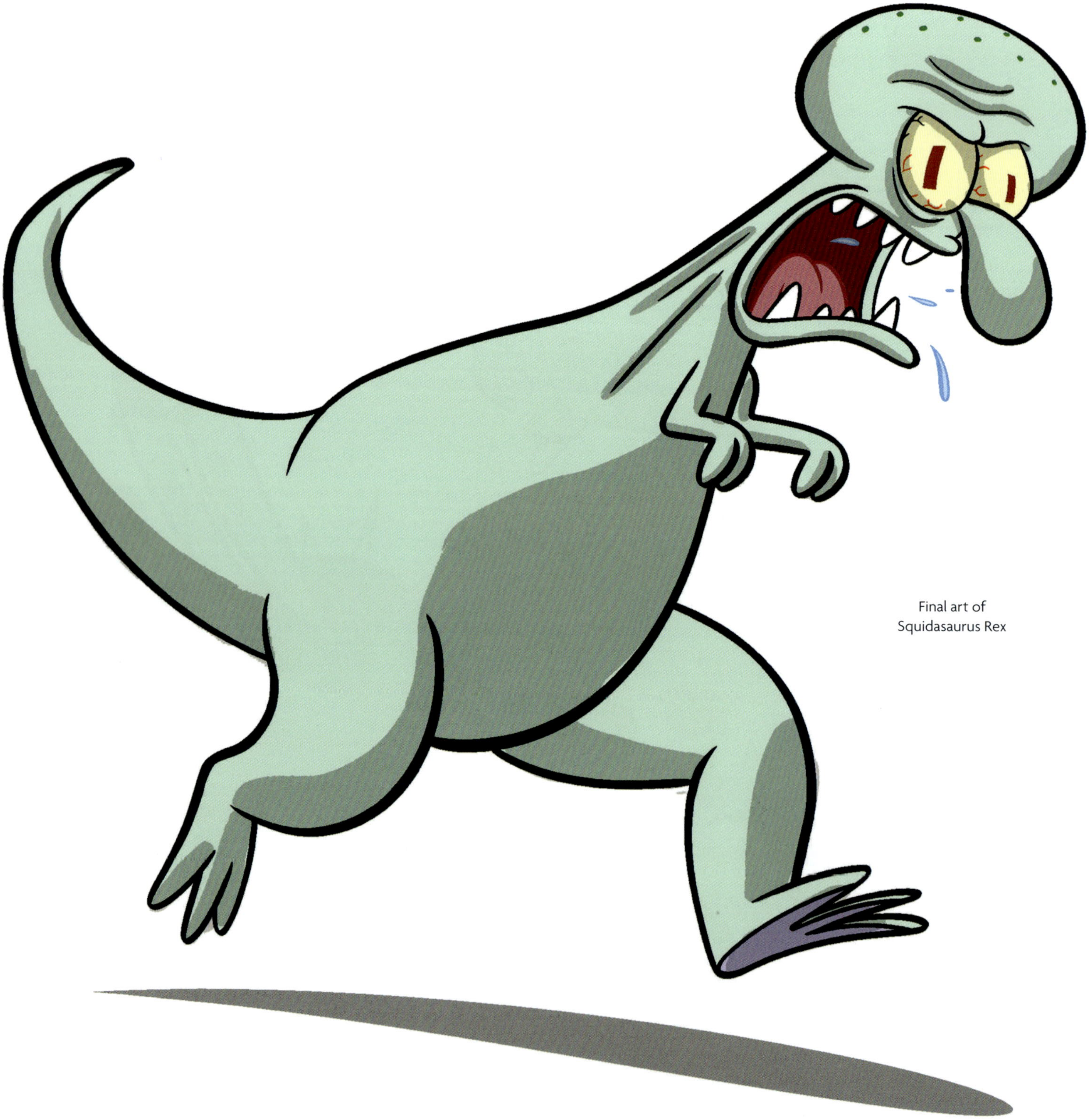

Final art of Squidasaurus Rex

CONSPIRACY SANDY

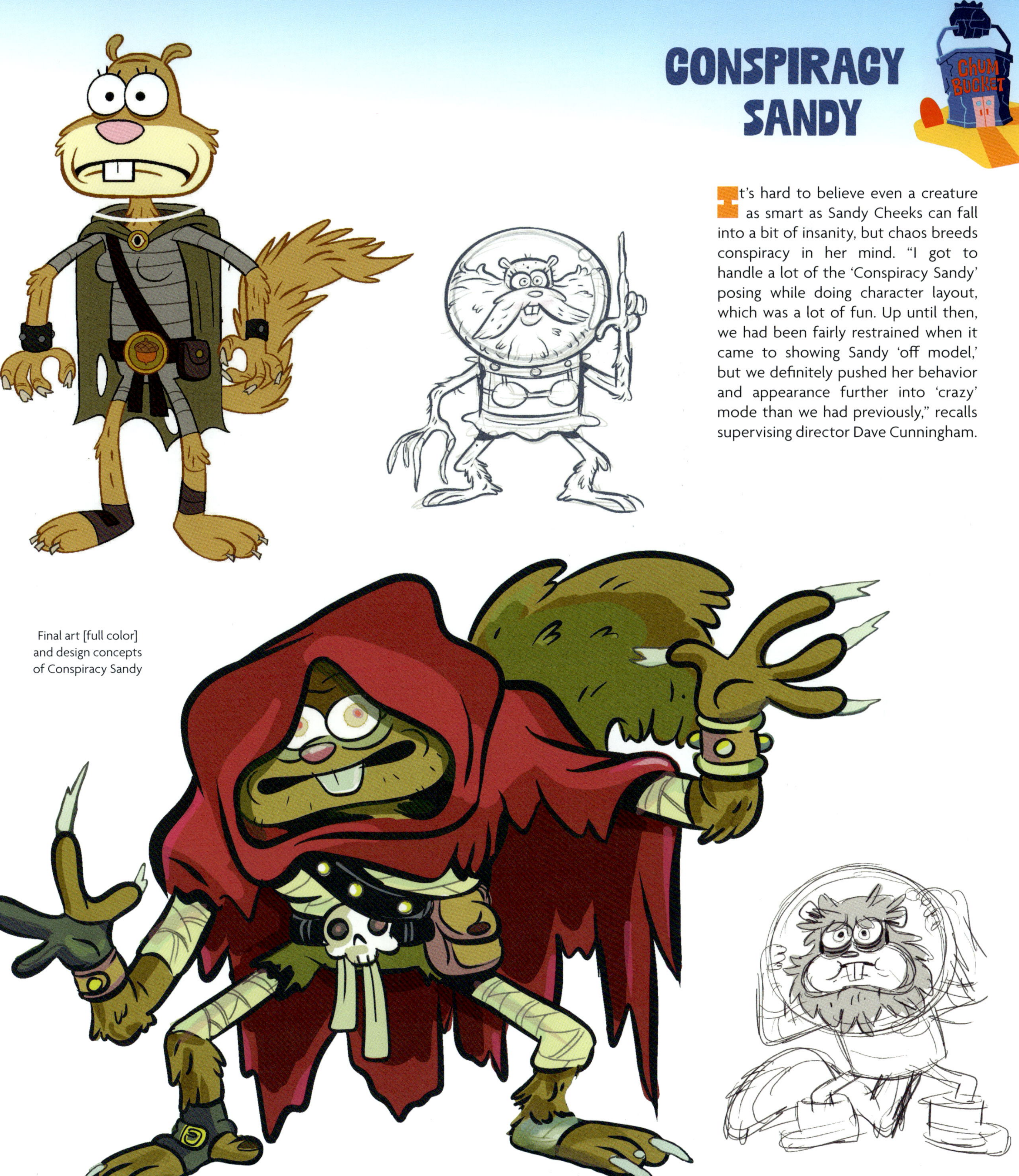

It's hard to believe even a creature as smart as Sandy Cheeks can fall into a bit of insanity, but chaos breeds conspiracy in her mind. "I got to handle a lot of the 'Conspiracy Sandy' posing while doing character layout, which was a lot of fun. Up until then, we had been fairly restrained when it came to showing Sandy 'off model,' but we definitely pushed her behavior and appearance further into 'crazy' mode than we had previously," recalls supervising director Dave Cunningham.

Final art [full color] and design concepts of Conspiracy Sandy

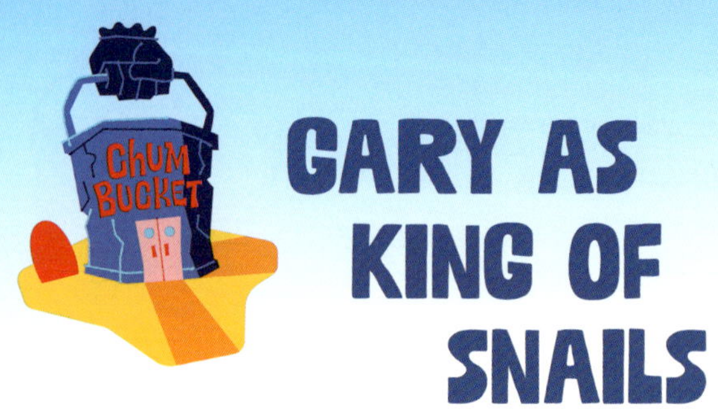

GARY AS KING OF SNAILS

Final frame images that inspire the phrase "All hail the King of Snails!"

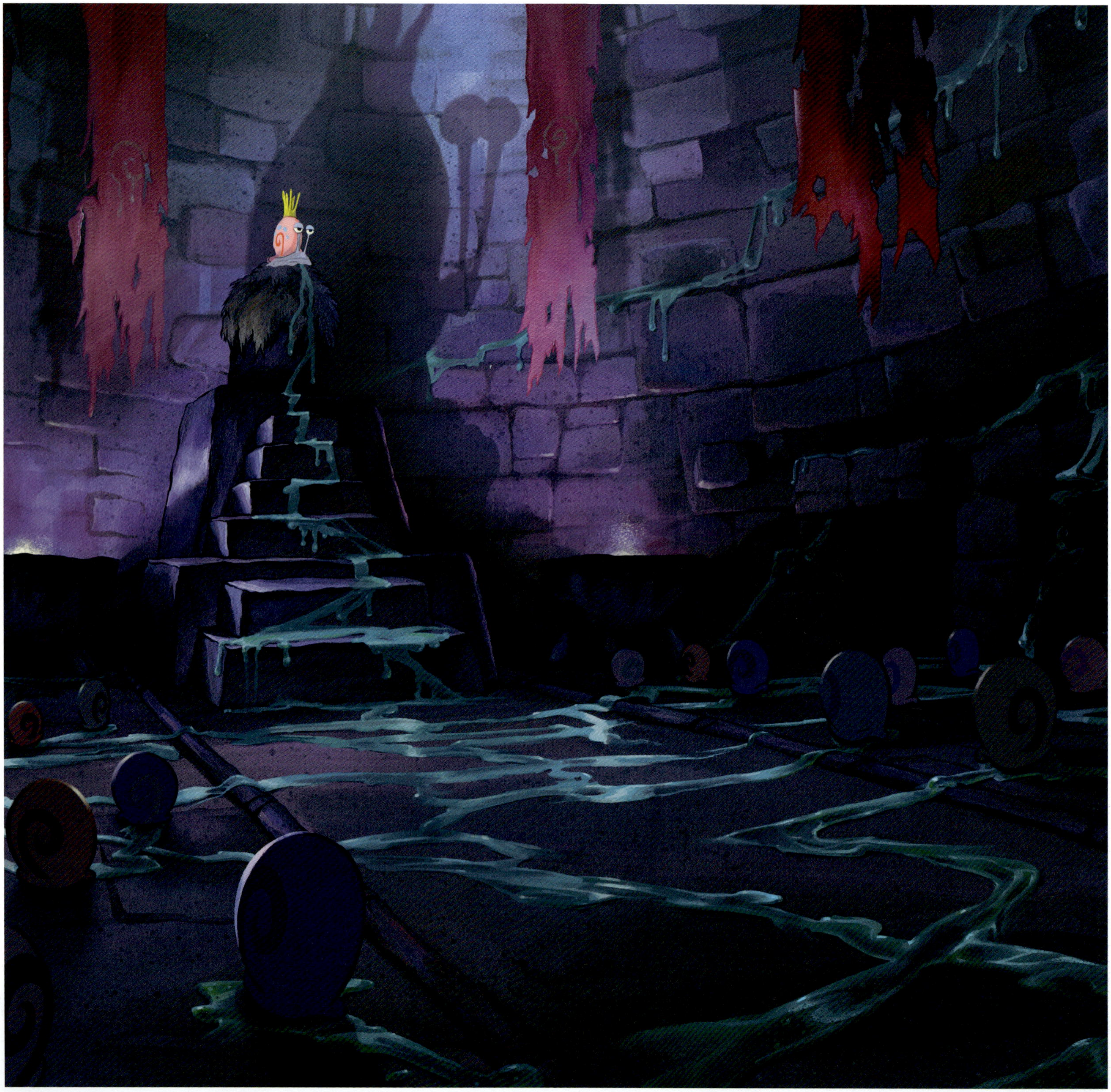

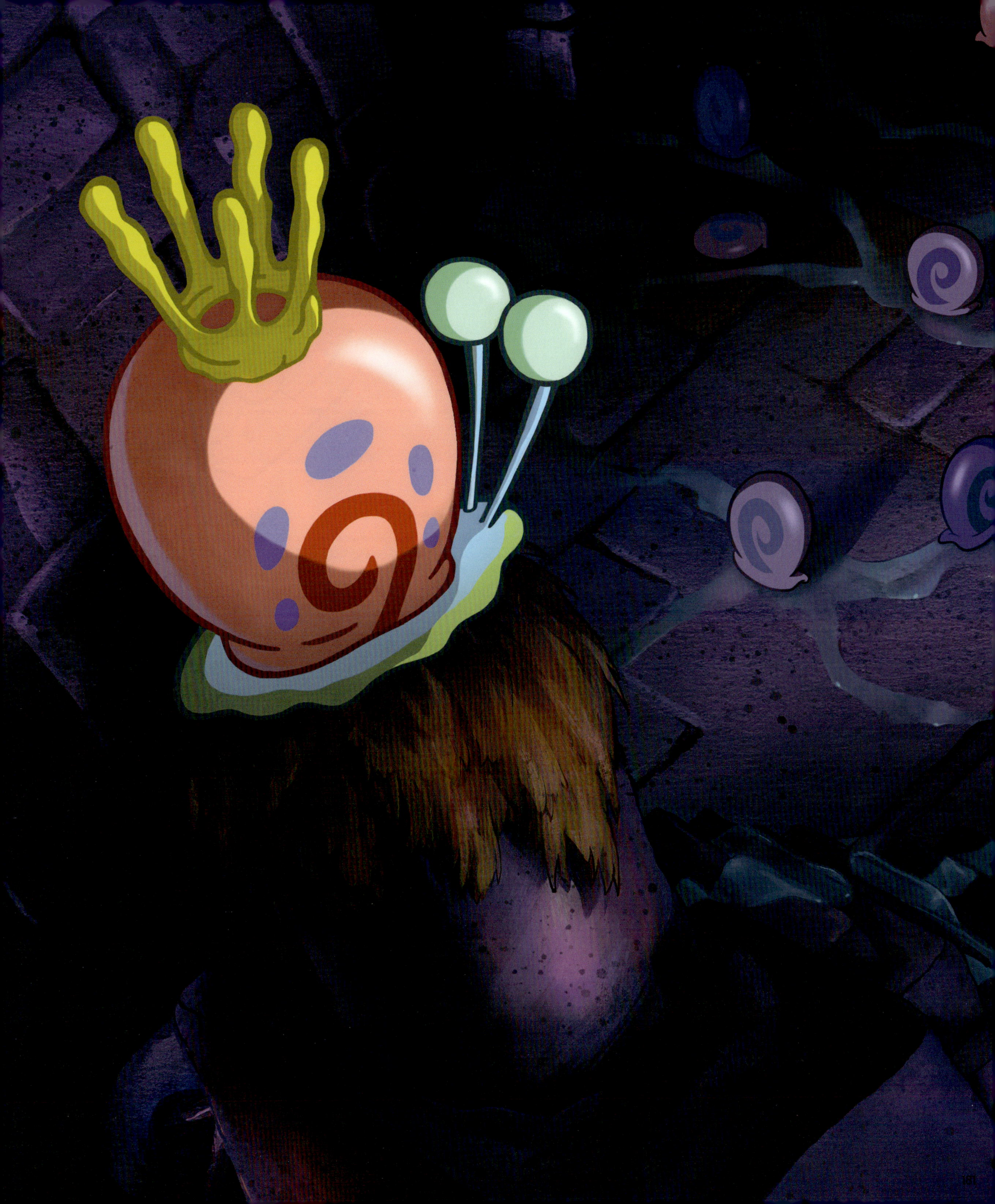

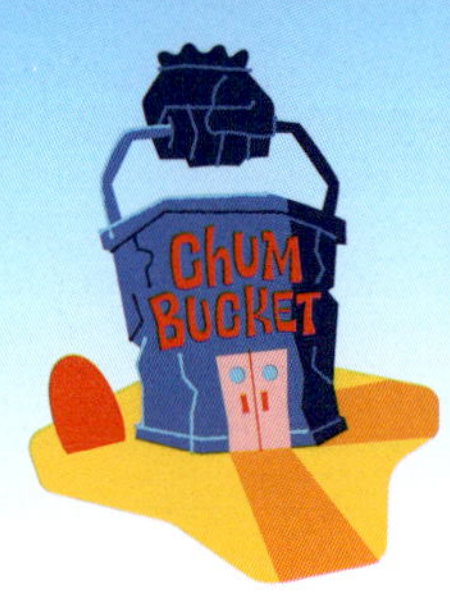

A STRANGE ALLIANCE & "TEAMWORK"

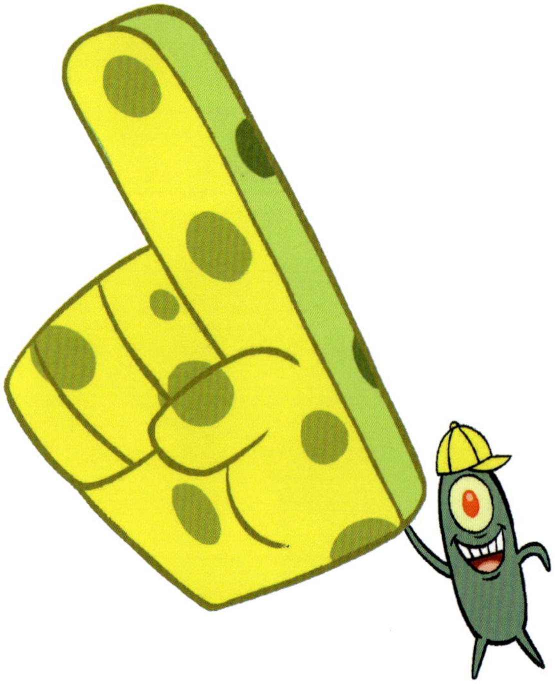

In chaotic times, sometimes the most unexpected partnerships can arise, and sometimes a song ensues to commemorate such "Teamwork." Artistic teamwork flows with the ebb as well, playing into what works best for the characters. "Our characters' personalities have remained consistent, but what has changed in some cases are the character designs. You can see that when you compare the pilot, for example, to later seasons. We sometimes evolved things even years later: When we were working on the second SpongeBob movie, Steve Hillenburg asked me to make a subtle change to Plankton's design, and [said] that it had been fifteen years since the show came out," recalls former storyboard supervisor Erik Wiese.

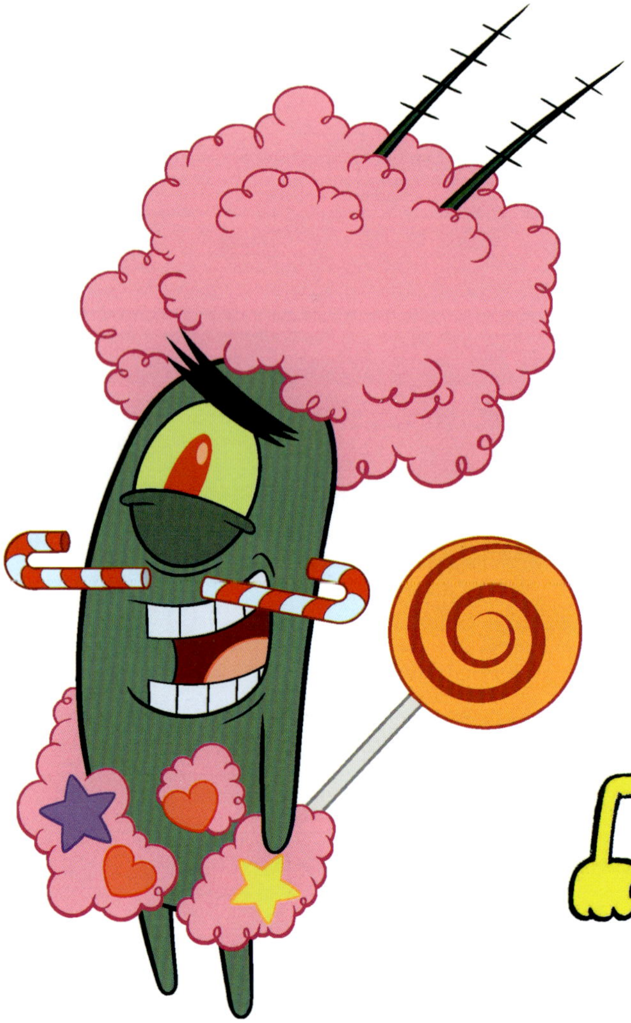

Final art of teammates Plankton and SpongeBob [left] and final frame image of a bonding bonfire moment [right]

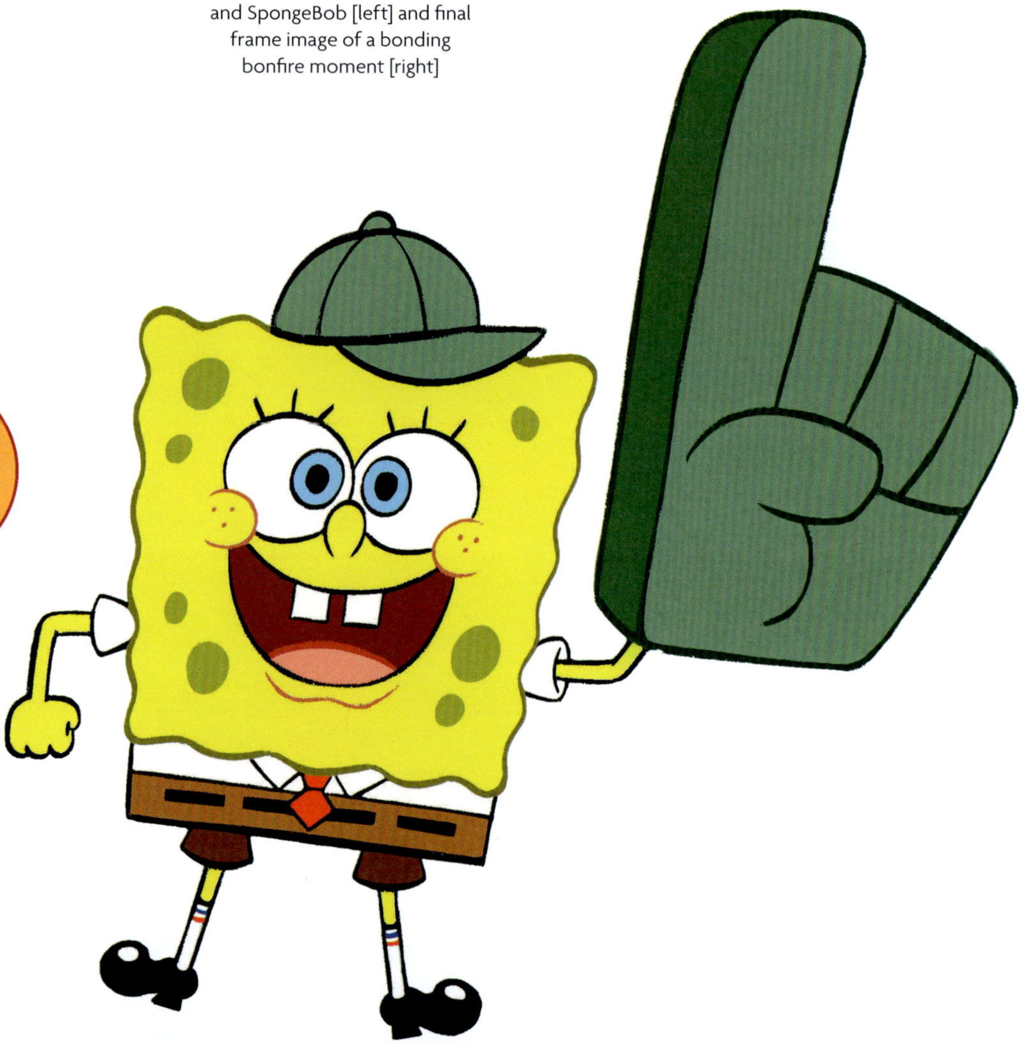

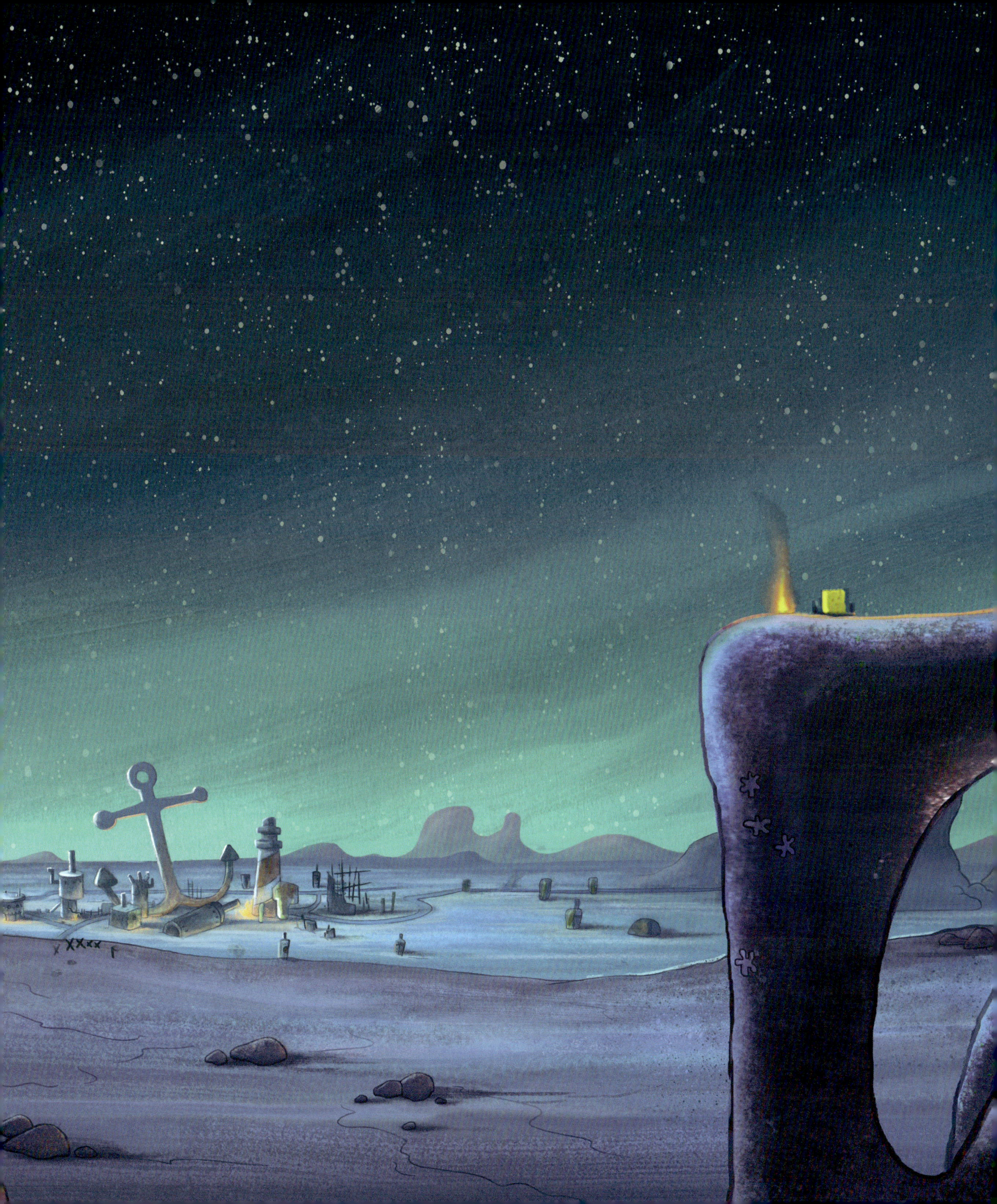

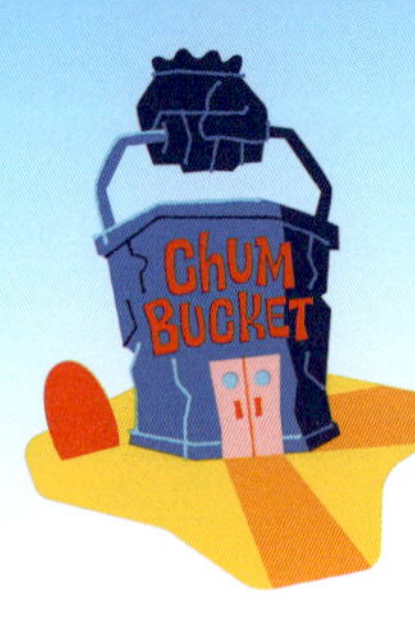

TIME TRAVEL & MEETING BUBBLES

Some groovy time travel leads SpongeBob and Plankton into stop-motion territory that introduces them to Bubbles, whose existence contains many levels of incredulity, but all of them intriguing and entertaining.

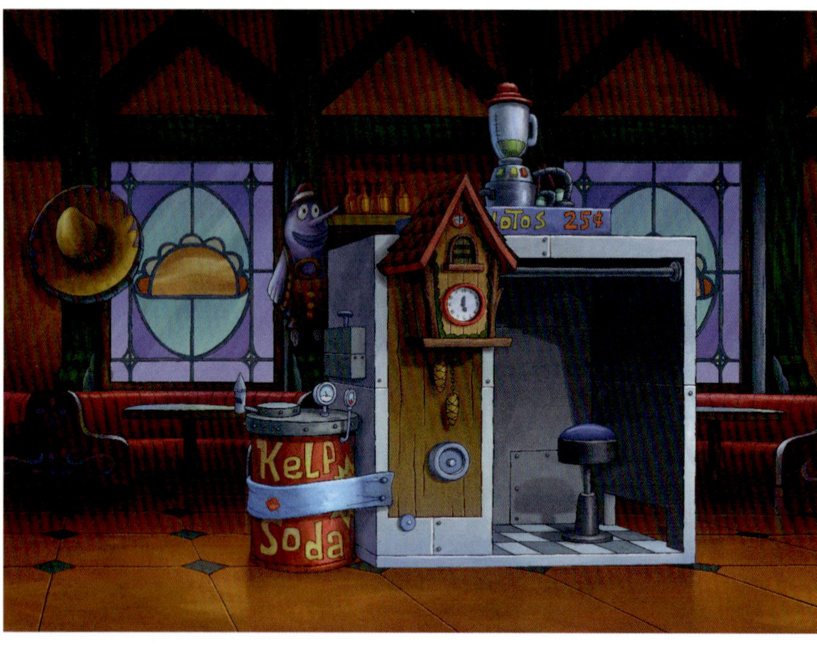

Final art of the time machine [upper left], final frame image of a bewildered Plankton and SpongeBob [right], and another view of the time machine [lower left]

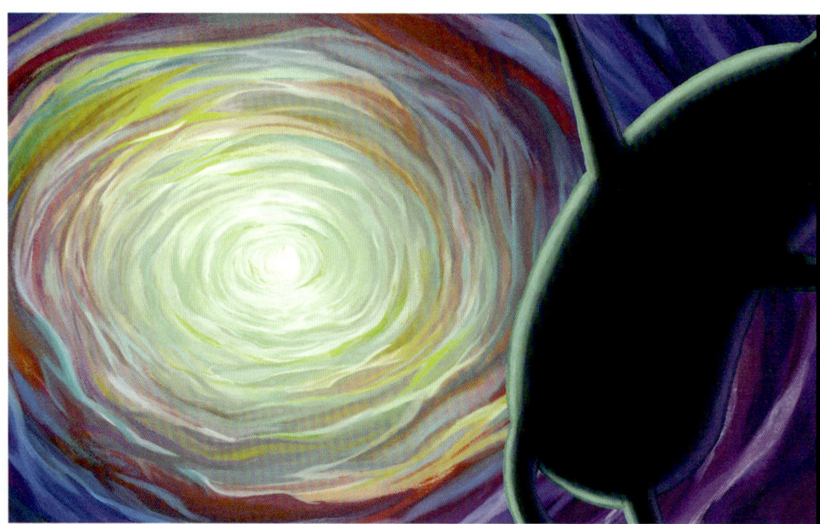

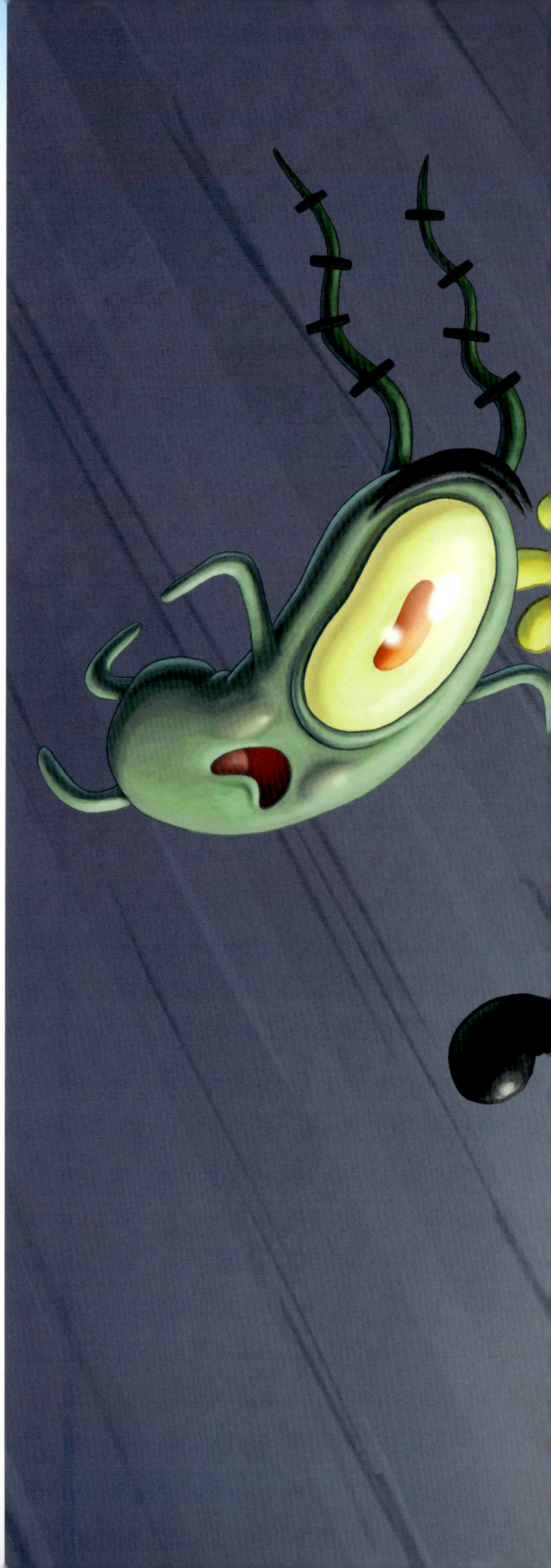

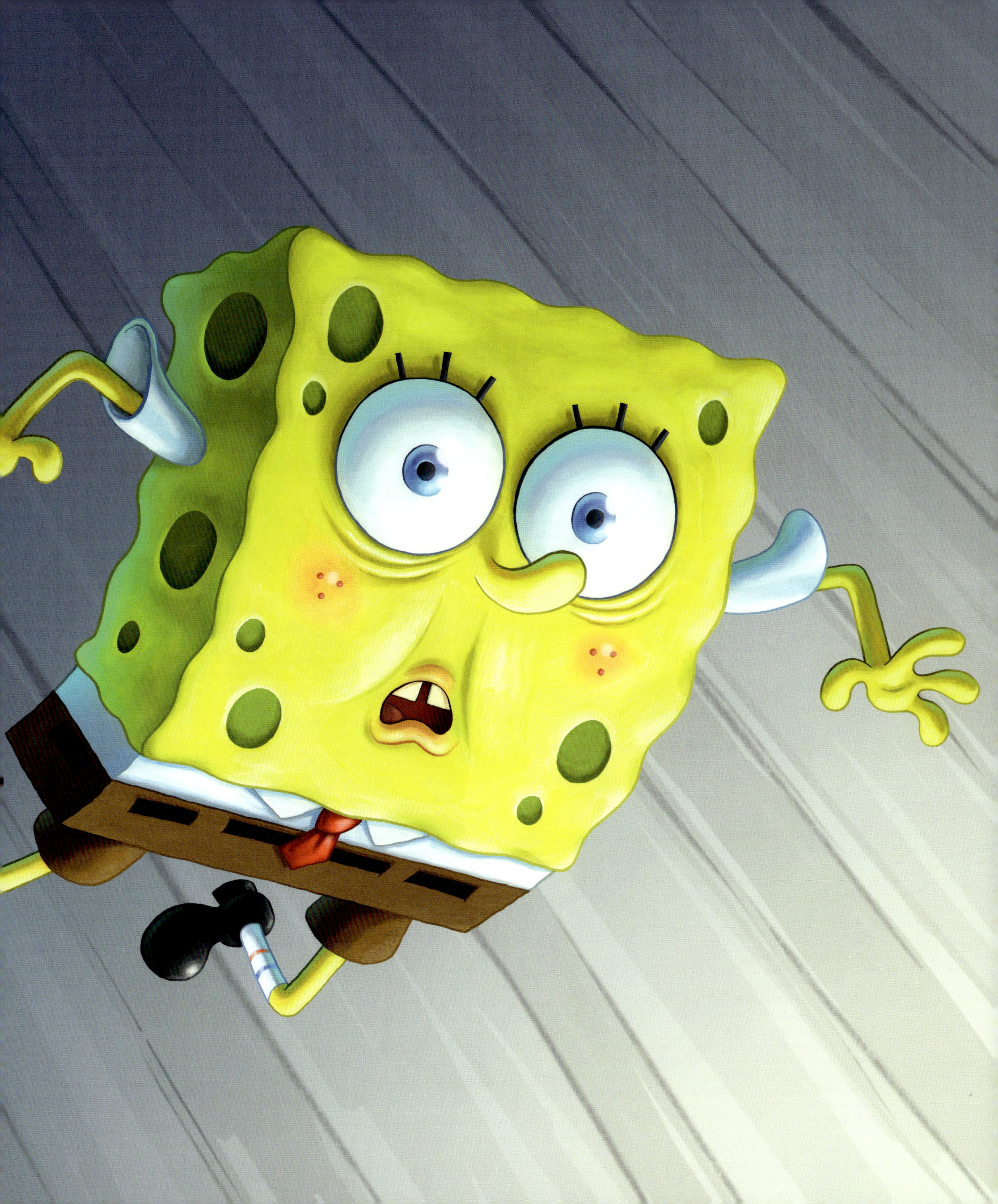

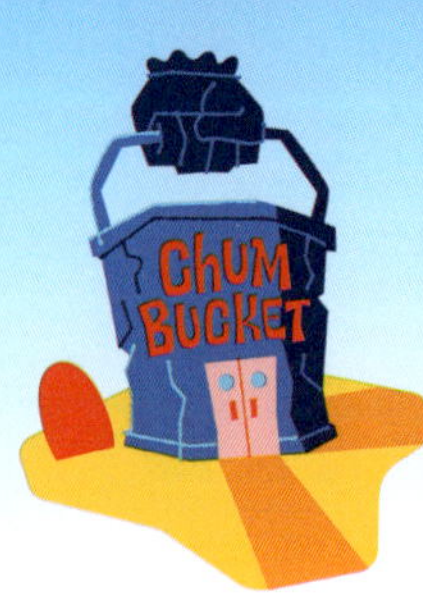

PIRATE STORYTELLING & SANDWICH SELLING

Portrayed by both a live-action actor and a CG model in the film, Burger Beard takes his cooking gig to new (and above sea-level) culinary heights with his Krabby Patty offering.

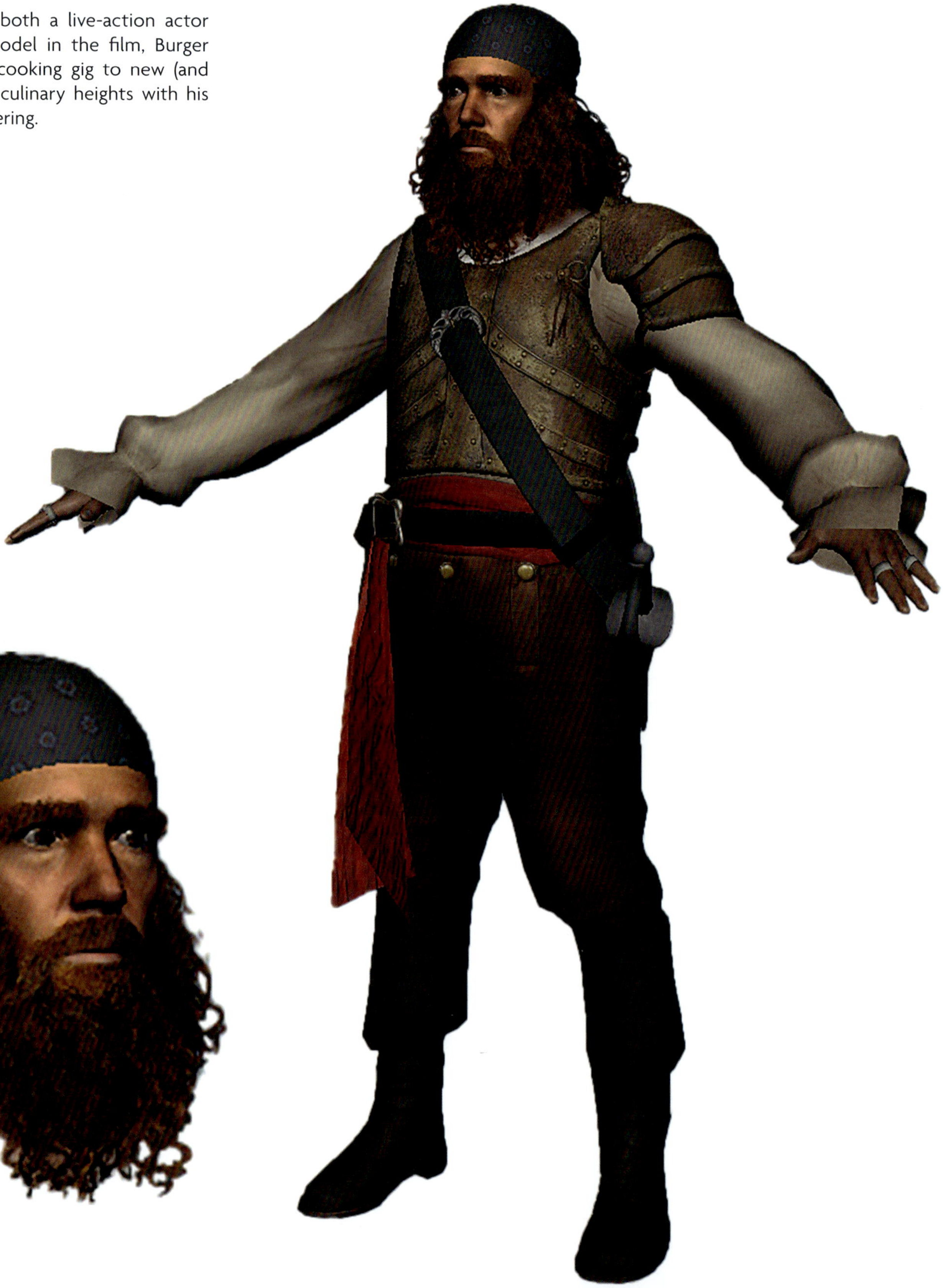

The CG version of Burger Beard

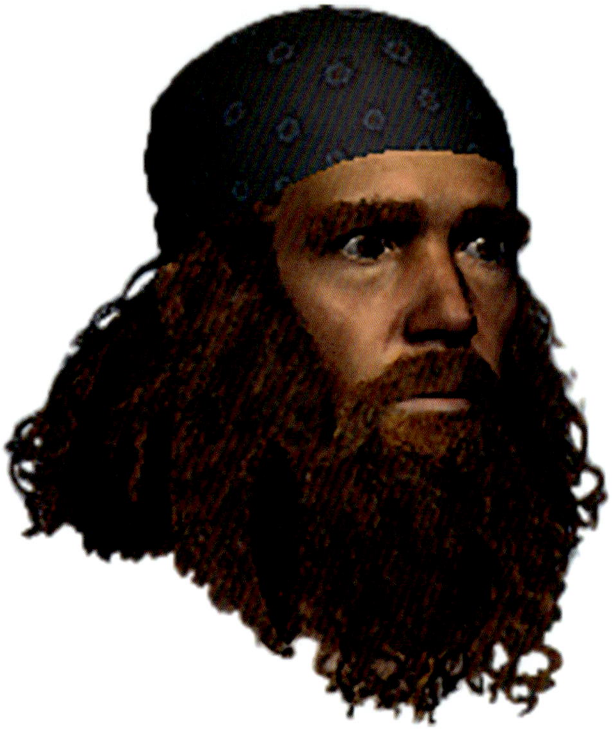

REWRITING THE ENDING

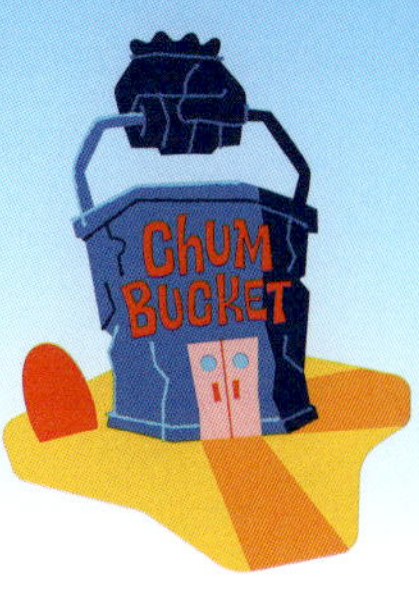

Such a powerful story moment and message were delivered to the audience through this story: "You are in charge of your story and CAN write your own ending!" The "happily ever after" effect of this film carried into other productions as well. "On the second film, we started pushing the character posing further than we had in recent seasons and everyone was pleased with the result. So when we returned to the show, we were encouraged to begin pushing the physical comedy and expressions, and we did just that," recalls supervising producer Dave Cunningham. "As a bonus, Steve Hillenburg enjoyed being back on the film so much that he decided to return to being a part of the show when we resumed production," he adds.

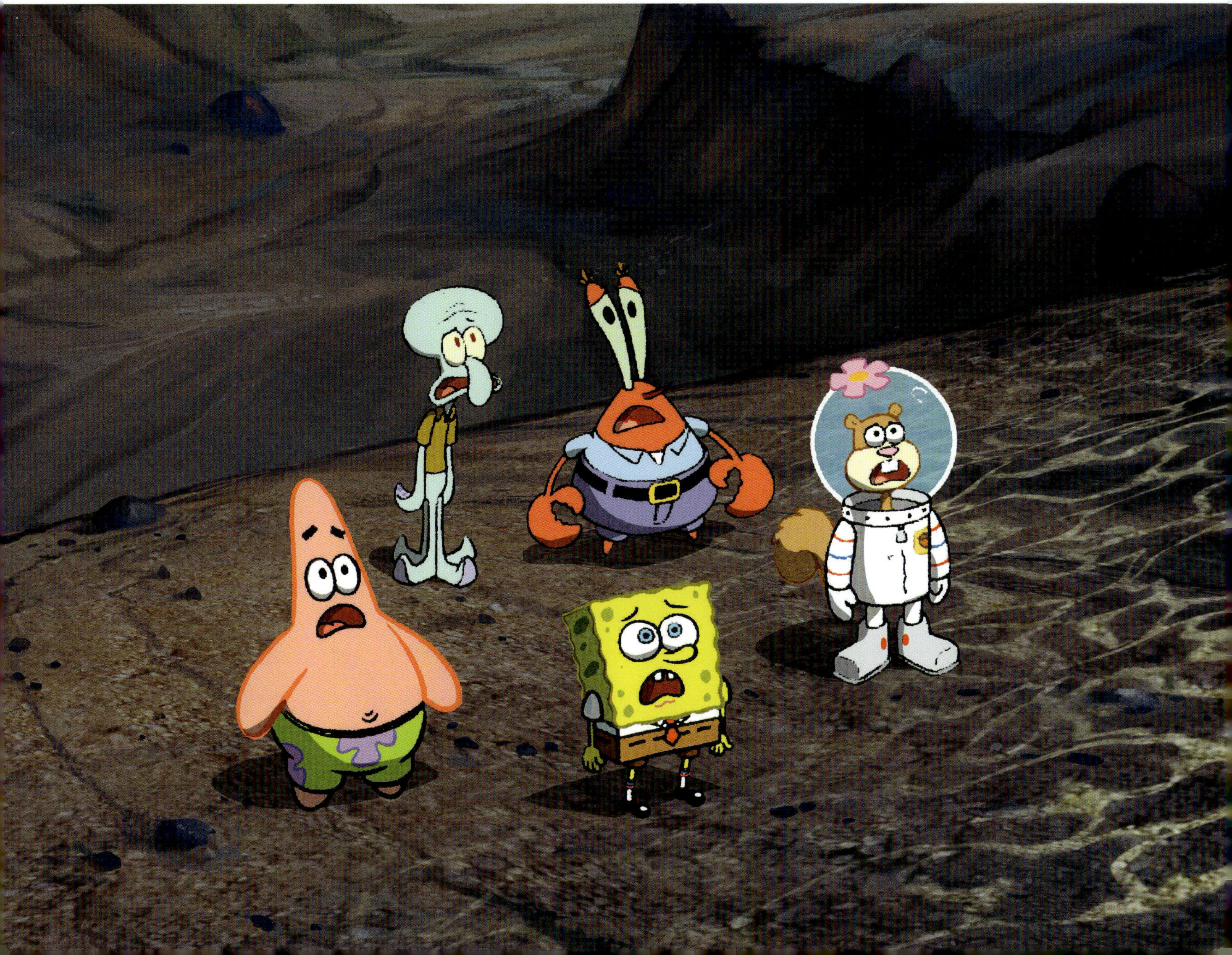

A jaw-dropping final frame image of the Bikini Bottom gang

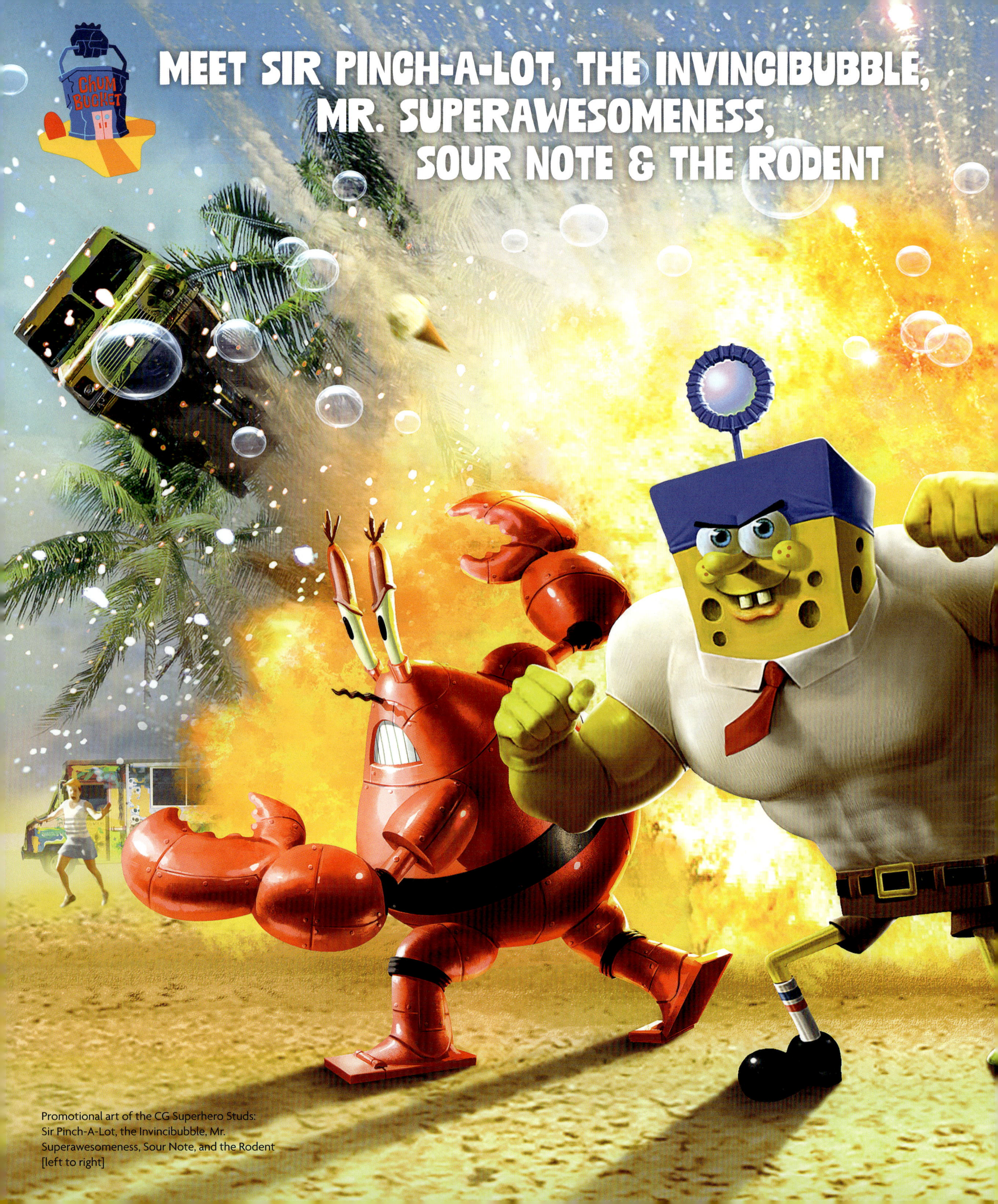

Promotional art of the CG Superhero Studs: Sir Pinch-A-Lot, the Invincibubble, Mr. Superawesomeness, Sour Note, and the Rodent [left to right]

To save the day, the mighty five from Bikini Bottom write themselves into heroes, spawning their transformation into bigger and better versions, unlike anything they (or the audience) have ever seen, through the magic of CG animation. "The CG work was the biggest challenge we faced while working on this film because of the pressure to 'compete' in the feature-film market with titans of CG like Pixar. We owed it to the fans to not do anything that didn't feel true to the original animation," explains former executive producer Paul Tibbitt.

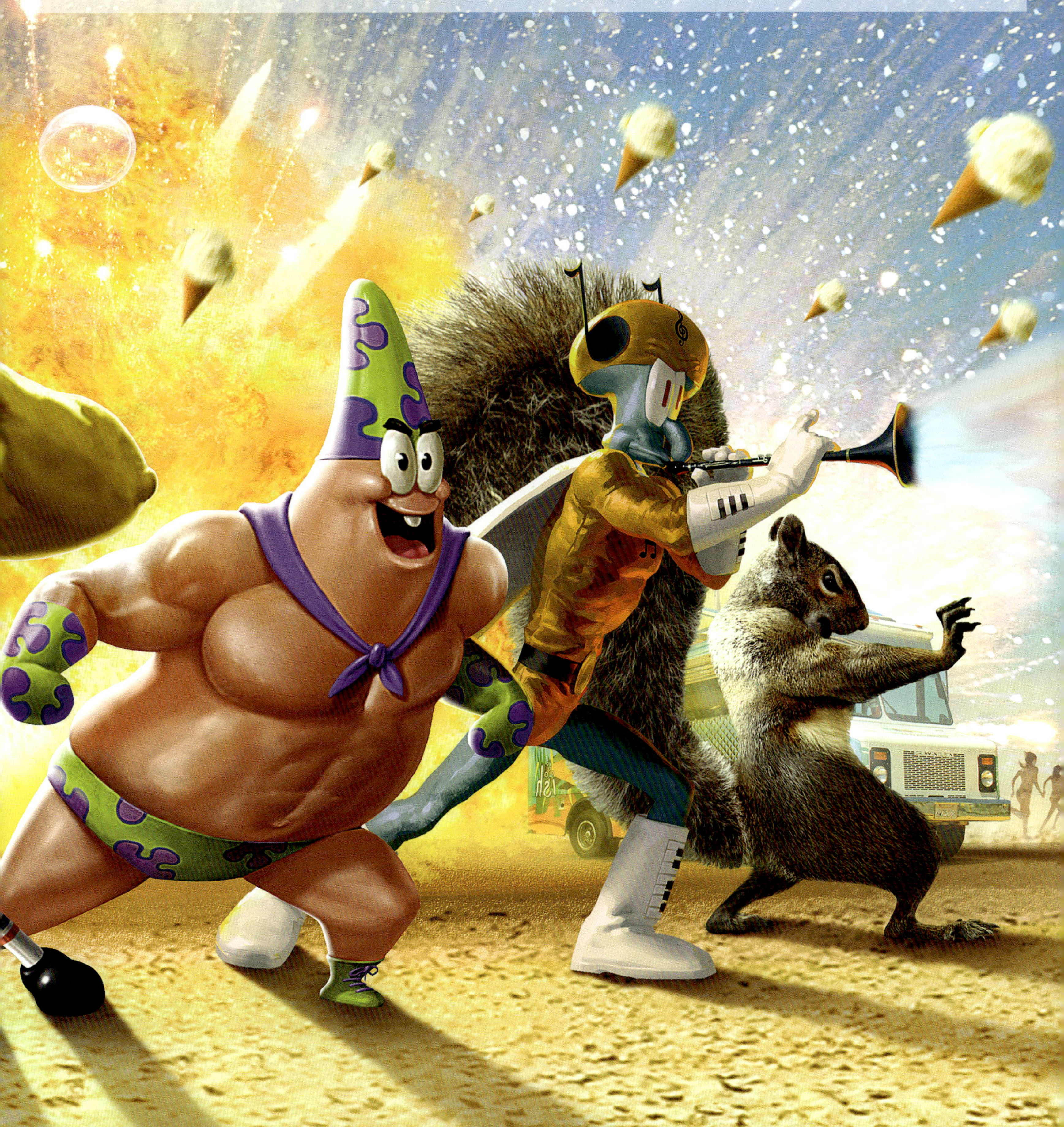

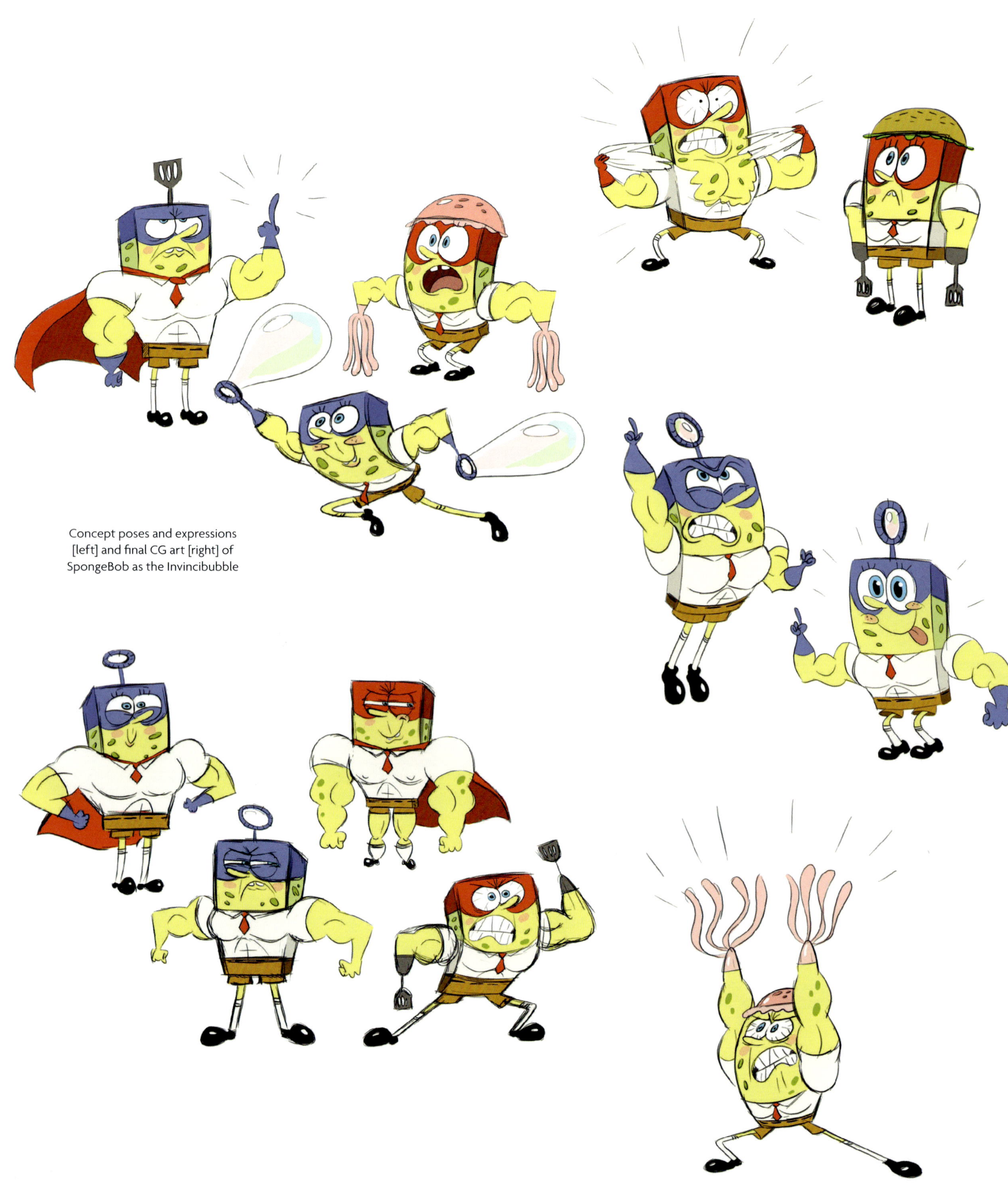

Concept poses and expressions [left] and final CG art [right] of SpongeBob as the Invincibubble

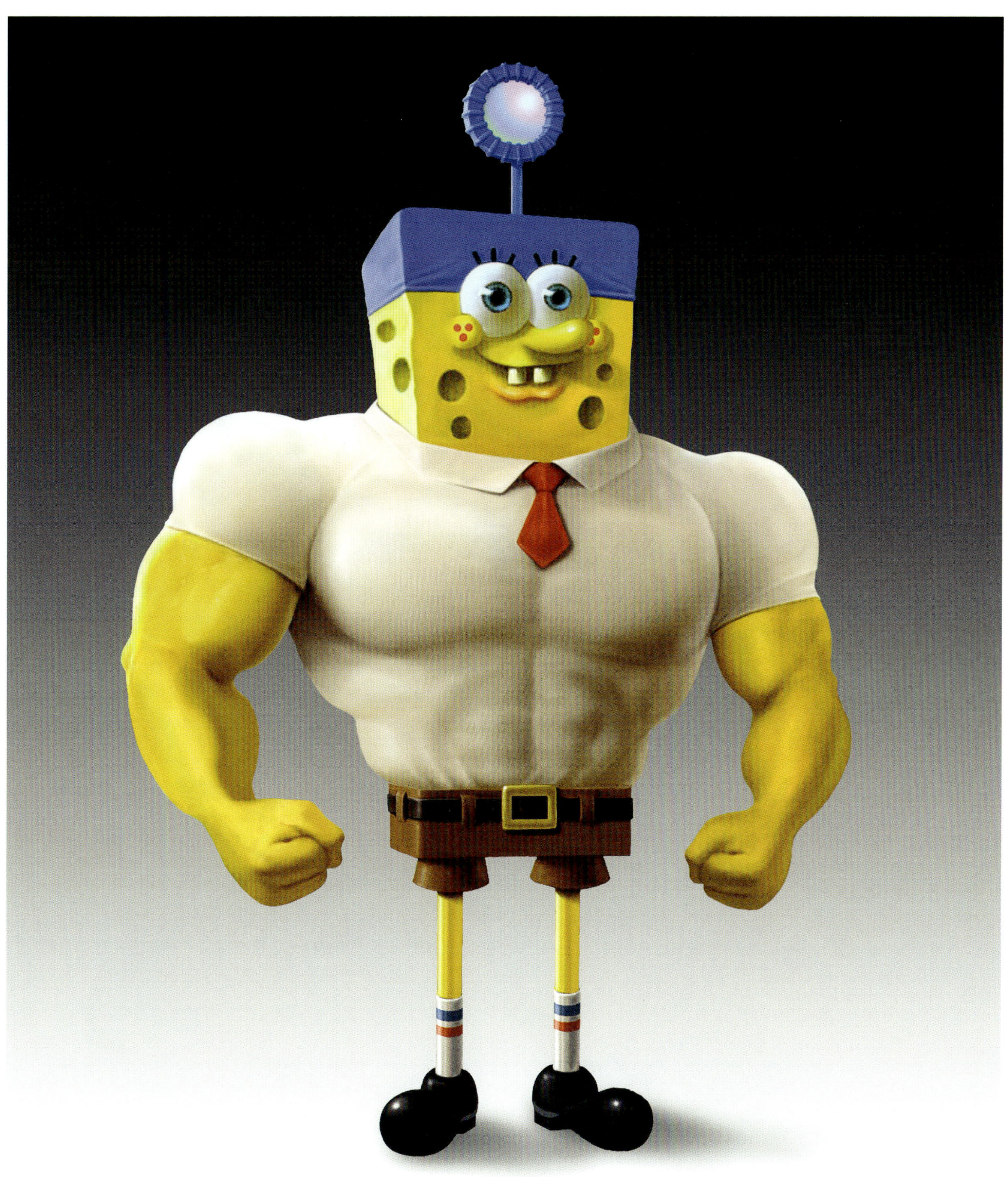

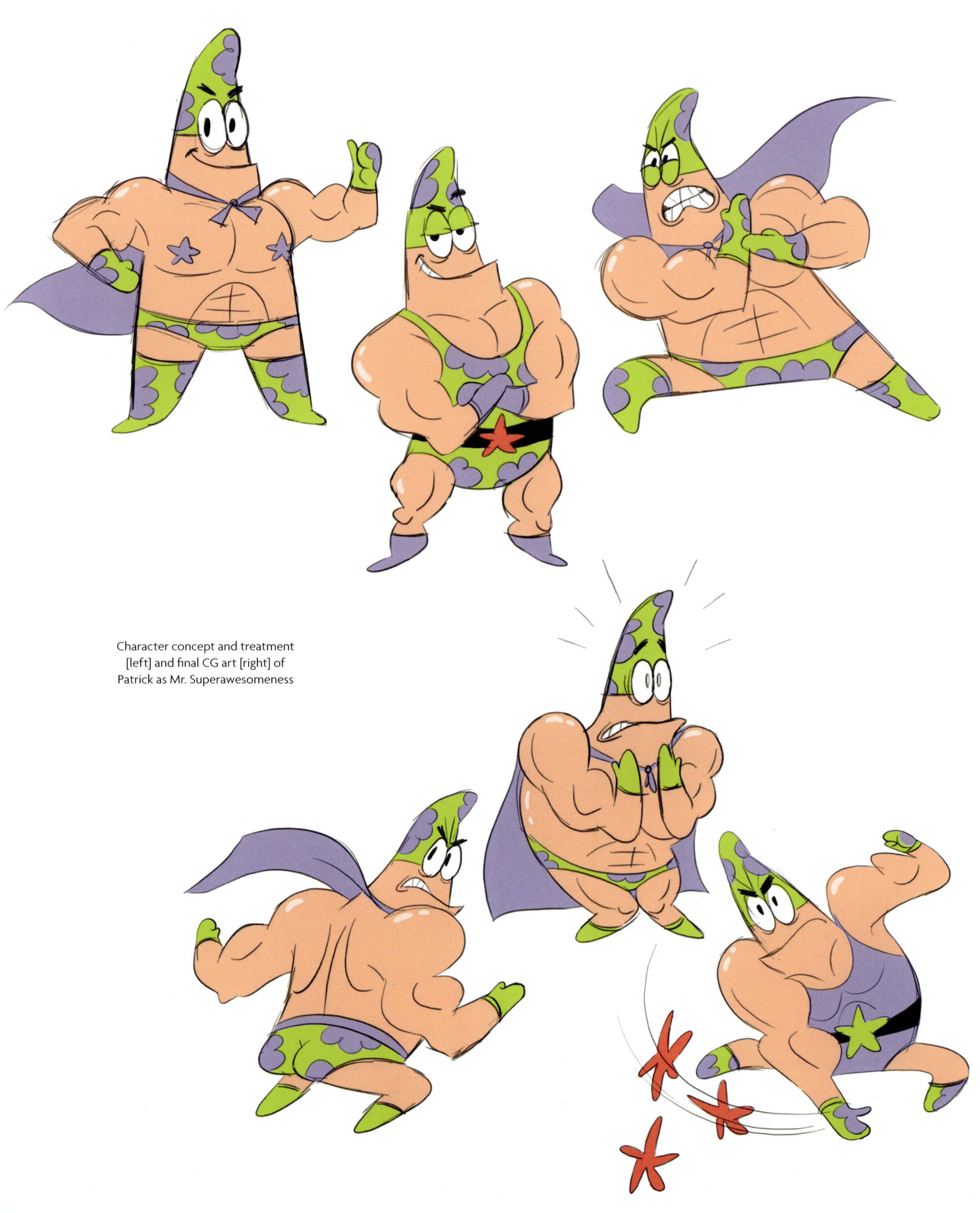

Character concept and treatment [left] and final CG art [right] of Patrick as Mr. Superawesomeness

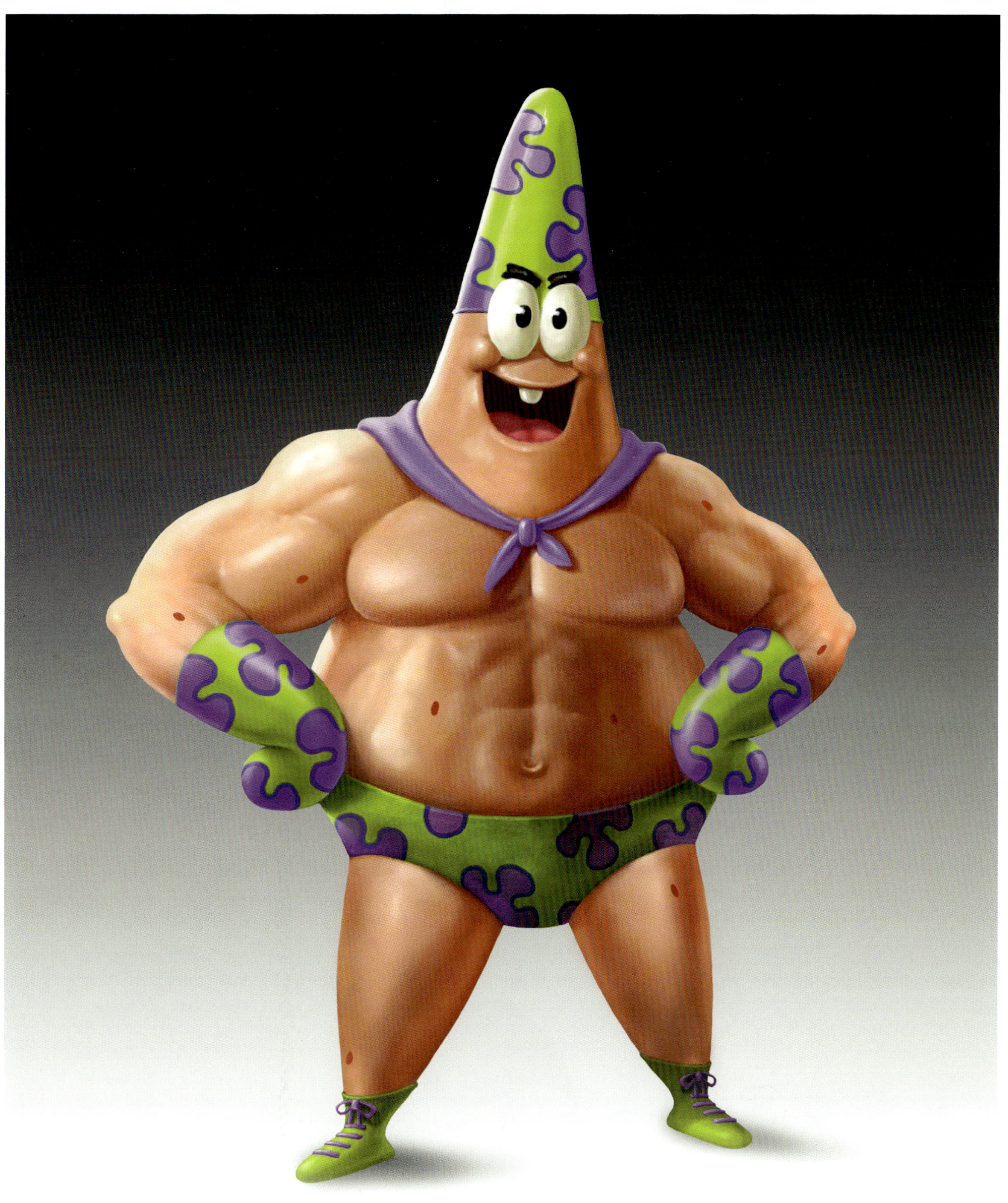

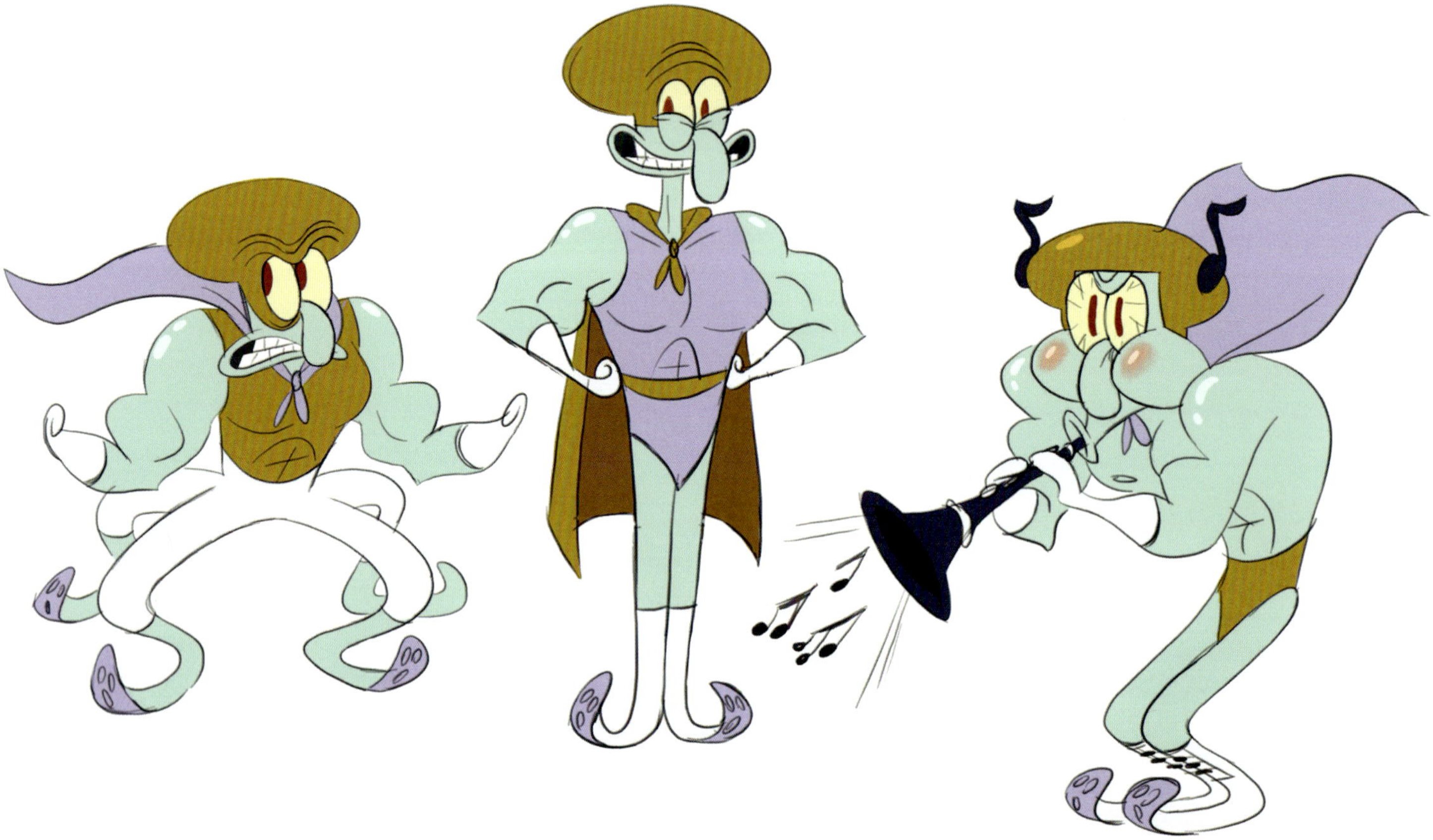

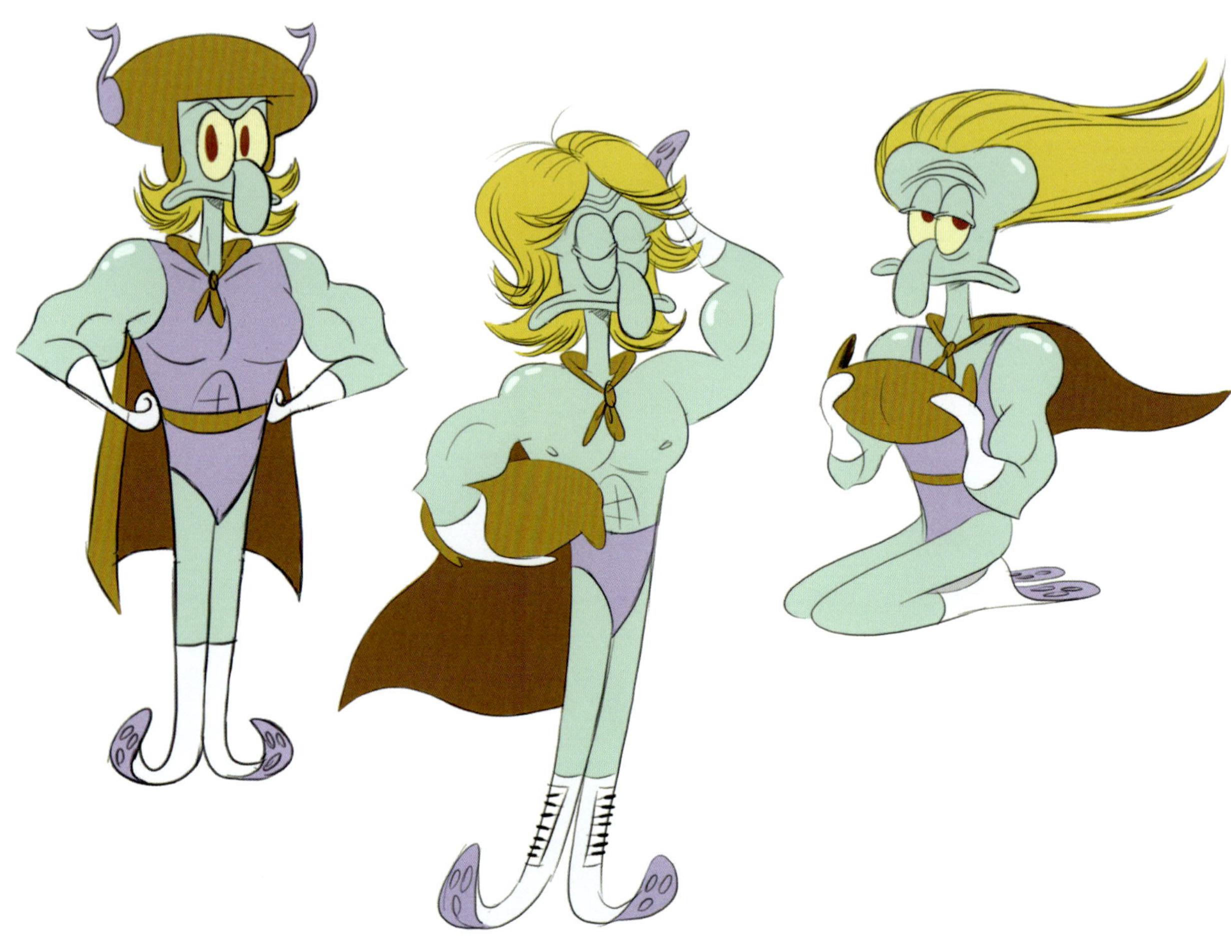

Concept poses and expressions [left] and final CG art [right] of Squidward as Sour Note

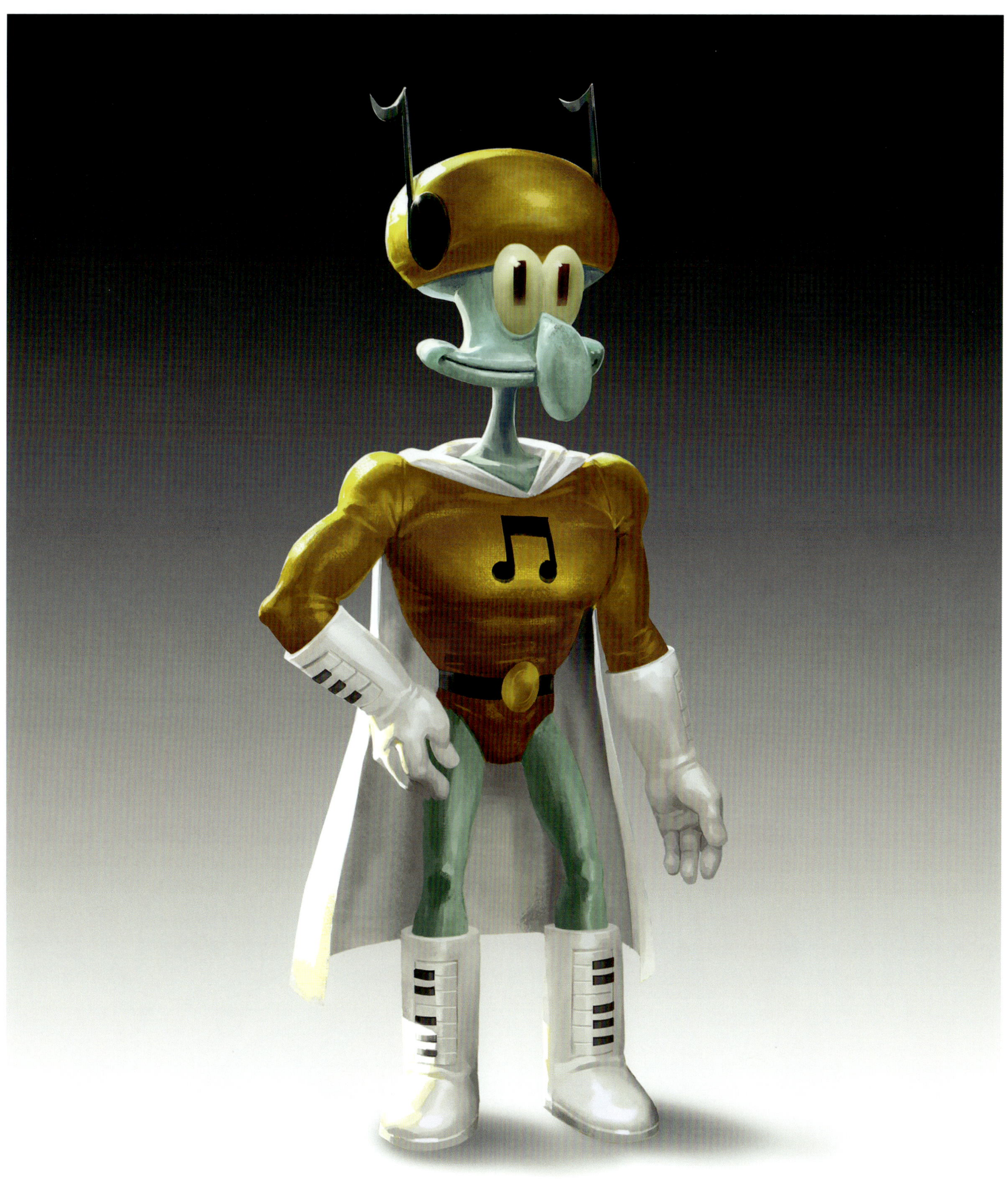

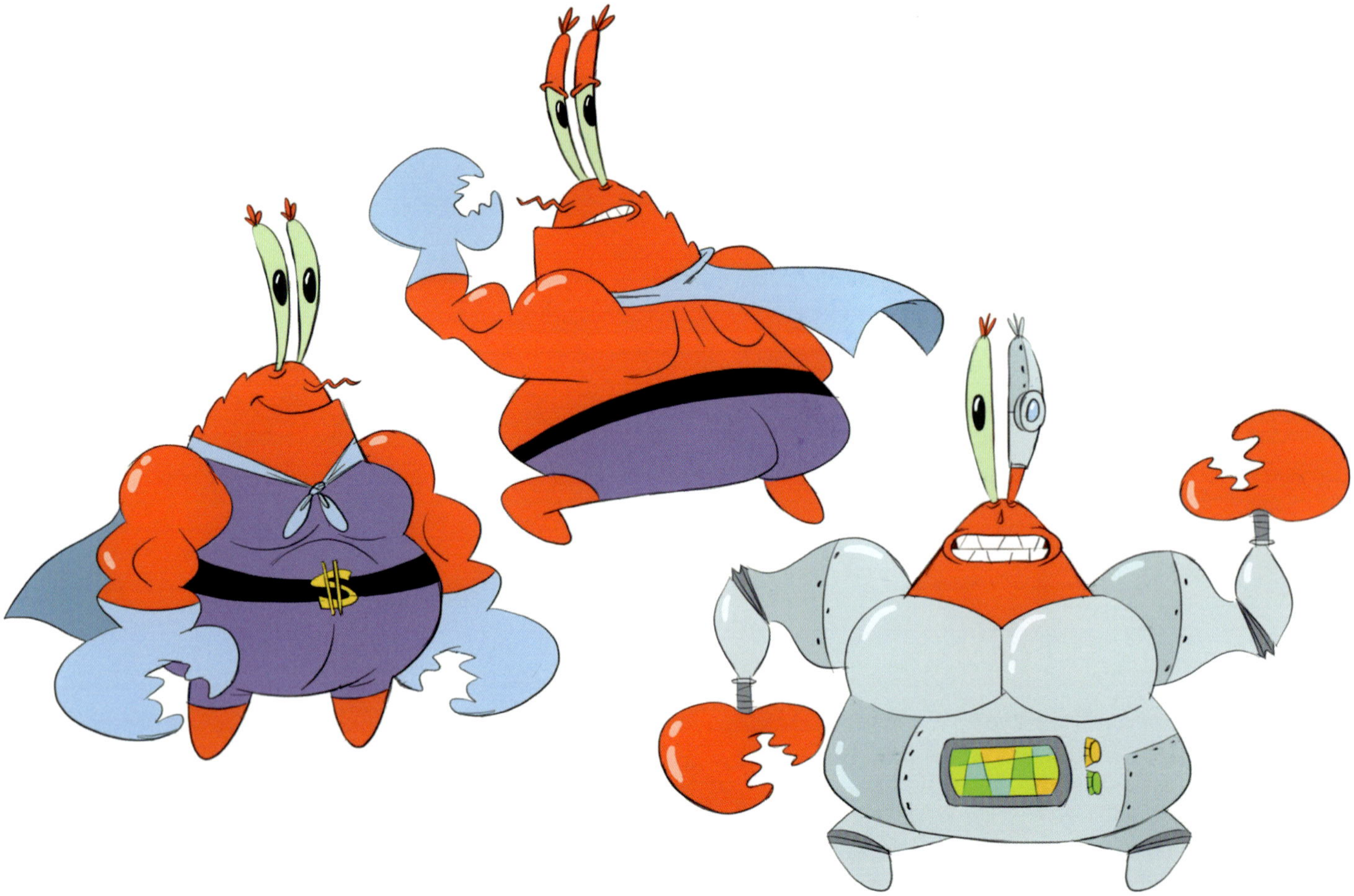

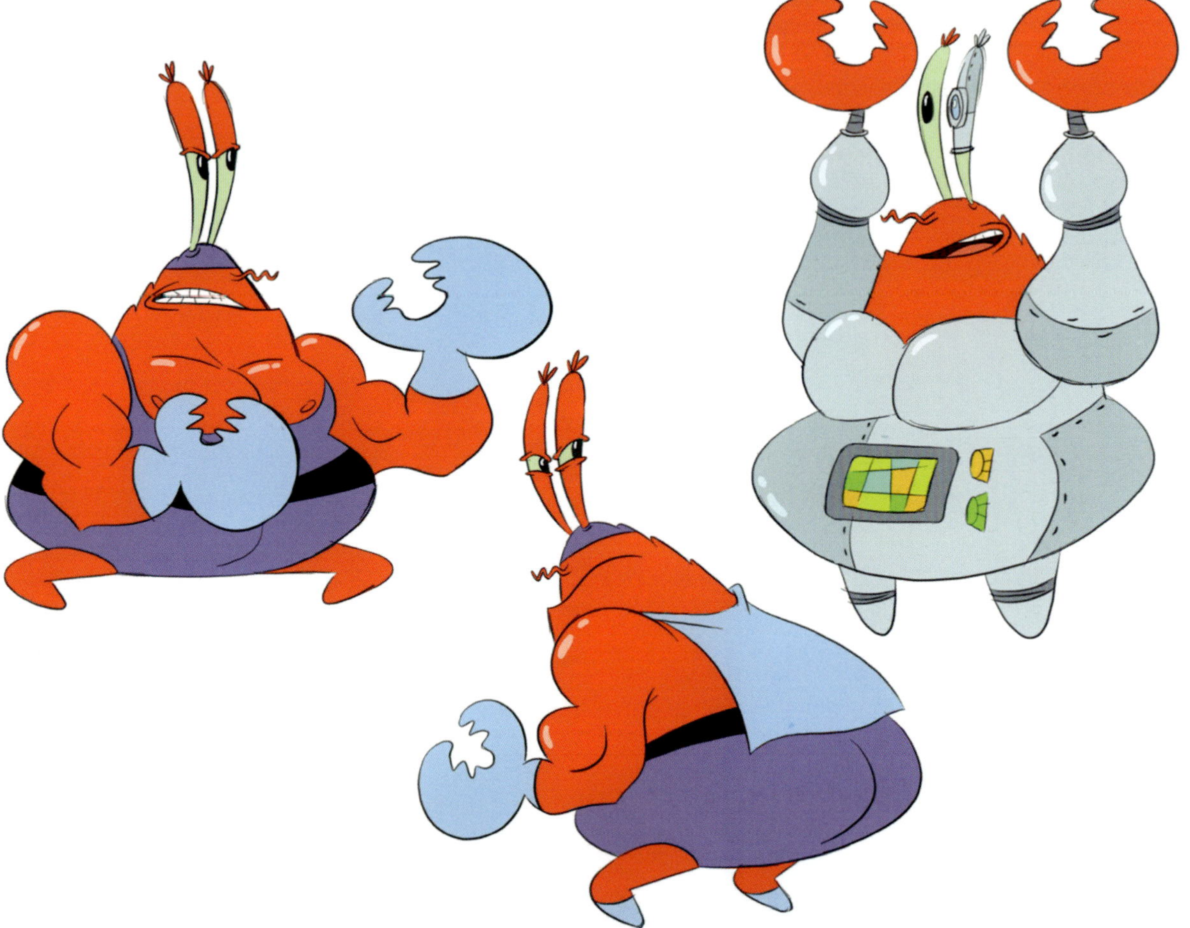

Character concept and treatment [left] and final CG art [right] of Mr. Krabs as Sir Pinch-A-Lot

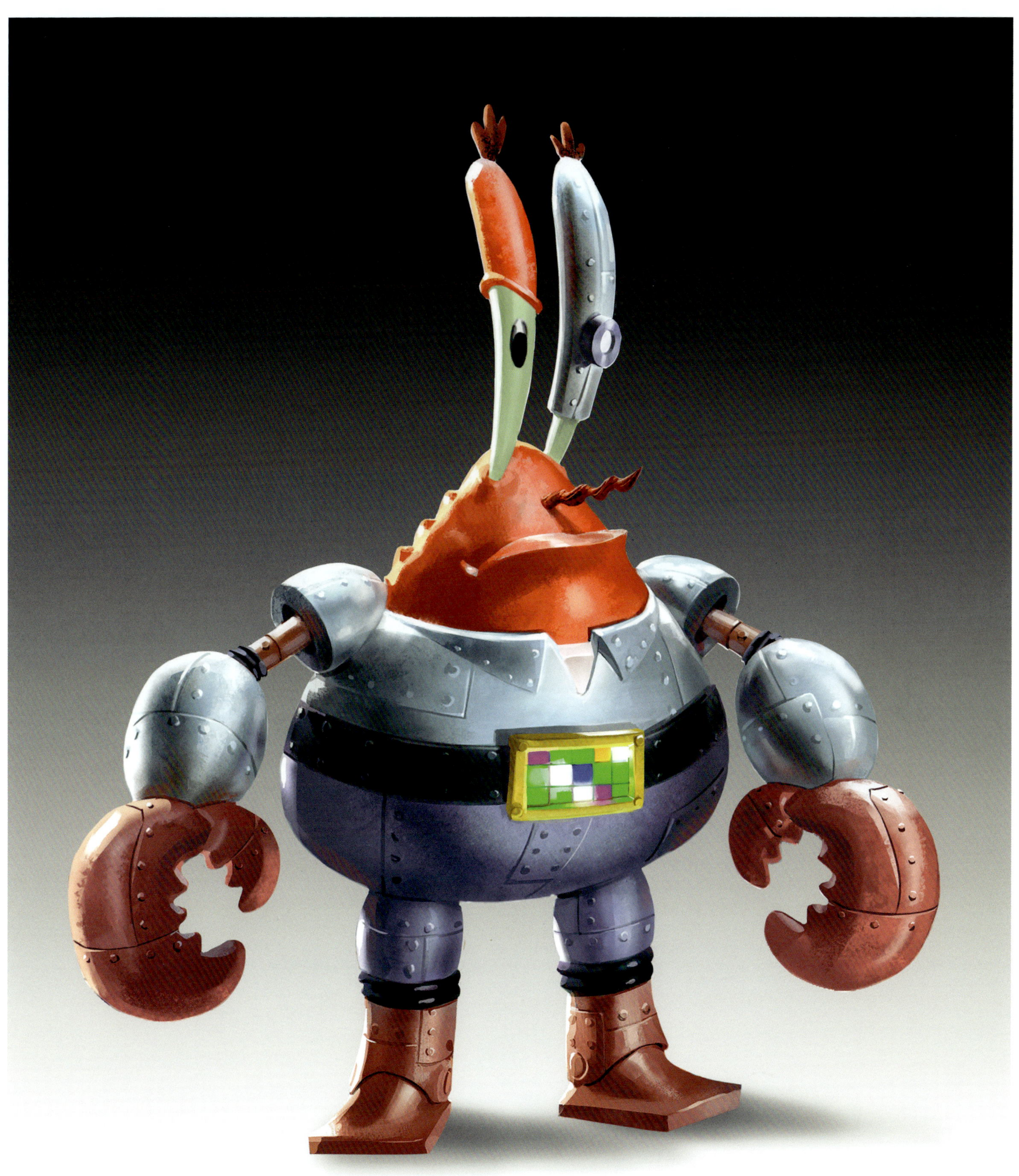

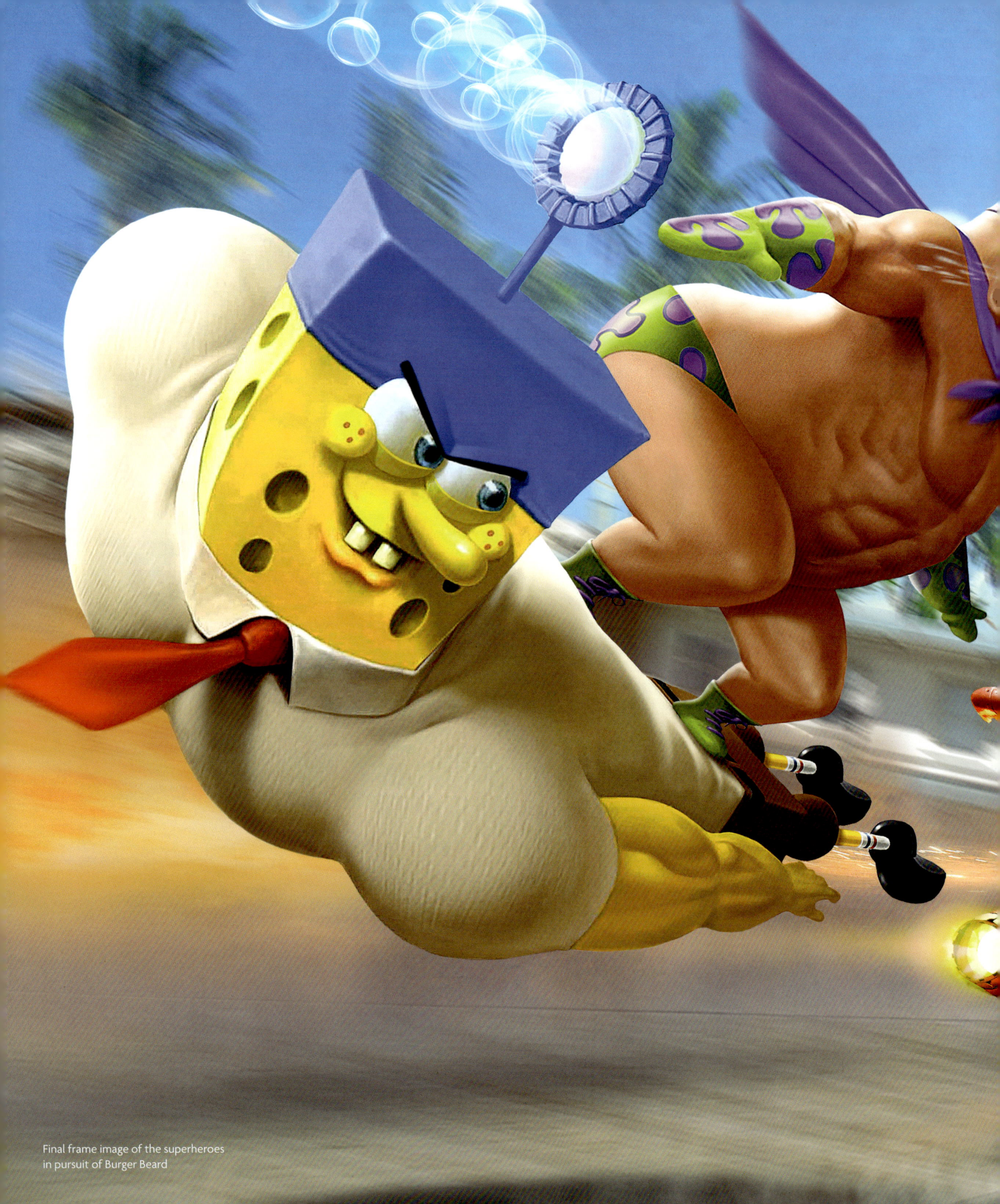

Final frame image of the superheroes in pursuit of Burger Beard

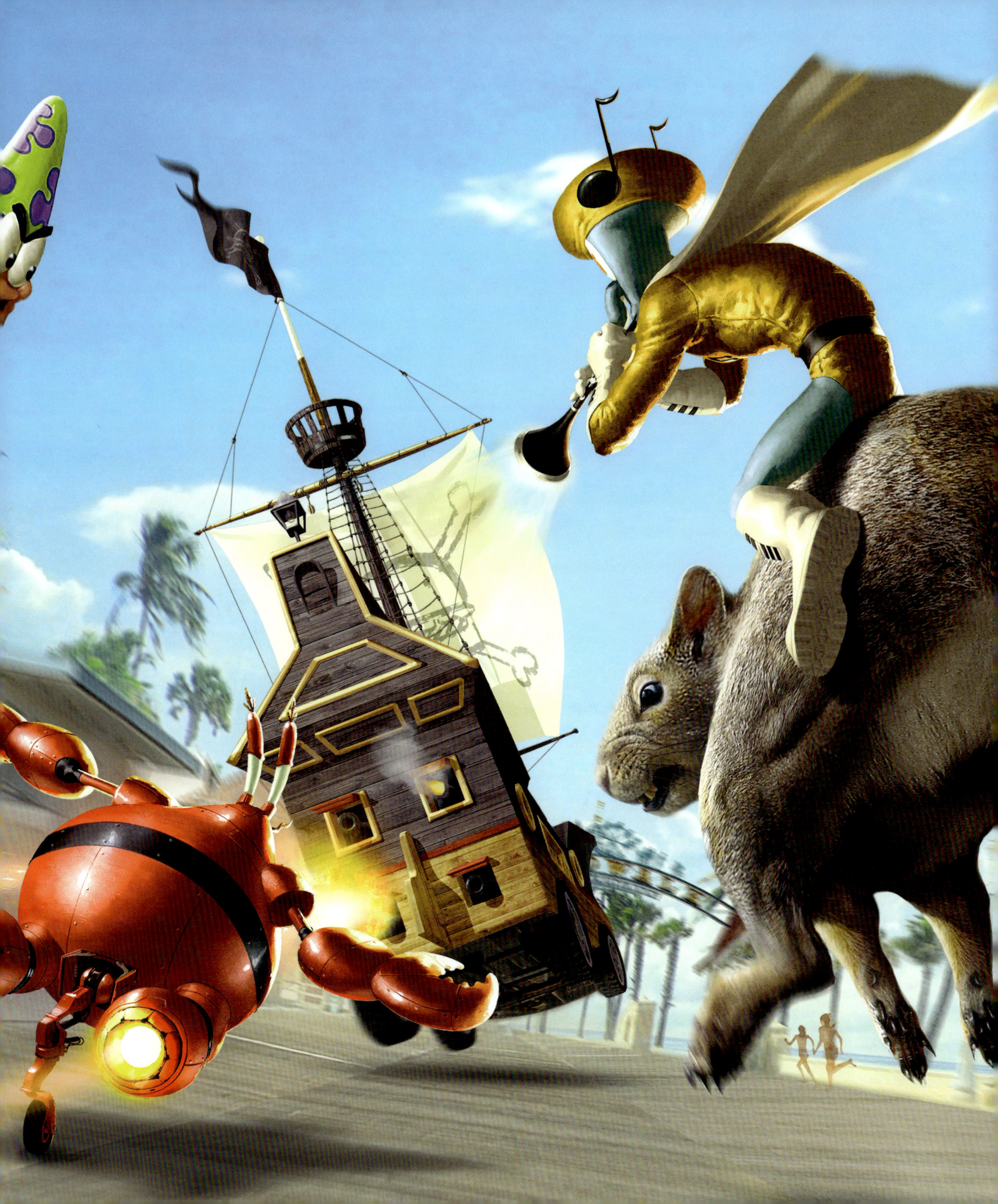

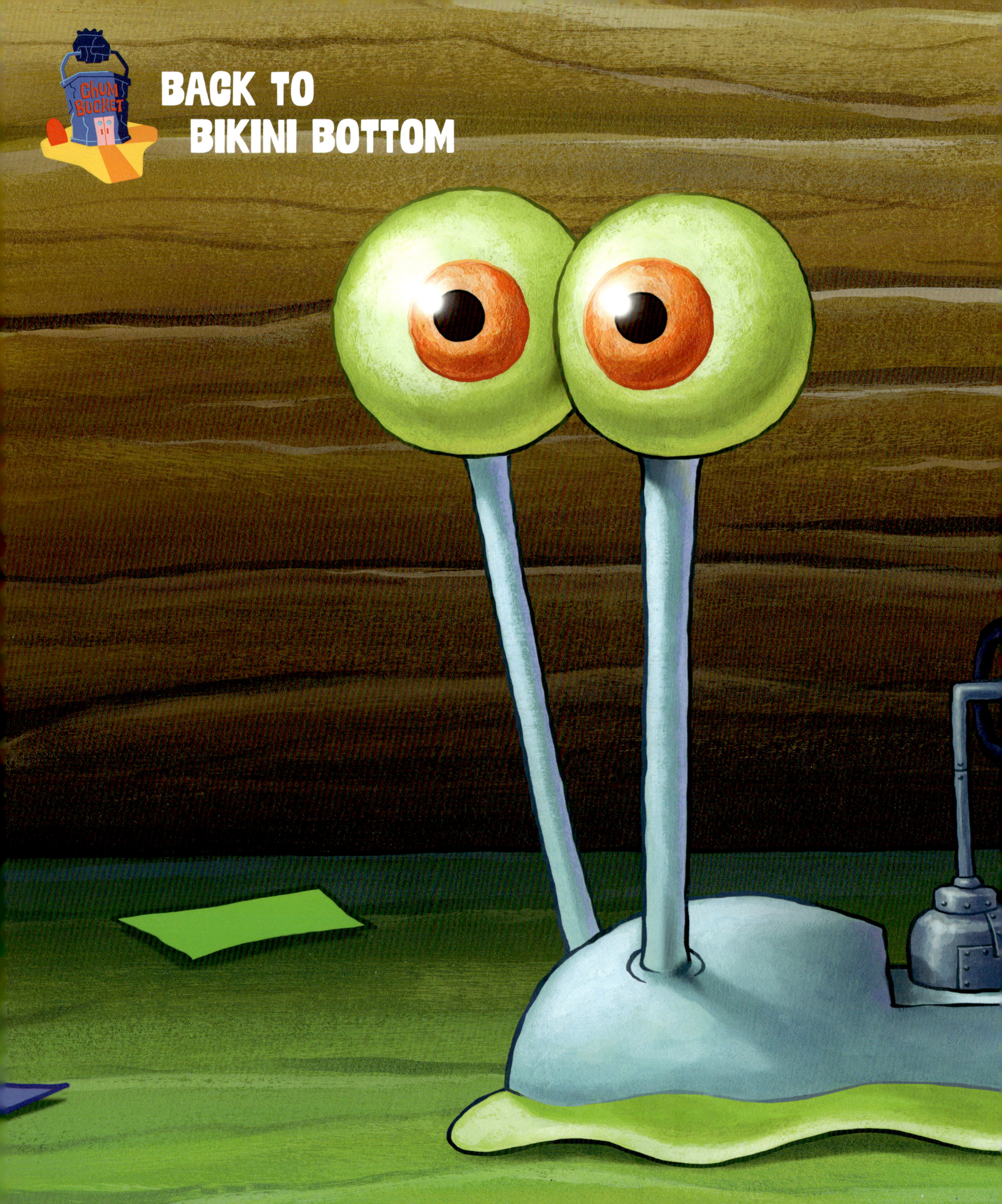

BACK TO BIKINI BOTTOM
CHUM BUCKET

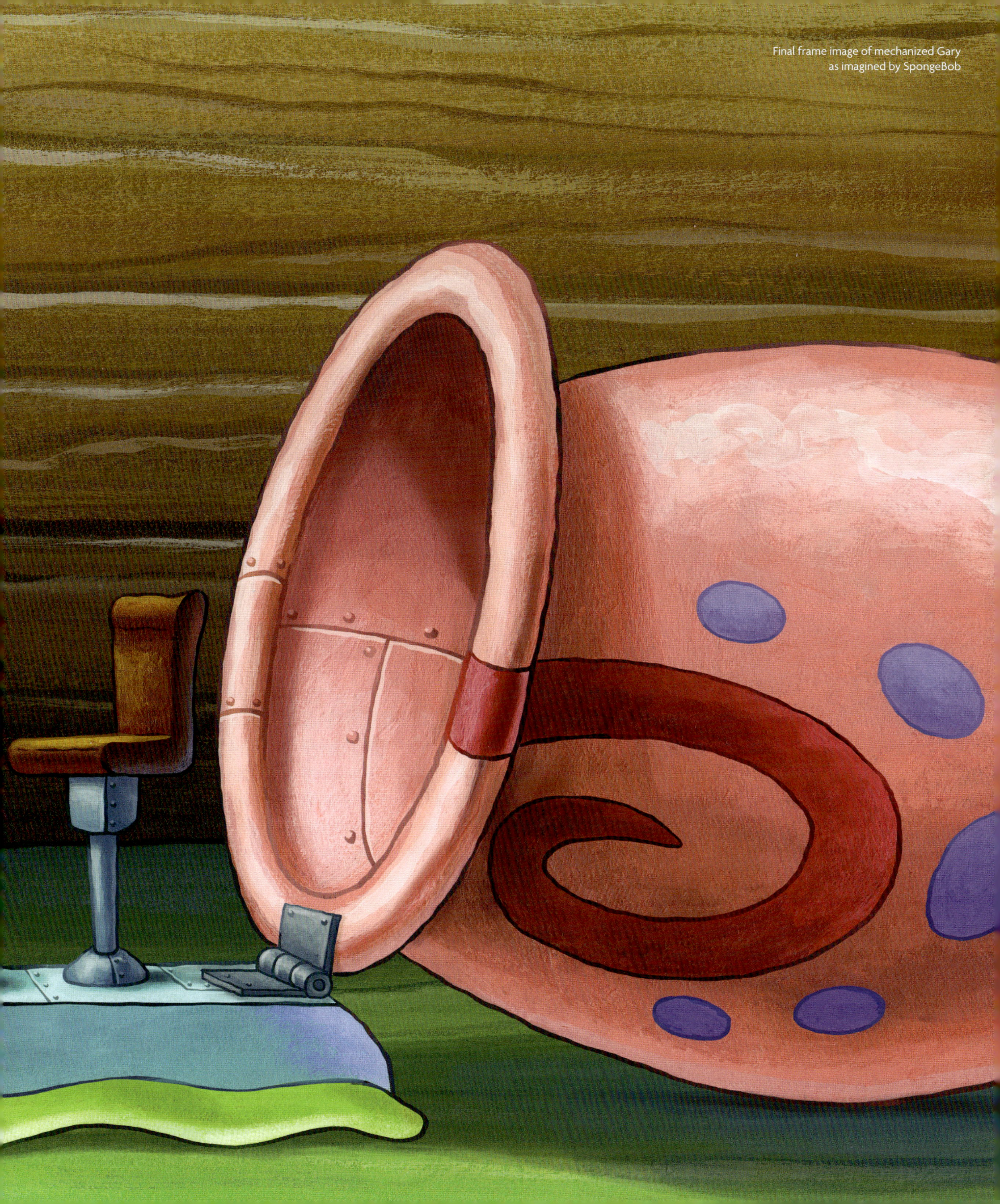

Final frame image of mechanized Gary
as imagined by SpongeBob

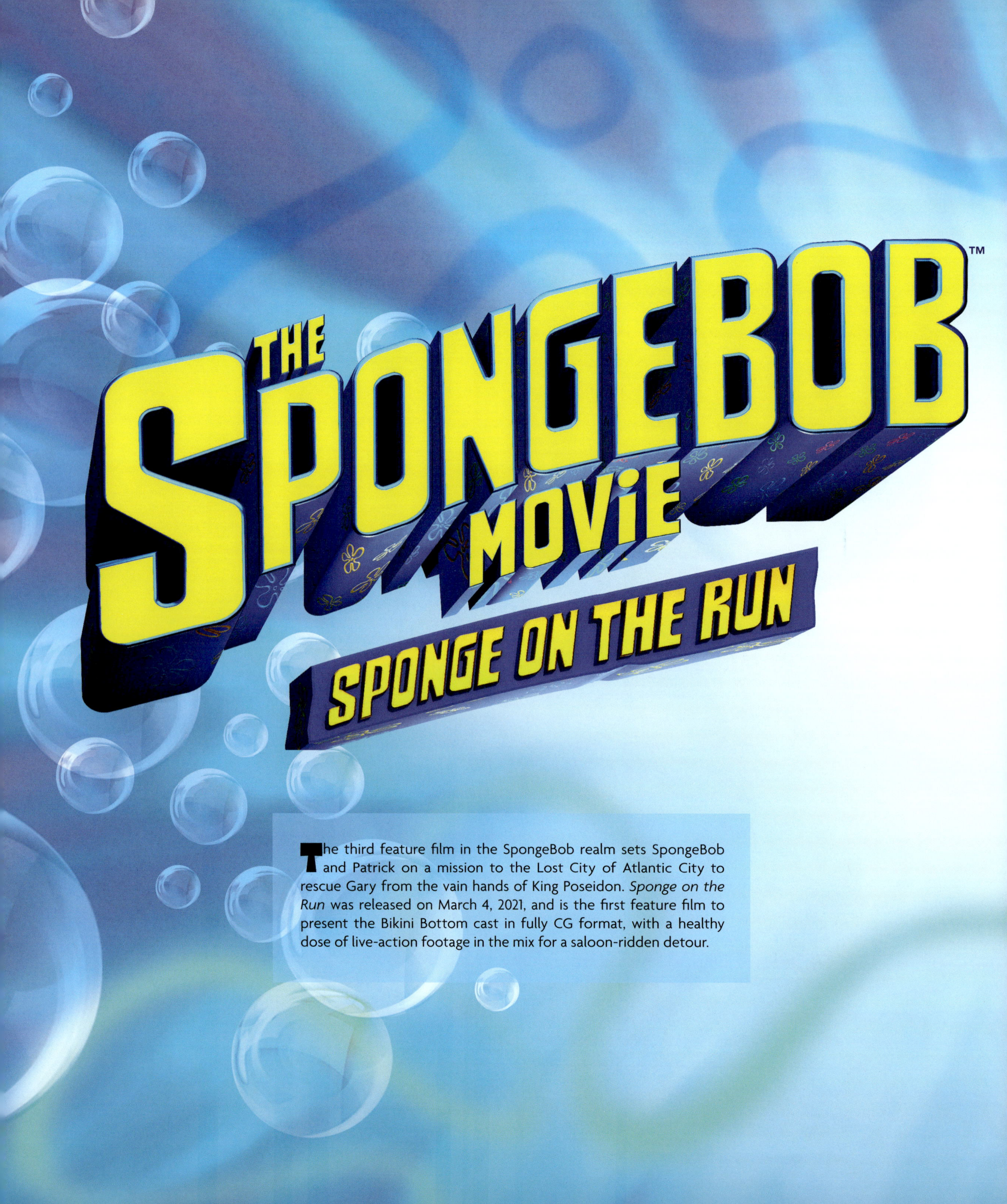

The third feature film in the SpongeBob realm sets SpongeBob and Patrick on a mission to the Lost City of Atlantic City to rescue Gary from the vain hands of King Poseidon. *Sponge on the Run* was released on March 4, 2021, and is the first feature film to present the Bikini Bottom cast in fully CG format, with a healthy dose of live-action footage in the mix for a saloon-ridden detour.

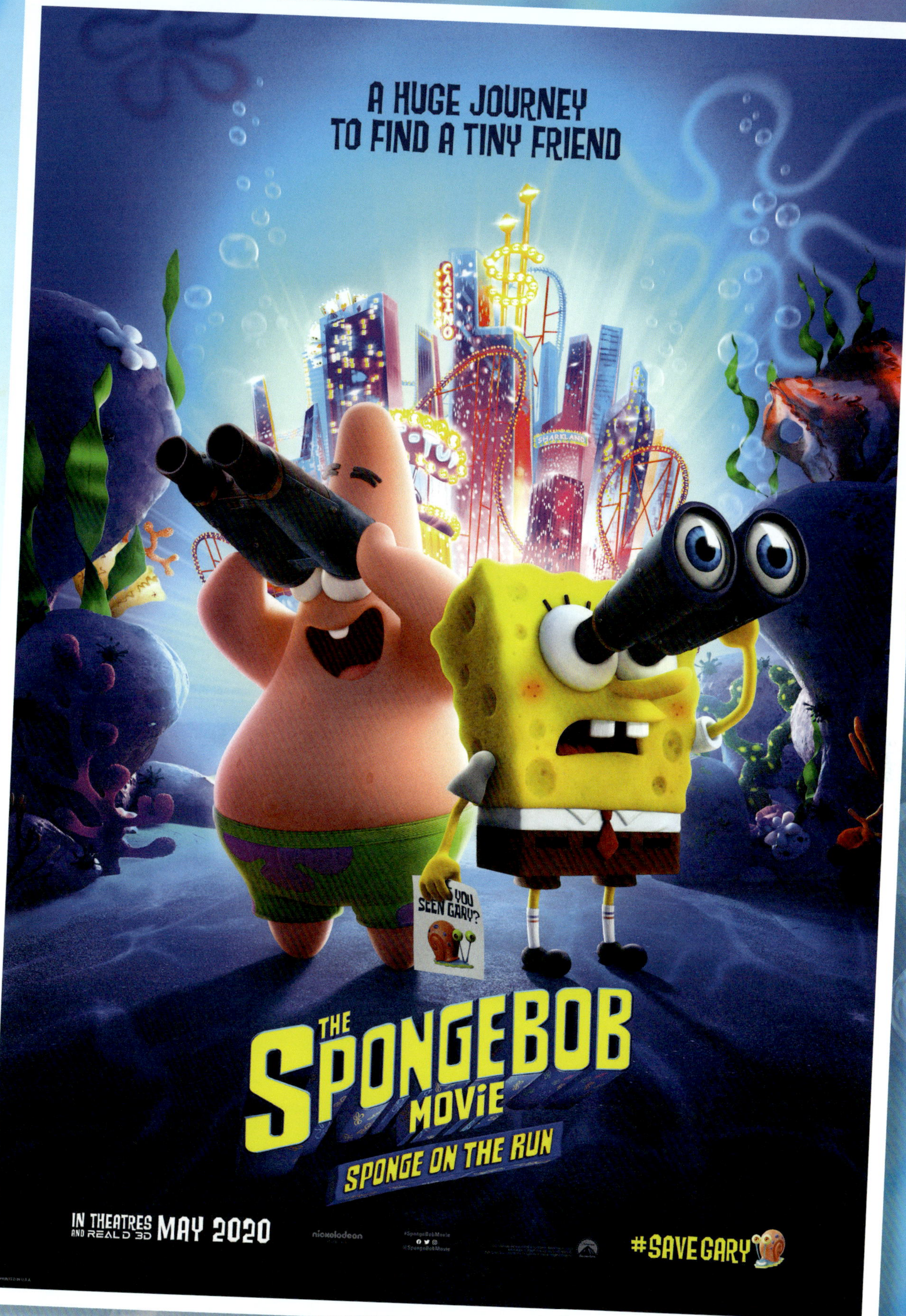
A HUGE JOURNEY
TO FIND A TINY FRIEND
CASINO
HAVE YOU SEEN GARY?
THE SPONGEBOB MOVIE
SPONGE ON THE RUN
IN THEATRES AND REAL D 3D MAY 2020
nickelodeon
#SAVEGARY

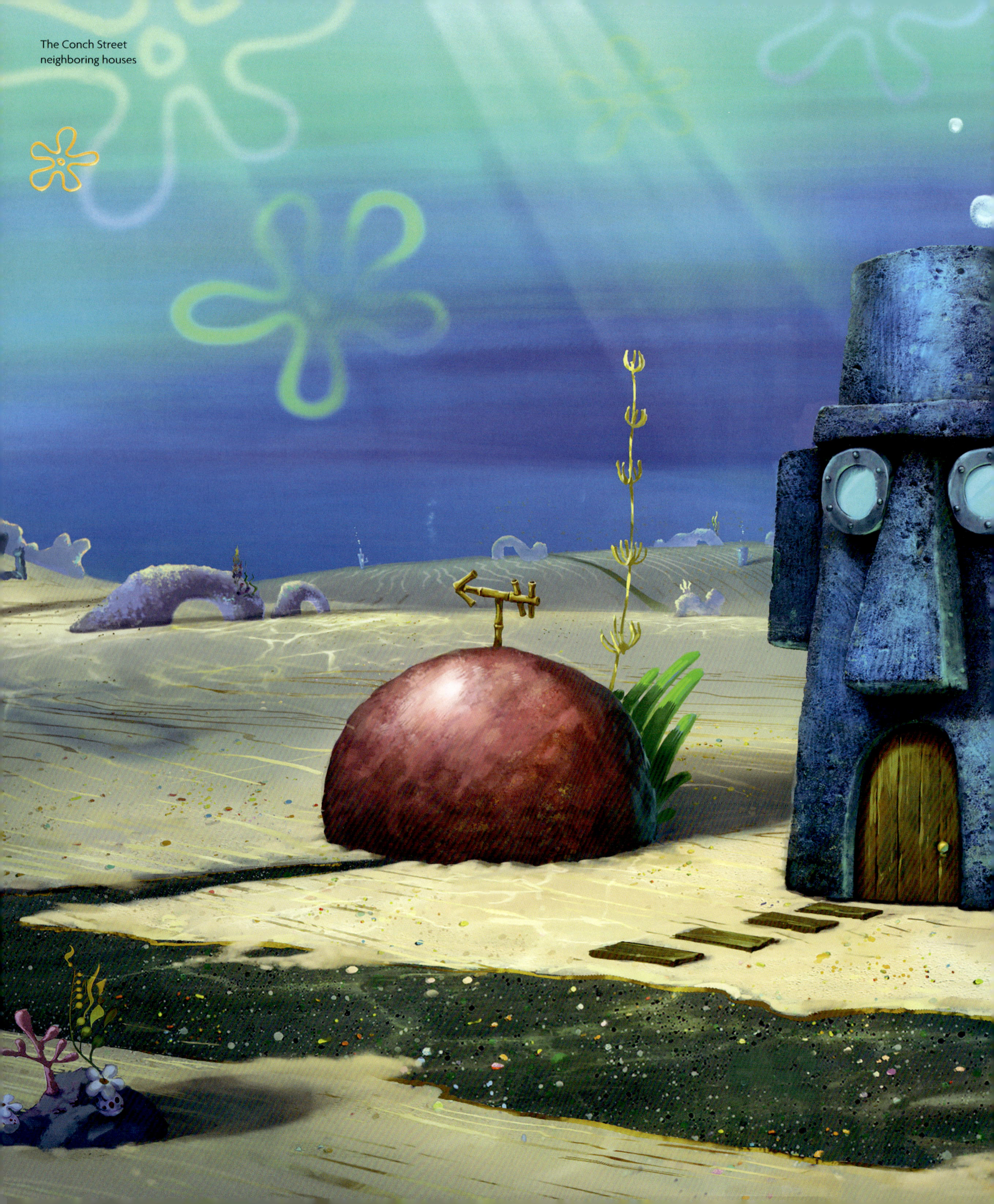
The Conch Street
neighboring houses

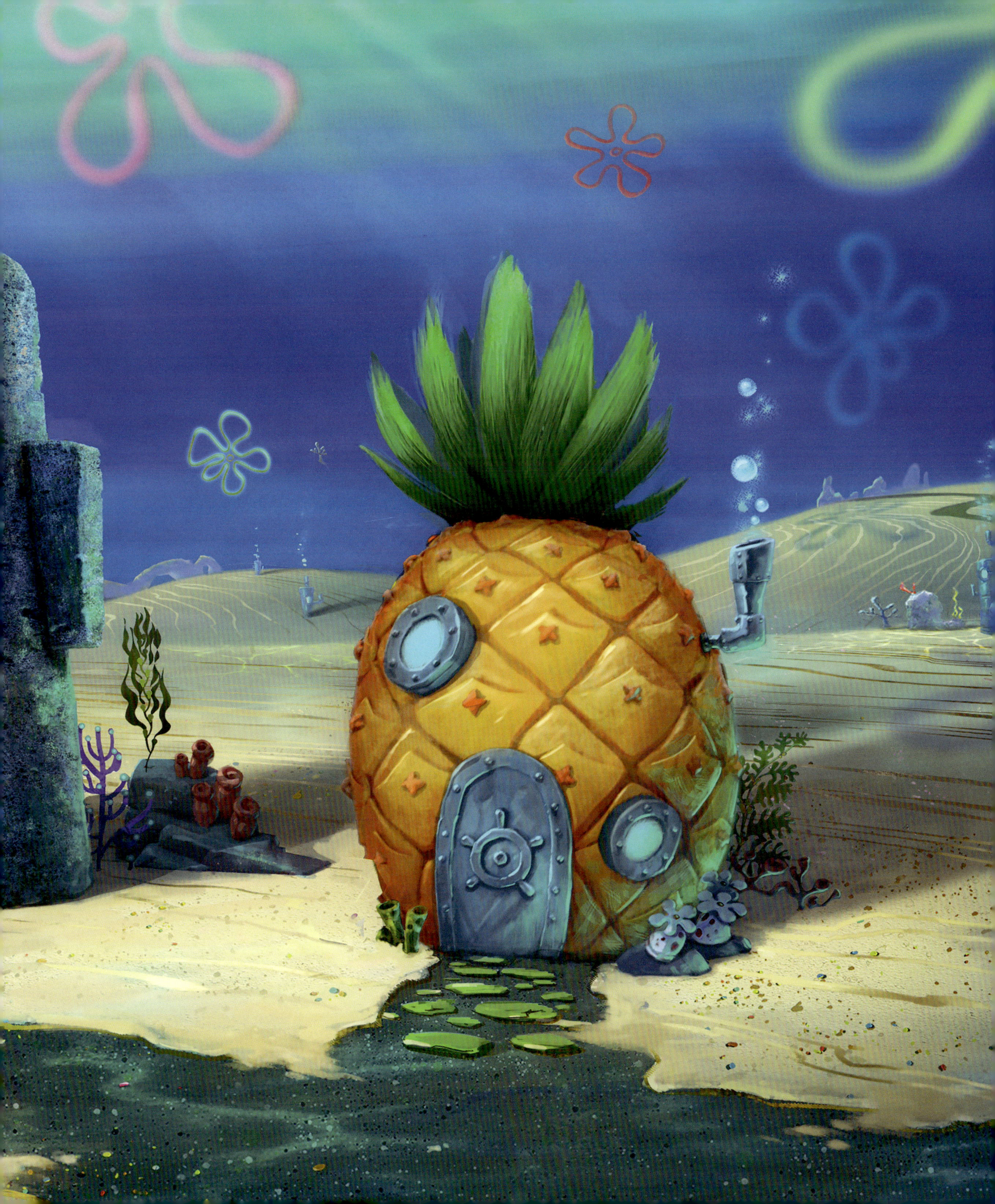

THE LATEST PLOT: SNAILNAPPING

Plankton's latest evil plan involves getting SpongeBob out of his way, and he does so by whisking Gary off to fulfill Poseidon's call for fresh snail slime as part of a royal skin-care regimen... and then setting up SpongeBob and Patrick to go on a high-stakes rescue effort.

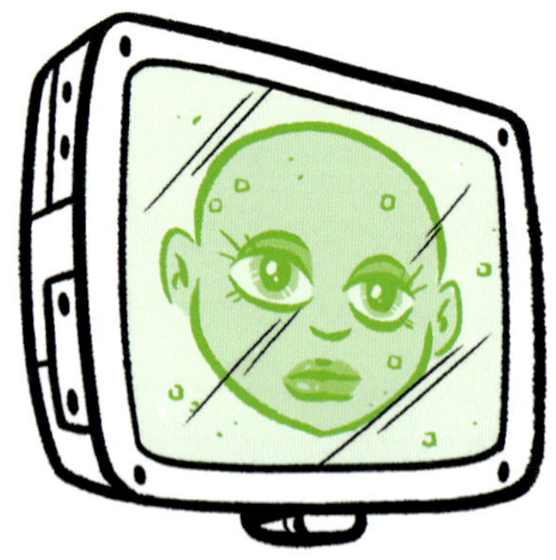

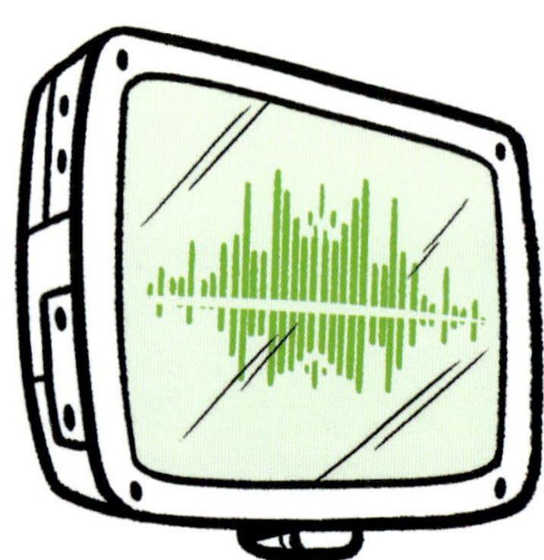

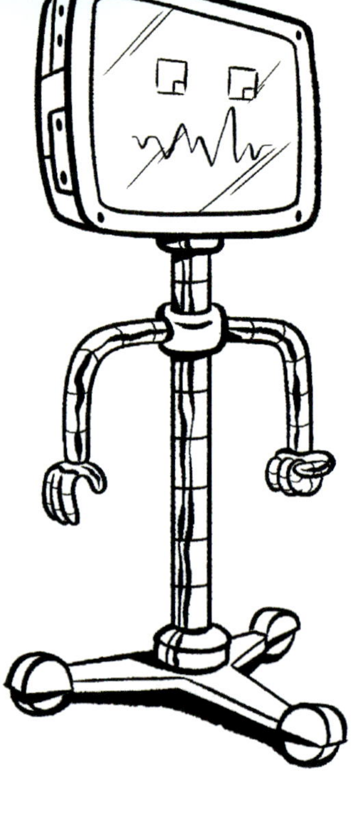

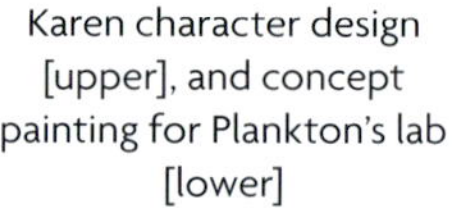

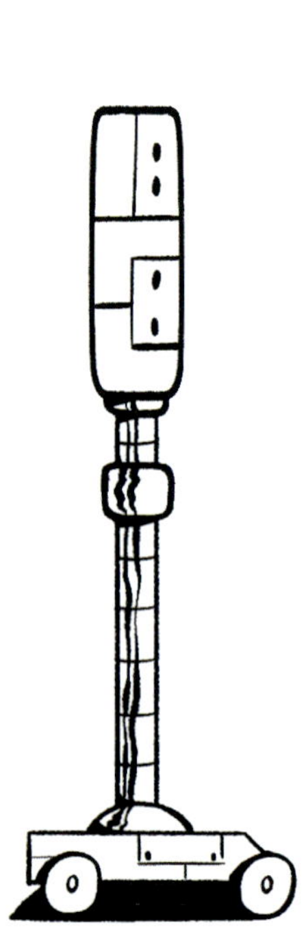

Karen character design [upper], and concept painting for Plankton's lab [lower]

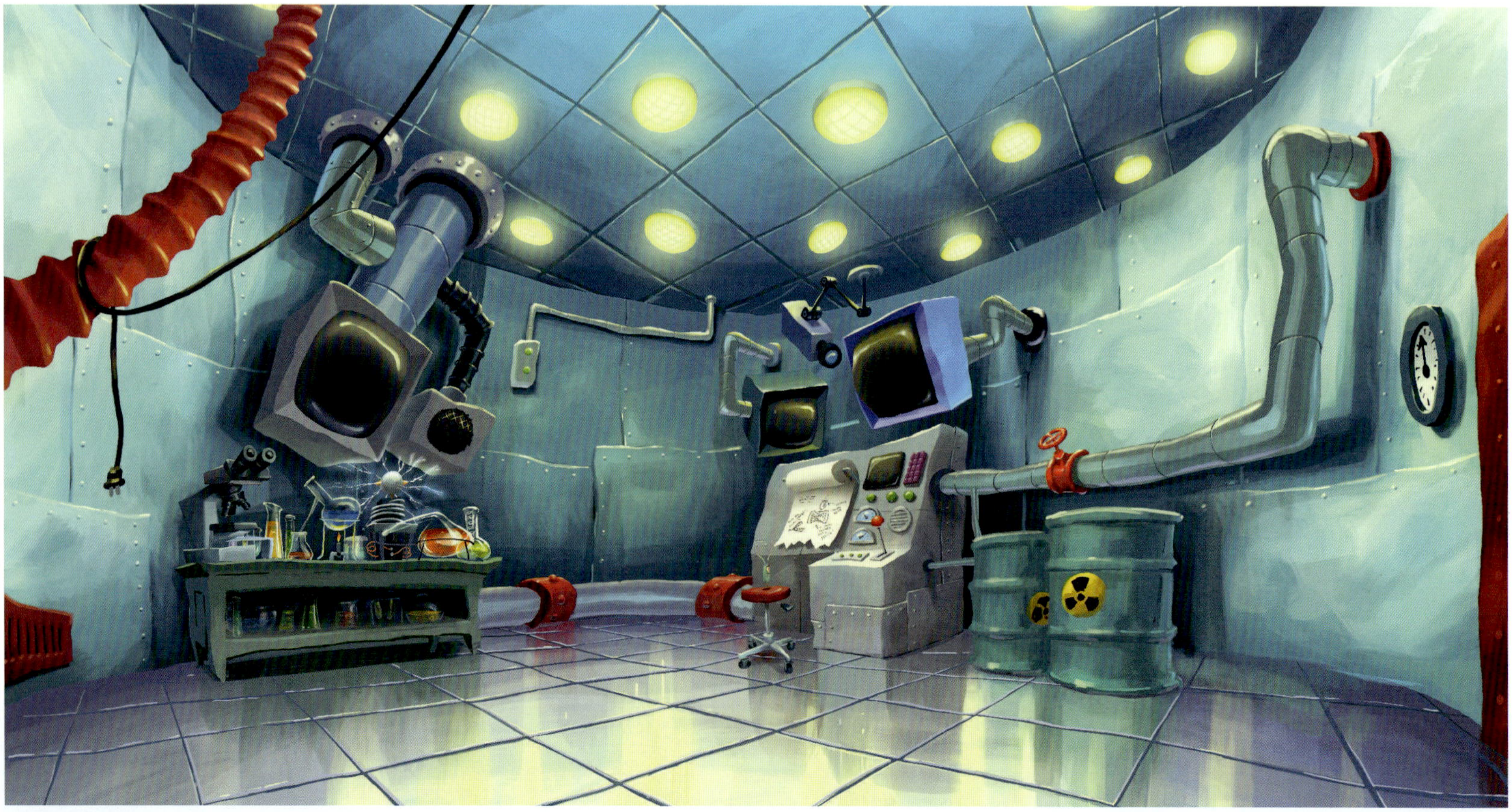

Examples of Squidward self-portraits

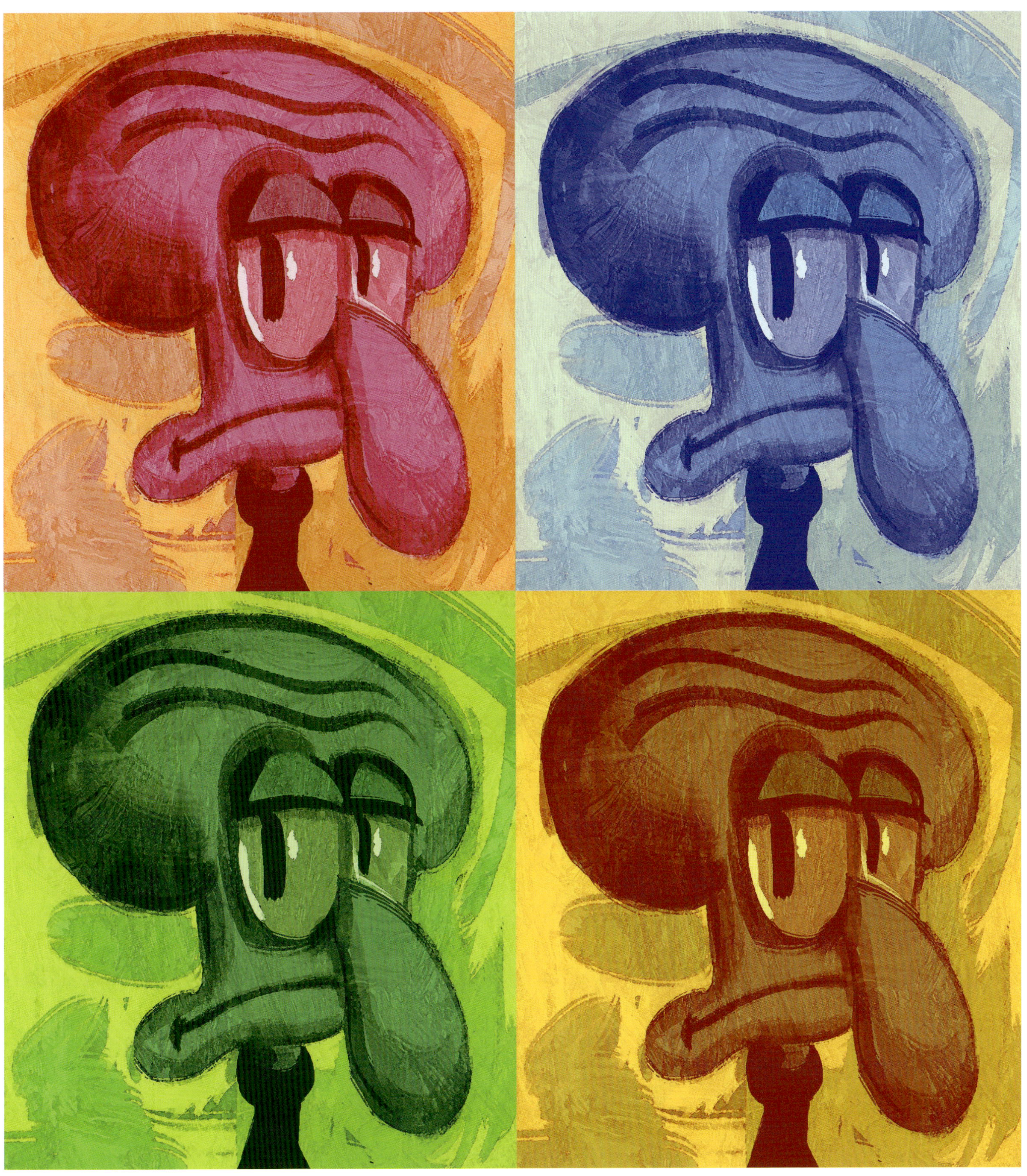

MEET KING POSEIDON

In trying to learn more about where this heroic trek will take them, SpongeBob reads in a guidebook that "King Poseidon has proven himself a whimsical tyrant, known for executing his subjects by beheading them in a flamboyant floor-show extravaganza."

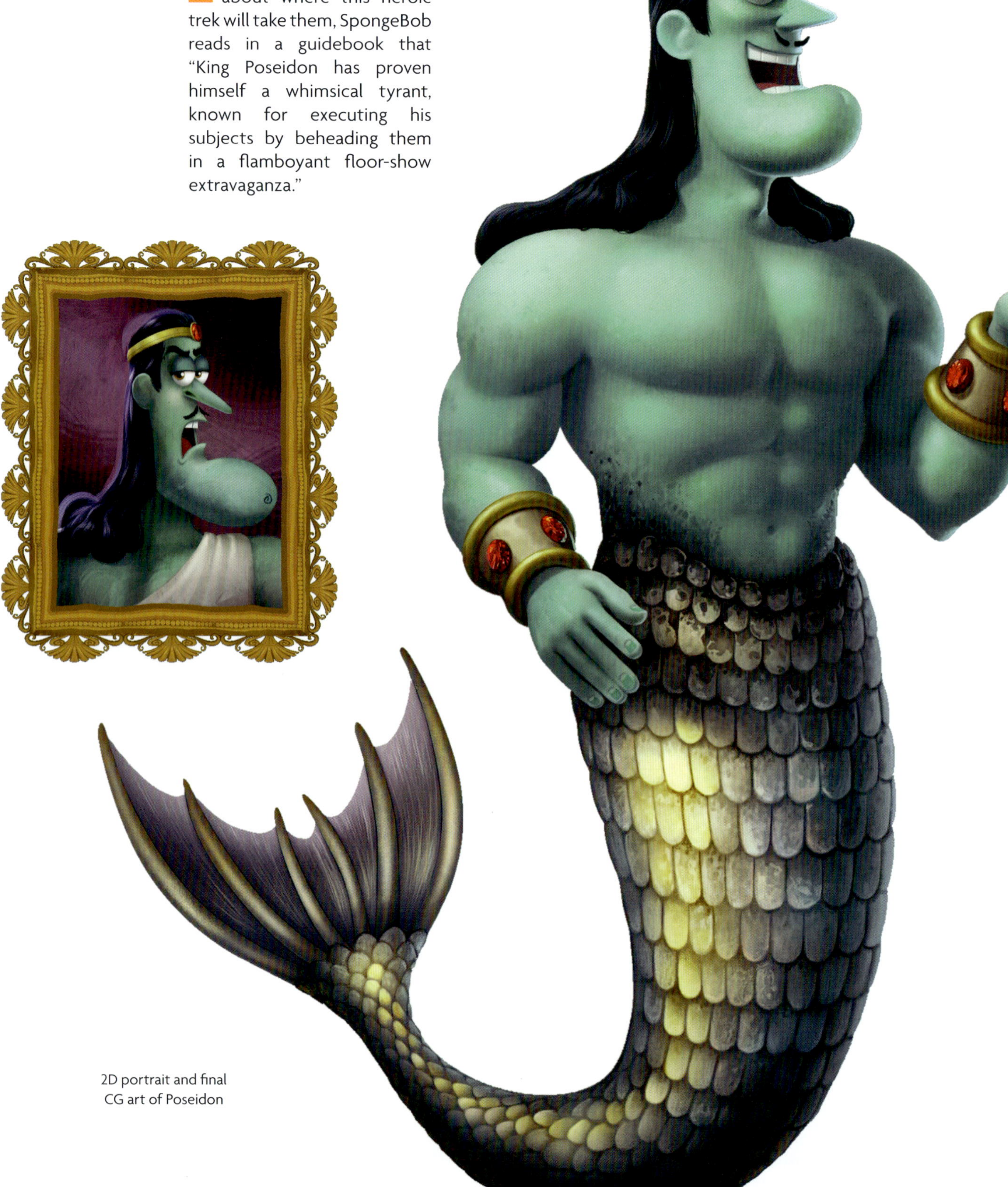

2D portrait and final CG art of Poseidon

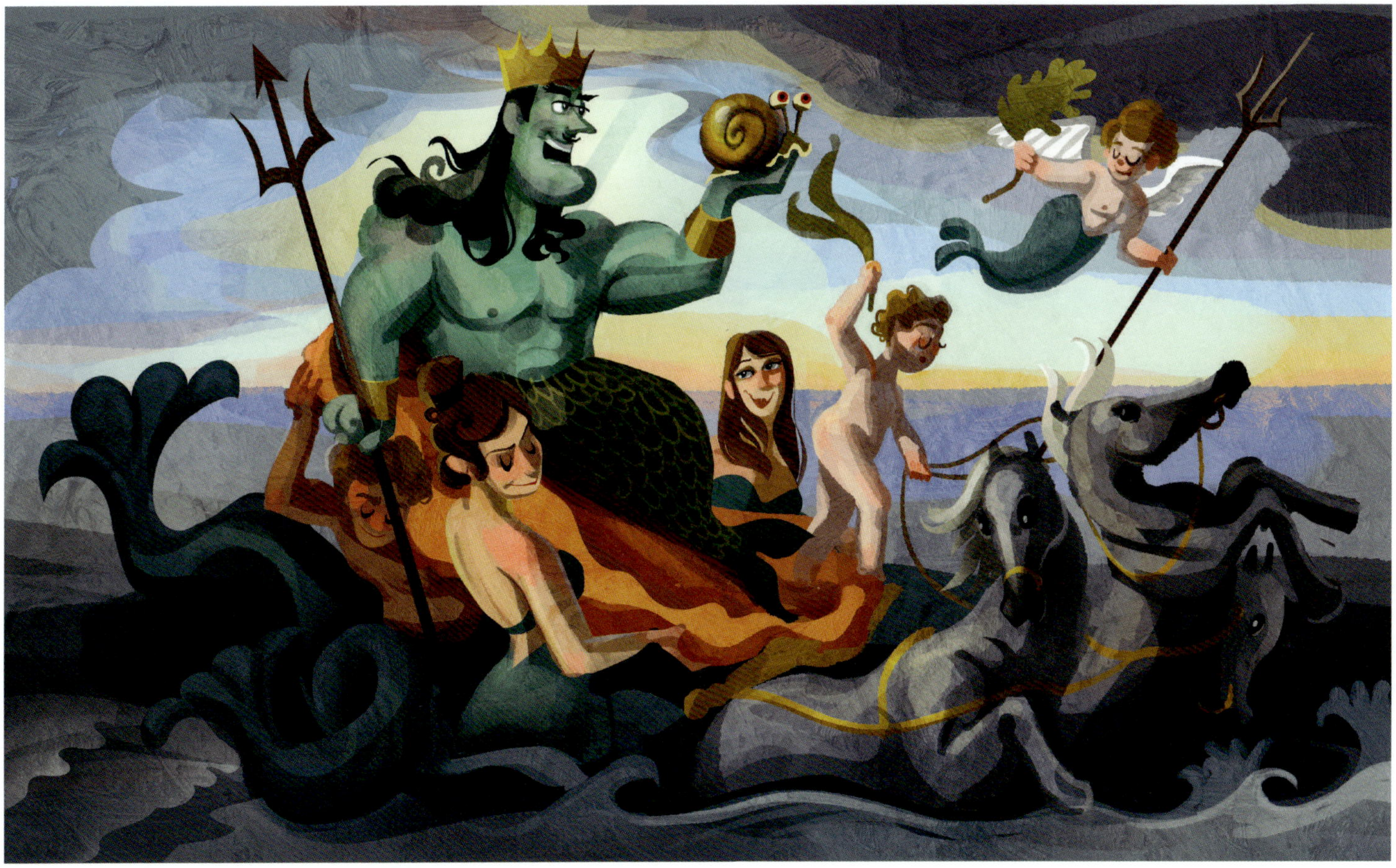

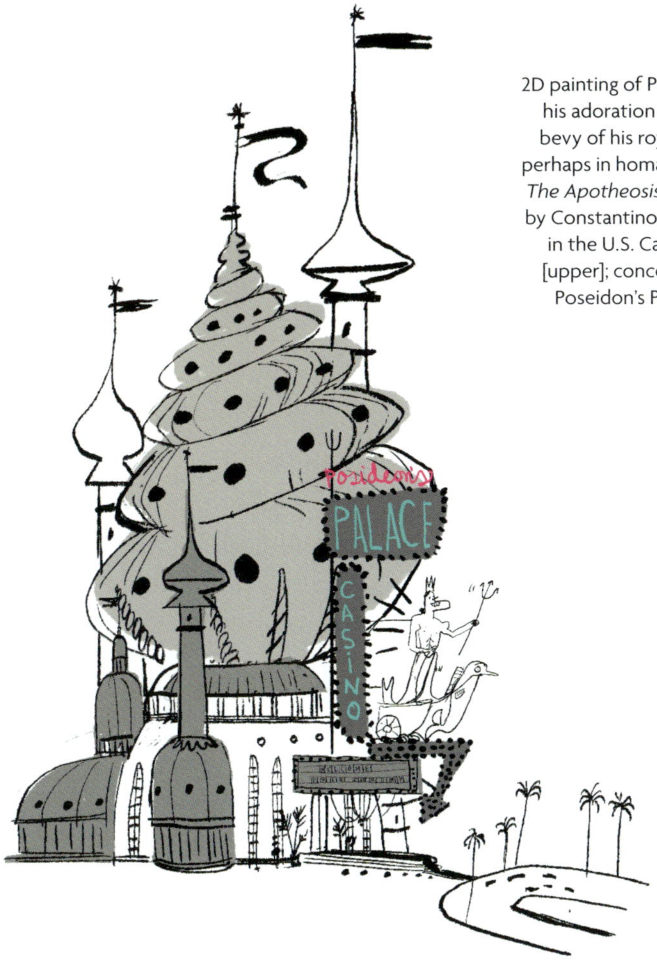

2D painting of Poseidon showing his adoration of snails and a bevy of his royal attendants, perhaps in homage to the fresco *The Apotheosis of Washington* by Constantino Brumidi housed in the U.S. Capitol rotunda [upper]; concept artwork of Poseidon's Palace [lower]

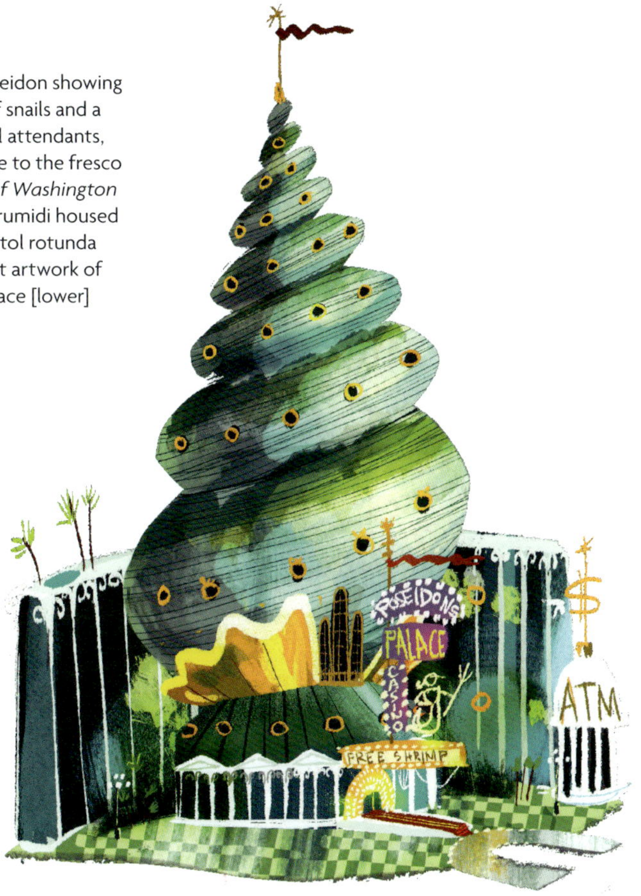

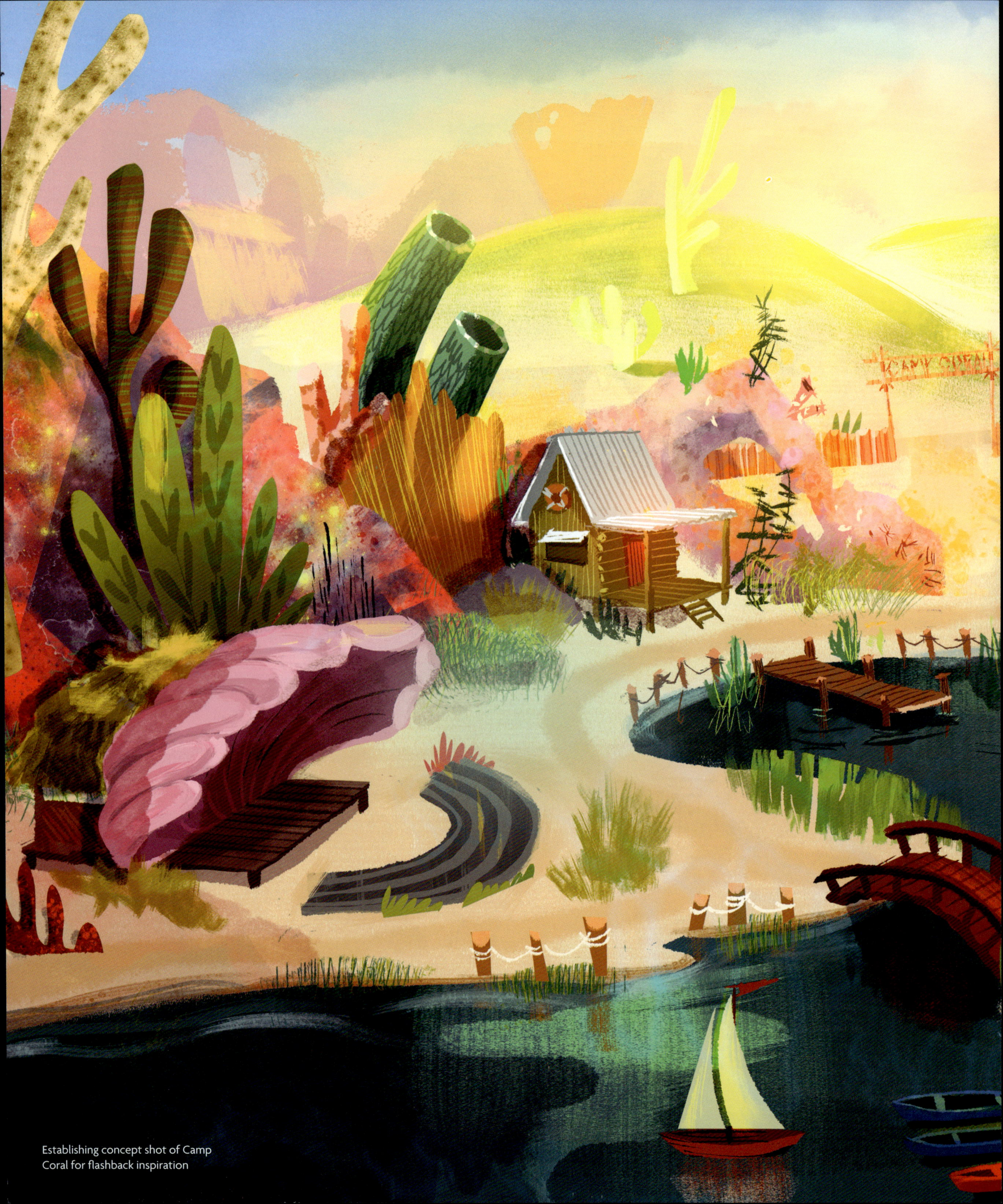

Establishing concept shot of Camp Coral for flashback inspiration

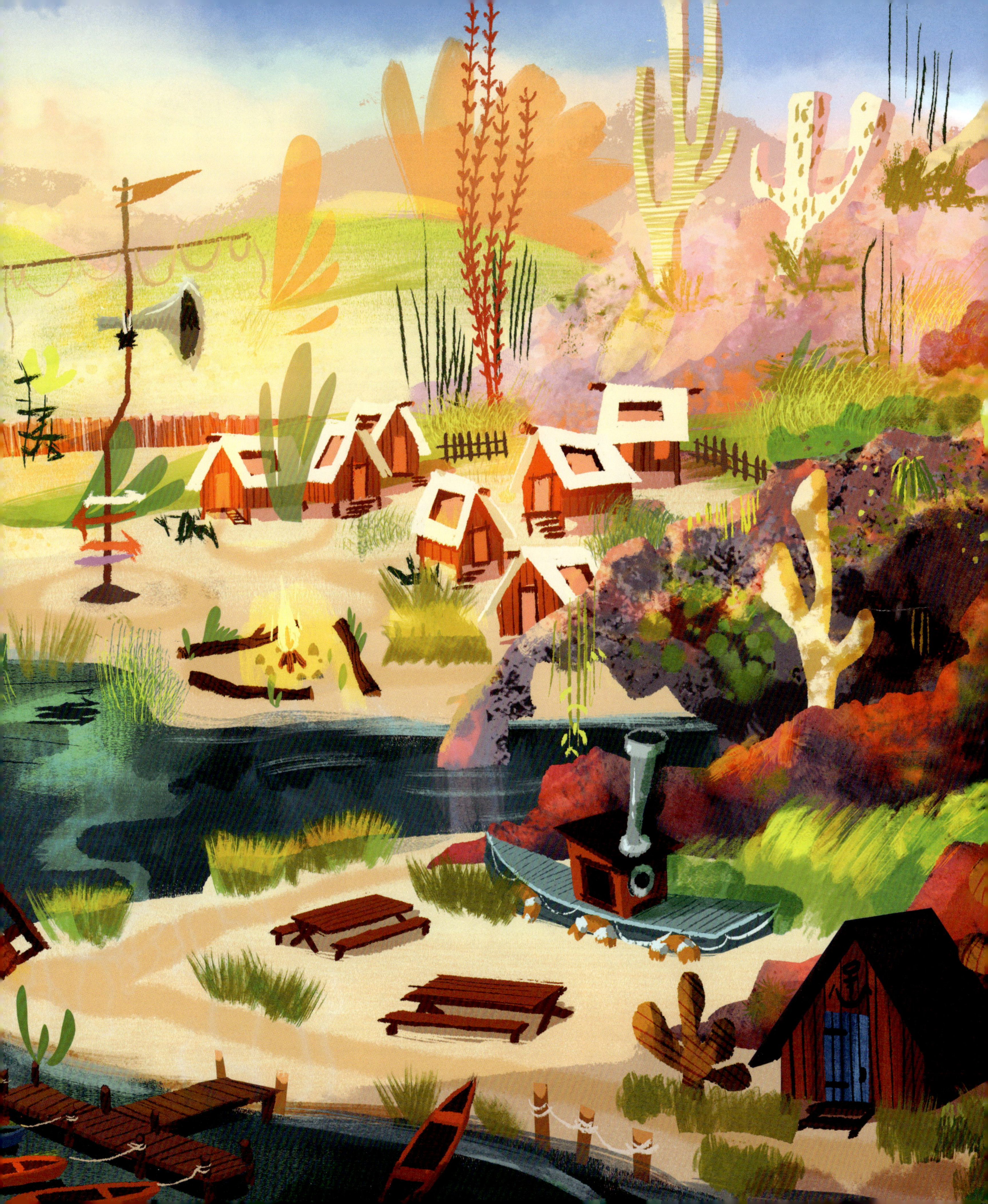

CAMP CORAL FLASHBACKS

In his weepy trip down memory lane, SpongeBob reminisces about when he first met Gary, at Camp Coral (which would get a spelling update later in the chronology, by the way, when the series *Kamp Koral* would be produced). Flashbacks to memories at Camp Coral take place throughout the film, sharing both a look at cute young versions of some of the Bikini Bottom residents and their deep history of friendship.

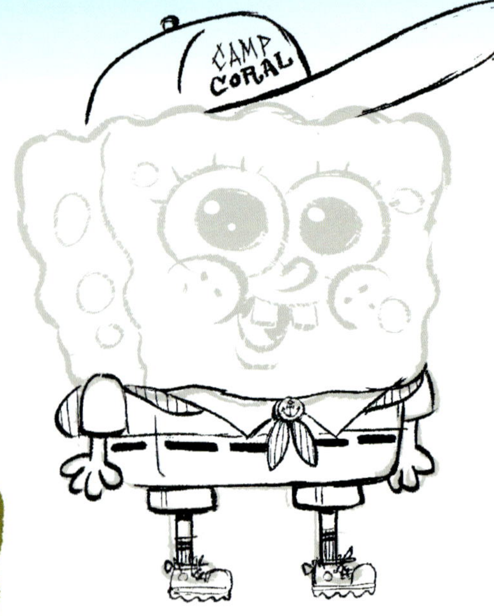

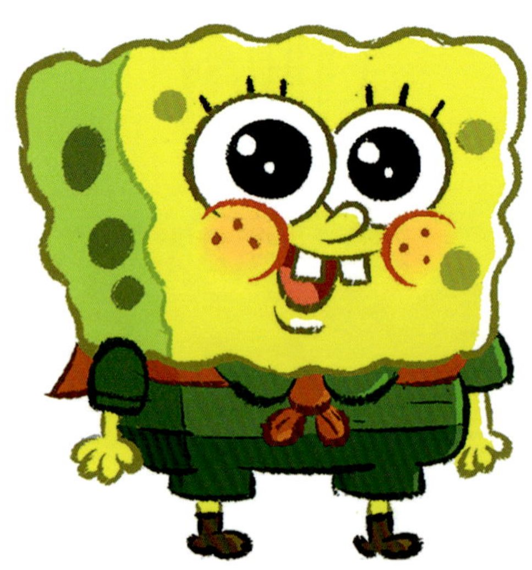

Visual development of young camper SpongeBob [upper] and final frame image of SpongeBob and Patrick among other campers

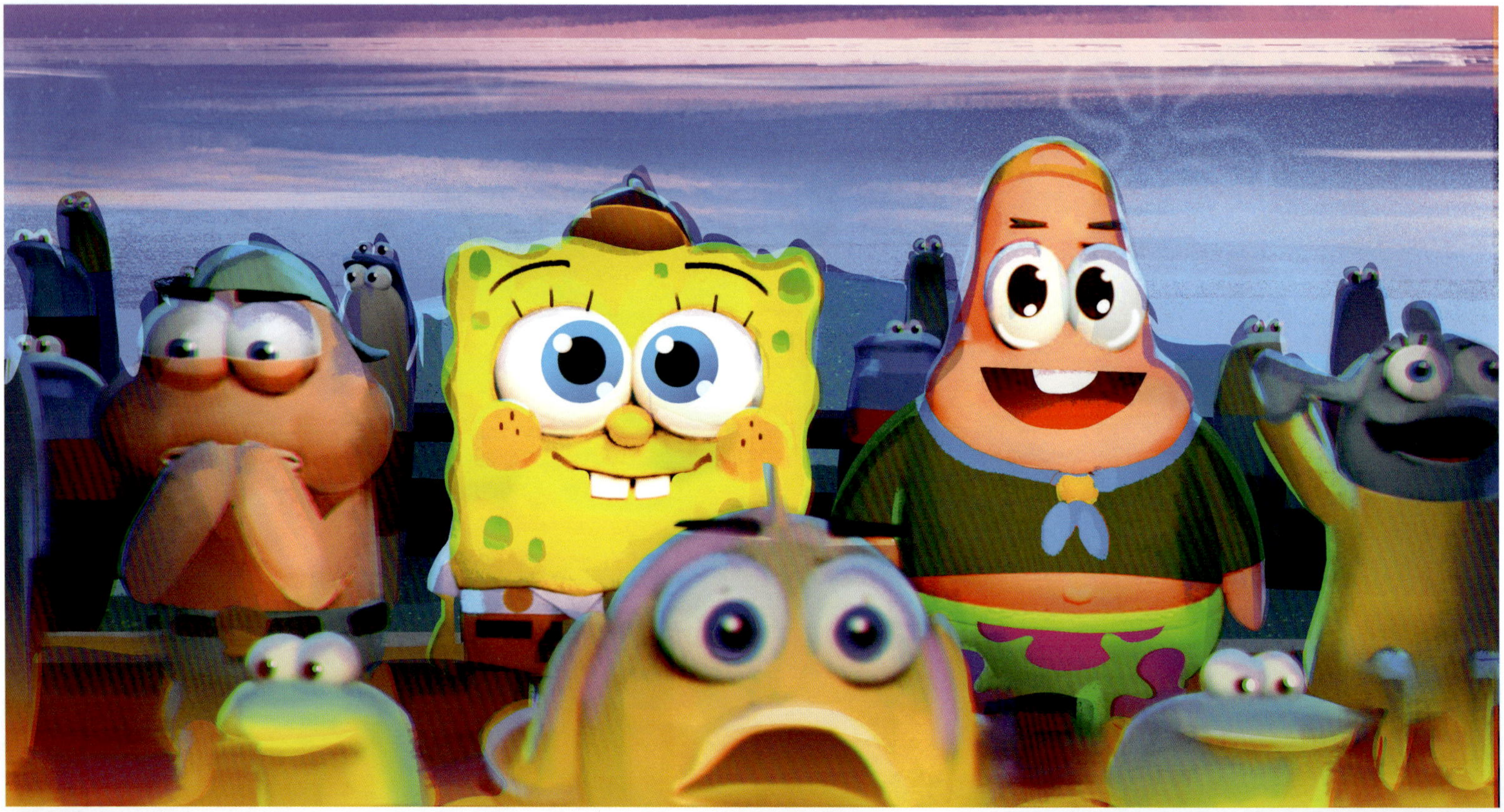

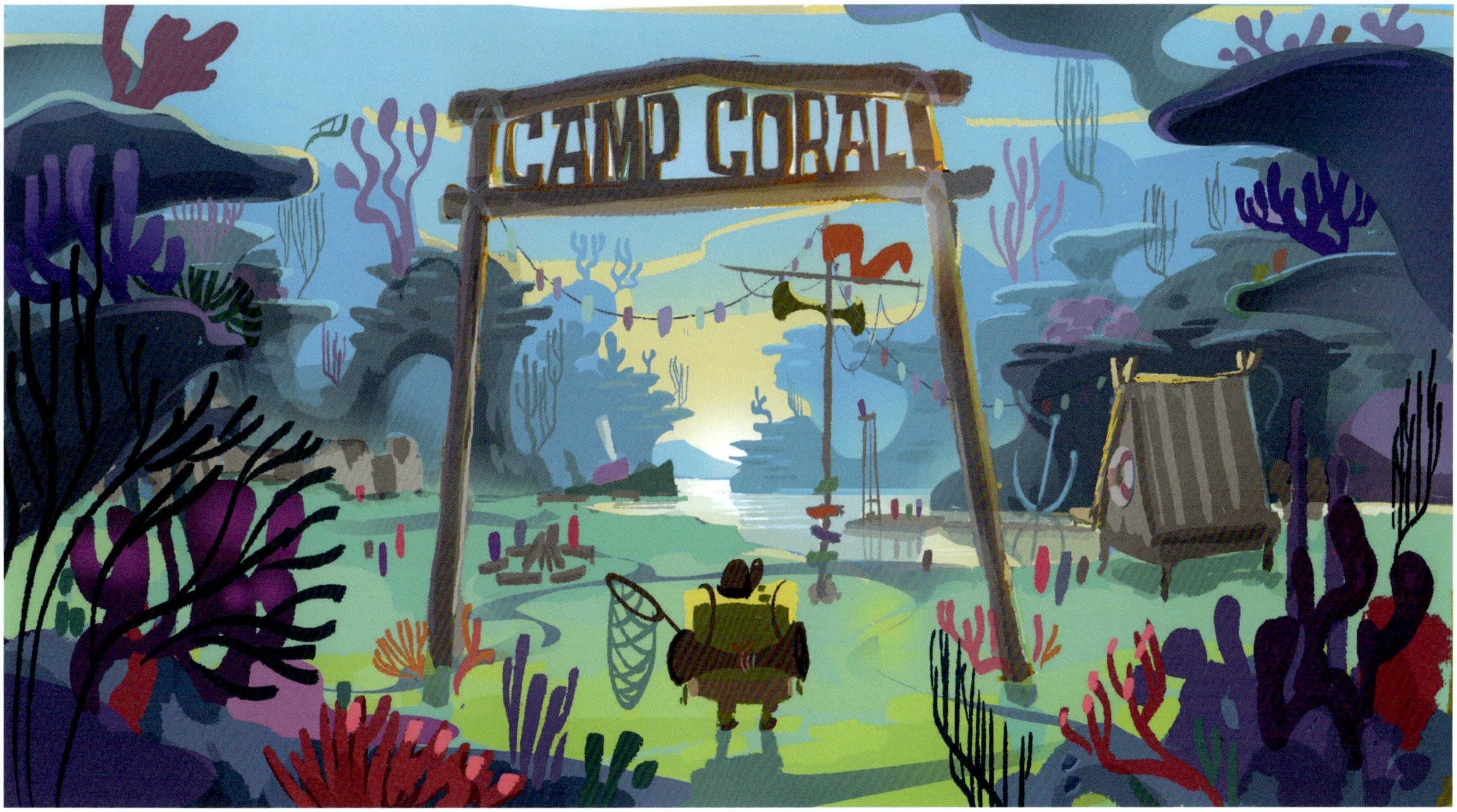

Look of pictures of Camp Coral

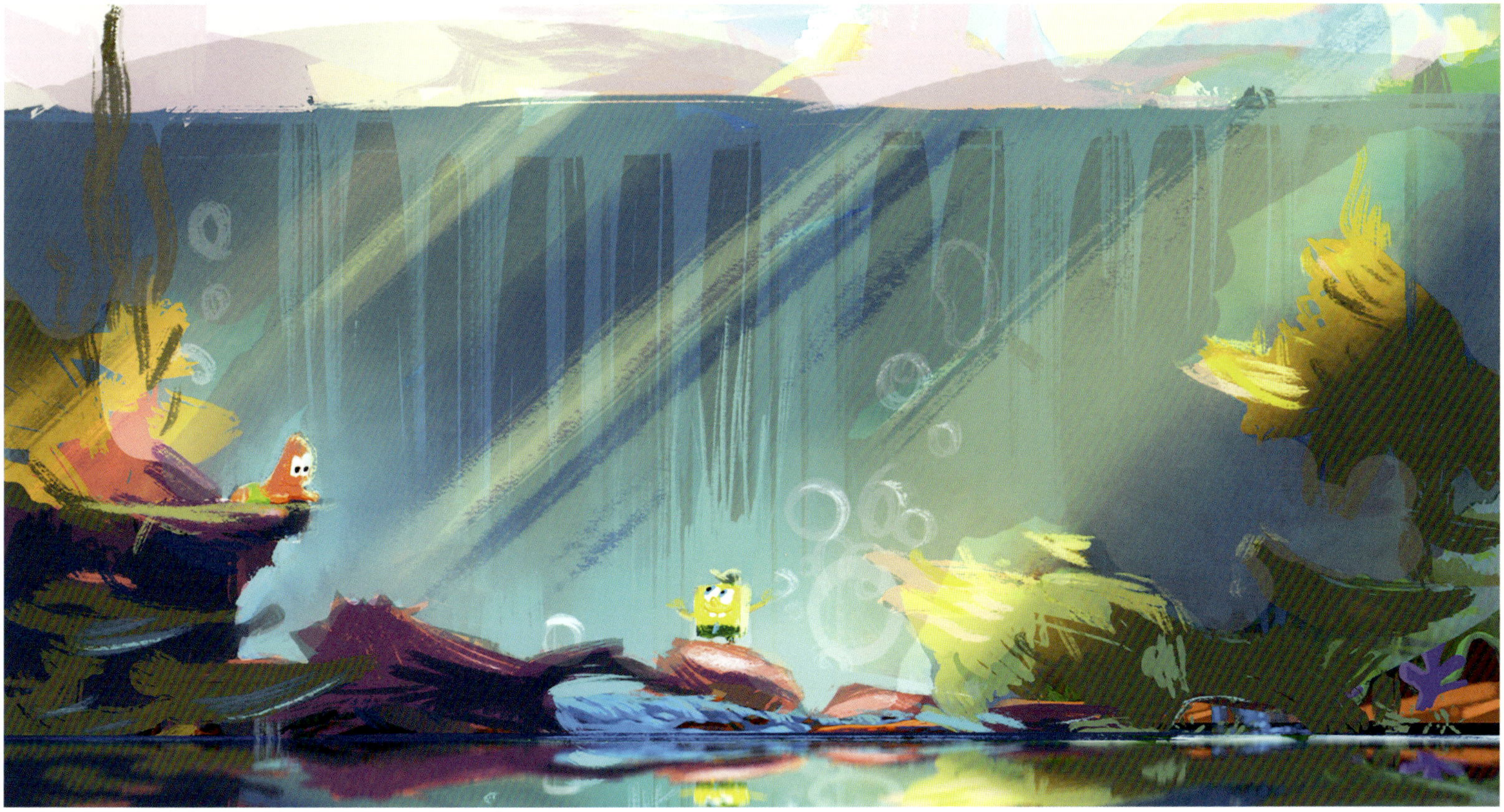

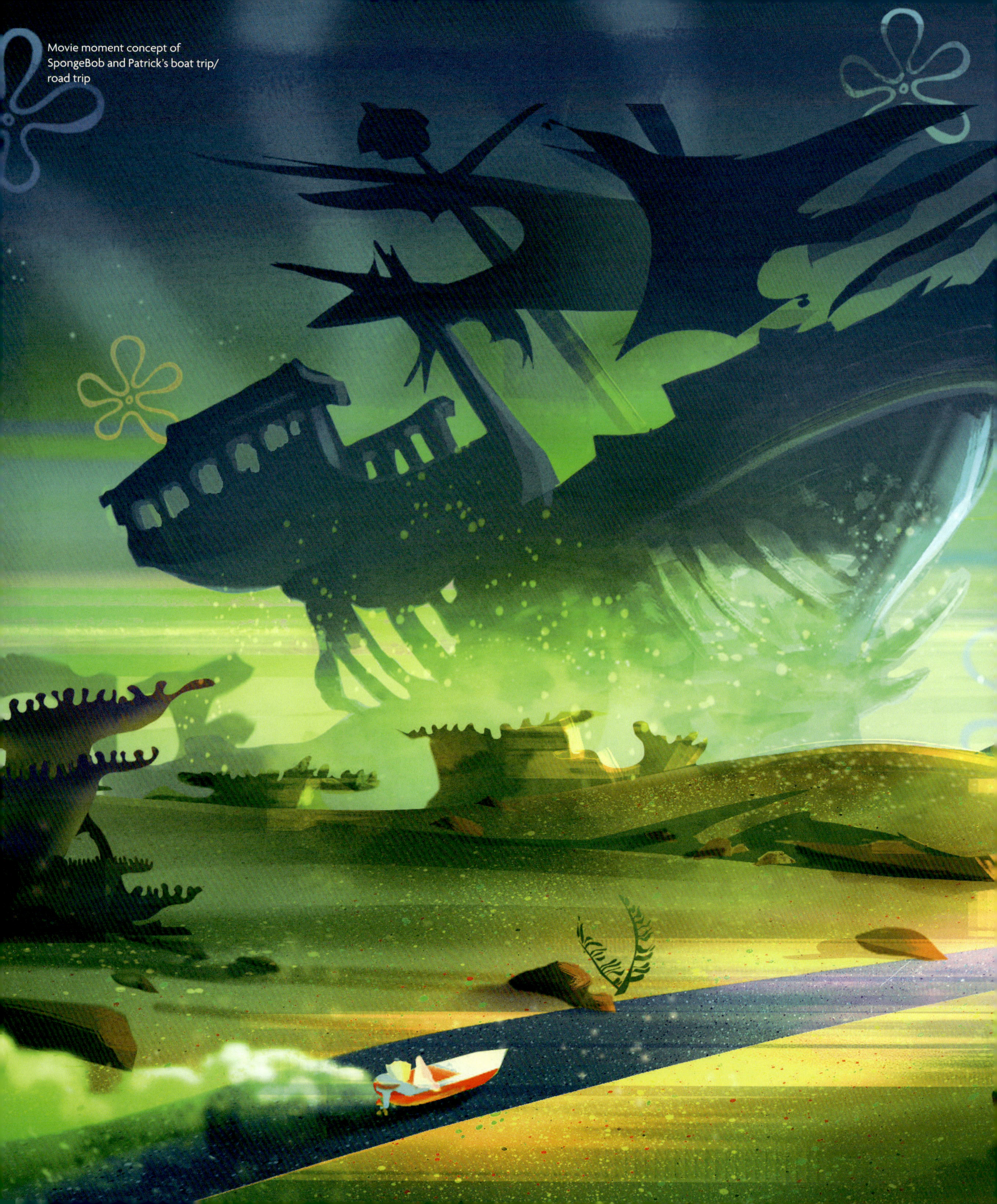

Movie moment concept of SpongeBob and Patrick's boat trip/road trip

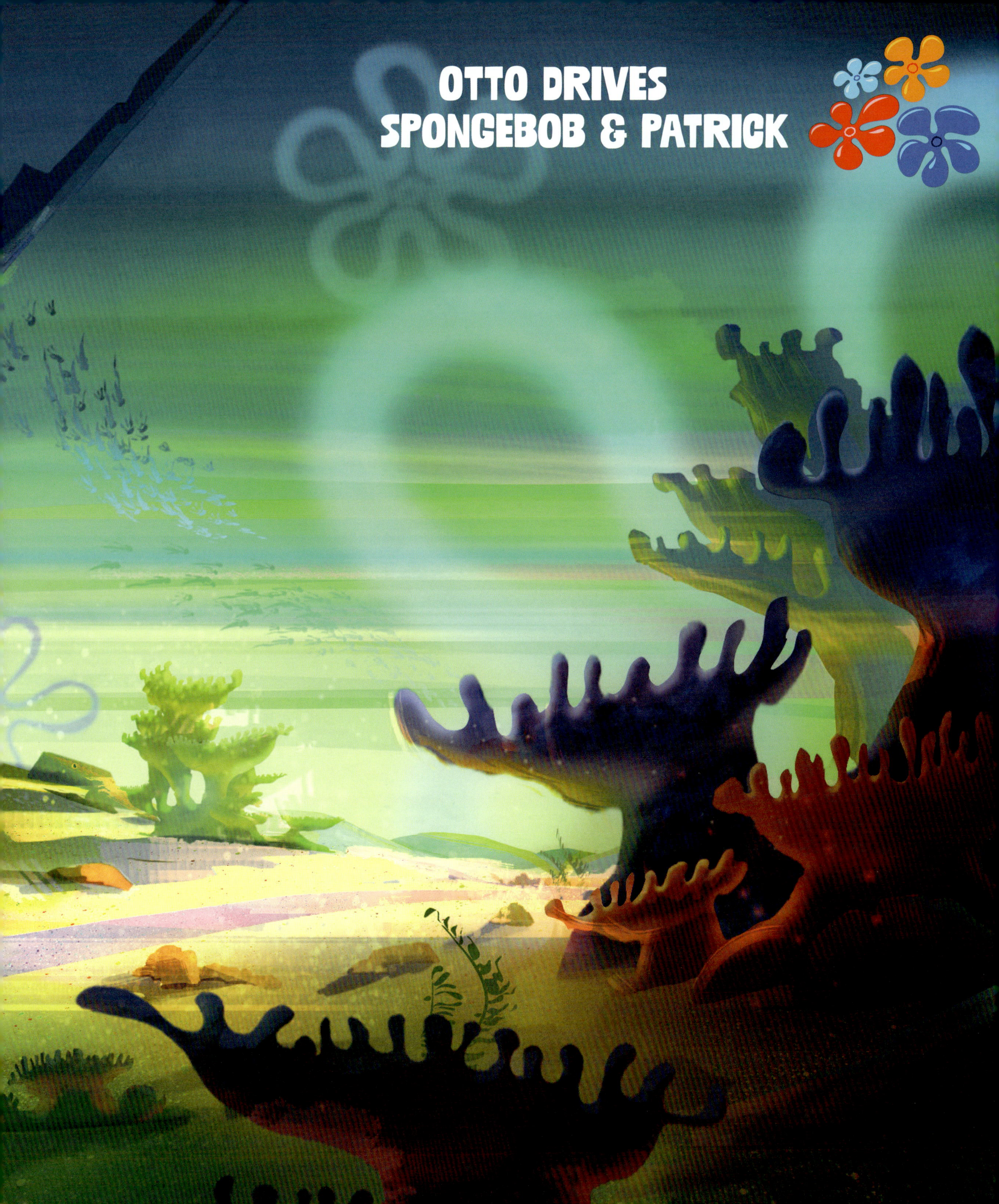
OTTO DRIVES
SPONGEBOB & PATRICK

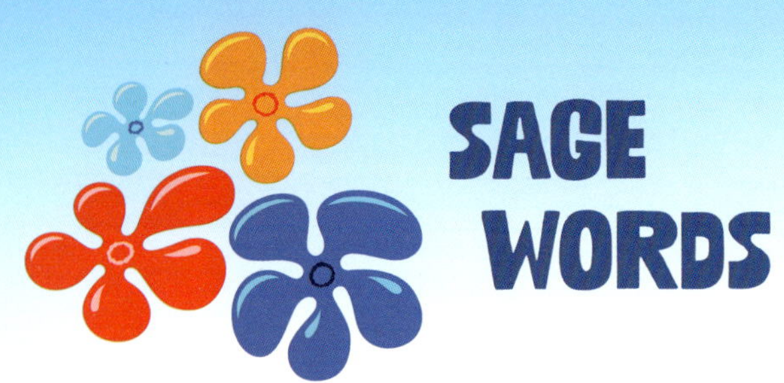

SAGE WORDS

While in Goner Gulch, SpongeBob and Patrick encounter an excellent adventure with a wise tumbleweed that gives them thoughtful yet cryptic advice and a Challenge Coin.

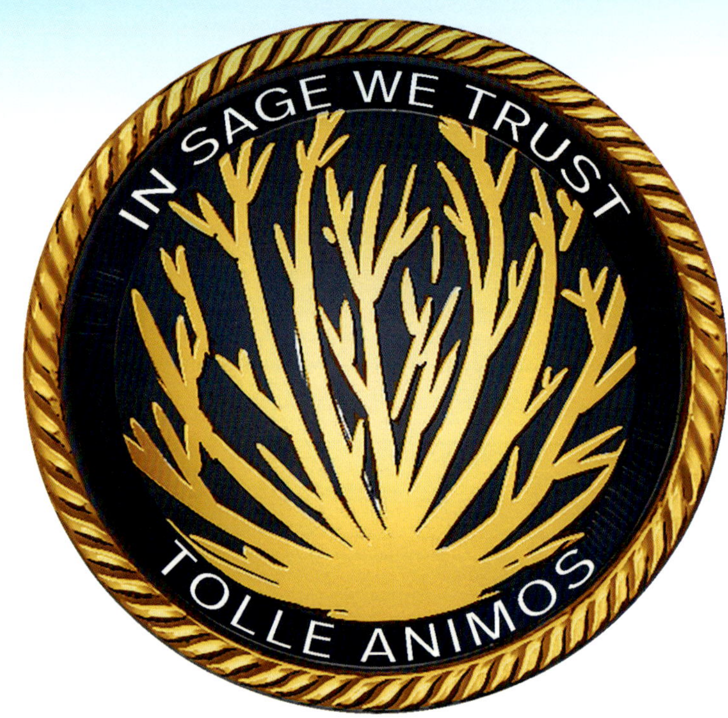

Textured render of the Challenge Coin [upper] and CG art of Patrick, SpongeBob, Sage, and Otto [lower]

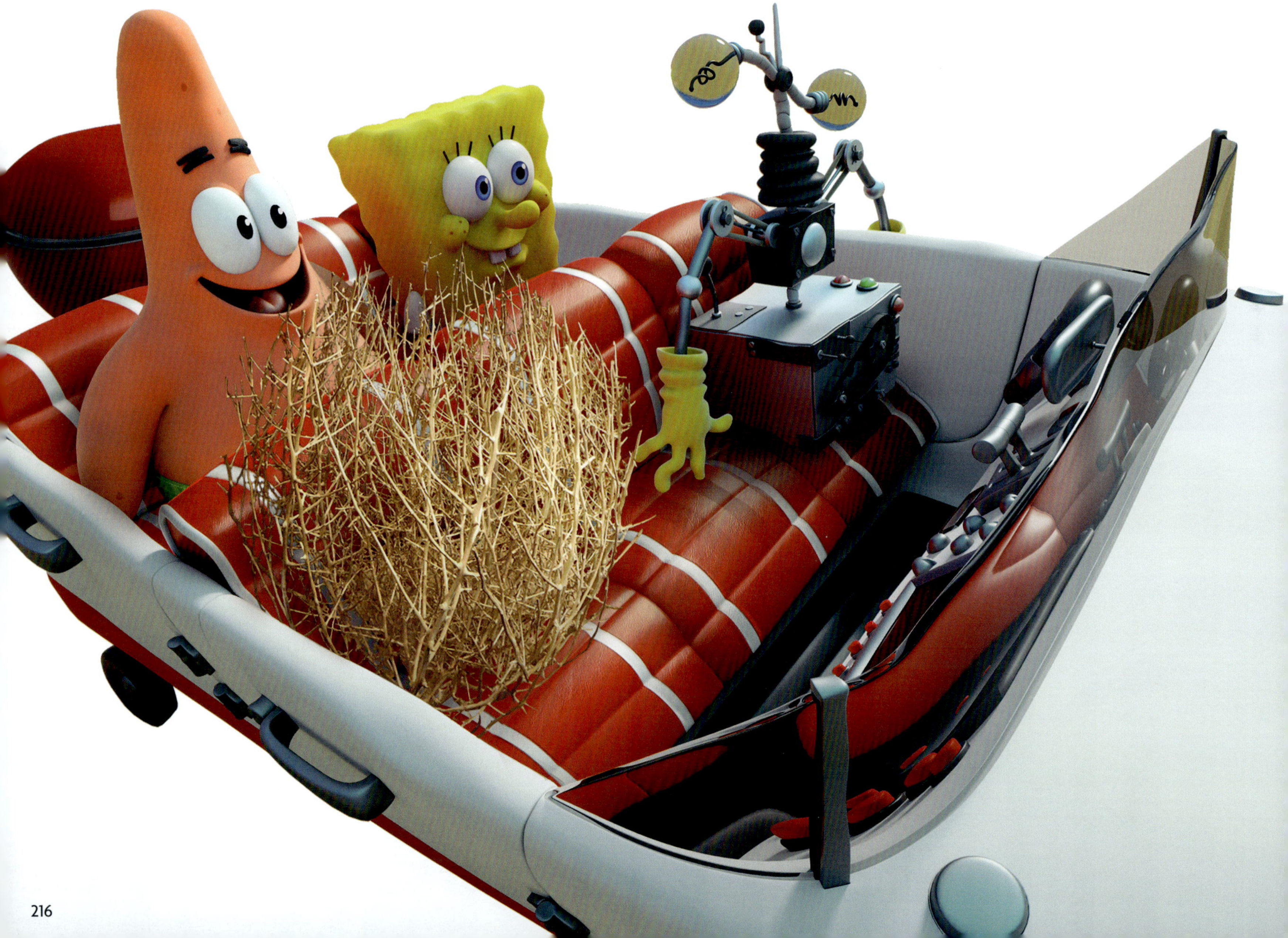

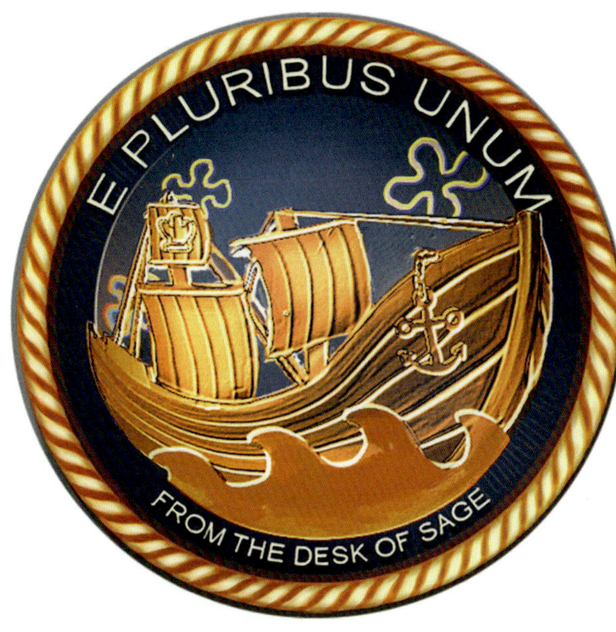

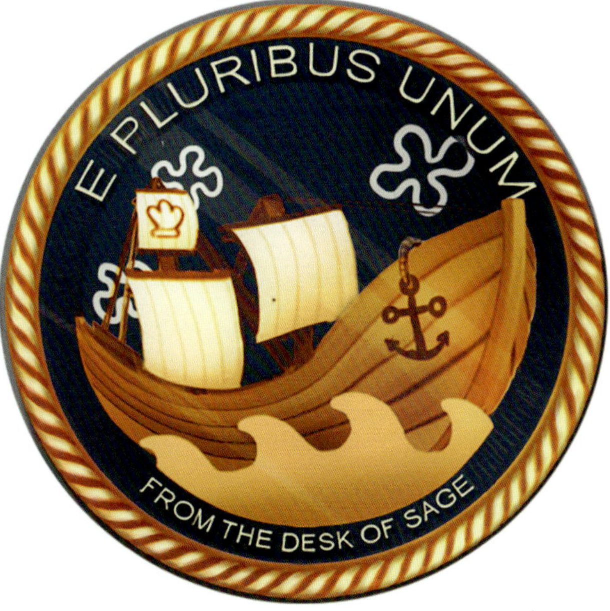

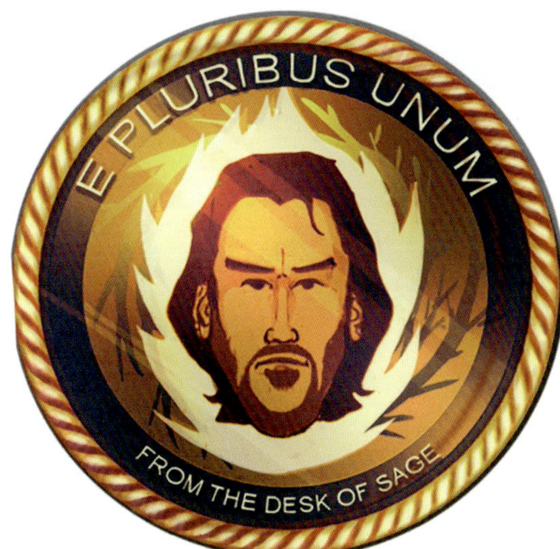

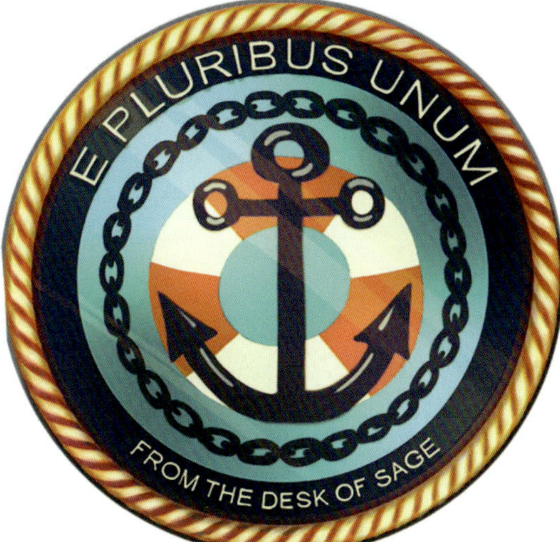

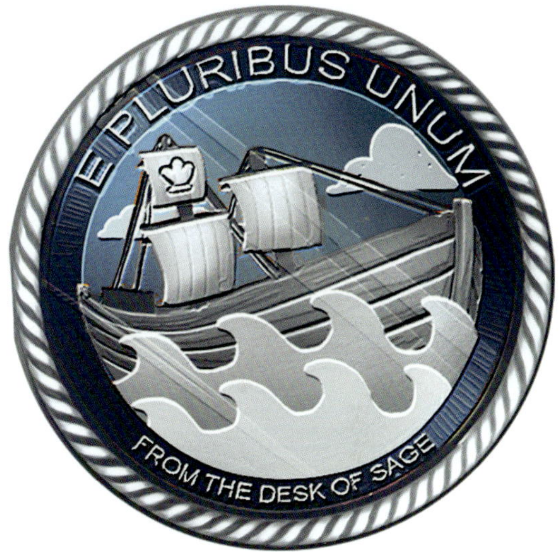

Alternative designs for the Challenge Coin

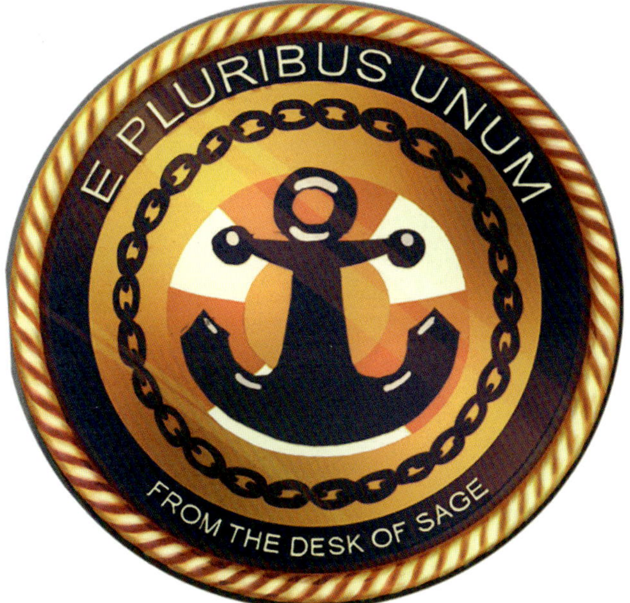

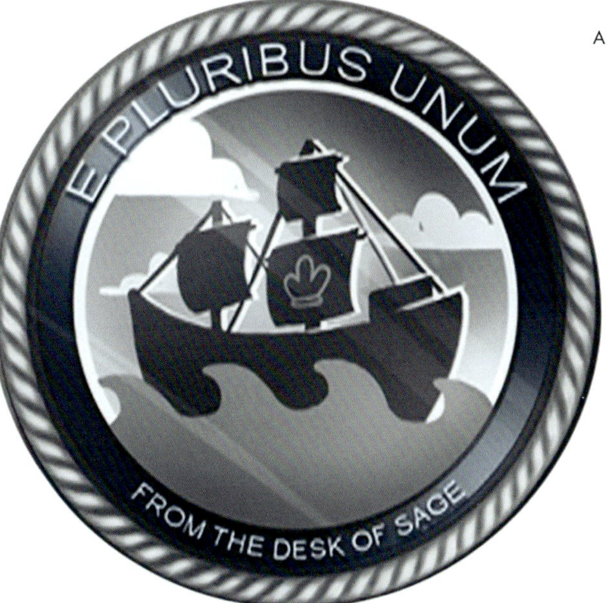

THE LOST CITY OF ATLANTIC CITY

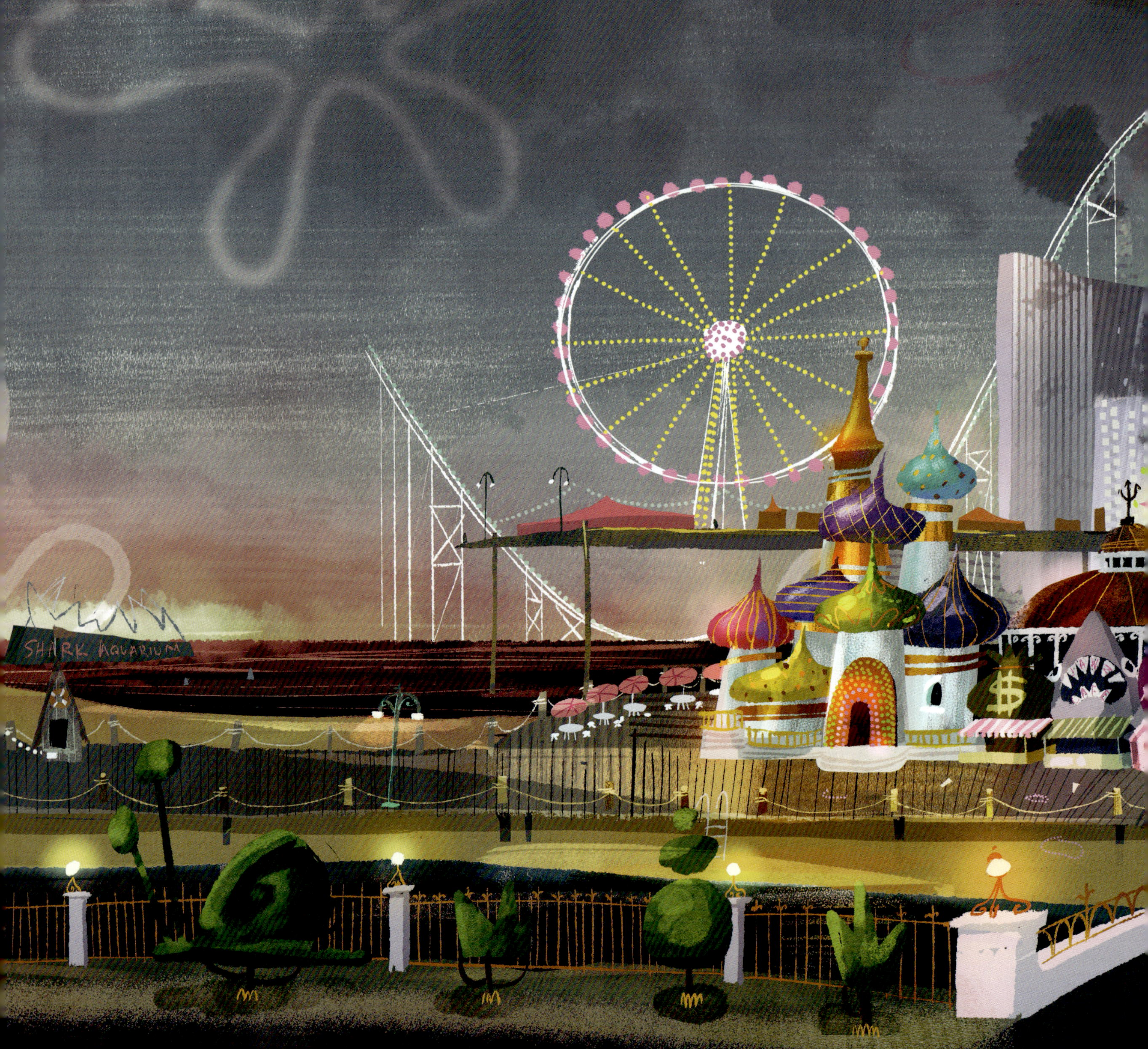

Visual development of the Lost City of Atlantic City, where bright lights and big sounds lure SpongeBob and Patrick into another detour, this time enrobed in neon and gluttony instead of dust and zombies

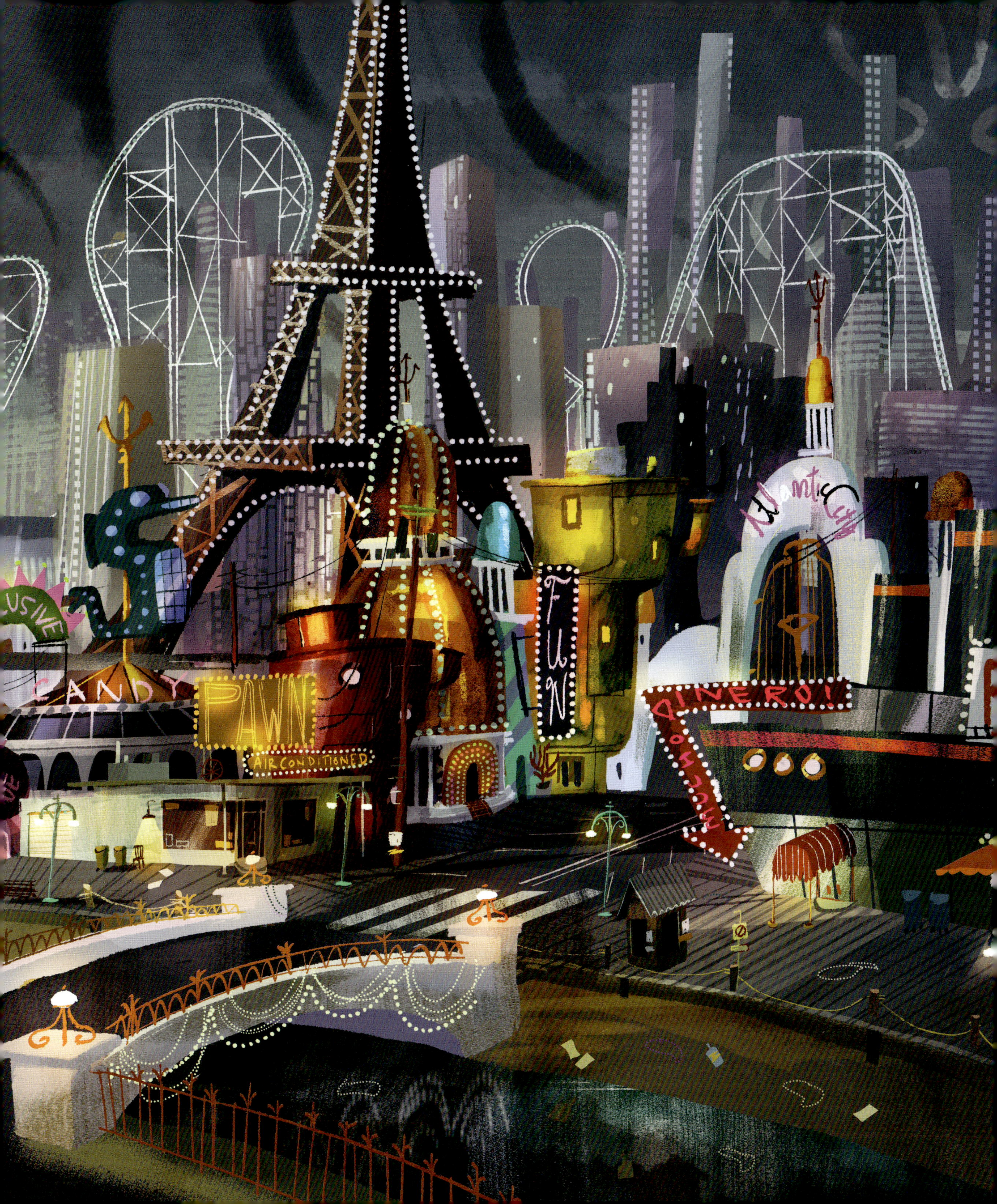
CANDY
PAWN
AIR CONDITIONED
FUN
Atlantic City
DINERO!

FOOD

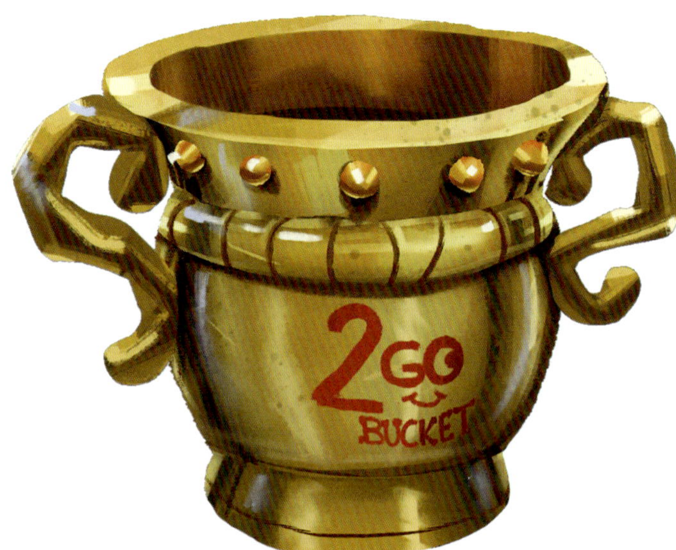

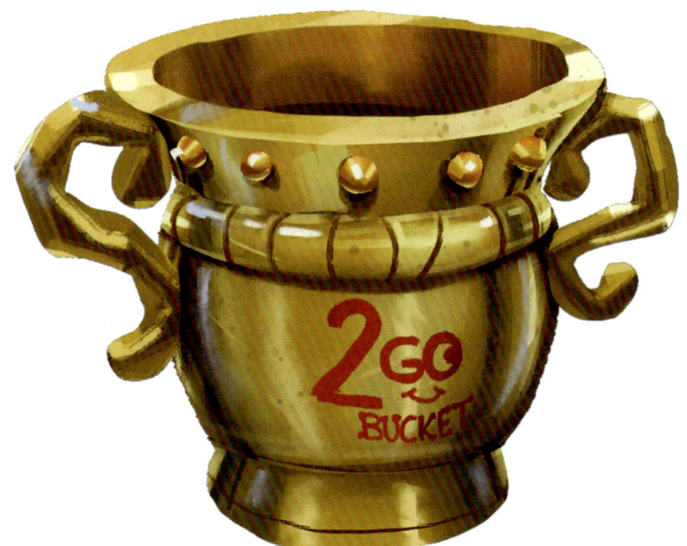

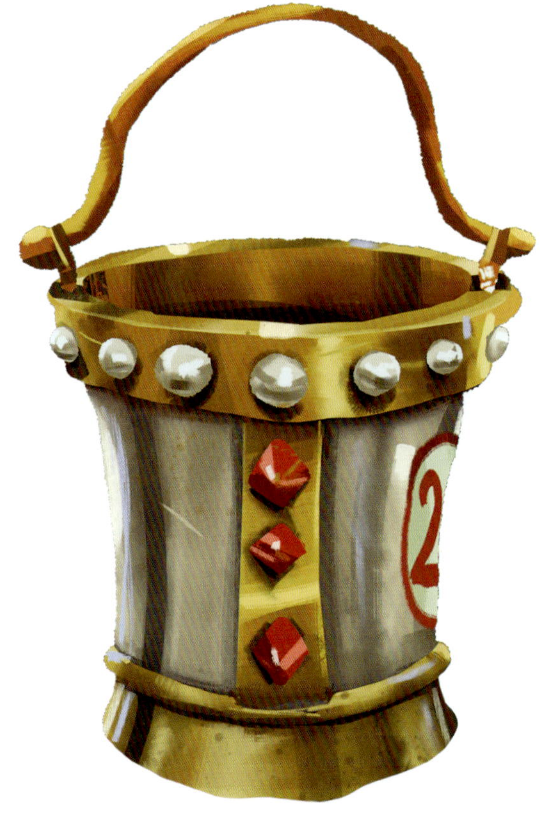

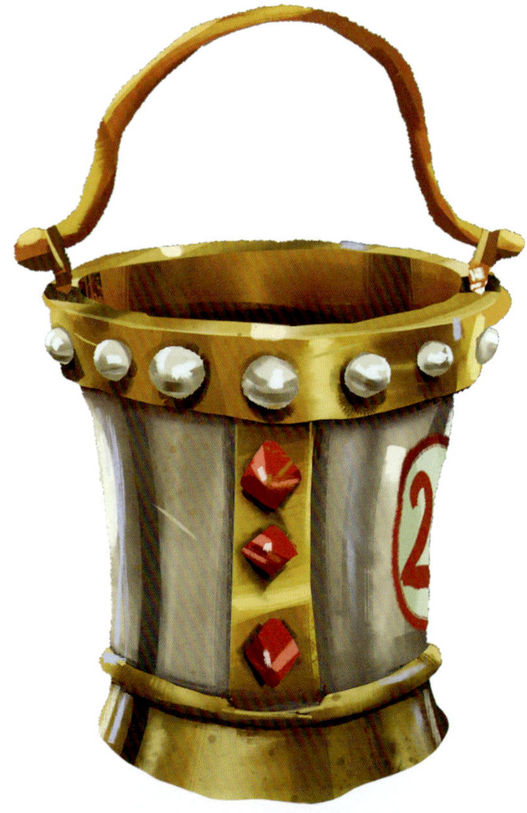

Prop design of the flashy dinnerware [left] and lavish food [right] available in the Lost City of Atlantic City

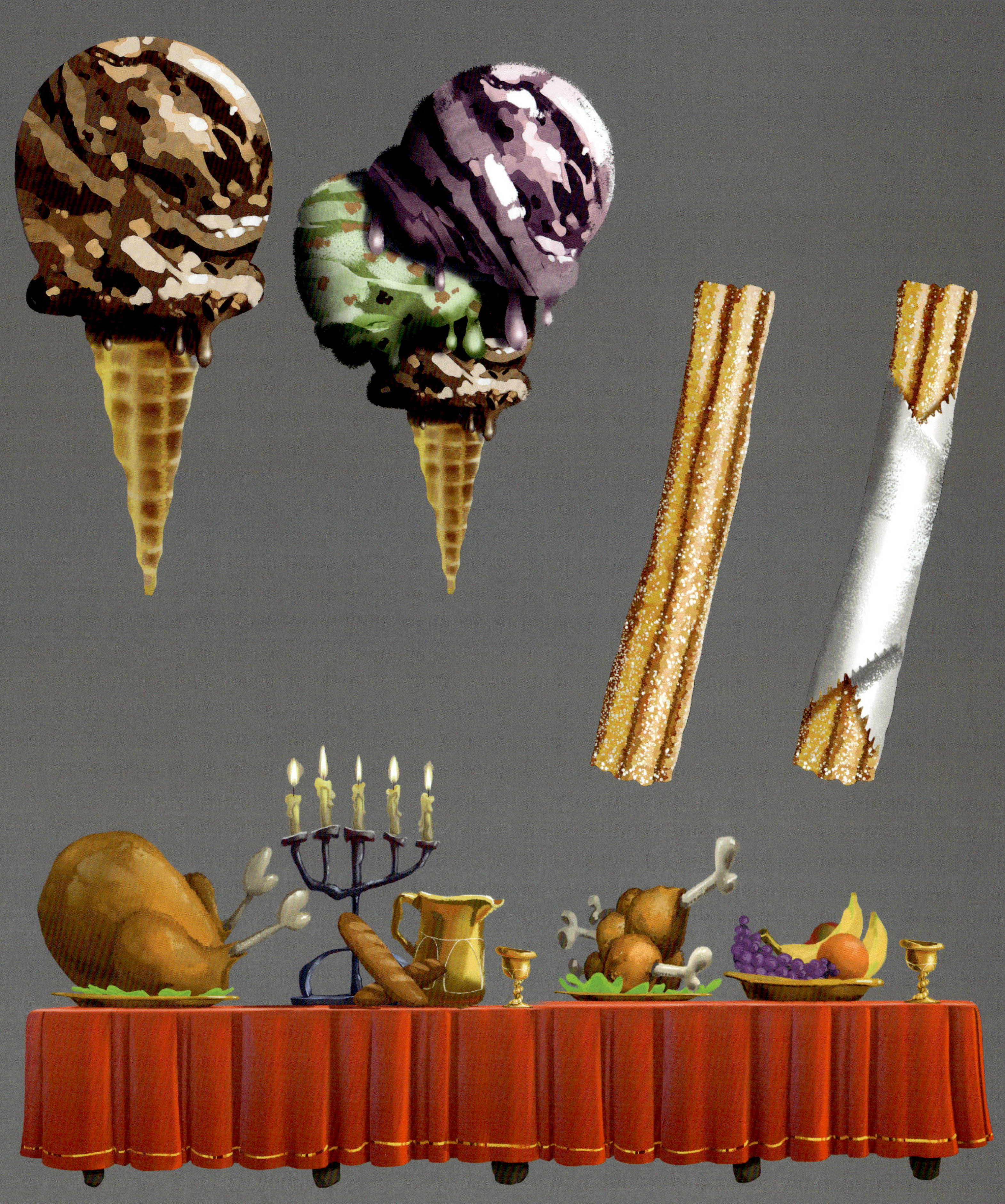

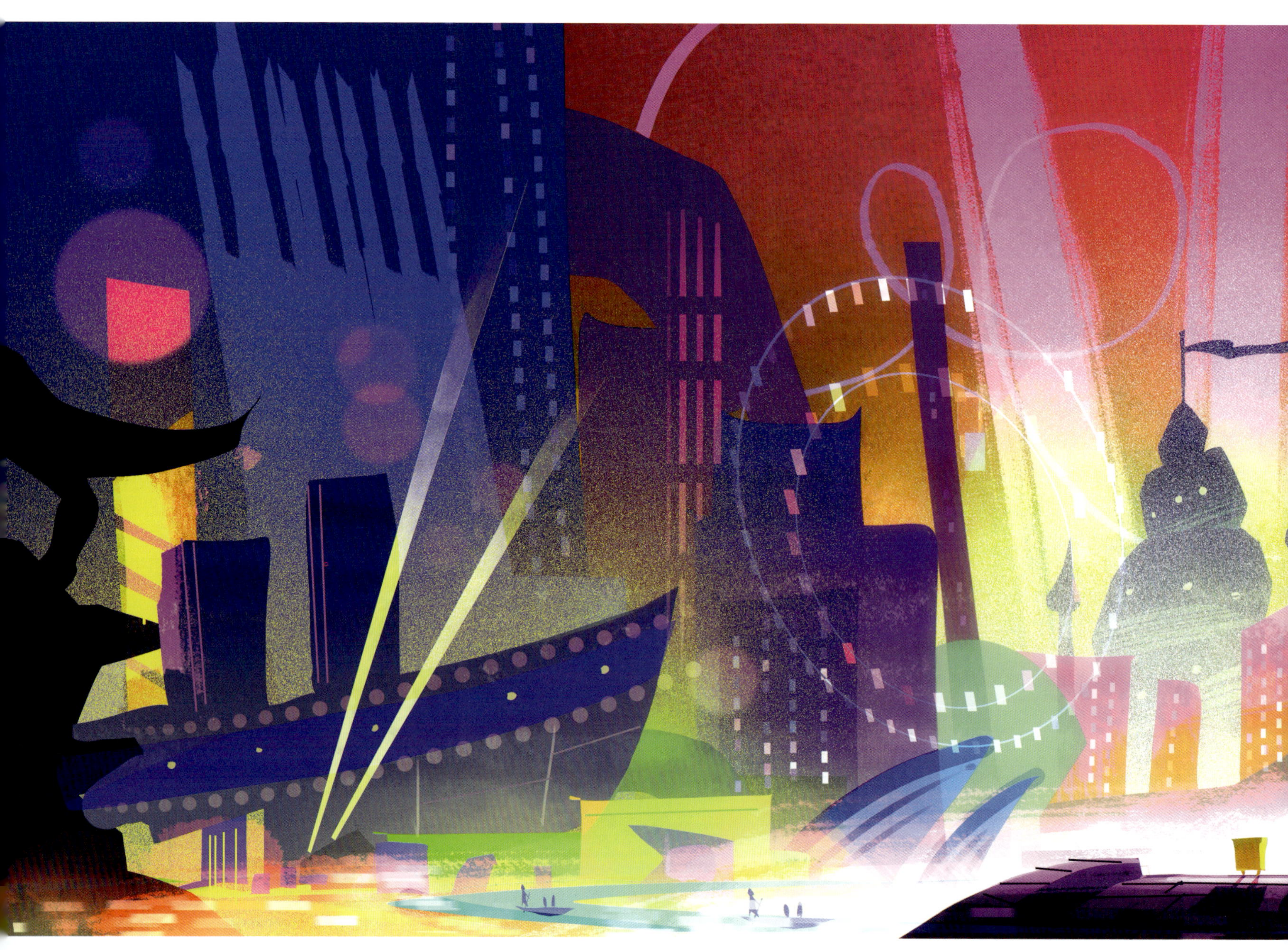

Look of picture concept of the
Lost City of Atlantic City

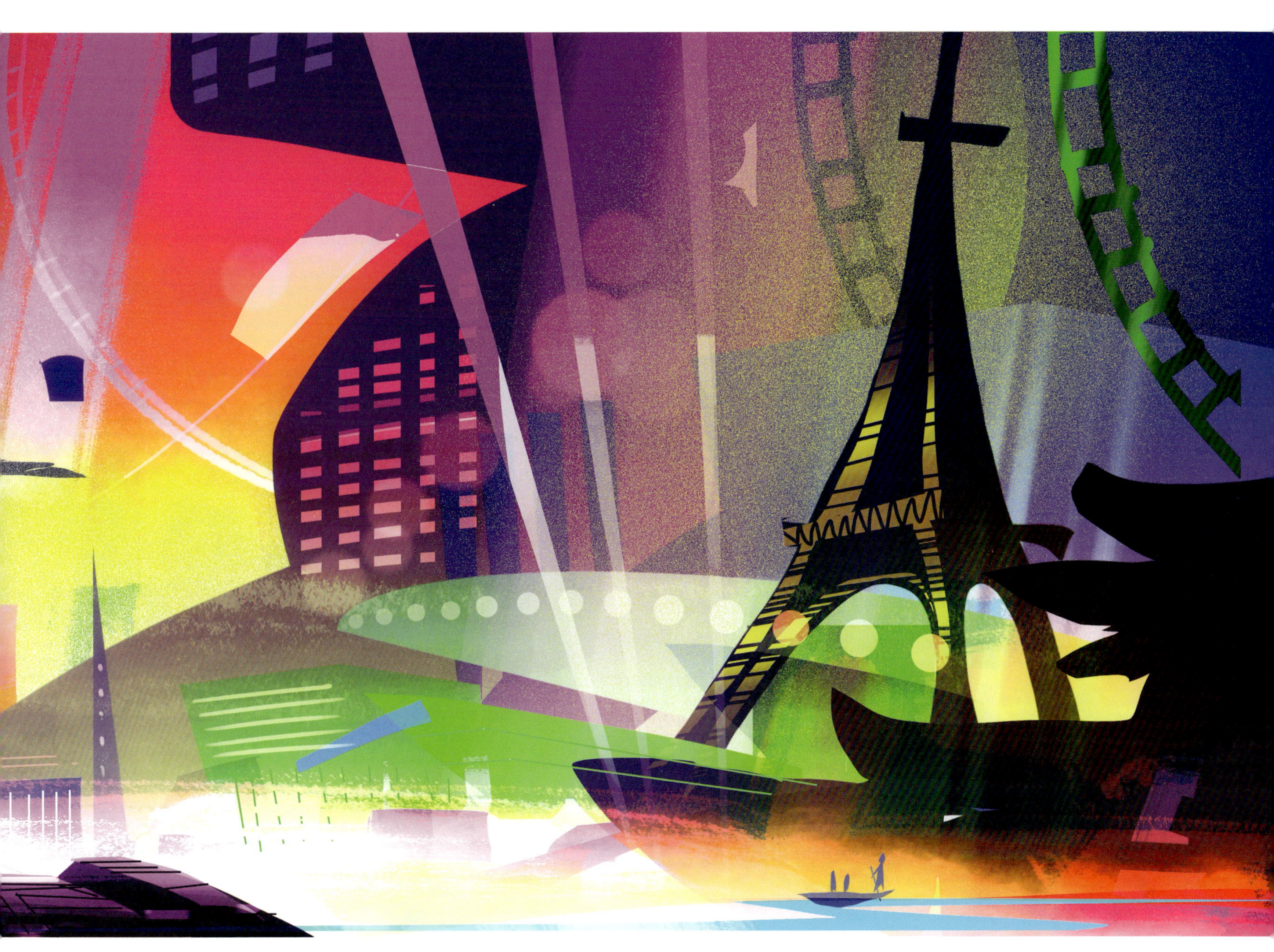

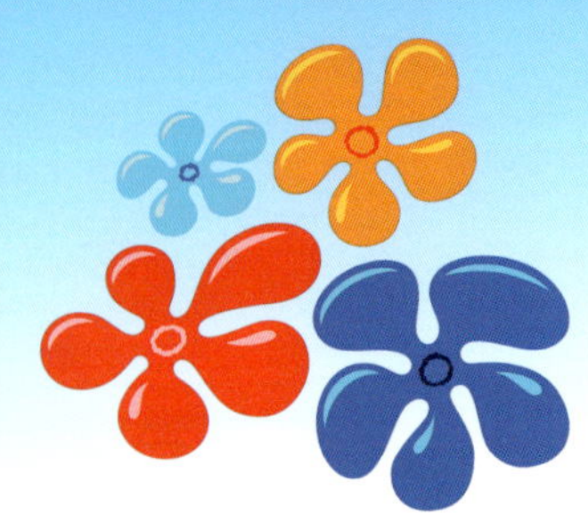

GAMBLING

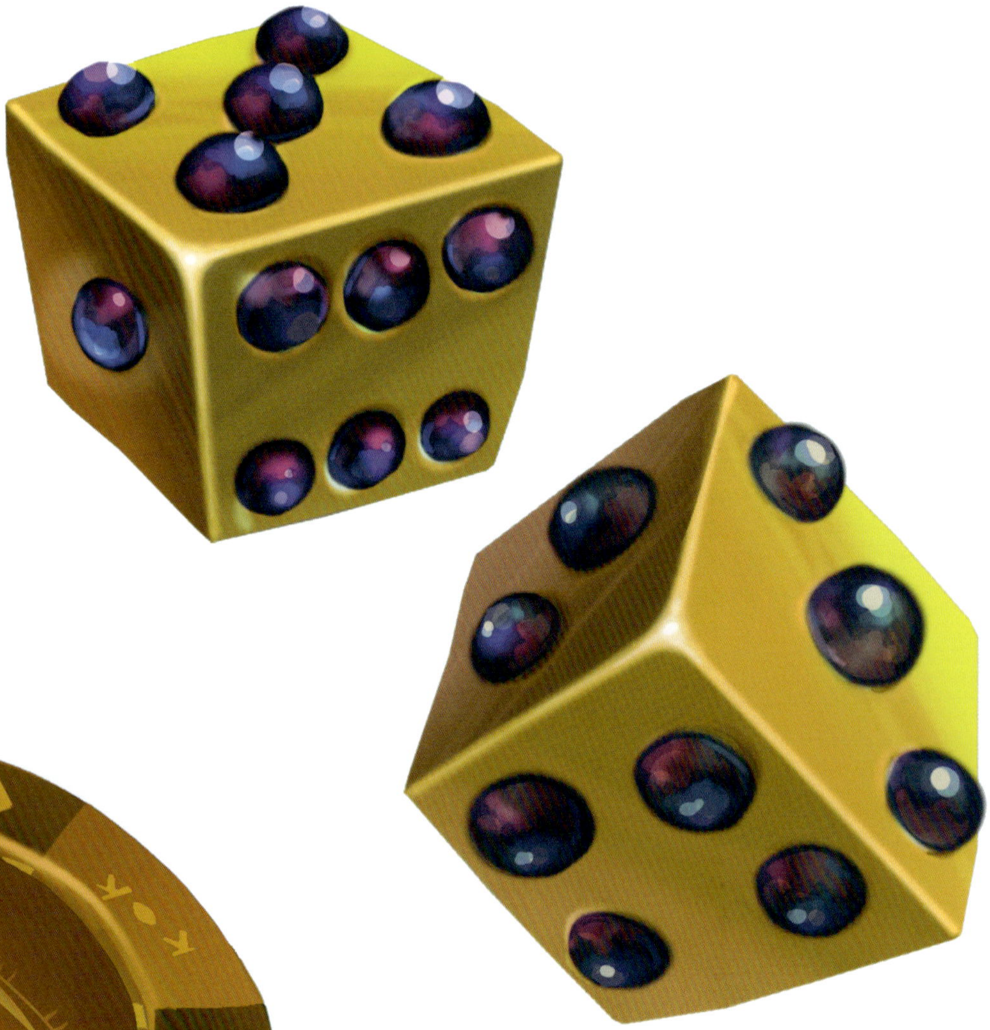

Prop design of accessories from the casino scene in the Lost City of Atlantic City

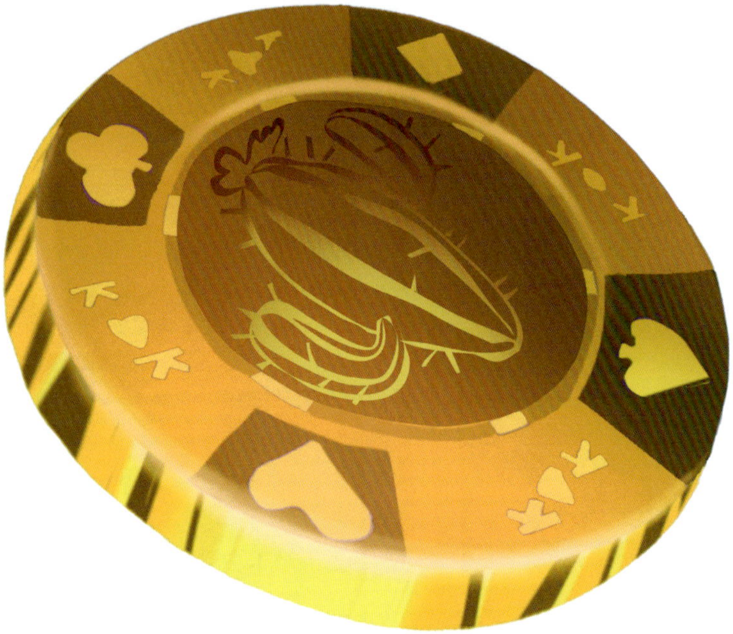

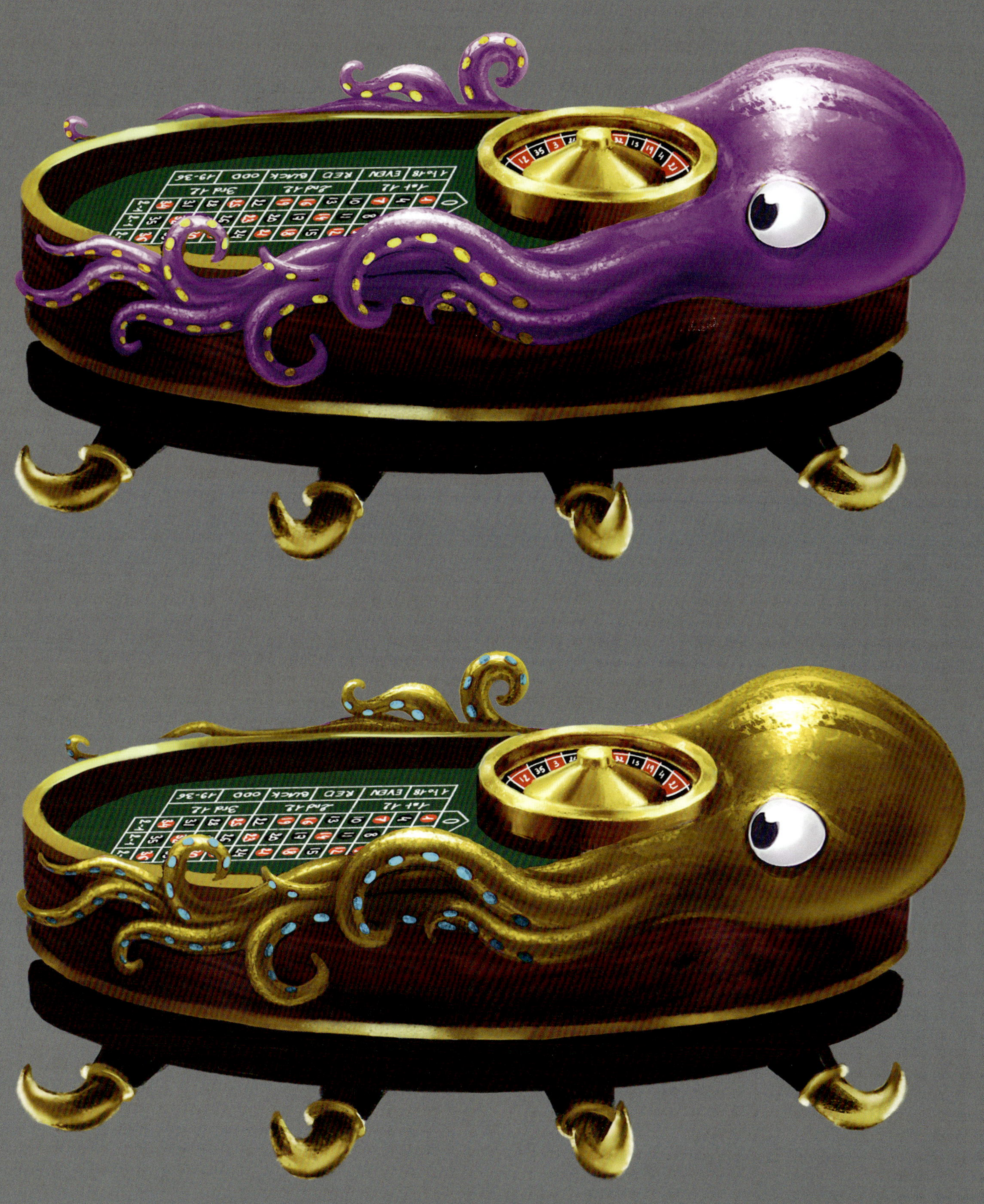

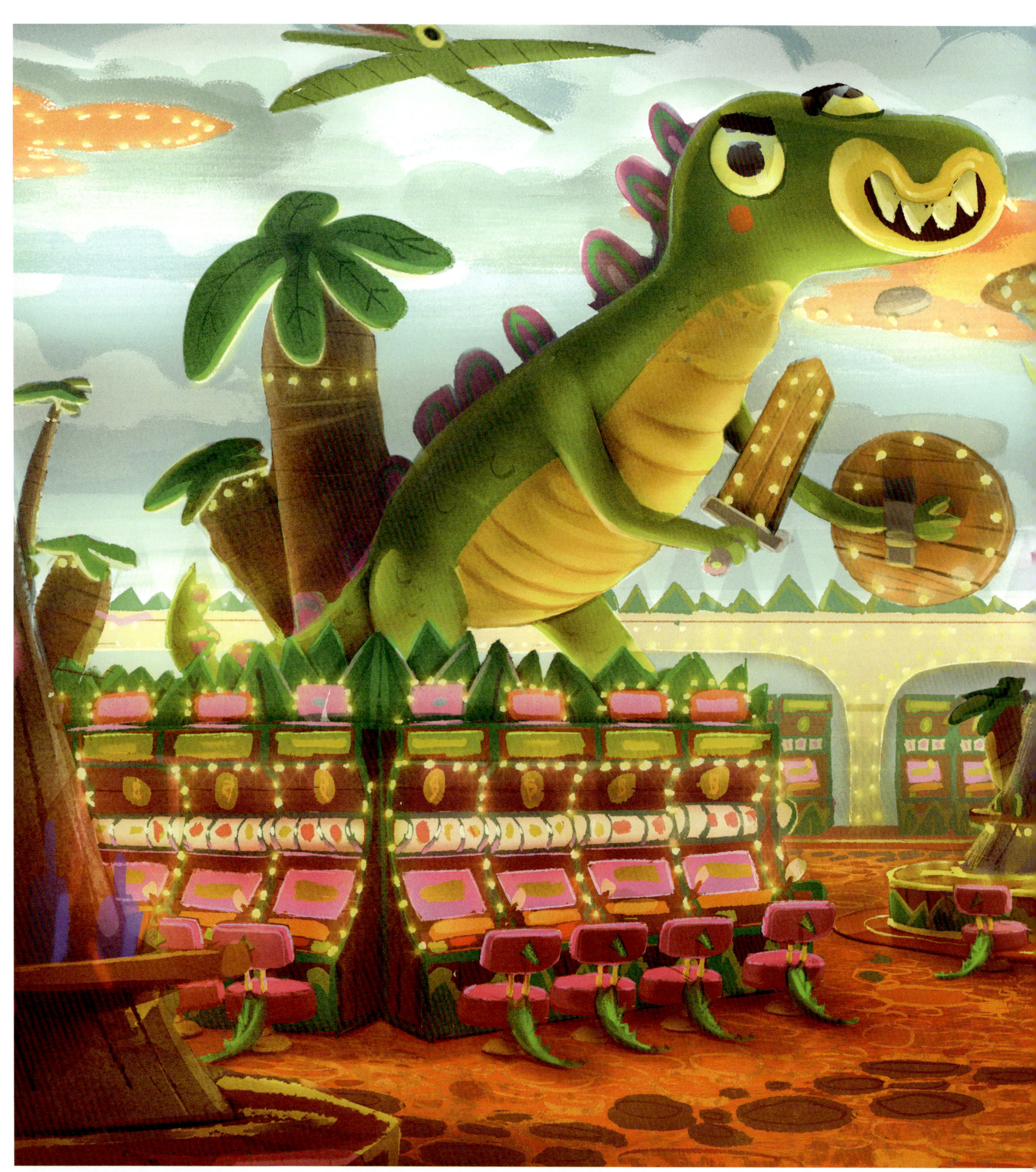

Look of picture concept of the casino
scene in the Lost City of Atlantic City

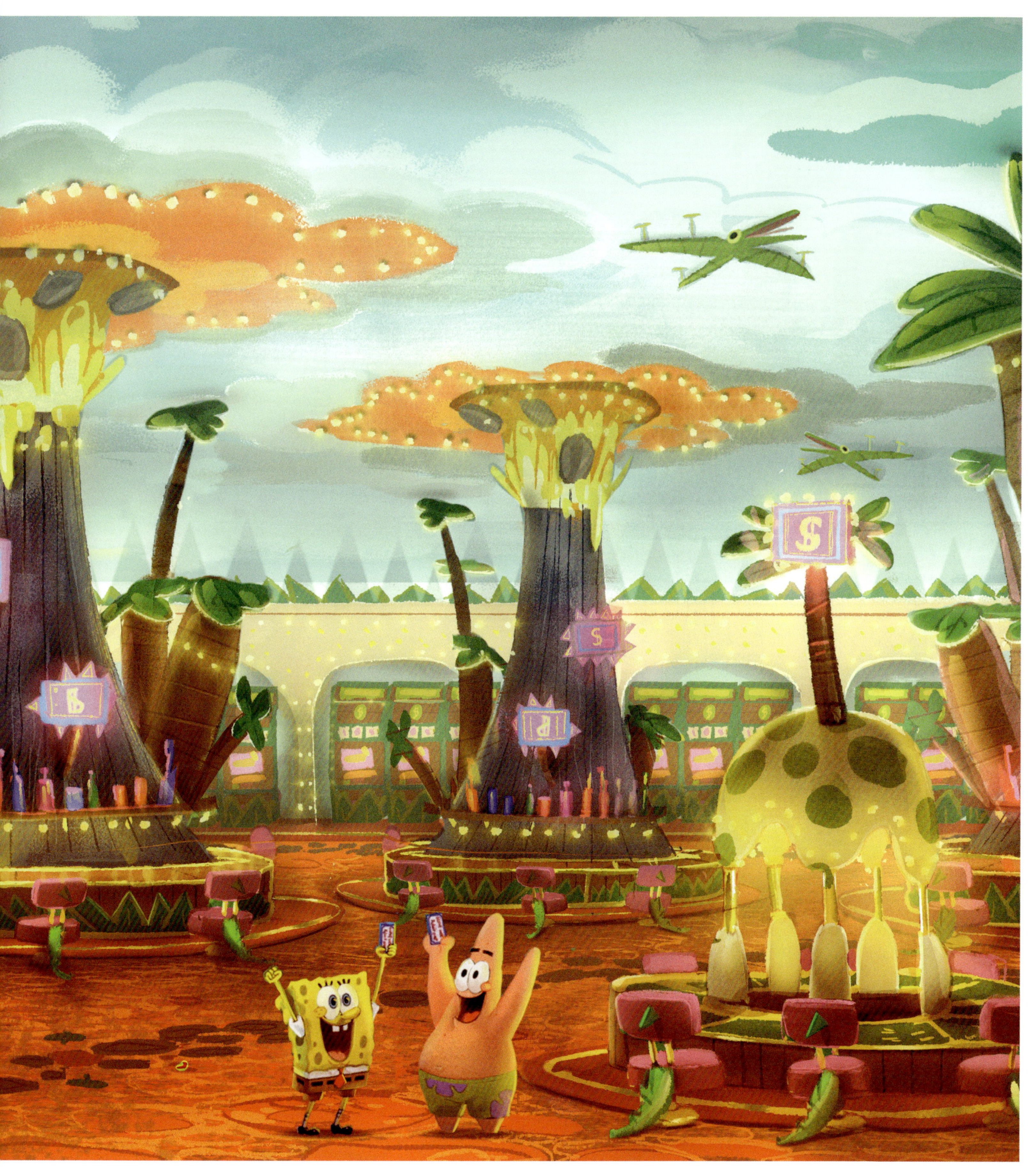

KELPY G

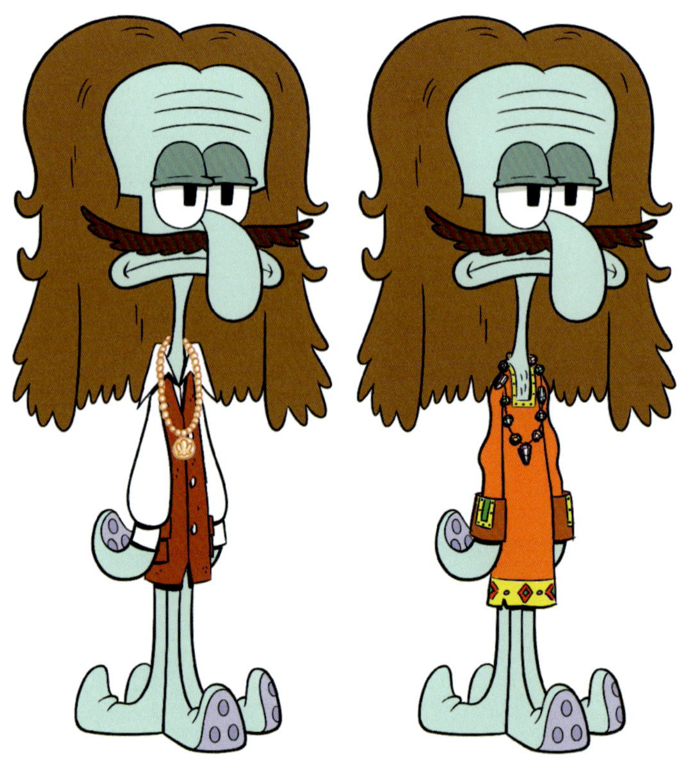

Character design variations [line art] and final CG art of Kelpy G [center], an homage to Kenny G and, not surprisingly, one of Squidward's favorites; plus prop design of musical instruments

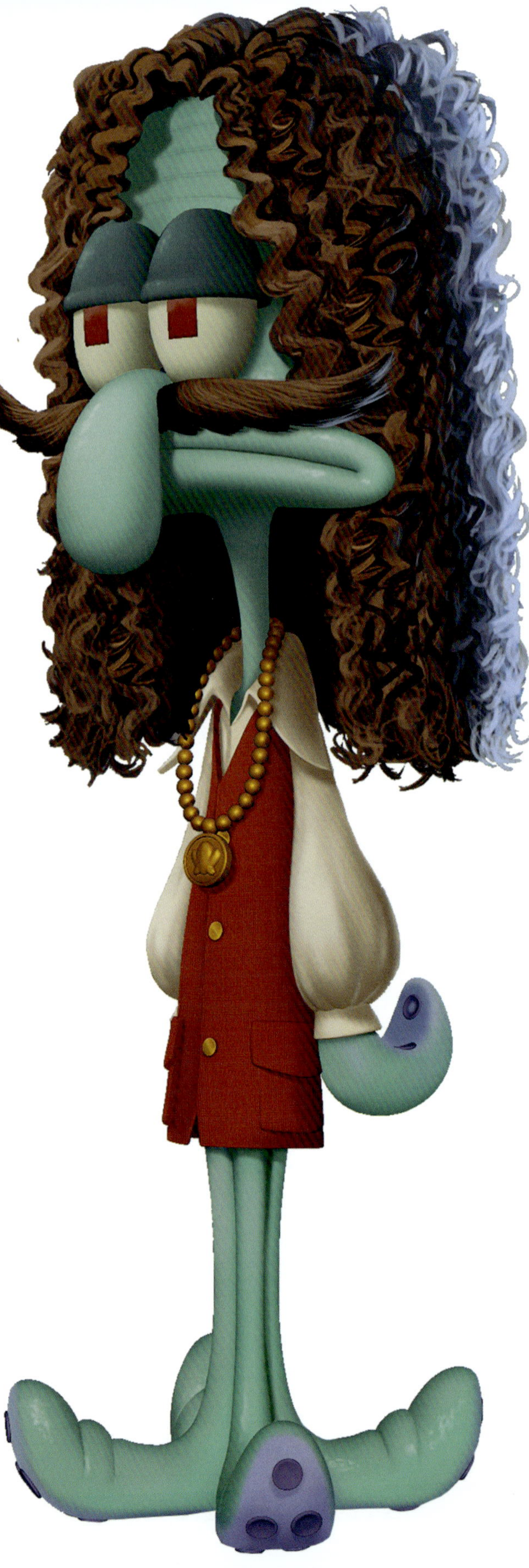

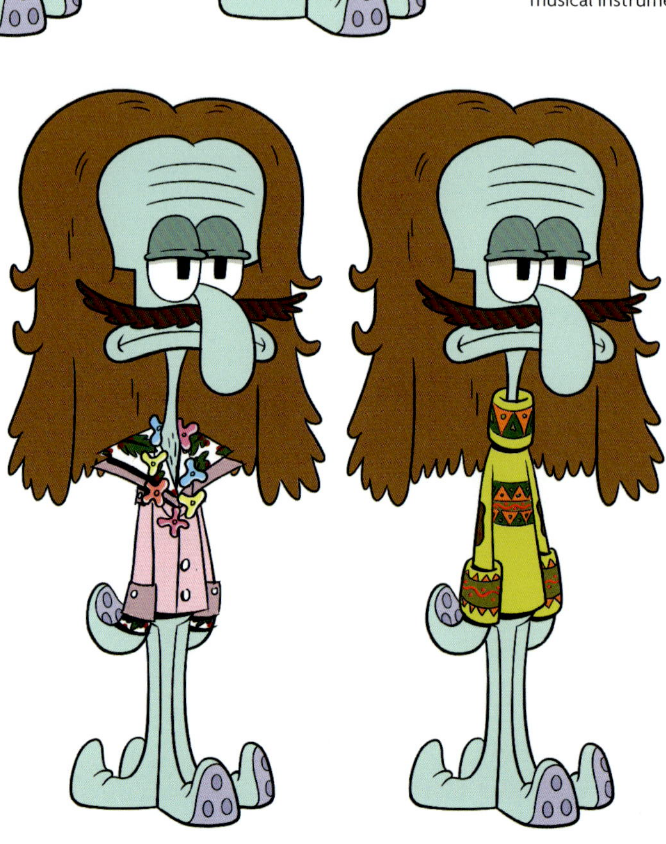

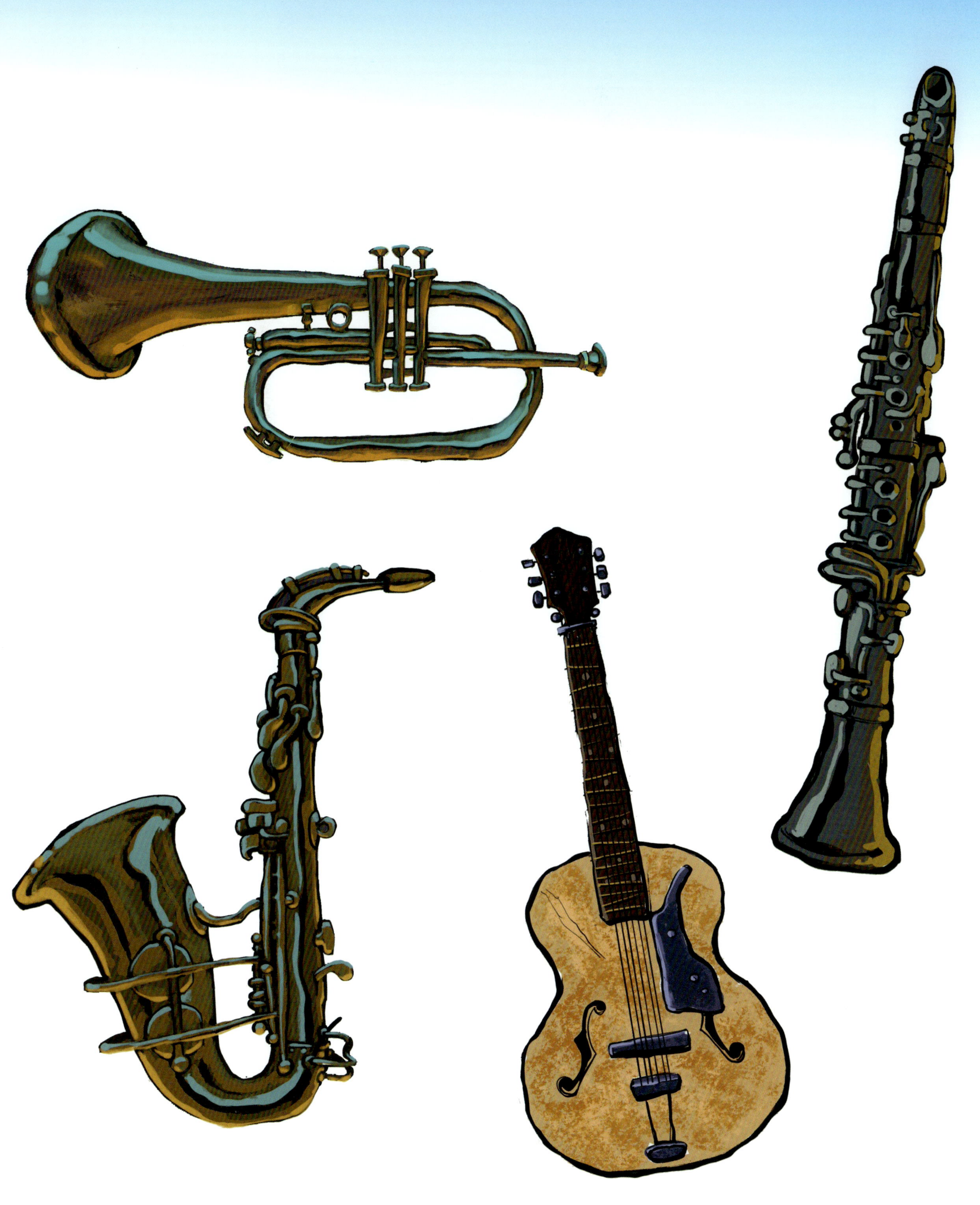

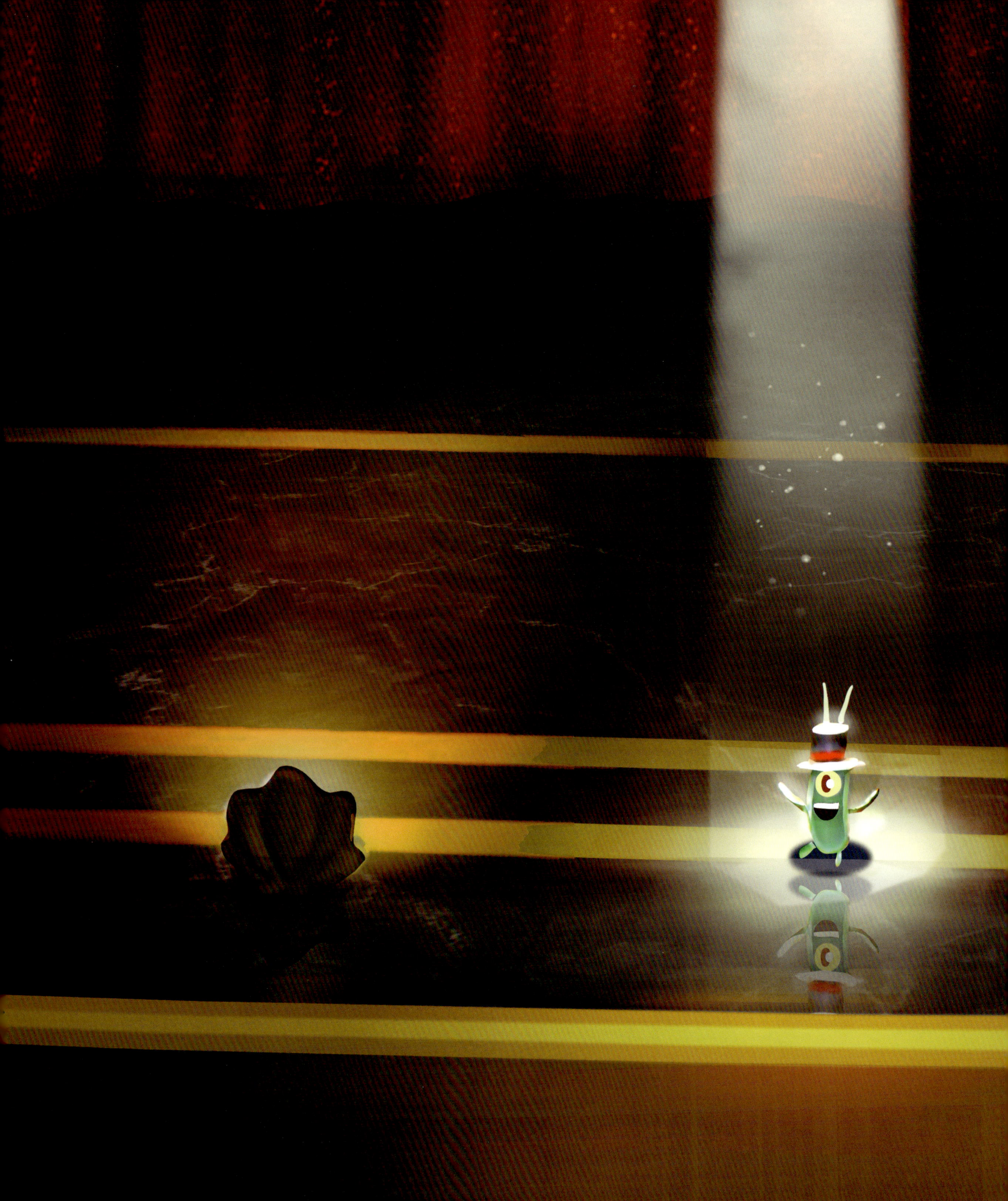

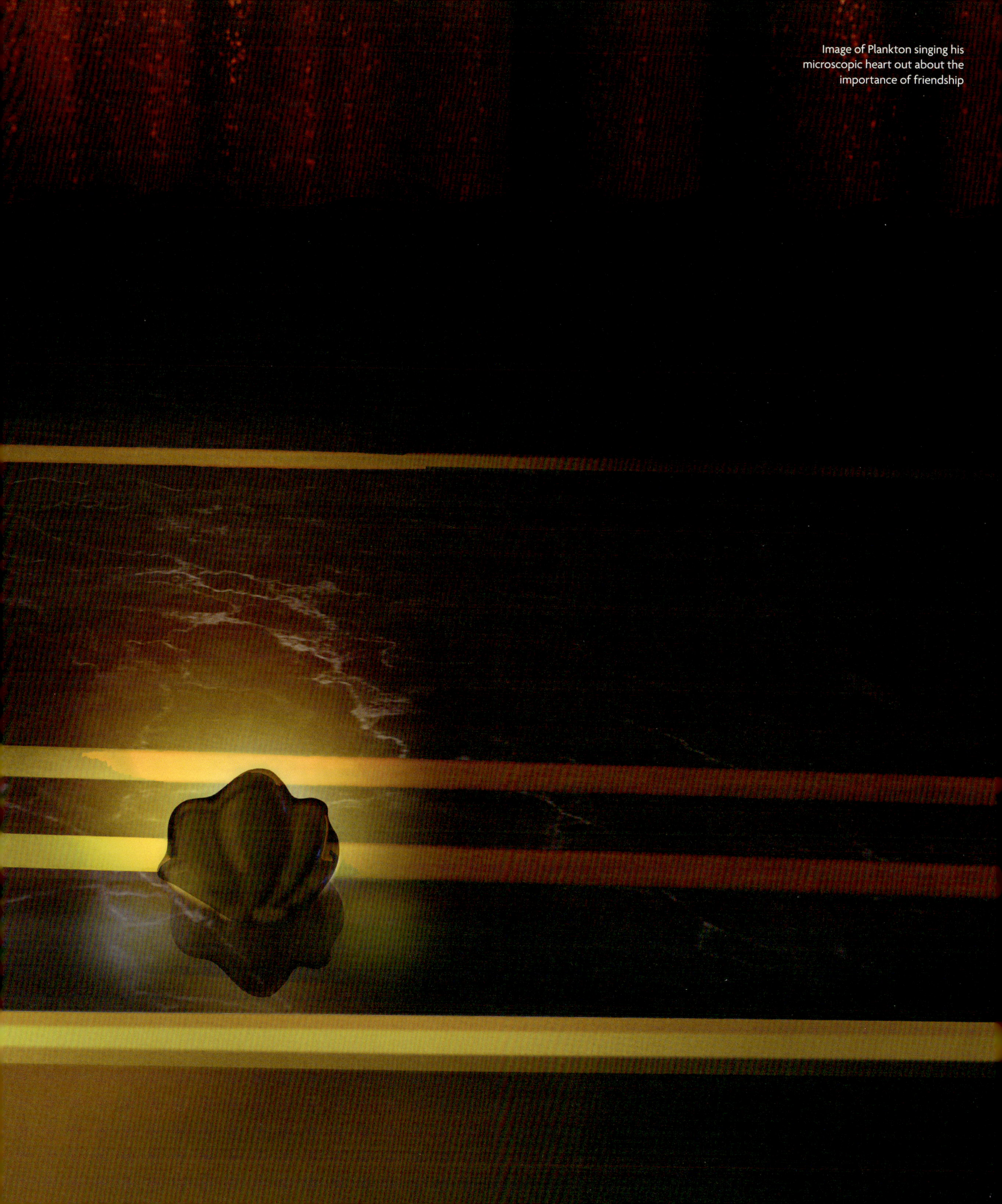

Image of Plankton singing his microscopic heart out about the importance of friendship

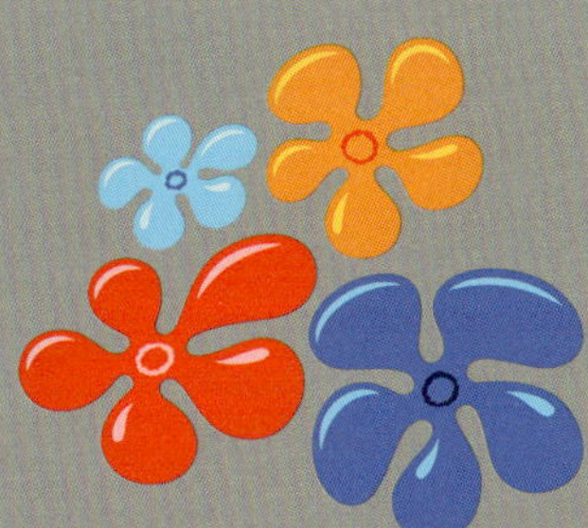

COURAGEOUS CONCLUSION

After fountainous tear-soaked realizations, all is resolved and life is even better for snail-kind.

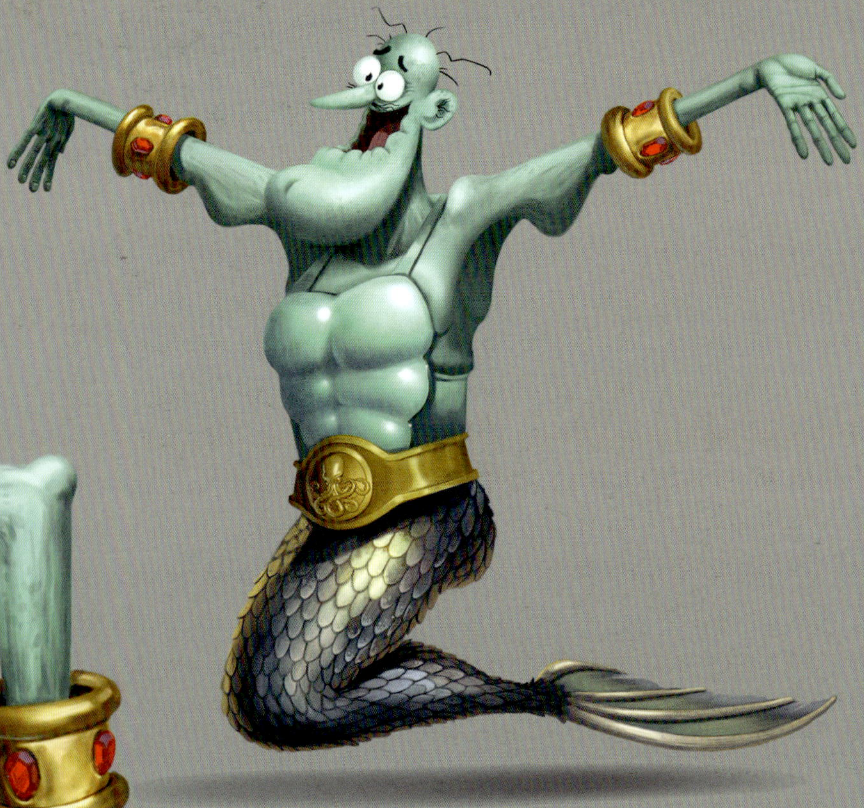

Character treatment of the true Poseidon

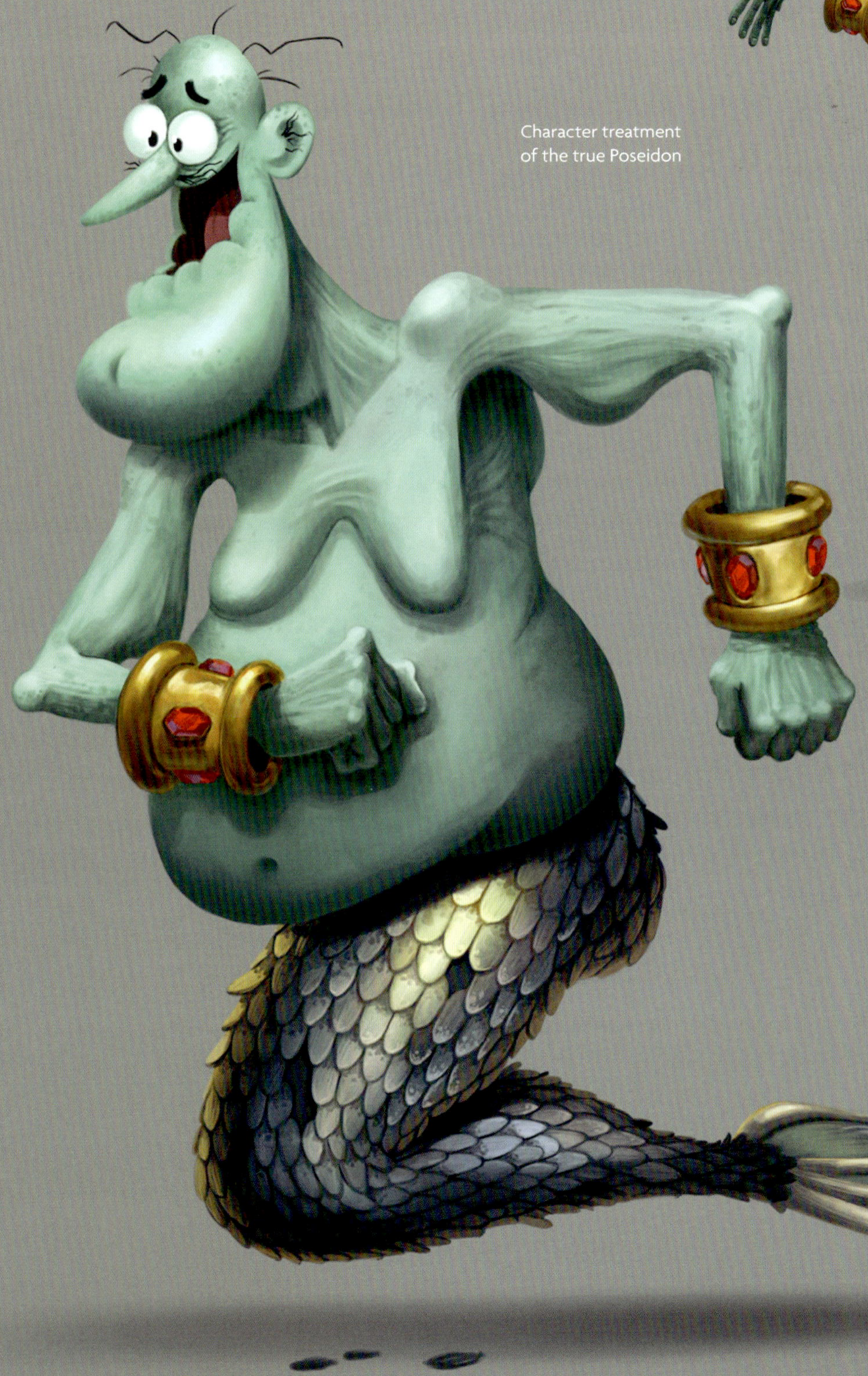

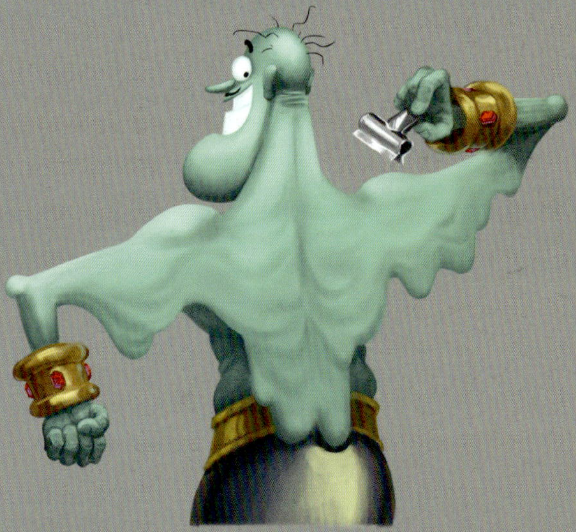

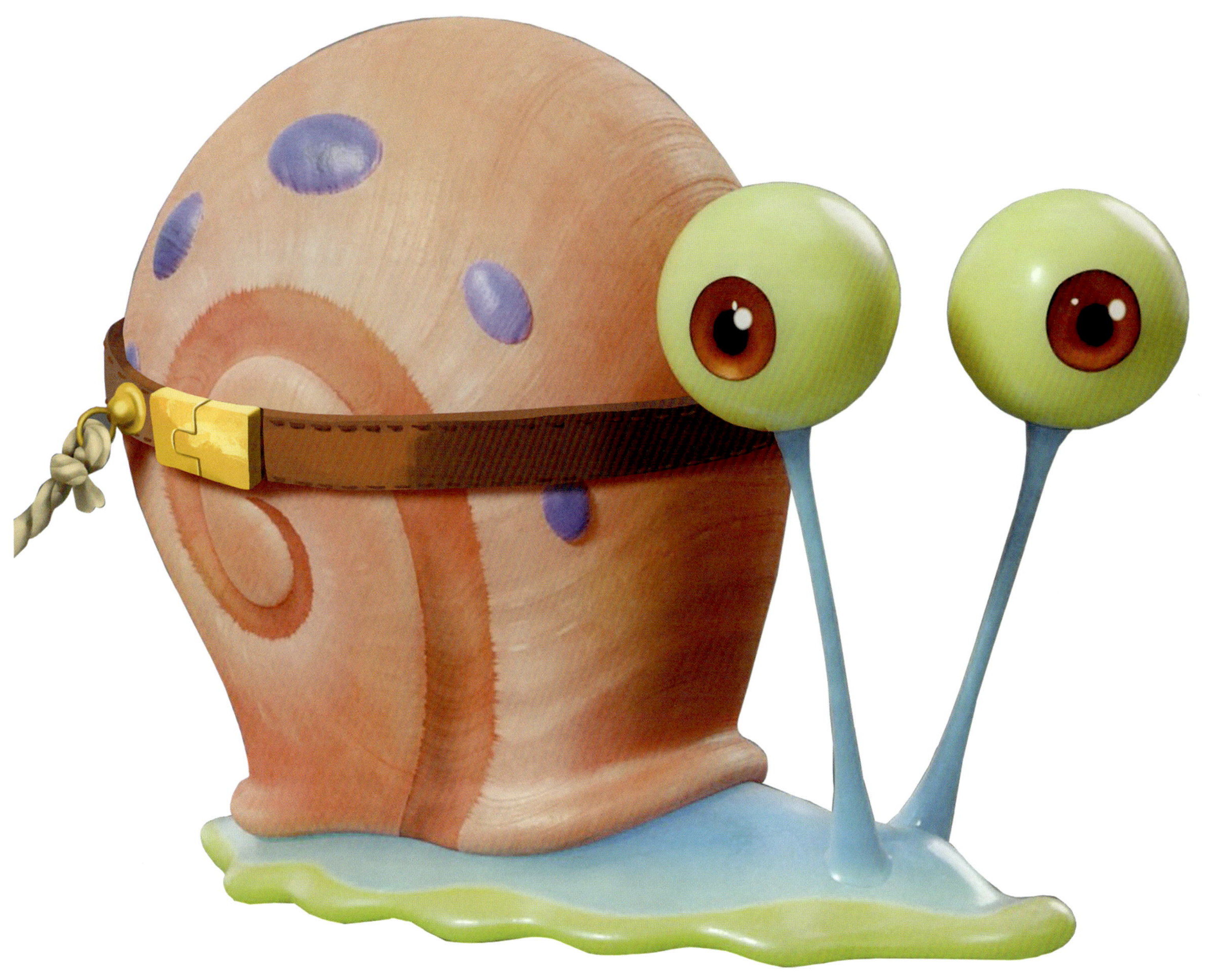

Final CG art of
Gary when in royal
possession

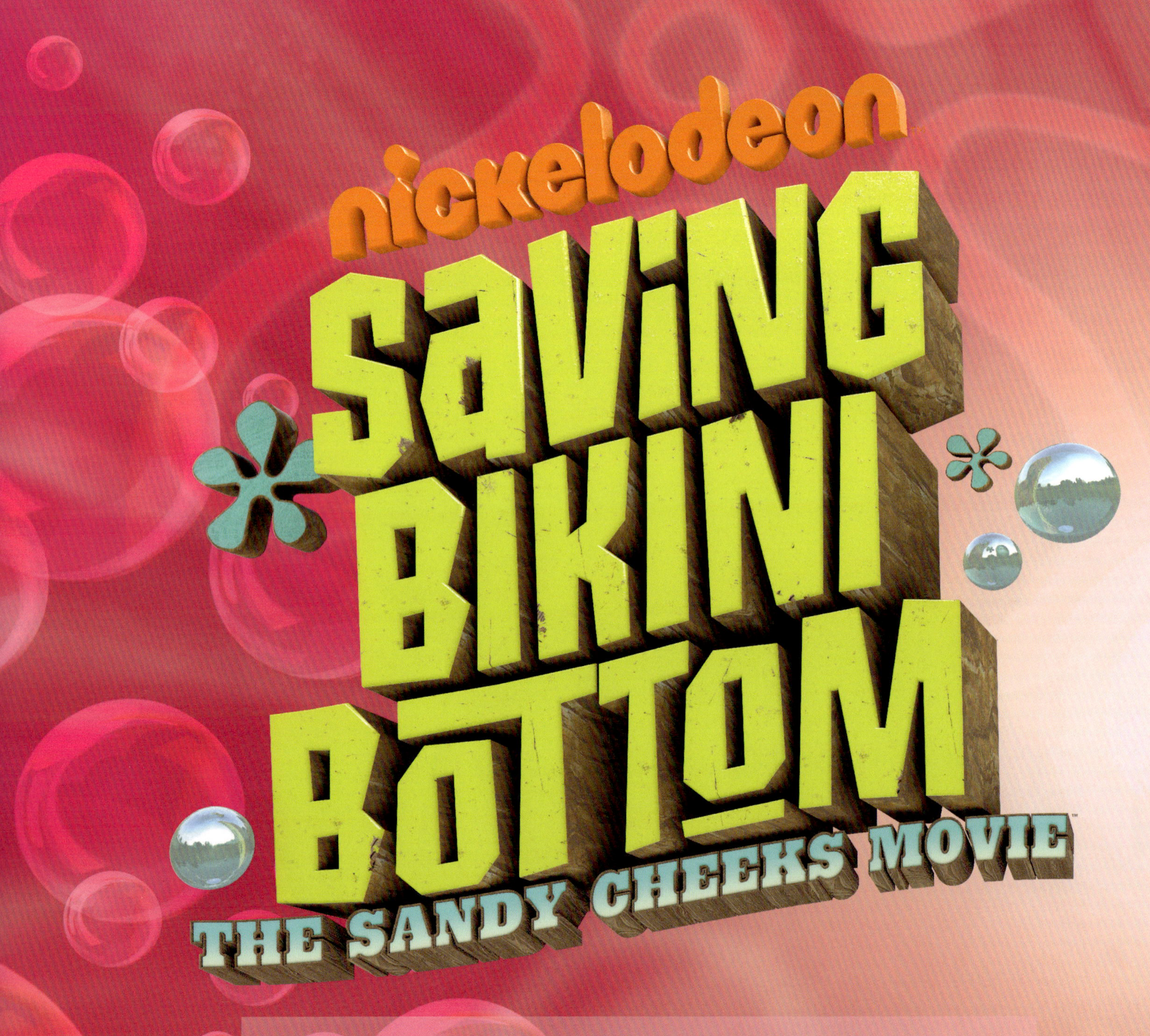

When Bikini Bottom is scooped out of the ocean and transported to a Texas laboratory, it's Sandy and SpongeBob to the rescue, with a little help from Mother Nature and the Cheeks family. *Saving Bikini Bottom: The Sandy Cheeks Movie*, a feature-length hybrid animation/live-action film, was released on Netflix on August 2, 2024.

Sandy Cheeks has long expressed her love of science, but in this film, she's a marine biologist... a wonderful detail in homage to her creator, Stephen Hillenburg, who unfortunately passed away before this film went into development. Carolyn Lawrence, the voice of Sandy Cheeks, says, "I'm glad that after twenty-five years, Sandy's getting her moment. She's been such a phenomenal character for girls and women, because she is an atypical animated character. She's highly capable. She is athletic. She is ridiculously smart. She's a lot of things that female animated characters traditionally haven't necessarily been able to be."

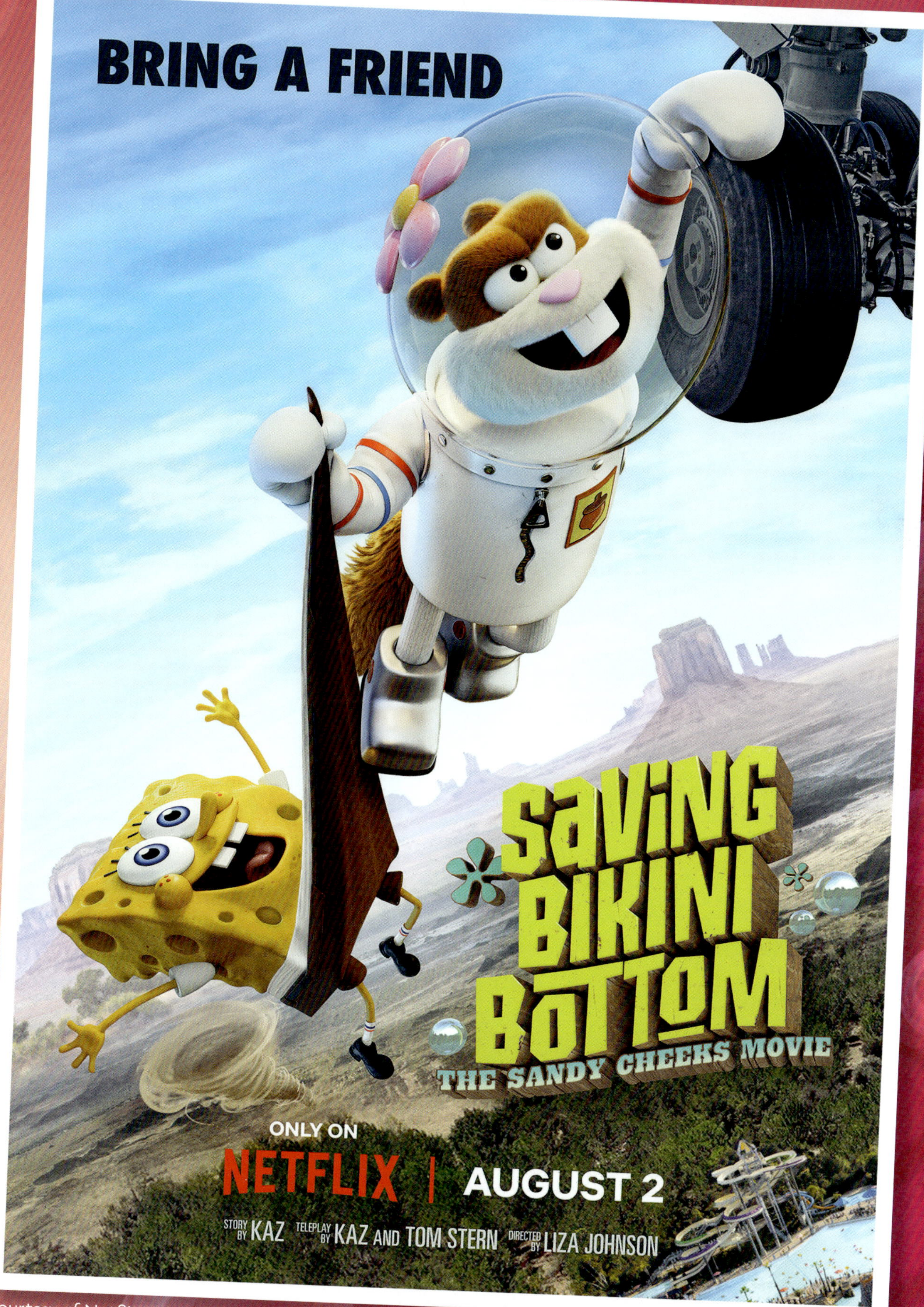

Courtesy of Netflix

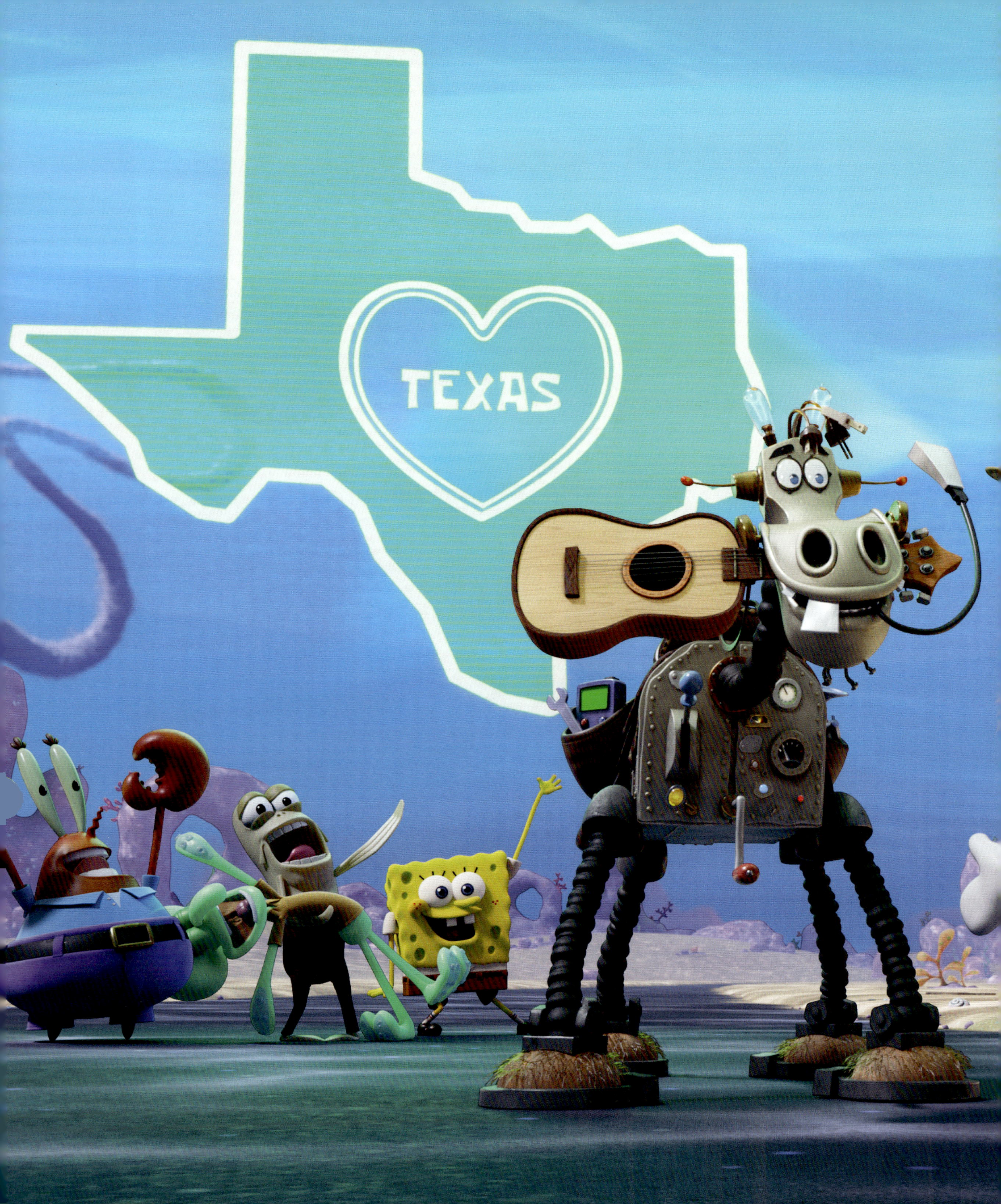
TEXAS

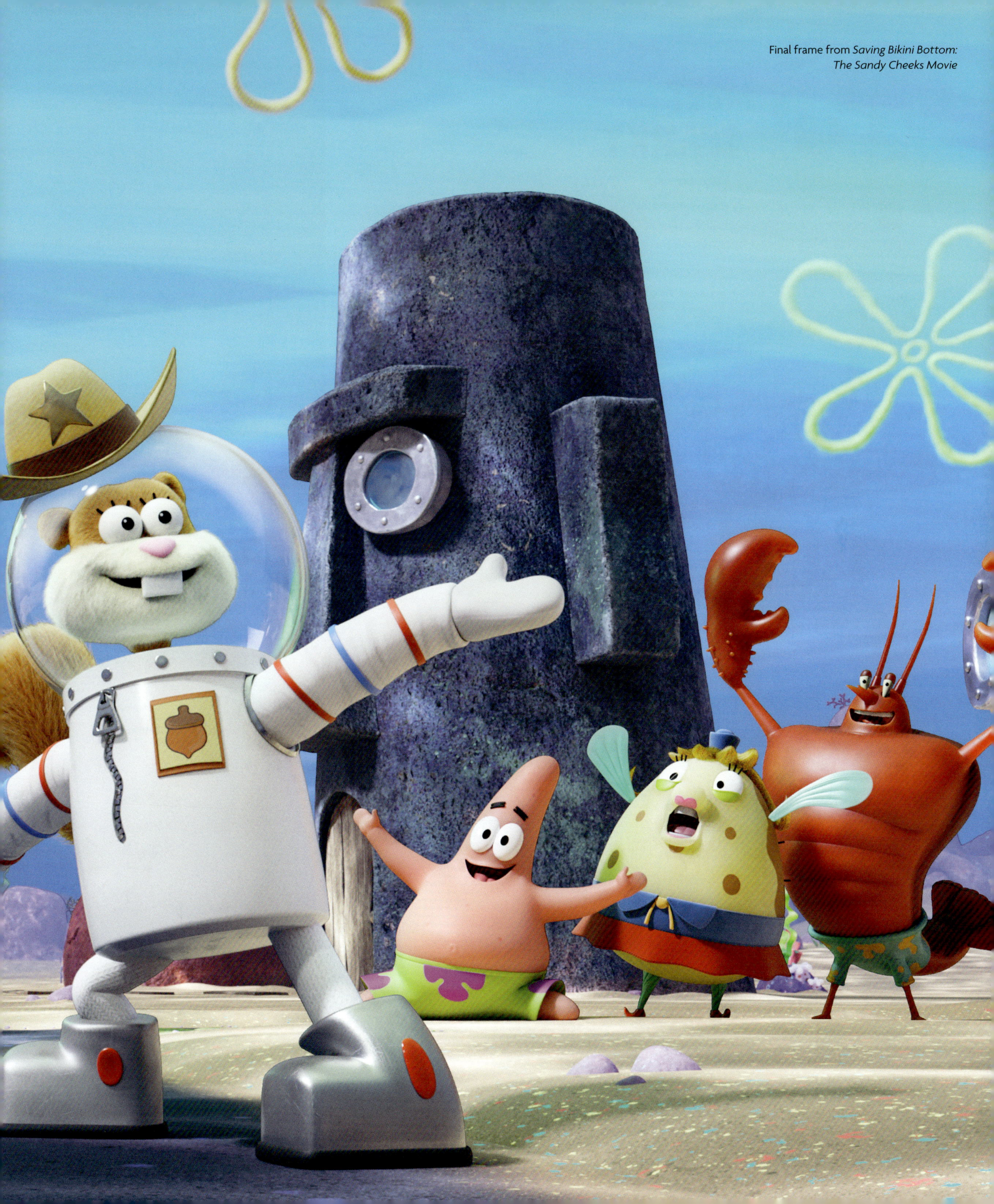

Final frame from *Saving Bikini Bottom: The Sandy Cheeks Movie*

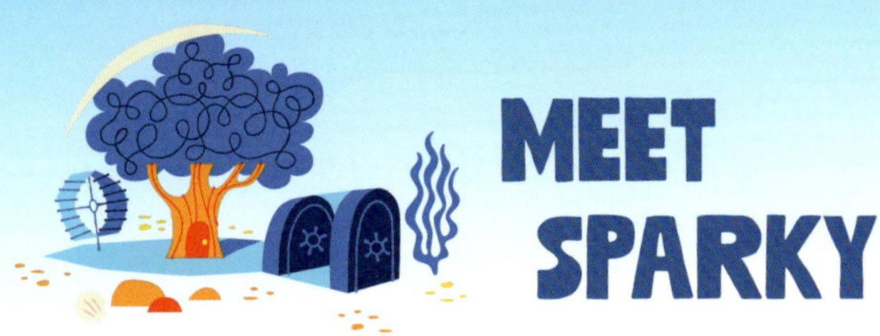

MEET SPARKY

Sparky is one of Sandy's inventions, a robotic horse that seems like a perfect partner for a Texas-born scientist.

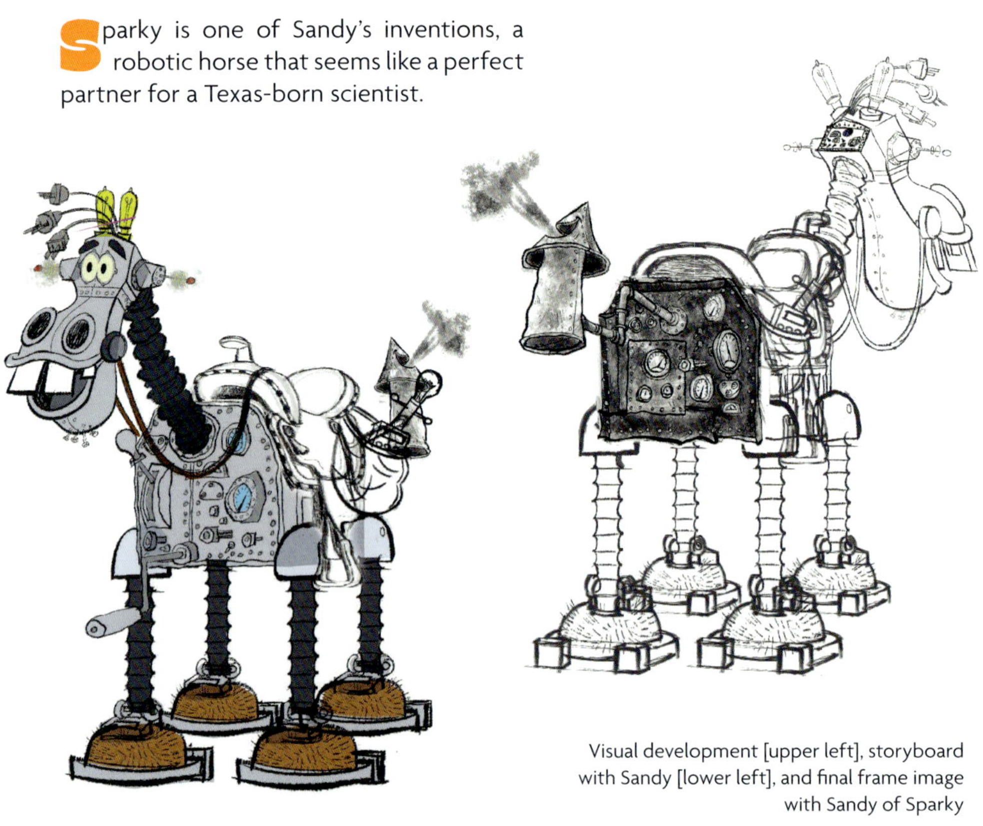

Visual development [upper left], storyboard with Sandy [lower left], and final frame image with Sandy of Sparky

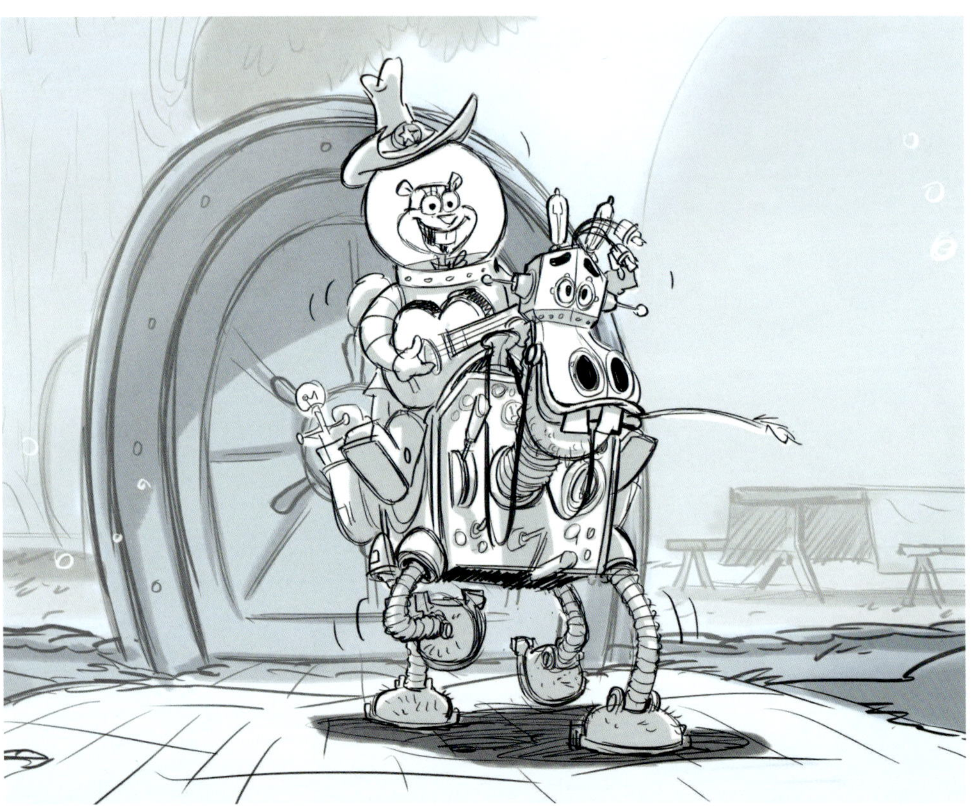

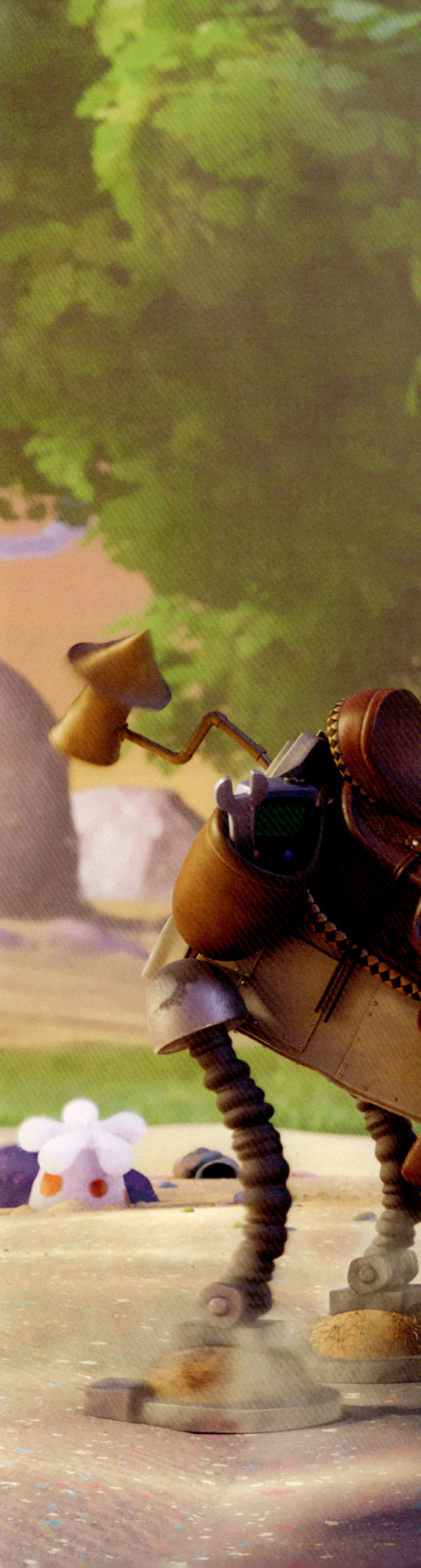

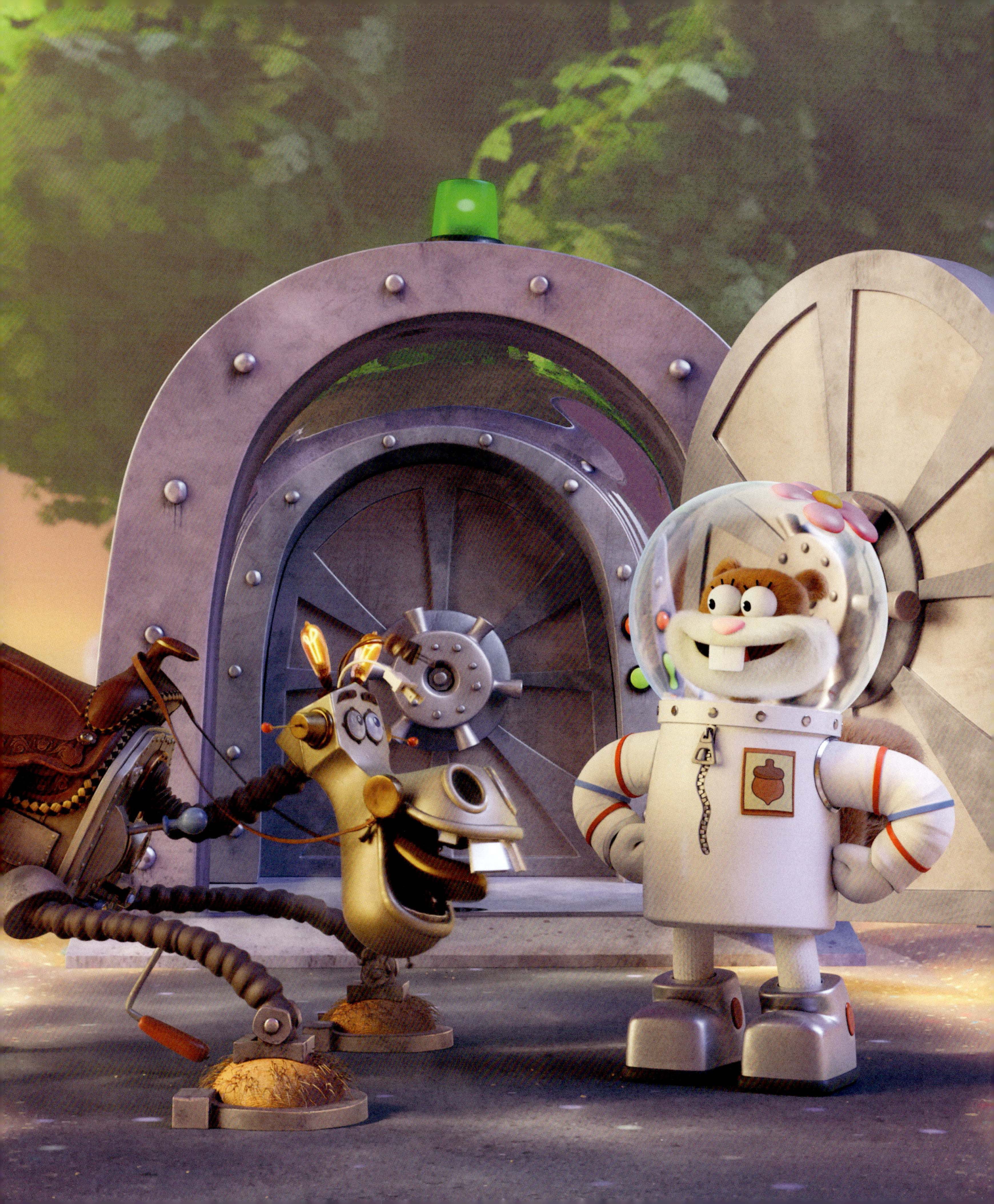

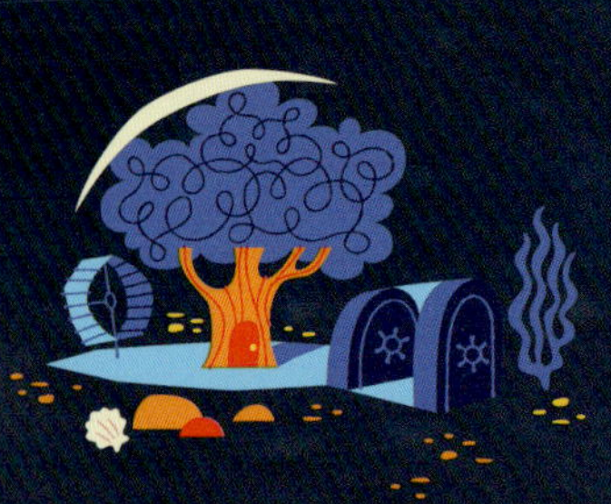

BACK TO TEXAS

The journey to rescue Bikini Bottom takes Sandy back to her old stomping grounds of Texas; the movie's production crew also went to Texas to shoot these scenes in live action. "For the live-action scenes, we shot in Santa Fe [New Mexico] in a desert that's intended to resemble Texas. When we were scouting for the movie, we found fossils of sea life in the desert in Santa Fe. I have an ammonite of a nautilus shell that came from the desert, because whatever millions of years ago, it was on the ocean floor. It was amazing to take that community from the ocean floor and put them on the old ocean floor, and then find old shells from the previous ocean floor, which it was once," says director Liza Johnson.

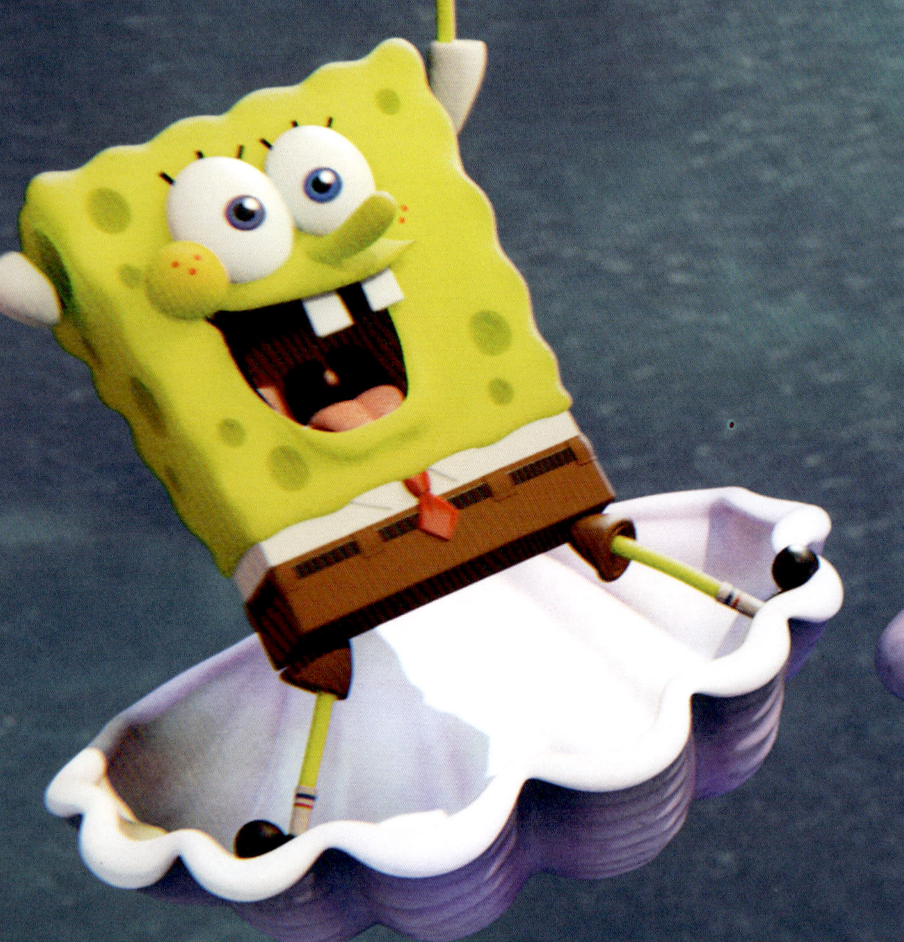

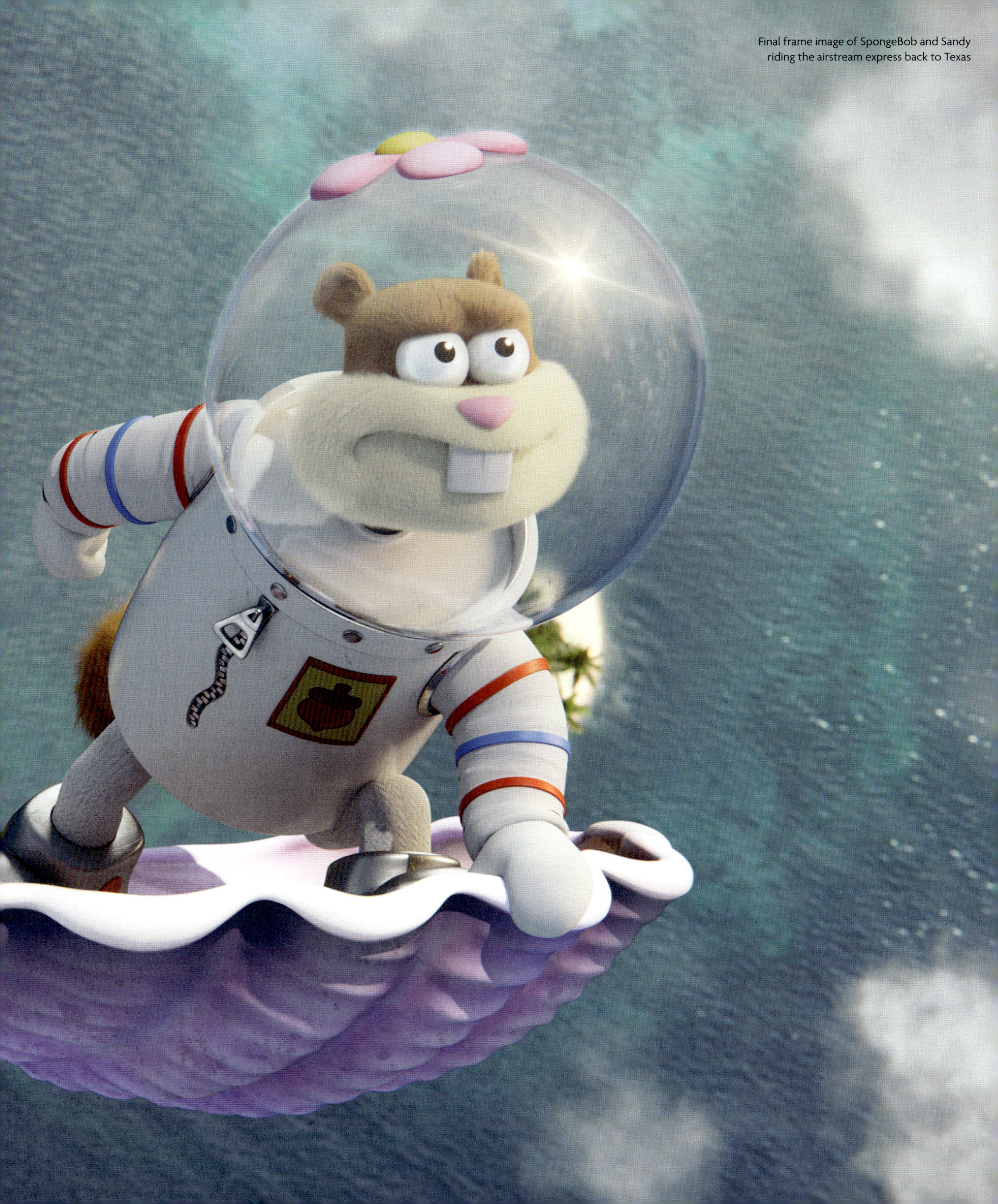

Final frame image of SpongeBob and Sandy riding the airstream express back to Texas

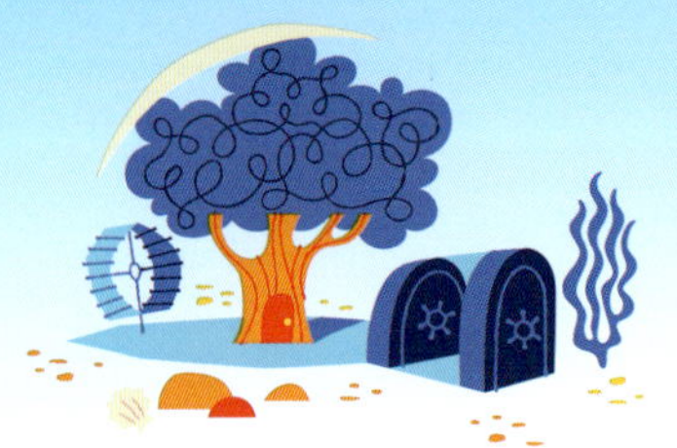

SANDY CHEEKS CAN FLY!

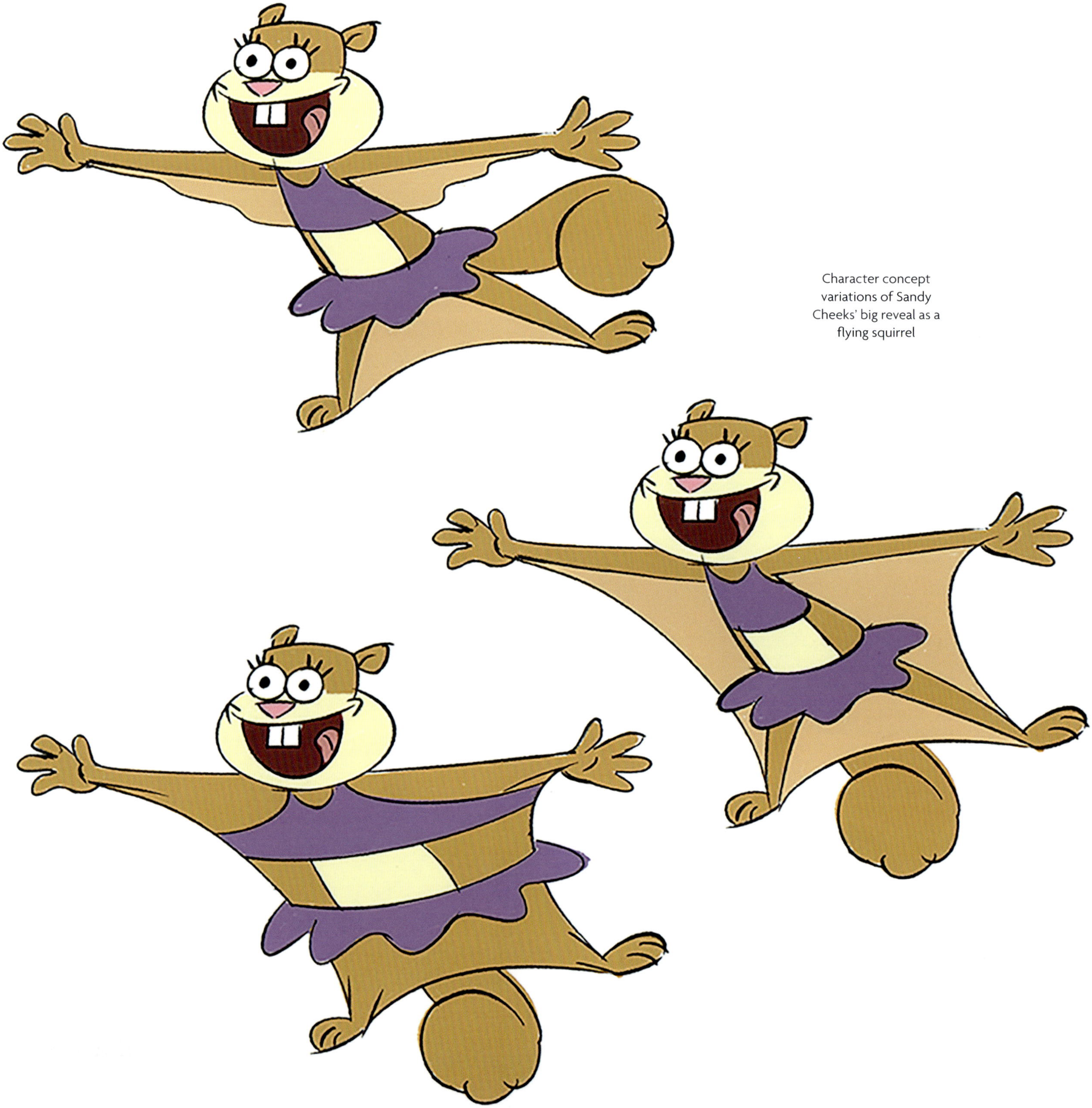

Character concept variations of Sandy Cheeks' big reveal as a flying squirrel

SNAKES

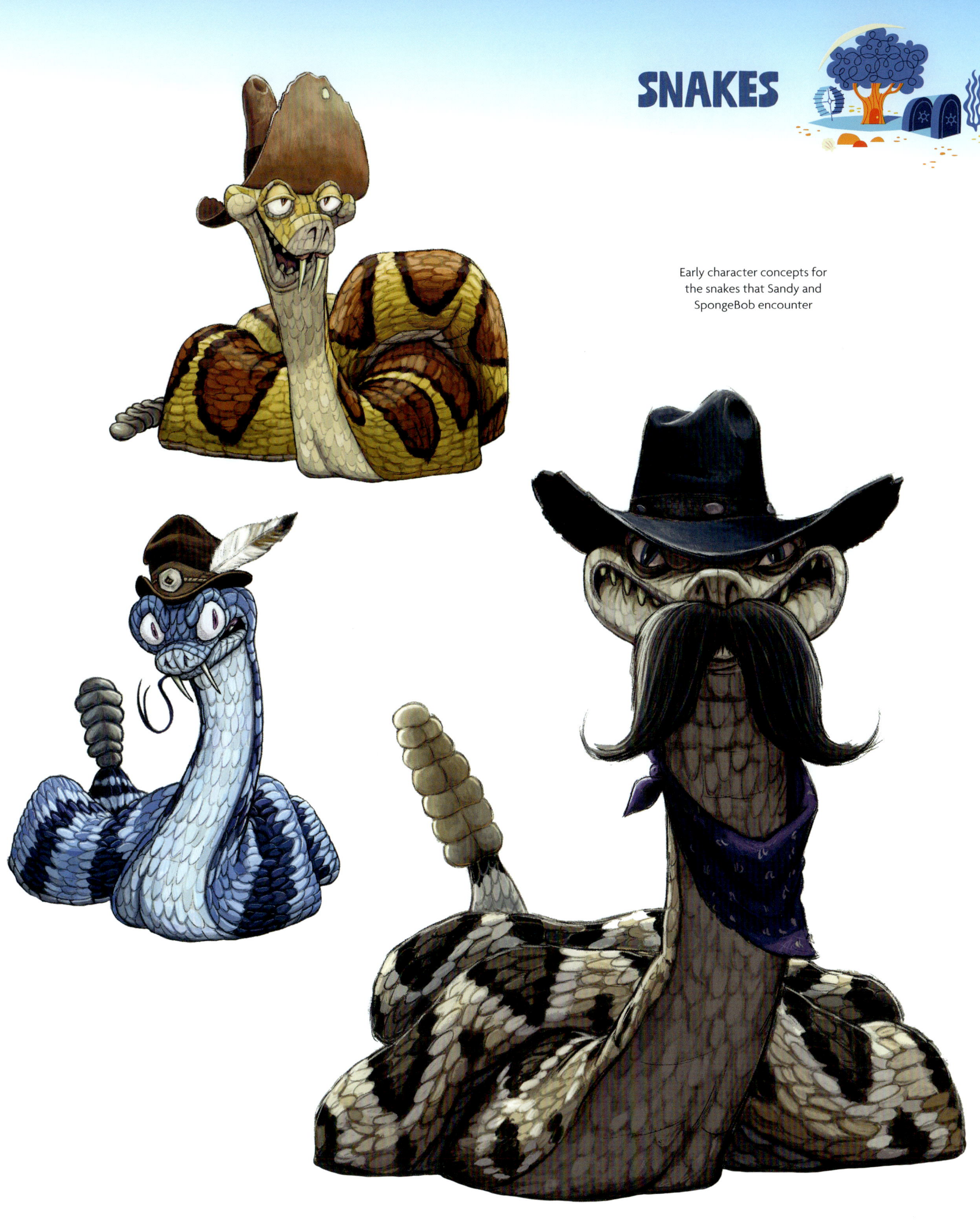

Early character concepts for the snakes that Sandy and SpongeBob encounter

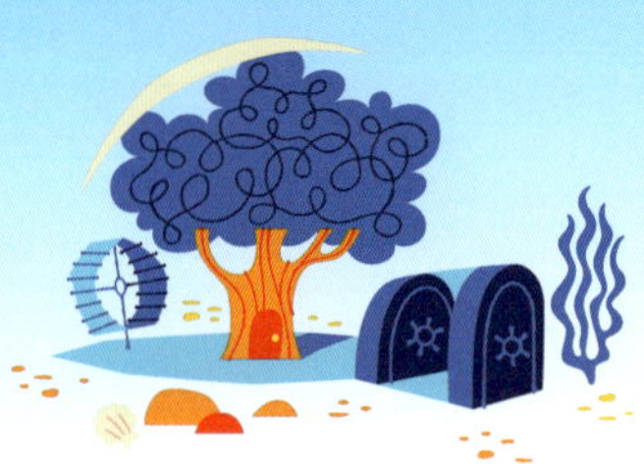

CHEEKS FAMILY TRAVELING CIRCUS

Visual development of the Cheeks family members: Pa [upper left], Ma [center], Randy [upper right], Granny [lower left], and Rosie and Rowdy [lower right]

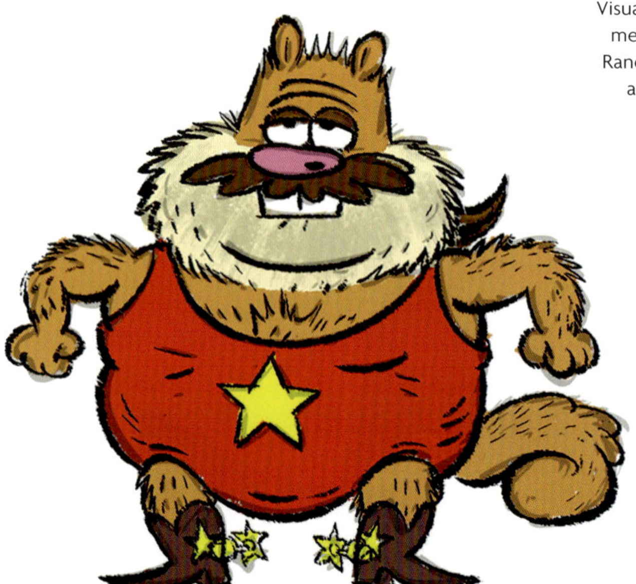

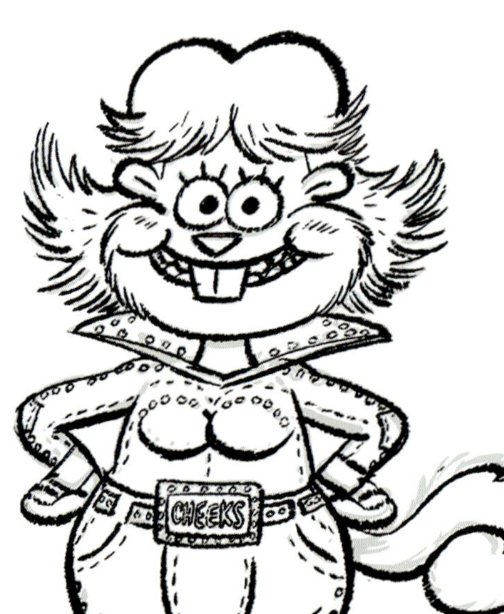

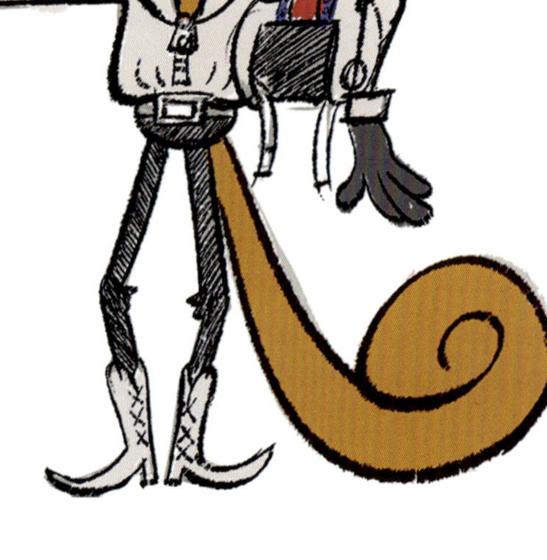

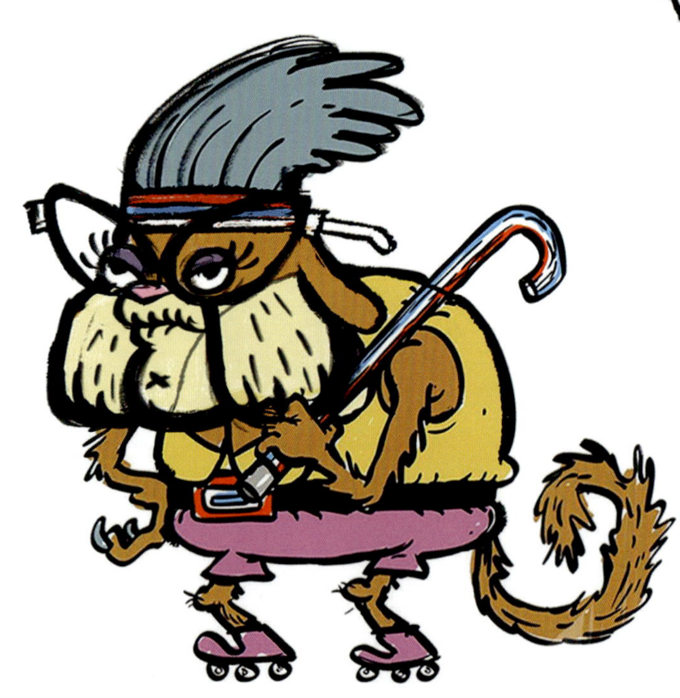

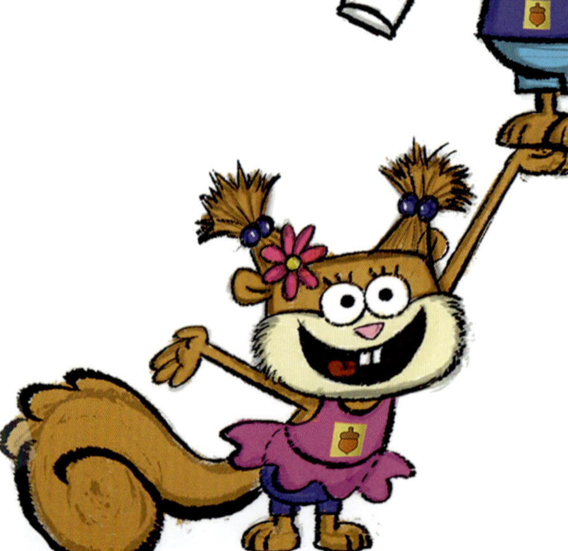

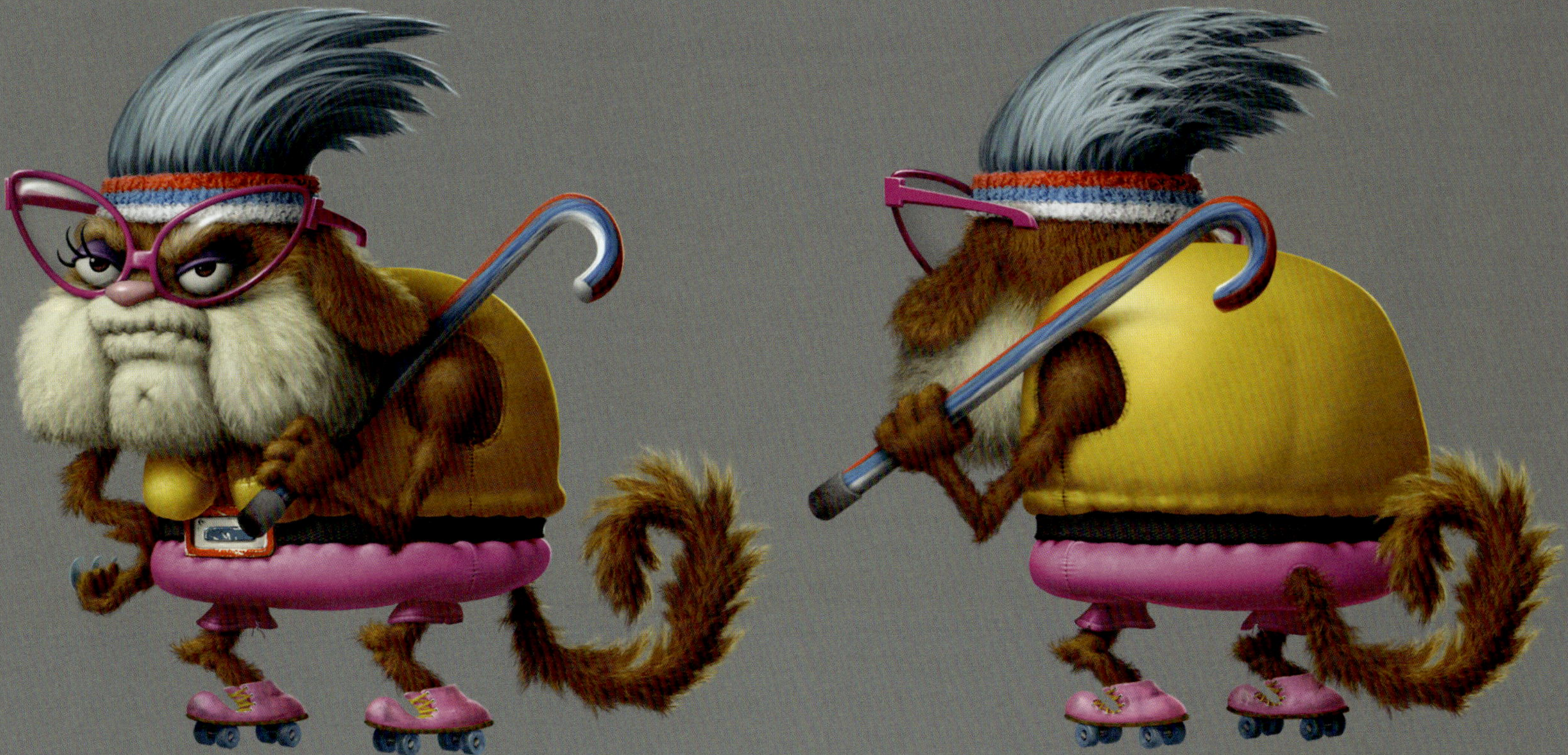

Final CG art of Granny [upper]; storyboard of Cheeks family making a grand entrance [lower]

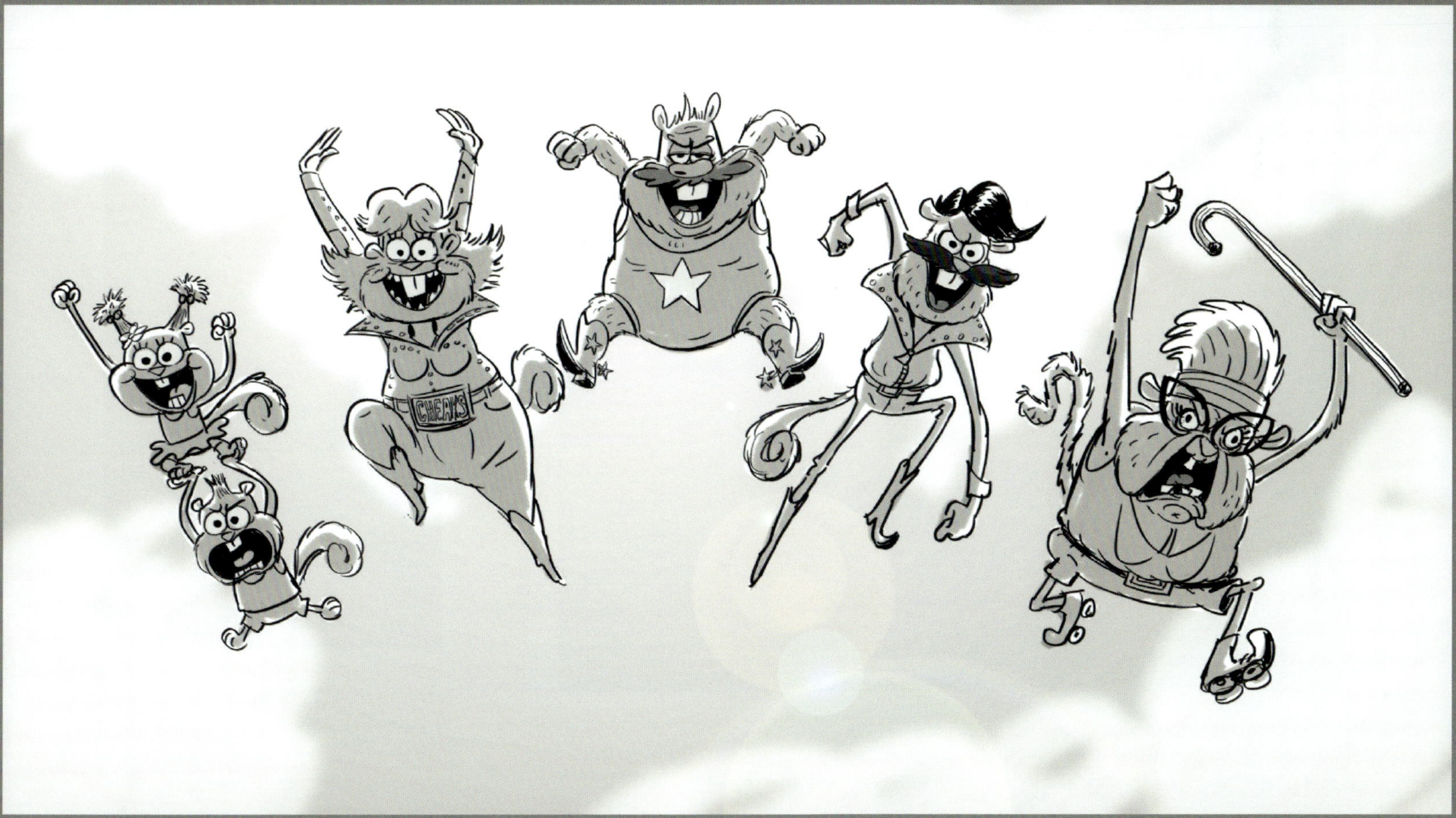

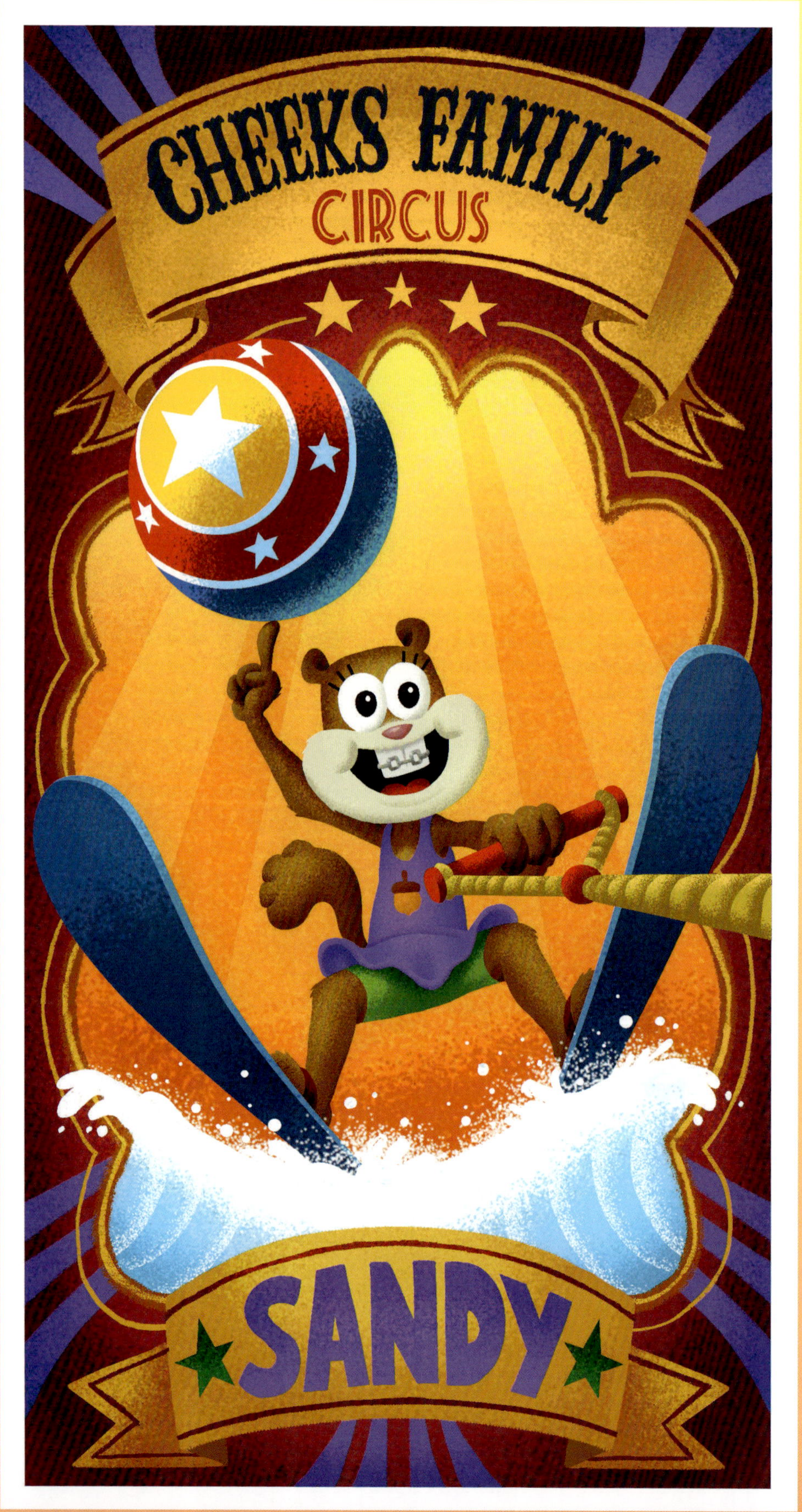

Heading back to her hometown, Sandy knows she can count on her family to back her up in a pinch, or more specifically in a rumble with rattlers and travel assistance.

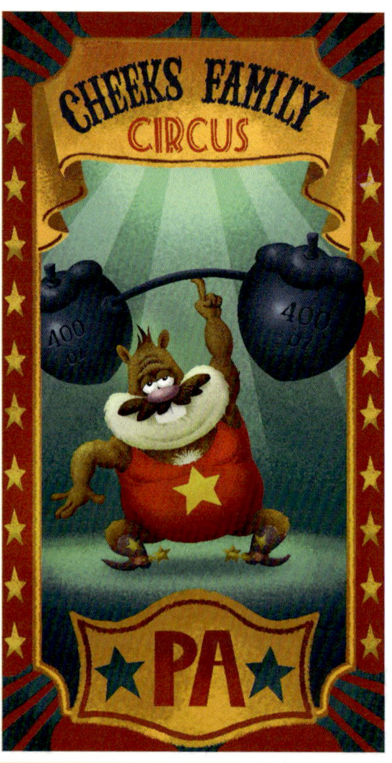

Pa Cheeks is the ultimate bodybuilder whose physical strength and love for Sandy are both impressive.

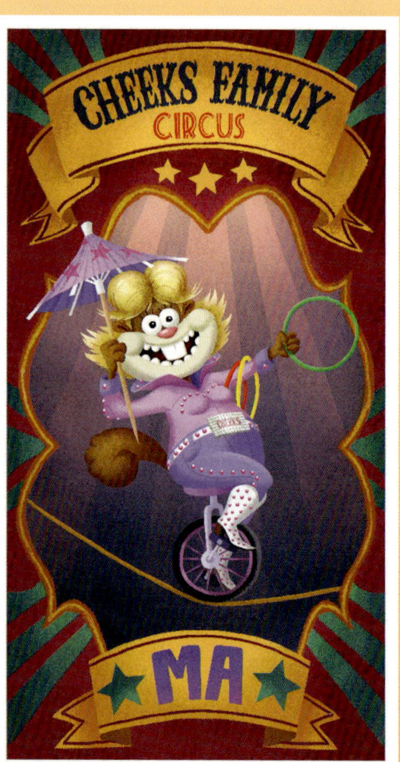

Ma Cheeks can spin plates like nobody's business but wishes she could spin a story to convince Sandy to rejoin their family business.

Historical Cheeks Family promotional posters, including Sandy's former circus performer role

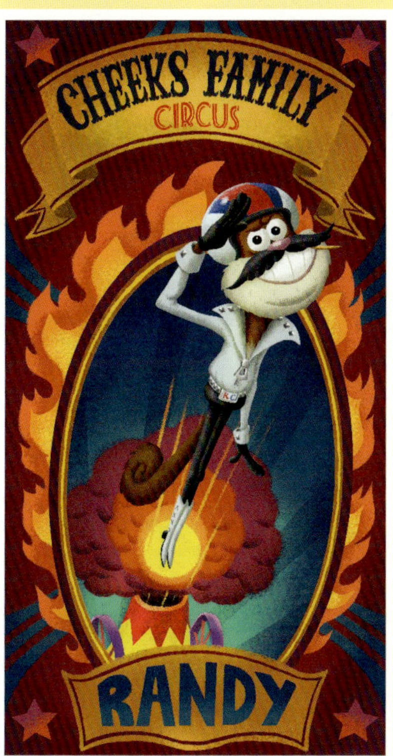

Randy is Sandy's twin brother, with charm enough to earn him the title of "Most Irresistible Wink in Texas" for eight years running.

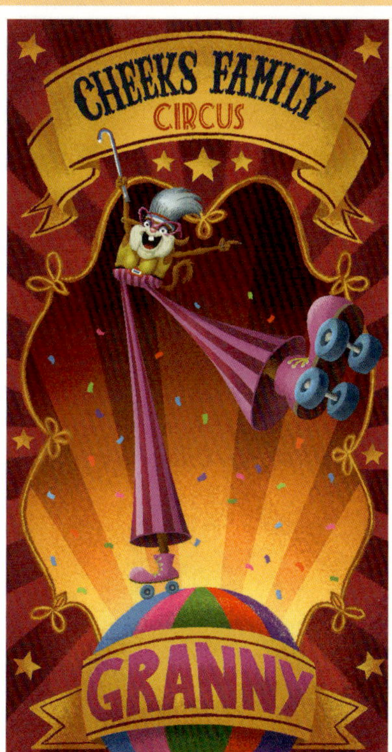

Granny Cheeks is still rocking the stilt-walk even at an advanced age, in between naps.

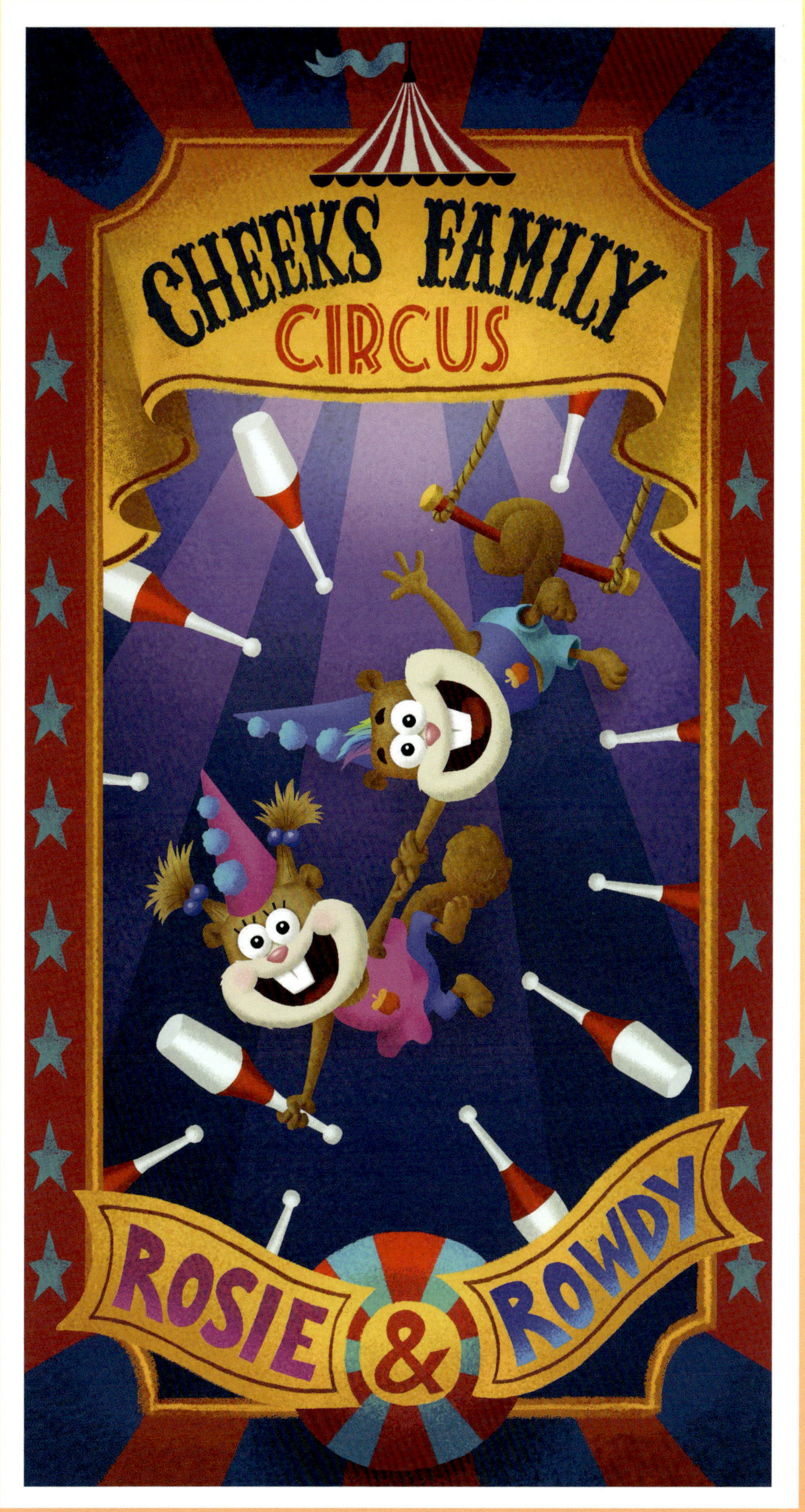

The twins Rowdy and Rosie round out the family with their youthful energy and creative looks.

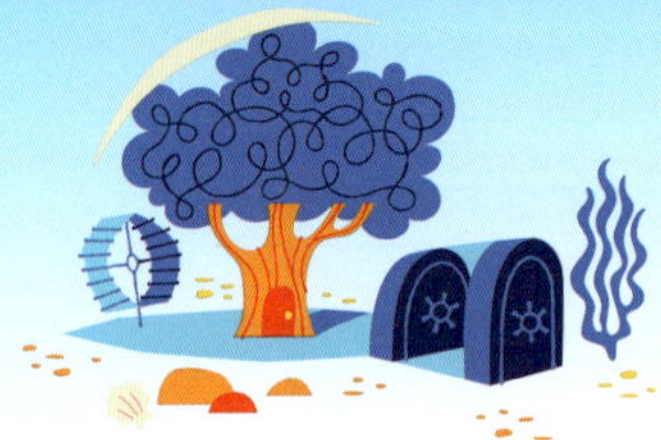

SEA PALS PROJECT

The residents of Bikini Bottom are abducted and taken to a Texas laboratory, where they are subjected to some interesting marine-centric experimentation. Under the leadership of the villainous Sue Nahmee, the Sea Pals project aims to turn the Bikini Bottom creatures into air breathers and clone them into off-brand toys for children to play with... what could possibly go wrong?

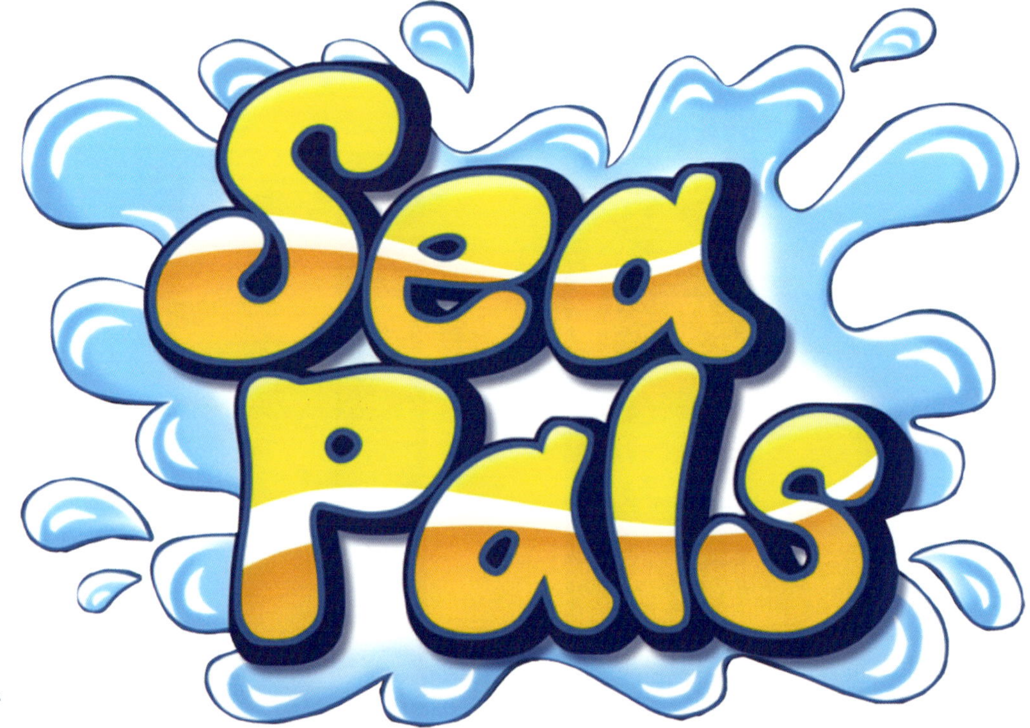

(Fictional) Sea Pals marketing materials

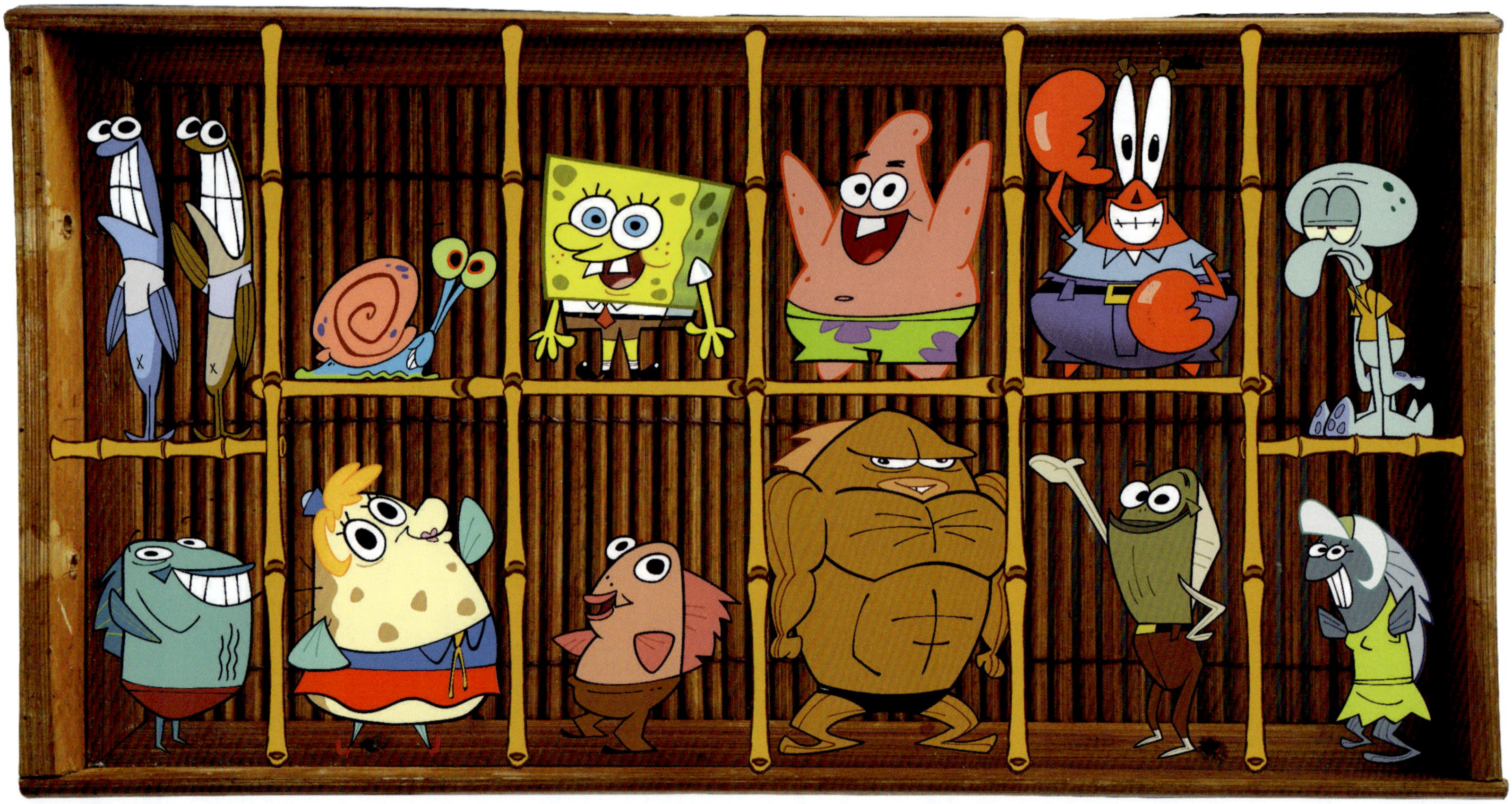

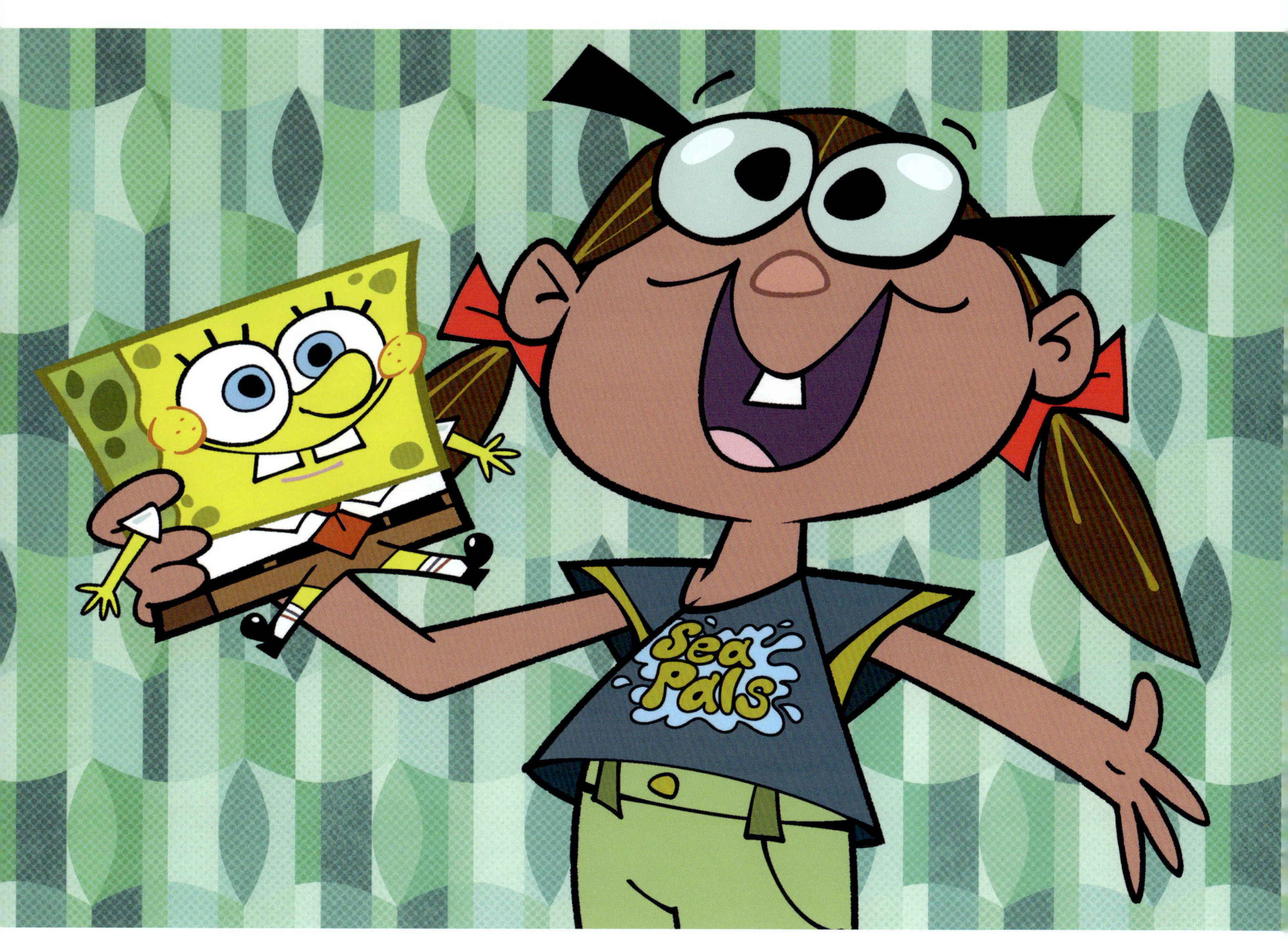
Sea Pals

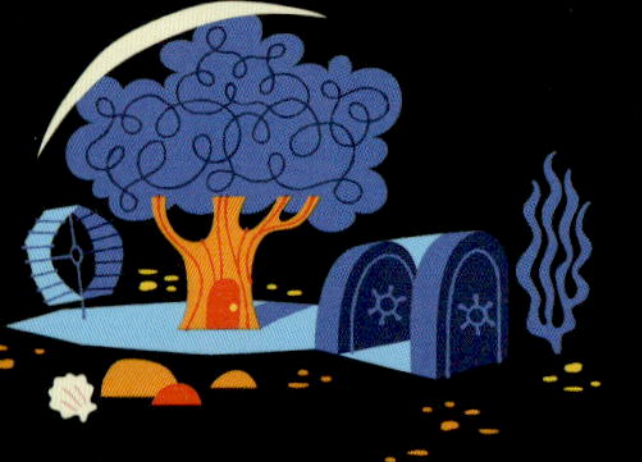

BOUNCED BACK TO BIKINI BOTTOM

After an electro-boost back to Bikini Bottom, all is well again as everyone celebrates the combination of "surf and turf" with special guest circus acts as part of the fun.

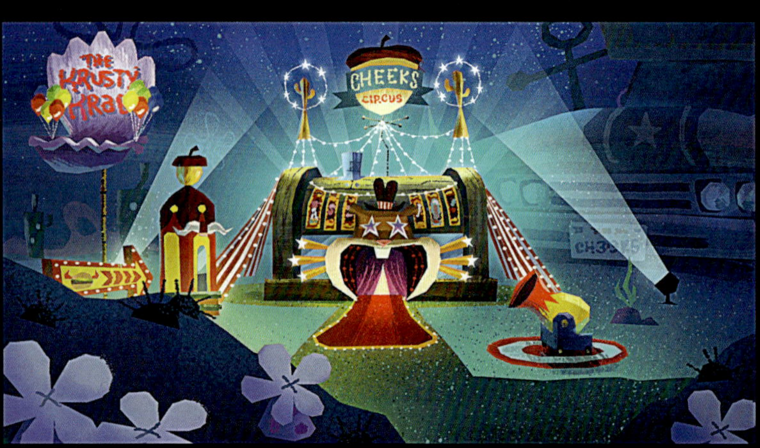

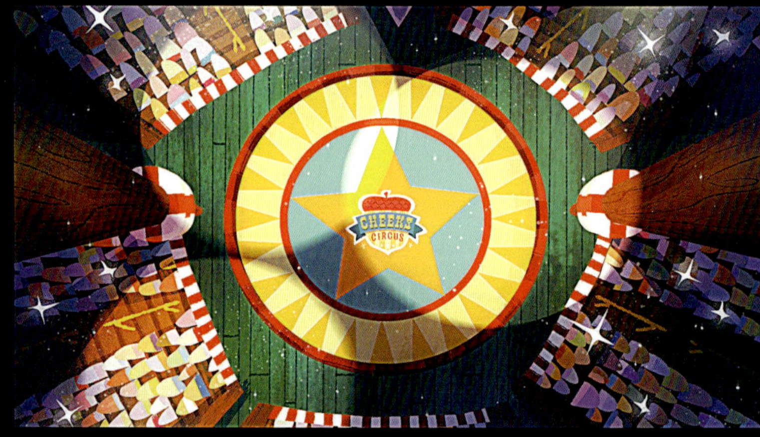

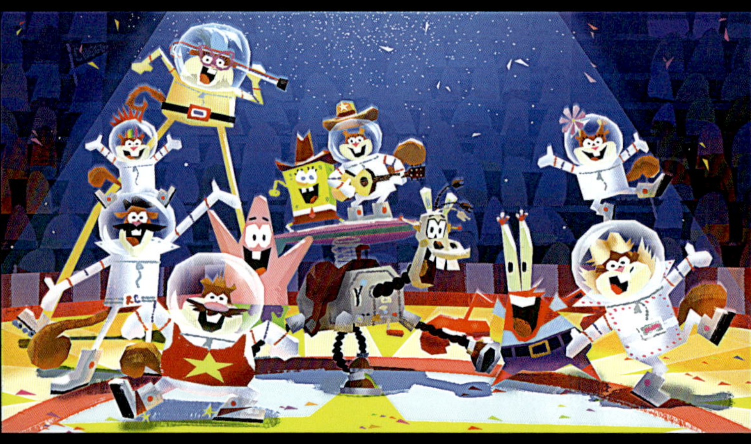

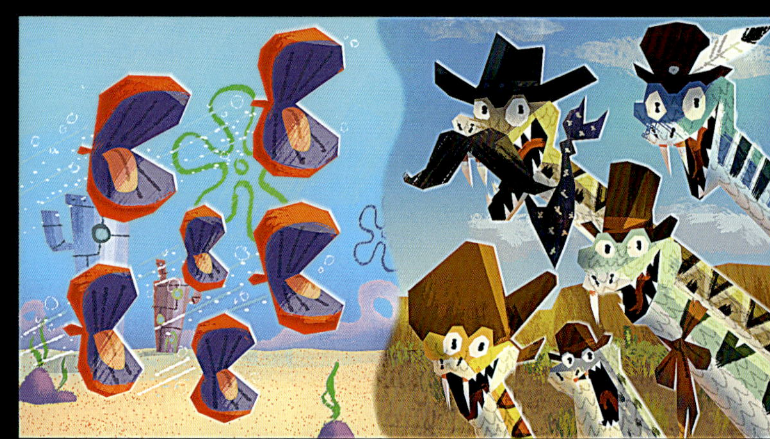

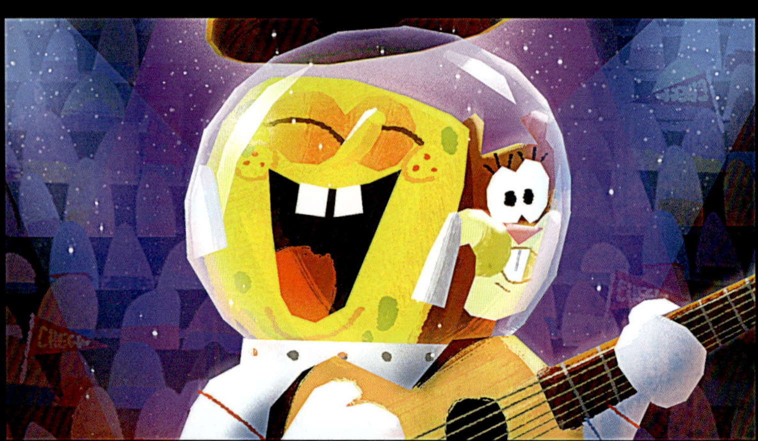

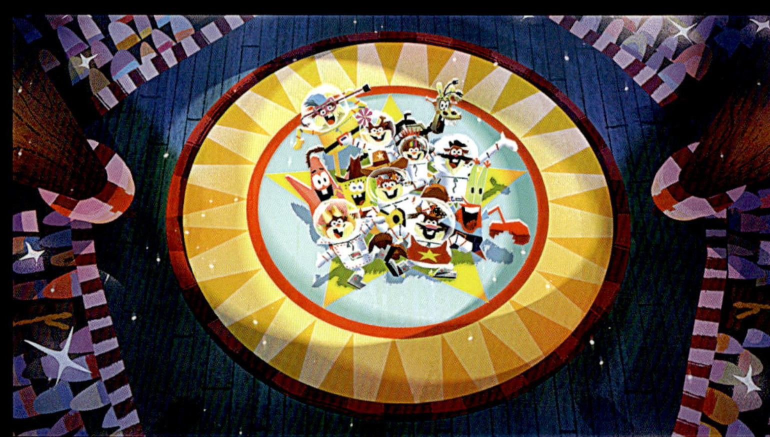

"SANDY CHEEKS IS SUCH A SWEET AND BELOVED CHARACTER IN THE SPONGEBOB UNIVERSE, SO WE WANTED TO MAKE SURE THIS FINAL SEQUENCE REFLECTED THAT, AND WHAT BETTER WAY TO DO SO THAN WITH A FINAL MUSICAL NUMBER SURROUNDED BY ALL HER LOVED ONES. IT HAD TO FEEL LIKE A CELEBRATION SPECIFIC TO HER, COMBINING BOTH WORLDS ABOVE AND BELOW THE SEA. THE LIGHTING IS MORE THEATRICAL THROUGHOUT OUR MUSICAL SEQUENCES, BUT THIS ONE NEEDED TO BE PUMPED UP A NOTCH OR TWO TO SEND HER OFF AS SHE DESERVED."

TRAVIS RUIZ,
ART DIRECTOR

Color key illustrating the movie's happy musical ending

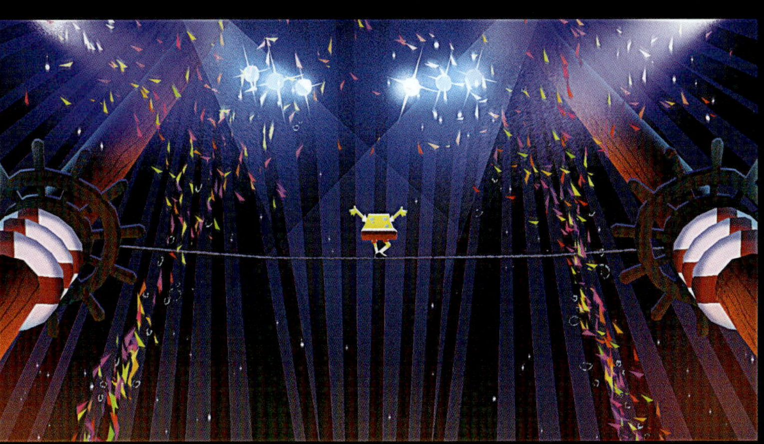

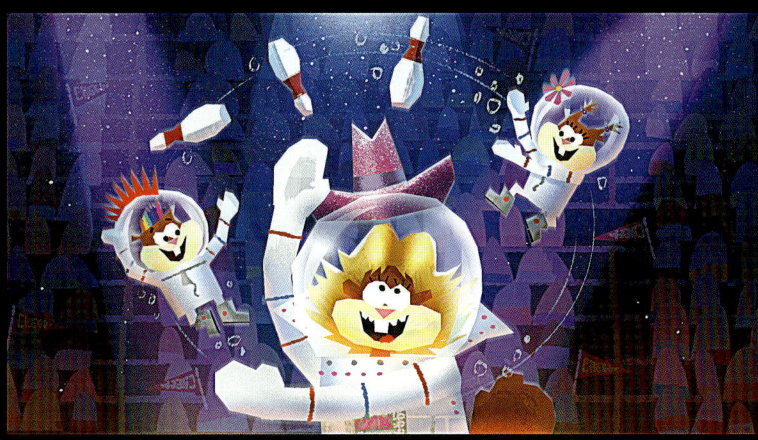

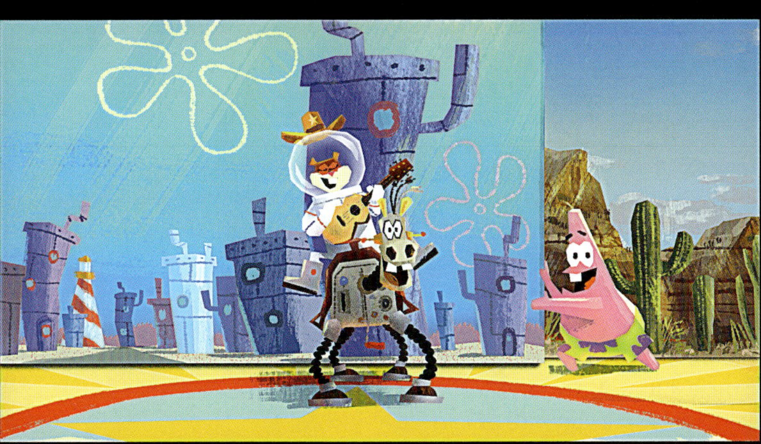

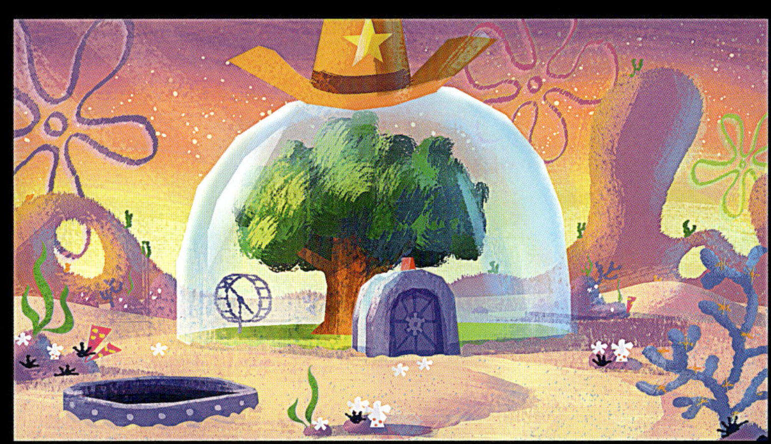

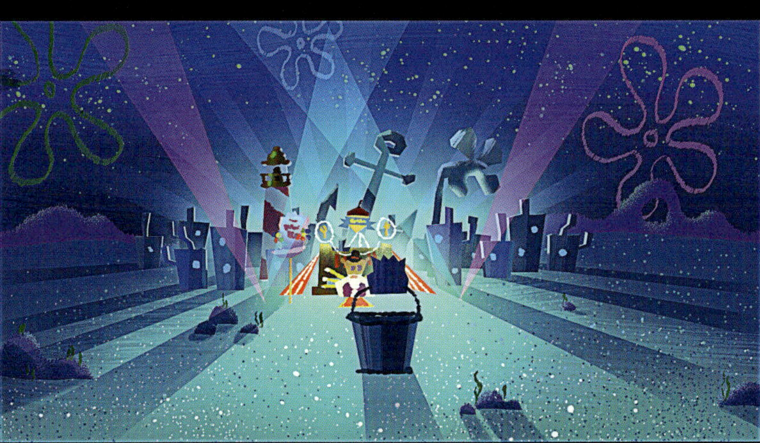

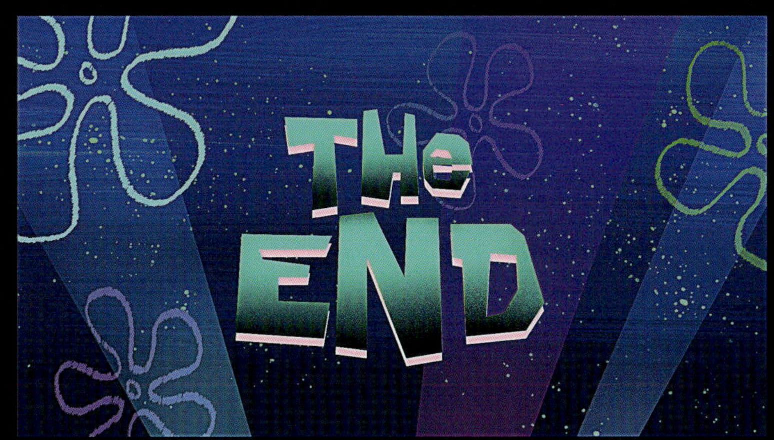

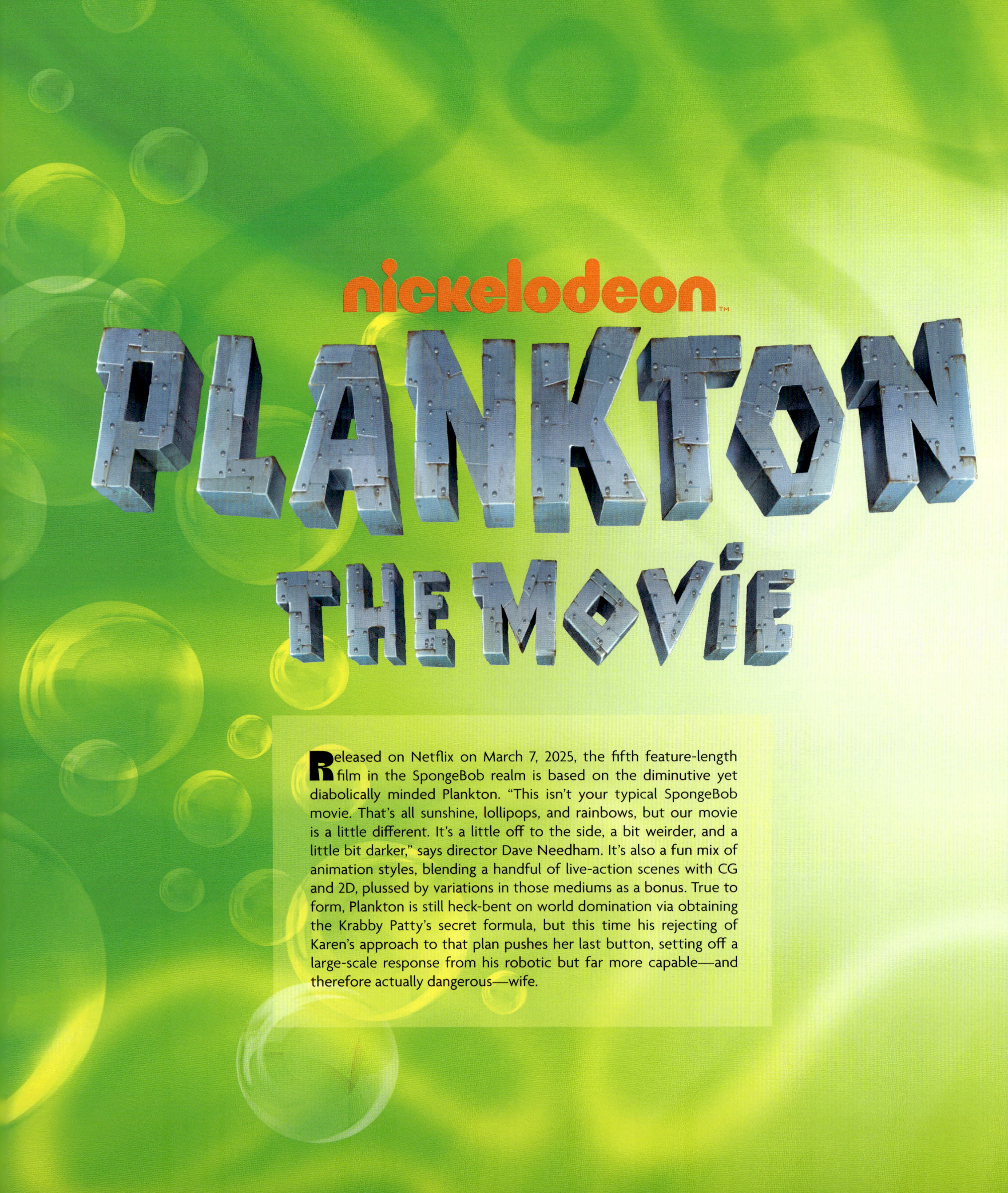

Released on Netflix on March 7, 2025, the fifth feature-length film in the SpongeBob realm is based on the diminutive yet diabolically minded Plankton. "This isn't your typical SpongeBob movie. That's all sunshine, lollipops, and rainbows, but our movie is a little different. It's a little off to the side, a bit weirder, and a little bit darker," says director Dave Needham. It's also a fun mix of animation styles, blending a handful of live-action scenes with CG and 2D, plussed by variations in those mediums as a bonus. True to form, Plankton is still heck-bent on world domination via obtaining the Krabby Patty's secret formula, but this time his rejecting of Karen's approach to that plan pushes her last button, setting off a large-scale response from his robotic but far more capable—and therefore actually dangerous—wife.

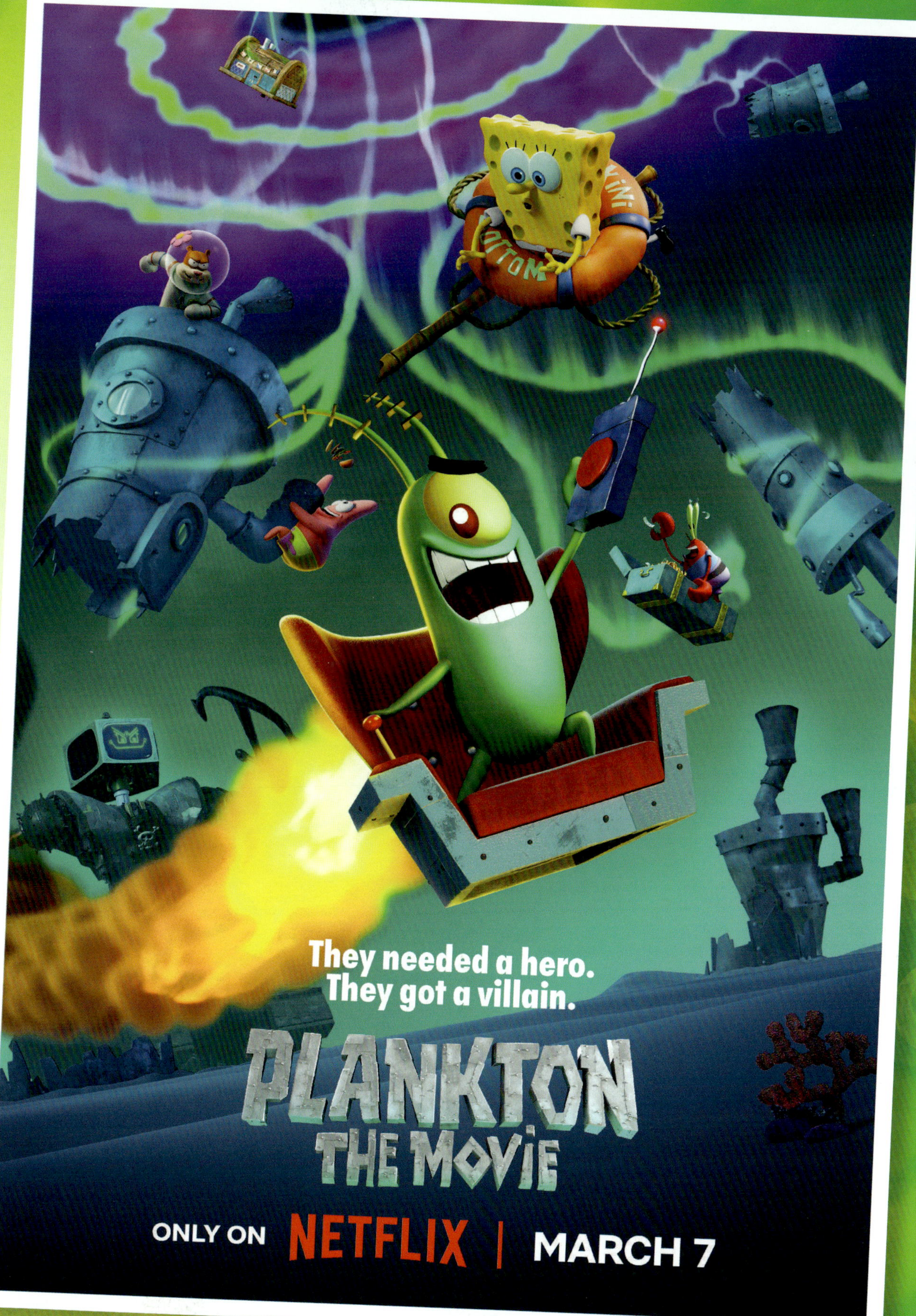

Courtesy of Netflix

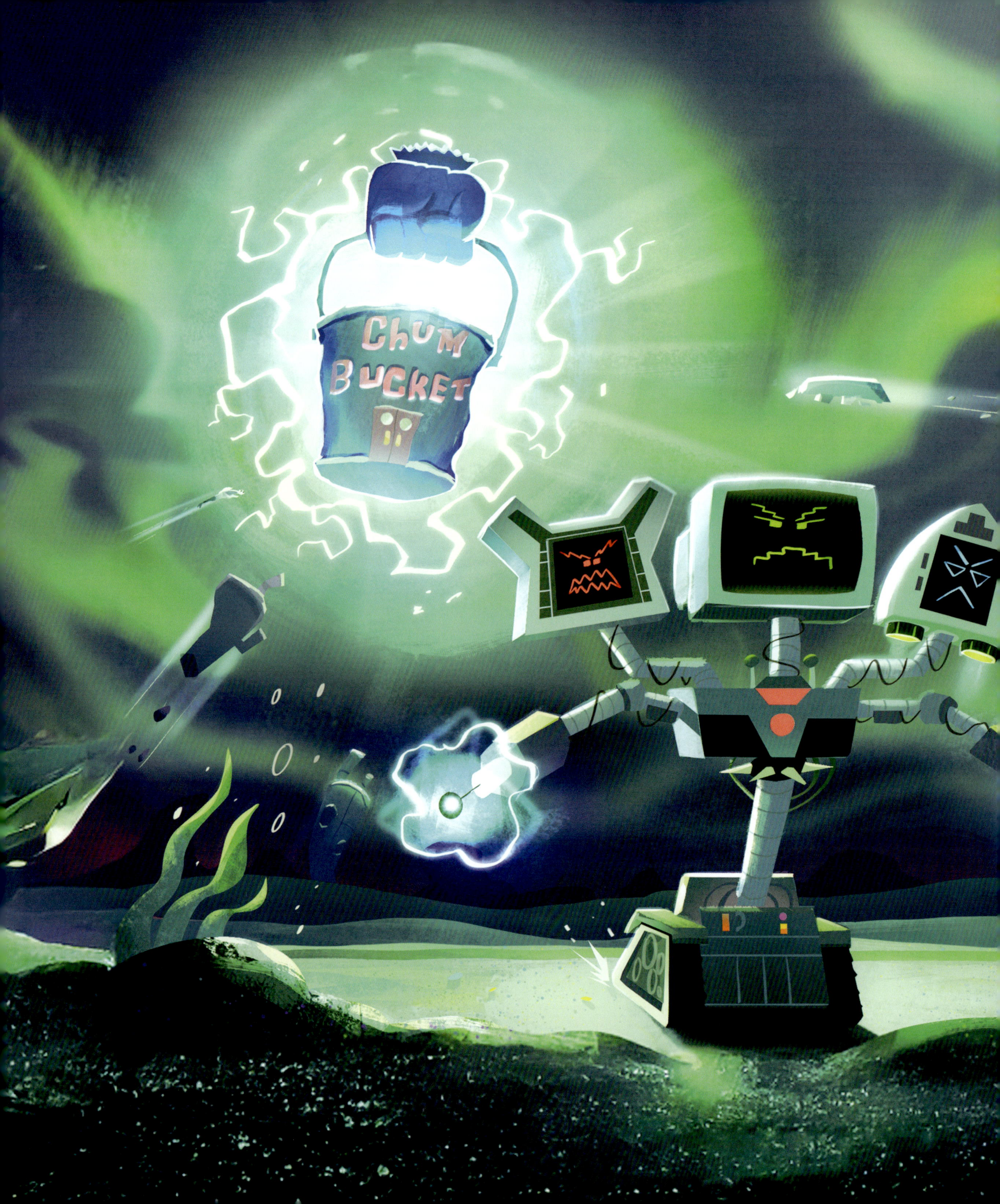
Chum Bucket

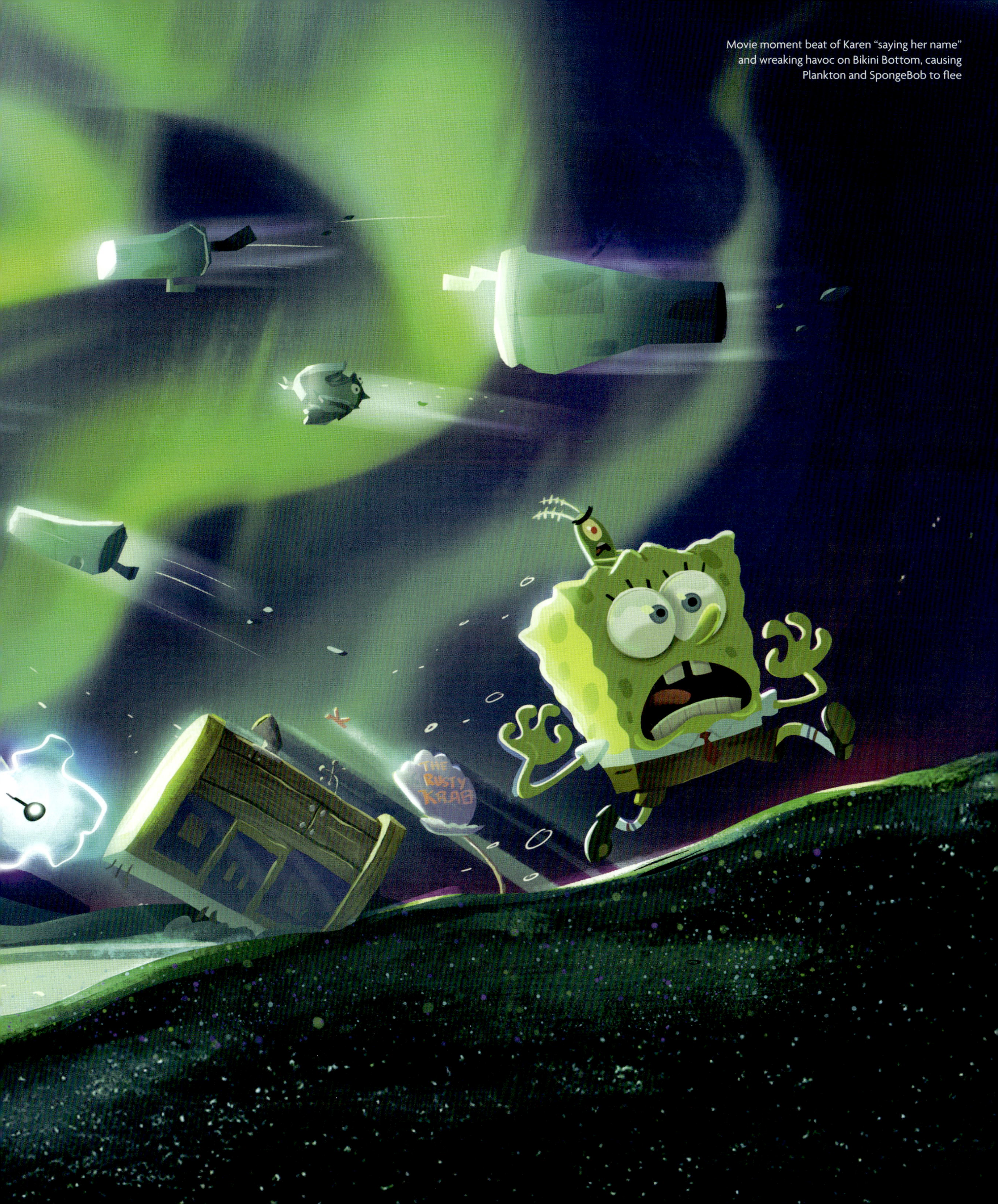

Movie moment beat of Karen "saying her name" and wreaking havoc on Bikini Bottom, causing Plankton and SpongeBob to flee

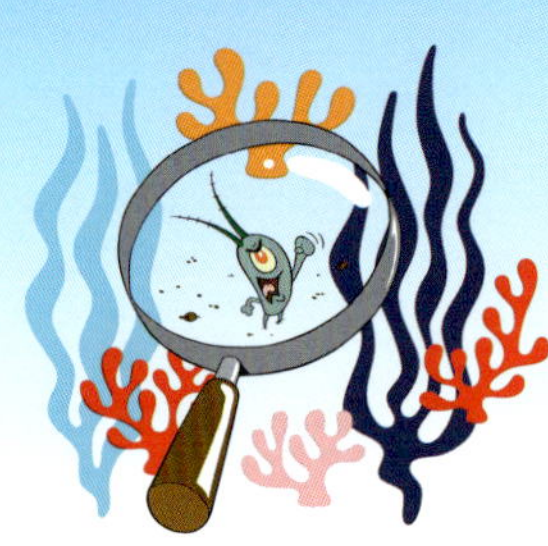

"I'M PLANKTON" WITH ANOTHER PLAN

This film has the touch of Mr. Lawrence all over it, channeling decades of Plankton's thoughts and voice talent into one focused storyline. "Because of his size and his ego, he never really wins or gets what he wants. He becomes sympathetic but easy to laugh at. People tell me sometimes that they feel Plankton's pain... and I guess that means I'm getting to the root of something very human with my portrayal," says Mr. Lawrence.

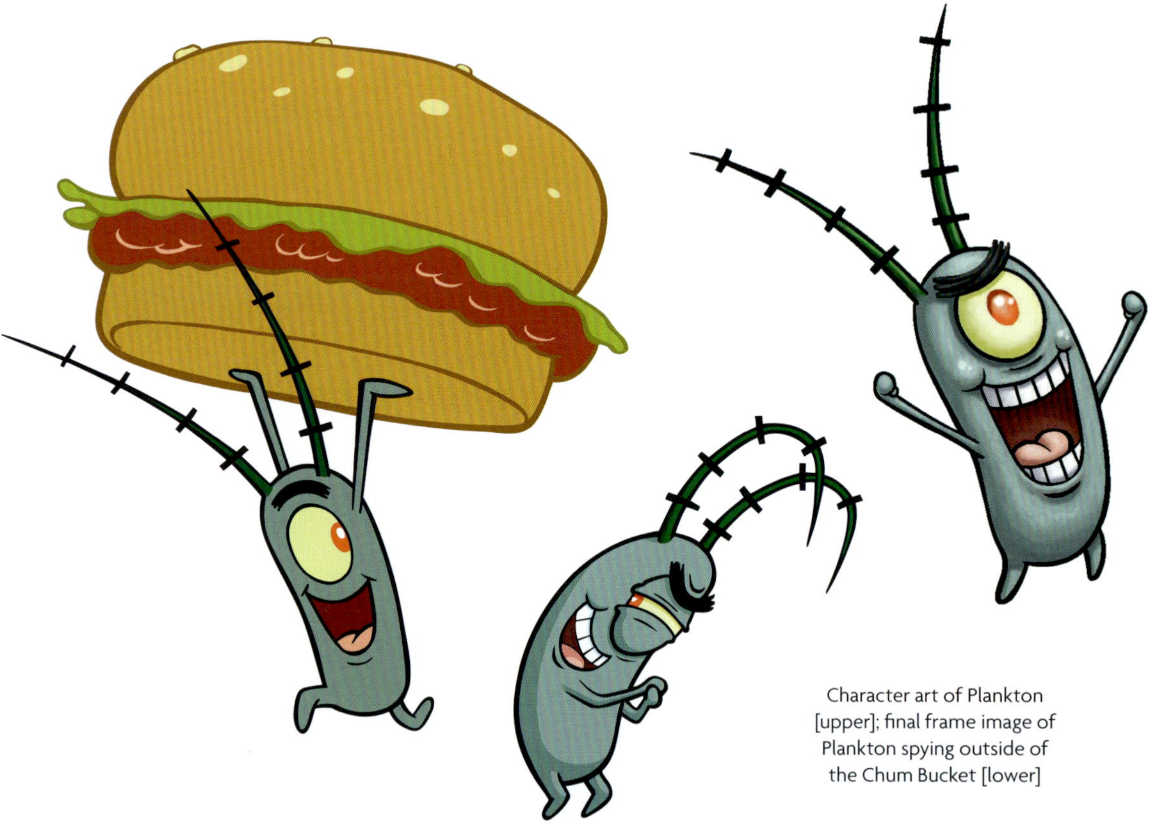

Character art of Plankton [upper]; final frame image of Plankton spying outside of the Chum Bucket [lower]

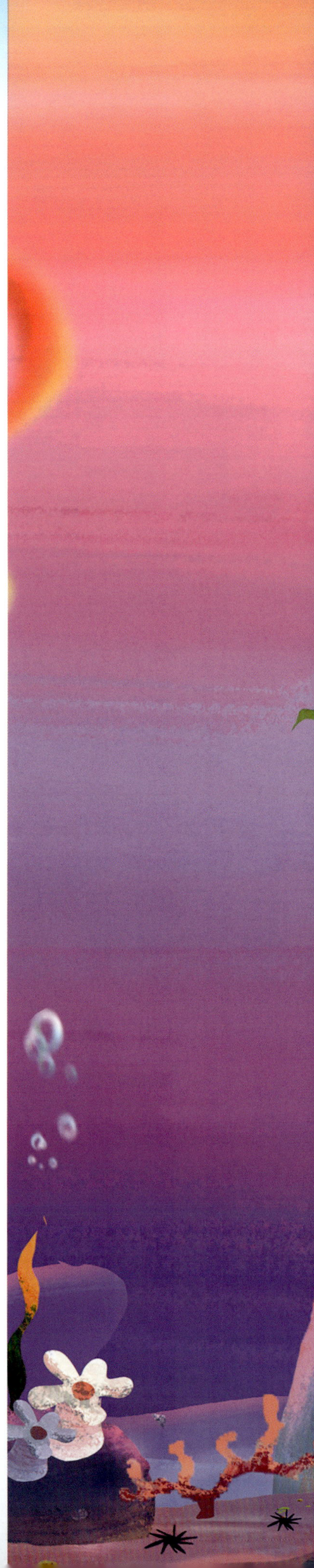

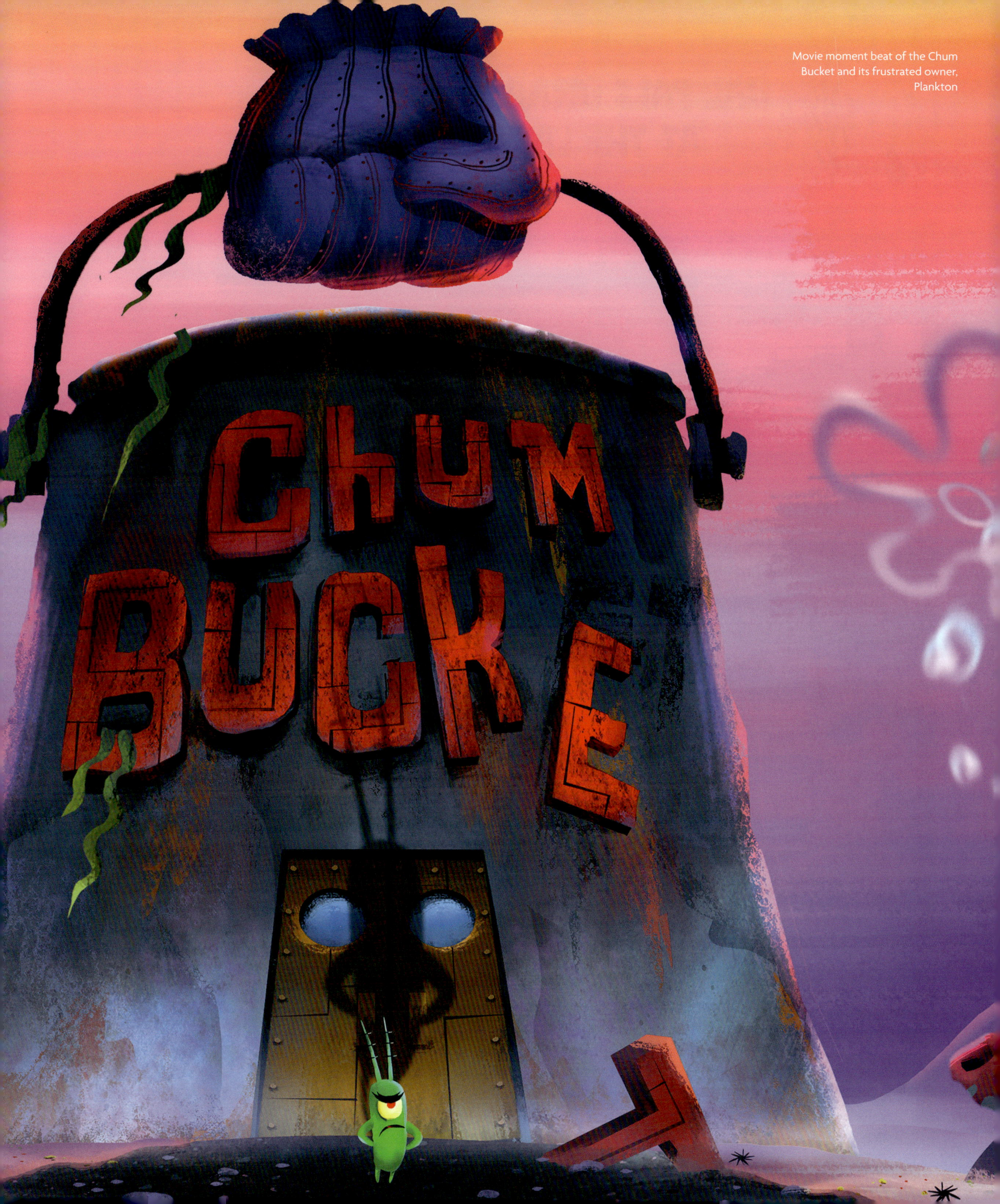

Movie moment beat of the Chum Bucket and its frustrated owner, Plankton

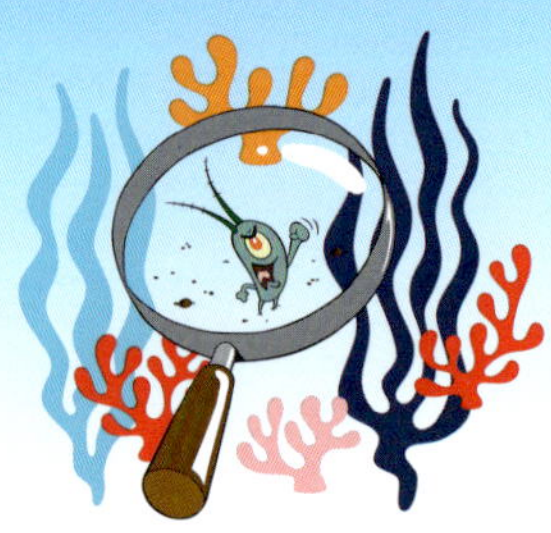

GAL PALS GRAB COFFEE AT THE LAST DRIP

The film provides a rare look at Karen out and about instead of at the lab or restaurant with Plankton. She's got plenty of ideas, and it's nice when her circle of friends (the Gal Pals) hears them, since her tiny-minded husband never seems to listen to her advice.

Final frame images of the Gal Pals coffee date in which Karen electrifyingly announces the impending reveal of her own world domination plan

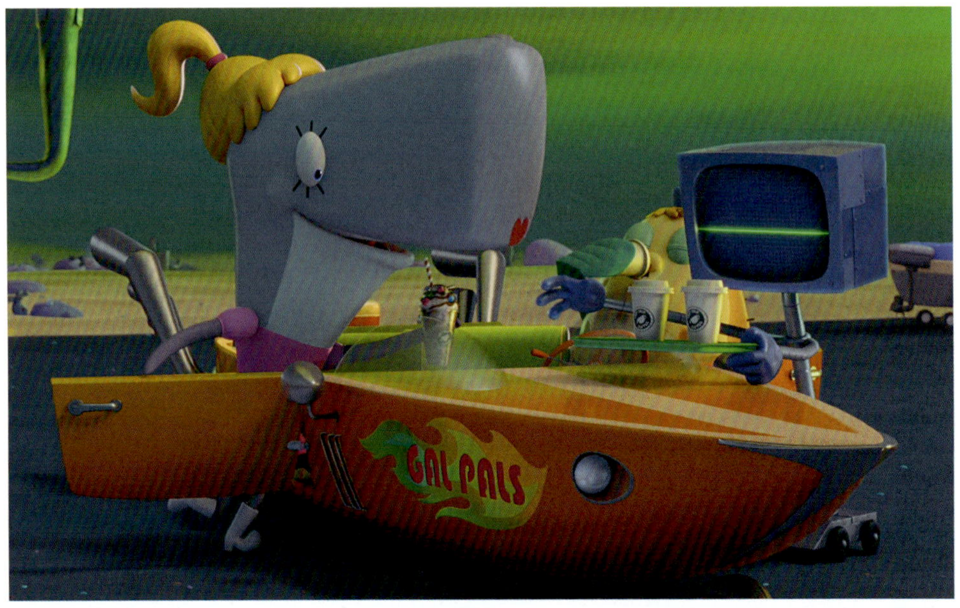

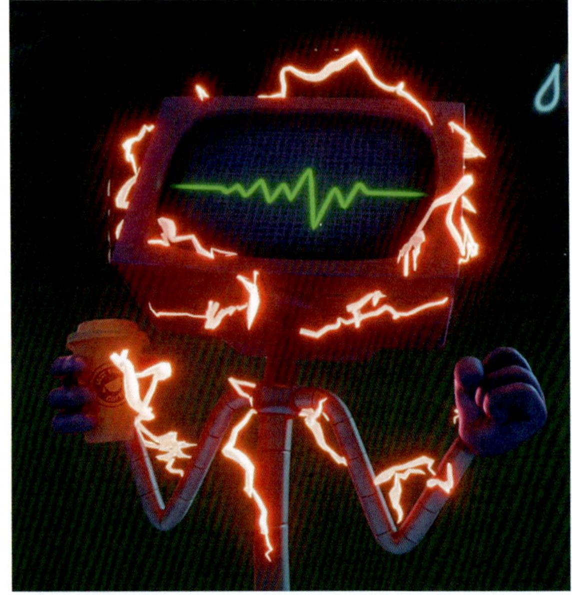

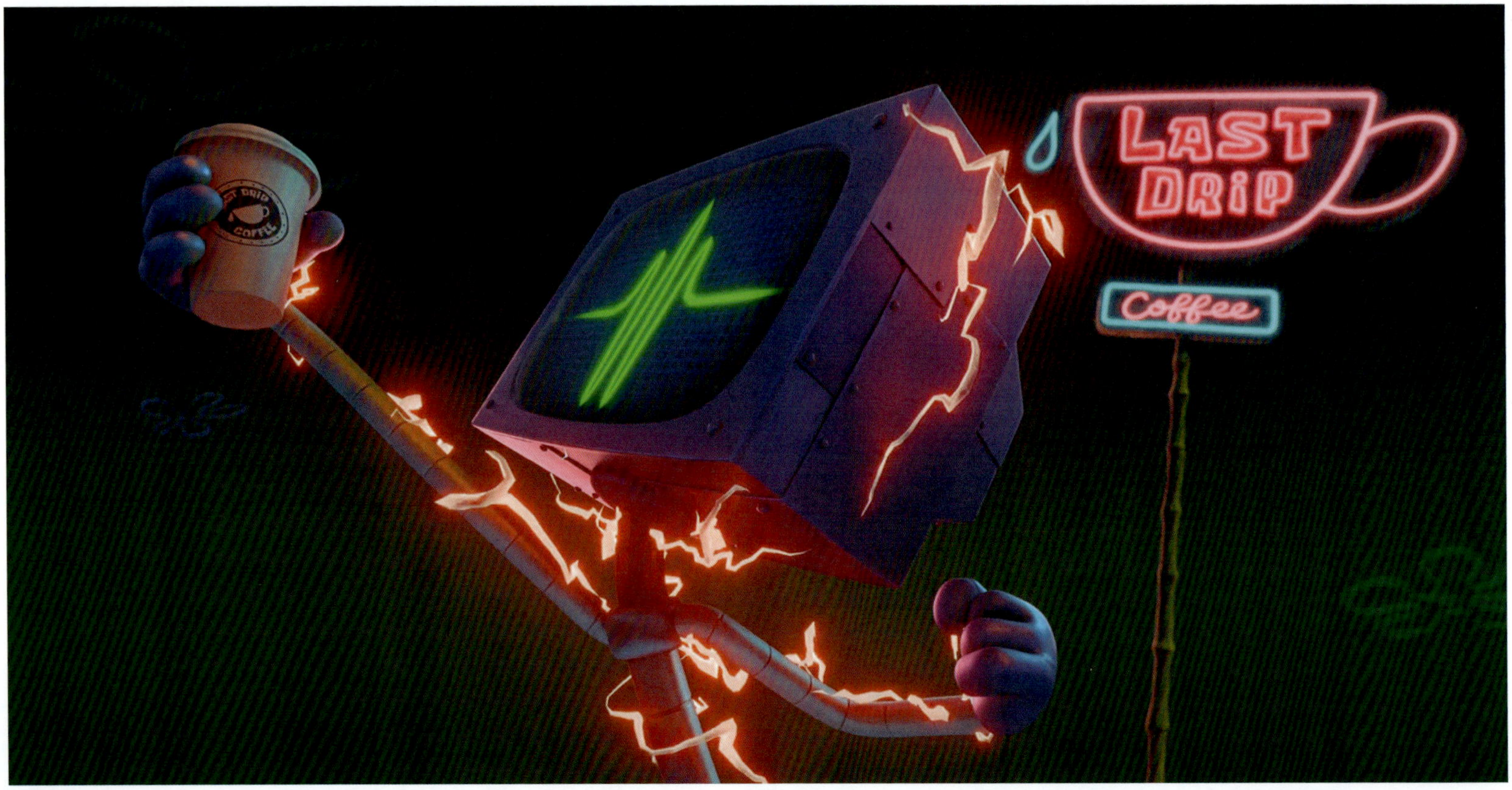

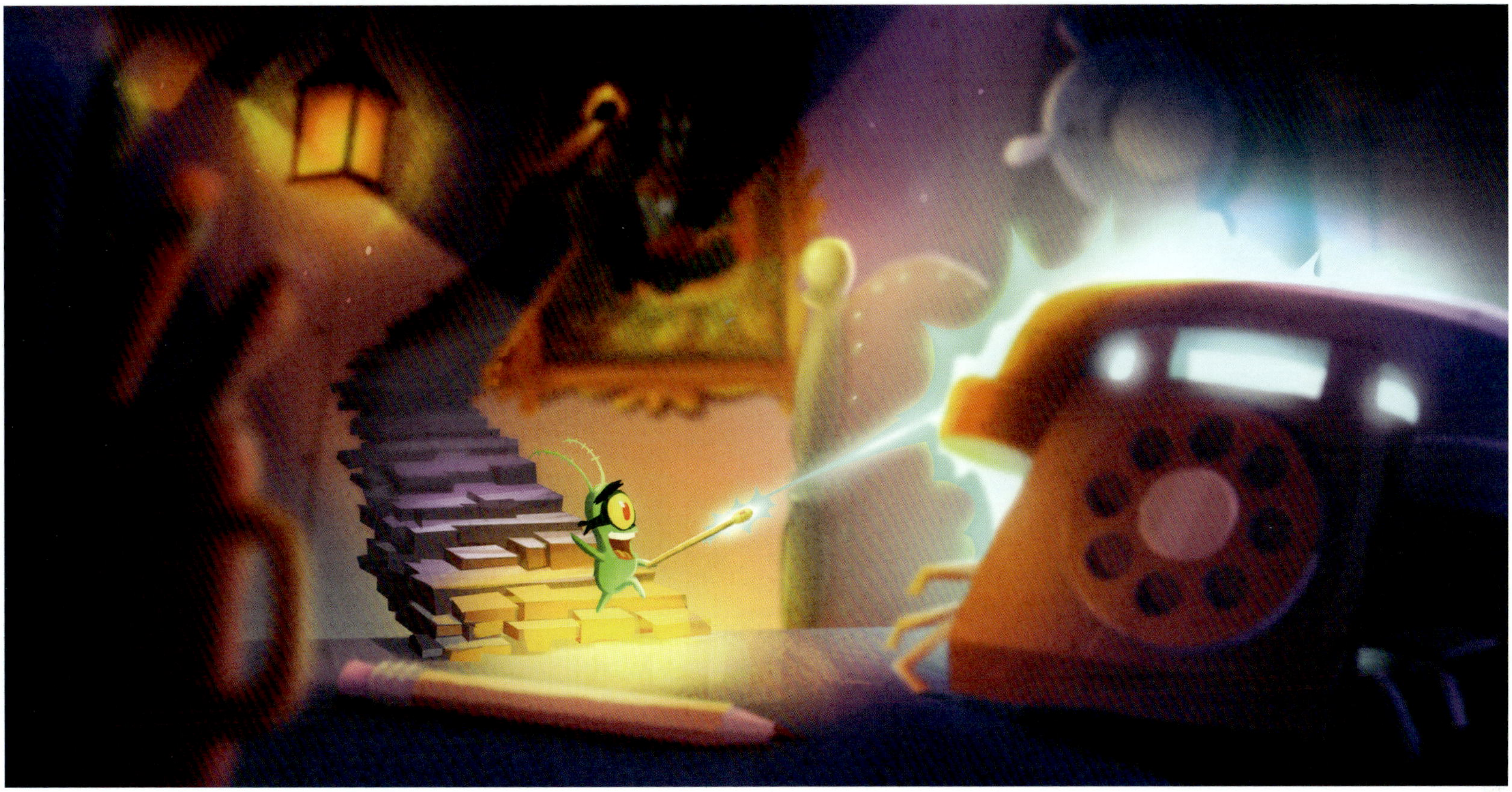

Visual development of Plankton ramping up for his latest attempt to obtain the Krabby Patty secret formula [upper]; artwork of SpongeBob and Mr. Krabs in the Crow's Nest while surveilling Plankton [lower]

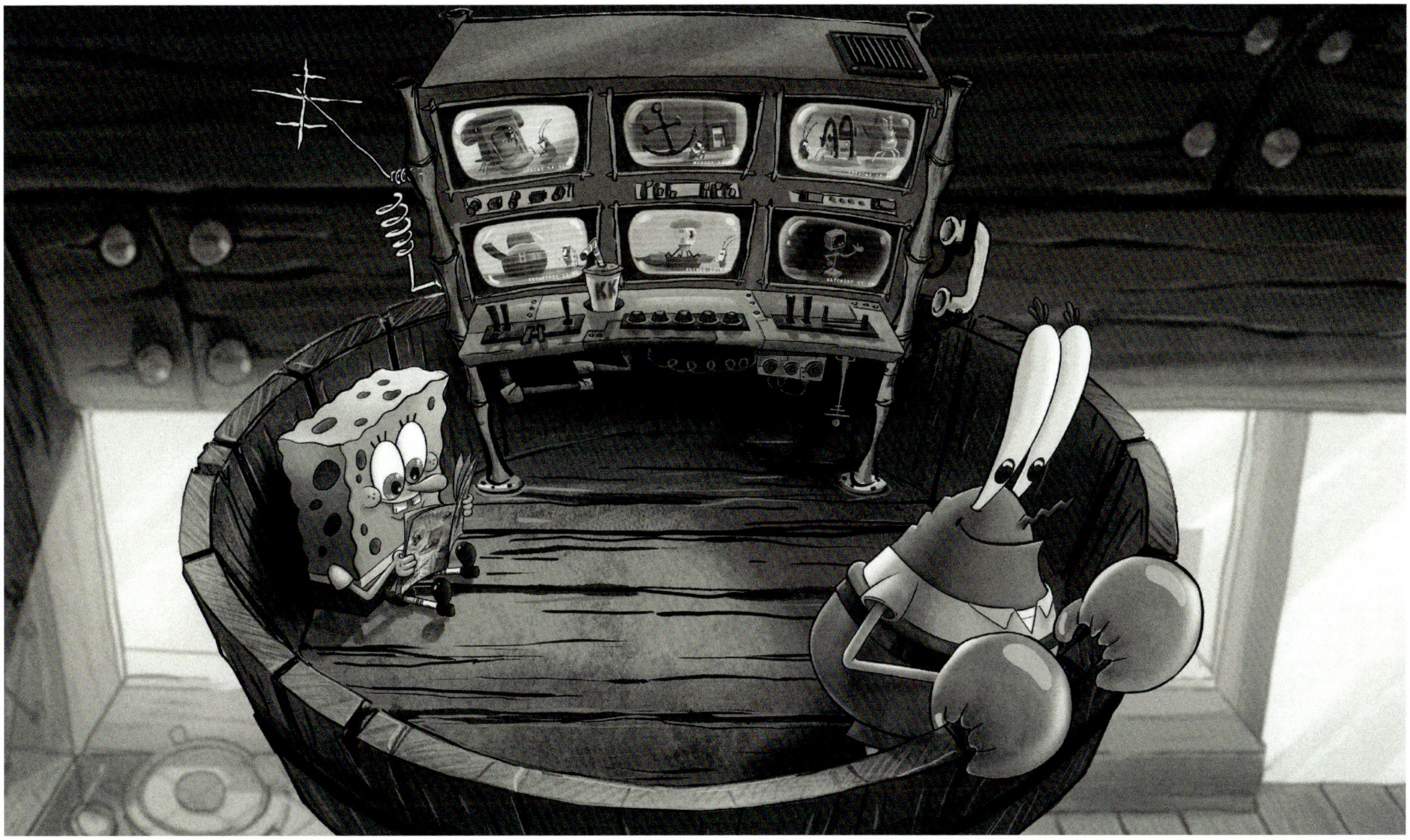

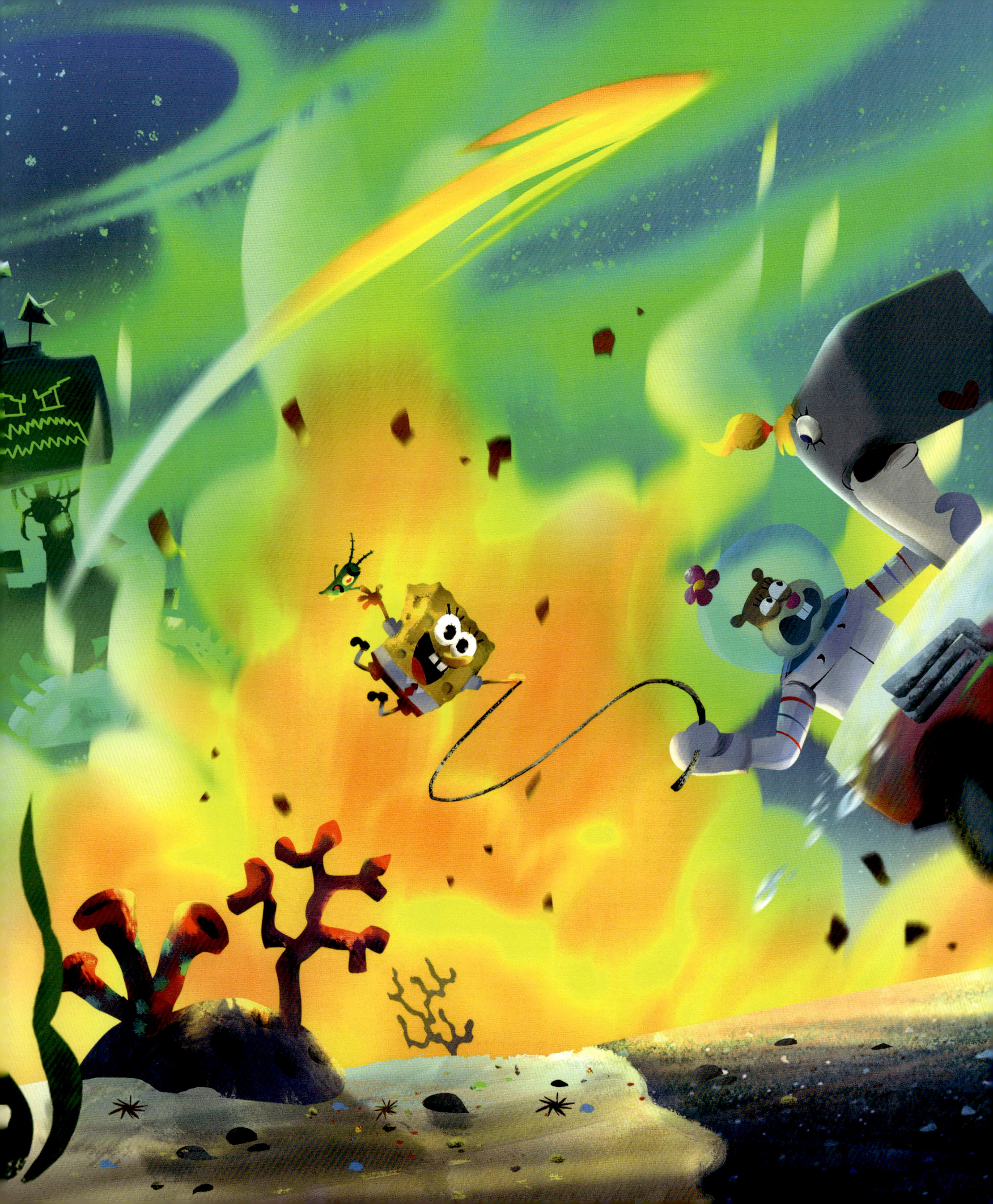

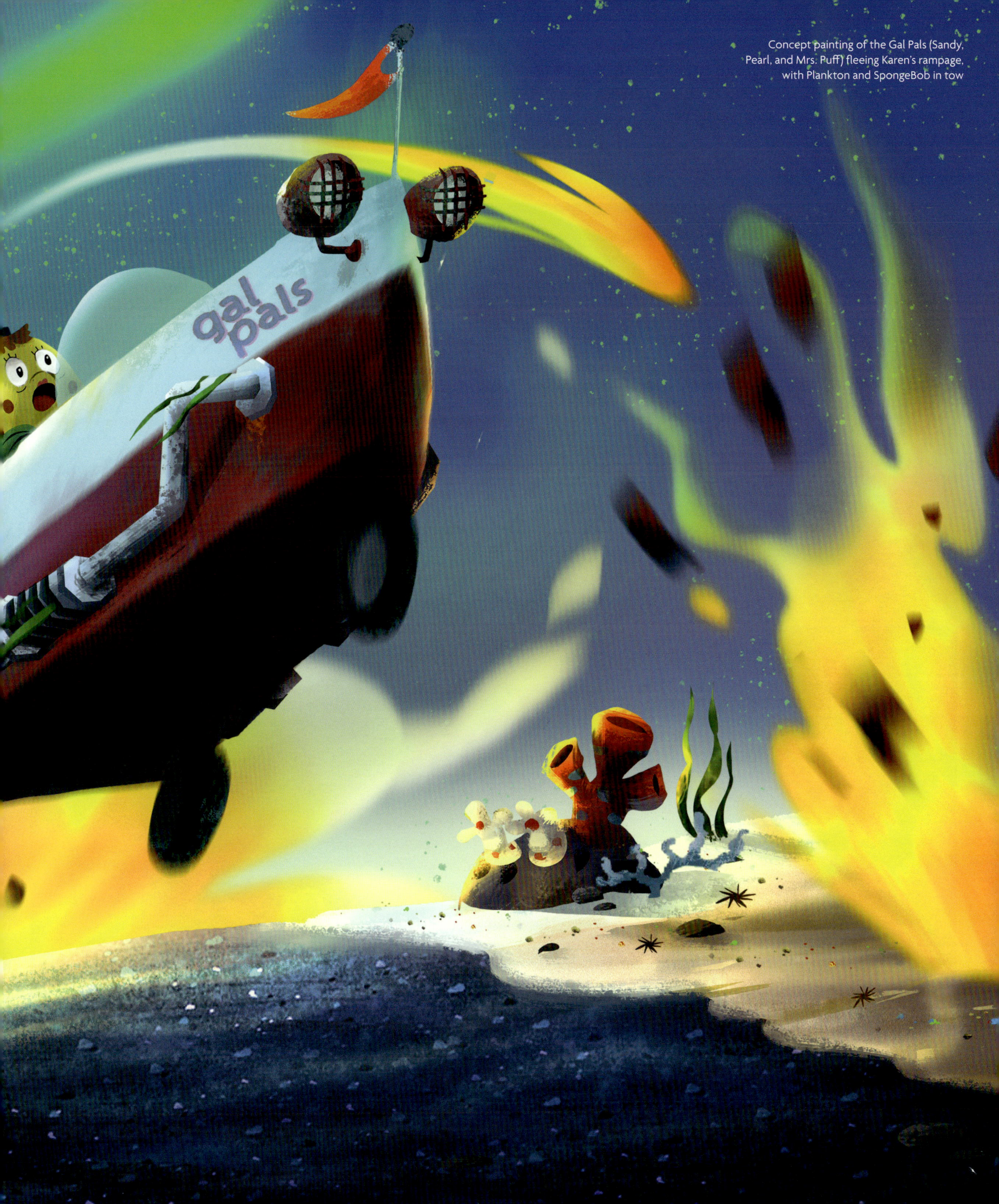

Concept painting of the Gal Pals (Sandy, Pearl, and Mrs. Puff) fleeing Karen's rampage, with Plankton and SpongeBob in tow

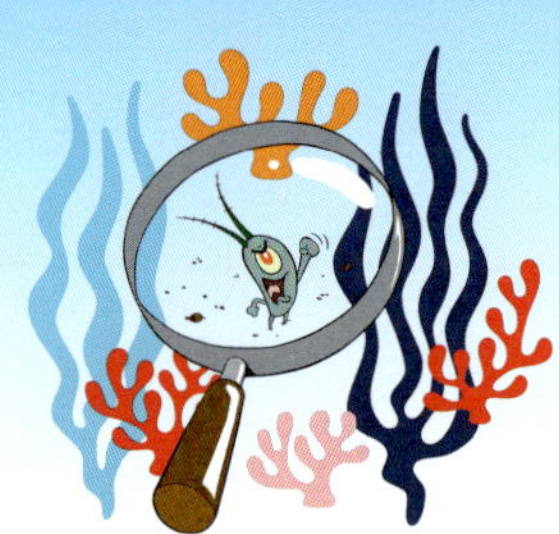

A PEEK AT THE GAL PALS' UNDERGROUND GETAWAY

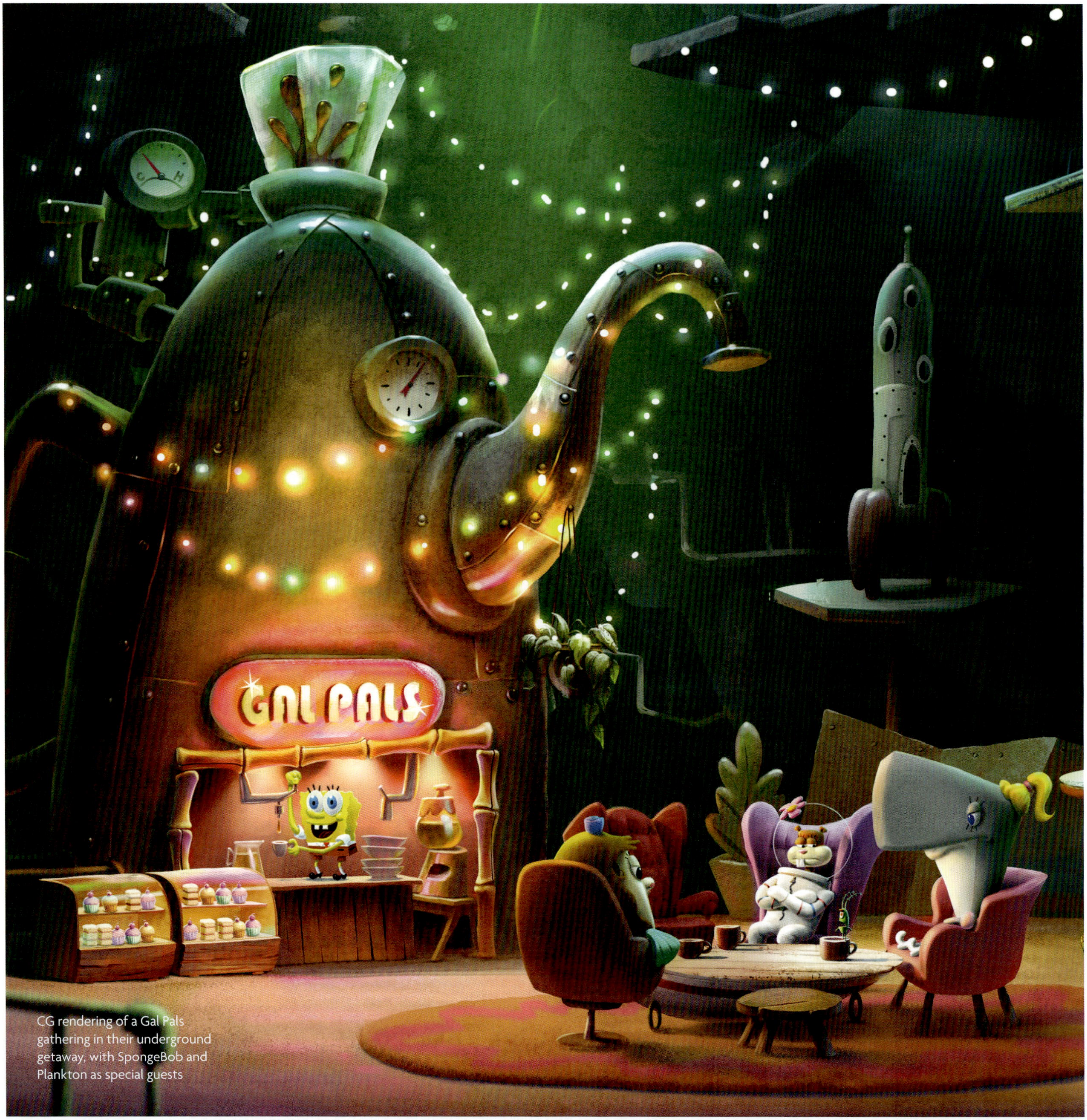

GAL PALS

CG rendering of a Gal Pals gathering in their underground getaway, with SpongeBob and Plankton as special guests

CHUM BUCKET'S MAIN COURSE

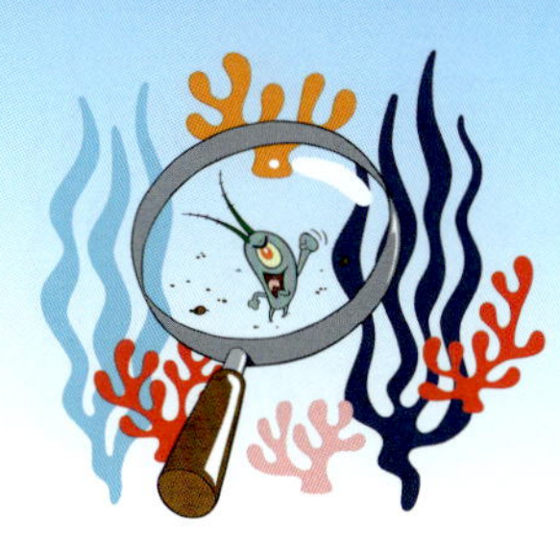

Final CG art of Chum as served at the Chum Bucket, with Karen for scale

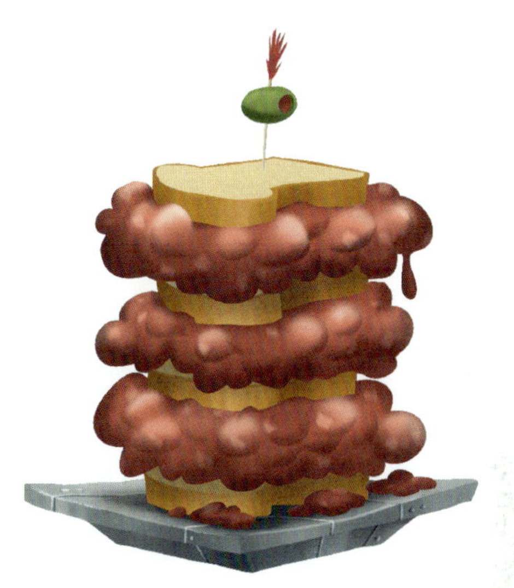

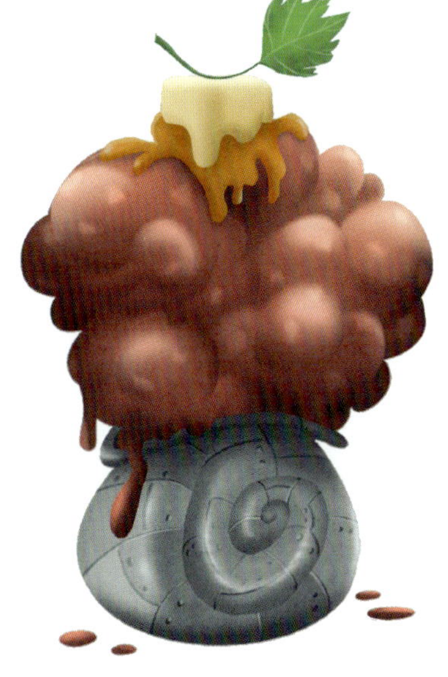

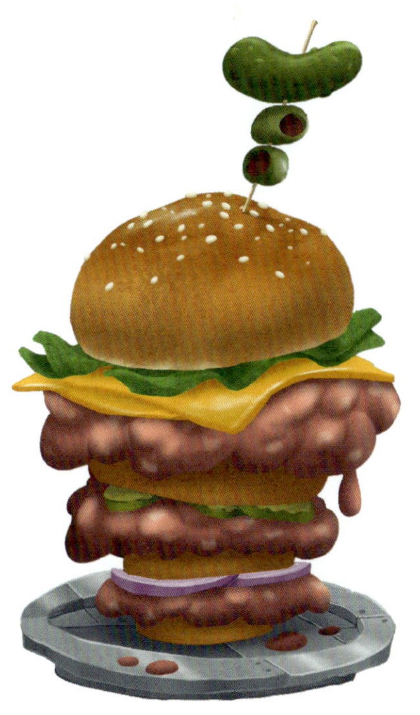

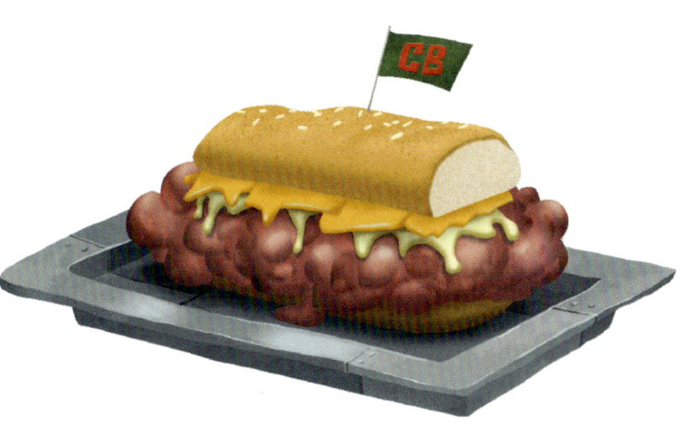

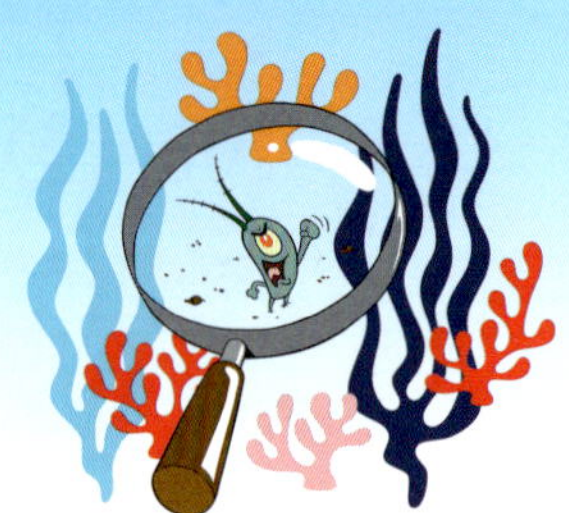

PLANKTON & KAREN'S HISTORY

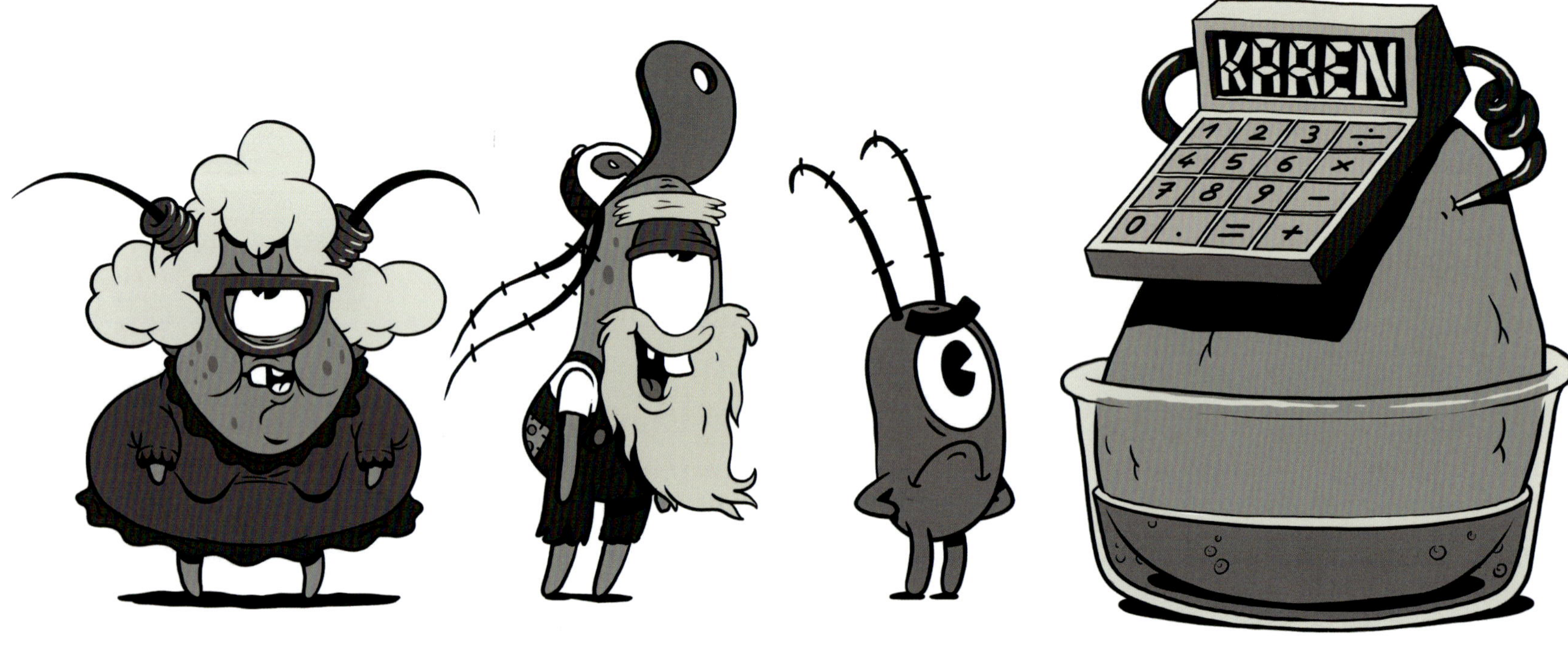

Final art of some of Plankton's family, plus the new friend he made from a potato and a calculator [upper], and black-and-white concept art [lower]

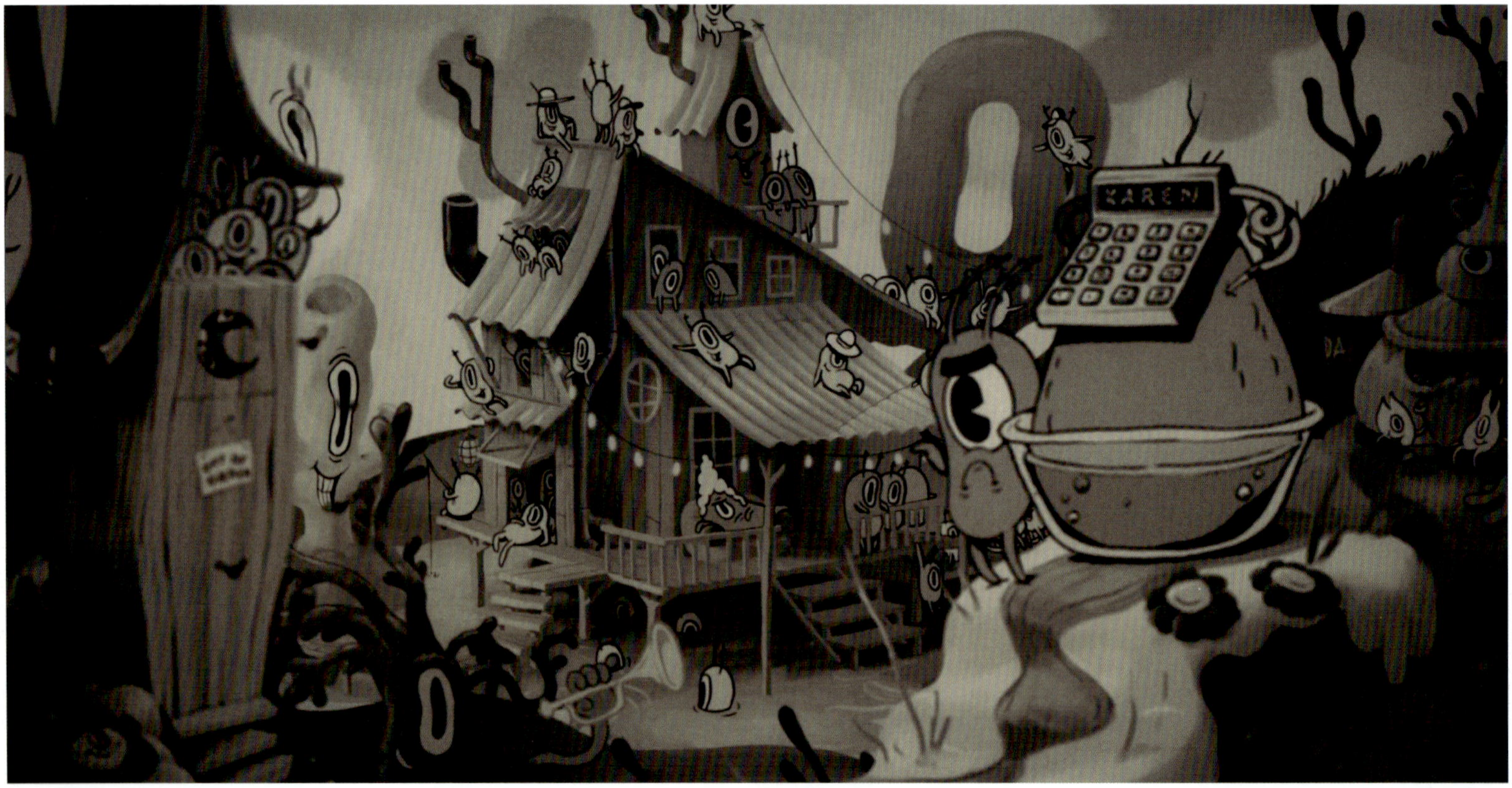

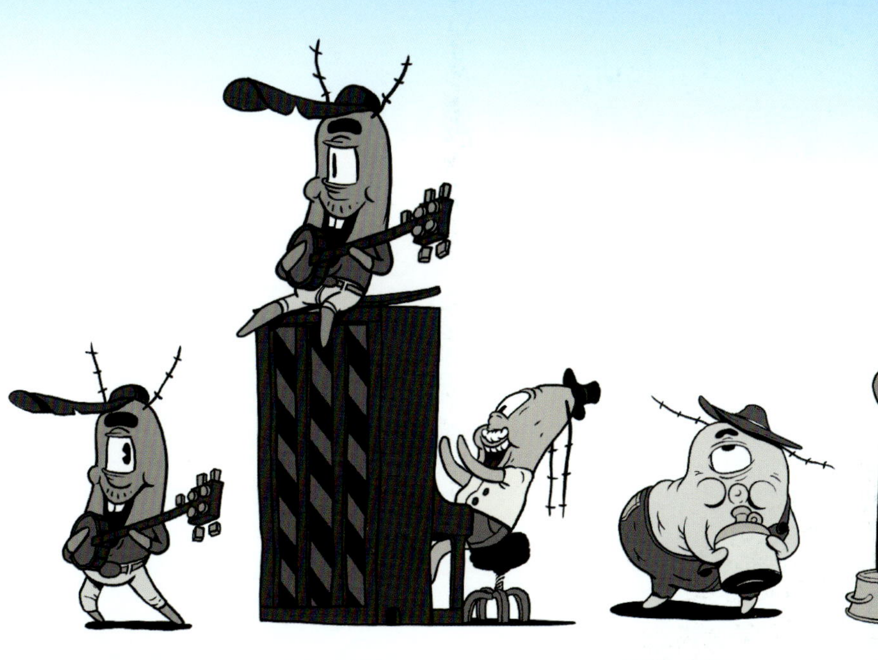

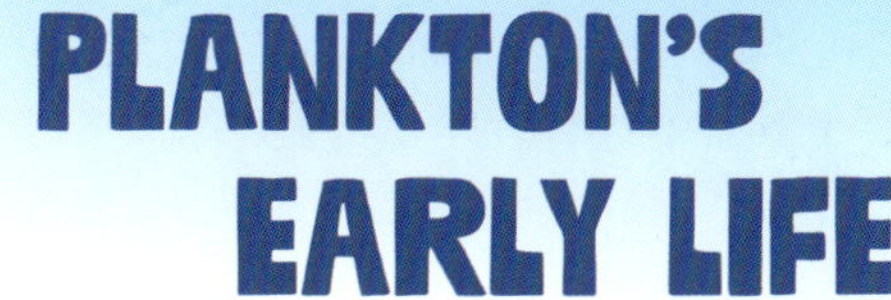

PLANKTON'S EARLY LIFE

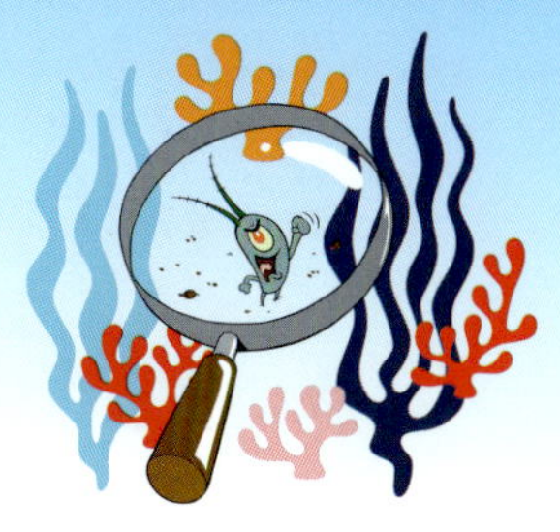

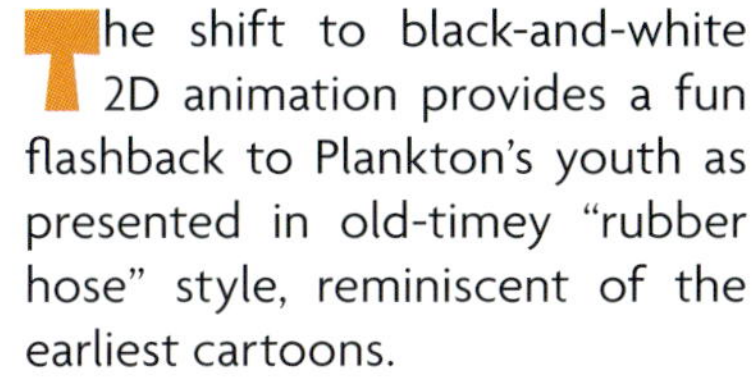

The shift to black-and-white 2D animation provides a fun flashback to Plankton's youth as presented in old-timey "rubber hose" style, reminiscent of the earliest cartoons.

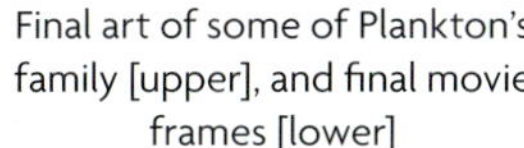

Final art of some of Plankton's family [upper], and final movie frames [lower]

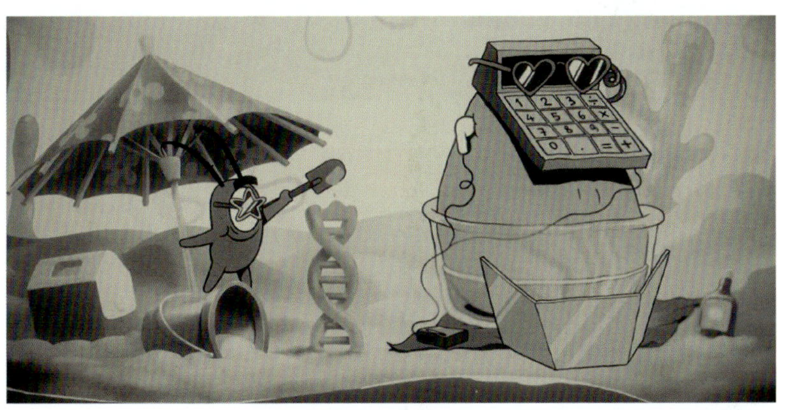

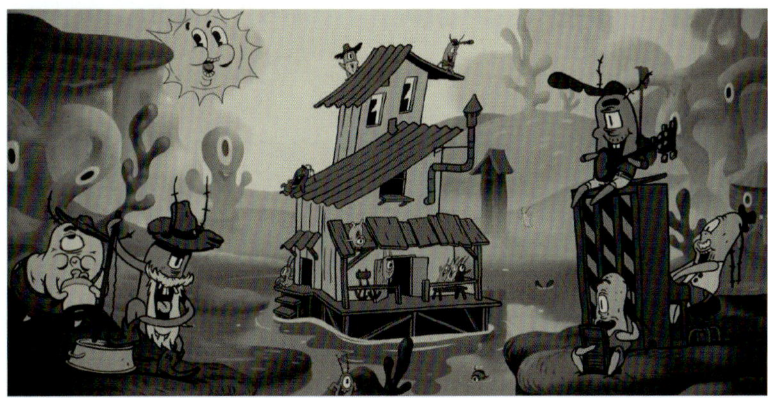

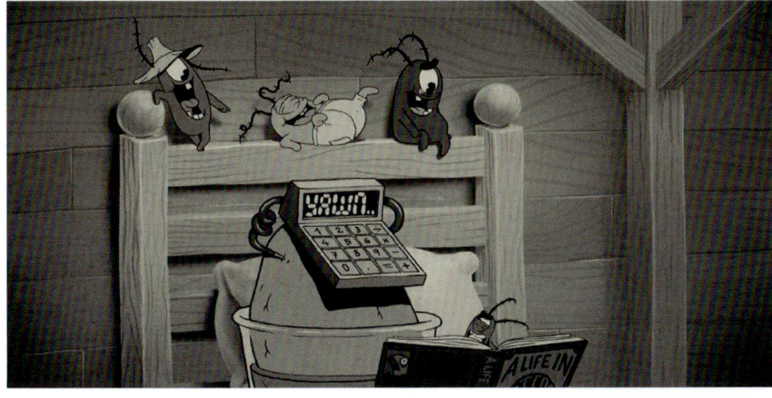

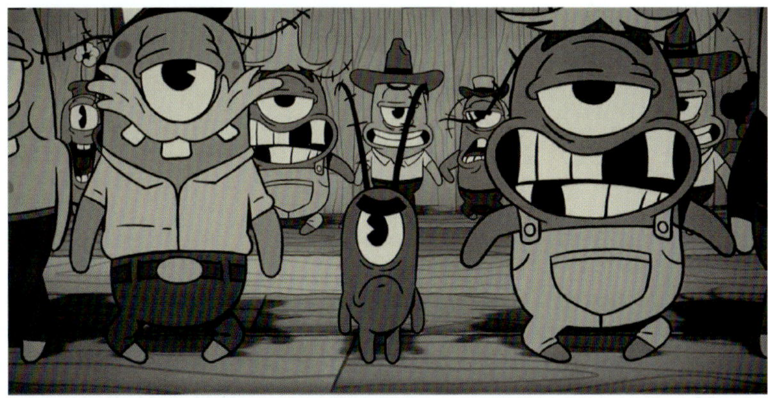

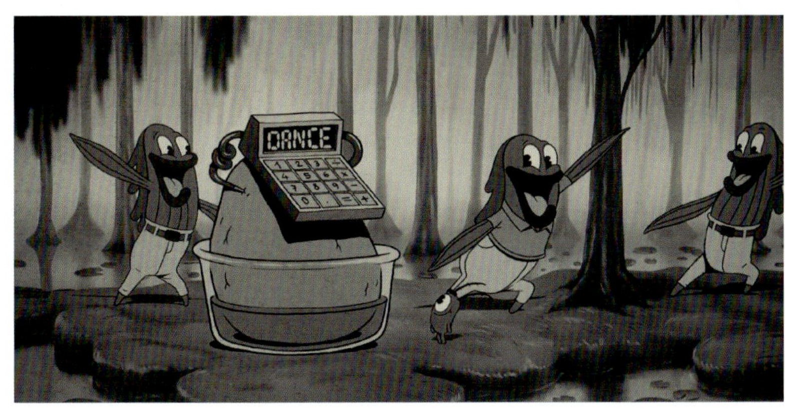

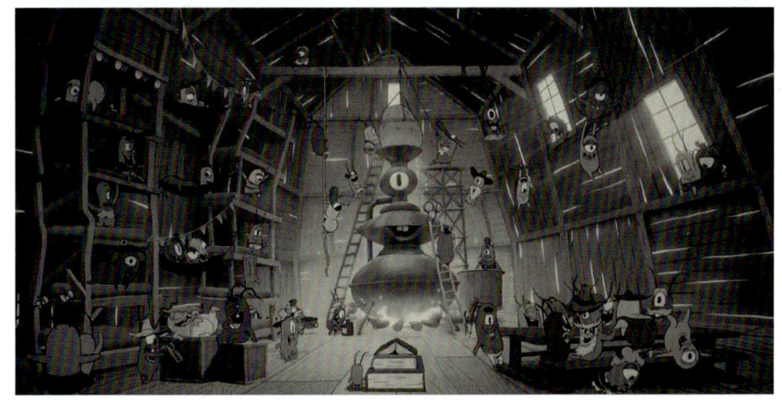

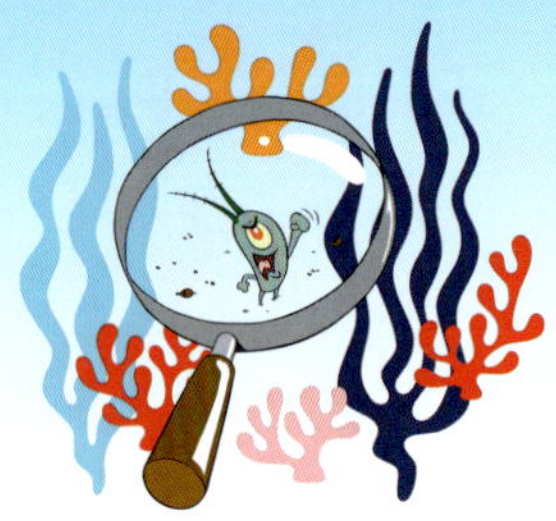

CALCULATOR + POTATO = LOVE

From their first moments of spudding love when Plankton built Karen, the numbers just added up that these two would make a nice pair.

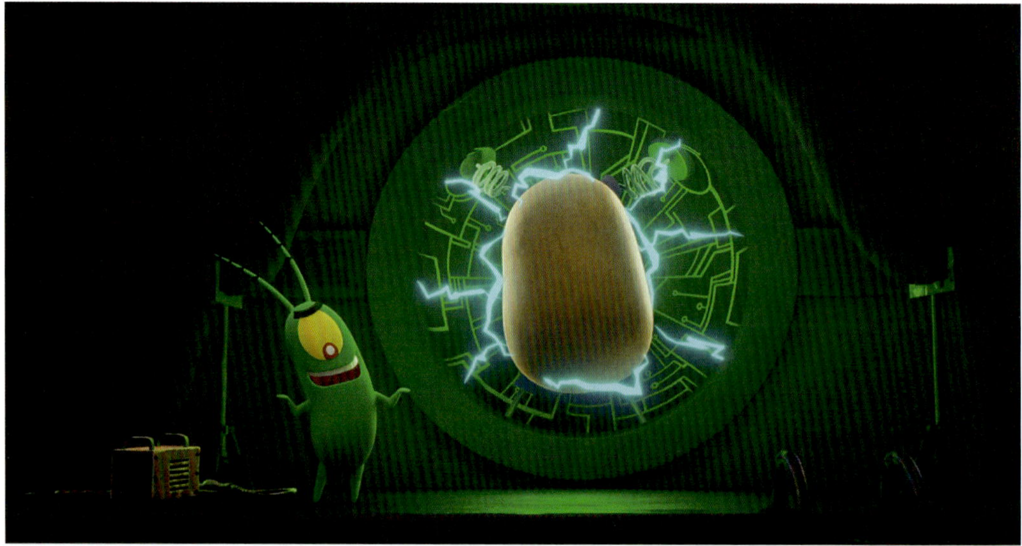

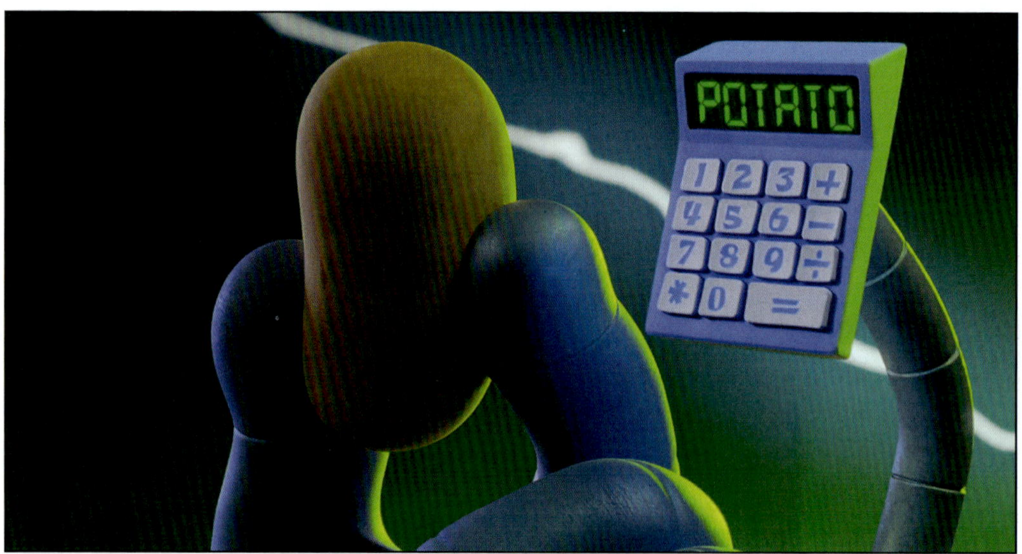

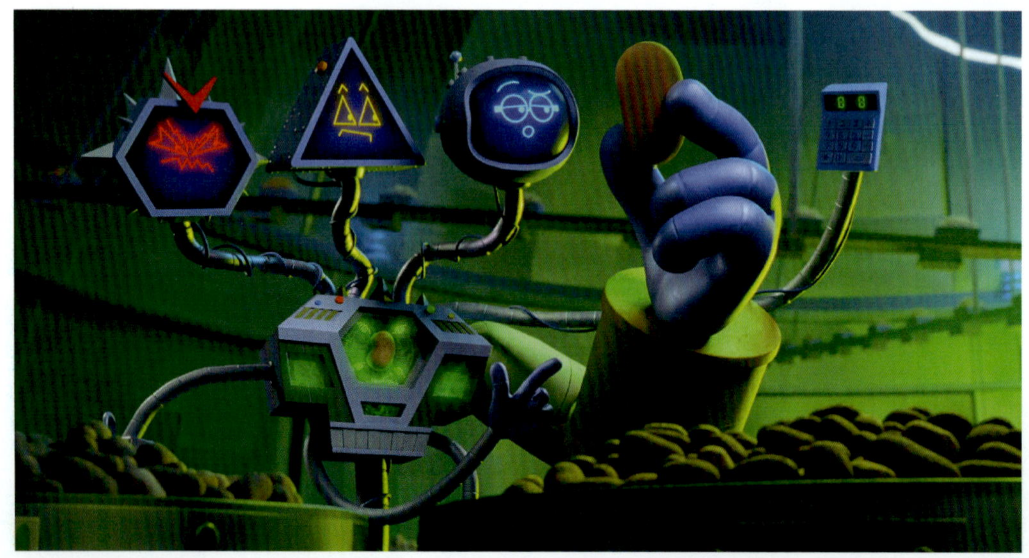

Final frame images of Plankton and Karen recognizing the power of the potato

BIKINI STATE UNIVERSITY

Final art expressions of Karen [upper]; movie moment beat of Plankton building Karen, with her Empathy Chip in hand [lower]

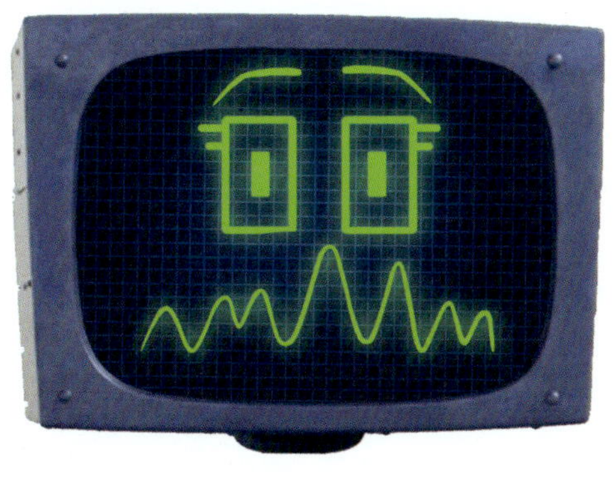

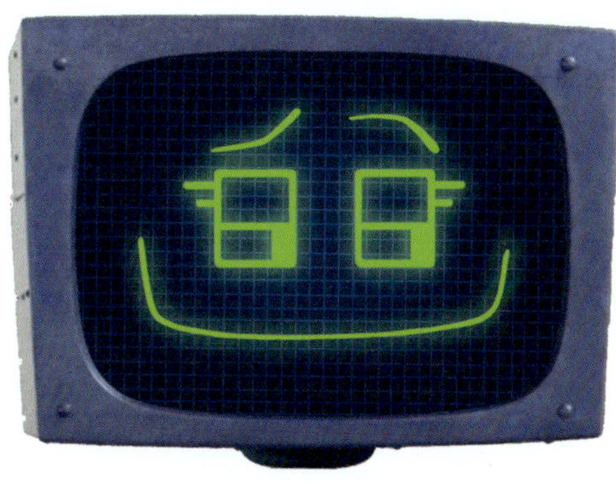

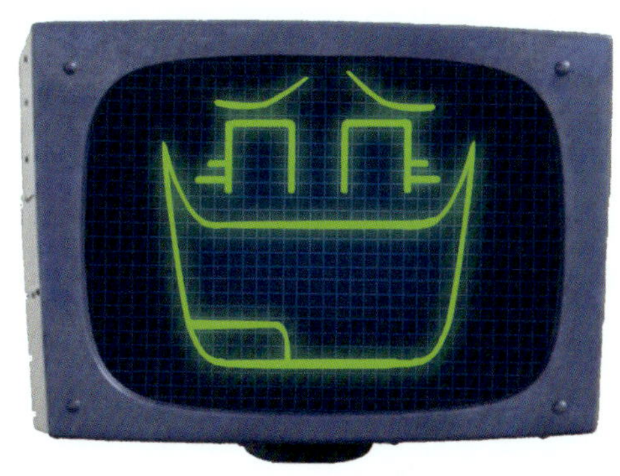

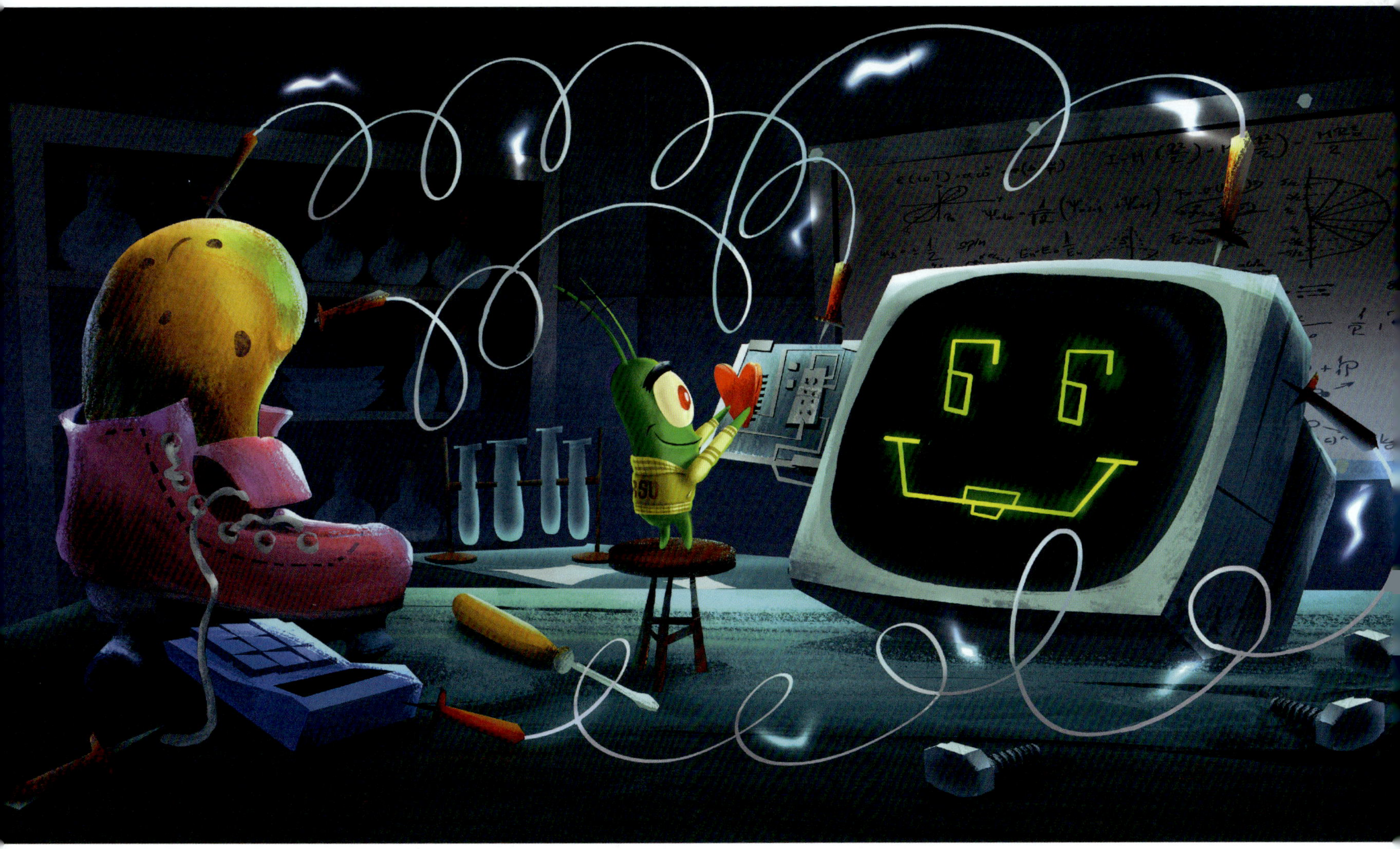

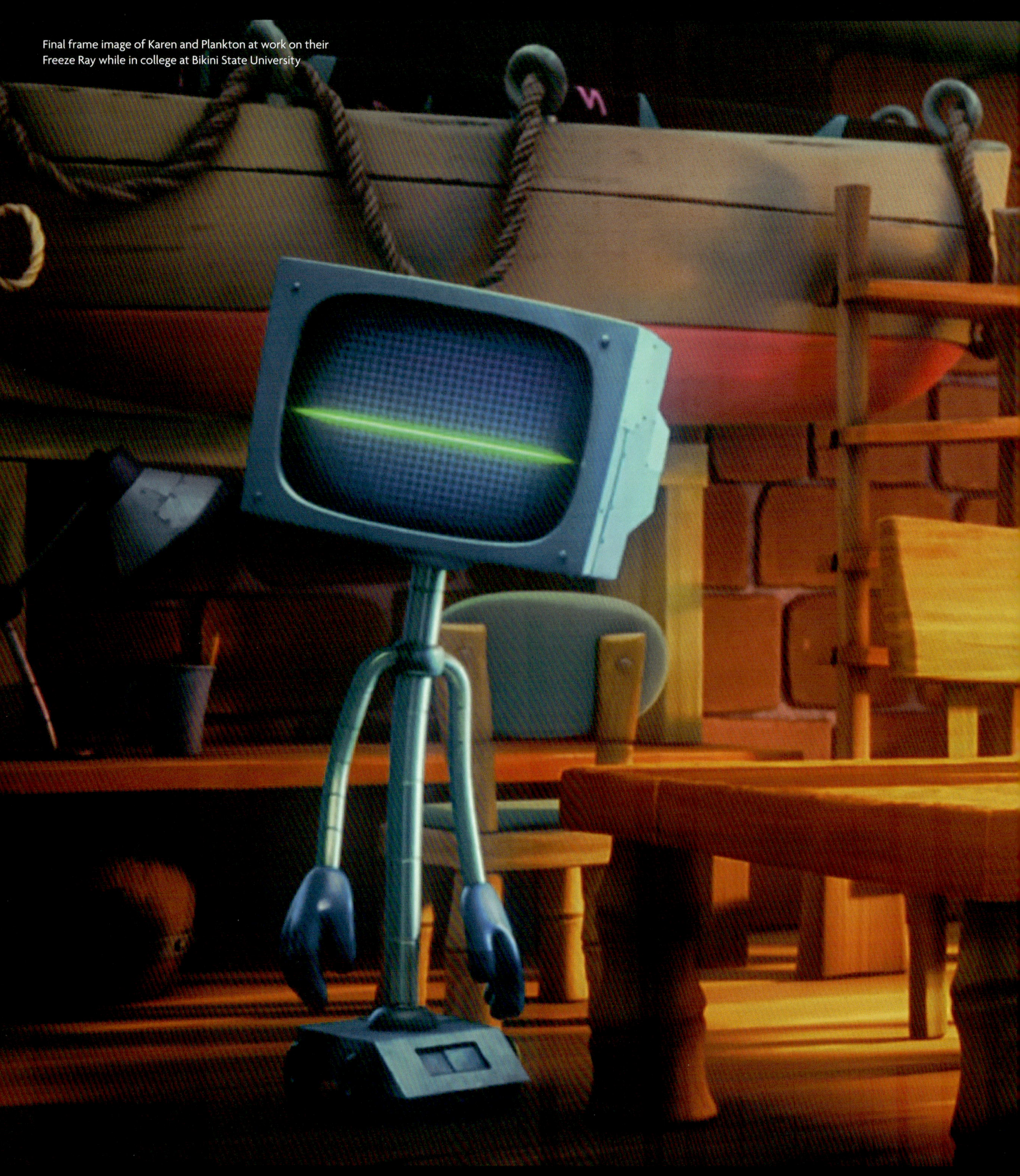

Final frame image of Karen and Plankton at work on their Freeze Ray while in college at Bikini State University

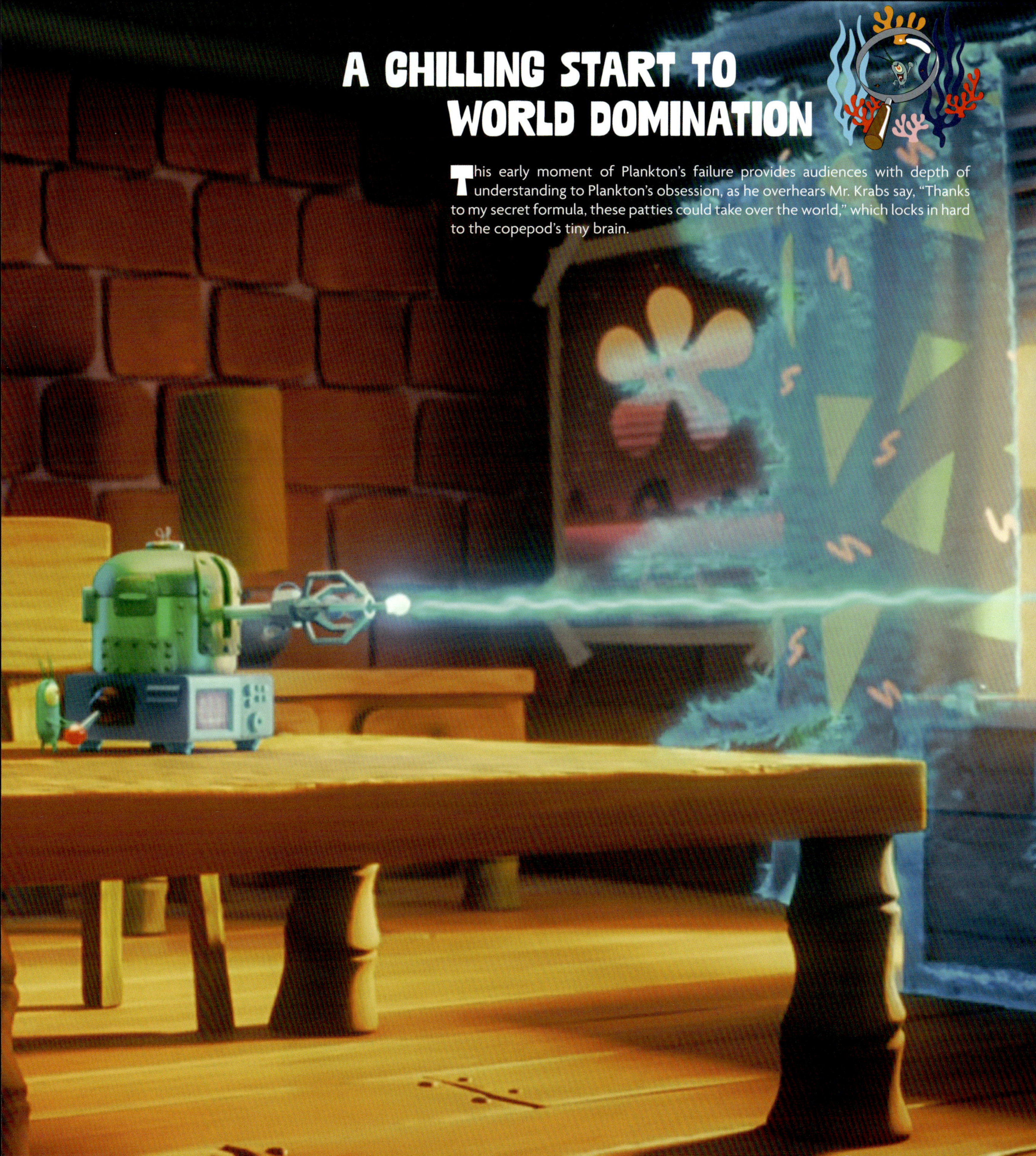

A CHILLING START TO WORLD DOMINATION

This early moment of Plankton's failure provides audiences with depth of understanding to Plankton's obsession, as he overhears Mr. Krabs say, "Thanks to my secret formula, these patties could take over the world," which locks in hard to the copepod's tiny brain.

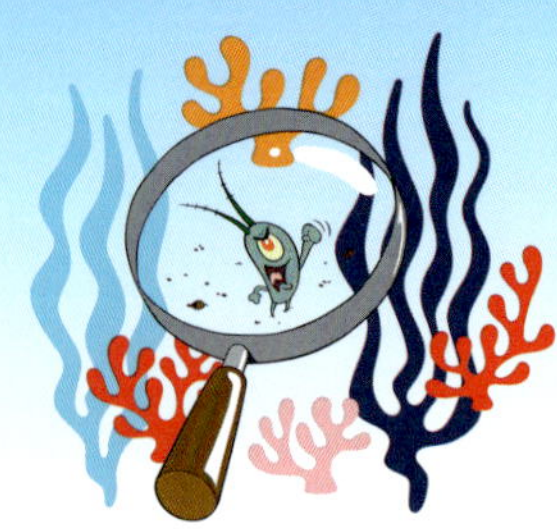

KAREN GOES FULL HYDRA

The stakes escalate quickly when Plankton gets on Karen's last wire... and the three-headed Karen is not afraid to sing about how she can be the real evil mastermind, in cool retro 2D style. "This movie was fun because the two main characters were adults and so their emotions and motivations were more mature—while at the same time exaggerated and comical," says writer Kaz.

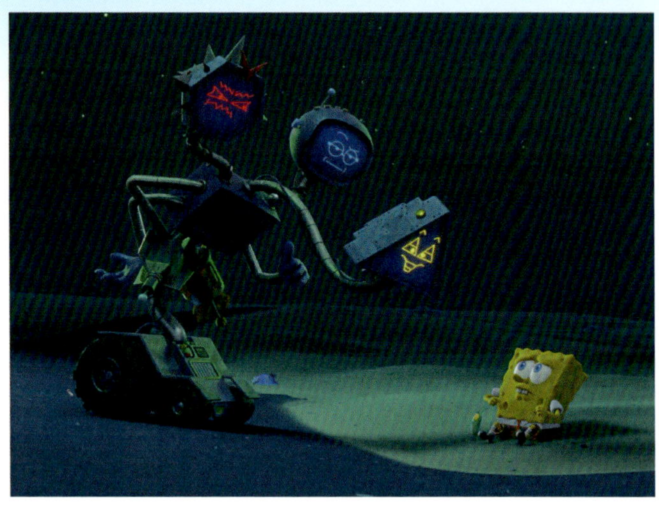

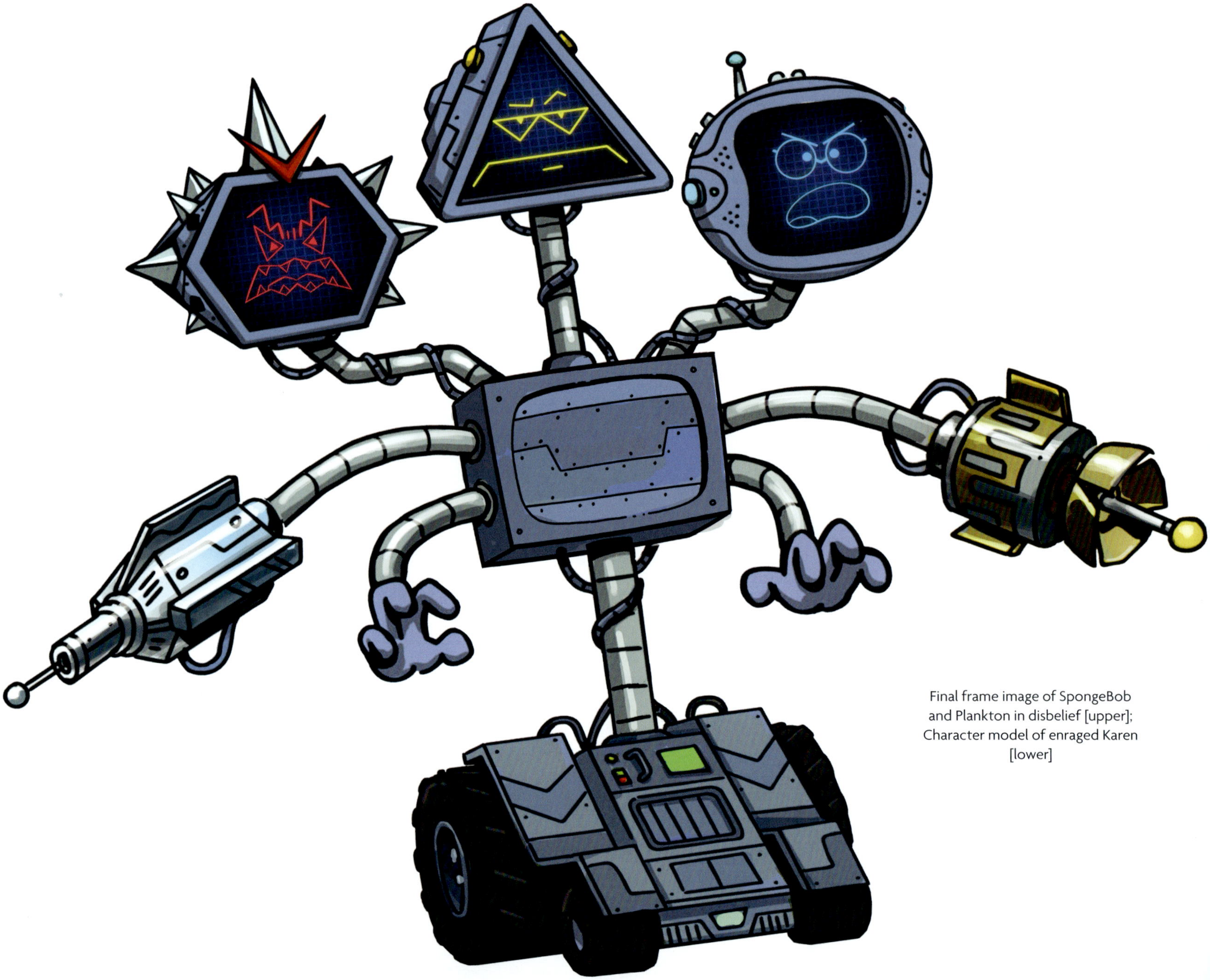

Final frame image of SpongeBob and Plankton in disbelief [upper]; Character model of enraged Karen [lower]

"SAY MY NAME"

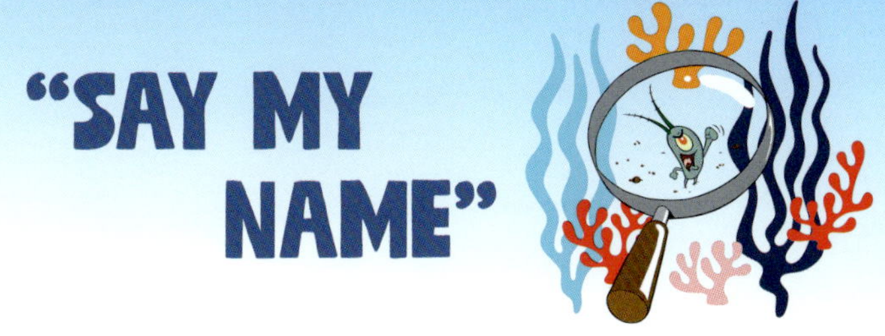

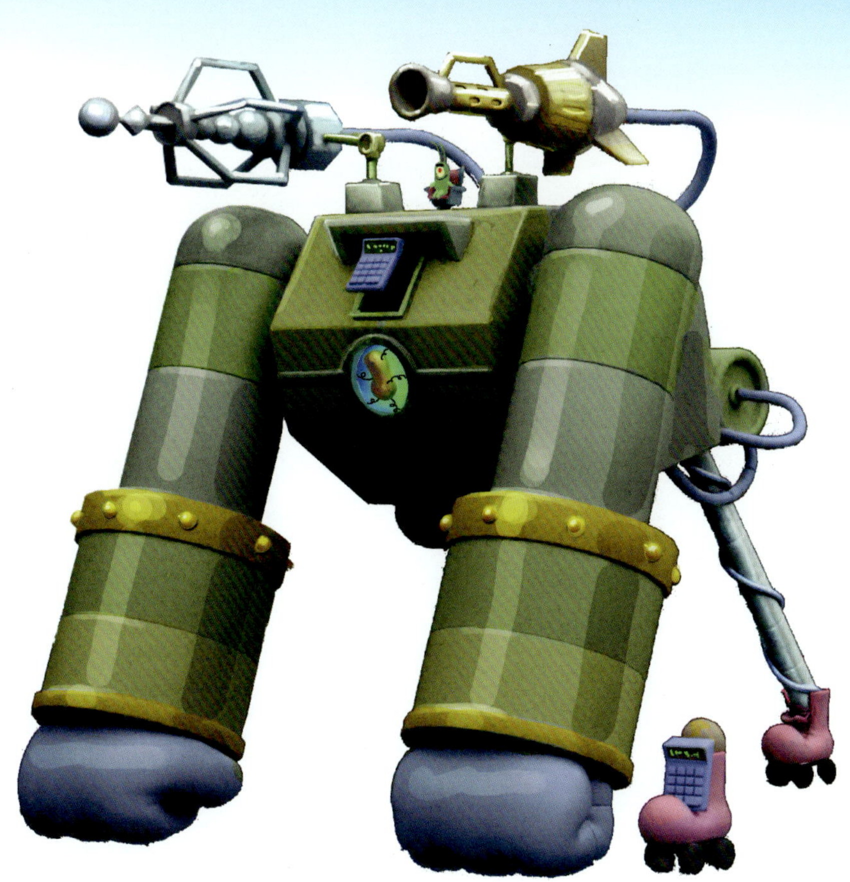

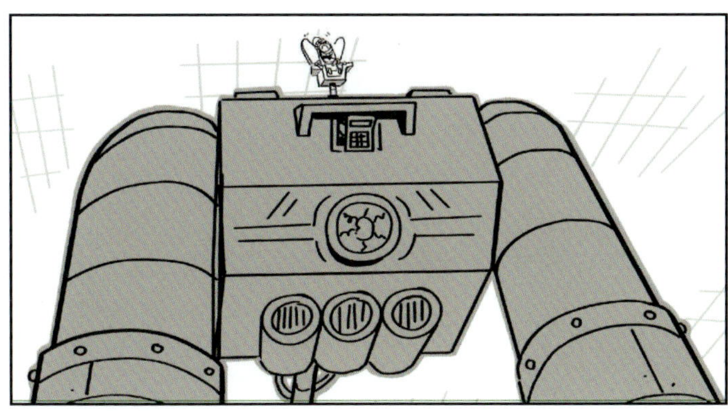

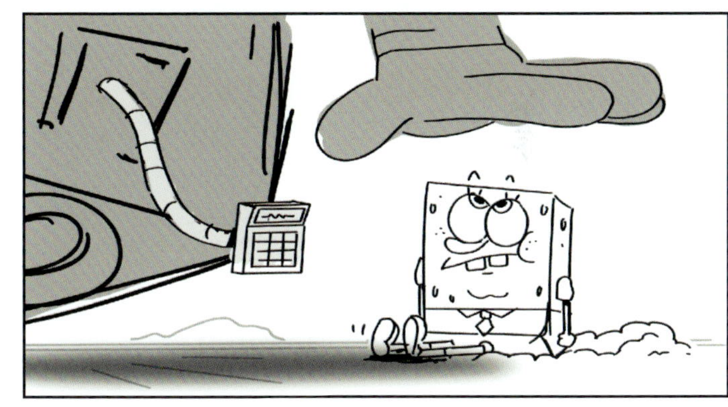

CG art of "New Karen" [upper] and old Karen elements [lower]

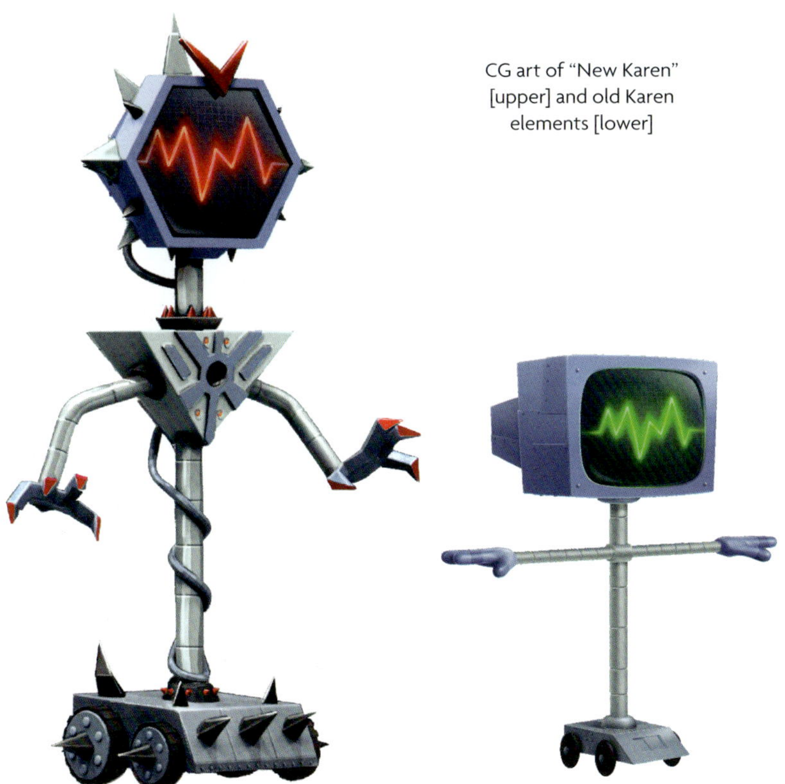

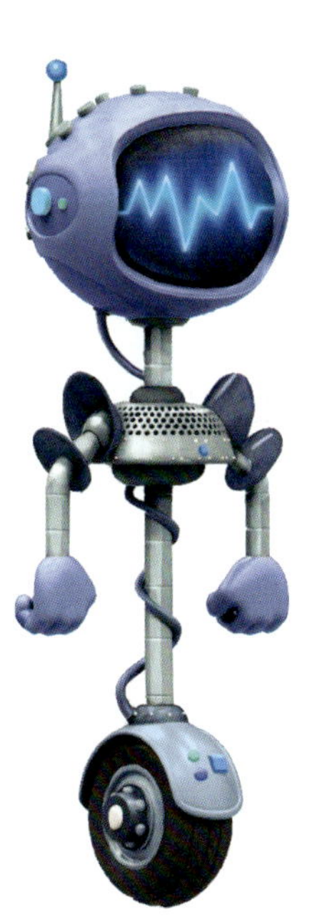

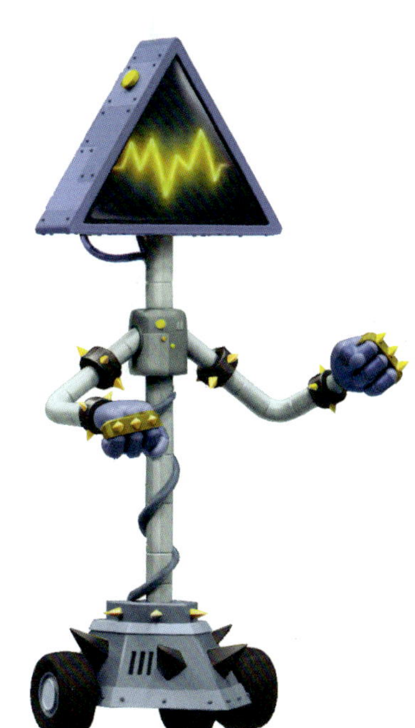

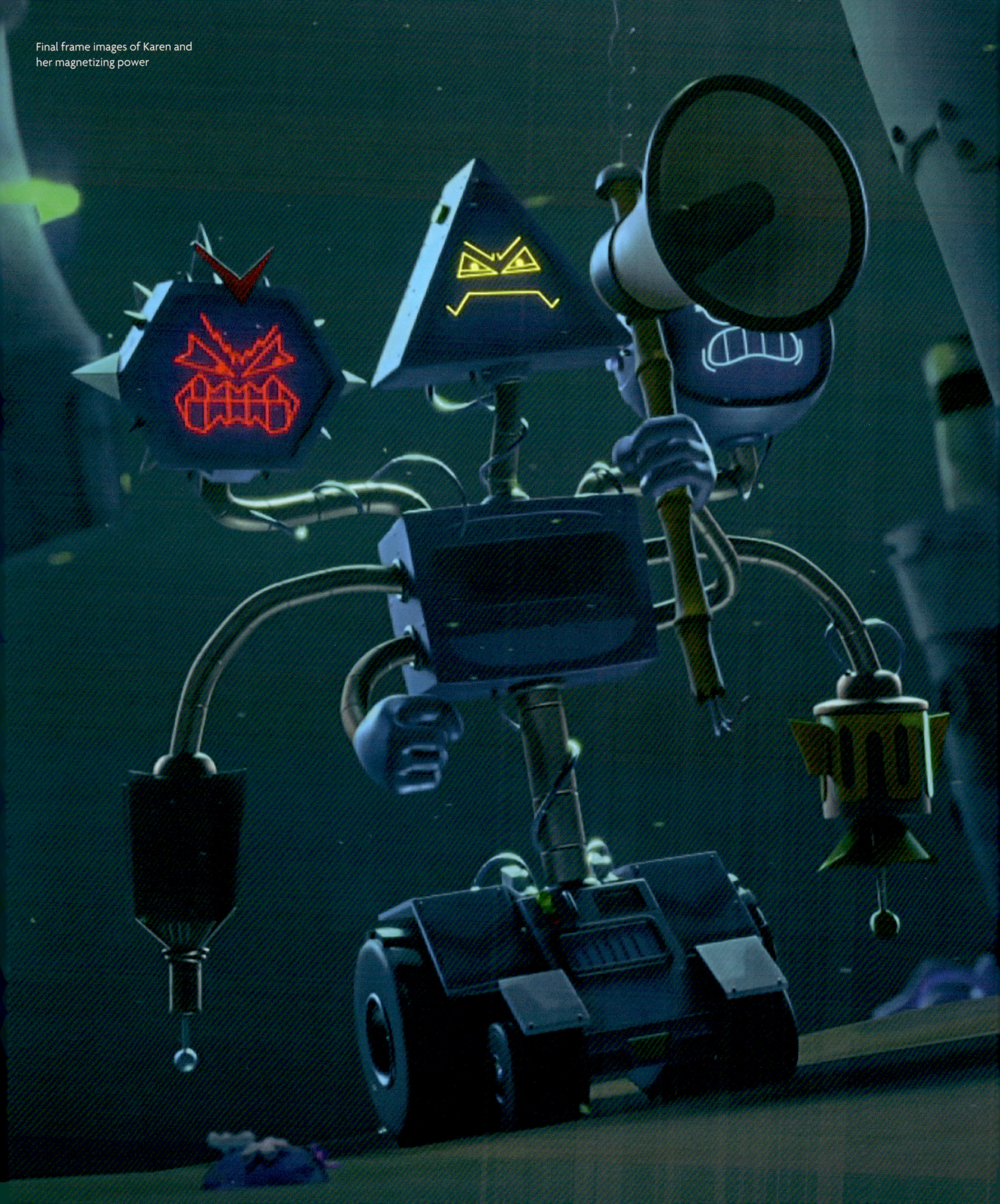

Final frame images of Karen and her magnetizing power

HEAVY METAL ACTION

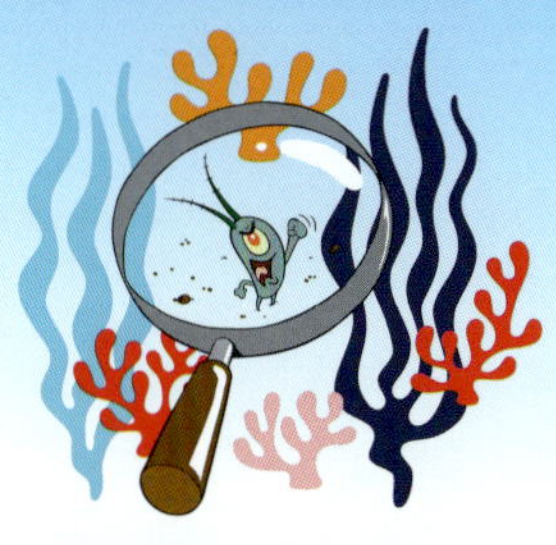

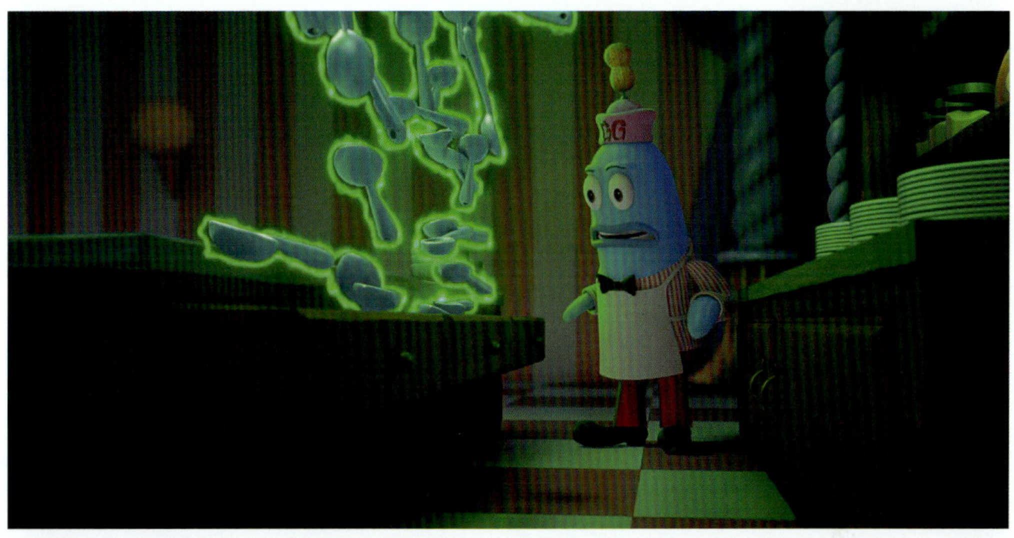

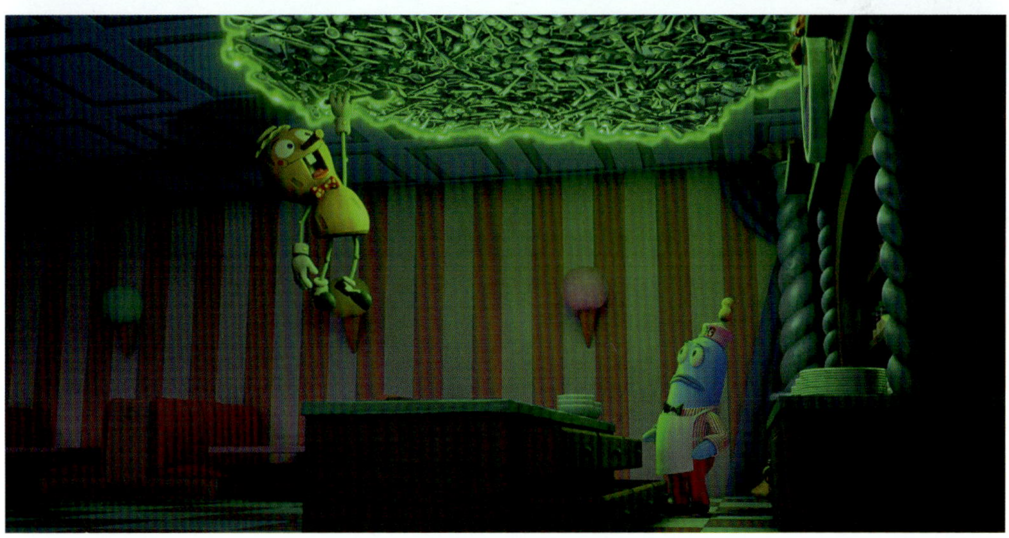

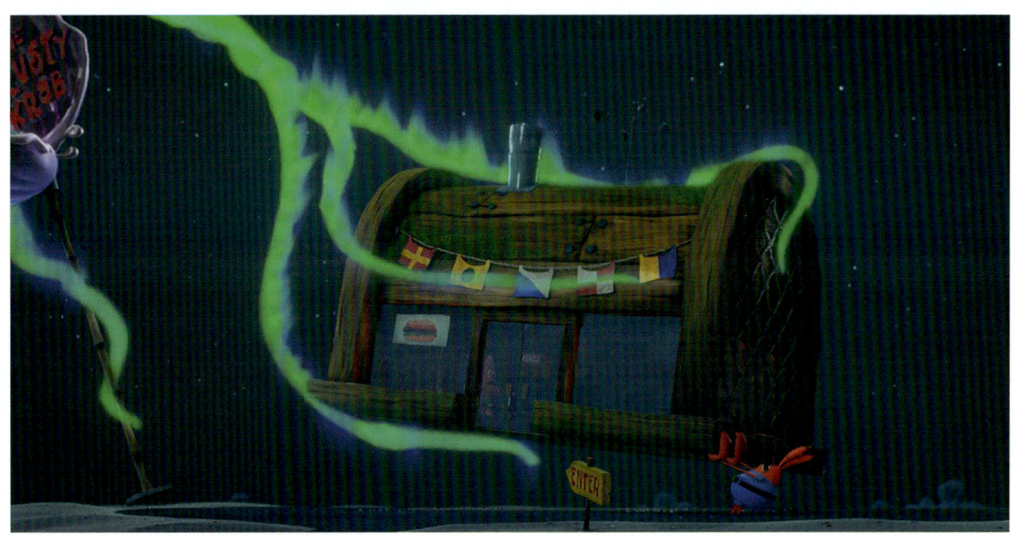

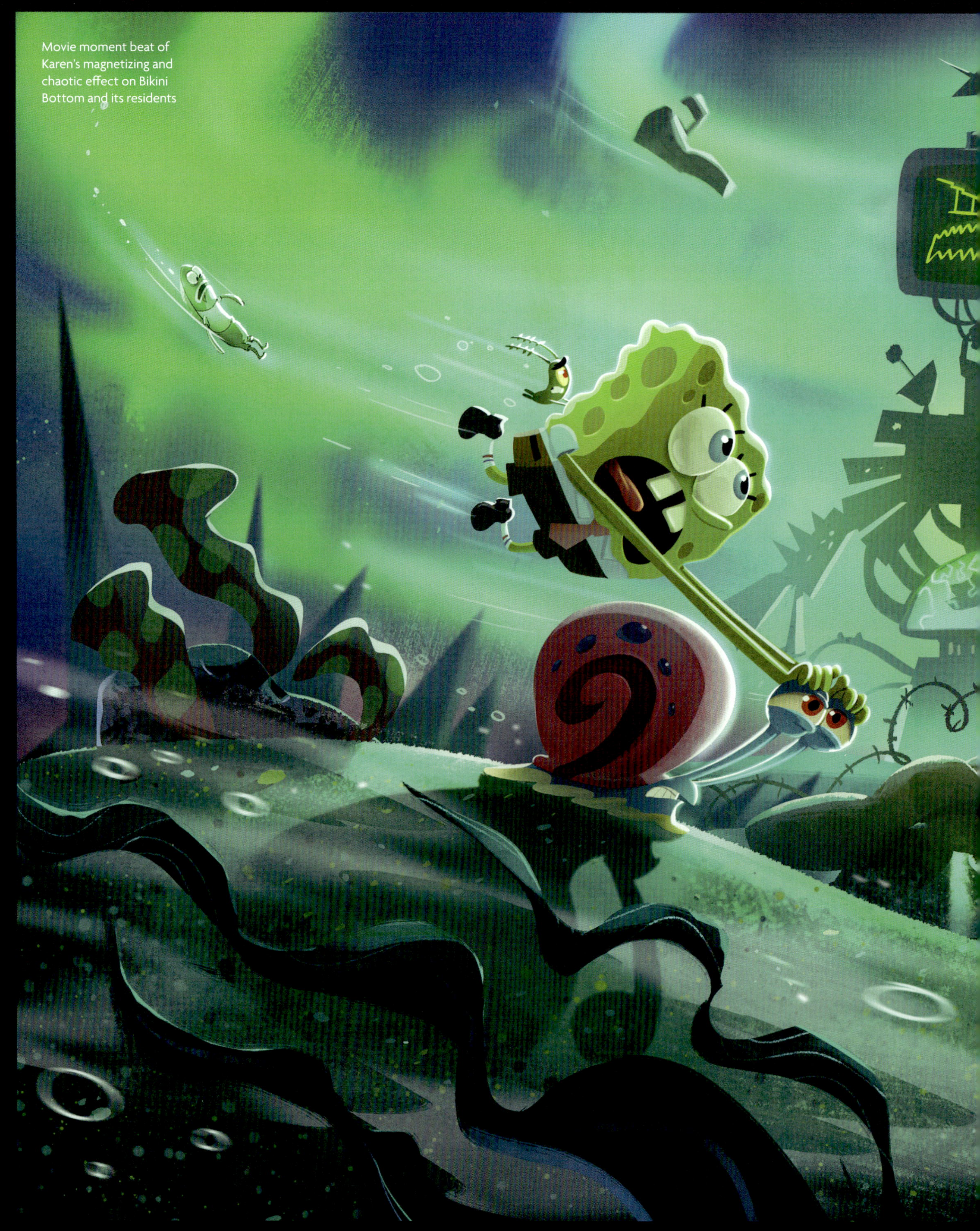

Movie moment beat of Karen's magnetizing and chaotic effect on Bikini Bottom and its residents

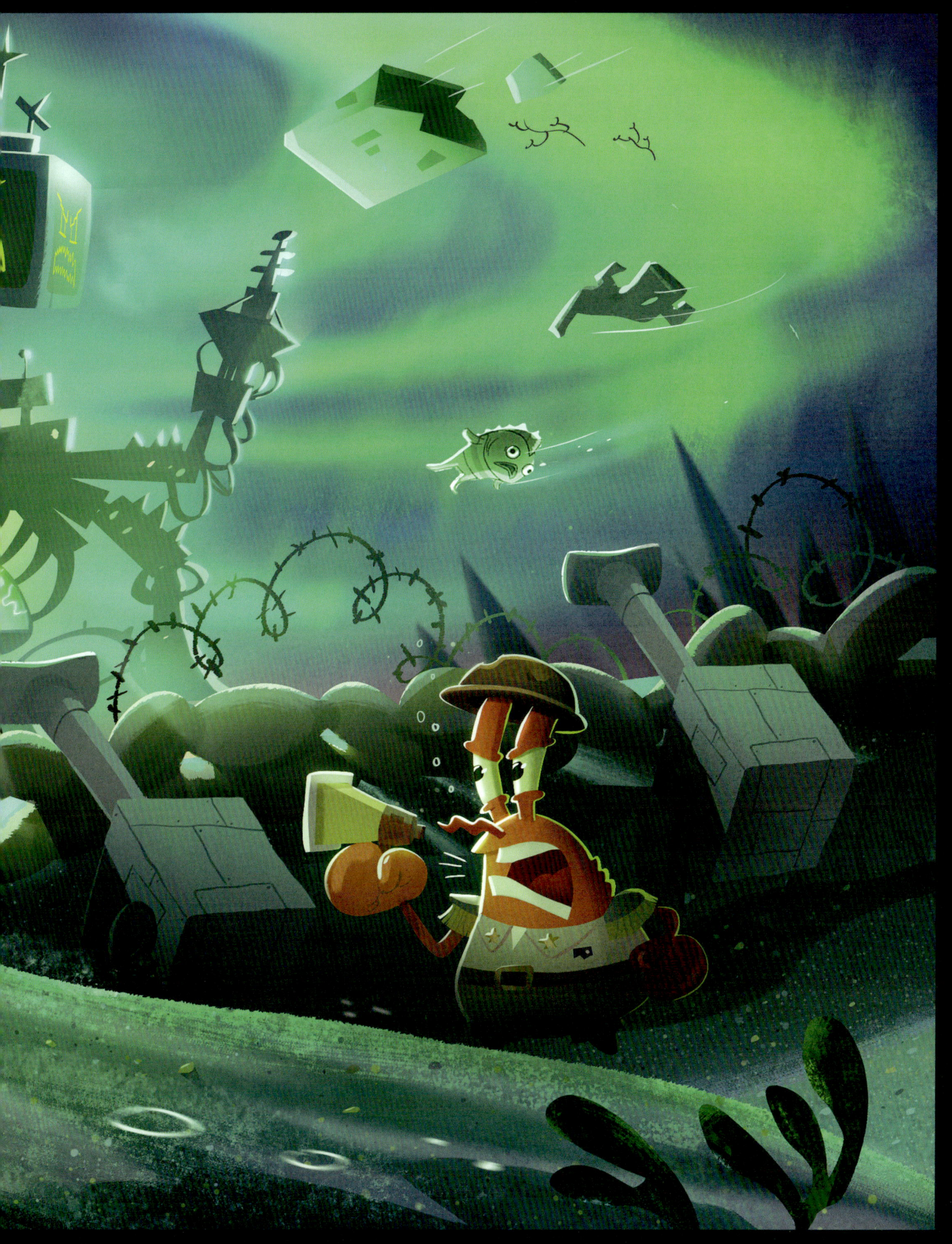

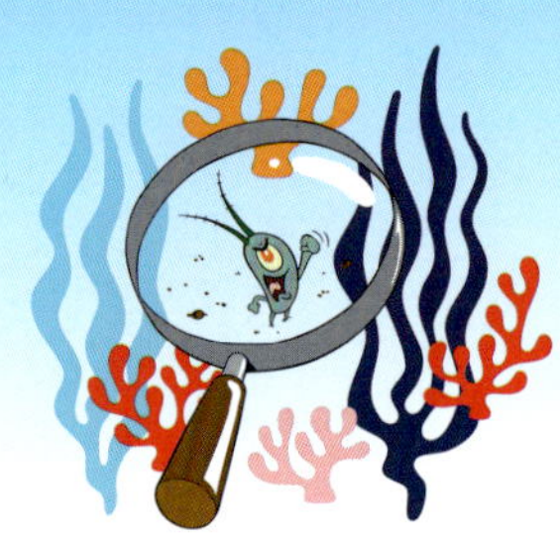

KRABS & TOWN IN UNIFORM

Final frame images of Krabs diving into his military past to lead his fellow Bikini Bottom recruits into battle against Karen

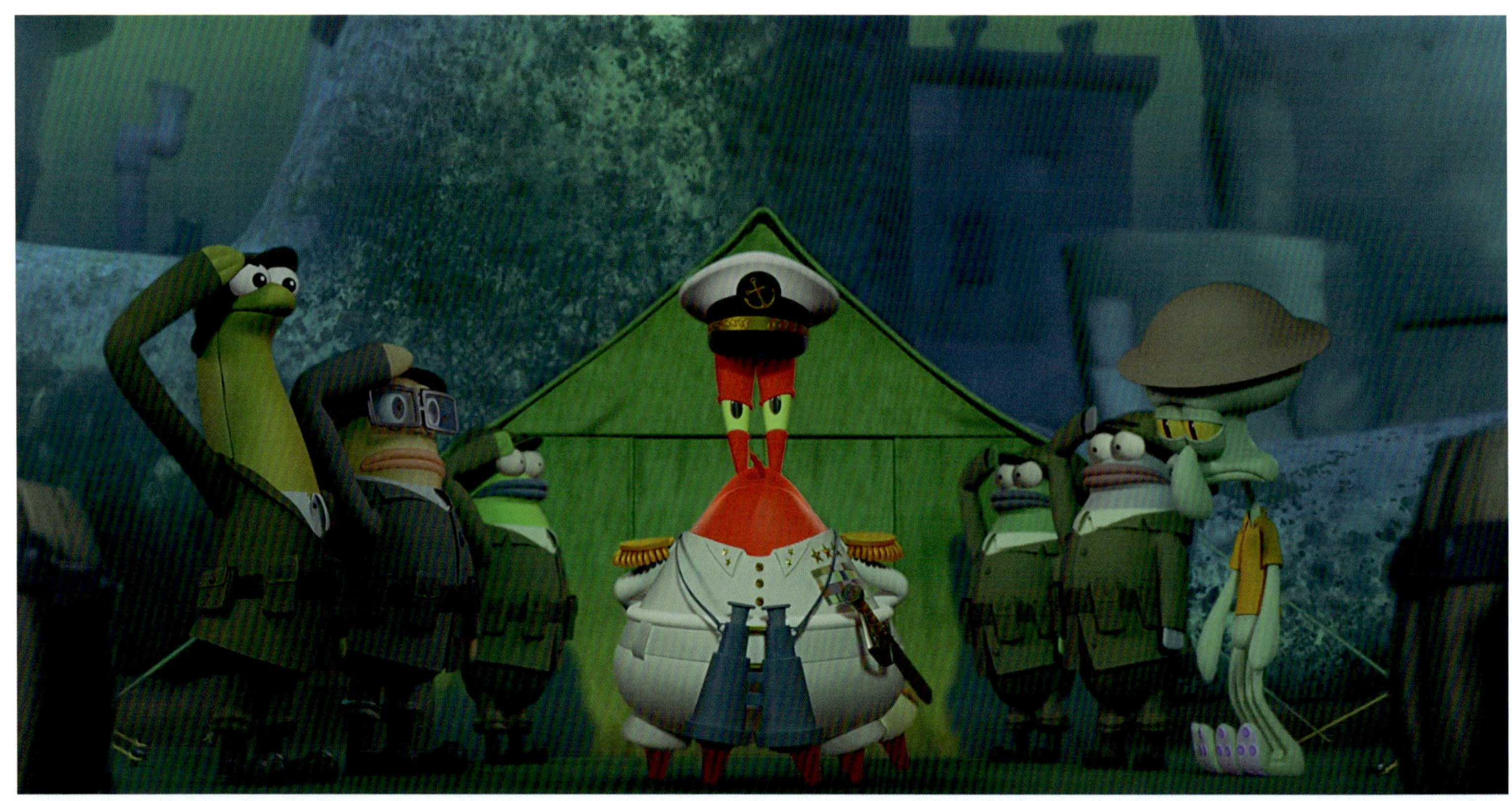

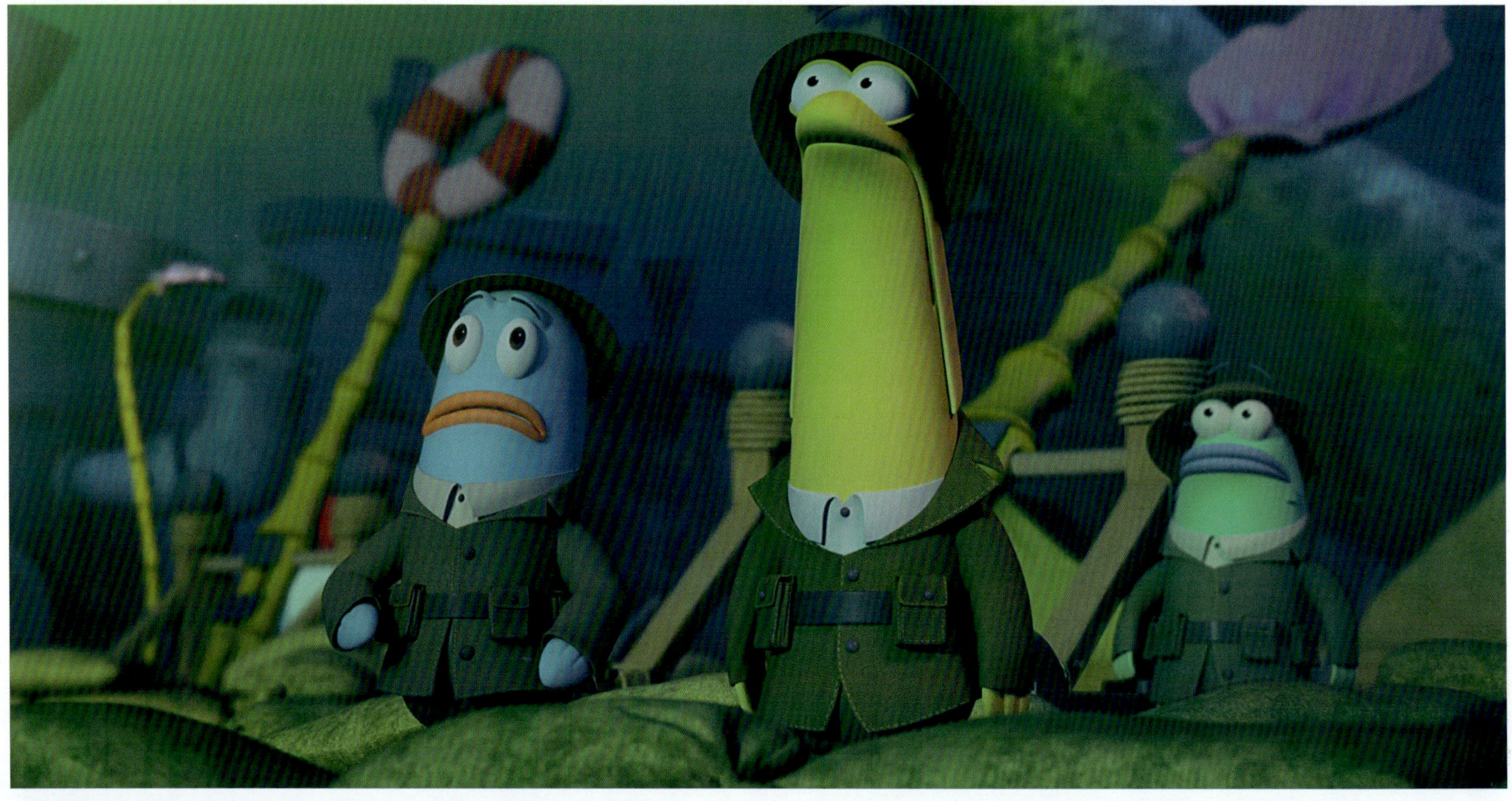

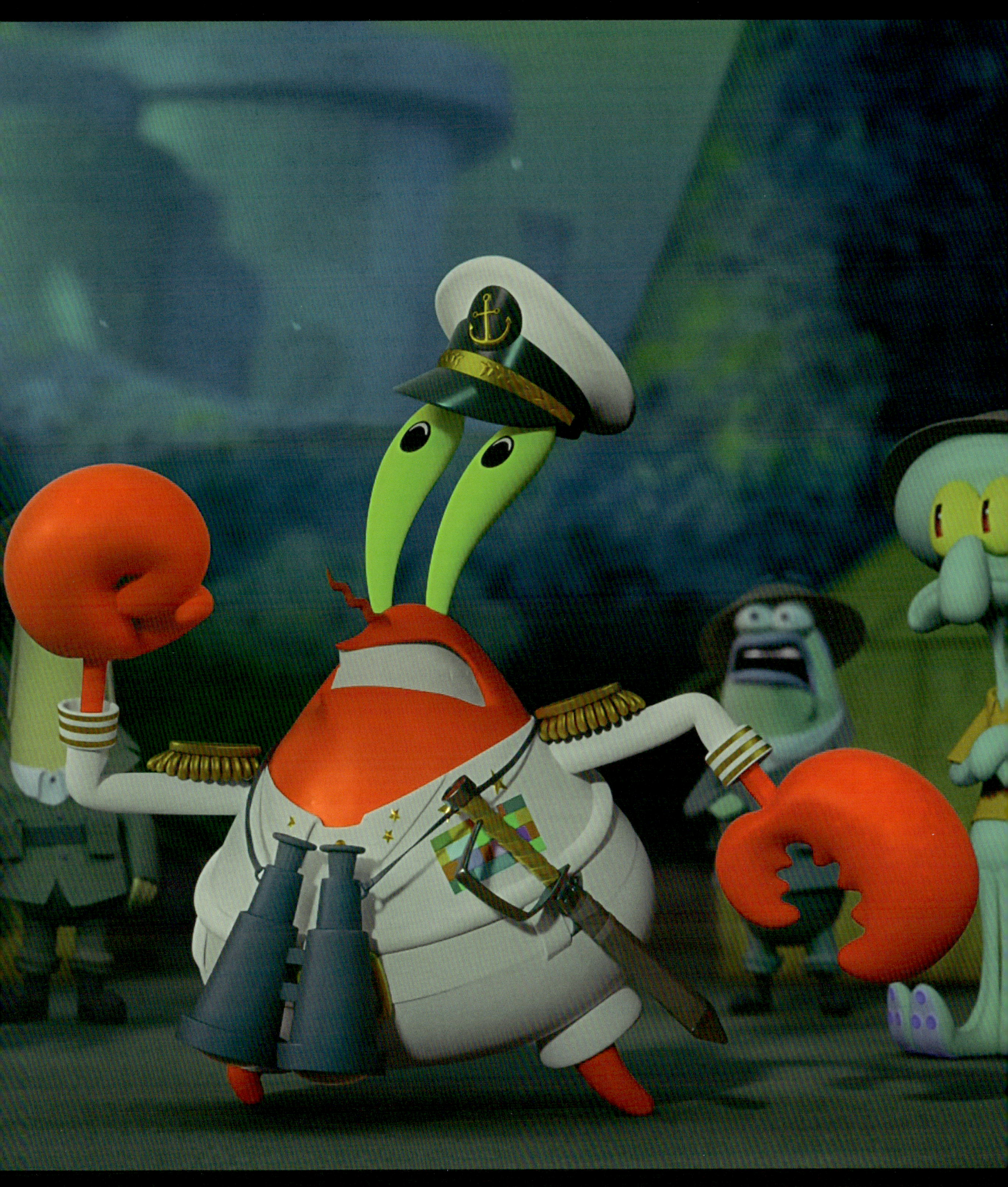

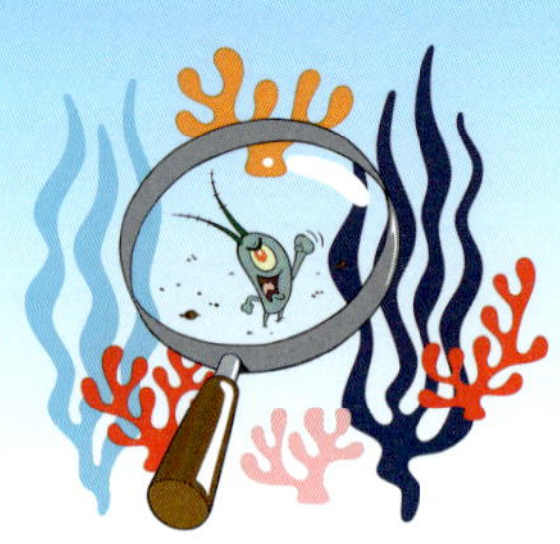

SPONGEBOB, FREUD & PLANKTON TEAM UP

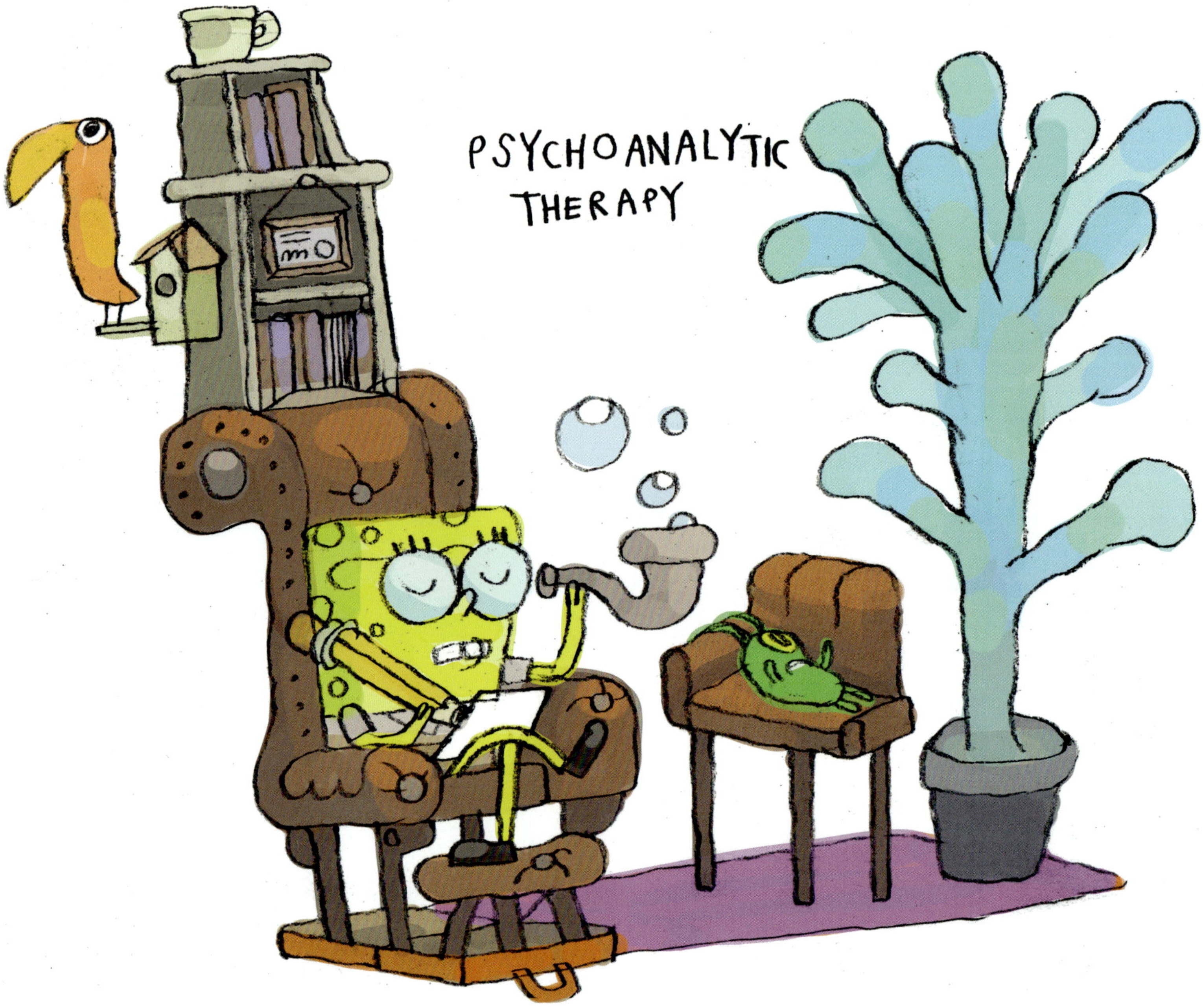

PSYCHOANALYTIC
THERAPY

Concept art of SpongeBob as psychoanalyst for Plankton [left]; Plankton being "nosy" after SpongeBob drags him along on a mission [right]

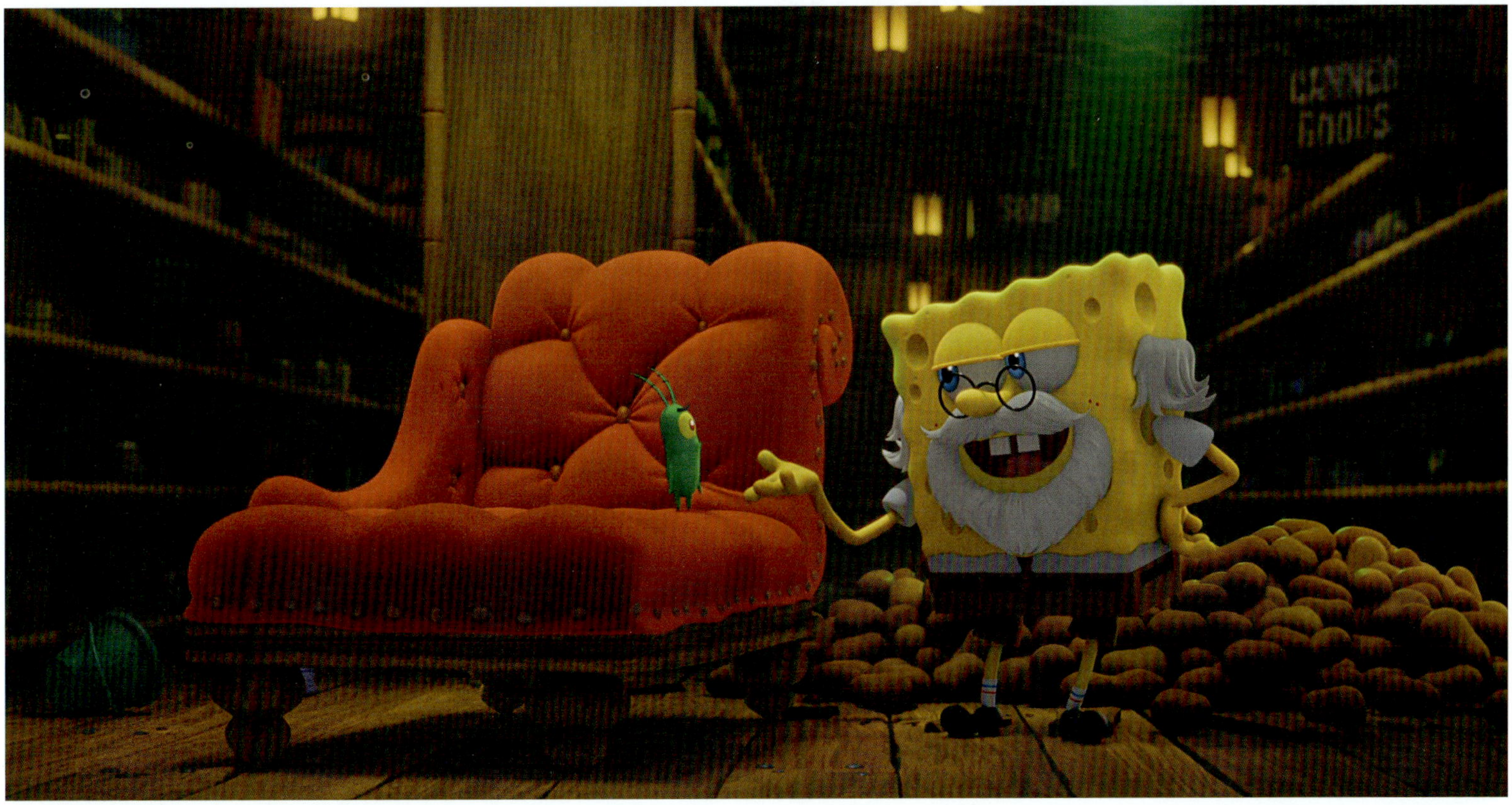

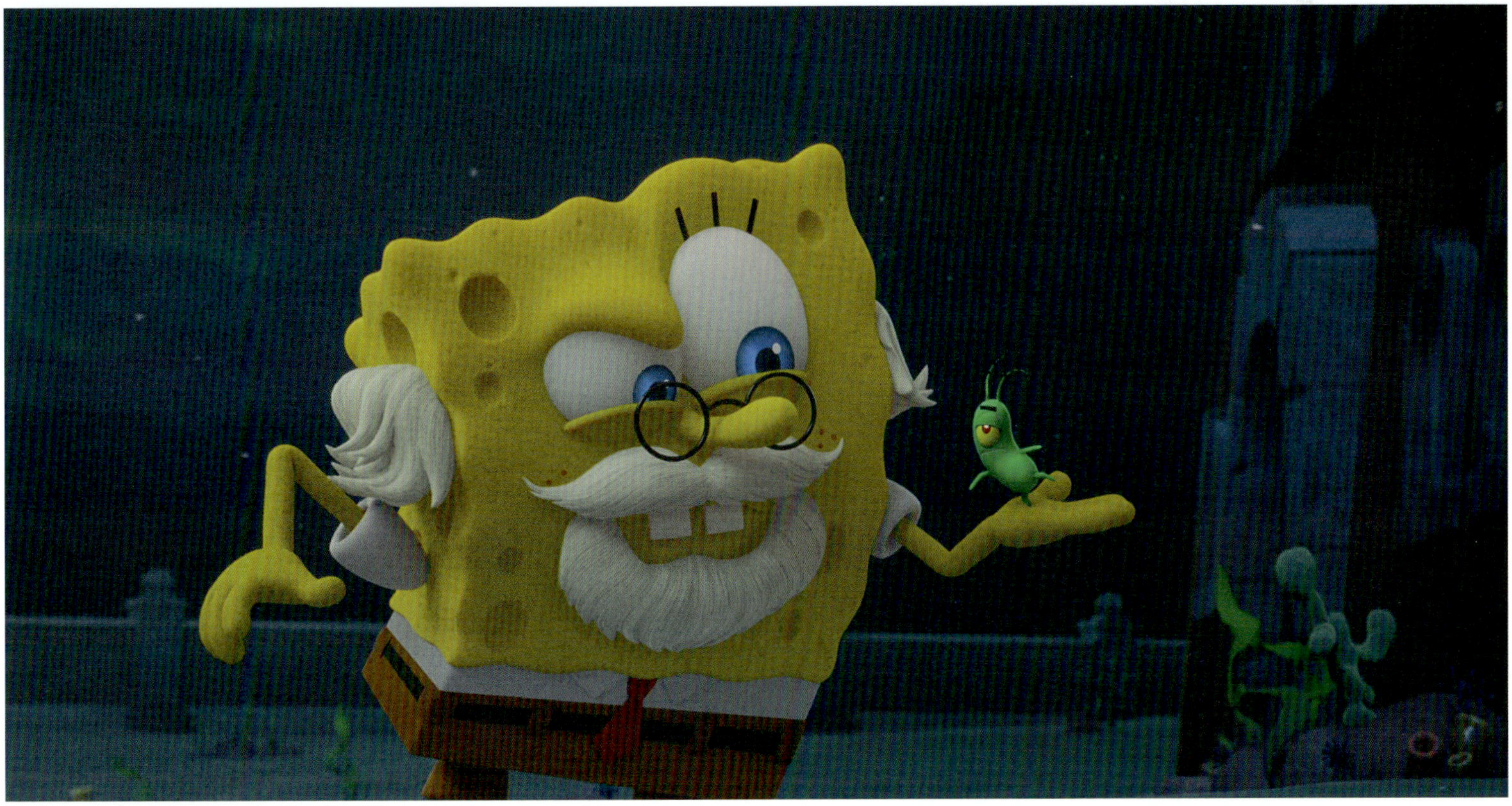

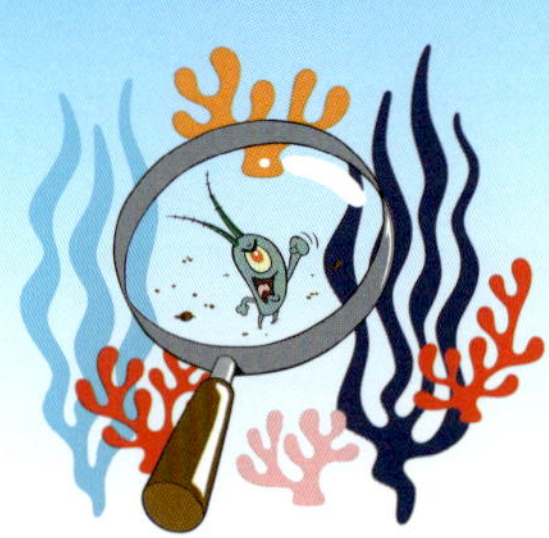

HYPNOSIS INTO HISTORY

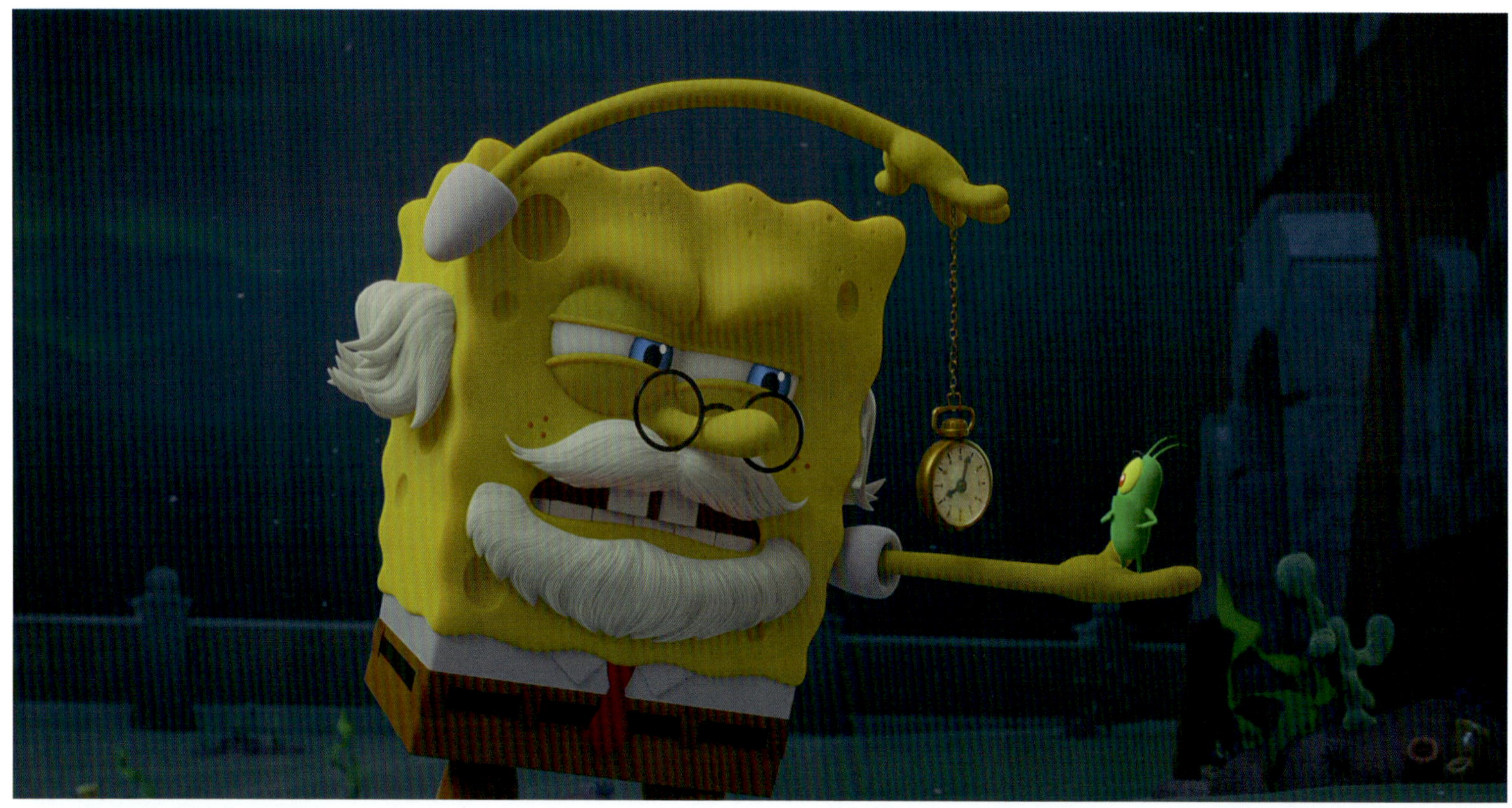

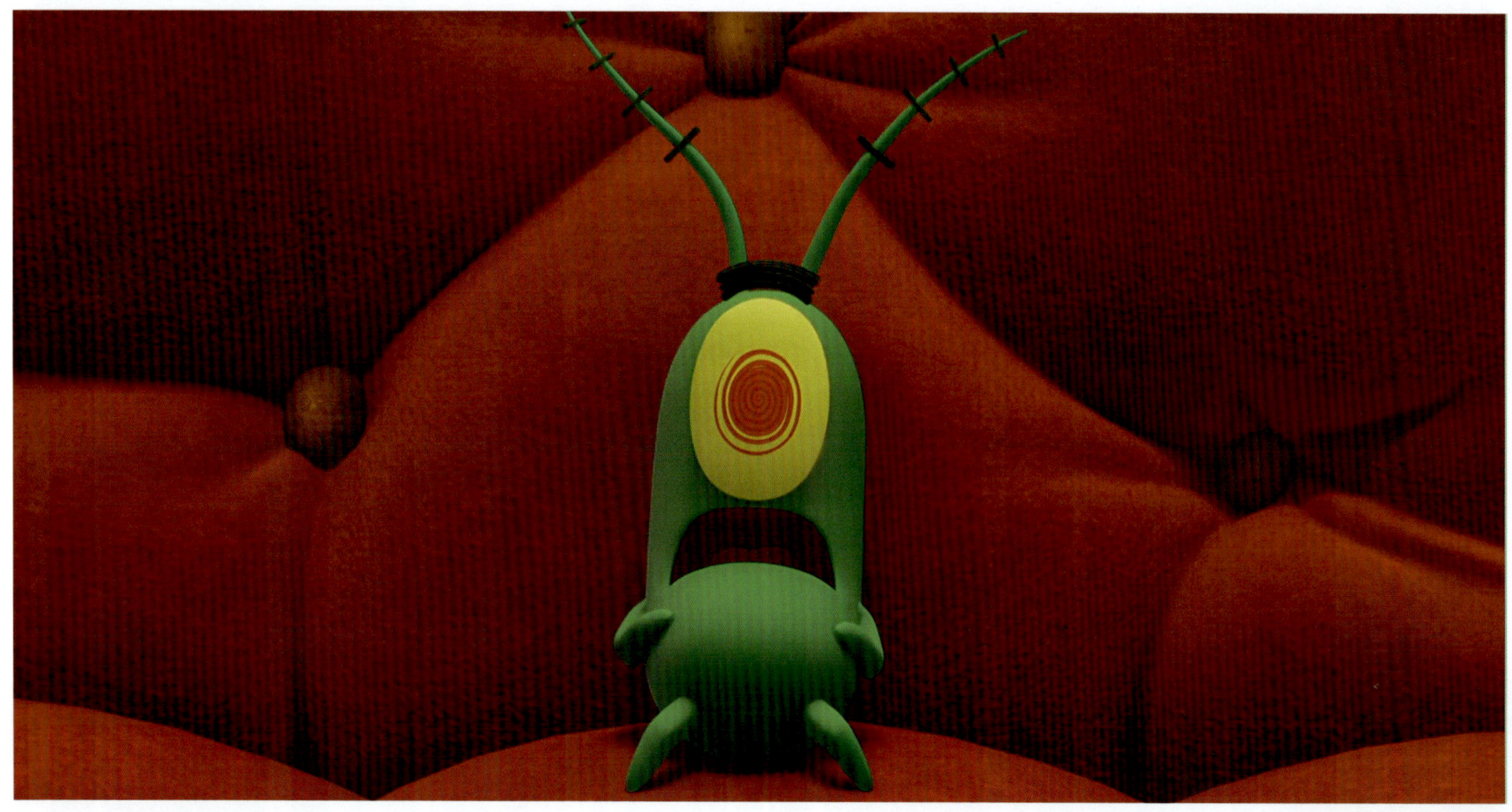

Final frame images of psychoanalyst SpongeBob hypnotizing Plankton into revisiting his history

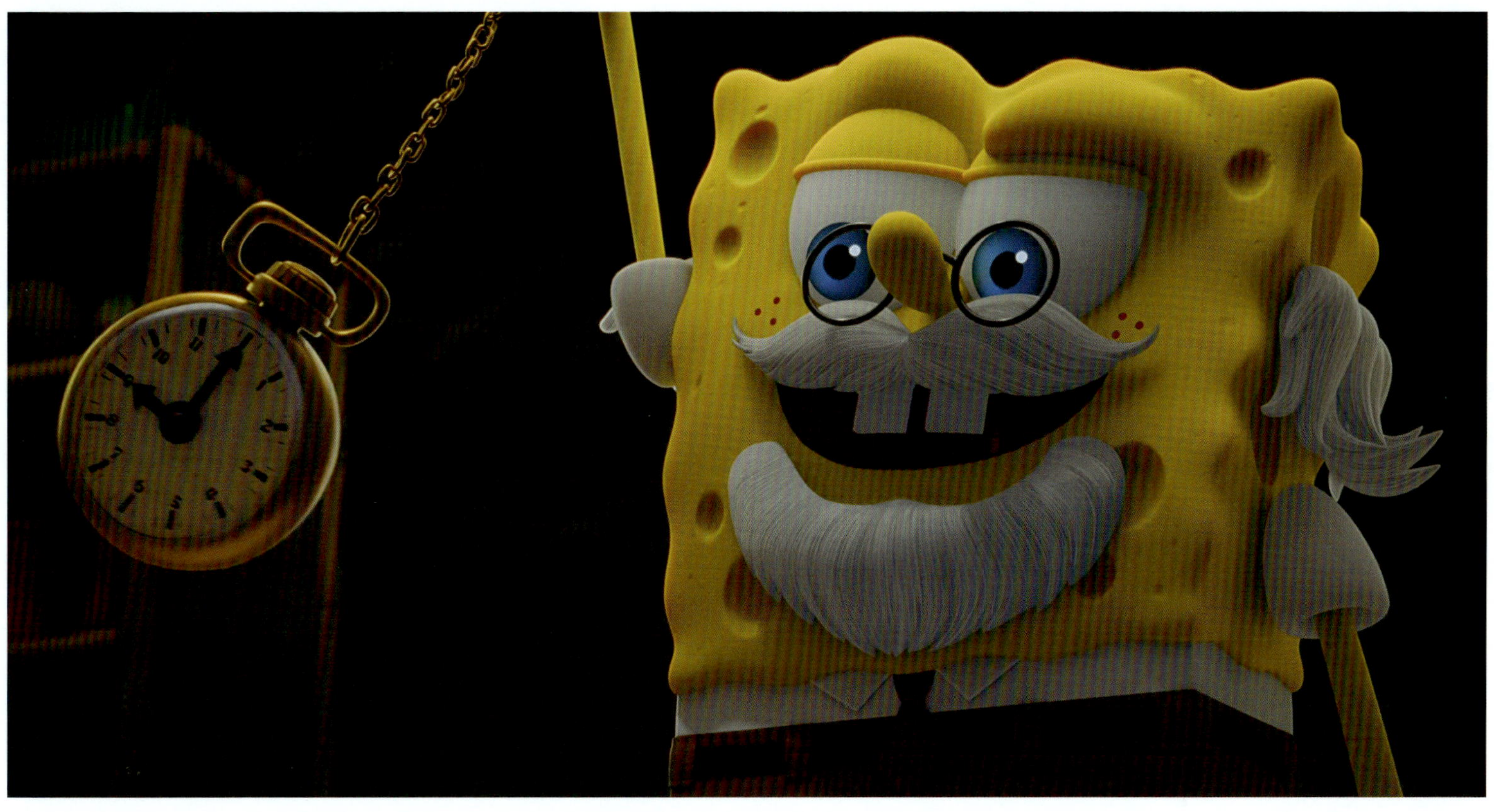

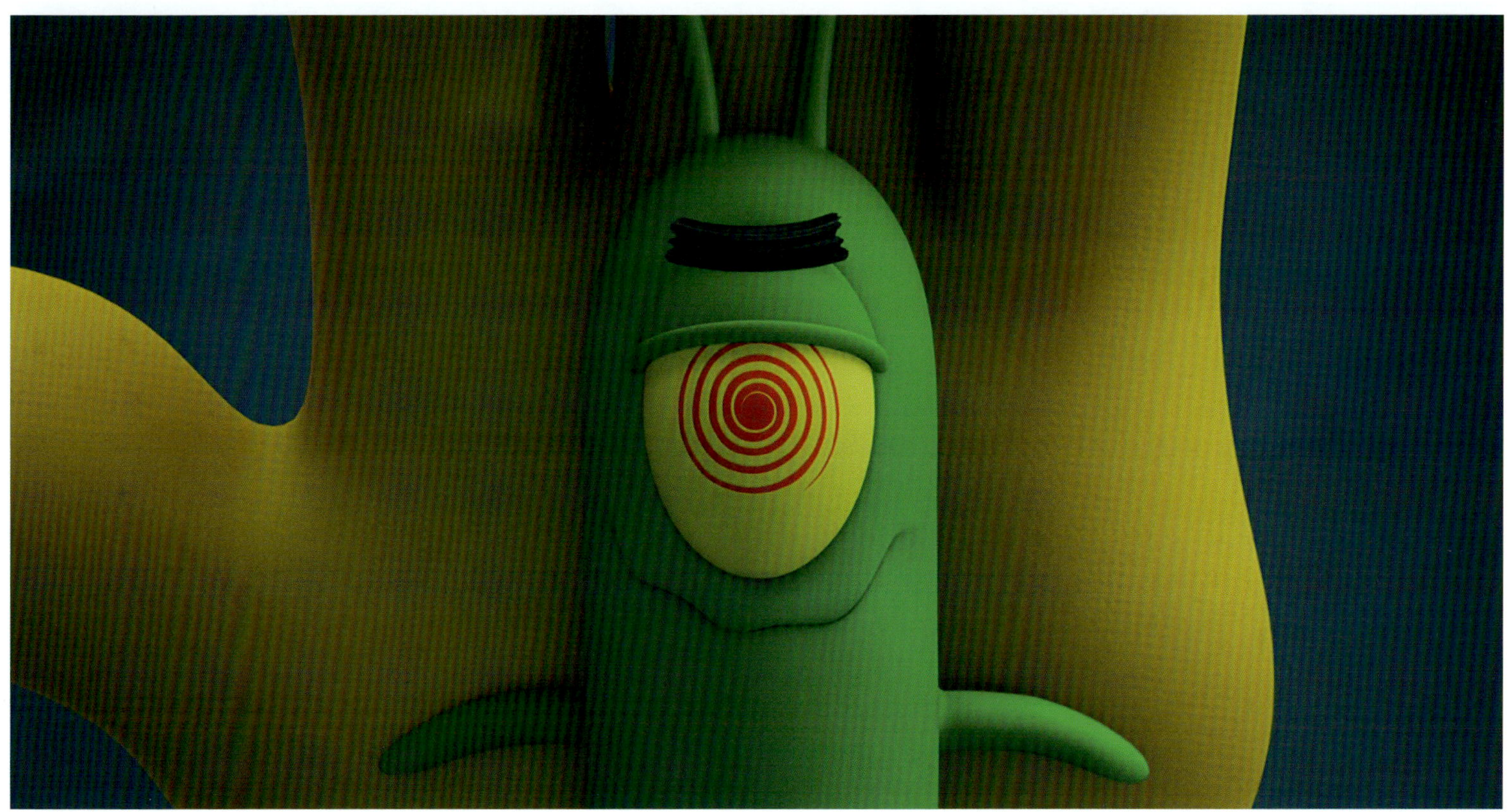

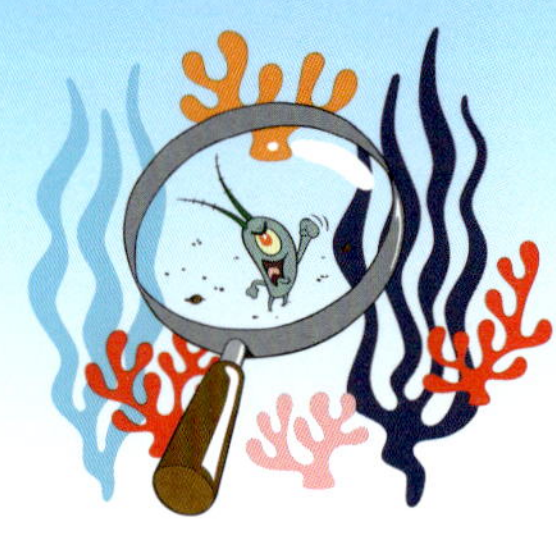

EMPATHY IS A TRIP

Another shift in 2D-animation style provides a groovy "tunnel of love" ride for Plankton as he embarks on an emotional roller coaster after having the Empathy Chip forcefully implanted in his tiny brain.

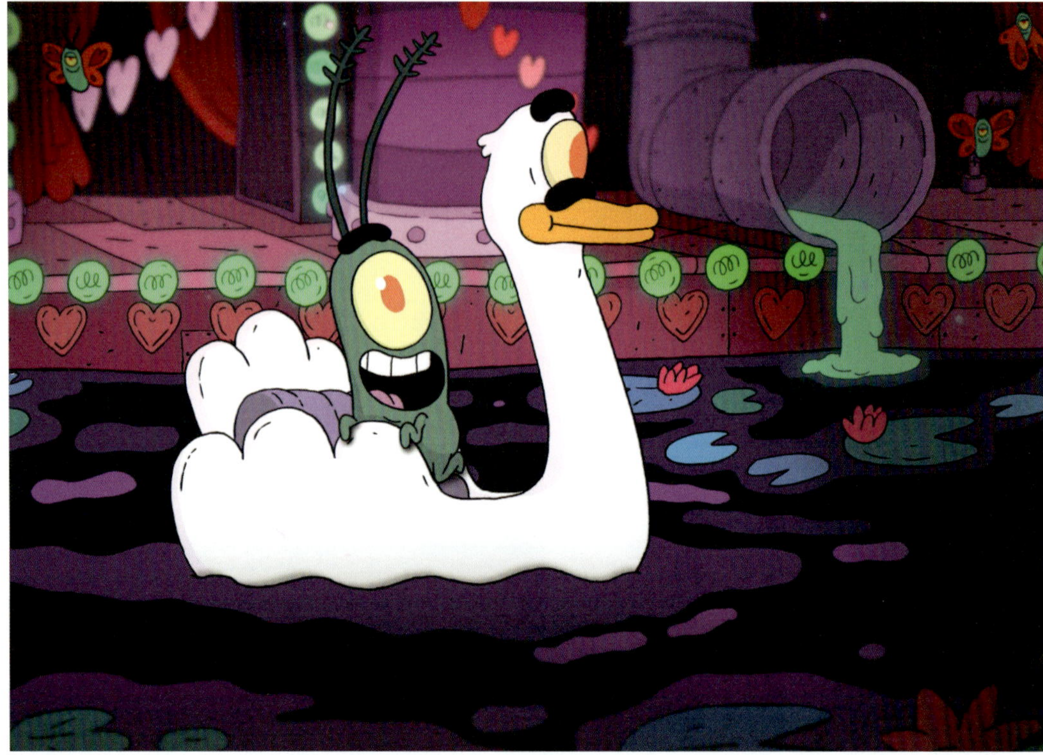

Final frame images of a trip down memory lane, guided by Plankton's newfound empathy

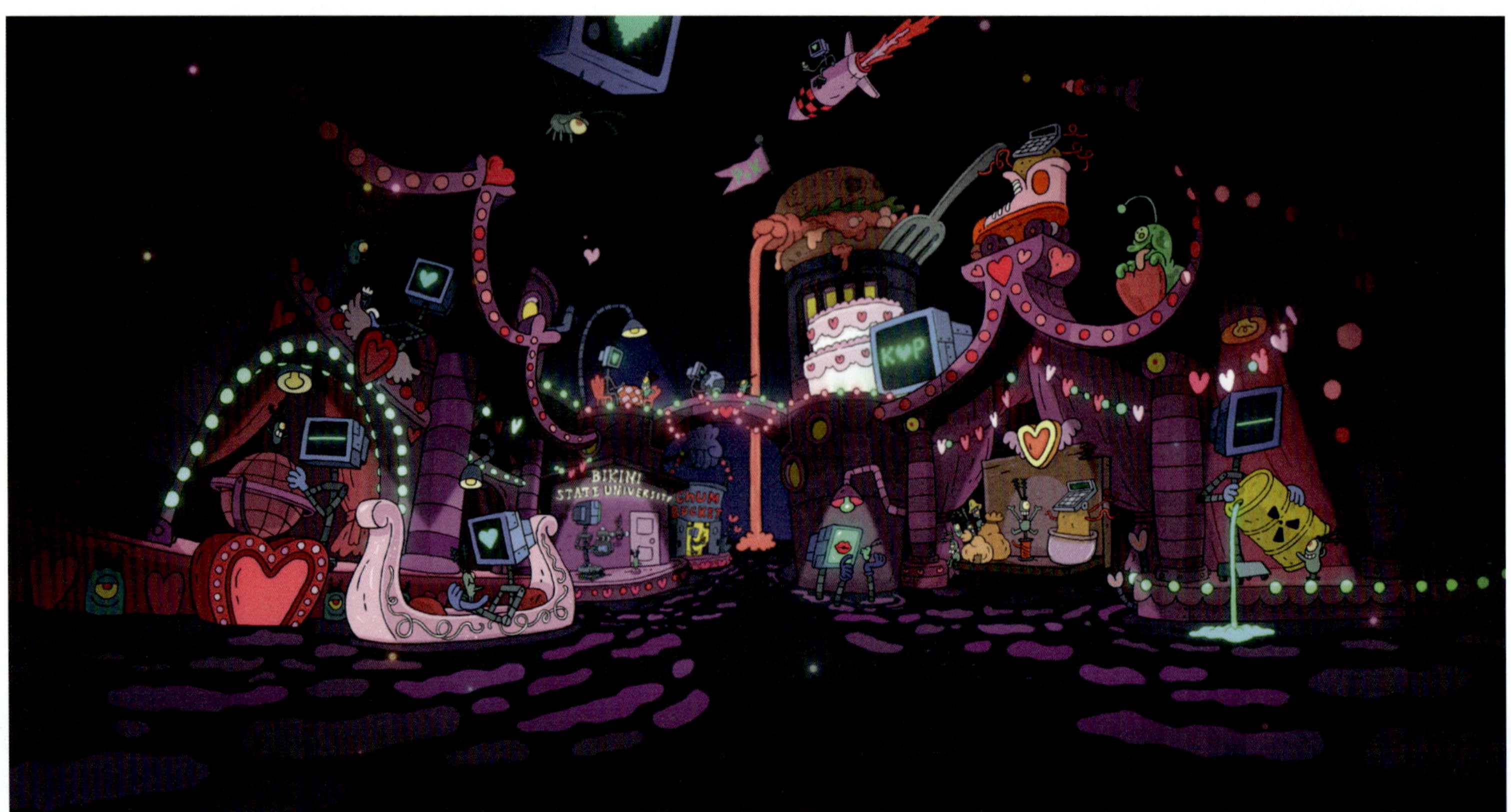

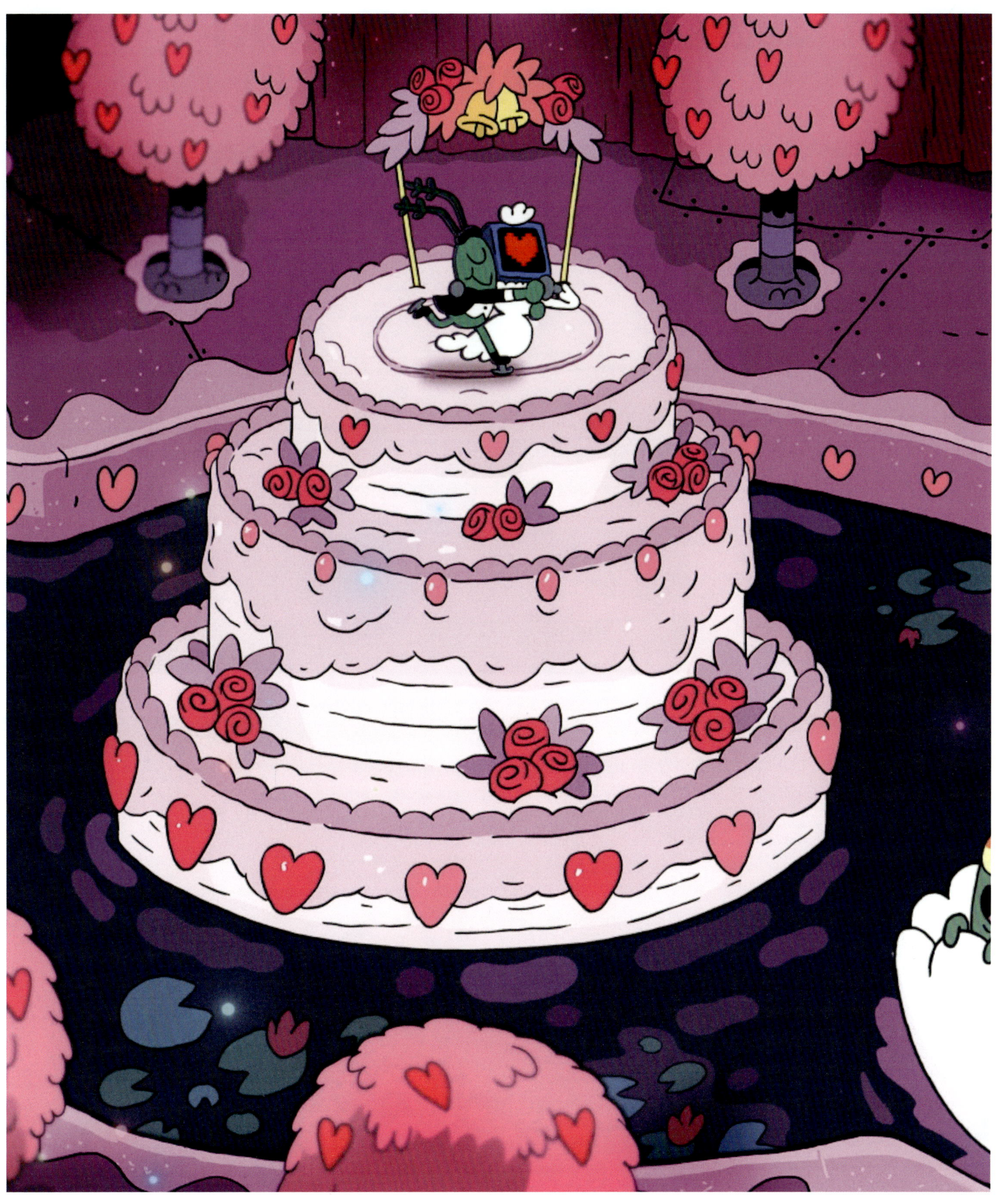

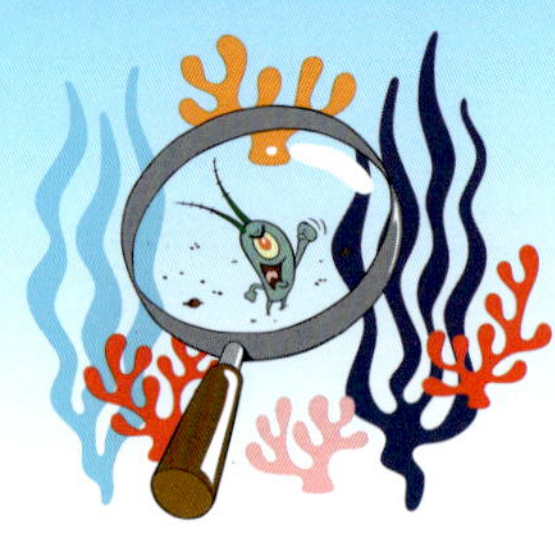

SUCKERS FOR A LOVE STORY (AND A HAPPY ENDING)

The pieces fall back into place in Bikini Bottom, as does an uplifting closing song in true *SpongeBob* fashion.

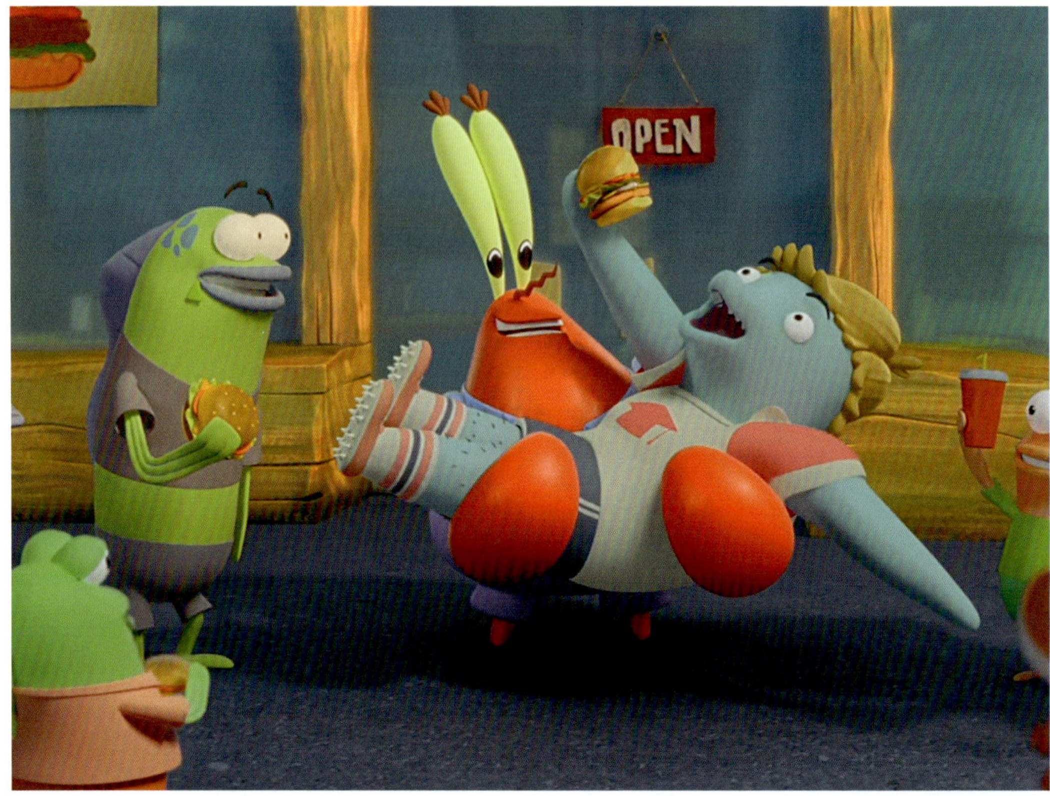

Final frame images of a harmonious happy ending [left, upper right, lower right]

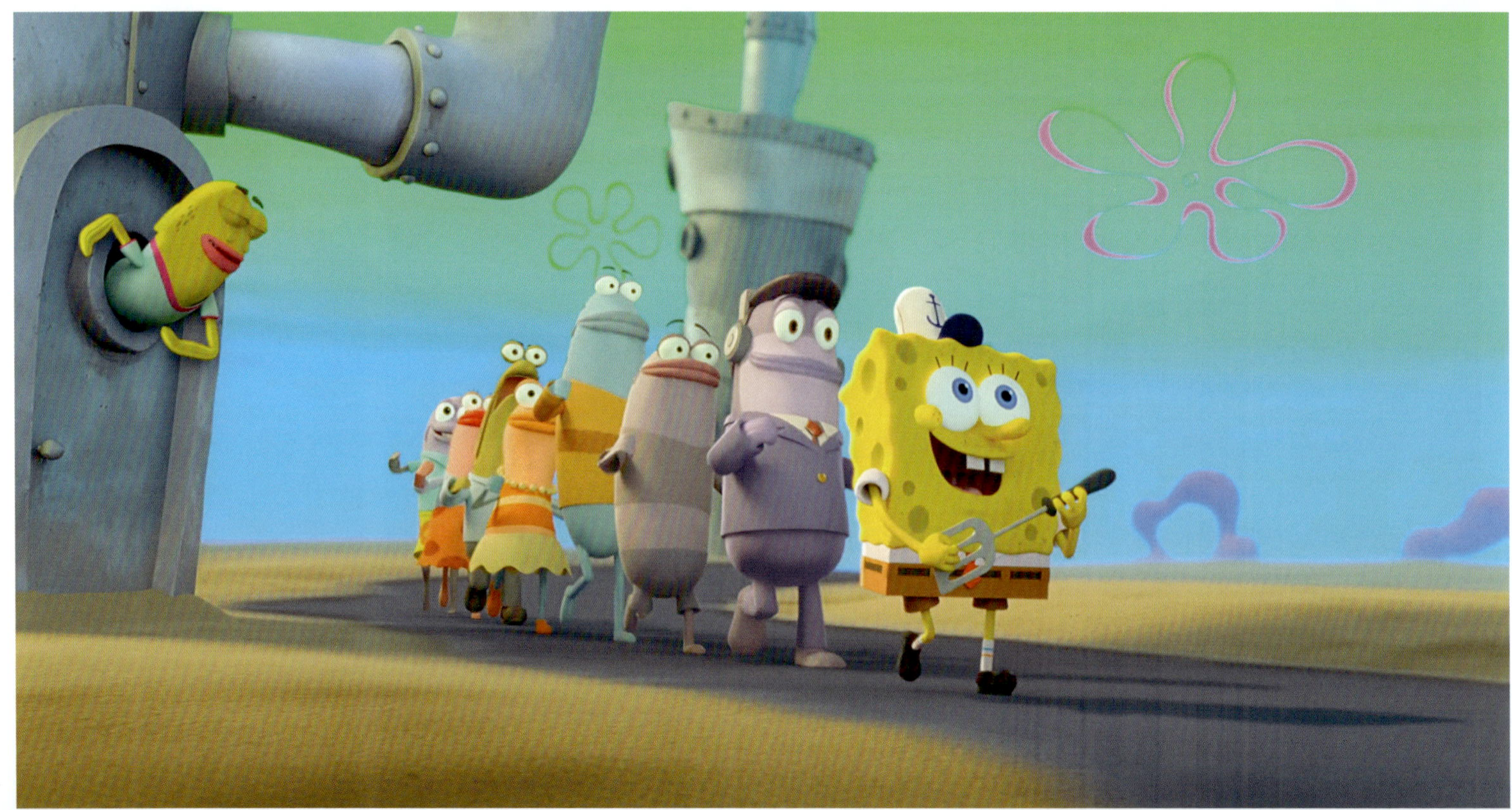

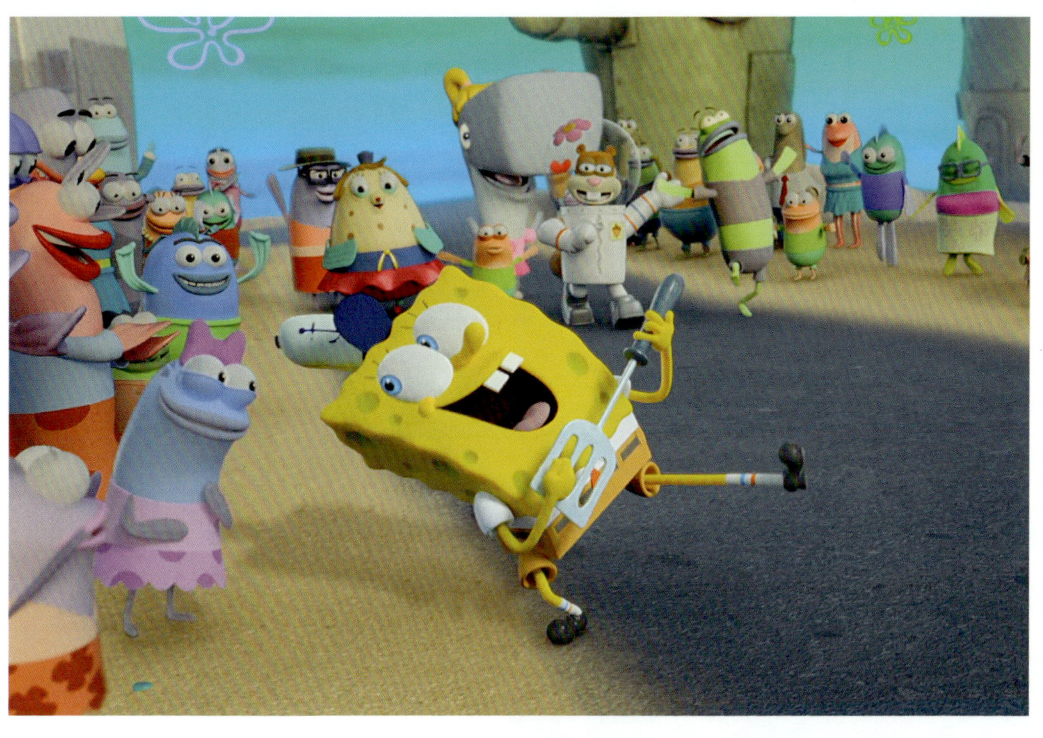

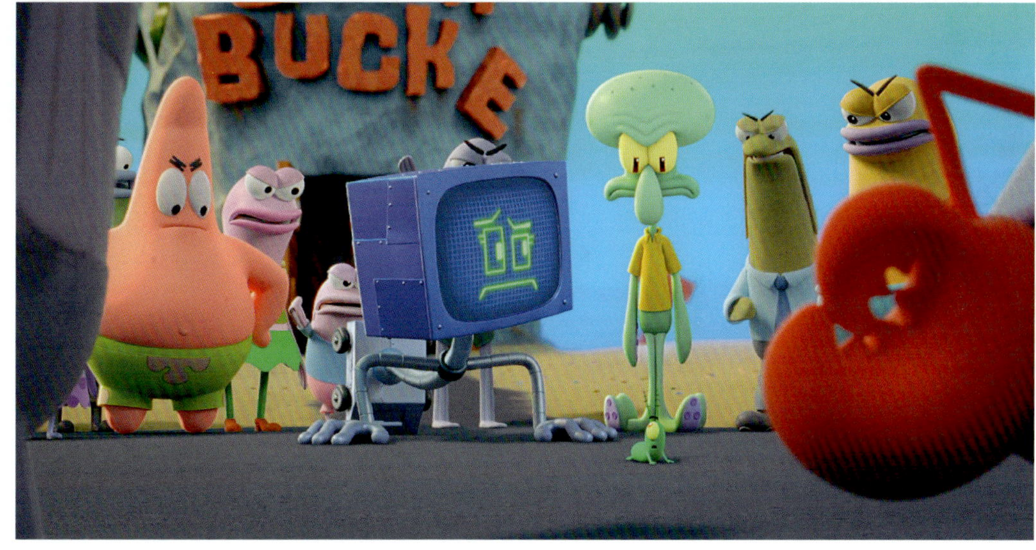

Final frame images of Karen and Plankton returning [right]

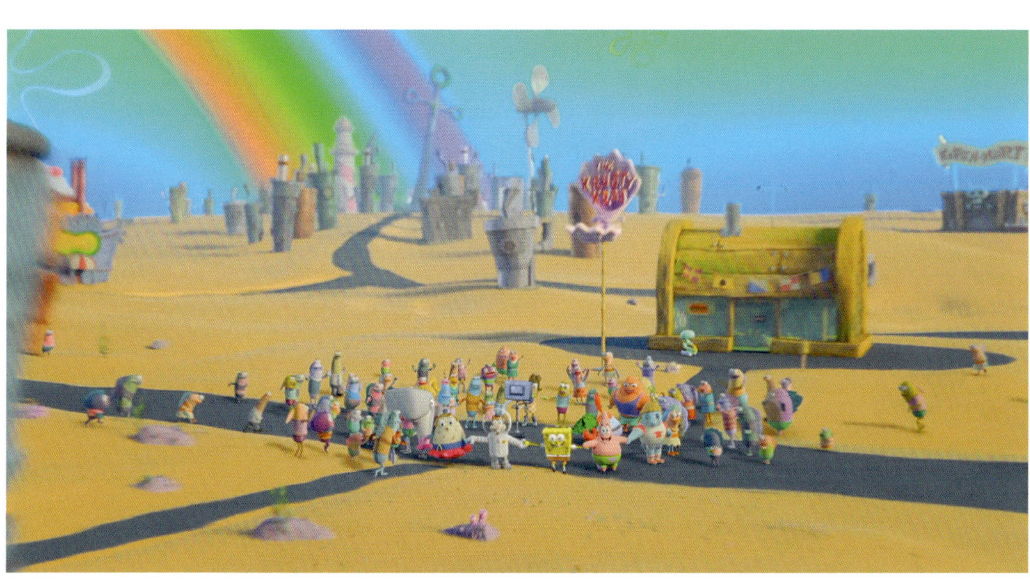

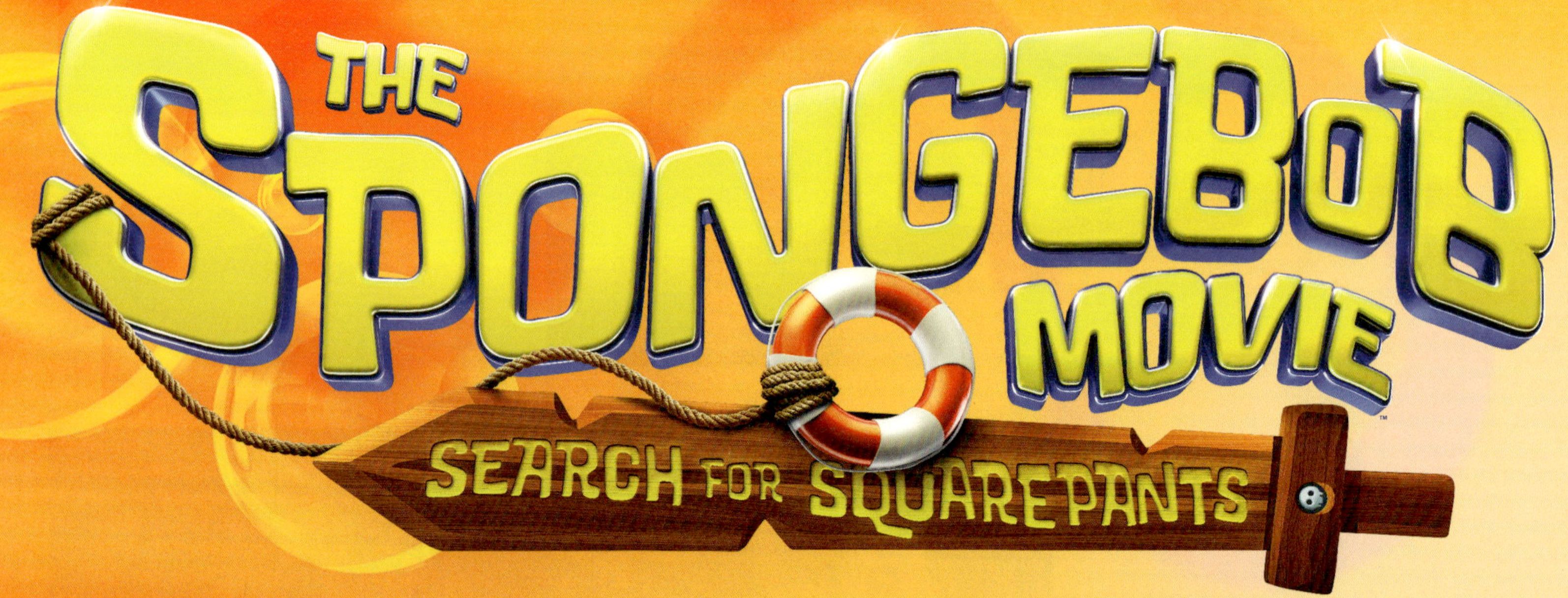

The sixth feature-length film in the SpongeBob realm was released on December 19, 2025, amping up the swashbuckling fun in SpongeBob's quest to prove himself to be a "big guy." In establishing the look of this CG film with 2D accents, animation production designer Pablo R. Mayer and animation art director Travis Ruiz wanted to serve the legions of SpongeBob fans while making the most of today's technology.

Director Derek Drymon "made it very clear he wanted it to feel like the original series, so that's where we started with everything. The thing that stood out to us most in the original 2D artwork were all the perfect imperfections. You can really see the handwork in every wobbly brush stroke and scattered texture. So knowing we needed to interpret that into a 3D world, our solution was to make everything feel as if it was molded by hand to give it that same wobbly imperfect feel," explains Ruiz.

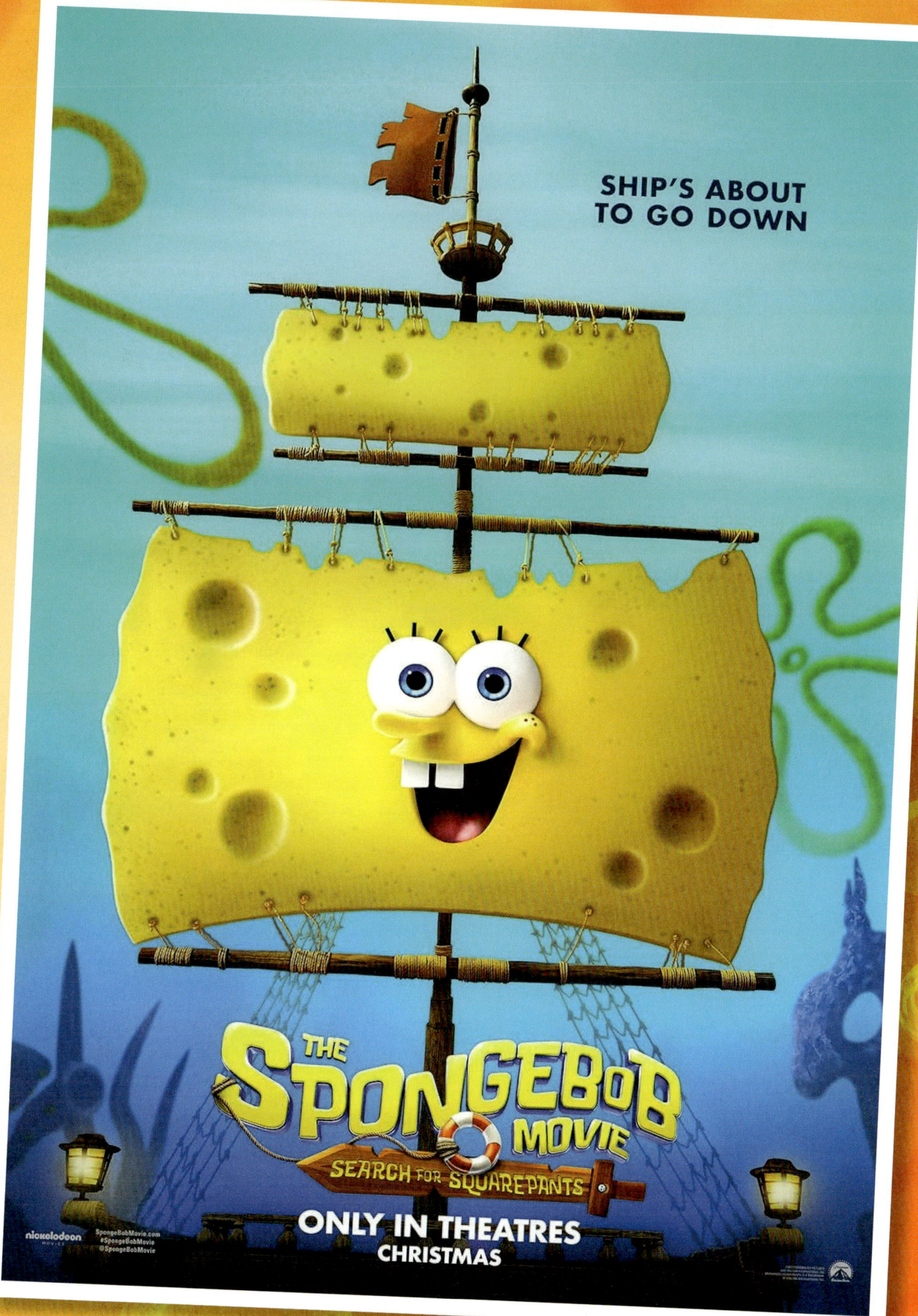
SHIP'S ABOUT
TO GO DOWN
THE SPONGEBOB MOVIE
SEARCH FOR SQUAREPANTS
ONLY IN THEATRES
CHRISTMAS
nickelodeon
MOVIES
SpongeBobMovie.com
#SpongeBobMovie
@SpongeBobMovie

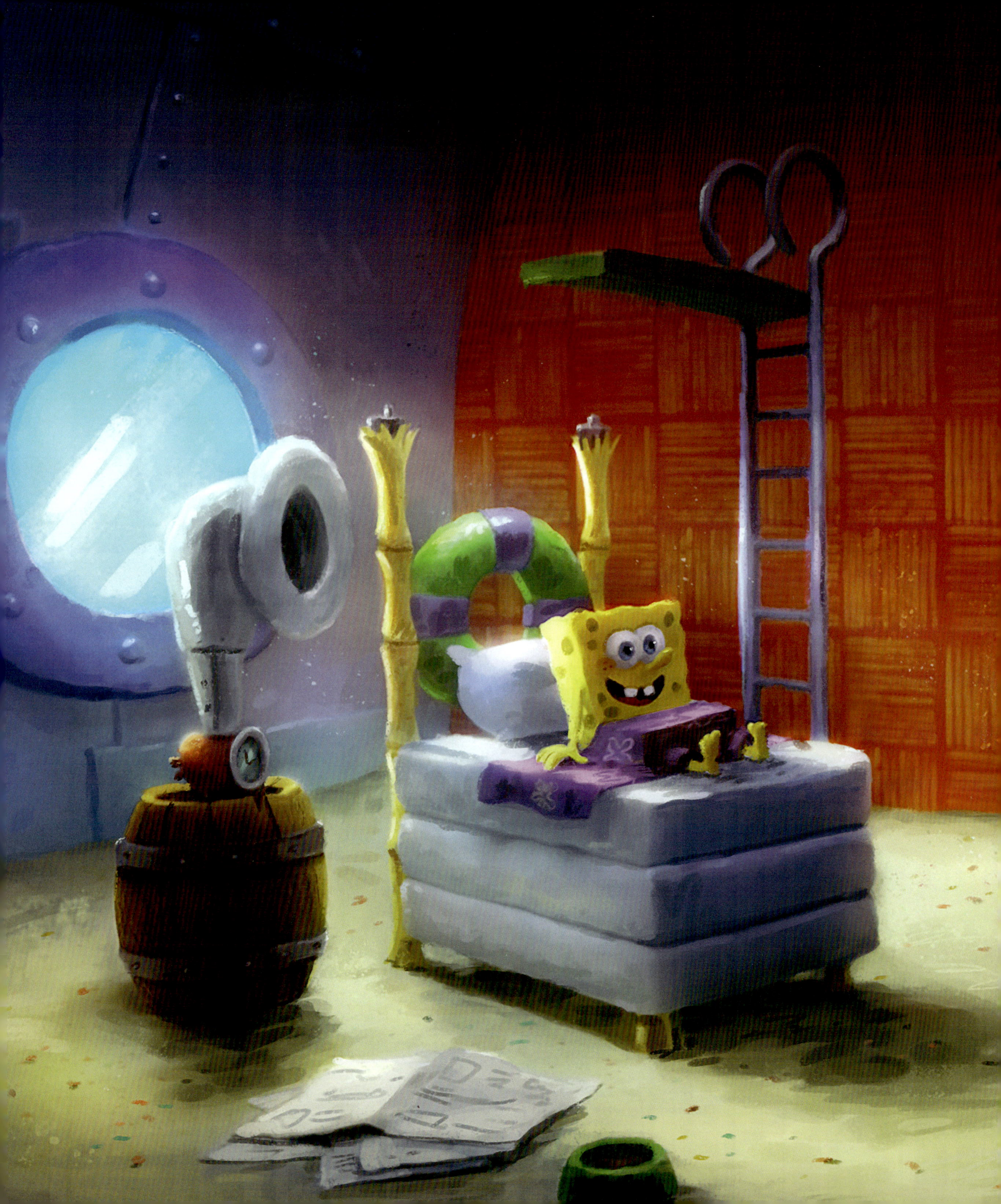

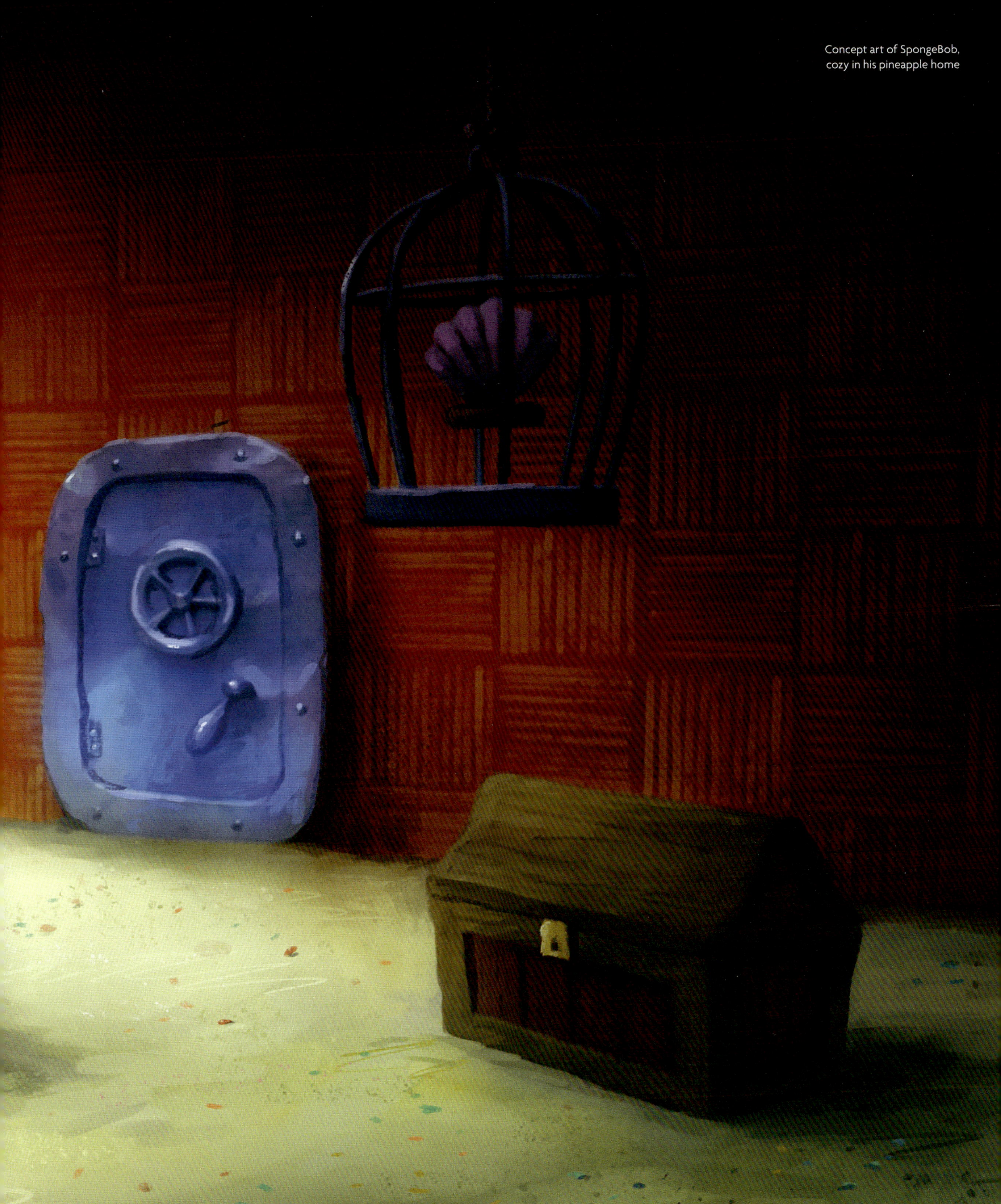

Concept art of SpongeBob,
cozy in his pineapple home

CURSE OF THE FLYING DUTCHMAN

Alas, there's a pirate tale about how an ancient, wicked curse befalls a sailor and marks him as the Flying Dutchman, and the only way to break out of that role is through the pure heart of an innocent… who might ye be thinking fits that bill?

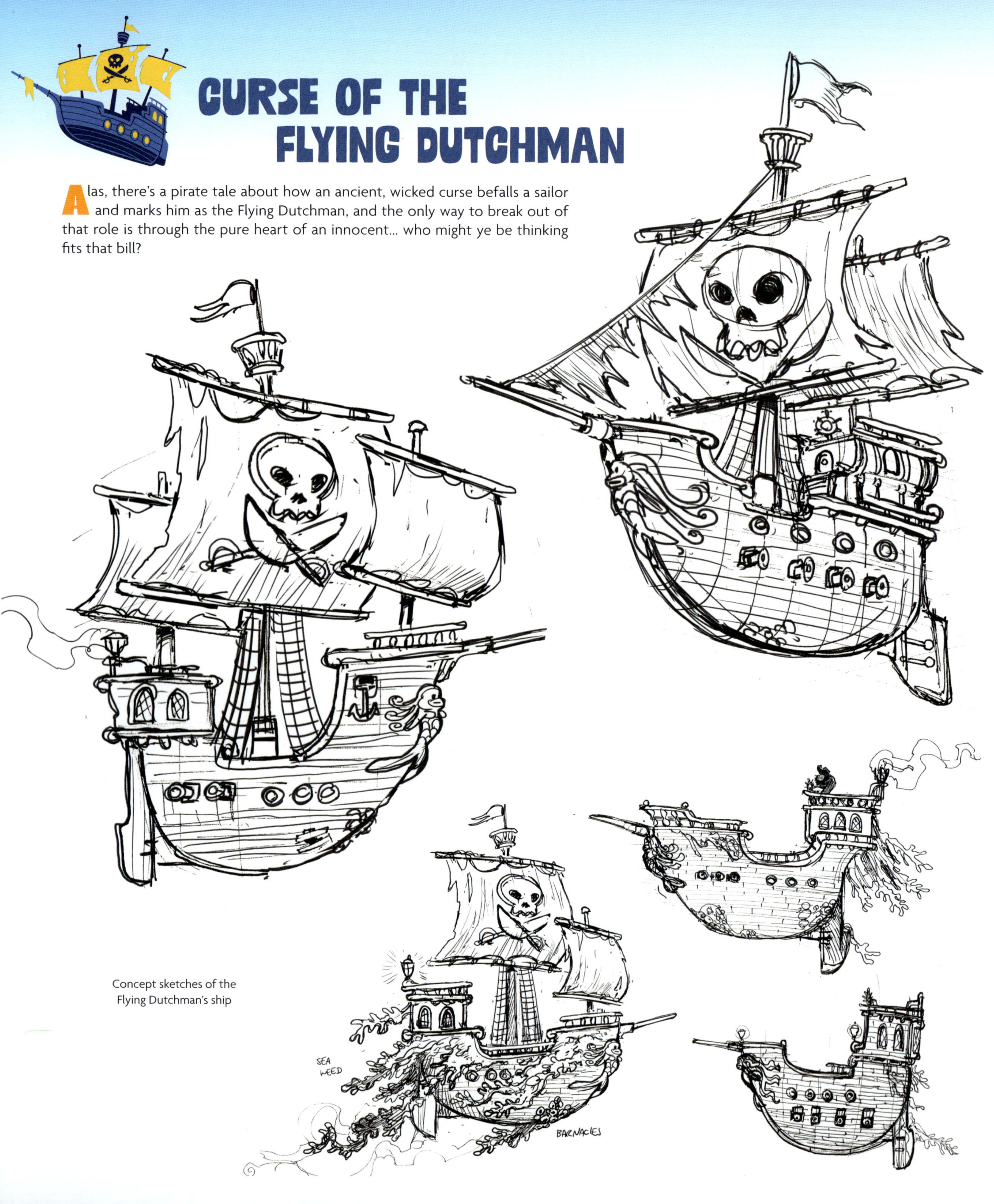

Concept sketches of the Flying Dutchman's ship

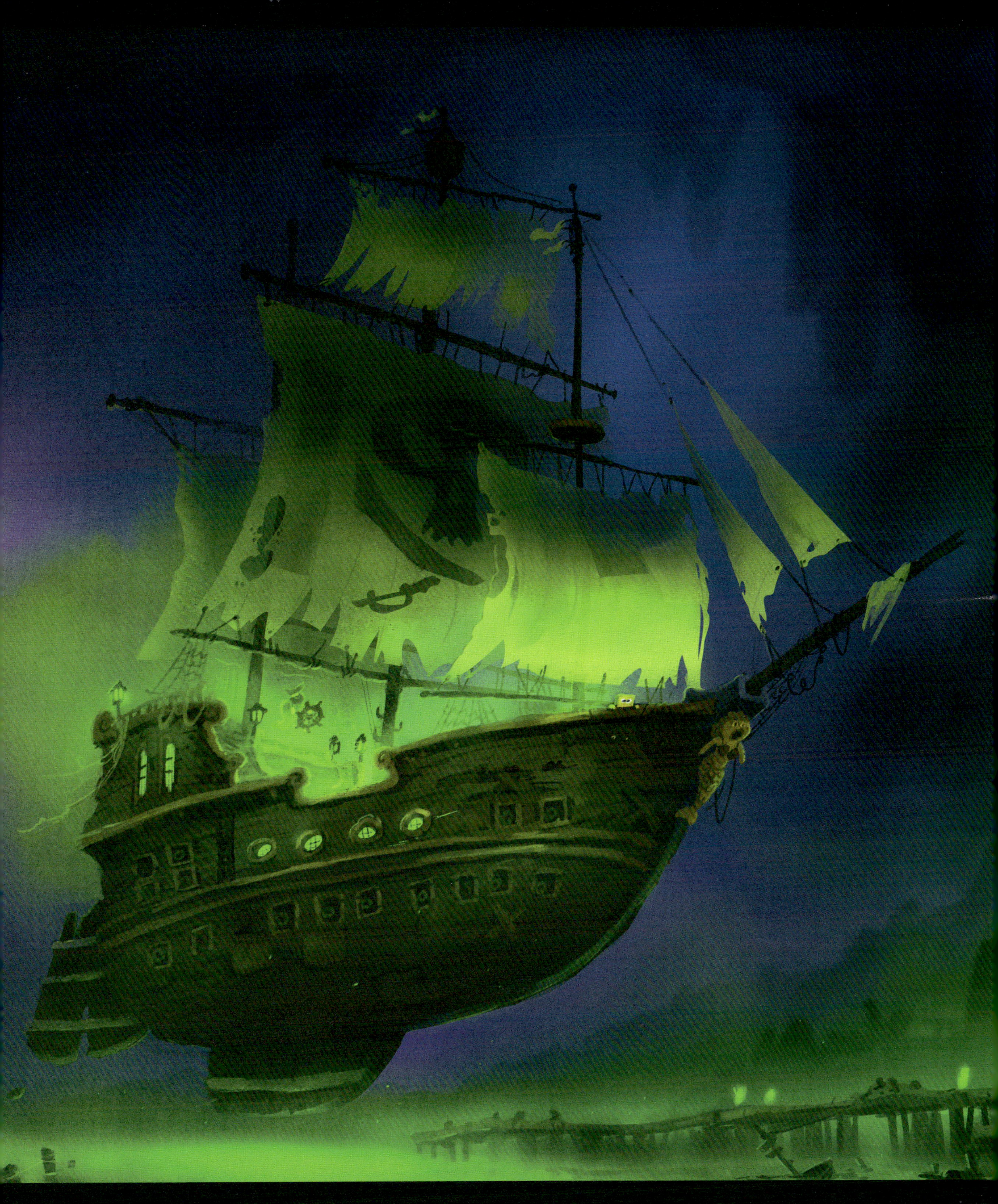

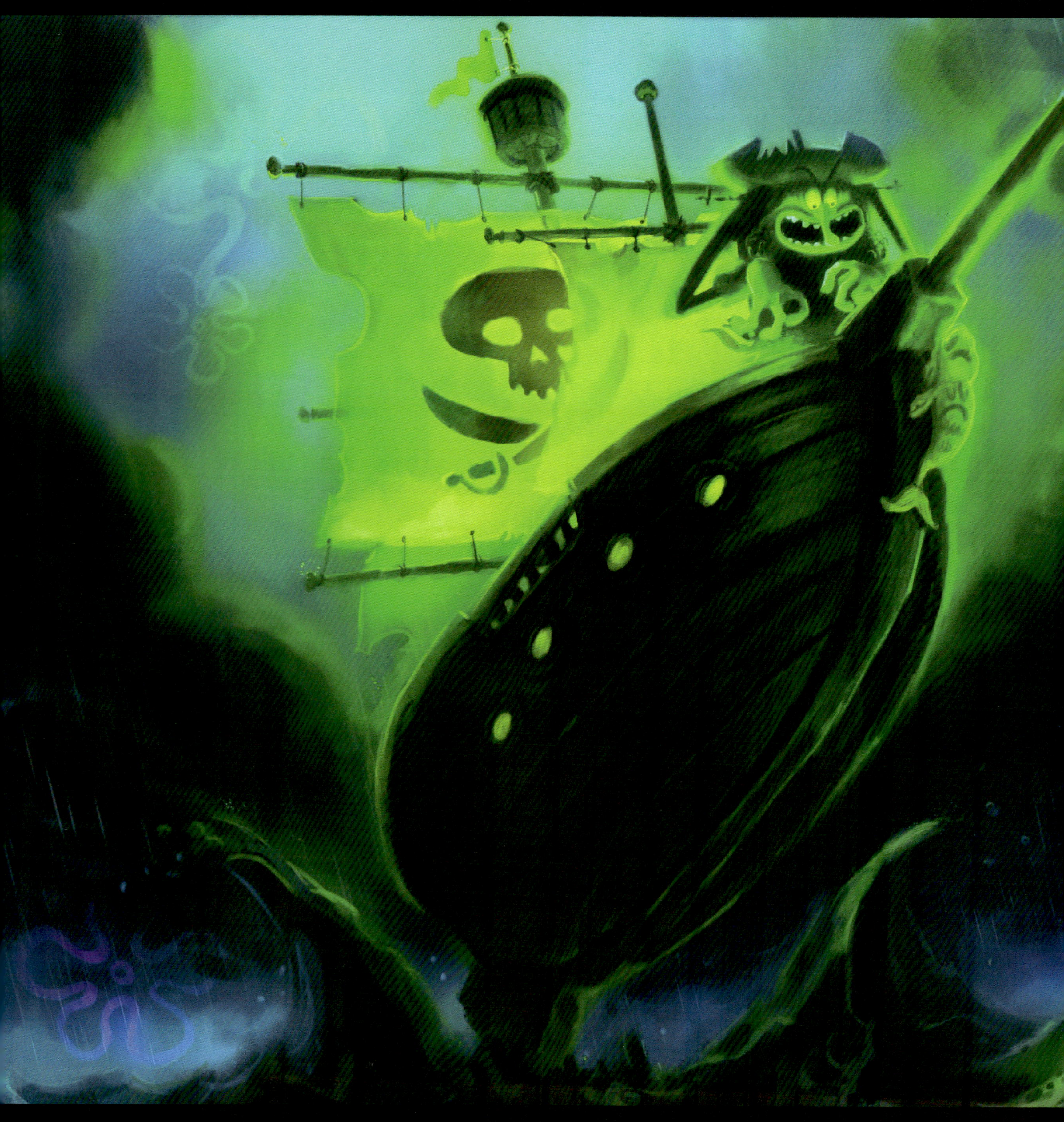

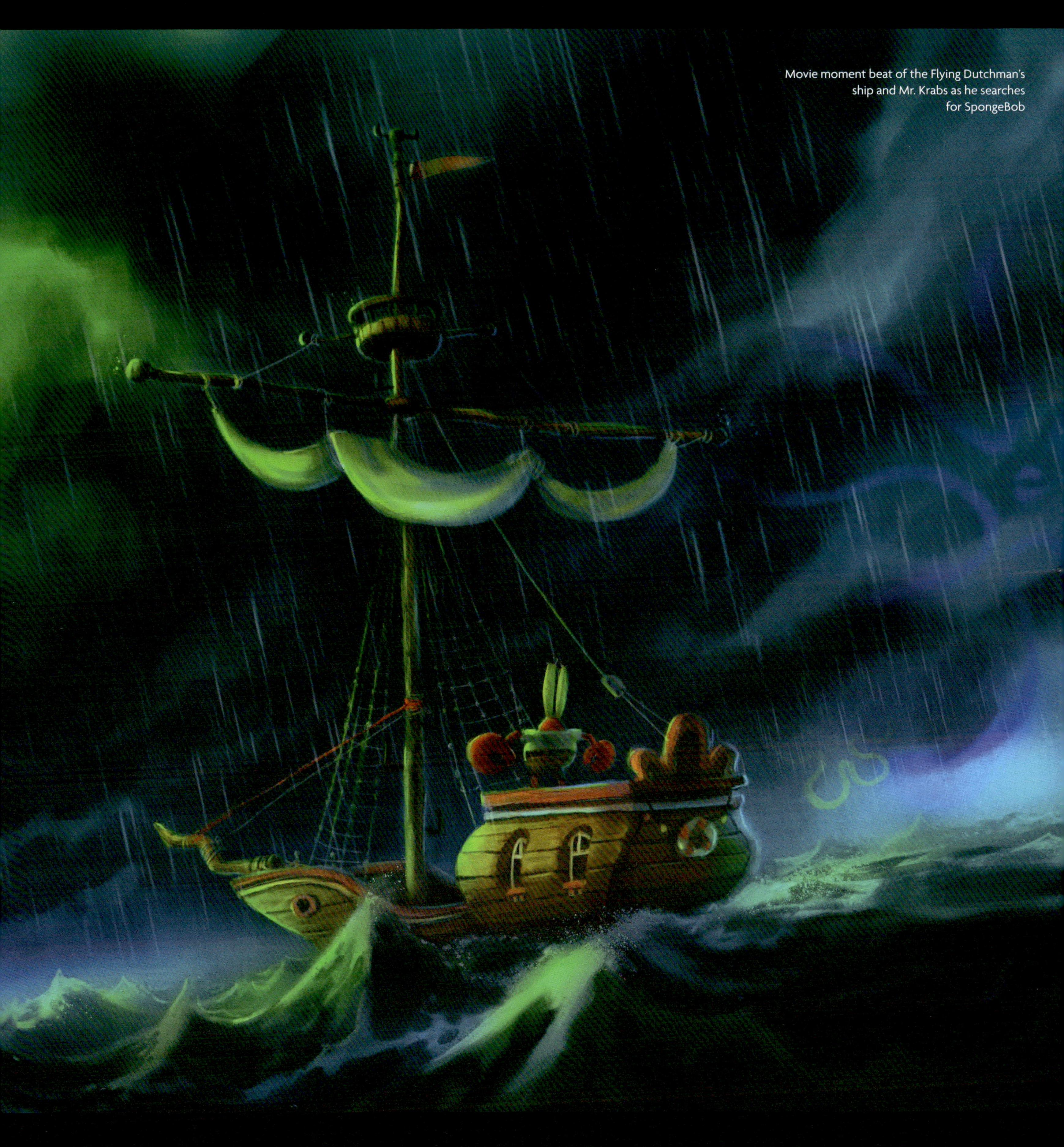

Movie moment beat of the Flying Dutchman's ship and Mr. Krabs as he searches for SpongeBob

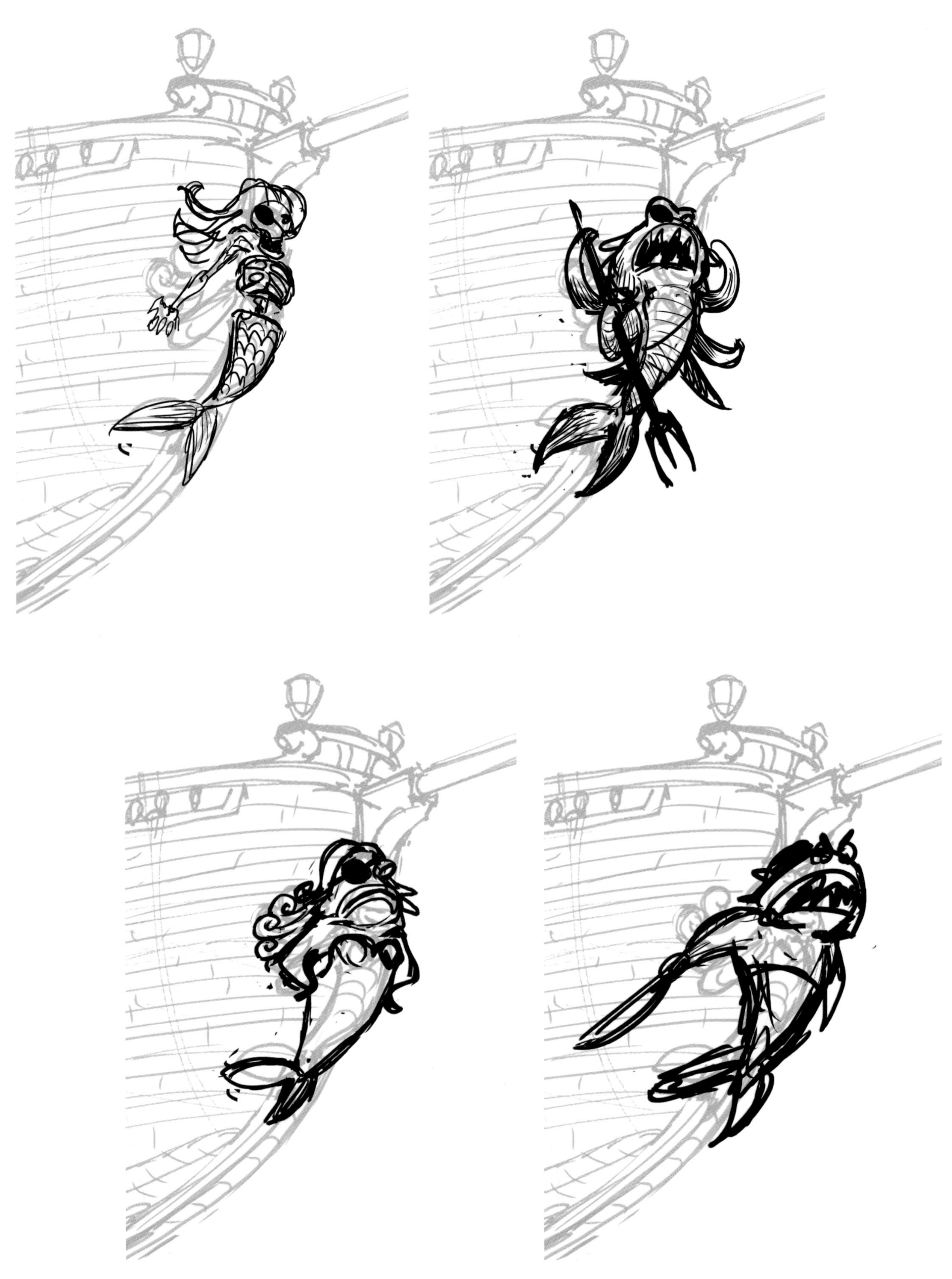

Prop design and treatment of the figurehead design on the Flying Dutchman's ship

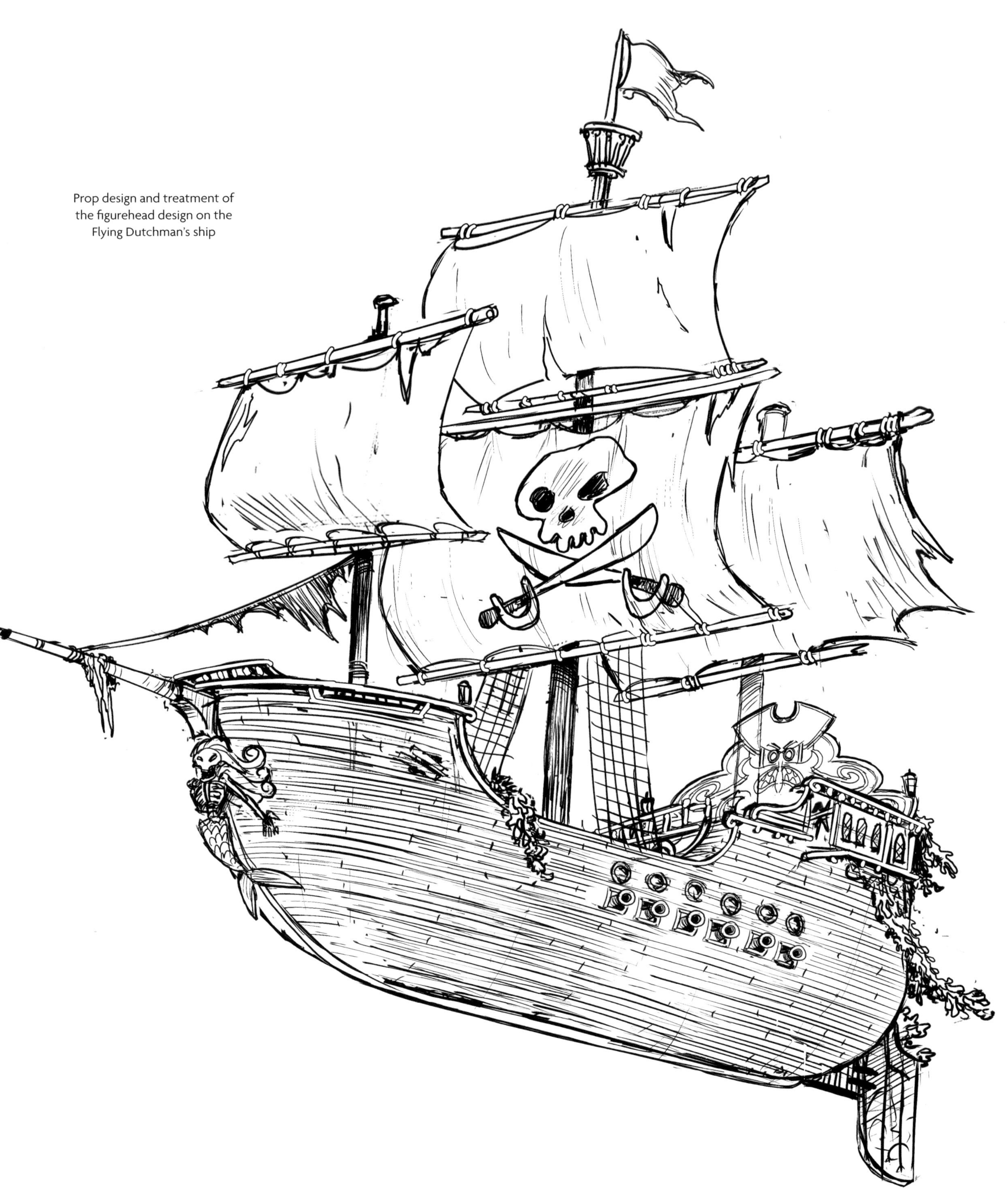

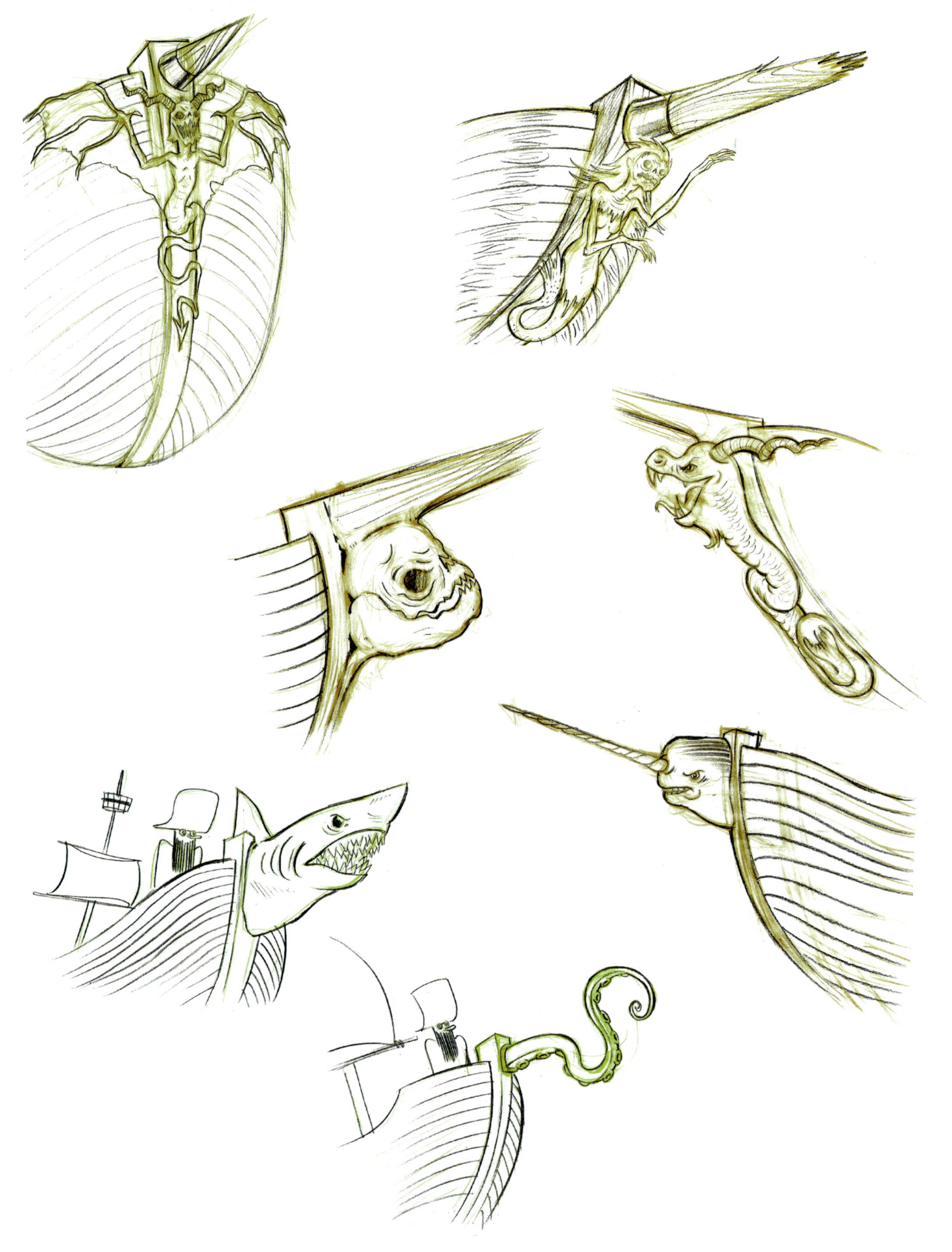

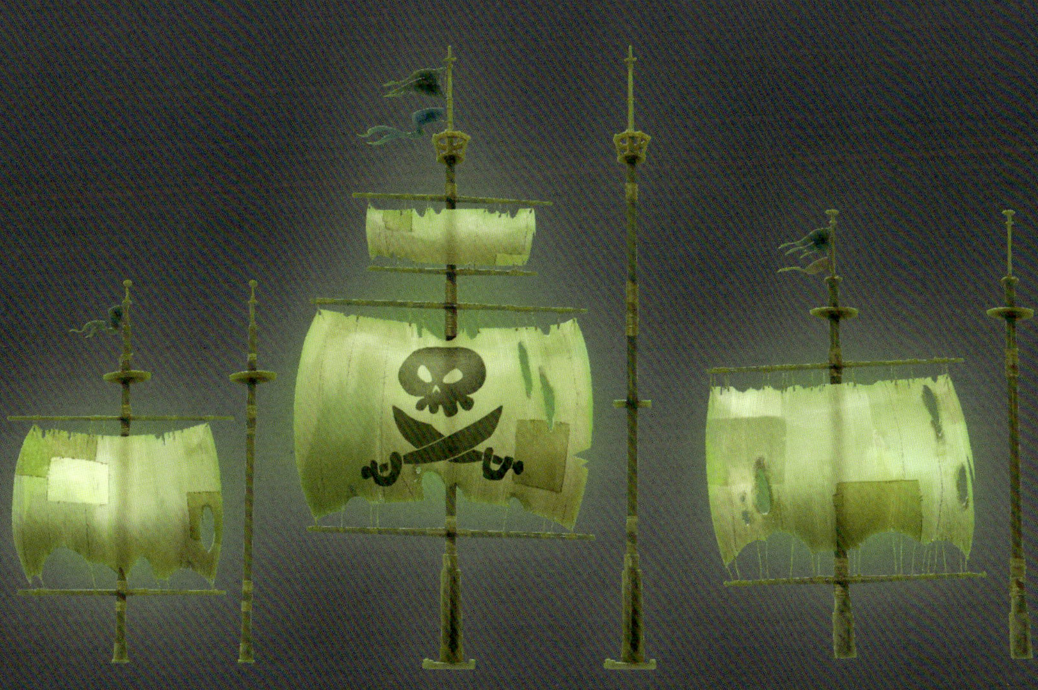

Textured render of the figurehead design [left] and partial element breakdown of the CG model of the Flying Dutchman's ship

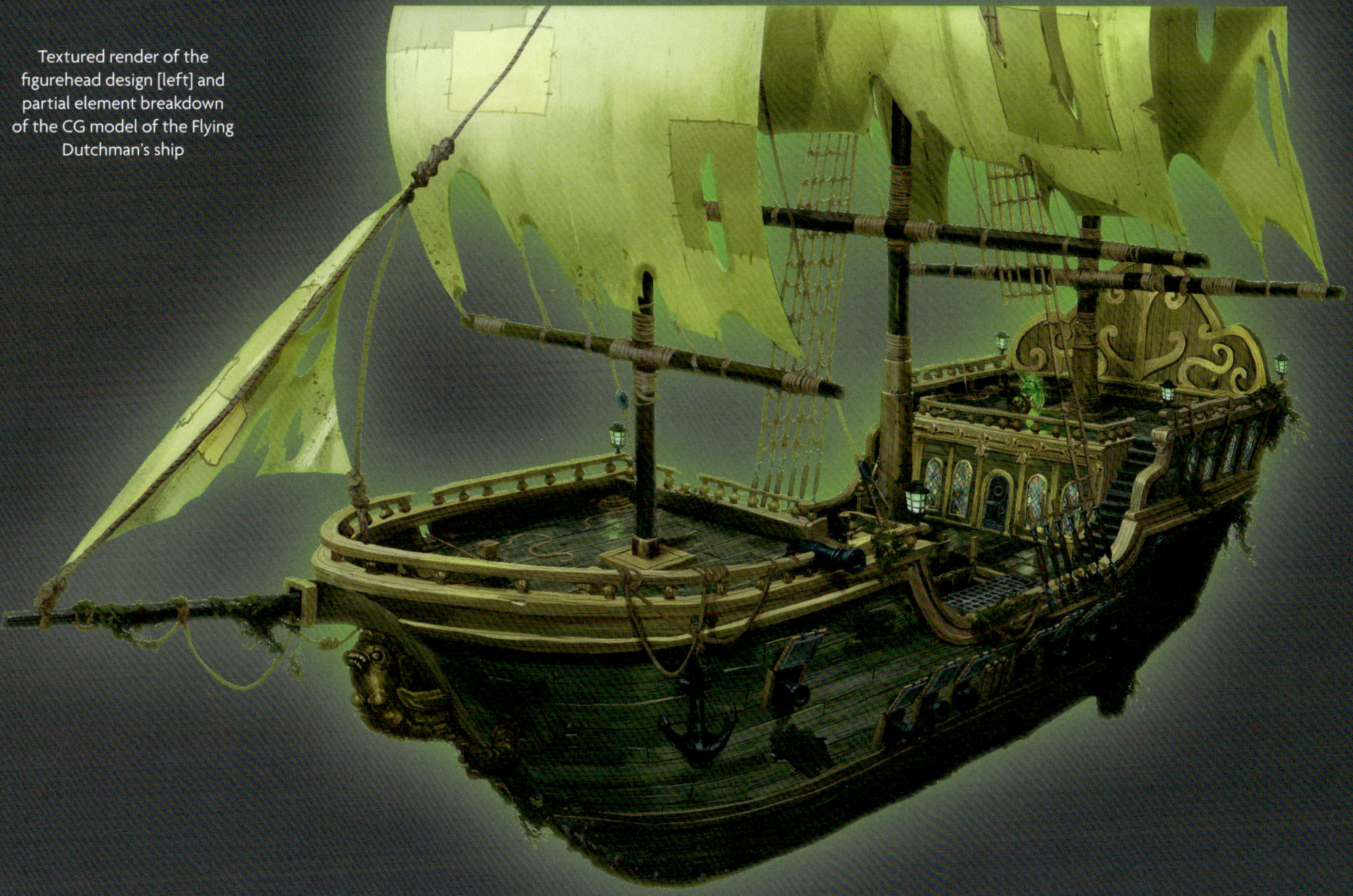

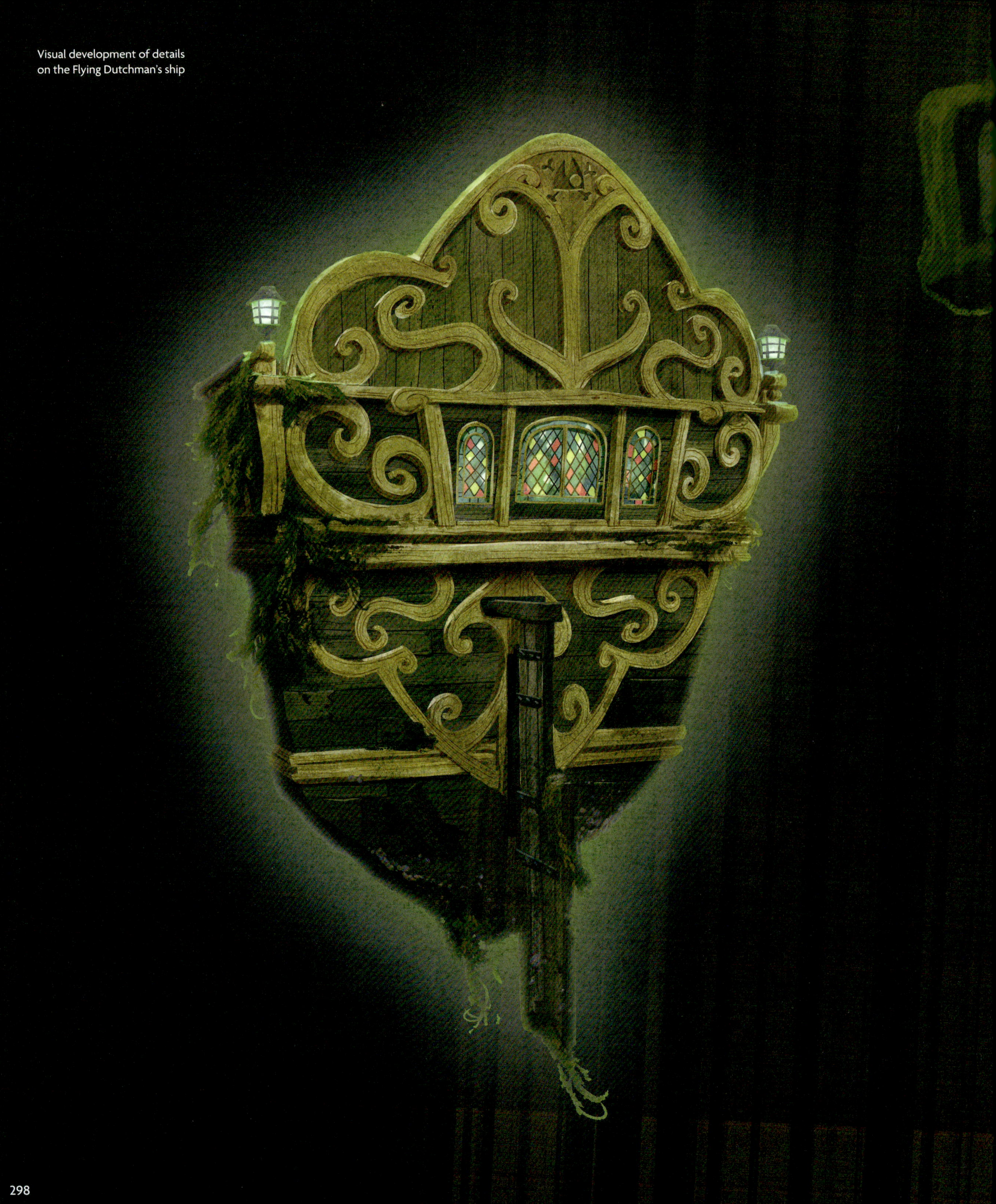

Visual development of details on the Flying Dutchman's ship

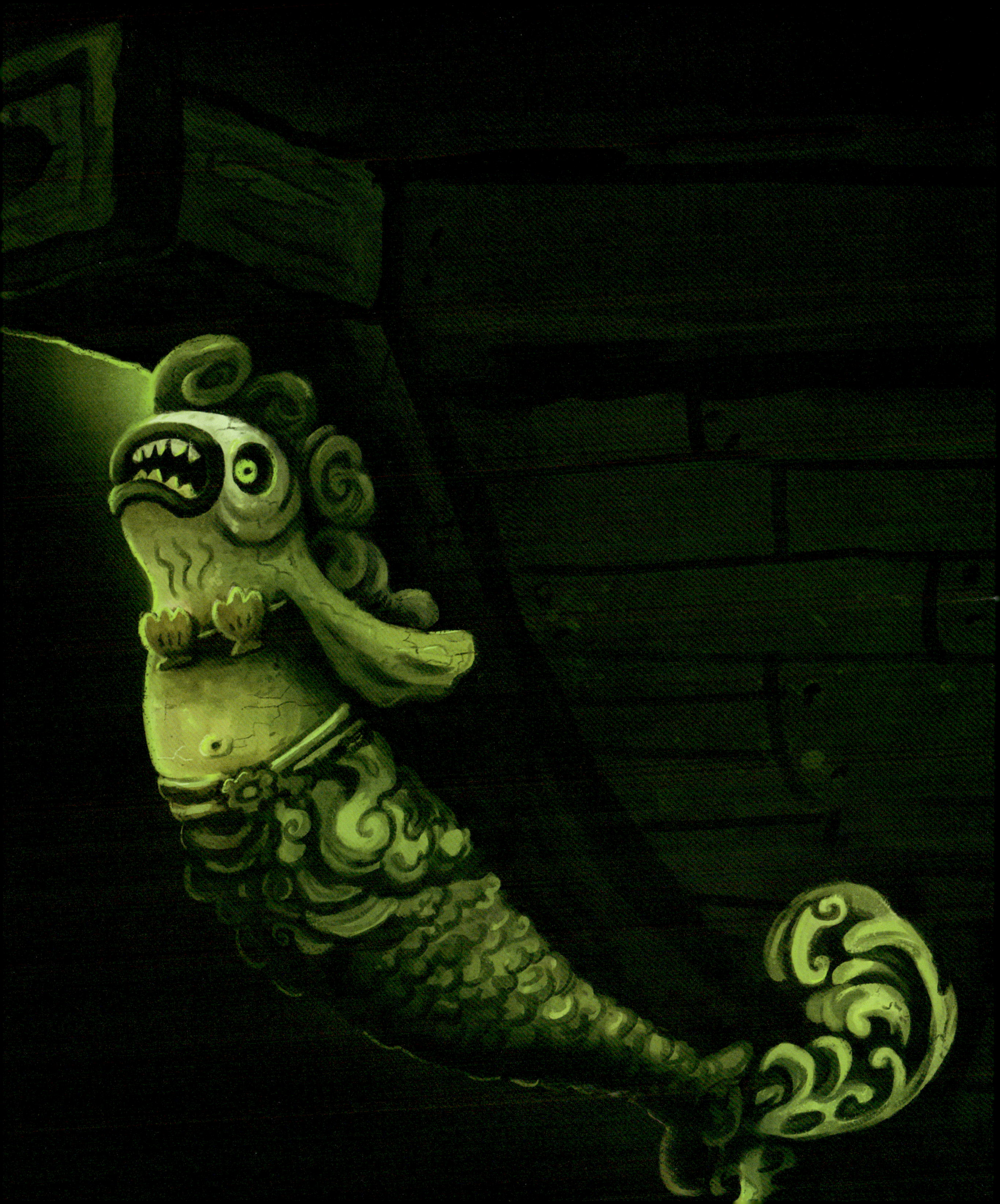

BIG GUY NOW!

That aforementioned bill-fitter is likely SpongeBob SquarePants, who has just realized he's reached the height of thirty-six clams tall and is ready to take on his greatest and loopiest and corkscrewiest challenge ever... riding the big roller coaster!

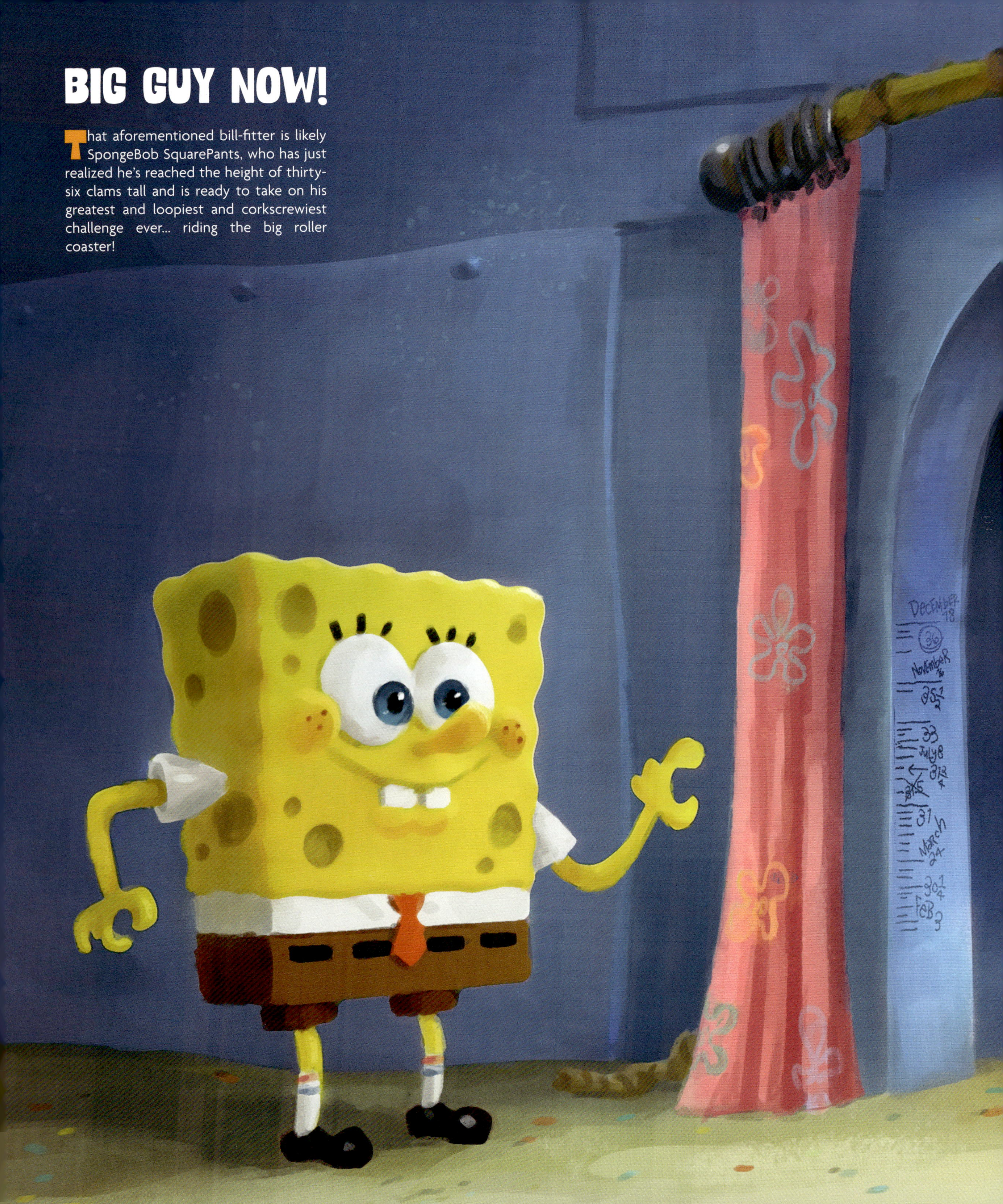

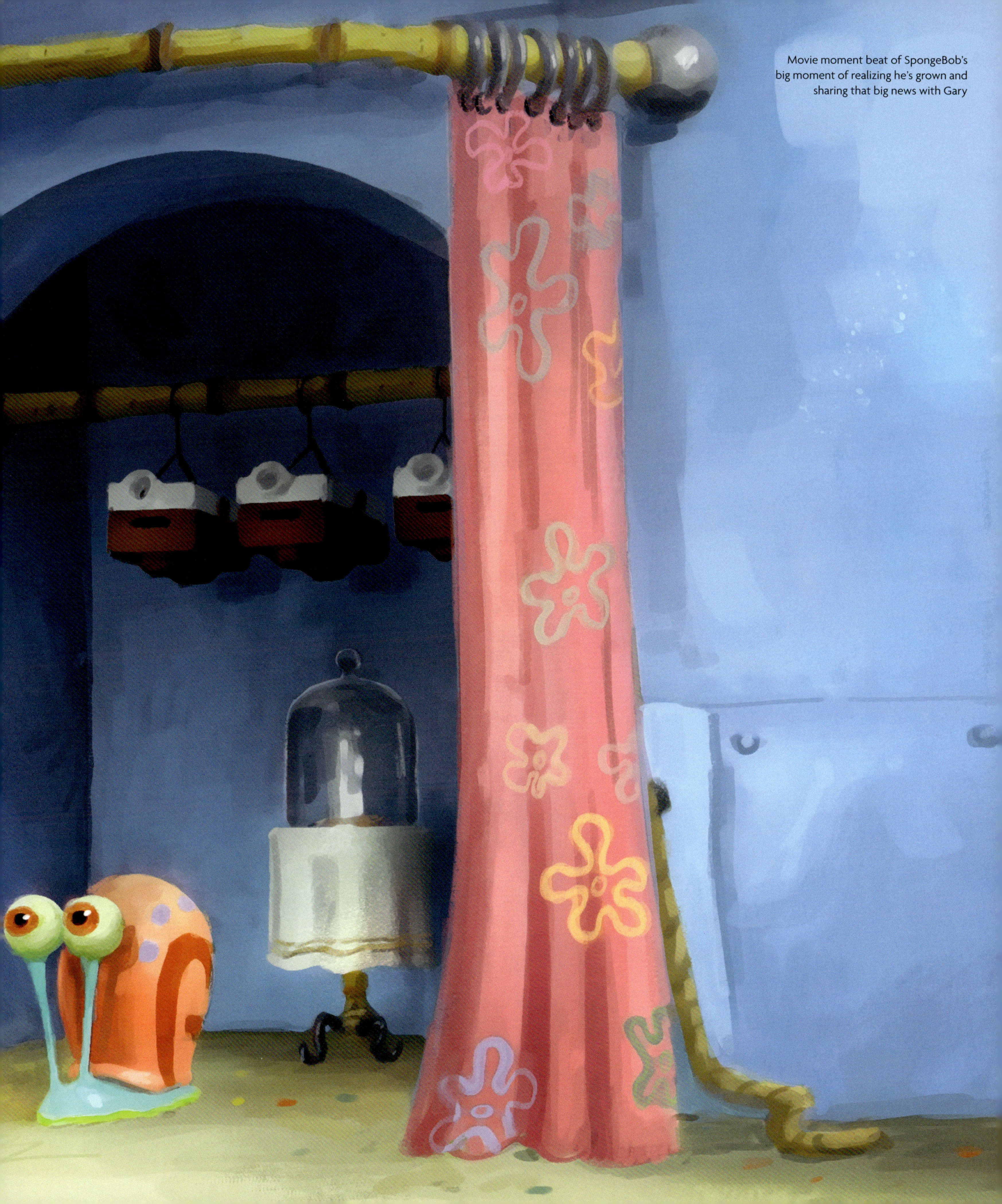

Movie moment beat of SpongeBob's big moment of realizing he's grown and sharing that big news with Gary

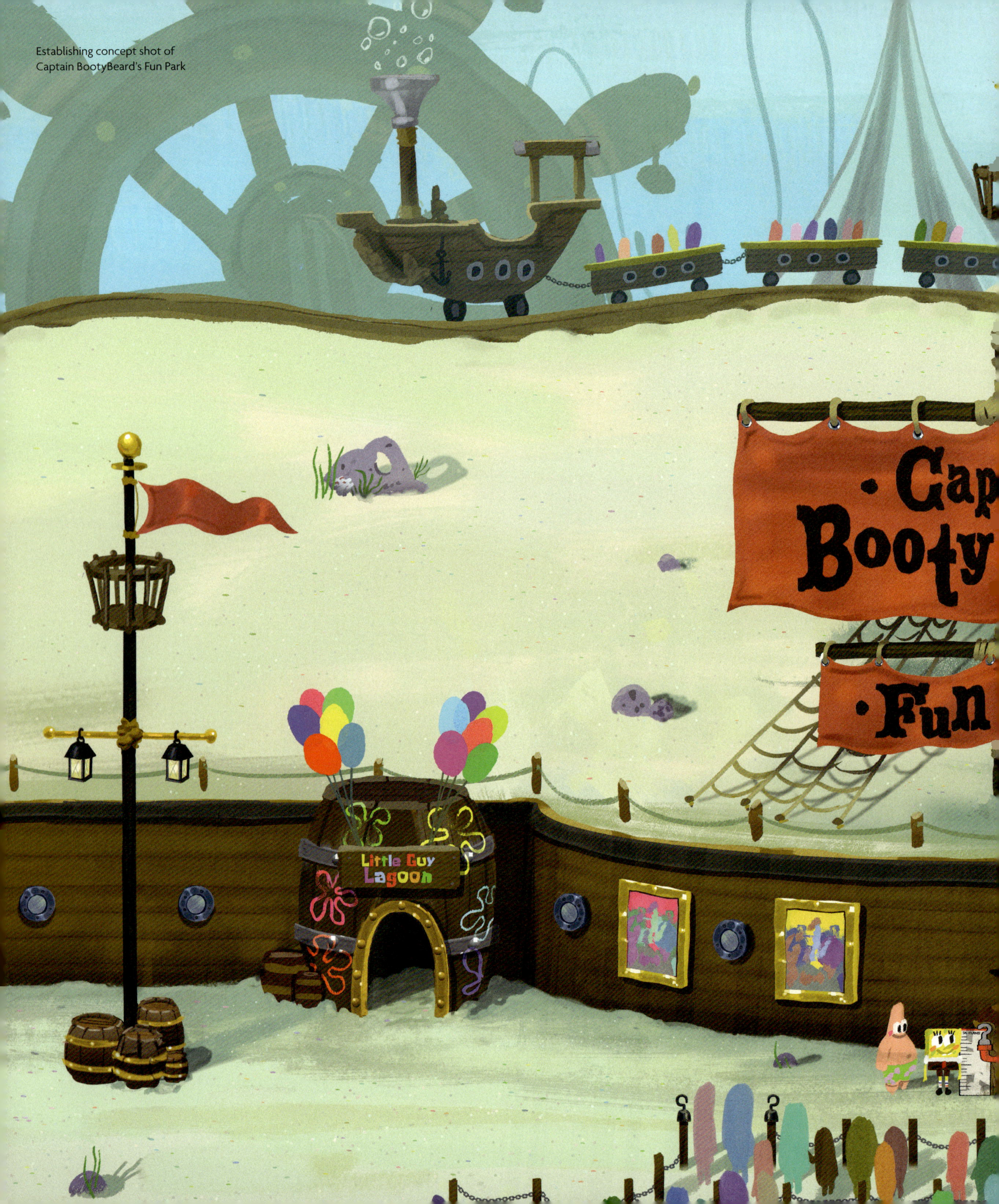

Establishing concept shot of Captain BootyBeard's Fun Park

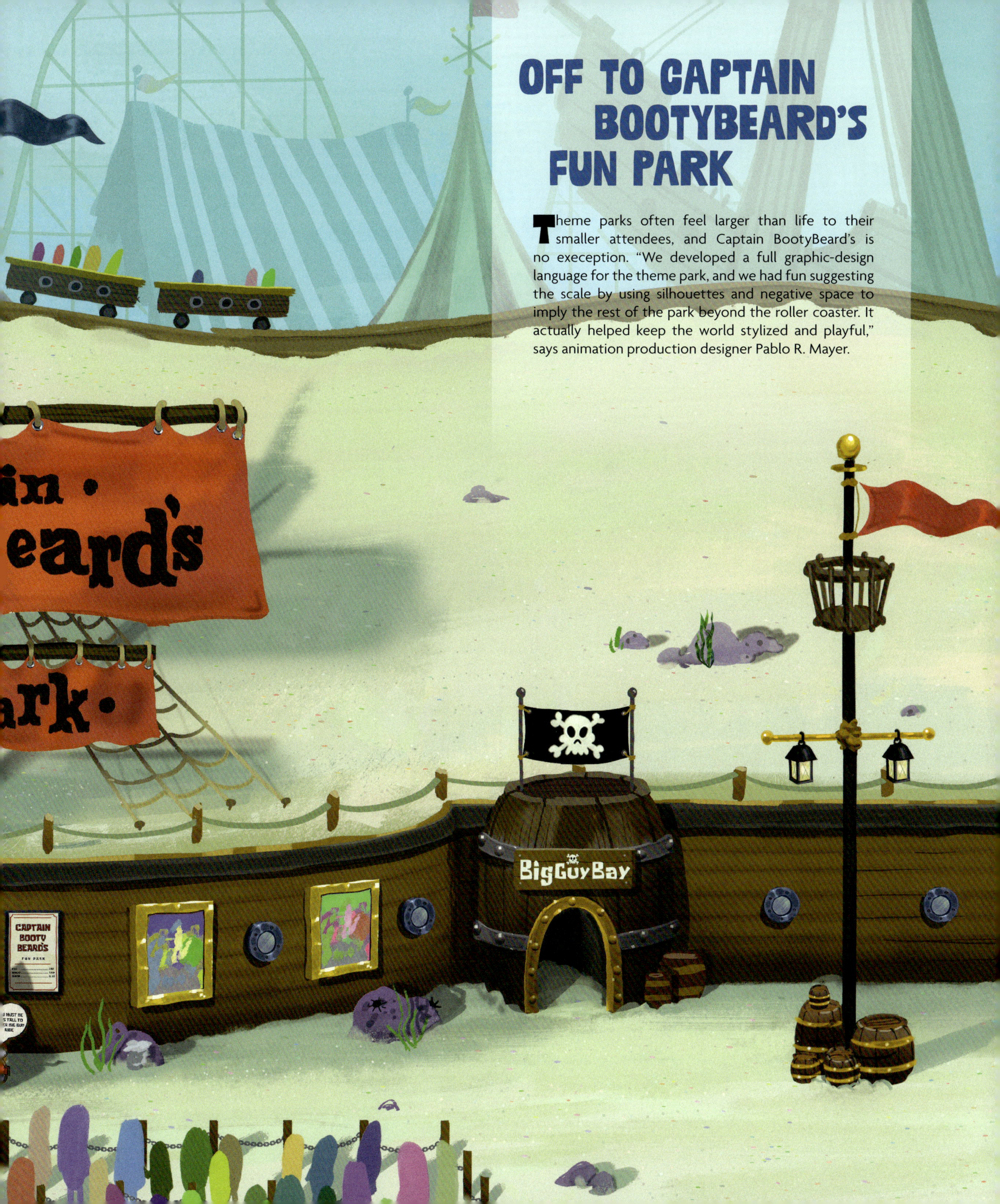

OFF TO CAPTAIN BOOTYBEARD'S FUN PARK

Theme parks often feel larger than life to their smaller attendees, and Captain BootyBeard's is no exeception. "We developed a full graphic-design language for the theme park, and we had fun suggesting the scale by using silhouettes and negative space to imply the rest of the park beyond the roller coaster. It actually helped keep the world stylized and playful," says animation production designer Pablo R. Mayer.

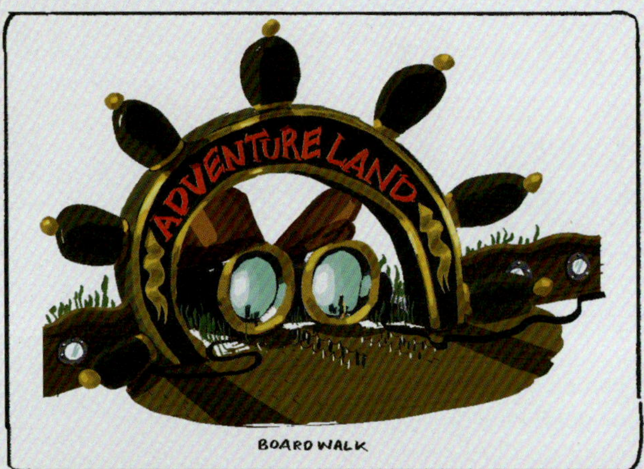

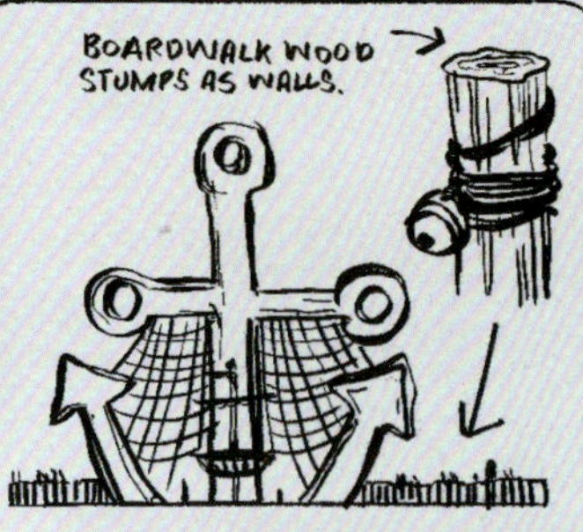

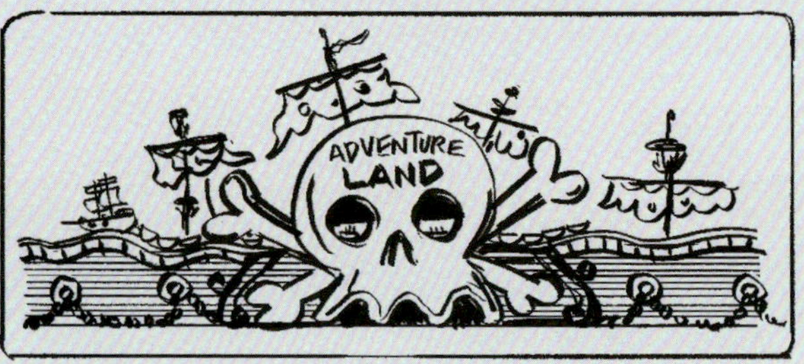

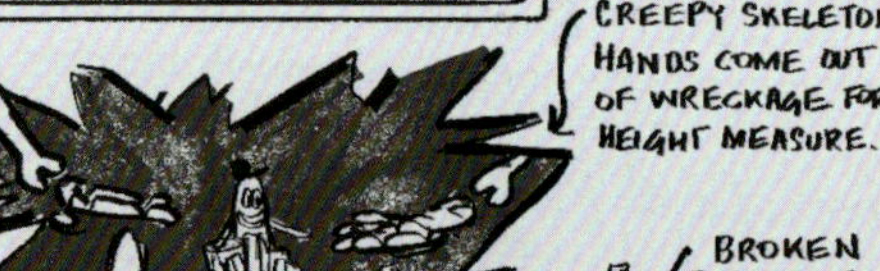

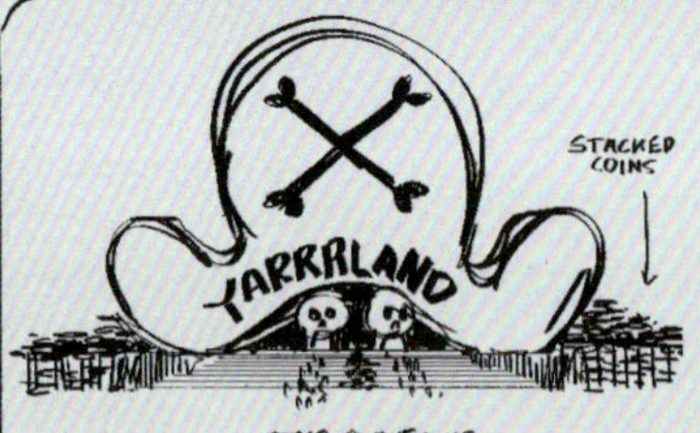

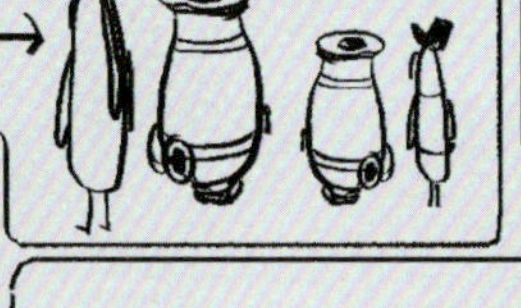

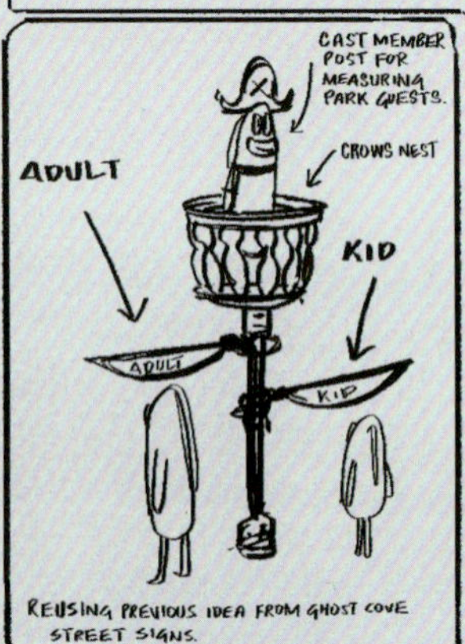

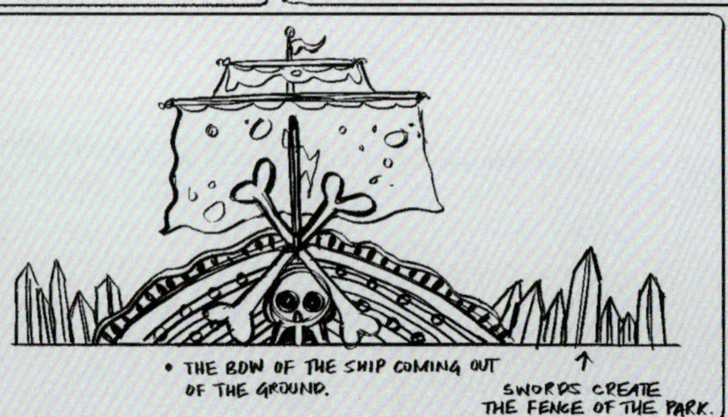

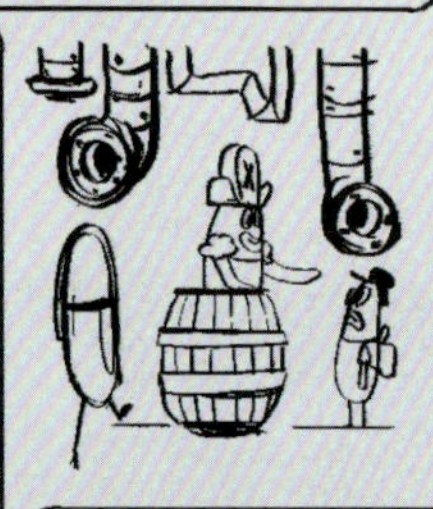

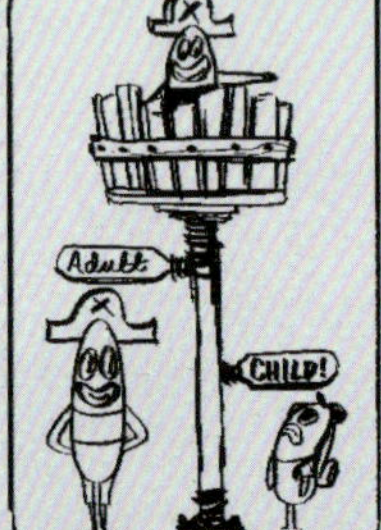

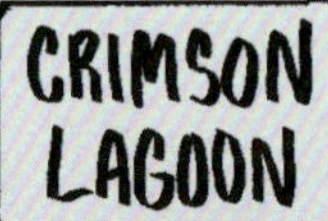

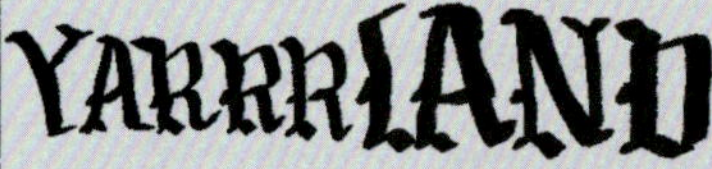

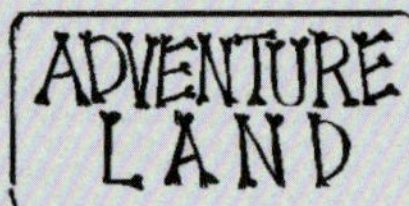

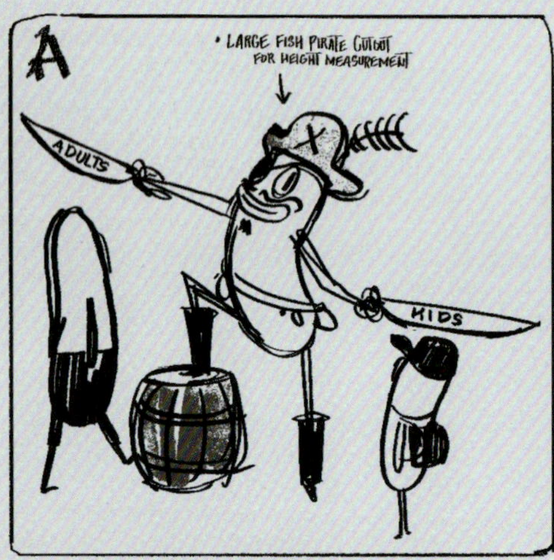

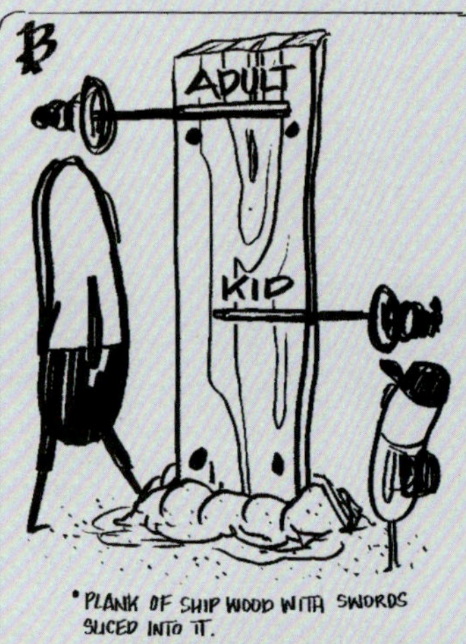

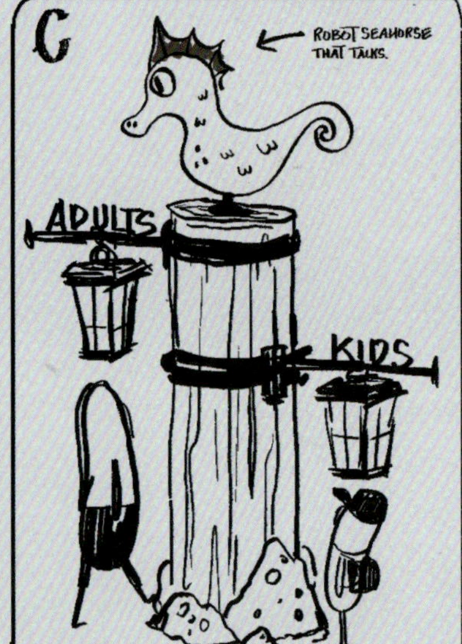

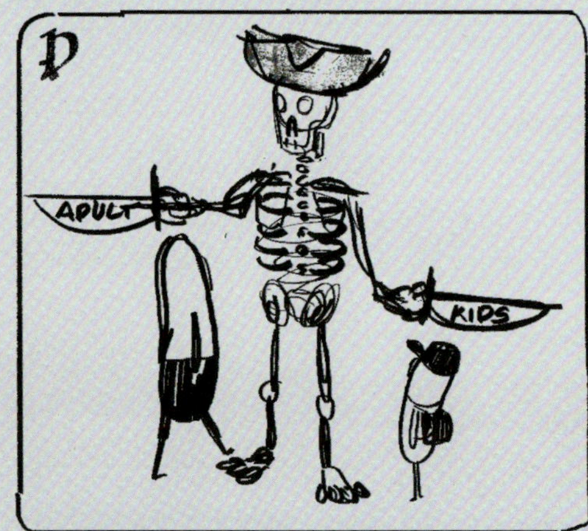

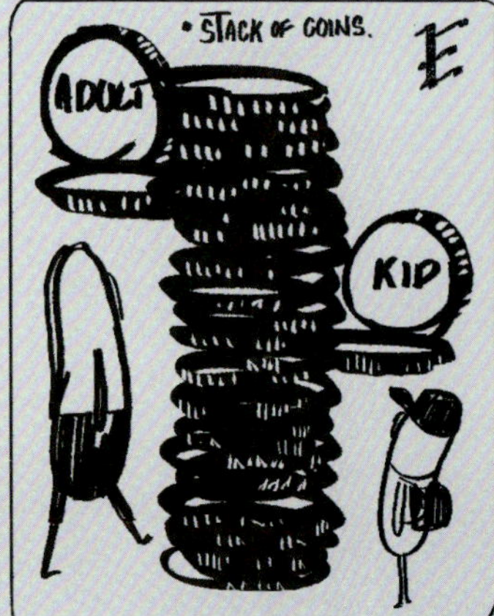

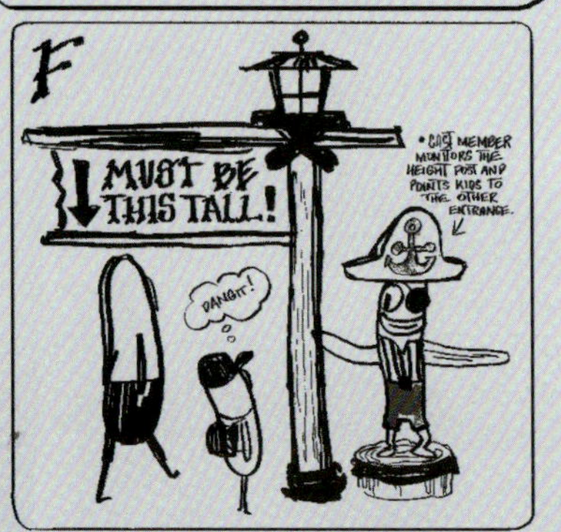

Rough designs of theme park signage and other décor elements

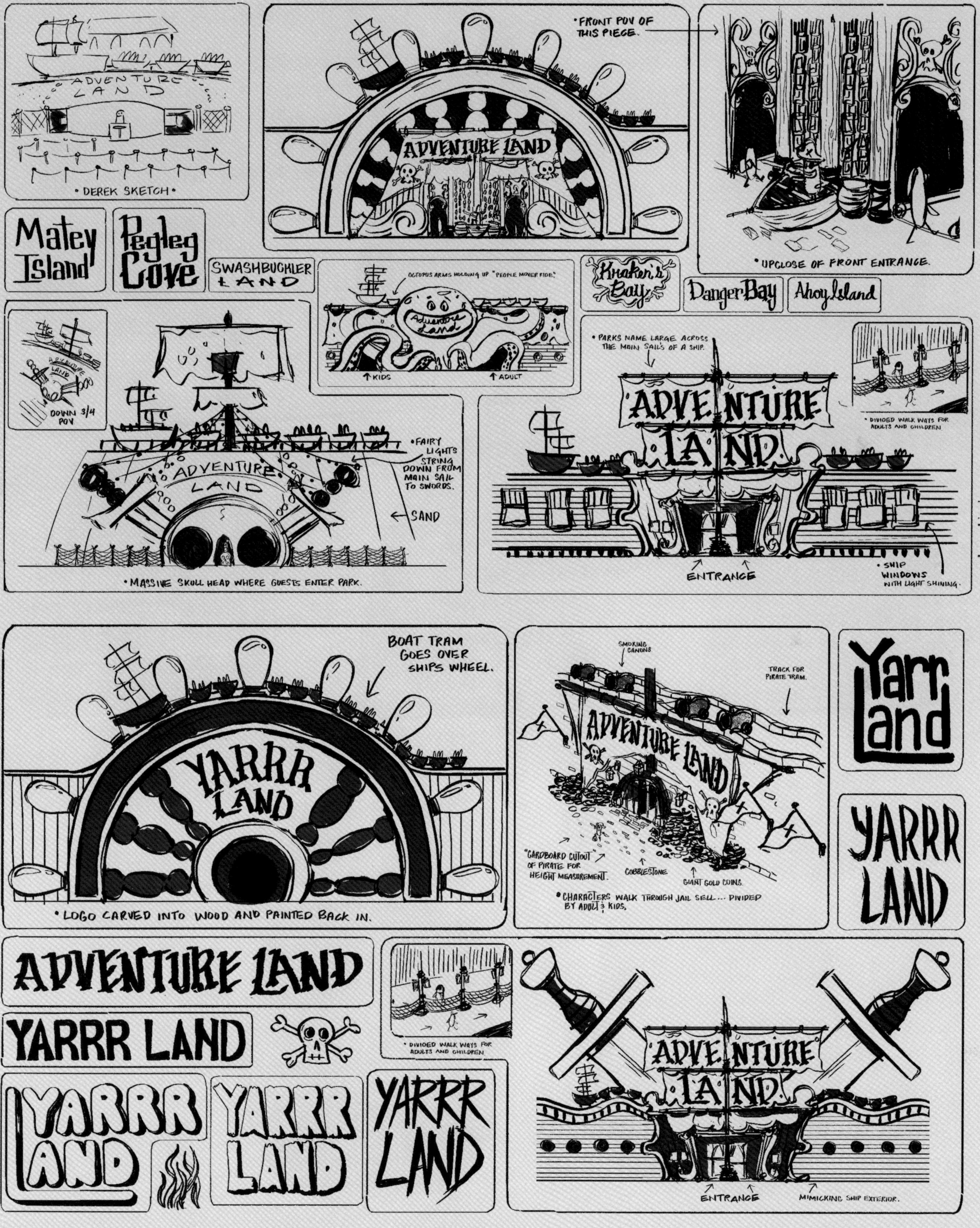

ADVENTURE LAND

• DEREK SKETCH •

• FRONT POV OF THIS PIECE.

ADVENTURE LAND

• UPCLOSE OF FRONT ENTRANCE.

Matey Island

Pegleg Cove

SWASHBUCKLER LAND

OCTOPUS ARMS HOLDING UP "PEOPLE MOVER RIDE"

Adventure Land

↑ KIDS

↑ ADULT

Kraken's Bay

Danger Bay

Ahoy Island

ADVENTURE LAND

DOWN 3/4 POV

ADVENTURE LAND

• FAIRY LIGHTS STRING DOWN FROM MAIN SAIL TO SWORDS.

← SAND

• MASSIVE SKULL HEAD WHERE GUESTS ENTER PARK.

• PARKS NAME LARGE ACROSS THE MAIN SAILS OF A SHIP.

ADVENTURE LAND

ENTRANCE

• SHIP WINDOWS WITH LIGHT SHINING.

• DIVIDED WALK WAYS FOR ADULTS AND CHILDREN.

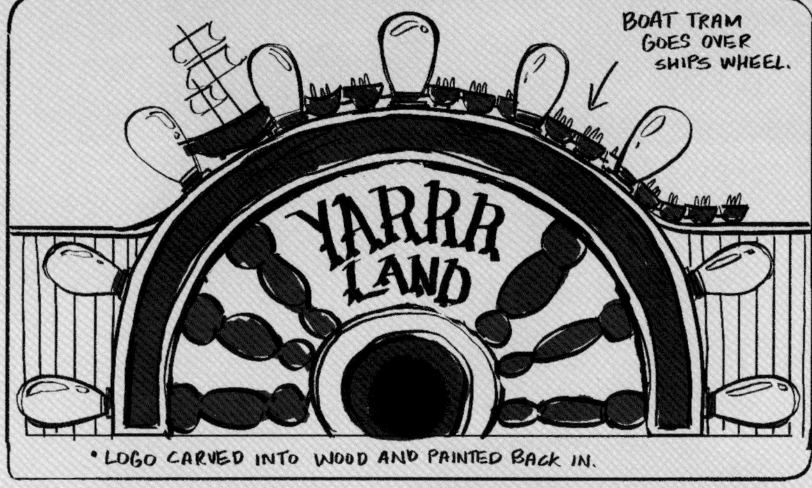

• LOGO CARVED INTO WOOD AND PAINTED BACK IN.

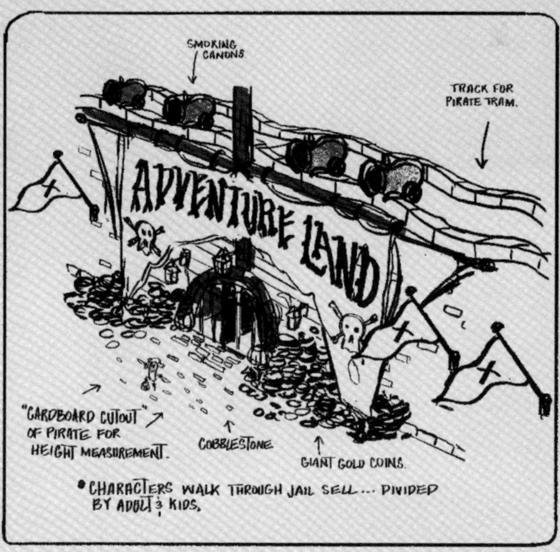

• CHARACTERS WALK THROUGH JAIL SELL... DIVIDED BY ADULT & KIDS.

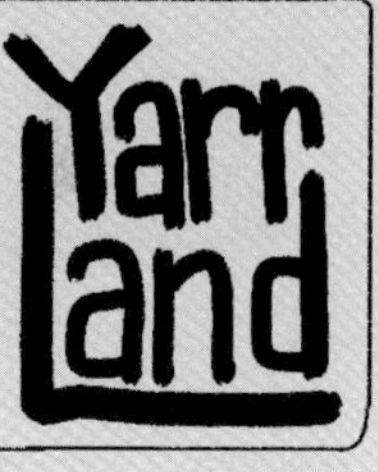

YARRR LAND

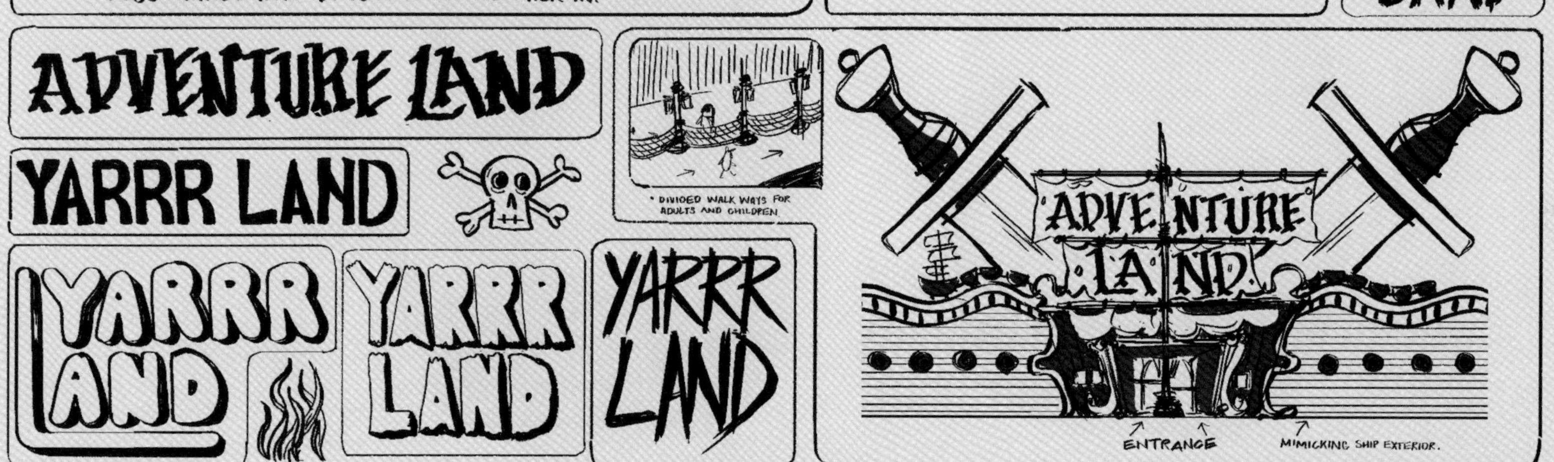

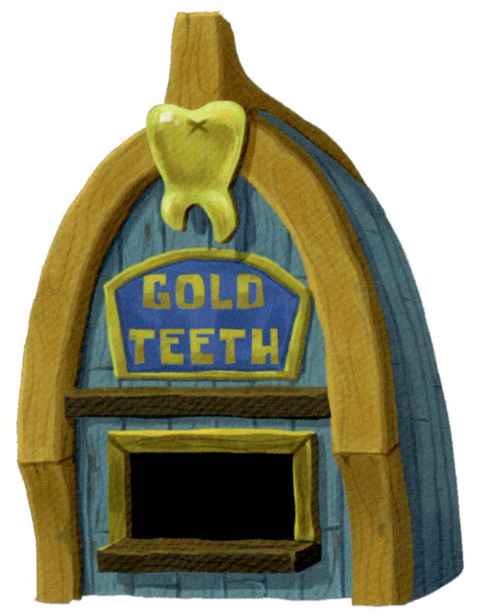

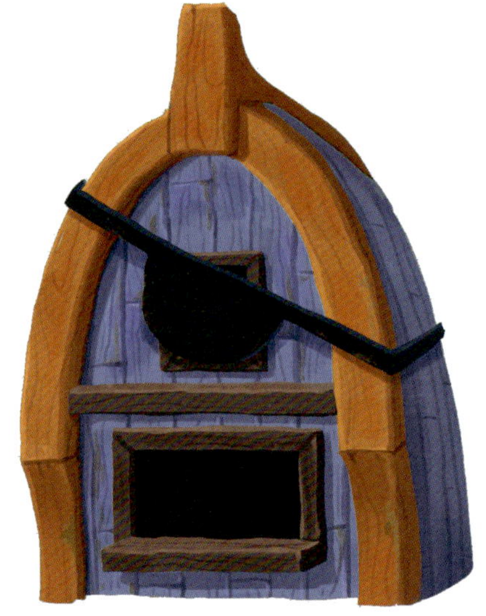

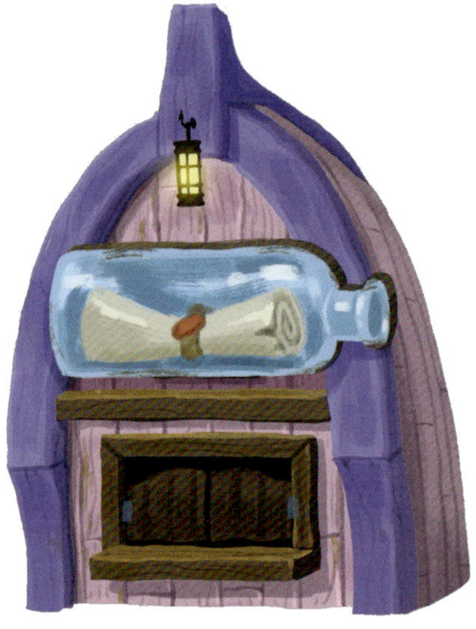

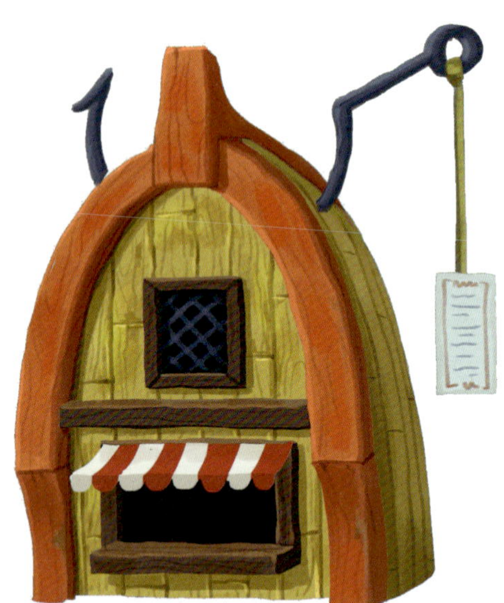

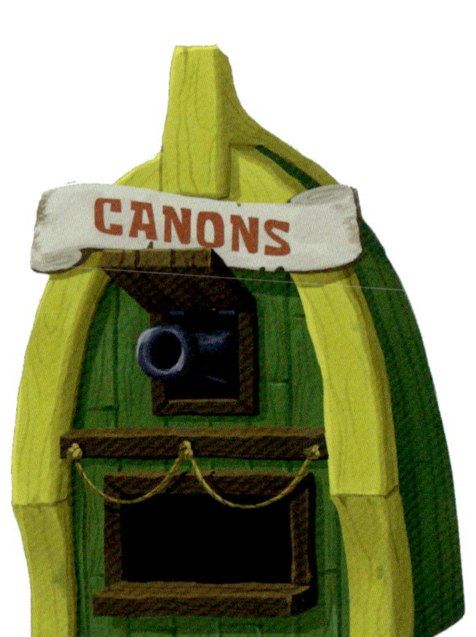

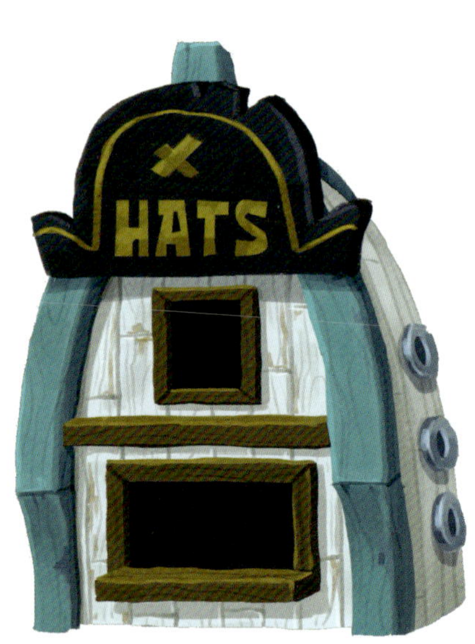

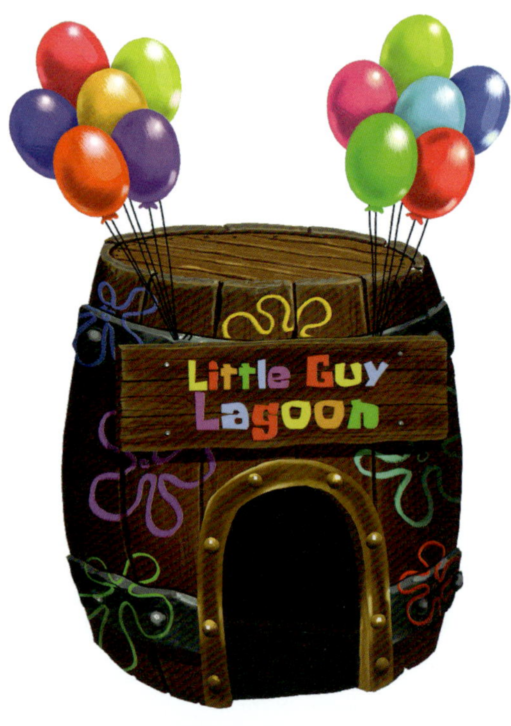

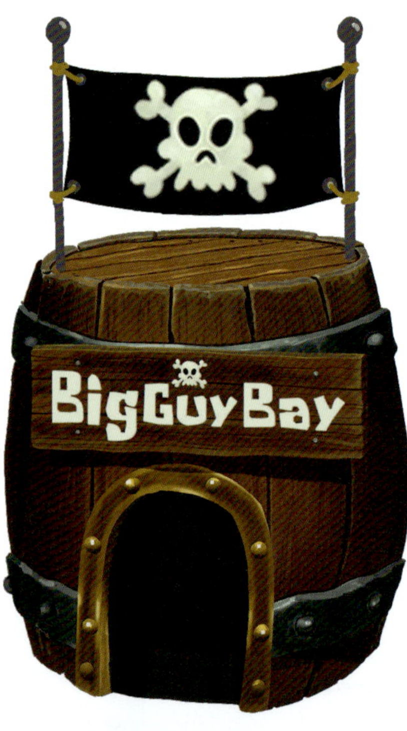

Prop design variations of theme park booths and points of entry [left]; design treatments of gateway, a theme park worker, and a balloon salesfish [right]

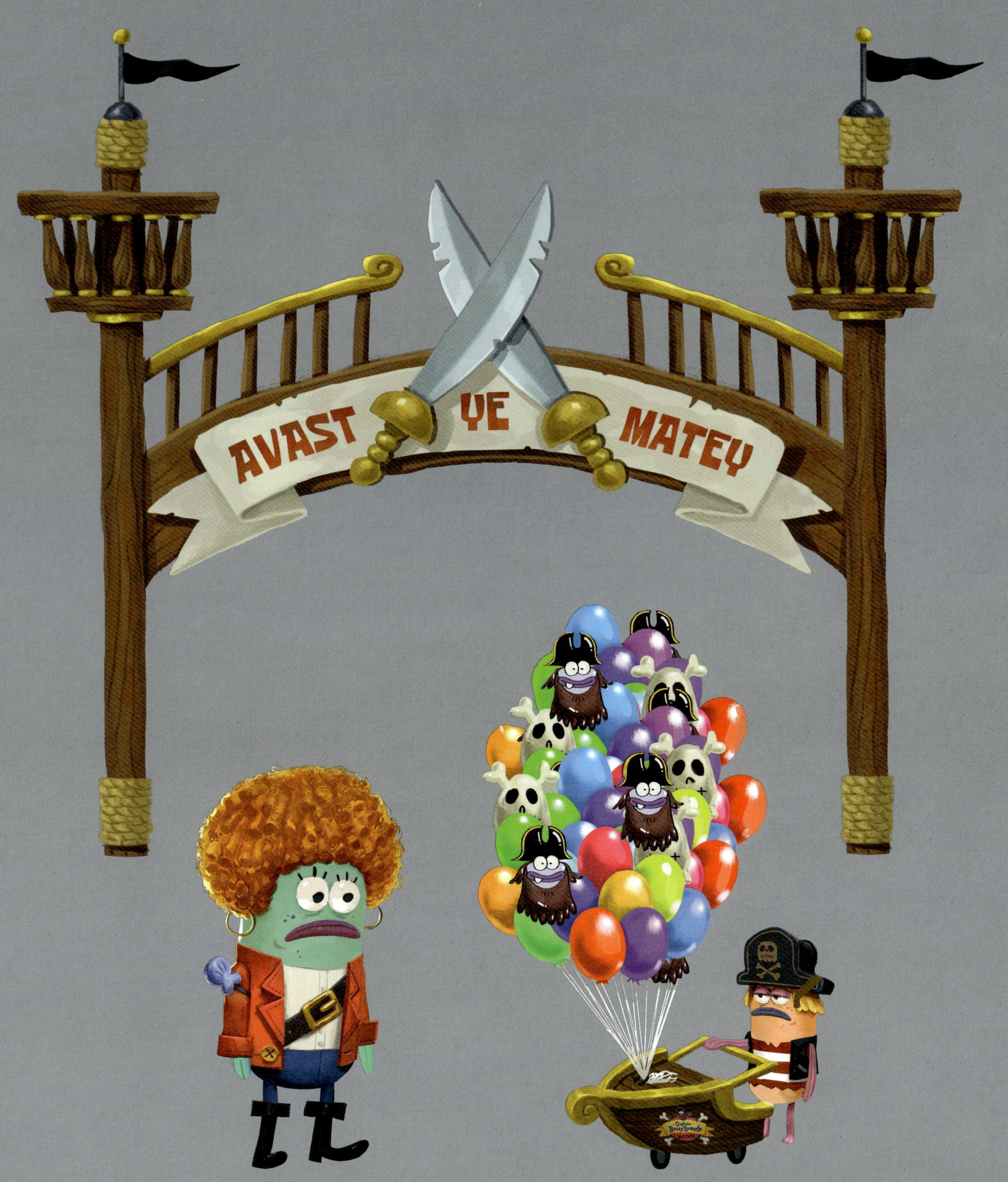
AVAST YE MATEY

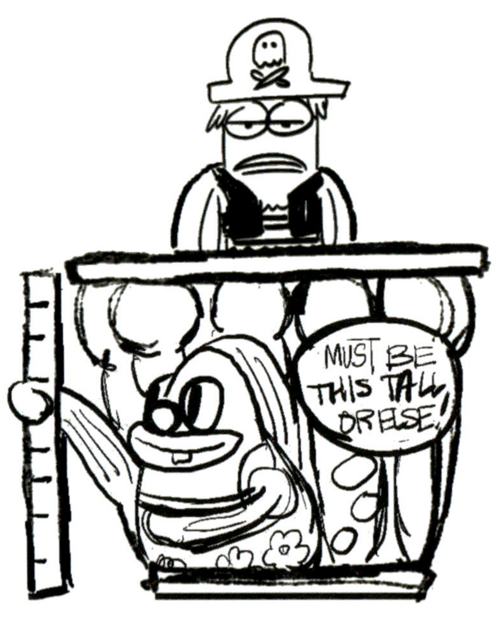

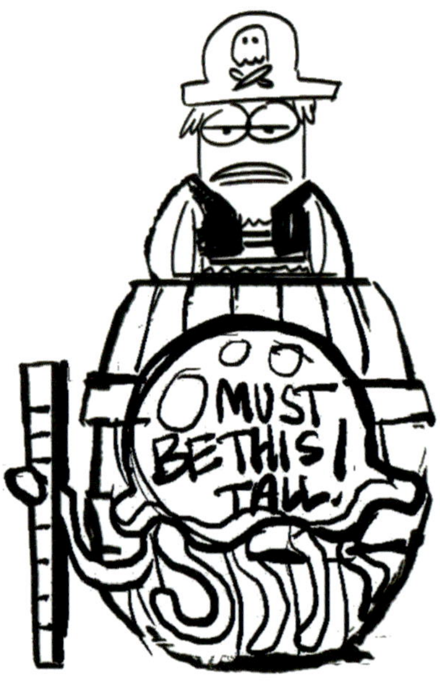

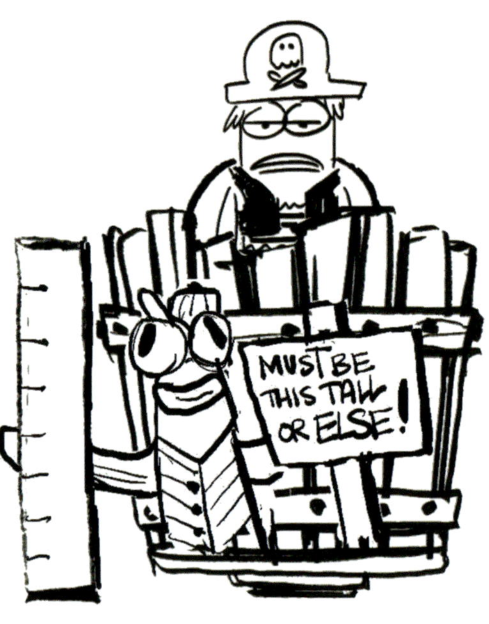

Rough design concepts of the point of measurement [left] and the theme park measurer [right]

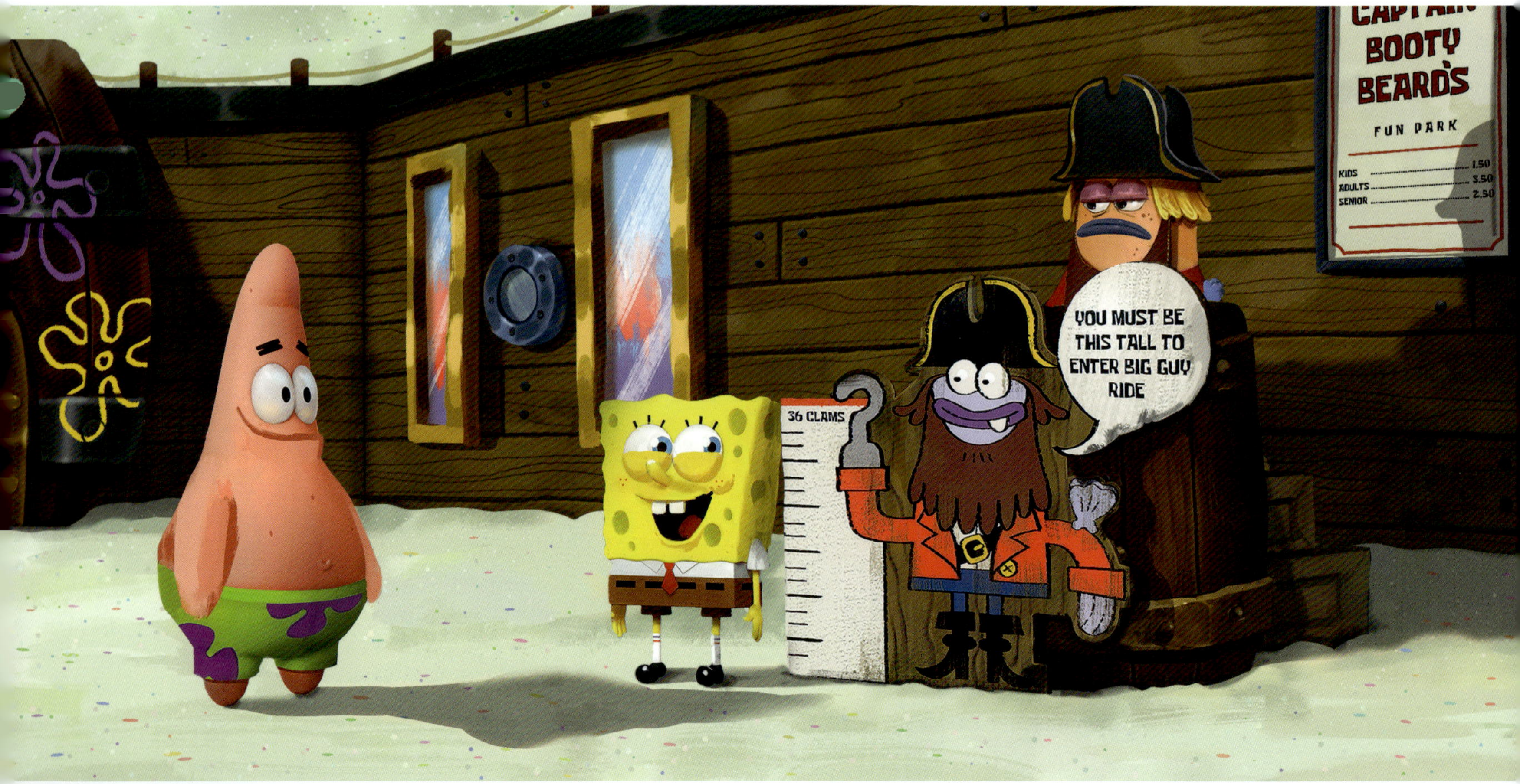

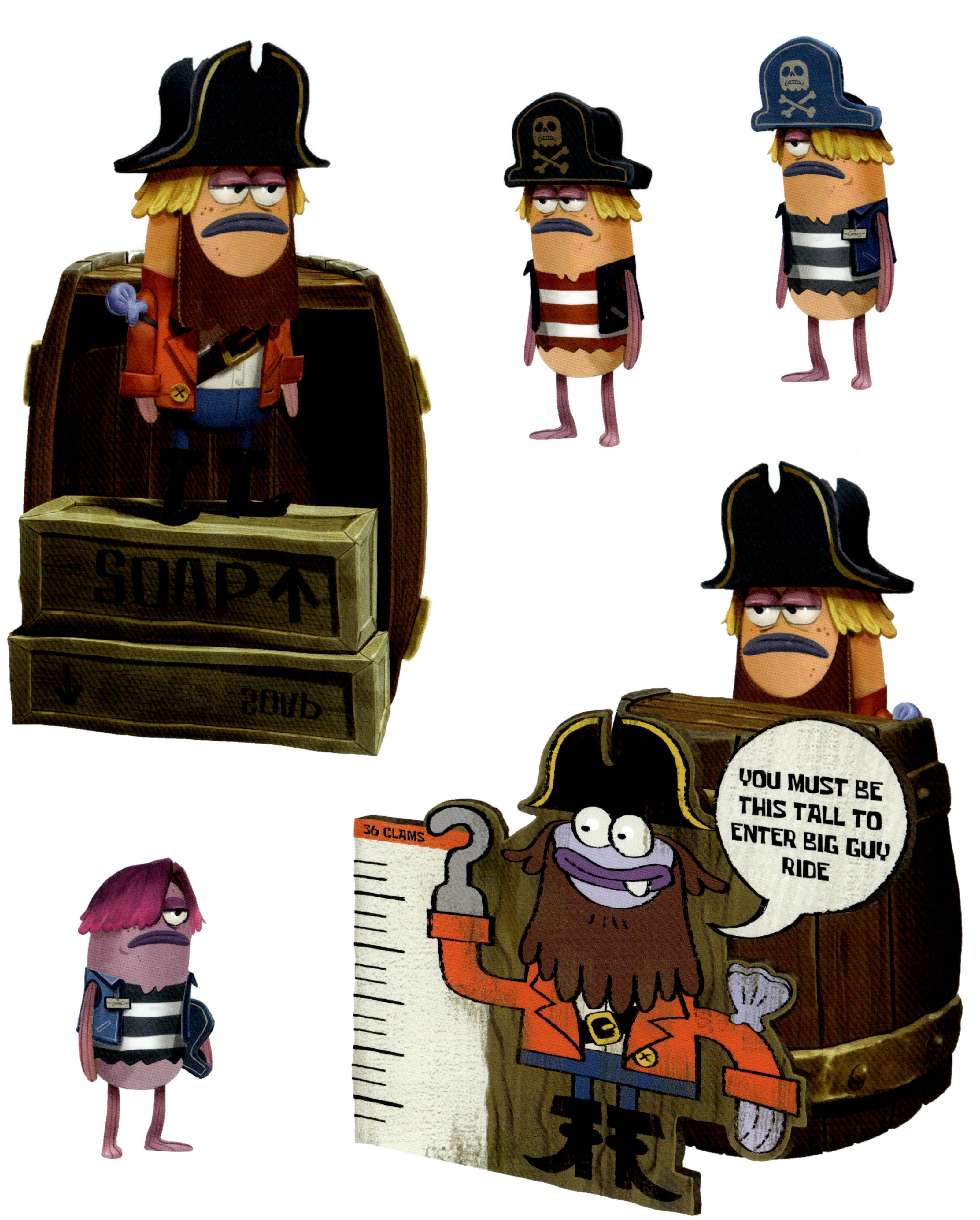
SOAP
SOAP
36 CLAMS
YOU MUST BE THIS TALL TO ENTER BIG GUY RIDE

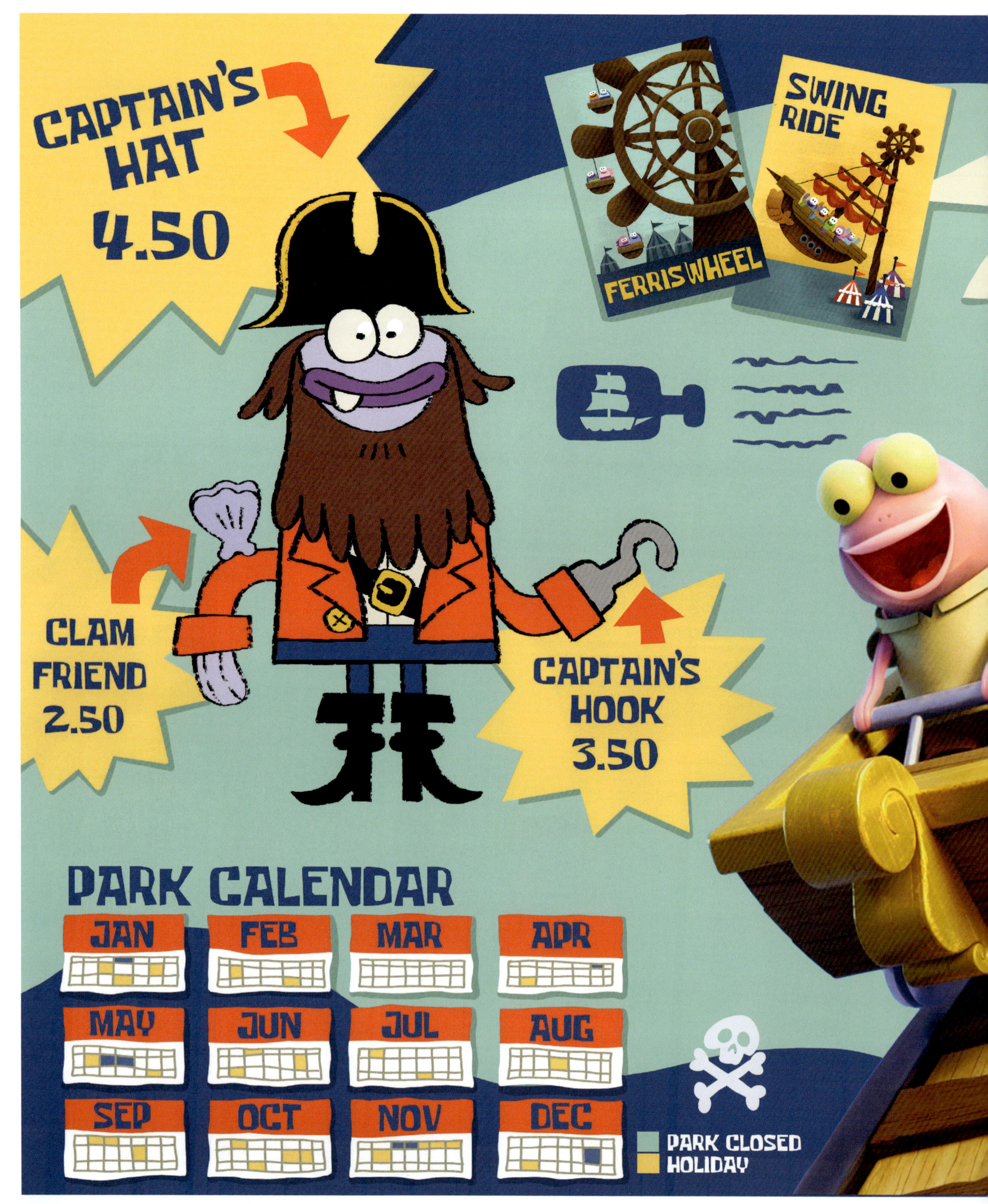

CAPTAIN'S HAT
4.50
FERRIS WHEEL
SWING RIDE
CLAM FRIEND
2.50
CAPTAIN'S HOOK
3.50
PARK CALENDAR
JAN
FEB
MAR
APR
MAY
JUN
JUL
AUG
SEP
OCT
NOV
DEC
PARK CLOSED
HOLIDAY

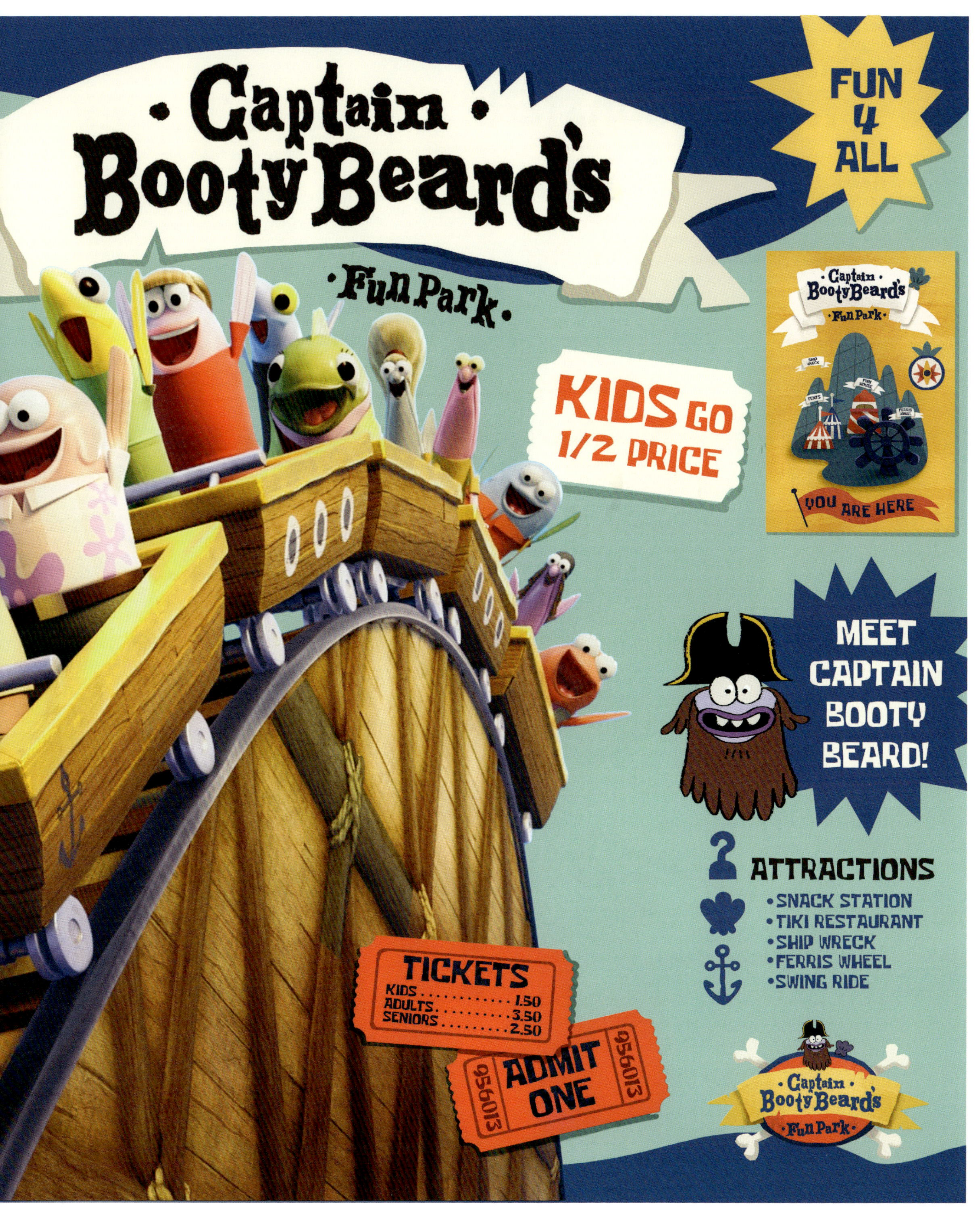

• Captain •
Booty Beard's
• Fun Park •
FUN
4
ALL
KIDS GO
1/2 PRICE
• Captain •
Booty Beard's
• Fun Park •
YOU ARE HERE
MEET
CAPTAIN
BOOTY
BEARD!
ATTRACTIONS
• SNACK STATION
• TIKI RESTAURANT
• SHIP WRECK
• FERRIS WHEEL
• SWING RIDE
TICKETS
KIDS 1.50
ADULTS 3.50
SENIORS 2.50
956013
ADMIT
ONE
956013
• Captain •
Booty Beard's
• Fun Park •

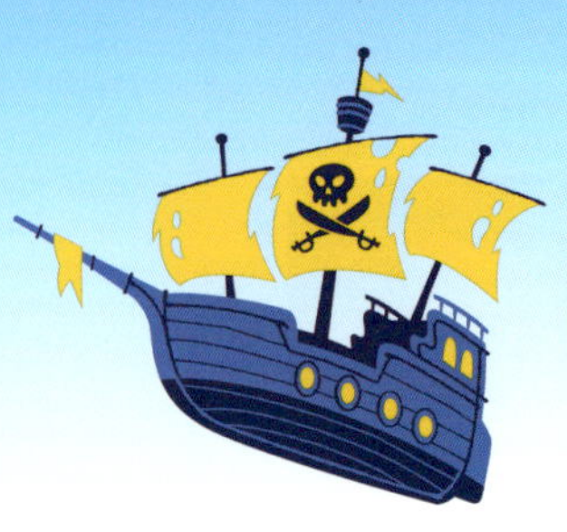

SHIPWRECK ROLLER COASTER

SpongeBob thinks he is ready to face the Shipwreck roller coaster, and what a ride it is! "Although we never see the entire roller coaster on screen, each shot was crafted to feel exaggerated and absurd as if part of SpongeBob's imagination. It didn't need to make logical sense, it just had to feel wild and fun," explains production designer Pablo R. Mayer.

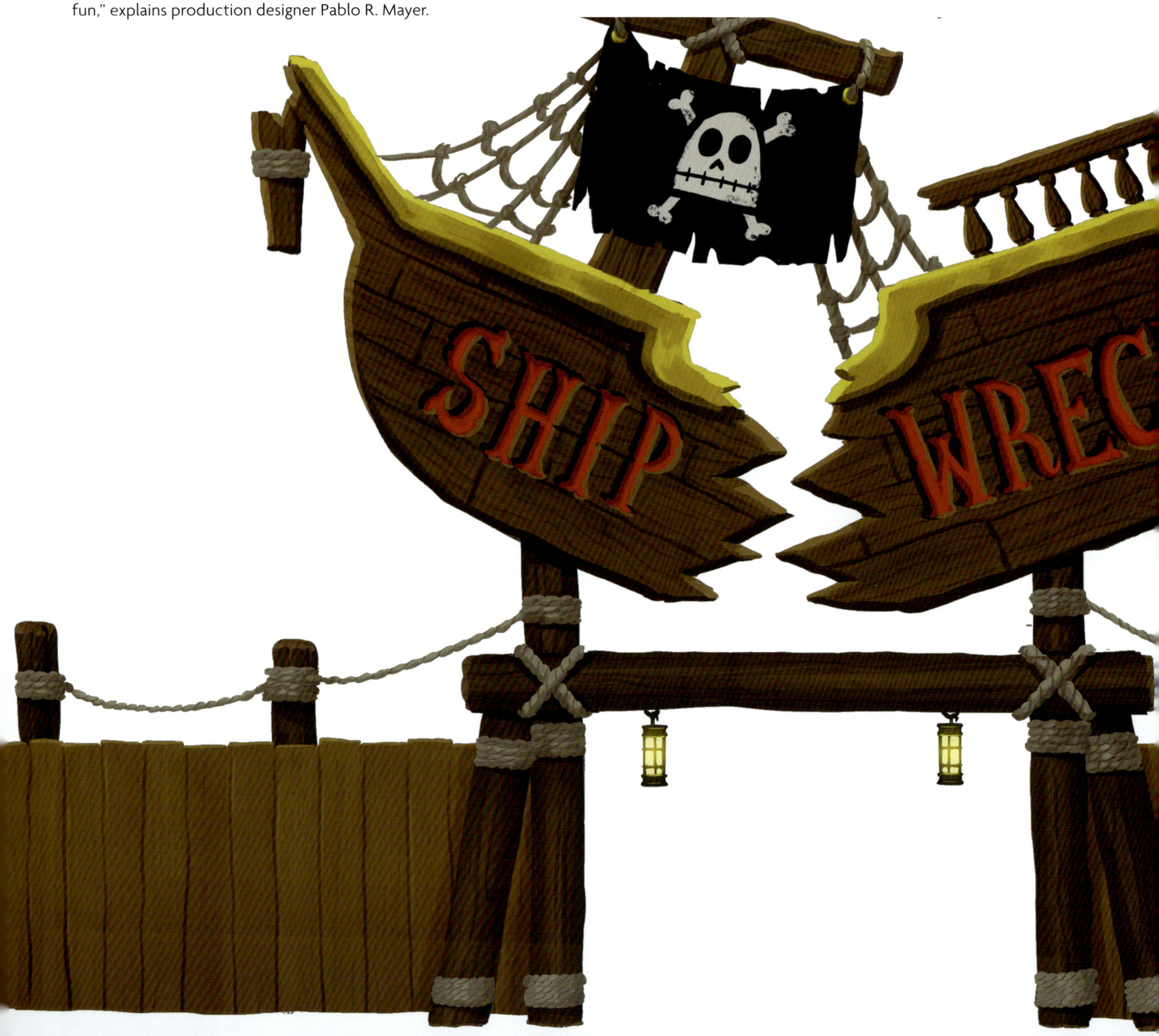

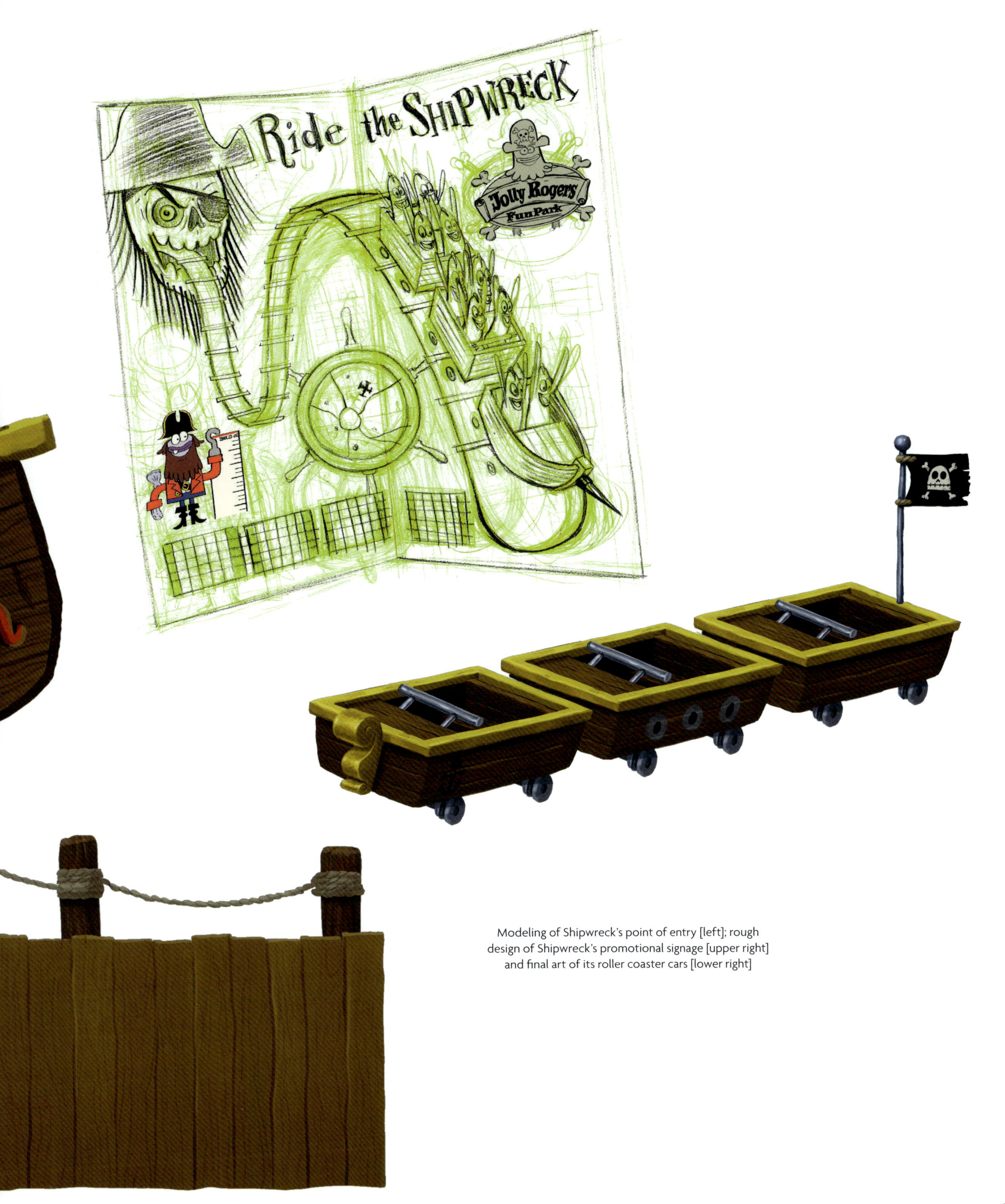

Modeling of Shipwreck's point of entry [left]; rough design of Shipwreck's promotional signage [upper right] and final art of its roller coaster cars [lower right]

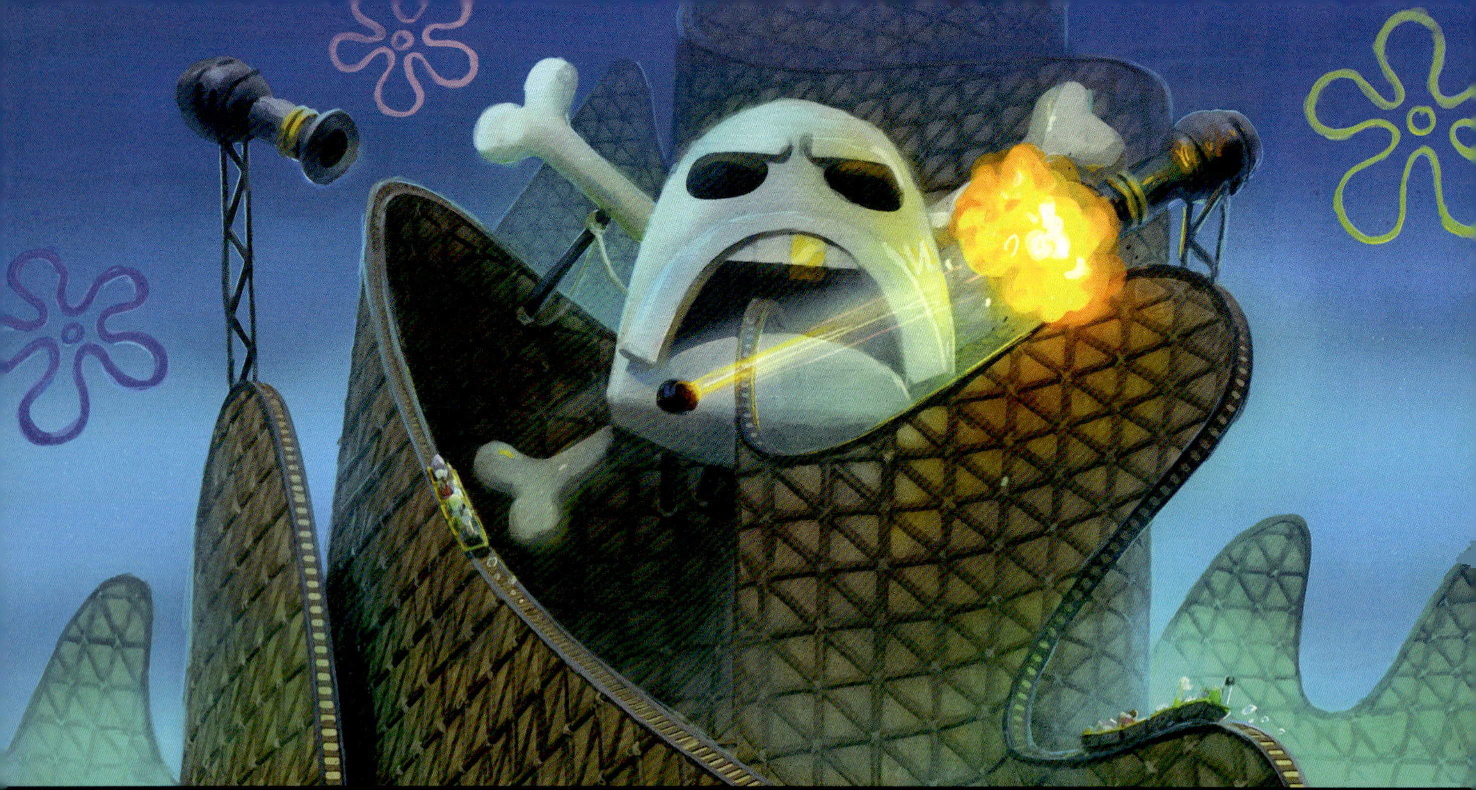

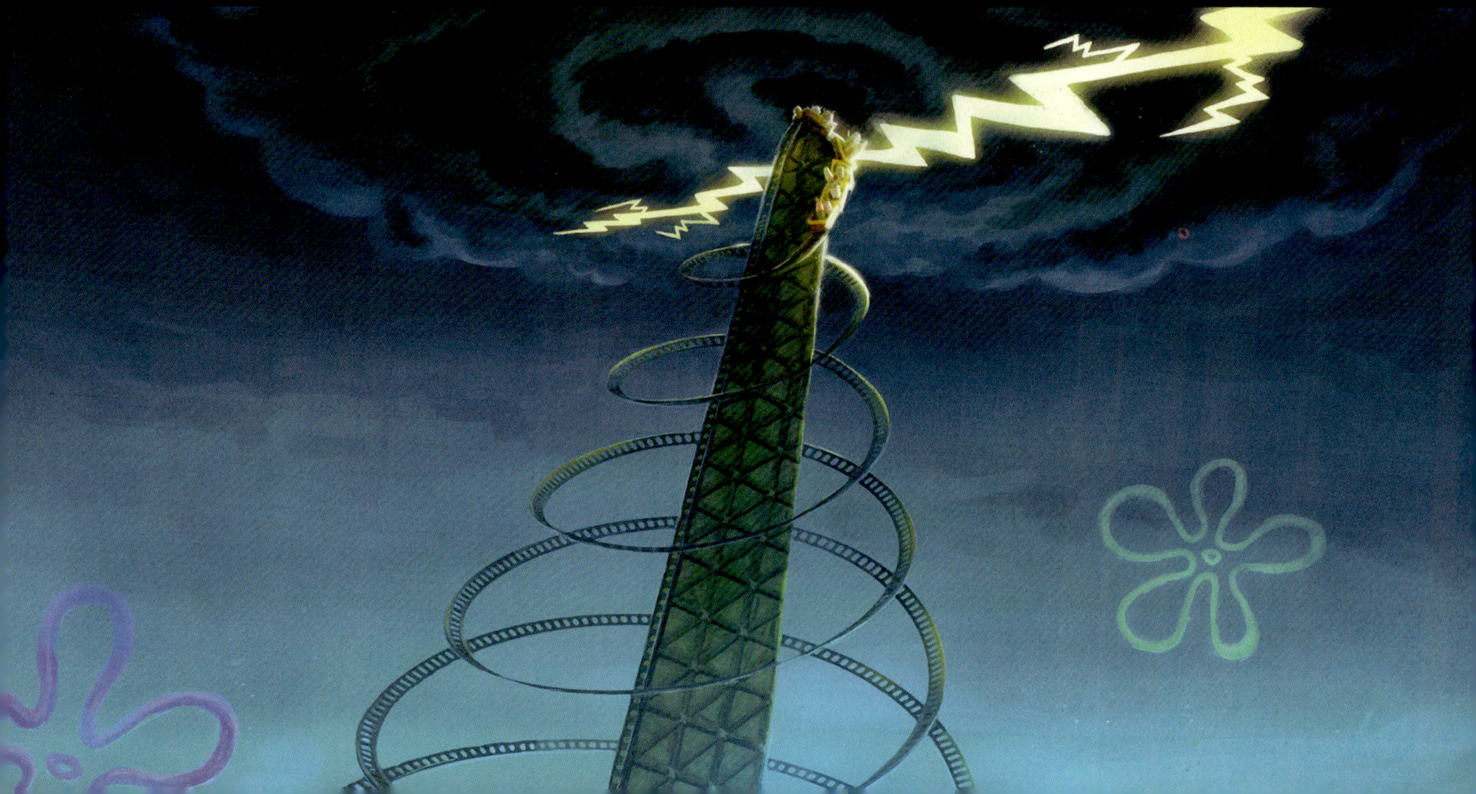

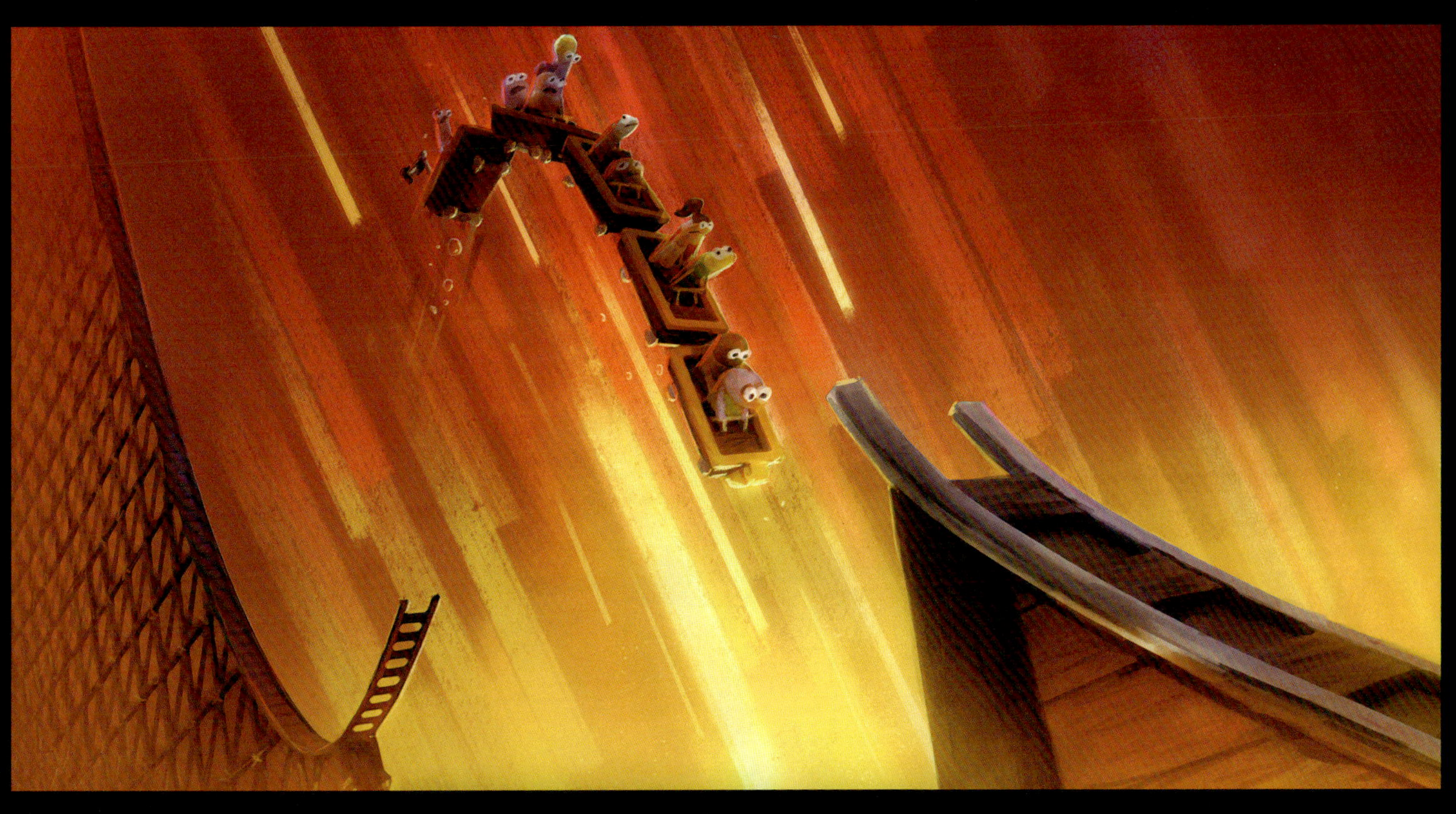

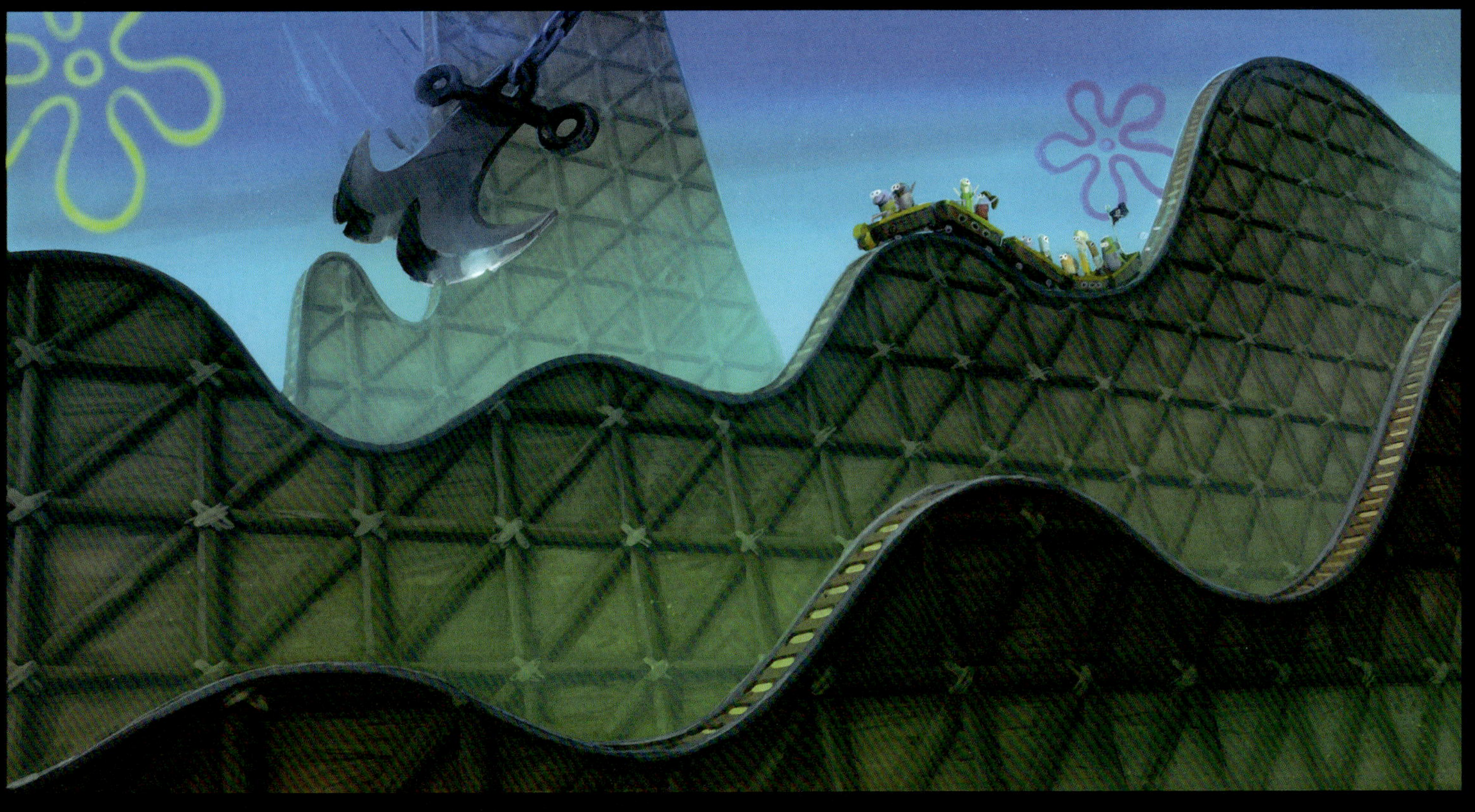

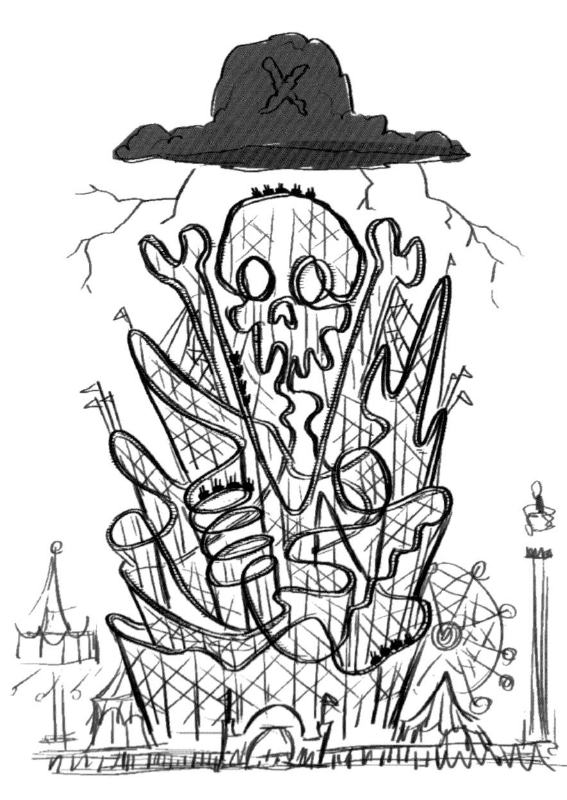

Design variations and effects of Shipwreck

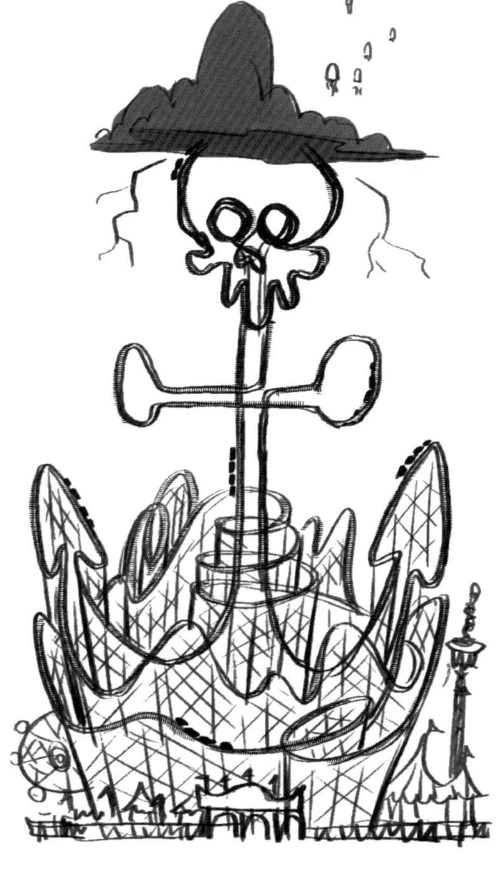

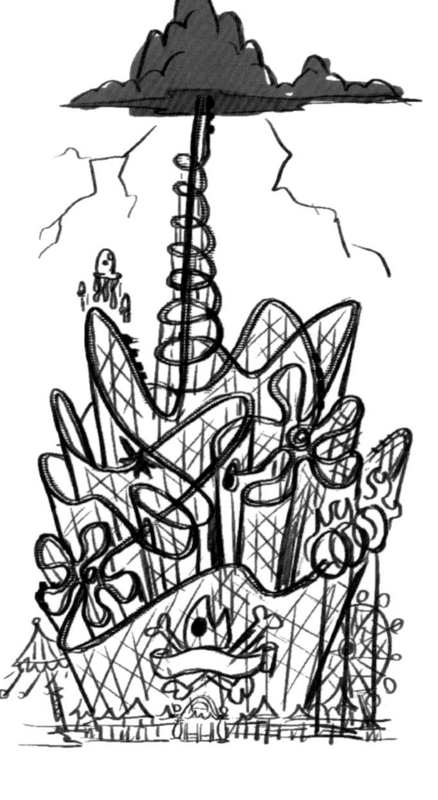

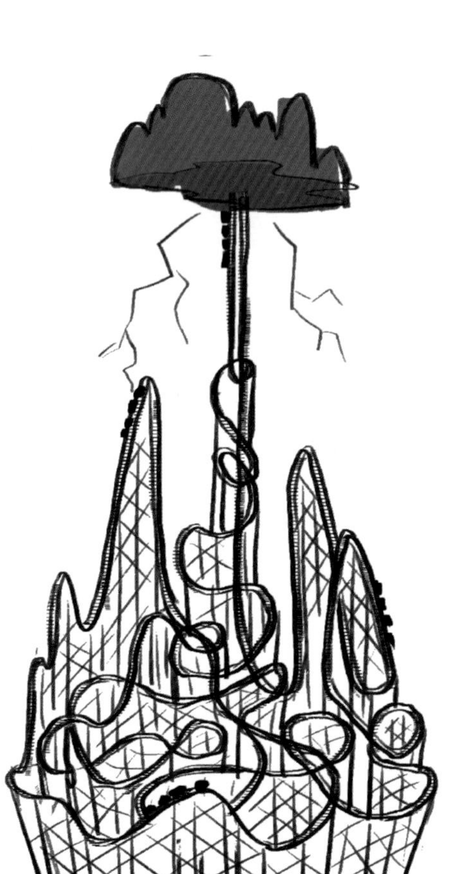

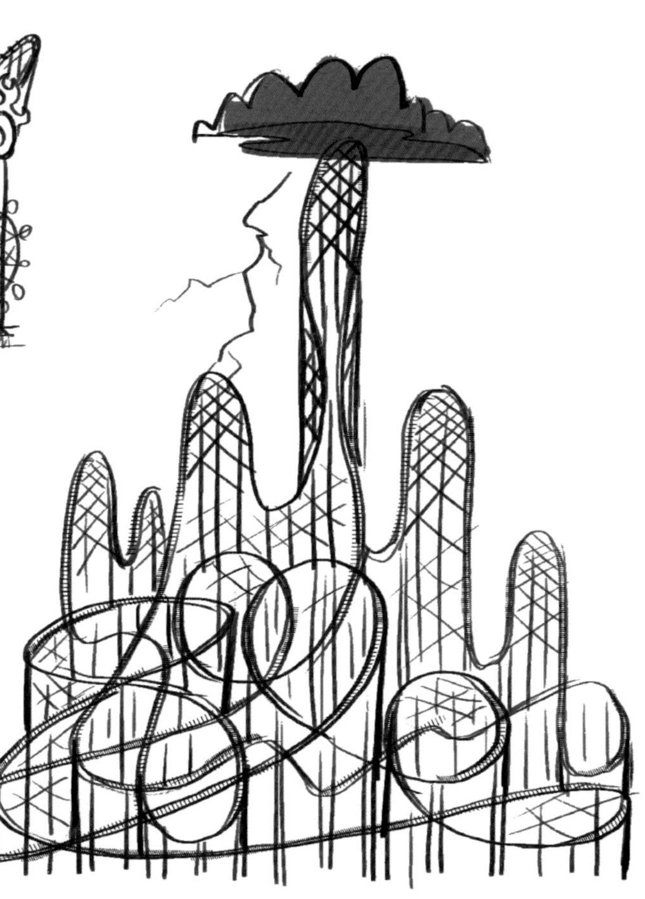

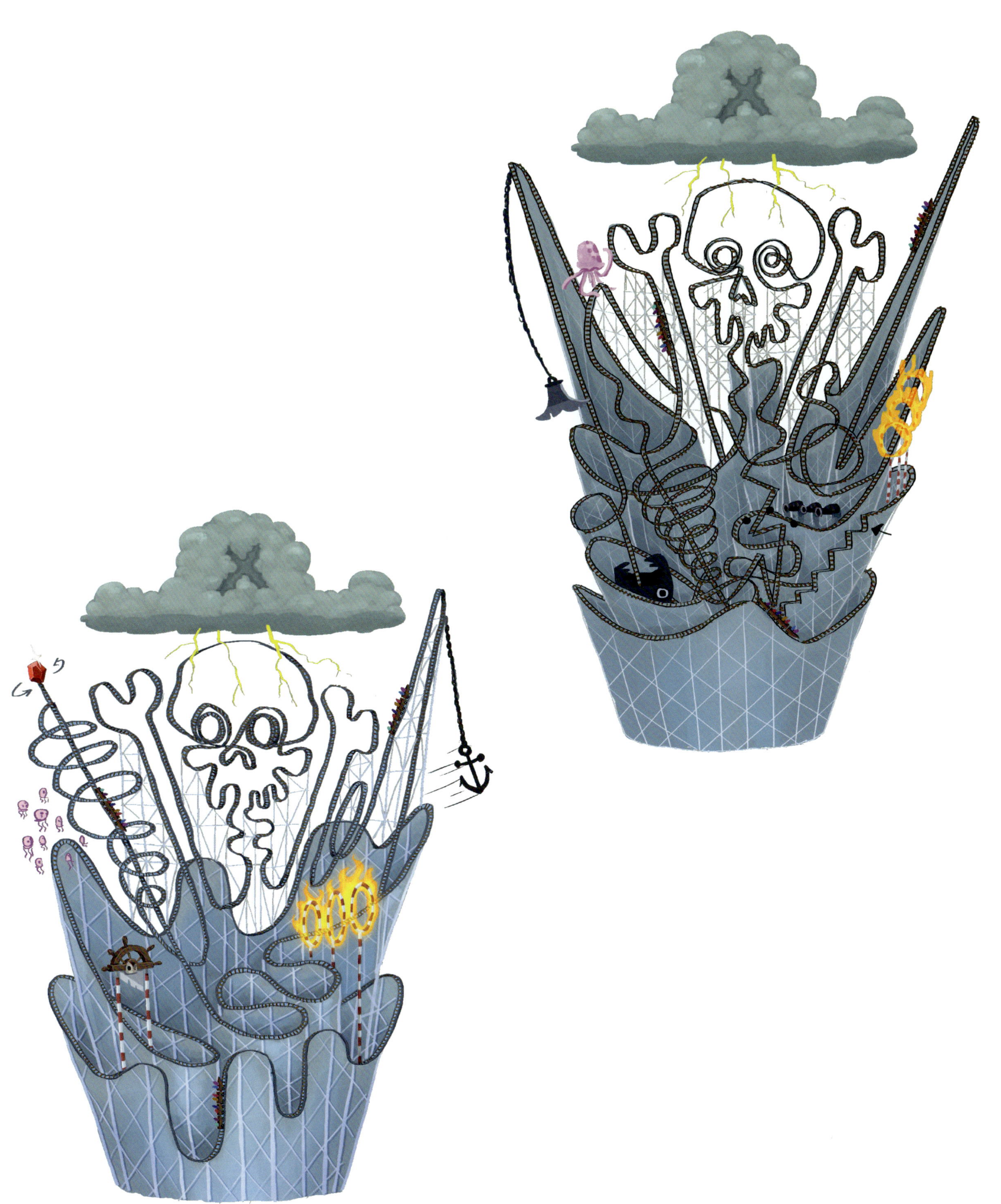

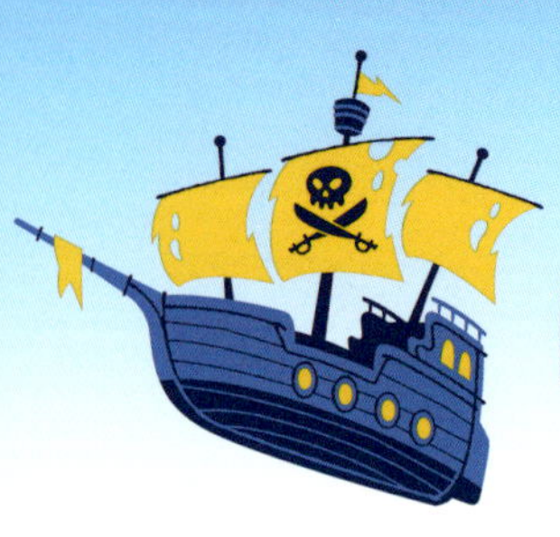

KRABS' TALE OF SWASHBUCKLING

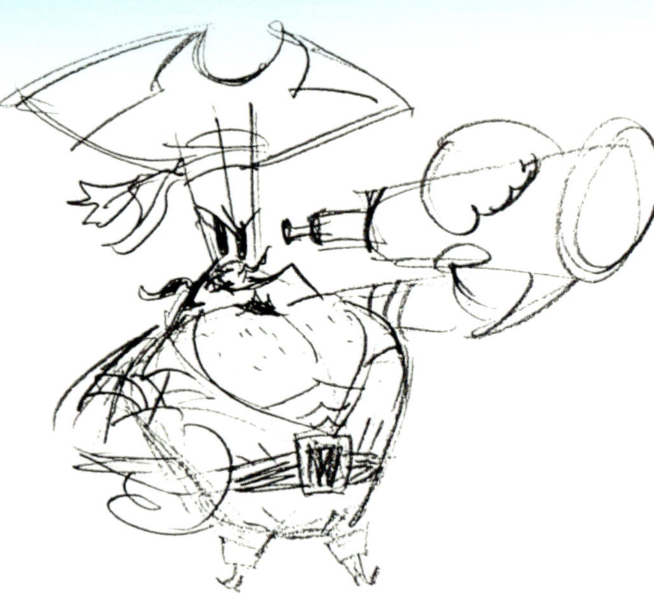

Flaunting his own bravery in a moment when SpongeBob questions how much of a big guy he himself is, Mr. Krabs tells SpongeBob how he earned his Swashbuckling Certificate, in a visually fun recollection of his mariner past.

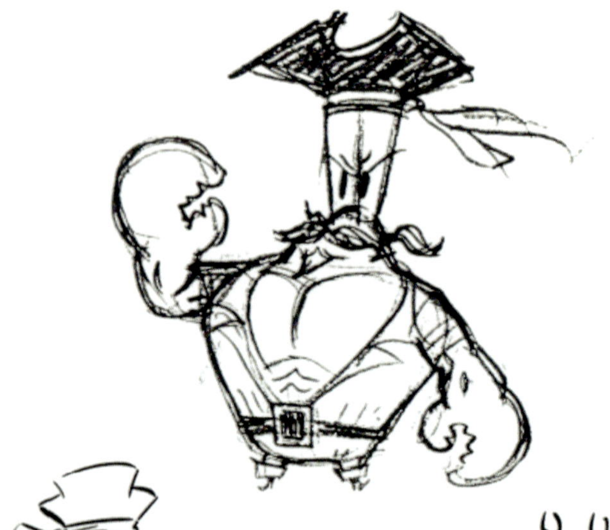

Character roughs and concepts of Mariner Mr. Krabs

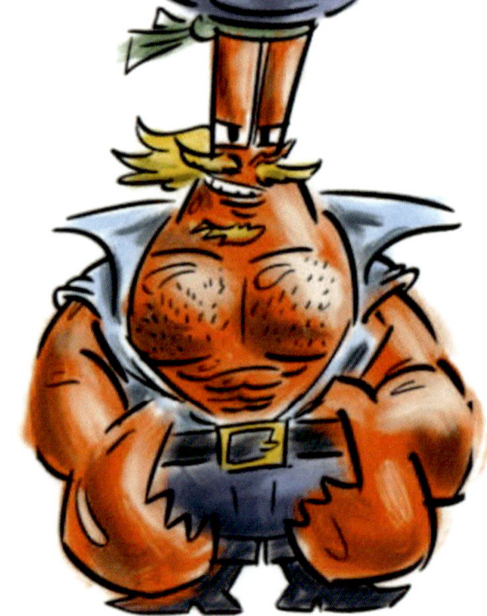

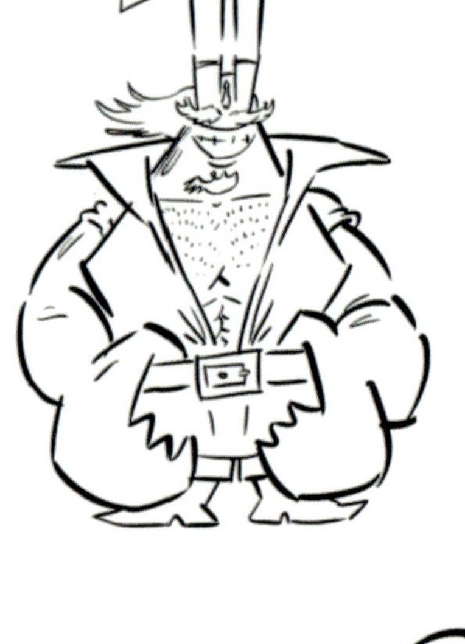

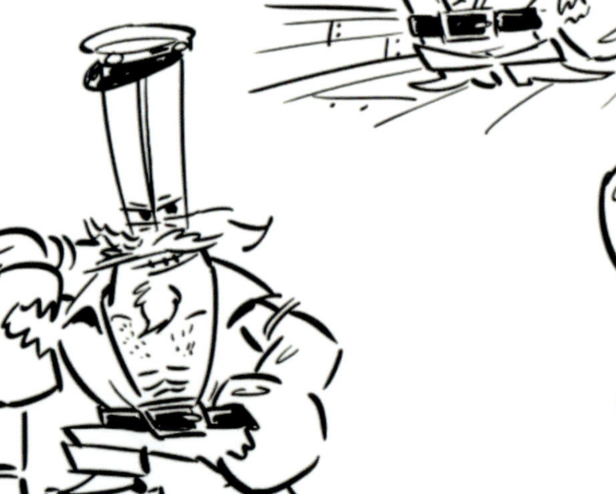

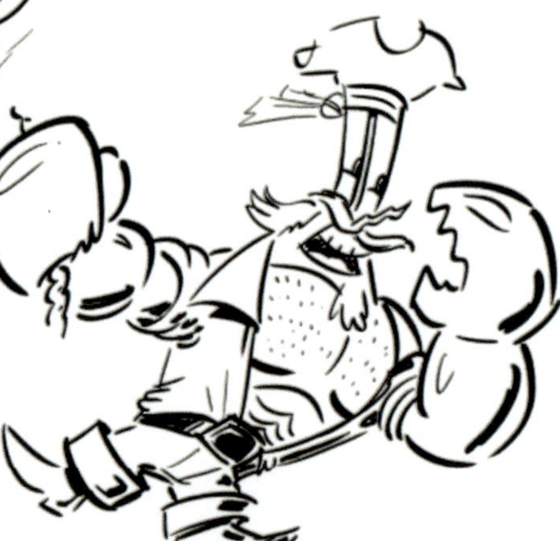

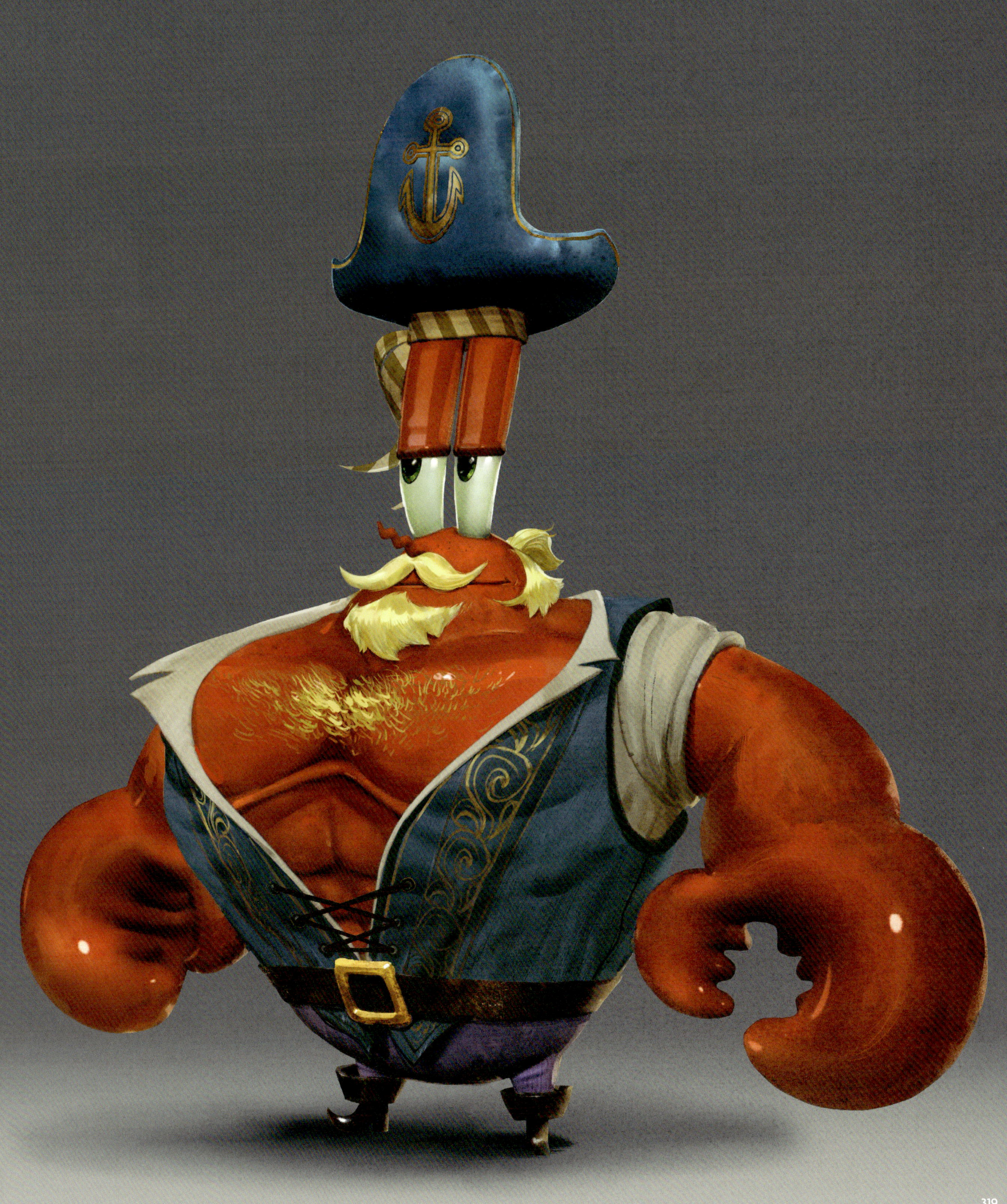

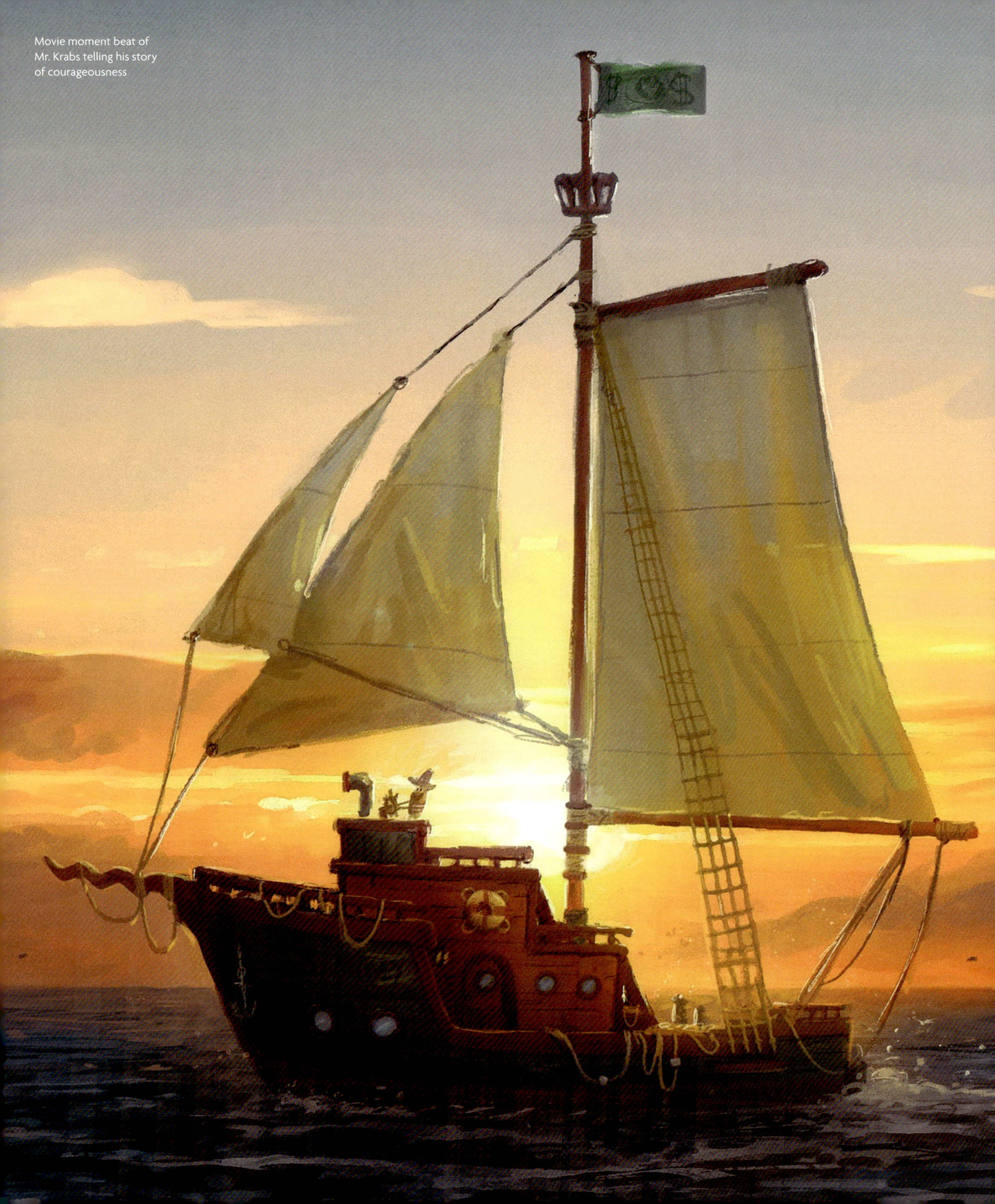

Movie moment beat of Mr. Krabs telling his story of courageousness

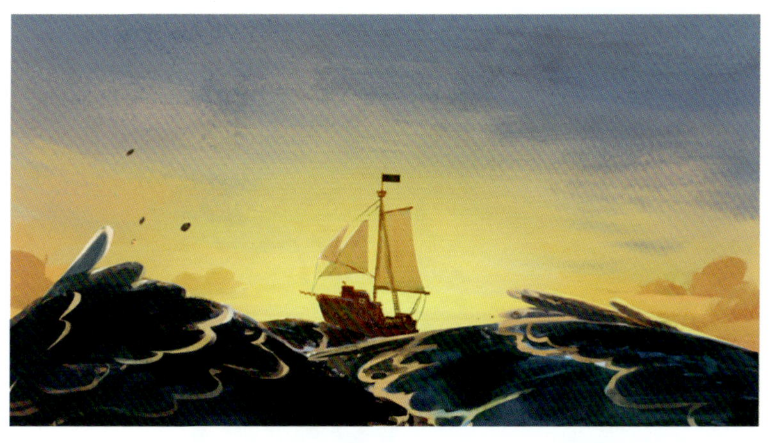
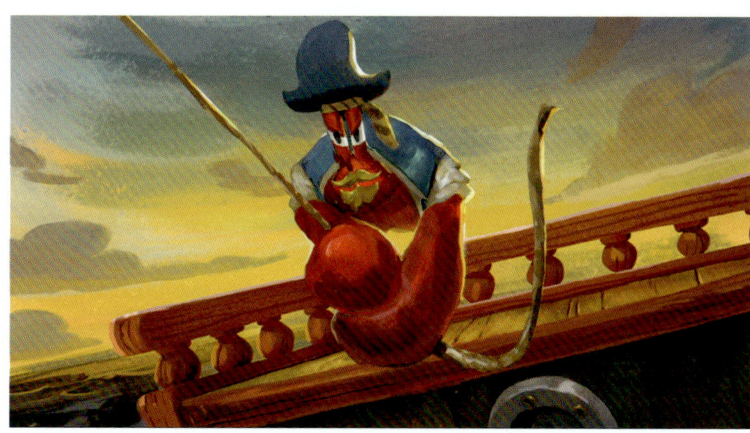
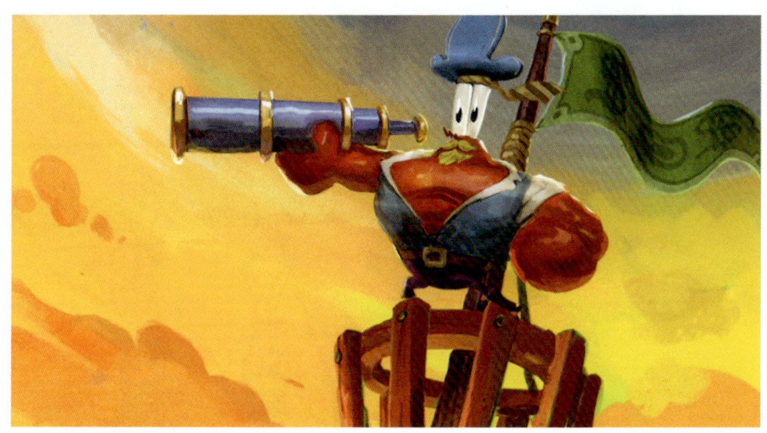
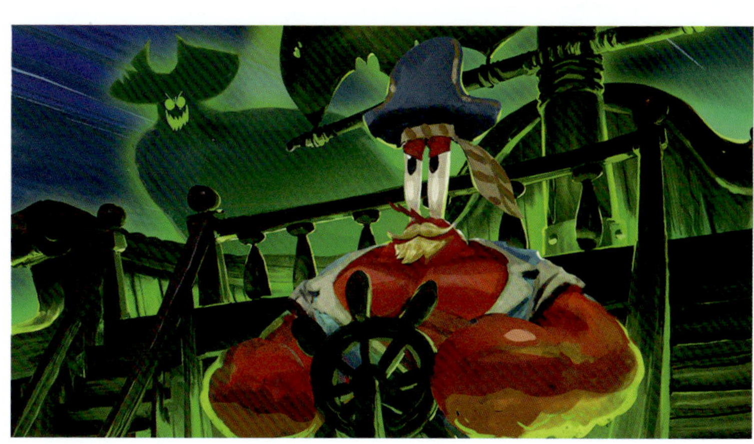
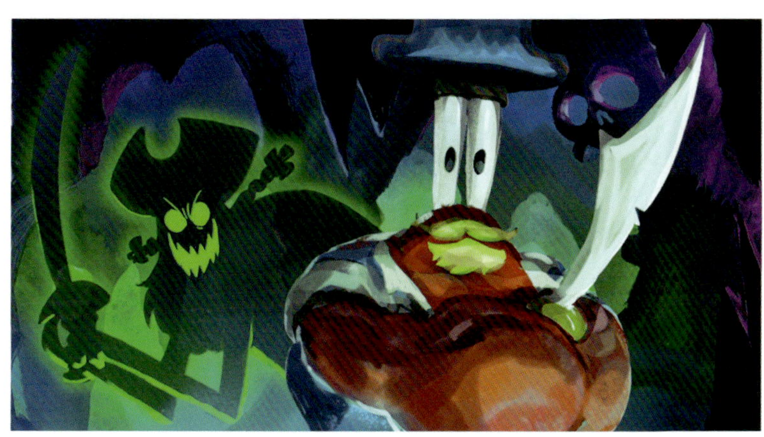
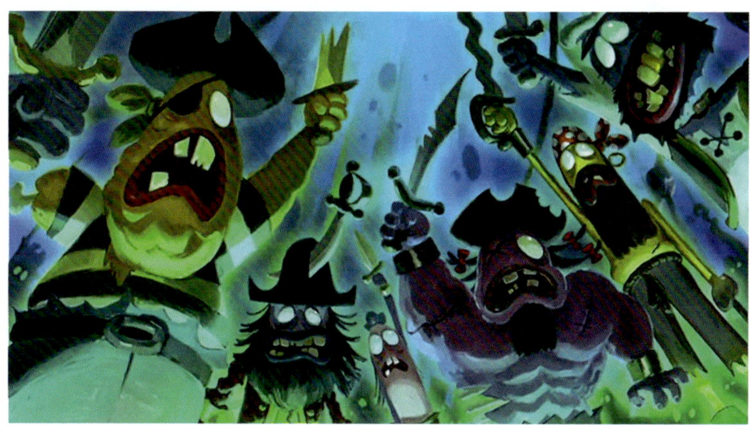
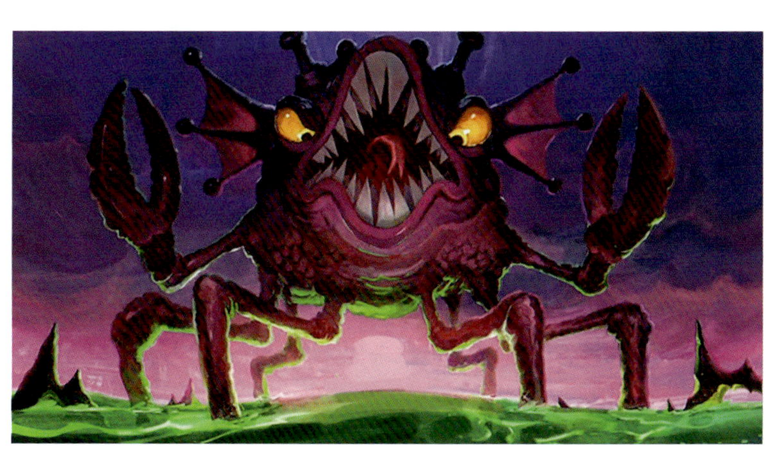
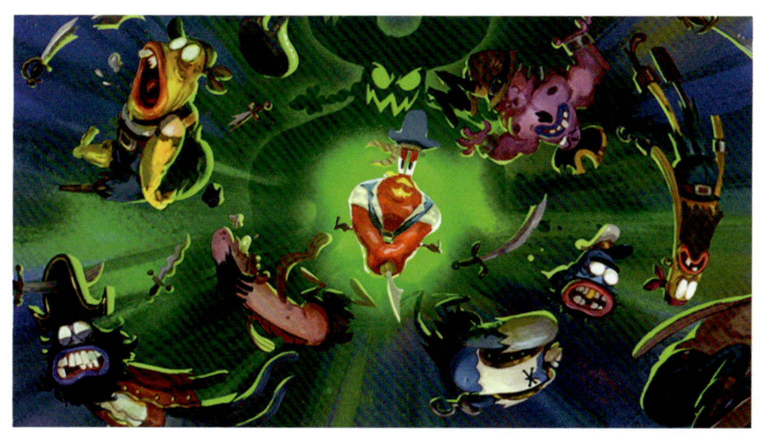

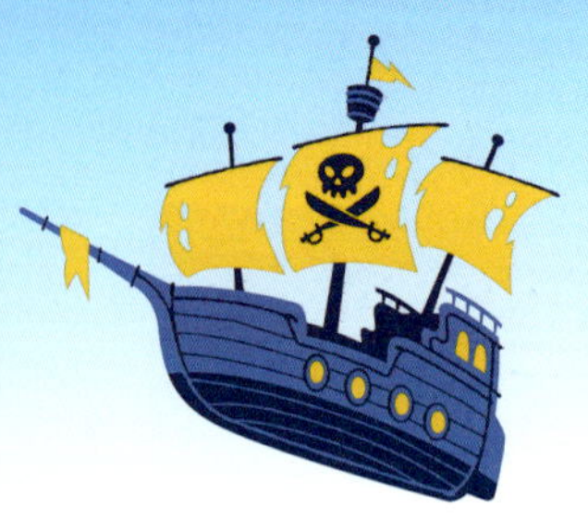

THE HORNPIPE

Sometimes tooting your own horn (or someone else's) leads to unexpected complications. That's exactly what happens when SpongeBob uses the legendary hornpipe. "We explored many iterations for this design, drawing inspiration from naval horns and artifacts. It needed to feel mysterious yet instantly recognizable," says production designer Pablo R. Mayer.

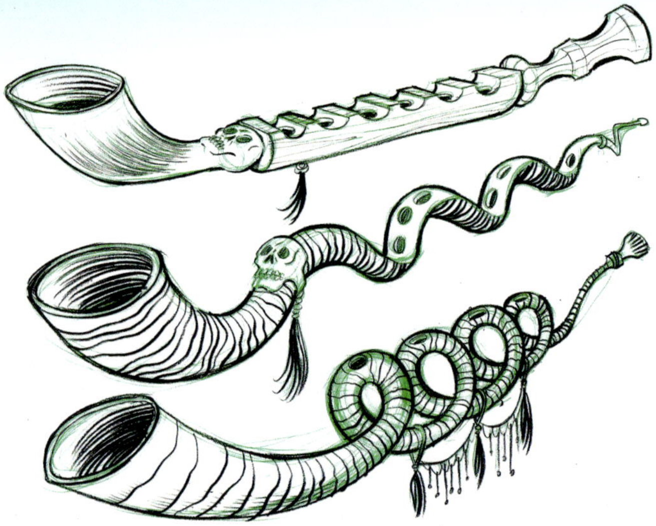

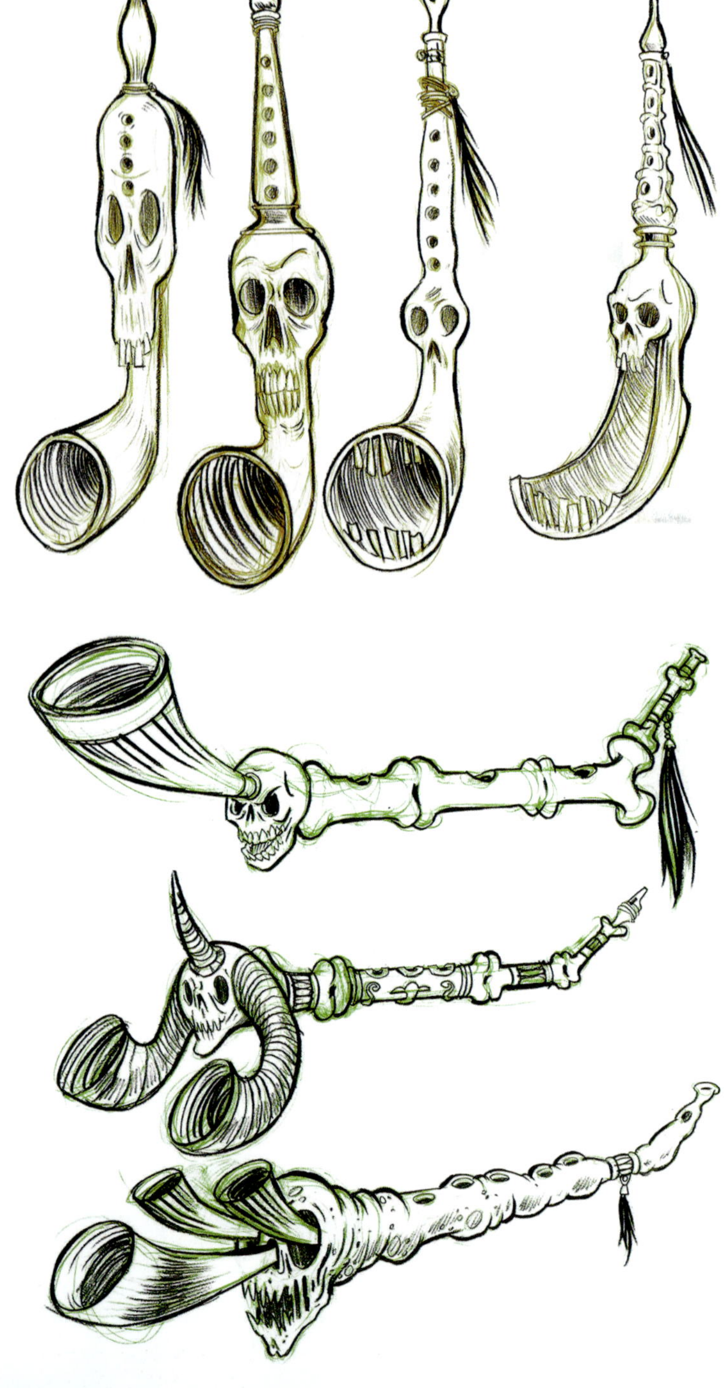

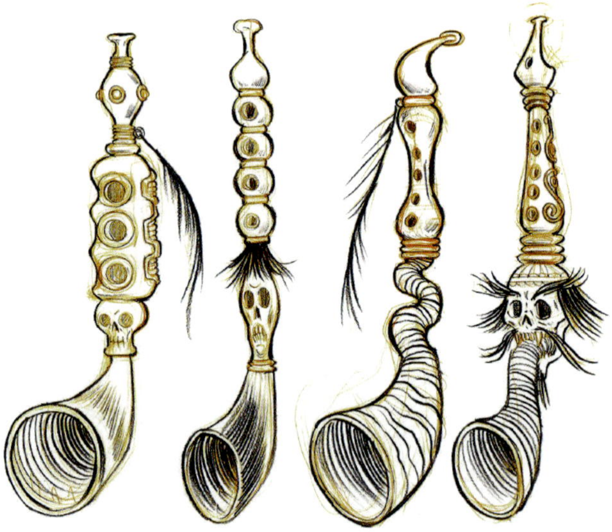

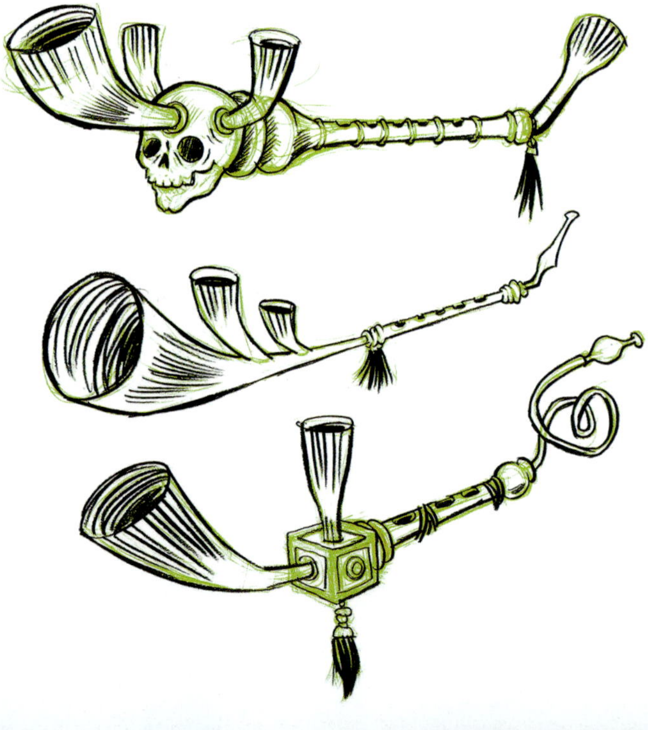

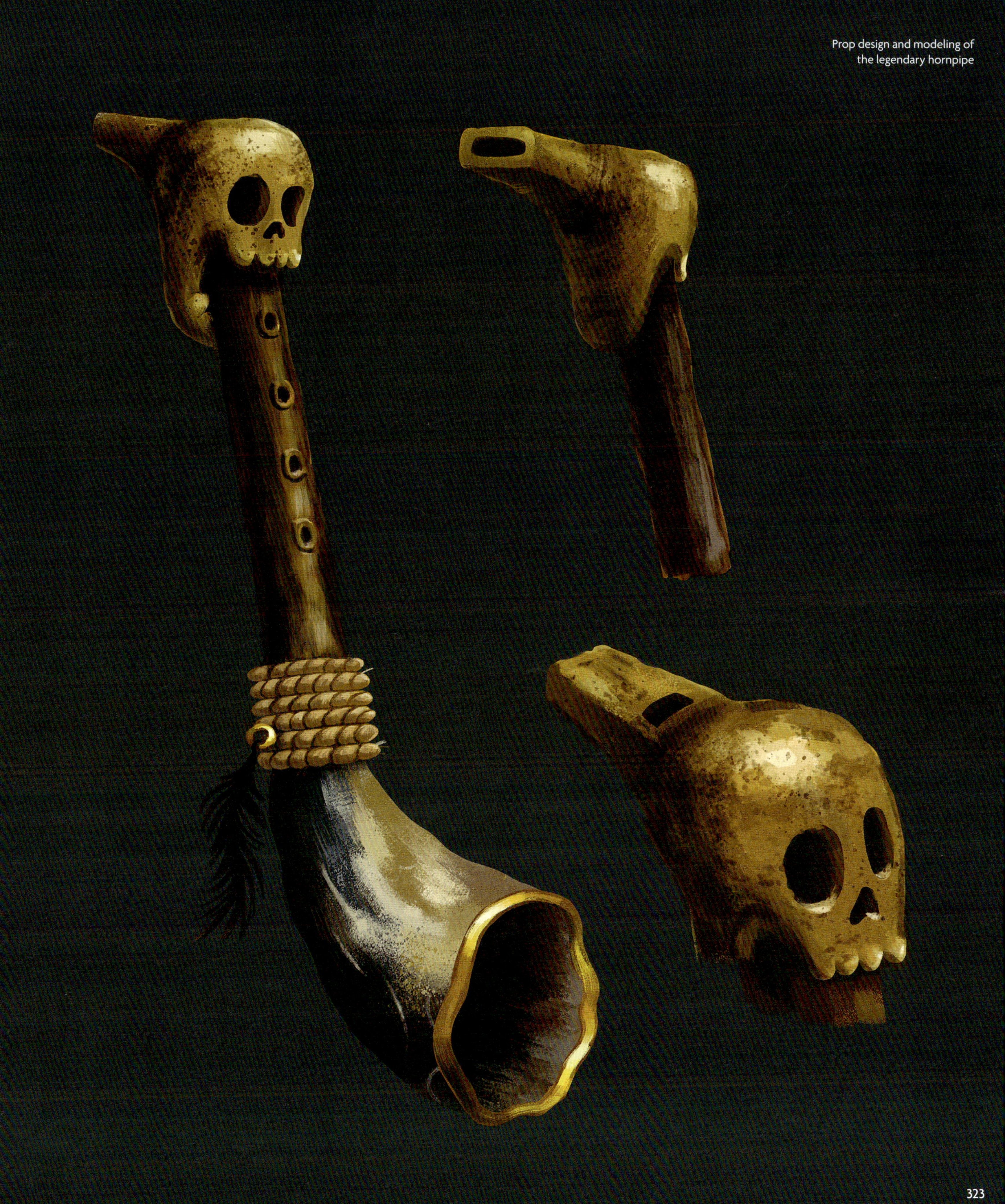

Prop design and modeling of the legendary hornpipe

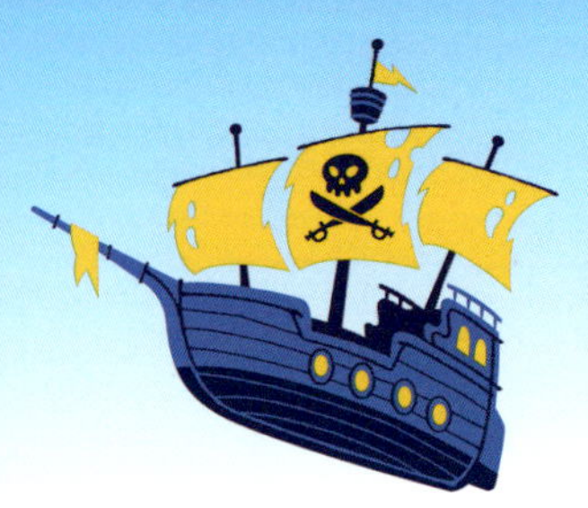

GHOSTLY PIRATES

When SpongeBob is whisked into the Underworld, "that entire sequence is probably the biggest, most cinematic thing that's ever happened in the SpongeBob world, with the fly-bys from the ship giving the audience an intense firsthand glimpse into this space," notes art director Travis Ruiz. The filmmakers had to steer this cinematic ship with great balance, introducing this spooky new environment in a digestible way while allowing the moving camera to create a somewhat disconcerting effect on the viewer, mimicking what SpongeBob must be feeling. "Designing the ghosts was a lot of fun, trying to make them appear undead and zombie-like without being too grotesque," adds Pablo R. Mayer.

The ghostly crew embody the essence of dead fish and every pirate trope possible, from peg legs to eye patches to bandanas and hooks, and maybe a partially headless guy to convey a zombie-esque vibe.

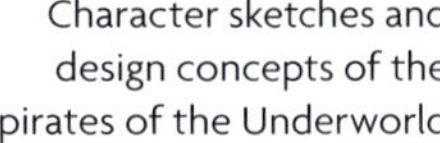

Character sketches and design concepts of the pirates of the Underworld

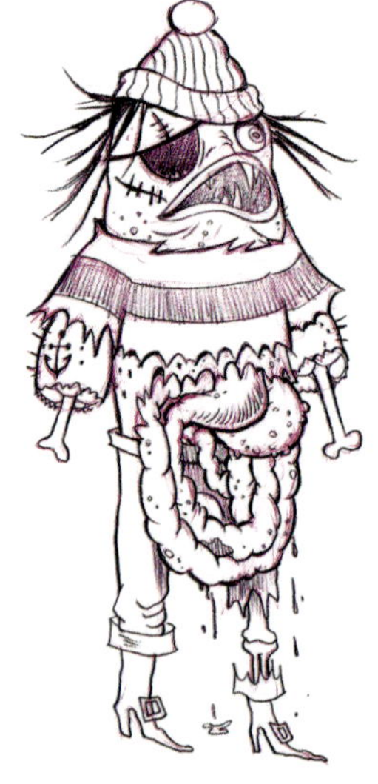

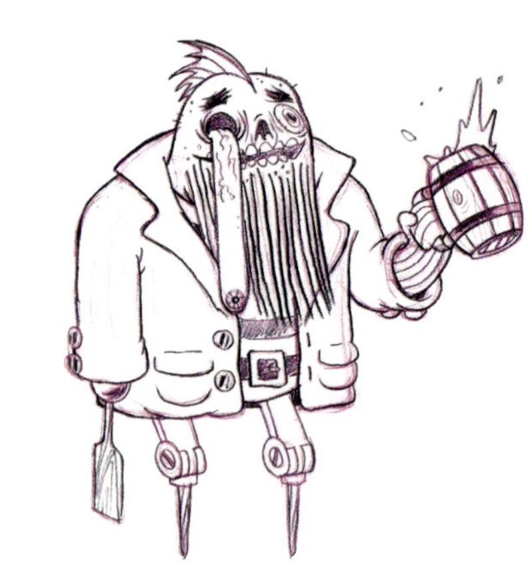

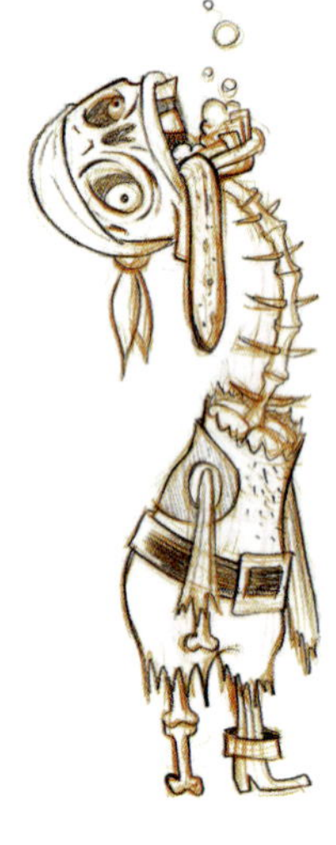

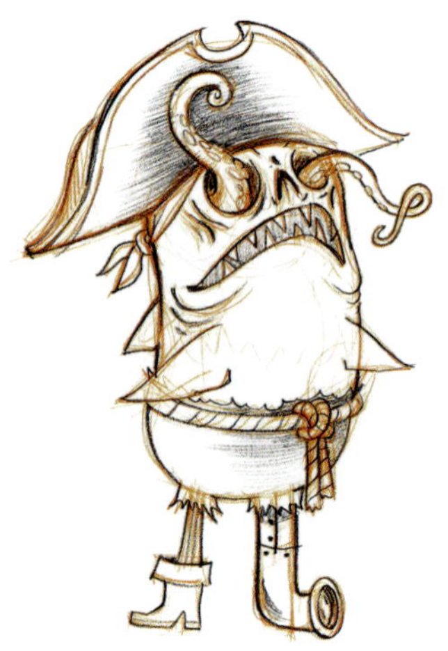

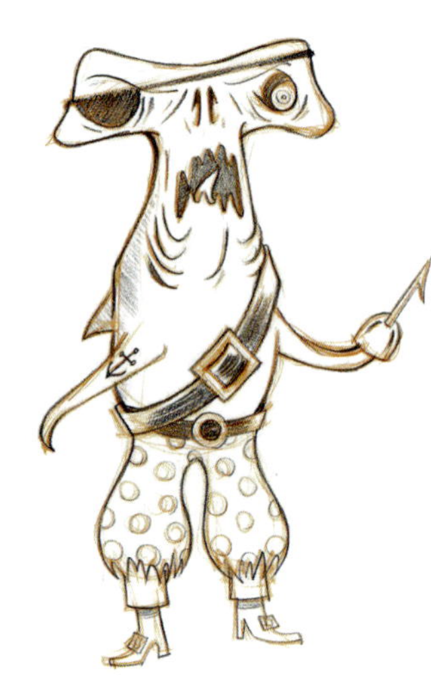

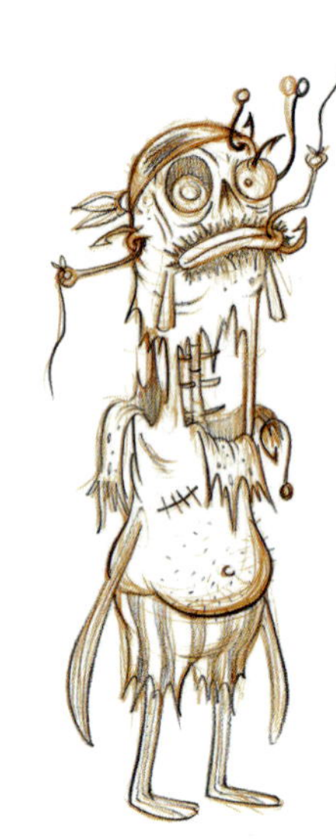

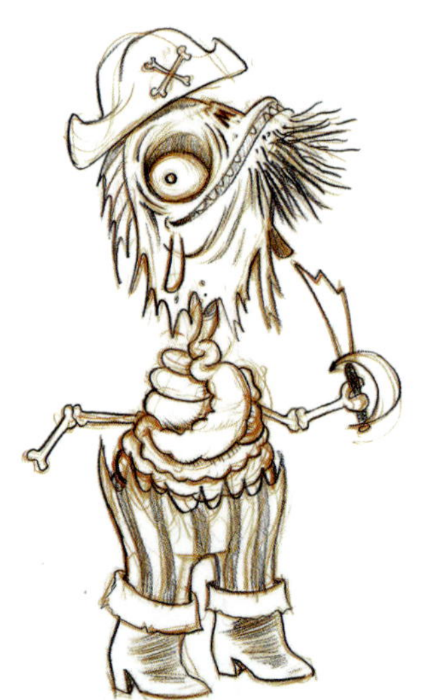

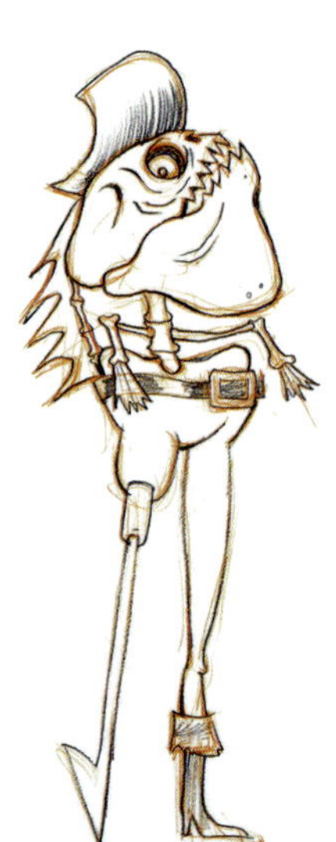

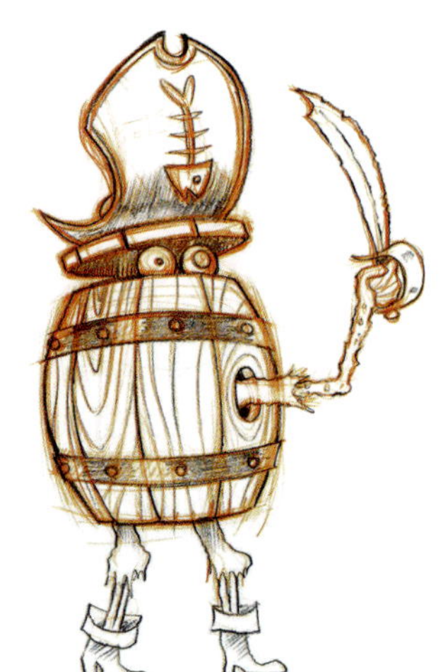

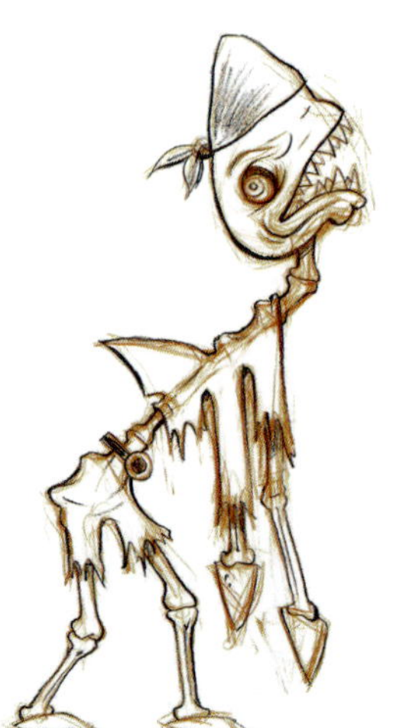

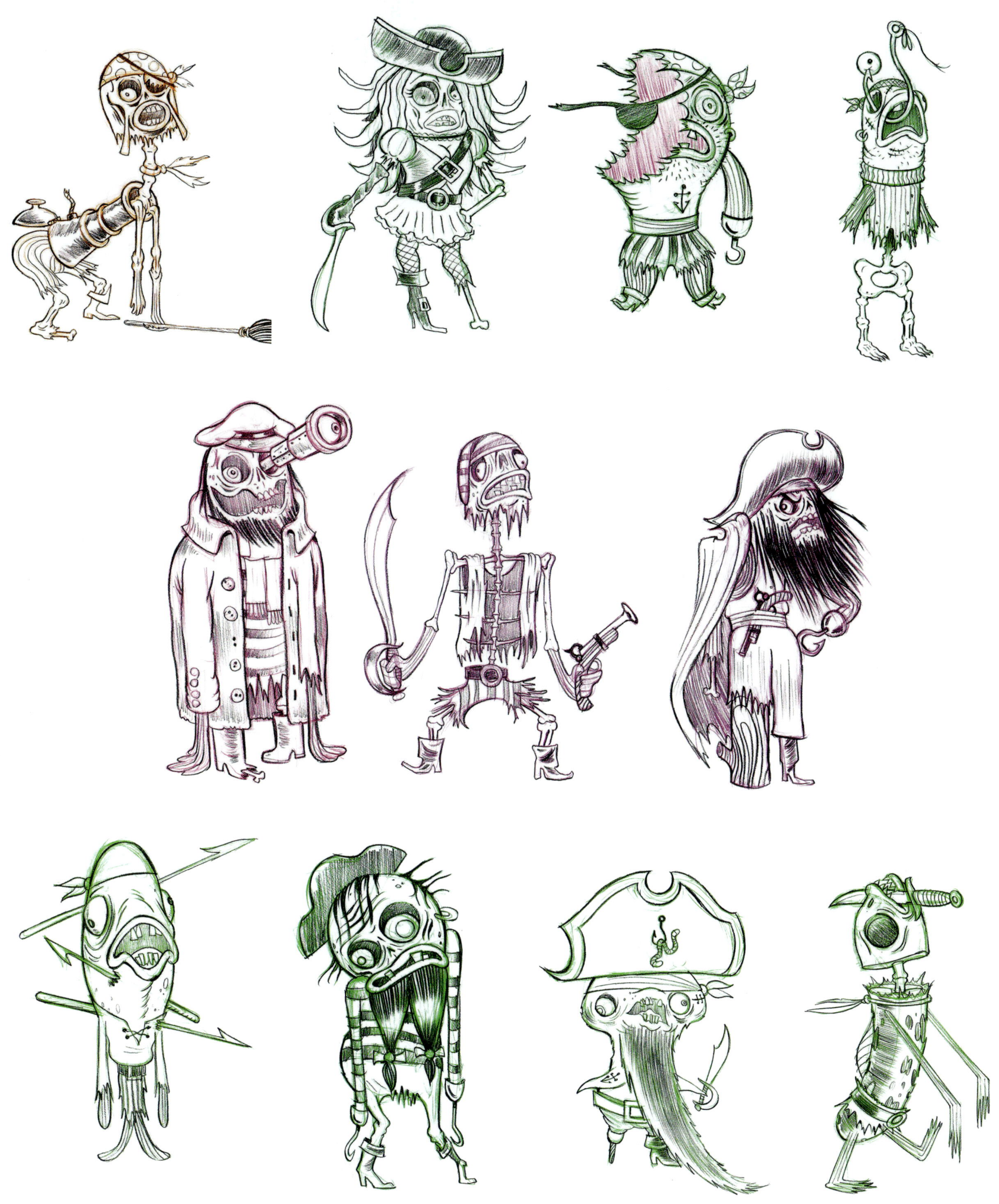

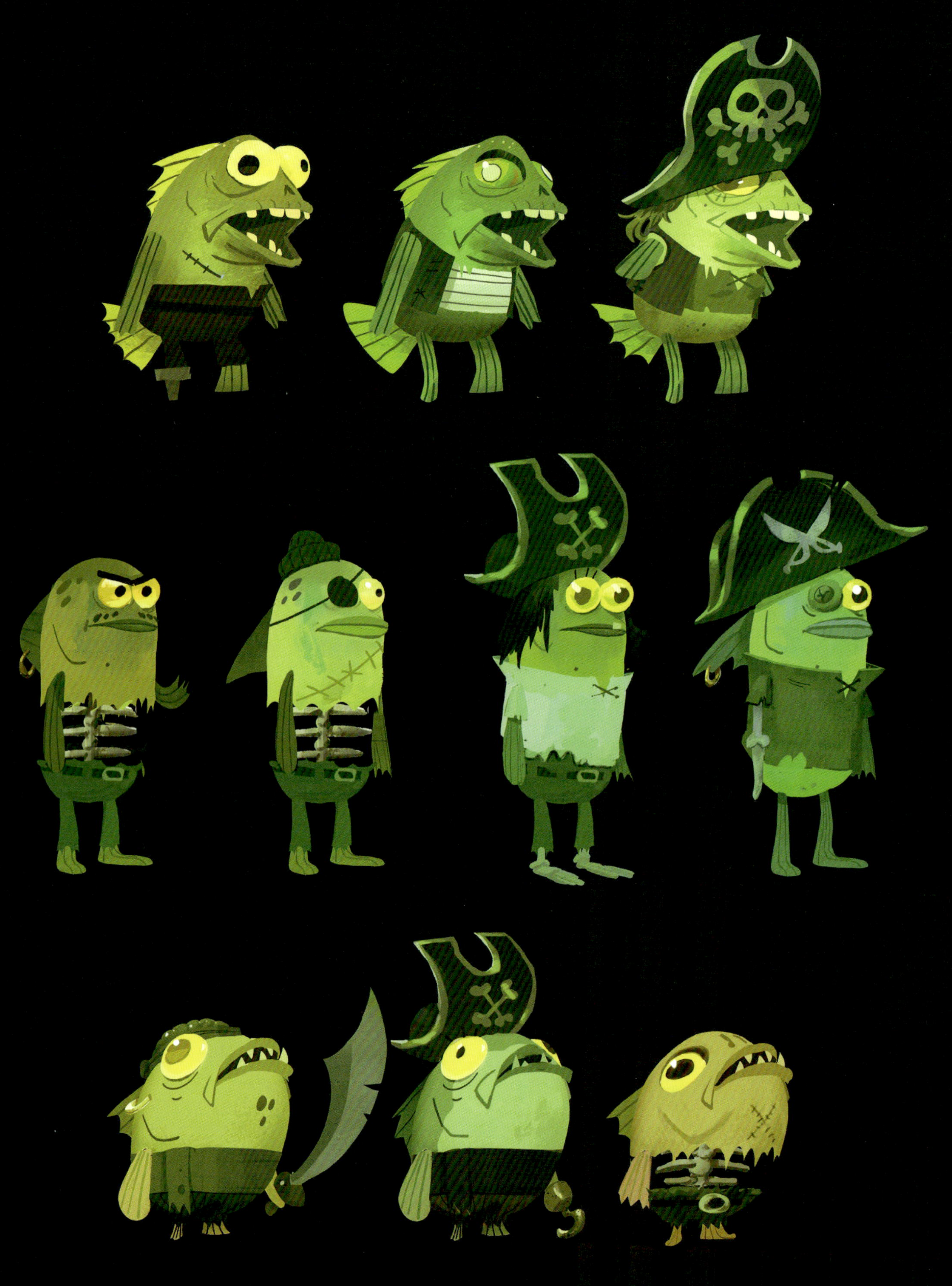

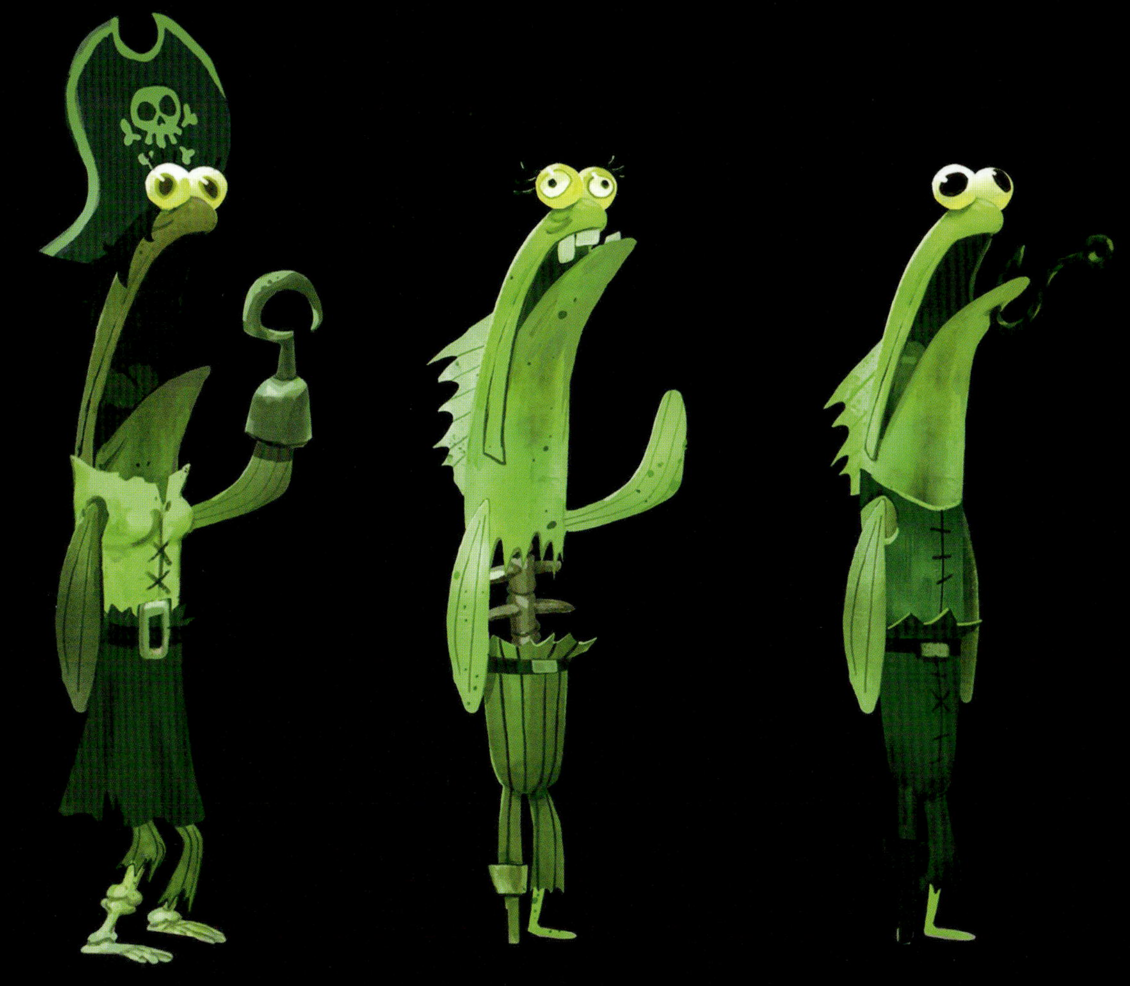

Character modeling of the pirates of the Underworld

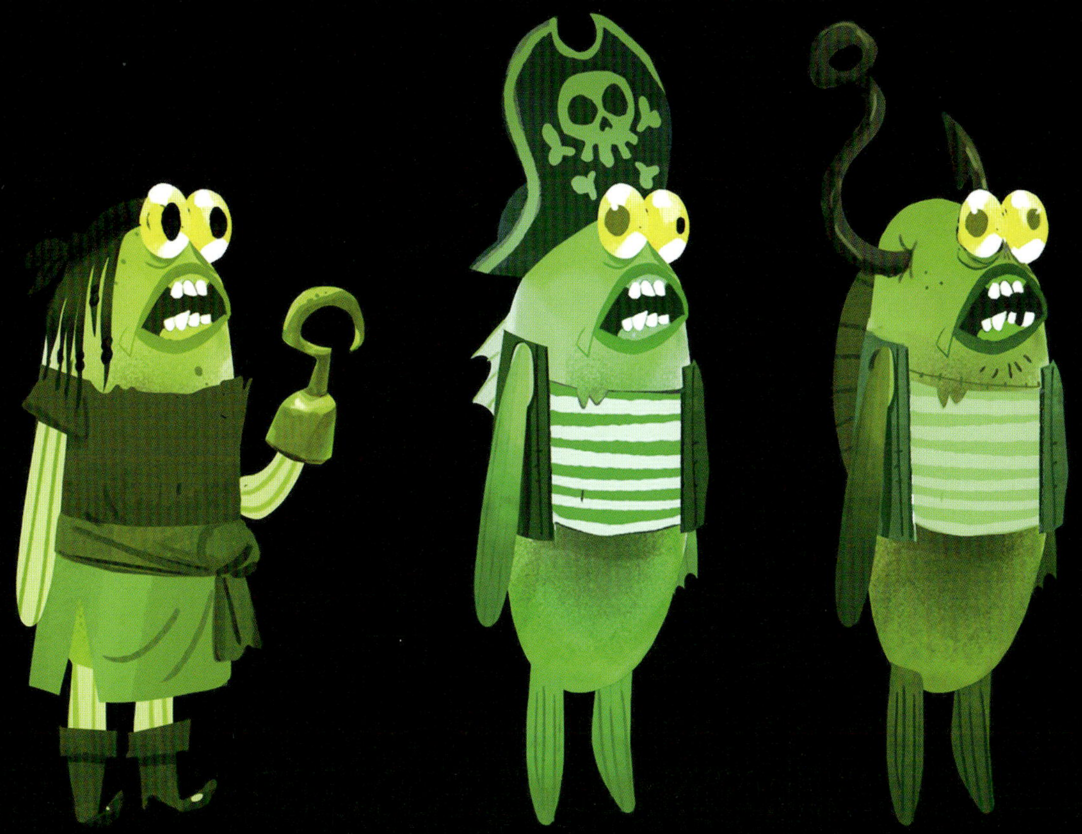

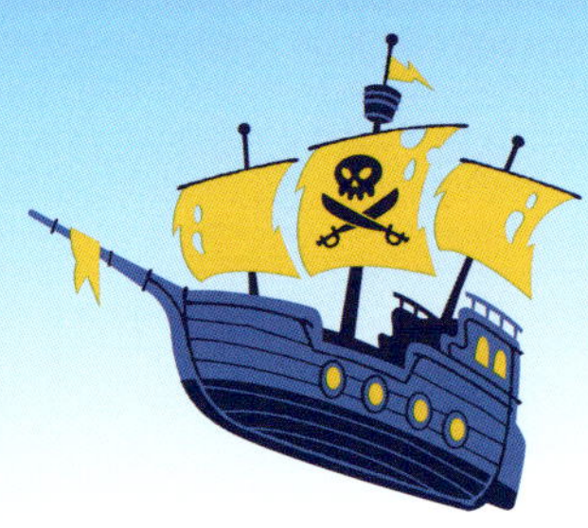

SWASHBUCKLING CERTIFICATE

This document causes more trouble than the glory it "earned" Mr. Krabs, but the design work by Mara Mitterstainer is worthy of recognition in itself. Its slip down the grate, highlighted with a green glow from below, is translated by SpongeBob to mean "destiny is squeezing my buns" and thus his buns thrust him towards that destiny.

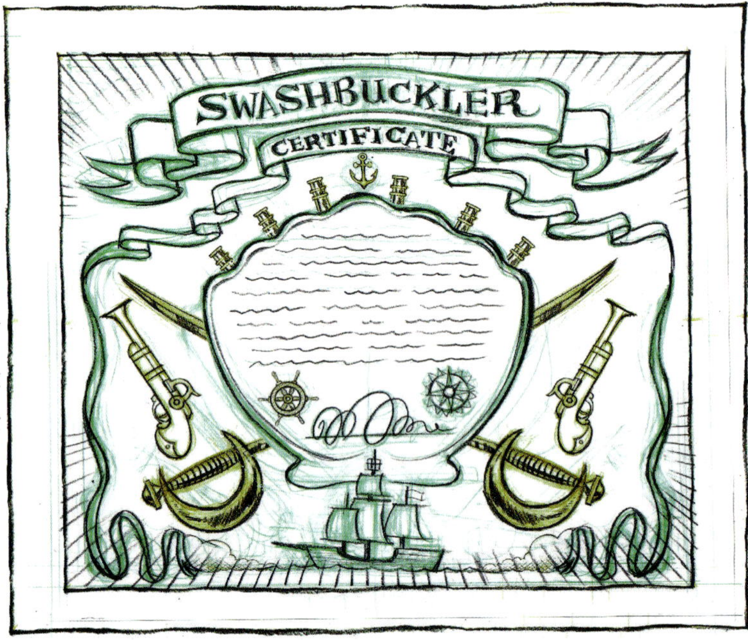

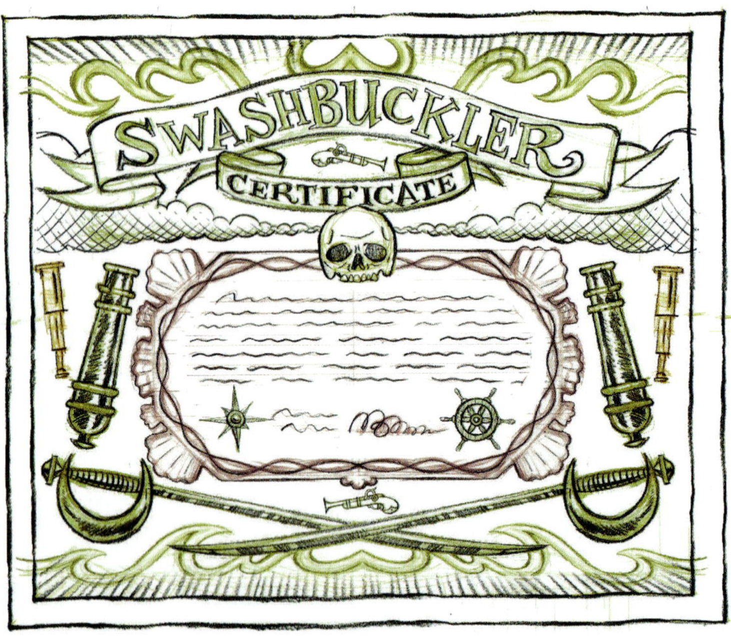

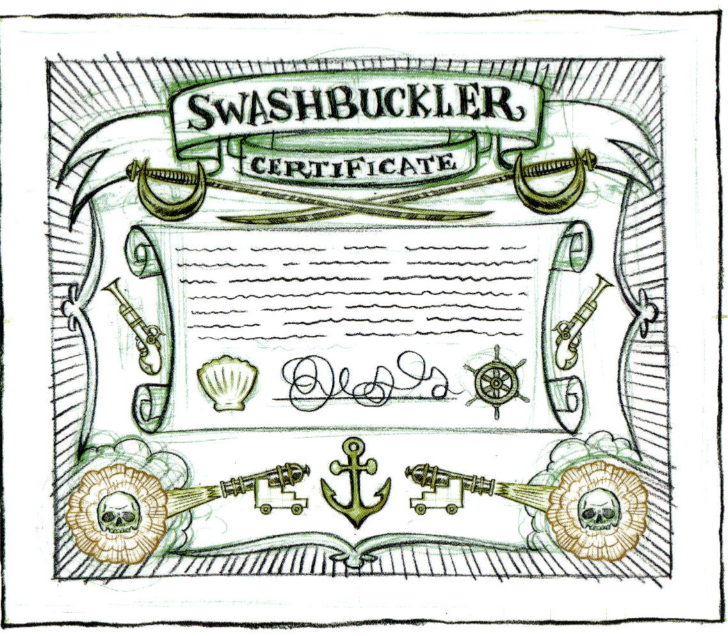

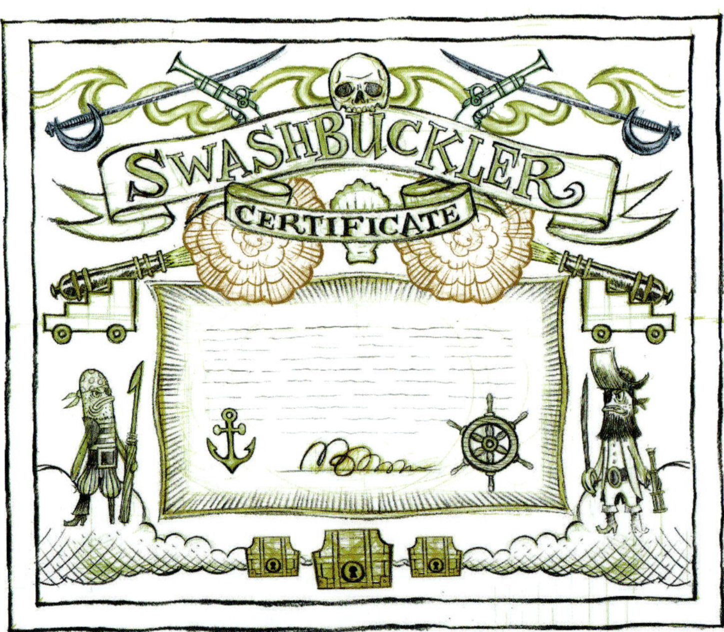

Prop design variations of the highly coveted Swashbuckler Certificate

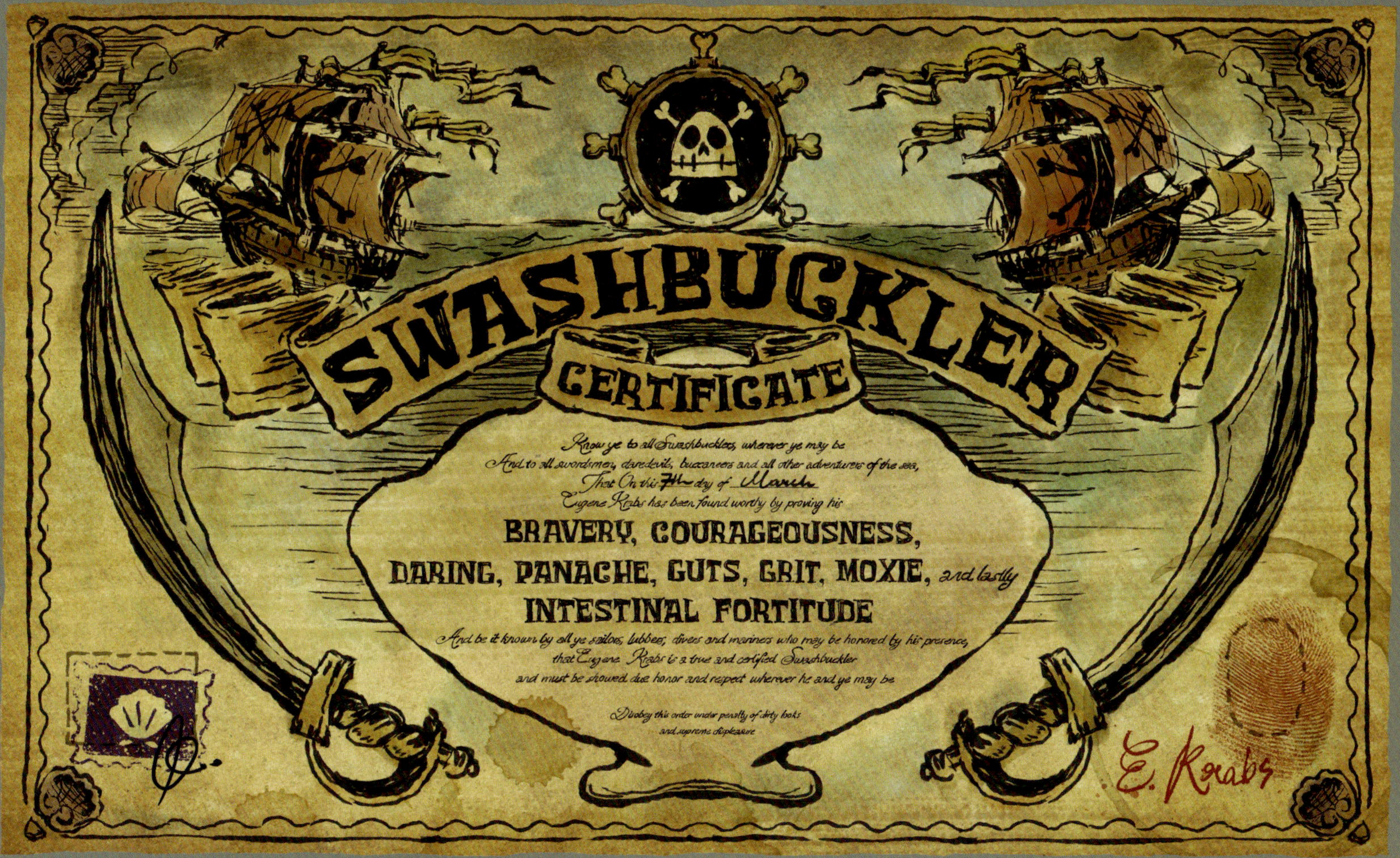

SWASHBUCKLER
CERTIFICATE
Know ye to all Swashbucklers, wherever ye may be
And to all swordsmen, daredevils, buccaneers and all other adventurers of the sea,
That On this 7th day of March
Eugene Krabs has been found worthy by proving his
BRAVERY, COURAGEOUSNESS,
DARING, PANACHE, GUTS, GRIT, MOXIE, and lastly
INTESTINAL FORTITUDE
And be it known by all ye sailors, lubbers, divers and mariners who may be honored by his presence,
that Eugene Krabs is a true and certified Swashbuckler
and must be showed due honor and respect wherever he and ye may be
Disobey this order under penalty of dirty looks
and supreme displeasure
E. Krabs

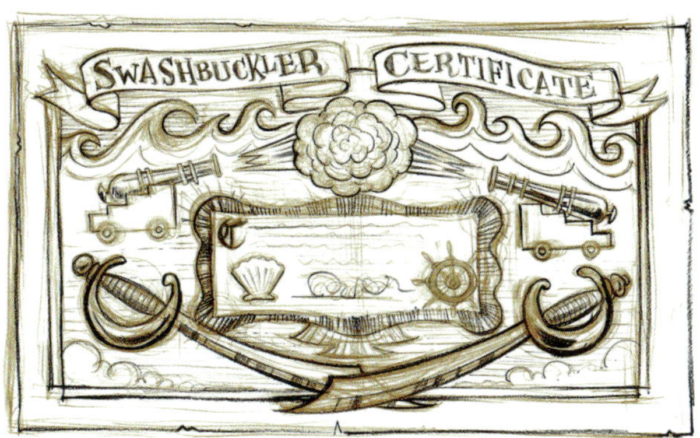

SWASHBUCKLER
CERTIFICATE

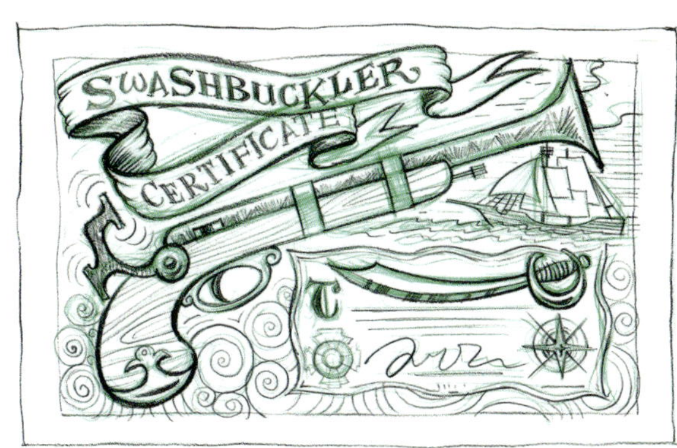

SWASHBUCKLER
CERTIFICATE

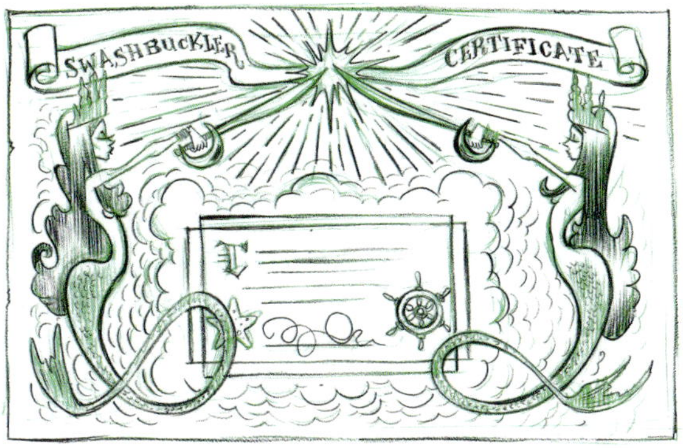

SWASHBUCKLER
CERTIFICATE

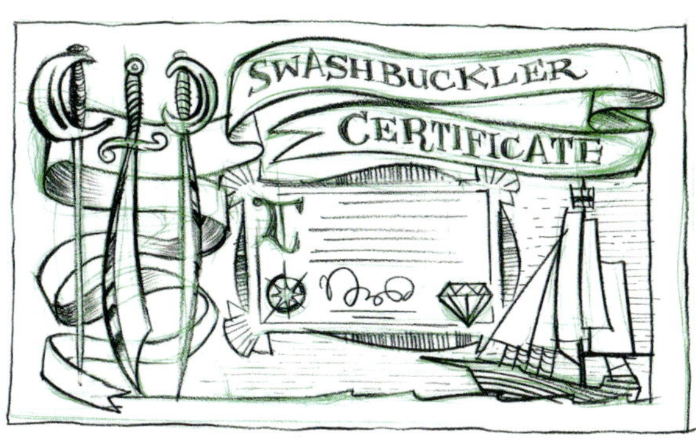

SWASHBUCKLER
CERTIFICATE

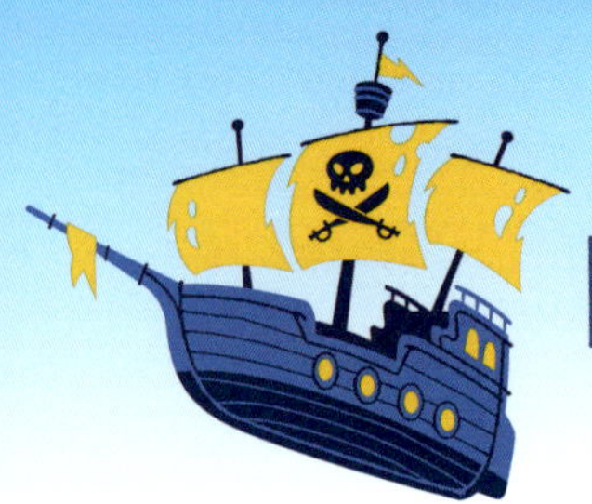

DOWN TO THE KRAB CAVE

The chase after that precious piece of paper leads SpongeBob and Patrick down into unimaginable depths that took great imagination on the part of the artistic team. In the Krab Cave, "every treasure and prop needed to feel like it had a story, like something unique and interesting. Thaddeus, one of our concept artists, went wild with absurd designs. It gave the whole place a kind of *Indiana Jones* treasure-hunter energy," explains production designer Pablo R. Mayer, who also oversaw the inclusion of some historical props that fans might enjoy discovering in this space.

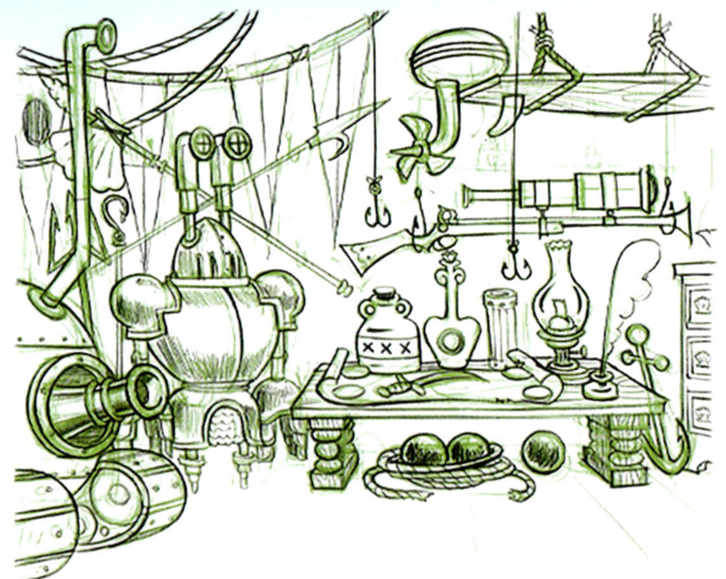

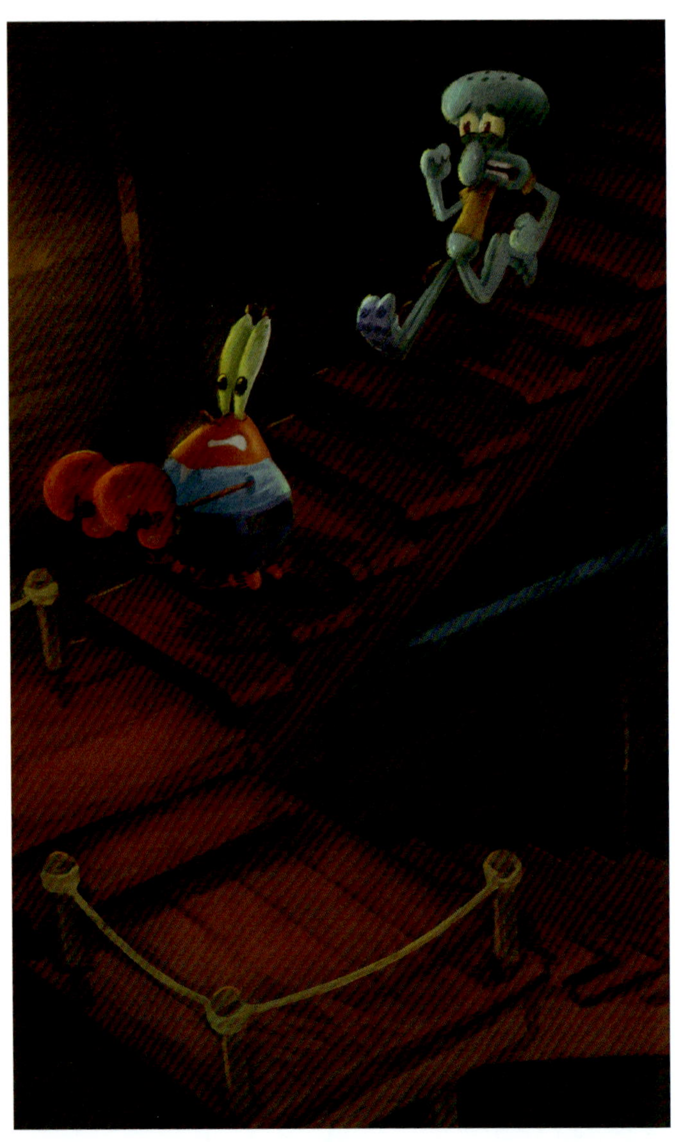

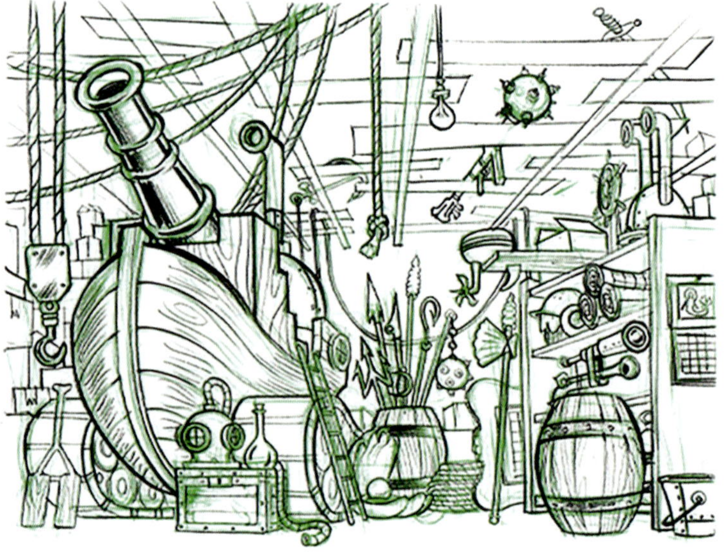

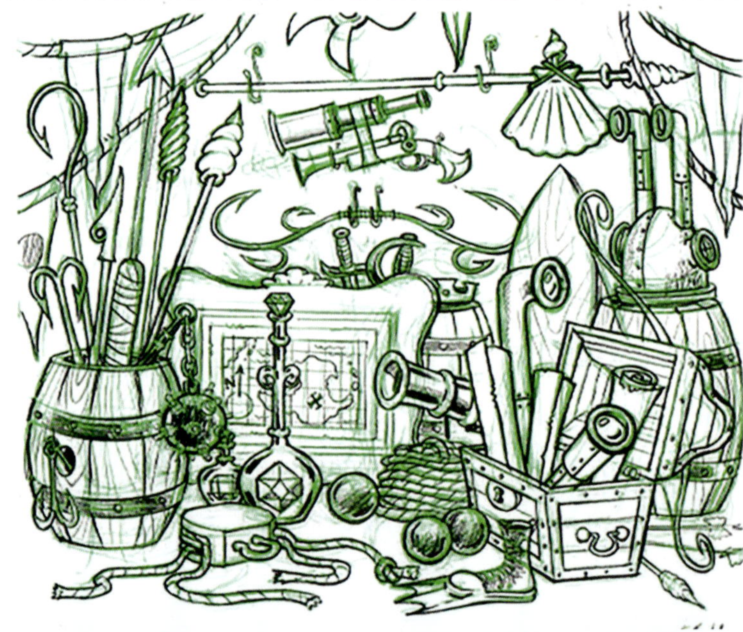

Rough background layouts of the Krab Cave, including a color key of Squidward and Mr. Krabs' race down into it [left] and layouts of the details [right]

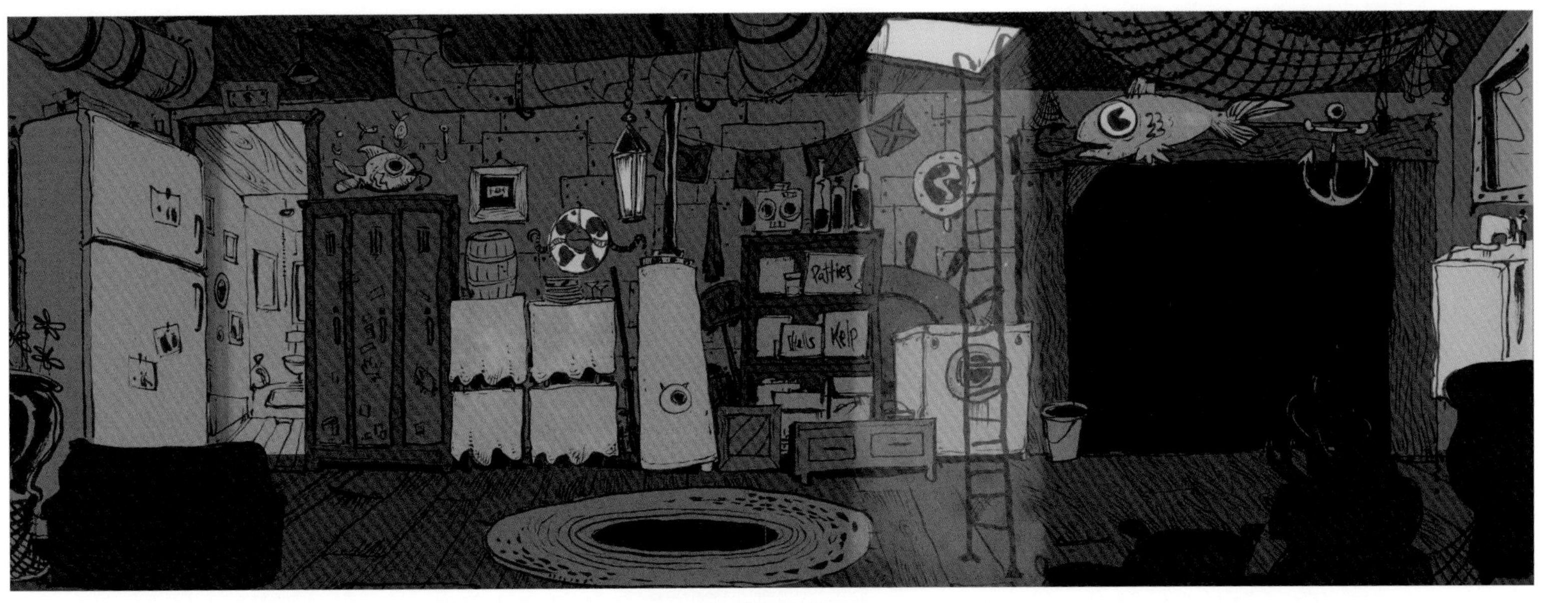

Tonals of the Krab Cave

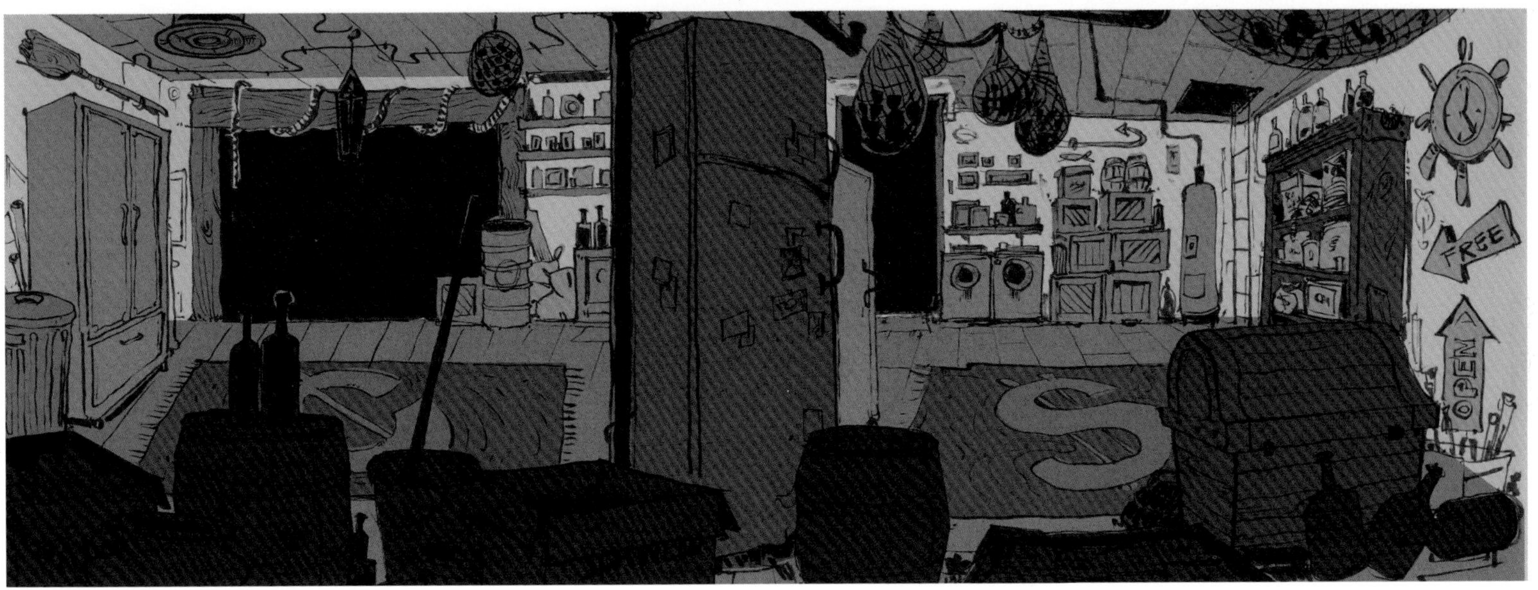

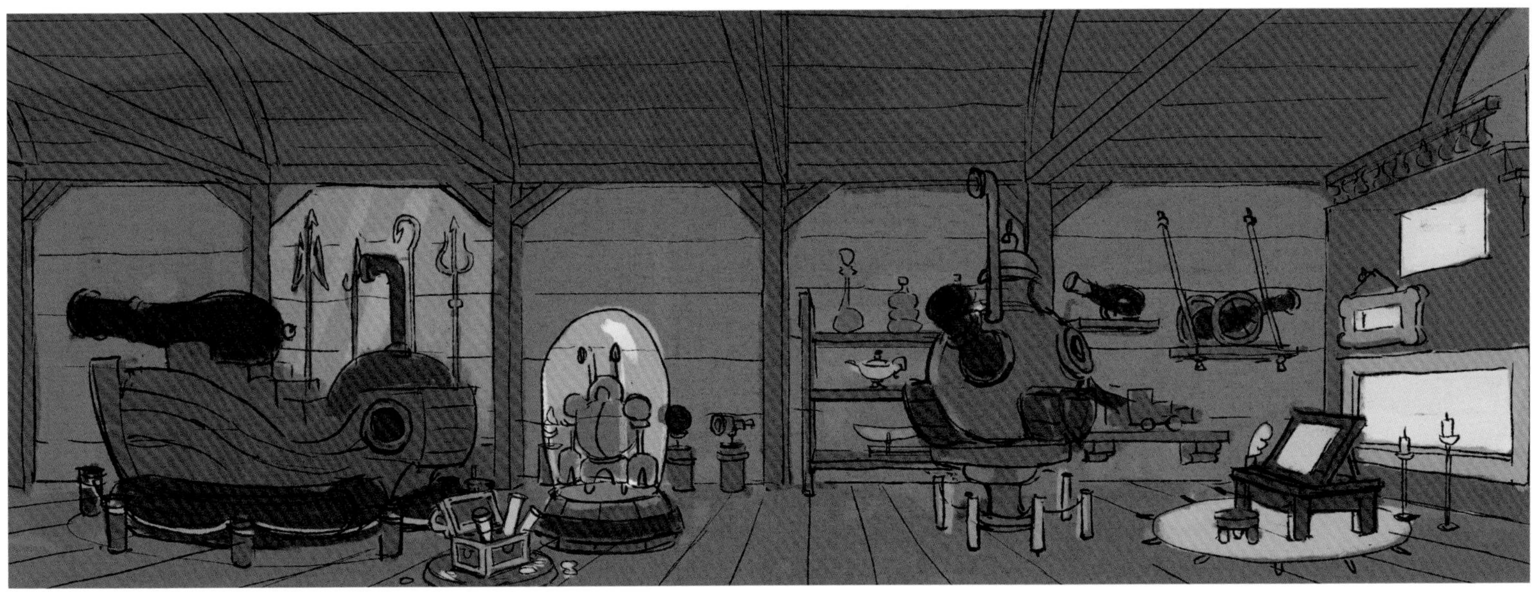

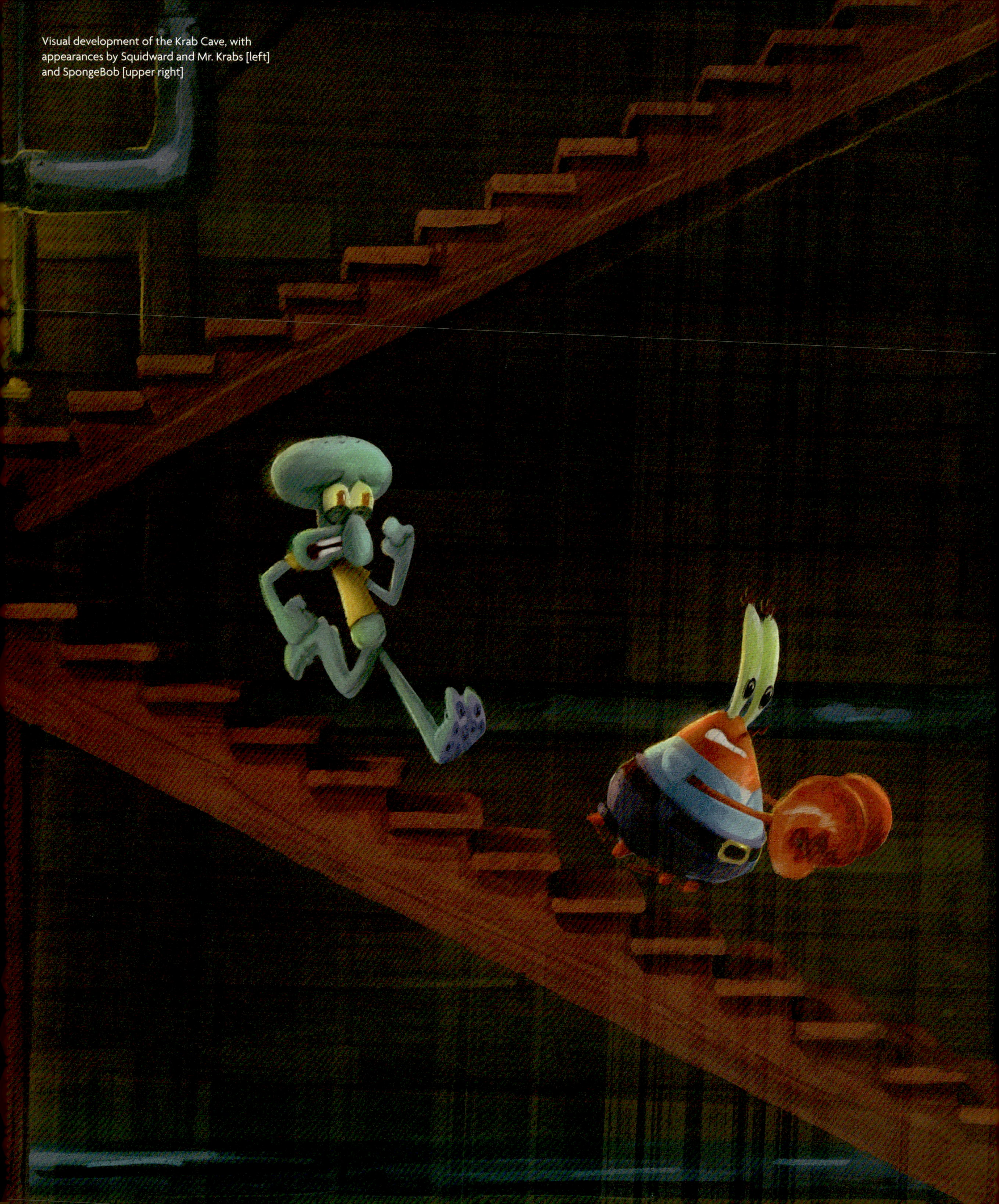

Visual development of the Krab Cave, with appearances by Squidward and Mr. Krabs [left] and SpongeBob [upper right]

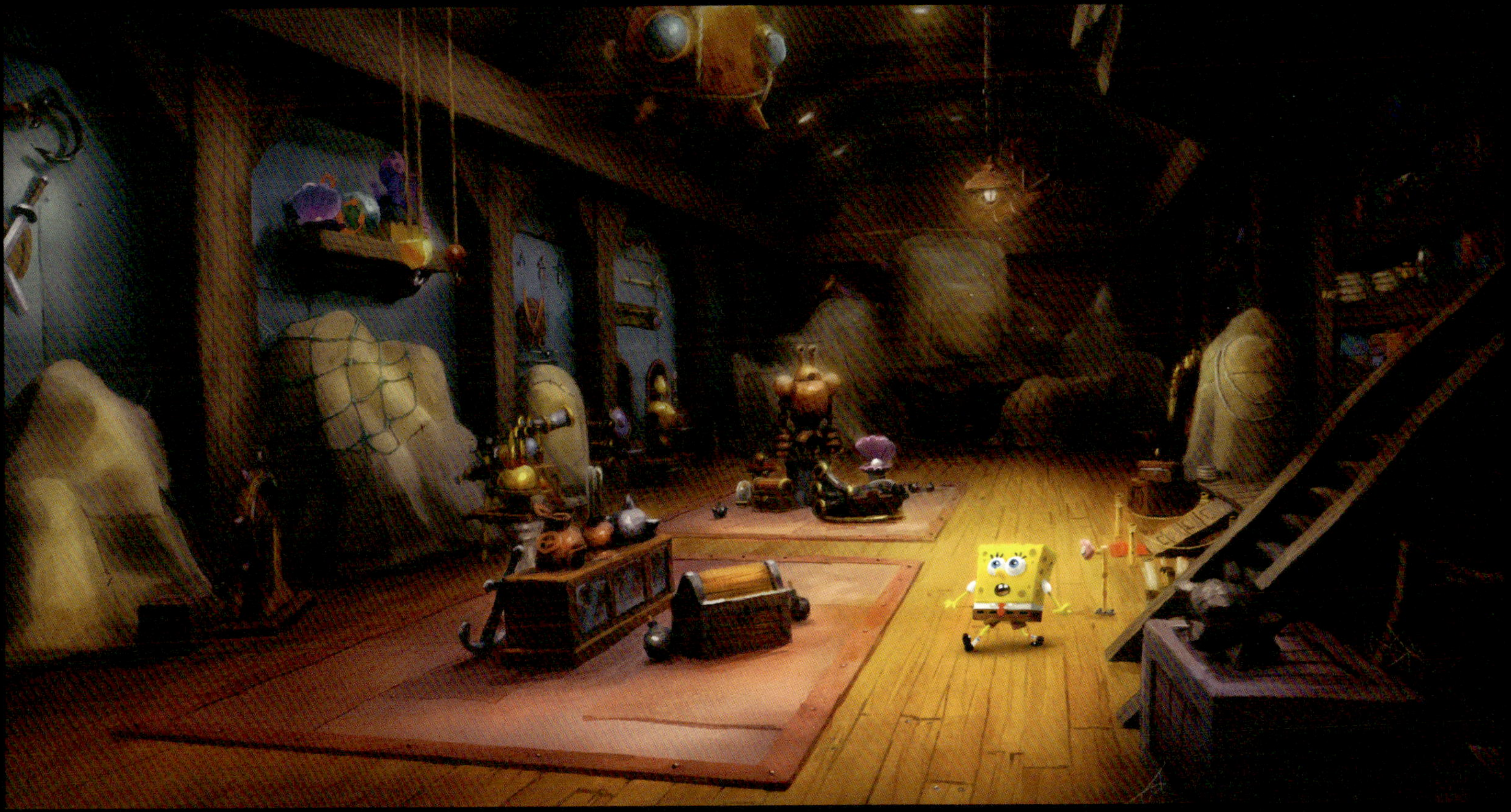

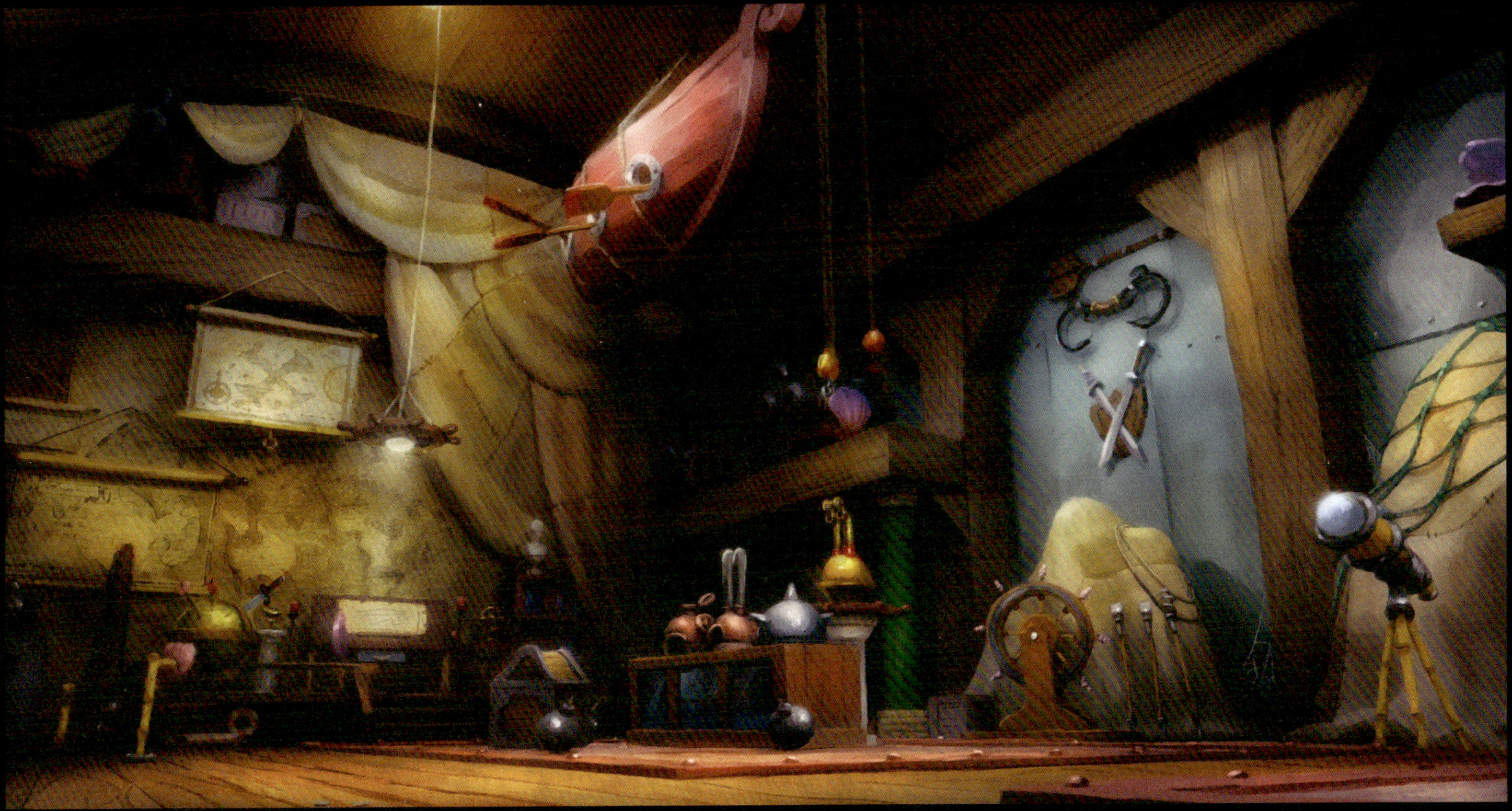

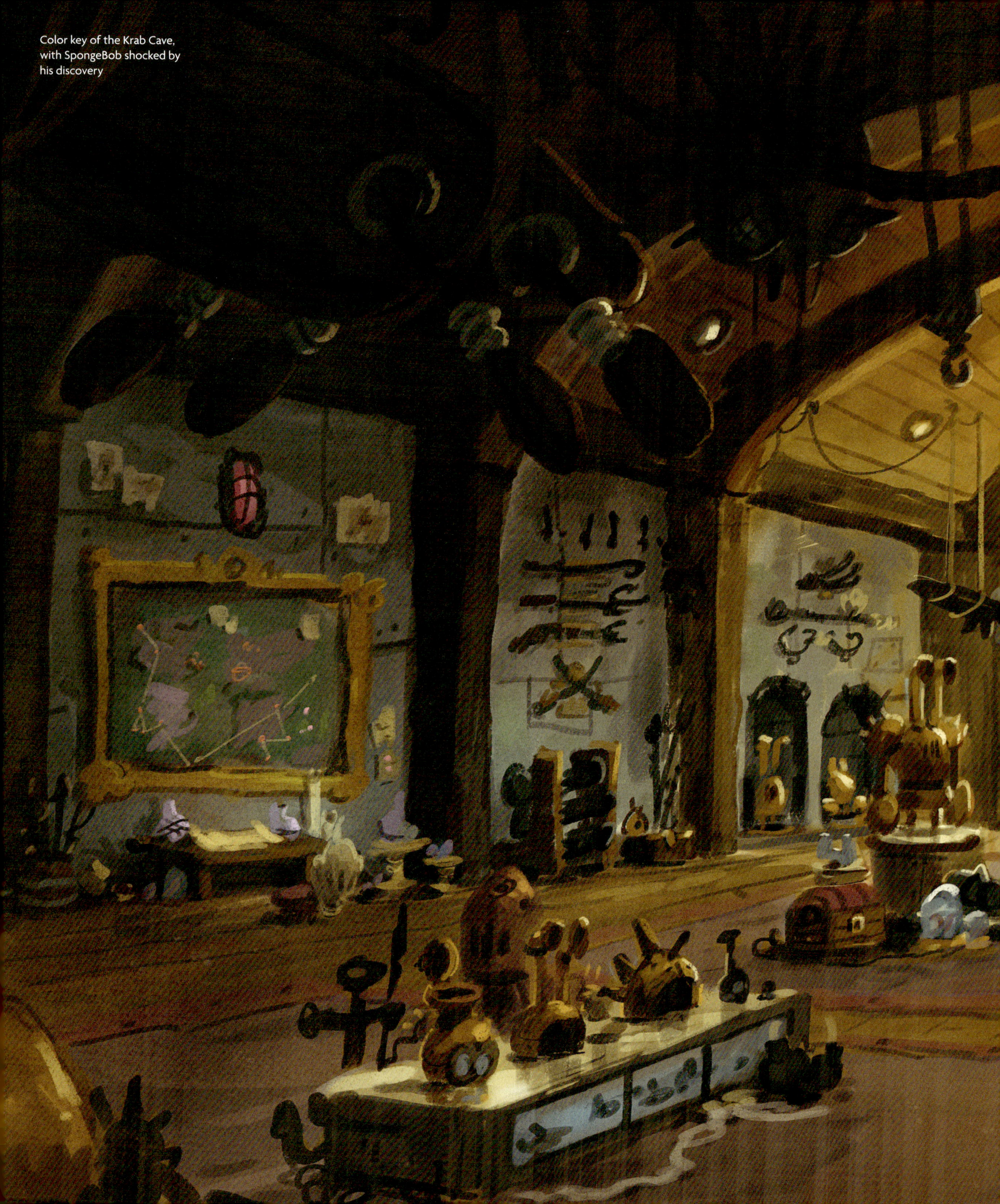

Color key of the Krab Cave, with SpongeBob shocked by his discovery

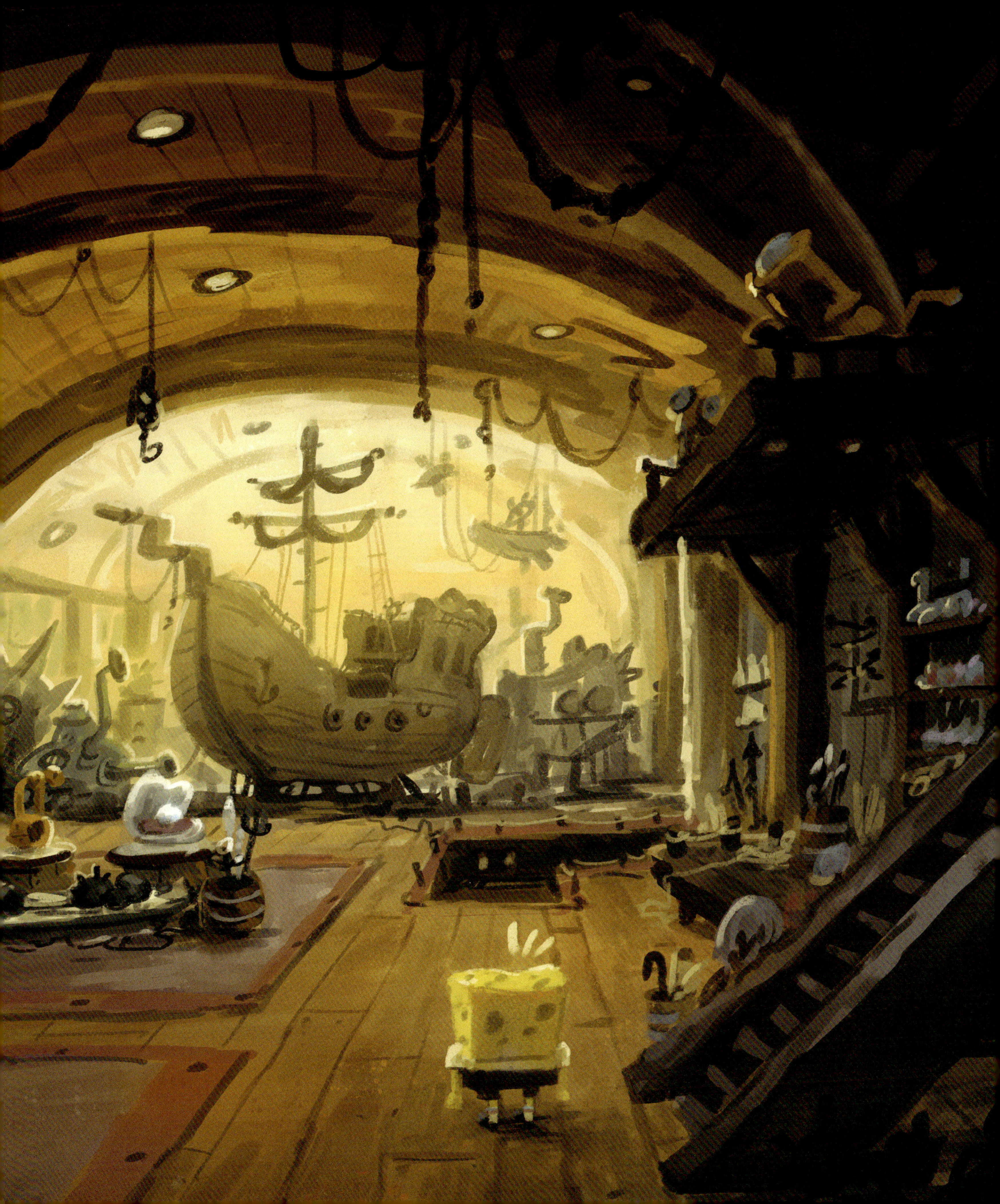

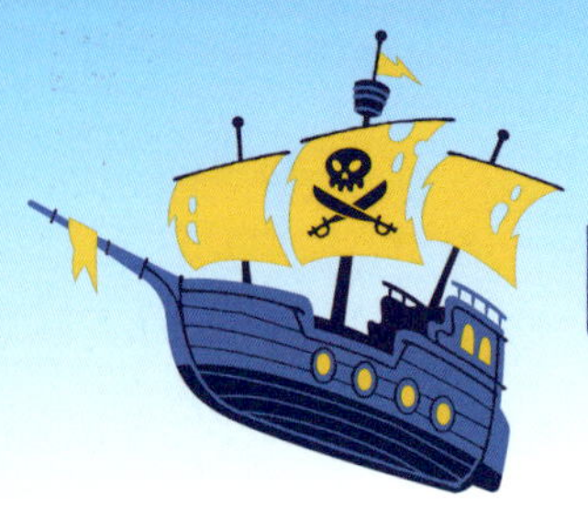

INTO THE UNDERWORLD

Director Derek Drymon knew he wanted to create an environment never before experienced in the SpongeBob realm, so the artistic team worked with three main visual cues to craft the Underworld: underwater caves, tiki bar colors, and surrealism. "We wanted the Underworld to contrast Bikini Bottom, so instead of a bright, sunny water/sky, we have a space with dramatically lit underwater caves made of volcanic rock surrounded by stalagmites and stalactites," says art director Travis Ruiz.

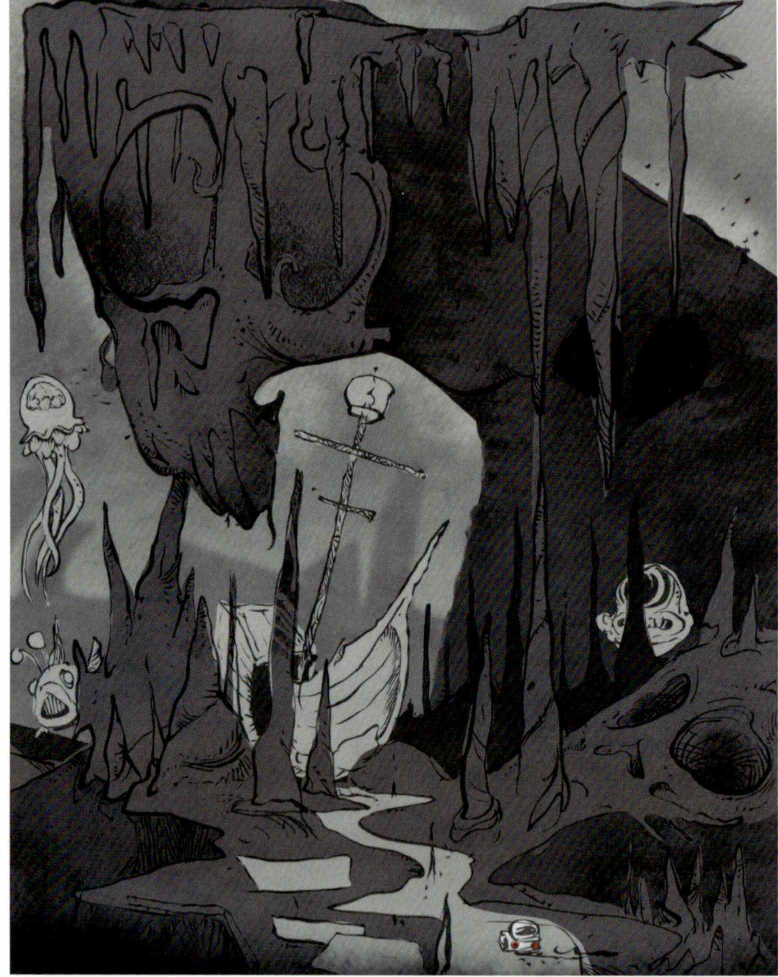

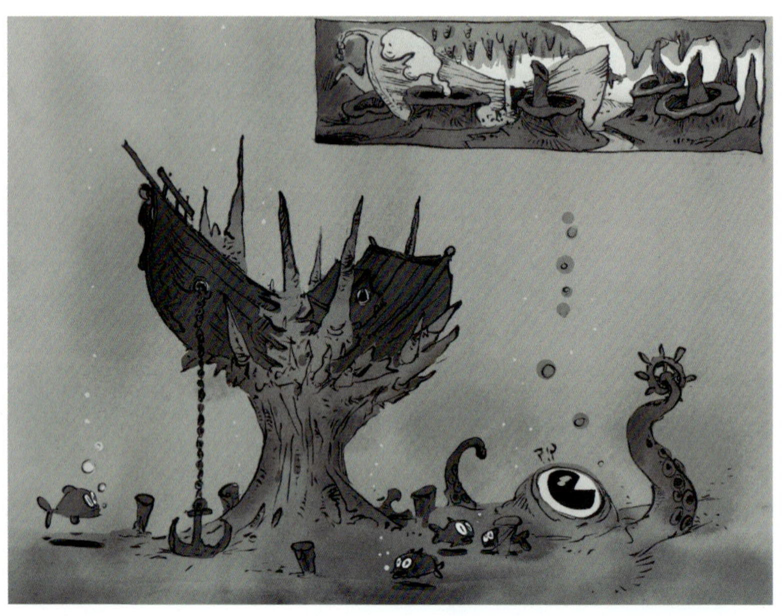

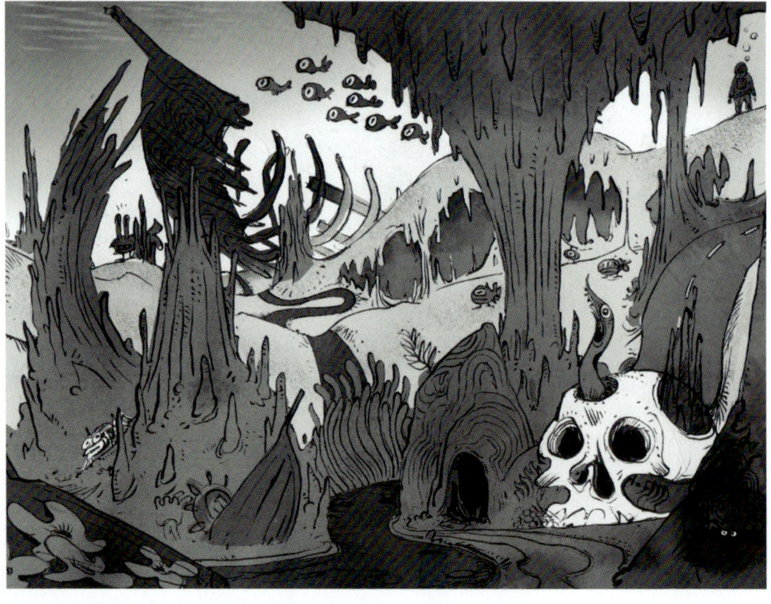

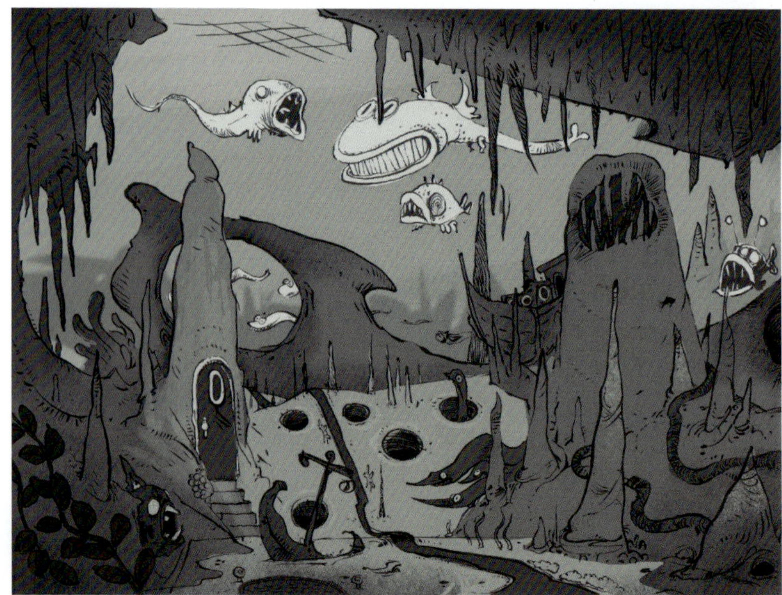

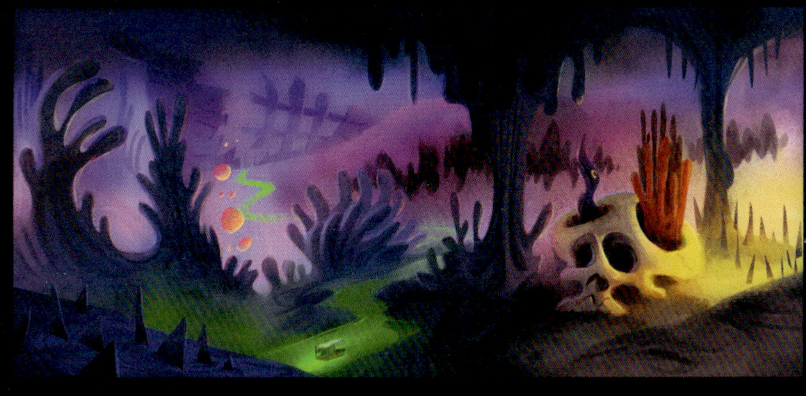
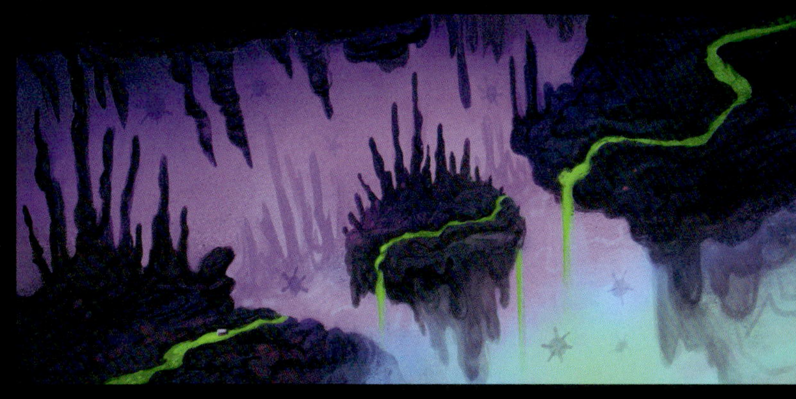
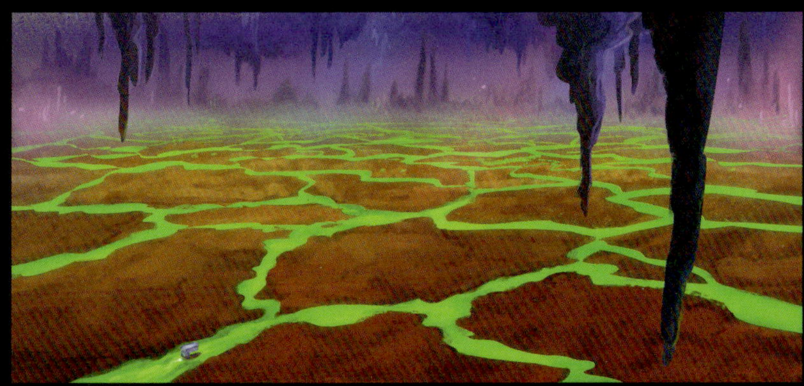
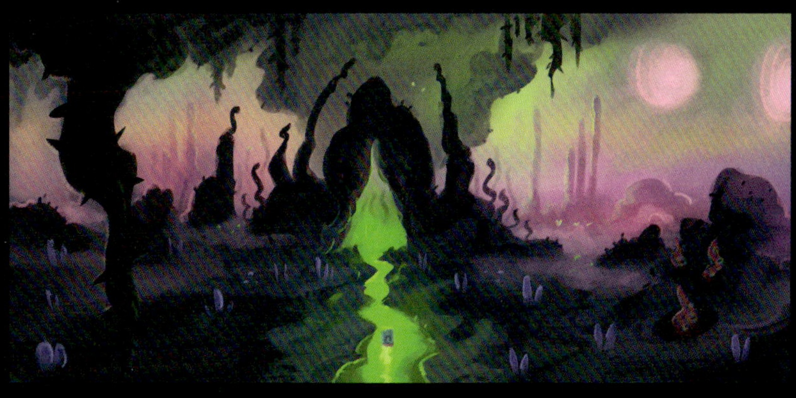
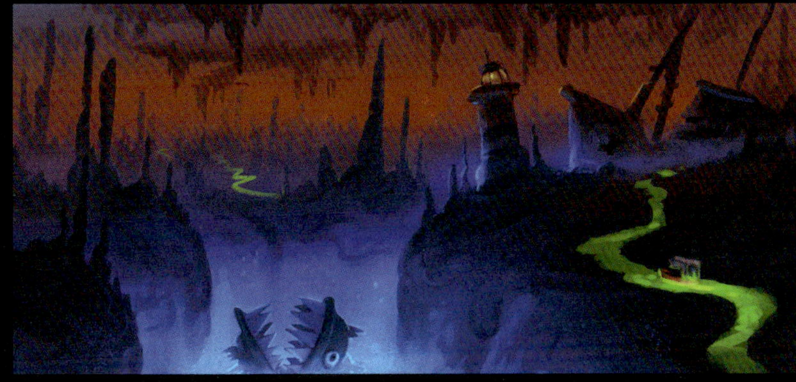
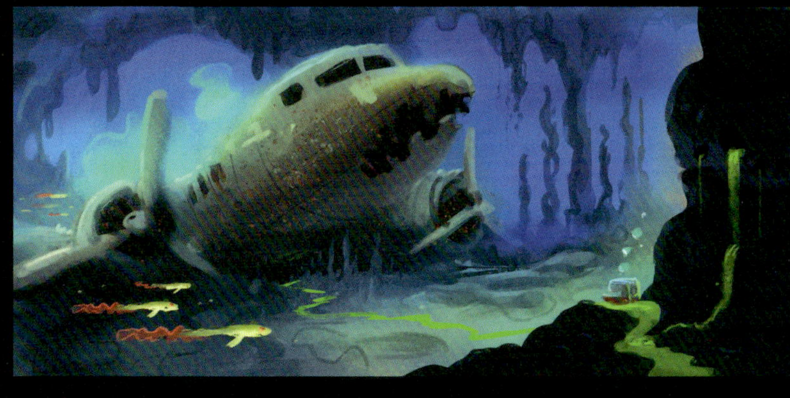
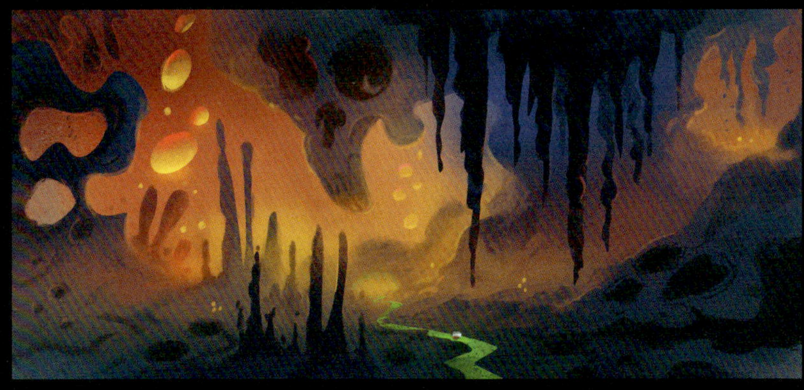
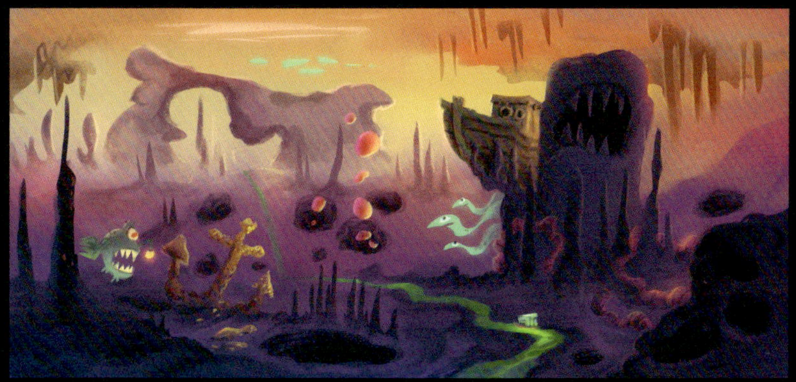

Tonals [left] and visual development art [right] of the Underworld

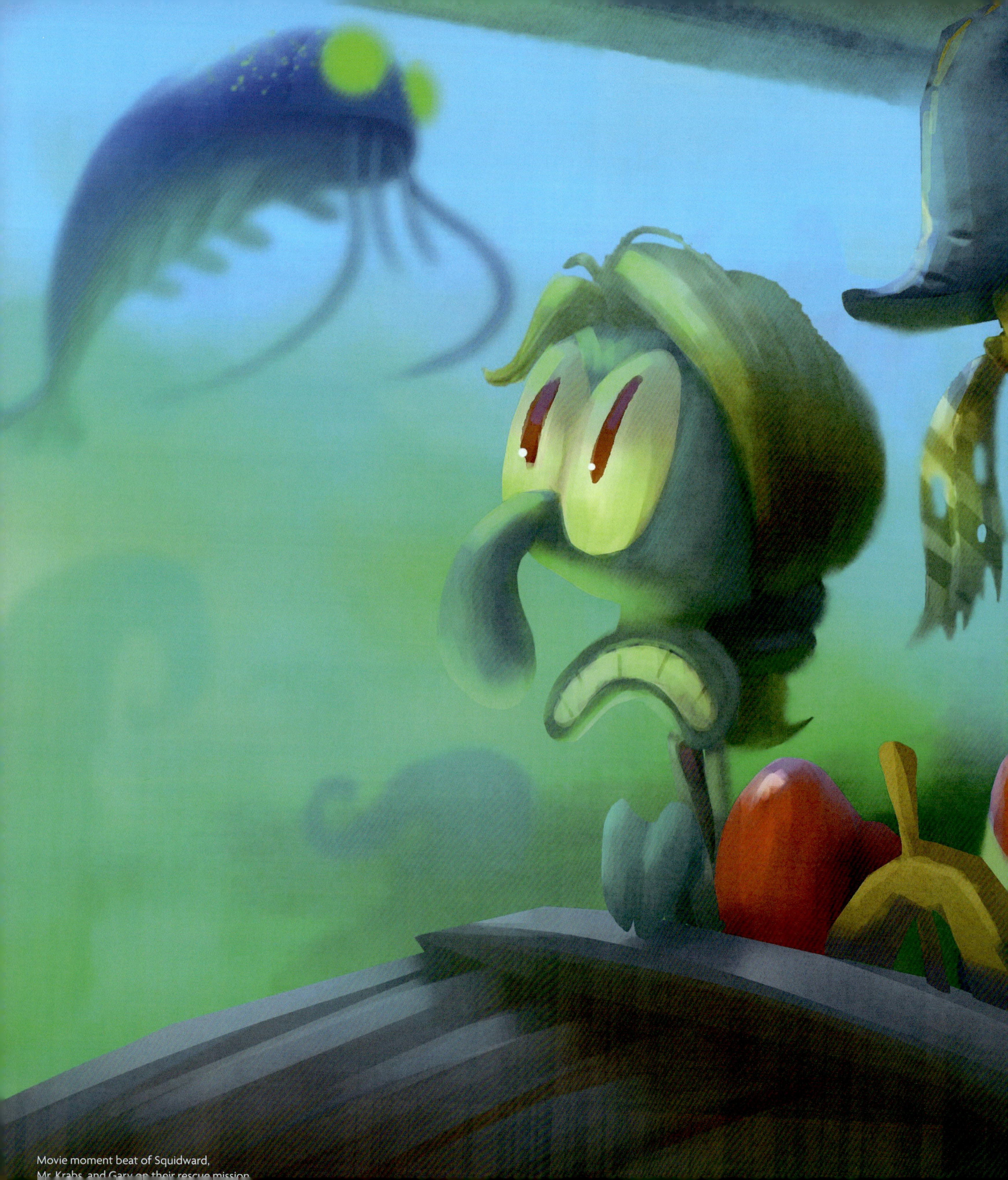

Movie moment beat of Squidward,
Mr. Krabs, and Gary on their rescue mission.

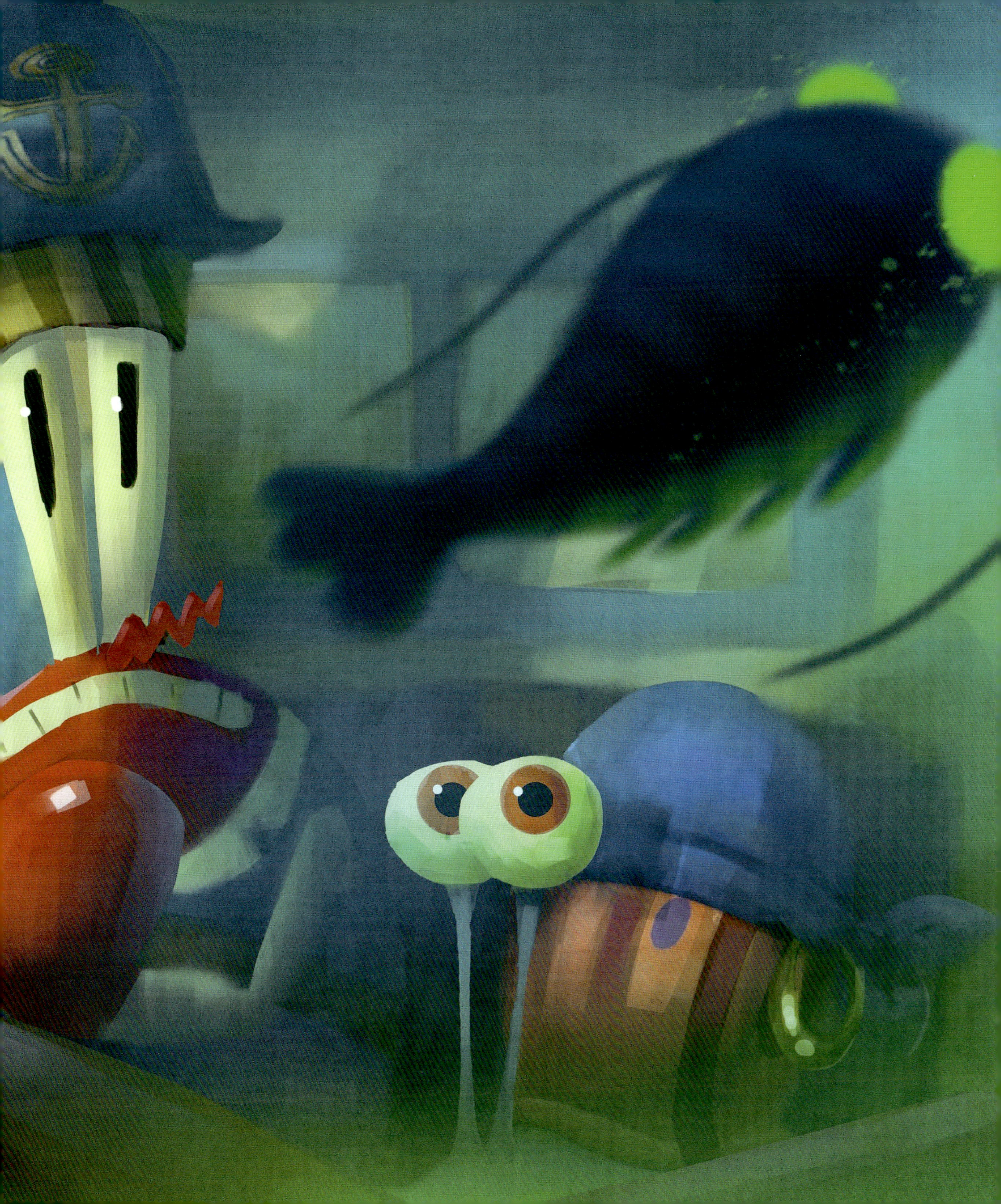

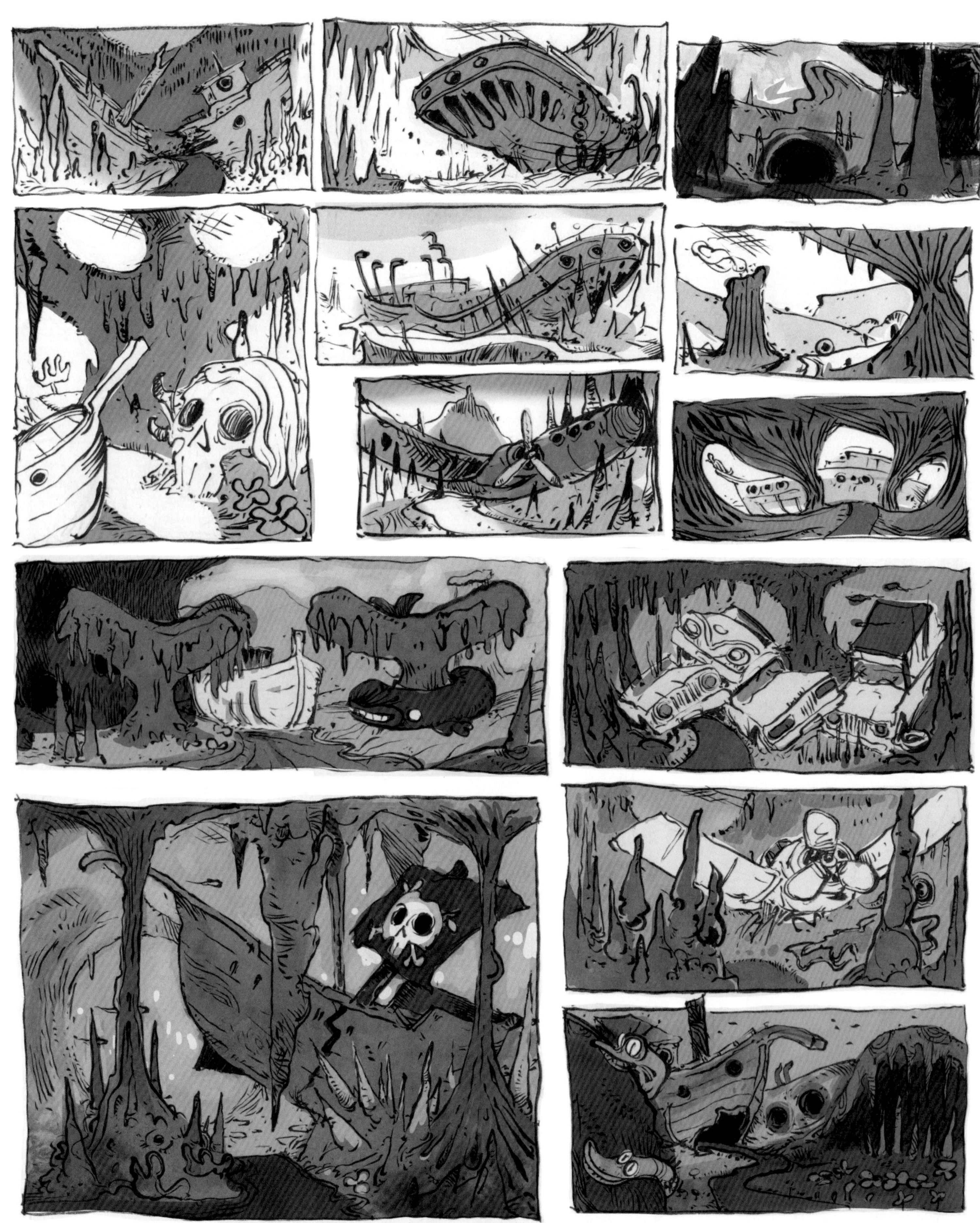

Tonals [left] and visual development art [right] of the Underworld

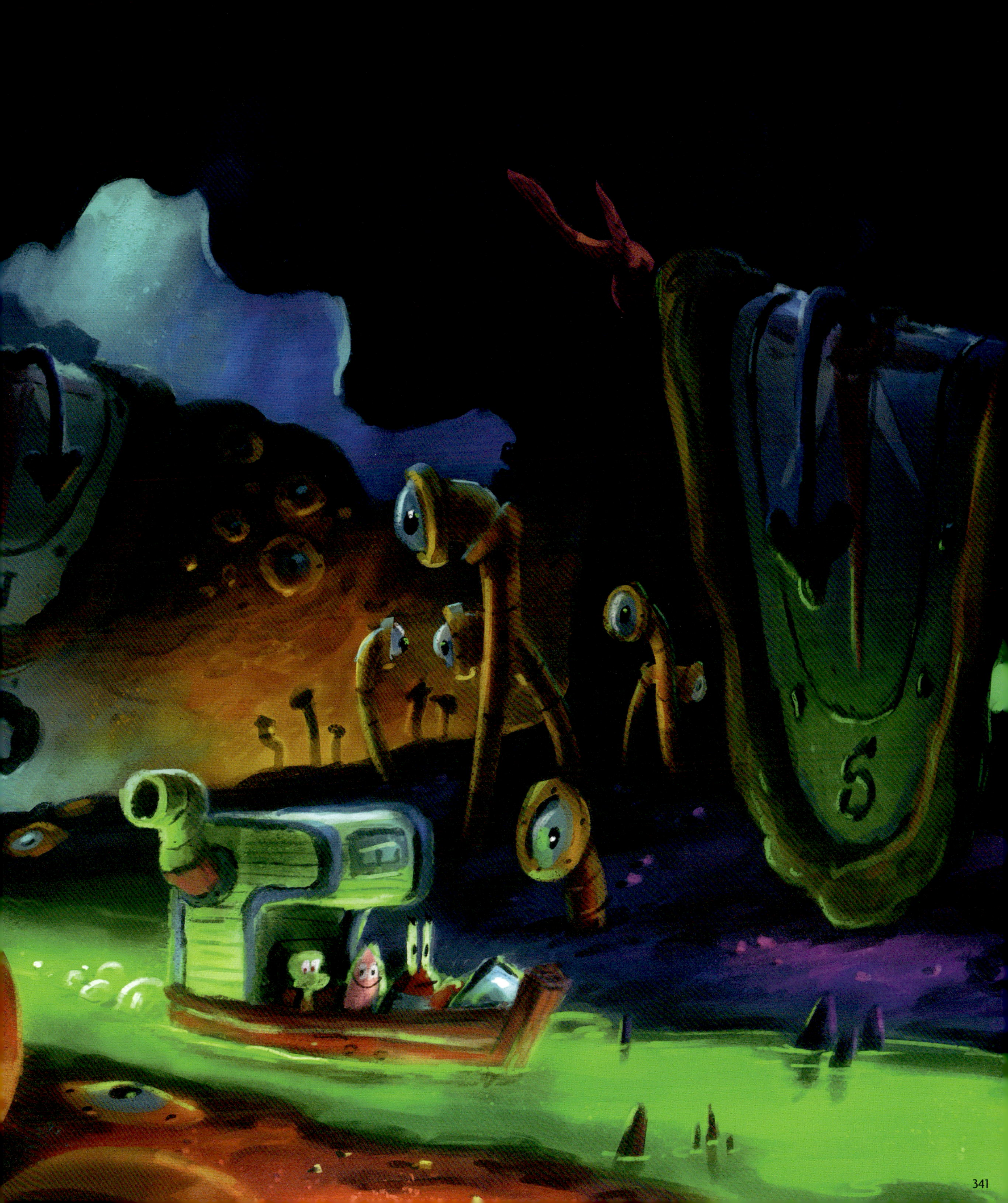

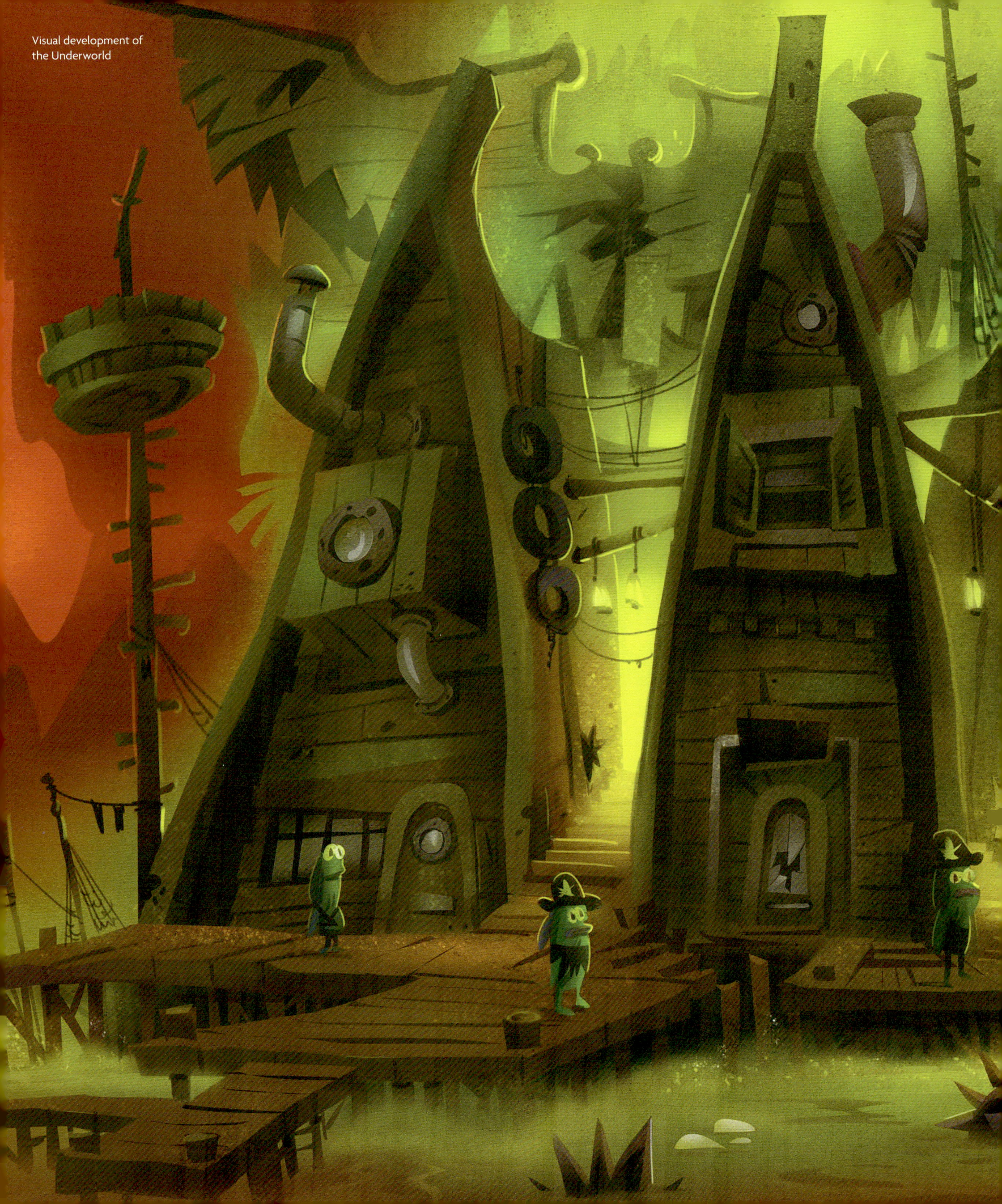

Visual development of the Underworld

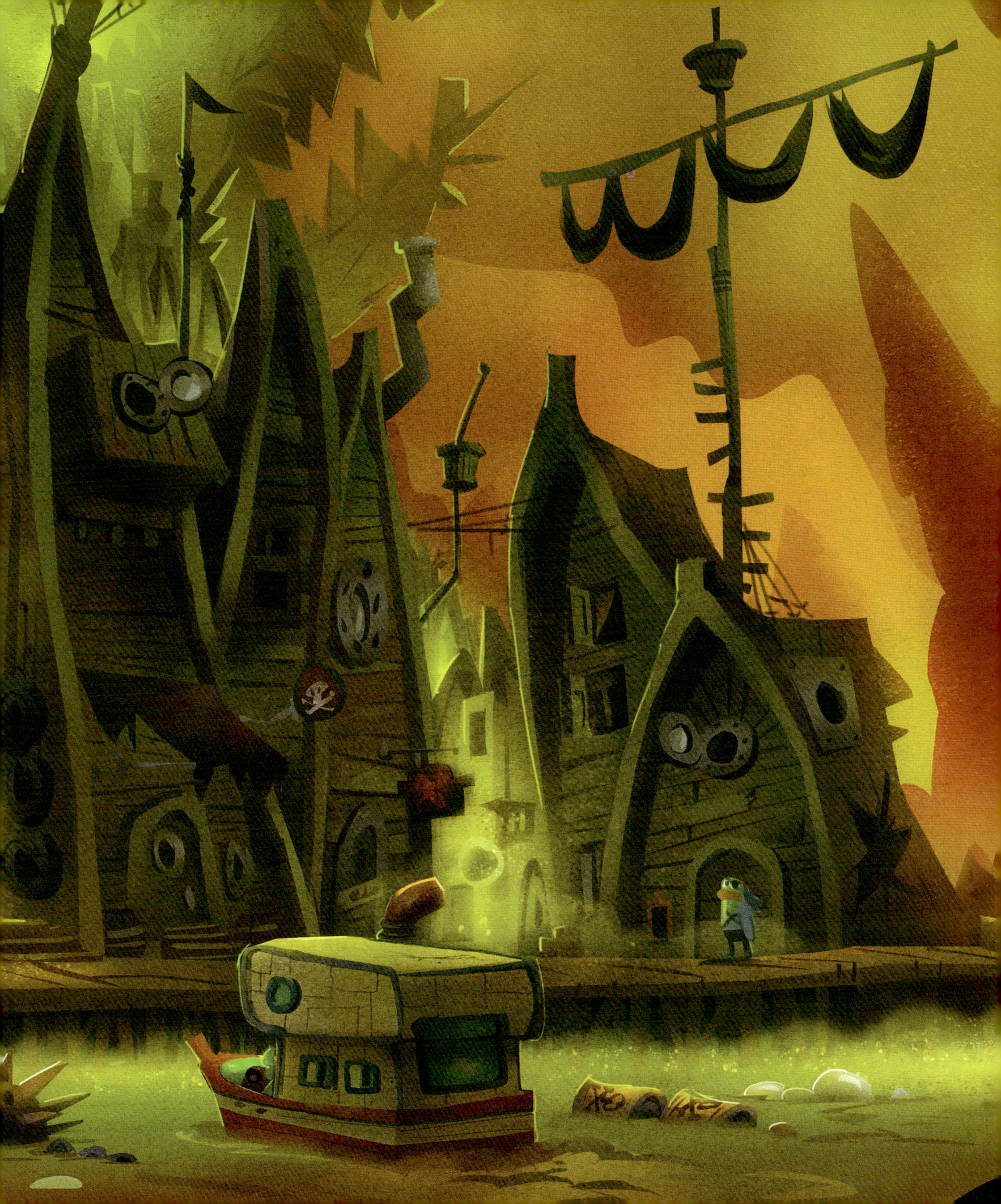

Prop design and treatments of the Pirate Law handbook

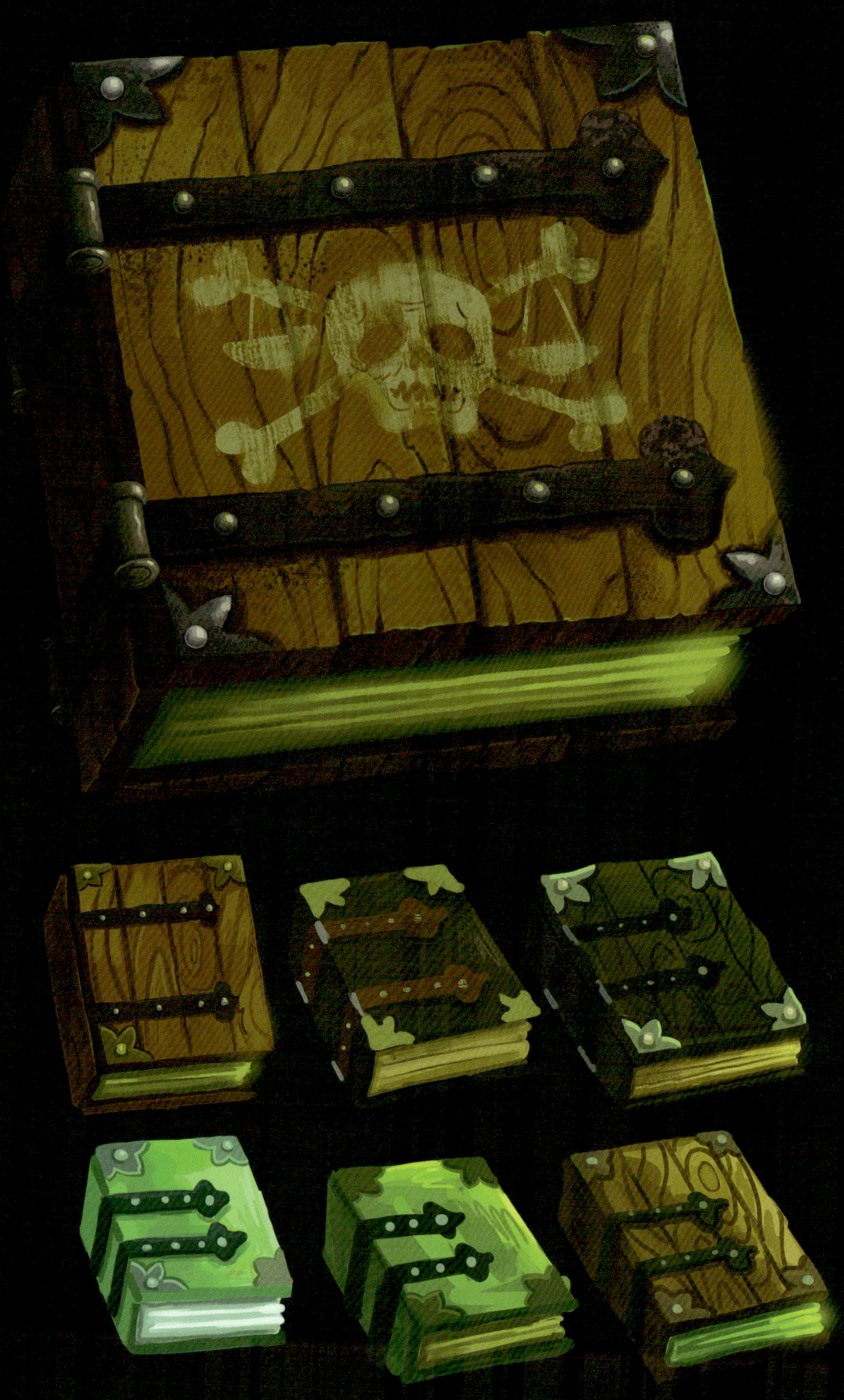

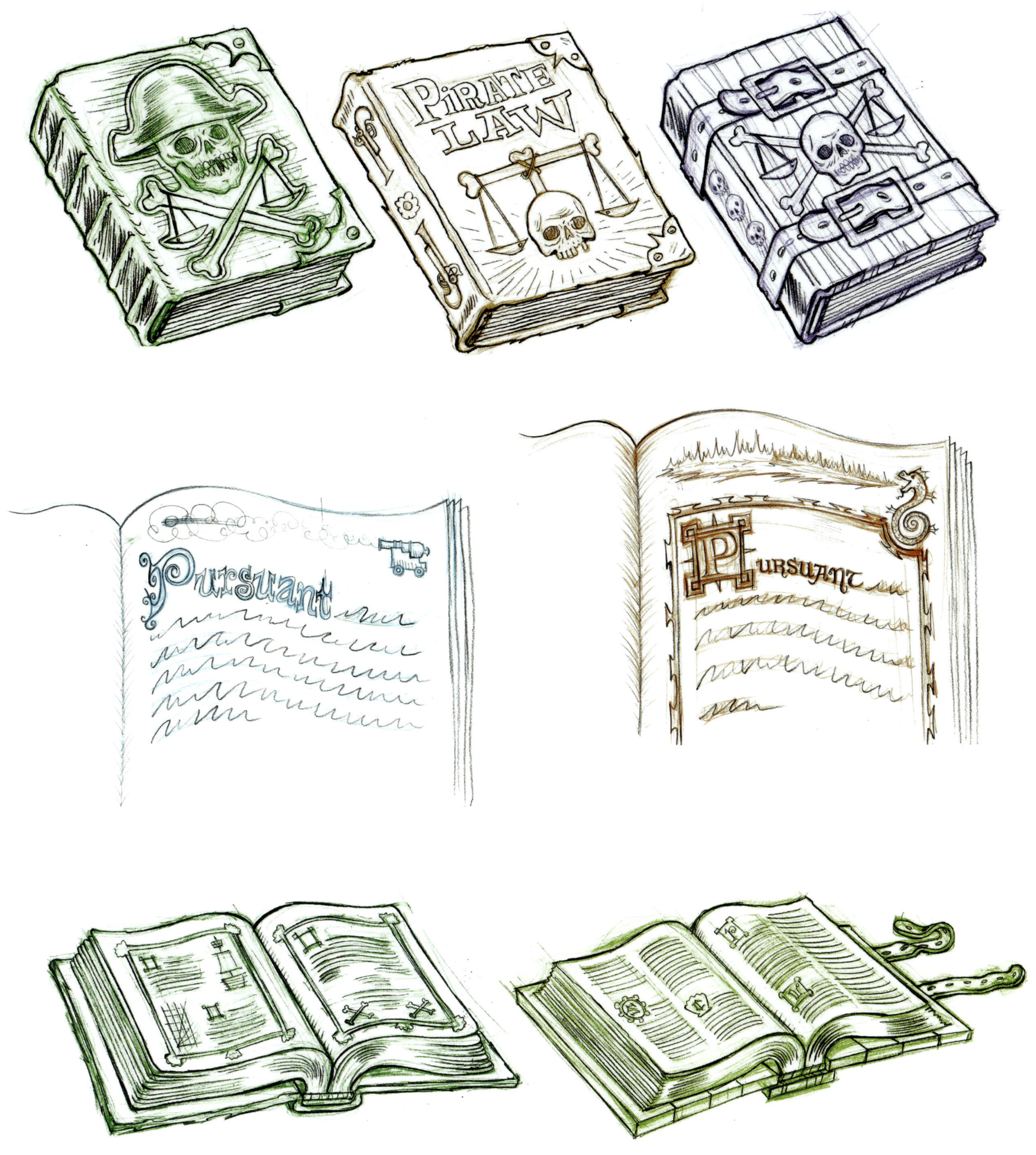
PIRATE LAW
Pursuant
PURSUANT

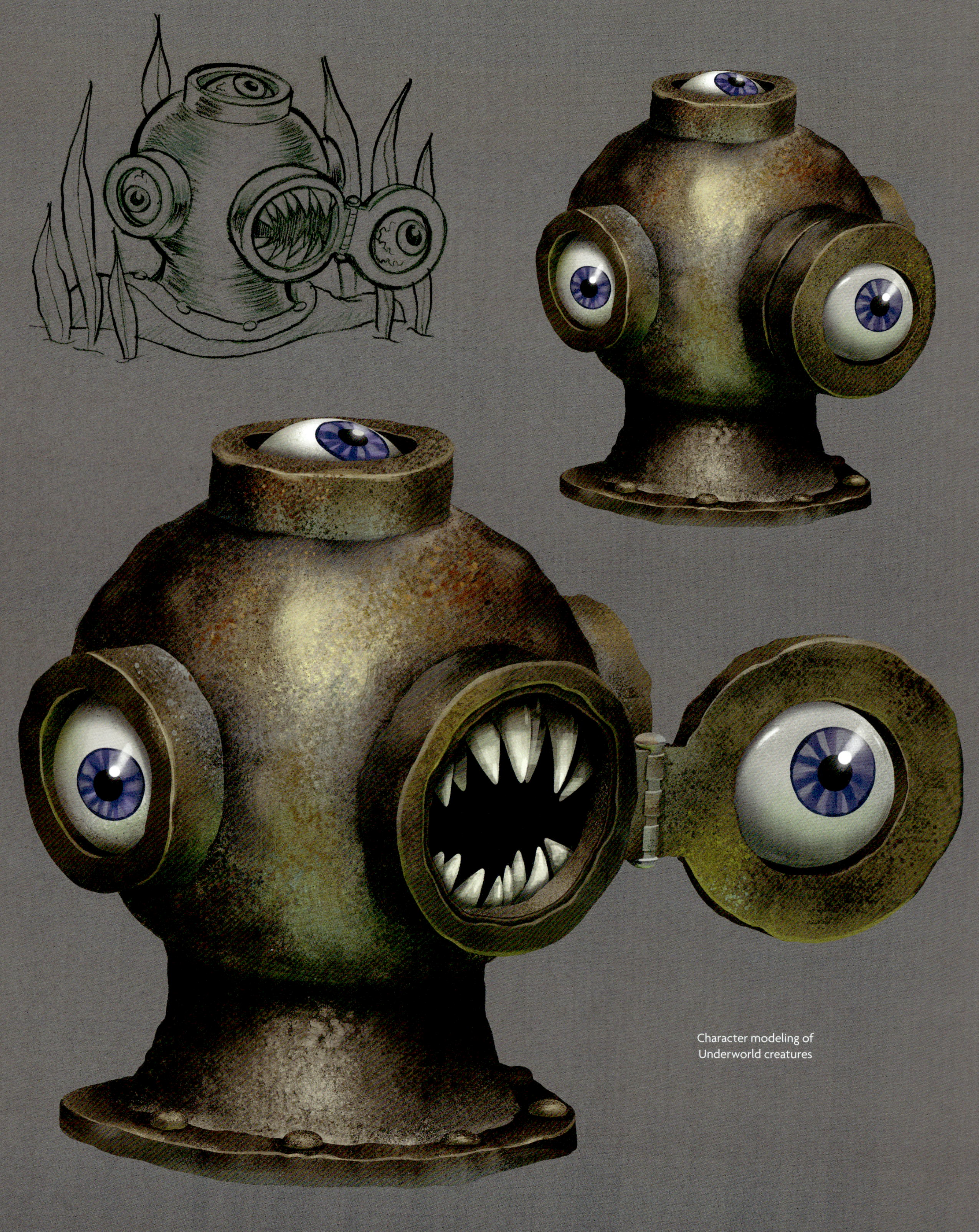

Character modeling of Underworld creatures

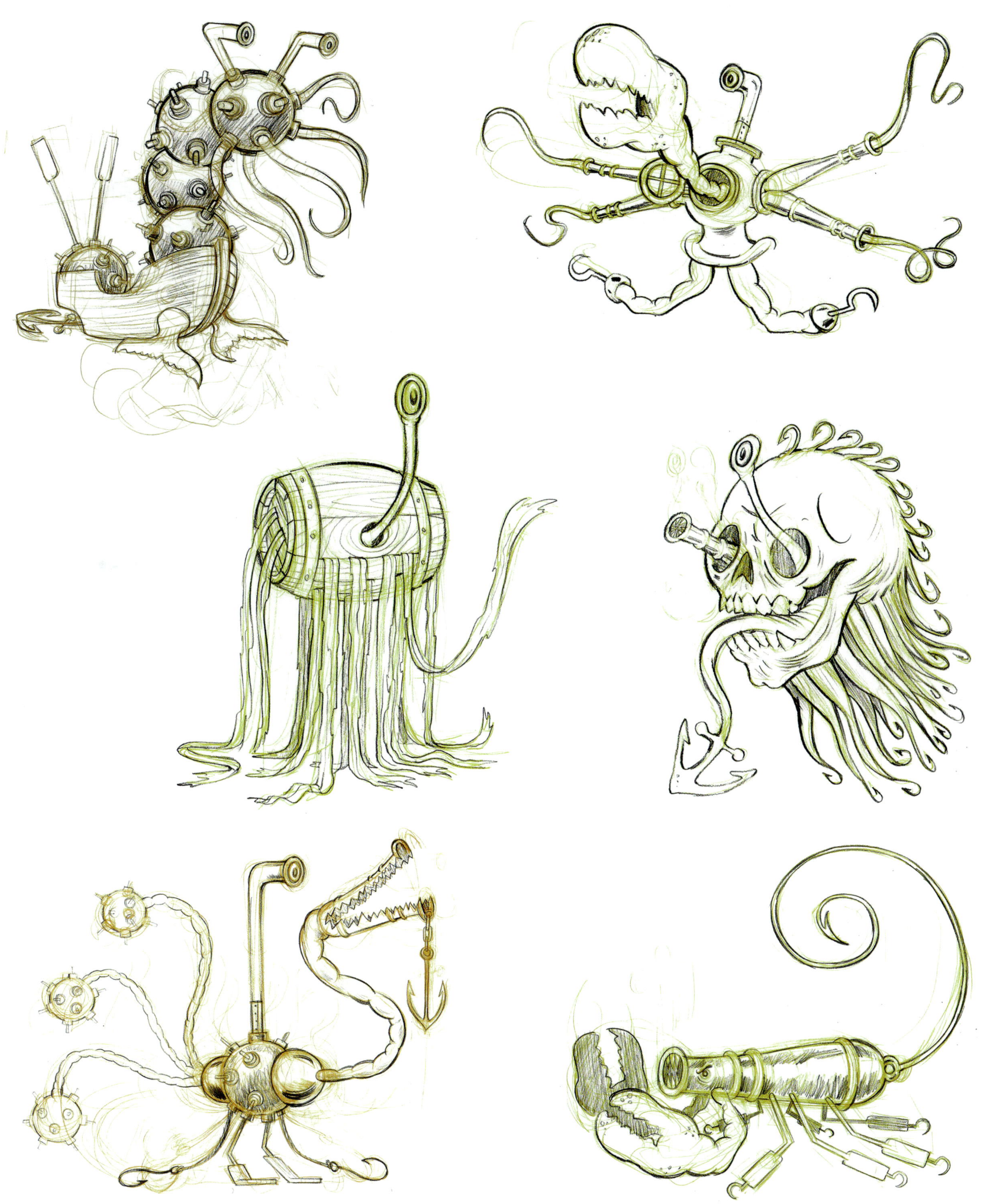

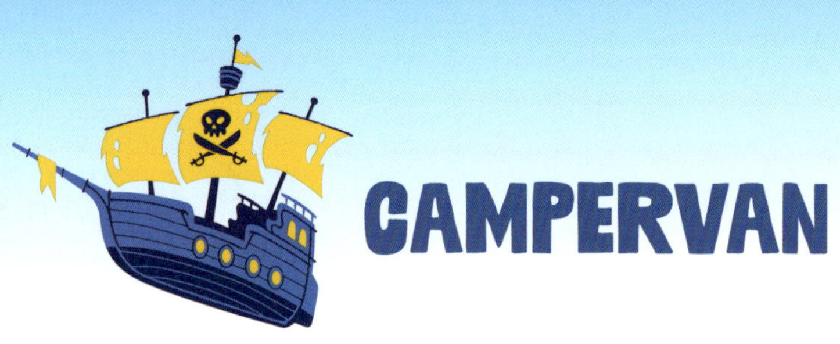

CAMPERVAN

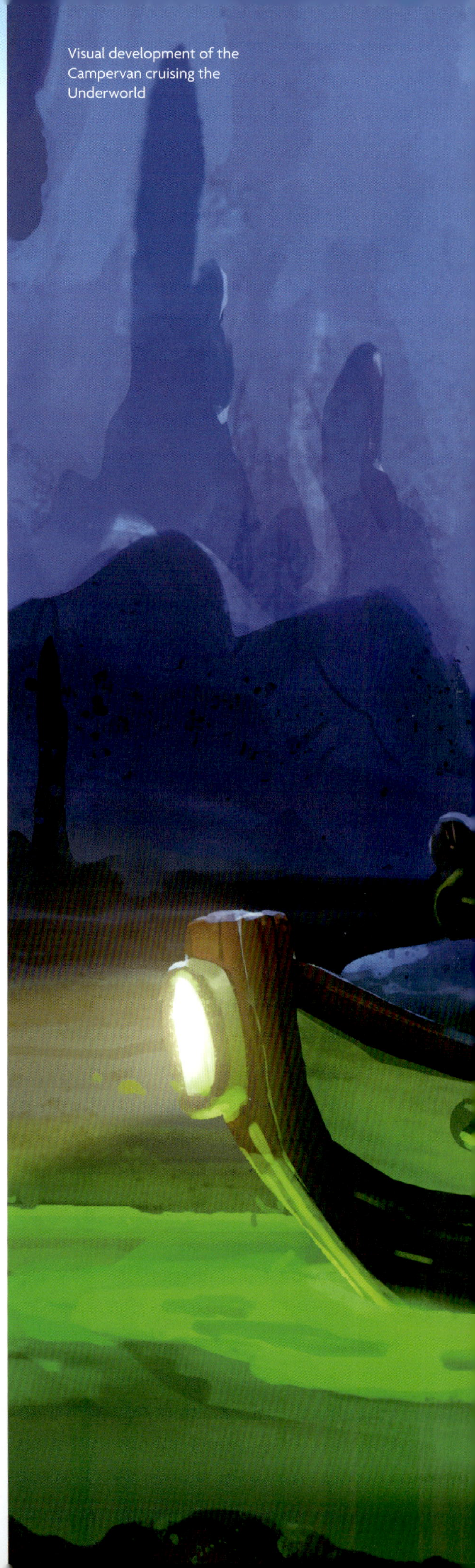

Visual development of the Campervan cruising the Underworld

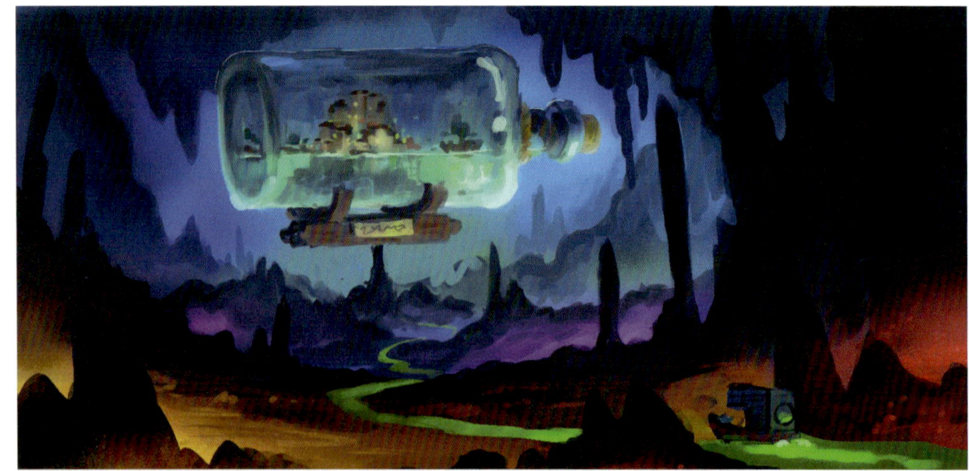

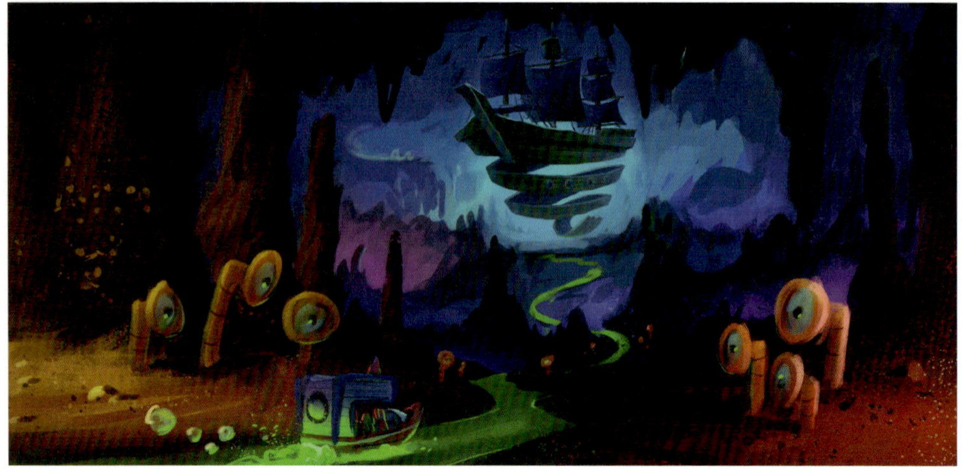

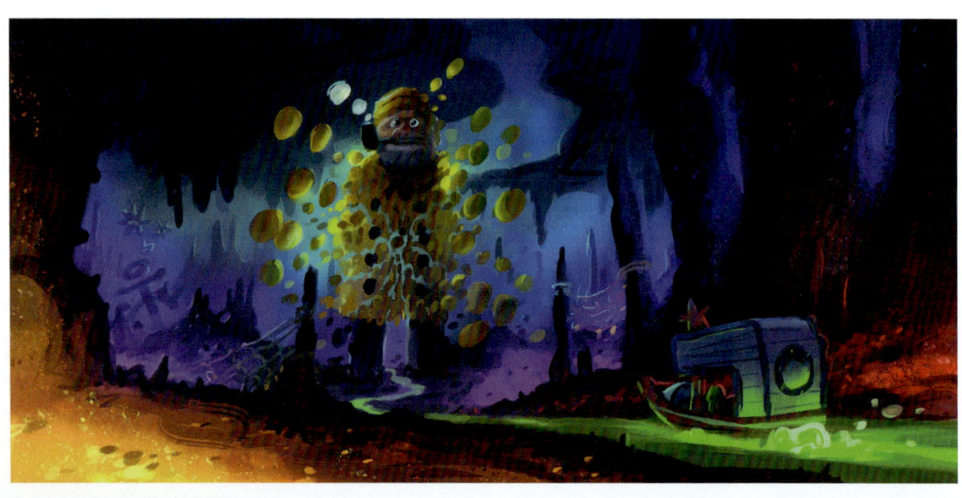

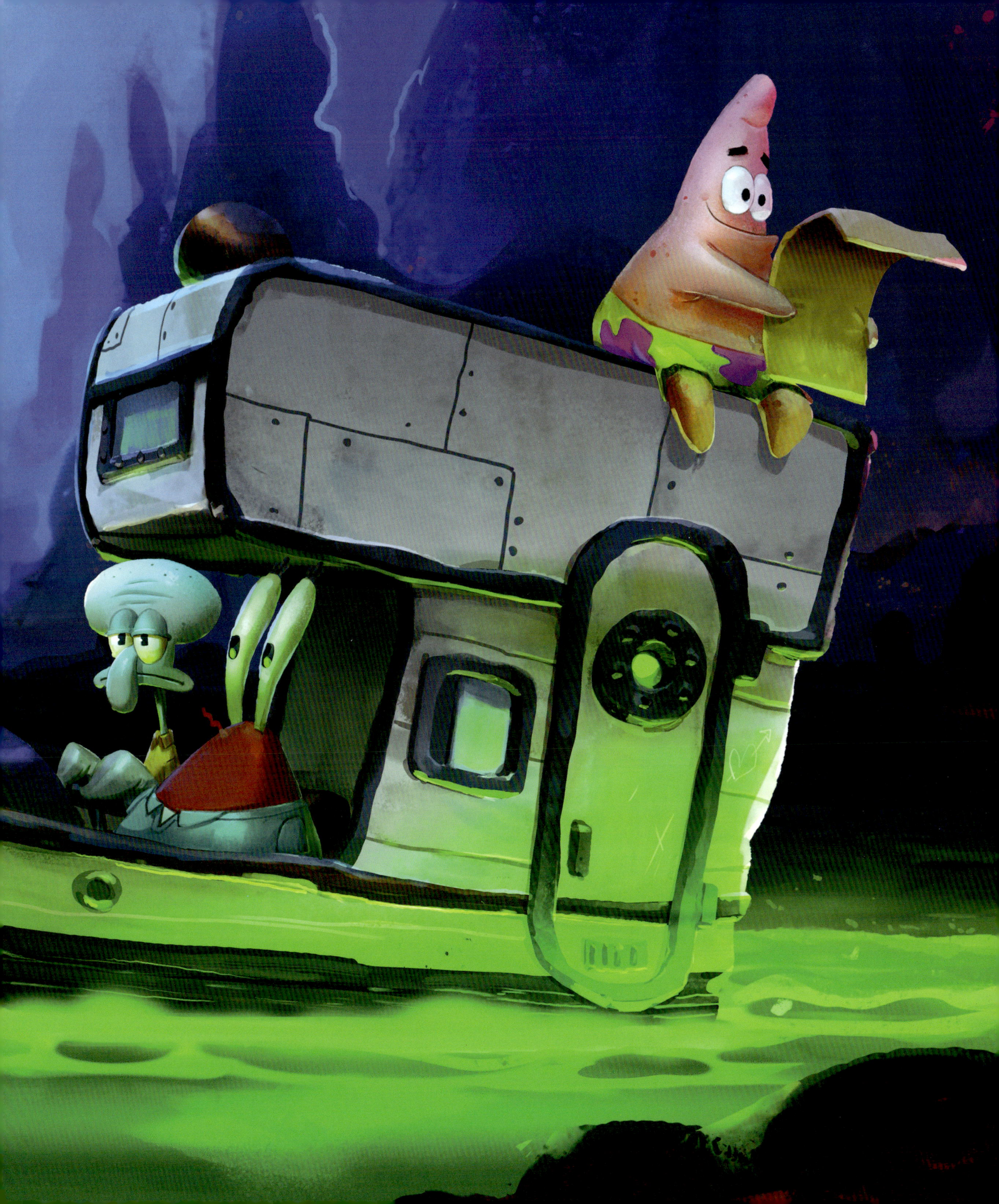

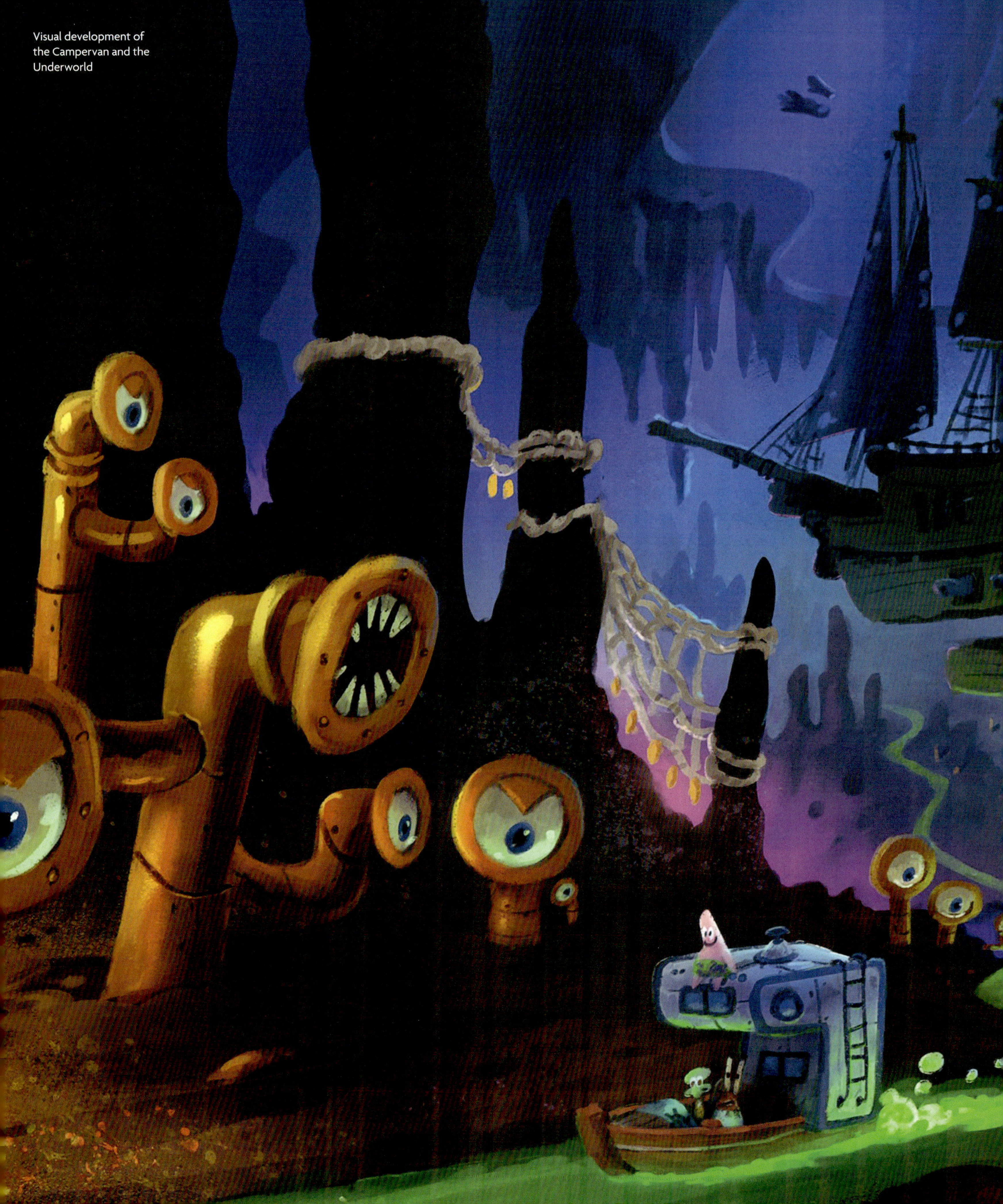

Visual development of the Campervan and the Underworld

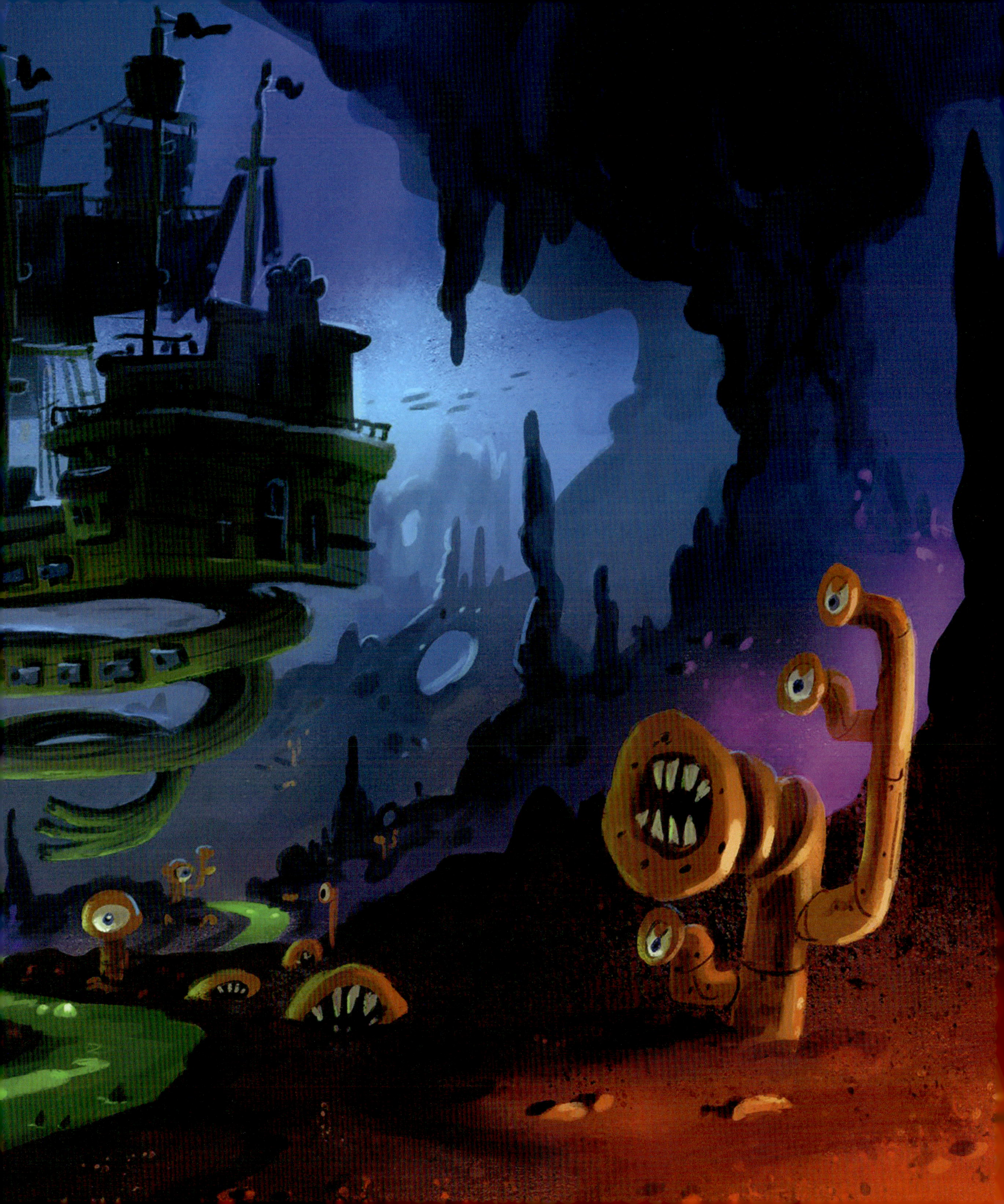

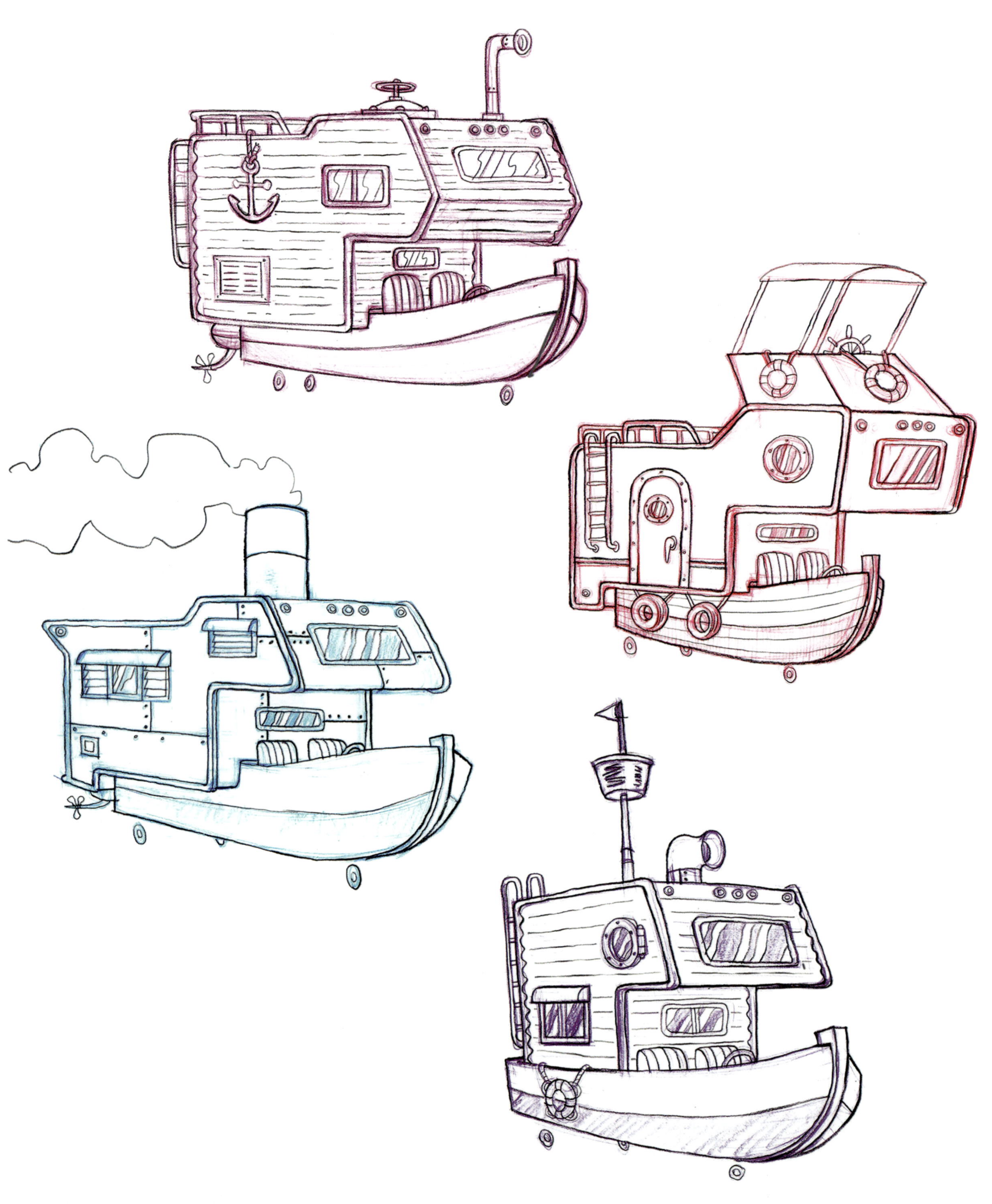

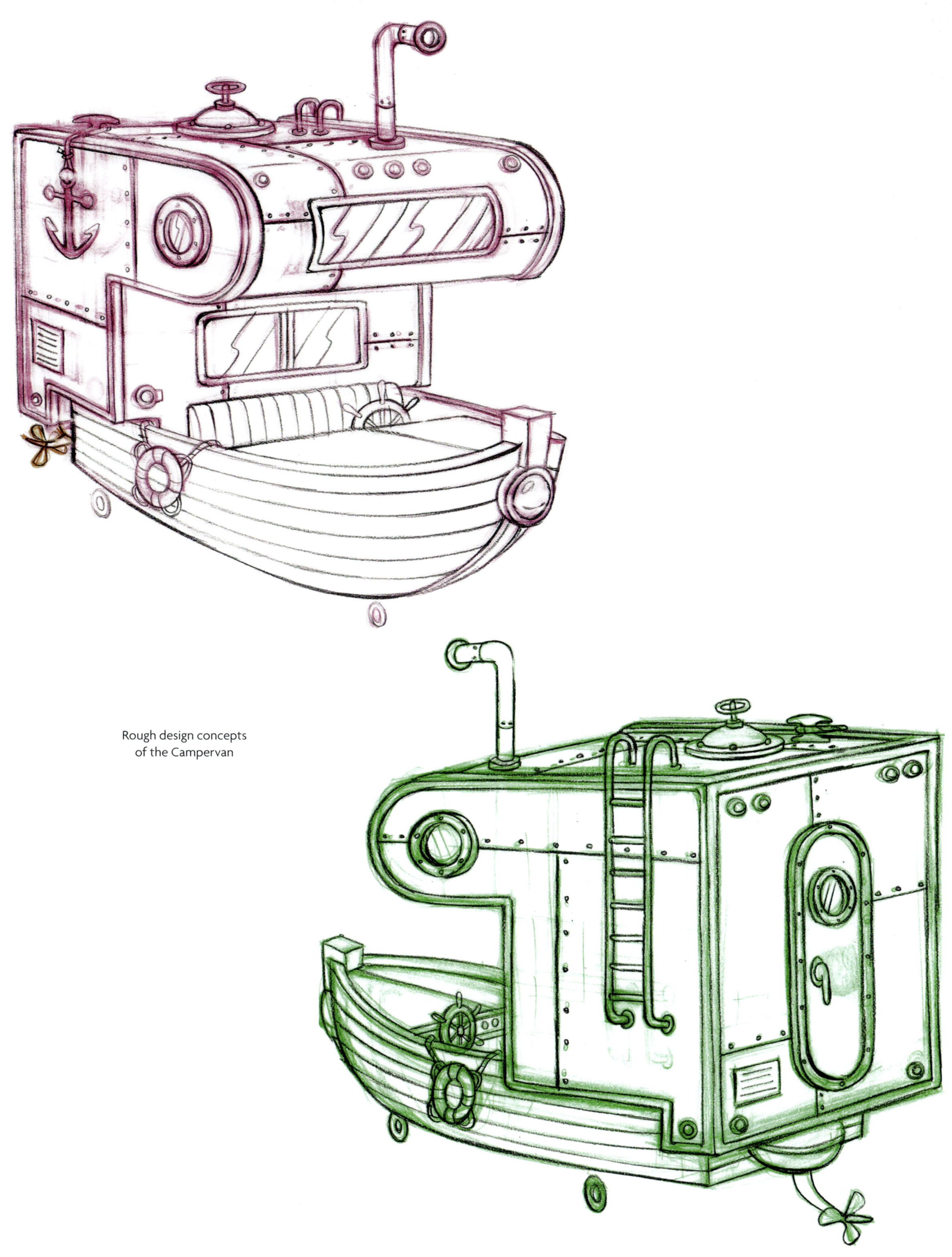

Rough design concepts
of the Campervan

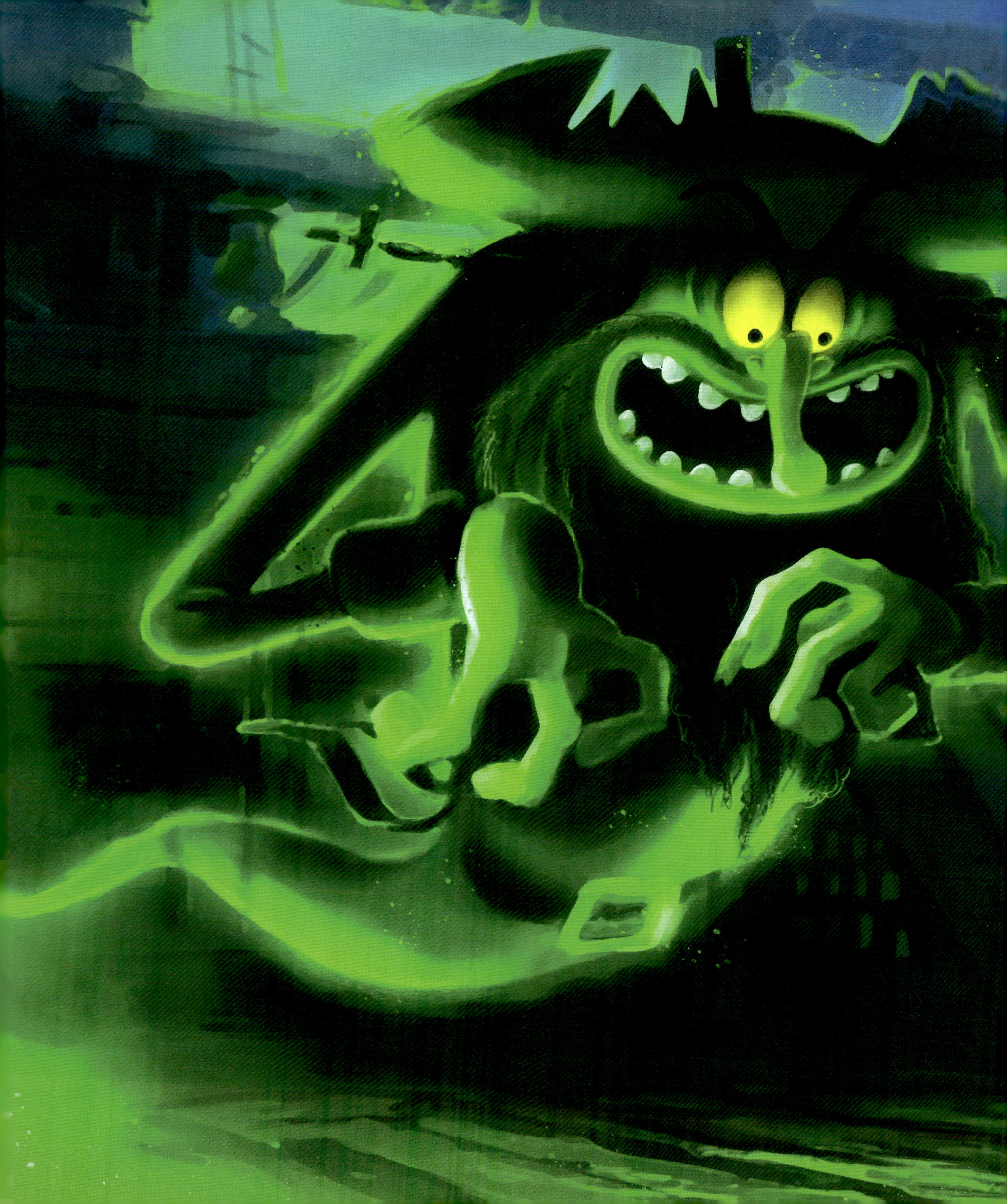

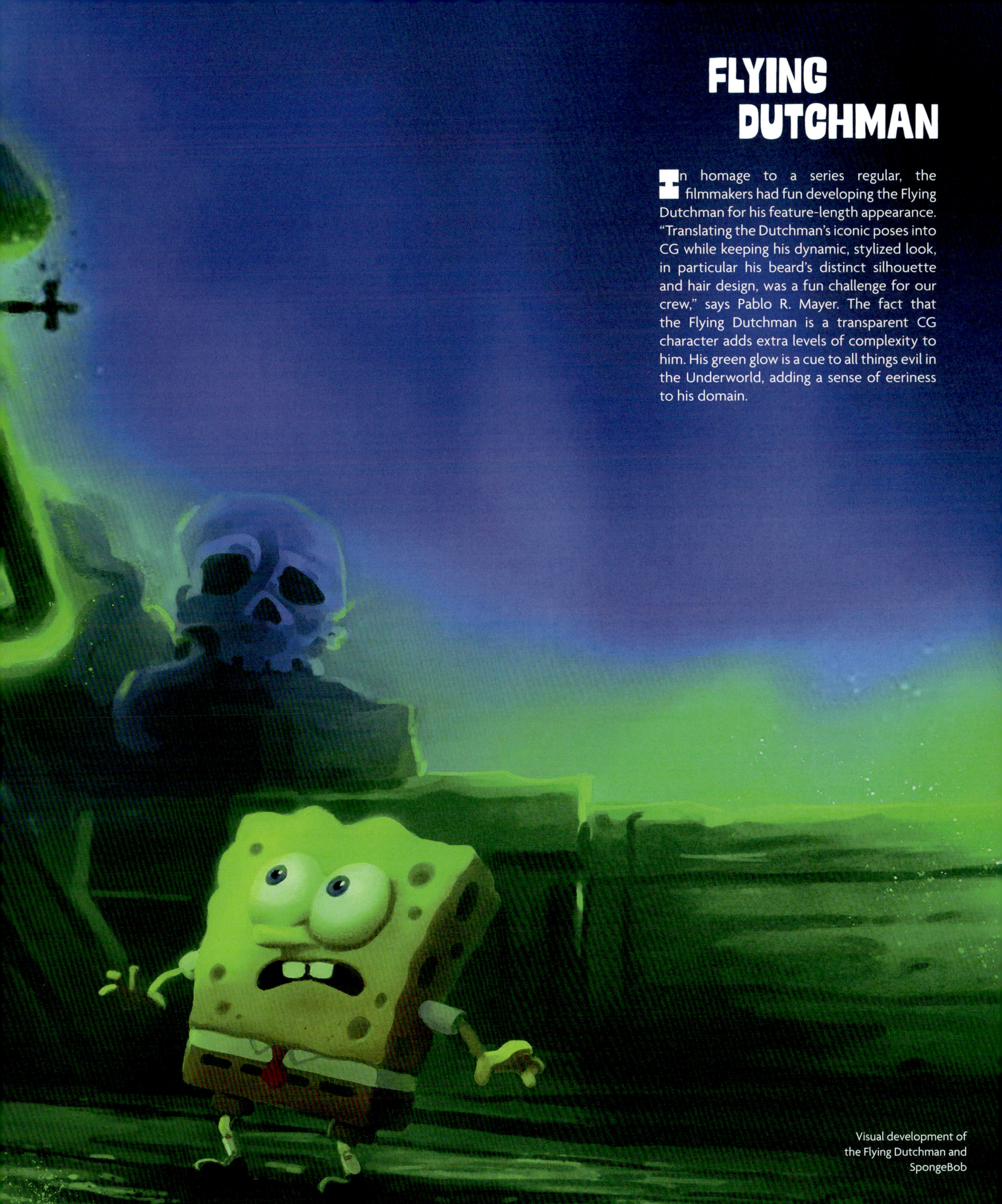

FLYING DUTCHMAN

In homage to a series regular, the filmmakers had fun developing the Flying Dutchman for his feature-length appearance. "Translating the Dutchman's iconic poses into CG while keeping his dynamic, stylized look, in particular his beard's distinct silhouette and hair design, was a fun challenge for our crew," says Pablo R. Mayer. The fact that the Flying Dutchman is a transparent CG character adds extra levels of complexity to him. His green glow is a cue to all things evil in the Underworld, adding a sense of eeriness to his domain.

Visual development of the Flying Dutchman and SpongeBob

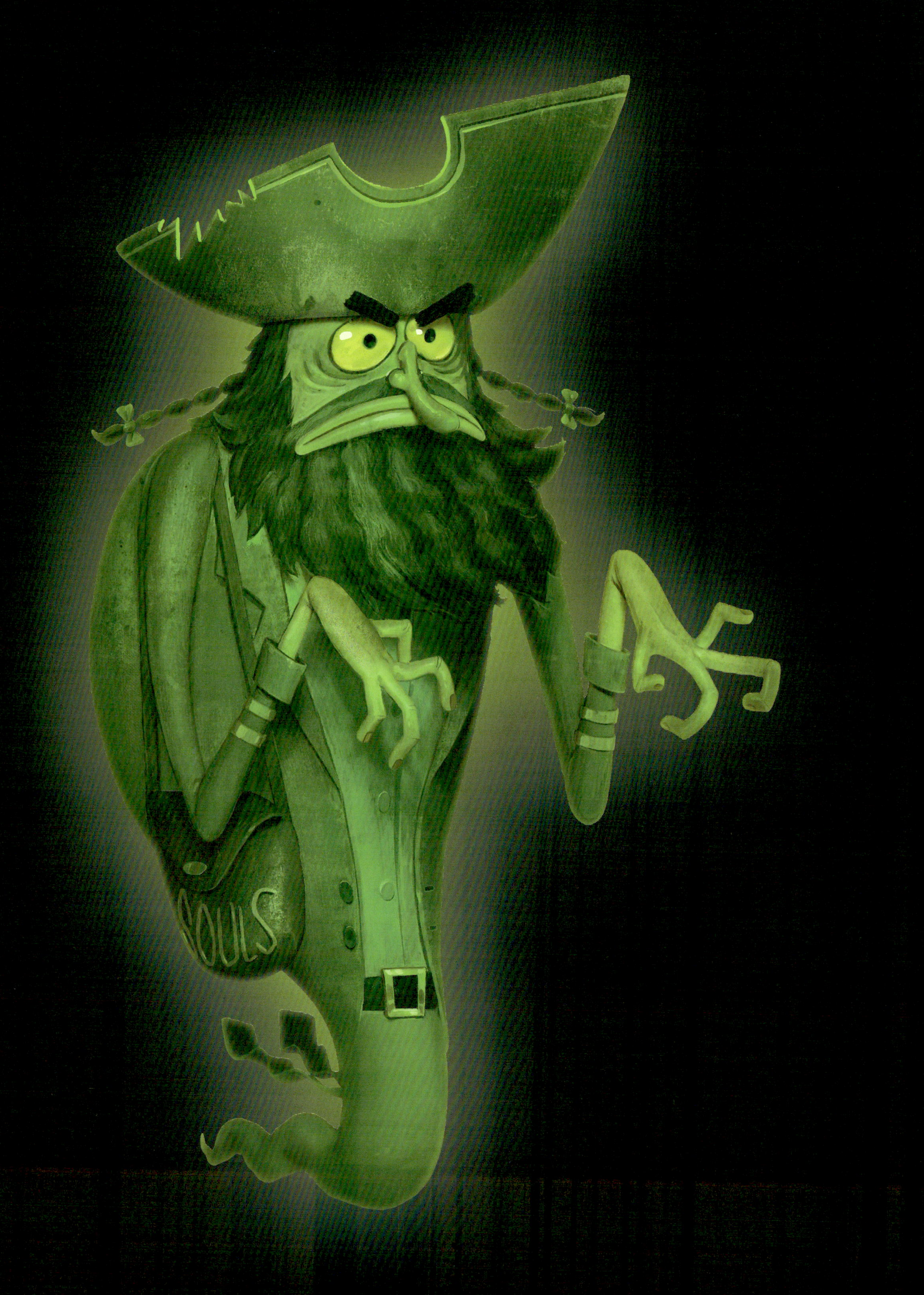
SOULS

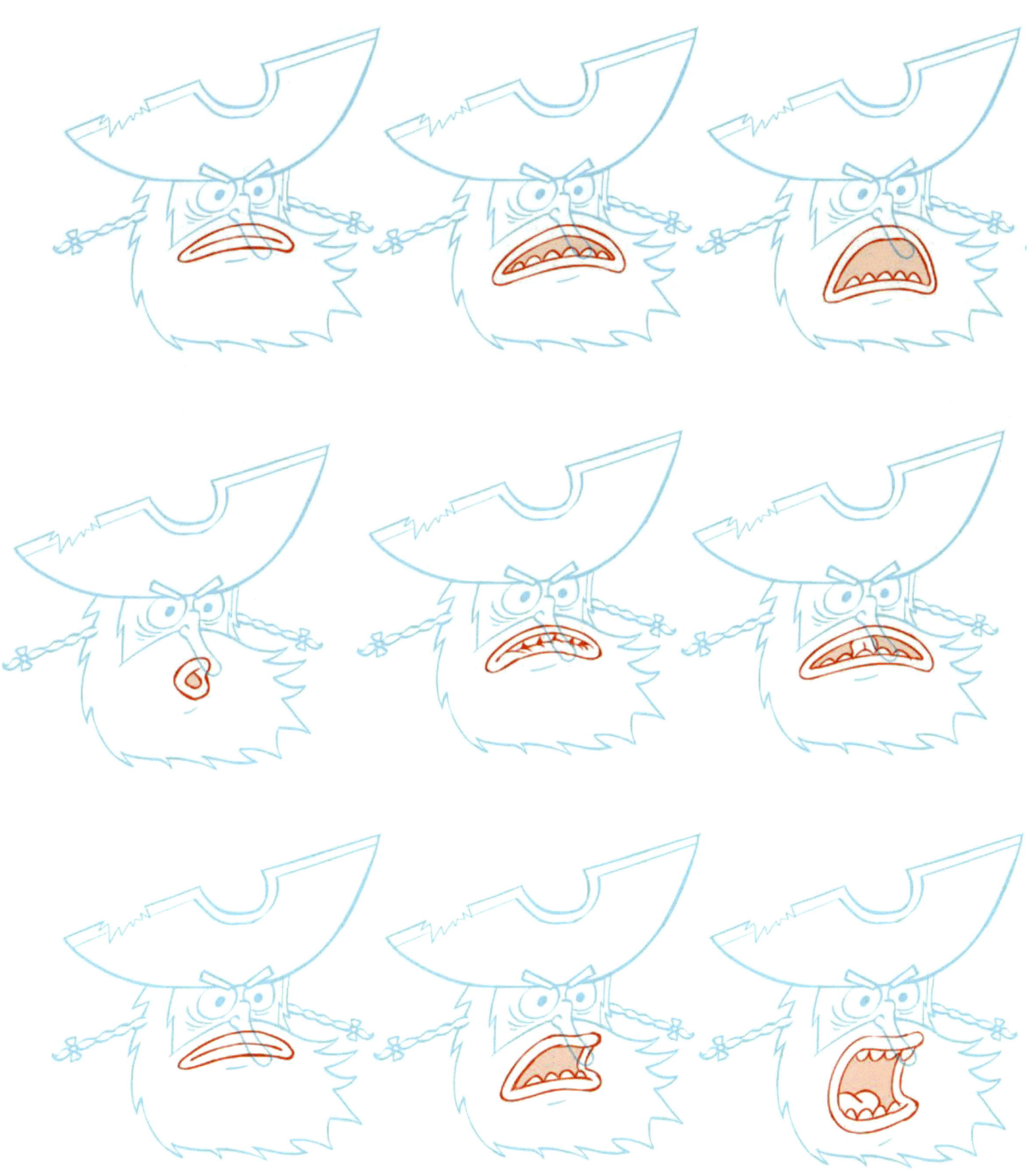

Final art [left] and mouth shapes [right] of the Flying Dutchman

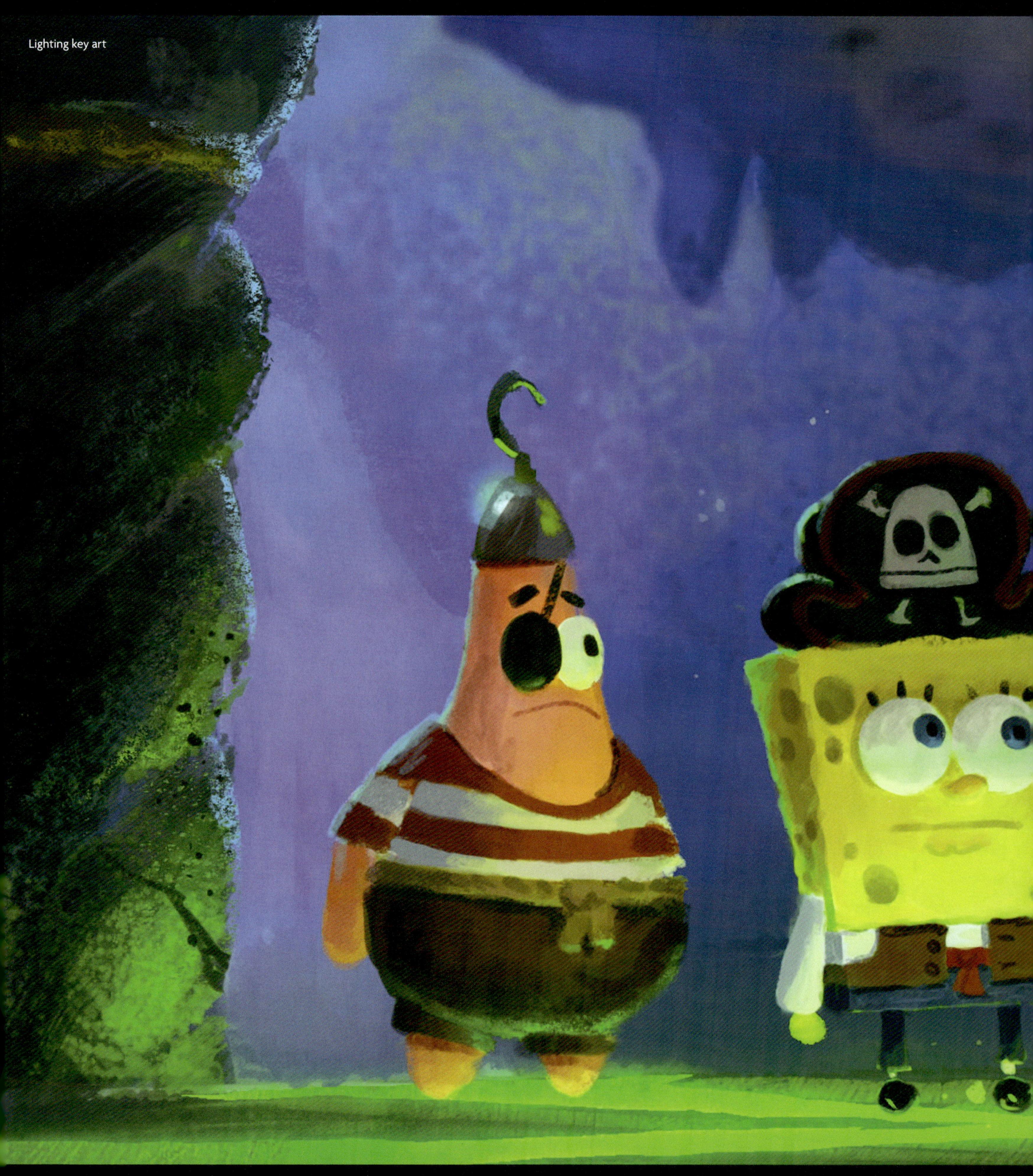

Lighting key art

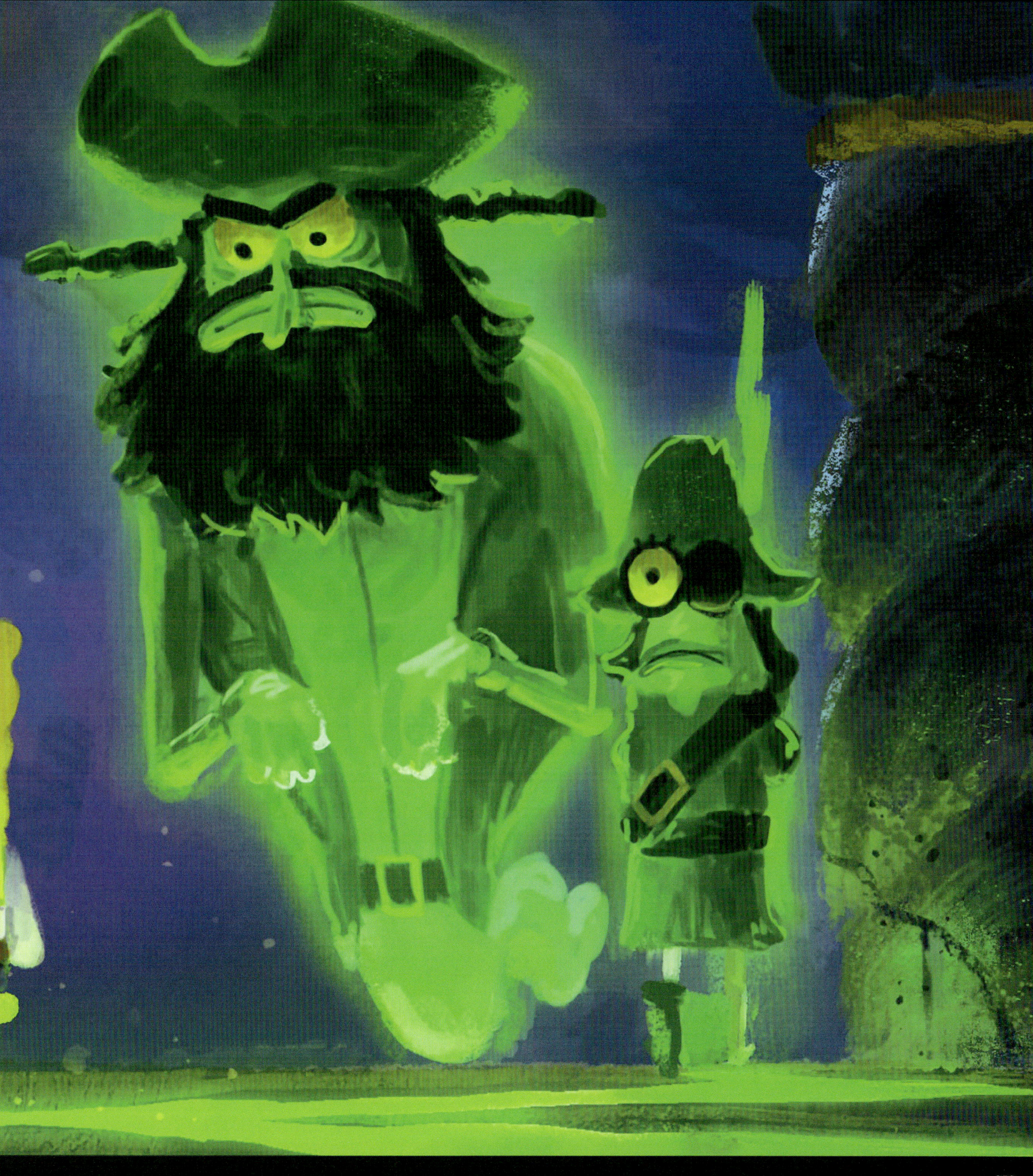

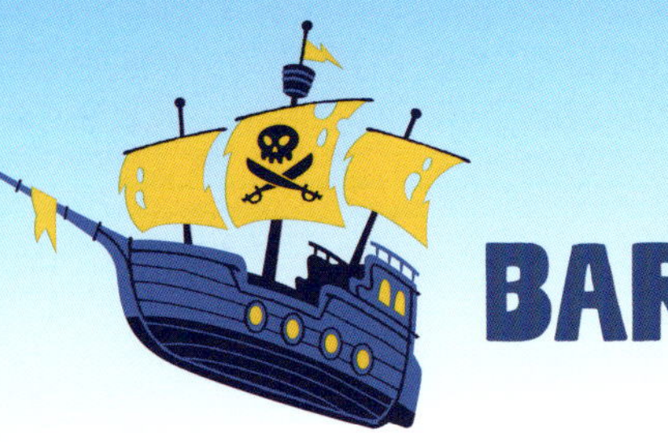

BARB

Another new addition to the SpongeBob realm is Barb, the Flying Dutchman's trusty first mate, also featured in ghost pirate form.

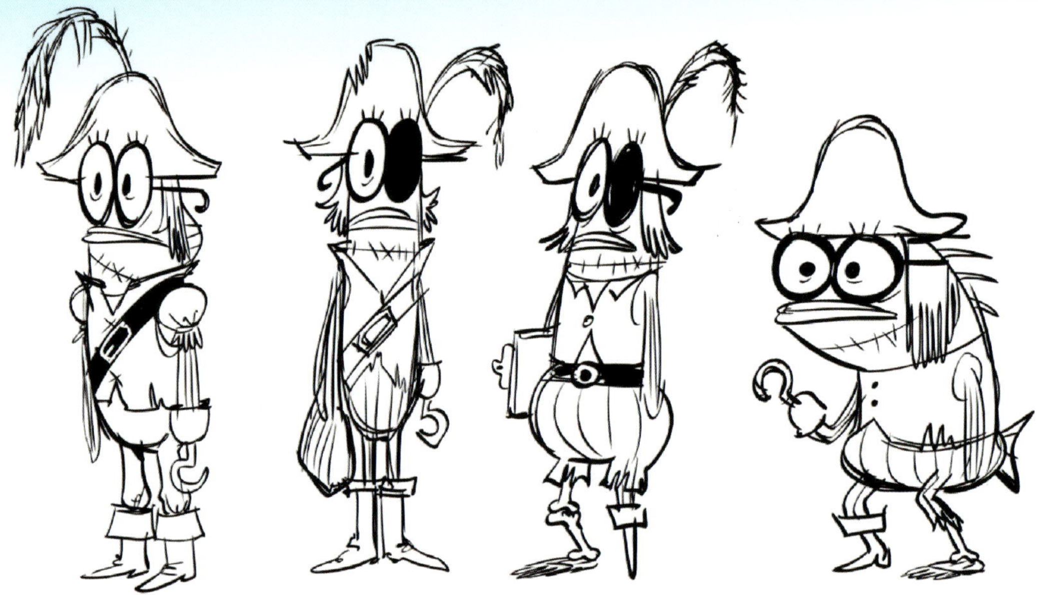

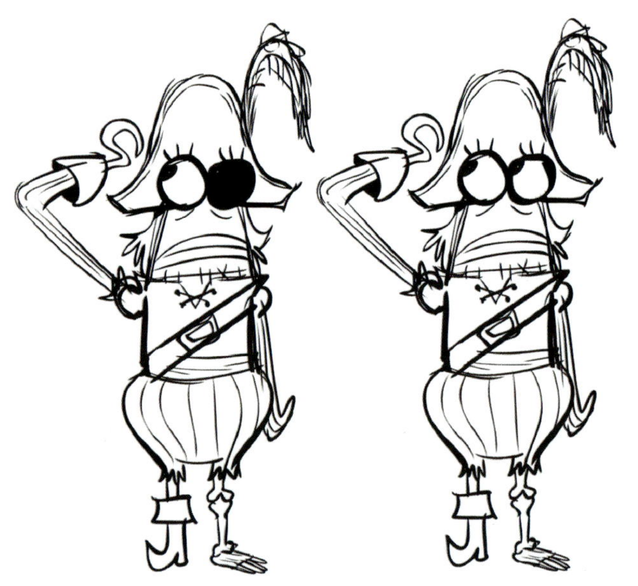

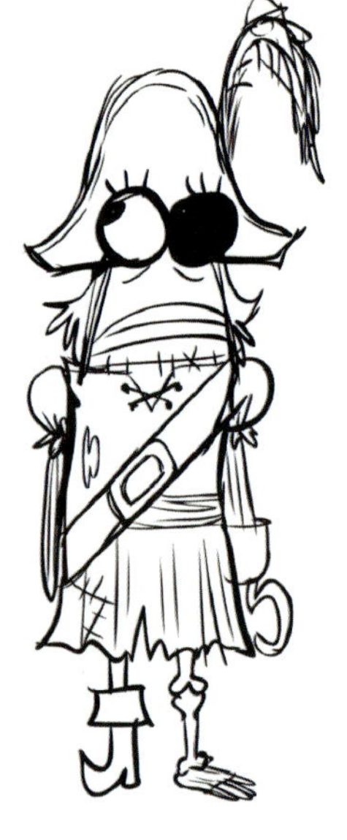

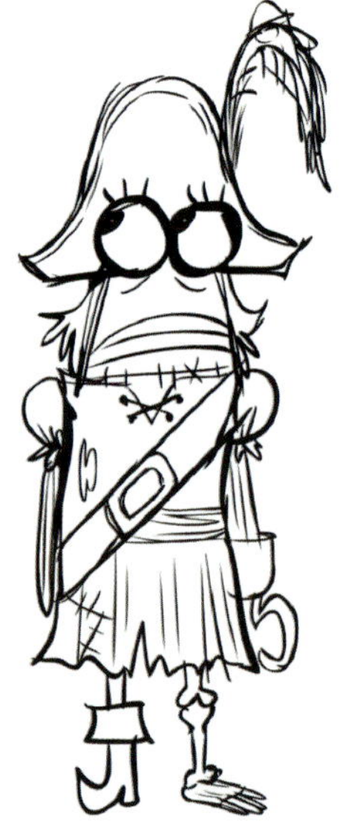

Rough character designs [left and far right] and final art [right] of Barb

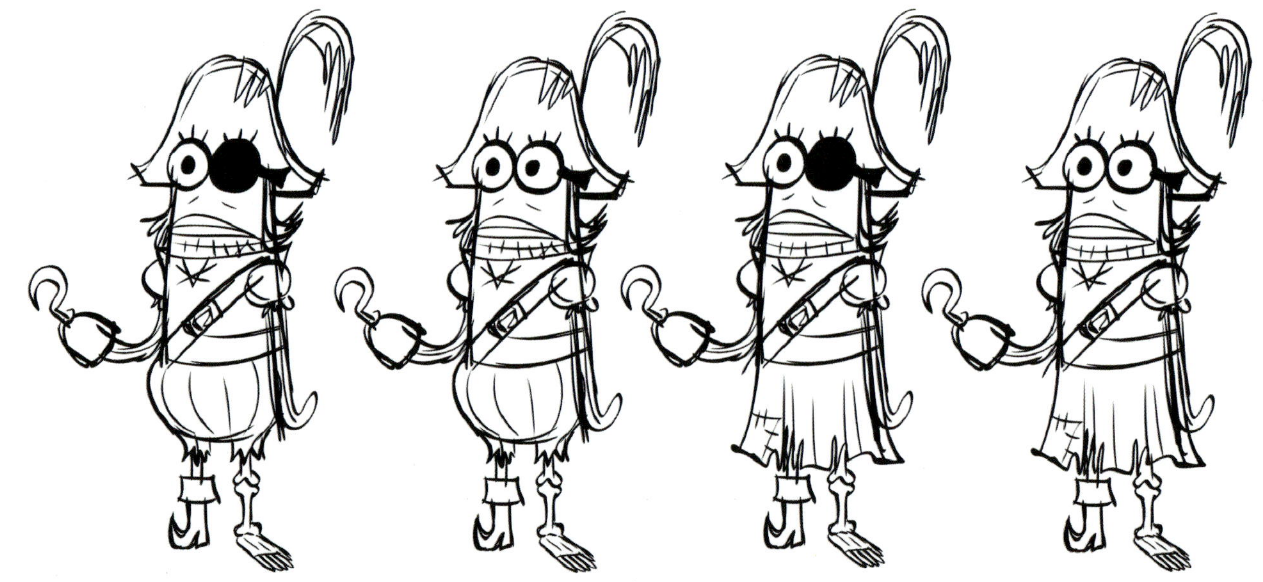

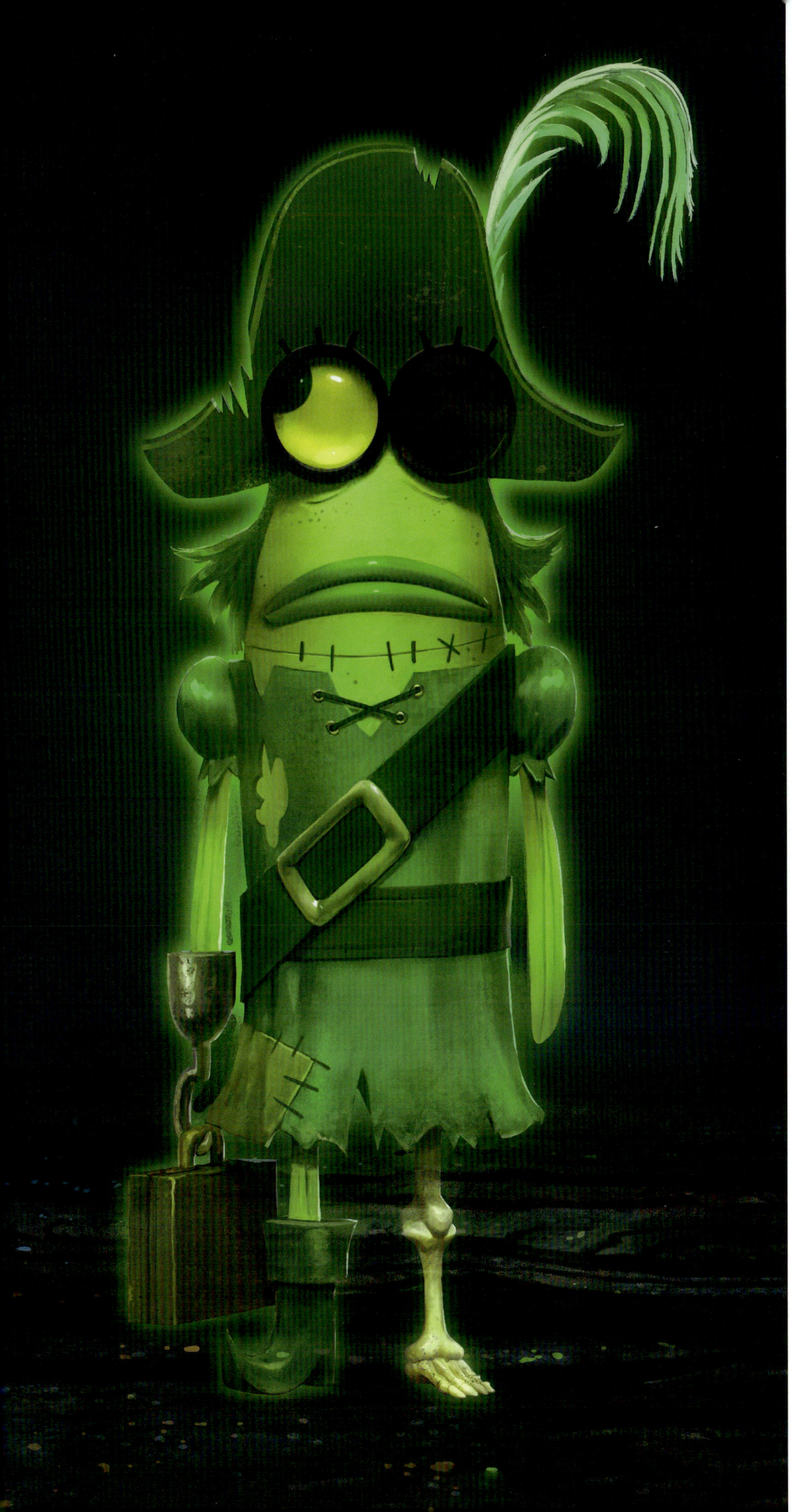

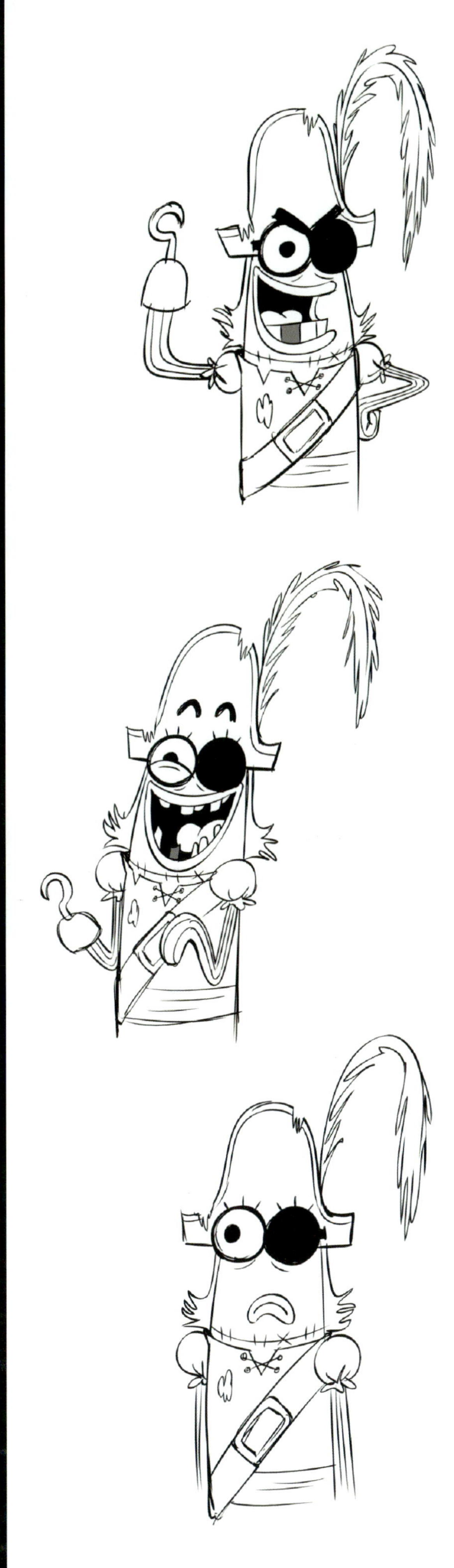

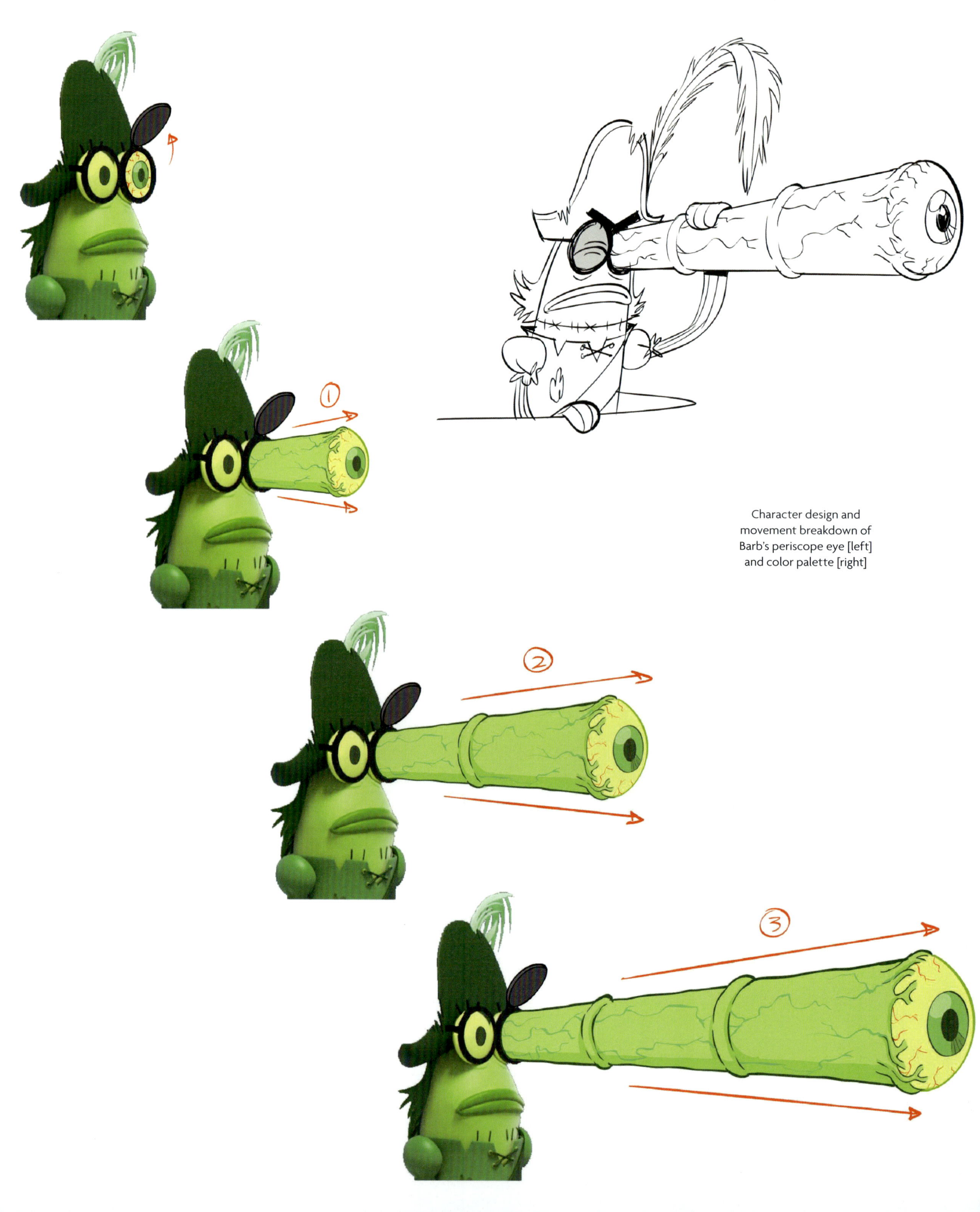

Character design and movement breakdown of Barb's periscope eye [left] and color palette [right]

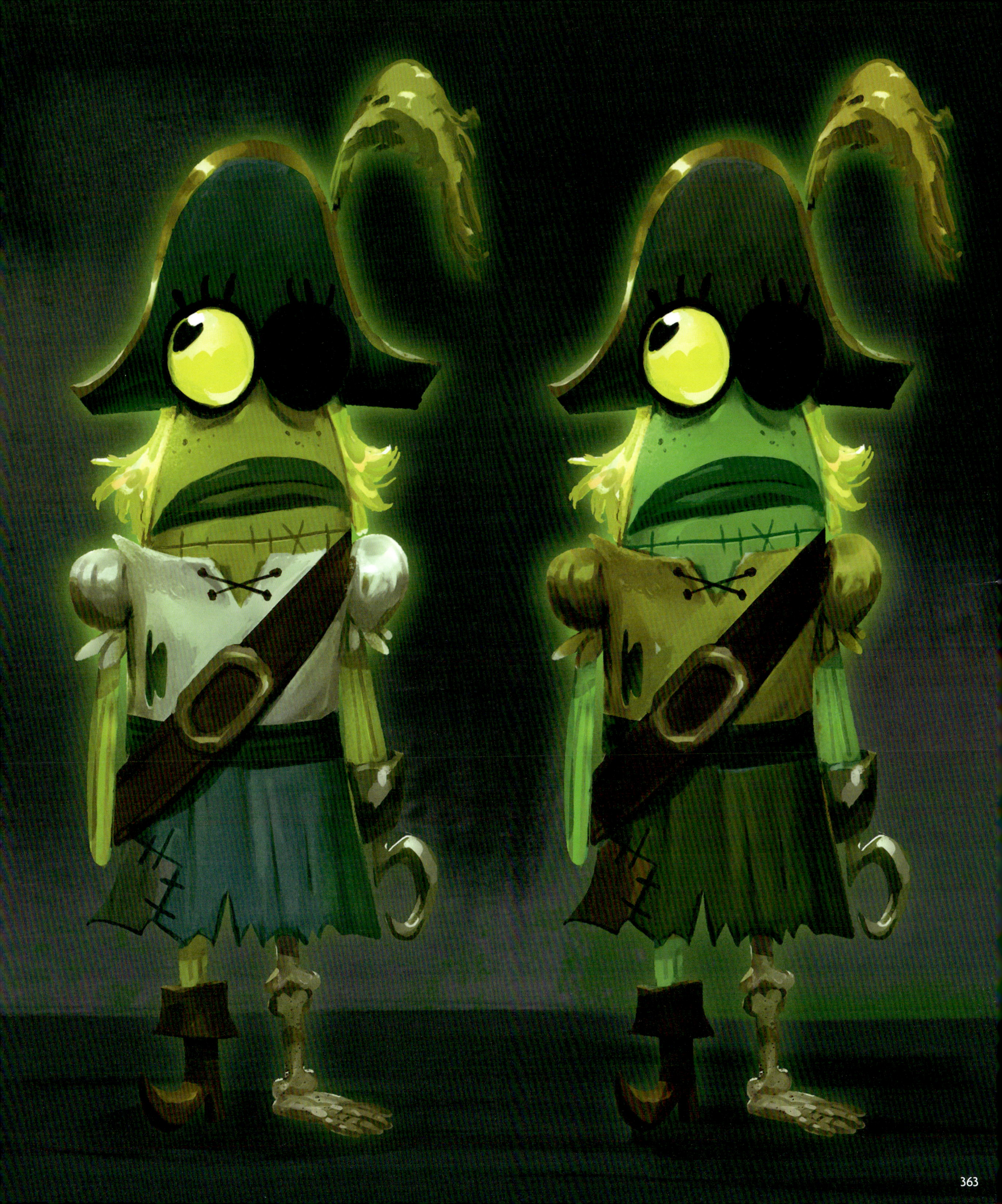

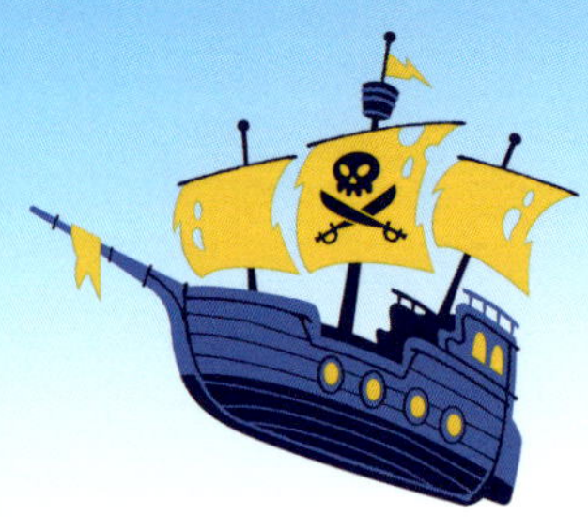

CHALLENGE COVE

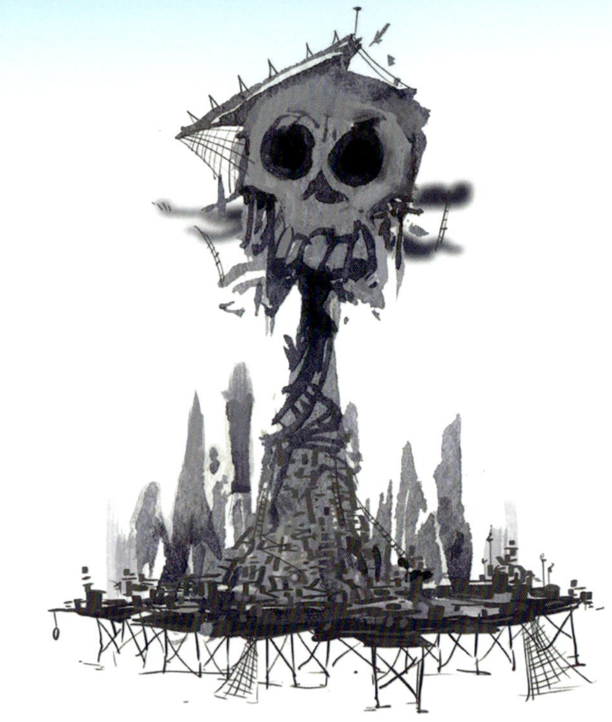

To prove himself in the Underworld, SpongeBob must face a series of challenges and monsters. "The concept was a layered island, where each victory unlocked access to the next tier. It had to feel game-like but grounded in the underwater world's logic," says production designer Pablo R. Mayer. The challenges blend a mix of sports, pirate, horror Western, and just plain silliness themes, with color-saturation lighting and timing that build to a big finish.

While use of the flat cards in this sequence harkens back to the original SpongeBob series dynamic, the creatures that appear in these challenges certainly do not. "Creatures in the Underworld were inspired by nautical elements, sea life, and surrealism. We aimed for them to fit seamlessly into the environment, sometimes even using them as part of the set design," explains Mayer. "We knew we wanted the monsters to be based off nautical and pirate-themed things, so we just started asking ourselves questions like 'Where would we put an eyeball? Could we put a mouth on that item? Could we make those things tentacles?' Then we would combine a few different concepts to make them even scarier or sillier," recalls art director Travis Ruiz.

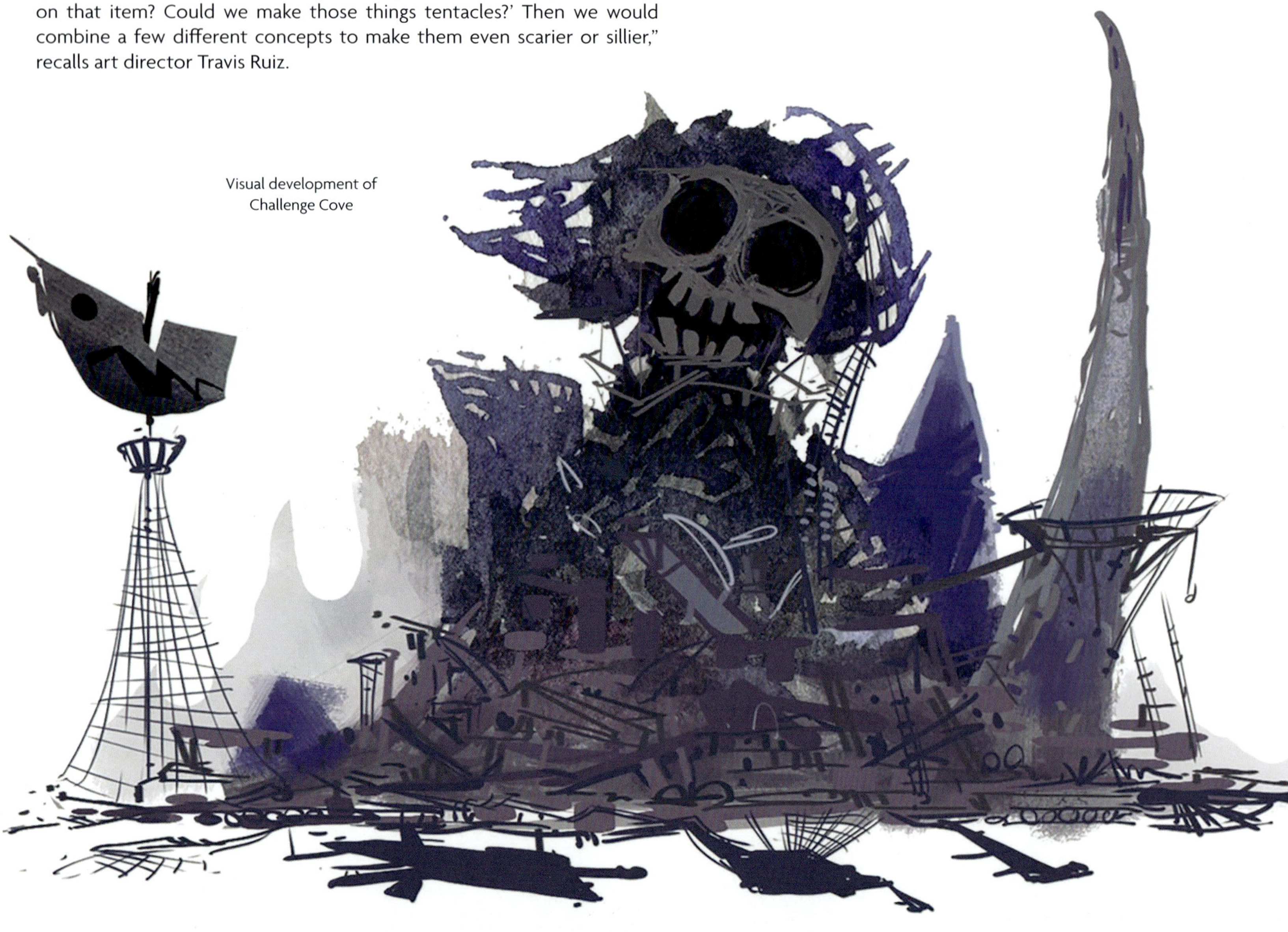

Visual development of Challenge Cove

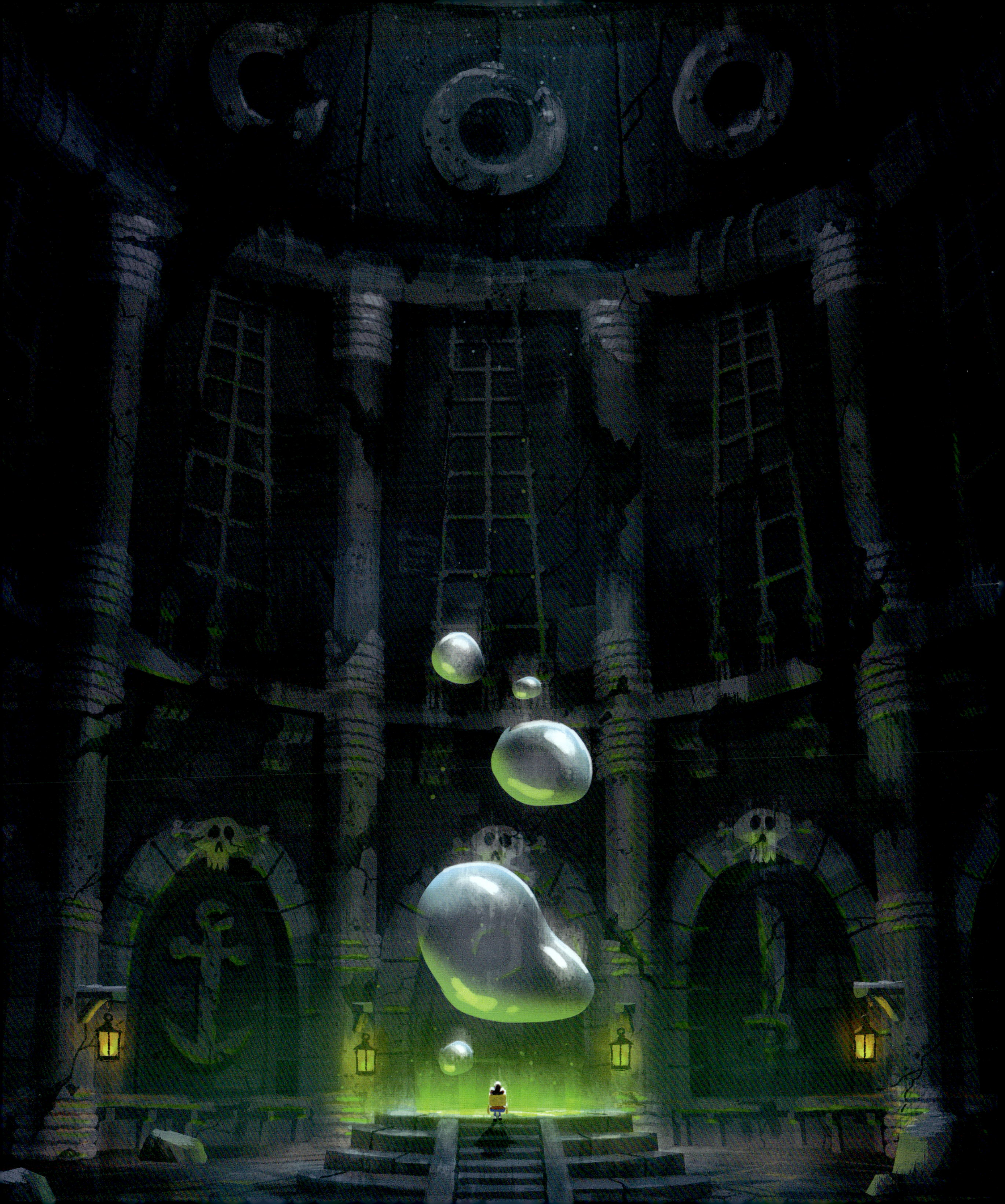

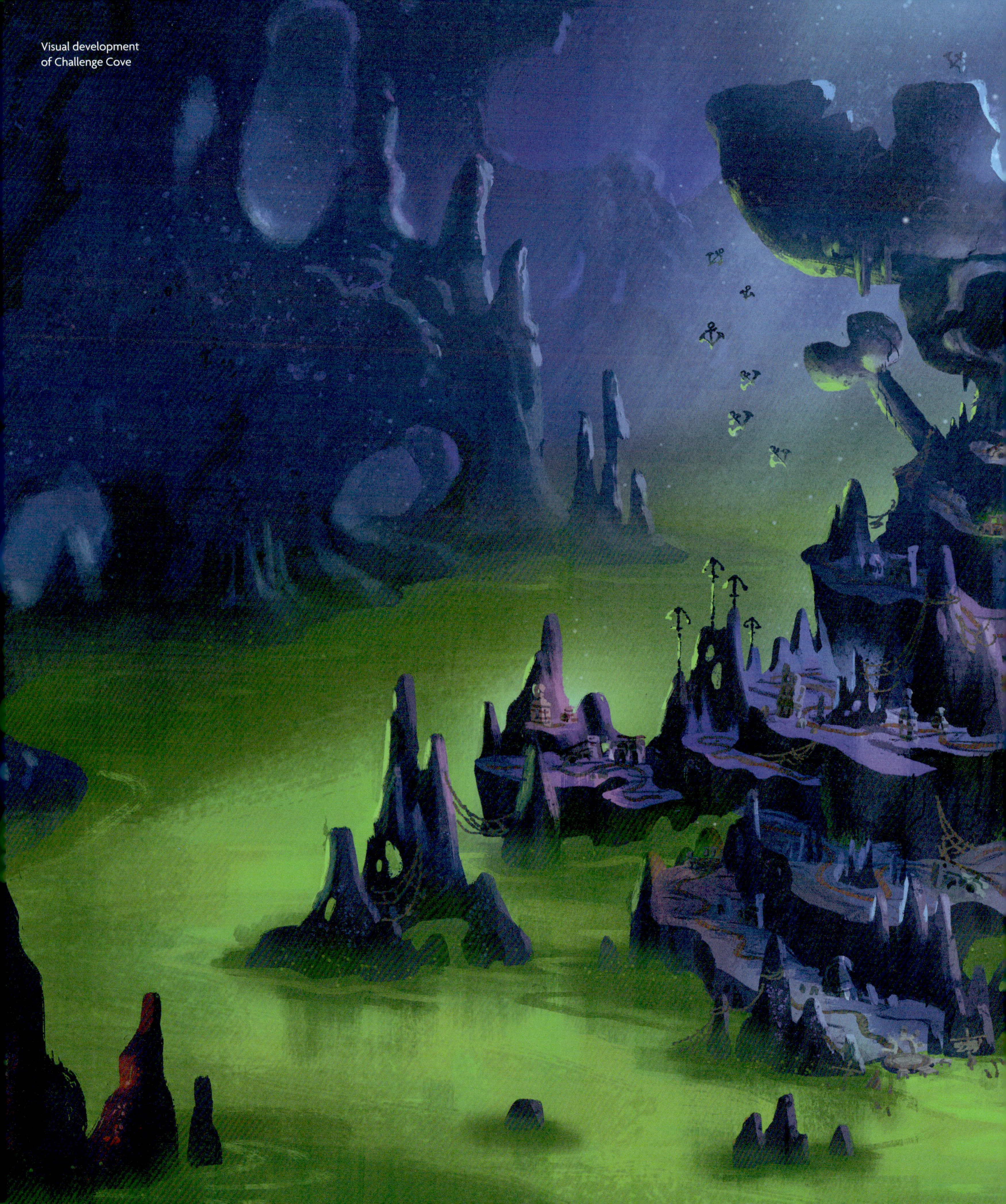

Visual development of Challenge Cove

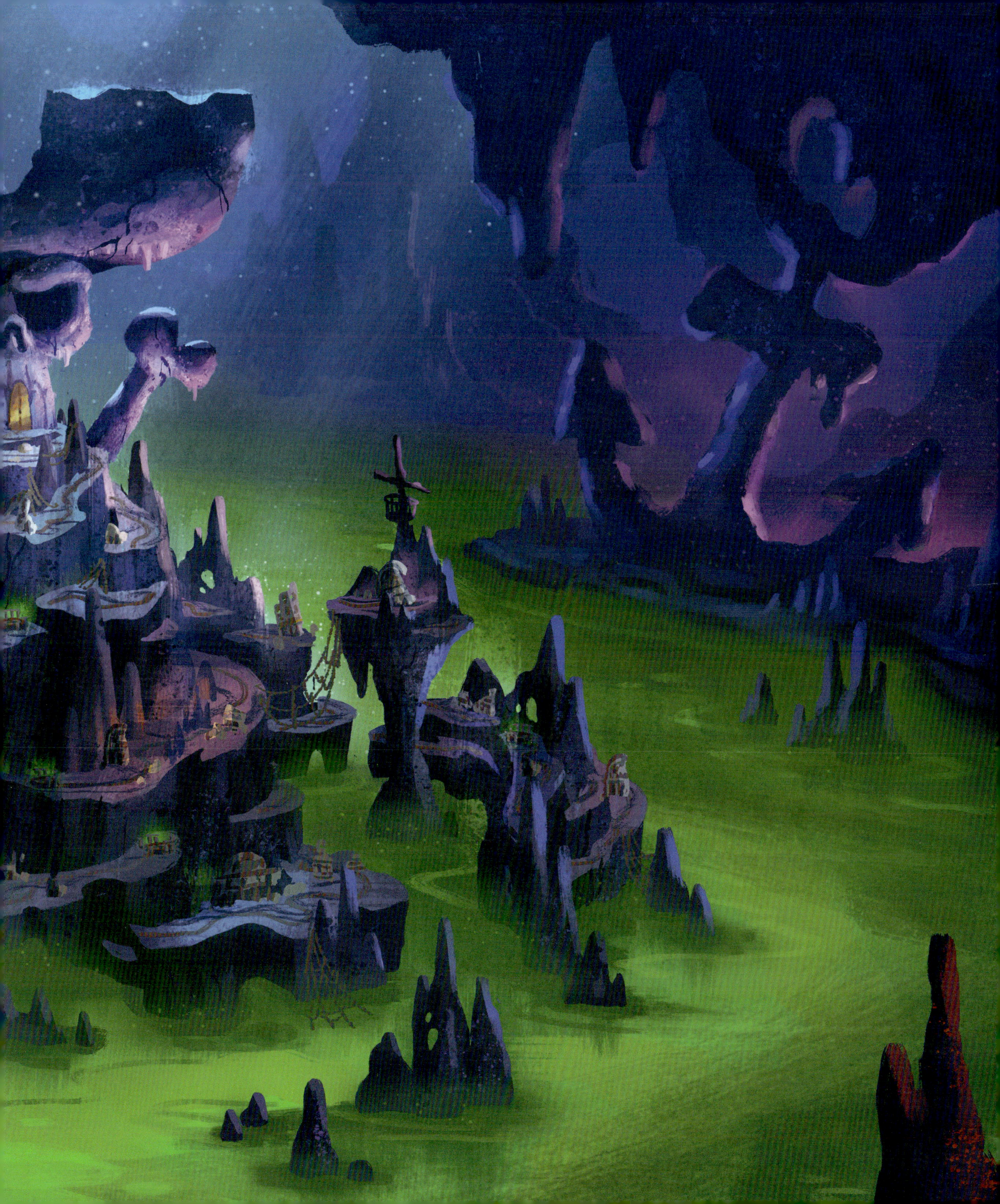

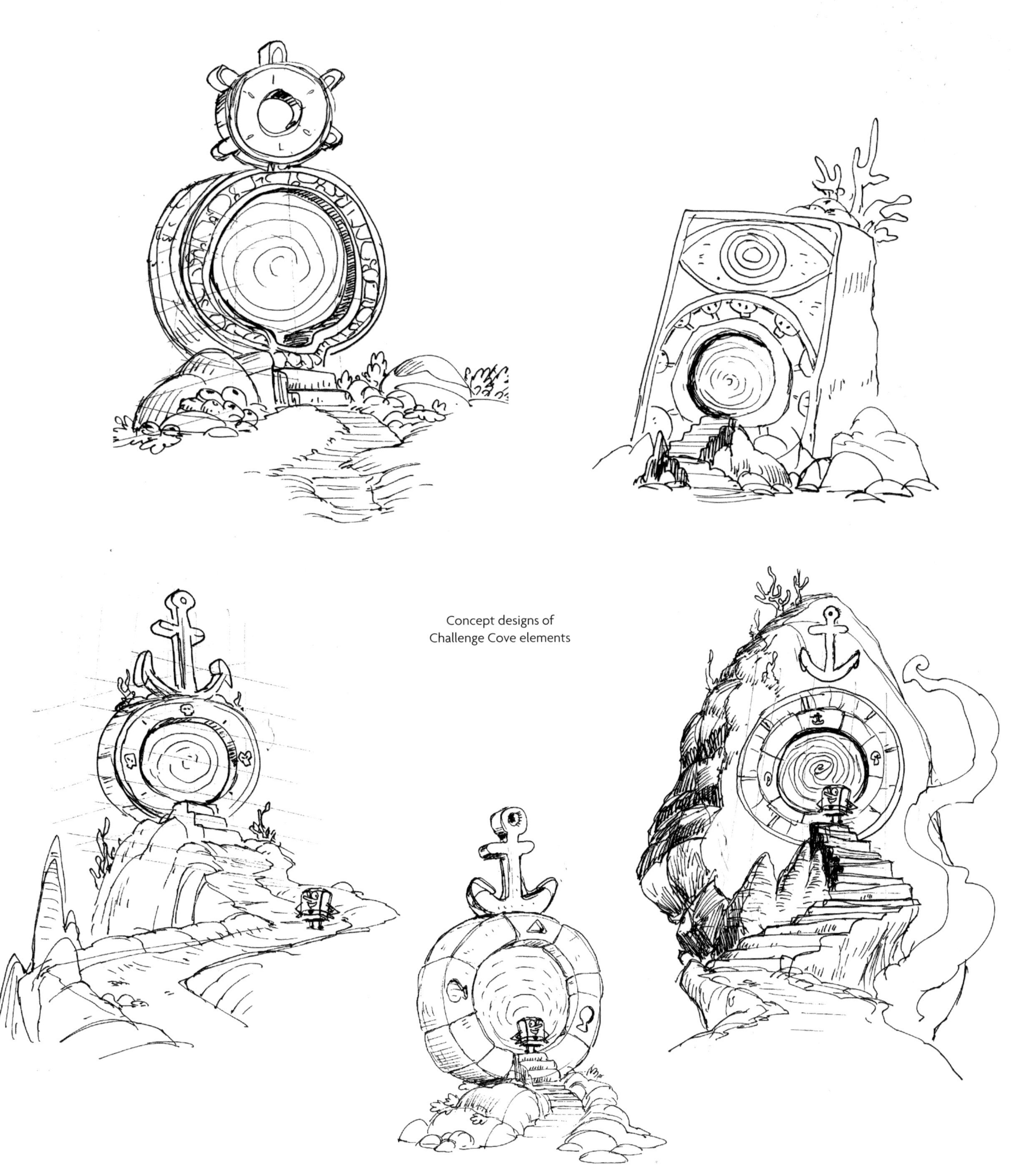

Concept designs of
Challenge Cove elements

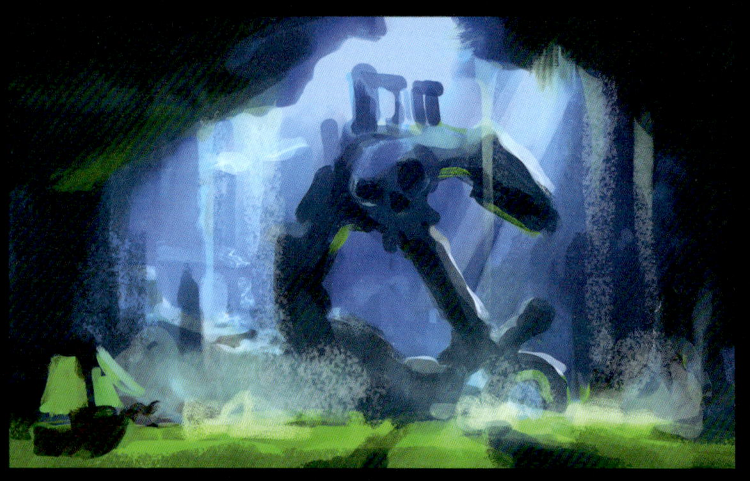
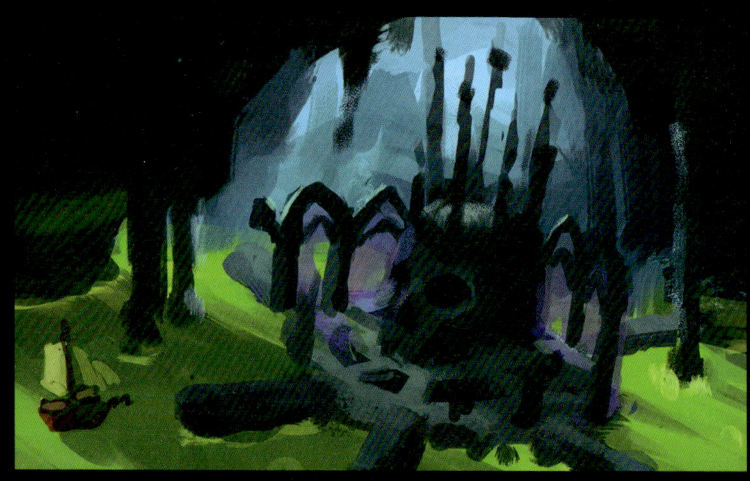
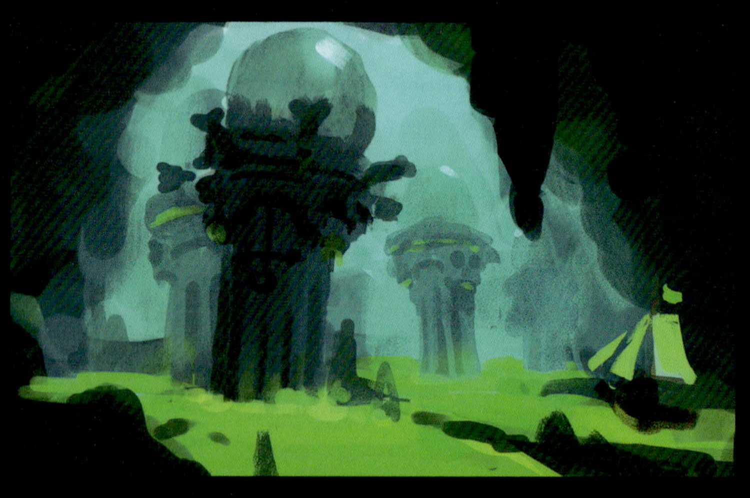
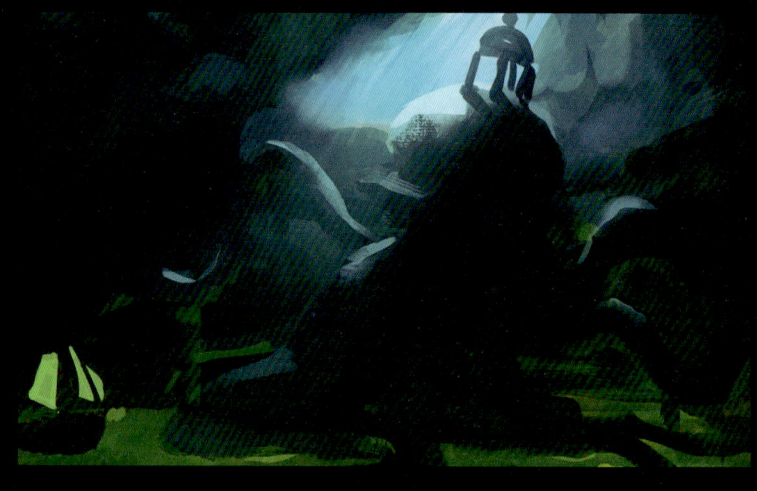
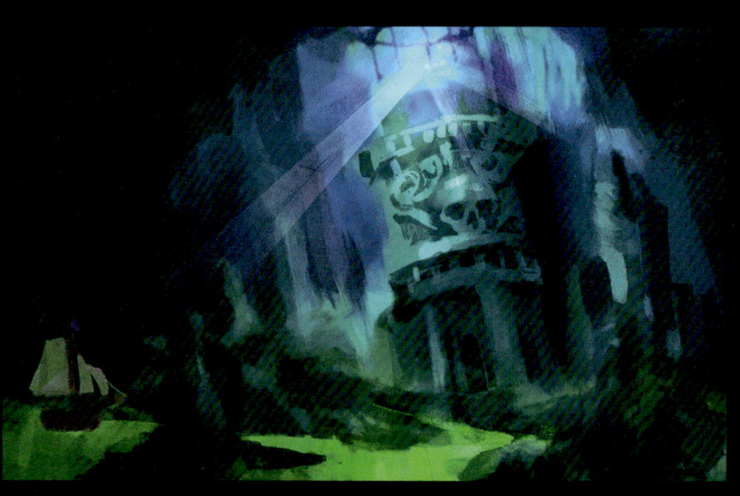
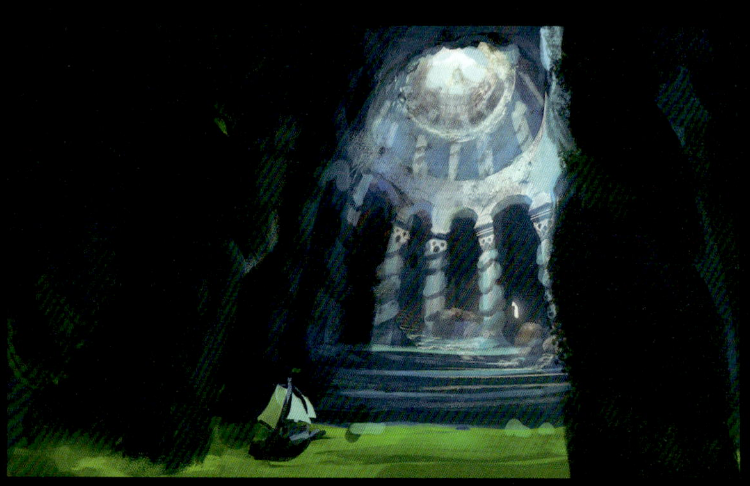

Visual development of
Challenge Cove

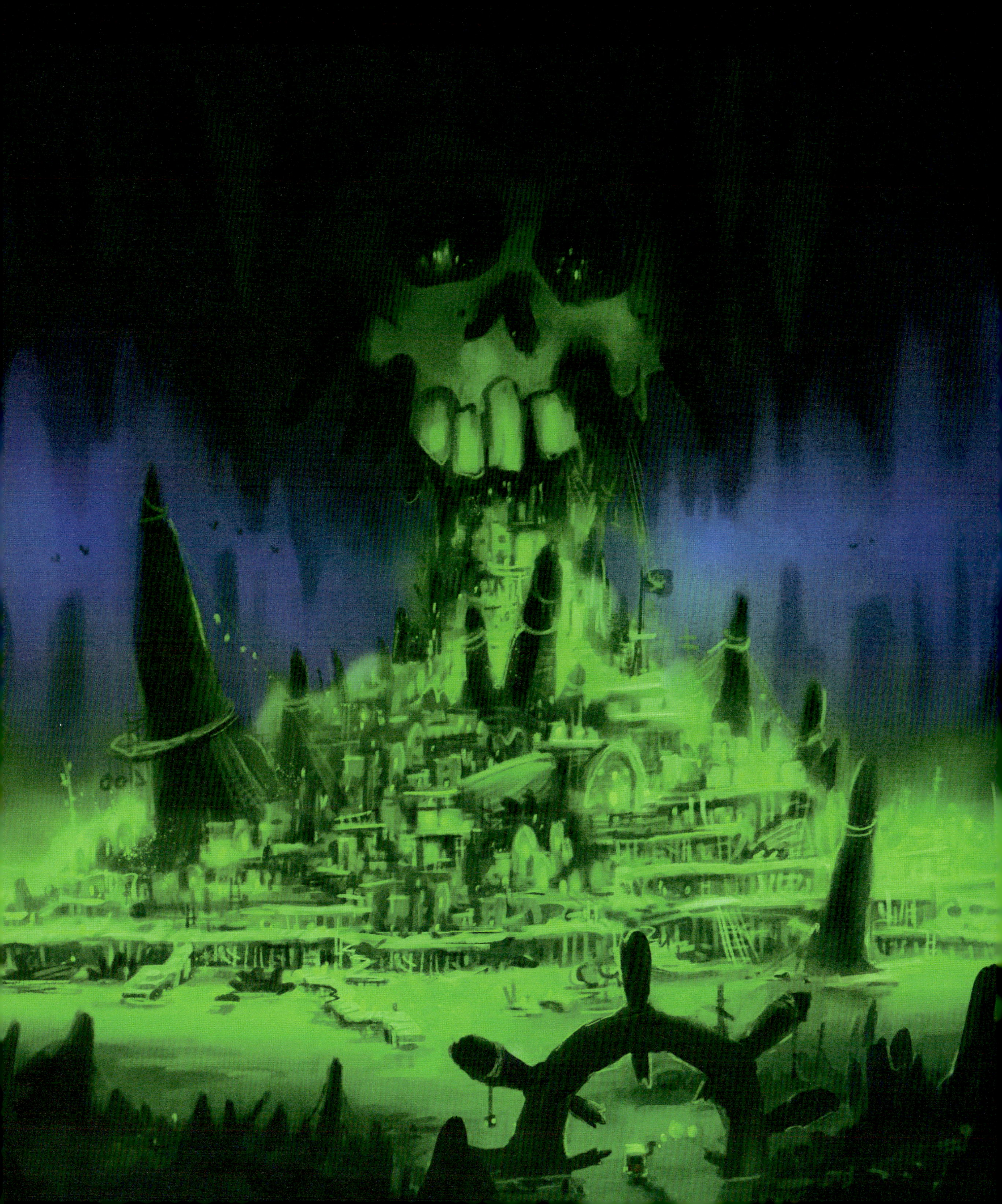

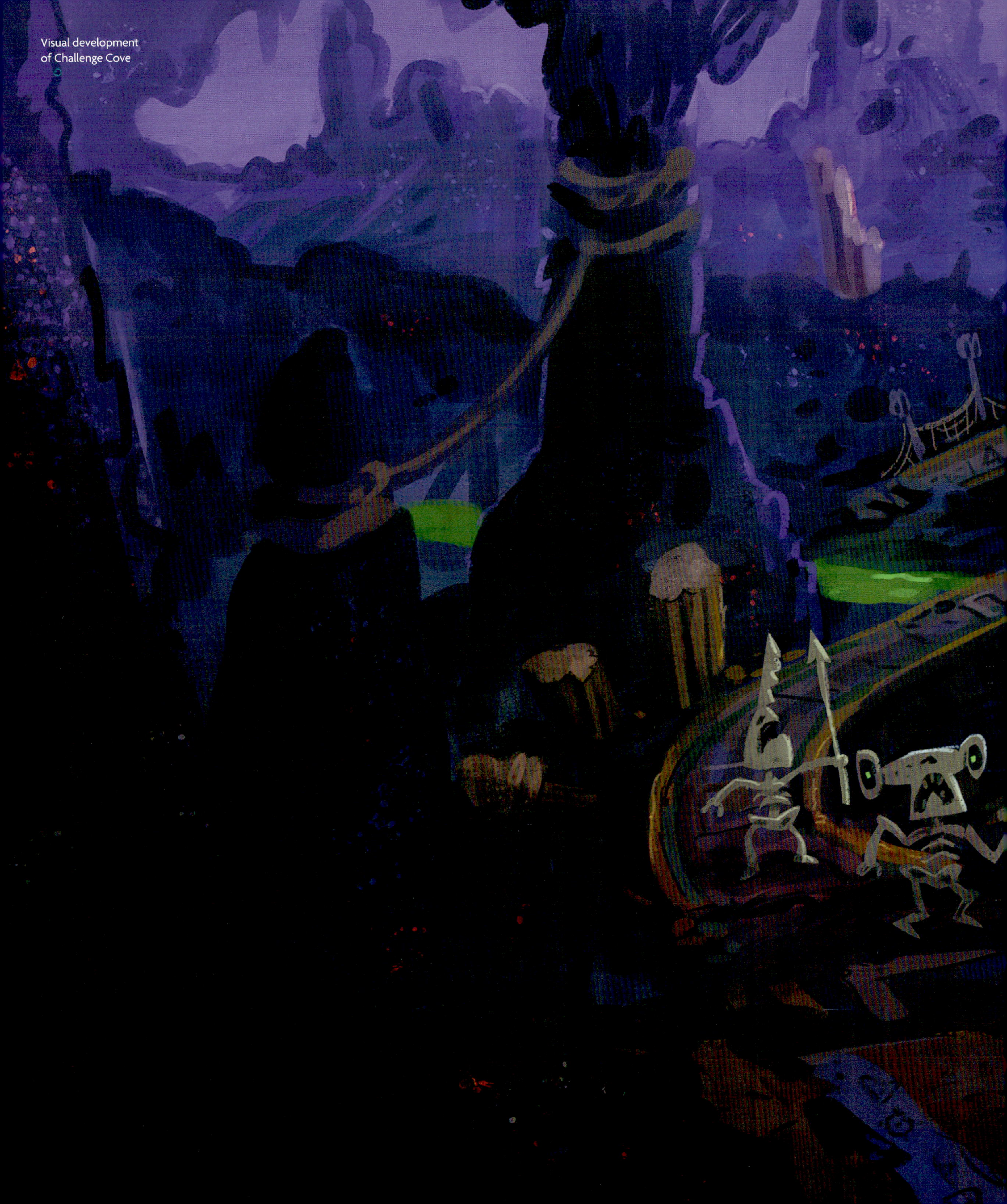

Visual development of Challenge Cove

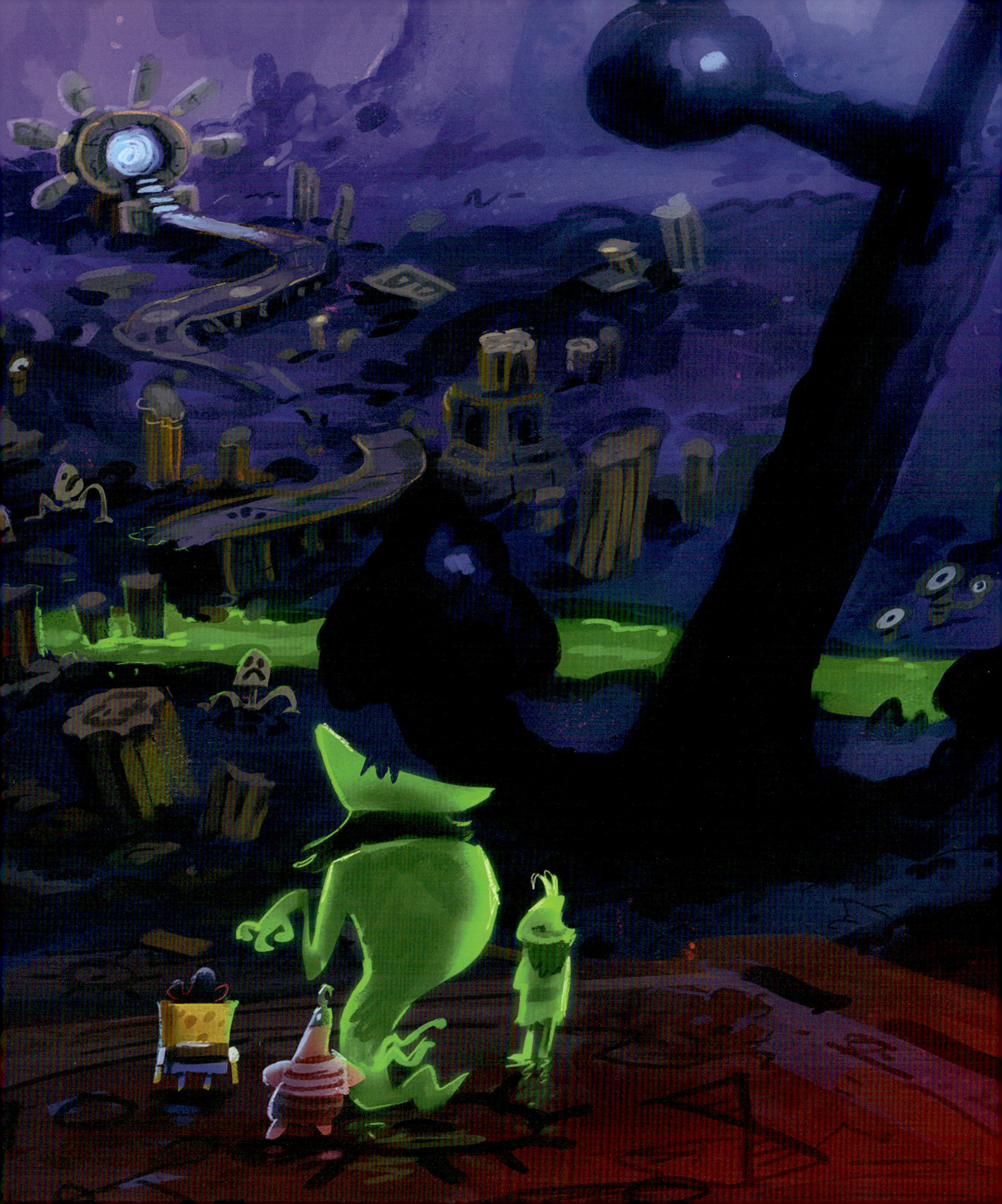

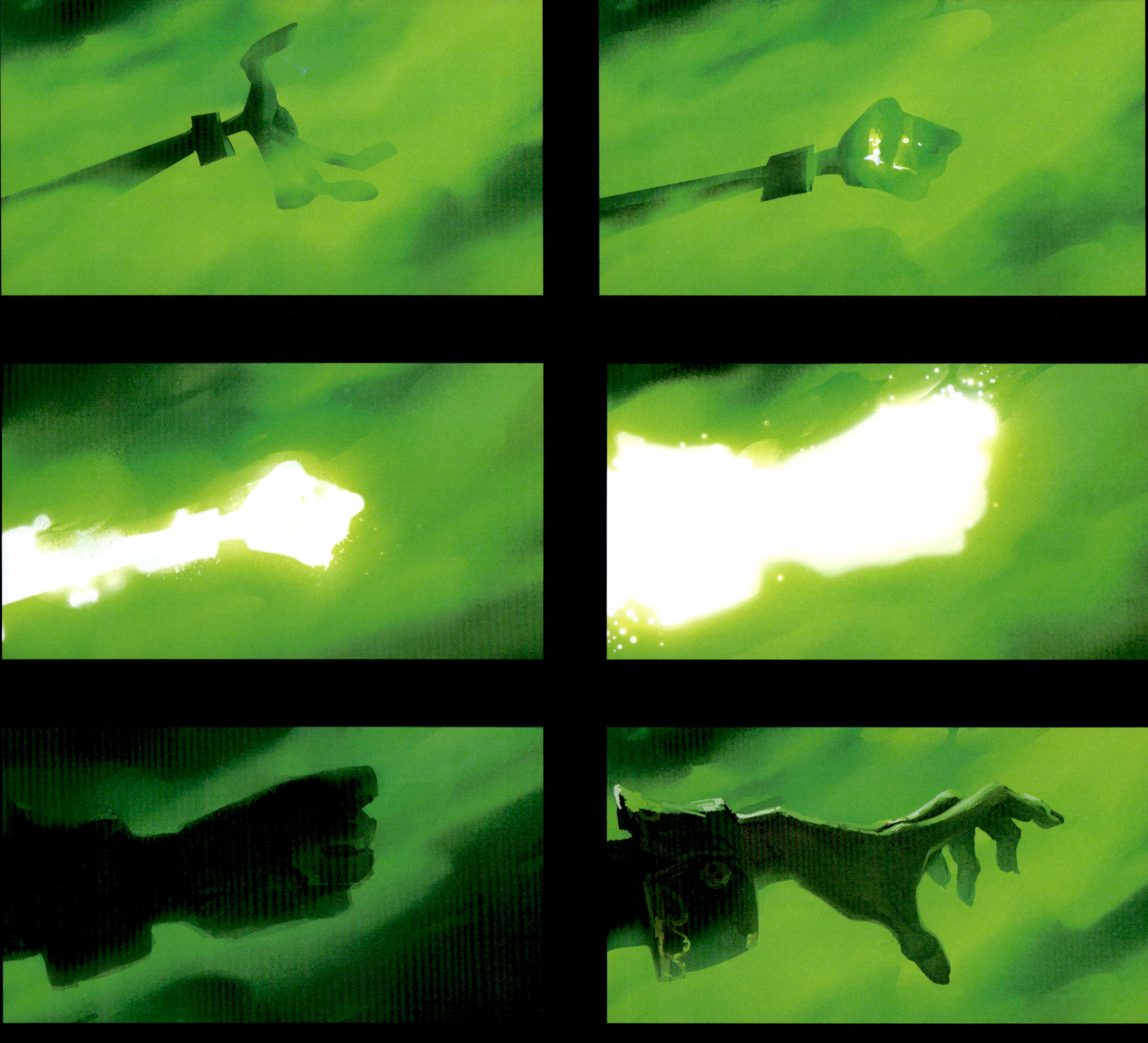

Visual development of Flying Dutchman
and SpongeBob confrontation

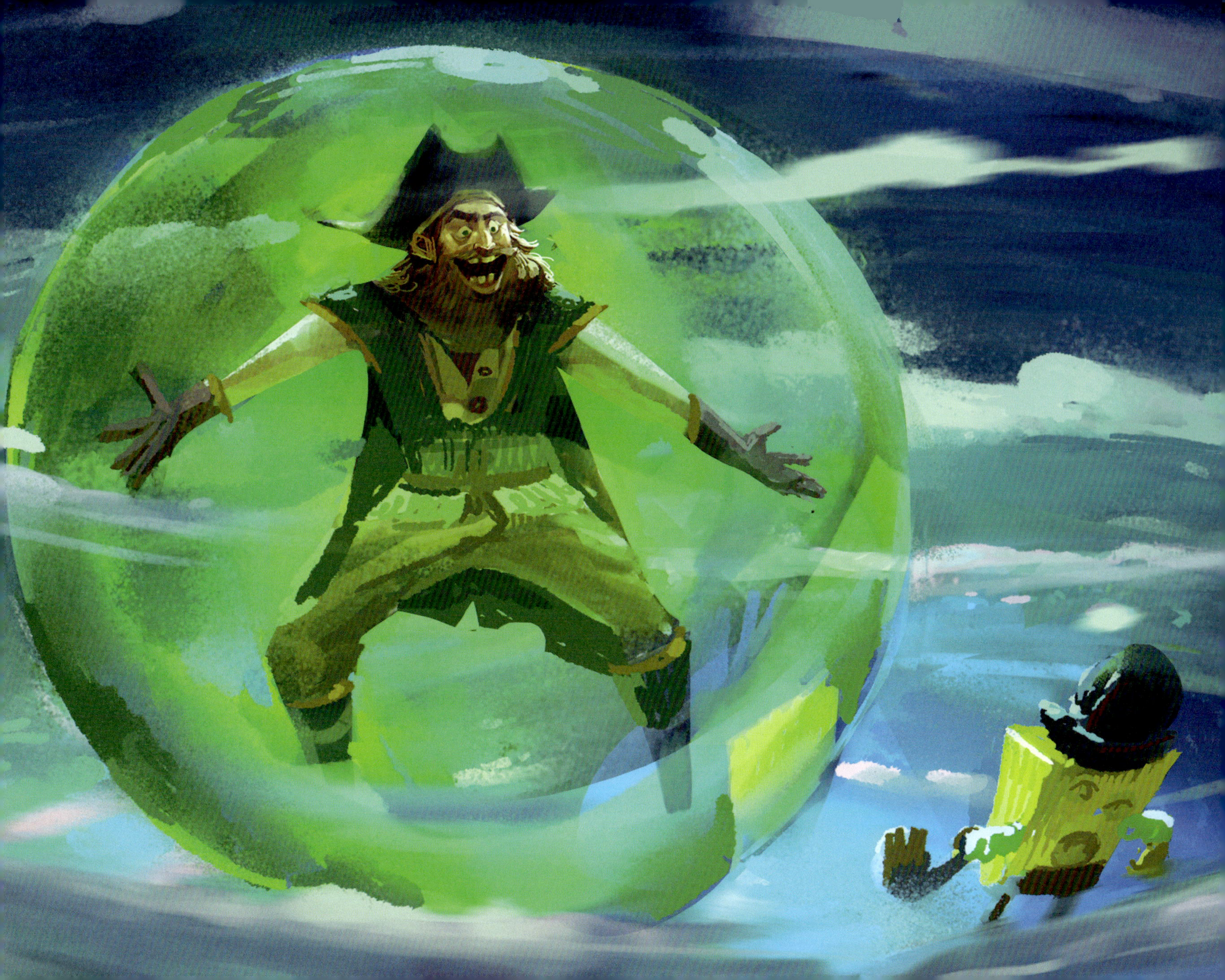

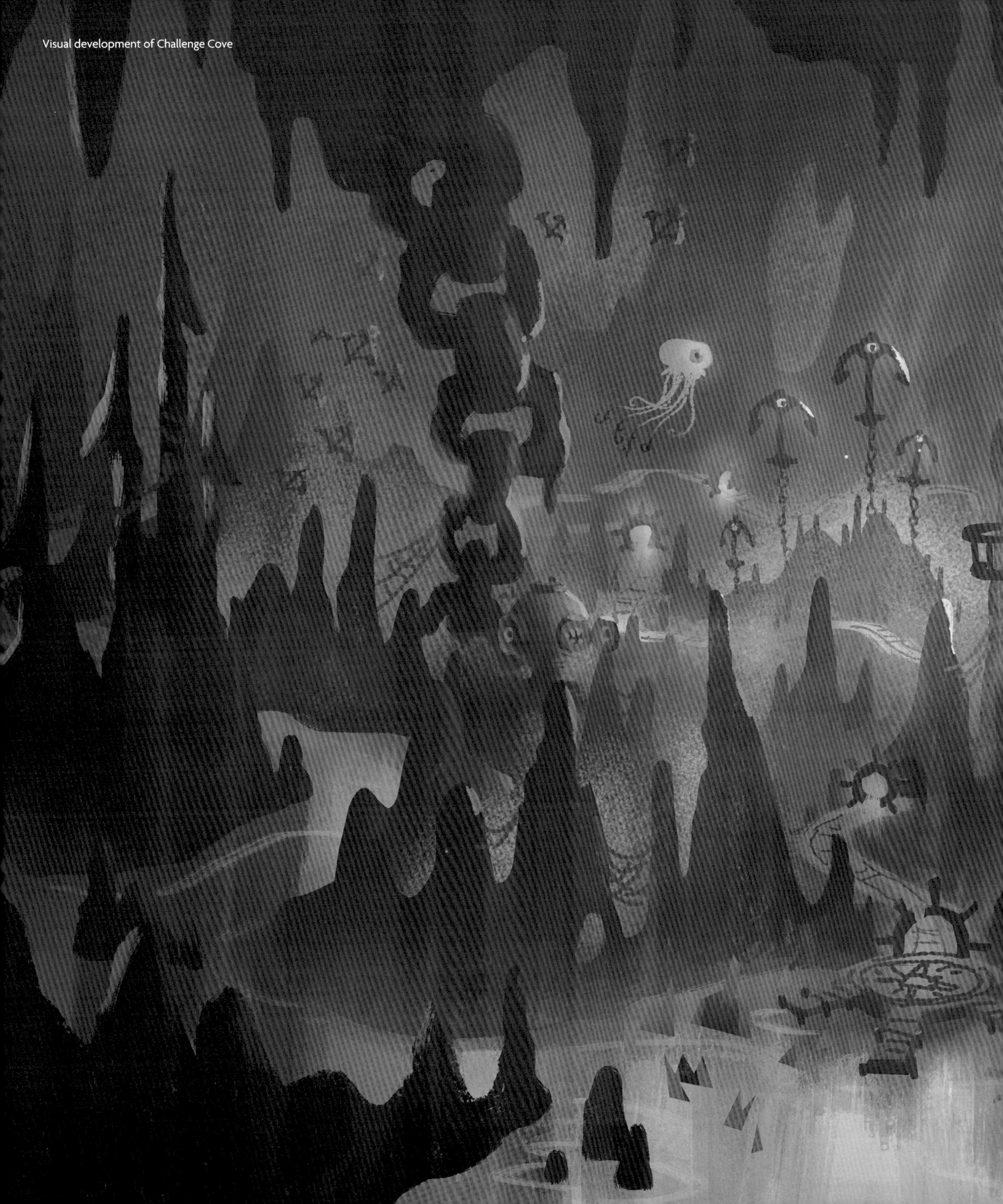

Visual development of Challenge Cove

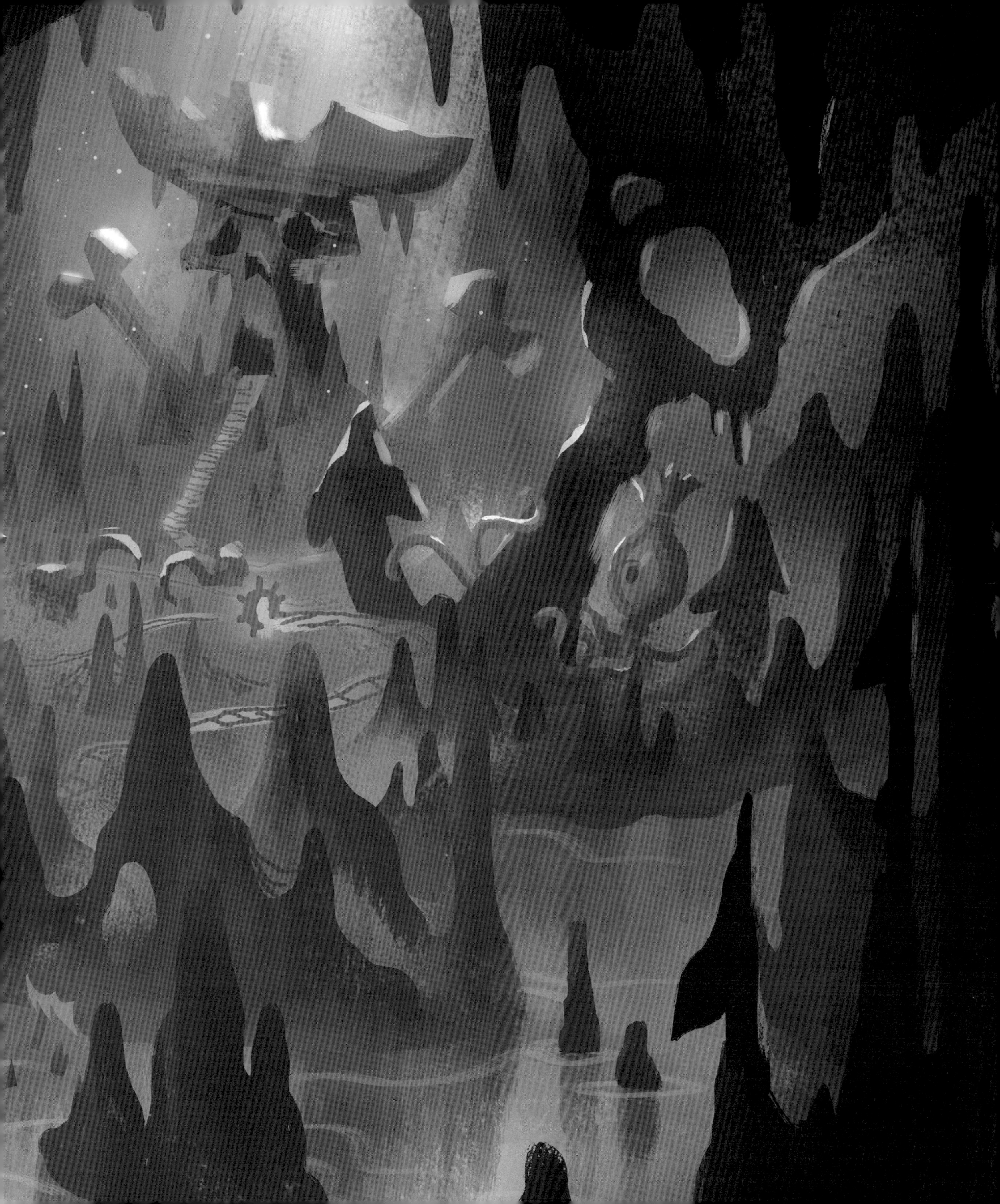

SKELETON GUARDIANS

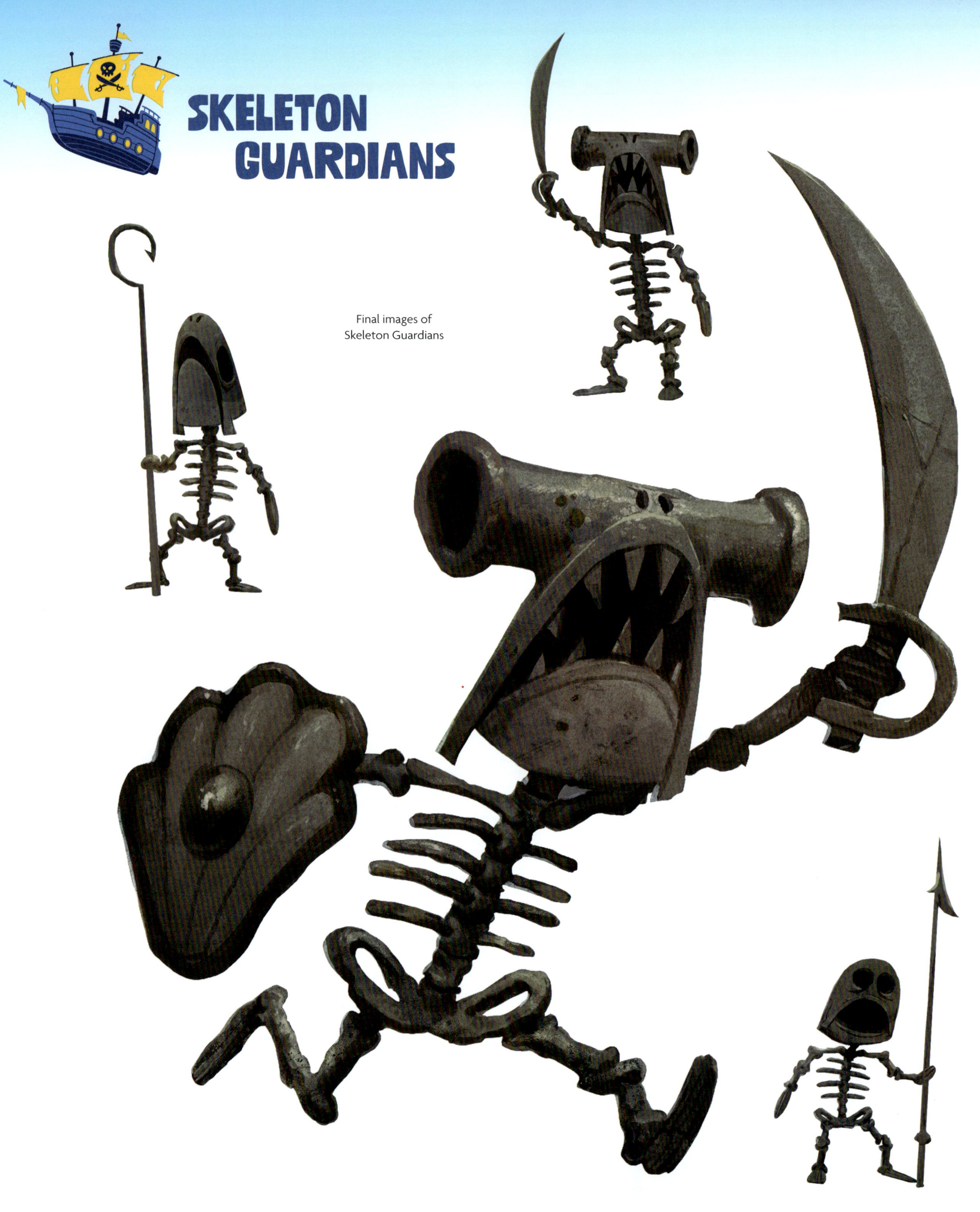

Final images of
Skeleton Guardians

CLAM MONSTER

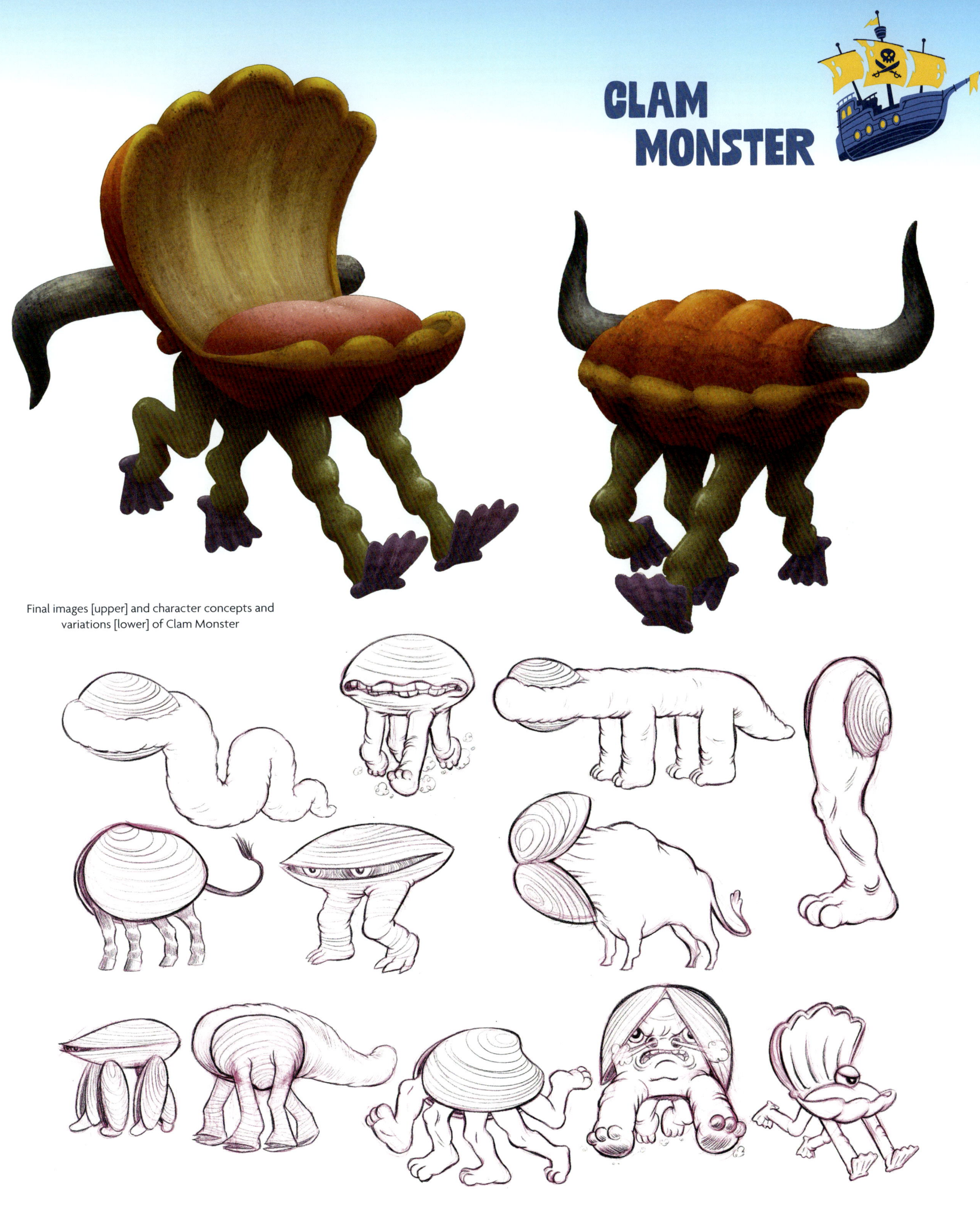

Final images [upper] and character concepts and variations [lower] of Clam Monster

SHIPWRECK HERMIT CRAB

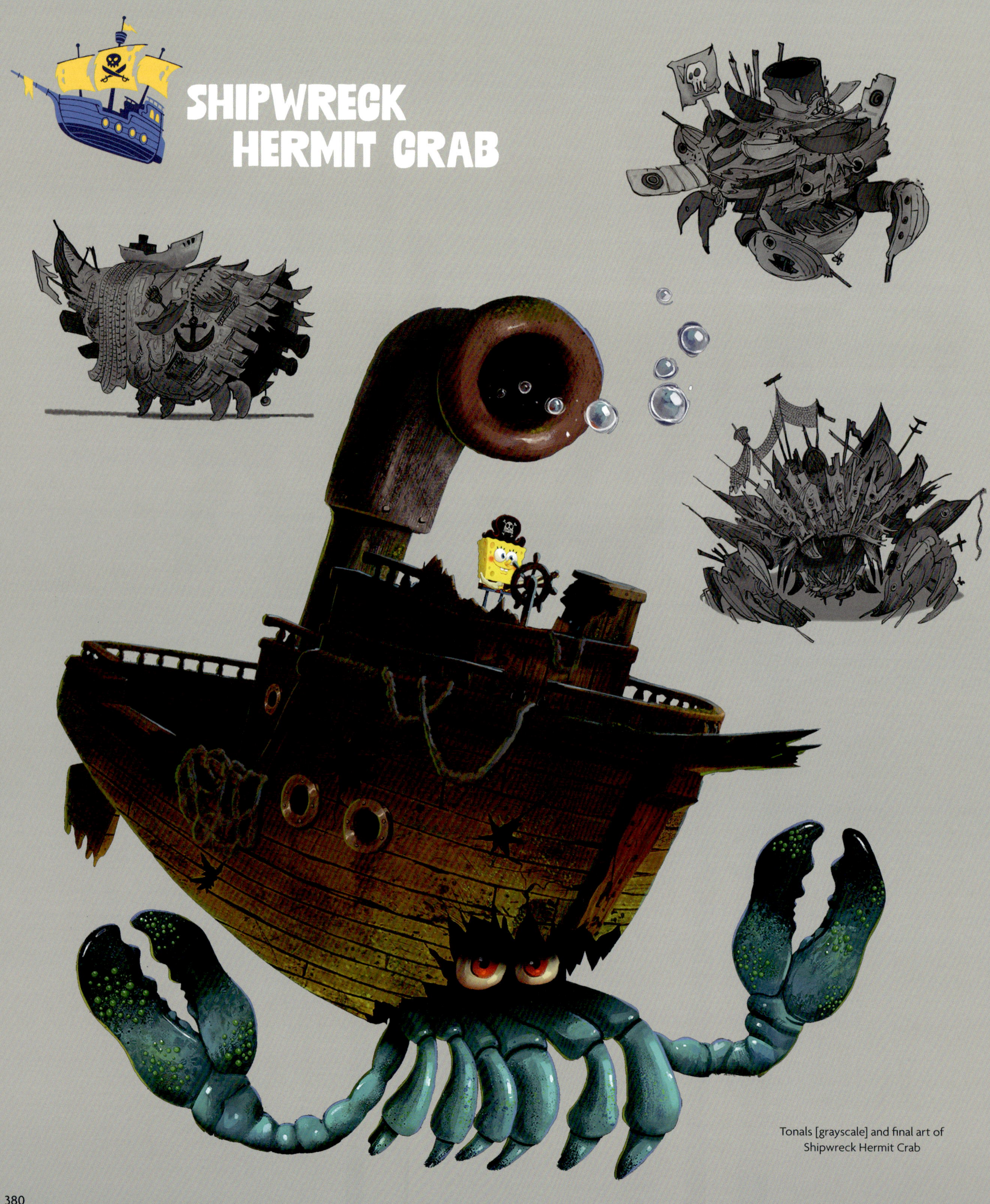

Tonals [grayscale] and final art of Shipwreck Hermit Crab

ANCHOR BAT

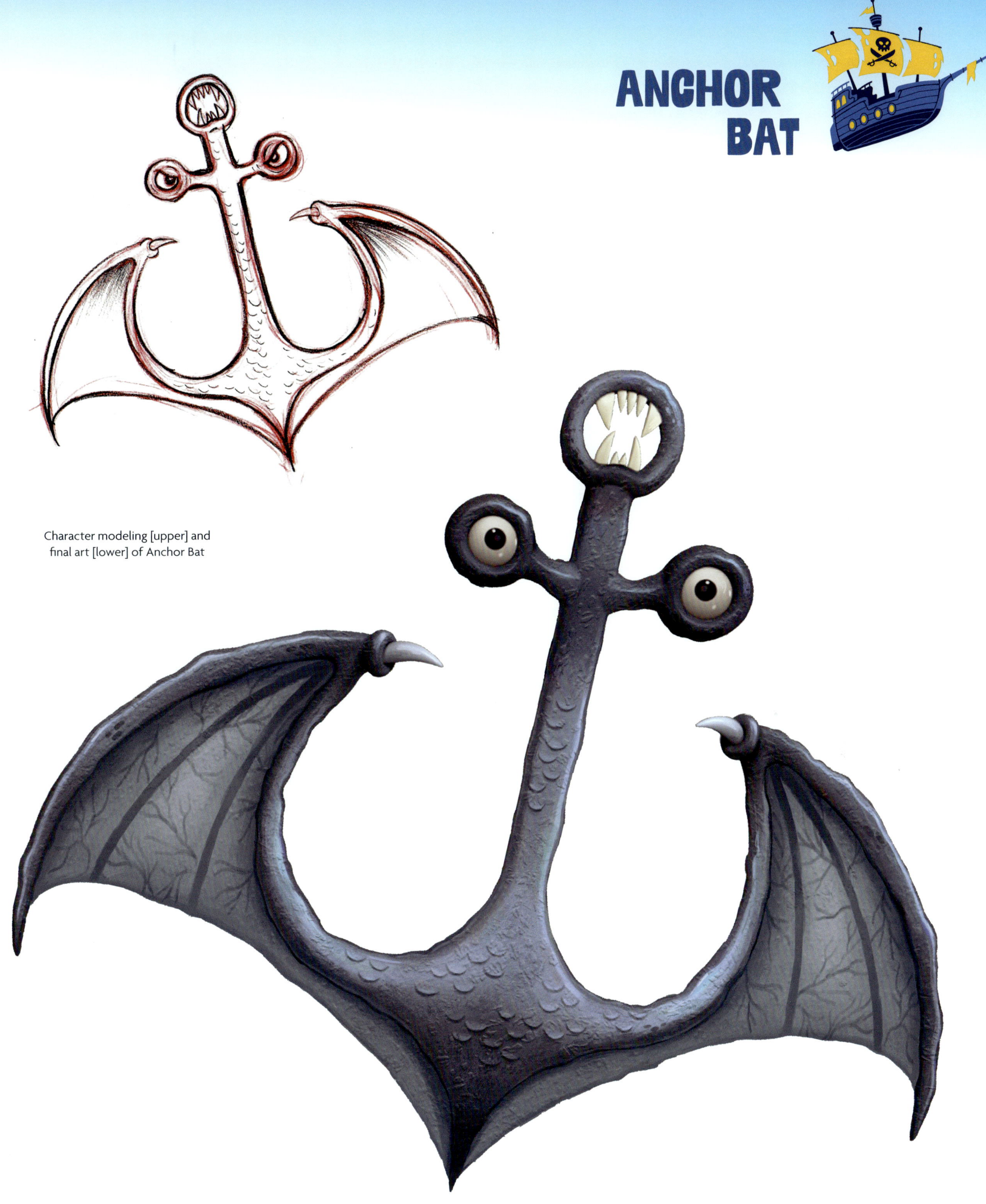

Character modeling [upper] and final art [lower] of Anchor Bat

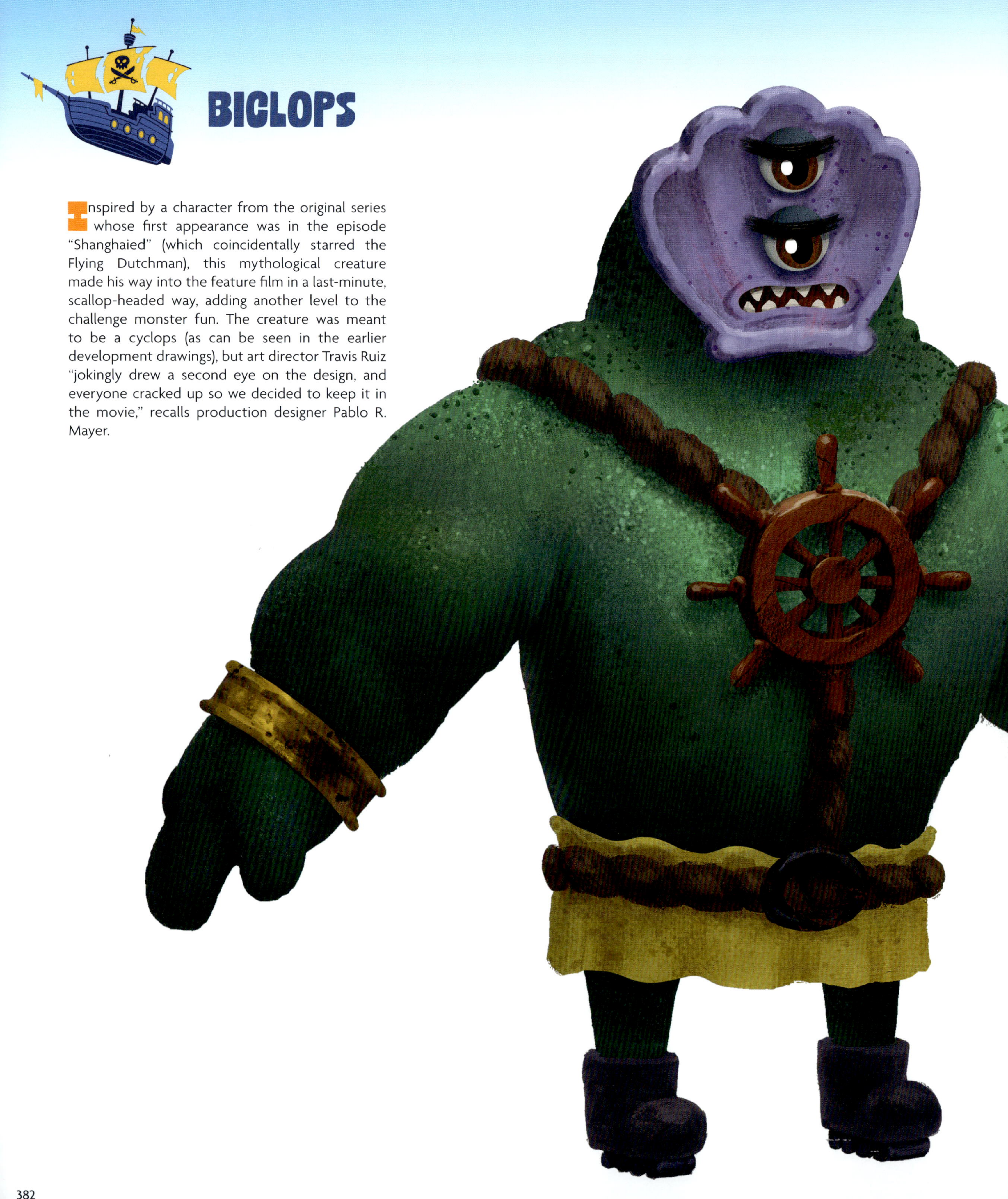

BIGLOPS

Inspired by a character from the original series whose first appearance was in the episode "Shanghaied" (which coincidentally starred the Flying Dutchman), this mythological creature made his way into the feature film in a last-minute, scallop-headed way, adding another level to the challenge monster fun. The creature was meant to be a cyclops (as can be seen in the earlier development drawings), but art director Travis Ruiz "jokingly drew a second eye on the design, and everyone cracked up so we decided to keep it in the movie," recalls production designer Pablo R. Mayer.

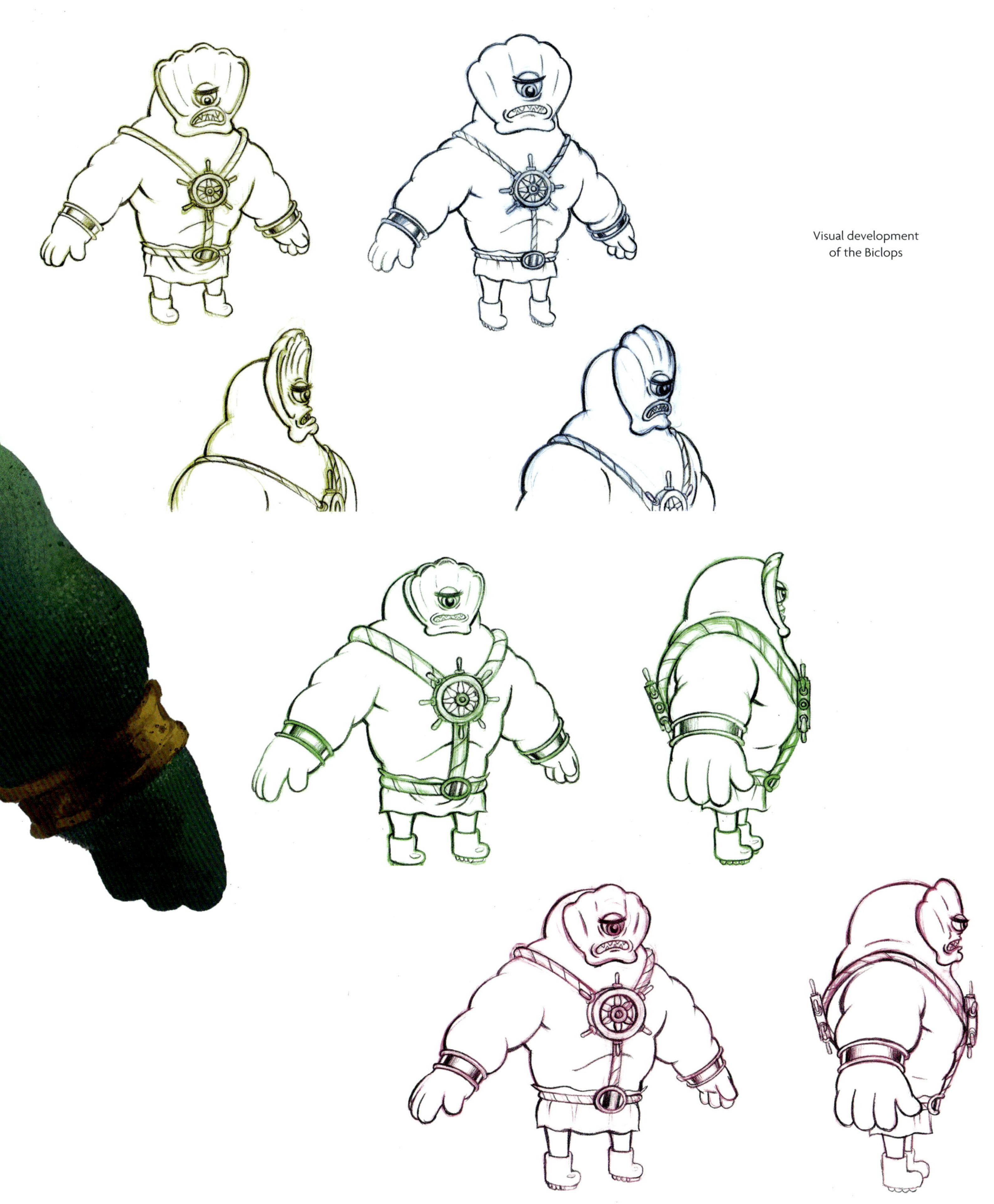

Visual development of the Biclops

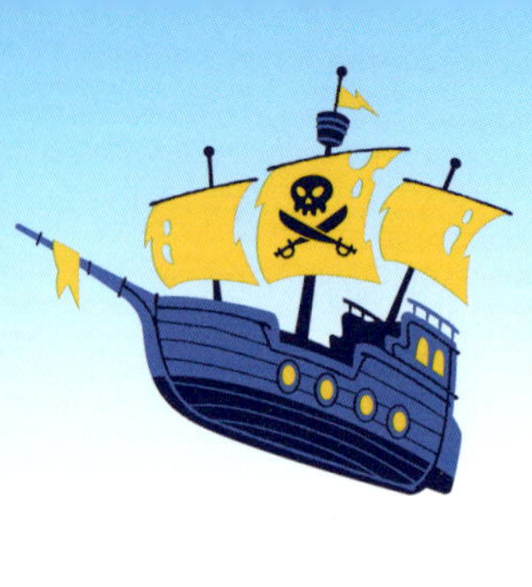

ROPE SQUID

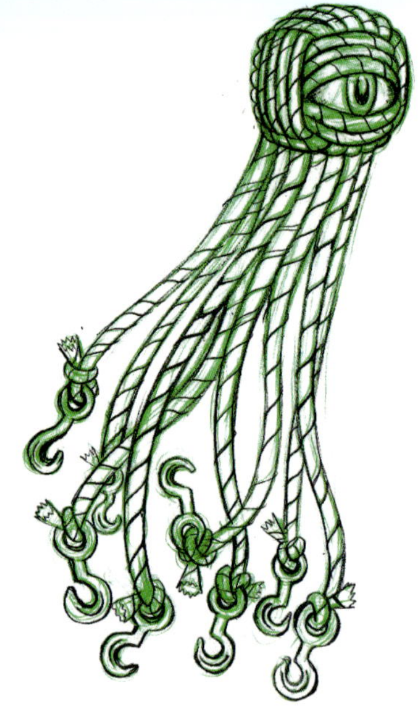

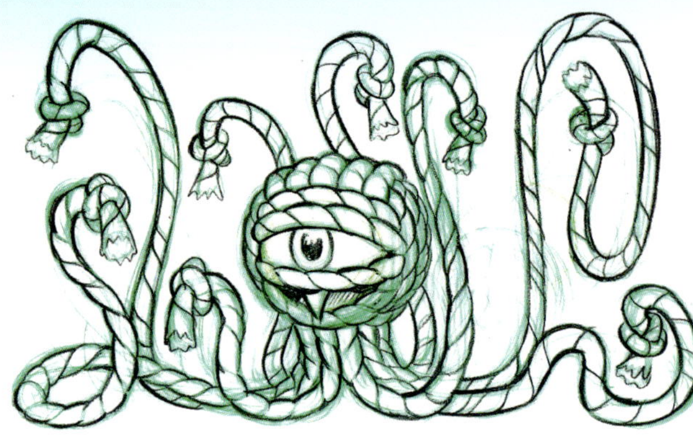

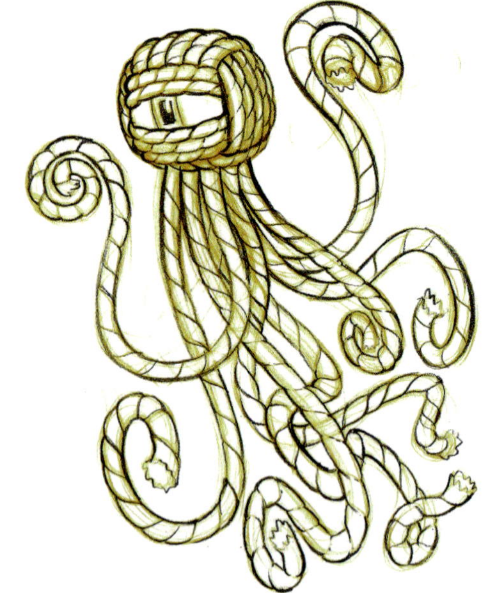

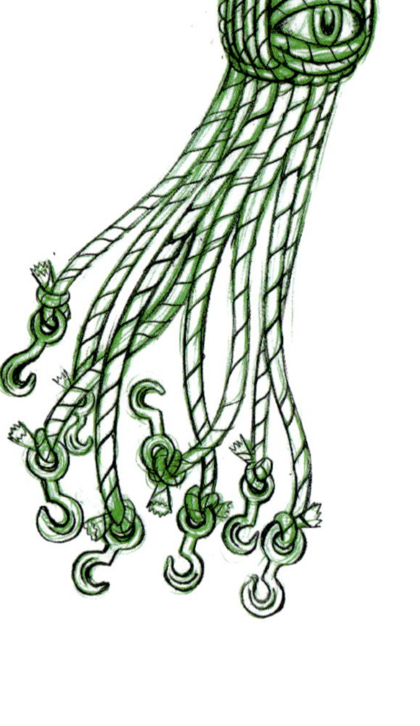

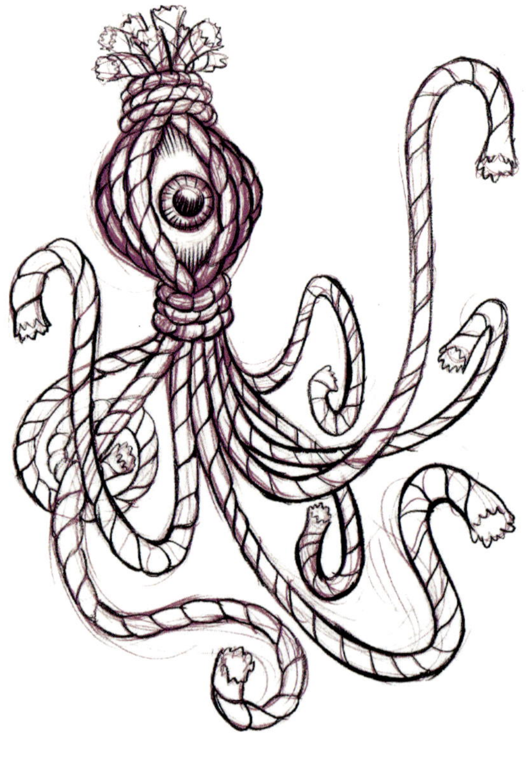

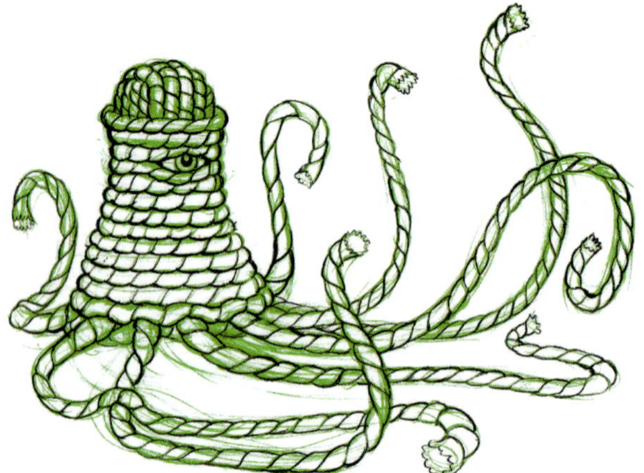

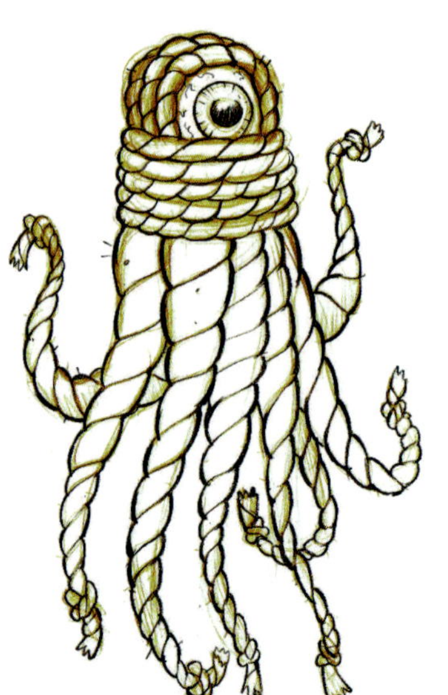

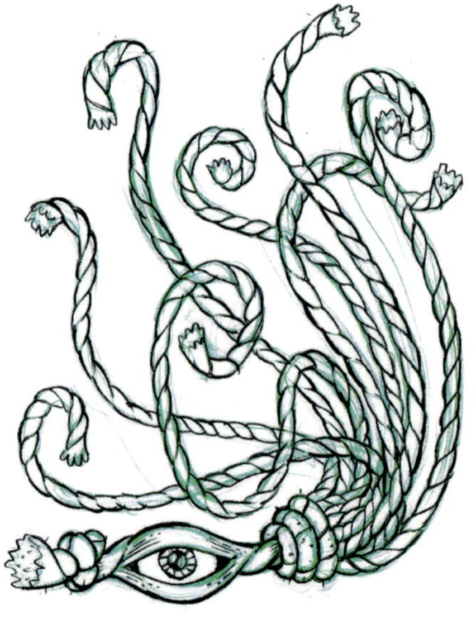

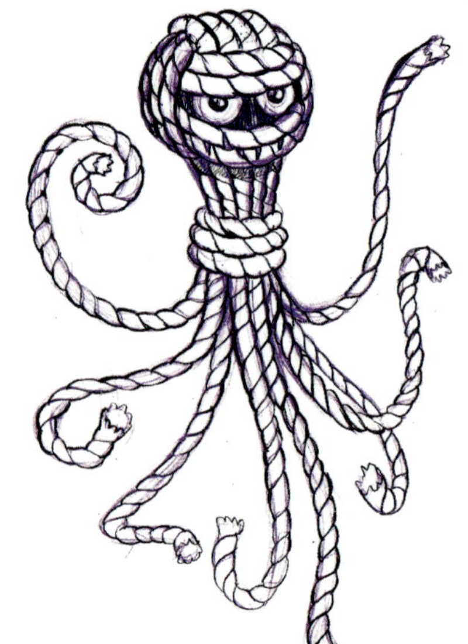

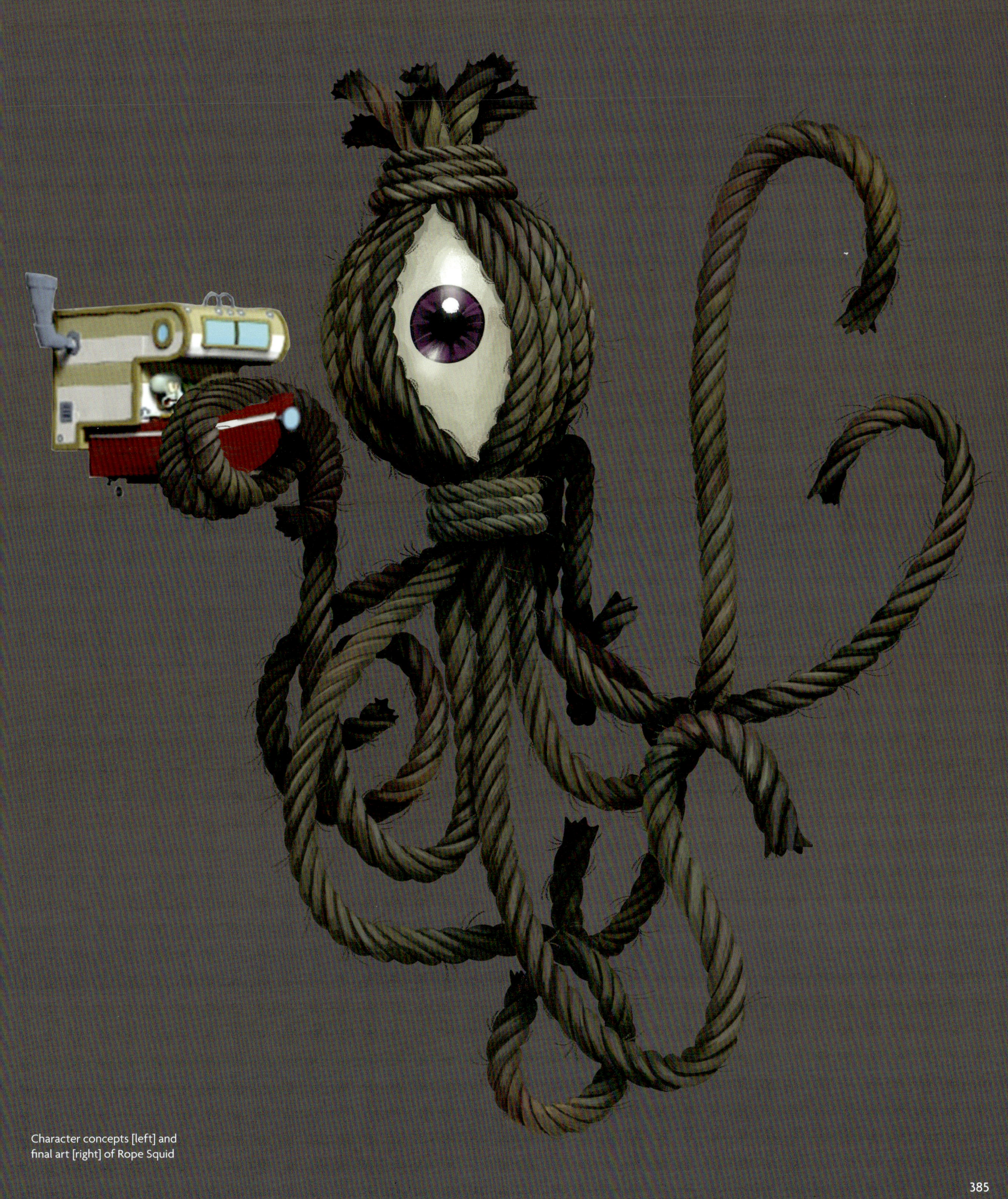

Character concepts [left] and final art [right] of Rope Squid

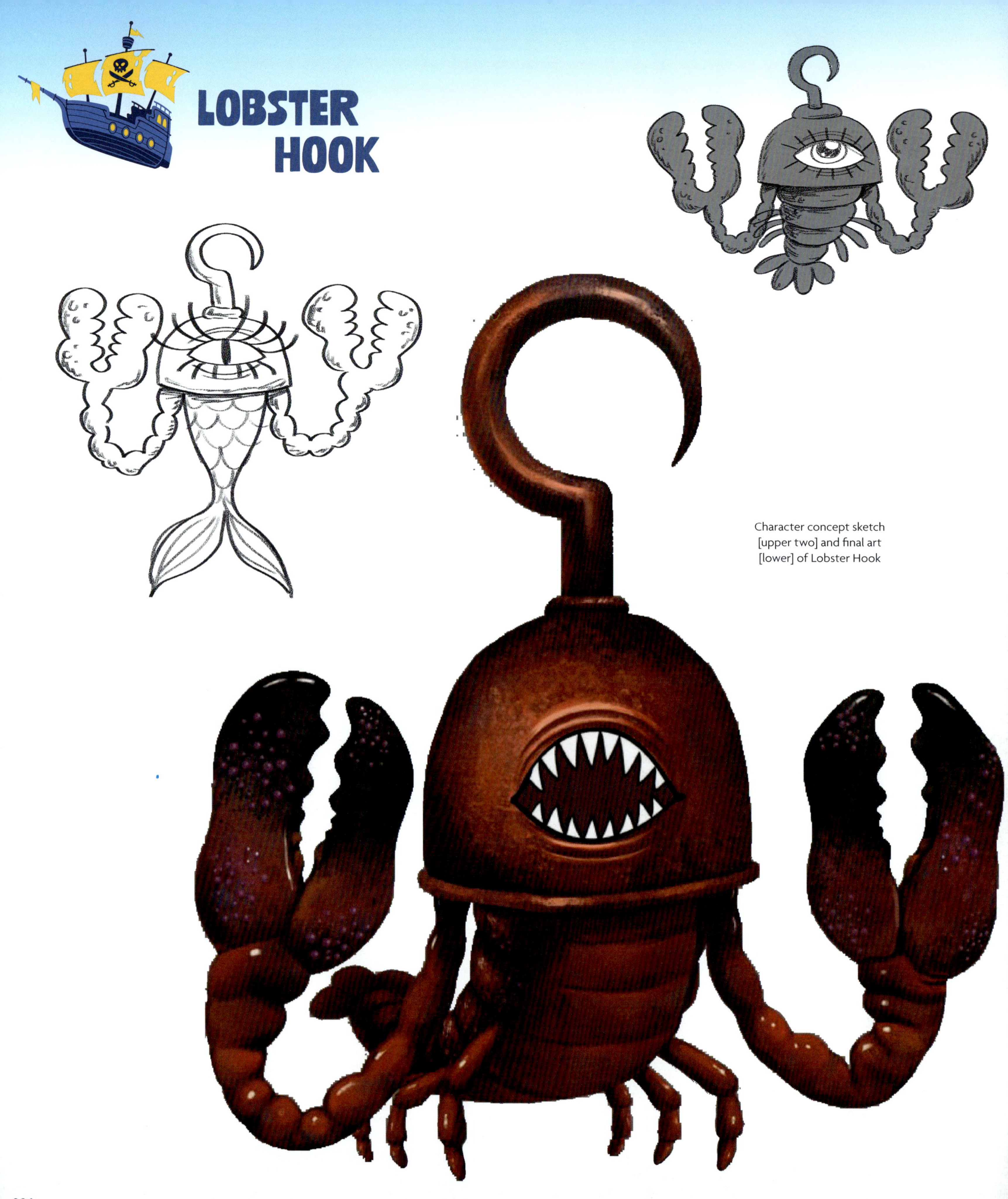

LOBSTER HOOK

Character concept sketch [upper two] and final art [lower] of Lobster Hook

JELLY HOOK

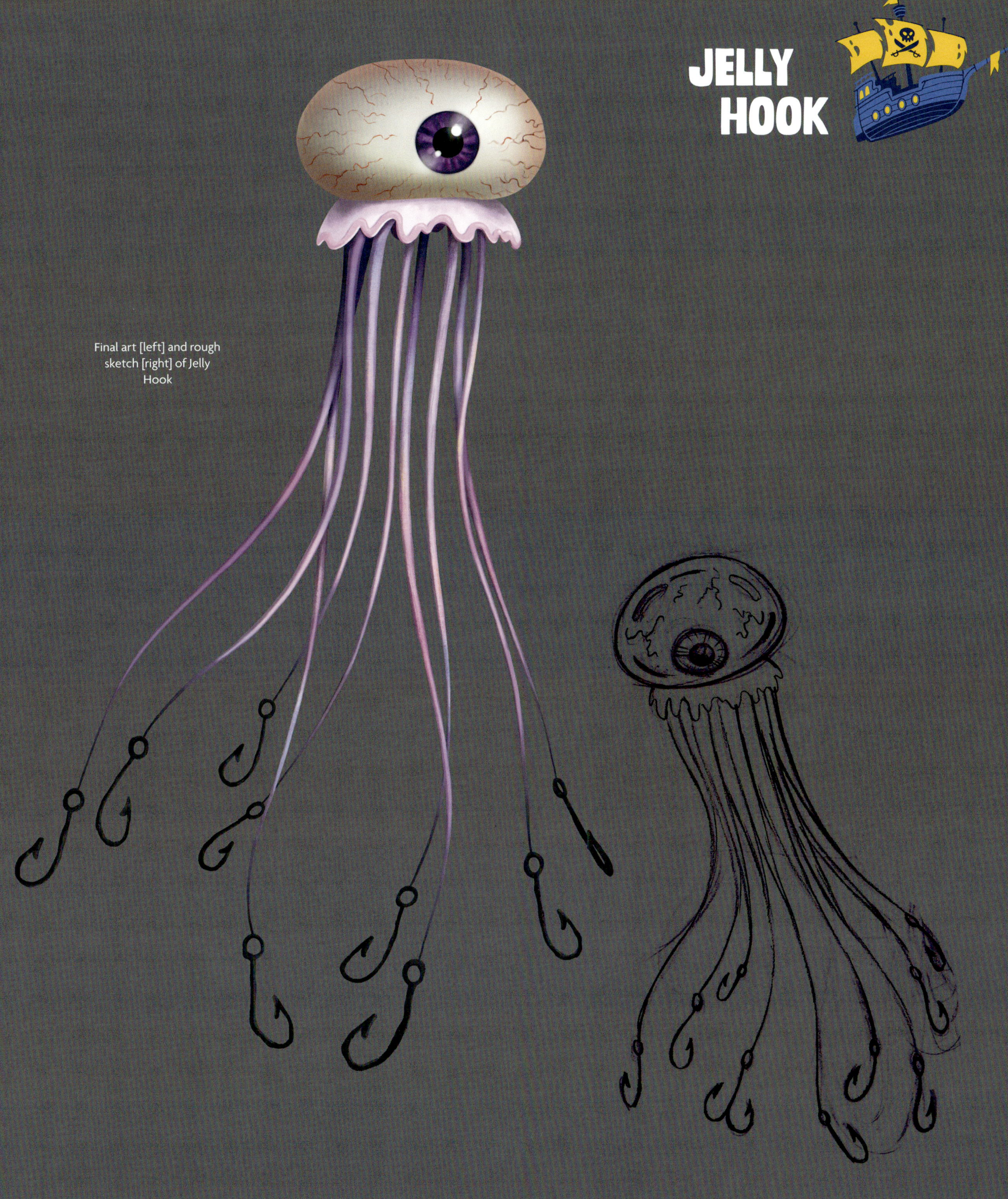

Final art [left] and rough sketch [right] of Jelly Hook

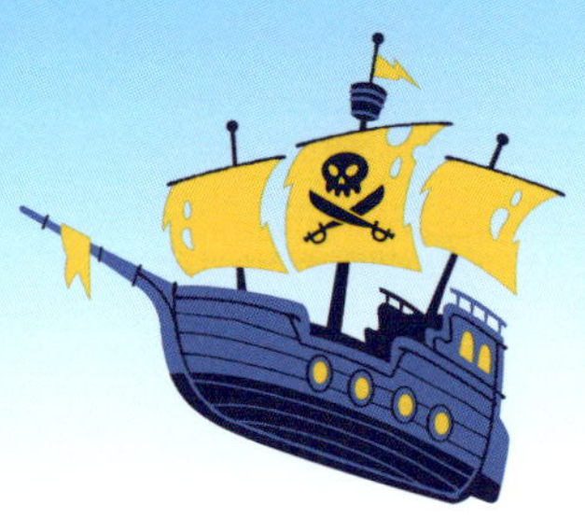

KRABS, SQUIDWARD & GARY TO THE RESCUE

After Mr. Krabs and Gary convince Squidward that the only way to keep himself from becoming the zit-laden fry cook is to help get SpongeBob back, he joins them on a road trip in the Patty Blaster, all attired in appropriate pirate garb. The rescue party involves a trip to Davey Jones' locker, which, in Bikini Bottom, happens to exist at the high school. "This sequence is one of the first we tackled, and where we really found the film's visual tone. It also has a nice variety of moods, like the gym standoff with a Western flair," says production designer Pablo R. Mayer.

When the Sirens come into play, their smooth jazz melodies are the soundtrack to complicated art direction decisions. "We wanted it to feel hypersaturated and psychedelic at the beginning of the sequence, which created a new challenge of trying to make characters and action stand out in a sea of color," adds Mayer.

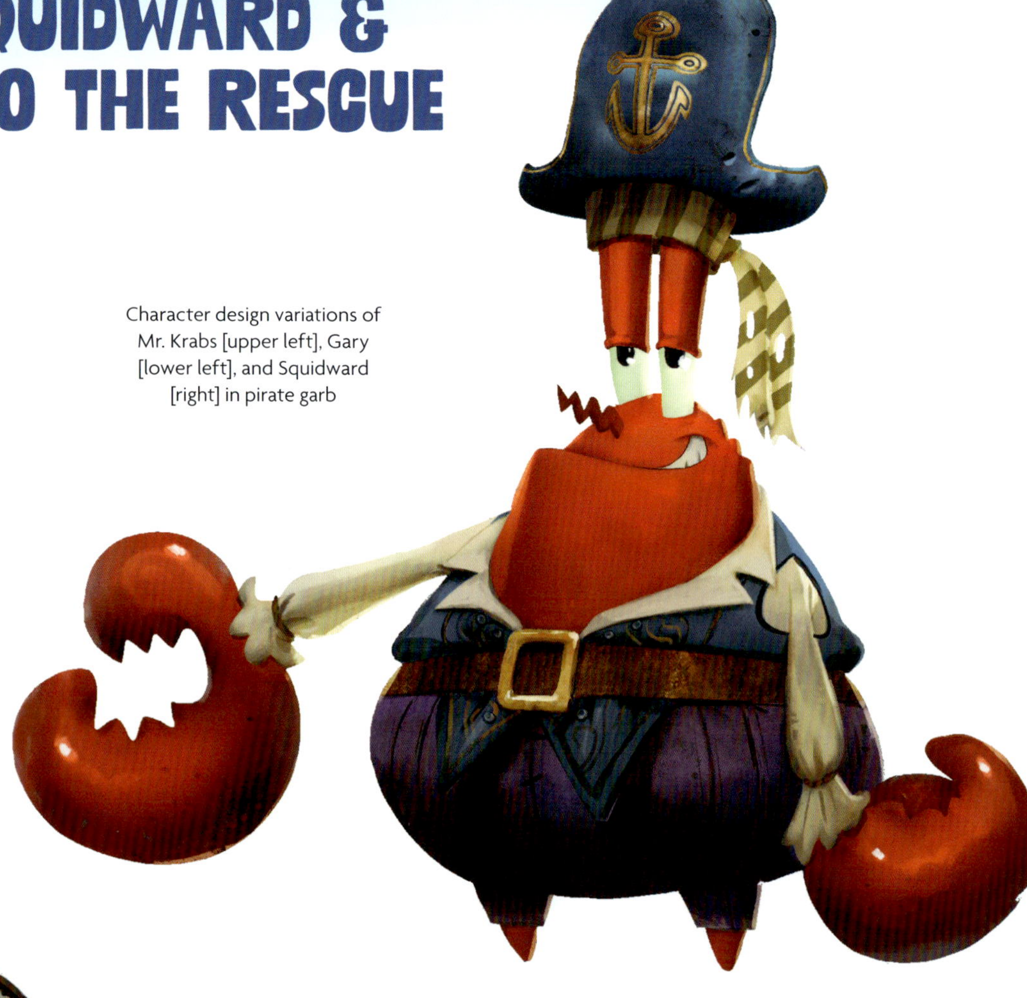

Character design variations of Mr. Krabs [upper left], Gary [lower left], and Squidward [right] in pirate garb

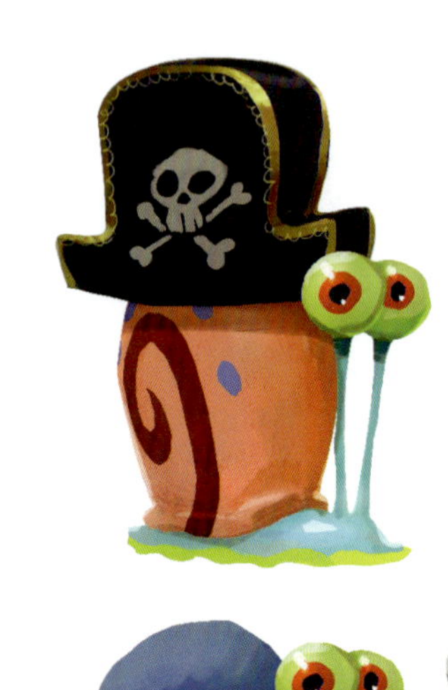

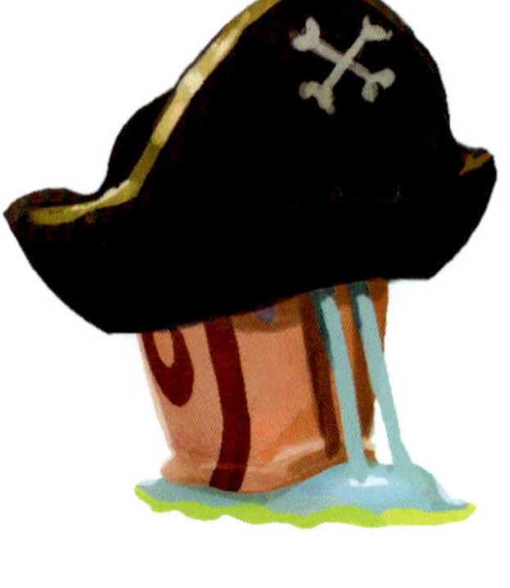

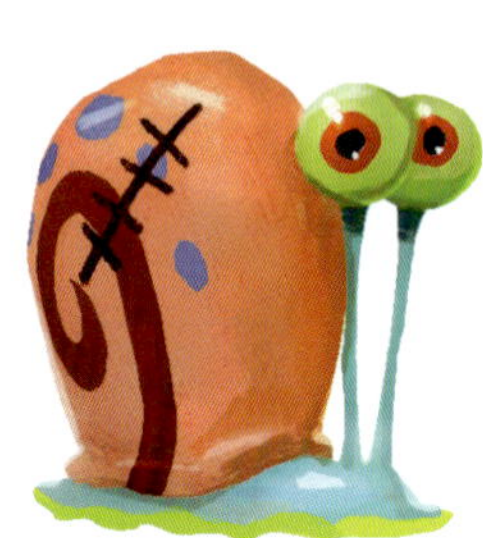

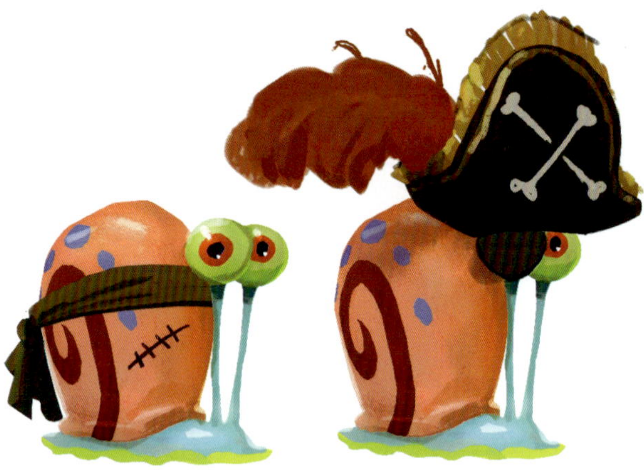

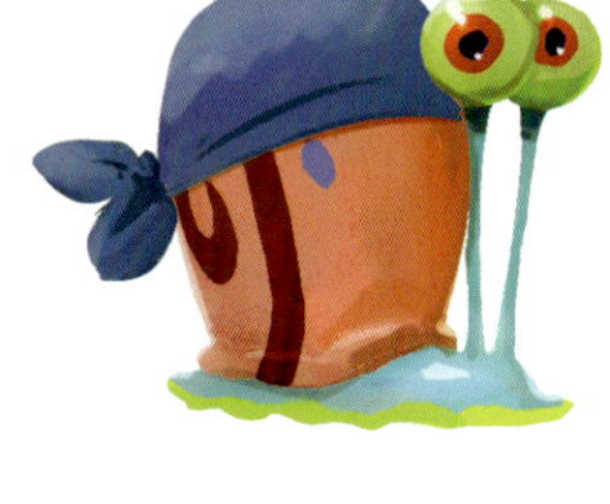

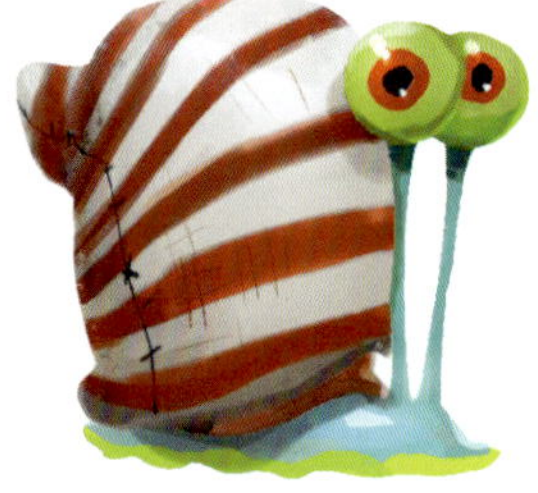

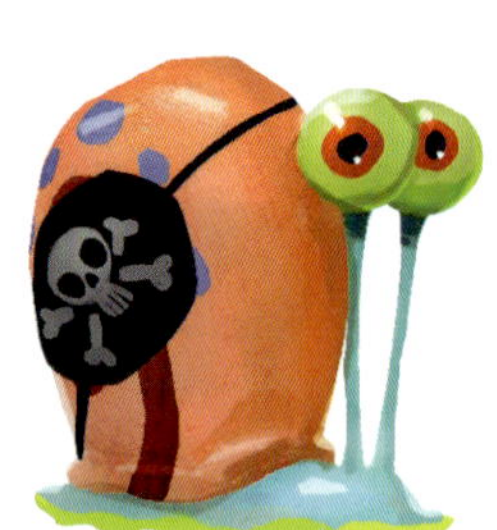

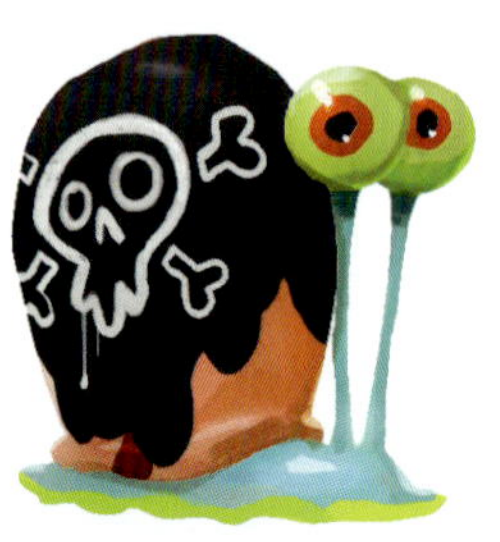

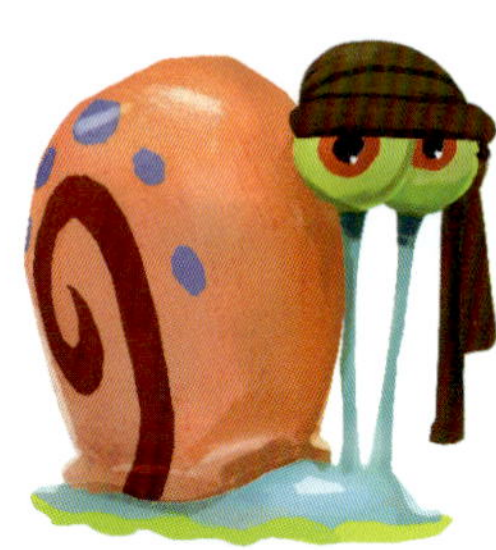

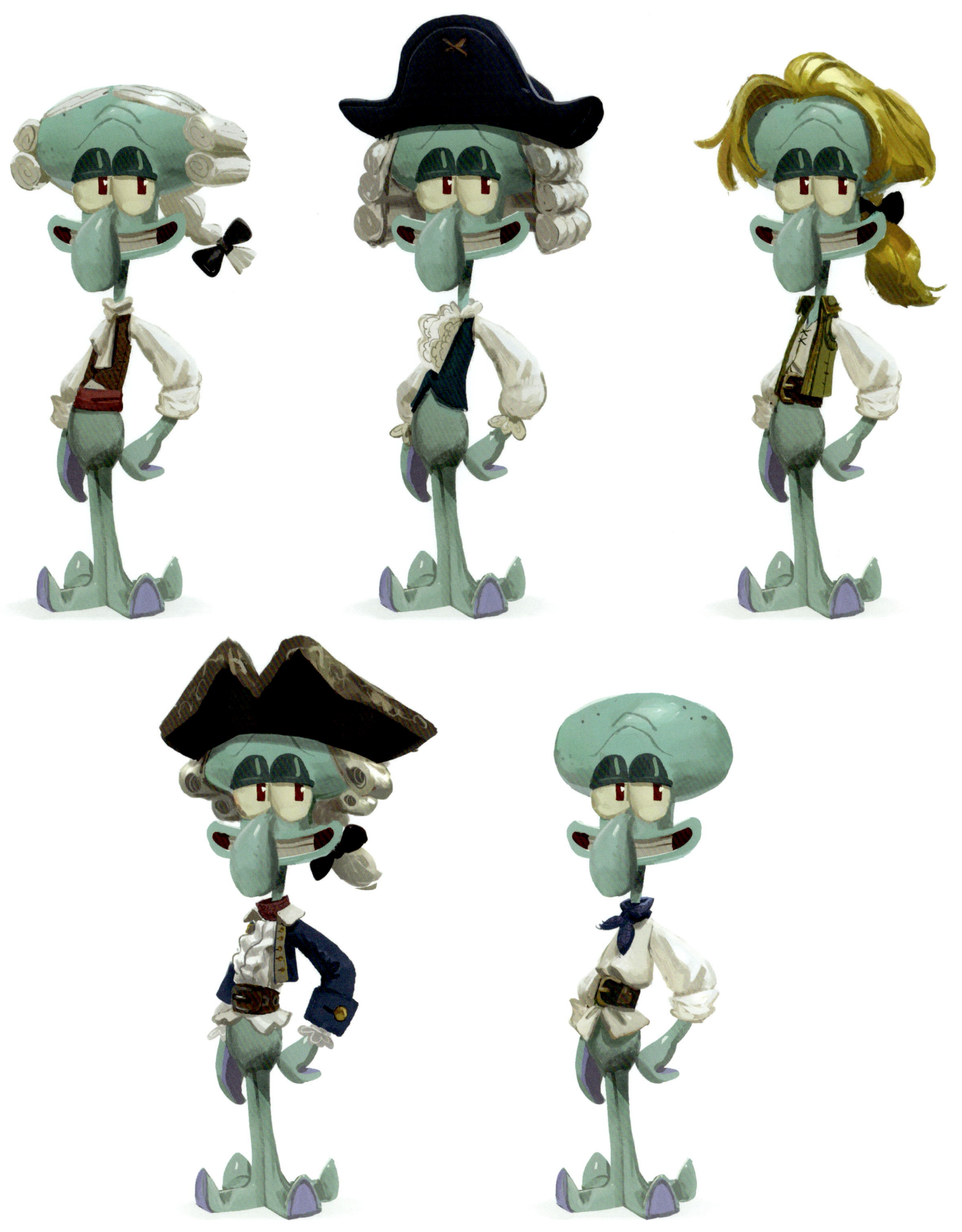

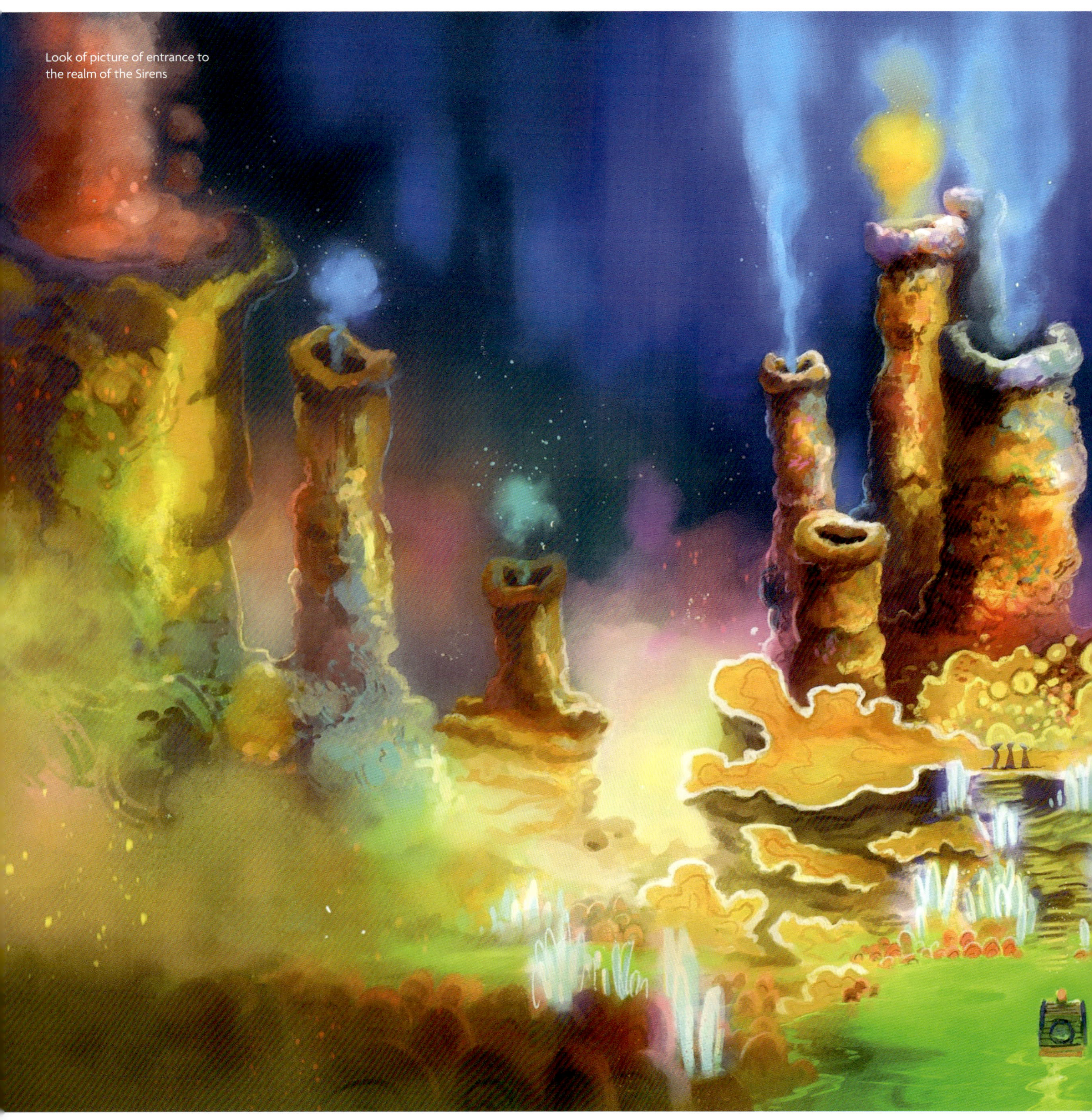

Look of picture of entrance to the realm of the Sirens

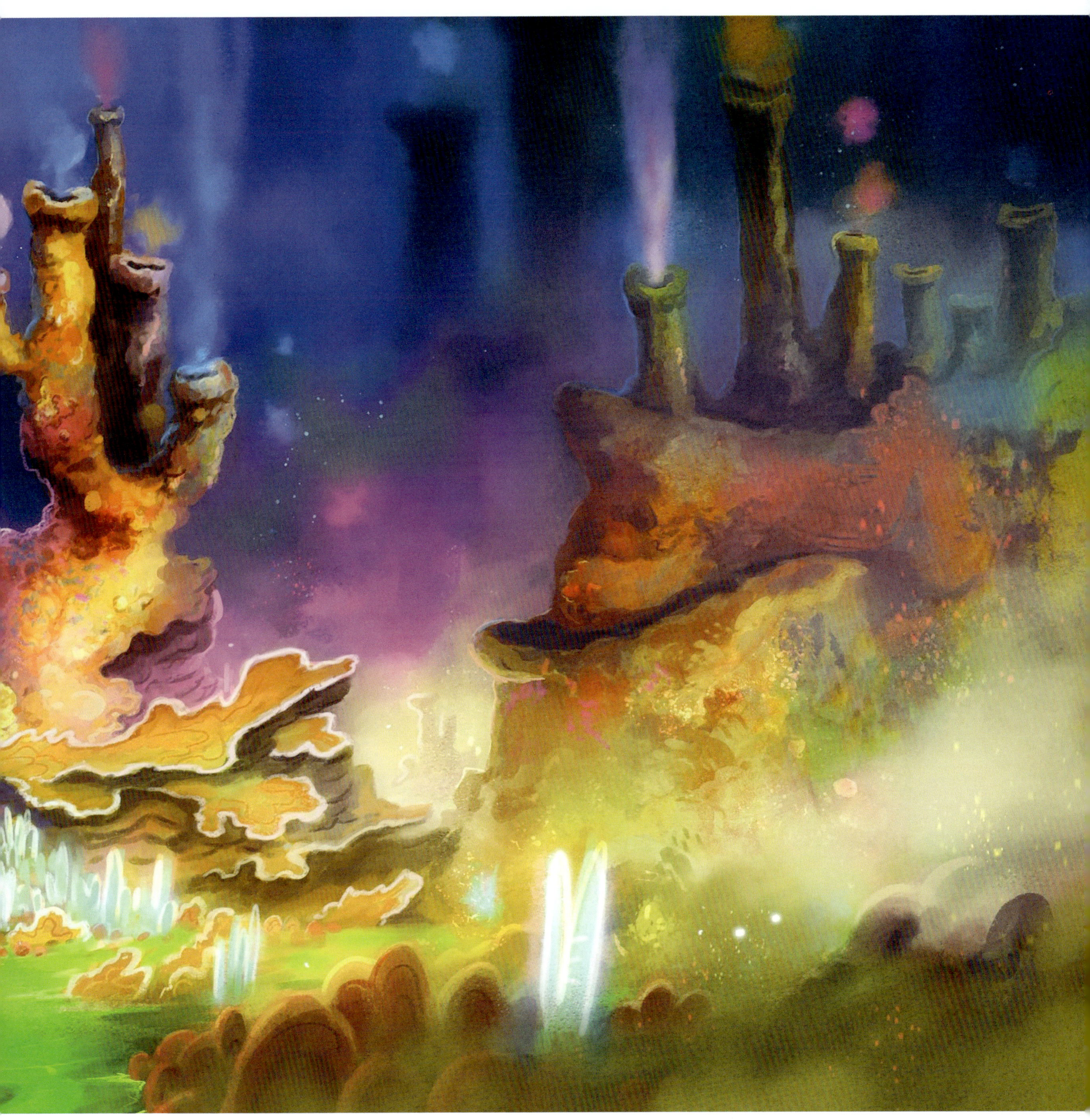

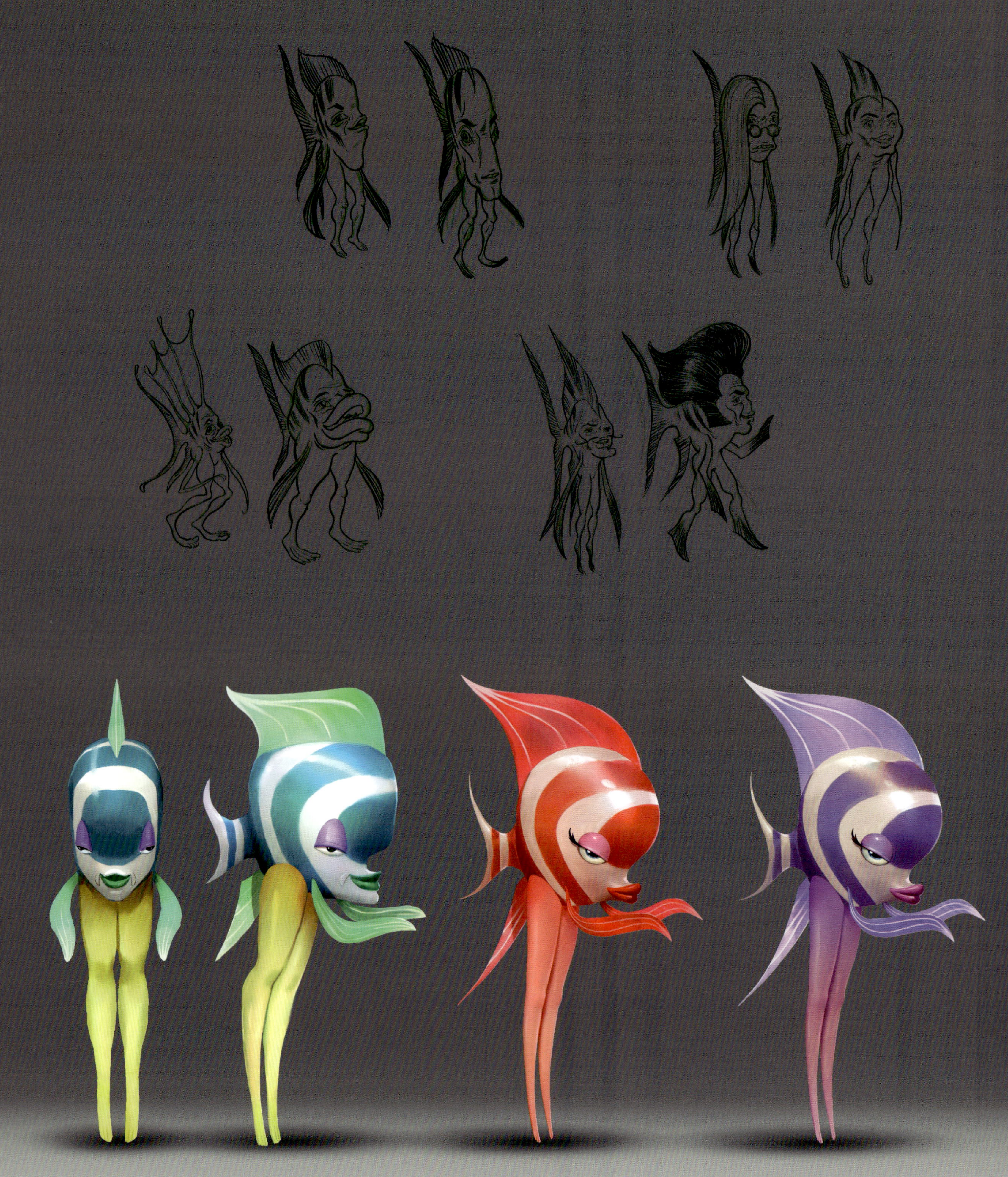

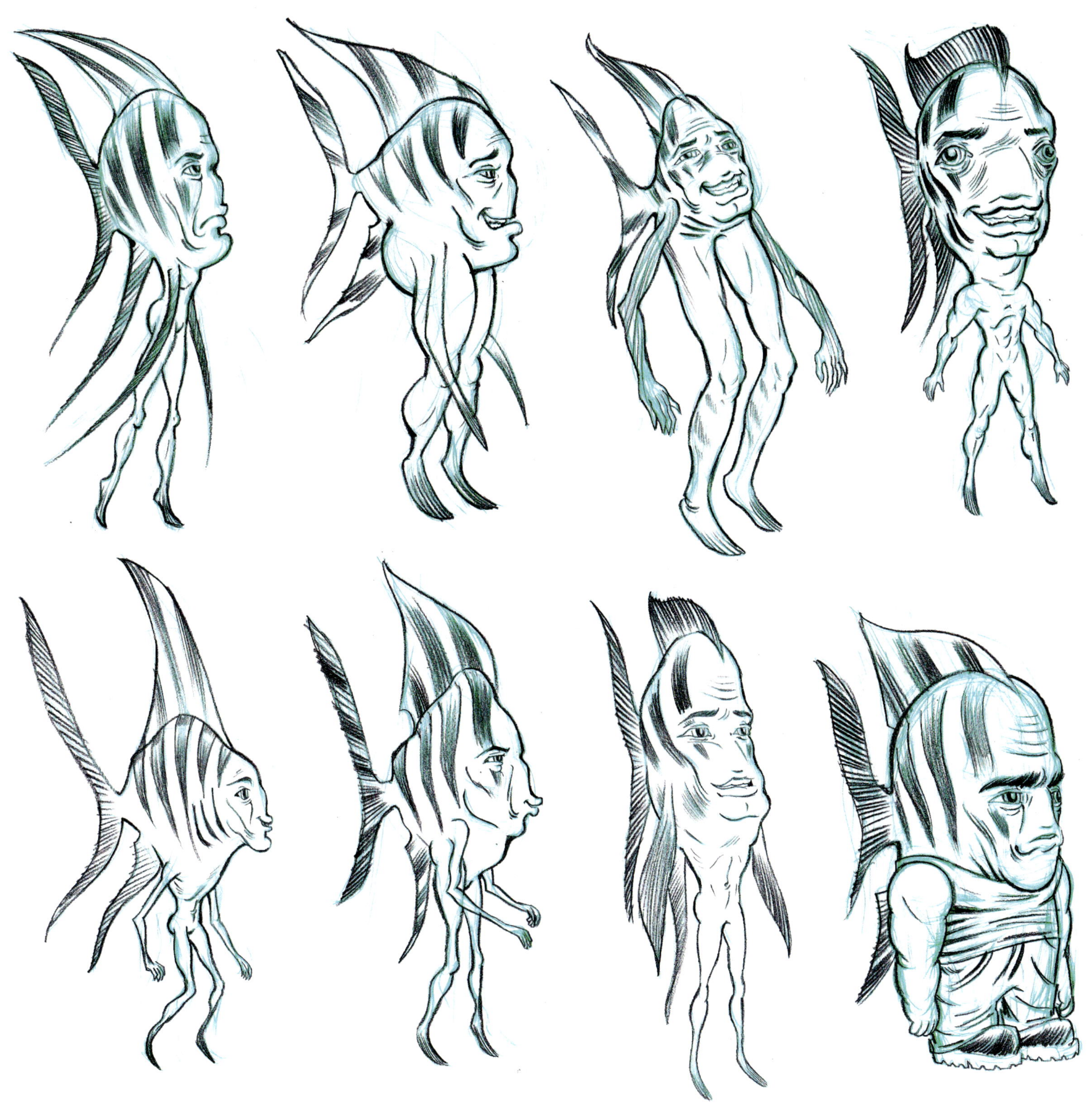

Character concepts of the Sirens

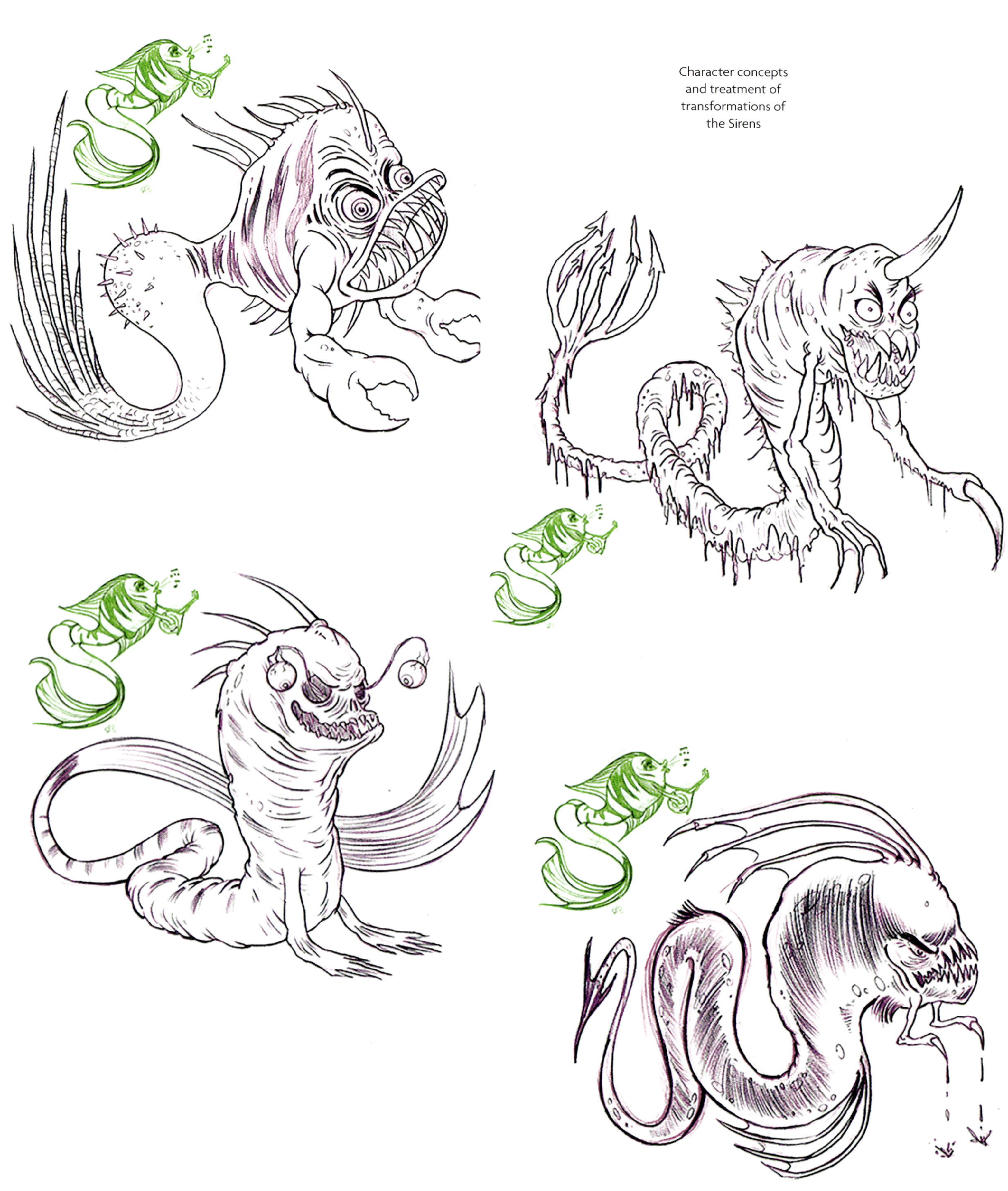

Character concepts and treatment of transformations of the Sirens

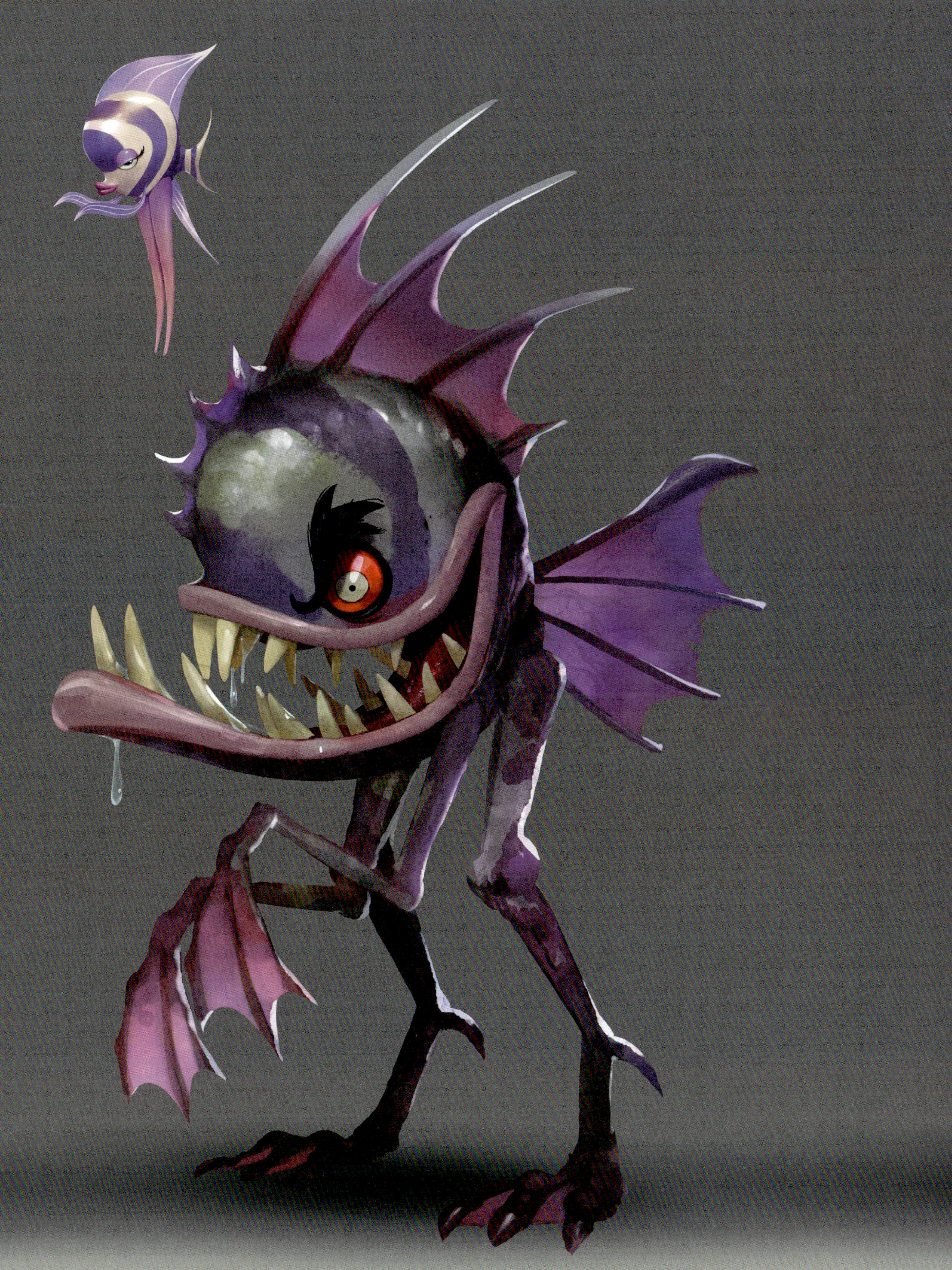

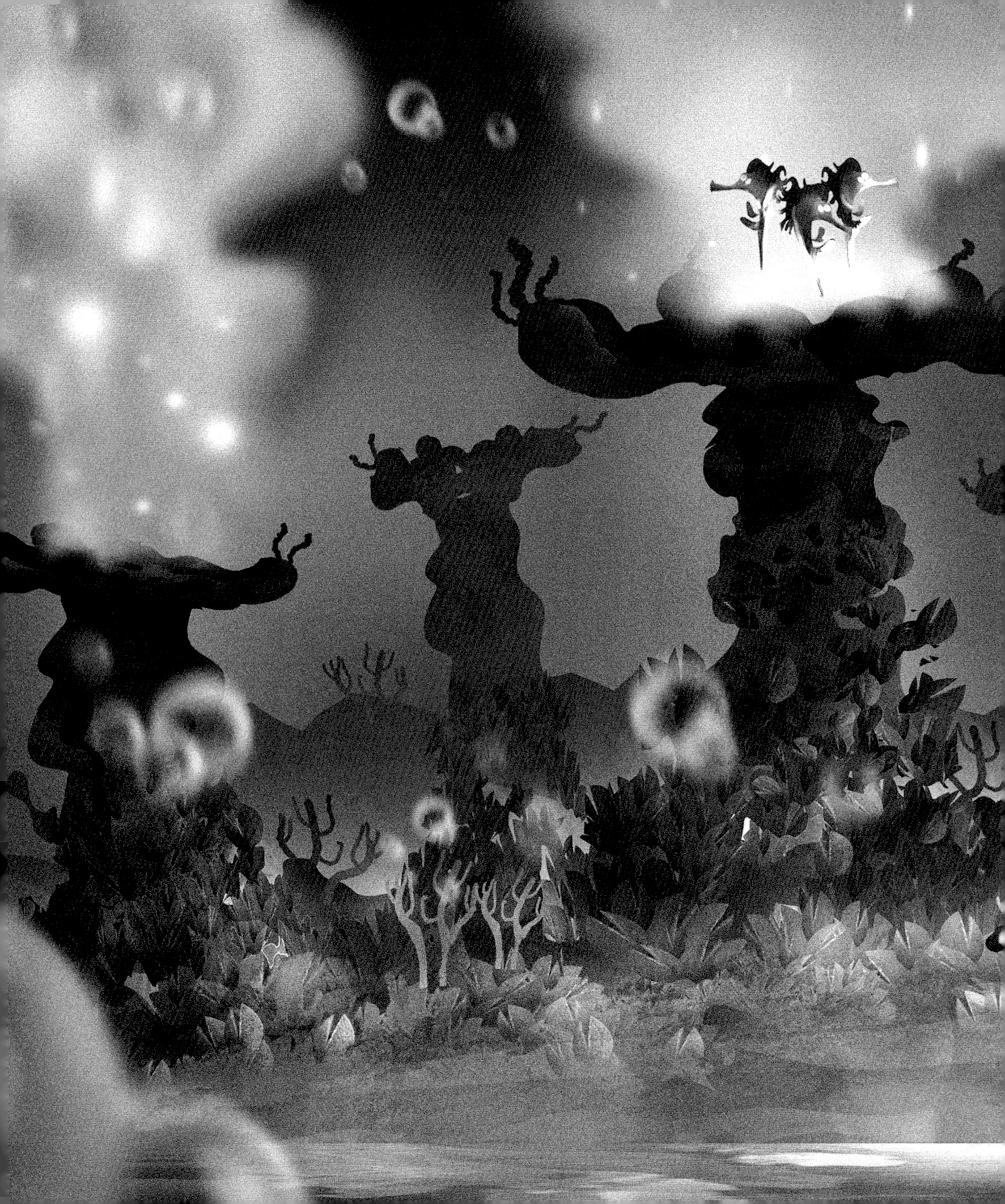

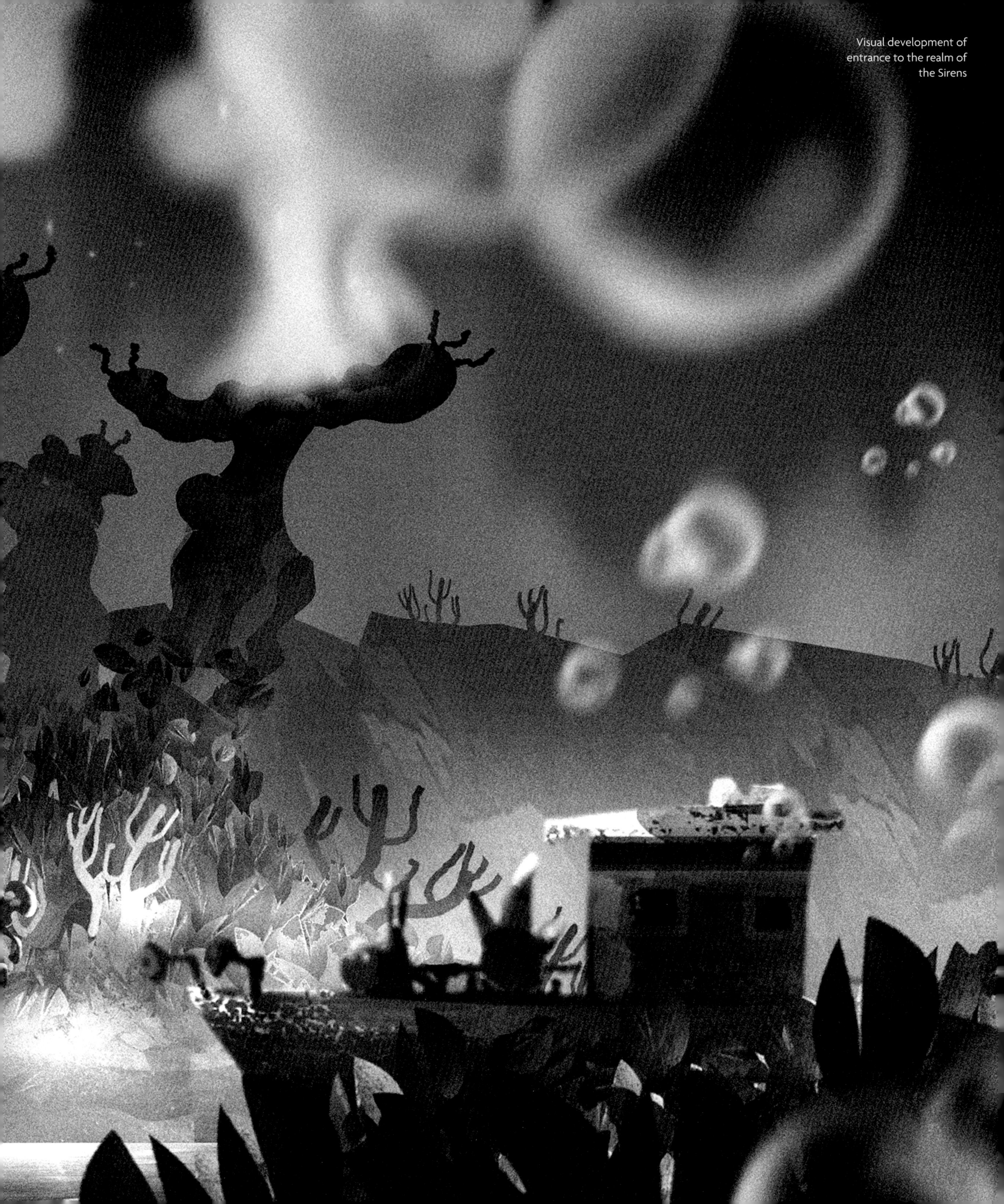

Visual development of entrance to the realm of the Sirens

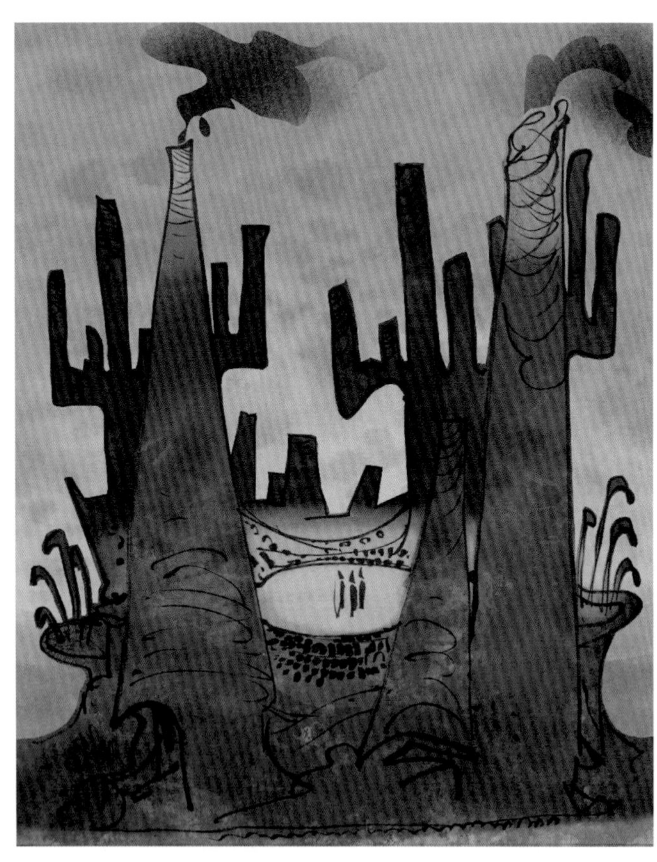

Set development and concept art of the realm of the Sirens

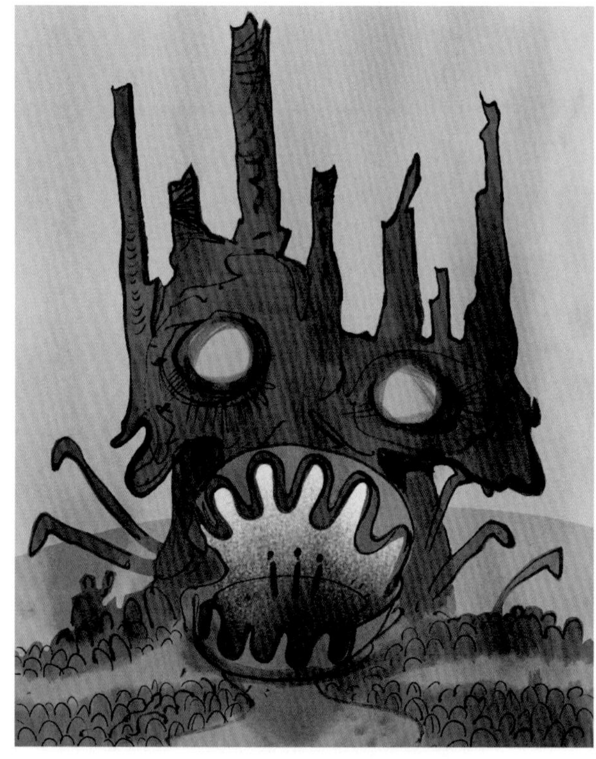

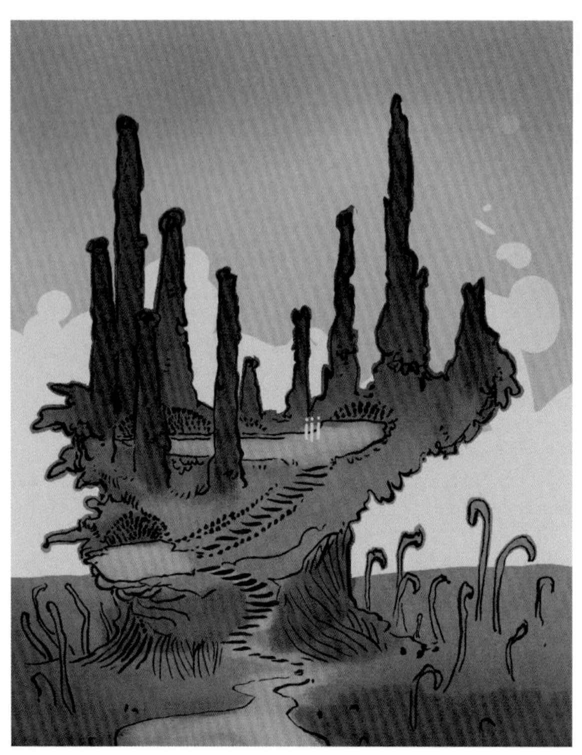

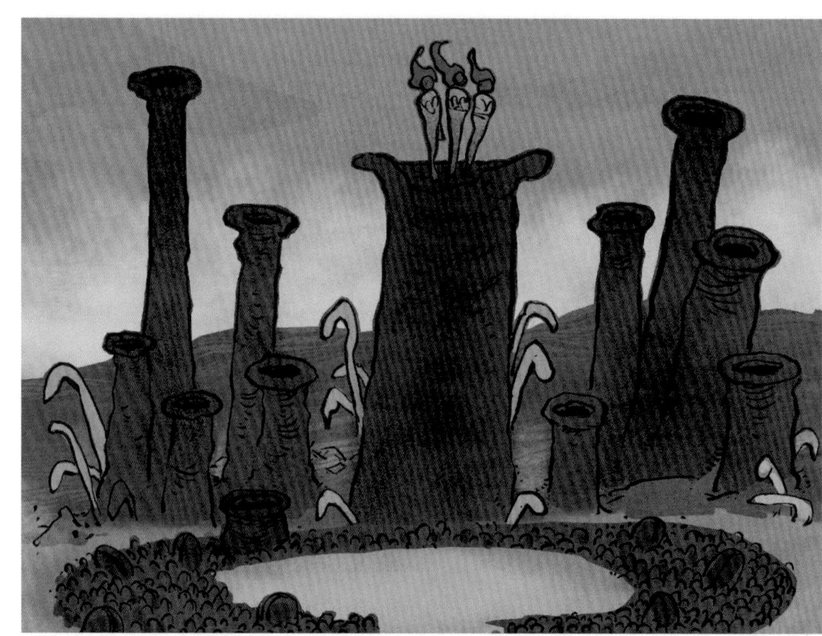

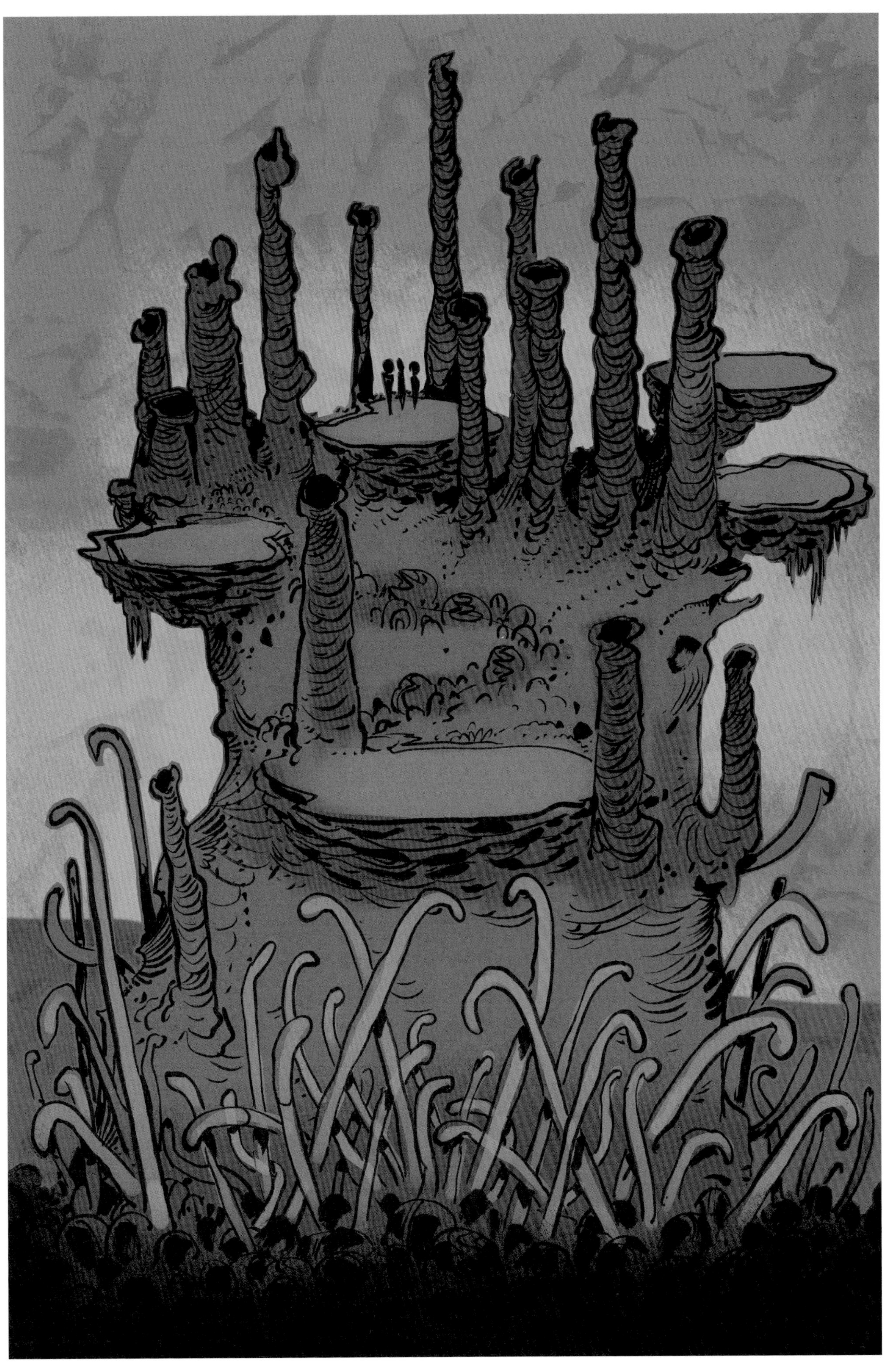

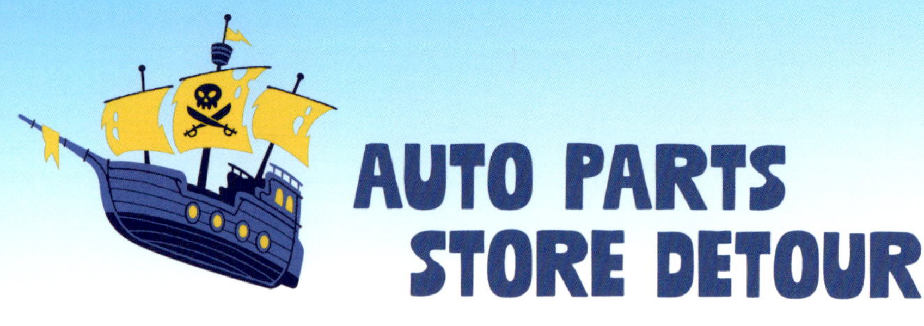

AUTO PARTS STORE DETOUR

The Patty Blaster breaks down on the rescue mission, requiring that Mr. Krabs, Squidward, and Gary cruise by the auto parts store, modeled after a sunken toolbox but containing more creepiness than serviceable items.

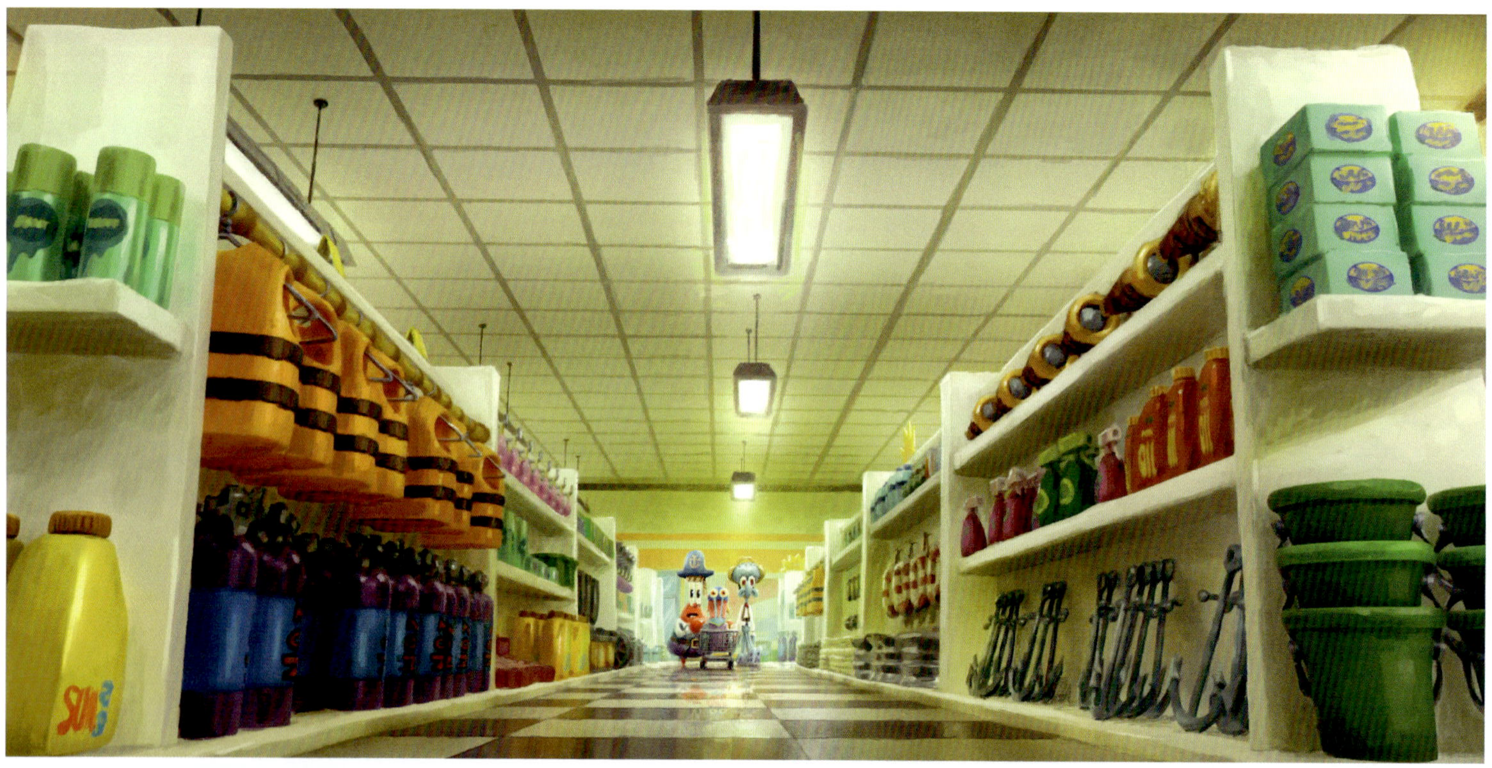

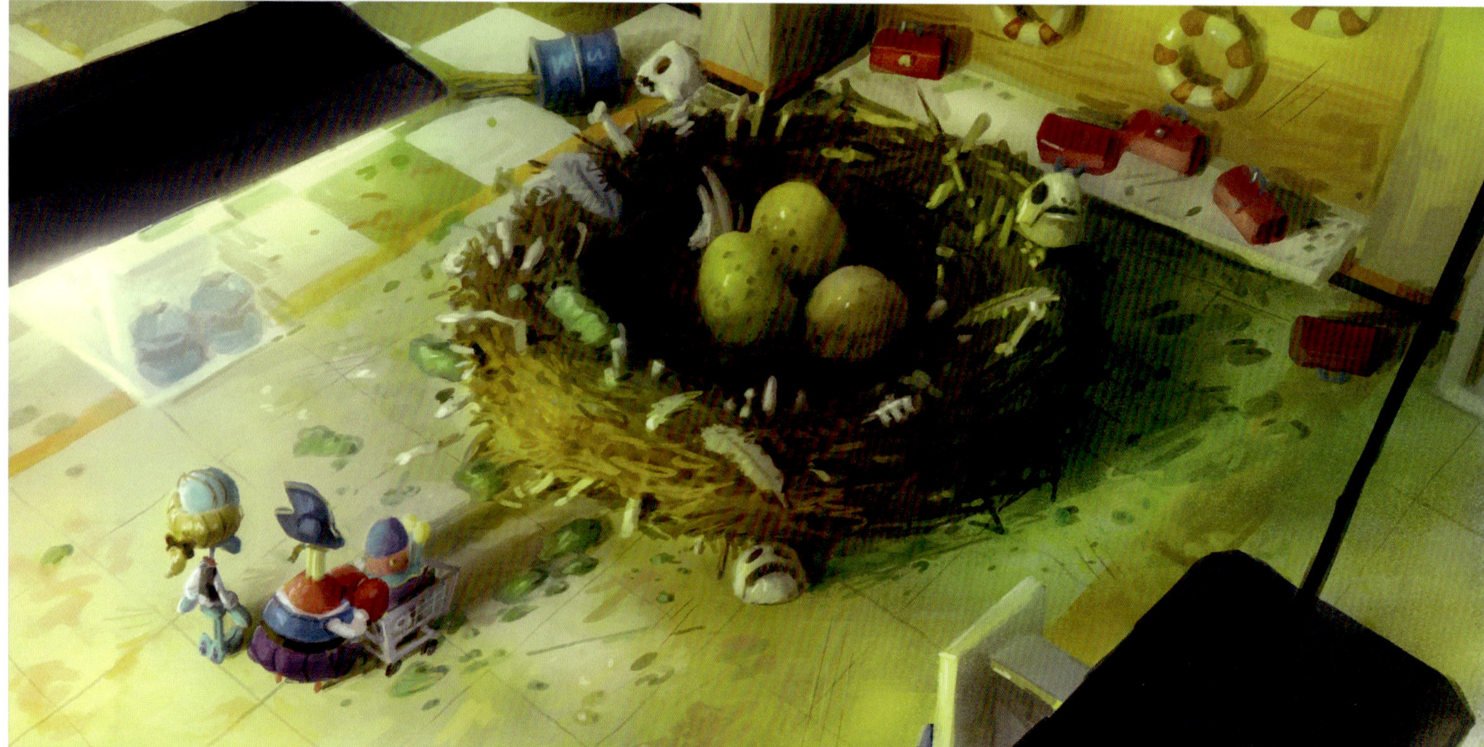

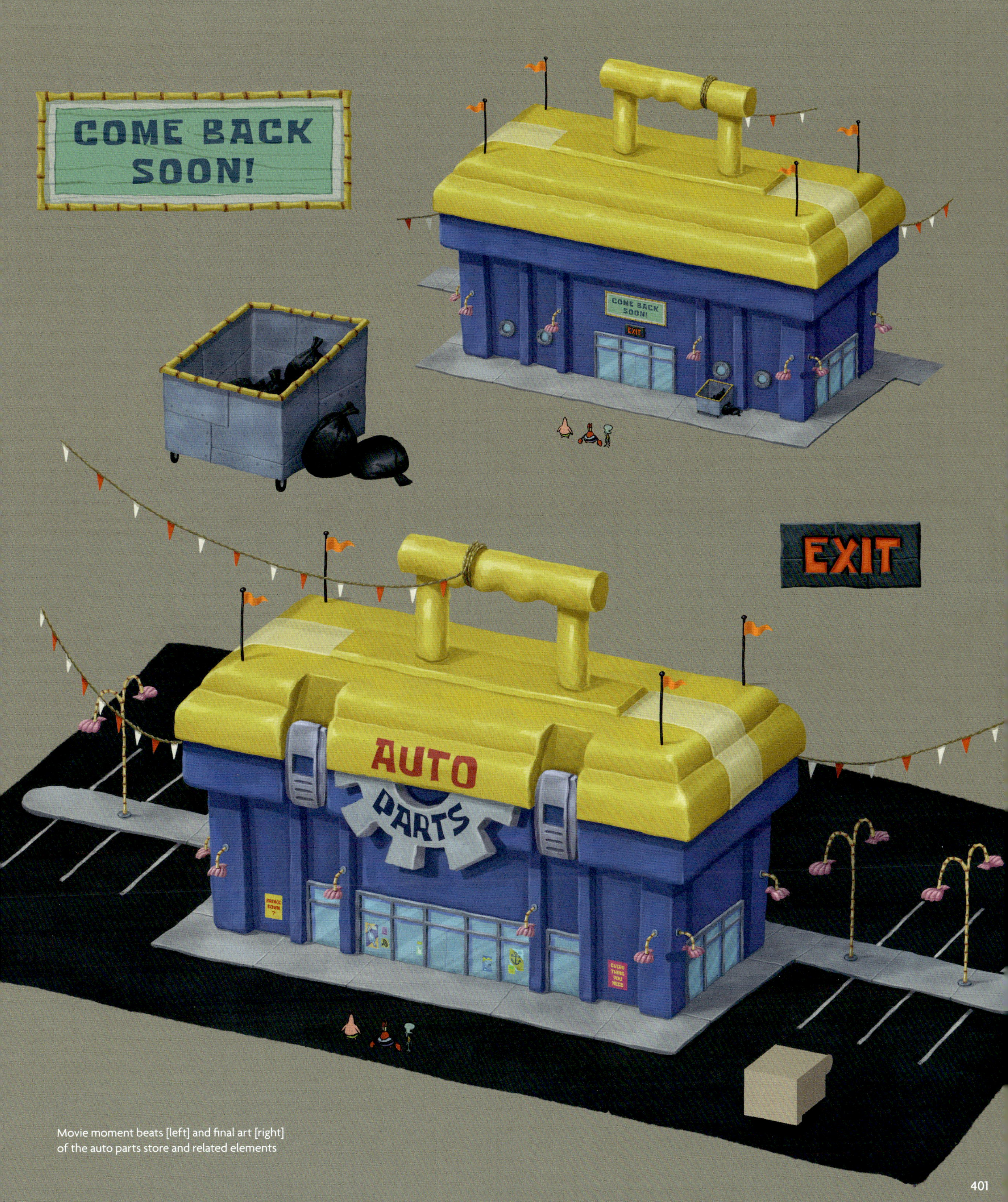

Movie moment beats [left] and final art [right] of the auto parts store and related elements

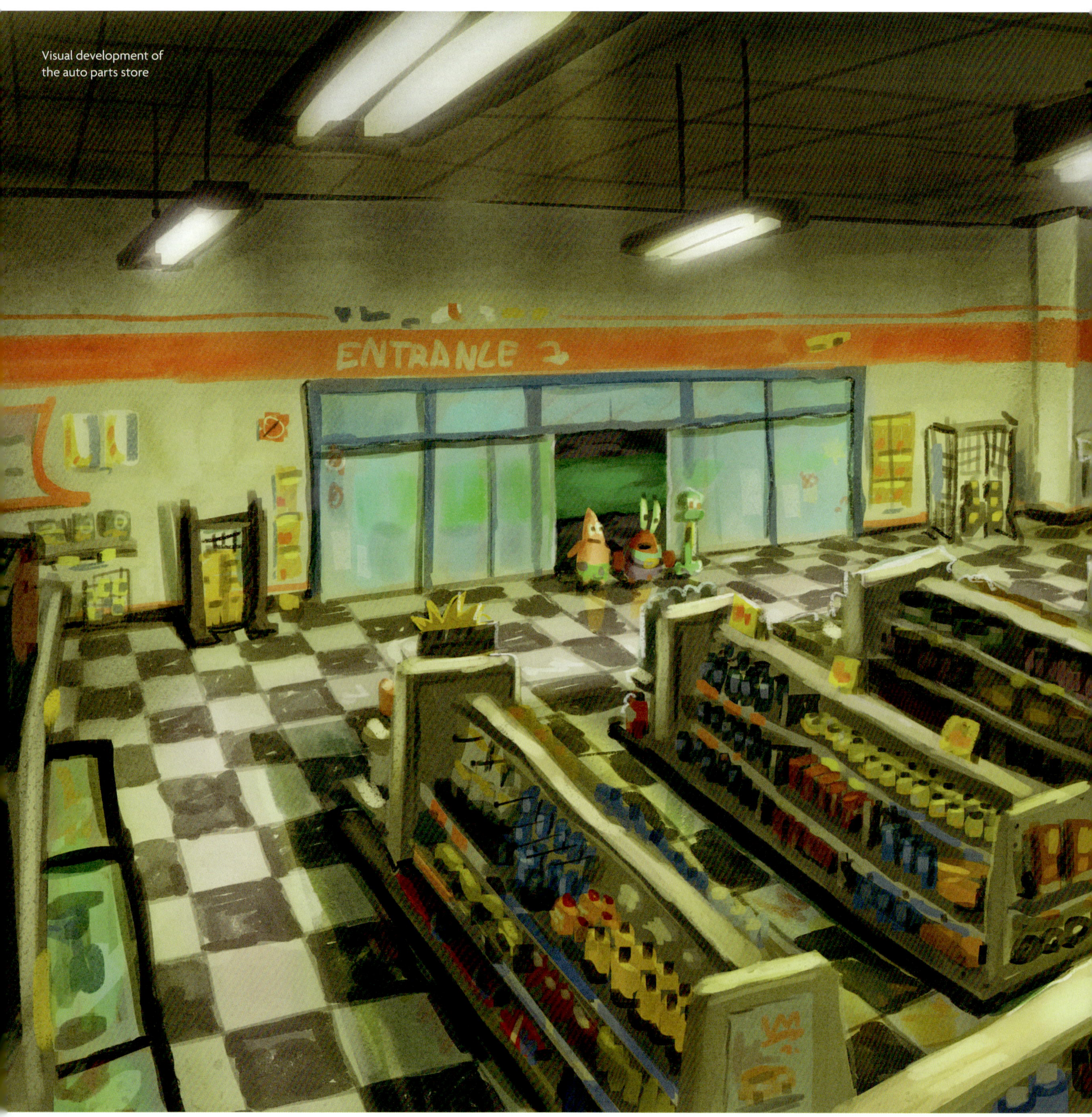

Visual development of the auto parts store

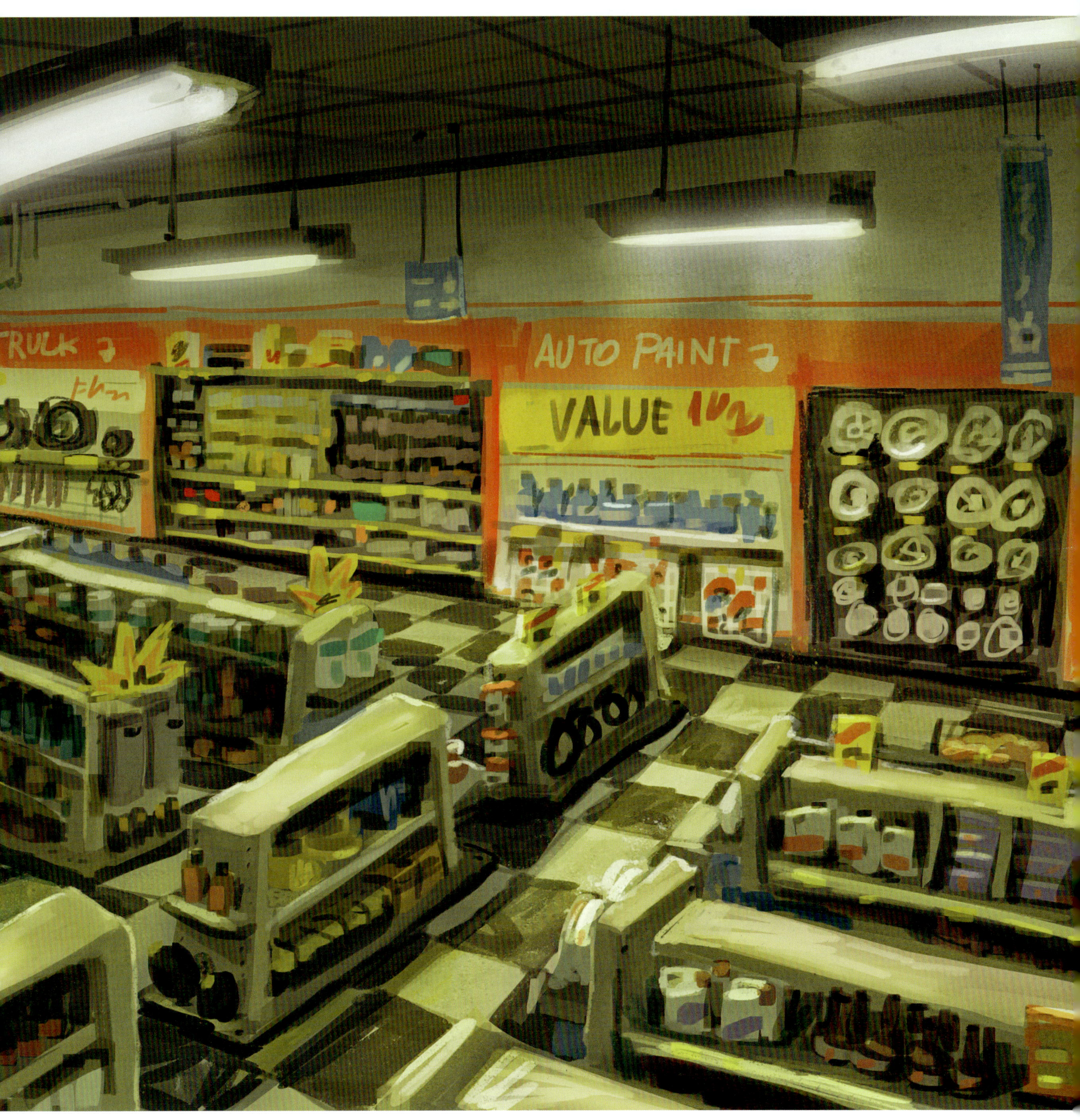

TRUCK
AUTO PAINT
VALUE

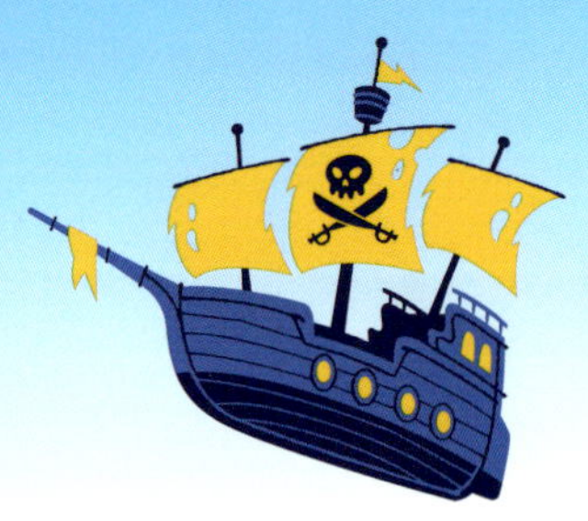

THREE-HEADED SEAGULL PARTNER

Essentially Cerberus with wings, the three-headed gull swoops in to add a horrifying but helpful presence to the rescue mission.

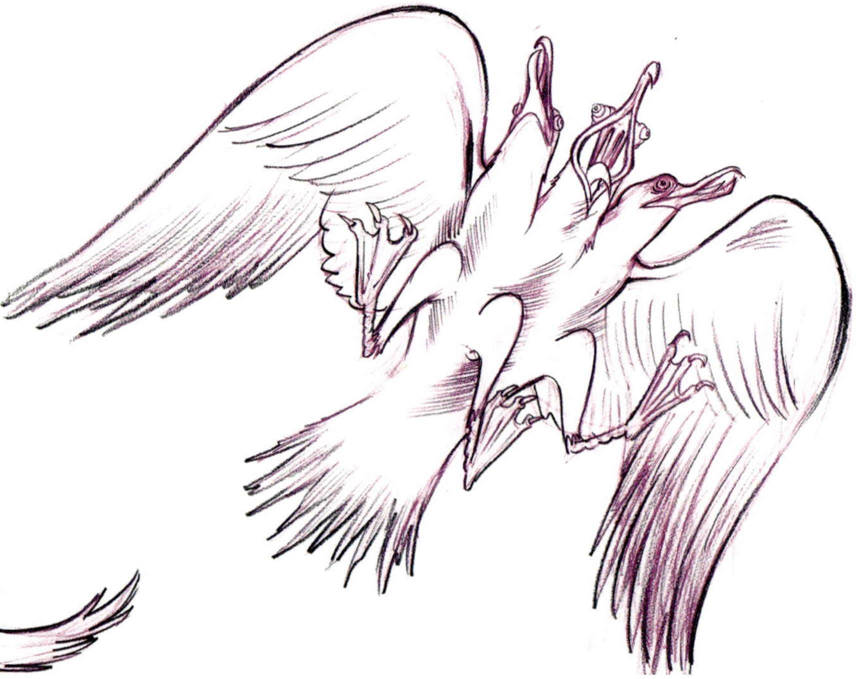

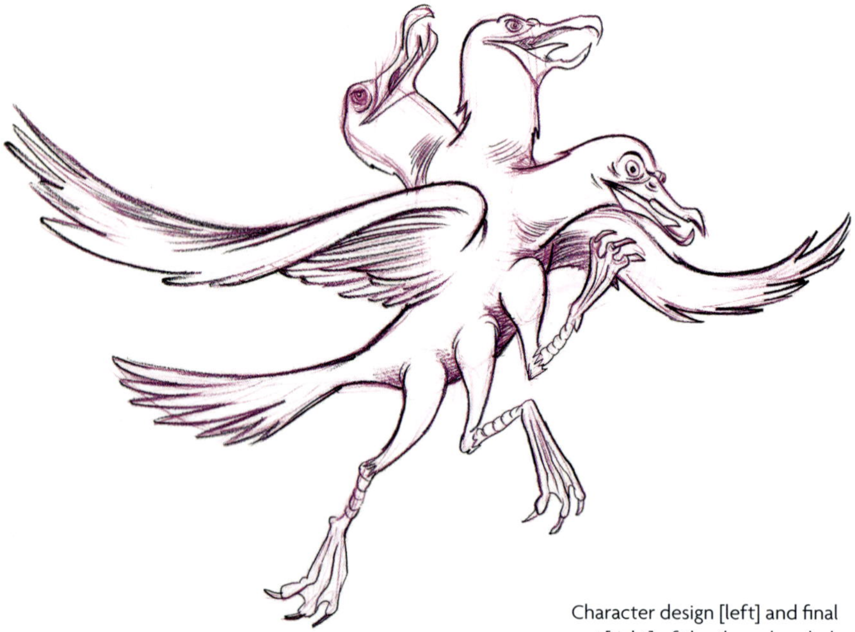

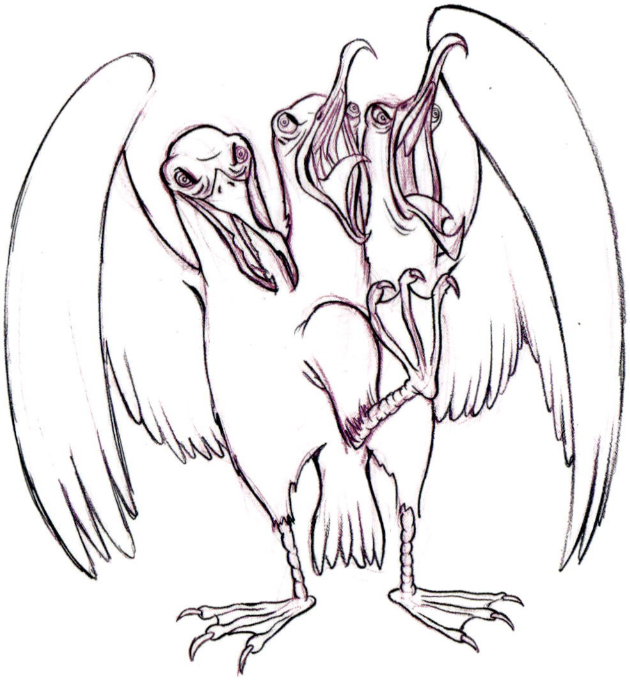

Character design [left] and final art [right] of the three-headed seagull

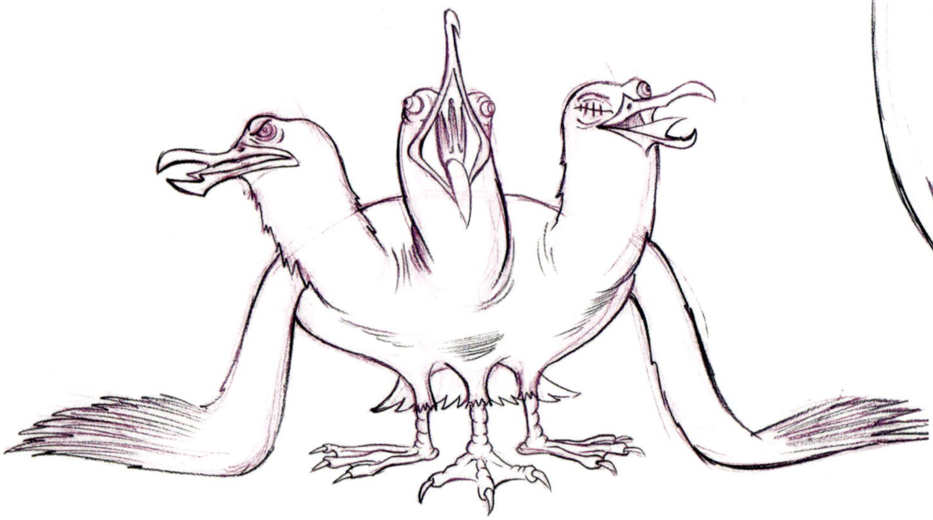

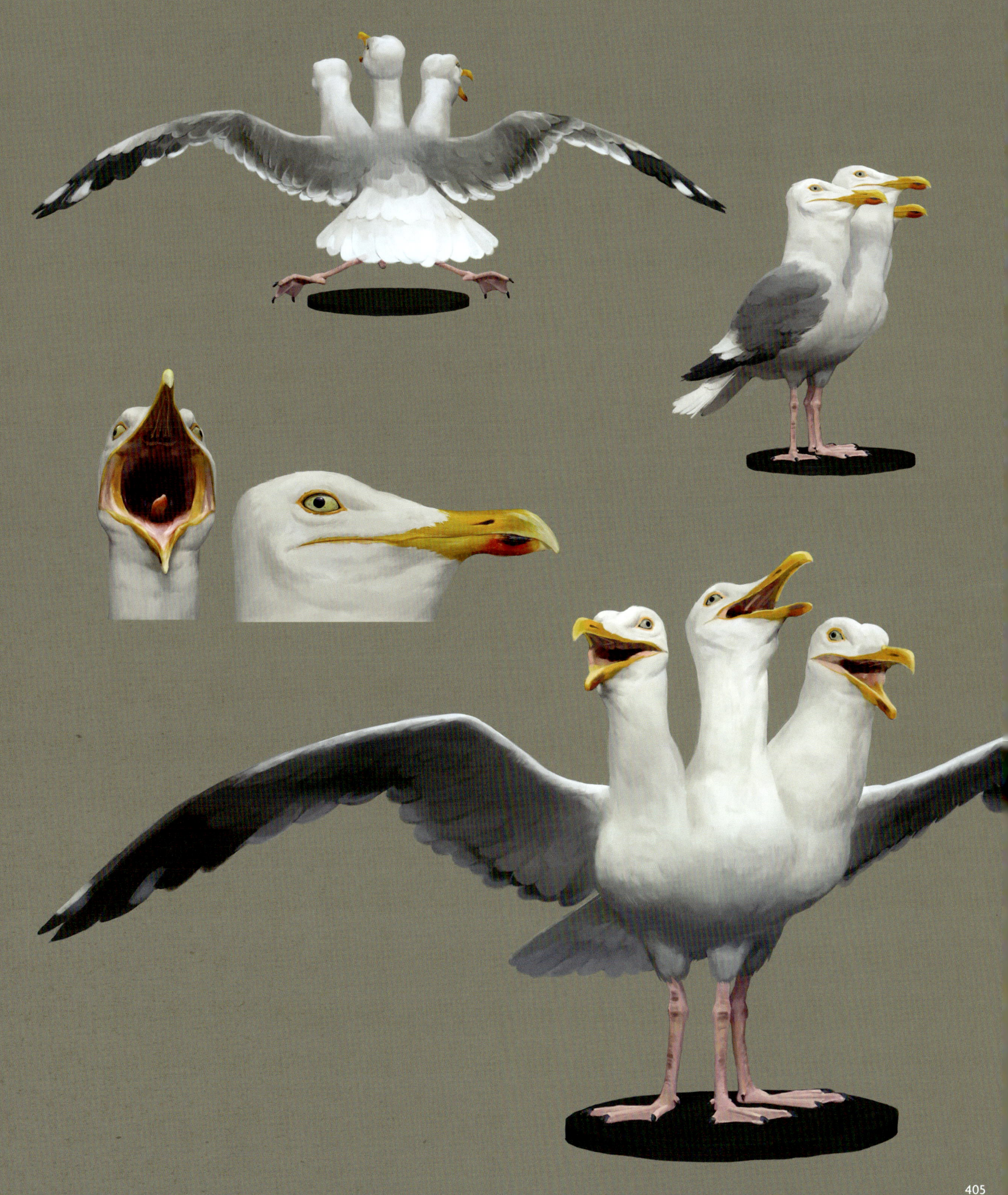

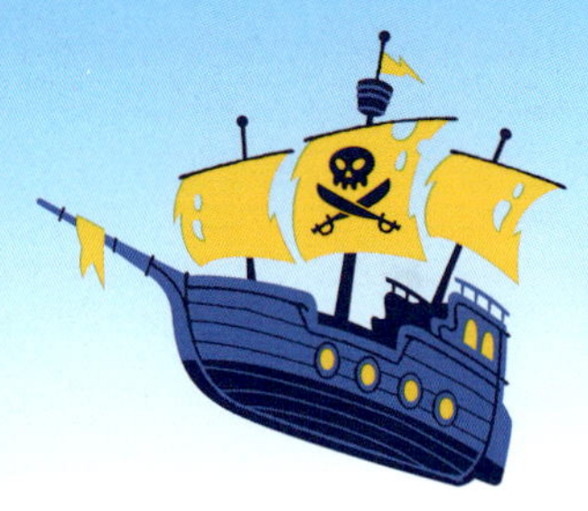

MEET FLYINGBOB DUTCHPANTS & GHOST KRABS

The curse is transferable, as SpongeBob and Mr. Krabs discover and fear that they might endure up through Tuesday the 4,732nd in the month of Forever in the year of Eternity... but luckily Barb knows how to read fine print to get them out of that fate!

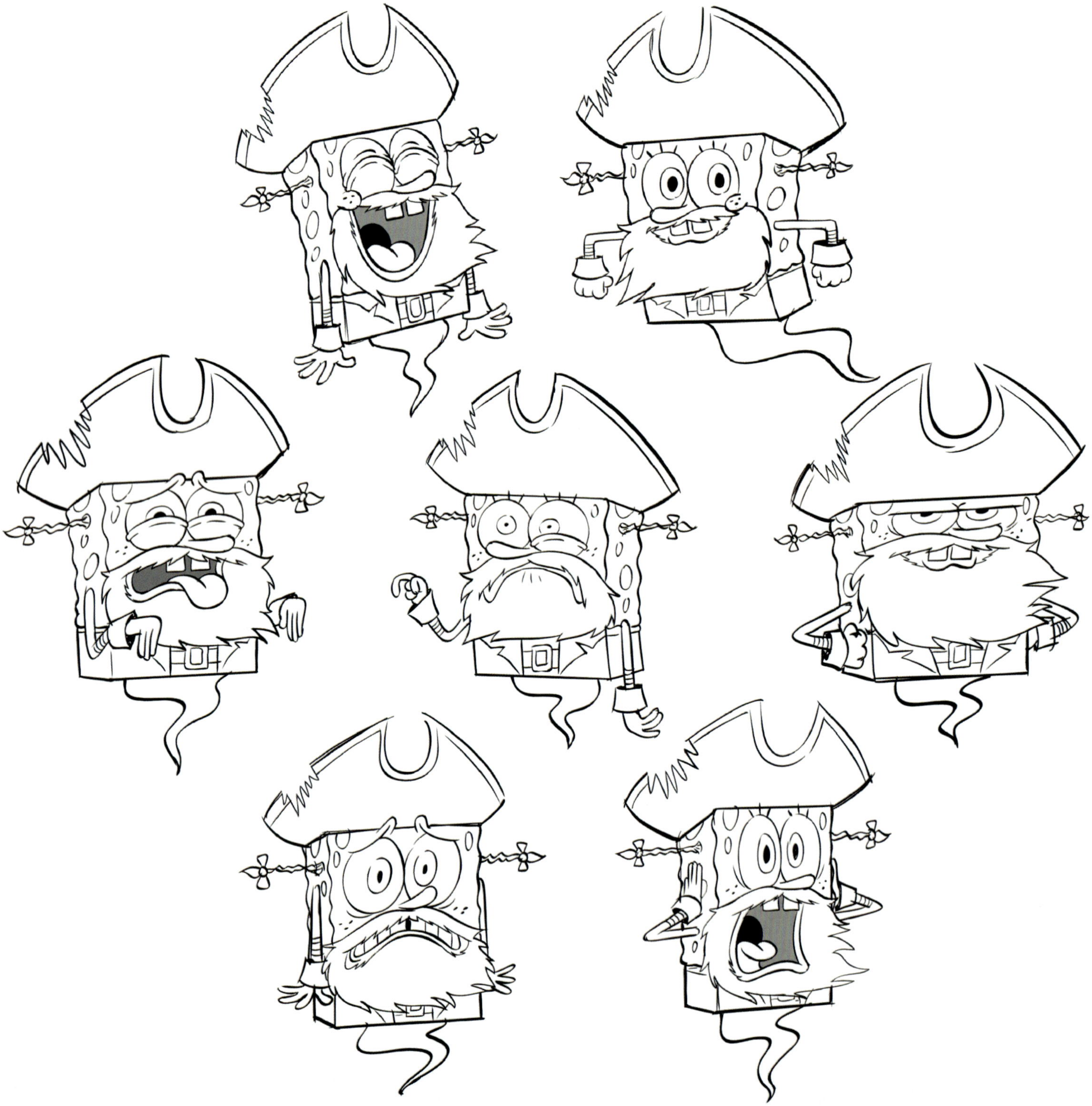

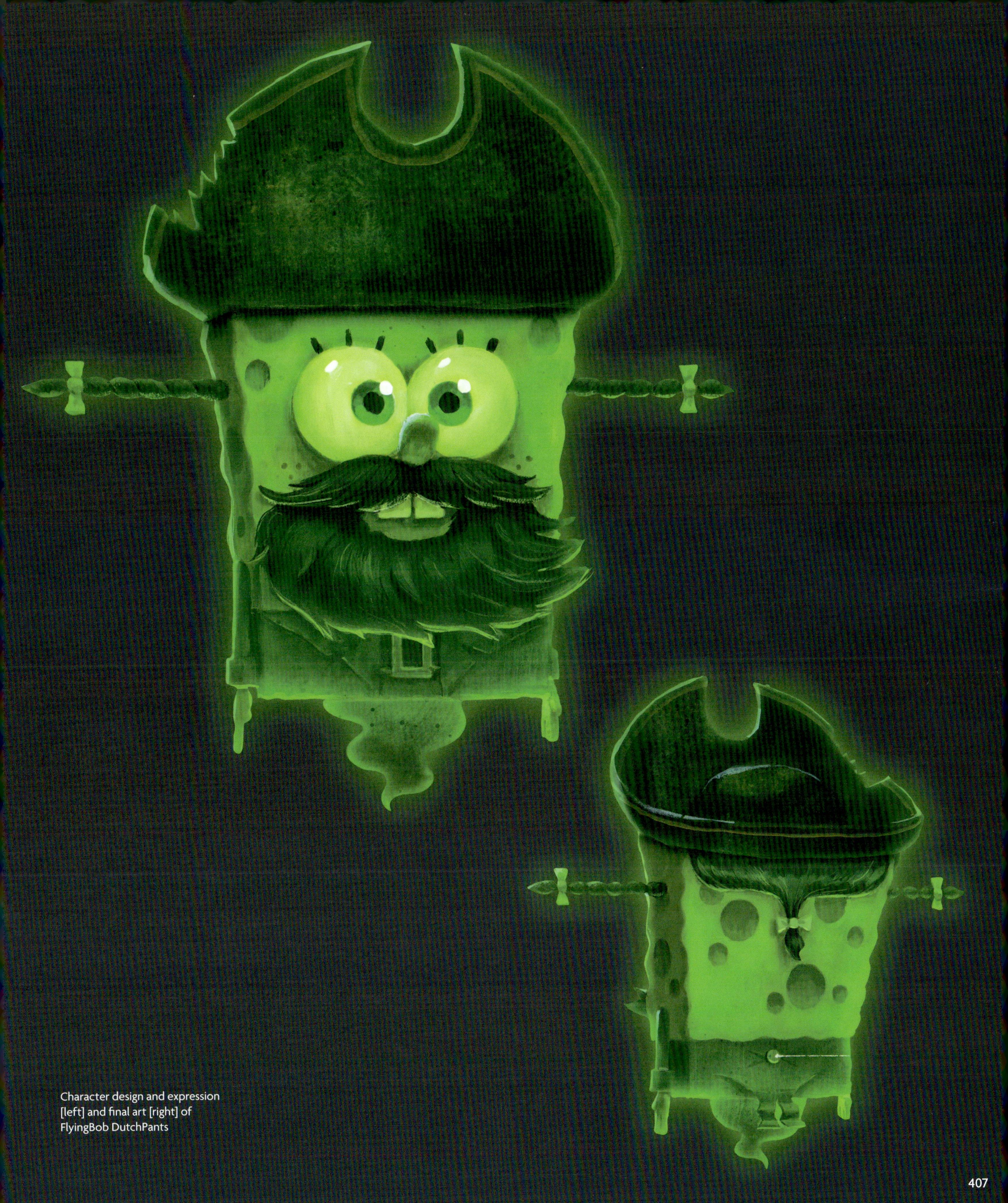

Character design and expression [left] and final art [right] of FlyingBob DutchPants

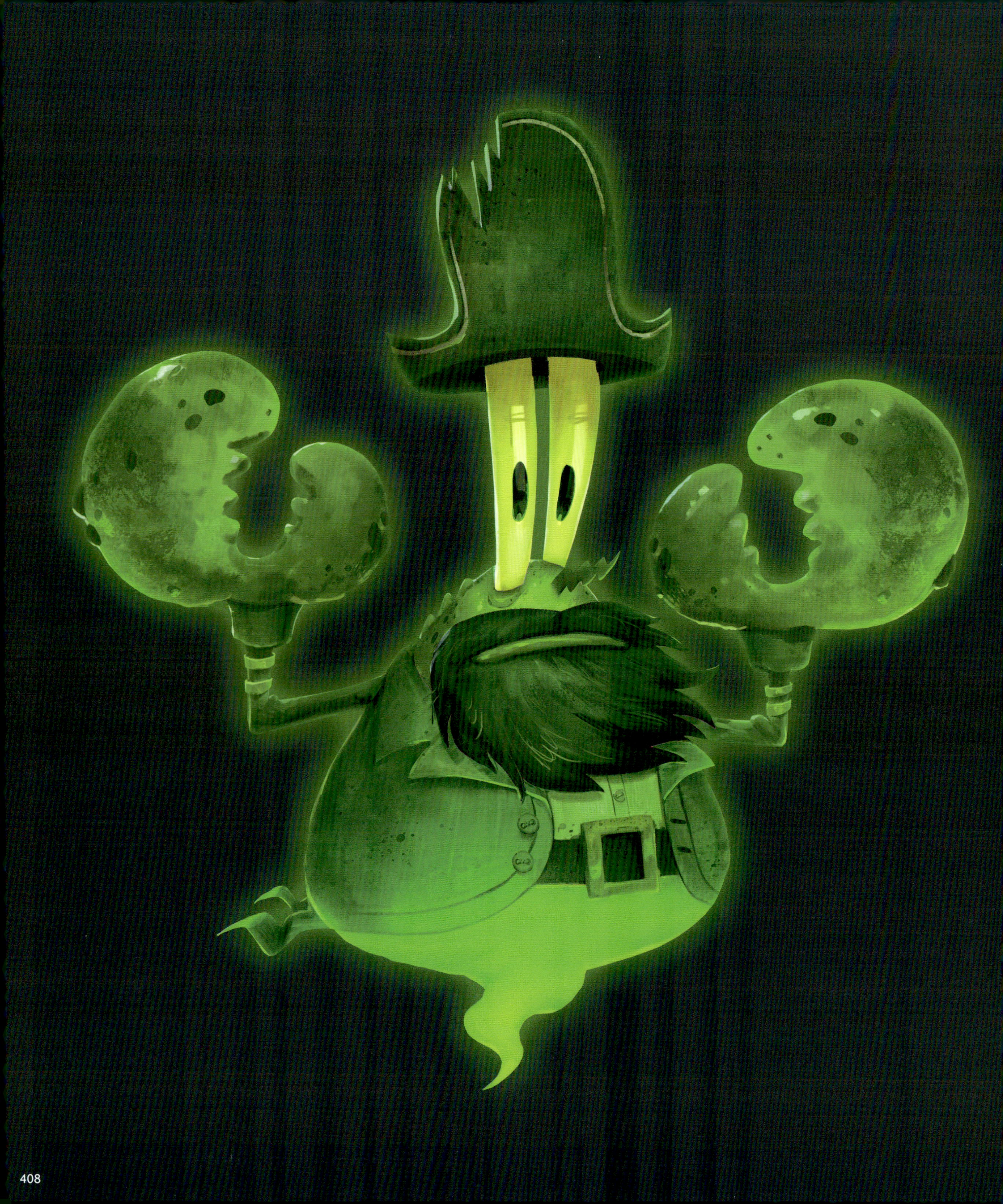

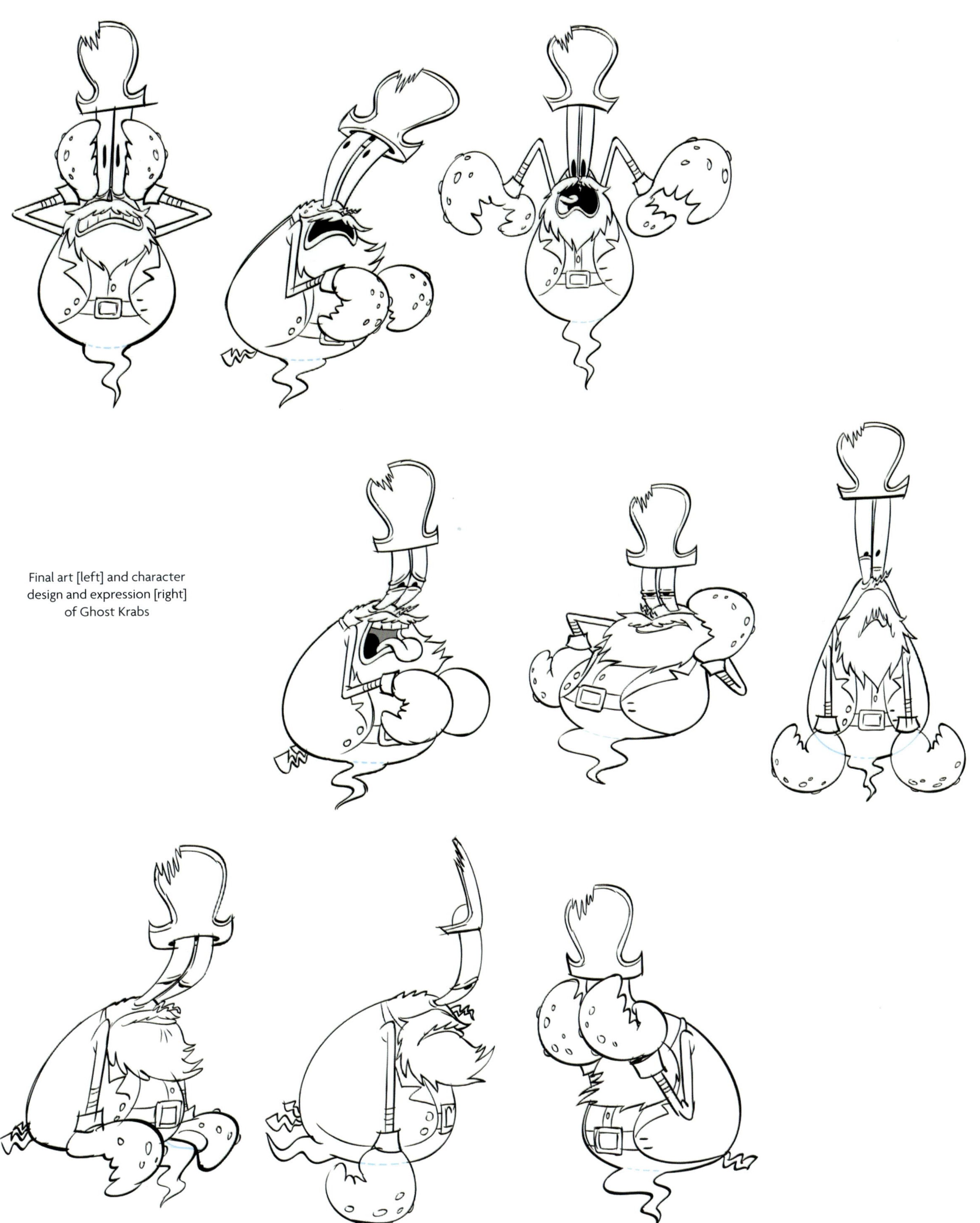

Final art [left] and character design and expression [right] of Ghost Krabs

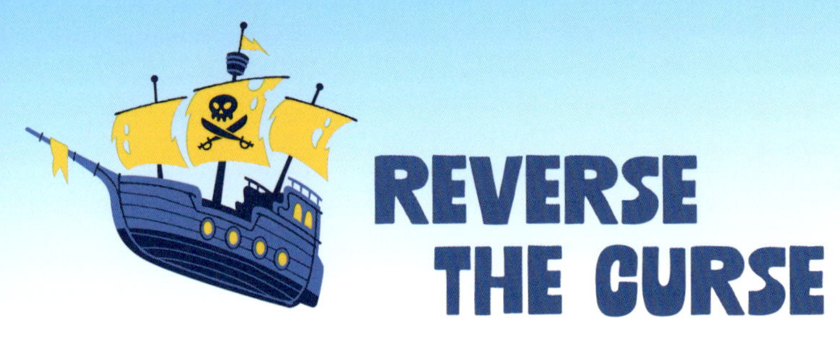

REVERSE THE CURSE

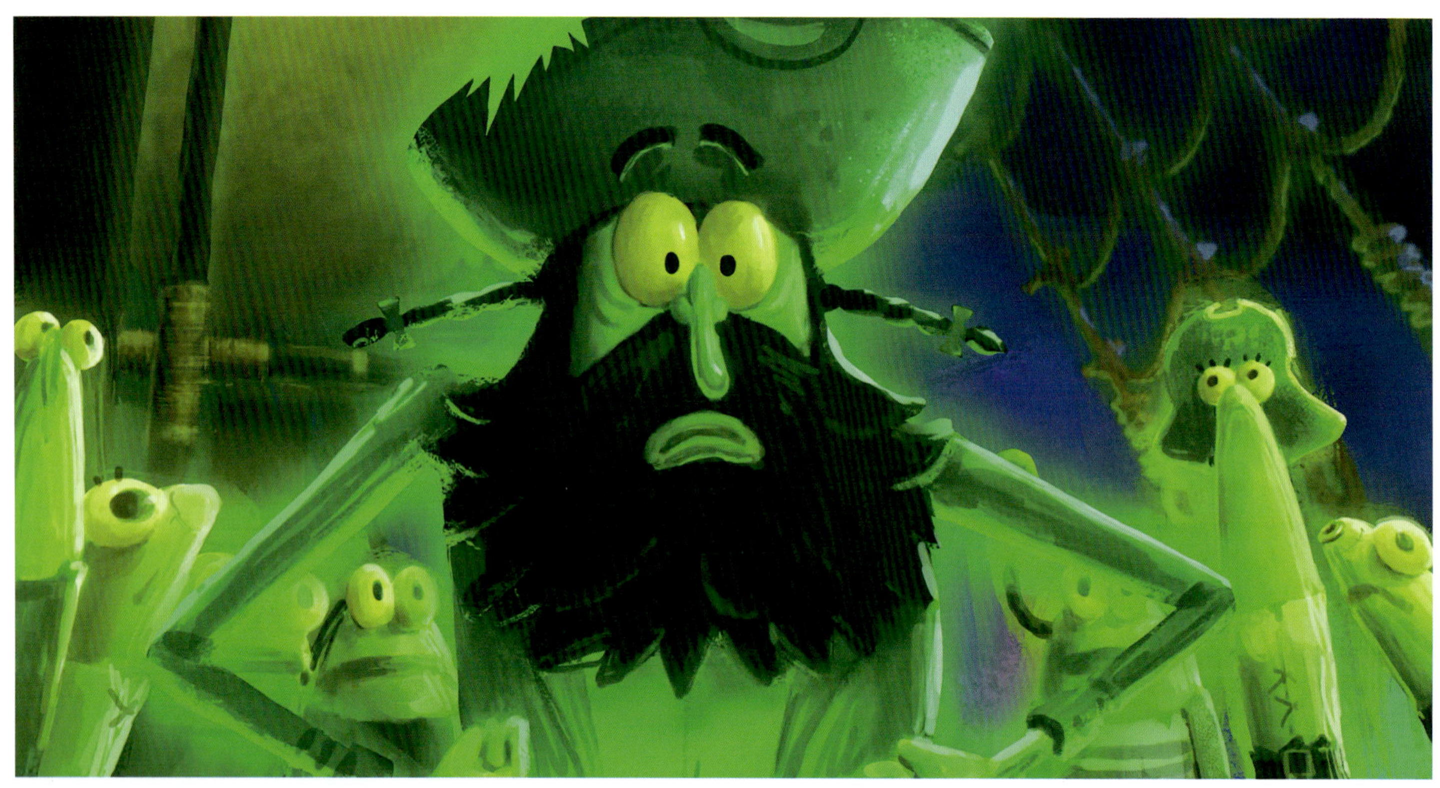

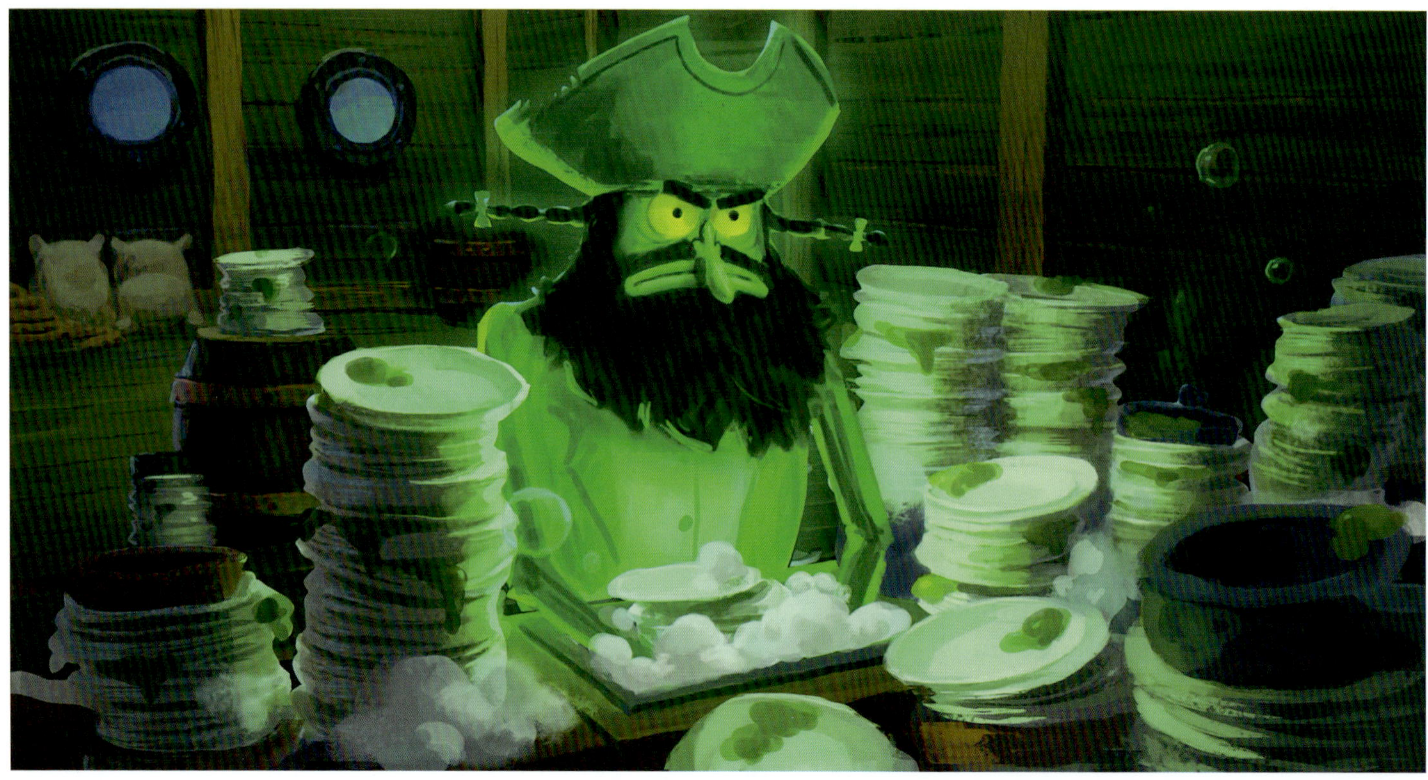

OFFICIAL BIG GUY

With almost everyone back to normal in Bikini Bottom, SpongeBob is finally recognized as being an Official Big Guy, and hugs abound to celebrate his thirty-six-clams-high milestone.

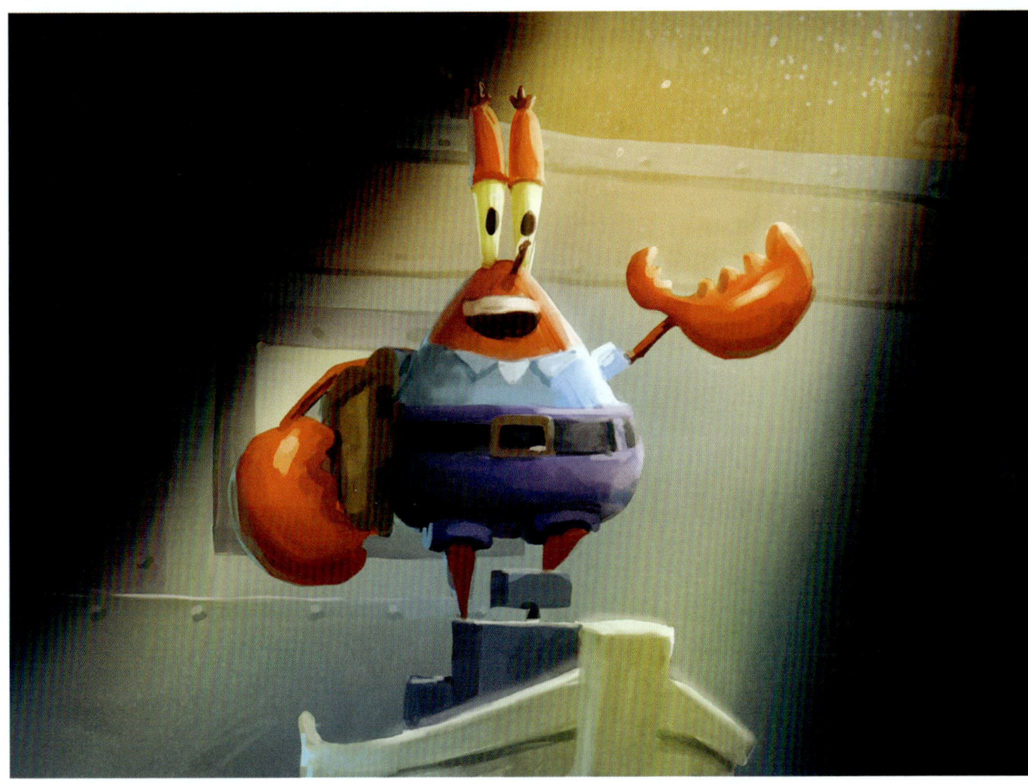

Color keys of the grand finale

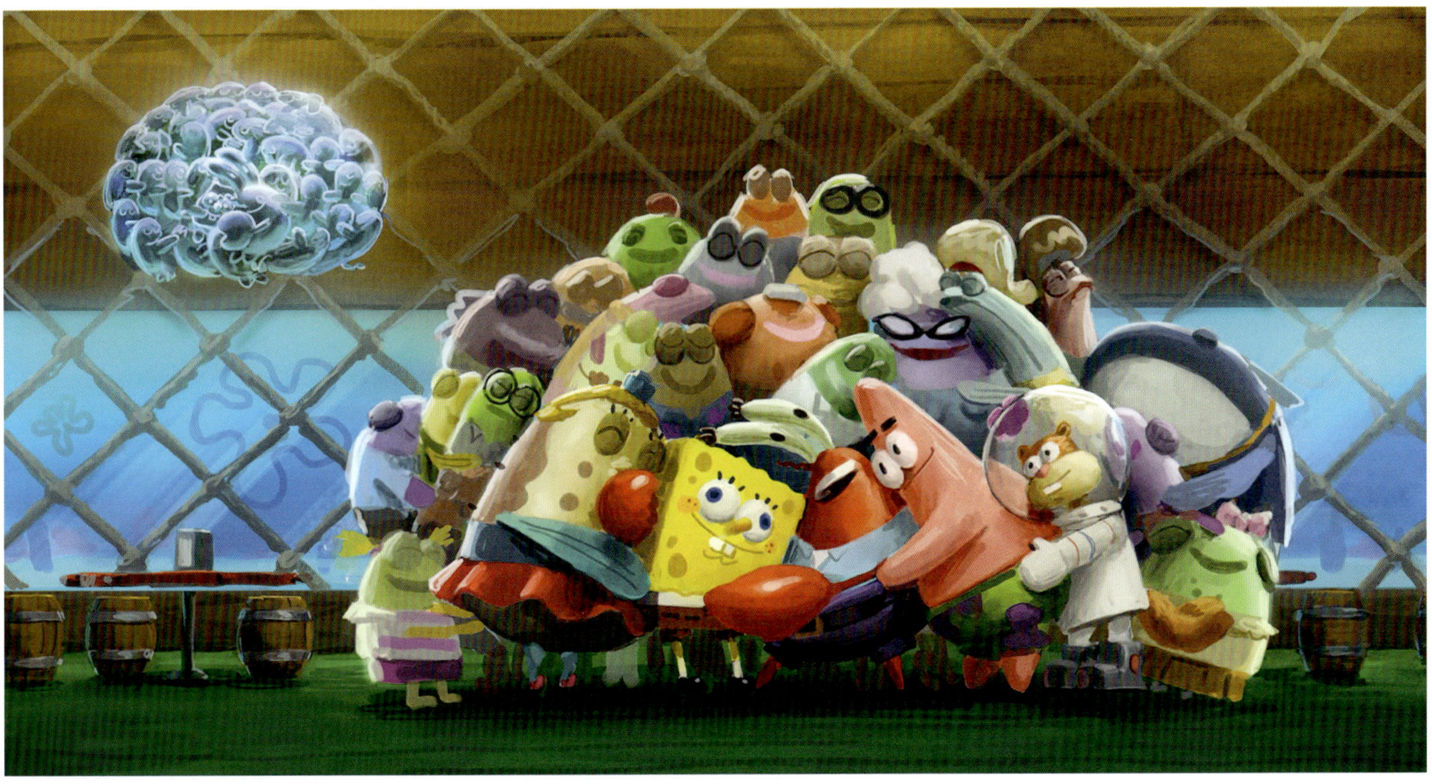

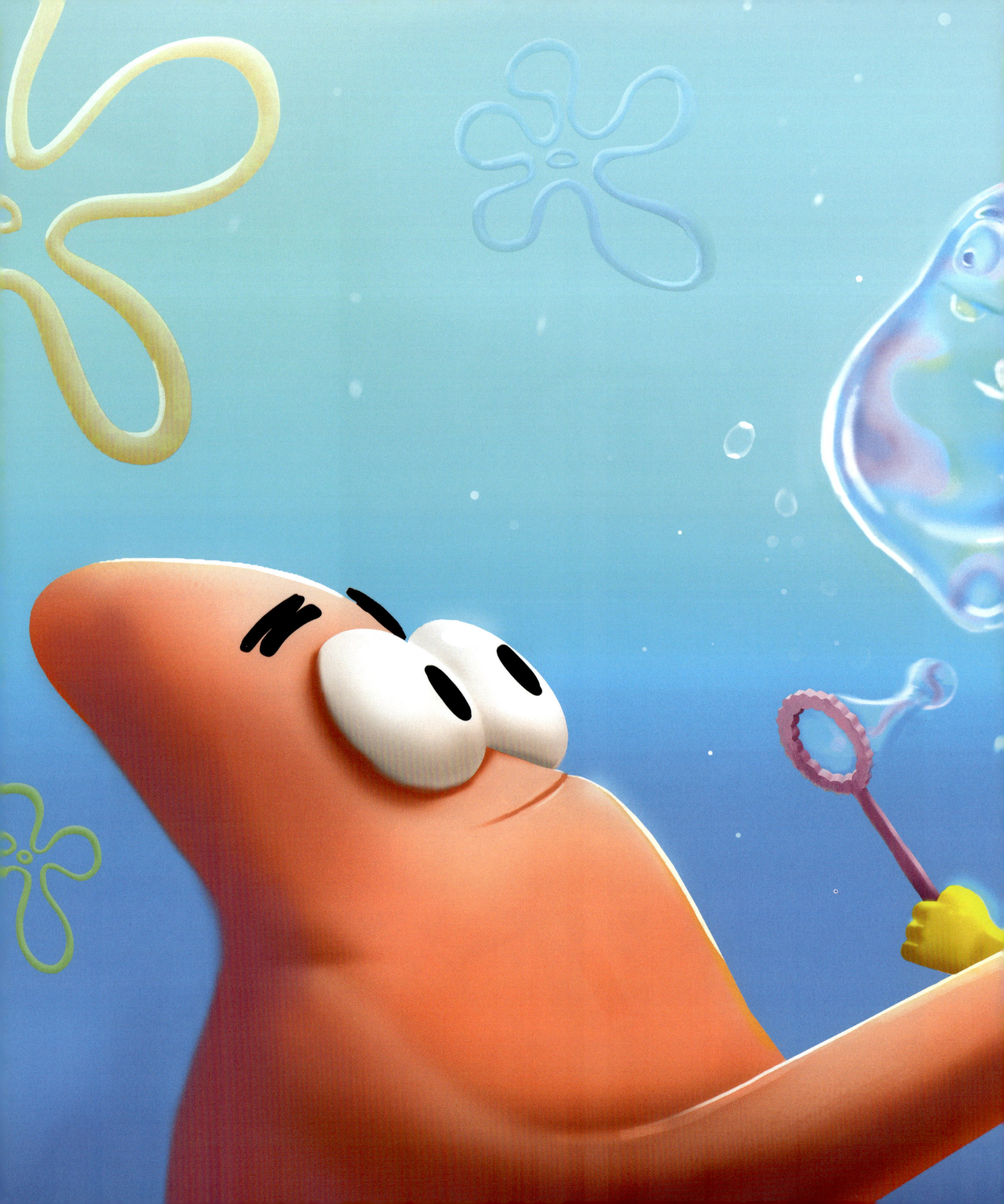

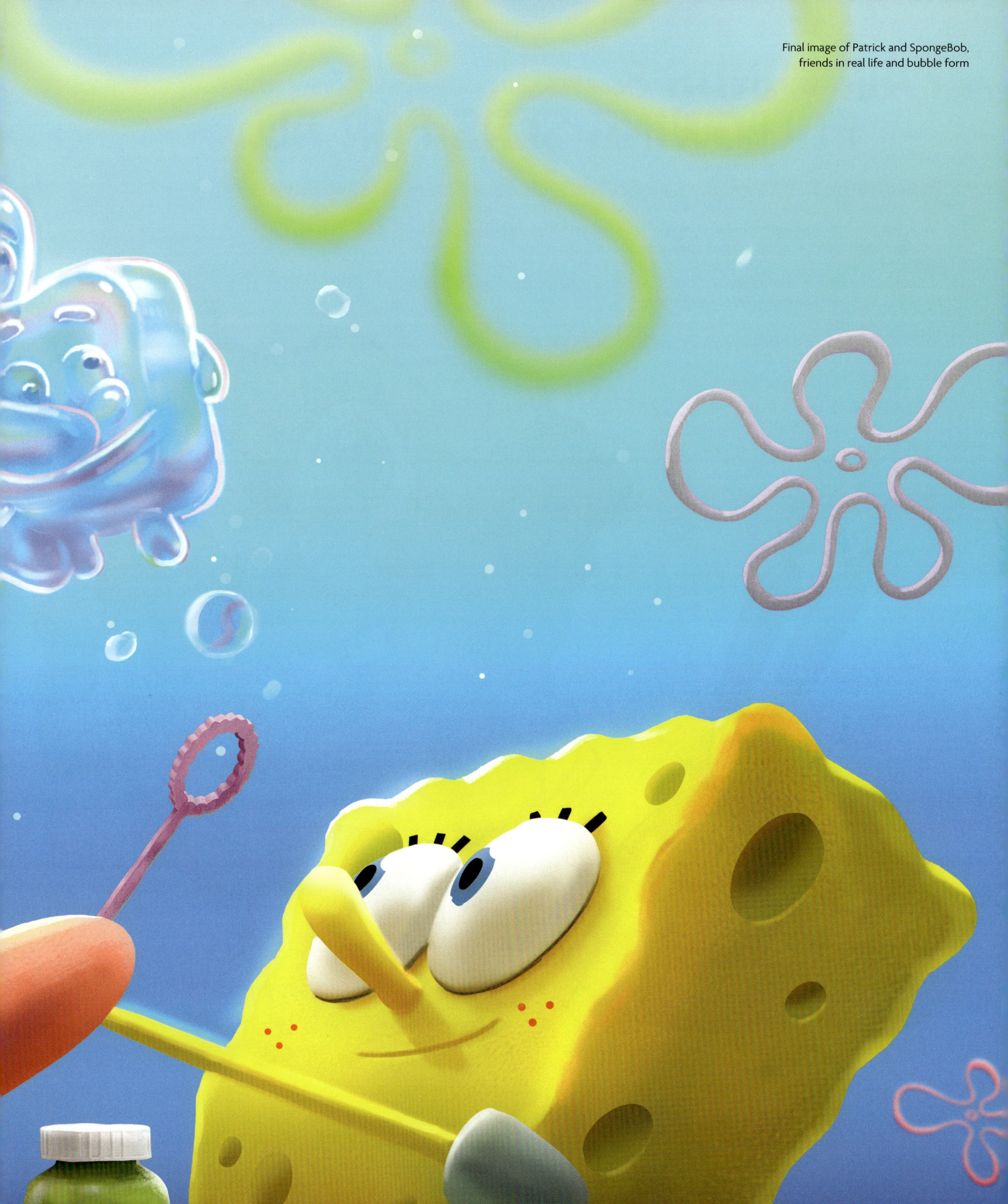

Final image of Patrick and SpongeBob, friends in real life and bubble form

FAIR WINDS & FOLLOWING SEAS FOR ALL

SpongeBob SquarePants has become a beloved part of culture around the globe over the last quarter of a century. Beyond the series and films, the effects of Bikini Bottom are clear and present in music, art, merchandising, Broadway theater, gaming, theme parks, cosplay, memes, parodies, tattoos, personalized license plates, wedding themes, and more. As long as there'll be fish in the sea and talented artists at Nickelodeon, may the nautical nonsense of SpongeBob continue to warm the hearts, imaginations, and screens of young and old alike!

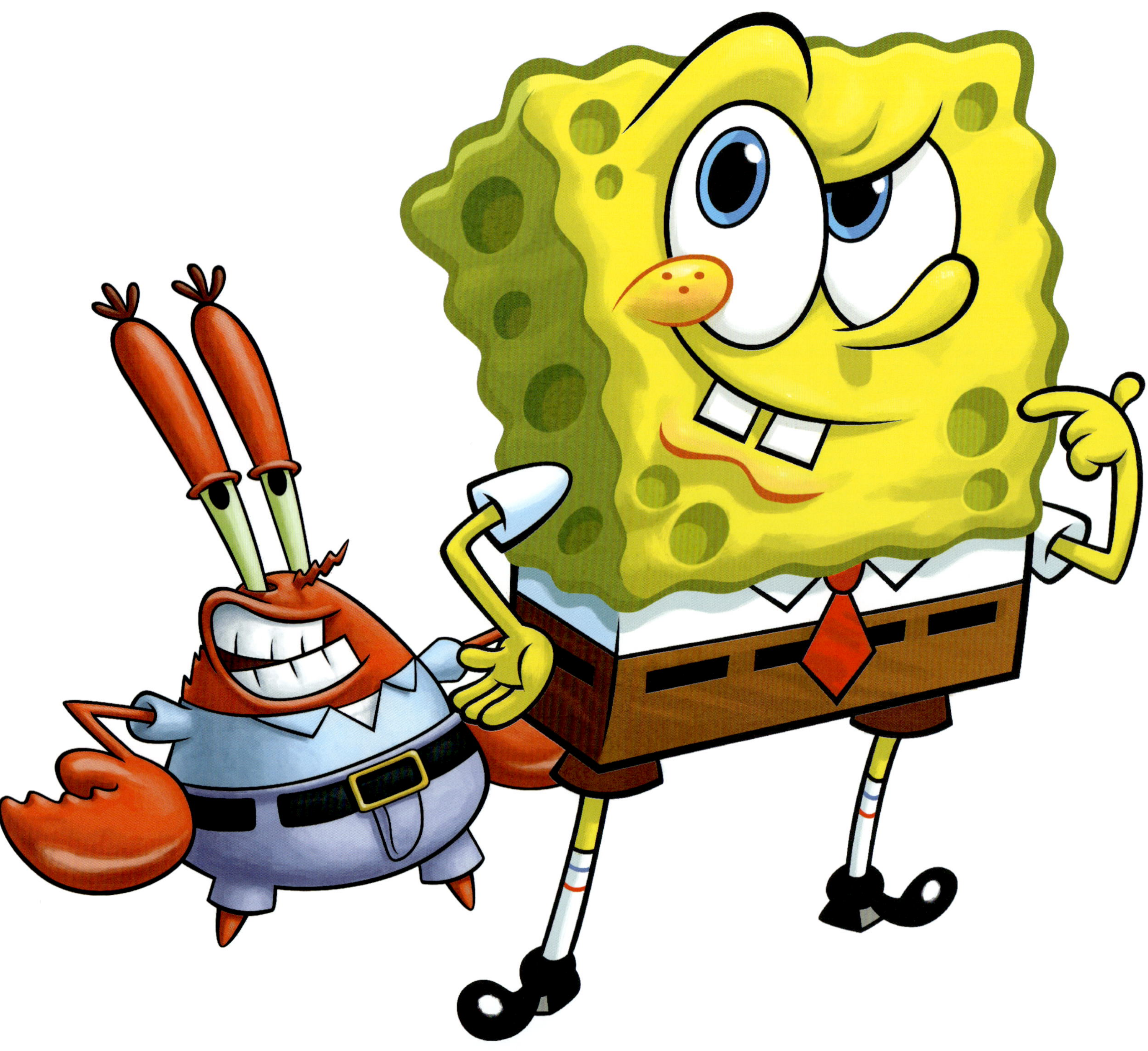

ACKNOWLEDGMENTS

Inspired by SpongeBob, I must express that I have been honored to stand up to the literary challenges and publishing limitations such as time, paper, and ink quantity and to invoke the spirit of all authors, writers, drafters, transcribers, fact finders, researchers, and good old animation fans before me as I have strived forward in the pursuit of life, literacy, and just storytelling in order to form a more perfect manuscript and an honest attempt to recount an animation legacy as deep and wide as the ocean within the pages of this humble book... I offer my gratitude to Alonzo Simon and the whole IDW Publishing team who heard me say "I'm ready, I'm ready, I'm ready to try!" Big thanks also to Benjamin Harper, Risa Kessler, and especially all the incredible *SpongeBob* creators who shared their time and reflections with me along this journey.

—Tracey Miller-Zarneke

A special thank-you to the following people, without whom this book would not have been possible.

Derek Drymon
Pablo R. Mayer
Marc Ceccarelli
Ramsey Naito
Daniel Wineman
Vincent Waller
Jennie Monica
Jaclyn Bender
Shawn Wong
Emily Nordwind
Roxanne Escatel
Caitlin Denny
Britany Valdez
Rebecca Rosenburgh
Claudia Spinelli
Hershel Davis
Amy Jarashow
Risa Kessler
Benjamin Harper
Evelyna Nazari
Emma Cooney

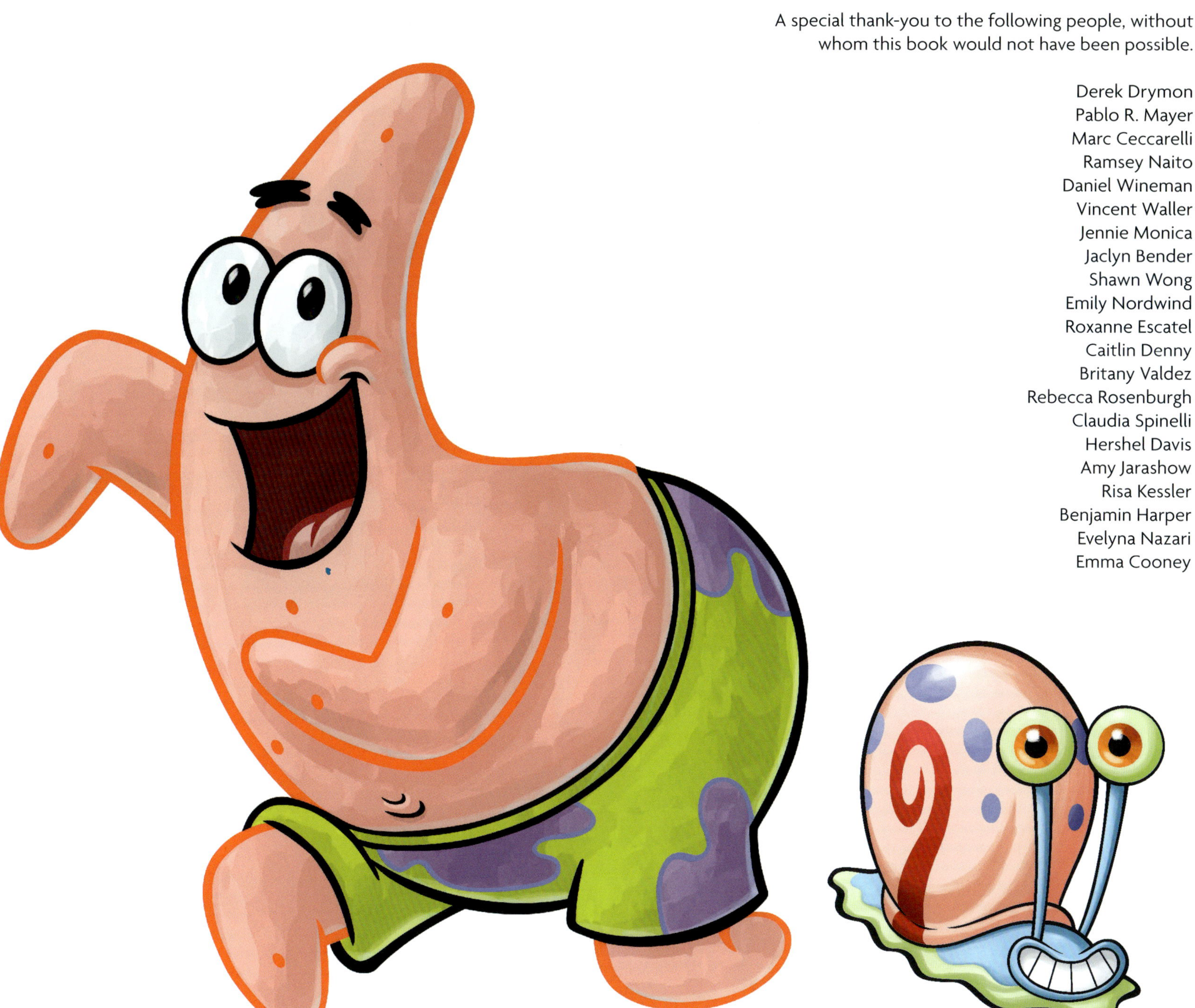

The publisher has to the best of its ability identified and credited those artists whose work is featured in this volume.

Aaron Painter
Aaron Springer
Abril Aello Fregozo
Adam Fay
Adam Paloian
Adam Reed
Ahn Bui
Alex Sokoloff
Alexander Cho
Alexandra Winters
Alexandre Blain
Alfredo Cruz
Allen Battino
Alvi Ramirez
Alyssa Brule
Amy Lewis
Amy Vatankul
Andre Medina
Andre Nieves
Andrea Coleman
Andrew Brandou
Andy "Spike" Clark
Andy Bialk
Andy Greiling
Ann Lee
Anna Chambers
April Borchelt
Arut Tantasirin
Audrey Stedman
Aurore Damant
Baptiste Lucas
Benjamin Chuang
Bill Kaufmann
Bill Waldman
Bob Camp
Bobby London
Brad Sutton
Brad Vandergrift
Bryan Sims
Calvin G. Liang
Carey Yost
Caroline Director
Carolyn Guske
Casey Alexander
Catherine Simmonds
CH Greenblatt
Chad Soren Harper
Chloe Bennett
Chloe Bristol
Chris DeRose
Chris L. Spellman
Chris Mitchell
Christian White
Christopher Leone
Christopher Near
Chu-Hui Song
Chuck Klein
Clint Bond
Craig Elliott
Craig Kellman
Damon Bard

Dave Alvarez
Dave Cunningham
Dave Needham
Dave Wasson
David Brueggeman
David Lu
David Wigforss
Dene Ann Heming
Derek Drymon
Derek L'estrange
Don Reich
Doug Allen
Doug Chiang
Dustin D'Arnault
Dylan Hoffman
Eduardo Acosta
Edward Georgian
Edwin Rhemrev
Elise Hatheway
Elsa Chang
Emily Merl
Eric Stanton
Ernie Gilbert
Ernie Rinard
Fei Xu
Fides Belmonte
Fides Gutierrez
Francesco Denicolo
Francis Boncales
Francisco Mora
Garvin Beltz
George Nachev
George P. Villaflor
Ghostshrimp
Ginny Hawes
Gordon Hammond
Grace P Young
Gregg Schigiel
Guillaume Fesquet
Harley Huang
Hena Hong
Ibrahim Corona Buenrostro
Image Asylum
Ingo Gudmundsson
Isaac Marzioli
Jackson Dryden
Jaclyn Scaramuzzo
Jason Hall
Jeff Palm
Jennifer Powell
Jeremiah Alcorn
Jerry Suh
Jessica Shih
Joann Chang
Joe Bluhm
Joe Orrantia
John Seymore
Joseph Jones
Joshua Stevens
Julio Vega
Junpei Takayama

Kali Fontecchio
Karen Hamrock
Kaukab Basheer
Kayla Jones
Kaz
Keith Chi Ming Lee
Kelly McGraw
Kendall Hale
Kenny Pittenger
Kim Knowles
Kimberly Knoll
Kit Boyce
Kris Kapp
Kristy Kay
Kyle A. Carrozza
Lauren Airriess
Leigh Rens
Leo Garcia
Leonard Robledo
Letia Lewis
Lucy Tanashian-Gentry
Luke Allen
Luke Freeborn
Lynn Wang
Maddie Carter
Madelaine Wilkinson
Madi Hodges
Mara Mitterstainer
Marc Ceccarelli
Marc Ellis
Marco Cinello
Mark Bachand
Mark Colangelo
Mark O'Hare
Marta Knudsen
Martin Wittig
Maryann Thomas
Maureen David Mascarina
Maximus Julius Pauson
mcbess
McBess Studios
Meg Hanna
Megan Ruiz
Michael Chen
Michael Defeo
Michael Humphries
Michelle Thies
Mick De Falco
Mike Fontanelli
Mike Geiger
Mikros Animation
Miles Thompson
Monica Davila
Monica Orange
Morgan Ngu
Nadia Vurbenova-Mouri
Natalie Franscioni-Karp
Nick Jennings
Nikita Chan
Olga Gerdjikov
Olga Stern

Pablo R. Mayer
Paige Woodward Scheier
Paul Tibbitt
Paula Spence
Paulette H. Emerson
Perry Dixon Maple
Peter Bennett
Piero Piluso
Pipeline Studios
Rachel Colucci
Rachel Tiep-Daniels
Rebekie Bennington
ReDefine
Rick Evans
Robertryan Cory
Ronnie Senteno
Rough Draft Korea Co., LTD.
Rough Draft Studios, Inc
Rozalina Tchouchev
Ruben Hickman
Ryan Jouas
Saeid Zameniateni
Sally Cruikshank
Sang Young Bang
Scott Fassett
Screen Novelties
Shakeh Haghnazarian
Shaun Bryant
Sherm Cohen
Simon Rodgers
Sinking Ship Entertainment
Spin VFX
Stephanie Gladden
Stephen Christian
Stephen DeStefano
Stephen Hillenburg
Stephen Russell Wells
Sterling Richter
Steven Kellams
Sue Mondt
Teale Reon Wang
Ted Seko
Thaddeus Paul Couldron
Thomas Wellmann
Tim Allen
Tim Hill
Timothy Björklund
Todd White
Travis Ruiz
Tristin Cole
Troylan B. Caro
Vanessa Morales
Virginia Hawes
Wesley T. Paguio
Will Terrell
Win Arayaphong
Yukfoo Animation
Yuriko Oto
Zach Heffelfinger
Zak Plucinski

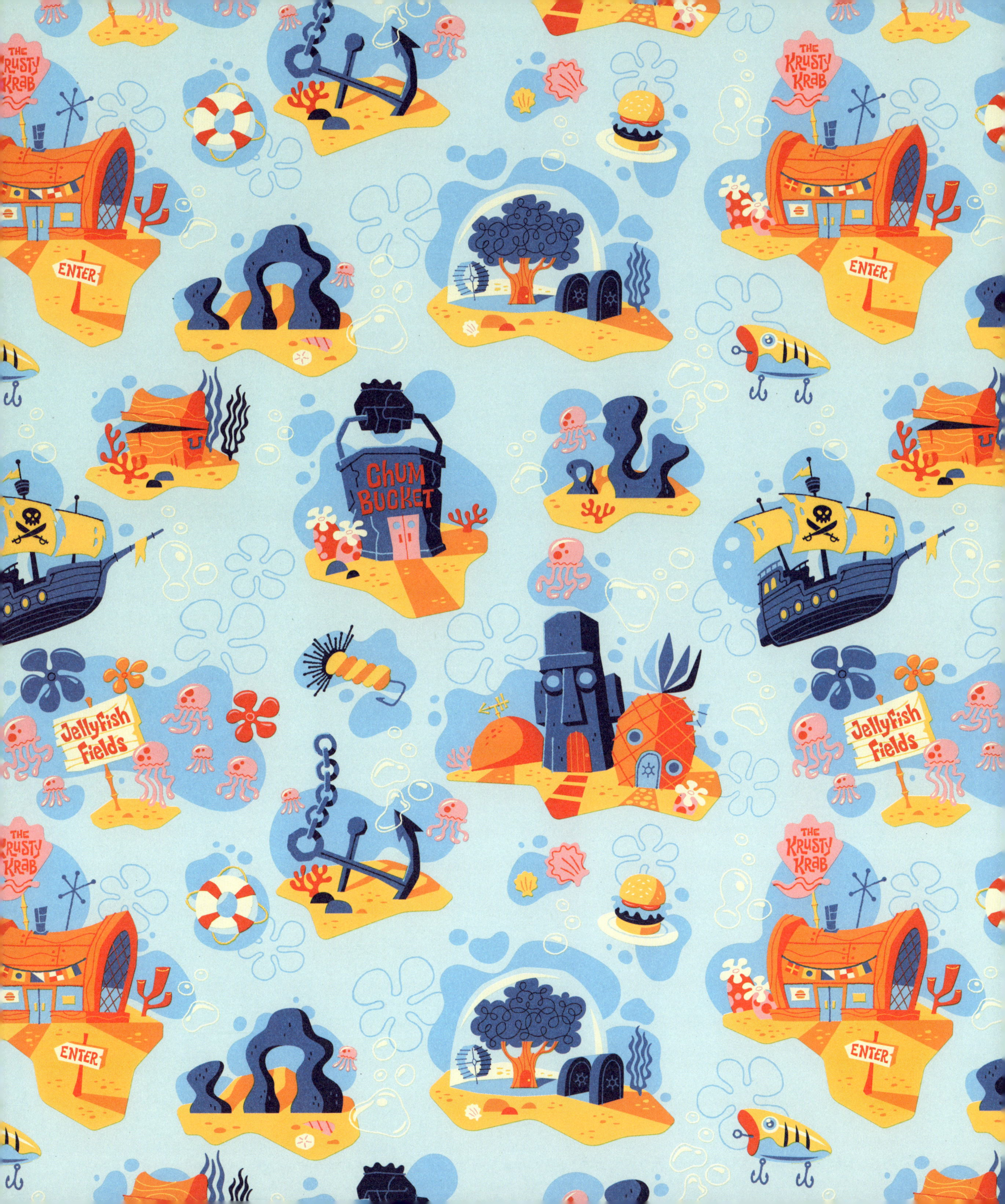
The Krusty Krab
Enter
Chum Bucket
Jellyfish Fields

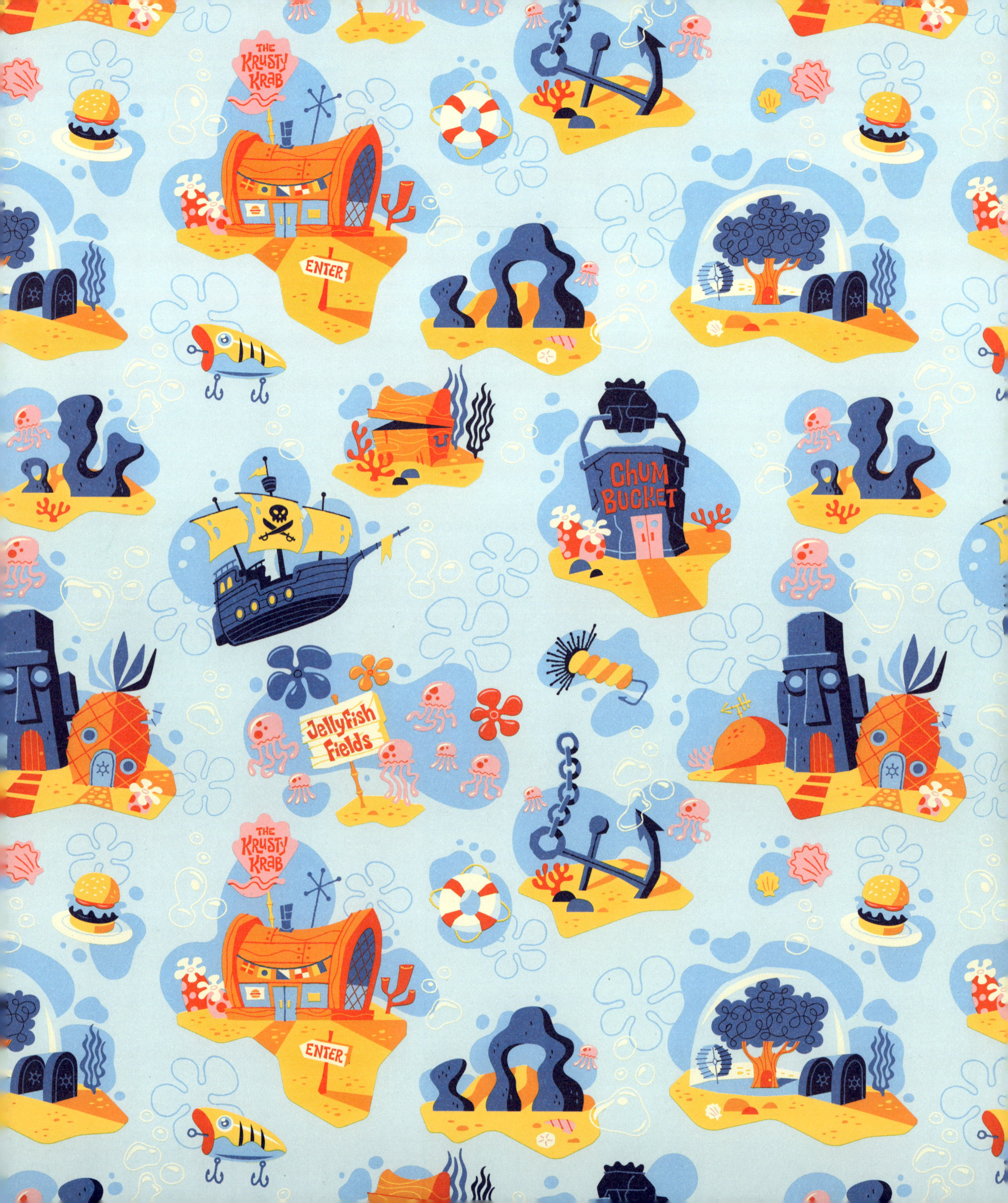
THE
Krusty
Krab
ENTER
Chum
Bucket
Jellyfish
Fields
THE
Krusty
Krab
ENTER